THE *unofficial* GUIDE®

TO Walt Disney World®

2018

BOB SEHLINGER *and* LEN TESTA

(Walt Disney World® is officially known as Walt Disney World® Resort.)

AdventureKEEN

Please note that prices fluctuate in the course of time and that travel information changes under the impact of many factors that influence the travel industry. We therefore suggest that you write or call ahead for confirmation when making your travel plans. Every effort has been made to ensure the accuracy of information throughout this book, and the contents of this publication are believed to be correct at the time of printing. Nevertheless, the publishers cannot accept responsibility for errors or omissions, for changes in details given in this guide, or for the consequences of any reliance on the information provided by the same. Assessments of attractions and so forth are based upon the authors' own experiences; therefore, descriptions given in this guide necessarily contain an element of subjective opinion, which may not reflect the publisher's opinion or dictate a reader's own experience on another occasion. Readers are invited to write the publisher with ideas, comments, and suggestions for future editions.

The Unofficial Guides
An imprint of AdventureKEEN
2204 First Ave. S., Ste. 102
Birmingham, AL 35233
theunofficialguides.com, facebook.com/theunofficialguides, twitter.com/theugseries

Cover design by Scott McGrew

Text design by Vertigo Design and Annie Long

For information on our other products and services or to obtain technical support, please contact us from within the United States at 888-604-4537 or by fax at 205-326-1012.

AdventureKEEN also publishes its books in a variety of electronic formats. Some content that appears in print may not be available in electronic formats.

ISBN: 978-1-62809-067-3; eISBN: 978-1-62809-068-0

Distributed by Publishers Group West

Manufactured in the United States of America

5 4 3 2 1

CONTENTS

LIST *of* MAPS *and* DIAGRAMS

THE
unofficial GUIDE®
TO Walt Disney World®

2018

INTRODUCTION

WHY "UNOFFICIAL"?

DECLARATION OF INDEPENDENCE

THE AUTHORS AND RESEARCHERS of this guide specifically and categorically declare that they are and always have been totally independent of the Walt Disney Company, Inc.; of Disneyland, Inc.; of Walt Disney World, Inc.; and of any and all other members of the Disney corporate family not listed.

The material in this guide originated with the authors and researchers and has not been reviewed, edited, or approved by the Walt Disney Company, Inc.; Disneyland, Inc.; or Walt Disney World, Inc.

This guidebook represents the first comprehensive *critical* appraisal of Walt Disney World. Its purpose is to provide the reader with the information necessary to tour Walt Disney World with the greatest efficiency and economy and with the least hassle.

In this guide, we represent and serve you, the reader. If a restaurant serves bad food or a gift item is overpriced or a ride isn't worth the wait, we say so, and in the process we hope to make your visit more fun and rewarding.

DANCE TO THE MUSIC

A DANCE HAS A BEGINNING and an end. But when you're dancing, you're not concerned about getting to the end or where on the dance floor you might wind up. In other words, you're totally in the moment. That's the way you should be on your Walt Disney World vacation.

You may feel a bit of pressure concerning your vacation. Vacations, after all, are very special events—and expensive ones to boot. So you work hard to make your vacation the best that it can be. Planning and organizing are essential to a successful Walt Disney World vacation, but if they become your focus, you won't be able to hear the music and enjoy the dance.

So think of us as your dancing coaches. We'll teach you the steps in advance so that when you're on vacation and the music plays, you'll move with effortless grace and ease.

THE IMPORTANCE OF BEING GOOFY

BOSCO, DISNEY'S SOCIAL MEDIA GURU, stares, perplexed, at a new report. "Since Donald Trump was elected, our characters are losing followers across the board but are really getting trounced on Twitter," he remarks.

"Which characters?" quizzes his assistant, Hubert.

"The number of Twitter followers is down just a little for most of our characters," Bosco replies, "but bird characters like Donald, Daisy, Huey, Dewey, Louie, and Uncle Scrooge have totally tanked."

"So it's just duck characters, then?" Hubert asks.

"Nope," Bosco replies. "Among our bird characters, José Carioca, Lago, Scuttle, and Zazu are losing followers *by the minute*. Even non-Disney characters—including Woody Woodpecker, Foghorn Leghorn, Daffy Duck, *and* Road Runner—are way down."

"Where are the followers going? Do you see an uptick for *anyone*?"

"No—hey, wait a minute. I'm seeing a huge gain in Twitter followers in the Looney Tunes column . . . but it's just one character who's cleaning up!"

"Who?" implores Hubert.

"Good grief—it's *Tweety Bird*! He's gained thousands of followers because of a string of tweets with 'Twump' arguing about cats' rights."

"Huh? Like what?"

"Whether a cat has to use the litter box corresponding to the sex on his birth certificate, for example," Bosco explains.

"Ooh, that's topical all right," Hubert concedes.

"Tweety told the president that he's pooped from tweeting all night but that he's on call 24/7 for matters of national security, which he prefers to tweeting about cats. And there's more—Trump invited Tweety to join him at a rally to sing a duet. You won't believe this, but they've even recorded a song together!"

Incredulous, Hubert asks, "What's the song?"

"It was commissioned by the tourism authorities of Louisiana and Mississippi: 'It's sweet to bleat your tweet in the Mississippi mud.' "

And so it goes. . . .

What really makes writing about Walt Disney World fun is that the Disney people take everything so seriously. Day to day, they debate momentous decisions with far-ranging consequences: Will Pluto look silly in a silver cape? Have we gone too far with The Little Mermaid's cleavage? With the nation's drug problem a constant concern, should we have a dwarf named Dopey?

Unofficially, we think having a sense of humor is important. This guidebook has one, and it's probably necessary that you do, too—not to use this book, but to have the most fun possible at Walt Disney World. Think of the *Unofficial Guide* as a private trainer to help get your sense of humor in shape. It will help you understand the importance of being Goofy.

HONEY, I BLEW UP THE BOOK!

THE FIRST EDITION OF *The Unofficial Guide to Walt Disney World* was fewer than 200 pages, a mere shadow of its current size. Since that edition, Disney World has grown tremendously. The *Unofficial Guide* has grown to match this expansion.

A mom from Streator, Illinois, is amazed by the size of the *Unofficial Guide,* writing not unsympathetically:

> *It had been 10 years since we'd been to WDW, and I was shocked by how the size of your book grew. After going, I'm surprised that it's so small.*

The good news is that we're working with leading scientists to put the entire book on a computer chip implanted directly in your brain! In the meantime, we offer a qualified apology for the bulk of this edition. We know it may be too heavy to carry comfortably, but we defend the inclusion of all the information presented. Not every diner uses ketchup, A.1. sauce, or Tabasco, but it's nice to have all three on the table.

Concerning *Unofficial Guide* content, readers have offered these suggestions for new material:

- *I think your guide should have a list of attractions that provide (1) seats, (2) air-conditioning, and (3) at least 15 minutes off your feet.*

- *I feel the* Unofficial Guide *should include a claustrophobia rating for each attraction.*

- *I wish you'd discuss restrooms more in the next edition. I found myself constantly searching for one.*

- *We think you need a rating system regarding water [i.e., how wet you can expect to get on specific attractions]. EW = Extreme Water; SW = Some Water; M = Mist.*

These comments are representative in that many of you would like more detailed coverage of one thing or another. We've debated adding hundreds of other things, but we haven't done so. Why? Because we don't have an infinite number of pages to work with, and we felt other information was more important. New ideas for book material are usually tested first at blog.touringplans.com, so check there to see what your fellow readers have suggested.

YOUR *UNOFFICIAL* WALT DISNEY WORLD TOOLBOX

WHEN IT COMES TO WALT DISNEY WORLD, a couple with two toddlers in diapers needs different advice than a party of seniors going to the Epcot International Flower & Garden Festival. Likewise, adults touring without children, families with kids of varying ages, and honeymooners all require their own special guidance.

To meet the varying needs of our readers, we've created the comprehensive guide before you. We call **The Unofficial Guide to Walt Disney World,** at about 850 pages, the "Big Book." It provides the detailed information that anyone traveling to Walt Disney World needs to have a super vacation. It's our cornerstone.

As thorough as we try to make the main guide, there just isn't sufficient space for all the tips and resources that may be useful to certain readers. Therefore, we've developed four additional guides that provide information tailored to specific visitors.

Here's what's in the toolbox:

The Unofficial Guide Color Companion to Walt Disney World, by Bob Sehlinger, Len Testa, Erin Foster, and Brian McNichols, proves that a picture is indeed worth a thousand words. In the Big Book, for instance, you can learn about the best guest rooms to request at Disney's Wilderness Lodge, but in the *Color Companion* you can *see* the rooms, along with the pool and the magnificent lobby. Full-color photos show how long the lines get at different times of day, how wet riders get on Splash Mountain, and how the parks are decked out for various holidays. Most of all, the *Color Companion* is for fun. For the first time, we're able to use photography to express our zany *Unofficial* sense of humor. Think of it as Monty Python meets Walt Disney . . . in Technicolor.

The Unofficial Guide to Disney Cruise Line, by Len Testa with Laurel Stewart, Erin Foster, and Ritchey Halphen, presents advice for first-time cruisers; money-saving tips for booking your cruise; and detailed profiles for restaurants, shows, and nightclubs, along with deck plans and thorough coverage of the ports visited by DCL.

The Unofficial Guide to Walt Disney World with Kids, by Bob Sehlinger and Liliane J. Opsomer with Len Testa, presents detailed planning and touring tips for a family vacation, along with more than 20 family touring plans that are exclusive to this book.

The Unofficial Guide to Universal Orlando, by Seth Kubersky, is the most comprehensive guide to Universal Orlando Resort in print. At almost 400 pages, it's the perfect tool for understanding and enjoying Universal's ever-expanding complex consisting of theme parks, a water park, five resort hotels, nightclubs, and restaurants. The guide includes field-tested touring plans that will save you hours of standing in line.

THE DEATH OF SPONTANEITY

ONE OF OUR ALL-TIME FAVORITE LETTERS came from a man in Chapel Hill, North Carolina:

> *Your book reads like the operations plan for an amphibious landing: Go here, do this, proceed to Step 15. You must think that everyone is a hyperactive, type-A theme park commando. What happened to the satisfaction of self-discovery or the joy of spontaneity? Next you'll be telling us when to empty our bladders.*

(We'd love to hear this reader's thoughts on FastPass+, which lets you reserve spots on popular rides two months in advance.)

As it happens, we *Unofficial Guide* researchers are a pretty existential crew who are big on self-discovery. But Disney World—especially for first-time travelers—probably isn't the place you want to "discover" the spontaneity of needless waits in line or mediocre meals when you could be doing better.

In many ways, Disney's theme parks are the quintessential system, the ultimate in mass-produced entertainment, the most planned and programmed environment anywhere. Lines for rides form in predictable ways at predictable times, for example, and you can either learn here how to avoid them or "discover" them on your own.

We aren't saying that you can't have a great time at Walt Disney World. What we *are* saying is that you should think about what you want to do before you go. The time and money you save by planning will help your family have more fun.

THE BIG HURT

THE TITLE OF THIS SECTION alludes to a pop song from the 1950s, when Bob was a teenager, but it's relevant in this sense: Planning a Walt Disney World vacation takes time, effort, and creativity. If you're lucky enough to have someone in your group to take on the responsibility of planning, don't throw them under the bus the second you hit the theme parks. Take to heart the experience of this Manassas, Virginia, mom:

> First, if you're allowing one member of your group to plan your days in the park, FOLLOW THEIR PLAN! This is not the time to decide that you know better. Secondly, a Disney vacation is not for being lazy or sleeping in. If that's what you want out of a vacation, then please go to the Caribbean and drink rum for three days. A Disney vacation takes planning, and a lot of it. Once you're there, it's doubtful that you'll do better on your own.

DON'T LET THE TAIL WAG THE DOG

SOME FOLKS BECOME SO INVESTED in their plan that it becomes the centerpiece of the vacation. Witness this Columbia, Missouri, mom:

> Getting to the park when it opens is the key to beating the lines. To make that happen: (1) Pack breakfast on the go—you can eat your Pop-Tarts once you're on the shuttle bus, then drink your juice while you wait in line for Dumbo. (2) Send the fastest runner in your party to jump on the bus or boat; the driver will wait if he sees you coming and one of your kids is already hanging on. (3) Showering wastes precious park and rest time; the pool will do. (4) Braid your daughter's hair. Seriously. My 8-year-old never had to brush her hair in the morning. (5) Ball caps for boys also avoid hair brushing.

The stress and doggedness of such an approach would push most of us over the edge. So remember the basics: Know thyself, nothing to excess, and concentrate on having fun.

WE'VE GOT ATTITUDE

SOME READERS DISAGREE with our attitude toward Disney. A woman from Golden, Colorado, lambastes us:

> I read your book cover-to-cover and felt you were way too hard on Disney. It's disappointing when you're all enthused about going to Walt Disney World to be slammed with all these criticisms.

A reader from Little Rock, Arkansas, takes us to task for the opposite prejudice:

> Your book was quite complimentary of Disney, perhaps too complimentary. Maybe the free trips you travel writers get at Disney World are chipping away at your objectivity.

And from a Williamsport, Pennsylvania, mother of three:

> Reading your book irritated me before we went to Disney World because of all the warnings and cautions. I guess I'm used to having

guidebooks pump me up about where I'm going. But once I arrived, I found I was fully prepared and we had a great time. In retrospect, I have to admit you were right on the money. What I regarded as you being negative was just a good dose of reality.

Finally, a reader from Phoenixville, Pennsylvania, prefers no opinions at all, writing:

While each person has the right to his or her own opinion, I didn't purchase the book for an opinion.

For the record, we've always paid our own way at Walt Disney World: Hotel rooms, admissions, and meals have always come out of our own pockets. We don't dislike Disney, and we don't have an ax to grind. Personally, we've enjoyed the Disney parks immensely over the years, both experiencing them and writing about them. But, as with any corporation, Disney is better at some things than others. Because our readers shell out big bucks to go to Walt Disney World, we believe they have the right to know in advance what's good and what's not.

For those who think we're overly positive, please understand that the *Unofficial Guide* is a guidebook, not an exposé. Our aim is for you to enjoy your visit. To that end, we report fairly and objectively. When readers disagree with our opinions, we, in the interest of fairness, publish their viewpoints alongside ours. To the best of our knowledge, the *Unofficial Guides* are the only travel guides in print that do this.

YOU'VE GOT ATTITUDE

WE READ THE COMMENTS ON EVERY READER SURVEY sent in. Those comments often express the mood of the average Disney World visitor better than a numbers-based rating scale. Being nerds, we were interested in seeing whether these moods, if they could be detected, were becoming more (or less) positive over time.

For that we turned to the field of *sentiment analysis,* a subset of computational linguistics that seeks to quantify the emotion displayed in a block of text. Using two commercially available analysis tools, we rated each comment received since 2010 on a scale of –1 (very negative) to 1 (very positive), with 0 representing neutral.

For comparison, here's a comment rated as very negative:

I was very disappointed with Pop Century Resort. The food court was a madhouse and was run poorly. The check-in process took forever—and I did online check-in! Many of the staff were helpful, while others could not answer any question and at some points were very rude.

Here's a neutral comment:

My family did not want to have such a planned trip, so I tried hard to just keep the touring plans to myself and use them as a gentle guide. I tried to be patient with what people wanted to do and tried not to be too attached to the idea of the plans.

And here's a comment rated as very positive:

We had an absolutely wonderful vacation staying at Shades of Green. We will most definitely stay there again and will recommend it to all our military friends!

We're still working through how best to analyze comments. For example, comments that contain both praise and criticism are probably better handled as separate sentences. But individual sentences may use contextual phrases such as "because of that," in which identifying the subject (and assigning a score) requires referring to another sentence. We hope to have more detailed analyses for you soon.

That said, here's a graph showing the results of our preliminary analysis of all reader comments received since 2010:

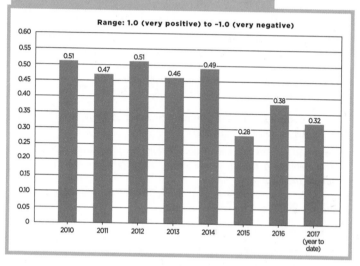

Mood of Reader Comments

Range: 1.0 (very positive) to –1.0 (very negative)

The past several years have seen significant drops in reader sentiment. Why? Our hypothesis is simple: Visitors see higher prices but don't see Disney spending that money to improve the theme parks.

The period from 2010 through 2014, which yielded the most positive reader comments, included the Magic Kingdom's largest expansion in history—New Fantasyland—smack-dab in the middle of Orlando's busiest theme park.; that project added six new attractions and two highly rated restaurants. In contrast, Disney opened just one major new ride—Epcot's Frozen Ever After, in 2016—until Pandora opened at Animal Kingdom in 2017. But Pandora is tucked into an obscure corner of Disney's least-visited theme park and is based on an 8-year-old non-Disney movie that doesn't seem to have many ardent fans. It may turn out to be an excellent addition to Animal Kingdom, but Disney had a hard row to hoe in persuading and demonstrating to its fans that Pandora was worth its share of seven years' price increases.

Where's the Beef?

Overall, Walt Disney World provides a great vacation experience. Even so, guests express dissatisfaction with many things. We are torn between keeping the tone of this guide positive and giving you a heads-up concerning various problems and deficits. At the risk of dampening your enthusiasm and anticipation, we believe that drawing your attention to the beefs of other readers will, in the end, provide a more realistic picture and enhance your vacation. So, here in rank order are the most common complaints, followed by representative comments:

1. Costs going up and value decreasing. Cost cuts are affecting the Disney guest experience negatively across the board. A Texas mother of a teen shared this example:

> We had previously been to 1900 Park Fare for dinner and enjoyed it. This time we did not. There were way less food choices (they had sushi last year), and the character interactions were not as good. It's way too expensive for bad food.

A dad from Holly Springs, North Carolina, commented:

> Every time we visit, our experience is less "magical" than the last. You can tell that Disney is a large corporation because they are making corporate decisions that take much of the fun out of the vacation. That's not to say that we still didn't have a lot of fun; it's just not as special anymore.

2. The complexity of the planning process. A Princeton, West Virginia, reader stated it succinctly:

> Disney World has become as complicated as doing your taxes. It is overwhelming. I feel like you almost have to get an expert to navigate all the Extra Magic Hours, FastPasses, parks to choose on what day, restaurant reservations, and hotels. Prepare for at least a year of research and bookings if you are going.

A woman from Springfield, Illinois, offered this:

> Very disappointing. There is no such thing as a spontaneous trip to Disney anymore. Every day must be planned as to what park you will attend on what day, and what rides you want and when you want to ride them, and [all] planned around any dining you might have.

3. Drinking. We've received complaints about intoxicated guests for quite a while, but they doubled over 2016–17. Ninety percent of them were about Epcot, where a "Drinking Around the World Showcase" pub crawl is popular.
From a Denver family:

> The Food & Wine Festival made the World Showcase unbearably crowded with intoxicated people who were rude and using language inappropriate for children. Although the guide mentions it's similar to a "beerfest" atmosphere, I think a little more emphasis could be made that it indeed affects the whole park every day as early as about 11 a.m. I would go as far as to discourage young families from visiting Epcot when the Food & Wine Festival is operating.

FYI, Disney is experimenting with selling beer in smaller quantities. Because the price has remained the same as for the larger pours, we see this as a way to cut costs and increase profitability rather than an attempt to curtail drunkenness. In direct conflict with Walt Disney's wishes, beer and wine have been introduced to the Magic Kingdom, but only at Be Our Guest and full-service restaurants.

4. Rude guests. Inconsiderate stroller pilots, along with aggressive scooter drivers lead the pack, followed by line-cutters and foreign tour groups evidently not accustomed to waiting in lines. Concerning the latter, Disney is doing a better job of reining them in.

5. The Disney bus transportation system. Four or five resorts receive the lion's share of reader complaints.

A woman from Houston, Texas, gave us the what for, writing:

I think you are much too easy on Disney with regard to the bus service. Considering the money we spent on Animal Kingdom Lodge, Park Hopper passes and sit-down restaurants, I think the least Disney could do is provide efficient, reliable transportation around its world. The bus service was terrible. Disney can have the best service and the most interesting attractions in the world, but if it takes 2 hours to get to them on crowded, unreliable buses, it just isn't worth it. We greatly prefer Disneyland California for this reason alone.

A reader from Central America shared her experience:

Caribbean Beach transportation was as bad as you said it would be, and we will avoid the resort in the future. Despite leaving a LOT of time, transportation was so poor we actually missed our friend's finish at the half marathon. Two other times, we waited over an hour at a theme park to return to the hotel, despite calling the front desk. We were told that each resort has a transportation budget. Clearly someone is using the CB budget for something other than transportation! One highlight was a bus driver named John—truly Disney at its best.

A big fan of Port Orleans Riverside won't be going back:

I absolutely love Port Orleans Riverside. It is a gorgeous resort. I have stayed there four times since 1997. However, as lovely as it is, I doubt I will go back because each time I do, I am very disappointed with the bus service to and from the Magic Kingdom. The bus service to the Magic Kingdom is pretty bad. You have people trying to make it to early dining reservations and leaving early enough, but whoever schedules these buses doesn't seem to care. . . . The bus service coming back from the Magic Kingdom is nothing short of abominable. The lines are incredibly long. They send out the short buses, rather than the longer, bendy buses. I waited 35+ minutes in a large crowd, only to have to stand on this bus every single night. It is for this reason I will not go back to this beautiful resort.

THE SUM OF ALL FEARS

EVERY WRITER WHO EXPRESSES an opinion is accustomed to readers who strongly agree or disagree: It comes with the territory. Extremely troubling, however, is the possibility that our efforts to be objective have frightened readers away from the World or made them apprehensive.

A mom from Avon, Ohio, was just such a person, writing:

After reading parts of the Unofficial Guide, *I seriously reconsidered going to WDW at all because I felt it required too much planning—too many things that could go wrong, too many horrible outcomes (like waiting for hours in scorching heat with kids), etc. A friend convinced me it wouldn't be that bad, so I kept on with planning the trip.*

We certainly understand the reader's feelings, but the key point was that, though apprehensive, she stayed the course. Here's what she said after returning home:

> *Let me tell you, your guide and touring plans were dead-on accurate! We didn't wait more than 10 or 15 minutes for almost every attraction in two days!*

For the record, if you love theme parks, Disney World is as good as it gets—absolute nirvana. If you arrive without knowing a thing about the place and make every possible mistake, chances are about 90% that you'll have a wonderful vacation anyway. The job of a guidebook is to give you a heads-up regarding opportunities and potential problems. We're certain we can help you turn a great vacation into an absolutely *superb* one.

TOO MANY COOKS IN THE KITCHEN?

WE RECEIVED THIS QUERY from a Manchester, Vermont, reader and feel it deserves a serious response:

> *I read a review criticizing the* Unofficial Guide *because it was "written by a team of researchers." The reviewer doesn't say why he thinks the team approach is inferior, but the inference is along the lines of "too many cooks spoil the soup." Why do you use this approach?*

There are several reasons. Most guidebooks do a reasonably good job with the what and where; *Unofficial Guide*s add the how and why. Describing attractions or hotels or restaurants (the what) at a given destination (the where) is the foundation of other travel guidebooks. We know from our research, though, that our readers like to know how things work.

unofficial **TIP**
Researching and writing this book as a team results in a more objective guidebook for you.

However, no individual author can possibly be qualified to write about every topic in the vast range of important subjects that make up a good guide to Walt Disney World. Our team approach enables us to provide deeper explanations of Disney's operations and undertake much more sophisticated and extensive research. Creating touring plans (see page 85), for example, requires statisticians who can analyze millions of attraction wait times to predict how and why lines will build throughout any day. Another project, monitoring the Disney transportation system, requires riding and timing every bus, boat, and monorail route, a task that takes four researchers almost a week to complete. Our Walt Disney World with Kids chapter (Part Five) was developed in consultation with three nationally respected child psychologists and an advisory group of parents. Similarly, our professional culinary experts ensure, say, that the *pollo al forno* you order at Epcot's Italy Pavilion is a decent approximation of what you might get in Rome.

We also conduct extensive research on you, the reader. Your tastes, preferences, and opinions—expressed in reader surveys, e-mails, and blog comments—dictate the subjects we research and the content of our books. Other guides are researched and developed by individual authors or coauthors, the content filtered through the lens of their tastes, preferences, and opinions. If the information is compatible with the needs of the reader, that's largely accidental.

Known and respected throughout the travel industry and academe, *Unofficial Guide* research has been recognized by the BBC, CNN, the *Dallas Morning News,* the *New York Times,* the Travel Channel, *USA Today,* and *Wired,* as well as numerous scholarly journals. We (Bob and Len) put the fruits of our research into words, but behind us is an organization unequaled in travel publishing.

THE *UNOFFICIAL* TEAM

SO WHO ARE THESE FOLKS? Allow us to introduce them all, except for our dining critic, who shall remain anonymous:

- BOB SEHLINGER Author and publisher • LEN TESTA Coauthor
- FRED HAZELTON Statistician • SARAH KELLETH **TouringPlans.com** webmaster, Lines developer
- LARRY OLMSTED Golf expert • TRAVIS BRYANT **TheUnofficialGuides.com** webmaster
- JIM HILL Entertainment reporter • KAREN TURNBOW, PʜD Child psychologist

• DATA COLLECTORS	• CONTRIBUTING WRITERS	• HOTEL INSPECTORS
Chantale Brazeau	Rich Bernato	Ritchey Halphen
Shane Grizzard	Liliane J. Opsomer	Kristen Helmstetter
Lillian Macko	Sue Pisaturo	Seth Kubersky
Richard Macko	Laurel Stewart	Lillian Macko
Cliff Myers	Darcie Vance	Richard Macko
Darcie Vance	Mary Waring	Darcie Vance
Rich Vosburgh	Deb Wills	
Kelly Whitman		

- • EDITORIAL, ART, AND PRODUCTION
- • RITCHEY HALPHEN Managing editor • KATE McWHORTER JOHNSON Production editor
- • ANNIE LONG Typesetter-designer • DARCIE VANCE, JAN VANCE Research editors
- • TAMI KNIGHT, CHRIS ELIOPOULOS Cartoonists
- • STEVE JONES, CASSANDRA POERTNER Cartographers
- • ANN WEIK CASSAR Indexer

Steve Bloom is the voice of reason in the wilderness that is statistical analysis. Gerelyn Reaves answers e-mail better than we could and generally keeps everyone in line. Seth Kubersky is our Universal Orlando guru, assisted by food *consigliere* Derek Burgan. David Davies is our jack-of-all-trades; Brad Huber assisted with software development. Brian McNichols does Disney bar "research" and whatever photographer Tom Bricker tells him. Todd Perlmutter and Bryan Klinck skillfully debugged our touring plan software. Our Lines app was created by Henry Work, who's now trying to perfect soccer-playing animatronics for Disney. Lines' chat is moderated by the fabulous Weasus and Camsdad.

Finally, we'd like to say thanks to the following folks for their assistance with fact-checking: Robert Bloom, Shannon Bohn, Dani Dennison, Anne Densk, Alyssa Drake, Erin Foster, Erin Jenkins, Richard and Lillian Macko, Lauren Macvane, Julia Mascardo, David McDonough, and Sara Moore.

THIS IS NOT A NOVEL!

THOUGH THIS GUIDE IS FULL OF CHARACTERS—and was created by a few more—it is at heart a reference work, and many readers do not read it cover-to-cover, as they would a piece of fiction. For some this causes problems—witness this angry reader who identified him/herself as "None of Your Business":

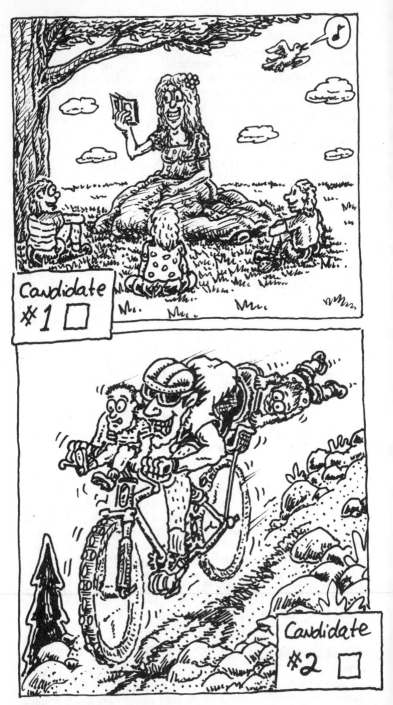

SURVEY: *Which author do you prefer to write your guidebooks? (Guess which ones you got?)*

I am very disappointed that the book doesn't mention that an additional fee is required to access the touring plans and crowd-level information on your website. . . . I don't mind paying, but I am disgusted that you would not mention it in your book. Shame on me for assuming this information would be free, even though I shelled out $23.99 [Canadian] for the book.

Don't you hate it when people hide their true feelings just to be polite? In any event, None of Your Business's complaint illustrates how readers use the guide in different ways. Here's our reply to NOYB:

Dear None,

Thanks for your letter. Here's the thing:

The Unofficial Guide to Walt Disney World is used by many readers as a reference work as opposed to a cover-to-cover read. Consequently, a reader might miss something, say, at the beginning of the guide, that provides information necessary for understanding references to the same subject elsewhere. For several editions, we've been explaining in Part One, Gathering Information, specifically what readers can access on our website at no cost and what they can access only with a paid subscription.

In the last edition, this information read as follows:

> Much of our web content, including new research, book updates, resort photos and video, and up-to-date dining menus, is completely free. Access to part of the site, most notably the Crowd Calendar, additional touring plans, and in-park wait times, requires a small subscription fee (current-book owners get a substantial discount). This nominal charge helps keep us online and costs less than lunch at Flame Tree Barbecue in Disney's Animal Kingdom. Plus, TouringPlans.com offers a 45-day money-back guarantee—something we don't think the Flame Tree can match.

In an 850-page book, it's unrealistic for us to think everyone will read every word. On the other hand, it's totally impractical to explain things that are mentioned multiple times each time they're referenced. So we don't blame you for being angry—you probably were using the guide as a reference and just missed the explanation.

All the best,
Bob and Len

If you use the guide like an encyclopedia or dictionary—say, you look something up in one of the indexes, then go to the cited page—you may overlook information presented in previous sections that is vital to understanding the subject. Likewise, if you skip or skim over explanatory material in the introductory chapters, that might lead to a misunderstanding later on.

CORRECTIONS, UPDATES, AND BREAKING NEWS

LOOK FOR THESE at **TouringPlans.com**; see page 28 for a complete description of the site. The e-book versions of the *Guide* (ePub and Kindle) are updated periodically between print editions.

THE *UNOFFICIAL GUIDE* PUBLISHING YEAR

WE RECEIVE MANY QUERIES asking when the next edition of the *Unofficial Guide* will be available. Usually our new editions are in stores by late August or early September. Thus, the 2019 edition will be on shelves in August or September 2018.

LETTERS AND COMMENTS FROM READERS

unofficial **TIP**
If you're up for having your comments quoted in the guide, be sure to tell us where you're from.

MANY OF YOU WHO USE *The Unofficial Guide to Walt Disney World* write us to comment or share your own strategies for visiting Disney World. Your comments and observations are frequently incorporated into future editions of the *Unofficial Guide* and have contributed immeasurably to its ongoing improvement. If you write us or complete our reader survey, please rest assured that we won't release your name or address to any mailing-list companies, direct-marketing advertisers, or other third parties.

Online Reader Survey

Our website hosts a questionnaire you can use to express opinions about your Walt Disney World visit. Access it here: touringplans.com /walt-disney-world/survey. The questionnaire lets every member of your party, regardless of age, tell us what he or she thinks about attractions, hotels, restaurants, and more.

You can also print out the survey and mail it to us here:

Reader Survey
The Unofficial Guide to Walt Disney World
2204 First Ave. S., Suite 102
Birmingham, AL 35233

Finally, if you'd like to review this book on Amazon, go to tinyurl .com/wdw2018reviews.

How to Contact the Authors

Bob Sehlinger and Len Testa
The Unofficial Guide to Walt Disney World
2204 First Ave. S., Suite 102
Birmingham, AL 35233
unofficialguides@menasharidge.com
facebook.com/theunofficialguides | twitter.com/theugseries

When you write, please put your address on both your letter and your envelope; the two sometimes get separated. It's also a good idea to include your phone number. If you e-mail us, please tell us where you're from. Also understand that, as travel writers, we're often out of the office for extended periods of time, so please bear with us if we're slow to respond. *Unofficial Guide* e-mail isn't forwarded to us when we're traveling, but we'll get back to you as soon as possible after we return.

WALT DISNEY WORLD:
An OVERVIEW

IF YOU'RE CHOOSING a US tourist destination, the question is not whether to visit Walt Disney World, but how to see its best offerings with some economy of time, effort, and finances.

WHAT WALT DISNEY WORLD ENCOMPASSES

WALT DISNEY WORLD COMPRISES 43 square miles, an area twice as large as Manhattan. Situated strategically in this vast expanse are the **Magic Kingdom, Epcot, Disney's Hollywood Studios,** and **Disney's Animal Kingdom** theme parks; 2 water parks; a sports complex; 4 golf courses; 41 hotels and a campground; more than 100 restaurants; 4 interconnected lakes; a shopping complex; 8 convention venues; a nature preserve; and a transportation system consisting of four-lane highways, elevated monorails, and a network of canals.

Walt Disney World employs around 70,000 people, or "cast members," making it the largest single-site employer in the United States. Keeping the costumes of those cast members clean requires the equivalent of 16,000 loads of laundry a day and the dry cleaning of 30,000 garments daily. (Mickey Mouse alone has 130 different sets of duds, ranging from a scuba wet suit to a tux; Minnie boasts more than 100 outfits.) Each year, Disney restaurants serve 10 million burgers, 7 million hot dogs, 75 million Cokes, 9 million pounds of French fries, and 150 tons of popcorn. In the state of Florida, only the cities of Miami and Jacksonville have bus systems larger than Disney World's. The Disney monorail trains have logged mileage equal to more than 30 roundtrips to the moon.

DISNEY-SPEAK POCKET TRANSLATOR
AND GUIDE TO COMMON ABBREVIATIONS

IT MAY COME AS A SURPRISE to many, but Walt Disney World has its own somewhat peculiar language. The charts below and on the next page list some abbreviations and argot you're likely to bump into, both in this guide and in the larger Disney (and Universal) community.

COMMON ABBREVIATIONS AND WHAT THEY STAND FOR	
CM Cast member	**FP+/FPP** FastPass+
DCL Disney Cruise Line	**I-DRIVE** International Drive (major Orlando thoroughfare)
DDV Disney Deluxe Villas	**IOA** Universal's Islands of Adventure theme park
DHS Disney's Hollywood Studios	**TTC** Ticket and Transportation Center
DSRA Disney Springs Resort Area	**USF** Universal Studios Florida theme park
DTS Disney Transportation System	**WDI** Walt Disney Imagineering
DVC Disney Vacation Club	**WDTC** Walt Disney Travel Company
EMH Extra Magic Hours	**WDW** Walt Disney World

THE DISNEY LEXICON IN A NUTSHELL
ADVENTURE Ride | **ATTRACTION** Ride or theater show
ATTRACTION HOST Ride operator | **AUDIENCE** Crowd
BACKSTAGE Behind the scenes, out of view of customers
CAST MEMBER Employee
CHARACTER Disney character impersonated by an employee
COSTUME Work attire or uniform | **DARK RIDE** Indoor ride
DAY GUEST Any customer not staying at a Disney resort
FACE CHARACTER A character who doesn't wear a head-covering costume (Snow White, Cinderella, Jasmine, and the like)
GENERAL PUBLIC Same as day guest
GREETER Employee positioned at an attraction entrance | **GUEST** Customer
HIDDEN MICKEYS Frontal silhouette of Mickey's head worked subtly into the design of buildings, railings, golf greens, attractions, and just about anything else
ON STAGE In full view of customers
PRESHOW Entertainment at an attraction before the feature presentation
RESORT GUEST A customer staying at a Disney resort
ROLE A cast member's job
SOFT OPENING Opening a park or attraction before its stated opening date
TRANSITIONAL EXPERIENCE An element of the queuing area and/or preshow that provides information essential to understanding the attraction

THE MAJOR THEME PARKS

The Magic Kingdom

When most people think of Walt Disney World, they think of the Magic Kingdom, opened in 1971. It consists of **Cinderella Castle** and adventures, rides, and shows featuring the Disney cartoon characters. It's only one element of Disney World, but it remains the heart.

The Magic Kingdom is divided into six "lands," with five arranged around a central hub. First you come to **Main Street, U.S.A.,** which connects the Magic Kingdom entrance with the hub. Arranged clockwise around the hub are **Adventureland, Frontierland, Liberty Square, Fantasyland,** and **Tomorrowland.** Five hotels (**Bay Lake Tower;** the **Contemporary, Polynesian Village,** and **Grand Floridian Resorts;** and **The Villas at the Grand Floridian**) are connected to the Magic Kingdom by monorail and boat. Three other hotels, **Shades of Green** (for the US military and their families), **Wilderness Lodge** (incorporating the new **Boulder Ridge Villas** time-share units), and **Fort Wilderness Resort & Campground,** are located nearby but aren't served by the monorail.

Epcot

Opened in October 1982, Epcot is twice as big as the Magic Kingdom and comparable in scope. It has two major areas: **Future World** consists of pavilions concerning human creativity and technological advancement; **World Showcase,** arranged around a 40-acre lagoon, presents the architectural, social, and cultural heritages of almost a dozen nations,

What's New at Walt Disney World Since Your Last Visit

LAST 2 YEARS

• **Disney's Hollywood Studios (DHS)** is undergoing major changes. The Studio Backlot Tour; *Lights, Motors, Action! Extreme Stunt Show;* the Streets of America; and the Osborne Family Spectacle of Dancing Lights holiday display have closed to make way for a Star Wars–themed land. Temporary attractions such as **Star Wars Launch Bay** and ***Symphony in the Stars: A Galactic Spectacular*** (Star Wars–themed fireworks) have been added, and **Toy Story Land** and its two new attractions will open in 2018.

• The remodeling of **Animal Kingdom** is complete with **Pandora—The World of Avatar,** with 2 new attractions and glowing bioluminescent plants. **Tiffins** restaurant opened, accompanied by **Nomad Lounge.** The nighttime spectacular ***Rivers of Light*** debuted, along with other evening activities such as **Kilimanjaro Safaris** and entertainment acts.

• At the **Magic Kingdom,** the longtime fireworks spectacular *Wishes* has been replaced by the fantastic ***Happily Ever After.*** The Muppets put on a hilarious history presentation in Liberty Square called ***The Muppets Present . . . Great Moments in American History.***

• Epcot saw the opening in 2016 of **Frozen Ever After,** a ride themed to *Frozen.*

• **Copper Creek Villas & Cabins at Disney's Wilderness Lodge Resort** was scheduled to open in summer 2017, adding refurbished Disney Vacation Club rooms and two-bedroom cabins along Bay Lake as well as the new **Geyser Point Bar & Grill.**

• **Disney Springs** continues to add highly rated dining, including **Chef Art Smith's Homecomin', Frontera Cocina by Chef Rick Bayless, Paddlefish,** and **The Edison.** DisneyQuest and Cirque du Soleil *La Nouba* closed in 2017.

LAST 5 YEARS

• **New Fantasyland** opened in the Magic Kingdom, including **Seven Dwarfs Mine Train; Under the Sea: Journey of the Little Mermaid;** *Enchanted Tales with Belle;* and **Be Our Guest Restaurant.** Also at the Magic Kingdom, **Jungle Navigation Co. Skipper Canteen** offers table-service dining in Adventureland with all the whimsy of the Jungle Cruise.

• The **FastPass+** ride-reservation system, with online and mobile apps, replaced the paper-based Fastpass system in use since 1998.

• *For the First Time in Forever: A Frozen Sing-Along Celebration* opened at DHS.

• **Festival of Fantasy** became the new daytime parade at the Magic Kingdom.

• **Disney's Polynesian Villas & Bungalows** opened, adding studios, suites, and over-the-water two-bedroom bungalows on 7 Seas Lagoon.

• New restaurants include **Trattoria al Forno** at the BoardWalk, **Spice Road Table** in Epcot's Morocco Pavilion, and **L'Artisan des Glaces** ice-cream parlor in the France Pavilion. Many dining options were added to Disney Springs, including **The Boathouse, Morimoto Asia,** and **Jock Lindsey's Hangar Bar.**

• Interactive games debuted at the Magic Kingdom (**Sorcerers of the Magic Kingdom**), Epcot (**Agent P's World Showcase Adventure**), and Disney's Animal Kingdom (**Wilderness Explorers**).

• **Disney's Art of Animation,** a Value resort, opened with many one-bedroom suites.

LAST 10 YEARS

• New attractions included *Monsters, Inc. Laugh Floor* at the Magic Kingdom; *Finding Nemo—The Musical* at Disney's Animal Kingdom; **Gran Fiesta Tour** at Epcot; and **Toy Story Mania!** and *Disney Junior—Live on Stage!* at Disney's Hollywood Studios. Also at DHS, Star Tours became **Star Tours—The Adventures Continue.**

• **Bay Lake Tower** at the Contemporary Resort, **The Villas at Disney's Grand Floridian Resort & Spa,** and **Kidani Village** at Animal Kingdom Lodge opened,.

• New restaurants included **Yak & Yeti** at Animal Kingdom and **La Cava del Tequila, Via Napoli,** and **Tutto Gusto** at Epcot.

each country represented by replicas of famous landmarks and settings familiar to world travelers.

The Epcot resorts—the **BoardWalk Inn & Villas, Dolphin, Swan,** and **Yacht & Beach Club Resorts and Beach Club Villas**—are within a 5- to 15-minute walk of the International Gateway, the World Showcase entrance to the theme park. The hotels are also linked to Epcot and Disney's Hollywood Studios by canal and walkway. Epcot is connected to the Magic Kingdom and its hotels by monorail. An elevated ski-lift–like gondola system should be completed by 2019 to link Epcot and Disney's Hollywood Studios to Disney's Pop Century, Art of Animation, and Caribbean Beach resorts.

Disney's Hollywood Studios

Opened in 1989 as Disney-MGM Studios in an area a little larger than the Magic Kingdom, Disney's Hollywood Studios (DHS) has two main sections. One area, occupying about 50% of the Studios, is a theme park focused on the motion picture, music, and television industries. Park highlights include a re-creation of Hollywood and Sunset Boulevards from Hollywood's Golden Age, several rides and musical shows, and a movie stunt show.

The rest of DHS is a giant construction zone and will remain that way through at least 2019. Disney has closed and demolished most of what used to be in the park's western and southwestern areas. In their places is an ambitious expansion plan that will add two new lands, dedicated to Disney's Toy Story and Star Wars franchises. We expect Toy Story Land to open in 2018, with two highly themed but relatively simple rides for small children. Star Wars Land will have two cutting-edge, large-scale rides for older children, teens, and adults. We expect it to open before July 2, 2019, because that's when current Disney CEO Bob Iger is scheduled to step down.

In the interim, we don't think DHS is worth its $100-plus admission cost. See Part Twelve for alternatives.

That said, DHS is connected to other Walt Disney World areas by highway and canal (and gondola soon; see above) but not by monorail. Guests can park in the Studios' pay parking lot or commute by bus. Guests at Epcot resort hotels can reach the Studios by boat or on foot.

Disney's Animal Kingdom

About five times the size of the Magic Kingdom, Disney's Animal Kingdom combines zoological exhibits with rides, shows, and live entertainment. The park is arranged in a hub-and-spoke configuration somewhat like the Magic Kingdom. A lush tropical rainforest serves as Main Street, funneling visitors to **Discovery Island,** the park's hub. Dominated by the park's central icon, the 14-story-tall, hand-carved **Tree of Life,** Discovery Island offers services, shopping, and dining. From there, guests can access the themed areas: **Africa, Asia,** and **DinoLand U.S.A.** Discovery Island, Africa, and DinoLand U.S.A. opened in 1998, followed by Asia in 1999. Africa, the largest themed area at 100 acres, is home to free-roaming herds in a re-creation of the Serengeti Plain.

The newly opened **Pandora—The World of Avatar** is the most significant recent expansion in Walt Disney World. Based on James Cameron's

2009 film *Avatar,* Pandora includes two headliner rides and two counter-service restaurants. The big draw, however, may be the animals and scenery—including "floating mountains" and glow-in-the-dark plants—which Disney has replicated here. See Part Eleven for full details.

Disney's Animal Kingdom has its own parking lot and is connected to other Walt Disney World destinations by the Disney bus system. Although no hotels lie within Animal Kingdom proper, the **All-Star Resorts, Animal Kingdom Lodge & Villas,** and **Coronado Springs Resort** are all nearby.

THE WATER PARKS

DISNEY WORLD HAS TWO MAJOR water parks: **Typhoon Lagoon** and **Blizzard Beach.** Opened in 1989, Typhoon Lagoon is distinguished by a wave pool capable of making 6-foot waves. Blizzard Beach, opened in 1995, features more slides. Both parks pay great attention to atmosphere and aesthetics. Typhoon Lagoon and Blizzard Beach have their own parking lots and can be reached by Disney bus.

OTHER WALT DISNEY WORLD VENUES

Disney Springs

Redevelopment of the sprawling shopping, dining, and entertainment complex formerly known as Downtown Disney was completed in 2017. Themed to evoke a Florida waterfront town, Disney Springs encompasses the **Marketplace,** on the east; the **West Side,** on the west; **The Landing,**on the waterfront; and **Town Center,** featuring shops and restaurants and a Florida–meets–Spanish Colonial architectural theme. Two desperately needed multistory parking garages have also opened.

The Marketplace contains the country's largest store selling Disney-character merchandise; upscale resort-wear and specialty shops; and numerous restaurants, including **Rainforest Cafe** and **T-REX.** The West Side is a diverse mix of nightlife, shopping, dining, and entertainment, most notably featuring a Disney outpost of **House of Blues,** encompassing a live-music venue and a restaurant serving Cajun-Creole cooking. The West Side may see significant remodeling over the next couple of years in a second wave of Disney Springs updates.

The Landing offers additional shopping and dining options. **The Boathouse,** an upscale waterfront seafood eatery, opened here in spring 2015. Also at The Landing are **Morimoto Asia,** a high-quality midpriced table-service restaurant from Iron Chef Masaharu Morimoto; **The Edison,** serving American cuisine in a faux electric power plant; and **Chef Art Smith's Homecomin',** a new restaurant from celebrity chef–Florida native Art Smith that features local-farm-to-table ingredients and traditional Southern cooking.

Disney Springs is accessed via Disney transportation from Disney resort hotels.

Disney's BoardWalk

Near Epcot, the BoardWalk is an idealized replication of an East Coast 1930s waterfront resort. Open all day, the BoardWalk features upscale restaurants, shops and galleries, a brewpub, and an ESPN sports bar. In the evening, a nightclub with dueling pianos and a DJ dance club join the lineup. Both are for guests ages 21 and up only. There's no admission fee for the BoardWalk, but the piano bar levies a cover charge at night. This area is anchored by the **BoardWalk Inn & Villas,** along with its adjacent convention center. The BoardWalk is within walking distance of the Epcot resorts, Epcot's International Gateway, and Disney's Hollywood Studios. Boat transportation is available to and from Epcot and Disney's Hollywood Studios; buses serve other Disney World locations.

ESPN Wide World of Sports Complex

The 220-acre Wide World of Sports is a state-of-the-art competition and training facility consisting of a 9,500-seat ballpark; two field houses; and venues for baseball, softball, tennis, track and field, beach volleyball, and 27 other sports. The spring-training home of the Atlanta Braves until 2019, the complex also hosts a mind-boggling calendar of professional and amateur competitions. Walt Disney World guests not participating in events may pay admission to watch any of the scheduled competitions.

Disney Cruise Line: The Mouse at Sea

In 1998, the Walt Disney Company launched (literally) its own cruise line with the 2,400-passenger **Disney Magic.** Its sister ship, the **Disney Wonder,** first sailed in 1999. Most cruises depart from Port Canaveral, Florida (about a 90-minute drive from Walt Disney World), or Miami on three-, four-, and seven-night itineraries. Bahamian and Caribbean cruises include a day at **Castaway Cay,** Disney's 1,000-acre private island. Cruises can be packaged with a stay at Disney World. In 2011 and 2012, respectively, two new ships, the **Disney Dream** and the **Disney Fantasy,** joined the fleet, enabling DCL to expand its sailings in the Caribbean as well as Alaska, California, Canada, Hawaii, the Mediterranean, and Northern Europe.

Disney offers a free online video that tells you all you need to know about DCL cruises and then some. View it at disneyplanning.com; note that you'll be asked to complete a short survey first.

To get the most out of your cruise, check out **The Unofficial Guide to Disney Cruise Line,** by Len Testa with Erin Foster, Laurel Stewart, and Ritchey Halphen.

THE PEOPLE

HOW YOU'RE TREATED BY THE CAST MEMBERS you encounter at Walt Disney World can make or break a vacation. Fortunately, Disney staff often go the extra mile to make your visit special, as the following three readers report. First, from a Paron, Arkansas, woman:

> We encountered a problem with FastPass+ midweek—somehow, only one of us had FastPass+ on our MagicBand and the other four did not. At the kiosk near Tower of Terror, an attendant pointed out the problem. No more passes were available for the day for Toy Story Mania!, and others wouldn't be available until evening during Fantasmic!, for which we had a dining package reserved. We were disappointed and confused, but we went to dinner determined to just wait in line later for Fantasmic! As we sat down to eat, customer service called—the

attendant had independently reported the issue for us, and we were given the three FastPasses we thought we had originally! And we were still able to enjoy dinner and Fantasmic! We were blown away by the service and communication on the part of the cast. Well done!

A family from St. Joseph, Michigan, has this to relate:

We had a very unexpected and wonderful surprise waiting in our stroller after the Country Bear Jamboree. Out of nearly 30 strollers, ours had been visited by Santa Mickey while we were in the show. We came out to a stroller decorated with silly bands, Christmas orna- ments, and a snowman Mickey plush toy. Our 5-year-old son was delighted, not to mention the rest of our party. Just another way that WDW goes one more step to make a magical experience.

Finally, from a suburban Philadelphia family:

At Expedition Everest, I witnessed expert handling of a group of teenage line-jumpers by Disney staff. Once they reached the loading area, cast members ushered them aside in a very calm and friendly fashion, causing no apparent disruption. I didn't see where they were ushered or what happened next, but I did not see them board the ride. It was as if they were never there.

UNIVERSAL ORLANDO

TIME TO TAKE OFF THE BLINDERS

READERS ASK US EVERY YEAR why we cover Universal theme parks in this guide. Simply stated, Universal is a high-quality direct competitor of Walt Disney World, and we think you should have detailed informa- tion on both the Disney and Universal parks so you can make an in- formed decision about where to spend your time. We also get comments from readers who are under the impression that Universal's offerings are inferior to Disney's. By any objective measure, they are not.

In many ways, Universal Orlando will never achieve true parity with Walt Disney World. It's minuscule compared with the 27,000-odd acres of the World. But in the areas where it *can* compete—namely, in theme park design and attraction quality—Universal has pulled even, if not ahead.

Universal has been technologically ascendant for several years, in- troducing revolutionary ride systems and special effects on both rides and in theater performances. While Disney relies conservatively on a combination of highly detailed themed areas, beloved characters, and inspiration from classic animated features (which many young people under age 16 have never seen), Universal takes more technological swings for the fences—the most notable examples being the spectacular **Harry Potter and the Forbidden Journey** at **Universal's Islands of Adven- ture (IOA)** and **Harry Potter and the Escape from Gringotts** at **Universal Studios Florida (USF).**

Granted, the Walt Disney World parks do have their share of high-tech attractions, and not all Universal attractions approach the creative genius of Forbidden Journey or Escape from Gringotts. But

STUFF UNIVERSAL SHOULD WIZARD-IZE TO MAKE MORE MONEY:

Chris Eliopoulos

while guests at both Disney and Universal report high levels of satis-faction, it's the next-gen technology manifested in Universal's headlin-ers that delivers true "Wow!" moments. Plus, **Port of Entry** and the new **Skull Island** at Islands of Adventure—along with **The Wizarding World of Harry Potter,** encompassing **Hogsmeade** at IOA and **Diagon Alley** at USF—clearly demonstrate that Universal can create exqui-sitely detailed and totally immersive themed areas.

We see the two Universal parks and the four Walt Disney World parks as rough equals—and every one a gem. There's more for little kids at Disney's Magic Kingdom than at the other parks, and more for teens and young adults at the Universal parks. In keeping with that young-adult demographic, Universal offers the **CityWalk** nightclub venue, just outside the park gates, for those with the energy to make a night of it; Disney World has nothing comparable. Both Universal and Disney have splendid on-site hotels, with Universal offering more perks to its guests. Disney parks have the edge in landscaping as well as full-service dining.

South Orlando & Walt Disney World Area

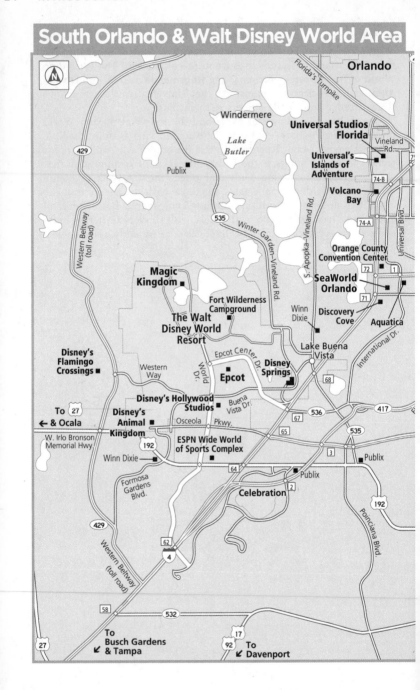

Orlando

Windermere

Lake Butler

Universal Studios Florida

Vineland Rd.

Universal's Islands of Adventure

74-B

Volcano Bay

74-A

Publix

429

535

Winter Garden–Vineland Rd.

S. Apopka–Vineland Rd.

Orange County Convention Center

72

1

Magic Kingdom

SeaWorld Orlando

71

Fort Wilderness Campground

Discovery Cove

The Walt Disney World Resort

Winn Dixie

Aquatica

Lake Buena Vista

International Dr.

Disney's Flamingo Crossings

Western Way

World Dr.

Epcot Center Dr.

Disney Springs

Epcot

68

Disney's Hollywood Studios

Buena Vista Dr.

536

417

To 27 & Ocala

Disney's Animal Kingdom

Osceola Pkwy.

67

65

535

W. Irlo Bronson Memorial Hwy

192

ESPN Wide World of Sports Complex

3

Publix

Winn Dixie

64

Publix

Formosa Gardens Blvd.

2

Celebration

192

429

62

Poinciana Blvd.

4

Western Beltway (toll road)

58

532

27

To Busch Gardens ↙ & Tampa

17

92

To ↙ Davenport

Western Beltway (toll road)

Florida's Turnpike

Universal Blvd.

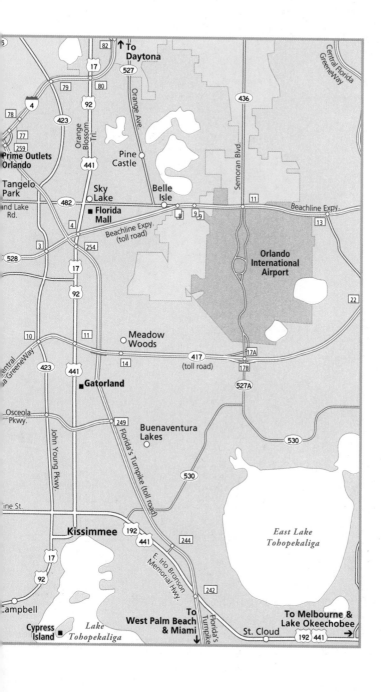

Walt Disney World

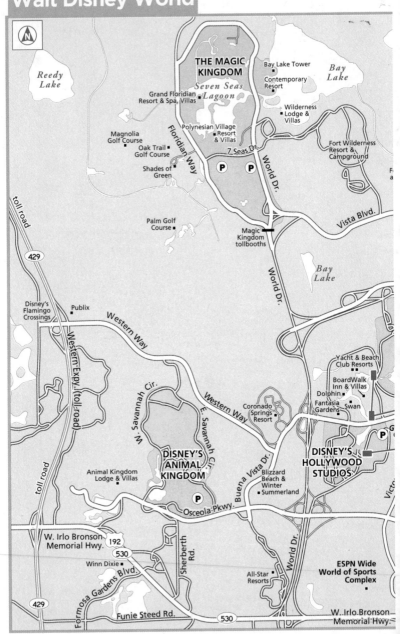

Reedy Lake

THE MAGIC KINGDOM

Seven Seas Lagoon

Bay Lake Tower

Contemporary Resort

Bay Lake

Grand Floridian Resort & Spa, Villas

Wilderness Lodge & Villas

Magnolia Golf Course

Polynesian Village Resort & Villas

Fort Wilderness Resort & Campground

Oak Trail Golf Course

7 Seas Dr.

Floridian Way

Shades of Green

World Dr.

Vista Blvd.

Palm Golf Course

Magic Kingdom tollbooths

Bay Lake

toll road

429

World Dr.

Disney's Flamingo Crossings

Publix

Western Way

Western Expy. (toll road)

Yacht & Beach Club Resorts

W. Savannah Cir.

E. Savannah Cir.

Western Way

Coronado Springs Resort

BoardWalk Inn & Villas

Dolphin

Fantasia Gardens

Swan

DISNEY'S ANIMAL KINGDOM

Animal Kingdom Lodge & Villas

DISNEY'S HOLLYWOOD STUDIOS

Buena Vista Dr.

Blizzard Beach & Winter Summerland

toll road

Osceola Pkwy.

W. Irlo Bronson Memorial Hwy.

192

530

Sherberth Rd.

Winn Dixie

ESPN Wide World of Sports Complex

Formosa Gardens Blvd.

All-Star Resorts

World Dr.

429

Funie Steed Rd.

530

Victory

W. Irlo Bronson Memorial Hwy.

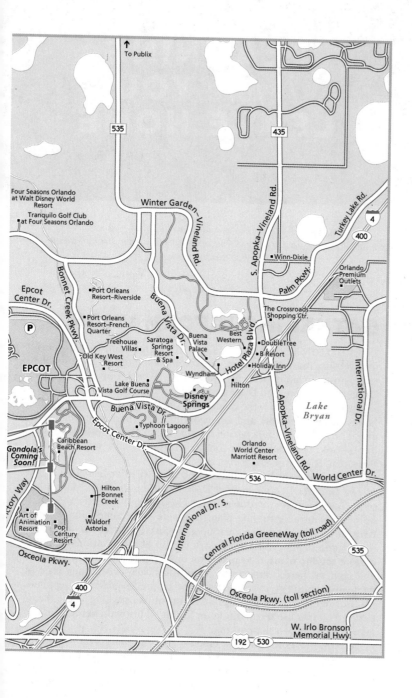

To Publix

535

435

Four Seasons Orlando
at Walt Disney World
Resort

Tranquilo Golf Club
at Four Seasons Orlando

Winter Garden–Vineland Rd.

S. Apopka–Vineland Rd.

Turkey Lake Rd.

4

400

Winn-Dixie

Palm Pkwy.

Orlando
Premium
Outlets

Bonnet Creek Pkwy.

Epcot
Center Dr.

P

EPCOT

Port Orleans
Resort–Riverside

Port Orleans
Resort–French
Quarter

Treehouse
Villas

Old Key West
Resort

Buena Vista Dr.

Saratoga
Springs
Resort
& Spa

Buena
Vista
Palace

Best
Western

The Crossroads
Shopping Ctr.

DoubleTree

B Resort

Holiday Inn

Hotel Plaza Blvd.

Wyndham

Lake Buena
Vista Golf Course

Buena Vista Dr.

Disney
Springs

Hilton

International Dr.

Lake
Bryan

S. Apopka–Vineland Rd.

Epcot Center Dr.

Typhoon Lagoon

Gondolas
Coming
Soon!

Caribbean
Beach Resort

Victory Way

Art of
Animation
Resort

Pop
Century
Resort

Hilton
Bonnet
Creek

Waldorf
Astoria

Orlando
World Center
Marriott Resort

536

World Center Dr.

535

International Dr. S.

Central Florida GreeneWay (toll road)

Osceola Pkwy.

400

4

Osceola Pkwy. (toll section)

W. Irlo Bronson
Memorial Hwy.

192   530

PART ONE

PLANNING *before* YOU LEAVE HOME

Visiting Walt Disney World is a bit like childbirth—you never really believe what people tell you, but once you have been through it yourself, you know exactly what they were saying!

—Hilary Wolfe, a mother and
Unofficial Guide reader from Swansea, Wales

GATHERING INFORMATION

IN ADDITION TO USING THIS GUIDE, we recommend that you visit our website, **TouringPlans.com.** The companion blog, blog.touringplans .com, posts breaking news for Walt Disney World, Universal Orlando, Disney Cruise Line, and Disneyland.

TouringPlans.com is the official website for all of our Disney guidebooks. It complements and augments the information in our books, and it provides *real-time personal services* that are impossible to build into a book. The book is your comprehensive reference source; Touring Plans.com is your personal concierge.

Occasionally, readers misunderstand what we offer. In a 2016 review of *The Unofficial Guide to Walt Disney World with Kids,* Marla Elsea of the *Baton Rouge Advocate* wrote, "The only drawback [is] the promise of customizable touring plans available on a companion website. Great in theory, but not so great upon discovering [a fee] to join."

To address her criticisms: First, a wealth of information, **including custom touring plans,** is available on our website absolutely free after you sign up here: touringplans.com/walt-disney-world/join/basic. A paid subscription gives you access to other, predesigned touring plans. (A TouringPlans.com subscription is sort of like parking at the theme parks: You can use self-parking or, for an additional charge, you can take advantage of valet parking.)

Second, our best and most efficient touring plans are those in the guidebooks. However, they depend on you arriving at the park before opening. For some families with small children and for those who balk at rising early while on vacation, being on hand for park opening is a nonstarter. For these families and others dealing with unique circumstances, we provide custom touring plans online. They're not as efficient as the plans in this book, but given the specific needs of your family, it might be worth it to trade ultimate efficiency for an extra hour or so of sleep or more time in the morning to get up and organized. If getting up early *isn't* an issue, you can customize the plans in the book yourself by simply skipping any attractions that don't interest you.

But customized touring plans are only the tip of the iceberg. Here are some other TouringPlans.com features:

DETAILED 365-DAY CROWD CALENDAR FOR EACH THEME PARK See which parks will be the least crowded every day of your trip, using a 1-to-10 scale. You can also view historical crowd data and check the accuracy of our predictions.

HOTEL-ROOM VIEWS AND ONLINE FAX SERVICE We have photos of the views from every hotel room in Walt Disney World—more than 30,000 images in all—and we'll give you the exact wording to use to request a specific room. We'll even automatically fax your request to Disney right before you arrive. A mother who used the fax service writes:

> *The fax-ahead feature was wonderful! We got a room with a GORGEOUS river view! My husband's jaw dropped when he saw what our view was like! He immediately gave me a big high-five. Thanks!*

Disney tries to accommodate your request, but its ability to do so depends on a number of variables that we can't control. The majority of the faxed requests we send on behalf of readers are honored in full or partially, but sometimes Disney just can't make it work. All this is to say that fulfilled requests are far from a given. Feel fortunate if you get what you asked for.

TICKET DISCOUNTS A customizable search helps you find the cheapest tickets for your specific needs. The average family can save $20–$80 by purchasing admission from one of our recommended ticket wholesalers.

FASTPASS+ INFORMATION We show every FastPass+ reservation available at every attraction in the parks on a single page of our site.

ANSWERS TO YOUR TRIP-PLANNING QUESTIONS Our online community includes tens of thousands of Disney experts and fans willing to help with your vacation plans. Ask questions and offer your own helpful tips.

Much of our online content, including new research, menus, and updates and changes to this book, is completely free. Access to parts of the site, including the Crowd Calendar, hotel-room views, and some custom touring plans, requires a small subscription fee (current-book owners get a substantial discount). This nominal charge—less than a meal at most Disney counter-service restaurants—subsidizes our research and keeps the site up and running day and night.

Our online app, **Lines,** available free to TouringPlans.com subscribers, is designed to accompany you in the parks. It provides ride and park information that Disney doesn't, including the following:

- **Posted and actual wait times at attractions.** Lines is the only Disney-parks app that displays both posted wait times and the actual times you'll wait in line. The wait time you see posted outside of a ride is often much longer than the real wait time, because Disney wants you to go to another part of the park—it's simple crowd control. With Lines, you can make better decisions about what to see.

- **"Ride now or wait" recommendations.** Lines shows you whether ride wait times are likely to get longer or shorter. If you find a long line at a particular attraction, Lines tells you the best time to come back.

- **Real-time touring plan updates while you're in a park.** Lines automatically updates your custom touring plan to reflect actual crowd conditions at a given moment. You can also restart your plan and add or change attractions, breaks, meals, and more.

- **In-park chat with our Lines community.** Do you have a question while you're in the parks? Ask our community of thousands of Liners and get a reply in seconds.

The *Unofficial Guide* and TouringPlans.com, along with the Lines app, are designed to work together as a comprehensive planning and touring resource. This mom from St. Louis used all of the tools in our toolbox:

> The *Unofficial Guide was the perfect place to start planning our vacation (actually our honeymoon). After reading the book, I had a good idea of what hotels I was interested in, and I had "must-do" and "must-eat" places somewhat picked out. I then took the knowledge from the book and switched to the website to personalize our touring plans and use as a reference when needed. The book and the website together made our trip* INCREDIBLE.

A mother from Lexington, South Carolina, echoes the sentiments of the mom above:

> The Lines app and the personalized tour plans were unbeatable! If we missed a step or took extra time on something, it was so easy to catch right back up. Wait times were extremely reliable. The book allowed me to preplan our entire trip, from what to pack to what to see and eat. It was priceless. We traveled during Thanksgiving week, so the parks were at very high crowd levels. The planning allowed us to maximize the use of our time and quietly rejoice that we weren't the ones standing in line for hours.

Our other website, **TheUnofficialGuides.com,** is dedicated to news about our guidebooks and features a blog with postings from *Unofficial Guide* authors. You can also sign up for the **Unofficial Guide Newsletter,** which contains even more travel tips and special offers.

Next, we recommend that you obtain the following:

1. **WALT DISNEY WORLD RESORT VACATION-PLANNING VIDEOS** Disney has discontinued mailing DVD-based vacation-planning toolkits, instead shifting to online videos advertising the resort's offerings. To view them, you'll need to fill out a short survey at disneyplanning.com. You can access videos about Walt Disney World, Disney Cruise Line, and other Disney destinations from the same website.

2. **HOTELCOUPONS.COM FLORIDA GUIDE** This is another good source of discounts on lodging, restaurants, and attractions. Sign up at hotelcoupons.com to have a free monthly guide sent to you by e-mail, or view the guide online. If you prefer a hard copy, you can request one by calling ☎ 800-222-3948 Monday–Friday, 8 a.m.–5 p.m. Eastern time. The guide is free, but you pay $4 for handling ($6 if it's shipped to Canada).

Important Walt Disney World Addresses

GENERAL INFORMATION
Walt Disney World Guest Communications
PO Box 10040, Lake Buena Vista, FL 32830-0040
wdw.guest.communications@disneyworld.com
General online help: disneyworld.disney.go.com/help/email

CONVENTION AND BANQUET INFORMATION
Walt Disney World Resort South
PO Box 10000, Lake Buena Vista, FL 32830-1000
☎ 321-939-7129, disneymeetings.com

MERCHANDISE MAIL ORDER (Guest Service Mail Order)
PO Box 10070, Lake Buena Vista, FL 32830-0070
☎ 877-560-6477, merchandise.guest.services@disneyparks.com

WALT DISNEY WORLD CENTRAL RESERVATIONS
PO Box 10100, Lake Buena Vista, FL 32830-0100
☎ 407-W-DISNEY (934-7639)

WALT DISNEY WORLD YOUTH PROGRAMS
PO Box 10000, Lake Buena Vista, FL 32830-1000
☎ 877-WD-YOUTH (939-6884), disneyyouth.com

WALT DISNEY WORLD TICKET MAIL ORDER
PO Box 10140, Lake Buena Vista, FL 32830-0140
☎ 407-566-4985, ticket.inquiries@disneyworld.com

3. *KISSIMMEE VISITOR'S GUIDE* This full-color guide is of particular interest to those who intend to lodge outside of Disney World, featuring ads for hotels, rental houses, time-shares, and condominiums, as well as a directory of attractions, restaurants, special events, and other useful info. To order a copy, call ☎ 800-333-5477, or view the guide at experiencekissimmee.com.

4. *GUIDEBOOK FOR GUESTS WITH DISABILITIES* Available at Guest Relations when entering the theme/water parks, at resort front desks, and wheelchair-rental areas (listed in each theme park chapter). More-limited information is available at disneyworld.disney.go.com/plain-text.

5. *VISIT ORLANDO DEALS* If you're considering lodging outside Disney World or if you think you might patronize out-of-the-World attractions and restaurants, obtain a Vacation Planner and the *Orlando Official Visitors Guide* (both free) from the **Visit Orlando Official Visitors Center.** The discounts cover hotels, restaurants, ground transportation, shopping malls, dinner theaters, and non-Disney theme parks and attractions. View the deals at tinyurl.com/visit orlando2017. To order the accommodations guide, call ☎ 800-643-9492. For more information and materials, call ☎ 407-363-5872 from 8:30 a.m. to 6:30 p.m. Eastern time on weekdays, or go to visitorlando.com.

YOUR DISNEY TRIP-PLANNING TIMELINE, A.K.A. THE QUICK-START GUIDE TO USING THE *GUIDE*

AS YOU GO THROUGH THIS BOOK, you'll see many references to date-specific planning milestones for your trip: You can start making Disney dining reservations 180 days before your arrival, for example, and you can make FastPass+ ride reservations 60 or 30 days before your visit, depending on whether you're staying on or off Disney property. All this got us thinking about other milestone dates that are important to know for your Disney trip.

Continued on page 34

Walt Disney World Phone Numbers

General Information	☎ 407-824-4321 or 407-824-2222
General Information for the Hearing-Impaired (TTY)	☎ 407-827-5141
Accommodations/Reservations	☎ 407-934-7639
All-Star Movies Resort	☎ 407-939-7000
All-Star Music Resort	☎ 407-939-6000
All-Star Sports Resort	☎ 407-939-5000
AMC Movies at Disney Springs	☎ 407-827-1308
Animal Kingdom Lodge & Villas *(Jambo House)* Animal Kingdom Lodge & Villas *(Kidani Village)*	☎ 407-938-3000 ☎ 407-938-7400
Art of Animation Resort	☎ 407-938-7000
Beach Club Resort	☎ 407-934-8000
Beach Club Villas	☎ 407-934-8000
Blizzard Beach Information	☎ 407-560-3400
BoardWalk Inn	☎ 407-939-6200
Caribbean Beach Resort	☎ 407-934-3400
Centra Care	
Kissimmee	☎ 407-390-1888
Lake Buena Vista	☎ 407-934-2273
Universal-Dr. Phillips	☎ 407-291-8975
Cirque du Soleil	☎ 407-939-1929
Contemporary Resort–Bay Lake Tower	☎ 407-824-1000
Convention Information	☎ 321-939-7129
Coronado Springs Resort	☎ 407-939-1000
Dining Advance Reservations	☎ 407-939-3463
Disabled Guests Special Requests	☎ 407-939-7807
Disney Institute	☎ 407-824-7997 or 321-939-4600
Disney Springs Information	☎ 407-939-6244
ESPN Wide World of Sports Complex	☎ 407-939-4263
Fantasia Gardens Miniature Golf	☎ 407-560-4870
Fort Wilderness Resort & Campground	☎ 407-824-2900
Golf Reservations and Information	☎ 407-939-4653
Grand Floridian Resort & Spa/Villas	☎ 407-824-3000
Group Camping	☎ 407-939-7807
Guided-Tour Information	☎ 407-939-8687

Guided VIP Solo Tours	☎ 407-560-4033
House of Blues Tickets & Information	☎ 407-934-2583
Lost and Found (for articles lost):	
Today at Disney's Animal Kingdom	☎ 407-938-2784
Today at Disney's Hollywood Studios	☎ 407-560-4668
Today at Epcot	☎ 407-560-7500
Today at the Magic Kingdom	☎ 407-824-4521
Today at Universal Orlando (Universal Studios, Islands of Adventure, and CityWalk)	☎ 407-224-4244
Yesterday or before (at all Disney parks)	☎ 407-824-4245
Merchandise Guest Services	☎ 877-560-6477
Old Key West Resort	☎ 407-827-7700
Outdoor Recreation Reservations & Information	☎ 407-939-7529
Polynesian Village Resort	☎ 407-824-2000
Polynesian Village Villas	☎ 407-824-3500
Pop Century Resort	☎ 407-938-4000
Port Orleans Resort–French Quarter	☎ 407-934-5000
Port Orleans Resort–Riverside	☎ 407-934-6000
Resort Dining	☎ 407-939-3463
Saratoga Springs Resort & Spa, Treehouse Villas	☎ 407-827-1100
Security	
Routine	☎ 407-560-7959
Urgent	☎ 407-560-1990
Shades of Green Resort	☎ 407-824-3400 or ☎ 407-824-3600
Telecommunication for the Deaf Reservations (voice)	☎ 407-939-7670
Telecommunication for the Deaf Reservations (TTY)	☎ 407-827-5141
Tennis Reservations & Lessons	☎ 321-228-1146
Walt Disney Travel Company	☎ 407-939-6244
Walt Disney World Dolphin	☎ 407-934-4000
Walt Disney World Swan	☎ 407-934-3000
Walt Disney World Ticket Inquiries	☎ 407-939-7679
Weather Information	☎ 407-827-4545
Wilderness Lodge/Boulder Ridge & Copper Creek Villas	☎ 407-824-3200
Winter Summerland Miniature Golf	☎ 407-560-3000
Wrecker Service *(if closed, call Security, above)*	☎ 407-824-0976
Yacht Club Resort	☎ 407-934-7000

Continued from page 31

Starting below is a comprehensive timeline that represents the major research, decisions, and tasks that come into play when preparing for a typical Walt Disney World vacation. Next to each milestone, we've put a reference to the section in this book that has the information you need for that milestone, and/or links to our website and blog for additional material like photos or video.

Most Disney trips involve about a dozen important dates to remember. If you've started planning more than 11 months before your trip, you'll have plenty of time to do research ahead of them. If you've just decided to visit Disney World within the next couple of months, you'll have a few more decisions to make a bit quicker.

Do you really need to do this? Absolutely—the demand for good rides and restaurants far exceeds their capacity, and you won't get near them without planning and reservations. Consider that around 55,000 people visit the Magic Kingdom on an *average* day. A hot restaurant such as Be Our Guest, running at full speed, can serve lunch to maybe 1 in 12 of them. A very popular character meet and greet, such as the Frozen princesses, may be able to handle 1 in 50 park guests during an entire day of operation. Those are not good odds.

Making dining and attraction reservations as soon as possible is vital if you want to eat at nice restaurants and avoid hours-long waits at popular rides. Other reservations, such as those for spas or recreational activities, can frequently be made when you arrive in Orlando, especially if you're visiting during a slower time of year or you're flexible with the date or time of your appointment. But your best bet is to research early and make reservations as soon as Disney allows.

12–9 Months Before Your Trip

You may already have a general idea of when you want to visit Disney World. What the trip will cost you, however, can be a surprise. Take a couple of evenings to plan a budget, an approximate time of year to travel, and narrow down your hotel choices.

- **Establish a budget.** See pages 59–62 in Part Two for an idea of how much Disney vacation you can get for $500, $1,000, $1,500, and $2,000, for various family sizes. More information is available at tinyurl.com/500-disney-vacation.
- **Figure out when to go and where to stay.** Begin researching resorts (see Part Three) and the best times of year to visit to avoid crowds (see page 41). Our own Erin Foster has devised an excellent method for finding the best vacation dates for your family: See her planning blog at tinyurl.com/wdwplanning.
- **Brush up on discounts.** Disney releases certain discounts around the same time every year. Check mousesavers.com for a list of these regular discounts, when they're usually announced, and the travel dates they cover at tinyurl.com/wdw-historic-discounts.
- **Create an account at mydisneyexperience.com** (see page 38). You'll need it to make hotel, dining, and ride reservations later.
- **Make a preliminary hotel reservation.** This typically requires a deposit equal to one night's cost, and it guarantees you a room. You

can change or cancel your reservation without penalty for several months while you continue your research.

Disney Vacation Club members can make reservations at their home resorts starting 11 months before their trip. See page 131 for information on how to rent points from a DVC member.

- **Investigate whether trip insurance makes sense for your situation.** If you'll be traveling to Disney World during peak hurricane season (August and September), it might be worthwhile. Third-party policies, such as those from insuremytrip.com, are usually cheaper than Disney's trip insurance, and often more comprehensive.

- **If you're not a US citizen, make sure your family's passports and visas are in order.** Passports typically need to be valid for six months beyond your travel dates. An electronic US visa is typically good for two years from the date of issue, if you need one. See esta.cbp.dhs.gov /esta for details.

9–7 Months Before Your Trip
Now is the time to start thinking about where you'll be eating and what you want to do in the theme parks.

- **Get familiar with Disney World restaurants** (see Part Four). When Disney's dining system opens at your 180-day mark, you can make reservations. See touringplans.com/walt-disney-world/dining for current menus and prices at every Disney restaurant, all searchable.

  Disney Vacation Club members can make reservations outside their home resorts starting seven months before their trip.

- **Also get familiar with the Disney Dining Plan** (see Part Three, page 242). If you're planning to stay at a Disney hotel, you'll need to figure out if the plan will save you money on the restaurants you've identified.

- **Check the best days to visit each park.** Use our Disney World Crowd Calendar to select the parks that you'll visit on each day of your trip: touringplans.com/walt-disney-world/crowd-calendar.

6–4 Months Before Your Trip
Become familiar with the rides, shows, and attractions at Disney World's four theme parks, and start planning what you'll see each day. This will help you identify any potential bottlenecks, which you can address using our touring plans and Disney's FastPass+ system. You'll be able to make FastPass+ reservations in a few weeks.

- **Review the attractions and shows** at the Magic Kingdom (page 514), Epcot (page 570, Disney's Animal Kingdom (page 609), and Disney's Hollywood Studios (page 641).

- **Make a list of must-see attractions in each park.** If you're unsure about your child experiencing a particular attraction, see our Small-Child Fright Potential Chart on pages 432–436. Every attraction is listed, along with information on its potential to scare children. Also see on page 437 a chart that shows height requirements for different attraction. Finally, you can preview attractions on YouTube at tinyurl.com /wdw-ride-videos.

- **Review our touring plans** (see page 85) and use them to begin putting together a preliminary touring strategy for each park. You can also use our touring plan software: See touringplans.com/walt-disney-world /touring-plans. By starting now, you'll be able to see which attractions would benefit from FastPass+, which you can reserve 60 or 30 days before your trip. You'll also see whether you'll need the Park Hopper option on your theme park tickets, which you'll purchase later.

180 Days Before Your Trip

Now you can start making dining, recreation, and other reservations.

- **Make sit-down-dining reservations** beginning at 6 a.m. Eastern time online at disneyworld.disney.go.com/dining or at 7 a.m. by telephone: ☎ 407-WDW-DINE (see page 321 for tips). If you're staying at a Disney resort, you can make reservations for up to 10 days of your trip today.
- **Revisit the economics of the Disney Dining Plan** after you've made dining reservations, to verify it's still worth the money. If not, call Disney to drop it from your reservation.
- **Make reservations for the following:**

  Theme park tours (page 741): ☎ 407-WDW-TOUR

  Recreational activities (such as boating): ☎ 407-WDW-PLAY

  Spa treatments (page 774): ☎ 407-WDW-SPAS

  Bibbidi Bobbidi Boutique (page 751): ☎ 407-WDW-STYLE

  Theme park dessert parties (pages 555 and 604): ☎ 407-WDW-DINE

120 Days Before Your Trip

As your vacation approaches, it's time to make concrete arrangements for your days in the theme parks.

- **Purchase your park admission** at least this far in advance (see pages 64 and 65 for ticket details and add-ons). Our online Least Expensive Ticket Calculator tool will find you the best discounts on Disney tickets: touringplans.com/walt-disney-world/ticket-calculator.
- **Link your tickets to your My Disney Experience account** so you can make FastPass+ reservations at the 30- or 60-day mark.
- **Save money on stroller rentals in the parks** (if needed) by renting from a third-party company; see page 426 for our recommendations. You can save on **wheelchair and ECV rentals** by using third-party companies, too; see page 465 for details and recommendations.

60 Days Before Your Trip

The theme for this week is "the three F's": **F**astPass+, **f**itness, and re**f**unds. (If you're a stickler for precision, substitute *funds retrieval* for *refunds*.)

- **Disney resort guests can make FastPass+ reservations** (see page 89) beginning at midnight Eastern time. Once that's done, update your touring plans. If you're using our online touring plans, we'll redo your schedule so that you get to your chosen attractions on time.
- **Start a walking regimen** to prepare for the 7–10 miles per day you may be walking in the parks. See page 414 for more on that.
- **If you decide not to go to Disney World,** you have 30 days to cancel most Disney vacation packages without penalty; room-only reservations can be canceled without penalty until five days before your trip. See page 126 for a review of Disney's cancellation policies. Otherwise, you can start your online check-in at Disney resorts 60 days before you arrive: disneyworld.disney.go.com/trip/online-check-in.

45 Days Before Your Trip

- **Final payment is due for Disney vacation packages that start in 2017.** Final payment for room-only reservations is due at check-in. If you book online within 45 days of arrival, however, full payment is required when you make the reservation.

- **Customize and order your MagicBands** (page 73) if staying on-site.
- **Make Disney's Magical Express reservations** (page 479) if flying, or make other transportation arrangements.
- **If you want to switch resorts** or make additional dining reservations, now is a good time to check, owing to cancellations at the 45-day mark.

30 Days Out

- **Off-site guests can make FastPass+ reservations** (see page 94) beginning at midnight Eastern time.
- **Confirm park hours** and finish preliminary touring plans.
- **Download our Lines app** so you can follow your touring plan and get updates in the parks: touringplans.com/disney-world-app.
- **Arrange to stop delivery of mail and newspapers.**
- **Arrange for pet or house sitters.**

2 Weeks Out

- **Arrange grocery delivery to your resort** (see Part Eight, page 512).
- **If you're flying to the US from another country,** complete the **Advance Passenger Information and Secure Flight** (**APIS**) process at least 72 hours before your flight. You should be able to do this through your airline's website; otherwise, make sure your travel agent has your information. You'll need to provide the address where you'll be staying in the US, so have that information handy when you complete this form. See tinyurl.com/ustravel-apis for details.
- **Check that you have enough prescription medication.**

6 Days Out

- This is your last chance to **cancel Disney room-only reservations** *booked online* without a penalty. Call ☎ 407-W-DISNEY to do so.
- **Check the weather forecast** for Orlando: tinyurl.com/wdw-weather.
- **Start packing.** See tinyurl.com/wdw-packing-tips for our tips.

5 Days Out

- **Fax your room request to Disney.** We can do this for you automatically—see tinyurl.com/wdw-hotel-fax for details.
- This is your last chance to **cancel Disney room-only reservations** *booked by phone or travel agent* without a penalty. Call ☎ 407-W-DISNEY to do so.

4 Days Out

- **Purchase Disney's Memory Maker photo package** (see Part Eight, page 510) at least three days in advance to ensure that all photos are linked as soon as you arrive. You'll also get a $20 discount if you buy your package ahead of time.

2 Days Out

- **Last chance to cancel reservations at Victoria & Albert's restaurant or any behind-the-scenes tours.**

The Day Before

- **Check in to your airline online.**
- **Finish Disney resort online check-in,** if you haven't already done so: disneyworld.disney.go.com/trip/online-check-in.

- **Cancel any unneeded dining or babysitting reservations.**
- **Do one last check of park hours and weather.**

How to Plan in a Hurry

We get variations on this e-mail a lot:

> *OMG! Our first Disney trip is in three weeks and I just found out about the* Unofficial Guide. *I had no idea about all the preparation I should have done! What do I do?*

One minute you're in the Taco Bell drive-through, the next you're throwing clothes in suitcases. We've all been there. But guess what? *Three weeks is plenty of time!* You'll still want to go through the timeline in the previous section, because those steps are important, if not mandatory—you'll just do most of them sooner.

If your preferred places to eat are already booked, check out our guide on page 322 that shows highly rated alternatives to hard-to-get restaurants. Also check TouringPlans.com for advice.

You'll also want to follow the touring plans in the back of this book—they're your insurance against long waits in line. They recommend which FastPass+ reservations to get, and when. If our recommendations aren't available, our free touring plan software can make alternative suggestions and work with whatever FastPasses you can get.

DISNEY ONLINE: OFFICIAL AND OTHERWISE

A SET OF HIGH-TECH ENHANCEMENTS to Disney's theme parks and hotels, officially known as **MyMagic+,** includes issuing rubber wristbands (**MagicBands**) with embedded computer chips that function as admission tickets and hotel keys; it also encompasses Disney's **FastPass+** ride-reservation system and its dining-reservation system.

MyMagic+ requires you to make detailed decisions about every day of your trip, up to two months in advance, if you want to avoid long waits in line (see the previous section for a complete trip-planning timeline). FastPass+ requires that you make reservations months in advance to ride Disney's headliner attractions, if you want any chance of avoiding long waits in line; other features, such as MagicBands and restaurant reservations, require you to provide detailed information about your traveling party.

The Walt Disney World website (disneyworld.com) and mobile app are the "glue" that binds all of this together. Because you've got to plan so much before you leave home, we cover the basics of the website and app in the following section. While we provide navigational instructions here, Disney's web designers change direction faster than hypercaffeinated squirrels in traffic, so you may have to hunt around to find some features. Full coverage of MagicBands starts on page 73; details on FastPass+ start on page 94.

My Disney Experience at DisneyWorld.com

A lot of work has gone into the Disney website. You can make hotel, dining, and some recreation reservations; buy admission; and get park hours, attraction information, and much more.

The most important of the site's features support My Disney Experience. To make use of some of these, you'll need to register by providing your e-mail address and choosing a password. You'll also need to have valid theme park tickets; if you've reserved a room at a Disney-owned hotel, have that reservation number handy as well.

GETTING STARTED In the upper-right corner of the homepage, click "My Disney Experience" to access a welcome page with links to existing hotel and dining reservations. Click the "My Family & Friends" link, then enter the names and ages of everyone traveling with you. You'll need this information when you make your FastPass+ and dining reservations.

Back on the "My Disney Experience" page, click "My Itinerary" in the top right corner of the page. A calendar will then appear—if you've got a Disney-hotel reservation, the calendar should display those dates of travel. If not, you'll need to manually enter your reservation number, then select your travel dates using the calendar.

For each day of your trip, the website will display operating hours for the theme and water parks. Select the theme park you'll be visiting on a particular day; if you're visiting more than one, select the one at which you want to make reservations now.

MAKING DINING RESERVATIONS From the "My Itinerary" page, click the "Reserve Dining" link. (You may have to reenter your travel dates.) A list of every Disney World eatery will be displayed. Use the filtering criteria at the top of the page to narrow the list.

Once you've settled on a restaurant, click the restaurant's name to check availability for your dining time and the number of people in your party. If space is available and you want to make a reservation, you'll need to indicate which members of your party will be joining you. If you want to make other dining reservations, you'll need to repeat this process for every reservation.

Once you've made your initial set of FastPass+ and dining reservations, you'll be able to view and edit them (along with your hotel reservation) in the "My Reservation" section of My Disney Experience.

MAKING FASTPASS+ RESERVATIONS Click the "FastPass+" link from the menu on the right side of your screen, then select "New FastPass+." On the next screen, indicate which members of your group will be with you. On the screen after that, choose the park and date on which you're visiting. *At press time, you could make advance FastPass+ reservations at just one park per day.*

Now you'll see a list of your chosen park's participating FastPass+ attractions. Select the ones you'd like to reserve; if an attraction isn't selectable, either all of its available FastPass+ reservations are gone or the attraction is closed at the time shown.

At this point, the website will give you a "Best Match" set of Fast-Pass+ reservations and return times for your attractions, plus three optional sets of return times. Select the set that most closely fits the rest of your plans for the day, or, if you're using our touring plans, select the set that most closely matches the suggested FastPass+ return times on the plans. After confirming your selections, you can check for alternative return-time windows for each attraction.

You'll need to repeat these steps for every day for which you want to use FastPass+ in the theme parks. Having fun yet?

If you're unsure of the attractions or times of day for which you should use FastPass+, our touring plan software can make recommendations that will minimize your time in line. See page 94 for details.

My Disney Experience Mobile App

Along with the website, Disney offers a companion app on iTunes, Google Play, and the Amazon Appstore for Android (search for "My Disney Experience"). It includes park hours, attraction operating hours and descriptions, restaurant hours with descriptions and menus, the ability to make FastPass+ and dining reservations online, GPS-based directions, the locations of park photographers, and more. My Disney Experience is optimized for the latest phones and tablets, so some features may not be available on all devices.

My Disney Experience has improved a lot since it was first rolled out, although it gives you only Disney's "official" information, including (we believe) intentionally wrong attraction wait times so you'll go elsewhere in the park. (Most other theme parks do the same thing.)

Our Recommended Websites

Searching online for Disney information is like navigating an immense maze for a tiny piece of cheese: There's a lot of information out there, but you may find a lot of dead ends before you get what you want. Our picks follow.

BEST Q&A SITE Walt Disney World's **Mom's Panel** consists of mothers chosen from among 10,000-plus applicants. Unpaid and unbiased, the panelists have a website, **disneyworldmoms.com,** where they offer tips and discuss how to plan a Disney World vacation. Several moms have specialized experience in areas such as Disney Cruise Line, runDisney, and traveling with sports groups; some speak Spanish, too.

BEST GENERAL UNOFFICIAL WALT DISNEY WORLD WEBSITE Besides TouringPlans.com, Deb Wills's **AllEars.net** is the first website we recommend to friends who want to make a trip to Disney World. Updated several times a week, the site includes breaking news, tons of photos, Disney restaurant menus, resort and ticket information, tips for guests with special needs, and more. We also check **wdwmagic.com** for news and happenings around Walt Disney World.

BEST MONEY-SAVING SITE MouseSavers (mousesavers.com) keeps an updated list of discounts for use at Disney resorts. Discounts are separated into categories such as "For the general public" and "For residents of certain states." Anyone who calls or books online can use a current discount. Savings can be considerable—up to 40% in many cases. MouseSavers also has deals on rental cars and non-Disney hotels in the area, along with a calendar showing when Disney sales typically launch.

BEST WALT DISNEY WORLD PREVIEW SITE TouringPlans.com offers free videos or photos of every Disney attraction. Videos of indoor ("dark") rides are sometimes inferior to those of outdoor rides due to poor lighting, but even the videos and photos of indoor rides generally provide a good sense of what the attraction is about. **YouTube** is also an excellent place to find videos of Disney and other Central Florida attractions.

SOCIAL MEDIA Facebook, Twitter, and **Instagram** are popular places for Disneyphiles to gather online and share tips and photos. **Disney World's**

official social-media outlets are **facebook.com/waltdisneyworld, twitter .com/waltdisneyworld,** and **instagram.com/waltdisneyworld.**

BEST THEME-PARK-INSIDER SITE If you have a yen for behind-the-scenes gossip, check out **Jim Hill Media (jimhillmedia.com).** Jim's got insider accounts of the politics, frantic project management, and pipe dreams that combine to create the attractions that Disney and Universal build.

BEST DISNEY DISCUSSION BOARDS There are tons of these; among the most active boards are **disboards.com, forums.wdwmagic.com,** our own **forum.touringplans.com,** and, for Brits, **thedibb.co.uk** (DIBB stands for "Disney Information Bulletin Board").

BEST SITE FOR GUESTS WITH FOOD ALLERGIES At **allergyeats.com /disney,** you put in your allergies and your park, and it shows you where and what you can eat.

BEST SITES FOR TRAFFIC, ROADWORK, CONSTRUCTION, AND SAFETY INFORMATION Visit **cfxway.com** for the latest information on roadwork in Orlando and Orange County.

A seven-year construction project to improve I-4 was launched in 2015. Information on the northern section between Kirkman Road (near Universal) and downtown Orlando can be found at **i4ultimate .com.** Construction updates on the southern section from Kirkman Road to US 27 in Polk County are available at **i4express.com.**

Check **tinyurl.com/childsafetyfl** to learn about state child-restraint requirements. Finally, we like **maps.google.com** for driving directions.

WHEN *to* GO *to* WALT DISNEY WORLD

Why do they call it tourist season if we can't shoot them?

—Palatka, Florida, outdoorsman

SELECTING THE TIME OF YEAR FOR YOUR VISIT

WALT DISNEY WORLD IS BUSIEST from Christmas Day through the first few days of January. Next busiest are spring break (mid-March through Easter week); Thanksgiving week; the first few weeks of June, when summer vacation starts; and the week of Presidents' Day.

The least-busy time *historically* is Labor Day through the beginning of October—but see our caveat below. Next slowest is mid-January, after the Martin Luther King Jr. holiday weekend, through Presidents' Day in February (except when the Walt Disney World Marathon is held after MLK Day). The weeks after Thanksgiving and before Christmas are less crowded than average, as is mid-April–mid-May, between spring break and Memorial Day.

Late February, March, and early April are dicey. Crowds ebb and flow according to spring-break schedules and the timing of Presidents' Day weekend. Besides being asphalt-melting hot, July brings throngs of South American tourists on their winter holiday.

In both the fall of 2016 and the late winter and spring of 2017, crowds at all parks far surpassed the attendance of previous years. A New Orleans couple describes their experience:

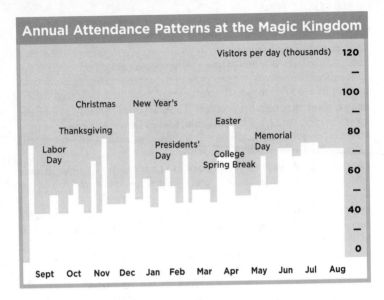

Annual Attendance Patterns at the Magic Kingdom

Visitors per day (thousands)

Everything we read led us to believe that October after Columbus Day and before Halloween week would be relatively uncrowded. Nothing prepared us for the crowds we experienced. I may not have understood the crowd estimates, but barely being able to move was not what I expected. At Epcot, people were sitting on the cement to eat—I felt like I was at an "Ungrateful Dead" concert! In fairness, the cast members were absolutely awesome, which went a long way toward at least giving Disney one more chance—just not in October.

The basic rule of thumb is that Walt Disney World is more crowded when school is out and less crowded when kids are in school. However, Disney has become increasingly adept at loading slow periods of the year with special events, conventions, food festivals, and the like; discounts on rooms and dining during slower periods also figure in, as does the number of employees Disney decides to use in the parks.

We thought the large crowds were an anomaly, but they've persisted into early 2017. We're reasonably confident that some of this is due to a reduction in the number of people running the rides. The employees we spoke to indicated that a hiring freeze began in fall 2016, for example, just as we saw a substantial increase in the average wait in line.

In short: The World can be packed at any time, and you need to dig a little deeper than merely the time of year to pinpoint the least crowded dates. For a calendar of scheduled Disney events, see touringplans.com /walt-disney-world/events#. Huge conventions at the Orange County Convention Center also contribute to the problem—go to occc.net /global/calendar.asp and click on any meeting slated during your Disney dates to view the expected attendance. (Don't worry about conventions with fewer than 10,000 attendees unless you want to book a hotel in the International Drive area.)

Other factors affecting crowding and long lines include a combination of closed rides and an improving US economy. As a result, we've added more data about ride closures and economic indicators to our Crowd Calendar forecasts.

The Downside of Off-Season Touring

Though we strongly recommend going to Disney World in the fall, winter, or spring, there are a few trade-offs. The parks often close early during the off-season, either because of low crowds or special events such as the Halloween and Christmas parties at the Magic Kingdom. This drastically reduces touring hours. Even when crowds are small, it's difficult to see big parks such as the Magic Kingdom between 9 a.m. and 7 p.m. Early closing also usually means no evening parades or fireworks. And because these are slow times, some rides and attractions may be closed. Finally, Central Florida temperatures fluctuate wildly during late fall, winter, and early spring; daytime highs in the 40s and 50s aren't uncommon.

Given the choice, however, smaller crowds, bargain prices, and stress-free touring are worth risking cold weather or closed attractions. Touring in fall and other "off" periods is so much easier that our research team, at the risk of being blasphemous, would advise taking children out of school for a Disney World visit. For the pros and cons of this approach, see page 412.

DON'T FORGET AUGUST Kids go back to school pretty early in Florida (and in a lot of other places, too). This makes mid- to late August a good time to visit Walt Disney World for families who can't vacation during the off-season. A New Jersey mother of two school-age children spells it out:

The end of August is the PERFECT time to go (just watch out for hurricanes; it's the season). There were virtually no wait times, 20 minutes at the most.

A family from Roxbury, New Jersey, agrees:

I recommend the last two weeks of August for anyone traveling there during the summer. We have visited twice during this time of year and have had great success touring the parks.

HIGH-LOW, HIGH-LOW, IT'S OFF TO DISNEY WE GO Though we recommend off-season touring, we realize that it's not possible for many families. We want to make it clear, therefore, that you can have a wonderful experience regardless of when you go. Our advice, irrespective of season, is to arrive early at the parks and avoid the crowds by using one of our touring plans. If attendance is light, kick back and forget the touring plans.

ATTENDANCE TRENDS Disney's theme parks showed small attendance drops in 2016, while Universal's parks showed solid gains (see chart on next page). Both still posted increases in revenue, however. In Disney's case, that money came from charging fewer people much higher prices.

WE'VE GOT WEATHER! Long before Walt Disney World, tourists visited Florida year-round to enjoy the temperate tropical and subtropical climates. The best weather months generally are October, November, March, and April (see chart on page 45). Fall is usually dry, whereas spring is wetter. December, January, and February vary, with average highs of 72°–73°F intermixed with highs in the 50°–65°F range. May is

TOP 10 NORTH AMERICAN THEME PARKS

	THEME PARK	2016 ATTENDANCE	CHANGE FROM 2015	DAILY AVERAGE
1.	The Magic Kingdom	20.39 million	-0.5%	55,877
2.	Disneyland	17.94 million	-1.8%	49,159
3.	Epcot	11.71 million	-0.7%	32,088
4.	Disney's Animal Kingdom	10.84 million	-0.7%	29,709
5.	Disney's Hollywood Studios	10.78 million	-0.5%	29,523
6.	Universal Studios Florida	9.99 million	+4.3%	26,260
7.	Universal's Islands of Adventure	9.36 million	+6.5%	25,649
8.	Disney California Adventure	9.29 million	-0.9%	25,466
9.	Universal Studios Hollywood	8.09 million	+13.9%	22,153
10.	SeaWorld Orlando	4.40 million	-7.9%	12,060

Source: *Themed Entertainment Association/AECOM Theme Index and Museum Index: The Global Attractions Attendance Report 2016* (released June 1, 2017)

hot but tolerable. June, July, August, and September are the warmest months. Rain is possible anytime, usually in the form of scattered thunderstorms. An entire day of rain is unusual.

CROWD CONDITIONS AND THE BEST AND WORST PARKS TO VISIT FOR EACH DAY OF THE YEAR We receive thousands of inquiries about crowd conditions on specific dates throughout the year.

Readers also want to know which park is best to visit on each day of their stay. To make things easier for you (and us), we provide at TouringPlans.com a calendar covering the next year (click "Crowd Calendar" on the homepage). For each date, we offer a crowd-level index based on a scale of 1–10, with 1 being least crowded and 10 being most crowded. Our calendar takes into account all holidays, special events, and more, as described on the next page.

Because Disney is constantly testing resort discounts and tinkering with park hours, it's just not possible to include an accurate calendar in this book. Keeping the online Crowd Calendar updated requires year-round work from our statisticians. Thus, we have to charge a modest subscription fee. The same fee also provides access to additional touring plans and other features. Owners of the current edition of this guide are eligible for a substantial discount on the subscription. See the beginning of this chapter for more information about our website.

A Bristol, Tennessee, couple had good luck with the calendar:

The UG Crowd Calendar is 100% accurate. We love it and will continue to use it every trip. We even tested it in heavy-duty crowds just to see if it worked, and you were dead-on correct!

But a Braintree, Massachusetts, woman cautions:

It should be emphasized that parks can still feel really crowded on a low-crowd day, especially the Magic Kingdom. But you will notice the difference when you see the wait times for the rides. Anyone

Walt Disney World Climate

	JAN	FEB	MAR	APR	MAY	JUN	JUL	AUG	SEP	OCT	NOV	DEC
AVERAGE DAILY LOW												
	47°F	50°F	54°F	59°F	65°F	71°F	73°F	73°F	72°F	66°F	58°F	51°F
AVERAGE DAILY HIGH												
	71°F	73°F	78°F	83°F	89°F	91°F	92°F	92°F	90°F	84°F	78°F	72°F
AVERAGE DAILY TEMPERATURE												
	60°F	61°F	67°F	71°F	77°F	81°F	82°F	83°F	81°F	75°F	68°F	62°F
AVERAGE DAILY HUMIDITY PERCENTAGE												
	62	73	71	70	71	70	74	76	76	75	74	73
AVERAGE RAINFALL PER MONTH												
	2.9"	2.7"	4.0"	2.3"	3.1"	8.3"	7.0"	7.7"	5.1"	2.5"	2.1"	2.9"
NUMBER OF DAYS OF RAIN PER MONTH												
	6	7	8	6	8	14	17	16	14	9	6	6

expecting to have room to roam freely in certain parts of the Magic Kingdom on a low attendance day will be disappointed. The same is true for Animal Kingdom: We went there on a "low" attendance day in the afternoon, and it was extremely congested and difficult to walk through some areas of the park.

Even on a slow day, you may find waits of 30–45 minutes or more on popular rides such as Seven Dwarfs Mine Train at the Magic Kingdom and Test Track at Epcot. To save on maintenance costs, Disney doesn't run most rides at 100% of their capacity when crowds are low. Instead, they run fewer mine trains, test cars, and other vehicles and assume that most people simply expect a certain amount of waiting at a theme park. Running fewer vehicles means less wear and tear on the track, cars, and other moving parts—which saves Disney money—without generating many complaints.

HOW WE DETERMINE CROWD LEVELS AND BEST DAYS A number of factors contribute to the models we use to predict both crowd levels and the best days to visit each theme park.

Data we use to predict crowd levels:

- Historical wait times from the same time period in past years
- Historical theme park hours from the same time period in past years
- Future hotel-room bookings in the Orlando area
- Disney's special-events calendar (for example, Mickey's Not-So-Scary Halloween Party)
- Legal holidays in the United States
- Public-school schedules (including spring-break schedules for the 100 largest school districts east of the Mississippi River, plus Massachusetts and Connecticut)

We collect thousands of wait times from every Disney park every day, including posted and actual times. Historical park hours include the actual operating hours for all of the theme parks over the past five years. Special events include everything from official Walt Disney World–sanctioned events to such independent events as Gay Days. Our Central

Florida tourism demographics cover everything from where Orlando visitors come from and how long they stay to how many people make up each party and which theme parks they visit.

CROWD-CALENDAR REASONING AND ACCURACY Our online Crowd Calendar explains why we rate the parks a specific way on a specific day, including how we weigh each of the factors listed on the previous page. The site also shows you our predictions versus actual crowd levels for past days, so you can see how we fared with our predictions.

A mom from Edmonds, Washington, however, thinks maybe we overlooked something, writing:

> Crowd level—in your estimates, are you sure you're including everyone from the country of Brazil? Because they're all there!

EXTRA MAGIC HOURS

EXTRA MAGIC HOURS (EMHS) is a perk for families staying at a Walt Disney World resort, including the Swan, Dolphin, and Shades of Green. On selected days of the week, Disney resort guests will be able to enter a Disney theme park 1 hour earlier or stay in a selected theme park about 2 hours later than the official park-operating hours. Theme park visitors not staying at a Disney resort may stay in the park for Extra Magic Hour evenings, but they can't experience any rides, attractions, or shows. In other words, they can shop and eat. The swimming theme parks, Typhoon Lagoon and Blizzard Beach, rarely offer EMHs. If they do, it's usually during the summer.

WHAT'S REQUIRED? A valid admission ticket or MagicBand wristband is required to enter the park, and you must show your Disney resort ID or have your MagicBand scanned when entering. For evening EMHs, you may be asked to show your Disney resort ID or MagicBand to experience rides or attractions.

WHEN ARE EMHS OFFERED? You can check the Crowd Calendar at TouringPlans.com for the dates of your visit, check the parks calendar at disneyworld.com, or call Walt Disney World Information at ☎ 407-824-4321 or 407-939-6244 (press 0 for a live representative).

In addition to these, it's common for Epcot to have evening EMHs on Wednesdays or Thursdays in September and October, and for Animal Kingdom to have morning EMHs on any day except Tuesday and Thursday later in the year.

TYPICAL EXTRA MAGIC HOURS SCHEDULE THROUGH OCTOBER 2017 *(frequently varies)*						
MORNING						
MON	TUES	WED	THUR	FRI	SAT	SUN
Animal Kingdom	–	–	Epcot	Magic Kingdom	Animal Kingdom	DHS
EVENING						
MON	TUES	WED	THUR	FRI	SAT	SUN
–	Epcot	Magic Kingdom	–	DHS	–	–

WHAT DO EXTRA MAGIC HOURS MEAN TO YOU? Disney seems to use EMHs in two ways: to provide Disney resort guests some extra park time on days when those parks are traditionally crowded, and as an incentive to visit one park on days when another park is typically more crowded.

Crowds range from slightly below average to average at Animal Kingdom and the Magic Kingdom on days when those parks host Extra Magic Hours. Crowds are larger than average at Disney's Hollywood Studios, and slightly higher than average at Epcot, on EMH days.

Not many families have the stamina to take advantage of morning and evening EMHs on consecutive days. If you have to choose between morning or evening sessions, consider first whether your family functions better getting up early or staying up late. Also, consider the time at which the parks close to day guests. Evening EMHs are most useful when the crowds are low and the parks close relatively early to the general public, so your family doesn't have to stay up past midnight to take advantage of the perk.

unofficial **TIP**
If you're going to get up early for one morning Extra Magic Hour session during your vacation, make sure that it's for the Magic Kingdom.

MORNING EXTRA MAGIC HOURS *(a.k.a. Early Entry)*

MORNING EXTRA MAGIC HOURS are offered at all four theme parks throughout the year, and rarely (during summer) at Blizzard Beach and Typhoon Lagoon water parks. Several days of the week, Disney resort guests are invited to enter a designated theme park 1 hour before the general public. During this hour, guests can enjoy selected attractions opened early just for them.

How Early Entry Affects Attendance at the Theme Parks

Morning Extra Magic Hours strongly affect attendance at Disney's Hollywood Studios and Epcot, especially during busier times of year. Crowds at those parks are usually larger than average, as a Winston-Salem, North Carolina, mom discovered:

> *Disney Hollywood Studios was a MADHOUSE. Do NOT go on Extra Magic Hours days. After spending about 3 hours to ride three rides, I just wanted to trample the people stampeding to the exit.*

Magic Kingdom crowds are about average when it has morning EMHs (usually Thursday). Because Disney's Animal Kingdom typically has two morning EMHs but no evening EMHs, crowds are spread out, resulting in lower-than-average waits on both days.

If you're staying at a Disney resort, remember these three things about Extra Magic Hours:

1. The Magic Kingdom has more attractions open for morning EMHs than any other park. Coupled with a good touring plan, we think the Magic Kingdom's morning session is the most worthwhile of any EMHs at any park.

2. Morning EMHs are least useful at Disney's Animal Kingdom because it has fewer rides overall. There's simply not as much benefit for the lost sleep.

3. If you think it unlikely that you'll be at the park offering morning Extra Magic Hours 30 minutes before it opens, visit another park instead.

During holidays and summer, when Disney hotels are full, getting in early makes a tremendous difference in crowds at the designated park. The program funnels so many people into the EMH park that it fills by about 10 a.m. and is practically gridlocked by noon. A mother of three from Lee's Summit, Missouri, writes:

> Our first full day at WDW, we went to the Magic Kingdom on an early-entry day for resort guests. We were there at 7:30 a.m. and were able to walk onto all the rides in Fantasyland with no wait. At 8:45 a.m. we positioned ourselves at the Adventureland rope and ran toward Splash Mountain when the rope dropped. We were able to ride Splash Mountain with no wait and then Big Thunder with about a 15-minute wait. We then went straight to the Jungle Cruise and the wait was already 30 minutes, so we skipped it. The park became incredibly crowded as the day progressed, and we were all exhausted from getting up so early. We left the park around noon. After that day, I resolved to avoid early-entry days and instead be at a non-early-entry park about a half-hour before official opening time.

Note that during holidays, the Magic Kingdom opens to regular guests at 8 a.m. Morning EMHs begin at 7 a.m., so you'll need to be at the Magic Kingdom entrance at around 6:30 a.m. You won't be alone, but relatively few people are willing to get up that early for a theme park, and your first hour in the parks will be (pardon us) magical.

This note from a North Bend, Washington, dad emphasizes the importance of arriving at the beginning of the early-entry period.

> We only used early entry once—to Disney's Hollywood Studios. We got there 20 minutes after early entry opened, and the wait for Tower of Terror was 1½ hours long without FastPass+. We skipped it.

Morning Extra Magic Hours and Park-Hopping

An alternative strategy for Disney resort guests is to take advantage of morning Extra Magic Hours, but only until the designated park gets crowded. At that time, move to another park.

A Dillsburg, Pennsylvania, mom has another tip:

> If you have FastPass+ opportunities [see page 94], schedule them for the park you're visiting second.

This works particularly well at the Magic Kingdom for families with young children who love the attractions in Fantasyland. However, it will take you about an hour to commute to the second park of the day. If, for example, you depart the Magic Kingdom for Disney's Hollywood Studios at 11 a.m., you'll find the Studios pretty crowded when you arrive at about noon, as this Texas mom found:

> We made the mistake of doing a morning at the Magic Kingdom and an afternoon at the Studios. Worst idea ever. By the time we got to the Studios, all the [FastPass+ reservations] were gone for Toy Story Mania!, the Tower of Terror, and Rock 'n' Roller Coaster. And all three rides had at least 90-minute waits.

Keeping these and other considerations in mind, here are some tips:

1. Use the morning-EMH-park-hopping strategy during the less busy times of year when the parks close early. You'll get a jump on the general public and add an hour to what, in the off-season, is an already short touring day.

2. Use the morning–EMH–park-hopping strategy to complete touring a second park that you've already visited on a previous day, or specifically to see live entertainment in the second park.

The Animal Kingdom's latest changes, including to Kilimanjaro Safaris and the new Pandora land, offer nighttime effects. Many guests make return or special trips back to the park after dark. Also, it may not be a good idea to hop to the Studios—so many attractions here are closed for construction that crowds often build very quickly.

On any day except its EMH days, hopping to Epcot is usually good. Epcot is equipped to handle large crowds better than any other Disney park, minimizing the effects of a midday arrival. Also, World Showcase has a large selection of interesting dining options, making it a good choice for evening touring.

Don't hop to the park with morning EMHs. The idea is to avoid crowds, not join them. Finally, limit your hopping to two parks per day. Hopping to a third park in one day would result in more time spent commuting than saved by avoiding crowds.

Evening Extra Magic Hours

The evening Extra Magic Hours program lets Disney resort guests enjoy a different theme park on specified nights for about 2 hours after it closes to the general public. Guests pay no additional charge to participate but must scan their MagicBands (see page 73) at each ride or attraction they wish to experience. You can also show up at the turnstiles at any point after evening Extra Magic Hours have started. Note that if you've been in another park that day, you'll need the Park Hopper feature on your admission ticket to enter. Evening Extra Magic Hours are offered at the Magic Kingdom, Epcot, and Disney's Hollywood Studios, but not (yet) at Disney's Animal Kingdom.

Evening sessions are usually more crowded at the Magic Kingdom and the Studios than at Epcot. Those evening EMH crowds can be just as large as those throughout the day. During summer, when the Magic Kingdom's evening EMH session runs until 1 a.m., lines at headliner attractions can still be long at midnight. A mom from Fairhaven, Massachusetts, doesn't mince words:

I say steer clear of a park that is open late. There are only a few attractions open and tons of people trying to get on them.

Hours are almost always offered at the Magic Kingdom, Epcot, and Disney's Hollywood Studios. Animal Kingdom offered evening EMHs during early summer 2017 but, as we went to press, not beyond that.

SUMMER AND HOLIDAYS

A READER FROM COLUMBUS, OHIO, once observed, "The main thing I learned from your book is not to go during the summer or at holiday times. Once you know that, you don't need a guidebook."

While we might argue with the reader's conclusion, we agree that avoiding summer and holidays is a wise strategy. That said, we also understand that many folks have no choice concerning the time of year they visit Disney World. Much of this book, in fact, is dedicated to making sure those readers who visit during busier times enjoy their experience. Sure, off-season touring is preferable, but, armed with knowledge and some strategy, you can have a great time whenever you visit.

To put things in perspective, early summer (up to about June 15) and late summer (after August 15) aren't nearly as crowded as the intervening period. And even midsummer crowds pale in comparison to the hordes during holiday periods. If you visit in midsummer or during a holiday, the first thing you need to know is that the theme parks' guest capacity is not infinite. In fact, once a park reaches capacity, only Disney resort guests arriving via the Disney transportation system are allowed to enter. If you're not staying in the World, you may find yourself in a situation similar to this Boise, Idaho, dad's:

> The Magic Kingdom and Hollywood Studios were so full they closed the parks. For three days we couldn't enter those parks, so we were forced to go to Epcot and use up two days of our four-day pass. We paid for another night at our hotel to see if the crowds would let up, but no luck. All we could do was drive around Orlando and sightsee.

We hasten to point out that this reader would've had no difficulty gaining admission to the parks of his choice had he committed to being at the turnstiles 40–60 minutes before official opening time.

Packed-Parks Compensation Plan

The thought of teeming throngs jockeying for position in endless lines under the baking Fourth of July sun is enough to wilt the will and ears of the most ardent Mouseketeer. Disney, however, feeling bad about those long lines and challenging touring conditions on packed holidays, compensates patrons with a no-less-than-incredible array of first-rate live entertainment and events.

Shows, parades, concerts, and pageantry continue throughout the day. In the evening, so much is going on that you have to make tough choices. Concerts, parades, light shows, laser shows, fireworks, and dance productions occur almost continuously. Disney also provides colorful decorations for most holidays, plus special parades and live entertainment for Christmas, New Year's, Easter, and the Fourth of July, among others. (See "The Walt Disney World Calendar," next, for specific holiday advice.) No question about it: You *can* go to Walt Disney World on the Fourth of July or any crowded extended-hours day, never get on a ride, and still have a good time.

Hit your favorite rides early using one of our touring plans, then go back to your hotel for lunch, a swim, and perhaps a nap. If you're interested in the special parades and shows, return to the park in late afternoon or early evening. Assume that unless you use FastPass+, early morning will be the only time you can experience the attractions without long waits. Finally, don't wait until the last minute in the evening to leave the park—the exodus at closing is truly mind-boggling. Above all, bring your sense of humor, and pay attention to your group's morale.

THE WALT DISNEY WORLD CALENDAR

DISNEY CELEBRATES SPECIAL EVENTS throughout the year. Some events commemorate major holidays, while others have been designed specifically by Disney to boost attendance during otherwise-slow times of year.

JANUARY Usually held the second weekend after New Year's, the **Walt Disney World Marathon** pulls in more runners and their families every year. Some 100,000 runners participate in the event—enough to affect crowd conditions and pedestrian traffic throughout Disney World. In the spirit of participatory journalism, *Unofficial Guide* coauthor Len Testa usually runs one of the 5K, 10K, half, or full marathons. (Bob ices Len's tequila.) Following the marathon by a few days is the **Castaway Cay 5K,** but you'll need passage on Disney Cruise Line to run it. Information on all Disney running events can be found at rundisney.com. Also check mickeymilespodcast.com for in-depth coverage and tips.

Added to the calendar in 2017 was the **Epcot International Festival of the Arts.** Running from mid-January through mid-February, the festival features art, including Disney Art, food, entertainment, and workshops to further your creative skills. In 2017 the festival was included as part of your park admission. A Conroe, Texas, reader thought the festival was super, writing:

> I loved the Festival of the Arts. It's a great addition to Epcot. I really enjoyed talking to the artists and getting a print signed that I purchased. We had a lot of fun looking for Figment, and the magnets are great. The Broadway performers were exceptional. I am a big music fan and have been to hundreds of concerts, but I was blown away by their talent.

FEBRUARY Black History Month is celebrated throughout Walt Disney World with displays, artisans, storytellers, and entertainers. The Kinsey Collection at Epcot's United States Pavilion is a highlight.

In 2018, **Presidents' Day** is Monday, February 19, and **Mardi Gras** is Tuesday, February 13. These holidays will bring increases in attendance starting the weekend before. Usually held the second weekend of the month is the **Princess Half-Marathon** event, February 22–25 in 2018. The schedule includes a health expo, kids' races, a family 5K, a 10K, and the big race. The event draws more than 20,000 runners, enough to increase park attendance and affect vehicular and pedestrian traffic.

MARCH The **Epcot International Flower & Garden Festival** runs annually from early March to mid-May. Expert horticulturists showcase exotic floral displays and share gardening tips. The 30 million blooms from some 1,200 species will make your eyes pop, and best of all, the event doesn't seem to affect crowd levels at Epcot. The festival features food and beverage kiosks, making it more like September's Food & Wine event (see page 53), only with flowers.

APRIL Easter is April 11, 2018, so expect the two weeks on either side of that to be peak Spring Break season. April also has a **Star Wars Half-Marathon** (April 18–22 in 2018), another running event that draws tens of thousands of visitors. Finally, Disney usually announces a **"free"** Disney Dining Plan promotion around the last week of April for travel dates starting in August. See page 241 for more details.

JUNE Gay Days, an unofficial gathering of lesbian, gay, bisexual, and transgender (LGBT) people from around the world, has been happening annually at Walt Disney World since 1991. The celebration will take place on May 29–June 4, 2018. Organizers expect Gay Days to attract more than 160,000 visitors and their friends and families. For additional information, visit gaydays.com.

AUGUST Held on 32 nights in 2017 (August 25–November 1), **Mickey's Not-So-Scary Halloween Party** runs from 7 p.m. to midnight at the Magic Kingdom. The festivities include trick-or-treating in costume, parades, live music, storytelling, and a fireworks show. Advance tickets usually go on sale in early May and increase substantially every year. The 2017 prices (including tax) were $79–$122 for adults and $73–$117 for kids. Ticket prices rise as the date gets closer to Halloween; the October 31 party is the most expensive. Discounts are available for members of the US military, Disney Annual Pass holders, and Disney Vacation Club members. The least-crowded events are typically in September and on Tuesdays; tickets for the late-October dates usually sell out one to four days in advance. See tinyurl.com/mickeysnotsoscary for more information.

If you're wondering what "really crowded" looks like, here's how an Atlanta reader describes it:

> *The only time the crowds were unbearable was during the Halloween party. When I say it was sold out—man, was it sold out! Just moving 20 feet took forever. My 72-year-old mom ended up renting a scooter at the end of the day because her hip was bothering her. Anytime we wanted to go somewhere, it was an ordeal. The lines for the characters were off the chain, so we skipped them entirely. We loved the parade and the people in costume, but the intense crowds made it way less fun than we expected. Candy lines stayed long until the end, and we were glad we rode The Haunted Mansion early, as the end of the line was way past the* Liberty Belle *boat all evening.*

Fortunately, the party isn't always jam-packed. A Maryland family of four had a great experience:

> *Went to Mickey's Not-So-Scary Halloween Party. Had read a lot of mixed reviews both in your book and online, mostly complaining about crowds, and based on these reviews we almost decided to skip it but were talked out of it by a friend. The event was fantastic— plenty of trick-or-treating, a great parade, and no problems with rides. We are very glad we took our 5- and 8-year-olds.*

SEPTEMBER Radio personality Tom Joyner hosts an extremely popular party at Walt Disney World. Held Labor Day weekend (August 31– September 4 in 2017), the **Allstate Tom Joyner Family Reunion** typically features live musical performances, comedy acts, and family-oriented discussions. For information, visit familyreunion.blackamericaweb.com.

Night of Joy, a Christian-music festival, is staged at the ESPN Wide World of Sports Complex the first or second weekend of the month (September 7–8, 2017). About 15–20 nationally known acts perform concerts on Friday and Saturday evenings after the Complex has closed. For information or to purchase tickets, call ☎ 407-W-DISNEY (934-7639) or visit tinyurl.com/wdwnightofjoy. One-day concert-only advance tickets cost $48 per person for adults and children, including tax; two-day concert-only tickets are $73 in advance. (Same-day ticket prices hadn't been announced at press time, so call or check online for the latest information.) A one-day admission to any Walt Disney World theme park can be added on to a one- or two-day ticket and costs $67, including tax.

Those who say Christmas is the most wonderful time of year have never been to the **Epcot International Food & Wine Festival.** Held in World Showcase from September through mid-November, the celebration represents 25 nations and cuisines, including demonstrations, wine seminars, tastings, and opportunities to see some of the world's top chefs. Although many activities are included in Epcot admission, some workshops and tastings are by reservation only and cost more than $100. Call ☎ 407-WDW-DINE starting around the beginning of August for more information. We think the culinary demos and the wine-and-beverage seminars (about $15–$20 each) are the best values at the festival. Because most of the food kiosks are set up around World Showcase, it can be difficult to walk through the crowds at some of the popular spots. Wait times at Epcot's attractions, however, are affected only slightly.

The Food & Wine Festival is an exceptional event, but as a woman from New Springs, Missouri, explains, it also has its downside:

> World Showcase is one of our favorite parts of Disney World, but we will NEVER go there during the Food & Wine Festival again. Warnings would have been in order for families with children. We were elbowed aside, bumped into, pushed out of the way by "guests" who had been sampling alcohol at EVERY Food & Wine location. I get that people enjoy trying out new food and drink—but after my teen granddaughters had unwelcome comments aimed their way by drunk people, we decided to stay away from Epcot.

NOVEMBER The **Wine and Dine Half-Marathon** early this month (November 1–5 in 2017) revolves around a 13.1-mile race that ends with a nighttime party amid Epcot's International Food & Wine Festival. A 10K race is held the Saturday before the Sunday half, too. The number of runners and their "cheer squads"—combined with the guests who descend upon Epcot for the food festival alone—blows up the crowd levels like an agitated pufferfish. Again, vehicular and pedestrian traffic is disturbed by the running courses throughout Disney property.

DECEMBER The **Pop Warner Super Bowl** and **Pop Warner National Cheer & Dance Championships** are held at Disney World's ESPN Wide World of Sports Complex each year in early December. The 2017 championships run December 2–9. The Value resorts, especially All-Star Sports, fill up fast with these participants. Because they're competing, the 20,000 or so participants and their families tend to spend more time at Wide World of Sports than the parks.

The annual **Disney Parks Christmas Day Parade,** televised on December 25, is usually taped at the Magic Kingdom in mid- to late November or the first week of December. The parade ties up pedestrian traffic on Main Street, U.S.A. all day.

In 2016, Disney introduced **Seasonal Tastes** (taking place in 2017 from November 25 to December 30), as part of the Epcot Holidays Around the World celebration. Seasonal Tastes will feature food and beverage booths scattered around the World Showcase area, offering holiday-themed tasting portions.

Christmas and New Year's at the Theme Parks

Don't expect to see all the attractions in a single day of touring at any park. That said, Disney's Animal Kingdom is usually the least crowded park during the winter holidays, especially on New Year's Eve, because the park doesn't have fireworks. Epcot is a good choice, too, because it typically has lower crowds and about twice the land of the Magic Kingdom. (It also has fewer attractions, but many of them are high-capacity shows and rides.)

As with summer, your best bet during winter holidays is to arrive early, take a midday break, and head back to the parks around dusk. Touring in the evening will reward you with stunning displays of holiday decorations and slightly smaller crowds than during the day. In particular, Disney's Hollywood Studios is a good choice for evening touring. Crowds will be larger than normal, but the decorations make up for it.

A Bridgewater, Massachusetts, mom loves Disney World during the holidays but warns that it's not the best time for everyone:

> Having just completed our first holiday trip, I would never recommend a Christmas-week vacation for first-time visitors. But for anyone who's visited enough to navigate the parks without a map, the opportunity to experience the beauty and joy of the holiday season outweighs the huge crowds. You must accept that access to rides and shows will be limited and instead concentrate on the unique offerings such as the parades and fireworks at the Magic Kingdom. Allow yourself time to visit the resorts—the gingerbread house at the Grand Floridian must be seen to be believed. And arrive early: We were in the MK by 7:10 a.m. on New Year's Eve and enjoyed all of the parades, shows, and fireworks, as well as all the major rides (except Splash Mountain—it was too cold).

The Magic Kingdom stages New Year's Eve fireworks on both December 30 and 31 for those who either wish to see fireworks in multiple parks or who don't wish to be caught in the largest crowds of the year on New Year's Eve.

MICKEY'S VERY MERRY CHRISTMAS PARTY This event is staged 7 p.m.–midnight (after regular hours) on 21 evenings in November and December. Advance tickets for the 2017 events went on sale in early May and cost (including tax) $95–$116 for adults and $89–$111 for kids. As with the Halloween events, tickets get more expensive for parties closer to the holiday. Tickets for busier dates usually sell out one to four days in advance. Included in the cost is the use of all attractions during party hours, holiday-themed stage shows featuring Disney characters, cookies and hot chocolate, performances of Mickey's Once Upon a Christmas-time Parade, carolers, "a magical snowfall on Main Street," white lights on Cinderella Castle, fireworks, and a new show for 2016 titled *Mickey's*

Most Merriest Celebration. The least crowded dates are usually the weeks before Thanksgiving week, and the week after. Tuesday (and the rare Wednesday) parties are the slowest, too. See tinyurl.com/mickeys verymerryxmas for more details.

A reader from Pineville, Louisiana, tried the Very Merry Christmas Party and found the guest list too large for her liking:

> *We went in early December to avoid crowds but were surprised to find wall-to-wall people. They offered some great shows, but we could not get to them. The parade at 9 p.m. and the fireworks at 10 p.m., then fighting our way back to the parking lot was all we could muster.*

A Hoffman Estates, Illinois, reader was likewise overwhelmed:

> *Everything was terrific except that our experience with Mickey's Very Merry Christmas was awful. Wristbands were not checked, too many people were in the park, things were disorganized, and the Christmas celebration that we waited 1½ hours for lasted only 5 minutes!*

But a woman from Buffalo, New York, says that, as with all things Disney, you need a plan:

> *I just wanted to note a counterpoint to the comments about Mickey's Very Merry Christmas Party and the crowds: If you go in with a plan (as you should with any park at any time) and avoid Main Street as much as possible, you'll be fine. We were able to meet the Seven Dwarfs, Aurora and Prince Philip, Snow White and Snow Prince, Winnie the Pooh and friends, Donald, Daisy, and Scrooge McDuck, as well as Santa Goofy and Peppermint Minnie during the party. Additionally, we saw the second parade in Frontierland, watched Celebrate the Magic and Holiday Wishes from the Adventureland bridge, and braved Main Street only for the castle lighting and Celebrate the Season shows. In short, we accomplished everything we set out to do and even squeezed in some dinner, because we had a plan beforehand.*

HOLIDAYS AT DISNEY SPRINGS   In an effort to funnel some holiday guest traffic out of the theme parks, Walt Disney World has introduced a new nighttime holiday show at Disney Springs. ***Starbright Holidays—An Intel Collaboration*** features drones flying in formation to form light sculptures depicting trees, stars, and other seasonal symbols. This is in addition to more low-key theming, such as a traditional Santa greeting station, musicians playing carols, and a "Christmas Tree Trail" of photo ops and merriment. If your schedule permits, we advise visiting in early December, when you can enjoy the decorations and festivities without the crowds. The area behind Bongos Cuban Cafe, on the West Side, is the best viewing location.

PART TWO

MAKING *the* MOST *of* YOUR TIME *and* MONEY

There is more to Orlando than Disney World. And that's a good thing, because increasingly, the only people who get to rub elbows with Mickey Mouse are rich ones.

—Sandra Tan, staff writer, *Buffalo News*

CROSSING *the* LINE

BOB HERE. I've been writing about Disney theme parks for many years. I was drawn to Disney by the quality of its products and a feeling of nostalgia for all Disney meant to me when I was a kid. I read the comic books, watched *The Mickey Mouse Club,* never missed a Disney movie. On television, I watched Walt preview the theme park he was building in Florida. There was never a place I wanted more to see.

When Walt Disney World opened in 1971, it truly was a wonder. And it was a good value. Now I look on with conflicted emotions as admission, hotel, and restaurant prices skyrocket while services, guest benefits, and many other aspects of the Disney World experience are cut back—or cut entirely.

Remember when appetizers and gratuities were included in the Disney Dining Plan, or when there was an option to buy park admission with no expiration date. Or when FastPass+ was easy and convenient to use? Or when there were no restaurant surcharges? Or when you didn't have to plan every minute of your vacation months in advance?

For several years, I taught corporation finance at the university level. One of the first things students learned was that the top priority of a corporation is to maximize shareholder wealth. But is that the whole story? Does a corporation owe anything to its customers? When does a governing policy of maximizing shareholder wealth alienate customers and damage the company's image? I still think the Disney product is, for the most part, excellent, but I take issue with Disney's continuing to charge so much more and delivering so much less.

Disney barrages children with an incessant drumbeat of advertising for its movies, toys, games, comics, television shows, and, of course, theme parks. But its pricing policies—its devotion to maximizing profit—exclude millions of families from their Disney World dream.

Disney has willingly thrown this population under the bus. Its inexorable pricing policies are like death by a thousand cuts: certainly not stark and dramatic, but just as calculated.

Imagine explaining that you can't afford Disney World to a disappointed 6-year-old. The truth is hard to hear: "Disney doesn't care. They've made everything so expensive that people like us can't afford to go. Now turn on the Disney Channel and watch other people's children enjoy Walt Disney World."

YOU AND US VS. AN ARMY OF PhDS—FOR MONEY

FOR OUR FIRST FEW VISITS TO ORLANDO, dear reader, our concept of the Walt Disney Company consisted of a group of talented artists earning a living through fine family films and who also happen to dabble in theme parks and television. Oh, the joy of those innocent years.

In reality, Disney has long been a leader in the use of operations research and quantitative analysis to make more money. The location of its first theme park, Disneyland, among rural orange groves in Anaheim, was no happy accident. It was the result of detailed analysis by Stanford-trained engineers of 1950s California's housing and population trends, along with forecasts of where the new interstate highway system would likely be built to accommodate that growth.

Type the words "Disney revenue optimization" into your favorite search engine today, and you'll see that Disney employs a small, growing army of mostly PhD-level statisticians and analysts in a group called Revenue and Profit Management (*management* used here as a euphemism for maximization).

The job of Disney's "revenue management" data scientists is to use immense computing power, sophisticated experiments done on consumers, and tons of behavioral data to increase prices to the point just below where you'd give up and vacation somewhere else. But even if you consider the high cost of a Disney vacation as exactly worth the entertainment you get, the hidden effect of this work is often to shift more financial risk from Disney to you.

As an example, consider the Disney Dining Plan (see page 242). When it debuted in 2005, it cost $39 per day per adult; a table-service meal included an appetizer, a main course, dessert, a drink, tax, and tip. We lauded the dining plan and noted that many families could see "fairly substantial savings" by using it—something like $5–$7 per person per day—even if you didn't eat everything you could.

Disney's analysts quickly identified your $5–$7 savings as money they could have instead and have been whittling away at the plan ever since. The price is now $67.37 for adults, and table-service meals no longer include an appetizer or gratuity. That's effectively a price increase of 110%. Over the same period, the cost of dinner in an average US restaurant went up 11%, according to Zagat.

We think that today's dining plan is essentially a break-even proposition for most families; you'll spend on the plan about what you'd spend anyway on meals during your vacation. But that means you'll lose money if you skip even one meal—the margins are that small.

In effect, Disney's data scientists have priced their dining plan so that they make money whether you use it or not, but you risk *losing* money if you make the wrong choice. And Disney's army of PhDs is doing the same kind of adjustment all the time with their ticket and hotel room prices. That's what you're up against.

The good news is that you've got us—a team of data scientists, programmers, and operations-research experts—to help show you how Walt Disney World works and how you can save time and money. Our favorite new tip this year, for low-cost Disney hotel stays, is on page 133. As for the rest, we're not saying that you and us planning your Disney vacation is like Buffy and Spike versus the Hellmouth. Bob does look good with short blond hair, though.

READERS SPEAK OUT

THE COST OF WALT DISNEY WORLD is the subject of thousands of letters, e-mails, and survey responses that we receive. The following comments are representative.

From a reader in Claremont, New Hampshire:

While I still enjoy a WDW vacation, the value is eroding. Between the crowds and the prices of everything, you can now do other types of vacations at a much more reasonable price and for a longer time period. The Mouse is getting way too greedy!

From a Louisville, Kentucky, dad:

Disney World definitely gouges you with their food and souvenir prices. We spent over $24 for a burger, a fistful of fries, and a few chicken nuggets (no drink), whereas we bought three Chick-fil-A combo meals for less the following day! We also purchased a picture album at Disney Springs for $20, only to find a similar one at Publix for $7! Although we love Disney—first-class in every way—they are a first-class rip-off when it comes to their food and gifts.

From a longtime Disney patron from New York:

There's nothing else like Disney, but we're actually part of the prob-lem—we keep buying tickets no matter how high the gate price gets, or how many attractions they close down without replacement.

A couple from New Paris, Ohio, has this to say:

The costs keep going up, but the original ideas of Walt Disney are going away—mainly customer service and good value for the money.

A group of four seniors from West Lafayette, Indiana, chimes in:

"Disney Magic" is really getting you to pay huge sums for travel, lodging, and meals so you can stand in line for 30–60 minutes for a 2-minute ride.

From a Falls Church, Virginia, reader:

Loved the trip—just one small hiccup. We asked for a late check-out and were told it shouldn't be too much of an issue. Then, the day before checkout, we were told they were booked solid and they couldn't let us check out late. As I started walking away, the cast mem-ber told me that we could *check out late if we were willing to pay the extra $300 or so for an extra night . . . so apparently they weren't* *booked solid, they just wanted extra money. It seemed like a money grab to me, and when I said as much, they said it was the policy—which struck me as really strange.*

From a 14-year-old reader from Harvest, Alabama:

My family is not rich (my dad is a pastor), but I saved up $3,000 to take me, my two cousins, and my mom to Disney World. I loved it, but I just wish they could make it cheaper, improve lines, improve everything a little more with all that money. Disney: PLEASE, PLEASE, PLEASE stop raising prices!

ALLOCATING MONEY

CAN YOU AFFORD A DISNEY VACATION? WE CRUNCH THE NUMBERS

EVERY YEAR, WE HEAR FROM tens of thousands of families who are either planning or just back from a Walt Disney World vacation, and we talk with travel agents who hear from thousands more. And the thing that surprises these families the most is how expensive their trip turned out to be.

So that you know what you're dealing with up front, we've created the chart on pages 60–62. It shows how much Disney vacation you get for $500, $1,000, $1,500, and $2,000, for families of various sizes.

Most cells in the chart contain a list of options, such as the type of hotel at which you stay or the restaurants at which you dine. These options illustrate the trade-offs you should consider when planning your trip—and there *will* be trade-offs. Here's an example for a family of two adults and one child with a $1,500 vacation budget, excluding transportation:

OPTION A One full day at Disney's theme parks, counter-service breakfast and lunch, a sit-down dinner, and one night at a Disney Deluxe resort

OPTION B Two full days at Disney's theme parks, counter-service meals every day, and two nights at a budget off-site motel

In this case (and in general), your choice is between (1) a nicer hotel or (2) a longer trip, including more time in the parks, plus more nights in a cheaper hotel. You may also get better meals every day.

If you'd like to try your own numbers, you can download our Excel spreadsheet at tinyurl.com/wdwyouget2018. All hotel prices are quoted for mid-June nights in 2017 and include tax.

Here are the assumptions we made to go along with actual prices from Disney's website:

- Children are ages 3–9; adults are ages 10 and up.
- The cost of Magic Your Way Base Tickets comes from Disney's website and includes tax.
- One night at our off-site budget hotel costs $80 via Expedia.
- One night at Disney's Pop Century Resort (Value) costs $168.75 on the WDW website.

Continued on page 62

WHAT YOU PAY AND WHAT YOU GET AT WDW

2 ADULTS $500 ($489)

• 1 day theme park admission • 1 counter-service breakfast, lunch, and dinner • 1 night at a budget off-site resort

2 ADULTS, 1 KID $500

Nothing

2 ADULTS $1,000

BUDGET OPTION ($992)
• 2 days theme park admission
• 2 counter-service breakfasts, lunches, parking, 2 sit-down dinners
• 3 nights at a budget off-site motel

VALUE OPTION ($1,049)
• 2 days theme park admission
• 2 counter-service breakfasts and lunches, 2 sit-down dinners
• 2 nights at a Disney Value resort

MODERATE OPTION ($1,048)
• Same as Value with 1 night and 1 day of meals at a Disney Moderate resort

DELUXE OPTION ($1,107)
• Same as Moderate with 1 night at a Disney Deluxe resort

2 ADULTS, 1 KID $1,000

BUDGET OPTION ($987)
• 2 days theme park admission and parking
• 2 counter-service breakfasts, lunches, and dinners
• 2 nights at a budget off-site motel

VALUE OPTION ($1,036)
• 2 days theme park admission
• 2 counter-service breakfasts, lunches, and dinners
• 1 night at a Disney Value resort

MODERATE OPTION ($963)
• 1 night at a Disney Moderate resort, 1 day admission, 2 days of counter-service meals

DELUXE OPTION ($944)
• 1 day theme park admission
• 1 counter-service breakfast and lunch, 1 sit-down dinner
• 1 night at a Disney Deluxe resort

2 ADULTS $1,500

BUDGET OPTION ($1,575)
• 4 days theme park admission
• 4 counter-service breakfasts, lunches, and dinners
• 4 nights at a budget off-site motel and parking

VALUE OPTION ($1,512)
• 3 days theme park admission
• 4 counter-service breakfasts, lunches, and 3 dinners, 1 sit-down dinner
• 3 nights at a Disney Value resort

MODERATE OPTION ($1,563)
Same as Value with 2 nights at a Disney Moderate resort and 3 sit-down dinners

DELUXE OPTION ($1,535)
• 2 days theme park admission
• 2 counter-service breakfasts, lunches, and 2 sit-down dinners
• 2 nights at a Disney Deluxe resort

2 ADULTS, 1 KID $1,500

BUDGET OPTION ($1,570)
• 3 days theme park admission
• 3 counter-service breakfasts, lunches, and dinners
• 3 nights at a budget off-site motel

VALUE OPTION ($1,546)
• 2 days theme park admission
• 3 counter-service breakfasts, lunches, and 2 dinners, 1 sit-down dinner
• 2 nights at a Disney Value resort

MODERATE OPTION ($1,484)
• 2 days theme park admission
• 2 counter-service breakfasts, lunches, and sit-down dinners
• 2 nights at a Disney Moderate resort

DELUXE OPTION ($1,381)
• 2 days theme park admission
• 2 counter-service breakfasts, lunches, and dinners
• 1 night at a Disney Deluxe resort

2 ADULTS $2,000

BUDGET OPTION ($1,943)
• 6 days theme park admission, parking
• 6 counter-service breakfasts, lunches, and dinners, plus 1 sit-down dinner
• 6 nights at a budget off-site motel

VALUE OPTION ($2,015)
• 5 days theme park admission
• 5 counter-service breakfasts, lunches, and 4 dinners, plus 1 sit-down dinner
• 4 nights at a Disney Value resort

MODERATE OPTION ($2,010)
• 4 days theme park admission
• 4 counter-service breakfasts, lunches, and 2 dinners, plus 2 sit-down dinners
• 3 nights at a Disney Moderate resort

DELUXE OPTION ($1871)
• 3 days theme park admission
• 3 counter-service breakfasts, lunches, and sit-down dinners
• 2 nights at a Disney Deluxe resort

2 ADULTS, 1 KID $2,000

BUDGET OPTION ($2,087)
• 4 days theme park admission, parking
• 4 counter-service breakfasts, lunches, and 2 dinners, plus 2 sit-down dinners
• 4 nights at a budget off-site motel

VALUE OPTION ($2,067)
• 3 days theme park admission
• 4 counter-service breakfasts, lunches, and dinners
• 4 nights at a Disney Value resort

MODERATE OPTION ($2,043)
• 3 days theme park admission
• 3 counter-service breakfasts, lunches, and dinners
• 3 nights at a Disney Moderate resort

DELUXE OPTION ($2,094)
• 3 days theme park admission
• 3 counter-service breakfasts, lunches, and dinners
• 2 nights at a Disney Deluxe resort

WHAT YOU PAY AND WHAT YOU GET AT WDW

2 ADULTS, 2 KIDS $500

Nothing

3 ADULTS $500

Nothing

2 ADULTS, 2 KIDS $1,000

- 1 day theme park admission, parking
- 1 counter-service breakfast and lunch,
  1 sit-down dinner, and
  (choose one of the following):

  ◆ 2 nights at a **budget** off-site motel ($855)
  ◆ 2 nights at a **DISNEY VALUE** resort ($1,012)
  ◆ 1 night at a **DISNEY MODERATE** resort ($932)
  ◆ 1 night at a **DISNEY DELUXE** resort ($1,027)

3 ADULTS $1,000

BUDGET OPTION ($979)
- 2 days theme park admission, parking
- 2 counter-service breakfasts, lunches, and
  sit-down dinners
- 2 nights at a budget off-site motel

VALUE OPTION ($1,011)
- 1 day theme park admission
- 2 counter-service breakfasts, lunches, and dinners
- 2 nights at a Disney Value resort

MODERATE OPTION ($841)
- 1 day theme park admission, 1 set of counter-
  service meals, 1 night at a Disney Moderate resort,
  1 sit-down meal

DELUXE OPTION ($813)
- 1 day theme park admission, 1 set of counter-service
  meals, 1 night at a Disney Deluxe resort,
  1 sit-down meal

2 ADULTS, 2 KIDS $1,500

BUDGET OPTION ($1,506:
- 2 days theme park admission, parking
- 3 counter-service breakfasts and lunches,
  2 sit-down dinners
- 3 nights at a budget off-site motel

VALUE OPTION ($1,405):
- 2 days theme park admission
- 2 counter-service breakfasts and lunches,
  2 sit-down dinners
- 2 nights at a Disney Value resort

MODERATE OPTION ($1,457):
Same as Value with 2 nights at a Disney Moderate resort
and 2 counter-service breakfasts, lunches, and dinners

DELUXE OPTION ($1,480):
Same as Moderate with 1 night at a Disney Deluxe resort,
2 sit-down dinners

3 ADULTS $1,500

BUDGET OPTION ($1,564):
- 2 days theme park admission, parking
- 2 counter-service breakfasts, lunches, and
  sit-down dinners
- 3 nights at a budget off-site motel

VALUE OPTION ($1,405):
- 2 days theme park admission
- 2 counter-service breakfasts, lunches, and
  sit-down dinners
- 2 nights at a Disney Value resort

MODERATE OPTION ($1,457):
- 2 days theme park admission
- 2 counter-service breakfasts, lunches, dinners
- 2 nights at a Disney Moderate resort

DELUXE OPTION ($1,480):
- 2 days theme park admission
- 2 counter-service breakfasts, lunches, and
  sit-down dinners
- 1 night at a Disney Deluxe resort

2 ADULTS, 2 KIDS $2,000

BUDGET OPTION ($2,039):
- 3 days theme park admission, parking
- 3 counter-service breakfasts, lunches, dinners,
  2 sit-down dinners
- 3 nights at a budget off-site motel

VALUE OPTION ($1,956):
- 3 days theme park admission
- 3 counter-service breakfasts, lunches, and dinners
- 2 nights at a Disney Value resort

MODERATE OPTION ($1,999):
- 2 days theme park admission
- 2 counter-service breakfasts, lunches, and
  sit-down dinners
- 3 nights at a Disney Moderate resort

DELUXE OPTION ($2,050):
- 2 days theme park admission
- 2 counter-service breakfasts and lunches,
  2 sit-down dinners
- 2 nights at a Disney Deluxe resort

3 ADULTS $2,000

BUDGET OPTION ($1,978):
- 3 days theme park admission, parking
- 3 counter-service breakfasts, lunches, 1 dinner,
  2 sit-down dinners
- 4 nights at a budget off-site motel

VALUE OPTION ($2,015):
- 3 days theme park admission
- 3 counter-service breakfasts, lunches, 1 dinner,
  2 sit-down dinners
- 3 nights at a Disney Value resort

MODERATE OPTION ($1,898):
- 3 days theme park admission
- 3 counter-service breakfasts, lunches, and dinners
- 2 nights at a Disney Moderate resort

DELUXE OPTION ($1,891):
- 2 days theme park admission
- 2 counter-service breakfasts, lunches, and
  sit-down dinners
- 2 nights at a Disney Deluxe resort

3 ADULTS, 1 KID $500

Nothing

(Table continued from previous page)

WHAT YOU PAY AND WHAT YOU GET AT WDW

3 ADULTS, 1 KID $1,000

• 1 day theme park admission, parking • 1 counter-service breakfast and lunch, 1 sit-down dinner, and (choose one of the following):	◆ 1 night at a budget off-site motel ($826) ◆ 1 night at a Disney Value resort ($895) ◆ 1 night at a Disney Moderate resort ($984)

3 ADULTS, 1 KID $1,500	3 ADULTS, 1 KID $2,000
BUDGET OPTION ($1,524) • 2 days theme park admission, parking • 2 counter-service breakfasts and lunches, 2 sit-down dinners • 2 nights at a budget off-site motel	**BUDGET OPTION ($2,031)** • 3 days theme park admission, parking • 3 counter-service breakfasts, lunches, and dinners • 3 nights at a budget off-site motel
VALUE OPTION ($1,518) • 2 days theme park admission • 2 counter-service breakfasts, lunches, and dinners • 2 nights at a Disney Value resort	**VALUE OPTION ($2,068)** • 3 days theme park admission • 3 counter-service breakfasts, lunches, and dinners • 2 nights at a Disney Value resort
MODERATE OPTION ($1,510) • 2 days theme park admission • 2 counter-service breakfasts and lunches, 1 counter-service dinner, 1 sit-down dinner • 1 nights at a Disney Moderate resort	**MODERATE OPTION ($1,953)** • 2 days theme park admission • 2 counter-service breakfasts, lunches, and dinners • 3 nights at a Disney Moderate resort
DELUXE OPTION ($1,383) • 1 day theme park admission • 2 counter-service breakfasts, lunches, and sit-down dinners • 1 night at a Disney Deluxe resort	**DELUXE OPTION ($2,004)** • 2 days theme park admission • 2 counter-service breakfasts, lunches, and dinners • 2 nights at a Disney Deluxe resort

Continued from page 59

- One night at Disney's Port Orleans Riverside Resort (Moderate) costs $257.63 using Disney's website.
- One night at Disney's Wilderness Lodge (Deluxe) costs $411.75 using Disney's website.
- A day's worth of counter-service meals, plus one snack, costs $51 for adults and $20 for kids.
- A counter-service breakfast and lunch, a snack, and a table-service meal costs $72 per adult and $29 per child.

In most places in the chart, theme park admission ranges from 30% to 60% of the cost of a trip, regardless of family size. If you're not staying at a Deluxe resort, it's safe to assume that ticket costs will take half of your budget (again, excluding transportation).

It's a different story for off-site hotels, which lack services like free shuttles and extra time in the theme parks. Excellent third-party resorts, such as the Waldorf Astoria, adjacent to Disney property, offer rates 30%–60% less than those of comparable Disney hotels. It helps considerably if you've got a car, even if you factor in the cost of gas.

How to Save $500 on Your Trip

THIS GUIDE DESCRIBES many techniques for saving money on a Walt Disney World vacation, including finding an inexpensive hotel, discounts on third-party admission tickets, and budget-friendly restaurants. But sometimes you can do all of that *and* still need to cut your budget.

TouringPlans.com blogger **Kristi Fredericks** has you covered with six simple ways to save more than $500 on your Disney vacation.

For each of these tips, assume a family of four traveling to Walt Disney World for a one-week (six-day, seven-night) vacation. Our sample family includes two adults and two children ages 3 and 9.

TIP #1: BRING YOUR OWN RAIN PONCHOS

Disney World can be a rainy place no matter what time of year you visit. Bring your own rain ponchos instead of buying at the parks to save some dough.

DON'T Buy 2 adult ponchos x $10 and 2 kids' ponchos x $9 = **$38**
DO Buy 4 ponchos at local dollar store = **$4**   **SAVINGS** $38 – $4 = **$34**

TIP #2: BRING YOUR OWN STROLLER

Our sample family will need a stroller for their 3-year-old in the parks, and it's handy to have a stroller for the airport and resort areas as well. Remember that most airlines will gate-check your stroller for free.

DON'T Rent a stroller for $14 per day (length-of-stay rate) x 6 days = **$84**
DO Buy 1 umbrella stroller on Amazon = **$29**   **SAVINGS** $84 – $29 = **$55**

TIP #3: DRINK FREE WATER

All Disney restaurants will give you a free cup of ice water. Instead of wasting money and calories on sugary drinks, this is an easy way to save some cash. For our sample family, let's assume that everyone wants something other than water to drink at breakfast and that the kids' meals will include a drink at lunch and dinner. Only the adults will drink free water, and only at lunch and dinner.

DON'T Buy 1 beverage at $3.50 each x 2 adults x 2 meals x 6 days = **$84**
DO Drink free water x 2 adults x 2 meals x 6 days = **$0**

SAVINGS $72 – $0 = **$84**

TIP #4: BRING YOUR OWN SNACKS

It's amazing how much you can save by bringing your own nonperishable snacks into the park. A zip-top bag filled with cereal bars, granola, raisins, and crackers goes a long way toward staving off hunger.

DON'T Buy 1 snack at $4 each x 4 people x 2 times x 6 days = **$192**
DO Bring your own snacks = **$35**   **SAVINGS** $192 – $35 = **$157**

TIP 5: EAT BREAKFAST IN YOUR ROOM

This saves you time and a small fortune in food costs. Let's assume our family will grab two coffees and two milks from their hotel's food court each morning, so we won't include beverages in either cost.

DON'T Buy one $11 breakfast platter + one $6 yogurt parfait + two kids' Mickey
    waffle meals x $5 x 6 days = **$162**
DO Bring your own breakfast, including paper bowls, napkins, plastic spoons,
    cereal, breakfast pastries, mini-doughnuts, and cereal bars = **$30**

SAVINGS $162 – $30 = **$132**

TIP #6: BUY TICKETS IN ADVANCE

Disney adds a $21.30 surcharge to every ticket bought at its theme parks. Why? Because they can; Disney knows you're not likely to turn the kids around and leave once you're that close.

DON'T Wait until you get to the parks to buy tickets.
DO Buy tickets in advance either from Disney or one of our recommended ticket wholesalers.

SAVINGS $21.30 x 4 tickets = **$85.20**

TOTAL SAVINGS $547.20 *(about $89 per day)*

WDW Theme Park Ticket Options

	1-DAY	2-DAY	3-DAY	4-DAY	5-DAY
BASE TICKET AGES 3-9					
MK: $108–126 EP/AK/DHS: $99–$120		$199.16	$288.62	$351.45	$372.75
—		($99.58/day)	($96.21/day)	($87.86/day)	($74.55/day)
BASE TICKET AGES 10 AND UP					
MK: $114–$132 EP/DHS/AK: $105–$127		$211.94	$307.79	$372.75	$394.05
—		($105.97/day)	($102.60/day)	($93.19/day)	($78.81/day)

Base Ticket admits guest to one theme park each day of use.

PARK HOPPER *(including tax) One-day ticket prices are shown as totals.*					
Ages 3-9: $166–$179 Ages 10+: $173–$185		$63.90	$63.90	$63.90	$63.90
—		($31.95/day)	($21.30/day)	($15.98/day)	($12.78/day)

Park Hopper option entitles guest to visit more than one theme park on each day of use.

PARK HOPPER PLUS *(including tax) 1-day ticket prices are shown as totals.*					
Ages 3-9: $182–$195 Ages 10+: $189–$201		$79.88	$79.88	$79.88	$79.88
—		($50.59/day)	($33.73/day)	($25.29/day)	($20.24/day)

Park Hopper Plus option entitles guest to a specified number of visits (between 2 and 10) to a choice of entertainment and recreation venues, plus the Park Hopper option described above.

Note: Check **TouringPlans.com** for the latest ticket prices, which are subject to change. All tickets expire 13 days after first use.

FOUR MORE TIPS FROM BOB

1. Buy your admission online from one of the sellers on page 70. Get tickets only for the number of days you plan to visit, and skip all add-ons.

2. Book a hotel outside of Walt Disney World. Hotels on US 192 (Irlo Bronson Memorial Highway) are usually the least expensive. Or consider renting a vacation home (see discussion starting on page 261) if you have four or more people in your group.

3. Avoid parking fees by using your hotel's shuttle service or by taking a Disney bus from the water parks (where—for the moment—parking is free) to a Disney hotel, then to a theme park. The second suggestion takes a lot of time, so do this only if budgeting to the penny.

4. Buy discounted Disney-brand apparel and souvenirs from one of Orlando's two **Disney Character Warehouse** outlets (see tinyurl.com/disneyoutlets).

MAGIC YOUR WAY

DISNEY OFFERS AN ARRAY OF theme park ticket options collectively known as Magic Your Way. These range from the humble **1-Day Base Ticket,** good for a single day's entry into one Disney theme park, to the blinged-out **Premium Annual Pass,** good for 365 days of admission into every Disney theme or water park, plus Disney's Oak Trail Golf Course and other attractions. See the chart above for a summary of the most common admission types.

Note: All ticket and add-on prices include 6.5% sales tax.				
6-DAY	**7-DAY**	**8-DAY**	**9-DAY**	**10-DAY**
BASE TICKET AGES 3–9				
$394.05	$415.35	$426.00	$436.65	$447.30
($65.68/day)	($59.34/day)	($53.25/day)	($48.52/day)	($44.73/day)
BASE TICKET AGES 10 AND UP				
$415.35	$436.65	$447.30	$457.95	$468.60
($69.23/day)	($62.38/day)	($55.91/day)	($50.88/day)	($46.86/day)
Park choices are Magic Kingdom, Epcot, Disney's Hollywood Studios, or Disney's Animal Kingdom.				
PARK HOPPER *(including tax) One-day ticket prices are shown as totals.*				
$63.90	$63.90	$63.90	$63.90	$63.90
($10.65/day)	($9.13/day)	($7.99/day)	($7.10/day)	($6.39/day)
Park choices are any combination of Magic Kingdom, Epcot, Disney's Hollywood Studios, or Disney's Animal Kingdom on each day of use.				
PARK HOPPER PLUS *(including tax) 1-day ticket prices are shown as totals.*				
$79.88	$79.88	$79.88	$79.88	$79.88
($16.86/day)	($14.45/day)	($12.65/day)	($11.24/day)	($10.12/day)
Choices are Disney's Blizzard Beach water park, Disney's Typhoon Lagoon water park, Oak Trail Golf Course, ESPN Wide World of Sports Complex, or Fantasia Gardens or Winter Summerland minigolf.				

The number of ticket options available makes it difficult to sort out which option represents the least expensive way to see and do everything you want. The average family staying for a week at an off-World hotel and planning a couple of activities outside the theme parks has about a dozen different ticket options to consider.

Adding to the complexity, Disney's reservation agents are trained to avoid answering subjective questions about which ticket option is "best." Many families, we suspect, become overwhelmed trying to sort out the different options and simply purchase an expensive ticket with more features than they'll use.

As an example, a family of two adults and two kids who want to visit the theme parks for five days and a water park for one day could buy everyone a 5-Day Base Ticket plus the Park Hopper Plus option at the gate, for $1,938 total. Or they could buy separate admissions to the theme and water parks in advance from a third-party vendor for $1,622, a savings of $316. Problem is, comparing options requires detailed knowledge of the myriad perks included with specific admissions.

THIS IS A JOB FOR . . . A COMPUTER!

IT'S COMPLICATED ENOUGH that we wrote a computer program to solve it. Visit TouringPlans.com and try our **Park Ticket Calculator,** on the homepage. It aggregates ticket prices from Disney and a number of online ticket vendors. Answer a few questions relating to the size of your party and the parks you intend to visit, and the calculator will identify your four cheapest ticket options. It'll also show you how much you'll save.

The program will also make recommendations for considerations other than price. For example, Annual Passes might cost more, but Disney often offers substantial resort discounts and other deals to Annual Pass holders. These resort discounts, especially during the off-season, can more than offset the price of the pass.

SEASONAL PRICING AND OTHER SURCHARGES

IN EARLY 2016, Disney introduced seasonal, demand-based pricing for single-day park admission. Each day of the year is now classified into one of three seasons according to how busy Disney thinks its parks will be on a given day. The cost to enter the park depends on the season:

Value season is Disney's term for the least-attended days of the year. There were 86 such days in 2017 (15%).

Regular season is the designation for days of average attendance. There were 162 regular days in 2017 (53%).

Peak season includes days of heaviest attendance, such as Easter, Memorial Day through late July, Thanksgiving, and Christmas. There were 117 peak days in 2017 (32%).

Disney releases a rolling calendar showing the next 8–11 months in advance, showing each day's seasonal classification.

Here's how it works in practice if you want to visit one Disney World theme park for one day: First, determine which theme park you want to visit. Next, determine the exact date on which you plan to visit. Then look up the park and date on Disney's calendar to see the price. The following chart shows what to expect (including tax):

SEASON	MAGIC KINGDOM	EPCOT, DHS, AK
Value	ADULT: $113.96 CHILD: $107.57	ADULT: $105.44 CHILD: $99.05
Regular	ADULT: $122.48 CHILD: $116.09	ADULT: $113.96 CHILD: $107.57
Peak	ADULT: $132.06 CHILD: $125.67	ADULT: $126.74 CHILD: $120.35

Multiday pricing is still uniform across the parks. The more days of admission you buy, the lower the cost per day. For example, if you buy an adult 5-Day Base Ticket for $394.05 (tax included), each day costs $78.81, compared with $105–$127 a day for a one-day pass to Epcot, the Studios, or Animal Kingdom and $114–$132 for the Magic Kingdom. Tickets can be purchased from 1 up to 10 days and admit you to exactly one theme park per day; you can reenter your chosen park as many times as you like on that day.

WHEN TICKETS EXPIRE

DISNEY SAYS ITS TICKETS EXPIRE within 14 days of the first day of use. In practice, they really mean 13 days after the first day of use. If, say, you purchase a 4-Day Base Ticket on June 1 and use it that day for admission to the Magic Kingdom, you'll be able to visit a single Disney theme park on any of your three remaining days from June 2 through June 14. After that, the ticket expires, and any unused days will be lost.

Tickets expire even if you don't use them. Tickets purchased in one year must be used by December 31 of the following year. After that, the value of a completely unused ticket can be applied to the purchase of a new ticket at the prevailing cost on that future date. This new restriction means you can no longer avoid more than one year of price increases by buying tickets way ahead of time.

TICKET ADD-ONS

TWO ADD-ON OPTIONS are offered with the Magic Your Way Ticket, each at an additional cost:

PARK HOPPER This add-on lets you visit more than one theme park per day. The cost is about $53–$59 (including tax) on top of the price of an adult 1-Day Base Ticket and a flat $63.90 tacked on to adult or child multiday tickets. The longer your stay, the more affordable it is: As an add-on to a 7-Day Base Ticket, for example, the flat fee works out to $10.50 per day for park-hopping privileges. If you want to visit the Magic Kingdom in the morning and eat at Epcot in the evening, this is the feature to request.

PARK HOPPER PLUS On top of the Park Hopper feature described above, the Park Hopper Plus (PHP) option gives you admission to one Disney water park (Blizzard Beach or Typhoon Lagoon), Oak Trail Golf Course, Fantasia Gardens or Winter Summerland minigolf, or the ESPN Wide World of Sports Complex. The PHP option costs $79.88—almost $16 per ticket more than the Park Hopper option alone, including tax.

Except for the single-day ticket, which gives you two admissions, the number of admissions equals the number of days on your ticket. If you buy an 8-Day Base Ticket, for example, and add the Park Hopper/PHP option, you get eight Park Hopper/PHP admissions.

You can't change how many Park Hopper/PHP admissions you can buy with either option; the number is fixed, and unused days aren't refundable. You *can,* however, skip Park Hopper/PHP entirely and buy an individual admission to any of the venues above—that's frequently the best deal if you're not park-hopping and, say, you'd like to visit just Typhoon Lagoon and/or Blizzard Beach.

If you buy a ticket but then decide later that you want to add the Park Hopper/PHP option, you can do so. Note, though, that Disney doesn't prorate the cost: If you add Park Hopper/PHP on the last day of your trip, you'll pay the same $63.90 or $79.88 as if you'd bought it before you left home.

Annual Passes

An Annual Pass provides unlimited use of the major theme parks for one year. Two versions are available: The **Disney Platinum Pass** ($830 with tax; ages 3 and up) includes free use of Disney's Memory Maker digital-photo service in addition to park access. The **Disney Platinum Plus Pass** ($925 with tax; ages 3 and up) also provides unlimited use of the minor parks, ESPN Wide World of Sports, and Disney's Oak Trail Golf Course. Holders of both types of Annual Passes also get perks, including free parking, dining and merchandise discounts, and seasonal offers such as room-rate discounts at Disney resorts or a dedicated entrance line at the theme parks. These passes are not valid for special events, such as admission to Mickey's Very Merry Christmas Party. Finally, the **Water Parks Annual Pass** costs $133 for adults and children ages 3–9, tax included.

Florida Resident Passes

Disney offers several special admission options to Florida residents and members of the Disney Vacation Club time-share program. The **Disney Gold Pass** ($595 with tax; ages 3 and up) offers unlimited admission and park-hopping privileges to the four major theme parks, free parking, and the discounts mentioned in the previous paragraph. The Gold Pass does specify blackout dates, during which it cannot be used for admission to the theme parks; these include December 18–January 2, plus the two weeks around Easter. The cheaper **Disney Silver Pass** ($446 with tax; ages 3 and up) offers the same park benefits as the Gold Pass but has additional blackout dates from the first week of June through the second week of August. There's also a **Weekday Select Pass** ($286 with tax; ages 3 and up), good for visits Monday–Friday, and an **Epcot After 4 Annual Pass** ($276 with tax; ages 3 and up), good for admission to Epcot after 4 p.m.

*un*official **TIP**
The break-even point for an Annual Pass is 12 days of theme park visits. With Annual Pass resort discounts, the break-even is about six days at a Deluxe resort.

4-Park Magic Tickets

In 2016, Disney introduced a new ticket type called the **4-Park Magic Ticket.** This ticket allows guests four days of park admittance, one day to each of the four primary theme parks, with no park hopping allowed. In other words, with the 4-Park Magic Ticket, guest can visit Epcot, Animal Kingdom, Disney's Hollywood Studios, and Magic Kingdom for one day each. Tickets are priced at $337 with tax for guests ages 10 and up, and $315 for children ages 3–9, compared with $373 for adults and $351 for traditional tickets of the same duration. The ticket comes with a number of caveats, including a use-by date and holiday-season blackout dates, which makes them unsuitable for many guests. However, if the available dates and park visit structure work for you, this ticket provides considerable savings.

*un*official **TIP**
Save money on tickets by planning ahead—buy them before the next price increase.

HOW TO GET THE MOST FROM MAGIC YOUR WAY

FIRST, BE REALISTIC about what you want out of your vacation. A seven-day theme park ticket with seven PHP admissions might seem like a wonderful idea when you're snowbound in February and planning your trip. But actually trying to visit all those parks in a week in July might end up feeling more like Navy SEAL training. If you're not park-hopping but going to visit just one or two water parks or the ESPN Wide World of Sports Complex, you're almost always better off purchasing that admission separately rather than in the PHP option. If you plan to visit two or more PHP venues, you're better off buying the add-on.

DISNEY PRICE INCREASES

DISNEY USUALLY RAISES PRICES ONCE A YEAR, Hikes were announced in February of 2017, 2016, 2015, and 2014; in June 2013, 2012, and 2011; and August 2010 back to 2006. We expect the next one in January or February 2018.

Prices on all tickets were up an average of 7% in 2017, and year-over-year hikes generally run around 5%. If you're putting together a budget, assume at least 5%. And with an improving economy and strong attendance, Disney may even increase prices twice per year.

A Georgia dad puts Disney's price hikes in perspective:

In the spring of 1983 as a working student, I purchased a [3-Day Park Hopper for $35 (including tax). Minimum wage was $3.35/hour, meaning it took less than 11 hours of work to pay for that ticket. With the latest increase, a 3-Day Base Ticket plus Park Hopper costs $372, or about 51 hours of work at today's minimum wage of $7.25/hour.

TICKETS, BIOMETRICS, WRISTBANDS, AND RFID

TO THIS POINT IN THE BOOK, we've used the word *ticket* to describe that thing you carry around as proof of your admission to the park. In fact, Disney admission media come in two forms—neither of which is a ticket. While we use *ticket* as shorthand for "admission medium," you'll be better prepared by knowing what you'll actually be handed when you plunk down your money.

If you're staying at a Disney resort, your admission medium is a rubber wristband about the size and shape of a small wristwatch. Called a **MagicBand,** it contains a tiny radio frequency identifier (RFID) chip, on which is stored a link to the record of your admission purchase in Disney's computers. Your MagicBand also functions as your hotel-room key, and it can (optionally) work as a credit card for most food and merchandise purchases.

If you don't want a MagicBand, you get a **Key to the World Card,** which looks like a credit card. If you're staying off-property or you bought your admission from a third-party vendor, your ticket is a flexible, credit card–sized piece of plastic. Both alternatives also contain an RFID chip; upgrading them to a MagicBand costs $13. The inner workings of RFID are discussed in detail starting on page 73.

In addition to using RFID chips, Disney computers store the dimensions of one finger (not a fingerprint) from your right hand, a reference to which is also stored on your MagicBand or laminated card. Recording this biometric information requires a quick and painless measurement, taken the first time you use the ticket. When you use it again, you'll be asked to scan the same finger to validate your identity. If the scans don't match—say, you use a different finger—you may be asked to present photo ID. Beginning in summer 2016, Disney began asking for biometric finger scans for children ages 3–9, as well as for adults and children ages 10 and older. Younger kids may have a parent or other adult provide their scans, or Disney may ask to photograph the child for admission-verification purposes.

If you're buying admission for your entire family and you're worried that you won't be able to keep everyone's tickets straight,

Disney's computer system should have every family member's data linked to every ticket, allowing anyone in your group to enter with anyone else's ticket. We've confirmed this by having a platoon of our researchers swap MagicBands with each other; all were admitted.

WHERE TO PURCHASE MAGIC YOUR WAY TICKETS

YOU CAN BUY YOUR ADMISSION PASSES on arrival at Walt Disney World (with a $21 per-ticket surcharge) or buy them in advance to avoid that fee. Passes are available at Walt Disney World resorts and theme parks, at some non-Disney hotels and shopping centers, and through independent ticket brokers. Because Disney admissions are only marginally discounted in the Walt Disney World–Orlando area, the chief reason for you to buy from an independent broker is convenience. Offers of free or heavily discounted tickets abound, but they generally require you to attend a time-share sales presentation.

unofficial **TIP**
If you order tickets in advance, allow enough time for them to be mailed to your home.

Magic Your Way tickets are available at Disney Stores and at disneyworld.com for the same prices listed in the chart on pages 64 and 65.

If you're trying to keep costs to an absolute minimum, consider using an online ticket wholesaler, such as **The Official Ticket Center, Park-Savers,** or **Boardwalk Ticketing,** especially for trips with five or more days in the parks. All tickets sold are brand-new, and the savings can range from $4 to more than $60, depending on the ticket and options chosen. If any options don't make sense for your specific plans, the representatives will tell you so. The Official Ticket Center will provide you with electronic tickets, as Disney does, so you'll be able to make FastPass+ reservations immediately through the My Disney Experience website. ParkSavers will e-mail you ticket vouchers within 24 hours to be redeemed at the park entrance, plus ticket-validation codes within three days to use with My Disney Experience.

All three companies offer discount tickets for almost all Central Florida attractions, including Disney, Universal, SeaWorld, and Cirque du Soleil. Discounts for the major theme parks range from about 6% to 12%; tickets for other attractions are more deeply discounted. **The Official Ticket Center** (3148 Vineland Road, Kissimmee; daily, 8 a.m.–6 p.m. Eastern time; ☎ 407-396-9020 or 877-406-4836; fax 407-396-9323; officialticketcenter.com) offers USPS Certified Mail for free or Priority Mail for $10. For the same price, they'll also deliver to area hotels; pickup at their office is free. **ParkSavers** (US: ☎ 877-226-3380; park savers.com) offers electronic ticket vouchers for three- to seven-day Magic Your Way tickets, usually at substantially discounted prices. Because they're vouchers, there are a couple of extra steps involved: You'll need to tell ParkSavers your approximate travel dates, you'll need to convert those vouchers to theme park tickets the first time you arrive at a Disney theme park, and you may need to wait up to 24 hours to register those vouchers on My Disney Experience and start making Fast-Pass+ reservations. Finally, **Boardwalk Ticketing** (boardwalkticketing.com) operates only online. They'll send actual tickets to you through the mail (free shipping), or you can pick them up at the park entrances (also free). Either way, within a few hours of your order, you'll receive a purchase confirmation code that can be used to make FastPass+ reservations on My Disney Experience.

Where *Not* to Buy Passes

unofficial TIP

Also steer clear of passes offered on eBay and Craigslist.

In addition to the many authorized resellers of Disney admissions, a number of unauthorized ones exist. They buy unused days on legitimately purchased park passes and resell them as if they were brand-new.

These resellers insist that you specify the exact days when you plan to use the ticket. They know, of course, how many days are left on the pass and when it expires. If you tell them you plan to use it tomorrow and the next two days, then they'll sell you a ticket that has three days left on it and expires in three days. Naturally, because they don't tell you this, you assume the usual 14-day expiration period applies from the date of first use. In the case of your tickets, however, the original purchaser triggered the 14-day expiration period. Skip a day instead of using the pass on the next three consecutive days, and you'll discover to your chagrin that it has expired.

FOR ADDITIONAL INFORMATION ON PASSES

IF YOU HAVE A QUESTION OR CONCERN regarding admissions that can be addressed only through a person-to-person conversation, phone **Disney Ticket Inquiries** at ☎ 407-566-4985 or e-mail ticket .inquiries@disneyworld.com. If you call, be aware that you may spend considerable time on hold; if you e-mail, be aware that it can take up to three days to get a response. In contrast, the ticket section of the Walt Disney World website—disneyworld.disney.go.com/tickets—is helpfully straightforward in showing how ticket prices break down.

WHERE THE REAL DEALS ARE

BOTH GREAT THEME PARKS, **Universal Studios Florida** and **Universal's Islands of Adventure** routinely offer admission discounts and specials at universalorlando.com. For a family of four—say, Mom, Dad, and two kids under age 10—the total cost to visit both Universal parks for two days is around $1,065, including tax. For the same family to spend two days at Disney parks with park-hopping privileges during the same period, it cost a whopping $1,341, tax included. Even in the absence of any discounts, two days of park hopping at Universal for our family of four cost $276 less than the same admission at Walt Disney World. But wait: Universal's current offer adds two more days to each pass—free! That same four-day pass at Disney world cost our family a whopping $2,200.

THE BRITISH ARE COMING!

IN THE UNITED KINGDOM, Disney offers advance-purchase tickets not available in the US. **Ultimate Tickets** cost £299 for adults and £284 for kids for 7- or 14-day passes (the 14-day passes are currently on sale) and £439 and £419 for 21-day passes. Ultimate Tickets provide unlimited admission to both major and minor parks along with park-hopping privileges to the major parks. The 7- and 14-day Ultimate Tickets expire

14 days after first use, and the 21-day Ultimate Ticket expires 21 days after first use. To find out more, call ☎ 0870-242-4900 UK or ☎ 407-566-4985 US (Monday–Friday, 9 a.m.–8 p.m.; Saturday, 9 a.m.–7 p.m.; and Sunday, 10 a.m.–4 p.m.), or see disneyholidays.co.uk/walt-disney-world/tickets or the **Disney Information Bulletin Board** at thedibb.co.uk.

MORE DISCOUNTS ON ADMISSIONS

Discounts Available to Certain Groups and Individuals

DISNEY VACATION CLUB Members get a discount on Annual Passes.

CONVENTION-GOERS Disney World, Universal, SeaWorld, and other parks sometimes set up a link cited in convention materials to purchase discounted afternoon and evening admissions. See tinyurl.com/disneyconventiontix and tinyurl.com/seaworldconventiontix2016.

DISNEY CORPORATE SPONSORS If you work for one of these, you may be eligible for discounted admissions or perks at the parks. Check with your workplace's employee-benefits office.

FLORIDA RESIDENTS get substantial savings on virtually all tickets. You'll need to prove residency with a driver's license or state ID card.

MILITARY, DEPARTMENT OF DEFENSE, CIVIL SERVICE Active-duty and retired military, Department of Defense (DOD) civilian employees, some civil-service employees, and dependents of these groups can buy Disney multiday admissions at a 9%–10% discount. Military personnel can buy discounted admission for nonmilitary guests as long as the military member accompanies the nonmilitary member. If a group seeks the discount, at least half must be eligible for the military discount.

DISNEY YOUTH EDUCATION SERIES Disney runs daily educational programs for K–12 students that also offer substantial ticket discounts (with substantial restrictions). See disneyyouth.com for more information.

Special Passes

See tinyurl.com/wdwdiscounttix for details on passes that are not known to the general public and are not sold at any Walt Disney World ticket booth.

HOW MUCH DOES IT COST PER DAY?

A TYPICAL DAY COSTS $828.32, excluding lodging and transportation, for a family of four—Mom, Dad, 12-year-old Abner, and 8-year-old Agnes—using their own car and staying outside of Disney World. They plan to stay a week, so they buy 5-Day Base Tickets with the Park Hopper option. The biggest outlay is usually food costs, which increase at least twice a year and account for almost half the price of a day in the parks.

HOW MUCH DOES A DAY COST?	
Breakfast for four at Denny's with tax and tip	**$53.61**
Epcot parking fee (free for pass holders and resort guests)	**$20.00**
Four days' admission on a 5-Day Ticket with Park Hopper (including tax)	**$362.10**
Dad: *$457.95 divided by five days* = $91.59 **Mom:** *$457.95 divided by five days* = $91.59	

Abner (child over 9): *$457.95 divided by five days* = $91.59 Agnes (child under 9): *$436.65 divided by five days* = $87.33	
Morning break (soda or coffee)	**$12.31**
Fast-food lunch (sandwich or burger, fries, soda), no tip	**$65.09**
Afternoon break (soda and popcorn)	**$33.02**
Dinner at Italy (3 appetizers, 4 entrées, 3 desserts), with tax and tip	**$229.08**
Souvenirs (Mickey T-shirts for Abner and Agnes) with tax*	**$53.14**
One-day total (without lodging or transportation)	$828.35
Increase over last year's total ($802.80)	3.18%

Cheer up—you won't have to buy souvenirs every day.

RFID: IT'S ALL IN THE WRIST

WITH ITS MYMAGIC+ CAMPAIGN (see page 38), Disney introduced the **MagicBand**—a reusable rubber wristband—as a sort of wearable theme park ticket. Small and reusable across trips, a MagicBand is imprinted with your first name, an ID number, and some legalese, along with a Mickey logo. A tiny radio-frequency-identification (RFID) chip embedded in the wristband holds your ticket and travel information.

unofficial **TIP**
Old-style tickets must be converted to RFID media before you can enter the parks or use FastPass+. Get the conversion done at Guest Relations, just outside each park.

Each RFID chip—not much larger than the end of a pencil—sends a unique serial number over short distances via radio waves. When you purchase theme park admission, Disney's computers will store that serial number, along with your ticket information. To enter a theme park, you touch your MagicBand to an RFID reader instead of going through a turnstile. The RFID reader collects your MagicBand's serial number, compares your biometric information, and verifies with Disney's computer systems that you've got the correct admission to enter the park.

Disney hotel guests get a MagicBand by default but may request a plastic **Key to the World (KTTW) Card** instead. If you're staying off-site or you bought your admission through a third party, you can upgrade to a MagicBand for $13; otherwise, you get a credit card–sized laminated ticket. Like the MagicBand, the two card options use RFID. Each member of your family gets his or her own MagicBand, each with a unique serial number. Along with the wristband, each family member will be asked to select a four-digit personal-identification number (PIN) for purchases—more on that on the next page.

The wristbands are resizable and waterproof, and they have ventilation holes for cooling. Eight colors are available: black, blue, green, orange, pink, purple, red, yellow, and gray (the default). You can choose your colors and personalize your bands when you book your resort stay at the Disney World website. Further customization is available at **MagicBand on Demand,** located at the exit to Space Mountain in Tomorrowland in the Magic Kingdom.

unofficial **TIP**
Get stickers of almost any color or design for your MagicBand at magicyourbands.com.

Some guests, particularly those with hand or wrist mobility issues, find using the MagicBand physically challenging. It sometimes takes a few tries to get the band's RFID chip (located under the Mickey head symbol) properly oriented on the reader stations or room doors. In January 2017, the MagicBands were redesigned so that the center portion of the band (essentially a puck the size of a quarter) became removable. The puck can be placed on a lanyard or clipped on a bag, making it easier to maneuver.

A Dublin, Ohio, woman finds MagicBands inconvenient to use:

> *You have to be ElastiGirl to use the MagicBand when driving up to the hotel. My husband was wearing the band on his right wrist and could never reach it over to the post without taking it off (and some of the posts had the electronic thing so high that it was doubly hard to reach from a car window).*

*un*official **TIP**
If you're driving, wear your MagicBand on your left wrist.

RFID for Payment, Hotel-Room Access, and Photos

Disney's hotel-room doors have RFID readers, allowing you to enter your room simply by tapping your wristband or KTTW Card against the reader. RFID readers are also installed at virtually every Disney cash register on-property, allowing you to pay for food, drinks, and souvenirs by tapping your MagicBand/KTTW Card against the reader. You'll be asked to verify your identity by entering your PIN on a small keypad to complete your purchase.

If you're using Disney's **Memory Maker** service (see page 510), your MagicBand/KTTW Card serves as the link between your photos and your family. Each photographer carries a small RFID reader, against which you tap your MagicBand after having your photo taken. The computers that run the Memory Maker system will link your photos to you, and you'll be able to view them on the Disney World website.

Disney's onboard ride-photo computers incorporate RFID technology, too. As you begin down the big drop near the finale of Splash Mountain, for example, RFID sensors read the serial number on your MagicBand and pass it to Splash Mountain's cameras. When those cameras snap your family plunging into the briar patch, they attach your MagicBands' serial number to the photo, allowing you to see your ride photos together after you've returned home. Because ride sensors may not pick up the signal from an RFID card sitting in a wallet or purse, we're fairly sure that onboard ride photos require MagicBands.

PRIVACY CONCERNS Many people are understandably wary of multinational corporations tracking their movements. As noted earlier, guests who prefer not to wear MagicBands can instead obtain KTTW Cards, which are somewhat harder to track (RFID-blocking wallets are available online). Disney says guests who opt out of MagicBands don't get the full range of ride experiences, though, so there's a trade-off.

DISNEY AND THE UPCHARGE

DURING THE PAST YEAR, Disney has experimented with adding products and events that involve a fee or service charge above and beyond the normal cost of a Disney theme park visit. Some of the upcharges are similar to previous park offerings. For example, the new **Star Wars Guided Tour** (page 745), at $129 per person with tax, is a pretty standard variation on the many backstage tours offered, and Epcot's *IllumiNations* Sparkling Dessert Party, at $49 per adult, is a variation on a similar event that's been offered for several years at the Magic Kingdom's *Happily Ever After* (formerly *Wishes*) fireworks show.

On the other end of the spectrum are experimental add-ons that some have found shocking. During the fall 2016–winter 2017 season, the Magic Kingdom offered $650 private cabanas located in Tomorrowland, $20 private water-taxi rides to and from points around Bay Lake; after-hours Magic Kingdom park access (initially tried at $150 per person, now listing at $120 per person), $15-per-day Express bus transportation between the theme parks for guests with Park Hopper tickets, an ice-cream social aboard the *Liberty Belle* riverboat ($49 per adult), and many more.

Some of these experiments have already been discontinued (bye-bye for now, cabanas), and others are likely to have short life-spans, but some will certainly stick around. We haven't yet found one new upcharge item that we'd say is a 100% must-do or an absolute game changer. We are concerned, however, about whether these add-ons will have a negative impact on regular guests. The Tomorrowland cabanas, as executed in their test run, were unsightly white tents assembled near Space Mountain; their shantylike appearance was out of place for the environment. The ice-cream social aboard the *Liberty Belle* takes that attraction offline for regular guests for about 3 hours every afternoon. That's a real loss for some.

If you're looking for ways to add convenience or excitement to your vacation, and you're willing to pay for it, Disney now has you covered in spades. But we'll continue to monitor whether Disney's formerly passive class stratification for guests is on its way to becoming an active nuisance.

ALLOCATING TIME

*un*official **TIP**
If you have only one day to tour, concentrate on one park and save the others for another visit.

DURING DISNEY WORLD'S FIRST DECADE, a family with a week's vacation could enjoy the Magic Kingdom and the now-closed River Country water park and still have several days left for the beach or other area attractions. Since Epcot opened in 1982, however, Disney World has steadily been enlarging to monopolize the family's entire vacation. Today, with the addition of Blizzard Beach, Typhoon Lagoon, Hollywood Studios, Animal Kingdom, and Disney Springs, you should allocate 6 days for a whirlwind tour (7–10 if you insist on a little relaxation during your vacation). If you don't have that much time, be prepared to make some hard choices.

This Arlington, Virginia, family recommends taking it slow and easy:

We spent eight days in Disney, and it was totally worth it. A longer trip, believe it or not, eliminates the happy death march—we cut our stress by 90 percent. Each day, we took some sort of break: a morning swim, an afternoon nap, a sit-down snack in a restaurant. The end result was that the kids got to see/ride everything they wanted without exhausting themselves (or us)—or spending most of their days in line. And we had almost zero tantrums (really!).

WHICH PARK TO SEE FIRST?

THIS QUESTION IS LESS ACADEMIC than it appears, especially if your party includes children or teenagers. Kids who see the Magic Kingdom first expect the same experience at the other parks. At Epcot, they're often disappointed by the educational orientation (as are many adults). Hollywood Studios offers some wild action along with family-friendly stage shows and attractions, but it can be seen in less than a day. Children may not find Animal Kingdom as exciting as the Magic Kingdom or the Studios—animals, after all, can't be programmed to entertain on cue.

First-time visitors should see Epcot first; you'll be able to enjoy it without having been preconditioned to think of Disney entertainment as solely fantasy or adventure.

See Disney's Animal Kingdom second. Like Epcot, it's educational, but its live animals provide a change of pace.

Next, see Disney's Hollywood Studios (DHS), which helps all ages transition from the educational Epcot and Animal Kingdom to the fanciful Magic Kingdom. Also, because DHS has few substantial attractions for the next several years, you won't walk as much or stay as long.

We recommend saving the Magic Kingdom for last, though we do recognize that for many readers the Magic Kingdom *is* Disney World.

OPERATING HOURS

THE DISNEY WORLD WEBSITE publishes preliminary park hours 180 days in advance, but schedule adjustments can happen at any time, including the day of your visit. Check disneyworld.com or call ☎ 407-824-4321 for the exact hours before you arrive. Off-season, parks may be open as few as 8 hours (9 a.m.–5 p.m.). At busy times (particularly holidays), they may operate 8 a.m.–2 a.m.

PARK SECURITY SCREENING

OVER THE PAST SEVERAL YEARS, Disney has been gradually increasing guest security screenings for park entry. In addition to full bag searches for all guests, some guests are also chosen for screening via walk-through metal detectors like you'd find at an airport. These increased screenings had created lengthy and frustrating backlogs at the park entrance gates. In an effort to decrease crowding at the gate area, in spring 2017 Disney began experimenting with moving security screenings to other areas of the resort, away from the park gates.

Guests arriving by car and boarding the Magic Kingdom–bound ferry or monorail will be screened at the Transportation and Ticket Center. Guests arriving at the Magic Kingdom via the resort loop monorail will be screened at the resorts before boarding. Guests arriving by bus will be screened closer to the bus drop point. Currently, the modified security process is only at the Magic Kingdom, but expect additions and changes to occur as Disney works out the specifics. It may be prudent to bake a few extra minutes into your park entry plan as Disney tinkers with their procedures.

OFFICIAL OPENING VERSUS REAL OPENING

WHEN YOU CHECK THE WEBSITE OR CALL, you're given "official hours." On many days, the parks open a bit earlier. If the official hours are 9 a.m.–9 p.m., for instance, Hollywood Boulevard at Disney's Hollywood Studios might open at 8:30 a.m., and the remainder of the park, at 9 a.m.

The Magic Kingdom is a special case in that Main Street, U.S.A., opens a full hour before the park's official opening time on days when Extra Magic Hours are *not* in effect. If the park's listed opening time is 9 a.m., then most of Main Street and the Central Plaza will be open for photos, shopping, and getting in line for rides by 8 a.m. (On days when the Magic Kingdom hosts morning EMHs, Main Street, Tomorrowland, and Fantasyland open at the same time.) This significantly alters the Magic Kingdom's early-morning traffic patterns by dumping, for example, up to 500 people at Seven Dwarfs Mine Train the instant the park opens. See page 89 for how to deal with this.

Rides and attractions shut down at approximately the official closing time. Some shopping venues, such as Main Street, U.S.A., in the Magic Kingdom, remain open 30 minutes to an hour after the rest of the park has closed.

THE VACATION THAT FIGHTS BACK

VISITING DISNEY WORLD REQUIRES levels of stamina more often associated with running a marathon. A British gentleman, thinking we exaggerated, measured his outings using a pedometer. His discovery:

> Our visits to the theme parks were spread over five days, during which my wife and I (ages 51 and 55) walked a total of 68 miles for an average of 13 miles per day!

At Walt Disney World, less is more. Take the World in small doses, with plenty of swimming, napping, reading, and relaxing in between. If you don't see everything, you can always come back.

An articulate Anchorage, Alaska, teen and her family found out the hard way the importance of building in time to decompress:

> We crammed our schedule a little too full, with seven parks—Disney, Universal, and SeaWorld—in eight full days. My older sisters would speed-walk from attraction to attraction while my parents straggled behind trying to keep up, while I was caught in the middle, both wanting to get to the next ride as fast as I could and wanting just to spend some quality time with my parents. No family should spend more than two consecutive days at the parks without a low-key day in the middle. I wish I'd known this going in.

Hitting the Wall

As you plan your time at Disney World, consider your physical limitations. It's exhausting to rise at dawn and run around a theme park for 8–12 hours day after day. Sooner or later (usually sooner), you hit the wall. To avoid that, use these two tips alone or in combination:

1. Take at least a morning off (preferably the entire day) after two consecutive days in the parks. See the "Full-Day/Sleep-In Alternating Days" section, next, for more details.

2. Return to your hotel for a 3- to 5-hour break each day you're in the theme parks.

FULL-DAY/SLEEP-IN ALTERNATING DAYS Throughout most of 2017, Animal Kingdom's longer evening hours and Hollywood Studios' construction closures make it possible to sleep in and still see everything in one day. That means you can alternate full days in Epcot and the Magic Kingdom with relaxed, late starts at the others, even on short trips. A sample four-day trip might look like this:

- Full day at Magic Kingdom
- Sleep late and visit the Studios or Animal Kingdom
- Full day at Epcot
- Sleep late and visit the park you've not yet seen

The key to those sleep-in days is setting up a touring plan with early-afternoon FastPass+ reservations. To get you started, we've created **late-start touring plans** for Animal Kingdom and Hollywood Studios. Check out the Animal Kingdom plan at tinyurl.com/sleepin-animal kingdom and the DHS plan at tinyurl.com/sleepin-hollywoodstudios.

THE PRACTICALITY OF RETURNING TO YOUR HOTEL FOR REST

MANY READERS WRITE ABOUT the practicality of departing the theme park for a nap and swim at the hotel. A dad from Sequim, Washington, made the following request:

> I would like to see nearness to the parks emphasized in your accommodation guide. We tried going back to the hotel for midday breaks, but it was too time-consuming. By the time you got to the car, negotiated traffic, rested, and reversed the process to get back to the park, it took 2–3 hours for a short rest and was not worth it!

We publish a chart in Part Three, Accommodations, that provides the commuting times to each of the Disney theme parks from many popular hotels within 20 miles of Walt Disney World. That said, we think this reader was overly anxious about being away from the parks. Two to 3 hours isn't make-or-break. Had he resigned himself to a 4- to 5-hour break, his family would've stayed rested and relaxed.

At Animal Kingdom, Hollywood Studios, and Epcot, you can get to your car in the parking lot in about 15–20 minutes. From the Magic Kingdom, it will take you 30–35 minutes. Obviously, if you're at the farthest point from the park entrance when you decide to return to the hotel, or you barely miss a parking-lot tram, it will take longer. But from most places in the parks, the previous times are correct. Once in your car, you'll be able to commute to most US 192 hotels, all Disney World hotels, all Lake Buena Vista hotels, and most hotels along the Interstate 4 corridor and south International Drive ("I-Drive") in 20 minutes or less. It will take about the same time to reach hotels on I-Drive north of Sand Lake Road and in the Universal Orlando area.

So, for most people, the one-way commute will average 35–40 minutes. But here's what you get for your time: a less-expensive lunch at a restaurant of your choosing, a swim, and a nap. If you add up the times, you'll be away from the parks about 4–5 hours, counting the commute. If you want, eat dinner outside the World before returning. Clearly, this won't work when the parks close early, but these aren't times when most families go to Disney World. If you visit when the parks close early, you'll see more attractions in less time *and* you'll be able to leave the parks earlier and take your break in the late afternoon or early evening.

ARRIVAL- AND DEPARTURE-DAY BLUES: WHAT TO DO WHEN YOU HAVE ONLY HALF A DAY

ON ARRIVAL AND DEPARTURE DAYS, you probably will have only part of a day for touring or other recreational pursuits. It's a common problem: You roll into the World about 1 p.m., excited and ready to go—but where?

The first question: Do you feel comfortable using a full day's admission to the parks when you have less than a full day to tour? The incremental cost to add another day of admission is small when you're visiting for three or more days, but significant if you're there for only a long weekend. Your arrival time and the parks' closing times are also considerations, but so is the touring disadvantage you suffer by not being on hand when a park opens. **FastPass+,** a reservation system for popular attractions (discussed starting on (page 94)), provides some relief from long afternoon lines, but it isn't available for every attraction, nor is there an unlimited supply of reservations.

Opting for a Partial Day at the Theme Parks

If you decide to use one day's admission on a half-day or less, refer to our *Unofficial Guide* Crowd Calendar at TouringPlans.com for the least-crowded park to visit.

You can make FastPass+ reservations for each park's most popular rides up to 60 days before your visit at disneyworld.com (it's 30 days in advance for Annual Pass holders and off-site guests with a valid ticket). You could try to obtain FastPass+ reservations when you arrive, but be aware that the daily allocation of FastPasses at popular rides may be gone by then.

One option, if you can reach the park before 1 p.m. and stay until closing (8–10 p.m., depending on season), is **Disney's Hollywood Studios,** which requires the least time to tour. Because guests who arrive at opening frequently complete their tour by about 3 p.m., crowds thin in late afternoon. Try to make FastPass+ reservations for Toy Story Mania! or Rock 'n' Roller Coaster in advance.

Whenever you arrive at a theme park (including Universal parks) after 10 a.m., you should go to higher-capacity attractions where waiting time is relatively brief, even during the most crowded part of the day. Besides FastPass+, another time-saver at Test Track in Epcot, Expedition Everest in Disney's Animal Kingdom, Rock 'n' Roller Coaster in Disney's Hollywood Studios, and several Universal Orlando attractions is the **singles line,** a separate line for individuals who are alone or don't mind riding alone. The objective is to fill odd spaces left by groups that don't quite fill the entire ride vehicle. Because there aren't many singles and most groups are unwilling to split up, singles lines are usually much shorter than regular lines.

Disney parks are better for partial-day touring than Universal parks because Disney parks generally operate more high-capacity attractions than Universal does. We like the Universal parks and admire their cutting-edge technology, but the best way to see them is to be there at opening and follow our touring plans.

Our clip-out Touring Plan Companions in the back of the book list attractions in each Disney park that require the least waiting during the most crowded part of the day. Although the queues for these attractions may seem humongous, they move quickly. Also check out parades, stage shows, and other live entertainment. Popular attractions generally stay packed until an hour or so before closing; however, they often require little waiting during evening parades, shows, or fireworks.

Alternatives to the Theme Parks on Arrival Day

Before you head out for fun on arrival day, you must check in, unpack, and buy admissions, and you probably will detour to the grocery or convenience store to buy snacks, drinks, and breakfast food. At all Disney resorts and many non-Disney hotels, you can't occupy your room until after 3 p.m. (4 p.m. for DVC resorts); however, many properties will check you in, sell you tickets, and store your luggage before that hour.

The least expensive way to spend your arrival day is to check in, unpack, do your chores, and relax at your hotel swimming pool.

Another daytime option is a trip to a local water park. Any one that stays open past 5 p.m. is worth a look because the crowds at all parks clear out substantially after 4 p.m. If the park is open late and you get hungry, you'll find ample fast food. See Part Fourteen for more info.

If you want something drier, we heartily recommend **Gatorland,** a quirky attraction on US 441 near Kissimmee (about 20 minutes from Walt Disney World). Gatorland, a slice of pre-Disney Florida, is exceptionally interesting and well managed. It's perfect for a half-day outing, provided you like alligators, snakes, and lizards. For information, call ☎ 800-393-5297 or go to gatorland.com.

If none of the previous fires your boiler, consider miniature golf (expensive in Walt Disney World, more reasonable outside it) or the entertainment lineup at Disney Springs (see Part Sixteen, page 753).

In the Evening

Dinner provides a great opportunity to plan the next day's activities. If you're hungry for entertainment too, take in a show at or after dinner. Disney also offers some dinner shows (see page 341), of which the *Hoop-Dee-Doo Musical Revue* is our pick. It's extremely popular, so make reservations well in advance. Note that the long-running Cirque du Soleil *La Nouba* is permanently closing on December 31, 2017.

Not up for a dinner show? Consider the nighttime-entertainment complexes at **Disney Springs** or Universal's **CityWalk.** Disney Springs includes The Edison (opens late 2017), which offers a burlesque show with dinner, and **Raglan Road,** an Irish pub with live music and good food. All are best appreciated by adults—energetic adults, at that.

Departure Days

Departure days don't seem to cause as much consternation as arrival days. If you want to visit a theme park on your departure day, get up early and be there when it opens. If you have a lot of time, check out and store your luggage with the bell desk or in your car. Or, if you can arrange a late checkout, you might want to return to your hotel for a shower and change of clothes before departing.

THE CARDINAL RULES FOR SUCCESSFUL TOURING

MANY VISITORS DON'T HAVE SIX DAYS to devote to Disney. Some are en route to other destinations or may wish to sample additional Central Florida attractions. For these visitors, efficient touring is a must.

Even the most time-effective touring plan won't allow you to comprehensively cover two or more major theme parks in one day. Plan to allocate an entire day to each park (an exception to this is when the parks close at different times, allowing you to tour one park until closing, then proceed to another).

One-Day Touring

A comprehensive one-day tour of the Magic Kingdom, Epcot, Disney's Animal Kingdom, or Disney's Hollywood Studios is possible, but it requires knowledge of the park, good planning, good navigation, and plenty of energy and endurance. One-day touring leaves little time for sit-down meals, prolonged browsing in shops, or lengthy breaks. Yes, it can be fun and rewarding, but allocating two days per park, especially for the Magic Kingdom and Epcot, is ideal.

A Connecticut couple in their 20s underscores the walking involved in seeing Walt Disney World:

> You don't realize how much you're going to walk on this vacation— take whatever amount you're thinking and double it.

Successfully touring the Magic Kingdom, Epcot, Animal Kingdom, or Disney's Hollywood Studios hinges on three rules:

1. Determine in Advance What You Really Want to See

Which attractions appeal to you most? Which ones would you like to experience if you have time left? What are you willing to forgo?

To help you set your touring priorities, we describe the theme parks and their attractions in detail. In each description, we include the authors' evaluation of the attraction and the opinions of Disney World guests expressed as star ratings. Five stars is the highest rating.

Finally, because Disney attractions range from midway-type rides and horse-drawn trolleys to high-tech extravaganzas, we've developed a hierarchy of categories to pinpoint an attraction's magnitude:

SUPER-HEADLINERS The best attractions the theme park has to offer. Mind-boggling in size, scope, and imagination, they represent the cutting edge of attraction technology and design.

HEADLINERS Multimillion-dollar, full-scale, themed adventures and theater presentations. Modern in technology and design and employing a full range of special effects.

MAJOR ATTRACTIONS More modestly themed adventures, but ones that incorporate state-of-the-art technologies. Or larger-scale attractions of older design.

MINOR ATTRACTIONS Midway-type rides, small "dark" rides (cars on a track, zigzagging through the dark), small theater presentations, transportation rides, and elaborate walk-through attractions.

DIVERSIONS Exhibits, both passive and interactive; include playgrounds, video arcades, and street theater.

Though not every attraction fits neatly into these descriptions, the categories provide a comparison of attraction size and scope. Remember that bigger and more elaborate doesn't always mean better. Peter Pan's Flight, a minor attraction in the Magic Kingdom, continues to be one of the park's most beloved rides. Likewise, for many young children, no attraction, regardless of size, surpasses Dumbo.

2. Arrive Early! Arrive Early! Arrive Early!

This is the single most important key to efficient touring and avoiding long lines. First thing in the morning, there are no lines and fewer people. The same four rides you experience in 1 hour in early morning can take as long as 3 hours after 10:30 a.m. Eat breakfast before you arrive; don't waste prime touring time sitting in a restaurant.

The earlier a park opens, the greater your advantage. This is because most vacationers won't make the effort to rise early and get to a park before it opens. Fewer people are willing to make an 8 a.m. opening than a 9 a.m. opening. If you visit during midsummer, arrive at the turnstile 30–40 minutes before opening. During holiday periods, arrive 45–60 minutes early.

Many readers share their experiences about getting to the parks before opening. From a 13-year-old girl from Bloomington, Indiana:

Please stress this to your readers: If you want to ride anything with a short wait, you have to get up in the morning! If this is a sacrifice you aren't willing to make, reconsider a Disney World vacation.

A Pennsylvania mom of two found that slacking didn't pay:

Be there at rope drop. I went during one of the slowest times of the year, and the morning I didn't wake up for rope drop I was able to experience less than half of what I did the other days.

A mom from Chatham, Virginia, discovered there's more to arriving at the parks before opening than she imagined:

There were several days in which we left for the parks 45–60 minutes prior to opening, which I had figured into the touring plans. However, due to long lines at the bus stop or buses not coming as often as expected; long lines for bag inspection; or long lines and congestion at the park entrance, we never arrived at the anticipated time, and I had to optimize my touring plan often. This often meant we couldn't see some of the more popular attractions.

If getting the kids up earlier than usual makes for rough sailing, don't despair: You'll have a great time no matter when you get to the park. Many families with young children have found that it's better to accept the relative inefficiencies of arriving at the park a bit late than to jar the children out of their routine. In our guide especially for families, *The Unofficial Guide to Walt Disney World with Kids,* we provide a number of special touring plans (including touring plans for sleepyheads) that we don't have room for in this guide.

3. Avoid Bottlenecks

Helping you avoid bottlenecks is what the *Unofficial Guide* is about. This involves being able to predict where, when, and why they occur. Concentrations of hungry people create bottlenecks at restaurants during lunch and dinner; concentrations of people moving toward the exit near closing time cause gift shops en route to clog; concentrations of visitors at new and popular rides, and at rides slow to load and unload, create logjams and long lines.

Our solution for avoiding bottlenecks is touring plans for the Magic Kingdom, Epcot, Disney's Animal Kingdom, Disney's Hollywood Studios, and the two Disney water parks. We also provide detailed information on rides and performances, enabling you to estimate how long you may have to wait in line and allowing you to compare rides for their crowd capacity.

All touring plans are in the back of this book, following the indexes. Plans for Magic Kingdom begin on page 819 and for Epcot on page 825. A one-day touring plan for Animal Kingdom and two different plans for Disney's Hollywood Studios follow, on pages 830–832. Next come one-day touring plans for Universal's Islands of Adventure and Universal Studios Florida, on pages 833 and 834, respectively; a plan for both parks is on pages 835 and 836. Touring plans for Blizzard Beach and Typhoon Lagoon water parks are found on pages 837 and 838, respectively.

WHAT'S A QUEUE?

ALTHOUGH USED MORE IN THE UK than in the United States, **queue** (pronounced "cue") is the universal English word for a line, such as one in which you wait to cash a check at the bank or to board a ride at a theme park. **Queuing theory,** a mathematical area of specialization within the field of operations research, studies and models how lines work. Because the *Unofficial Guide* draws heavily on this discipline, we use some of its terminology. In addition to the noun, the verb **to queue** means to get in line, and a **queuing area** is a waiting area that accommodates a line. When guests decline to join a queue because they perceive the wait to be too long, they're said to **balk.**

OF UTMOST IMPORTANCE: READ THIS!

IN ANALYZING READER SURVEYS, we're astonished by the percentage of readers who *don't* use our touring plans. Scientifically tested and proven, these plans can save you **4 entire hours** or more of waiting in line in a single day—4 fewer hours of standing, 4 hours freed up to do something fun. Our groundbreaking research that created the touring plans has been the subject of front-page articles in the *Dallas Morning News* and *The New York Times* and has been cited in numerous scholarly journals. So why would you *not* use them?

We get a ton of reader mail—98% of it positive—commenting on our touring plans. First, from a mother who planned a last-minute trip:

We rode all of the main attractions in Epcot, Magic Kingdom, and Hollywood Studios over a three-day period, and we didn't wait more than 10 minutes for any ride—and this was during spring break!

An Ohio family felt the wind in their sails:

The whole time we were in the Magic Kingdom, following the touring plan, it seemed that we were traveling in front of a hurricane—we'd wait 10 minutes or so for an attraction (or less—sometimes we just walked right on), but when we got out and started moving on to the next one, we could see the line building for what we just did.

A family of four from Louisville, Kentucky, had this to say:

If there is one cult in this world I could join, it would be the staff of the Unofficial Guide. *I tell everyone going to Disney to use this book, and the awesome app. Years ago, we tried to convince friends to use the book, but they were scared off by the highly structured nature of the touring plans. We happened to see them at Disney during a late summer afternoon. Our family had enjoyed a full day with lots of rides and no more than a 20-minute wait. They had been on two total rides, standing in line over 1½ hours each time. They were miserable, and already considering escaping back to the hotel.*

A mom from Warren, Arkansas, gave the touring plans a shot:

This is our fifth family trip to WDW, and this was my first time to use a touring plan. I have read the books and been a member of Lines for years. However, I never bought into the demands of the touring plan. After this last trip, I am officially a fan! I cannot express to you how much better our trip was since we followed a plan. We accomplished more in the first hour of Magic Kingdom than we used to accomplish in 3 hours. My family will use touring plans from now on.

A woman from Westminster, Colorado, chimed in with this:

I love the Unofficial Guides. *I love the humor, and I feel like I get a real idea of what to expect. When I first told my family I wanted to use the touring plans to maximize our theme park experience, they thought I was crazy. I secretly cut the plans out of the book and stowed them in my day pack, then urged us in the direction of the plans. After the first day they were shocked at how much we got done and how few huge lines we had to wait in. When I told them that we had actually followed your touring plans, they happily followed them the rest of the trip. It made a huge difference with the crowds and heat of summer!*

A 30-something mom of two from Oconomowoc, Wisconsin, found that the touring plans fanned the flames of *amour:*

My husband was a bit doubtful about using a touring plan, but on our first day at Magic Kingdom, after we'd done all the Fantasyland attractions and ridden Splash Mountain twice before lunch, he looked at me with amazement and said, "I've never been so attracted to you."

Finally, from an Edmonds, Washington, family who used the touring plans for Universal's Islands of Adventure:

This trip was the first time we were actually going to leave the property (gasp!) and go to Universal, and I was very happy that you included a touring plan for Islands of Adventure. It worked like a charm! I've always wondered how it feels to follow your plans not ever having seen the park before, and now I know—it was easy!

TOURING PLANS: WHAT THEY ARE AND HOW THEY WORK

See More, Do More, Wait Less

From the first edition of the *Unofficial Guide*, minimizing our readers' waits in line has been a top priority. We know from our research and that of others that theme park patrons measure overall satisfaction based on the number of attractions they're able to experience during a visit: the more attractions, the better. Thus, we developed and offered our readers field-tested touring plans that allow them to experience as many attractions as possible with the least amount of waiting in line.

> *unofficial* **TIP**
> The facts and figures in our books come from years of data collection and analysis by expert statisticians, programmers, field researchers, and lifelong Disney enthusiasts.

Our touring plans have always been based on theme-park-traffic flow, attraction capacity, the maximum time a guest is willing to wait (called a **balking constraint**), walking distance between attractions, and waiting-time data collected at every attraction in every park, every day of the year. The plans derived from a combinatorial model (for anyone who cares) that approximated the most time-efficient sequence in which to visit the attractions of a specific park. After we created a preliminary touring plan from the model, we field-tested it in the park, using a test group (who followed our plan) and a control group (who didn't have our plan and who toured the park using their own best judgment).

The two groups were compared, and the results were amazing. On days of heavy attendance, the groups touring without our plans spent an average of 4 hours more in line and experienced 37% fewer attractions than did those who did use the plans.

Over the years, this research has been recognized by both the travel industry and academe, having been cited by such diverse sources as the *Atlanta Journal-Constitution, Bottom Line,* the *Dallas Morning News,* the Mathematical Association of America, *Money,* the *New York Times, Operations Research Forum, Travel Weekly, USA Today,* and *Wired,* along with the BBC, CBS News, Fox News, and the Travel Channel. The methodology behind our touring plans was also used as a case study in the 2010 book *Numbers Rule Your World,* by Kaiser Fung, professor of statistics at New York University.

So how good *are* the touring plans in the *Unofficial Guide?* Our computer program typically gets within about 2% of the optimal touring plan and finds an optimal plan for most straightforward situations around 70% of the time. If, for instance, the hypothetical "perfect" Adult One-Day Touring Plan took about 10 hours to complete, then the *Unofficial Guide* touring plan would take around 10 hours and 12 minutes.

In the 2003 edition of this guidebook, we noted the possibility of using our software to see every attraction in the Magic Kingdom in one day. We dubbed this the **Ultimate Magic Kingdom Touring Plan** and offered it free to anyone up for the challenge. Dozens of otherwise-sane families have completed this plan since that time, and hundreds have come close. The current record-holders are Jordyn and Kenny White of Gun Barrel City, Texas, who saw 98 attractions in 23 hours and 54 minutes on May 23, 2014 (the Magic Kingdom was open for 24 consecutive hours). That works out to roughly 1 attraction every 15 minutes. Other "ultimate" plans exist for Epcot, DHS, and Disney's Animal Kingdom. Drop us a line or visit touringplans.com/ultimate if you're up for the challenge. *Note:* These plans are serious business—more akin to running a marathon than to merely touring the parks.

Customize Your Touring Plans

The attractions included in our touring plans are the most popular as determined by almost 72,000 reader surveys. If you've never been to Walt Disney World, we suggest using the plans in this book. Not only are they the best our program can produce, they've been field-tested by tens of thousands of families. They'll ensure that you see the best Disney attractions with as little waiting in line as possible.

If you're a return visitor, your favorite attractions may be different. One way to customize the plans is to go to TouringPlans.com to create personalized versions. Tell the software the date, time, and park you've chosen to visit, along with the attractions you want to see. Your custom plan will tell you, for your specific travel date and time, the exact order in which to visit attractions to minimize your waits in line. Our touring plans also support "switching off" on thrill rides (see page 439). Besides attractions, you can schedule meals, breaks, character greetings, and more. You can even tell your plans how fast you plan to walk, and they'll make the necessary adjustments. Plus, the plans can handle any FastPass+ reservations you've already got and tell you which attractions would benefit most from using them.

Our custom touring plans get rave reviews from readers and website subscribers. From an Edmonton, Alberta, reader:

We love the ability to personalize the touring plans! Because we rarely arrive at park opening we can't use the ones printed in the book. The personalized plans let us reduce wait times and eliminate arguing about what we are going to do next. Everyone can see their "big" attraction coming up on the plan and we know we'll get to them all.

From a mother of two from Halifax, Nova Scotia:

I was hesitant to pay additional money to get the TouringPlans.com membership, but boy, am I glad I did! My husband was hesitant about needing to have a plan for the park, but when we got there and he saw how we beat all the lines by following it and using the FastPasses suggested in the book, he was happy we had the plan. We also used the Lines app in the park to see the waiting times for rides, which were much more accurate than the Disney posted times. Next time we go to Disney World, the very first thing we will do is get a website membership!

From an Alexandria, Virginia, mom:

The touring plans helped make our vacation perfect! We visited WDW over spring break, the week before Easter. It was CROWDED. We saw signs for 90- to 120-minute waits on some of the rides. Using our touring plans, we only waited for 30 minutes once. Other than that, our longest wait was 20 minutes and most of our other waits were 0–10 minutes. We would have had a completely different vacation without the touring plans. They were life-savers!

From a couple across the pond in London:

The personalized touring plans and the Lines app worked really well. In our five days at the parks, we managed to ride everything we wanted to multiple times. Even though there were posted waits of up to and over 120 minutes for some rides at peak times, we very rarely waited more than 15 minutes, and most times we just walked straight up to the rides.

Finally, from a Chelsea, Alabama, reader:

The book and the personal touring plans are like a one-two punch. Between them we were completely covered

Alternatively, some changes are simple enough to make on your own. If a plan calls for an attraction you're not interested in, simply skip it and move on to the next one. You can also substitute similar attractions in the same area of the park. If a plan calls for, say, riding Dumbo and you'd rather not, but you would enjoy the Mad Tea Party (which is not on the plan), then go ahead and substitute that for Dumbo. As long as the substitution is a similar attraction—substituting a show for a ride won't work—and is pretty close by the attraction called for in the touring plan, you won't compromise the plan's overall effectiveness.

A family of four from South Slocan, British Columbia, found they could easily tailor the touring plans to meet their needs:

We amended your touring plans by taking out the attractions we didn't want to do and just doing the remainder in order. It worked great, and by arriving before the parks opened, we got to see everything we wanted, with virtually no waits!

As did a Jacksonville, Florida, family:

We used a combination of the Two-Day Touring Plan for Parents with Small Children and the Two-Day Touring Plan for Adults. We were able to get on almost everything with a 10-minute wait or less.

OVERVIEW OF THE TOURING PLANS

OUR TOURING PLANS ARE STEP-BY-STEP guides for seeing as much as possible with a minimum of standing in line. They're designed to help you avoid crowds and bottlenecks on any day of the year.

What You Can Realistically Expect from the Touring Plans

Though we present one-day touring plans for each theme park, be aware that the Magic Kingdom and Epcot have more attractions than you can reasonably expect to see in one day. Because the two-day plans for the Magic Kingdom and Epcot are the most comprehensive, efficient, and relaxing, we strongly recommend them over the one-day plans. However, if you must cram your visit into a single day, the one-day plans will allow you to see as much as is humanly possible.

Variables That Affect the Success of the Touring Plans

*un*official **TIP**
Because construction at Disney's Hollywood Studios has closed many attractions, seeing the ones that remain open there in a single day is doable. Likewise, Disney's Animal Kingdom is a one-day outing.

The plans' success will be affected by how quickly you move from ride to ride; when and how many refreshment and restroom breaks you take; when, where, and how you eat; and whether you have young children in your tour group, among other factors. Switching off (page 439), also known as "The Baby Swap," among other things, inhibits families with little ones from moving expeditiously among attractions. Plus, some folks simply cannot conform to the plans' "early to rise" conditions, as this reader from Cleveland Heights, Ohio, recounts:

Our touring plans were thrown totally off by one member who could not be on time for opening. Even in October, this made a huge difference in our ability to see attractions without waiting.

The Disney Dining Plan's required restaurant reservations impose a rigid schedule that can also derail a touring plan, as this Wichita, Kansas, mom attests:

The [printed] touring plans were impractical if used with the dining plan. The hourlong meals wreaked havoc on the itinerary, and we never seemed to be able to get back on track.

Along with dining breaks, the appearance of a Disney character usually stops a touring plan in its tracks. While some characters stroll the parks, it's equally common that they assemble in a specific venue where families queue up for photos and autographs. Meeting characters, posing for photos, and getting autographs can burn hours of touring time.

If your kids love characters, you need to anticipate these interruptions by including character greetings when creating your online touring plans, or else negotiate some understanding with your children about when you'll collect autographs. Note that queues for autographs, especially in the Magic Kingdom and Disney's Animal Kingdom, are sometimes as long as or longer than the queues for major attractions. The only time-efficient ways to collect autographs are to use FastPass+ where available (such as for Mickey Mouse and the Disney princesses at the Magic Kingdom) or to line up at the character-greeting areas first thing in the morning. Early morning is also the best time to experience popular attractions, so you may have some tough choices to make.

Some things are beyond your control. Chief among these are the manner and timing of bringing a particular ride to capacity. For example, Big Thunder Mountain Railroad, a roller coaster in the Magic Kingdom, has five trains. On a given morning, it may begin operation with two of the five, then add the other three when needed. If the waiting line builds rapidly before operators go to full capacity, you could have a long wait, even in early morning.

A variable that can give your touring plans a boost is the singles line (see page 79), as this English reader explains:

> *We found that the touring plans worked even better in conjunction with single-rider queues. The only rides that we queued up for normally were ones with a 20-minute-or-less queue time and wet rides.*

Another variable is your arrival time for a theater show: You'll wait from the time you arrive until the end of the presentation in progress. The sooner you arrive after the show has started, the longer you'll wait; conversely, the later you arrive, the shorter your wait will be.

While we realize that following the touring plans isn't always easy, we nevertheless recommend continuous, expeditious touring until around noon. After that, breaks and diversions won't affect the plans significantly.

What to Do if You Lose the Thread

If unforeseen events interrupt a plan:

1. If you're following a touring plan in our **Lines** app (**touringplans.com/lines**), just press "Optimize" when you're ready to start touring again. Lines will figure out the best possible plan for the remainder of your day.

2. If you're following a printed touring plan, skip a step on the plan for every 20 minutes' delay. For example, if you lose your wallet and spend an hour hunting for it, skip three steps and pick up from there.

3. Forget the plan and organize the remainder of your day using the standby wait times listed in Lines or the Clip-Out Touring Plan Companions in the back of this book.

What to Expect When You Arrive at the Parks

Because most of the touring plans are based on being present when the theme park opens, you need to know about opening procedures. Disney transportation to the parks begins 1½–2 hours before official opening. The parking lots open at around the same time. Each park has an entrance plaza outside the turnstiles, where you'll be held until the next stage in the park-opening process happens.

That next step depends on the park you're visiting, the season, and the day's crowds:

1. **STANDARD OPENING PROCEDURES** At the Magic Kingdom on days when morning Extra Magic Hours are not in effect, you'll be admitted past the turnstiles about an hour before park opening, but you'll be confined to Main Street, U.S.A., and the Central Plaza until official opening time. Ropes and a human wall of Disney cast members keep you there until opening, when the wall speed-walks you back to the headliner attractions (to prevent anyone from running or getting trampled). The effect of this procedure is to cause instant, hourlong waits at Seven Dwarfs Mine Train as soon as the park opens, and more-moderate waits at other headliners. See the Magic Kingdom chapter (Part Nine, page 515) for more details on how to deal with this.

    Animal Kingdom starts admitting guests past the turnstiles about 30 minutes prior to official opening. This crowd is either stopped at the Oasis or led up to the base of the Tree of Life on Discovery Island, depending on the crowd size. Guests are held there until a few minutes before the park's official opening. A short announcement is played, possibly accompanied by the arrival of Disney characters to mark the event. After that, you'll be released to head to your first attraction.

Epcot allows guests past the main entrance turnstiles anywhere from 15 to 30 minutes before official opening. Most of the time, guests are held in Future World Plaza until about 10 minutes before official opening, at which time the rides start running and guests are released to enjoy them. Epcot's International Gateway typically starts admitting guests about 10 minutes before official opening, so guests arriving at the park entrance often have a sizable head start to their first attraction.

At Disney's Hollywood Studios, you'll be admitted past the turnstiles and onto Hollywood Boulevard about 15 minutes prior to official opening. Some shops and food carts will be open. If your child wants to participate in the *Jedi Training: Trials of the Temple* stage show, you'll be directed to that sign-up location immediately. Ropes will be set up to hold everyone else on Hollywood Boulevard until the park officially opens.

2. HIGH-ATTENDANCE DAYS   When large crowds are expected, you'll usually be admitted through the turnstiles up to 30 minutes before official opening at Epcot, the Studios, and Animal Kingdom, and at least an hour at the Magic Kingdom. (We've experienced a 6:25 a.m. opening for an official 7 a.m. start.) Much of the park may be operating, and Disney may permit you to head to your first attraction immediately upon entering.

In the first scenario above, you gain a big advantage if you're already past the turnstiles when the park opens. While everyone else is stuck in line waiting for the people ahead to find their tickets and figure out how the biometric scans work, the lucky few (hundreds) already in the park will be in line for their first attraction. You'll probably be done and on your way to your second before many of them are even in the park, and the time savings accrue throughout the rest of the day.

Clip-Out Touring Plans

For your convenience, we've prepared graphical clip-out copies of all touring plans. These pocket versions combine touring plan itineraries with maps and directions. Select the plan appropriate for your party, and get familiar with it. Then clip the pocket version from the back of this guide and carry it with you as a quick reference at the theme park.

Will the Plans Continue to Work Once the Secret Is Out?

Yes! First, all the plans require that a patron be there when a park opens. Many Disney World patrons simply won't get up early while on vacation. Second, less than 2% of any day's attendance has been exposed to the plans—too few to affect results. Last, most groups tailor the plans, skipping rides or shows according to taste.

How Frequently Are the Touring Plans Revised?

We revise these touring plans each time the book is printed, and updates are always available at TouringPlans.com. If you're using an online version of a plan, our app will even adjust for ride breakdowns and changes to show schedules.

Things Beyond Our Control: Weather and Staffing

The two biggest unaccounted-for factors that determine your waits in line are the weather and Disney's staffing of the rides. We know, for example, that crowds will be substantially lower than usual on a day where Disney World gets more than half an inch of rain. Crowds bounce back to higher than expected on the first nice day after that rain. We're working to model this in our short-term crowd forecasts.

The other thing we can't predict is how many people Disney will use to staff the rides. Here's some background: The touring plan software uses some fairly sophisticated machine-learning algorithms to predict how long you'll wait in line. Into those models, we feed millions and millions of wait times we've collected from Disney World's rides. To each of those wait times, we attach up to 600 other pieces of information, including everything from the day of week, the parks' operating schedules, public school calendars, and various US financial metrics (such as three- to nine-month CPI and unemployment trends) to similar measures for the economies of Canada, the UK, and Brazil.

After adjusting for those hundreds of factors we track, we noticed two spikes in wait times, one in September 2015 and another, larger peak that began around September 2016 and is ongoing as we went to press. These spikes can't be explained by school calendars, changes in the US economy, or anything else we're aware of. We're reasonably sure—because we've asked around—that they represent Disney's using fewer people to run the rides. With fewer employees, it takes longer to load and unload the rides and more time to handle FastPass+ returns at the rides at which it's offered. We've heard various theories about why Disney does this, from trying to make up for cost overruns at other parks to trying to make up for losses at ESPN. The point is that it's hard for us to know ahead of time that these things are coming or how long they'll last.

"Bouncing Around"

Some readers object to crisscrossing a theme park as our touring plans sometimes require. A woman from Decatur, Georgia, told us she "got dizzy from all the bouncing around." Believe us, we empathize.

We've worked hard over the years to eliminate the need to crisscross a theme park in our touring plans. (In fact, our customized software can minimize walking instead of waiting in line, if that's important to you.) Occasionally, however, it's possible to save a lot of time in line with a few extra minutes of walking.

unofficial **TIP**
Because an attraction's FastPass+ availability is limited by its hourly rider capacity, those who book last-minute trips or buy admission at the gate may find that reservations are no longer available at their favorite attractions.

The reasons for this are varied. Sometimes a park is designed intentionally to require walking. In the Magic Kingdom, for example, the most popular attractions are positioned as far apart as possible—in the north, east, and west corners of the park—so that guests are more evenly distributed throughout the day. Other times, you may be visiting just after a new attraction has opened that everyone wants to try. In that case, a special trip to visit the new attraction may be required earlier in the day than normal, in order to avoid longer waits later.

And live shows, especially at the Studios, sometimes have performance schedules so at odds with each other (and the rest of the park's schedule) that orderly touring is impossible.

If you want to experience headliner attractions in one day without long waits, you can see those first (requires crisscrossing the park), use FastPass+ (if available), or hope to squeeze in visits during parades and the last hour the park is open (may not work).

If you have two days to visit the Magic Kingdom or Epcot, use their respective Two-Day Touring Plans (see pages 822 and 823 for the Magic Kingdom, pages 828 and 829 for Epcot). These spread the popular attractions over two mornings and work great even when the parks close early.

Touring Plans and the Obsessive-Compulsive Reader

We suggest sticking to the plans religiously, especially in the mornings, if you're visiting during busy times. The consequence of touring spontaneity in peak season is hours of standing in line. When using the plans, however, relax and always be prepared for surprises and setbacks.

If you find your type-A brain doing cartwheels, reflect on the advice of a woman from Trappe, Pennsylvania:

I had been planning for this trip for two years and researching it using guidebooks, websites, videos, and information from WDW. On night three of our trip, I ended up taking an unscheduled trip to the ER. When the doctor asked what seemed to be the problem, I responded, "I don't know—but I can't stop shaking and I can't stay here very long, because I have to get up in a couple hours to go to Disney's Hollywood Studios." Diagnosis: an anxiety attack caused by my excessive itinerary.

An Omaha, Nebraska, couple devised their own way to cope:

We created our own 4.25 x 5.5 guidebook for our trip that included a number of pages from the TouringPlans.com website. This was the first page:

The Type-A Spouse's Bill of Rights
1. We will not see everything in one vacation, and any attempt to do so may be met with blunt trauma.
2. Len Testa will not be vacationing with us. His plans don't schedule time for benches. Ours may.
3. We may deviate from the touring plans at some point. Really.
4. Even if it isn't on the Disney Dining Plan, a funnel cake or other snack may be purchased without a grouchy face from the nonpurchasing spouse.
5. Sometimes, sitting by the pool may sound more fun than going to a park, show, or other scheduled event. On this vacation, that will be fine.
6. "But I thought we were going to . . ." is a phrase that must be stricken from the discussion of any plans that had not been previously discussed as a couple.
7. Other items may be added as circumstances dictate at the parks.

It was a much happier vacation with these generally understood principles in writing.

Touring Plan Rejection

Some folks don't respond well to the regimentation of a touring plan. If you encounter this problem with someone in your party, roll with the punches, as this Maryland couple did:

The rest of the group was not receptive to the use of the touring plans. I think they all thought I was being a little too regimented about planning this vacation. Rather than argue, I left the touring plans behind as we ventured off for the parks. You can guess the outcome.

A reader from Royal Oak, Michigan, ran into trouble by not getting her family on board ahead of time:

The one thing I will suggest is if one member of the family is doing most of the research and planning (like I did), that they communicate what the book/touring plans suggest. I failed to do this and it led to some, shall we say, tense moments between my husband and me on our first day. However, once he realized how much time we were saving, he understood why I was so bent on following the plans.

Touring Plans for Low-Attendance Days

We receive a number of letters each year similar to the following one from Lebanon, New Jersey:

The guide always assumed there would be large crowds. We had no lines. An alternate tour for low-traffic days would be helpful.

There are, thankfully, still days on which crowds are low enough that a full-day touring plan isn't needed. However, some attractions in each park bottleneck even if attendance is low:

MAGIC KINGDOM *Enchanted Tales with Belle,* The Many Adventures of Winnie the Pooh, Peter Pan's Flight, Seven Dwarfs Mine Train, Space Mountain, Splash Mountain

EPCOT Frozen Ever After, Soarin', Test Track

DISNEY'S ANIMAL KINGDOM Avatar Flight of Passage, Dinosaur, Expedition Everest, Kilimanjaro Safaris, Na'Vi River Journey

DHS Rock 'n' Roller Coaster, Toy Story Mania!, The Twilight Zone Tower of Terror

Huge lines also build for meet and greets involving characters from Disney's latest films. When the Frozen princesses first appeared at the Magic Kingdom, for example, 2-hour waits were common from the moment the park opened. For this reason, we recommend following a touring plan through the first five or six steps. If you're pretty much walking onto every attraction, scrap the remainder of the plan. Alternatively, experience the attractions above right after the park opens, or use FastPass+.

EXTRA MAGIC HOURS AND THE TOURING PLANS

IF YOU'RE A DISNEY RESORT GUEST and use your morning Extra Magic Hours privileges, complete your early-entry touring before the general public is admitted, then position yourself to follow the touring plan. When the public is admitted, the park will suddenly swarm. A Wilmington, Delaware, mother advises:

The early-entry times went like clockwork. We were finishing up the Great Movie Ride when Disney's Hollywood Studios opened to the public, and we had to wait in line quite a while for Voyage of the Little Mermaid, *which sort of screwed up everything thereafter. Early-opening attractions should be finished up well before regular opening time so you can be at the plan's first stop as early as possible.*

In the Magic Kingdom, early-entry attractions currently operate in Fantasyland and Tomorrowland. At Epcot, they're in the Future World section. At Disney's Animal Kingdom, they're in DinoLand U.S.A., Asia, Africa, and Pandora. At Disney's Hollywood Studios, they're dispersed. Practically speaking, see any attractions on the plan that are open for early entry, crossing them off as you do. If you finish all early-entry attractions and have time left before the general public is admitted, sample early-entry attractions not included in the plan. Stop touring about 10 minutes before the public is admitted, and position yourself for the first attraction on the plan that wasn't open for early entry. During early entry in the Magic Kingdom, for example, you can almost always experience Seven Dwarfs Mine Train and Under the Sea: Journey of the Little Mermaid in Fantasyland, plus Space Mountain in Tomorrowland. As official opening nears, go to the boundary between Fantasyland and Liberty Square and be ready to blitz Splash and Big Thunder Mountains according to the touring plan when the rest of the park opens.

Evening Extra Magic Hours, when a designated park remains open for Disney resort guests 2 hours beyond normal closing time, have less effect on the touring plans than early entry in the morning. Parks are almost never scheduled for both early entry and evening Extra Magic Hours on the same day. Thus a park offering evening Extra Magic Hours will enjoy a fairly normal morning and early afternoon. It's not until late afternoon, when park hoppers coming from the other theme parks descend, that the late-closing park will become especially crowded. By that time, you'll be well toward the end of your touring plan.

FASTPASS+

THE LATEST EVOLUTION of this 18-year-old ride-reservation system, FastPass+ is a milestone in Disney's never-ending quest to create something more complicated than the US tax code or the Affordable Care Act.

unofficial **TIP**
Disney offers FastPass+ only for select attractions —around 70 in all. Specific FastPass+ information for each Disney theme park is provided in its respective chapter.

The original iteration of FastPass was introduced in 1999 as a way to moderate high wait times at some of Disney's headliner attractions. A new version of the system, called FastPass+, completely replaced the old one in January 2014. Where the old system printed your reservation times on small slips of paper dispensed from ATM-like kiosks next to each attraction, the current FastPass+ system is (with one exception described later) entirely electronic: You must use a computer, mobile device, or in-park terminal to make and modify FastPass+ reservations, and you must use your RFID-enabled MagicBand, Key to the World Card, or day-guest card to redeem the reservation. As before, FastPass+ is free of charge to all Walt Disney World guests.

Because FastPass+ has a learning curve, understanding how to use it is important for success when using our touring plans, especially if you want to experience lots of attractions or you're unable to arrive at park opening. Somewhat like making a dinner reservation at a restaurant, FastPass+ allows you to reserve a ride on an attraction at a Disney theme park. You can request a specific time, such as 7:30 p.m., or you can let the system give you its "first available" reservation.

Although we take issue with the current system's complicated rules and procedures, we do concede that FastPass+ can help you see more with less waiting, **provided you know how to use it.** Like the old Fast-Pass, it reduces waits for designated attractions by distributing guests at those attractions throughout the day. Also like the old system, FastPass+ provides an incentive—a shorter wait—for guests who are willing to postpone experiencing a given attraction until later in the day. The system also, in effect, imposes a penalty—standby status—on guests who don't use it. However, spreading out guest arrivals sometimes decreases waits for standby guests as well.

FastPass+ does **not** eliminate the need to arrive early at a theme park. Because each park offers a limited number of FastPass+ attractions, you still have to make an early start if you want to avoid long lines at non-FastPass+ attractions.

Making a FastPass+ Reservation

Anyone with an upcoming stay at a Walt Disney World hotel can make FastPass+ reservations up to 60 days in advance at disneyworld.com and through the My Disney Experience app; Annual Pass holders staying off-property may reserve up to 30 days in advance, as may day guests with a valid ticket.

unofficial **TIP**
You'll be notified of any issues with FastPass+ reservations through the My Disney Experience mobile app.

If you buy your admission the day you arrive at the park or you want to change your previous FastPass+ selections once you're inside, you can do so using the mobile app or new in-park computer terminals.

You should set aside **at least** 30–40 minutes to complete the advance-booking process. Before you begin, make sure that you have the following items on hand:

- A valid admission ticket or purchase-confirmation number for everyone in your group
- Your hotel-reservation number, if you're staying on-site
- A computer, smartphone, or tablet connected to the Internet
- An e-mail account that you can access easily while traveling
- An account at mydisneyexperience.com
- A schedule of the parks you'll be visiting each day, including arrival and departure times, plus the times of any midday breaks
- The dates, times, and confirmation numbers of any dining or recreation reservations you've already made
- A fistful of Xanax
- The patience of Job

If you're coordinating travel plans with friends or family who live elsewhere, the following information is also good to have:

- The names and (optionally) e-mail addresses of the people you're traveling with
- A schedule of the parks these folks are visiting on each day of their trip, including their arrival, departure, and break times
- The dates and times of any dining or recreation reservations these folks have made

Again, the only way to make FastPass+ reservations before your trip is to use the My Disney Experience (MDE) website or app—you can't make them by phone, the way you would for a restaurant reservation. We think it's easier to use the website, so we'll describe that here; the steps for the app are similar.

1. E-MAIL ACCESS Because the MDE site uses your e-mail address to identify you and send you new login credentials should you forget your old ones (see next step), you need to make sure you'll have easy access to your account while you're in the parks. If you don't have a mobile app for your e-mail account, download and configure it before you leave home. And if you don't have an account with a web-based service such as Gmail, go ahead and set one up—webmail is much easier to configure for mobile devices than e-mail you get through your ISP.

2. MY DISNEY EXPERIENCE ACCESS Now go to the MDE site and click "Sign In or Create Account" in the upper-right corner; then click "Create

Account" on the screen that follows. You'll be asked for your e-mail address, along with your name, home address, and birth date. (Disney uses your home address to send your MagicBands and, if applicable, hotel-reservation information.) You'll also be asked to choose two security questions and answers—write these down and store them in a safe place, or save them as a text file. If you forget your MDE login information, Disney will ask you these questions to verify your identity.

3. DISNEY HOTEL INFORMATION Next, MDE asks whether you'll be staying at a Disney hotel. If you are, enter your reservation number. This associates your MDE account with your hotel stay in Disney's computer systems. If you've booked a travel package that includes theme park admission, Disney computers will automatically link the admission to your MDE account, allowing you to skip Step 5 below.

4. REGISTER FRIENDS AND FAMILY You'll now be asked for the names, ages, and e-mail addresses of everyone traveling with you. This is so you can make dining and FastPass+ reservations for your entire group at the same time later in the process. You can add family and friends at any time, but you might as well do it now.

5. REGISTER TICKETS If you've bought your admission from a third-party ticket reseller or you have tickets or MagicBands left over from a previous trip, you'll be asked to register those next. On each ticket is printed a unique ID code, usually a string of 12–20 numbers, located at one corner on the back; on MagicBands, look for a 12-digit number printed inside the band. Enter the ID code for each ticket you have.

You can make FastPass+ reservations for as many days as there are on your ticket. If you decide later to extend your stay, you'll be able to make reservations for additional days. If you've got a voucher that needs to be converted to a ticket at the parks, you can still register it by calling Disney tech support at ☎ 407-939-7765.

6. SELECT A DATE AND A PARK Click on the My Disney Experience logo in the upper-right corner of your screen. A menu should appear, with "FastPass+" as one of the choices. Click on "Make New FastPass+ Reservation."

The next screen should display a monthly seven-day calendar, beginning around the start of your trip's dates. Select one of these dates and click "Next."

7. SELECT TRAVEL PARTY On the screen that follows, you'll choose which of your friends and family will use the FastPass+ reservations you're making. Note that everyone you select during this step will get the same set of FastPass+ attractions and times: If your FastPass+ choices include, say, Space Mountain and your father-in-law doesn't do roller coasters, you'll need to tweak his selections in Step 10. For now, choose all the members of your group and click "Next."

8. SELECT ATTRACTIONS On this screen you choose your FastPass+ experiences from a list of eligible attractions. Because Disney has rules governing the combinations of FastPasses you can get at Epcot and Disney's Hollywood Studios (see page 100), the attractions will be grouped into the correct tiers for those parks, and you'll see how many opportunities you have in each tier. If all FastPasses for an attraction have been distributed, the message "FastPass+ distribution has ended for selected day" will appear next to its name.

If you don't choose an attraction for every opportunity MDE gives you—for instance, if you choose only two attractions when MDE says you can choose three—you'll be prompted to confirm that you don't want the remaining opportunities.

9. CHOOSE INITIAL RETURN TIMES Next, MDE will give you four different sets of FastPass+ return times, grouped as Options 1 (Best), 2, 3, and 4, plus Best Match. Each option contains one return time for each attraction that you selected in Step 8. Again, we're not sure how Disney assigns the return times or what Disney thinks "Best Match" means. We do know that you have to choose all of the return times in Options A–C and Best Match. For now, choose the set of return times that's closest to what you want, and you'll be able to modify them in the next step. To underscore a point, the "Best" designation is meaningless. Just forget about it and select times from whatever option best fits your plans.

10. MODIFY RETURN TIMES OR ATTRACTIONS If the initial set of Fast-Pass+ return times conflicts with your plans, you can check whether alternate times are available that better fit your schedule. The good news is that you can change each attraction's return times separately. Plus, if none of the return times for a particular attraction work for you, you can pick another attraction at this stage without having to start over.

unofficial **TIP**
To see how Adolf Hitler feels about FastPass+, go to tinyurl.com/hitler fastpass.

OK, you've booked one set of FastPasses for one park visit—now you'll need to repeat Steps 6–10 for every park you plan to visit, on every day of your trip. Simple, no?

A reader from White Plains, New York, found it all too much work:

> It was tough to set up for a big group—we ended up just getting the same FastPasses for everyone.

You've gotta hand it to Disney—making FastPass+ reservations online combines the efficiency of a third-world bureaucracy with the excitement of double-entry bookkeeping.

Buying Tickets and Making FastPass+ Reservations On Arrival

If (1) you buy your admission the day you arrive at the parks or (2) you have to delay making your FastPass+ selections until you're inside, Disney has placed new computer terminals throughout the parks where you can make on-the-spot reservations; we've listed the specific locations in each theme park's chapter. Each set of terminals—look for the FP+ KIOSK signs—is staffed by a group of cast members who can walk you through the reservation process.

If you're tech-challenged, not to worry: A cast member will help you navigate the kiosk. You'll still need to provide your MagicBand or ticket, however.

Be aware that the number of kiosks is limited, and most locations can process reservations for no more than 150 people per hour, as a Cleveland family found out:

On our first day, I had to wait in line for around a half-hour at a FastPass+ kiosk, and by the time it was my turn they had run out of passes for two of the three selections I had wanted: Peter Pan's Flight and Enchanted Tales with Belle. I was a pro by our third day there, but I miss the old system, which was much more user-friendly.

RETURNING TO RIDE Each FastPass+ reservation lasts for an hour, and Disney officially enforces the ride return time. Thus, if you make a Fast-Pass+ reservation to ride Space Mountain at 7:30 p.m., you have until 8:30 p.m. to either use it or change it to something else. Just like a restaurant reservation, your FastPass+ may be canceled if you don't show up on time. In practice, however, we've found that you can usually be up to 15 minutes late to use your reservation.

When you return to Space Mountain at the designated time, you'll be directed to a FASTPASS+ RETURN line. Before you get in line, you'll have to validate your reservation by touching your MagicBand or RFID ticket to a reader at the FastPass+ Return entrance. Then you'll proceed with minimal waiting to the attraction's preshow or boarding area.

If technical problems cause an attraction to be closed during your return time, Disney will automatically adjust your FastPass+ reservation in one of three ways:

1. If it's early in the day, Disney will offer you the chance to return to the attraction at any point in the day after it reopens.

2. Alternatively, Disney may let you choose another FastPass+ attraction in the same park, on the same day.

3. If it's late in the day, Disney will automatically give you another selection good for any FastPass+ attraction at any park the following day.

At a number of FastPass+ attractions, listed in the following chart, the time gap between getting your pass and returning to ride can range from 3 to 7 hours. To ensure that you have enough time to ride on the day of your visit, either book FastPass+ in advance for these attractions or reserve them in the parks as early in the day as possible.

GET FASTPASS+ *BEFORE 11 A.M.* FOR THE FOLLOWING:
MAGIC KINGDOM All character meet and greets, *Enchanted Tales with Belle*, Peter Pan's Flight, Seven Dwarfs Mine Train, Space Mountain, Splash Mountain
EPCOT Character Spot, Frozen Ever After, Mission: Space (Orange), Soarin', Test Track
ANIMAL KINGDOM Expedition Everest, Festival of the Lion King, Kilimanjaro Safaris, Meet Mickey and Minnie at Adventurers Outpost, Avatar Flight of Passage, Na'Vi River Journey
DHS Rock 'n' Roller Coaster, Slinky Dog Dash, Tower of Terror, Toy Story Mania!, Star Tours

FastPass+ Rules

Disney has rules in place to prevent guests from obtaining certain combinations of FastPass+ reservations before they get to the parks:

RULE #1: You can obtain only one advance FastPass+ reservation per attraction, per day, but you can get more once you're in the park and you've used your first set of three. You can't make multiple advance FastPass+ reservations for, say, Toy Story Mania!—you have to select three different attractions. But once you've entered Hollywood Studios for the day and your first three reservations have been used or have expired, you can obtain more for Toy Story Mania! if they're available.

RULE #2: FastPass+ reservation times can't overlap—Disney's computer system doesn't allow it. If you have a FastPass+ reservation for 2–3 p.m., for instance, you can't make another reservation later than 1 p.m. or earlier than 3 p.m. in the same park.

FASTPASS+ TIERS Disney also prohibits guests from using FastPass+ on all of a park's headliner attractions. The practice, known informally as "FastPass+ tiers," was in effect only at Epcot, Animal Kingdom, and Disney's Hollywood Studios at press time.

At Epcot, by way of example, the FastPass+ attractions are divided into the following two tiers:

TIER A (*Choose* 1)	
• Frozen Ever After	• Soarin'
• *IllumiNations*	• Test Track
TIER B (*Choose* 2)	
• Disney & Pixar Short Film Festival	• Mission: Space
• Epcot Character Spot	• Spaceship Earth
• Journey into Imagination	• The Seas with Nemo & Friends
• Living with the Land	• *Turtle Talk with Crush*

FastPass+ lets you choose only one attraction from Tier A and two attractions from Tier B. Note that Tier A comprises the attractions with the longest lines: This ensures that most guests get to choose either Soarin' or Test Track. Also, note that few of the attractions in Tier B actually require FastPass+ for most of the year. In practice, it's difficult to score a FastPass+ at the park for the Tier A attractions you didn't select in advance. The only reliable strategy for avoiding long waits is to be on hand at park opening and experience these attractions before the park gets crowded.

Again, though, the tiers don't apply beyond your first three advance FastPass+ reservations—any reservations you make beyond the first three when you're in the parks are totally up to you.

Clearly, these rules are designed to do three things: encourage you to stay at a Disney resort, book your trip well in advance, and tell Disney exactly where you plan to be every day. These three things not only increase Disney's revenue, they decrease its operating expenses because Disney can adjust its staffing levels at each park based on how many people have made FastPass+ reservations. And by promising lower wait times in advance, Disney encourages you to spend more time at its parks versus Universal's and others.

How FastPass+ Affects Your Waits in Line

Since it was introduced in early 2014, FastPass+ has had the effect of lowering wait times at Disney's headliner attractions and raising wait times at the parks' second-tier attractions. In effect, FastPass+ spreads guests out across the park.

To determine this, we analyzed more than 2 million standby wait times collected at Walt Disney World with FastPass+ running. We compared those with 8 million standby wait times collected across Walt Disney World since 2009.

For example, we think standby wait times are down significantly at these attractions:

- Rock 'n' Roller Coaster
- Toy Story Mania!
- Expedition Everest
- Test Track

Wait times are *up* at these attractions:

- Pirates of the Caribbean
- The Haunted Mansion
- The Magic Carpets of Aladdin
- Primeval Whirl
- Dinosaur
- Spaceship Earth
- Journey into Imagination

One possible reason for the decrease in wait times at headliners is that before FastPass+, guests would use legacy FastPass much more often. Now that there are limits on the number of FastPass+ reservations that guests can obtain in advance, coupled with the byzantine process for obtaining FastPasses online, people are riding these attractions less frequently.

We think waits are up at the secondary attractions because Disney encourages guests to choose three FastPass+ attractions, and many secondary attractions appear at the top of the alphabetical list of attractions to choose from. For example, in the past, people would have had to hike to a remote corner of the park to find Dinosaur's FastPass+ machines. Now that Dinosaur is a more visible choice in the app, it's getting more traffic.

If you're using FastPass+ at an attraction, you'll still wait to actually board the ride. The time you'll wait varies considerably, from almost nothing to 45 minutes or more (see the next section for possible reasons why). A reasonable estimate is that your wait to ride with FastPass+ will be 15%–25% of the posted wait time when you return.

How FastPass+ Affects Your Touring Plans

We think most *Unofficial Guide* readers probably spend fewer minutes per day walking around the parks because they no longer need to walk to an attraction's FastPass machines. The time saved by walking is a little more than the overall increases in standby waits at secondary attractions, so FastPass+—when it works—is roughly a break-even proposition for folks using our touring plans.

> *un*official **TIP**
> Generally, attractions are immensely popular when they're new, and thus have longer lines.

We say "when it works" because on a recent trip to Disney World, we (Bob and Len) spent the better part of a day at the Magic Kingdom observing just how wrong things can go at a FastPass+ return point. The most common snafu we saw was a family arriving too early or too late for their reservation. That's understandable because MagicBands don't display reservation times, and they're a hassle to find on My Disney Experience.

The next most frequent issue we saw was from families, particularly those who don't

> *un*official **TIP**
> Assume that using the FastPass+ line will take 10%–20% as long as the posted standby time— about 6–12 minutes for an attraction with a 60-minute posted wait.

speak English as their first language, who simply didn't get how Fast-Pass+ works. For example, many families seemed to think that simply wearing the MagicBand allowed them access to the FastPass+ line, without their having to make a reservation.

When a MagicBand doesn't work at a FastPass+ return point, a cast member can usually resolve the problem fairly quickly. When the problem is more complex, the line stops while the issue is sorted.

Consider what happens when an issue occurs at Pirates of the Caribbean, which can handle around 2,800 people in a good hour. Roughly half the ride's capacity is dedicated to FastPass+, so on busy days about two new guests arrive at the FastPass+ entrance every 5 seconds. If the cast member at the FastPass+ return point takes 30 seconds to resolve a problem, then a line of 12 guests will have formed by time the issue is fixed. When the guest experiencing the issue needs to get his or her MagicBand serviced somewhere else in the park or doesn't understand English very well, then the interaction can easily take more time.

unofficial **TIP**
The Magic Kingdom offers the greatest variety in capacity and popularity, with vastly differing rides and shows.

On the upside, Disney has made a lot of progress in streamlining these "recovery" processes, and we expect them to continue to pour resources into further speed-ups.

Your FastPass+ Priorities at Each Park

Including the touring plans in this book and on our website, we've updated almost 200 touring plans to use FastPass+ exclusively. Each plan now lists the suggested FastPass+ start times for the attractions that will save you the most time in line, like this:

SUGGESTED START TIMES FOR FASTPASS+ RESERVATIONS

- Peter Pan's Flight: 10 a.m.
- Buzz Lightyear's Space Ranger Spin: 5 p.m.
- *Enchanted Tales with Belle:* 7 p.m.

When we updated the plans, we kept count of how many times each attraction was identified as needing FastPass+. It turns out that this is a prioritized list of the attractions for which you should use FastPass+ to avoid long waits in line. We've added this information to the FastPass+ section in each theme park's chapter.

Customized Touring Plans and FastPass+

The touring plans in this guide, which have all been revised to incorporate FastPass+, are our most efficient, provided you're willing to arrive at the park 35–60 minutes before opening. Likewise, both our custom plans and our Lines app support FastPass+.

You can update your reservations while you're in the park, too. If, say, you decide to change a reservation from Splash Mountain to Big Thunder Mountain Railroad, you can tell Lines to reoptimize your plan based on your new FastPass+ times.

That said, most of the Studios' and Animal Kingdom's shows never require FastPass+. The touring plans already do a good job of getting you to the show at least 15 minutes in advance (or earlier for

Fantasmic!), in which case you'll almost always be able to get in to see that performance. In the worst-case scenario, you'll have to wait only until the next show. Also, because you can get FastPass+ for either *Fantasmic!* or Toy Story Mania! at the Studios, you'll almost always end up with a shorter wait if you use the Toy Story FastPass+.

Likewise, we don't usually recommend using FastPass+ for *Illumi-Nations* at Epcot, *Fantasmic!* at the Studios, or many theater shows (unless you've got extra FastPasses at the end of your second day). Using FastPass+ for these usually guarantees you only somewhere to sit or stand. Because you still have to arrive early to claim a prime viewing location, you end up not saving much time—as this Charleston, South Carolina, reader figured out:

> *FastPass+ for* IllumiNations *and shows like* Beauty and the Beast *is a waste. They give away many more reservations for* IllumiNations *than actually provide a good view, so unless you arrive early and stake out a place (which you can do without FastPass+), there really is no point.*

Readers React to FastPass+

FastPass+ generates more comments than anything we've seen in years. A mother from Kansas likes the ability to schedule rides in advance:

> *It was great to schedule our FastPasses ahead of time and know when and where we were going to be. If a ride was closed during our scheduled time, we got an e-mail, and we were able to go back at any time the rest of the day or switch the attraction or time.*

Other readers speak less fondly of FastPass+. This woman from Minneapolis says that it's made her rethink her opinion of Disney:

> *FastPass+ has made my trips less enjoyable, to the point that I've decided not to renew my Annual Pass. You were absolutely correct when you predicted that the new system would rescind privileges. If you ask me, they should rename it "FastPass Minus."*

A dad from Port St. Lucie, Florida, minces no words:

> *The only people who like FastPass+ are the ones who didn't know how to use the old system.*

From a Round Rock, Texas, reader:

> *I am a type-A pre-planner, and even I can't stand the rigidity and stress involved with this system! Finally, the choices you have to make in the tiers are ridiculous. The only two rides in Epcot's Future World that need a FastPass are Soarin' and Test Track, and with FastPass+ you have to pick one and stand in line for the other. Even with the touring plans (which I love), we have to wait 30–40 minutes for one or the other! Two thumbs down and two more from my husband.*

A woman from Shoreview, Minnesota, offered this:

> *This was my first trip with FastPass+, and it was a nightmare. I don't think we used all of our passes on any given day. I really don't like the added lines—we go at off-times of the year, and [on previous trips] we had NEVER seen a line of more than 5 or 10 minutes at It's a*

Small World. This time, lines of 40 minutes were not uncommon—for Small World? Give me a break!

From a Columbus, Ohio, mother of two:

Disney has added a lot of stress with FastPass+. It's harder to have a flexible, go-with-the-flow trip because you constantly have an FP+ reservation or ADR, both of which are very difficult to get and which you have to rush through heat and crowds to get to. I just had to let go of a few FastPasses for the sake of my family's sanity.

A woman from Scottsdale, Arizona, puts it bluntly:

We will not be returning to WDW due to FastPass+, increased prices, and increased crowds. FP+ is the major factor—it sucks all spontaneity out of a WDW visit. We do not enjoy choosing what park we will visit on a specific day, let alone make a ride reservation! This is a major fail. I think WDW should use this slogan, "WDW: Pay more and experience less," or "WDW: You'll love it if you lower your expectations."

From a Disney fan in Brandon, Mississippi:

The Unofficial Guide *was especially helpful in navigating the Gordian knot of FastPass+. I had the old system down pat and could just about finish my ideal day in any park by midafternoon and head back to the room to crash awhile. Now it seems we're forced to spend more time in the parks. On our next visit in March, I think I won't be so bewildered. I'm hardcore Disney, but I swear, it can be a tortured relationship some days!*

To the reader above: FastPass+ was designed to make touring less efficient and hook you for the days when you have reservations. When it comes to enriching Disney's coffers, the more time you spend in the park the better.

From a Little Rock, Arkansas, family:

The thing we hated most was FastPass+. The agony of trying to schedule rides months in advance and having limitations, as well as having the last bit of flexibility removed from a WDW trip, nearly made me insane.

In a similarly frazzled vein, a reader in a multigenerational Las Vegas family comments:

After I tried to explain FastPass+ tiers to my parents, they agreed that if it had been this complicated when they took us for the first time over 35 years ago, we never would have been back. And I do think that's the real shame of it all, both for Disney and the people who love it. For people of a certain age, Disney is rapidly sucking all the joy out of a vacation. If you plan ahead, you could have a nervous breakdown before you even get there. If you don't plan ahead, you'll likely have one while you're there.

A mom from Edinburg, Texas, writes:

FastPass+ has ruined our way of experiencing the parks. We used to be able to experience a ride two or three times a day if we wanted to, but this time around, we were very limited in our experiences. Did not like it—not one bit.

From a grandma in the Midwest:

We probably will return to Disney World—but I can say for certain that I would never bring children. Trying to keep kids happy with the current FastPass+ system in operation would be an absolute nightmare. No one can tell months in advance what ride a child will want to ride on a certain day and time!

From a Mexico City family:

Vacation: tiring, stressful, fun, expensive and rewarding. Definitely not enough FastPass+ availability for non-Disney guests, even on the very early beginning of each of the corresponding 30-day windows (for each park).

A reader from Richmond Hill, Ontario, liked the simplicity still available at Disneyland:

I had a lot more fun on a last-minute trip to Disneyland [California] because the only thing you had to do to get good FastPasses was to show up early in the morning.

And a reader in central Ohio makes no bones about it:

I hate the new FastPass+—hate it, hate it, hate it! At least with the old system, everyone in the park had the same chance of obtaining a FastPass. By the way, we never overheard any conversations praising FastPass+—only the opposite.

We've been getting lots of good reader tips and advice about using FastPass+. First, from a Springfield, Oregon, senior:

One suggestion I have for those using mobile devices in the parks: Use your data plan rather than Wi-Fi when accessing My Disney Experience. I found Disney's Wi-Fi to be unpredictable when trying to adjust FastPasses at the last minute. Also, if you can't get an attraction or don't get the time you want, definitely try again the week or two before you leave, and even the day of your visit. People change their minds—I know I did—and FastPasses do become available even for the most sought-after rides.

A Decatur, Georgia, woman offers this tip:

The Wi-Fi in the parks is so crappy that you might not be able to access your FastPass+ reservations. My suggestion is to take a screen shot of them before heading to the parks.

UNDERSTANDING WALT DISNEY WORLD ATTRACTIONS

DISNEY WORLD'S PRIMARY APPEAL IS IN ITS rides and shows. Understanding how these are engineered to accommodate guests is interesting and invaluable to developing an efficient itinerary.

All attractions, regardless of their location, are affected by two elements: capacity and popularity. Capacity is how many guests the attraction can serve at one time. Popularity shows how well visitors like an attraction. Capacity can be adjusted at some attractions. It's possible, for example, to add trucks to Kilimanjaro Safaris at Disney's Animal Kingdom or put extra boats on the Magic Kingdom's Jungle Cruise. Generally, however, capacity remains relatively fixed.

Designers try to match capacity and popularity as closely as possible. A high-capacity ride that isn't popular is a failure. Lots of money, space, and equipment have been poured into the attraction, yet there are empty seats. Ellen's Energy Adventure at Epcot fits this profile.

It's extremely unusual for a new attraction not to measure up, but it's fairly common for an older ride to lose appeal. Some attractions, such as Space Mountain at the Magic Kingdom, have sustained great appeal years beyond their debut, while others declined in popularity after a few years. Most attractions, however, work through the honeymoon, then settle down to handle the level of demand for which they were designed. When this happens, there are enough interested guests during peak hours to fill almost every seat, but not so many that long lines develop.

Sometimes Disney correctly estimates an attraction's popularity but fouls the equation by mixing in a third variable such as location. Spaceship Earth, the ride inside the geosphere at Epcot, is a good example. Placing the ride squarely in the path of every person entering the park ensures that it will be inundated during morning when the park is filling. On the flip side, *The American Adventure,* at the opposite end of Epcot, has huge capacity but plays to a partially filled theater until midafternoon, when guests finally reach that part of the park.

If demand is high and capacity is low, large lines materialize. The Studios' Toy Story Mania!, for instance, is the only headliner attraction that is open during morning Extra Magic Hours and has no minimum height requirement. Thus, it's the only headliner many families can experience, so demand quickly outstrips the ride's capacity. The result of this mismatch is that children and parents often suffer hour-long waits for a 6½-minute ride.

Capacity design is predicated on averages: the average number of people in the park, the normal distribution of traffic to specific areas, and the average number of staff needed to operate the ride. On a holiday weekend, when the averages are exceeded, all but a few attractions operate at maximum capacity, and even then they're overwhelmed by huge crowds. On days of low attendance in the fall, capacity is often not even approximated, and guests can ride without a wait.

Only the Magic Kingdom and Disney's Animal Kingdom offer low-capacity midway rides and spook-house "dark" rides. They range from state-of-the-art to antiquated. This diversity makes efficient touring of the Magic Kingdom much more challenging. If guests don't understand the capacity–popularity relationship and don't plan accordingly, they might spend most of the day in line.

Although Epcot, Animal Kingdom, and Disney's Hollywood Studios have fewer rides and shows than the Magic Kingdom, almost all their attractions are major features on par with the Magic Kingdom's

Pirates of the Caribbean and The Haunted Mansion in scope, detail, imagination, and spectacle. All but a few Epcot, Animal Kingdom, and DHS rides are fast-loading, and most have large capacities. Because Epcot, Animal Kingdom, and DHS attractions are generally well engineered and efficient, lines may appear longer than those in the Magic Kingdom but usually move more quickly. There are no midway rides at Epcot or DHS, and fewer attractions at those parks are intended for children.

In the Magic Kingdom, crowds are more a function of the popularity and engineering of individual attractions; at Epcot, Animal Kingdom, and DHS, traffic flow and crowding are more affected by park layout. For touring efficiency, it's important to understand how Magic Kingdom rides and shows operate. At Epcot and Animal Kingdom, this knowledge is less important.

To develop an efficient touring plan, it's necessary to understand how rides and shows are designed and function. We'll examine both.

CUTTING YOUR TIME IN LINE BY UNDERSTANDING THE RIDES

WALT DISNEY WORLD HAS MANY TYPES OF RIDES. Some, such as The Great Movie Ride at Disney's Hollywood Studios, can carry more than 3,000 people an hour. At the other extreme, TriceraTop Spin at Animal Kingdom can handle only around 500 people an hour. Most rides fall somewhere in between. Many factors figure into how long you'll wait to experience a ride: its popularity; how it loads and unloads; how many persons can ride at once; how many units (cars, rockets, boats, flying elephants, and the like) are in service at a time; and how many cast members are available to operate the ride. Let's take the factors one by one.

1. How Popular Is the Ride?

Newer rides such as Animal Kingdom's Avatar Flight of Passage attract a lot of people, as do such longtime favorites as the same park's Expedition Everest. If a ride is popular, you need to know how it operates in order to determine the best time to ride. But a ride need not be especially popular to generate long lines; in some cases, such lines are due not to a ride's popularity but to poor traffic engineering. This is the case at the Mad Tea Party and The Barnstormer (among others) in Fantasyland. Both rides serve only a small percentage of any day's attendance at the Magic Kingdom, yet because they take so long to load and unload, long lines form regardless.

2. How Does the Ride Load and Unload?

Some rides never stop. They're like conveyor belts that go around and around. These are "continuous loaders." The Haunted Mansion and Under the Sea: Journey of the Little Mermaid at the Magic Kingdom, along with Spaceship Earth at Epcot, are continuous loaders. The number of people that can be moved through in an hour depends on how many cars—"doom buggies" or whatever—are on the conveyor. The Haunted Mansion and Spaceship Earth have lots of cars on the conveyor, and each consequently can move more than 2,000 people an hour.

Other rides are "interval loaders." Cars are unloaded, loaded, and dispatched at set intervals (sometimes controlled manually, sometimes by computer). Space Mountain in Tomorrowland is an interval loader. It has two tracks (the ride has been duplicated in the same facility). Each track can run as many as 14 space capsules, released at 36-, 26-, or 21-second intervals. (The bigger the crowd, the shorter the interval.)

In one kind of interval loader, empty cars, as in Space Mountain's space capsules, return to where they reload. In a second kind, such as Splash Mountain, one group of riders enters the vehicle while the previous group departs. Rides of the latter type are referred to as "in and out" interval loaders. As a boat docks, those who have just completed their ride exit to the left; at almost the same time, those waiting to ride enter the boat from the right. The reloaded boat is released to the dispatch point a few yards down the line, where it's launched according to the interval being used.

Interval loaders of both types can be very efficient people-movers if (1) the dispatch (launch) interval is relatively short and (2) the ride can accommodate many vehicles at one time. Because many boats can float through Pirates of the Caribbean at one time, and the dispatch interval is short, almost 3,000 people can see this attraction each hour.

The least efficient rides, in terms of traffic engineering, are "cycle rides," also called "stop and go" rides. Those waiting to ride exchange places with those who have just ridden. Unlike in-and-out interval rides, cycle rides shut down during loading and unloading. While one boat is loading and unloading in It's a Small World (an interval loader), many other boats are advancing through the ride. But when Dumbo touches down, the whole ride is at a standstill until the next flight launches (ditto Prince Charming Regal Carrousel and the Mad Tea Party).

In cycle rides, the time in motion is "ride time." The time the ride idles while loading and unloading is "load time." Load time plus ride time equals "cycle time," or the time from the start of one run of the ride until the start of the next. The only cycle rides in Disney World are in the Magic Kingdom and Disney's Animal Kingdom.

3. How Many Persons Can Ride at One Time?

This figure expresses "system capacity," or the number of people who can ride at one time. The greater the carrying capacity of a ride (all other things being equal), the more visitors it can accommodate per hour. Some rides can add extra units (cars, boats, and such) as crowds build, to increase capacity; others, such as the Astro Orbiter in Tomorrowland, have a fixed capacity (it's impossible to add more rockets).

4. How Many Units Are in Service at a Given Time?

Unit is our term for the vehicle in which you ride. At the Mad Tea Party the unit is a teacup, at Peter Pan's Flight a pirate ship. On some rides (mostly cycle rides), the number of units operating at one time is fixed. There are always 32 flying elephants at Dumbo and 90 horses on Prince Charming Regal Carrousel. There's no way to increase the capacity of such rides by adding units. On a busy day, the only way to carry more people each hour on a fixed-unit cycle ride is to shorten the loading time or decrease the ride time. The bottom line: On a busy day for a cycle ride, you'll wait longer and possibly be rewarded with a shorter ride. This is why we steer you away from cycle rides unless you're willing to ride them early in the morning or late at night. These are the cycle rides:

THE MAGIC KINGDOM Astro Orbiter, The Barnstormer, Dumbo the Flying Elephant, Mad Tea Party, The Magic Carpets of Aladdin, Prince Charming Regal Carrousel

DISNEY'S ANIMAL KINGDOM TriceraTop Spin

Many other rides throughout Disney World can increase their capacity by adding units as crowds build. For example, if attendance is light, Big Thunder Mountain Railroad in Frontierland can start the day by running only one of its five mine trains from one of two available loading platforms. If lines build, the other platform is opened and more mine trains are placed into operation. At capacity, the five trains can carry about 2,400 persons an hour. Likewise, Star Tours at Disney's Hollywood Studios can increase its capacity by using all its simulators, and the Gran Fiesta Tour boat ride at Mexico in Epcot can add more boats. Sometimes a long queue will disappear almost instantly when new units are brought online. When an interval loader places more units into operation, it usually shortens the dispatch intervals, allowing more units to be dispatched more often.

5. How Many Cast Members Are Available to Operate the Ride?

Adding cast members to a ride can allow more units to operate or additional loading or holding areas to open. In the Magic Kingdom, Pirates of the Caribbean and It's a Small World can run two waiting lines and loading zones. The Haunted Mansion has a 1½-minute preshow staged in a "stretch room." On busy days, a second stretch room can be activated, permitting a more continuous flow of visitors to the actual loading area.

Additional staff makes a world of difference to some cycle rides. Often, the Mad Tea Party has only one attendant. This person alone must clear visitors from the ride just completed, admit and seat visitors for the upcoming ride, check that each teacup is secured, return to the control panel, issue instructions to the riders, and finally activate the ride (whew!). A second attendant divides these responsibilities and cuts loading time by 25%–50%.

CUTTING YOUR TIME IN LINE BY UNDERSTANDING THE SHOWS

MANY FEATURED ATTRACTIONS AT WALT DISNEY WORLD are theater presentations. While they aren't as complex as rides, understanding them from a traffic-engineering standpoint may save you touring time.

Most theater attractions operate in three phases:

1. Guests are in the theater viewing the presentation.

2. Guests who have passed through the turnstile wait in a holding area or lobby. They will be admitted to the theater as soon as the show in progress concludes. Several attractions offer a preshow in their lobby to entertain guests until they're admitted to the main show. Examples include *Enchanted Tiki Room* and *Stitch's Great Escape!* in the Magic Kingdom and *Muppet-Vision 3-D* at DHS.

3. A line waits outside. Guests in line enter the lobby when there's room and will ultimately move into the theater.

Theater capacity, the presentation's popularity, and park attendance determine how long lines will be at a show. Except for holidays and other days of heavy attendance, the longest wait for a show usually doesn't exceed the length of one performance. As almost all theater attractions run continuously, stopping only long enough for the previous audience to leave and the waiting audience to enter, a performance will be in progress when you arrive. *O Canada!* at Epcot's Canada

Pavilion lasts 18 minutes; your longest wait under normal circumstances is about 18 minutes if you arrive just after the show has begun.

A WORD ABOUT DISNEY THRILL RIDES

READERS OF ALL AGES should try to be open-minded about Disney "thrill rides." In comparison with those at other theme parks, the Disney attractions are quite tame, with more emphasis on sights, atmosphere, and special effects than on the motion, speed, or feel of the ride. While we suggest you take Disney's pre-ride warnings seriously, we can tell you that guests of all ages report enjoying rides such as Tower of Terror, Big Thunder Mountain, and Splash Mountain.

The Rock 'n' Roller Coaster and Expedition Everest, however, are a different story. Both are serious coasters that share more in common with Revenge of the Mummy at Universal Studios than they do with Space Mountain or Big Thunder Mountain.

Mission: Space, a high-tech simulation ride at Epcot, is a toss-up (pun intended)—it absolutely has the potential to make you sick. After many guest incidents, Disney made half of the ride a tamer, no-spin experience—one that's less likely to launch your lunch.

CENTRAL FLORIDA ROLLER COASTERS

IF YOU EVER GO to a party where folks are discussing Immelmanns, heartline rolls, dive loops, and LIM launchers, don't mistake the guests for fighter pilots. Incredibly, you'll be among the intelligentsia of roller-coaster aficionados. This growing population, along with millions of other not-quite-so-fanatical coaster lovers, is united in the belief that roller coasters are—or ought to be—the heart of every theme park.

Though Disney pioneered the concept of super-coasters with the **Matterhorn Bobsleds** at Disneyland in 1959, it took them 16 years to add another roller coaster, **Space Mountain** at Walt Disney World, to their repertoire. In relatively quick succession followed Space Mountain at Disneyland and **Big Thunder Mountain Railroad** at both Disneyland's and Walt Disney World's Magic Kingdoms. Irrespective of the Mountains' popularity, Disney didn't build another coaster in the United States for almost 20 years. In the interim, coasters enjoyed a technical revolution that included aircraft carrier–type launching devices and previously unimaginable loops, corkscrews, vertical drops, and train speeds. Through all this, Disney sat on the sidelines. After all, Disney parks didn't offer "rides" but, rather, "adventure experiences" in which the sensation of the ride itself was always secondary to storylines and visuals. But when archrival Universal announced plans for its Islands of Adventure theme park, featuring an entire arsenal of thrill rides, Disney—spurred by competition—went to work.

The upshot was a banner year in 1999 for Central Florida coasters, with **The Incredible Hulk Coaster, Dueling Dragons: Fire** and **Ice** (now **Dragon Challenge: Chinese Fireball** and **Hungarian Horntail**) opening at Universal's Islands of Adventure; **Rock 'n' Roller Coaster**

Our Top 18 Central Florida Roller Coasters

COASTER	HOST PARK
MANTA	SeaWorld
MAKO	SeaWorld
EXPEDITION EVEREST	Animal Kingdom
CHINESE FIREBALL	Islands of Adventure
CHEETAH HUNT	Busch Gardens
MONTU	Busch Gardens
INCREDIBLE HULK COASTER	Islands of Adventure
KUMBA	Busch Gardens
HUNGARIAN HORNTAIL	Islands of Adventure
KRAKEN	SeaWorld
SHEIKRA	Busch Gardens
HOLLYWOOD RIP RIDE ROCKIT	Universal Studios Florida
ROCK 'N' ROLLER COASTER	Disney's Hollywood Studios
REVENGE OF THE MUMMY	Universal Studios Florida
SPACE MOUNTAIN	Magic Kingdom
BIG THUNDER MOUNTAIN	Magic Kingdom
ESCAPE FROM GRINGOTTS	Universal Studios Florida
SEVEN DWARFS MINE TRAIN	Magic Kingdom

coming online at Disney's Hollywood Studios; and **Gwazi,** a wooden coaster, premiering at Busch Gardens Tampa. Close on their heels in early 2000 was **Kraken** at SeaWorld. These six coasters made Space and Big Thunder Mountains look like cupcakes and wienie buns. All except Gwazi featured inversions, corkscrews, and rollovers. Best of all for coaster lovers, none of the players were content to rest on their laurels: Universal Studios came back with **Revenge of the Mummy** in 2004, followed by **SheiKra** at Busch Gardens in 2005 and the awe-inspiring **Expedition Everest** at Disney's Animal Kingdom in 2006.

The spring and summer of 2009 marked the debut of **Manta** at Sea World Orlando and **Hollywood Rip Ride Rockit** at Universal Studios Florida. Manta is an inverted steel coaster on which riders are suspended under the tracks, prone and facedown; Rip Ride Rockit is also a steel coaster, only here you sit as opposed to being suspended. The first hill is a 16-second *vertical* climb, followed by a 65-mph plunge. Two years later, **Cheetah Hunt,** a launched coaster, opened at Busch Gardens.

The spring and summer of 2014 witnessed the unveiling of two new coasters: **Seven Dwarfs Mine Train** at the Magic Kingdom and **Harry Potter and the Escape from Gringotts** at Universal Studios Florida. Seven Dwarfs Mine Train, a family coaster, offers modest speeds, small hills, and a slow-mo look at the Dwarfs' cottage and gem mine; its ride vehicles swing slightly, almost imperceptibly, from side to side. Gringotts is a 3-D steel coaster ride through the bank vaults made famous in the

TYPE	LENGTH (FEET)	HEIGHT (FEET)	INVERSIONS	SPEED (MPH)	RIDE TIME	RIDE FEEL
Steel/inverted	3,359	140	4	56	2:35	Very smooth
Steel/sit-down	4,760	200	0	73	3:13	Very smooth
Steel/sit-down	4,424	199.5	0	50	2:50	Very smooth
Steel/inverted	3,200	125	5	60	2:25	Very smooth
Steel/sit-down	4,429	102	1	60	3:30	Smooth
Steel/inverted	3,983	150	7	60	3:00	Smooth
Steel/sit-down	3,700	110	7	67	2:15	Smooth
Steel/sit-down	3,978	143	7	60	2:54	Slightly rough
Steel/inverted	3,200	125	5	55	2:25	Very smooth
Steel/sit-down	4,177	151	7	65	2:02	Smooth
Steel/sit-down	3,188	200	1	70	3:00	Very smooth
Steel/sit-down	3,800	167	2	65	2:30	Rough
Steel/sit-down	3,403	80	3	57	1:22	Very smooth
Steel/sit-down	2,200	45	0	40	3:00	Very smooth
Steel/sit-down	3,196	90	0	27	2:35	Rough
Steel/sit-down	2,780	45	0	36	3:30	Smooth
Steel/sit-down	2,000	27	0	26	4:00	Smooth
Steel/sit-down	2,000	41	0	34	2:15	Very smooth

Harry Potter books and movies. Stunning visual effects are emphasized over raw speed or height—there are no loops or inversions. And, unlike Seven Dwarfs Mine Train, Escape from Gringotts is totally indoors.

White Lightning debuted in 2013 at Orlando's Fun Spot America theme park. It offers a surprising amount of airtime for a small wooden coaster. With a max vertical of 58 feet and reaching speeds of 44 mph, it delivers a surprisingly smooth and satisfying thrill experience for a family coaster. Its Fun Spot sibling is **Freedom Flyer,** a low-to-the-ground inverted steel coaster. Also a family coaster, it hits speeds of 34 mph (the same as Seven Dwarfs Mine Train) as your feet dangle over pedestrian traffic below. It's known for its tight whiplash turns.

New for 2016, Busch Gardens' **Cobra's Curse** is a combination roller coaster, wild mouse, and spin coaster that hits top speeds of 40+ mph over its 2,100-foot layout. The ride is zippy enough, but the real Cobra's Curse is that it can handle only 1,000 riders an hour, a paltry number in the world of modern coasters.

The big coaster news in 2016 was the opening of **Mako** at SeaWorld. Overnight it became the longest, highest, and fastest coaster in Central Florida. It doesn't have any inversions, but it's an air-time supercoaster. On tap for 2019 is the **Skyscraper,** to be located at the new Skyplex entertainment development off International Drive. Designed to minimize the attraction's footprint, the track wraps around and down a 5,000-foot-high vertical tower. Highlights of the descent include seven inversions, a drop with an angle of 123 degrees, and a top speed of 65 mph. Construction was supposed to begin in 2015 but hadn't started as of spring 2017.

The next horizon for roller coasters is when the ride is synchronized with a virtual reality (VR) program by means of a headset, either portable or attached to the ride. Cedar Point theme park in Sandusky, Ohio, along with several Six Flags parks, has operational VR coasters. In Central Florida, Kraken at SeaWorld is undergoing an extensive redesign that includes the addition of VR. The enhancement is expected to be commonplace worldwide within four years.

Today there are 16 big-time roller coasters in Central Florida, 26 if you want to include the tamer Space Mountain, Seven Dwarfs Mine Train, and Big Thunder Mountain Railroad at Walt Disney World; **Flying School, Lego Technic Test Track,** and **Coastersaurus** at Legoland Florida; Escape from Gringotts at Universal Studios; Cobra's Curse at Busch Gardens; and White Lightning and Freedom Flyer at Fun Spot America. Cheetah Hunt, The Incredible Hulk Coaster, Revenge of the Mummy, and Rock 'n' Roller Coaster feature accelerated launch systems in which the train is hurled, slingshotlike, up the first hill; Rock 'n' Roller Coaster and Revenge of the Mummy are indoor coasters augmented by mind-blowing visuals, special effects, and soundtracks. Expedition Everest is the most fully realized attraction of the 16, with a storyline, astounding attention to detail, and a track that plunges in and out of the largest (albeit artificial) mountain in Florida. Mako, Kraken, Cheetah·Hunt, and Expedition Everest are the longer roller coasters of the lot, their tracks exceeding 4,000 feet long. **Montu** at Busch Gardens, along with Dragon Challenge at Universal, is inverted, meaning the track is overhead and your feet dangle.

Having ridden all of these until we could no longer walk straight, we rank them as follows. (We included Space Mountain, Seven Dwarfs Mine Train, and Big Thunder Mountain Railroad in the list for sentimental reasons and because they're good for families.) *Note:* International and US roller coaster polls and rankings were not conducted last year, so the following ranking is based on the opinions of the authors and research team. For a glossary of roller-coaster terminology, see ultimaterollercoaster.com/coasters/glossary.

1. MANTA, SEAWORLD There are coasters you barely survive and coasters you savor. Manta is clearly among the latter: a supersmooth experience that leaves you grinning from ear to ear. An inverted flying steel coaster, Manta gently lowers you into a suspended Superman position and you, well, fly. Many coaster fans consider the most memorable moments a sweeping loop in the first half of the ride and near-misses of a pond or rock wall (depending where you're sitting) in the second half. Technically, Manta has it all. After a first drop of 113 feet, it zooms through a pretzel loop, a 360-degree incline roll, and two corkscrews while reaching a height of 140 feet and speeds of 56 mph.

2. MAKO, SEAWORLD As the tallest, fastest, longest coaster in Florida, Mako makes a strong case for being number one. It all depends on what you like. Mako is a hypercoaster, meaning its sole purpose is to serve up air time—that weightless feeling on downhills that lifts you out of your seat. Mako has, count 'em, nine drops that induce this sensation of flying. At 4,760 feet long, Mako plunges from a soaring height of 200 feet and reaches a speed of 73 miles an hour. This combination of length, height, and speed translates into near continuous air time. There are no inversions, and the ride is downy-smooth—so smooth, in fact, that the only restraint is a lap bar. The mako shark is one of the fastest predators in the sea, and the coaster layout is designed to emulate the fast, sweeping motions of the shark on the hunt.

3. EXPEDITION EVEREST, DISNEY'S ANIMAL KINGDOM This coaster offers such a complete package, with something to dazzle each of the senses, that it overcomes its lack of loops and inversions. The segment where the train corkscrews downward in the dark may be the most unusual in roller-coaster annals. Though you begin the segment in reverse, you soon succumb to an almost disembodied and dreamlike state of drifting in a void, with an exhilarating sense of speed but with no certain sense of direction. When you can see, there's plenty to look at: The mountain, with its caverns, cliffs, and crags, is a work of art; then there's that pesky yeti who menaces you throughout the ride. And for those of you who hate rough coasters, Expedition Everest is oh-so-smooth.

4. DRAGON CHALLENGE: CHINESE FIREBALL, UNIVERSAL'S ISLANDS OF ADVENTURE Dragon Challenge has two trains, Chinese Fireball and Hungarian Horntail, which are launched in short succession, creating a sense of chase between the two. Though both trains have identical lift hills, their respective layouts are different, and Chinese Fireball offers the superior ride, with a 115-foot drop, five inversions, and speeds of 60 mph. Because this is an inverted coaster, your feet dangle throughout.

5. CHEETAH HUNT, BUSCH GARDENS With a 4,429-foot track, Cheetah Hunt is the second-longest coaster in Florida. A complete experience both tactilely and visually, Cheetah Hunt hurls you through the scenic, wildlife-rich Serengeti Plain section of the park. The ride emulates the hunting style of the cheetah with sudden bursts of speed, accomplished with linear-synchronous-motor launches similar to the accelerated launch systems of The Incredible Hulk Coaster at Universal and Rock 'n' Roller Coaster at DHS. With Cheetah Hunt, however, you're launched three times—once at the start of the ride and twice more during the circuit. The layout includes a 130-foot drop into a shallow canyon, overbanked turns, parabolas, and a heartline-roll inversion. The linear out-and-back course allows more opportunity for viewing the animals than would the more common concentric, twisting layouts from which it's almost impossible to take in your surroundings.

6. MONTU, BUSCH GARDENS Montu is a little longer than Chinese Fireball and features seven inversions—including loops of 104 and 60 feet and a 0-g roll—on a layout distinguished by very tight turns. With an initial drop of 128 feet, Montu posts top speeds of 60 mph and pulls 3.8 g's. Also inverted, Montu is intense and exhilarating but less visually interesting than and not as smooth as Chinese Fireball.

7. THE INCREDIBLE HULK COASTER, UNIVERSAL'S ISLANDS OF ADVENTURE No weak points here. A tire-propelled launch system takes you from 0 to 40 mph in 2 seconds up the first hill, hurling you into a twisting dive of 105 feet. From there it's two loops, two flat-spin corkscrews, a cobra roll, and a plunge through a 150-foot-long tunnel to the end. You hit speeds of 67 mph and pull as many as 4 g's. Unequivocally, the Hulk has the best start of any roller coaster in Central Florida. In 2016, Hulk was fitted with a new track and ride vehicles, a new sound system, and an enhanced queuing area. The ride's pretty much the same, but the storyline is improved.

8. KUMBA, BUSCH GARDENS With a track of almost 4,000 feet, seven inversions, a 135-foot first drop, g-forces of 3.8, a top speed of 60 mph, and a very tight layout, Kumba can hold its own with any coaster. Features include a 114-foot-tall vertical loop, two rolls, and interlocking corkscrews, among others. We find Kumba a little rough, but sitting toward the back of the train mitigates the problem somewhat.

9. DRAGON CHALLENGE: HUNGARIAN HORNTAIL, UNIVERSAL'S ISLANDS OF ADVENTURE Hungarian Horntail is Chinese Fireball's slightly less evil twin, with speeds of 55 mph and a first drop of 95 feet, compared with Chinese Fireball's 60 mph and 115 feet. Hungarian Horntail's design elements are different as well, though both coasters hit you with five inversions bundled in a mix of rolls, corkscrews, and a loop. Like Chinese Fireball, Hungarian Horntail is an inverted coaster.

10. KRAKEN, SEAWORLD The Kraken was a ferocious sea monster kept caged by Poseidon, Greek god of the sea. Much of this Kraken's track is over water, and it takes a number of sweeping dives into subterranean caverns. A very fast coaster, Kraken hits speeds of 65 mph with one drop of 144 feet, and it boasts loops, rolls, and corkscrews for a total of seven inversions. Though not inverted, the cars are open-sided and floorless.

11. SHEIKRA, BUSCH GARDENS While the higher-rated coasters do a lot of things well, SheiKra is pretty much one-dimensional—it drops like a rock straight down (a *sheikra* is an African hawk known for diving vertically on its prey). After scaling the 200-foot lift hill, the coaster descends over the lip of the first drop and brakes to a stop. There you're suspended, dangling for a few anxious moments until the train is released. On the way down, you hit speeds of 70 mph and enjoy the best airtime of any Florida coaster. Following a loop, the drill is repeated on a second, more modest drop. The cars on SheiKra are the widest we've seen, seating eight people across in each of three rows. Accordingly, the track is very wide. This width, among other things, makes for a plodding, uninspiring ride except during the two big drops.

12. HOLLYWOOD RIP RIDE ROCKIT, UNIVERSAL STUDIOS "The Triple R," as some locals call it, opened in August 2009 as Universal's second roller coaster. A steel sit-down coaster, RRR trades full inversions for steep dives and tight corkscrew turns. The ride is a lot more jarring than we expected, with a fair amount of lateral shaking. The gimmick here is that you can select your own music to accompany the ride. Views from the top of the 167-foot lift hill are killer. The Triple R reaches top speeds of 65 mph.

13. ROCK 'N' ROLLER COASTER, DISNEY'S HOLLYWOOD STUDIOS Rock 'n' Roller Coaster reaches a height of only 80 feet, lasts just 1 minute and 22 seconds, and incorporates just a couple of design elements, but that 0- to 57-mph launch in 2 seconds is totally sweet. Rock 'n' Roller

Coaster is a dark ride (that is, it's indoors), and the story is that you're on your way to an Aerosmith concert in Hollywood in a big stretch limousine. Speakers in each car blast a soundtrack of the group's hits synchronized with the myriad visuals that erupt out of the gloom. The ride is smooth. Not the biggest or baddest coaster in the realm, but like Expedition Everest, it'll put a big grin on your face every time.

14. REVENGE OF THE MUMMY, UNIVERSAL STUDIOS If we were ranking attractions as opposed to coasters, this one would rank much higher. Revenge of the Mummy is a super-headliner hybrid, of which its coaster dimension is only one aspect. A complete description of the attraction can be found starting on page 703; for the moment, however, we can tell you that it's a dark ride full of tricks and surprises, and in roller-coaster mode only for about a third of the ride. The ride is wild, and the visuals and special effects are among the best you'll find.

15. SPACE MOUNTAIN, THE MAGIC KINGDOM When you strip away the theme of this beloved Disney favorite, you're left with a souped-up version of the Wild Mouse, a midway staple with sharp turns and small, steep drops that runs with two- or four-passenger cars instead of trains. But when you put a Wild Mouse in the dark—where you can't anticipate the turns and drops—it's like feeding the mouse steroid-laced cheese. With Space Mountain, Disney turned a dinky coaster with no inversions and a top speed of 27 mph into a fairly robust attraction that set the standard for Disney thrill rides until the debut of The Twilight Zone Tower of Terror. Space Mountain may be close to the bottom of our ranking, but in the hearts of many theme park guests, it remains number one.

16. BIG THUNDER MOUNTAIN RAILROAD, THE MAGIC KINGDOM With its runaway-mine-train storyline, Big Thunder is long on visuals but ranks as a very innocuous roller coaster: It offers no inversions and has a top speed of just 36 mph. Though many riders consider it jerky and rough, it's a Rolls-Royce compared with the likes of Gwazi and Kumba at Busch Gardens. Unlike on Gwazi, you can ride with your arms in the air.

17. HARRY POTTER AND THE ESCAPE FROM GRINGOTTS, UNIVERSAL STUDIOS This indoor steel coaster incorporates 3-D projection, amazingly detailed sets, and a storyline of the Potter Fab Three rumbling through the underground vaults of Gringotts Wizarding Bank as they try to escape archenemy Voldemort. There's a load of action, some nifty track-switching, and a free-fall simulation, but the ride itself is tame: There's one 27-foot drop and one big up-launch, with no change in track elevation in between.

18. SEVEN DWARFS MINE TRAIN, THE MAGIC KINGDOM The mildest roller coaster on this list, Seven Dwarfs is designed to be the first or second roller-coaster experience for grade-schoolers. Its unique feature is that the ride vehicles swing slightly from side to side, which amplifies the turning sensation you feel in the ride's tight curves. Like Big Thunder, Seven Dwarfs is a steel coaster with no inversions, and it has a top speed of around 34 mph. Because the track is much smoother than Big Thunder's or Space Mountain's, you may not feel as if you're moving very fast.

PART THREE

ACCOMMODATIONS

The **BASIC CONSIDERATIONS**

LOCATING A SUITABLE HOTEL OR CONDO is critical to planning any Walt Disney World vacation. The basic question is whether to stay inside the World. Luxury lodging can be found both in and out of Disney World. Budget lodging is another story. In the World, room rates range from about $100 on a weeknight during what Disney calls Value season to more than $1,600 per night during the holidays. Outside, rooms are as low as $35 a night.

Beyond affordability is convenience. We've lodged both in and out of Disney World, and there's a special magic and peace of mind associated with staying inside the World. "I feel more a part of everything and less like a visitor," one guest writes.

There's no real hardship in staying outside Disney World and driving or taking a hotel shuttle to the theme parks. Meals can be less expensive, and rooming outside the World makes you more receptive to other Orlando-area attractions and eating spots. **Universal Studios** and **Universal's Islands of Adventure, Kennedy Space Center Visitor Complex, SeaWorld,** and **Gatorland** are well worth your attention.

Because Walt Disney World is so large, some off-property hotels are closer in both time and distance to many of the theme parks than are some Disney resorts. Check our Hotel Information Chart on pages 291–306, which lists commuting times from both Disney and non-Disney hotels. Lodging prices can change, but it's possible to get a hotel room comparable to one at a Disney Moderate resort for half the cost during holidays, or a room twice the size for the same money, all within a 15-minute drive of the Magic Kingdom.

If you have young children, read Part Five, Walt Disney World with Kids, before choosing lodging. Seniors, couples on a honeymoon or romantic holiday, and disabled guests should read the applicable sections of Part Six, Special Tips for Special People, before booking.

THE LATEST IN LODGING

OUR FOCUS FOR THIS UPDATE was on the construction and refurbishment of Disney's on-site hotels. Based on our survey results, the majority of readers stay at a Disney resort, making these changes even more relevant.

Disney's quest to market to high-income families is obvious in the new focus on resort amenities. And while we're not fans of the ever-increasing rates, we love the improved pools, expanded activities, and more sophisticated decor Disney has added. The resorts, especially in the Deluxe and Villa categories, are destinations in themselves, with plenty to entertain guests outside the parks.

Disney's recent trend is to pour money into the Disney Vacation Club (DVC) time-share resorts—a popular cash-generating machine with high occupancy rates. Not only has Disney converted traditional hotel rooms to DVC at many of its resorts, but massive upgrades to rooms, pools, and restaurants have also been done. A case in point is the beautiful **Wilderness Lodge & Boulder Ridge Villas** (page 172), just emerging from a couple-year pool, playground, and restaurant project to coincide with its DVC expansion. (The Lodge also got a convoluted naming scheme for its various DVC wings, which is explained later.)

In last year's edition, we warned against staying at **Disney's Caribbean Beach Resort** because of poor reader reviews. Guess what? In 2017 Disney decided to overhaul it, demolishing old buildings and adding new DVC rooms, new dining options, and high(er)-end amenities. The resort will be a construction zone for the next couple of years, with only makeshift dining options—so don't stay there just yet.

The big news at Caribbean Beach, however, is the imminent start of construction on an enclosed, ski lift–like **gondola** system to link it, Pop Century, and Art of Animation with Disney's Hollywood Studios and Epcot. It should be faster than buses, with options for reduced carbon emissions. Expect to see it before mid-2019. We're not sure where Disney is storing Walt's frozen head these days, but we're confident that it's nodding in approval over this idea. (We wouldn't be surprised to see self-driving cars on Disney property by then, either.)

Likewise, **Disney's Coronado Springs Resort** is undergoing a major transformation, adding a 13-story tower and more luxe rooms to its lineup, along with more dining options. Unlike the Caribbean Beach expansion, Coronado's is limited to a small section of the resort and doesn't affect dining or recreation. We'd still stay there, especially if Disney offers discounts or other things to sweeten the deal.

We speculated last year that **Disney's Pop Century Resort** might remodel its rooms. That effort has begun. The new look is clean and modern, with less Disney kitsch than in the other Value resorts. You'll find hardwood floors instead of carpets, a space-saving drop-down bed, a new bathroom design, and lots of storage nooks. It should be done by the end of 2017, with many rooms available earlier.

As mentioned above, Pop Century and Art of Animation are being linked by gondola to Disney's Hollywood Studios and Epcot. We expect Disney to charge more for rooms closest to the gondola. And that, coupled with the segmentation described above at Wilderness Lodge, Caribbean Beach, and Coronado Springs, is part of **Disney's plan to blur the lines** between its Value, Moderate, Deluxe, and DVC categories. We think there will be Moderate-like rooms at Values, and Deluxe-like rooms at Moderates, rendering obsolete the fixed classification system used for decades. The new system will operate more like market-based restaurant pricing: The cost will vary considerably by date, availability, and amenities, even within the same hotel.

THE TAX MAN COMETH

SALES AND LODGING TAXES can add a chunk of change to the cost of your hotel room. Cumulative tax in Orange County is 13.5%, and in adjacent Osceola County, 13%. Lake Buena Vista, the Universal Orlando area, International Drive, and all the Disney hotels except the All-Star Resorts are in Orange County.

ABOUT HOTEL INSPECTIONS

WE INSPECT SEVERAL HUNDRED HOTELS in the Disney World area to compile the *Unofficial Guide*'s list of lodging choices. Each year we call each hotel to verify contact information and inquire about renovations or refurbishments. If a hotel has been renovated or has refurbished its guest rooms, we reinspect it, along with any new hotels, for the next edition of the *Guide*. Hotels reporting no improvements are rechecked every two years. We inspect most Disney-owned hotels every 6–12 months, and no less than once every two years.

Getting a Room That Meets Your Expectations

Many of us have had the experience of booking a room in what we thought was a four-star hotel and getting a room with chipped furniture, worn carpeting, or any number of other defects inconsistent with four-star status. That's simply because rooms in properties more than a few years old show wear and tear, some more than others. It's disappointing, to be sure, but there are ways to maximize your chances of getting a room you'll enjoy.

Hotels naturally want to offer their guests a good experience and are sensitive to their star ratings. Consequently, they keep tabs on the condition of their rooms and schedule attention for those that could use some TLC. This attention comes in various forms.

Refurbishing a room may include upgrading TVs and Wi-Fi; replacing mattresses and/or carpets, other soft goods, and wall coverings; and painting. It may or may not include changing the decor. Depending on the scope, a refurbish usually takes one to two weeks. In contrast, **remodeling** is a big deal and often includes structural reconfigurations, major changes to the bathroom, and new furniture, plus most of the items involved in a refurbish. Remodels generally take three to five weeks.

At any moment in any hotel, there will be rooms that require no attention, newly refurbished or remodeled rooms, rooms currently undergoing a refurbish/remodel, and rooms scheduled for such. Newly refurbished/remodeled rooms are most desirable, followed by rooms that are OK as is. Least desirable are rooms awaiting a refurb/remodel.

In most properties, a range of prices is offered, generally with little explanation, but if you dig, you'll find upcharges for newly remodeled rooms, followed by newly refurbished rooms, with rooms awaiting attention at the lower end of the price range. Booking with the hotel directly (not through its 800 number) lets you ask reservationists exactly what you get for certain rates advertised online and else-where—and it largely prevents getting stuck with a room that doesn't live up to the hotel's star rating.

Beyond the room's intrinsic qualities, you might be interested in a room on a higher floor or a room facing a certain direction. Make these preferences known when booking, and then follow up with a call, an e-mail, or a fax to the hotel. Always mention anything you're celebrating, such as an anniversary or birthday, and sign up, prefer-ably before you book, for the hotel's loyalty program. Hotels rarely guarantee that requests will be honored but will try their best to accommodate you.

At most properties, your room is not assigned until you arrive. There's been a lot of press about tipping the desk clerk $20 or so to get an upgrade or have a special request honored. Our researchers have tested this technique many times, and we can tell you that it's not as straightforward as it seems.

Large hotels with varying room categories offer the best return for your tip—at smaller hotels, the rooms tend to be the same. Also, a front-desk clerk is limited by what rooms are available: More rooms will be unassigned and available at 3 p.m. than after 6 p.m. or later, when the hotel begins to fill. What's more, the latitude afforded front-desk staff varies considerably from hotel to hotel.

The approach that works best is to fold a $20 bill and hand it to the clerk along with your credit card (even if you prepaid for your room, he or she will ask for a credit card to cover incidentals). Say something like, "This is really a special trip for me. Anything you can do to make it more special would really be appreciated."

Though other travel specialists disagree, we find this works better than asking for an upgrade or special request outright, plus it leaves you some opportunity for tweaking after your room is assigned—for example, you might like the room type but would prefer a higher floor. Sometimes the clerk will ask you what you're looking for, in which case have a reply ready and be reasonable.

Things the clerk might have latitude to grant are room upgrades; rooms on floors with the best views; rooms situated out of earshot of traffic, ice machines, or elevators; amenities such as wine or fruit sent to your room; and coupons for the hotel bar or breakfast buffet. If you're hoping for a room upgrade at check-in, book a midpriced room or suite when you make your reservation so there's room to move up.

Remember, you're risking just $20, so temper your expectations. Be happy, friendly, and upbeat, addressing the clerk by name if she or he has a name tag. If you've patronized the hotel before, say so.

Before you approach the front desk, look for a similarly upbeat person with obvious experience and seniority. Young, unseasoned clerks are sometimes confused if they haven't confronted the situation before; they also may be wary of accepting a tip when a supervisor is around. In our experience, offering the $20 the way we describe is in no way offensive. The clerk might return your cash, but she or he will do so graciously and thank you for the overture.

Using these strategies will almost always eliminate disappointing surprises as well as offer the best chances for upgrades.

BENEFITS OF STAYING IN THE WORLD

GUESTS WHO STAY on Disney property enjoy privileges and amenities unavailable to those staying outside the World. Though some of these perks are advertising gimmicks, others are real and potentially valuable.

Here are the benefits and what they mean:

1. CONVENIENCE If you don't have a car, commuting to the parks is easy via the Disney transportation system. This is especially advantageous if you stay in a hotel connected by monorail or boat service. If you have a car, however, dozens of hotels outside Disney World are within 5–10 minutes of theme-park parking lots.

2. EARLY ACCESS TO RIDE AND RESTAURANT RESERVATIONS Disney hotel and campground guests, along with guests staying at the Swan and Dolphin resorts, can make FastPass+ ride reservations 60 days before they arrive, or 30 days earlier than the general public. Guests at Disney resorts *except* the Swan, the Dolphin, Shades of Green, and the hotels of the Disney Springs Resort Area can also make dining reservations up to 190 days before their visit, or 10 days earlier than the general public.

3. EXTRA MAGIC HOURS AT THE THEME PARKS Disney World lodging guests are invited to enter a designated park 1 hour earlier than the general public each day or to enjoy a designated theme park for up to 2 hours after it closes to the general public in the evening.

Extra Magic Hours can be valuable if you know how to use them. They can also land you in gridlock. (See our detailed discussion of EMHs starting on page 46.)

4. BABYSITTING AND CHILD-CARE OPTIONS Disney hotel and campground guests have several options for babysitting, child care, and children's programs. The **Polynesian Village Resort** and **Animal Kingdom Lodge,** along with several other Disney hotels, offer "clubs"—themed child-care centers for potty-trained children ages 3–12.

Though somewhat expensive, the clubs are highly regarded by children and parents. On the negative side, they're open only in the evening, and not all Disney hotels have them. If you're staying at a Disney hotel without a club, you're better off using a private in-room babysitting service (see page 454). In-room babysitting is also available at hotels outside Disney World.

5. DISNEY'S MAGICAL EXPRESS If you arrive in Orlando by air, Disney will collect your checked baggage and send it by bus directly to your Walt Disney World resort, allowing you to bypass baggage claim. Magical Express is available daily, 5 a.m.–10 p.m.; free bus service to your hotel is available 24 hours a day. Transportation to your resort hotel will usually include stops at other resorts. The time from deplaning to arriving at your resort will be anywhere from 45 to 90 minutes depending on your resort (35 minutes of that will be driving to Walt Disney World property).

unofficial **TIP**
You'll be asked to show your MagicBands (see page 73) to board Disney's Magical Express, so pack them in your carry-on stuff rather than your checked bags.

When it's time to go home, you can check your baggage and pick up your boarding pass at the front desk of your Disney resort. This service is available to all guests at Disney hotels (excluding the Swan, the Dolphin, Shades of Green, and hotels of the Disney Springs Resort Area), even those who don't use Magical Express (folks who have rental cars, for example). Resort check-in counters are open 5 a.m.–1 p.m., and you must check in no later than 3 hours before your flight (within the US and Puerto Rico) or 4 hours for international flights. Participating airlines are **AirTran, Alaska, American, Delta, JetBlue, Southwest, United,** and **US Airways.** All of the preceding airlines have restrictions on the number of bags, checking procedures, and related items; consult your carrier before leaving home for specifics. For an in-depth discussion of Disney's Magical Express, see Part Seven, Arriving and Getting Around.

6. PRIORITY THEME PARK ADMISSIONS On days of unusually heavy attendance, Disney may restrict admission into the theme parks for all customers. When deciding whom to admit into the parks, priority is given to guests staying at Disney resorts. In practice, no guest is turned away until a park's parking lot is full. When this happens, that park will be packed to gridlock.

7. CHILDREN SHARING A ROOM WITH THEIR PARENTS There's no extra charge per night for children younger than 18 sharing a room with their parents. Many hotels outside Disney World also offer this perk.

8. FREE PARKING Disney resort guests with cars pay nothing to park in theme park lots or hotels. This saves $20 per day at the parks and up to $20 per day at the hotel.

9. RECREATIONAL PRIVILEGES Disney guests get preferential treatment for tee times at the golf courses.

STAYING IN OR OUT OF THE WORLD: WEIGHING THE PROS AND CONS

1. COST If cost is a primary consideration, you'll lodge much less expensively outside Disney World. Our ratings of hotel quality, cost, and commuting times to the theme parks encompass hotels both in and out of the World (see How the Hotels Compare and the Hotel Information Chart, pages 291–306).

2. EASE OF ACCESS Even if you stay in Disney World, you're dependent on some mode of transportation. It may be less stressful to use the Disney transportation system, but with the single exception of commuting to the Magic Kingdom, the fastest, most efficient, and most flexible way to get around is usually a car. If you're at Epcot, for example, and want to take the kids back to Disney's Contemporary Resort for a nap, forget the monorail. You'll get back much faster by car.

A reader from Raynham, Massachusetts, who stayed at the Caribbean Beach Resort writes:

> *Even though the resort is on the Disney bus line, I recommend renting a car if it fits one's budget. The buses don't go directly to many destinations, and often you have to switch buses. Getting a bus back to the hotel after a hard day can mean a long wait in line.*

Readers complain about problems with the Disney transportation system more than most topics. The following comments from a Havertown, Pennsylvania, dad are typical:

WDW bus transportation is quite inefficient. When traveling from the BoardWalk to anywhere else, we had to pick up other passengers at the Swan, Dolphin, and Yacht & Beach Clubs before heading off to the parks. Same story upon return.

Although it's only for the use and benefit of Disney guests, the Disney transportation system is nonetheless public, and users must expect inconveniences: conveyances that arrive and depart on their schedule, not yours; the occasional need to transfer; multiple stops; time lost loading and unloading passengers; and, generally, the challenge of understanding and using a large, complex transportation network.

If you plan to have a car, consider this: Disney World is so large that some destinations within the World can be reached more quickly from off-property hotels than from Disney hotels. For example, guests at lodgings on US 192 (near the so-called Walt Disney World Maingate) are closer to Disney's Hollywood Studios, Animal Kingdom, and Blizzard Beach water park than guests at many hotels inside Disney World.

A Kentucky dad overruled his family about staying at a Disney resort and is glad he did:

My wife read in another guidebook that it can take 2 hours to commute to the parks if you stay outside Walt Disney World. I guess it could take 2 hours if you stayed in Tampa, but from our hotel on US 192 we could commute to any of the parks except the Magic Kingdom and have at least one ride under our belt in about an hour.

For commuting times from specific non-Disney hotels, see our Hotel Information Chart on pages 291–306.

3. YOUNG CHILDREN Although the hassle of commuting to most non-World hotels is only slightly (if at all) greater than that of commuting to Disney hotels, a definite peace of mind results from staying in the World. Regardless of where you stay, make sure you get your young children back to the hotel for a nap each day.

4. SPLITTING UP If you're in a party that will probably split up to tour (as frequently happens in families with teens or children of widely varying ages), staying in the World offers more transportation options and, thus, more independence. Mom and Dad can take the car and return to the hotel for a relaxed dinner and early bedtime while the teens remain in the park for evening parades and fireworks.

5. FEEDING THE ARMY OF THE POTOMAC If you have a large crew that chows down like cattle on a finishing lot, you may do better staying outside the World, where food is far less expensive.

6. VISITING OTHER ORLANDO-AREA ATTRACTIONS If you'll be visiting SeaWorld, Kennedy Space Center Visitor Complex, Universal Orlando, or other area attractions, it may be more convenient to stay outside the World.

The DISNEY RESORTS

DISNEY RESORTS 101

BEFORE YOU MAKE ANY DECISIONS, understand these basics regarding Disney resorts.

1. RESORT CLASSIFICATIONS Disney loves to categorize, so it's not surprising that they've developed a hierarchy of resort classifications and subclassifications:

Deluxe resorts are Disney's top-of-the-line hotels, with extensive theming, luxurious rooms, and superior on-site dining, recreation, and services. **Disney's Wilderness Lodge & Boulder Ridge Villas** and **Animal Kingdom Lodge & Villas** are popular for their theming and their price, which is at the low end of this category. (Their rooms are also the smallest among the Deluxes.)

Disney Deluxe Villa (DDV) resorts, also known as **Disney Vacation Club (DVC) resorts,** offer suites, some with full kitchens. DDV resorts, several of which are attached to Deluxe resorts, equal or surpass Deluxe resorts in quality. They can also be a better value: Unlike other Disney resorts, DDV resorts don't levy a nightly surcharge for each additional adult (age 18+) in a room beyond the standard two.

Moderate resorts are a step down from Deluxes in guest-room quality, amenities, and cost. The price difference among most Moderates is perhaps a few dollars per night at most, so choosing a resort in this category generally comes down to which theme you prefer.

Also classified by Disney as a Moderate resort, **Fort Wilderness Resort & Campground** offers both campsites and fully equipped cabins.

At the bottom of the list are **Value resorts,** with the smallest rooms, most limited amenities, and lowest rates of any Disney-owned hotels. Because this category is so popular with budget-conscious families, Disney has four separate Value price tiers:

- The **All-Star Sports, Music,** and **Movies Resorts** are Disney's oldest and least-expensive Value resorts.

- **Disney's Pop Century Resort** sits in the middle of the Value price range—about $10 per night more than the All-Stars.

- **Disney's Art of Animation Resort** is the newest Value property, with the largest rooms, best food court, and best pools in this category. Standard rooms here cost about $25 per night more than those at the All-Stars.

- Two-room **Family Suites** are available at the All-Star Music and Art of Animation Resorts, from around $240 to $510 per night.

2. MAKING RESERVATIONS Whether you book through Disney, a travel agent, online, with a tour operator, or through an organization like AAA, you'll frequently save by booking the room exclusive of any vacation package. This is called a *room-only reservation.* Though later in this chapter we'll scrutinize the advantages and disadvantages of buying a package, we'll tell you now that Walt Disney World packages at list price rarely save you any money (though they can certainly be convenient).

In dealing with Disney for rooms only, use disneyworld.com instead of calling the Disney Reservation Center (DRC) at ☎ 407-W-DIS-NEY (934-7639). Because of some administrative and operational consolidation, reservationists at the DRC are trained to sell only Walt Disney Travel Company packages. Even if

unofficial **TIP**
Understand that Disney Reservation Center and Walt Disney Travel Company representatives don't have detailed personal knowledge of resorts.

you insist that all you want is a room, they'll try to persuade you to bundle it with some small extra, like a miniature-golf pass, so that your purchase can be counted as a package. Seems innocuous enough, but that little upgrade allows Disney to apply various restrictions and cancellation policies that you wouldn't be saddled with if you bought a room by itself—for example, Disney might add trip insurance to your package automatically.

Regarding cancellation, know that there are trade-offs. If you book a package and cancel 2–30 days before arrival, you lose your $200 deposit. If you cancel a day or less before arrival, you lose the entire package cost, including airfare and insurance. If you reserve only a room and cancel fewer than five days before arrival (six days if you booked through Disney's website), you lose your deposit of one night's room charge, which can easily be more than $200 if you booked at a Moderate, Deluxe, or DDV resort. Further, Disney imposes a $65 fee for changing your package's details, including travel dates, moving to a cheaper resort, or adding a discount code.

If you call, tell the agent what you want in terms of lodging and get a room-only rate quote. Then tell the agent what you're looking for in terms of admissions. When you've pinned down your room selection and lodging costs, ask the agent if he or she can offer any packages that beat the à la carte prices. But don't be swayed by little sweeteners included in a package unless they have real value for you. If the first agent you speak to isn't accommodating, hang up and call back. There are a couple hundred agents, some more helpful than others.

unofficial **TIP**
Booking online is *much* faster than calling DRC. If you must call, do so before 11 a.m. or after 3 p.m. Eastern.

When dealing with Disney reservations, a careful shopper from West Lafayette, Indiana, advises both wariness and toughness:

> Making reservations through W-DISNEY is like buying a car: You need to know the sales tricks, have a firm idea of what you want, and be prepared to walk away if you don't get what you want at a price you want to pay.

If you need specific information, call the resort directly, ask for the front desk, and pose your question before phoning the DRC. If your desired dates aren't available, keep calling back or check online. Something might open up.

3. A MOST CONFUSING VIEW Rates at Disney hotels vary from season to season (see the next section) and from room to room according to view. Further, each Disney resort has its own seasonal calendar. Seasons such as "Regular," "Value," "Peak," and "Holiday" vary depending on the resort instead of that tired old January–December calendar that the rest of us use. But as confusing as Disney seasons are, they're logic personified compared to the panoply of guest-room views the resorts offer. Depending on the resort, you can choose standard views, water views, pool views, lagoon views, garden views, or savanna views, among others. Standard view, the most ambiguous category, crops up at about three-fourths of Disney resorts. It's usually interpreted as a view of infrastructure or unremarkable scenery. At Animal Kingdom Lodge, for example, you have savanna views, pool views, value views, and standard views. Savanna views overlook the replicated African savanna, pool views overlook the swimming pool, and value and standard views offer stunning vistas of . . . rooftops and parking lots.

With a standard view, however, you can at least pinpoint what you *won't* be seeing. Every resort defines views of water differently. At the Grand Floridian Resort & Spa, for example, rooms with views of Seven Seas Lagoon are sensibly called lagoon-view rooms, while those with views of the marina or pools are enigmatically called garden-view rooms.

Zip over to the Yacht Club Resort, another Deluxe property. Like the Grand Floridian, the Yacht Club is on a lake and has a pool and a marina. Views of all three are lumped into one big lagoon- or pool-view category—anything wet counts! If somehow you can glimpse the lake or a swimming pool, you have a water view.

It's worth noting that scoring a Grand Floridian room with a view of the Magic Kingdom requires exacting verbiage, as a mom from Pontefract, England, attests:

> We stayed at the Grand Floridian, which was lovely. However, I paid extra for a Magic Kingdom view. I was soooo disappointed when all I could see from the balcony was Space Mountain (unless I hung out so far I risked falling over). I was so looking forward to sitting on the balcony with a glass of wine and watching the fireworks. I know that next time I will have to ask for a view of Cinderella Castle, not just a Magic Kingdom view.

For many readers a good view is considered essential to the enjoyment of their hotel room. Getting the view you want, however, doesn't necessarily mean that you'll have the experience you want, as a Rochester, New York, couple points out:

> We stayed in the Conch Key building at the Grand Floridian. The view was lovely, but all we heard was the boat's horn blasting every 20 minutes, 7 a.m.–midnight. It was obnoxious and kept us up.

Our favorite water views are at the Contemporary Resort's Garden Building, which extends toward Bay Lake to the east of the giant A-frame. Rooms in this three-story structure, such as room 6109, afford some of the best lake vistas in Disney World (see tinyurl.com/contemporary6109 for a view from one of these rooms). Many rooms are so near the water, in fact, you could spit a prune pit into the lake from your window. And their category? Garden views.

We could go on and on, but pinning Disney down on precisely what will be outside your window is the point. In our discussion of individual resorts later in this chapter, we'll tell you which rooms have the good views.

Our website's **Hotel Room View** project uses more than 31,000 photos to show the view you get from every hotel room in Walt Disney World, plus instructions on how to request each specific room. It uses interactive maps for every building in every resort, so that you can search for rooms by cost, view, walking distance, noise, handicap accessibility, and more. As you read this chapter, visit touringplans.com/walt-disney-world/hotels to see photos of the rooms we recommend.

4. HOW TO GET THE ROOM YOU WANT Disney won't guarantee a specific room when you book but will post your request on your reservation record. The easiest way to make a request is to use our **Hotel Room View** tool, described above. Select the room you want, and we'll automatically fax your request to Disney five days before you arrive.

unofficial **TIP**
Disney will guarantee connecting rooms if your party includes more children than adults. (In Disney terms, *adjoining rooms* are next to each other and *connecting rooms* have a door between them.)

Our experience indicates that making a request by room number confuses the Disney reservationists; as a result, they're unsure where to place you if the room you've asked for is unavailable. To increase your odds of getting the room you want, tell the reservationist exactly what characteristics and amenities you desire—for example: "I'd like a room with a balcony on the second or third floor of the Contemporary Resort's Garden Building with an unobstructed view of the lake." (It's unnecessary to ask for a nonsmoking room at a Disney resort—all rooms were designated smoke-free in 2007.)

Be direct and politely assertive when speaking to the Disney agent. At Port Orleans Riverside, for example, rooms with king beds have options for standard-, garden-, pool-, preferred-, and river-view rooms. If you want to overlook the river, say so; likewise, if you want a pool view, speak up. Similarly, state clearly such preferences as a particular floor, a corner room, a room near restaurants, or a room away from elevators and ice machines. If you have a long list of preferences, type it in order of importance and e-mail, fax, or snail-mail it to the hotel. Include your contact information and reservation-confirmation number. Use abbreviations where possible—we're told Disney's reservation system may hold only around 80 characters of preference text.

It will be someone from the resort who actually assigns your room. Call back in a few days to make sure your preferences were posted to your record.

We'll provide info needed for each resort to frame your requests, including a resort layout map and our recommendations for specific rooms or buildings. We'll use a dash (–) to indicate a range of rooms. Thus, "rooms 2230–2260" refers to the 31 rooms within that range. Sometimes we'll specify even- or odd-numbered rooms within a range, for example, "odd-numbered rooms 631–639." In this case we're referring to rooms 631, 633, 635, 637, and 639.

Again, note that our Hotel Room View tool (see previous page) will give you the exact wording to use when requesting a specific room, and it can automatically send your request to Disney at the appropriate tine before you arrive.

Readers say our hotel-request service works a bit more than two out of three times. Disney's room assigners tell us that the most common reasons for not getting the exact room requested are as follows:

- **Someone is already in the requested room.** This is common during holidays and other busy times. It helps to list several alternatives.

- **Asking to get into your room early (before 3 or 4 p.m.).** Unless you say otherwise, the front desk will assume that any room currently available overrides your earlier requests.

- **Listing only rooms that are more expensive than the one you paid for.** It doesn't hurt to ask for an upgrade, but make sure you've given the room assigners a fallback option based on what you've bought.

HOW TO GET DISCOUNTS ON LODGING

THERE ARE SO MANY GUEST ROOMS in and around Disney World that competition is brisk, and everyone, including Disney, wheels and deals to fill them. Disney, however, has its own atypical way of managing its room inventory. To uphold the brand integrity of its hotels, Disney prefers to use inducements rather than discounts per se. For example, Disney might include free dining if you reserve a certain number of nights at rack rate, or offer special deals only by e-mail to returning guests. Con-

unofficial **TIP**
Three to four days before you arrive, call the resort front desk. Call late in the evening when they're not so busy, and reconfirm the requests that by now should be appearing in their computers.

sequently, many of the strategies for obtaining discounted rates in most cities and destinations don't work well for Disney hotels. We'll explore these strategies in-depth when we discuss booking non-Disney hotels near Walt Disney World; for the moment, though, here are some tips for getting price breaks at Disney properties:

1. SEASONAL SAVINGS Save 15%–35% per night or more on a Disney hotel room by visiting during the slower times of year. However, Disney uses so many adjectives (Regular, Holiday, Peak, Value, and the like) to describe its seasonal calendar that it's hard to keep up. Plus, the dates for each "season" vary among resorts. Disney also changes the price of its hotel rooms with the day of the week, charging more for the same room on Friday and Saturday nights. The increased rates range from $20 to $90 or more per room, per night.

2. ASK ABOUT SPECIALS When you talk to Disney reservationists, ask specifically about specials. For example, "What special deals or discounts are available at Disney hotels during the time of our visit?" Being specific and assertive paid off for a Warren Township, New Jersey, dad:

> *Your tip on asking Disney employees about discounts was invaluable. They will not volunteer this information, but by asking we saved almost $500 on our hotel room.*

A family from West Springfield, Massachusetts, discovered that if you keep on shopping even after you've booked, your efforts can really pay off:

> *I booked our trip online with Disney using a special-offer discount we had received in the mail. Two months before our trip, and after I had already paid in full, Disney ran a special that was actually better than the one I had booked. I gave them a call, and they politely, quickly, and efficiently credited me with the difference.*

Be aware that specials can include discounts on vacation packages in addition to discounts on rooms. Discounts on park admission or dining packages (see "Spring for 'Free Dining' " in "Disney Lodging for Less," pages 240 and 241) can be substantial, depending on the number of people in your traveling party or where you're staying.

3. TRADE-UP OR UPSELL RATES If you request a room at a Disney Value resort and none are available, you may be offered a discounted room in the next category up (Moderate resorts, in this example). Similarly, if you ask for a room in a Moderate resort and none are available, Disney will usually offer a deal for Disney Deluxe Villa rooms or a Deluxe resort. You can angle for a trade-up rate by asking for a resort category that's more likely to be sold out.

4. KNOW THE SECRET CODE The folks at **MouseSavers** (mousesavers .com) maintain an updated list of discounts and reservation codes for Disney resorts. The codes are separated into categories such as "for anyone," "for residents of certain states," and "for Annual Pass holders." Anyone calling ☎ 407-w-DISNEY (934-7639) can use a current code and get the discounted rate.

Be aware that Disney targets people with PIN codes in e-mails and direct mailings. PIN-code discounts are offered to specific individuals and are correlated with a given person's name and address. When you try to make a reservation using the PIN, Disney will verify that the street or e-mail address to which the code was sent is yours.

unofficial **TIP**
To enhance your chances of receiving a PIN-code offer, you need to get your name and street or e-mail address into the Disney system.

MouseSavers has a great historical list of when discounts were released and what they encompassed at mouse savers.com/historicalwdwdiscounts.html. You can also sign up for the MouseSavers newsletter, with discount announcements, Disney news, and exclusive offers not available to the general public.

To get your name in the Disney system for a PIN code, call ☎ 407-w-DISNEY and request written info or the free trip-planning DVD. If you've been to Walt Disney World before, your name and address will of course already be on record, but you won't be as likely to receive a PIN-code offer as you would by calling and requesting that information be mailed to you. On the web, go to disneyworld.com and sign up (via the trip-planning DVD) to automatically be sent offers and news at your e-mail address. You might also consider getting a **Disney Rewards Visa Card,** which entitles you to around two days' advance notice when a discount is released (visit disney.go.com/visa for details).

5. INTERNET SELLERS Online travel sellers **Expedia** (expedia.com), **One Travel** (onetravel.com), **Priceline** (priceline.com), and **Travelocity** (travel ocity.com) offer discounted rooms at Disney hotels, but usually at a price approximating the going rate obtainable from the Walt Disney Travel Company or Walt Disney World Central Reservations. Most breaks are in the 7%–25% range, but they can go as deep as 40%. Always check these websites' prices against Disney's. While updating this book, we saw Disney selling its luxe Yacht Club concierge lounge rooms for $492 per night (with tax) during summer, while Orbitz wanted $7 more for a standard Yacht Club room.

6. WALT DISNEY WORLD WEBSITE Disney still offers deals when it sees lower-than-usual future demand. Go to disneyworld.com and look for "Explore Our Special Offers" on the homepage. In the same place, also look for seasonal discounts, usually listed as "Summertime Savings" or "Fall Savings" or something similar. You can also go to "Places to Stay" at the top of the homepage, where you'll find a link to Special Offers. You must click on the particular special to get the discounts: If you fill out the information on "Price Your Vacation," you'll be charged the full rack rate. Reservations booked online are subject to a penalty if canceled fewer than 45 days before you arrive. Before booking rooms on Disney's or any website, click "Terms and Conditions" and read the fine print.

7. RENTING DISNEY VACATION CLUB POINTS The Disney Vacation Club (DVC) is Disney's time-share-condominium program. DVC resorts (a.k.a. Disney Deluxe Villa [DDV] resorts) at Walt Disney World are **Animal Kingdom Villas, Bay Lake Tower at the Contemporary Resort,** the **Beach Club Villas, BoardWalk Villas, Grand Floridian Villas, Old Key West Resort, Polynesian Villas & Bungalows, Saratoga Springs Resort & Spa, Treehouse Villas at Saratoga Springs,** and **Boulder Ridge** (formerly Wilderness Lodge) **Villas.** Each DVC resort offers studios and one- and two-bedroom villas; some resorts also offer three-bedroom villas. (The new Polynesian Village DVC resort is limited to studios and two-bedroom bungalows.) Studios are equipped with kitchenettes, wet bars, and fridges; villas come with full kitchens. Most accommodations have patios or balconies.

DVC members receive a number of points annually that they use to pay for their Disney accommodations. Sometimes members elect to "rent" (sell) their points instead of using them in a given year. Though Disney is not involved in the transaction, it allows DVC members to make these points available to the general public.

unofficial **TIP**
We think renting points for a **one-bedroom DVC villa** is the best hotel value on Disney property.

The going rental rate is usually in the neighborhood of $14 per point when you deal with members directly; third-party brokers often charge more for acting as a middleman. Renting a studio for a week during Summer season at Animal Kingdom Lodge & Villas currently costs a DVC member 95 points, or $2,753 with tax. If you rented those points at $14 per point, the same studio would cost you $1,330 with tax—more than $1,400 less.

You have two options when renting points: go through a third-party broker or deal directly with a DVC member. For a fixed rate of around $16 per point, the folks at **David's Disney Vacation Club Rentals** (dvcrequest.com) will match your request for a specific resort and dates to their available supply. Their per-point rate is a bit higher than if you did the legwork yourself, but they take requests months in advance and notify you as soon as something becomes available; plus, they take credit cards. We've used David's for huge New Year's Eve events and last-minute trips, and they're tops.

In addition to David's, some readers, like this one from St. Louis, have had good results with **The DVC Rental Store** (dvcrentalstore.com):

We rented DVC points for this trip through the DVC Rental Store, and we had a wonderful experience. Unlike David's, they don't make you pay the entire cost upon booking. For our stay at [Boulder Ridge] Villas, we paid just over half what we were planning to pay for the Wilderness Lodge.

When you deal directly with the selling DVC member, you pay him or her directly, such as by certified check (few members take credit cards). The DVC member makes a reservation in your name and pays Disney the requisite number of points. Arrangements vary, but again, the going rate is around $14 per point. Trust is required from both parties. Usually your reservation is documented by a confirmation sent from Disney to the owner and then passed along to you. Though the deal you cut is strictly up to you and the owner, you should always insist on receiving the aforementioned confirmation before making more than a one-night deposit.

We suggest checking online at one of the various Disney discussion boards (such as mouseowners.com) if you're not picky about where you stay and when you go and you're willing to put in the effort to ask around. If you're trying to book a particular resort, especially during a busy time of year, there's something to be said for the low-hassle approach of a points broker.

8. TRAVEL AGENTS are active players and particularly good sources of information on limited-time programs and discounts. We believe a good travel agent is the best friend a traveler can have. And though we at the *Unofficial Guide* know a thing or two about the travel industry, we always give our agent a chance to beat any deal we find. If she can't beat it, we let her book it anyway if she can get commission from it, thus nurturing the relationship.

Each year we ask our readers to rate the travel agents who helped them plan their Disney vacations. This year we received surveys on more than 1,900 agents. We can't emphasize enough how good these agents are at Disney trip planning. We use them for our own trips, and we often engage them to help shape our research projects. They are among the first travel professionals to see the results of that research, too, meaning they'll pass it on to you. If Disney releases a new discount, they'll try to rebook you at the lower rate automatically. Plus, none of them charge a fee for their services. Our top 12 are as follows:

SUE PISATURO of Small World Vacations, who contributes to this guide (sue@smallworldvacations.com)

Kathy Achue (kathy@smallworldvacations.com)

Lori Bandera (lori@smallworldvacations.com)

Amelia Haywood (amelia@smallworldvacations.com)

Kristin Moore (kristin@magicalvacationstravel.com; see next page)

Jan Pepe (janp@mei-travel.com)

Brandi Pold (brandi@magicalvacationstravel.com)

Mike Rahlmann (mike.rahlmann@themagicforless.com)

Jason Rowe (jason@magicalvacationstravel.com; see next page)

Candice Stoves (candice@magicalvacationstravel.com; see next page)

Amber Vaughan (amber@smallworldvacations.com)

Darren Wittko (darren@magicalvacationstravel.com; see next page)

Our reader-survey results indicate that for Walt Disney World, you'll be much more satisfied using a travel agent who specializes in Disney and much more likely to recommend those agents to a friend. While the agents listed above are among the ones most consistently recommended in our surveys, you'll find good Disney specialists throughout the country if you prefer to work with someone close to home.

9. ORGANIZATIONS AND AUTO CLUBS Disney has developed time-limited programs with some auto clubs and organizations. AAA, for example, can often offer discounts on hotels and packages comparable to those Disney offers its Annual Pass holders. Such deals come and go, but the market suggests there will be more. If you're a member of AARP, AAA, or any travel or auto club, ask whether the group has a program before shopping elsewhere.

10. ROOM UPGRADES Sometimes a room upgrade is as good as a discount. If you're visiting Disney World during a slower time, book the least expensive room your discounts will allow. Checking in, ask very politely about being upgraded to a water-view or pool-view room. A fair percentage of the time, you'll get one at no additional charge or at a deep discount. Understand, however, that a room upgrade should be considered a favor. Hotels are under no obligation to upgrade you, so if your request is not met, accept the decision graciously. Also, note that suites at Deluxe resorts are exempt from discount offers.

11. MILITARY DISCOUNTS The **Shades of Green Armed Forces Recreation Center,** near the Grand Floridian Resort & Spa, offers luxury accommodations at rates based on a service member's rank, as well as attraction tickets to the theme parks. For rates and other information, call ☎ 888-593-2242 or see shadesofgreen.org.

12. YEAR-ROUND DISCOUNTS AT THE SWAN AND DOLPHIN RESORTS Government workers, teachers, nurses, military, and AAA and *Entertainment Coupon Book* members can save on their rooms at the Dolphin or Swan (when space is available, of course). Call ☎ 888-828-8850.

Our Favorite Money-Saving Find This Year: Magical Vacations Travel

In July 2016, we paid $253 per night, with tax, for a room at Disney's Polynesian Resort. That's more than 50% less than the $533 rack rate Disney was asking for similar rooms. It was less than Disney was charging for the same room in 2001. And we didn't have to listen to a time-share presentation or be a personal friend of Disney CEO Bob Iger to do it. All we had to do was believe what we read on the Internet.

In this case, we'd seen a lot of talk in our Lines Chat forum about a company called Magical Vacations Travel (MVT), whose Disney World room offers were far below the prices we were seeing everywhere else. And that was unusual because we have relationships with some very large travel companies that you'd expect would be able to match any offer a smaller company could come up with. But the big travel companies weren't matching MVT's offers. To understand why, we needed to learn some background.

GROUP SALES CONTRACTS: THE MAGICAL VACATIONS TRAVEL MODEL If you're a travel agency looking to get the lowest prices for your clients' Disney World vacations, there are a couple of ways to go. One is to wait for Disney to announce a "special offer" and book your clients at those rates—for our July trip, the best rate available to the general public was

COSTS PER NIGHT OF DISNEY HOTEL ROOMS, 2017 (rack rate)

Rates are for standard rooms except where noted.

All-Star Resorts	$106–$205
All-Star Music Resort Family Suites	$255–$459
Animal Kingdom Lodge	$359–$575
Animal Kingdom Villas *(studio, Jambo/Kidani)*	$358–$621
Art of Animation Family Suites	$338–$570
Art of Animation Resort	$140–$248
Bay Lake Tower at Contemporary Resort *(studio)*	$515–$798
Beach Club Resort	$421–$695
Beach Club Villas *(studio)*	$470–$730
BoardWalk Inn	$459–$730
BoardWalk Villas *(studio)*	$470–$730
Boulder Ridge Villas *(studio)*	$440–$642
Caribbean Beach Resort	$187–$300
Contemporary Resort *(Garden Building)*	$425–$666
Coronado Springs Resort	$191–$300
Dolphin *(Sheraton)*	$189–$435
Fort Wilderness Resort & Campground *(cabins)*	$348–$606
Grand Floridian Resort & Spa	$646–$934
Grand Floridian Villas *(1-bedroom)*	$839–$1,329
Old Key West Resort *(studio)*	$371–$550
Polynesian Village Resort	$508–$793
Polynesian Villas & Bungalows *(studio)*	$529–$840
Pop Century Resort	$118–$225
Port Orleans Resort *(French Quarter & Riverside)*	$213–$323
Saratoga Springs Resort & Spa *(studio)*	$371–$550
Swan *(Westin)*	$189–$430
Treehouse Villas	$893–$1,484
Wilderness Lodge	$345–$612
Yacht Club Resort	$421–$695

*Copper Creek Villas & Cabins not open at press time

WHAT IT COSTS TO STAY IN THE DISNEY SPRINGS RESORT AREA

Best Western Lake Buena Vista Resort Hotel	$80–$233
B Resort & Spa	$89–$329
DoubleTree Suites by Hilton Orlando	$119–$291
Hilton Orlando Buena Vista Palace	$139–$342
Hilton Orlando Lake Buena Vista	$161–$278
Holiday Inn in the WDW Resort	$104–$282
Wyndham Lake Buena Vista Resort	$104–$370

around $468 per night with tax. And many clients would be satisfied simply knowing they got the lowest advertised rate. But there's another option that often results in even better offers, if your agency is willing to sign a contract with Disney's Group Sales department. But those contacts come with risks.

Here's how it works: Your travel agency tells Group Sales that you're going to sell a minimum of 10 rooms for a least three nights each, at some Disney hotel, during specific dates in the future. For example, let's say you're willing to commit to selling 30 "room nights" (10 rooms for three nights each) at Disney's Polynesian Resort between November 10 and November 16.

Disney's Group Sales department has two kinds of contracts your agency can sign, each with different levels of risk. Your price for the rooms depends on which contract you sign, and thus on the risk your agency is willing to accept:

In one contract, you commit to selling 30 room nights, but Disney gives you the option of "returning" any unsold rooms back to Disney without penalty. Let's call this the "standard" contract, because it's the most common one used, by far. We're told that a typical per-night room cost for the Polynesian with this contract might be around $325 per night during busy times of the year.

In the other contract option, you guarantee to Disney that you will pay for all 30 room nights and give up the option of returning unsold rooms to Disney. In that case, Disney is willing to provide better offers because you're guaranteeing it the revenue. We hear that per-room rates for these contracts are similar to the $253 per night we got at the Polynesian. Let's call this the "risk–reward" contract, because your travel agency now has to sell those rooms or lose money.

There's one other notable condition on the risk–reward contract: Disney doesn't allow the contracts to cover certain dates. (For example, December 11 to December 20, 2017, aren't available on MVT's agency-exclusive offers.) That means that clients have to be willing to take their vacations during the dates that are covered, if they want the best offers. Some resorts or room types may also be excluded from the contract.

The vast majority of travel agencies we've spoken to will sign only the standard contract. Why? The smaller agencies typically can't risk thousands of dollars on clients who might cancel at the last minute. Larger agencies, especially those with hundreds of thousands of clients, say that most of their clients can't make their vacation dates fit the offer dates because of work, school, or family commitments. The number of clients who are willing to do this doesn't offset the risk that comes with the contract.

Magical Vacations Travel is using the risk–reward contract. They also let clients cancel, with refunds, using Disney's standard cancellation policy (that is, up to 5 or 6 days in advance), not the 30-day policy they're being held to in their contract. Again, that's part of the risk that Magical Vacations accepts in return for less expensive rooms. But if you can work around their available dates, the savings can better than anything else.

Finally, a disclaimer: We have no business relationship of any kind with MVT. We think it's an interesting, innovative business model that some people might appreciate. It's possible, of course, that MVT could become popular enough for Disney to curtail these kinds of programs. If you try it, let us know how it worked for you.

CHOOSING A WALT DISNEY WORLD HOTEL

IF YOU WANT TO STAY IN THE WORLD but you don't know which hotel to choose, consider these factors:

1. COST Consider your budget. Hotel rooms start at about $100 a night at the **All-Star** and **Pop Century Resorts** during Value season and top out above $1,700 at the **Grand Floridian Resort & Spa** during Holiday season. Suites, of course, are more expensive than standard rooms.

Disney's Animal Kingdom Villas, Bay Lake Tower, Beach Club Villas, BoardWalk Villas, Grand Floridian Villas, Old Key West Resort, Saratoga Springs Resort & Spa, and **Boulder Ridge Villas** offer condo-type accommodations with one-, two-, and (at Saratoga Springs, BoardWalk Villas, Old Key West, Animal Kingdom Villas, Grand Floridian Villas, and Bay Lake Tower) three-bedroom units with kitchens, living rooms, DVD players, and washers and dryers. The **Polynesian Villas & Bungalows** consist solely of studios and two-bedroom freestanding units.

Studios have a kitchenette (with microwave, mini-fridge, and sink) but no washer or dryer. Prices range from $358 per night for a studio suite at Animal Kingdom Villas to more than $3,400 per night for a two-bedroom bungalow at Polynesian Village Villas. Fully equipped cabins (minus a washer and dryer) at **Fort Wilderness Resort & Campground** cost $348–$606 per night. The Family Suites at **All-Star Music** and **Art of Animation** have kitchenettes, separate bedrooms, and two bathrooms. A few suites without kitchens are available at the more expensive Walt Disney World resorts.

unofficial **TIP**
If you plan to use Disney transportation to visit all four major parks and one or both of the water parks, book a centrally located resort that has good transportation connections. The Epcot resorts and the **Polynesian Village, Caribbean Beach, Art of Animation, Pop Century, Coronado Springs,** and **Port Orleans Resorts** fill the bill.

For any extra adults in a room (more than two), the nightly surcharge for each extra adult is $10 at Value resorts, $15 at Moderates, and $25 at Deluxes, plus tax. *DDV resorts levy no surcharge.*

Also at Walt Disney World are the seven hotels of the **Disney Springs Resort Area** (**DSRA**). The accommodations range from fairly luxurious to motel-like. While the DSRA is technically part of Disney World, staying there is like visiting a colony rather than the motherland. Free parking at theme parks isn't offered, and the hotels operate their own buses rather than use Disney transportation. For more information on DSRA properties, see the discussion starting on page 229.

IS IT MORE THAN A PLACE TO SLEEP? Many families headed to Disney World opt for the Value resorts not because of cost, but because (in their words) "it's only a place to sleep." But do those families feel the same way at the end of their trip? We designed an experiment to find out.

We surveyed more than 11,000 families about the brand of hotel they typically stay at when *not* vacationing at Walt Disney World. We categorized those hotels as follows:

- **Budget:** Days Inn, Motel 6, Super 8, etc.
- **Moderate:** Best Western, Hampton Inn, Holiday Inn Express, etc.
- **Upscale:** Crowne Plaza, Radisson, SpringHill Suites, Wyndham, etc.
- **Luxury:** Four Seasons, Hyatt, Ritz-Carlton, Westin, etc.

We grouped Disney's hotels into Disney's own Value, Moderate, Deluxe, and DVC categories. Then we asked the families three questions, each on a five-point scale:

- How satisfied were you with your Disney hotel?
- Would you recommend this hotel to a friend?
- Would you stay at this hotel again?

Here's how the results shook out among those families who were "very satisfied" with their Disney hotel, would recommend it to a friend, and would stay at that hotel again:

CATEGORY (Off-Site and Disney)	DISNEY VALUE (% Positive Responses)	DISNEY MODERATE (% Positive Responses)	DISNEY DELUXE (% Positive Responses)	DVC (% Positive Responses)
Budget	71%	57%	85%	78%
Moderate	70%	61%	74%	78%
Upscale	65%	59%	74%	78%
Luxury	65%	51%	76%	81%

The takeaway? No matter what kind of hotel you stay at outside of Walt Disney World, **you'll probably be most satisfied at a Disney Deluxe or DVC resort.** So even if you stay at a low-cost Microtel Inn on other trips, you'll still be happier if you stay at Disney's Animal Kingdom Lodge than All-Star Music.

After doing these surveys for 30 years, we're convinced that most people add the words "for the money I paid" to the end of every question we ask. So when you read the survey results above, it's safe to assume that they take into account the higher cost of the hotel rooms. If you've got the budget, we think you'll have a better trip by booking a Deluxe hotel or DVC.

For the second year in a row, **Disney's Caribbean Beach Resort** dragged down the entire Moderate hotels segment. Adding to that in 2017 and 2018 is Caribbean Beach's ongoing, extensive renovation project. If you're a family (or a travel agent booking other families), we suggest avoiding Caribbean Beach until construction is done.

2. LOCATION Once you determine your budget, think about what you want to do at Disney World. Will you go to all four theme parks or concentrate on one or two?

If you're going to be driving, your Disney hotel's location isn't especially important unless you plan to spend most of your time at the

Magic Kingdom. (Disney transportation is always more efficient than your car in this case, because it bypasses the Transportation and Ticket Center, the World's transportation hub, and deposits you at the theme park entrance.) If you haven't decided whether you want a car for your Disney vacation, see "How to Travel Around the World" (page 486).

Most convenient to the Magic Kingdom are the three resort complexes linked by monorail: the **Grand Floridian** and its **Villas,** the **Contemporary** and **Bay Lake Tower,** and the **Polynesian Village, Villas, & Bungalows.** Commuting to the Magic Kingdom by monorail is quick and simple, allowing visitors to return to their hotel for a nap, swim, or meal.

Contemporary Resort and Bay Lake Tower, in addition to being on the monorail, are only a 10- to 15-minute walk to the Magic Kingdom. Guests reach Epcot by monorail but must transfer at the Transportation and Ticket Center. Buses connect the resorts to Disney's Hollywood Studios, Disney's Animal Kingdom, the water parks, and Disney Springs. No transfer is required, but the bus makes several stops before reaching either destination.

The Polynesian Village, Villas, & Bungalows are served by the monorail and are an easy walk from the transportation center, where you can catch an express monorail to Epcot. This makes the Polynesian Village the only Disney World resort that has direct monorail access to both Epcot and the Magic Kingdom. To minimize your walk to the transportation center, request a standard room in Raratonga or a DVC studio in Tokelau, Pago Pago, or Moorea.

Wilderness Lodge & Boulder Ridge Villas, along with **Fort Wilderness Resort & Campground,** are linked to the Magic Kingdom by boat and to everywhere else in the World by somewhat-convoluted bus service. The **Four Seasons Resort Orlando at Walt Disney World,** behind the former Osprey Ridge Golf Course, has its own bus service to the Magic Kingdom.

The most centrally located resorts in Walt Disney World are the Epcot hotels—the **BoardWalk Inn, BoardWalk Villas, Yacht & Beach Club Resorts, Beach Club Villas, Swan,** and **Dolphin**—and **Coronado Springs,** near Disney's Animal Kingdom. The Epcot hotels are within easy walking distance of Disney's Hollywood Studios and Epcot's International Gateway. Except at Coronado Springs, boat service is also available at these resorts, with vessels connecting to DHS. Epcot hotels are best for guests planning to spend most of their time at Epcot or DHS.

Caribbean Beach Resort, Pop Century Resort, and **Art of Animation Resort** are just south and east of Epcot and DHS. Along Bonnet Creek, **Disney's Old Key West** and **Port Orleans Resorts** also offer quick access to those parks.

Also along Bonnet Creek, pretty much surrounded by Walt Disney World, is a parcel of land that Disney was unable to acquire and that went undeveloped for decades. Now that property is home to the 70-acre **Bonnet Creek Resort,** comprising four non-Disney hotels: the **Waldorf Astoria Orlando;** the **Hilton Orlando Bonnet Creek;** and two **Wyndham** properties, the **Wyndham Bonnet Creek Resort** and its more luxurious sibling, the **Wyndham Grand Orlando Resort Bonnet Creek.** Technically, the complex isn't in Walt Disney World, but you can access it only via Disney property and roads—a real sore spot with Disney. The hotels of the Bonnet Creek Resort are as close to the theme parks as Disney's own, offer transportation to the parks and Disney Springs, and are every bit as good as Disney's best, often at around half the price. We profile the Hilton, the Waldorf Astoria, and the Wyndham Bonnet Creek later in this chapter in "Hotels Outside Walt Disney World."

Though not centrally located, the **All-Star Resorts** and **Animal Kingdom Lodge & Villas** have very good bus service to all Disney World destinations and are closest to Animal Kingdom.

Continued on page 144

"OK, next let's do Port Orleans to Blizzard Beach."

DISNEY DELUXE RESORTS ROOM DIAGRAMS

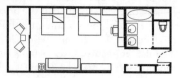

CONTEMPORARY RESORT
Typical room, 394 sq. ft., accommodates
5 guests plus 1 child under age 3 in a crib.

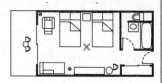

POLYNESIAN VILLAGE RESORT
Typical room, 415 sq. ft., accommodates
5 guests plus 1 child under age 3 in a crib.

GRAND FLORIDIAN RESORT & SPA
Typical room, 440 sq. ft., accommodates
5 guests plus 1 child under age 3 in a crib.

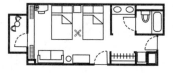

BOARDWALK INN
Typical room, 371 sq. ft., accommodates
4 guests plus 1 child under age 3 in a crib.

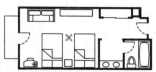

BEACH CLUB RESORT
Typical room, 381 sq. ft., accommodates
5 guests plus 1 child under age 3 in a crib.

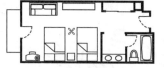

YACHT CLUB RESORT
Typical room, 381 sq. ft., accommodates
4 guests plus 1 child under age 3 in a crib.

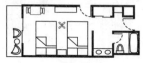

WILDERNESS LODGE
Typical room, 344 sq. ft., accommodates
4 guests plus 1 child under age 3 in a crib.

ANIMAL KINGDOM LODGE
Typical room, 344 sq. ft., accommodates
4 guests plus 1 child under age 3 in a crib.

COPPER CREEK VILLAS & CABINS
(not open at press time)
Studio
(gray area; sleeps 4): 350 sq. ft.
1-bedroom
(sleeps 4): 760 sq. ft.
2-bedroom
(sleeps 8): 1,100 sq. ft.
Cabin
(2 bedrooms; sleeps 8): 1,740 sq. ft.
Grand Villa (3 bedrooms):
3,000 sq. ft. (estimate)

DISNEY DELUXE VILLA RESORTS ROOM DIAGRAMS

OLD KEY WEST RESORT
Studio: (gray area) 376 sq. ft.; **1-bedroom:** 942 sq. ft.;
2-bedroom: 1,333 sq. ft.; **Grand Villa:** 2,202 sq. ft.

**BAY LAKE TOWER
AT CONTEMPORARY RESORT**
Studio: (gray area) 339 sq. ft.
1-bedroom: 803 sq. ft.; **2-bedroom:** 1,152
sq. ft.; **Grand Villa:** 2,044 sq. ft.

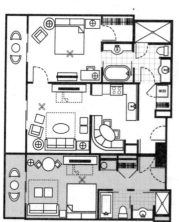

THE VILLAS AT GRAND FLORIDIAN RESORT & SPA
Studio: (gray area) 374 sq. ft.; **1-bedroom:**
(white area) 844 sq. ft.; **2-bedroom lock-off:**
(gray and white) 1,232 sq. ft.

**TREEHOUSE VILLAS AT
SARATOGA SPRINGS
RESORT & SPA**
3-bedroom:
1,074 sq. ft.

DDV GUEST-OCCUPANCY LIMITS

• **Studios:** 4 persons at all but Grand Floridian, Polynesian, and Boulder Ridge Villas (5). • **One-bedroom villas:** 4 at Beach Club, BoardWalk, Saratoga Springs, and Boulder Ridge; 4 or 5 at Animal Kingdom Lodge (Jambo House); 5 everywhere else. • **Two-bedroom villas:** 8 or 9 at Animal Kingdom Lodge (Jambo House); 9 at Animal Kingdom Lodge (Kidani Village), Bay Lake Tower, and Old Key West; 9 or 10 at Grand Floridian; 8 everywhere else. **Three-bedroom and Grand Villas:** 9 at Treehouse Villas; 12 everywhere else. *Note:* To all these limits you may add 1 child under age 3 in a crib.

BOARDWALK VILLAS
Studio: (gray area) 412 sq. ft.
1-bedroom: 814 sq. ft.; **2-bedroom:**
1,236 sq. ft.; **Grand Villa:** 2,491 sq. ft.

DISNEY DELUXE VILLA RESORTS ROOM DIAGRAMS (continued)

ANIMAL KINGDOM VILLAS
JAMBO HOUSE
Studio: (gray area) 316–365 sq. ft.
1-bedroom: 629–710 sq. ft.
2-bedroom: 945–1,075 sq. ft.
Grand Villa: 2,349 sq. ft.

KIDANI VILLAGE
Studio: (gray area) 366 sq. ft.
1-bedroom: 807 sq. ft.
2-bedroom: 1,173 sq. ft.
Grand Villa: 2,201 sq. ft.

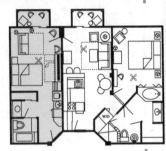

BOULDER RIDGE VILLAS
Studio: (gray area) 356 sq. ft.
1-bedroom: 727 sq. ft.
2-bedroom: 1,080 sq. ft.

BEACH CLUB VILLAS
Studio: (gray area) 356 sq. ft.
1-bedroom: 726 sq. ft.
2-bedroom: (gray and white)
1,083 sq. ft.

SARASOTA SPRINGS RESORT & SPA
Studio: (gray area) 355 sq. ft.
1-bedroom: 714 sq. ft.
2-bedroom: 1,075 sq. ft.
Grand Villa: 2,113 sq. ft.

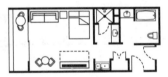

POLYNESIAN VILLAGE VILLAS
Studio: 460 sq. ft.

POLYNESIAN
VILLAGE
BUNGALOWS
1,650 sq. ft.

DISNEY MODERATE RESORTS ROOM DIAGRAMS

CORONADO SPRINGS RESORT
Typical room, 314 sq. ft.,
accommodates 4 guests plus 1 child
under age 3 in a crib.

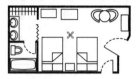

CARIBBEAN BEACH RESORT
Typical room, 314 sq. ft.,
accommodates 4 guests plus 1 child
under age 3 in a crib.

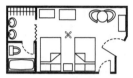

**PORT ORLEANS RESORT–
FRENCH QUARTER**
Typical room, 314 sq. ft.,
accommodates 4 guests plus 1 child
under age 3 in a crib.

**PORT ORLEANS RESORT–
RIVERSIDE**
Typical room, 314 sq. ft., accommodates
4 guests plus 1 child under age 3 in a crib.
Alligator Bayou has trundle bed for child
(54" long) at no extra charge.

DISNEY VALUE RESORTS ROOM DIAGRAMS

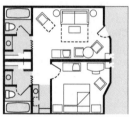

ALL-STAR RESORTS FAMILY SUITE
Typical suite, 520 sq. ft.,
accommodates 6 guests, plus 1 child
under age 3 in a crib.

ART OF ANIMATION RESORT
Little Mermaid standard room
Typical room, 277 sq. ft., accommodates
4 guests, plus 1 child under age 3 in a crib.

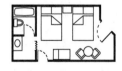

ALL-STAR RESORTS
Typical room, 260 sq. ft., accommodates
4 guests, plus 1 child under age 3 in a crib.

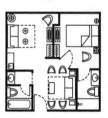

ART OF ANIMATION RESORT
Finding Nemo Family Suite
Typical suite, 565 sq. ft.,
accommodates 6 guests, plus 1 child
under age 3 in a crib.

POP CENTURY RESORT
Typical room, 260 sq. ft., accommodates
4 guests, plus 1 child under age 3 in a crib.

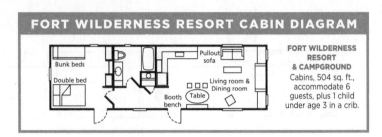

FORT WILDERNESS RESORT CABIN DIAGRAM

Bunk beds

Double bed

Pullout sofa

Living room & Dining room

Booth bench

Table

FORT WILDERNESS RESORT & CAMPGROUND Cabins, 504 sq. ft., accommodate 6 guests, plus 1 child under age 3 in a crib.

Continued from page 139

If you plan to play golf, book **Old Key West Resort** or **Saratoga Springs Resort & Spa,** both of which are built around golf courses, or the **Four Seasons,** which has its own course and is a short drive to Disney's Palm and Magnolia courses. The military-only **Shades of Green** resort is adjacent to the Palm and Magnolia as well. Nearby but not on a golf course are the **Contemporary** and **Bay Lake Tower,** along with the **Grand Floridian, Polynesian Village,** and **Port Orleans Resorts.**

For boating and water sports, try the **Polynesian Village, Contemporary,** or **Grand Floridian Resort; Fort Wilderness Resort & Campground;** or **Wilderness Lodge & Boulder Ridge Villas.** The lodge and campground are also great for hikers, bikers, and joggers.

3. ROOM QUALITY Few Disney guests spend much time in their hotel rooms, though these rooms are among the best designed and most well appointed anywhere. Plus, they're meticulously maintained. At the top of the line are the luxurious rooms of the **Contemporary, Grand Floridian,** and **Polynesian Village Resorts;** bringing up the rear are the small rooms of the **All-Star Resorts.** But even these Value rooms are sparkling-clean and quite livable.

The chart on the opposite page shows how Walt Disney World hotels (along with the **Swan** and **Dolphin,** which are Westin and Sheraton hotels, respectively) stack up for quality.

4. THE SIZE OF YOUR GROUP Larger families and groups may be interested in how many persons a Disney resort room can accommodate, but only Lilliputians would be comfortable in a room filled to capacity. Groups requiring two or more guest rooms should consider condo or villa accommodations in or out of the World. The most cost-efficient Disney resorts for groups of five are the **Alligator Bayou** section of **Port Orleans–Riverside** and **Caribbean Beach Resort.** The cheapest digs for six are the **All-Star Music Family Suites.** If your party includes more than six people, you'll need two hotel rooms, a suite, a villa, or a condo. The Disney room-layout diagrams on the previous pages show the rooms' relative sizes and configurations, along with the maximum number of persons per room.

5. THEME All Disney hotels are themed. Each is designed to make you feel you're in a special place or period of history.

Some resorts carry off their themes better than others, and some themes are more exciting. **Wilderness Lodge & Boulder Ridge Villas,** for example, is extraordinary, reminiscent of a grand national-park lodge from the early 20th century. The lobby opens eight stories to

HOTEL	ROOM-QUALITY RATING
1. BAY LAKE TOWER	95
2. CONTEMPORARY RESORT	93
3. GRAND FLORIDIAN VILLAS	93
4. POLYNESIAN VILLAGE RESORT	92
5. ANIMAL KINGDOM VILLAS *(studio)*	91
6. BEACH CLUB RESORT	90
7. BEACH CLUB VILLAS *(studio)*	90
8. BOARDWALK VILLAS *(studio)*	90
9. DOLPHIN	90
10. GRAND FLORIDIAN RESORT & SPA	90
11. OLD KEY WEST RESORT *(studio)*	90
12. POLYNESIAN VILLAS & BUNGALOWS *(studio)*	90
13. SARATOGA SPRINGS RESORT & SPA *(studio)*	90
14. SWAN	90
15. TREEHOUSE VILLAS	90
16. BOULDER RIDGE VILLAS *(studio)*	90
17. ANIMAL KINGDOM LODGE	89
18. BOARDWALK INN	89
19. YACHT CLUB RESORT	89
20. FORT WILDERNESS CABINS	86
21. WILDERNESS LODGE*	86
22. CORONADO SPRINGS RESORT	85
23. SHADES OF GREEN	85
24. PORT ORLEANS FRENCH QUARTER	84
25. PORT ORLEANS RIVERSIDE	83
26. CARIBBEAN BEACH RESORT	80
27. ART OF ANIMATION RESORT *(standard rooms)*	78
28. ALL-STAR RESORTS	73
29. POP CENTURY RESORT	71

*Copper Creek Villas & Cabins not open at press time.

a timbered ceiling supported by giant columns of bundled logs. One look eases you into the Northwest-wilderness theme. The lodge is a great choice for couples and seniors and is heaven for children.

Animal Kingdom Lodge & Villas replicates grand safari lodges of Kenya and Tanzania and overlooks its own African game preserve. By far the most exotic Disney resort, it's made to order for couples on romantic getaways and for families with children. Likewise dramatic, the **Polynesian Village, Villas, & Bungalows** conveys the feeling of the Pacific Islands. It's great for romantics and families. Many waterfront rooms on upper floors offer a perfect view of Cinderella Castle and the Magic Kingdom fireworks across Seven Seas Lagoon.

Grandeur, nostalgia, and privilege are central to the **Grand Floridian Resort & Spa, Grand Floridian Villas, Yacht & Beach Club Resorts,**

DISNEY HOTELS BY THEME

ALL-STAR RESORTS: Sports, music, and movies

ANIMAL KINGDOM LODGE & VILLAS: African game preserve

ART OF ANIMATION RESORT: Disney's animated films

BAY LAKE TOWER: Upscale, ultramodern urban hotel

BEACH CLUB RESORT & VILLAS: New England beach club of the 1870s

BOARDWALK INN: East Coast boardwalk hotel of the early 1900s

BOARDWALK VILLAS: East Coast beach cottage of the early 1900s

CARIBBEAN BEACH RESORT: Caribbean islands

CONTEMPORARY RESORT: Future as perceived by past, present generations

CORONADO SPRINGS RESORT: Northern Mexico and the American Southwest

DOLPHIN: Modern Florida resort

GRAND FLORIDIAN RESORT & SPA, VILLAS: Turn-of-the-20th-century luxury hotel

OLD KEY WEST RESORT: Key West

POLYNESIAN VILLAGE RESORT, VILLAS, & BUNGALOWS: Hawaii–South Seas

POP CENTURY RESORT: Icons from various decades of the 20th century

PORT ORLEANS RESORT–FRENCH QUARTER: Turn-of-the-19th-century New Orleans

PORT ORLEANS RESORT–RIVERSIDE: Antebellum Louisiana plantation, bayou-side retreat

SARATOGA SPRINGS RESORT & SPA: 1880s Victorian lake

SWAN: Modern Florida resort

TREEHOUSE VILLAS: Rustic vacation homes with modern amenities

WILDERNESS LODGE & BOULDER RIDGE VILLAS*: National-park grand lodge of the early 1900s

YACHT CLUB RESORT: New England seashore hotel of the 1880s

Copper Creek Villas & Cabins not open at press time

BoardWalk Inn, and **BoardWalk Villas.** Though modeled after Eastern-seaboard seaside hotels of different eras, the resorts are similar. **Saratoga Springs Resort & Spa,** supposedly representative of an upstate New York country retreat, looks like what you'd get if you crossed the Beach Club with the Wilderness Lodge. For all the resorts inspired by Northeastern hotels, thematic distinctions are subtle and lost on many guests.

Port Orleans Resort–French Quarter lacks the mystery and sultriness of the real New Orleans French Quarter but captures enough of its architectural essence to carry off the theme. **Port Orleans Resort–Riverside** likewise succeeds with its plantation and bayou setting. **Old Key West Resort** gets the architecture right, but cloning its inspiration on such a large scale totally glosses over the real Key West's idiosyncratic patchwork personality. The **Caribbean Beach Resort**'s theme is much more effective at night, thanks to creative lighting. By day, it looks like a Miami condo development.

Coronado Springs Resort features several styles of Mexican and Southwestern American architecture. Though the lake setting is lovely and the resort is attractive and inviting, the theme (with the exception of the main swimming area) isn't especially stimulating—more like a Scottsdale, Arizona, country club than a Disney resort. Like Caribbean Beach, though, Coronado Springs is beautiful at night.

The **All-Star Resorts** comprise 30 three-story, T-shaped hotels with almost 6,000 guest rooms. There are 15 themed areas: 5 celebrate sports (surfing, basketball, tennis, football, and baseball), 5 recall Hollywood movies, and 5 have musical motifs. The resort's design, with entrances shaped like giant Dalmatians, Coke cups, footballs, and the like, is pretty adolescent, sacrificing grace and beauty for energy and novelty. Guest rooms are small, with decor reminiscent of a teenage boy's bedroom. Despite the theme, there is neither sports nor music; however, movies are shown nightly at all three resorts. **Pop Century Resort** is pretty much a clone of All-Star Resorts, only here the giant icons symbolize decades of the 20th century (Big Wheels, 45-rpm records, silhouettes of people doing period dances, and such), and period memorabilia decorates the rooms. Across the lake from Pop Century Resort is the **Art of Animation Resort,** with icons and decor based on four animated features: *Cars, Finding Nemo, The Lion King,* and *The Little Mermaid.*

Pretense aside, the **Contemporary, Swan,** and **Dolphin** are essentially themeless though architecturally interesting. The original Contemporary Resort is a 15-story A-frame building with monorails running through the middle. Views from guest rooms here and in **Bay Lake Tower** are among the best at Disney World. The Swan and Dolphin are massive yet whimsical. Designed by Michael Graves, they're excellent examples of "entertainment architecture."

6. DINING The best resorts for dining quality and selection are the Epcot resorts: the **Beach Club Villas, BoardWalk Inn & Villas, Dolphin, Swan,** and **Yacht & Beach Club Resorts.** Each has good restaurants and is within easy walking distance of the others and of the 15 restaurants in Epcot's World Showcase section. If you stay at an Epcot resort, you have more than 30 restaurants within a 5- to 12-minute walk.

The only other place in Disney World where restaurants and hotels are similarly concentrated is in the **Disney Springs Resort Area.** In addition to restaurants in the hotels themselves, **B Resort & Spa, Best Western Lake Buena Vista Resort Hotel, Hilton Orlando Buena Vista Palace,** the **Hilton, Holiday Inn at Walt Disney World,** and **Wyndham Lake Buena Vista Resort,** along with **Saratoga Springs Resort & Spa,** are within walking distance of restaurants in Disney Springs.

Guests at the **Contemporary, Polynesian Village,** and **Grand Floridian** can eat in their hotels, or they can commute to restaurants in the Magic Kingdom (not recommended) or in other monorail-linked hotels. Riding the monorail to another hotel or to the Magic Kingdom takes about 10 minutes each way, plus waiting for the train.

The other Disney resorts are somewhat isolated. This means you're stuck dining at your hotel unless (1) you have a car or (2) you're content to eat at the theme parks or Disney Springs.

Here's the deal. Disney transportation works fine for commuting from hotels to theme parks and Disney Springs, but it's useless for getting from one hotel to another. If you're staying at Port Orleans and you want to dine at the Swan, forget it—it could take you up to an

DISNEY RESORT AMENITIES

RESORT	SUITES	CONCIERGE FLOOR	NUMBER OF ROOMS	ROOM SERVICE (full)	FREE IN-ROOM WI-FI	FRIDGE/ MINI-FRIDGE
ALL-STAR RESORTS	•	—	5,406	—	•	•
ANIMAL KINGDOM LODGE	•	•	972	•	•	•
ANIMAL KINGDOM VILLAS	•	•**	458	•	•	•
ART OF ANIMATION RESORT	•	—	1,984	—	•	•
BAY LAKE TOWER	•	—	295	•	•	•
BEACH CLUB VILLAS	•	—	282	•	•	•
BOARDWALK INN	•	•	371	•	•	•
BOARDWALK VILLAS	•	—	532	•	•	•
CARIBBEAN BEACH RESORT*	—	—	2,112	—	•	•
CONTEMPORARY RESORT	•	•	655	•	•	•
CORONADO SPRINGS RESORT*	•	•	1,915	•	•	•
DOLPHIN	•	—	1,509	•	—	•
FORT WILDERNESS CABINS	—	—	409	—	•	•
GRAND FLORIDIAN RESORT & SPA, VILLAS	•	•	1,067	•	•	•
OLD KEY WEST RESORT	•	—	761	—	•	•
POLYNESIAN VILLAGE, VILLAS, & BUNGALOWS	•	•	866	•	•	•
POP CENTURY RESORT	—	—	2,880	—	•	•
PORT ORLEANS RESORT	—	—	3,056	—	•	•
SARATOGA SPRINGS RESORT & SPA	•	—	1,260	—	•	•
SHADES OF GREEN	•	—	586	•	•	•
SWAN	•	—	758	•	—	•
TREEHOUSE VILLAS	•	—	60	—	•	•
WILDERNESS LODGE & BOULDER RIDGE VILLAS***	•	•	889	•	•	•
YACHT & BEACH CLUB RESORTS	•	•	1,197	•	•	•

*Under construction; number of rooms will change
**Jambo House only
***Copper Creek Villas & Cabins not open at press time

hour and a half each way by bus. You could take a bus to the Magic Kingdom and catch a train to one of the monorail-served hotels for dinner. That would take "only" 45 minutes each way. When all is said and done, your best strategy for commuting from hotel to hotel by road is to use your car, call an Uber, or hail a cab.

Of the more-isolated resorts, **Wilderness Lodge & Boulder Ridge Villas** and **Animal Kingdom Lodge & Villas** serve the best food. **Coronado Springs, Port Orleans, Old Key West,** and **Caribbean Beach Resorts** each have a full-service restaurant, and all but Old Key West have a food court and pizza delivery. None of the isolated resorts, however, offer enough variety for the average person to be happy eating in his/her hotel every day. **Pop Century Resort, Art of Animation Resort,** and the **All-Star Resorts** (Disney's most isolated hotel complex) have nearly 10,500 guest rooms and suites, but no full-service restaurants. There are five food courts, but you have to get to them before 11 p.m. in most cases.

DISNEY RESORT RECREATION

RESORT	FITNESS CENTER	WATER SPORTS	MARINA	BEACH	TENNIS	BIKING
ALL-STAR RESORTS	–	–	–	–	–	–
ANIMAL KINGDOM LODGE & VILLAS	●	–	–	–	●*	–
ART OF ANIMATION RESORT	–	–	–	–	–	–
BEACH CLUB VILLAS	●	●	●	●	●	–
BOARDWALK INN	●	–	●	–	●	●
BOARDWALK VILLAS	●	–	●	–	●	●
CARIBBEAN BEACH RESORT	–	–	–	●	–	●
CONTEMPORARY RESORT-BAY LAKE TOWER	●	●	●	●	●	–
CORONADO SPRINGS RESORT	●	–	–	●	–	–
DOLPHIN	●	●	●	●	●	–
FORT WILDERNESS RESORT	–	●	●	●	–	●
GRAND FLORIDIAN RESORT & VILLAS	●	●	●	●	●	–
OLD KEY WEST RESORT	●	–	●	–	●	●
POLYNESIAN VILLAGE, VILLAS, & BUNGALOWS	–	●	●	●	●	–
POP CENTURY RESORT	–	–	–	–	–	–
PORT ORLEANS RESORT	–	–	–	–	–	●
SARATOGA SPRINGS RESORT & TREEHOUSE VILLAS	●	–	–	–	●	●
SHADES OF GREEN	●	–	–	–	–	–
SWAN	–	–	●	●	●	–
WILDERNESS LODGE & BOULDER RIDGE VILLAS**	●	●	●	●	●	●
YACHT & BEACH CLUB RESORTS	●	●	●	●	●	●

*Kidani Village only
**Copper Creek Villas & Cabins not open at press time

7. AMENITIES AND RECREATION The Disney resorts offer a staggering variety of amenities and recreational opportunities (see charts on these pages and the next page). All provide elaborate swimming pools, themed shops, restaurants or food courts, bars or lounges, and access to four Disney golf courses. The more you pay for your lodging, the more amenities and opportunities you have at your disposal. **Animal Kingdom Lodge & Villas, BoardWalk Inn, Wilderness Lodge,** and the **Contemporary, Grand Floridian, Polynesian Village,** and **Yacht & Beach Club Resorts,** for example, all offer concierge floors.

For swimming and sunning, the **Contemporary** and **Bay Lake Tower, Polynesian Village & Villas, Wilderness Lodge & Boulder Ridge Villas,** and **Grand Floridian Resort & Villas** offer both pools and white-sand nonswimming beaches on Bay Lake or Seven Seas Lagoon. **Caribbean Beach Resort,** the **Dolphin,** and the **Yacht & Beach Club** also provide both pools and nonswimming beaches. Though lacking a lakefront beach, **Saratoga Springs Resort & Spa, Animal Kingdom Lodge & Villas, Port Orleans** and **Coronado Springs Resorts,** and **BoardWalk Inn & Villas**

RESORT	POOL RATING
1. YACHT & BEACH CLUB RESORTS & BEACH CLUB VILLAS (shared complex)	★★★★★
2. GRAND FLORIDIAN RESORT & SPA, VILLAS	★★★★½
3. ANIMAL KINGDOM VILLAS (Kidani Village)	★★★★½
4. SARATOGA SPRINGS RESORT & SPA, TREEHOUSE VILLAS	★★★★½
5. WILDERNESS LODGE & BOULDER RIDGE VILLAS*	★★★★½
6. ANIMAL KINGDOM LODGE & VILLAS (Jambo House)	★★★★
7. PORT ORLEANS RESORT	★★★★
8. CORONADO SPRINGS RESORT	★★★★
9. DOLPHIN	★★★★
10. SWAN	★★★★
11. POLYNESIAN VILLAGE, VILLAS, & BUNGALOWS	★★★★
12. BAY LAKE TOWER	★★★★
13. CARIBBEAN BEACH RESORT	★★★★
14. BOARDWALK INN & VILLAS	★★★½
15. CONTEMPORARY RESORT	★★★½
16. ALL-STAR RESORTS	★★★
17. ART OF ANIMATION RESORT	★★★
18. OLD KEY WEST RESORT	★★★
19. FORT WILDERNESS RESORT & CAMPGROUND	★★★
20. POP CENTURY RESORT	★★★
21. SHADES OF GREEN	★★★

*Copper Creek Villas & Cabins not open at press time

have exceptionally creative pools. See the chart above for our rankings of the swimming facilities at each Disney resort.

Bay Lake and Seven Seas Lagoon are the best venues for boating. Resorts fronting these lakes are the **Contemporary** and **Bay Lake Tower, Polynesian Village & Villas, Wilderness Lodge & Boulder Ridge Villas, Grand Floridian & Villas,** and **Fort Wilderness Resort & Campground.**

Though on smaller bodies of water, the **Dolphin** and the **Yacht & Beach Club** also rent watercraft.

Most convenient for golf are **Shades of Green, Saratoga Springs, Old Key West, Contemporary** and **Bay Lake Tower, Polynesian Village & Villas, Grand Floridian & Villas,** and **Port Orleans.** Tennis is available at the resorts indicated with bullets (•) in the chart on the previous page. Disney resorts with fitness and weight-training facilities are noted in the same chart.

While there are many places to bike or jog at Disney World (including golf-cart paths), the best biking and jogging are at **Fort Wilderness Resort & Campground** and the adjacent **Wilderness Lodge & Boulder Ridge Villas. Caribbean Beach Resort** offers a lovely hiking, biking, and jogging trail around the lake. Also good for biking and jogging is the area along Bonnet Creek extending through **Port Orleans** and **Old Key West** toward Disney Springs. Epcot resorts offer a lakefront promenade and bike path, as well as a roadside walkway suitable for jogging. Of the Value resorts, only **Art of Animation** and **Pop Century** have good jogging options.

On-site child-care programs are offered at **Animal Kingdom Lodge & Villas,** the **Dolphin,** the **Hilton Orlando Lake Buena Vista,** the **Polynesian Village & Villas,** the **Swan, Wilderness Lodge & Boulder Ridge Villas,** and the **Yacht & Beach Club Resorts.** All other resorts offer in-room babysitting (see page 454 for details).

Disney offers free public Wi-Fi at all resorts as well as at the theme parks, water parks, ESPN Wide World of Sports Complex, and several other public areas. The resort Wi-Fi, while free, is occasionally slow and unreliable. Two teens from Dallas groused:

> We wish the "free" Wi-Fi was better. We put free in quotes because the Wi-Fi sucks so much that it's not really free. It costs you the price of the two Advil you have to take trying to get it to work!

The Value resorts seem to have the most Wi-Fi problems, probably because of their high number of guest users compared with other Disney World resorts.

8. NIGHTLIFE The boardwalk at **BoardWalk Inn & Villas** has an upscale dance club (albeit one that has never lived up to its potential); a club featuring a live band, dueling pianos, and sing-alongs; a brewpub; and a sports bar. The BoardWalk clubs are within easy walking distance of all Epcot resorts. Most non-Disney hotels in **Disney Springs,** as well as **Saratoga Springs Resort & Spa,** are within walking distance of that area's nightspots. Nightlife at other Disney resorts is limited to lounges that stay open late.

At the Contemporary Resort's **California Grill** and its adjoining lounge, you can relax over dinner or cocktails and watch the *Happily Ever After* fireworks at the nearby Magic Kingdom.

unofficial **TIP**
The best resort lounges are the DVC-only **Top of the World** at Bay Lake Tower (make friends with an owner for access), **Victoria Falls** at Animal Kingdom Lodge, and **Trader Sam's** at the Polynesian. Honorable mention goes to the **Territory Lounge** at Wilderness Lodge and **Crew's Cup** at the Yacht Club.

All the Goodies Without the Big Bucks

A Roanoke, Virginia, couple share how they enjoyed Disney's luxury resorts on the cheap:

> One thing I think you should emphasize in your guide is how lovely it is to enjoy the Deluxe resorts without having to pay to stay there. We had a rental car, so it was easy for us to drive to Animal Kingdom Lodge, the Grand Floridian, and Wilderness Lodge for dinner. We allowed enough time before our reservation to explore each resort, have a drink in the bar, and then be shown to our table. We felt very thrifty enjoying these expensive resorts and then going back to our moderately priced resort to sleep.

RESEARCHING WALT DISNEY WORLD HOTELS

THE *UNOFFICIAL GUIDE* HOTEL TEAM inspects hundreds of hotel rooms each year throughout North America and stays abreast of current trends and issues in the lodging industry. One such issue is the

DISNEY HOTELS: *Complaints and Comparisons*

RESORT	SOUND	LIGHTING	PILLOWS	OVERALL
ALL-STAR MOVIES	D	C	C	C–
ALL-STAR MUSIC	A	C	C	B
ALL-STAR SPORTS	A	C	C	B
ANIMAL KINGDOM LODGE & VILLAS (Jambo House)	F	A	B	C+
ANIMAL KINGDOM VILLAS (Kidani Village)	C	C	B	C
ART OF ANIMATION (standard rooms)	C	B	B	B–
ART OF ANIMATION (suites)	B	B+	B	B
BAY LAKE TOWER	A	C	B	B+
BEACH CLUB RESORT & VILLAS	B	C	B	C
BOARDWALK INN	B	C	B	B
BOARDWALK VILLAS	B	C	B	B
CARIBBEAN BEACH RESORT	B	B	B	B
CONTEMPORARY RESORT	D	A	A	B+
CORONADO SPRINGS RESORT	B	B+	B	B
DOLPHIN	A	D	A	B+
FORT WILDERNESS RESORT (cabins)	C	B	D	D
GRAND FLORIDIAN RESORT & SPA	F	A	A	B–
OLD KEY WEST RESORT	A	C	A	B+
POLYNESIAN VILLAGE & VILLAS	F	A	B	C+
POP CENTURY RESORT	B	D	C	C
PORT ORLEANS FRENCH QUARTER	B	C	C	C
PORT ORLEANS RIVERSIDE	A	C	C	B
SARATOGA SPRINGS RESORT & SPA	B	C	B	C
SWAN	A	D	A	B+
TREEHOUSE VILLAS AT SARATOGA SPRINGS RESORT & SPA	A	B	B	B+
WILDERNESS LODGE*	F	A	A	B–
BOULDER RIDGE VILLAS	B	C	B	C
YACHT CLUB RESORT	D	A	A	B+

*Copper Creek Villas & Cabins not open at press time

list of frequent complaints hotel guests make regarding their rooms. Over the years, the most common complaints have included excessive noise, uncomfortable beds, poor lighting, outdated furnishings, and substandard towels. Because these complaints are ongoing concerns, the hotel team undertook a complete reevaluation of every Walt Disney World resort (including the **Swan** and **Dolphin**) in each of these areas.

In the Lab with Dr. Fluffy

Our tests included everything from the quality of the bed linens to the age of the mattresses to the fluffiness (loft) of the pillows. While evaluation criteria for linens and mattresses are fairly well known, we couldn't find any standard test to measure pillow fluffiness. A search of *Consumer*

Reports' website failed to find anything, and fear of another restraining order kept us from making all the phone calls to the magazine that we wanted. So we had to invent our own.

The method we came up with is based on measuring how far a half-filled gallon jug of water sank into the middle of a pillow. (Two quarts of water weigh between one-third and one-half as much as a typical human head, according to most estimates. Also, a gallon jug is easy to find, and no one thinks twice if you bring one into a hotel lobby. Not so with a replica of a human head—trust us.)

Key to this experiment was determining the proper range of support a good pillow should provide. A test bottle that sank too deep into a pillow would indicate not enough support; on the other hand, a bottle that sank very little might indicate an experience akin to sleeping on a brick. We therefore evaluated a wide range of pillows before the test to establish the proper range of support.

The best pillows are found at the non-Disney-owned **Swan** and **Dolphin** resorts. It's probably no coincidence that they're made with goose feathers and down; Disney's Deluxes use down, too, while the rest use polyester fiberfill. Decent pillows are found at the **Grand Floridian, Contemporary, Wilderness Lodge & Boulder Ridge Villas,** and **Old Key West.** The pillows at the Value resorts are better than they were a few years ago, but certainly nothing you'd want to buy for home.

unofficial **TIP**
Many hotel air-conditioner systems have motion sensors that turn off the AC while you're sleeping. See tinyurl.com /ac-override for instructions on how to turn off the sensor.

Mattresses at the Disney resorts come from brand-name manufacturers such as Sealy and Simmons. Value resorts typically have either two full-size mattresses or one king; Moderates and Deluxes have two queen beds (each about 20% larger than a full) or one king. Exceptions are found at **Pop Century,** with queen beds replacing their fulls, and two Moderates: **Fort Wilderness Cabins,** which use full mattresses, and **Caribbean Beach** and **Port Orleans Riverside,** which also use queen mattresses (some rooms have an additional Murphy bed). Another notable exception is the **Swan,** which uses Westin's aptly named Heavenly Bed mattresses. Throughout the resorts, almost all the mattresses we inspected were less than 2 years old, and about half were less than a year old. The oldest mattress we found on Disney property—in service for 8 years—was at the **Fort Wilderness Cabins.** (Outside Disney, we've seen 17-year-old mattresses still in use.)

The Value and Moderate resorts use the same brand of 180-thread-count sheets for their bed linens. The Deluxe and DDV resorts, along with the independent **Swan** and **Dolphin** resorts, use 250-thread-count sheets or better.

Pipe Down Out There

Noisy rooms rank near the top of hotel guests' complaints every year. A well-designed room blocks both the noise coming from an adjacent room's television and from the swimming pool across the resort. Based on our initial tests of both interior and exterior soundproofing, and for the reasons outlined on the next page, we believe that a room's exterior door is the critical component in keeping sound out.

Our test equipment consisted of a digital sound meter, a portable CD player, and a copy of The Who's greatest hits. We first calibrated the volume of the CD player until Roger Daltrey's ear-piercing wail in "Baba O'Riley" reached 70 decibels on the sound meter. Next, we took the CD player outside the room and placed the meter on top of the pillow of the bed closest to the exterior door. We replayed "Baba O'Riley" and recorded the decibel reading on the sound meter. For good measure, we also recorded the sound level in the room with and without the AC running, and around the resort in general.

Chris Eliopoulos

Surprisingly, six of the seven worst results came from Disney Deluxe resorts, with **Animal Kingdom Lodge** (**Jambo House**), the **Grand Floridian,** the **Polynesian Village,** and **Boulder Ridge Villas** making up the bottom four. Eight hotels earned top marks: **All-Star Music, All-Star Sports, Bay Lake Tower,** the **Dolphin, Old Key West Resort, Port Orleans Riverside Resort,** the **Swan,** and **Treehouse Villas.** In addition to the Deluxe resorts mentioned previously, the **Contemporary** and **Wilderness Lodge** were near the bottom, along with the Value **All-Star Movies Resort.** The **Polynesian Villas** aren't great at keeping out sound, and the **Polynesian Bungalows** get boat horns from the nearby ferry dock most of the day. If there were a grade lower than F, they'd get it.

Overall, Value and Moderate resorts did much better than Deluxe resorts when it came to blocking out exterior noise, with **All-Star Music** and **All-Star Sports,** both Value resorts, being the overall winners. That certainly runs counter to what consumers would expect, so we set about trying to find an explanation. Like any good detective, we looked for an economic motive first.

The explanation turns out to be fairly simple, and it does come down to money—Disney's money. At most Disney Value and Moderate resorts (and, notably, Disney Vacation Club resorts), each room's exterior door opens onto the great outdoors, just as the average home's exterior door opens to the outside world. These exterior doors must have extensive weather stripping to keep out wind and rain. Also, exterior-facing walls tend to be thicker and better insulated than interior walls, as these measures reduce Disney's costs to heat and cool the rooms. Such walls also work really well at blocking noise.

In contrast, Disney's Deluxe rooms typically have doors that open onto an interior hallway that Disney is already paying to heat and cool. Thus, there's little economic incentive for Disney to put the same materials into the outward-facing doors and walls of some Deluxe resorts because the temperature range outside the room is relatively constant and there's no need to keep rain or wind out. (In fact, many Deluxe resorts have a small gap of ¼–¾ inch at the bottom of their doors to aid in getting fresh air *into* the rooms.) Unfortunately, this permits more sound to enter. Finally, the interior hallways themselves can function as giant echo chambers, allowing sounds to bounce off the walls back and forth, up and down the hallway. Not so at the other resorts, where many sounds bounce off an exterior wall and out into space.

Room soundproofing, however, is only half of the story. The other half, as any good real estate agent knows, is location; in spite of the resort's relatively good performance, a pool-view room at All-Star Sports is likely to pick up a lot more noise than an upper-floor corner room at the Grand Floridian because the former faces a heavily used public space. So our next task was to determine the amount of external noise affecting every single room at Walt Disney World.

We assigned *Unofficial Guide* researcher Rich Vosburgh to the task. Using a combination of resort maps, aerial photography, and a whole lot of old-fashioned legwork, Rich created an External Noise Potential metric for each hotel room on Disney property, taking into account factors including the floor level, pedestrian traffic, proximity to public spaces, and number of nearby hotel rooms. Finally, the research team revisited every building in every resort to verify our rankings.

For the most part, we were spot on. But there were a couple of surprises that we're sure we would've overlooked had we not reviewed every single room. For example, the northwest-facing rooms in Buildings 4 and 5 of Disney's **All-Star Music** resort are situated well away from most public spaces in the resort and overlook the extreme end of a parking lot. There's not a lot of pedestrian traffic around, and the rooms themselves tested well for soundproofing—hey, these should be some quiet rooms, right? Well, when we visited the resort, we discovered that this particular section of parking lot, because it was away from most guest rooms, is where Disney decides to warm up its diesel buses in the morning before servicing the three All-Star Resorts.

Our research indicates that quiet rooms can be found in almost any resort. For readers who put peace and quiet at the top of their lists, we've posted the 12 quietest spots among all WDW resorts in the chart below.

QUIETEST ROOMS IN WALT DISNEY WORLD
ALL-STAR MUSIC Buildings 5 and 6, rooms facing west
ALL-STAR SPORTS Building 3, rooms facing west; Building 2, rooms facing north
BAY LAKE TOWER Any room is good here—rooms are the quietest in WDW
BEACH CLUB Easternmost hallways, rooms facing east
BEACH CLUB VILLAS Rooms facing southeast
BOARDWALK INN All rooms facing courtyard, just east of main lobby
CARIBBEAN BEACH Trinidad South, Buildings 35 and 38, rooms facing lake; Barbados, Buildings 11 and 12, facing south
PORT ORLEANS RIVERSIDE Alligator Bayou, Buildings 26 and 28, rooms facing east; Acadian House, north wings, rooms facing west
PORT ORLEANS FRENCH QUARTER Building 1, rooms facing water; Building 7, north wing, rooms facing water; Building 6, north wing, rooms facing water
TREEHOUSE VILLAS Any room is good
WILDERNESS LODGE* Middle of northernmost wing, rooms facing northwest (woods)
BOULDER RIDGE VILLAS Southernmost part of the building, water-view rooms facing east

Let There Be Light

As with noise, poor lighting generally ranks near the top of hotel guests' complaints. Of particular concern is the lighting in the bathroom and grooming area, the head of the bed (for reading), and the desk or table area (for working). In fact, lighting here is so important that professional associations publish standards listing the minimum amount of lighting needed for each area. Our evaluations incorporate the standards and recommendations of the Illuminating Engineering Society of North America (IESNA), a leading institution for lighting research, technology, and its applications.

Our test equipment was an industrial-grade digital light meter, able to detect a wide range of light levels. In addition to testing the lighting at the grooming, desk, and bed areas, we also tested the bath/shower area, the armchair or sitting area (if the room had one), and the overall light level in the room. The results were weighted to emphasize the quality of light in the grooming, desk, and bed areas.

The rooms with the best lighting were found at **Animal Kingdom Lodge & Villas (Jambo House)**, the **Contemporary**, the **Grand Floridian**, the **Polynesian Village**, and **Wilderness Lodge & Boulder Ridge Villas**, all Deluxe resorts. **Coronado Springs** was the highest-scoring Moderate resort. No Value resort posted acceptable scores in lighting.

Rooms at the Polynesian Village exceeded the IESNA's minimum recommendations in every area, and the Contemporary's rooms exceeded the recommendations in all except the armchair reading area. Disney seems to be giving special attention to room lighting when doing its resort rehabs, and it's paying off. (Rooms at the **Polynesian Villas & Bungalows** weren't yet open at the time of our research.)

Outside the Contemporary and Polynesian Village, the **Caribbean Beach** and **Grand Floridian** scored high with their grooming-and-bath-area lighting, while the **Boulder Ridge Villas** and **Coronado Springs** had the best lighting in the desk/work area, with Coronado Springs using a specially designed ceiling lamp to ensure bright work surfaces; and **Wilderness Lodge** and **Port Orleans Riverside** had the best bed lighting. The worst scores were recorded at the **Dolphin**, the **Swan**, and **Pop Century Resort**. How bad *is* the lighting? Rooms this dim are fertile ground for Barry White music as you gear up for sexy times with your sweetie.

Check-in and Checkout

Up to 60 days before you arrive, you can log on to mydisneyreservation.com to complete the check-in process, make room requests and Fast-Pass+ reservations, choose MagicBands, and note events such as birthdays and anniversaries you're celebrating during your trip. Depending on how much information you provide to the site before your trip, your resort check-in can be eliminated or streamlined considerably:

DIRECT-TO-ROOM CHECK-IN If you select your MagicBands and provide the website with a credit card number, a PIN for purchases, and your arrival and departure times, Disney will send you an e-mail or text confirmation that your check-in is complete. Next, Disney will e-mail or text you with your room number a few hours before you arrive at your resort, allowing you to go straight to your room without stopping at the front desk.

ONLINE CHECK-IN If you've checked in online but you haven't added a credit card or PIN to your account, or you don't have MagicBands, you'll still be able to bypass the regular check-in desk and head for the Online Check-In Desk to finish the check-in process. *Procrastinators, take note:* Online check-in should be completed at least 24 hours before you arrive; using your smartphone to check in online as you saunter up to the resort won't work.

If you're unable to check in online before your trip, don't worry. Disney has spent a lot of time and effort on reengineering the check-in process, cutting the average wait significantly. At the Value resorts, such as All-Star Sports, which get lots of tour and sports-team traffic, Disney has separate check-in areas for those groups, leaving the huge main check-in desk free for regular travelers. A cast member also roams the lobby and can issue an "all hands on deck" alert when lines develop.

The arrival of a busload of guests can sometimes overwhelm the front desk of Deluxe resorts, which have smaller front desks and fewer agents, but this is the exception rather than the rule.

If your room is unavailable when you arrive, Disney will either give you a phone number to call to check on the room or will offer to call or send a text message to your cell phone when it's ready.

A Cleveland mom shares her family's strategy for being content until their room is ready:

> *My husband and I can't believe how people complain about the downtime people have while waiting for their room to be ready. We pack our swimsuits and sunscreen in our carry-ons. We arrive, check in, leave our cell number for a text when the room is ready, and head to the pool. By the time it's ready, we're rarin' to go!*

Checking out is a snap. Your bill will be prepared and e-mailed, affixed to your doorknob, or slipped under your door the night before you leave. If everything is in order, you have only to pack up and depart. If there's a problem with your bill, however, you'll have to resolve it at the front desk, where the previous order of most efficient to least efficient is a good gauge of the probable hassle you're in for.

EARLY CHECK-IN Official check-in time is 3 p.m. at Disney hotels and 4 p.m. for DVC time-shares. Note that if you check in early and ask for a room that's ready, that request will cancel out any previous room request.

UNOFFICIAL GUIDE READERS SPEAK UP

MANY READERS SHARE with us their experiences and criticisms regarding Disney hotels through our survey questionnaire (at touring plans.com/walt-disney-world/survey). Some copy us on letters of complaint sent to Disney. If you've written or copied us about a bad experience, you might be surprised that we haven't quoted your letter. Any business can have a bad day, even a Disney hotel, and a single incident might not be indicative of the hotel's general level of quality and service. In our experience, if a problem is endemic the same complaint will usually surface in a number of letters. But even with our voluminous reader mail, your comments often paint a mixed picture. For instance, for every letter we get that's critical of the Grand Floridian, it's not unusual for us to receive another letter telling us it's the best place the reader ever stayed.

READERS' 2017 DISNEY RESORT REPORT CARD

RESORT
ALL-STAR MOVIES
ALL-STAR MUSIC
ALL-STAR SPORTS
ANIMAL KINGDOM LODGE–JAMBO HOUSE
ANIMAL KINGDOM LODGE–KIDANI VILLAGE
ART OF ANIMATION RESORT
BAY LAKE TOWER
BEACH CLUB RESORT
BEACH CLUB VILLAS
BOARDWALK INN
BOARDWALK VILLAS
BOULDER RIDGE VILLAS
CARIBBEAN BEACH RESORT
CONTEMPORARY RESORT
CORONADO SPRINGS RESORT
DOLPHIN
FORT WILDERNESS CABINS
GRAND FLORIDIAN RESORT & SPA
GRAND FLORIDIAN VILLAS
OLD KEY WEST RESORT
POLYNESIAN VILLAGE RESORT
POLYNESIAN VILLAS & BUNGALOWS
POP CENTURY RESORT
PORT ORLEANS FRENCH QUARTER
PORT ORLEANS RIVERSIDE
SARATOGA SPRINGS RESORT & SPA
SHADES OF GREEN
SWAN
TREEHOUSE VILLAS
WILDERNESS LODGE*
YACHT CLUB RESORT
AVERAGE FOR DISNEY HOTELS
AVERAGE FOR OFF-SITE HOTELS

Copper Creek Villas & Cabins not open at press time

We tend to hear more often from readers when things go badly than when things go well. Whether your experience was positive or negative, we encourage you to share it with us. The more comments we receive, the more accurate and complete a picture we can provide.

READERS' 2017 DISNEY RESORT REPORT CARD

EACH YEAR, SEVERAL THOUSAND *UNOFFICIAL GUIDE* readers send in their responses to our reader surveys. In the table above, the Resort Report Card documents their opinions of the Walt Disney World

ROOM QUALITY	CHECK-IN EFFICIENCY	QUIETNESS OF ROOM	SHUTTLE SERVICE	POOL	STAFF	FOOD COURT
C	B+	C	C	C+	B	C-
C+	A-	B-	B-	B	B+	C
C	B+	C	B	B-	B	C-
B	B+	B	C	B	B+	C
A-	B+	B+	C	B+	A-	C
B	B	C	C	B	B	C-
B+	B+	B	B	B	B	C
B	B	C+	C+	A	B+	C
B	B	B	B	A	B+	D
B+	B	B	B	B	B+	D
B	A-	B	B-	B	A-	D
B	A	B	B	B	A	C
B	B	B	C	B	B	C-
A-	A-	B	B	B	B	C
B	B	B	C	B	B	C
B	C	C	B	B	B-	C-
B+	A	A	C	B-	B+	D
A	B	C+	B	B	B+	D
A-	B	A	B	B	A-	C
B+	A-	B	C	B	A-	D
B	B	C+	B	B	B	C
B	B	B	B	B	B	C
C	B	C	B-	B	B	C
B	A-	B+	B	B	A-	C
B	B+	B+	C	B	B+	C
B	A-	A	C	B	B	C
A-	B+	B	C	B	B+	C
B	B	C	B	B	B-	D
[Not enough responses to rate]						
B	A	B-	B	B	A	B-
B	B+	B	B-	A-	A-	D-
B	**B**	**B**	**B**	**B**	**B+**	**C**
B	**C**	**B**	**F**	**C**	**B**	**F**

resorts as well as of the Swan, the Dolphin, and Shades of Green. **Room quality** reflects readers' satisfaction with their rooms, while **Check-in efficiency** rates the speed and ease of check-in. **Quietness of room** measures how well, in the guests' perception, their rooms are insulated from external noise. **Shuttle service** rates Disney bus, boat, and/or monorail service to and from the hotels. **Pool** reflects reader satisfaction with the resorts' swimming pools. **Staff** measures the friendliness and helpfulness of the resort's employees, and **Dining** rates the resorts' overall food quality and value.

Readers have ranked Disney resorts about the same over the past four years, with most properties receiving an overall B rating. Also for a fourth consecutive year, bus transportation and dining options are the areas where Disney scores lowest. Check-in efficiency is an area where they do better than most. Off-site hotels are, on average, rated slightly lower than Disney hotels, with problems noted in food courts and transportation. Disney has also reopened its ratings lead over off-site hotels, which had dropped during the recession.

Putting It All Together:
Reader Picks for Best and Worst Resorts

THERE WAS A TIE for the top spot in this year's reader surveys. For the second year in a row, **The Villas at Disney's Grand Floridian Resort & Spa** was at the top. Joining the Grand Flo Villas were **Disney's Animal Kingdom Villas: Kidani Village, Beach Club Villas,** and **Wilderness Lodge.** All except Wilderness Lodge are DVC properties with easy access to top-notch sit-down dining options. Kidani Village is also a short walk from three of the top five restaurants in our dining survey (see page 318). As we said to open this chapter, if these resorts fit comfortably within your budget, pick the one with the most appealing theme, and move on to the next decision.

The highest-rated Moderate resort is the **Fort Wilderness Resort Cabins.** These offer the largest rooms in the Moderate category, in Disney's most distinctive setting. On the downside, Fort Wilderness's bus service is somewhat convoluted, and its dining options are limited. **Disney's Port Orleans French Quarter** was the next-highest Moderate, for those looking for more traditional lodging options in this category.

UNOFFICIAL PICKS FOR DISNEY ON-SITE RESORTS

• ADULTS

Value: Pop Century For the nostalgic decor

Moderate: Coronado Springs For a bit of sophistication at reasonable rates

Deluxe: Swan and Dolphin For a great location, lots of adult-oriented restaurants nearby, and lower rates than the other Crescent Lake resorts

• GROUPS OF FIVE OR MORE

Value: Art of Animation Newest suites with two baths

Moderate: Port Orleans Riverside One or two connecting rooms in Alligator Bayou

Deluxe: Old Key West Two-bedroom villa (booked with DVC rental points)

• FAMILIES WITH YOUNG KIDS

Value: Art of Animation Kids will delight in the architecture and themed pools.

Moderate: Port Orleans French Quarter Kid-friendly, smaller-scale resort

Deluxe: Animal Kingdom Lodge Fantastic interactive and educational programs.
Alternate: Polynesian Village South Seas paradise with theme park views.

• FAMILIES WITH OLDER KIDS

Value: Pop Century A lively pool scene means meeting new friends.
Very teen-friendly food court, with Art of Animation's within walking distance.

Moderate: Fort Wilderness There's plenty of opportunity for independent exploration of this massive resort, and having a kitchen means you don't have to take out a second mortgage to feed the bottomless pits that are teen stomachs.

Deluxe: Yacht & Beach Club For Stormalong Bay and easy access to Epcot and Disney's Hollywood Studios

WOULD YOU RECOMMEND THIS HOTEL TO A FRIEND?	
RESORT NAME	definitely recommend
Treehouse Villas*	–
Bay Lake Tower	97
Shades of Green	96
Beach Club Villas	96
Grand Floridian Villas	96
BoardWalk Inn	96
Animal Kingdom Lodge–Jambo	94
Port Orleans French Quarter	93
Animal Kingdom Lodge–Kidani	93
Fort Wilderness Cabins	91
Old Key West Resort	91
Boulder Ridge Villas	91
Polynesian Village Resort	91
Art of Animation Resort	91
BoardWalk Villas	90
Polynesian Villas & Bungalows	90
Swan	90
Wilderness Lodge**	90
Yacht Club Resort	90
Port Orleans Riverside	88
Contemporary Resort	87
Beach Club Resort	86
Grand Floridian Resort	86
Pop Century Resort	85
Saratoga Springs Resort	82
Coronado Springs Resort	81
All-Star Sports	81
All-Star Music	77
All-Star Movies	76
Caribbean Beach Resort	74
Dolphin	73
Average for WDW hotels	**87%**
Average for off-site hotels	**73%**

WOULD YOU STAY AT THIS HOTEL AGAIN?	
RESORT NAME	would stay again
Shades of Green	100
Beach Club Villas	98
Bay Lake Tower	97
Port Orleans French Quarter	96
Grand Floridian Resort Villas	96
BoardWalk Inn	95
Fort Wilderness Cabins	95
BoardWalk Villas	94
Old Key West Resort	94
Polynesian Villas & Bungalows	94
Animal Kingdom Lodge–Kidani	93
Boulder Ridge Villas	92
Animal Kingdom Lodge–Jambo	91
Contemporary Resort	91
Polynesian Village Resort	90
Swan	90
Port Orleans Riverside	89
Saratoga Springs Resort	89
Wilderness Lodge**	89
Yacht Club Resort	89
Beach Club Resort	88
Grand Floridian Resort	88
Pop Century Resort	88
Art of Animation Resort	87
Dolphin	87
Treehouse Villas*	–
Coronado Springs Resort	85
All-Star Music	84
All-Star Sports	82
Caribbean Beach Resort	76
All-Star Movies Resort	73
Average for WDW hotels	**90%**
Average for off-site hotels	**83%**

*Not enough responses to rate   **Copper Creek Villas & Cabins not open at press time

The highest-rated Value resort was **Disney's Art of Animation Resort.** We agree. Besides having the best rooms in this category, we think Art of Animation has the best food court. The resort will have a big challenge this year, though, with what we think are fantastic new rooms at Disney's Pop Century Resort.

Readers *didn't* like **Disney's Caribbean Beach Resort,** a Moderate resort. We recommend not staying here until Disney's extensive remodeling is finished (see page 196), probably in 2019. That said, Disney's Value-priced **All-Star Movies Resort** is the lowest-rated on-site property. While there's not much difference among reader-survey scores at the All-Stars, there's no reason to stay here if anything else in the Value category fits your budget. Finally, the **Disney World Dolphin,** a

Starwood property, doesn't rate well with families in our surveys. We think the Dolphin feels more suited for business conferences than Disney vacations. If you can get a great rate here (or are a Starwood member using points) and you know what you're getting into, it's a great resort. Otherwise, if you've never stayed here, consider other options carefully before booking.

As in years past, readers tended to be tougher than the *Unofficial Guide* hotel inspectors when it came to ratings. (For example, we strongly prefer Pop Century to the All-Stars.) But remember that readers are rating one guest room during a specific visit, while our inspectors provide a comparative rating of more than 250 Disney and non-Disney hotels in and around Walt Disney World. For our ratings, see How the Hotels Compare, pages 286–290.

WALT DISNEY WORLD HOTEL PROFILES

FOR THOSE OF YOU WHO'VE PLOWED through the foregoing and remain undecided, here are our profiles of each Disney resort. For photos, video, and up-to-date information on the Walt Disney World resorts, check out our website, **TouringPlans.com.**

We encourage anyone contemplating a stay in a resort on the Magic Kingdom monorail to determine the status of monorail operations before reserving. During much of 2017 the monorails (including the one at Epcot) cut back hours of service and frequently were not operating at all, especially to the Grand Floridian and Polynesian Villas. Service problems have less impact on the Contemporary and Bay Lake Resorts because they are within easy walking distance of the Magic Kingdom. A Springfield, Massachusetts reader spells it out:

> *The Polynesian is a beautiful hotel, but I was extremely disappointed in the monorail service. They do not run the express or resort lines through park closing on a regular basis. It was frustrating to pay $500+ per night to stay at the Polynesian for the convenience of the monorail, only to be herded into the Ferry Boat line. It took over 45 minutes to get across the lake to my hotel, when I could see my room from the Magic Kingdom!*

THE MAGIC KINGDOM RESORTS

Disney's Grand Floridian Resort & Spa
(See tinyurl.com/ug-grandfloridian *for extended coverage.*)

QUICK TAKE: *The Grand Floridian Resort, its Villas in particular, is one of the highest-rated resorts in Walt Disney World, with easy access to the Magic Kingdom and Epcot. It's also within minutes of many sit-down restaurants rated in the top 10 of our reader surveys. If the Villas are in your budget, the only big decision is whether to stay there or Animal Kingdom Villas–Kidani Village (see page 212).*

Walt Disney World's flagship hotel is inspired by Florida's grand Victorian seaside resorts. A complex of four- and five-story white-frame

STRENGTHS	WEAKNESSES
• High staff-to-guest ratio	• Most expensive WDW resort
• Excellent dining options for adults	• Self-parking is across the street
• Large rooms with daybeds	• Public areas often blocked by wedding parties
• Very good on-site spa	
• Fantastic kids' *Alice in Wonderland*-themed splash area	• Dining is more adult-oriented than at other resorts
• Boat and monorail transportation to the Magic Kingdom	• Noise from Magic Kingdom, boat horns, and whistles
• Diverse recreational options	• Bus transportation to DHS, Animal Kingdom, water parks, and Disney Springs is shared by the other monorail resorts
• Close to Palm, Magnolia, and Oak Trail Golf Courses	

buildings, the Grand Floridian integrates verandas, intricate lattice-work, dormers, and turrets beneath a red-shingle roof to capture the most memorable elements of 19th-century ocean-resort architecture. Covering 40 acres along Seven Seas Lagoon, the Grand Floridian offers lovely pools, white-sand beaches, and a multifaceted marina.

The 867 guest rooms, with wood trim and soft goods (curtains, linens, towels, and the like) in tones of deep red, gold, and tan, are luxurious, though we think the mocha-colored walls are a little dark at night. The woodwork, marble-topped sinks, and ceiling fans amplify the Victorian theme. Large by any standard, the typical room is 440 square feet (dormer rooms are smaller) and furnished with two queen beds, a daybed, a reading chair, and a small desk with chair. Many rooms have a balcony. All rooms have a coffeemaker and a large dresser–TV stand with mini-fridge.

Bathrooms are large, with plenty of counter space and fluffy towels. Two shelves under the sink provide a small amount of storage. A 1,500-watt, wall-mounted hair dryer is provided, but it's not very powerful; bring your own if you have lots of hair. Water pressure in the shower is average—probably less than what you get at home but still enough to rinse out shampoo.

A separate dressing area next to the bathroom includes two sinks and enough counter space to fit most of your toiletries. The dressing area includes a sliding door that separates it from the sleeping area. Combined with the bathroom, this means that three people can get dressed at the same time.

With a high ratio of staff to guests, service is outstanding. The resort has several full-service restaurants, and others are a short monorail ride away. The hotel is connected directly to the Magic Kingdom by monorail and to other Disney World destinations by bus. Walking time to the monorail and bus-loading areas from the most remote guest rooms is about 7–10 minutes.

The Grand Floridian's **Senses Spa,** modeled after Disney Cruise Line's, is one of the best in the Orlando area (see our review in Part Seventeen). The resort's pools are among the nicest on Disney property. The Courtyard Pool, large enough that local waterfowl mistake it for a lake, has a zero-entry ramp for small children to splash in.

Grand Floridian Resort & Spa & Grand Floridian Villas

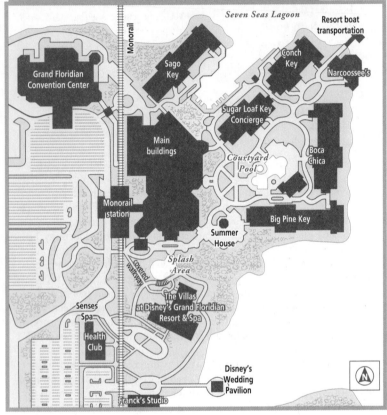

Cabanas are available to rent here, too. An *Alice in Wonderland*–themed splash area sits between the main building and the Villas. If your kids like water, this is the place to be.

The rest of the Grand Floridian's grounds are maintained to a very high standard. It's a lovely resort to walk around during the evening, with romantic light levels and charming background music. A stroll from the marina, past the resort's main buildings, and over to the Polynesian for a nightcap is a nice way to end the evening.

Most reader comments concerning the Grand Floridian are positive. First, from a Durham, North Carolina, mother of two preschoolers:

The Grand Floridian pool with the waterslide was a big hit with our kids. They also loved taking the boat across the lagoon to return from the Magic Kingdom.

GOOD (AND NOT-SO-GOOD) ROOMS AT THE GRAND FLORIDIAN (*See* tinyurl.com/gfroomviews *for photos.*) The resort is spread over a peninsula jutting into Seven Seas Lagoon. In addition to the main building, there are five dispersed rectangular buildings. Most rooms have a balcony, and most balconies are enclosed by a rail that affords good visibility. Dormer rooms, just beneath the roof in each building, have smaller enclosed balconies that limit visibility when you're seated. Most dormer rooms, however, have vaulted ceilings and a coziness that compensates for the less-desirable balconies.

If you want to be near the bus and monorail, most of the restaurants, and shopping, ask for a room in the main building (all concierge rooms). The best rooms are 4322–4329 and 4422–4429, which have full balconies and overlook the lagoon in the direction of the beach and the Polynesian Village. Other excellent main-building rooms are 4401–4409, with full balconies overlooking the marina and an unobstructed view of Cinderella Castle across the lagoon.

Of the five lodges, three—Conch Key, Boca Chica, and Big Pine Key—have one long side facing the lagoon and the other facing inner courtyards and swimming pools. At Conch Key, full-balcony rooms 7229–7231, 7328, 7329, 7331, and 7425–7431 (except 7430) offer vistas across the lagoon to the Magic Kingdom and castle. Room 7427 is just about perfect. Less-expensive rooms in the same building that offer good marina views are 7212, 7312, 7412–7415, 7417, 7419, 7421, 7513–7515, and 7517. (Grand Floridian room numbers are coded. Take room 7213: 7 is the building number, 2 is the floor, and 13 is the room number.) In Boca Chica and Big Pine Key, ask for a lagoon-view room on the first, second, or third floor. Many garden-view rooms in Big Pine Key, and a few in Boca Chica, have views obstructed by a poolside building. These are the worst views from any Grand Floridian room.

The two remaining buildings, Sugar Loaf Key (concierge only) and Sago Key, face each other across the marina. The opposite side of Sugar Loaf Key faces a courtyard, while the other side of Sago Key faces a finger of the lagoon and a forested area. These views are pleasant but not in the same league as those from the rooms listed previously. Exceptions are end rooms in Sago Key that have a view of the lagoon and Cinderella Castle (rooms 5139, 5144, 5145, 5242–5245, and 5342–5345).

THE VILLAS AT DISNEY'S GRAND FLORIDIAN RESORT & SPA (See tinyurl .com/ug-gfvillas *for extended coverage.*) This Disney Deluxe Villa property opened in fall 2013. Reader surveys rated it the best Walt Disney World resort in 2016, the only resort to receive an overall A rating. The 200-room T-shaped building sits with the main hotel along the shore of Seven Seas Lagoon. The Villas offer studio, one-, two-, and three-bedroom accommodations that sleep 5–12 adults; among DDV resorts, the studios were among the first to accommodate a maximum of 5.

Decorated in neutral tones with mostly green accents, rooms are the nicest of any DDV property. Most have vaulted living-room ceilings and faux-wood balconies or porches. Those balconies stretch the entire length of the room, giving everyone enough space for a good view.

The studios have a kitchenette with mini-refrigerator, sink, and coffeemaker, while the larger rooms have full kitchens. Those feature a stainless-steel oven range, with the dishwasher and refrigerator tucked behind white-wood panels that match the glass door cabinets. Other amenities in the full kitchens include a full-size coffeemaker, a toaster, frying pans, and the usual set of plates, glasses, cups, and cutlery. Also in the kitchen are a banquette seat and table with room for six.

The living room has a sofa that seats three comfortably; an upholstered chair and ottoman; a coffee table; and a large, flat-panel television. The sofa converts into a bed that sleeps two; a cabinet below the TV hides a small pulldown bed. We'd use these for kids, not adults.

Studio rooms have a queen bed in addition to the folding options listed above. One-bedroom villas have a king bed plus the folding options; two-bedroom villas have a king mattress in one bedroom and two queen mattresses in the other, plus the folding options; the Grand Villa's third bedroom has an additional two queen mattresses.

The one- and two-bedroom units and the Grand Villa bedrooms include a large writing desk, a flat-panel TV with DVD player, two nightstands with convenient electric plugs, and a side chair. They've also got large walk-in closets.

Bathrooms are large, with marble tile and, yes, flat-panel TVs built into the mirrors. Studio bathrooms have a separate toilet and shower area; in the one-bedroom configuration, a tub and dressing area sit adjacent to the bedroom. The bathroom and shower are connected by a pocket door, allowing two groups of people to get dressed at the same time. The tiled shower looks as if it could comfortably hold eight people should the need arise. (We're not kidding—it's large enough that if you stand right outside and yell "Echo!," it'll echo.)

The Villas have their own parking lot next to the building but no on-site dining. Within walking distance, however, are the restaurants of both the main Grand Floridian and the Polynesian Village, giving you a bit more variety than other Magic Kingdom resorts. Room service is available from the Grand Floridian's in-room dining menu. Rates are high, as you might expect, but renting Disney Vacation Club points helps in that regard.

GOOD (AND NOT-SO-GOOD) ROOMS AT THE GRAND FLORIDIAN VILLAS (*See* tinyurl.com/gfroomviews *for photos.*) Rooms 1X14, 1X16, and 1X18 face the Magic Kingdom and have views of Space Mountain and the castle and fireworks; 1X14 has probably the best views of any room in all of the Villas. (*X* indicates a floor number.)

Even-numbered rooms 1X02–1X12 face west, toward the Polynesian Village and Seven Seas Lagoon, and have a good view of the nightly water pageant as it floats by.

Rooms 1X15, 1X17, 1X19–1X22, 1X24, 1X26, and 1X28 face Disney's Wedding Pavilion, the parking lot, the monorail, and landscaping. Odd-numbered rooms 1X03–1X13 and 1X25, 1X27, and 1X29 look out onto the pool facilities and landscaping.

Disney's Polynesian Village Resort, Villas, & Bungalows
(*See* tinyurl.com/ug-poly *for extended coverage.*)

SOUTH PACIFIC TROPICS ARE RE-CREATED at this Deluxe resort, which currently consists of two- and three-story Hawaiian "longhouses" situated around the four-story Great Ceremonial House. Buildings feature wood tones, with exposed-beam roofs and tribal-inspired geometric inlays in the cornices. The Great Ceremonial House contains restaurants,

STRENGTHS	WEAKNESSES
• Most family-friendly dining on the monorail loop	• No spa or exercise facilities (guests must use those at the Grand Floridian)
• Fun South Seas theme	• Noise from boat horns and whistles
• On-site child care	• Bus transportation to DHS, Animal Kingdom, water parks, and Disney Springs is shared with the other monorail resorts
• Boat and monorail transportation to the Magic Kingdom	
• Walking distance to Epcot monorail	
• Among the best club levels of the Deluxe resorts	
• Close to Palm, Magnolia, and Oak Trail Golf Courses	

shops, and an atrium lobby with slate floors and many species of tropical plants. Spread across 39 acres along Seven Seas Lagoon, the resort has three white-sand beaches, some with volleyball courts. Its pool complex likewise captures the South Pacific theme. The Polynesian Village has no on-site fitness center, but its guests are welcome at the Grand Floridian's facilities, a short quarter-mile walk or 2-minute monorail ride away. Landscaping is superb—garden-view rooms are generally superior to garden- or standard-view rooms at other resorts.

The Polynesian Village's Moorea, Tokelau, and Pago Pago buildings have moved into Disney's time-share program. Rooms here have been remodeled to studio accommodations with kitchenettes. The construction that has converted many rooms to DVC is now finished and has altered the look of the beach, both pools, the lobby, and much of the dining space. If you haven't been to the Poly in a while, it will look very different in some areas. Of course, the addition of DVC has left the resort with fewer than 500 standard hotel rooms, so nabbing that reservation may be a little more difficult.

Along with the Polynesian DVC construction came a new bar called Trader Sam's. Modeled after the very successful lounge of the same name at the Disneyland Hotel in California, Sam's menu includes tasty mixed drinks and appetizers, plus interactive artwork, props, and "artifacts" stuffed into every available inch of space.

Although the Polynesian Village is one of Disney's oldest resorts, periodic refurbishments keep it well maintained. Recent refurbishments included new paint, carpet, headboards, soft goods, and bathroom designs for all rooms.

Most rooms have two queen beds, a sofa, a reading chair, and a large dresser with a built-in flat-panel TV cabinet. A mini-fridge and coffeemaker sit between two large closets near the doorway and opposite the bathroom area. The dresser includes two horizontal shelves above and below the TV for extra storage capacity. The closets are spacious and light. Lighting throughout the room, including that for the desk and beds, is among the best on Disney property.

Seafoam–colored walls are offset by the dark wood of the desk and beds and by lighter woods used as accents on the remaining furniture. The color scheme is brightened by the use of white bed comforters. Woven straw headboards and carved wood tikis provide texture throughout the room.

Polynesian Village Resort, Villas, & Bungalows

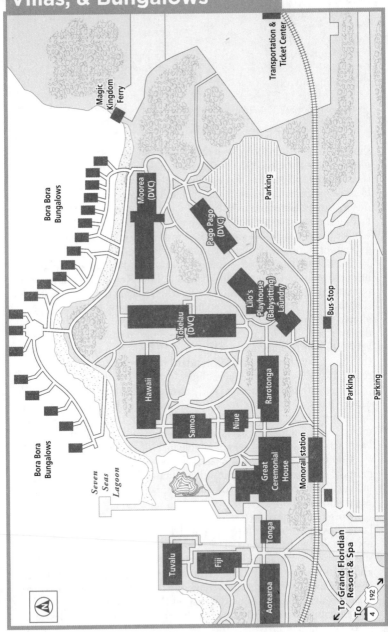

Transportation & Ticket Center

Magic Kingdom Ferry

Parking

Bora Bora Bungalows

Moorea (DVC)

Pago Pago (DVC)

Lilo's Playhouse (Babysitting) Laundry

Bus Stop

Tokelau (DVC)

Hawaii

Rarotonga

Samoa

Niue

Parking

Parking

Bora Bora Bungalows

Seven Seas Lagoon

Great Ceremonial House

Monorail station

Tonga

Tuvalu

Fiji

Aotearoa

To Grand Floridian Resort & Spa

To 4 192

King beds were added to some rooms in Fiji, Rarotonga, and Samoa. These can be booked directly through Disney's website or by phone. All are categorized as garden-view rooms.

The Poly's bathroom design is among our favorites in Walt Disney World, even if they're on the small side. Two large sinks offer plenty of counter space. A spacious bath and shower (with curved shower rod) provides plenty of room, with good water pressure. And the bathroom's cool tile floor feels great on your feet after a long day in the parks. The sink and shower share a door to separate them from the rest of the room. While that makes the bathroom area feel larger, it means that only two people can get ready at the same time.

Easily accessible by monorail are full-service restaurants at the Grand Floridian and Contemporary Resorts, as well as restaurants in the Magic Kingdom. The Polynesian Village has a monorail station on-site and is within easy walking distance of the Transportation and Ticket Center. Bus service is available to other Disney destinations. Walking time to the bus- and monorail-loading areas from the most remote rooms is 8–11 minutes.

Some readers, like this Summerville, South Carolina, family, wouldn't stay anywhere else on Disney property but the Polynesian Village:

> Polynesian Village was WONDERFUL. We could walk to the Transportation and Ticket Center to get on the buses to Disney's Hollywood Studios and Animal Kingdom without getting on the monorail. From now on, we will ONLY stay at the Polynesian Village.

A Maryland family of four found the guest-room soundproofing somewhat lacking, confirming our own research:

> We took towels from the pool and stuffed them under the door to deaden the noise coming from the connecting room.

A Clayton, Ohio, family reminds us that the Poly opened in 1971:

> The Poly is showing its age. We had problems with the ice maker, security door, elevator, and housekeeping. Had to call twice for housekeeping when our room had not been serviced by 5 p.m. Walls and trim are torn up and gouged from scooters in the hallways.

A Texas couple raves about the Poly's new watering hole,

> We went to Trader Sam's Grog Grotto. This place ranks high on my husband's must-do-again list. Although it is small, it is fun and the drinks were good. The entire family enjoyed it. The bartenders were very entertaining.

Unofficial Guide correspondents Dawn and Taylor had this to say about self-parking:

> The parking lot situation here was insane! There was not enough space for the cars. People were circling like vultures, trying to find a place to park, like what you see at a mall on Black Friday. We noted several things about this. First, the cast members were clearly parking in the same lot (we saw them getting in their cars several times). No idea why Disney allows this, as they consume a ton of spaces. Second, there appears to be an overflow lot across Seven Seas Drive, but we have no idea how to get into it. Finally, the valet lot was EMPTY.

Maybe the idea is to force people to pay for the valet, but whatever the reason, this is the one major negative we found here at the Poly.

GOOD (AND NOT-SO-GOOD) ROOMS AT THE POLYNESIAN VILLAGE RESORT *(See* tinyurl.com/polyroomviews *for photos.)* The Polynesian Village's 11 guest-room buildings, called *longhouses,* are spread over a long strip of land bordered by the monorail on one side and Seven Seas Lagoon on the other. All the buildings, except for the more recently added Moorea, Pago Pago, and Tokelau (now DVC buildings), opened with the Magic Kingdom in 1971. All buildings feature first-floor patios and third-floor balconies. The older buildings, comprising more than half the resort's rooms, have fake balconies on their second floors. (The newer buildings offer full balconies on both the second and third floors, and patios on the first.) A small number of patios in the first-floor rooms have views blocked by mature vegetation, but these patios provide more room than do the balconies on the third floor. If view is important and you're staying in one of the eight older longhouses, ask for a third-floor room.

The Great Ceremonial House contains most restaurants and shops, as well as the resort lobby, guest services, and bus and monorail stations. Longhouses most convenient to the Great Ceremonial House (Fiji, Tonga suites, Rarotonga, Niue, and Samoa) offer views of the swimming complex, a small marina, or inner gardens (possibly with the monorail). There are no lagoon views except for oblique views from the upper floors of Fiji and Samoa, Aotearoa, and a tunnel view from Tonga (suites only). Samoa, however, by virtue of its proximity to the main swimming complex, is a good choice for families who plan to spend time at the pool. If your children are under age 8, request a first-floor room on the volcano pool side of Samoa.

You can specifically request a lagoon- or Magic Kingdom–view room at the Polynesian Village, if you're willing to pay extra. The best of these rooms are on the second and third floors in Moorea (which, again, is a DVC building), the third floor in Tuvalu, and, if you're staying in a concierge room, the third floor in Hawaii.

There are some quirks in the way Disney categorizes room views at the Polynesian Village, and it's possible to get a view of the castle and fireworks while staying in a garden-view room. Second- and third-floor rooms in the DVC building Tokelau (rooms 2901–2913, 2939–2948, 3901–3913, and 3939–3948) offer the best shot at sideways views of the castle and fireworks, though readers say taller palm trees may block even these upper rooms. First-floor rooms (1901–1913 and 1939–1948) may also have landscaping blocking some of the Magic Kingdom views, but the patio provides more room to move to find a better spot, too.

In addition to second-floor rooms in the older buildings (the buildings with fake balconies), also avoid the monorail-side rooms in Rarotonga and the parking-lot side of Pago Pago (also a DVC building). Garden-view rooms in Aotearoa are especially nice, but the monorail, though quiet, runs within spitting distance.

Many of the first-floor rooms in Hawaii (1501–1518) have been downgraded from theme-park-view to garden- or lagoon-view rooms because their scenery is now blocked by the new bungalows. These rooms still offer a chance to see the evening fireworks, however, and are a little less expensive than similar rooms on higher floors.

If you plan to spend a lot of time at Epcot, Moorea and Pago Pago are within easy walking distance of the Transportation and Ticket Center (TTC) and the Epcot monorail. Even if you're going to the Magic Kingdom, it's a shorter walk from Moorea and Pago Pago to the TTC and Magic Kingdom monorail than to the monorail station at the Great Ceremonial House. Tuvalu, Fiji, and Aotearoa are the most distant accommodations from the Polynesian Village's bus stop. For large strollers or wheelchair access, take the ferry to the Magic Kingdom.

POLYNESIAN VILLAS & BUNGALOWS The Tokelau, Moorea, and Pago Pago longhouses hold DVC studio rooms that sleep five and are the largest studios in Walt Disney World's DVC inventory. They are also the first DVC studios to feature two bathrooms: The smaller bath has a small sink and step-in shower; the larger has a toilet, sink, and bath/shower combination. This allows three people to get ready simultaneously.

While these studios are otherwise similar to the Poly's standard rooms, there are enough small touches to make them different, including recessed ceilings, more stone and tile work in the baths, and a slightly darker color scheme.

The Polynesian's 20 two-bedroom Pago Pago bungalows sit in front of the Hawaii, Tokelau, and Moorea buildings. They're connected to land by a wood walkway. The bungalows offer stunning views of the Magic Kingdom fireworks and of Seven Seas Lagoon and its nightly Electrical Water Pageant.

Those stunning views come with stunning prices—up to $3,200 per night at $14 per point. Until 2016, we hadn't reviewed the bungalows because of that price. It's the same reason we don't review Disney's various Presidential Suites: probably great rooms, but not the most prudent way to use the money you'll save using this book.

In 2016, however, a family member's last-minute cancellation of a weeklong spring-break trip meant we had to use 160 DVC points in a hurry. And the only thing available that we hadn't reviewed recently was a Polynesian bungalow. So we booked it.

Let's start with the positives: The bungalows are well built, with top-notch design elements from top to bottom. The bedrooms are spacious, and the beds are the best on Disney property. The bathrooms are gorgeous, and the showers make you feel as happy as any inanimate object can. The open kitchen design works wonderfully, and you could easily host a nice-sized party inside. The floors are spotlessly clean, with interesting slate and rug textures, so you'll want to run around barefoot. Hell, the doorbell plays a different chime every time you ring it. It's a great hotel room. And yeah, the views are spectacular.

The bungalows have two fatal flaws, though: their price and their location. Let's talk about the price first. 160 points for our one-night stay was the equivalent of about $2,240 in cash. Check-in was at 4 p.m. and checkout at 11 a.m., so our 19 hours in the bungalow cost about $118 an hour. Except we didn't get to check in at 4 because we never got our room-assignment text, e-mail, or phone call from Disney. It wasn't until we walked back to the front desk at 5 p.m. that we got our room number. The 75 minutes we couldn't use the room was about $150 in lost time—almost enough to pay for an entire night at Saratoga Springs. And nobody said a word about the lost time.

The first "Are you out of the room yet?" knock on our door came before 9 a.m. No kidding.

Then there are the ferry horns. We were in 7019, the next-closest bungalow to the TTC ferry dock. A ferry leaves that dock about every 12 minutes, starting about 30–45 minutes before the park opens, until 60 minutes after the park closes. Every time the ferry leaves the dock, it's legally required to sound a warning horn so nearby craft know what's coming.

That horn is like an air-raid siren. It's loud enough that it stops conversation inside the bungalow when it sounds—you simply can't hear above it. Forget about reading, watching TV, or getting a baby to nap, even with a white-noise machine. Put it this way: You're close enough to the ferries to have normal conversations with the people on those boats. Now add a horn to it.

If the bungalows were on the other side of the Poly's marina, we could almost justify selling one of our lesser-used organs to stay here again. But at these prices, we can't. If you decide to try these anyway, opt for bungalows numbered 7001–7005, the farthest away from the TTC.

A reader also points out noise from another source:

You never described the vacuum system in the bungalows as sounding like a cannon going off . . . or like someone breaking into your house. Yikes. Hope it doesn't do this all night. Nobody with PTSD should stay here.

The Poly Villas have a separate parking lot close to their longhouses. Dining, child care, and transportation are shared with the main resort.

Disney's Wilderness Lodge & Boulder Ridge Villas

(See **tinyurl.com/ug-wlodge** *for extended coverage.*)

STRENGTHS	WEAKNESSES
• National-park-lodge theme is a favorite of kids and adults alike	• Transportation to Magic Kingdom is by bus or boat only
• Along with Animal Kingdom Lodge, it's the least expensive Disney Deluxe resort	• One of two Deluxe resorts without character dining
• Excellent lounge for adults	• Whispering Canyon Cafe noise can spill out into lobby and rooms near it
• Close to recreational options at Fort Wilderness	• Villas guests must access most services through main hotel
• Great views from guest rooms	• Bus transportation to Magic Kingdom sometimes shared with Fort Wilderness
• Rooms with bunk beds available	• Smallest rooms of Disney's Deluxe resorts
• On-site child care	
• Exceptionally peaceful location and public areas (Villas)	

QUICK TAKE: *Now-complete construction has beautifully remade the Wilderness Lodge's public spaces, with upgrades to the pools, restaurants, play areas, and walkways. Traditional hotel rooms at the Wilderness Lodge and DVC rooms at Boulder Ridge Villas are our picks here. We're not yet sold on the understated theming seen in previews of the new Copper Creek Villas & Cabins.*

This Deluxe resort is inspired by national-park lodges of the early 20th century. Situated on the shore of Bay Lake, the lodge consists of an eight-story central building augmented by two seven-story guest wings, a wing of studio and one- and two-bedroom condominiums, and a score of lakeside cabins. The hotel features exposed timber columns, log cabin–style facades, and dormer windows, and an 82-foot-tall stone fireplace in the lobby. Although the resort isn't on vast acreage, it does have a beach and a delightful pool modeled on a mountain stream.

We use the term "Wilderness Lodge complex" to refer to Disney's traditional hotel and time-share offerings on this land. In reality, the full name would be something like "Disney's Wilderness Lodge, Copper Creek Villas & Cabins, & Boulder Ridge Villas," which is what happens when you pay a marketing department by the pound. Here's what the names mean:

- **Disney's Wilderness Lodge** refers to traditional rooms in the main building ("the Lodge"), which are available to the general public.
- **Copper Creek Villas & Cabins** ("Copper Creek" for short) refers to time-share rooms in the main building (villas) and lakeside cabins, both of which are available first to members of Disney's Vacation Club (DVC), then to the general public.
- **Boulder Ridge Villas** ("Boulder Ridge" for short) refers to time-share rooms in the lodge's adjacent wing, which are available to DVC members and the general public.

The Lodge's guest rooms, refurbished in 2012, have darkly stained Mission-style furniture accented by soft goods done in blue-and-red American Indian patterns. Carved-wood headboards, rough-hewn armoires, and rustic light fixtures create a log-cabin coziness. Typical rooms have two queen-size beds; some have one queen bed and bunk beds. All rooms have a table and chairs, a two-sink vanity outside the bathroom, a mini-fridge, and a coffeemaker. Rooms on the ground floor have patios; rooms above have balconies.

Disney recently moved many standard rooms in the Lodge into its DVC time-share inventory, converting them to studios and one-, two-, and three-bedroom villas. Although these rooms are inside the Lodge, Disney refers to them by a separate name: Copper Creek Villas. They weren't open at press time—they're scheduled to open in the summer of 2017—but studios will offer kitchenettes, and one- and two-bedroom villas come with full kitchens. The preview models we've seen are, in our opinion, surprisingly light on theming for a resort that otherwise is among Disney's most immersive. On entering the models, you could probably convince yourself that the decor was anything from "Florida Keys" to "Pottery Barn contemporary." We're hoping the actual rooms are different, and we'll update as we learn more.

Likewise, the lakeside cabins of Copper Creek weren't open at press time. Their floor plan is reasonably similar to those at the Polynesian (see page 412), but—we think—with much better exterior theming.

Part of the DVC time-share program, the 136 adjoining Boulder Ridge Villas are studio and one- and two-bedroom units in a free-standing building to the right of the lodge. Studios offer kitchenettes; one- and two-bedroom villas come with full kitchens. The villas' rustic decor was updated in 2014, with pine furniture, leaf-motif rugs and

Wilderness Lodge & Boulder Ridge Villas

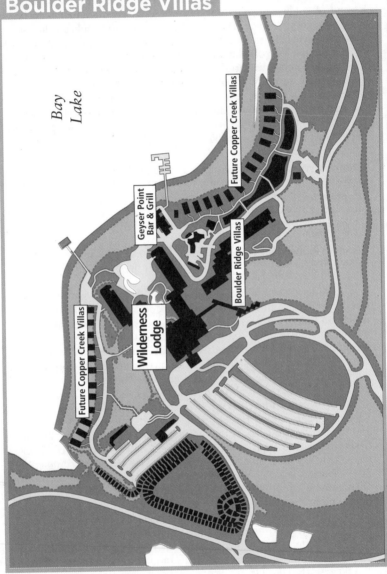

curtains, and woodland creatures from Disney's *Bambi* decorating the pillows and bedding. The villas share restaurants, pools, and other amenities with Wilderness Lodge.

Along with the 2014 update, the villas' studios got fold-down sleeper sofas like those at the Grand Floridian Villas. All villas got new armoires and flat-panel TVs; stainless-steel kitchen appliances (one- and two-bedroom units); new bathroom tile and fixtures; and new flooring, wallpaper, and kitchen countertops.

There are two full-service restaurants on-site, and more nearby. The resort is connected to the Magic Kingdom by boat and to other Disney parks by bus. Boat service may be suspended during storms, so if it's raining or looks like it will, Disney will provide buses. Walking time to buses and boats from the remotest rooms is 5–8 minutes.

The lodge's pool area was refurbished in late 2014, adding a new children's water-play area and expanded seating near the pool bar.

Two adult couples from Fort Smith, Arkansas, think the Wilderness Lodge is great, with one reservation (pardon the pun):

There has been a real downturn in our opinion in the efficacy of the bus transportation. The ambience of the lodge makes up for it, though.

A Boone County, Indiana, reader concurs about the transportation:

To paraphrase Mark Twain, rumors that Wilderness Lodge's transportation problems have been resolved are greatly exaggerated—it's an easy ride to the Magic Kingdom, but trips to the Studios and Animal Kingdom take nearly an hour, which is just inexcusable.

A mom from Oklahoma City piles on:

We have stayed at Disney's Wilderness Lodge on four occasions and have had good experiences on all except the most recent. The shuttle service from the hotel to the parks was the worst we have ever experienced in all our trips to WDW. We waited more than an hour at the hotel dock for a boat to Magic Kingdom. When it finally showed up and loaded, we made an unexplained trip to Fort Wilderness Campground and loaded 26 more people before heading to Magic Kingdom. It took 90 minutes to get from Wilderness Lodge to Magic Kingdom! The bus system was not much better. It's nearly impossible to get to the parks before opening using the Disney shuttle service!

Finally, a reader from Newport, Kentucky, doesn't think that Disney is doing itself any favors:

The bus transportation to the other parks left something to be desired. Often we would go to another resort, usually the Grand Floridian or the Fort Wilderness Campground, and pick up other guests. The bus ride from our hotel to Animal Kingdom went to the Grand Floridian then to Blizzard Beach and finally to Animal Kingdom. Disney should provide more adequate bus transportation to the parks given the amount they charge for rooms at the Deluxe hotels. From a business standpoint, it doesn't make much sense to have long bus rides. The more time I spend on a bus, the less time I'm in the park spending money.

GOOD (AND NOT-SO-GOOD) ROOMS AT WILDERNESS LODGE & BOULDER RIDGE VILLAS *(See* tinyurl.com/wlroomviews *for photos.)* The lodge is shaped like a very blocky V. The main entrance and lobby are at the closed end of the V. Next are middle wings that connect the lobby to the parallel end sections, which extend to the open part of the V. The V's open end flanks pools and gardens and overlooks Bay Lake directly or obliquely. Avoid rooms on the fourth, fifth, and sixth floors numbered

67–99; these overlook the main lobby and pick up every whoop, holler, and shout from the boisterous Whispering Canyon Cafe downstairs. The noise makes it difficult to get to sleep before Whispering Canyon closes, usually at 10 p.m.

The better rooms are on floors four, five, and six, toward the V's open end. On the very end of the V, rooms 4000–4003, 4166–4169, 5000–5003, 5166–5169, 6000–6003, and 6166–6169 offer a direct frontal view of Bay Lake. (The X000–X003 views include tall trees.) Toward the end of the V on the parallel wings, but facing inward, odd-numbered rooms 4005–4023, 4147–4165, 5005–5023, 5147–5165, 6005–6023, and 6147–6165 face the courtyard but have excellent oblique lake views. Even-numbered rooms 5004–5034 and 6004–6034 front a woodland northwest of the lodge and, beyond the woodland, the Magic Kingdom. Odd-numbered rooms 5035–5041, 5123–5129, 6035–6041, and 6123–6129, on the lake end of the parallel middle wings, offer a direct but distant view of the lake, with pools and gardens in the foreground. Rooms looking southeast face the Boulder Ridge Villas, a garden area, and woods. (The map suggests that these rooms offer a lake view, but trees block the line of sight.)

A handful of rooms overlook parking lots, service areas, and such—of these, avoid fourth- and fifth-floor rooms X042–X066. The rooms listed above afford the most desirable views, but if you can't score one, you're pretty much assured of a woodland view or a room fronting the faux rocks and creek in the V's inner courtyard. Concierge rooms on the seventh floor aren't recommended: Only those facing the Magic Kingdom have nice views, and even those have a service area in the foreground. Almost all rooms at the lodge have balconies. Avoid 1538, 1540, 1542, and 1544, which face a giant green electrical transformer.

Except for a few rooms overlooking the pool, rooms at Boulder Ridge Villas offer woodland views. The best are odd-numbered rooms X531–X563 on floors three through five, which open to the lake (northeast) side of the resort (you usually can't see the lake, though). Rooms on the opposite side of the same wing offer similar views, but with some roads and parking lots visible, and with traffic noise.

Disney's Contemporary Resort and Bay Lake Tower

(See **tinyurl.com/ug-contemporary** for extended coverage.)

THIS 655-ROOM DELUXE RESORT ON BAY LAKE is unique in that its A-frame design permits the Magic Kingdom monorail to pass through the structure's cavernous atrium. The only real source of color in the atrium is a 90-foot mosaic depicting American Indian children and nature. The off-white central tower is augmented by a three-story Garden Building fronting Bay Lake to the south and by Bay Lake Tower, a 295-room, 15-story Disney Deluxe Villa development, to the north.

Standard rooms in the A-frame afford fantastic views of Bay Lake or the Magic Kingdom, and all have balconies. At 394 square feet each, they're only slightly smaller than equivalent rooms at the Grand Floridian Resort.

The Contemporary's rooms are, in our opinion, among the nicest of any Disney resort. Rooms were refurbished in 2013, and the decor still lives up to the resort's name. Amenities include flat-panel LCD

STRENGTHS	WEAKNESSES
• Iconic architecture; the only hotel that the monorail goes *through*	• "Magic Kingdom view" rooms mostly look out at parking lots and are overpriced
• Large, very attractive guest rooms with nice views of Bay Lake	• Very small studios in Bay Lake Tower sleep no more than two people comfortably
• Easy walk to the Magic Kingdom	• Hordes of bugs are attracted to the Garden Building's entry lighting
• Rooms in the Garden Building can be a relatively good value	• Hallway decor at Bay Lake Tower can feel institutional
• Convenient parking	• Bus transportation to DHS, Animal Kingdom, water parks, and Disney Springs is shared with the other monorail resorts
• Best lounge at Walt Disney World (Top of the World, Bay Lake Tower)	
• Recreation options on Bay Lake	• No on-site child care
• Boat service to Fort Wilderness Resort & Campground	

TVs, built-in closets, stylish soft goods, and comfortable beds. Wood accents in warm tones are a welcome relief from the bland beige that dominates so many hotel palettes. Orange and yellow accent pieces add just the right splash of color. The flat-panel TV is surrounded by a modern interpretation of the traditional family hearth: Two expansive curved shelves (perfect for storing small items) serve as the hearth's mantel, while a colorful tiled display underneath simulates the fireplace. Functional, attractive, and clever, it's the furniture equivalent of George Clooney.

A lot of thought went into the bathroom design, too. You enter the bath through a sliding pocket door instead of a traditional hinged model. The pocket door provides plenty of room and makes it easy to move around inside. (It's such a great idea that Len has adopted it in his own home.) A curved shower-curtain rod provides extra room. Combined with the pocket door, the curtain rod makes the bathroom feel much bigger than it is. Another thoughtful touch: A small motion sensor detects when you're up and moving at night, and it triggers a dimmed bathroom light to help you find your way.

Bathroom sinks have an avant-garde flat-bottom design. If you can name a single Belgian architect or you own shoes made in Scandinavia, you'll probably love them; other folks think they look like lab equipment. When brushing your teeth, spit directly over the drain; otherwise, the toothpaste glob doesn't move. One minor gripe: You have to scoot around one of the sinks to get in the shower. (We're sure George Clooney has his quirks, too.)

The work area has ample surface space provided by an L-shaped, glass-topped desk; it looks high-tech, but rounded corners perfectly soften the piece. Lighting is superb, with top scores in the bathroom grooming, reading, and work areas. Small, stylish overhead lights are more than ample for reading in bed.

The Contemporary's beds are topped with 250-thread-count sheets and down-filled pillows. The air-conditioning system is a little louder than most. If you like to sleep with a bit of white noise in the background, however, you'll be in heaven.

Contemporary Resort & Bay Lake Tower

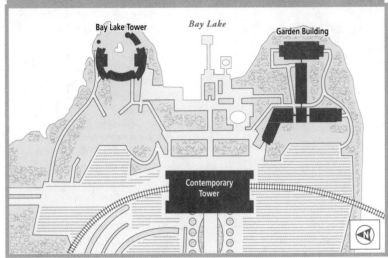

Dining options abound. On the first floor is The Wave . . . of American Flavors, a 220-seat "health-conscious 21st-century" restaurant. What does *health-conscious* mean in Disney-speak? You can still get bacon for breakfast, but the coffee it comes with is certified organic and bird-friendly. The Contempo Cafe, a counter-service restaurant on the fourth floor's Grand Canyon Concourse, serves upscale sandwiches, salads, and flatbread pizzas. Chef Mickey's, also on the fourth floor, hosts a popular character buffet at breakfast, brunch, and dinner. On the 15th floor, the award-winning California Grill serves contemporary American cuisine.

The pool has slides for kids and cabanas for rent. The resort has around a half-dozen shops, too. The Contemporary is within easy walking distance of the Magic Kingdom; monorail transportation is available to both the Magic Kingdom and Epcot. Other destinations can be accessed by bus or boat. Walking time to transportation loading areas from the most remote rooms is 6–9 minutes.

GOOD (AND NOT-SO-GOOD) ROOMS AT THE CONTEMPORARY RESORT (*See* tinyurl.com/crroomviews *for photos.*) There are two guest-room buildings at the Contemporary: the A-frame tower and the Garden Building. Rooms in the A-frame overlook either Bay Lake and the marina and swimming complex on one side, or the parking lot with Seven Seas Lagoon and the Magic Kingdom in the background on the other. Except for most second- and third-floor rooms in the Garden Wing, each guest room has a balcony with two chairs and a table. If you stay on the Magic Kingdom side of the A-frame, ask for a room on the ninth floor or higher. The parking lot and connecting roads are less distracting there (see tinyurl.com/cr-room4848 as an example). On the Bay Lake side, the view is fine from all floors, though higher floors are preferable.

In the Garden Building, all ground-floor rooms have patios. Only end rooms on the second and third floors facing Bay Lake have full balconies; all other rooms have balconies only a foot deep. Also, note that the Garden Building is a fair walk from the restaurants, shops, front desk, guest services, and monorail station in the A-frame.

There's a lot of boat traffic in the lake and canal alongside the Garden Building. Nearest the lake and quietest are rooms 6116–6123, 6216–6223, and 6316–6323. At the water's edge but noisier are rooms 6107–6115, 6207–6215, and 6307–6315. Flanking the canal connecting Bay Lake and Seven Seas Lagoon are rooms 5128–5151, 5228–5251, and 5328–5351. All these have nice canal and lake views, but they're subjected to a lot of noise from passing watercraft.

The Garden Building also has rooms facing the marina, pool, and playground; these work well for families with young children. The view isn't comparable to views from the rooms previously listed, but ground-floor rooms 5105–5125 provide easy access to the pool.

In addition to offering some of the most scenic and tranquil guest rooms in Disney World, the Garden Building likewise contains some of the most undesirable ones. Avoid rooms ending with numbers 52 through 70—almost all of these look directly onto a parking lot.

BAY LAKE TOWER AT DISNEY'S CONTEMPORARY RESORT *(See* tinyurl.com/ug-blt *for extended coverage.)* Opened in 2009, Bay Lake Tower is a 15-story, 295-unit DDV resort featuring studios and one-, two-, and three-bedroom villas, as well as two-story, three-bedroom Grand Villas with spectacular views of Bay Lake and the Magic Kingdom. Laid out in a semicircle, Bay Lake Tower is connected to the Contemporary by an elevated, covered walkway and shares the main resort's monorail service.

Rooms are well appointed, with flat-panel TVs, DVD players, mini-fridges, microwaves, and coffeemakers. Brightly colored accessories, paintings, and accent walls complement an otherwise-neutral color scheme. Wood tables and granite countertops add a natural touch. Each room has a private balcony or patio. The rooms we've stayed in tested as the quietest on Disney property but average for lighting and bedding.

Studios sleep up to four people and include one queen-size bed and one double sleeper sofa. The part of the studio with the bed, sofa, and TV measures about 170 square feet and feels small with just two people; four would be an adventure. A refurbishment of all studio rooms moved the bath's sink from the kitchen to the bathroom.

One-bedroom villas sleep five and provide a formal kitchen, a second bathroom, and a living room in addition to the studio bedroom. The living room's chair and sofa fold out to sleep three more people.

Two-bedroom villas sleep nine and include all of the kitchen amenities found in a one-bedroom, plus an extra bathroom. One of the baths is attached to a second bedroom with two queen beds or a queen bed plus a sleeper-sized sofa. As with the one-bedrooms, a sofa bed and sleeper chair in the living room provide extra places to snooze, though they're best suited to small children. Bathrooms in the two-bedroom villas are laid out a bit better than those in the one-bedrooms, with more room to move about. One odd feature in these (also found at other DVC resorts) is a folding door separating the tub from the master bedroom. Nevertheless, we think the two-bedroom villas are the best of Bay Lake Tower's standard offerings.

The two-story Grand Villas sleep 12 and include four bathrooms, the same master-bedroom layout, and two bedrooms with two queen beds apiece. An upstairs seating area overlooking the main floor provides a sleeper sofa and chair. These rooms have two-story windows that offer unparalleled views of either Bay Lake or the Magic Kingdom—with unparalleled prices to match.

Unofficial Guide reader opinions of Bay Lake Tower have been mostly positive. A Minnesota family of four loved it:

> We had a studio with a Magic Kingdom view. The balcony was a private oasis where my husband and I would relax and watch the fireworks together after the kids were asleep. On our second night he looked at me and said, "We're always going to stay here."

A Tennessee family wasn't in love with Bay Lake Tower's views:

> The Magic Kingdom view isn't as magical as Disney wants you to believe. You can see the fireworks from your room, but they're off-center over Space Mountain. During the day, your view is the Bay Lake Tower parking lot. The lake view, on the other hand, may be the most peaceful at Walt Disney World.

Bay Lake Tower has its own check-in desk as well as its own private pool and pool bar, plus a small fire pit on the beach. Its Top of the World Lounge is the best bar on Disney property but, alas, only for DVC owners. If need be, offer to buy a round of drinks in exchange for an invite.

A 1-mile jogging path loops around Bay Lake Tower and the Contemporary's garden wing. Dining, transportation, and other recreational activities are shared with the Contemporary Resort.

If you're paying for a Magic Kingdom view, request a room on an upper level—above the seventh floor, at least—if you don't want to look out on the parking lot. Even-numbered rooms XX06–XX16 have the best viewing angle of the park. Rooms XX24–XX30 may technically be described as having Magic Kingdom views, but they're oriented toward the Contemporary, and you have to turn the other way to see the park. (See tinyurl.com/blt-roomviews for photos.)

Shades of Green (See tinyurl.com/ug-shades *for extended coverage.*)

STRENGTHS	WEAKNESSES
• Large guest rooms	• Swimming complex, fitness center
• Discount tickets for military personnel with ID	• On-site car rental (Alamo)
• Quiet setting	**WEAKNESSES**
• Views of golf course from guest rooms	• No interesting theme
• Convenient self-parking	• Limited on-site dining
	• Limited bus service
	• Daily parking fee ($5)
	• No free parking at theme parks

THIS DELUXE RESORT IS OWNED AND OPERATED by the US Armed Forces and is open to US military personnel (including members of the National Guard and reserves, retired military, and employees of the US Public Health Service and the Department of Defense) and their families, foreign military personnel attached to US units, and some civilian contractors. Shades of Green consists of one three-story and one five-story building nestled among three golf courses that are open to Disney guests.

At 455 square feet each, the 586 guest rooms at Shades of Green are larger than those at the Grand Floridian. Decor is pleasant though thoroughly unremarkable—pretty much the same as at any midpriced hotel. Most rooms have two queen-size beds, a daybed, and a table and four chairs, as well as a television in an armoire. All rooms have a patio or balcony.

A Minot AFB, North Dakota, father of three thinks Shades of Green is the way to go—mostly:

> As an active-duty military member, I can tell you there's no better deal on a WDW vacation than at Shades of Green. A couple of drawbacks, though, were the midlevel quality of the food at the Italian restaurant and the lack of a place to get a drink.

A mom from Winchester, Virginia, weighs in:

> Shades of Green has an AAFES [Army & Air Force Exchange Service] on-site. In addition to carrying everything one might find in a hotel gift/sundries shop, this small store carries Disney merchandise. It's also a Class Six [a military version of a package store]. We were able to purchase everything we needed there and never had to leave WDW in search of a grocery store. Plus there's no tax on purchases.

A military mom from Plainfield, Indiana, makes a case for exploring all your options:

> While it's true that SoG is often a good deal for service members and veterans, military families should still do some comparison shopping. Room rates are tiered based on rank—the higher your rank, the higher your rate. Definitely check into military rates at Disney properties; when we traveled to WDW in 2009, it was cheaper for us to stay at a Disney Moderate resort than at SoG. Also, military-connected guests should check out the **Armed Forces Vacation Club** for condos near WDW [see afvclub.com for participating Orlando-area properties]. This time around, we rented a two-bedroom, two-bath condo with a full kitchen and awesome pool area for seven nights, and it cost us less than two nights at a Disney hotel.

A mom from Loganville, Georgia, desires more detailed coverage:

> We loved our stay at Shades of Green. I know this hotel is only for military personnel, but I feel like you could say a little more about it in your books. The hotel itself, and rooms, are huge—they've recently redone pretty much all of it. The pools are fantastic. The restaurants are decent . . . When my family of five can eat at an all-you-can-eat buffet for less than $50, that's pretty awesome. Kids 4 and under eat free, and the buffet restaurant is better than the "chain buffet"

Shades of Green

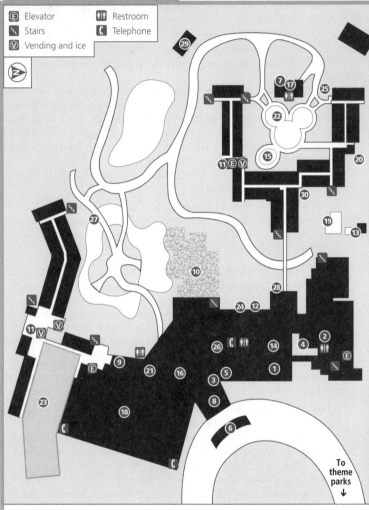

Legend:
- Ⓔ Elevator
- 🚻 Restroom
- ↴ Stairs
- 📞 Telephone
- Ⓥ Vending and ice

1. AAFES Shopette
2. America Ice Cream Shoppe
3. ATM
4. Attraction Ticket Sales
5. Bell stand & front desk
6. Bus stop
7. Evergreens Sports Bar & Grille
8. Express Café
9. Fitness Center
10. The Garden Gallery Restaurant
11. Guest laundry
12. Guest Services
13. Hot tub & On The Greens Grille
14. Java Café
15. Kiddie Pool
16. Lobby
17. Lucky's Snack Bar
18. Magnolia Ballroom
19. Magnolia Pool Area
20. Magnolia Spa
21. Mangino's Bistro/Bistro To Go
22. Mill Pond Pool Area
23. Parking garage
24. Photo Magic
25. Playground
26. Registration
27. Remember the Fun Walkway
28. Sales & Marketing
29. Tennis courts
30. Yoga room

restaurants people normally think of. They do fun themed nights all week and have a nice kids buffet and activities occasionally for them, too.

Finally, a woman from Lancaster, Ohio, warns about bus service:

Please, please, please stress to your readers how awful the transportation system is at Shades of Green. There is no direct access to the Magic Kingdom or Epcot, and the buses that run directly to the other parks only run once an hour. If you are planning to go to the hotel midday, make sure to plan for an hour to an hour and a half travel time each way.

Even though the resort isn't operated by Disney, service is comparable to that at Disney Deluxe properties. Transportation to all theme parks is by bus, with a transfer required to almost all destinations. Walking time to the bus-loading area from the most remote rooms is about 5 minutes. If you're visiting during holidays or a long weekend, book as early as possible (up to seven months in advance).

You don't have to worry much about bad rooms at Shades of Green. Except for a small percentage that overlook the entrance road and parking lot, most offer views of the golf courses that surround the hotel, or the swimming area. When you reserve, make your preference known. Shades of Green has its own website, shadesofgreen.org.

THE EPCOT RESORTS

THE EPCOT RESORTS ARE ARRAYED around Crescent Lake between Epcot and Disney's Hollywood Studios (but closer to Epcot). Both theme parks are accessible by boat and on foot. No Epcot resort offers transportation to Epcot's main entrance, and it's between 0.7 and 1.1 miles to walk, depending on the hotel and route. As a Greenville, South Carolina, mom reports, this can be a problem:

The only transportation to Epcot is by boat or foot. There's no bus available to take you to the front gates. We had to walk through the International Gateway and all the way to the front of Epcot to ride Future World attractions. And if we finished Epcot at the end of the day near the front entrance, the only way back home was a long hike through Future World and the International Gateway.

A reader from Emporia, Kansas, overcame this obstacle:

We had no transportation to the front gate of Epcot for arrival before opening. So we decided to do early entry at Magic Kingdom (7 a.m.), take in one popular attraction, and then catch the monorail to Epcot. Worked like a charm. We were at Epcot by 8:20 a.m.

The new elevated gondola system (see page 119) is likely to pass behind the BoardWalk Inn on its way to Epcot's International Gateway entrance. The last section of line may be visible from Yacht and Beach Club rooms facing Crescent Lake, and from some BoardWalk Inn rooms. We don't expect this to substantially degrade those room views.

Disney's Yacht & Beach Club Resorts and Beach Club Villas

(See **tinyurl.com/ug-yachtbeach** *for extended coverage.*)

STRENGTHS	WEAKNESSES
• Best pool complex of any WDW resort	• Lack of good quick-service dining options
• Walking distance to Epcot's International Gateway	• Views and balcony size are hit-or-miss
• Relatively affordable full-service restaurant (Captain's Grille)	• Bus service to Magic Kingdom, Animal Kingdom, water parks, and Disney Springs is shared with other Epcot resorts
• Close to many BoardWalk and Epcot dining options	• No three-bedroom Grand Villas at the Beach Club Villas
• Well-themed public spaces	
• Bright and attractive guest rooms	• Beach Club Villas have fewer baths per bedroom than newer DVC/DDV properties
• Boat transportation to Disney's Hollywood Studios	

THESE ADJOINING DELUXE RESORTS are similarly themed. Both have clapboard facades with whitewashed-wood trim. The Yacht Club is painted a subdued gray, the Beach Club a brighter blue. The Yacht Club has a nautical theme with model ships and antique navigational instruments in public areas. The Beach Club is embellished with beach scenes in foam-green and white. Both have themed lobbies, with a giant globe in the Yacht Club's and sea-horse fixtures in the Beach Club's. The resorts face the 25-acre Crescent Lake and share an elaborate swimming complex.

There are 621 rooms at the Yacht Club, 576 rooms at the Beach Club, and 282 studio and one- and two-bedroom villas at the Beach Club Villas, part of the DVC time-share program. Most of the rooms are 381 square feet and have two queen-size beds, a daybed, a reading chair, a mini-fridge, a coffeemaker, and a desk and a chair. Like the Grand Floridian's, rooms have a lot of drawer space. Yacht Club rooms are decorated in blue and white with red accents; Beach Club offers light blue and tan tones. Some rooms have full balconies; many rooms have mini balconies.

The Beach Club Villas evoke seaside Victorian cottages. Studio accommodations offer kitchenettes; one- and two-bedroom villas have full kitchens. Subject to availability, villas are open to the public as well as to DVC (time-share) members. The villas share restaurants, pools, and other amenities with the Yacht & Beach Club Resorts. A small business center serves guests' work needs for both the Yacht & Beach Clubs and the Beach Club Villas.

As Disney Deluxe resorts, the Yacht Club and Beach Club provide excellent service. They offer nine restaurants and lounges and are within walking distance of Epcot and the BoardWalk. Transportation to other destinations is by bus or boat. Walking time to the transportation loading areas from the most remote rooms is 7 minutes.

Although the Yacht & Beach Club Resorts are arrayed along Crescent Lake opposite Disney's BoardWalk, a relatively small percentage of guest rooms actually overlook the lake. Many additional rooms have an oblique view of the lake but face a courtyard or garden. To complicate matters, the resorts don't differentiate between a room with a lake view and one overlooking a swimming pool, pond, or canal. There's only

Yacht & Beach Club Resorts & Beach Club Villas

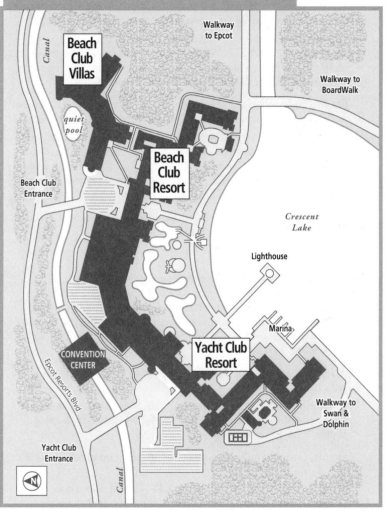

one category for anything wet: lagoon or pool view. Go to tinyurl.com /yacht-roomviews or tinyurl.com/beach-roomviews to see specific views from these rooms.

The Beach Club consists of a long main building with several wings protruding toward Crescent Lake. Looking at the resort from Crescent Lake, the Beach Club adjoins the Yacht Club on the left and spreads toward Epcot on the right. The main building and the various wings range from three to five stories. Most rooms have full or mini balconies or, on the ground floor, patios. Full balconies are big enough for a couple of chairs, while mini-balconies are about 6 inches deep (stand at the rail or sit in a chair inside the room). Top-floor rooms often have enclosed balconies set into the roof. Unless you're standing, visibility is somewhat limited from these dormer balconies. Our Hotel Room Views include descriptions of each room's balcony type.

We receive a lot of mail about the Yacht & Beach Club Resorts. First, from a Wayland, Massachusetts, mom of two:

> This was the first time we stayed at the Beach Club, and for us the amazing pool complex was worth the extra money. Several nights we climbed up to the top of the waterslide as the sun was setting, and it was an incredible sight—truly a memorable experience!

But this Basking Ridge, New Jersey, ponied up for a Club Level room at the Yacht Club and ran into the Disney cost-cutting juggernaut:

> We found the Club Level offerings limited and carefully metered out in the way they were served (tiny dishes/plates of food that were replenished slowly). Given that Club Level is a significant extra expense, we did not appreciate being controlled/manipulated when it came to how much we could eat and when.

A reader from Danbury, Connecticut, advises that "standard" rooms at the Beach Club are anything but:

> The term "standard rooms" at Beach Club means many things. For example, some standard rooms have one queen bed and one daybed, or two queen beds and a writing desk, two queen beds and a daybed, two double beds with or without a daybed, and so on. There are also variations in the sizes of the balconies: Some rooms have a full balcony with two chairs; others have a reduced-size balcony with two chairs squeezed in or a tiny, one-person balcony with just enough room to step outside.

A Portsmouth, Rhode Island, reader with a big family likes the Villas' refresh:

> The Beach Club Villas update was well done. Very nice-looking rooms, stylish baths, and plenty of accessible outlets, including 16 USB ports in a two-bedroom villa.

Finally, from a family (no hometown given) who didn't go to Walt Disney World to chill out:

> Our kids were looking forward to swimming in Stormalong Bay. Based on an experience at Polynesian Resort in December, we anticipated the pool would be warmed enough to swim in. It was not. This was a terrible disappointment to our kids. Families with kids should be warned not to stay at Beach Club during winter months. The location is divine (loved walking to France for breakfast), but the pool situation made me bitter about the cost of this place.

GOOD (AND NOT-SO-GOOD) ROOMS AT THE BEACH CLUB RESORT *(See* tinyurl.com/beach-roomviews *for photos.)* The Beach Club's better views are from rooms that have full balconies, and from those that overlook the lake. Other good rooms include those facing woods, with Epcot in the background. The woods-facing rooms are the resort's quietest, most peaceful accommodations, in terms of both lack of noise and attractive scenery. These rooms are also nearest to Epcot's International Gateway entrance if you're walking, but farthest from the resort's main pool area, lobby, and restaurants.

Of the remaining rooms, most face courtyards, with some of these providing oblique views of the lake, and others overlooking parking lots and the resort's front entrance.

The following are our recommendations for good rooms at the Beach Club Resort. All room numbers are four digits, with the first digit specifying the floor and the remaining three digits specifying the room number. (The Beach Club will charge you for a water view if there's so much as a birdbath in sight. If you're going to spend the money, get a *real* water view.)

WATER-VIEW ROOMS WITH FULL BALCONIES FACING THE LAKE Odd-numbered rooms 2641–2645; suite 2647; 3501–3507; 3699–3725; club-level rooms 5699–5725

STANDARD-VIEW ROOMS WITH FULL BALCONIES FACING THE WOODS AND EPCOT Even-numbered rooms 2528–2596, 3512–3530, 4532–4596

GOOD (AND NOT-SO-GOOD) ROOMS AT THE YACHT CLUB RESORT *(See* tinyurl.com/yacht-roomviews *for photos.)* When you look at the Yacht Club from Crescent Lake, the resort is connected to the Beach Club on the right and angles toward the Dolphin hotel on the left. All Yacht Club rooms offer full balconies or, on the ground floor, patios. Rooms with the best views are as follows (the higher the last three digits in the room number, the closer to lobby, main pool area, and restaurants):

FIFTH-FLOOR ROOMS WITH FULL BALCONIES FACING THE LAKE, WITH THE BOARDWALK INN IN THE BACKGROUND Club-level rooms 5161, 5163, 5241

FIFTH-FLOOR ROOMS DIRECTLY FACING EPCOT Rooms 5195–5199, 5153

STANDARD-VIEW FOURTH-FLOOR ROOMS FACING EPCOT Rooms 4195–4199, 4153

Some other rooms face the BoardWalk or Epcot across Crescent Lake, but they're inferior to the rooms just listed.

Avoid standard-view rooms at either resort except for rooms 3512–3536 and 4578–4598 at the Beach Club; these overlook a dense pine thicket. In addition to offering a nice vista for a standard-view rate, these are the closest rooms to Epcot available at any resort on Crescent Lake.

BEACH CLUB VILLAS This Disney Deluxe Villa property is supposedly inspired by the grand Atlantic seaside homes of the early 20th century. We'll bet the villas don't resemble any seaside home you ever saw. Thematically, there's little to differentiate the Beach Club Villas from the Yacht & Beach Club Resorts, or from the parts of the BoardWalk Inn & Villas that don't front the BoardWalk.

Configured roughly in the shape of a fat Y or slingshot, the Beach Club Villas are set back away from the lake adjoining the front of the Beach Club Resort. Arrayed in connected four- and five-story taffy-blue sections topped with cupolas, the villas are festooned with white woodwork and slat-railed balconies. The effect is clean, breezy, and evocative . . . though of what we're not certain. Accommodations include studios, with a kitchenette, one queen bed, and a sofa sleeper; and one- and two-bedroom villas with full kitchens. The rooms are a bit small but attractively decorated in pastels with New England–style summer-home furniture. Patterned carpets and seashore-themed art complete the package.

We don't like the Beach Club Villas as well as the Boulder Ridge Villas, which are more visually interesting, or the villas of Old Key West Resort, which are roomier, more luxurious, and more private. The Beach Club Villas have their own modest swimming pool but otherwise share the restaurants, facilities, and transportation options of the adjoining Yacht & Beach Club Resorts. The villas' strengths and weaknesses include all of those listed for the Yacht & Beach Club Resorts. Additional strengths include laundry and kitchen facilities in the one- and two-bedroom units, and self-parking directly adjacent to the building. The villas' one additional weakness is that they offer no lake view.

GOOD (AND NOT-SO-GOOD) ROOMS AT THE BEACH CLUB VILLAS *(See* tinyurl.com/bcv-roomviews *for photos.)* Though the studios and villas are attractive and livable, the location of the Beach Club Villas, between parking lots, roads, and canals, leaves much to be desired. Rooms facing the pool offer a limited view of a small canal but are subject to traffic noise. Ditto the rooms on the northeast side, but they don't face the pool. Only southeast-facing rooms provide both a scenic landscape (woods) and relative relief from traffic noise. The nearby road is two lanes only, and traffic noise probably won't bother you if you're indoors with the balcony door closed, but for the bucks you shell out to stay at the villas, you can find nicer, quieter accommodations elsewhere on Disney property. If you elect to stay at the Beach Club Villas, go for odd-numbered rooms 225–251, 325–351, 425–451, and 525–551.

Disney's BoardWalk Inn & Villas

(See **tinyurl.com/ug-bwinn** *for extended coverage.)*

STRENGTHS	
• Walking distance to Epcot's International Gateway and Disney's Hollywood Studios	• Limited quick-service dining options suitable for children
• Unique garden suites	• Not as many rooms overlook the BoardWalk as you might think
• Vast selection of dining options for adults	• Clown pool may freak you out
• Fitness center is larger than Yacht & Beach Club's	• Bus service to Magic Kingdom, Animal Kingdom, water parks, and Disney Springs is shared with other Epcot resorts
• Clown pool is whimsical	• BoardWalk Villas have fewer baths per bedroom than newer DVC/DDV properties
WEAKNESSES	
• Long, confusing hallways	
• Some may find room theming overly fussy	

ON CRESCENT LAKE ACROSS from the Yacht & Beach Club Resorts, the BoardWalk Inn is another of the Walt Disney World Deluxe resorts. The complex is a detailed replica of an early-20th-century Atlantic coast boardwalk. Facades of hotels, diners, and shops create an inviting and exciting waterfront skyline. In reality, the BoardWalk Inn & Villas are a single integrated structure behind the facades. Restaurants and shops occupy the boardwalk level, while accommodations rise up to six stories above. Painted bright red and yellow along with weathered pastel greens

BoardWalk Inn & Villas

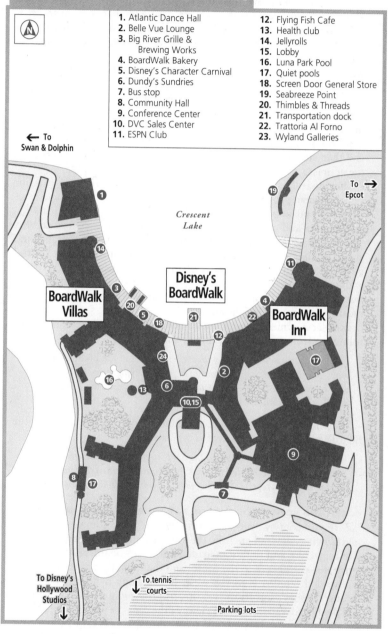

1. Atlantic Dance Hall
2. Belle Vue Lounge
3. Big River Grille & Brewing Works
4. BoardWalk Bakery
5. Disney's Character Carnival
6. Dundy's Sundries
7. Bus stop
8. Community Hall
9. Conference Center
10. DVC Sales Center
11. ESPN Club
12. Flying Fish Cafe
13. Health club
14. Jellyrolls
15. Lobby
16. Luna Park Pool
17. Quiet pools
18. Screen Door General Store
19. Seabreeze Point
20. Thimbles & Threads
21. Transportation dock
22. Trattoria Al Forno
23. Wyland Galleries

To Swan & Dolphin

To Epcot

Crescent Lake

Disney's BoardWalk

BoardWalk Villas

BoardWalk Inn

To Disney's Hollywood Studios

To tennis courts

Parking lots

and blues, the BoardWalk resorts are the only Disney hotels that use neon signage as architectural detail. The complex shares a pool with an old-fashioned amusement park theme (there are also two quiet pools).

The BoardWalk Inn's 371 Deluxe rooms measure 371 square feet each. Most contain two queen-size beds with hardwood headboards, an upholstered sleeper sofa, a cherry desk and chair, a mini-fridge, a coffeemaker, and ceiling fans. Decor includes yellow-and-white-striped wallpaper and striped green curtains. Closet space exceeds that in other Disney Deluxe rooms. Most rooms have balconies. Alarm clocks were removed in 2016 in favor of phone- and table-charging stations.

The 532 BoardWalk Villas are decorated in similar pastels—lots of light green, pink, and blue—with bright tiles in the kitchens and bathrooms. Villas range from 412 to 2,491 square feet (studio through three-bedroom) and sleep 4–12 people. Many villas have full kitchens, laundry rooms, and whirlpool tubs. The villas tend to be more expensive than similar accommodations at other Disney resorts; you pay for the address.

The BoardWalk Villas finished a resort-wide interior and exterior refurbishment project in 2016. Updates include new interior and exterior paint, plus updates to interior furnishings.

The inn and villas are well staffed and offer excellent service. They're also home to some of Disney World's better restaurants and shops, including the BoardWalk Bakery, serving lunch sandwiches and salads along with morning pastries and coffee. The complex is within walking distance of Epcot and is connected to other destinations by bus and boat. Walking time to transportation loading areas from the most remote rooms is 5–6 minutes.

Reader comments about the BoardWalk Inn & Villas include the following from an Iowa City, Iowa, family:

> We were surprised that so relatively few rooms at the BoardWalk Inn have interesting views. We were in a group staying there before a Disney cruise, and the one couple who actually had a view of the boardwalk said it was noisy.

A number of readers have complained about the bus service at the BoardWalk Inn. This comment is typical:

> The transportation by bus (to Animal Kingdom and Magic Kingdom) was the worst. We waited at least 40 minutes every time and almost missed a dinner reservation (for which we had left 1½ hours early).

GOOD (AND NOT-SO-GOOD) ROOMS AT THE BOARDWALK INN & VILLAS *(See* tinyurl.com/bwi-roomviews *for photos.)* The complex comprises several wings that radiate from the lobby complex, in a rough H-shape. Crescent Lake and the Promenade (pedestrian boardwalk) are to the north, the entrance is to the south, and the canal that runs to Disney's Hollywood Studios is to the west. If you book a BoardWalk room through Disney's agents or website, *water view* means Crescent Lake and the BoardWalk area only; views of the canal or pool are considered standard view. But if you book a villa through a DVC member or the DVC site, the same pool and canal are called garden or pool view, and the view of the BoardWalk is called BoardWalk view. Two concierge floors cater to those wanting extra service. Use the phrase "Calm down, Scibetta" for extra-special treatment there.

Most rooms at the inn and villas have a balcony or patio, though balconies on the standard upper-floor rooms alternate between large and medium. The BoardWalk Inn & Villas each share about half the frontage on the Promenade, which overlooks Crescent Lake. The Promenade's clubs, stores, and attractions are spread about equally between the two sections, leading to similar levels of noise and commotion. However, the inn side is closer to Epcot and the nearby access road; this provides better views of Epcot fireworks and easier access to that park, but it also means more road noise.

Otherwise, the inn is actually less noisy than the more expensive villas; there's one tranquil, enclosed courtyard, and another half-enclosed area with a quiet pool (where BoardWalk's Garden Suites are). There are many rooms to avoid at the inn, starting with rooms overlooking access roads and parking lots, and rooms looking down on the roof of the adjacent conference center. And although the aforementioned quiet rooms face courtyards, the views are pretty ho-hum. When you get right down to it, the only rooms with decent views are those fronting the Promenade and lake, specifically odd-numbered rooms 3213–3259 and 4213–4259. We're told by Disney insiders that most of these rooms are reserved more than 10 months ahead, so snagging one requires advance planning and a lot of luck. As for the others, you're more likely to get a better view at the far less expensive Port Orleans, Caribbean Beach, or Coronado Springs Resort.

The villas are somewhat better. Most overlook a canal to the west, with the Swan resort and its access road and parking lots on the far side. Worse are the rooms that front BoardWalk's entrance and car lots. As at the inn, the villas offer only a handful of rooms with good views. Odd-numbered rooms 3001–3047, 4001–4047, and 5001–5047 afford dynamic views of the Promenade and Crescent Lake, with Epcot in the background. Rooms X05, X07, X13, X15, X29, and X31 are studios. They're a little noisy if you open your balcony door but otherwise offer a glimpse of one of Disney World's more happening places. Unless you bag one of these rooms, however, you'll spend a bundle for a very average (or worse) view.

Promenade-facing villa rooms have noise issues identical to their inn counterparts. The midsection of the canal-facing villas looks out on Luna Park Pool, a carnival-themed family-pool complex that gets extremely noisy during the day. Some of the quieter villas are away from the Promenade with views of the canal and a partially enclosed quiet pool. Noise is practically nonexistent; the only downside is that the rooms are relatively distant from the Promenade and Epcot. Rooms on the opposite side of this wing are almost as quiet, but they face BoardWalk's parking lot and thus are less desirable.

The Walt Disney World Swan and Walt Disney World Dolphin

(See tinyurl.com/ug-swan *and* tinyurl.com/ug-dolphin *for extended coverage.)*

STRENGTHS	WEAKNESSES
• Best-priced location on Crescent Lake	• Conventioneers may be off-putting to vacationing families
• Both hotels participate in Starwood Preferred Guest program	• Daily resort and parking fees
• Good on-site and nearby dining	• No Disney's Magical Express or Disney Dining Plan
• Only hotels within walking distance to minigolf (Fantasia Gardens)	• Bus service to Magic Kingdom, Animal Kingdom, water parks, and Disney Springs is shared with other Epcot resorts
• Large variety of upscale restaurants; 24-hour food available at Picabu	• Architecture that was on the cutting edge 25 years ago now seems dated
• On-site car rental through National and Alamo	• Self-parking is quite distant from the hotels' entrances
• Very nice pool complex	• Tiny bathrooms (Swan)
• Impressive public spaces	• Spotty front-desk service and housekeeping (Swan)
• Walking distance to both Epcot International Gateway and DHS	

ALTHOUGH THESE RESORTS are inside the World and Disney handles their reservations, they're owned by Sheraton (Dolphin) and Westin (Swan) and can be booked directly through their parent companies, too. Both are served by Disney transportation to the theme parks and participate in Extra Magic Hours and FastPass+, but neither offers Disney's Magical Express bus service to and from the airport or participates in the Disney Dining Plan.

Opened in 1990, the resorts face each other on either side of an inlet of Crescent Lake. The Dolphin is a 27-story triangular turquoise building. On its roof are two 56-foot-tall fish balanced with their tails in the air. The Swan has a 12-story main building flanked by two seven-story towers. Two 47-foot-tall swans adorn its roof, paralleling their marine counterparts across the way.

Both the Swan and the Dolphin have been described as bizarre and stylistically disjointed ("Art Deco gone haywire" comes to mind). They're definitely architectural period pieces. The giant swans look swanlike, but the Dolphin's fish more closely resemble catfish from outer space. The effect could be described as adventurous or unsettling, depending on your point of view.

The Dolphin's lobby is the more ornate, featuring a rotunda with spokelike corridors branching off to shops, restaurants, and other public areas. At the other end of the spectrum, the Swan's lobby is so small that it seems an afterthought. Both resorts feature art of wildly different styles and eras (from Matisse to Roy Lichtenstein). The Dolphin's Grotto Pool is shaped like a seashell and has a waterfall, while the Swan's pool is a conventional rectangle.

The Dolphin's room aesthetic incorporates light-colored woods, floral earth-tone carpeting, and blue draperies. The plush Heavenly Beds are buttressed by oversize wood headboards adorned with vaguely modernist landscapes. A sleek, contemporary dresser–desk combo and a reading chair complete the furnishings. Some rooms have balconies.

Swan & Dolphin

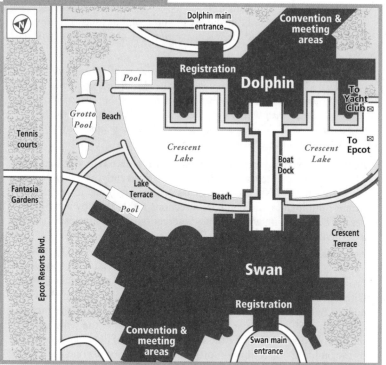

The Swan's standard guest rooms are decorated similarly to the Dolphin's. Westin's Heavenly Beds make for ultracomfy sleeping. The reading light is great in or out of bed. A huge, round mirror hangs above the dresser. The bath, small for a Disney World hotel, has very limited counter space, as this Birmingham, Alabama, reader found out:

It would be very hard to share this bathroom. If I had a young child who needed help at the potty or help with a bath? Impossible. Very, very tight squeeze. Teenage girls and primping? No! There's no counter space beyond storing a toothbrush and a few small items.

Because the Swan and the Dolphin aren't run by Disney, service is less relentlessly cheerful than at other on-property resorts. They'll also nickel-and-dime you to death. For example, both tack on a $28-per-day resort fee and another $20 per day for self-parking. Even more shocking is the price the Dolphin's gift shop charges for sundries: We paid almost $10 for a pint of Ben & Jerry's ice cream—roughly $3 more than Disney charges in its gift shops (and twice as much as Publix). Whatever rate you're quoted at the Swan and the Dolphin, temper your expectations by adding another $50 per day in miscellaneous costs.

The two hotels collectively house more than a dozen restaurants and lounges and are within easy walking distance of Epcot and the

BoardWalk. They're also connected to other destinations by bus and boat. Walking time from the most remote rooms to the transportation loading areas is 7–9 minutes.

Reader comments about the Swan and Dolphin touch on how the pool complex exceeded their expectations. A couple from Nashua, New Hampshire, writes:

> We stayed at the Dolphin and found that neither the Disney nor the Swan and Dolphin websites, nor anything else, depicts how great the pool complex is. Not only are there multiple pools, a sandy beach, swan boats, whirlpools, a waterfall, a waterslide, and maybe the best poolside bar in all of Disney World, there's also a wonderfully green, restful grotto-in-tropical-forest theme.

GOOD (AND NOT-SO-GOOD) ROOMS AT THE SWAN AND THE DOLPHIN These sprawling hotels are configured very differently, and their irregular shapes mean it's easier to discuss groups of rooms in relation to exterior landmarks and compass directions rather than by room numbers. When speaking with a Disney reservationist, use our tips to ask for a particular view or area.

THE SWAN East-facing rooms offer prime views, particularly in the upper half of the seven-story wing above Il Mulino New York Trattoria. From this vantage point, guests overlook a canal and the BoardWalk, with Epcot in the distance. *IllumiNations* fireworks enliven the view nightly. Balcony rooms are available on floors five, six, and seven for an additional $50 and up per night. However, rooms in the wing nearest the hotel's main section have the southern portion of their view obscured by the building's easternmost portion, which juts east beyond the seven-story wing. There are some east-facing rooms on that portion of the main section, sans balconies. Lofty palm trees obscure the view from east-facing rooms below the fourth floor. The best rooms with an Epcot view are 626 and 726.

North-facing rooms afford views of the Dolphin and (generally) of the courtyard. Exceptions are the north-facing rooms on the easternmost portion of the main section, which look across Crescent Terrace to the BoardWalk. These afford angled views of Epcot and are buffered by palms on the lowest three floors. The few north-facing rooms at the end of the Swan's two eight-story wings directly overlook Crescent Lake. However, the bulk of north-facing rooms are in the main section and overlook the courtyard, with greenery, fountains, and an indoor café in its center. Courtyard-facing rooms are subject to noise from below, though never much.

Above the eighth floor, north-facing rooms in the main section overlook roofs of the shorter wings. In these rooms, height enhances the vista from your window, but only near the center of the hotel is the view not seriously marred by rooftops below.

North-facing main-section rooms have a more direct view of the Dolphin across the lake than the courtyard-facing rooms in either eight-story wing. However, most wing rooms can view the lake at an angle. Those on the northern edge of the western wing also view the BoardWalk at an angle.

Most courtyard-facing rooms have balconies; 224 rooms are so equipped, and these balconies offer panoramic 180-degree views. Of course, from most rooms at the Swan, part of any 180-degree view will include another section of the hotel.

The Swan's worst views are from west-facing rooms above the fourth floor, which overlook the unsightly roof of the hotel's western wing. The northernmost rooms in the wing directly above Kimonos restaurant are an exception—their balconies overlook the pool and the beach on Crescent Lake's western shore. Rooms 680–691 offer nice pool views.

Above the Swan's main entrance, south-facing rooms overlook the parking lot, with forest and the Hollywood Studios in the distance. However, the canal is also visible to the east. These rooms lack balconies.

THE DOLPHIN Consisting of a central A-frame with large wings jutting off each side and four smaller arms extending from the rear of the building, the Dolphin is attached to a large conference center, which means that the majority of guests are ostensibly there on business. The same amenities found at Disney Deluxe resorts are found at the Dolphin. All parks are accessible from a shuttle stop or a boat dock between the Dolphin and the Swan.

If you want a room with easy access to shopping, dining, and transportation to and from the parks, almost any Dolphin room will do. The shuttle (outside the main entrance) and the boat dock are equidistant from the main front and rear exits. Restaurants and shopping are primarily on the first and third floors.

If, however, you also want a view of something other than parking-lot asphalt, your choices narrow considerably. Rooms in the Dolphin with pleasant views are in the four arms on the rear of the building. Rooms on all the arms sport balconies from the first through fourth floors, then offer balconies or windows alternately on floors five through nine.

One of the Dolphin's best views overlooks the Grotto Pool on the far west side of the building. An artificial beach with a small waterfall is visible from rooms at the very end of the large west wing. None of these rooms has a balcony, but that might be a blessing because the pool comes with canned music and a bar. A better bet would be to ask for a room on the far west side of the first rear arm. These outer rooms have balconies and are more removed from the pool. Rooms on the inner, west part of that arm overlook a bladderwort-encrusted reflecting pool; these aren't recommended. Nor are the facing rooms on the next arm.

Between the second and third arms looms the monstrous Dolphin fountain; the better room choices here are on the top two floors. Here, from arm two you can see the BoardWalk (including any nighttime fireworks at Epcot), and from arm three you can see the Grotto Pool. Otherwise, you may find you have a view of massive green-concrete fish scales. The noise from the water is loud, and the fountain gushes continuously—it's either soothing or maddening depending on your temperament.

Arms three and four are situated around a reflecting pool. A concern for rooms in this area is that the ferry toots its horn every time it approaches and departs the dock. Its path runs right by these rooms, and the horn blows just as it passes. The first time that happens, it's quaint. By the 117th, your hair will be coming out in clumps.

The Crescent Lake side of arm four, and the small jut of the large Dolphin wing perpendicular to it, offer arguably the best views. You have an unobstructed view of the lake and Epcot fireworks, a fine BoardWalk view for people-watching, and, from higher floors, a view of the beach at Beach Club. There's ferry noise, but these rooms still have the most going for them. The best of the best in this arm are rooms 8015, 7015, 5015, 4015, and 3015. Rooms with balconies at the Dolphin generally run upwards of $40 a night more than rooms without.

Disney's Caribbean Beach Resort

(See **tinyurl.com/ug-caribbean** *for extended coverage.)*

STRENGTHS	
• Colorful Caribbean theme	• Murphy beds in select rooms increase capacity to five people
• Rooms with *Pirates of the Caribbean* and *Finding Nemo* themes	**WEAKNESSES**
• Lakefront setting	• Check-in is far from rest of resort
• Large food court	• Sit-down dining is mediocre at best
• New queen bed mattresses replaced double beds	• Multiple bus stops
	• Some "villages" are a good distance from restaurants and shops

QUICK TAKE: *Caribbean Beach was the lowest-rated Disney hotel in this year's reader surveys (see page 158). Disney has announced plans to create a new waterfront dining and shopping area at the resort. This will be constructed in a central location to improve guest access to services and dining. The existing restaurant experiences at Caribbean Beach are closing, to be replaced with temporary grab-and-go stands. Resort amenities may be disrupted during the resort refurbishment. Expect construction to be finished sometime in 2019. In the meantime, we advise against staying here; try Port Orleans French Quarter or Riverside (see page 207) instead.*

The Caribbean Beach Resort occupies 200 acres surrounding a 45-acre lake called Barefoot Bay. This midpriced resort, modeled after resorts in the Caribbean, consists of the registration area ("Custom House") and six two-story "villages" named after Caribbean islands. Each village has its own pool, laundry room, and beach. The Caribbean motif is maintained with blue metal roofs, widow's walks, and wooden railed porches. The atmosphere is cheerful, with buildings painted blue, lime green, and sherbet orange. In addition to the six village pools, the resort's main swimming pool is themed as an old Spanish fort, complete with slides and water cannons.

Most of the 2,112 guest rooms are 314 square feet. After a renovation in 2015, Caribbean Beach replaced its two double beds with two queen mattresses and added a fold-down Murphy bed to select rooms. Most rooms are decorated with neutral beach tones accented by bright tropical colors. All are outfitted with the same light-oak furniture. Rooms don't have balconies, but the access passageways are external and have railings. Rooms in Trinidad South are themed to a *Pirates of the Caribbean* motif. These rooms cost about $50–$75 more than comparable

Caribbean Beach Resort

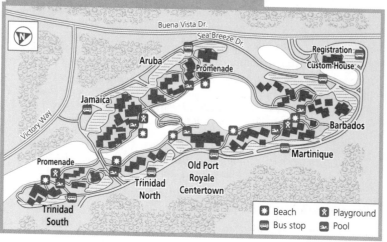

ones elsewhere in the resort. The soft goods and headboards in all non-*Pirates*-themed rooms have a subtle *Finding Nemo* theme.

South and east of Epcot and the Studios, Caribbean Beach offers transportation to all Disney World destinations by bus. We expect the Custom House check-in area to be demolished and its function moved to a temporary location sometime soon. In addition, all of Caribbean Beach's former restaurants at Old Port Royale were demolished in 2017 for new construction projects. Temporary, soft-sided structures dubbed "Old Tent Royale" were erected to provide food, and rooms in each island section of the resort were also turned into makeshift grab-and-go stations. The visual effect is a mildly realistic version of what an upscale, post-hurricane Caribbean-island recovery would look like, if the UN had stylish disaster coordination. This is, obviously, not where you should be paying to vacation. Walking time to the transportation loading area from the most remote rooms can be 7–9 minutes, so guests should seriously consider having a car.

This 20-something couple from Kansas City, Missouri, wished they'd had a car:

> The Caribbean Beach Resort is incredibly hard to navigate, and the bus service is horrendous. It often felt like there was only one bus running at a time, and we experienced several 30-plus-minute waits for the bus to and from parks. The resort is huge, and the bus circled the entire resort before it headed to the destination, so if you were unlucky enough to be on one of the last stops during a rush to the parks, the bus would pass right by if it was full. On multiple occasions we arrived at the bus stop 1-plus hour before our dining reservations but still found ourselves running from the park gates to make it to the restaurant on time!

A mom from Fenton, Michigan, found bus service lacking:

We recommend renting a car and/or paying for a preferred room location—especially if you're going in the hotter months or are impatient. The buses just take way too long with all the stops, and we thought it was a long hike to the food court and pools in the heat.

A woman from Colombia adds this:

Caribbean Beach transportation was as bad as you said it would be, and we will avoid the resort in the future. Despite leaving a lot of time, transportation was so poor we actually missed our friend's finish at the half marathon. Two other times, we waited over an hour at a theme park to return to the hotel, despite calling the front desk. We were told that each resort has a transportation budget. Clearly someone is using the CB budget for something other than transportation! One highlight was a bus driver named John—truly Disney at its best.

Despite these limitations, some readers love Caribbean Beach. An Edgewater, Colorado, couple comes to its defense:

Caribbean Beach was great. The hotel was full, but we saw very few people. It's laid out so you have some privacy, even though there was a bit of walking.

A Philadelphia dad with two tots in tow also had mostly positive things to say:

The Caribbean Beach Resort was beautiful. Our island (Barbados) was very quiet and relaxing on the courtyard/garden side, but the walk to the bus stop with a child was a bit of a haul.

A Kingwood, Texas, family of five also found the resort to be overly large but lucked out with the location of their room:

The Caribbean Beach Resort is a lovely property with a great pool and splash pad for our little guy. Fortunately, we had our own car with us because the thought of walking a half-mile for food, drink, or the pool was daunting after a day in the parks. We felt like offering rides to others for a buck!

From a Ridgeway, Virginia, mother of one:

The Caribbean Beach Resort was great—especially the housekeeping staff, who creatively rearranged my daughter's toys every day. Made coming back to the room much more fun. My only complaint with CBR was the inefficiency of checkout—although express checkout was available, someone had to be present to have luggage moved from the room to the main house for transport via Magical Express. We had scheduled a late-afternoon flight on our last day so we could all spend one last morning in the park—I missed most of it because I had to go and sit with the luggage. I was not happy AT ALL.

GOOD (AND NOT-SO-GOOD) ROOMS AT THE CARIBBEAN BEACH RESORT *(See* tinyurl.com/cbrroomviews *for photos.)* The resort's grounds are quite pleasant. Landscaping—lots of ferns and palm trees—is verdant, especially in the courtyards. The six "islands," or groups of buildings clustered around Barefoot Bay, are identical. The two-story motel-style structures are arranged in various ways to face courtyards, pools, the bay, and so forth. The setup is similar to Disney's Coronado Springs Resort in nearly every way but theme.

In general, corner rooms are preferable because they have more windows. Standard-view rooms face either the parking lots or court-yards, and the usual broad interpretation of water views is in play here. Beyond that, your main choices will revolve around your preference for proximity to (or distance from) the Custom House, pools, parking lots, pirates, or beaches on Barefoot Bay. Each island has direct access to at least one beach, playground, bus stop, and parking lot.

The island of Barbados is nearest the Custom House, but its central location guarantees that it also experiences the most foot traffic and road noise. It also shares its only beach and playground with Marti-nique, which probably is the best area for families. Martinique has access to two beaches, is adjacent to the main pool and playground at Old Port Royale Centertown, and yet is removed enough from the Custom House to offer a little serenity for parents.

The islands of Aruba and Jamaica are similar in character to Marti-nique, but each has only one beach, and guests must cross a footbridge to reach Old Port Royale center. Trinidad North comprises three buildings, and its thin layout means that noise penetrates its court-yard from surrounding roads and from rambunctious kids at Old Port Royale next door. The quietest island is Trinidad South, which is most remote from resort facilities. It has its own playground and beach, and the beach has a bonus—the view across Barefoot Bay is of wild, undeveloped Florida forest, a rarity on Disney property.

After you've sorted out your convenience and location priorities, think about the view. Avoid the standard-view rooms; all look onto a parking lot, road, or tiny garden. Water views at the Caribbean overlook swimming pools or Barefoot Bay. Pool views are less than enchanting, and there's lots of noise and activity around the pools. Bay views are the pick of the litter at the Caribbean. Such rooms in Barbados, Martinique, Trinidad North, and Trinidad South catch the afternoon sun. Bay-view rooms in Aruba and Jamaica catch the morning sun. Because we like the sun at our back in the evening, we always go for rooms 4246–4252 in Jamaica, 1246–1248 in Barba-dos, or 5256–5260 and 5541–5548 (but not 5542 or 5545) in Aruba. If you don't mind the sun in your eyes during cocktail time, rooms 2254–2256, 2413–2416, and 2445–2448 in Martinique are good bets, as are lake-facing rooms 3533–3534, 3853–3858, and 3949 in Trinidad South. We're not crazy about any room in Trinidad North. Be aware that the aging air-conditioning units for individual buildings are pretty loud. One room with an especially nice bay view (2525 in Martinique) is nonetheless not recommended because of its proximity to a clunky AC unit. Try room 2558 instead.

THE BONNET CREEK RESORTS

Not to be confused with the Disney resorts that follow, the **Bonnet Creek Resort** *is a 70-acre hotel, golf, and convention complex along Bonnet Creek. Although adjacent to and accessible from the World, it is not owned by Disney. Two of its four hotels are reviewed in "Hotels Outside Walt Disney World."*

Disney's Saratoga Springs Resort & Spa
Treehouse Villas at Disney's Saratoga Springs Resort & Spa

(See tinyurl.com/ug-ssr for extended coverage.)

SARATOGA SPRINGS RESORT & SPA

STRENGTHS	WEAKNESSES
• Often available at discounted rates or as a DVC/DDV rental	• Very nice spa and fitness center
• Attractive main pool; multiple well-themed quiet pools with snack bars	• On-site dining is limited for a resort of this size
• Closest resort to Disney Springs and Typhoon Lagoon	• Theme is dull compared with those of other Disney resorts
• Convenient parking	• Fewer baths per bedroom than newer DVC/DDV properties
• Only WDW-owned resort with dedicated golf (Lake Buena Vista Golf Course)	• Bus service can take some time to get out of the (huge) resort
• Grocery options in gift shop	

TREEHOUSE VILLAS

STRENGTHS	WEAKNESSES
• Spectacular stand-alone three-bedroom villas	• Long distance from Saratoga Springs services such as check-in and dining
• Quiet location	• Kids may find all that quiet boring
• Historical connection to the Treehouses from the 1970s	• Lackluster pool
• Innovative round design feels more spacious than other villas with the same square footage	• Limited number of units makes the Treehouses among the most difficult accommodations to book at WDW
	• Only two baths per villa
	• Bus travelers connect through Saratoga Springs

QUICK TAKE: *The completion of Disney Springs has markedly increased Saratoga Springs' appeal to readers and to us. Within a short walk of this resort are a week's worth of good dining options, plus enough people-watching and entertainment for everyone. Disney has responded by charging 15%–20% more for rooms closest to Disney Springs, naturally. We think the cost isn't worth the few extra minutes of walking. If you have a car to help avoid the resort's sometimes slow bus service to the theme parks, we recommend giving Saratoga Springs a try.*

Saratoga Springs, a Disney Deluxe Villa resort, has a theme wordily described by Disney as recalling an "1880s, Victorian, upstate New York lakeside retreat" amid "pastoral landscapes, formal gardens, bubbling springs, and natural surroundings." Saratoga Springs consists of 1,260 studio and one-, two-, and three-bedroom villas across the lake from Disney Springs. Housed in 12 buildings, most accommodations are of recent vintage, while the fitness center and check-in building are retooled vestiges of the erstwhile Disney Institute Resort. An adjacent 60-unit DDV complex, **Treehouse Villas at Disney's Saratoga Springs Resort & Spa,** opened in 2009.

The fitness center is by far the best at Walt Disney World. The Senses spa, like the Grand Floridian's, was refurbished in 2013 along

Saratoga Springs Resort & Spa

ACCOMMODATIONS
1. The Carousel (7101–7836)
2. Congress Park (1101–2836)
3. The Grandstand (8101–9836)
4. The Paddock (4501–6836)
5. The Springs (3101–4436)

AMENITIES
6. The Artist's Palette
7. Backstretch Pool Bar
8. BBQ Grill Area
9. On the Rocks Pool Bar
10. The Paddock Grill
11. Turf Club Bar & Grill

Boat dock
Bus stop

the lines of those on Disney's cruise ships. Service and decor are very good, and this Senses location is easier to get to than the one at the Grand Floridian if you're staying east of the World. See page 777 for a full review.

Treehouse Villas at Saratoga Springs Resort & Spa

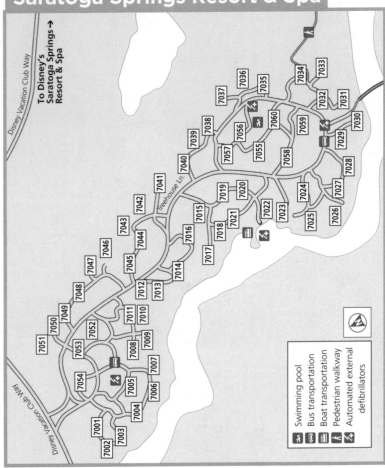

Surrounded on three sides by golf courses, Saratoga Springs is the only Disney-owned resort that affords direct access to the links (the military-only Shades of Green also provides golf on-property).

Furnishings and soft goods are less whimsical and more upscale and masculine than at other Disney resorts. Chairs, sofas, and tables are substantial—perhaps a little too substantial for the rooms they inhabit. The overall effect, however, is sophisticated and restful. A Gulf Shores, Alabama, family, however, takes a slight exception to the restful part:

Saratoga Springs Resort was beautiful, comfortable, and exactly what we needed for our family of five. It was VERY quiet . . . except for the toilets. When you flushed, it sounded like the space shuttle launching.

A couple from Peru, Indiana, is more critical:

Saratoga Springs is our least favorite resort. We didn't enjoy the theming, and unless you have a car, getting around by bus is a real hassle. The food court is very small and the food expensive. Also, checkout was very slow, and our room seemed smaller than comparable rooms at BoardWalk Villas and Old Key West.

A Cartersville, Georgia, reader echoes the previous complaint about bus service:

No matter when we tried to leave a park for Saratoga Springs, there were no buses—45 minutes was the norm. Why pay the premium when you end up driving or taking cabs so as not to waste 2–3 hours per day?

Finally, this from a Jeddo, Michigan, mom:

I would not recommend Saratoga Springs Resort. It is too vast, and there is only one place (at the main lobby) to fill your resort mugs. We stayed in Congress Park, and while it was quiet and a quick walk to Disney Springs, it is way too far from the other amenities of the hotel. This hotel is also starting to look a bit shabby and needs a bit of a facelift.

GOOD (AND NOT-SO-GOOD) ROOMS AT SARATOGA SPRINGS RESORT & SPA *(See* tinyurl.com/ssrroomviews *for photos.)* This resort's sprawling size puts some of its best rooms very far away from the main lobby, restaurants, and shops. If you don't have a car, the best rooms are those in The Springs, numbered 3101–3436 and 3501–3836. Ask for a room toward the northeast side of these buildings (away from the lobby), as the southwest rooms border a well-traveled road. Avoid rooms 4101–4436 in Building 14; a pedestrian walkway runs behind the patios of this building and gets a lot of use in the early morning from guests headed to breakfast.

If you have a car or you don't mind a couple of extra furlongs' walk to the lobby, rooms 1101–1436 and 2501–2836 in Congress Park offer quietness, a view of Disney Springs, and a relatively short walk to the bus stop. Also good are rooms 4501–4826, 6101–6436, and 6501–6836 in The Paddock. Avoid rooms on the northeast side of the 5101–5435 building of The Paddock, as well as the northwest side of the 5501–5836 building; these border a swimming pool and bus stop.

In addition to being quiet, rooms 1101–1436 of Congress Park and rooms 6101–6436 and 6501–6836 of The Paddock afford the closest walks to Disney Springs shops, restaurants, and entertainment.

TREEHOUSE VILLAS AT DISNEY'S SARATOGA SPRINGS RESORT & SPA Opened in 2009, this complex of 60 three-bedroom villas lies between Old Key West Resort and the Grandstand section of Saratoga Springs proper, with a separate entrance off Disney Vacation Club Way. The treehouses are bordered by Lake Buena Vista Golf Course to the northeast and a waterway to the southwest that feeds into Village Lake.

True to their name, the villas stand on stilts 10 feet off the ground (ramps provide wheelchair access) and are surrounded by a densely wooded landscape. Each villa is an eight-sided structure with three bedrooms and two full bathrooms in about 1,074 square feet.

Each villa holds nine people, about the same number as comparably sized rooms at the other DVC/DDV resorts. The master and second bedrooms have queen beds, and the third bedroom has bunk beds. A sofa bed and sleeper chair in the living room round out the mattress lineup. As with sleeper sofas and chairs in general, we think these are more appropriate for kids than adults.

The three-bedroom Treehouses usually cost about $130–$230 more per night than a comparably sized two-bedroom villa elsewhere at Saratoga Springs. The trade-off, however, is that you get an extra bedroom and give up some living space elsewhere. You probably won't notice the missing space because the layout of the kitchen, dining, and living areas is so open. Beware the master-bathroom shower, which is next to the tub in an enclosed glass wall: Tilt down to shave your legs or grab a bottle of shampoo, and you could bang your head on the side of the tub.

The interior of each villa is decorated with natural materials, such as stone floors in the kitchen, granite countertops, and stained wood furniture. End tables, picture frames, and bunk beds are made from rustic logs. Bathrooms, outfitted in modern tile, have showers and tubs plus a decent amount of counter space.

Because of its location, Treehouse Villas has few amenities of its own: Each villa has a large wooden deck with grill, and all villas share a small pool with spa. A walking path connects the complex to the rest of Saratoga Springs; Treehouse guests can use all of the main resort's facilities. Two dedicated bus stops serve the Treehouses.

A family from Columbus, New Jersey, thinks a stay at the Treehouse Villas is money well spent:

> *I give them five stars for value. We were trying to be economical, as there were nine people in our party and it saved us about $700–$1,000 per night. Our villa had three rooms and a pullout couch that comfortably housed our group. It had a great eat-in kitchen as well, which further helped us save money on breakfast.*

Treehouses 7024–7034 and 7058–7060 are closest to one of the villas' two dedicated bus stops and the walkway to Saratoga Springs; 7026–7033 also have water views. Treehouses 7001–7011 and 7045–7054 are closest to the other bus stop; 7020–7023 are closest to the boat docks. Finally, Treehouses 7035–7037, 7055, 7056, and 7060 surround the pool.

Disney's Old Key West Resort

*(See **tinyurl.com/ug-okwest** for extended coverage.)*

STRENGTHS	
• Largest villas of the DCV/DDV resorts	• Grocery selection in gift shop
• Often available at discounted rates or as DVC rental	• Convenient parking
• Mature landscaping	**WEAKNESSES**
• Homey, well-themed lounge (The Gurgling Suitcase)	• Multiple bus stops
• Close to Lake Buena Vista Golf Course	• No elevators in many buildings
• Boat service to Disney Springs	• Highway noise
	• Fewer baths per bedroom than newer DVC/DDV properties
	• Mediocre on-site dining

Old Key West Resort

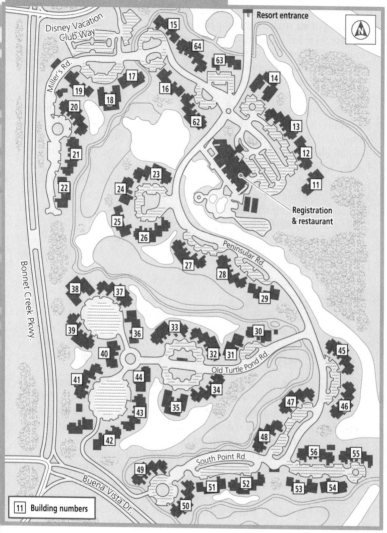

THIS WAS THE FIRST DVC/DDV PROPERTY. Although the resort is a time-share property, units not being used by owners are rented on a nightly basis. Old Key West Resort is a large aggregation of two- to three-story buildings modeled after Caribbean-style residences and guesthouses of the Florida Keys. Set subdivision-style around a golf course and along Bonnet Creek, the buildings are arranged in small, neighborhood-like clusters. They feature pastel facades, white trim, and shuttered windows. The registration area is in Conch Flats Community Hall, along with a full-service restaurant, modest fitness center, marina, and sundries shop. Each cluster of accommodations has a quiet pool; a larger pool is at the community hall. (A waterslide in the shape of a giant sand castle highlights the main pool.)

This resort offers some of the roomiest accommodations at Walt Disney World, with all rooms having been refurbished in 2010. Studios are 376 square feet; one-bedroom villas, 942; and two-bedroom villas, 1,333. Studios contain two queen-size beds, a table and two chairs, and an extra vanity outside the bathroom. One-bedroom villas have a king-size bed in the master bedroom, a queen-size sleeper sofa in the living room, a laundry room, and a full kitchen with coffeemaker. Two-bedroom villas feature a king-size bed in the master bedroom, a queen-size sleeper sofa and fold-out chair in the living room, and two queen beds in the second bedroom. All villas have enough closet space to contain your entire wardrobe. Studios and villas are tastefully decorated with leather and upholstered furniture in neutral tan or green color schemes. The wood kitchen table and chairs are painted white. One-bedroom and larger villas have wood flooring instead of carpet. Each villa has a private balcony that opens to views of the golf course, the landscape, or a waterway.

Transportation to other Disney World destinations is by bus. Walking time to transportation loading areas from the most remote rooms is about 6 minutes.

An Erie, Pennsylvania, reader thinks Old Key West is Walt Disney World's best-kept secret:

> Old Key West has the most spacious rooms and villas and the easiest access to your car—right outside your door! It's in a great location and built around a gorgeous golf course. There are a number of small, almost private pools, so you don't have to go to the main pool to swim.

GOOD (AND NOT-SO-GOOD) ROOMS AT OLD KEY WEST RESORT *(See* tinyurl.com/okw-roomviews *for photos.)* Old Key West is huge, with 49 three-story villa buildings offering a mix of studio and multiroom villas. Views are nice from almost all villas; all multiroom villas and some studios have a large balcony furnished with a table and chairs. Though nice vistas are easy to come by, quiet is more elusive. Because the resort is bordered by busy Bonnet Creek Parkway and even busier Buena Vista Drive, the best villas are those as far from the highway noise as possible. For quiet isolation and a lovely river view, ask for Building 46 or 45, in that order. For a lake and golf-course view away from road noise but closest to restaurants, recreation, the marina, the main swimming complex, and shopping, ask for Building 13. Nearby, Buildings 12 and 11 are likewise quiet and convenient but offer primarily golf-course views. Next-best choices are Buildings 32 and 34. Building 32 looks onto a lake with the golf course in the background, while 34 faces the golf course with tennis courts to the left and a lake to the right. None of the buildings recommended is more than a 2- to 5-minute walk to the nearest bus stop or pool. Avoid Buildings 19–22, 38 and 39, 41 and 42, and 49–54, which border Bonnet Creek Parkway and Buena Vista Drive.

Finally, if you want to use your balcony without the sun in your face, use the map on page 205 to check out the position of your building relative to sunrise and sunset. If you want to use your balcony in the afternoon, ask for an east-facing building. Conversely, request a west-facing building if you primarily want to use your balcony in the morning. We like to enjoy a drink on the balcony in the afternoon or evening, so we ensure shade by asking for an east-facing villa.

Disney's Port Orleans Resort–French Quarter
(See tinyurl.com/ug-pofq *for extended coverage.)*

Disney's Port Orleans Resort–Riverside
(See tinyurl.com/ug-por *for extended coverage.)*

PORT ORLEANS RESORT–FRENCH QUARTER

STRENGTHS
- Most compact of the WDW Moderate resorts
- One bus stop
- Live entertainment in Scat Cat's Club
- Beignets in food court!
- Attractively themed lobby
- Short walk to Port Orleans Riverside's restaurants and bars
- Good place to walk or run for fitness

WEAKNESSES
- Ho-hum pool
- Shares bus service with Port Orleans Riverside during slower times of year
- No full-service dining

PORT ORLEANS RESORT–RIVERSIDE

STRENGTHS
- Interesting narrative to theming
- Disney princess–themed rooms in Magnolia Bend
- Live entertainment in River Roost Lounge
- A Moderate resort that can sleep five, the fifth in a Murphy bed, at Alligator Bayou
- Very nice feature pool
- Close driving distance to the Magic Kingdom
- Good place to walk or run for fitness
- Recreation options (bikes, boats)

WEAKNESSES
- Multiple bus stops; shares service with Port Orleans French Quarter during slower times of year
- Mediocre full-service restaurant

A MODERATE RESORT, Port Orleans is divided into two sections. The smaller, southern part is called the French Quarter; the larger section is labeled Riverside.

PORT ORLEANS RESORT–FRENCH QUARTER The 1,008-room French Quarter section is a sanitized Disney version of New Orleans's Vieux Carré. Consisting of seven three-story guest-room buildings next to the Sassagoula River, the resort suggests what New Orleans would look like if its buildings were painted every year and garbage collectors never went on strike. The prim pink-and-blue guest buildings are festooned with wrought-iron filigree, shuttered windows, and old-fashioned iron lampposts. In keeping with the Crescent City theme, French Quarter is landscaped with magnolia trees and overgrown vines. The centrally located Mint contains the registration area and food court and is a reproduction of a turn-of-the-19th-century building where Mississippi Delta farmers sold their harvests.

unofficial **TIP**
Readers rate French Quarter higher than all other Moderate resorts and several Deluxe ones.

Port Orleans Resort–French Quarter

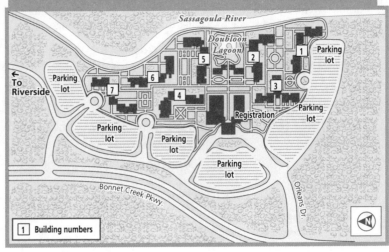

The registration desk features a vibrant Mardi Gras mural and old-fashioned bank-teller windows. Doubloon Lagoon surrounds a colorful fiberglass creation depicting Neptune riding a sea serpent.

French Quarter rooms measure 314 square feet. Most contain two queen beds, a table and two chairs, a dresser–credenza, a mini-fridge, a coffeemaker, and a vanity outside the bathroom. With their cherry headboards, Mardi Gras–purple coverlets, cherry-wood credenzas, and olive carpet, the rooms are themed but tasteful. A privacy curtain separates the dressing area from the rest of the room, allowing three people to get ready at once. No rooms have balconies, but ornamental iron-railed accessways on each floor provide a good (though less private) substitute.

There's a food court but no full-service restaurant. The closest full-service eatery is in the adjacent Riverside section of the resort, about a 15-plus-minute walk. The commute to restaurants in other hotels may be 40–60 minutes each way. The Disney bus system links the French Quarter to all Disney World destinations. Walking time to bus-loading areas from the most remote French Quarter rooms is 5 minutes or less.

Most readers really like Port Orleans French Quarter. This comment from a Wynnewood, Pennsylvania, father of two is typical:

> I highly recommend Port Orleans French Quarter. We stayed at All-Star Movies on our last trip and didn't think it made sense to stay anywhere else. Well, we were wrong. The price difference wasn't that big, and what we got for the difference was well worth it: uncrowded pool, bellhop service, front-door greeters with great tips for touring, and a bigger, more comfortable room. Totally worth the extra money.

One Philadelphia Gen Xer wasn't flush with joy about his stay:

Port Orleans Resort–Riverside

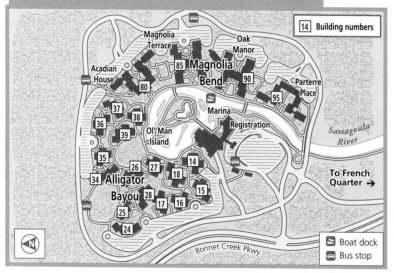

The in-room toilets seem to be powered by jet thrusters. We were woken up far too many times in the night when someone in a neighboring room would flush.

An unidentified e-mailer backs him up:

The reader comment about the toilets is 100% correct. They're air-pressure-forced rather than water-flow-and-gravity-operated—like an airplane toilet, only MUCH louder. Every morning I was woken up at 7:30 a.m. with an hour's worth of whoooshing.

From a Beaufort, South Carolina, mom:

We did a split stay between POFQ and one night in DVC Animal Kingdom Lodge Kidani. I fell in love with POFQ, liked it much more than I thought I would. Things I loved about POFQ—smaller size; so easy to get around; only one bus stop, so we went straight from resort to our destination without making more stops; boat to Disney Springs.

GOOD (AND NOT-SO-GOOD) ROOMS AT PORT ORLEANS RESORT–FRENCH QUARTER *(See* tinyurl.com/pofq-roomviews *for photos.)* Seven guest-room buildings flank the pool, Guest Relations building, and bus stop. The best views are from rooms facing the river and pine forest on the opposite bank. Wings of Buildings 1, 2, 5, 6, and 7 flank the river and provide the best river views in all of Port Orleans. River-view rooms in Buildings 1, 6, and 7 are a long walk from French Quarter public facilities, but they're the most tranquil. Families with children should request river-view rooms in Buildings 2 and 5, nearest the swimming complex. Make sure the reservationist understands that you're requesting a room with a river view, not just a water view. All river-view rooms are also water-view rooms, but not vice versa. Note that standard-view rooms look onto a courtyard or a parking lot.

Following are the best river-view rooms in each building:

BUILDING 1 Rooms 1127-1132, 1227-1232 (except 1229), 1327-1332

BUILDING 2 Rooms 2227-2232, 2327-2332

BUILDING 5 Rooms 5118-5123, 5218-5224, 5318-5325

BUILDING 6 Rooms 6123-6126, 6223-6226, 6323-6326, 6138-6139, 6236-6240, 6335-6340, 6145-6148, 6245-6248, 6345-6348

BUILDING 7 Rooms 7142-7147, 7242-7247, 7342-7347

Note that room 6X23 in Building 6 is a corner room with two windows, one of which faces the river. But Disney puts it in the less expensive garden-view category.

PORT ORLEANS RESORT-RIVERSIDE This resort draws on the lifestyle and architecture of Mississippi River communities in antebellum Louisiana. Spread along the Sassagoula River, which encircles Ol' Man Island (the section's main swimming area), Riverside is subdivided into two more themed areas: the mansion area, which features plantation-style architecture, and the bayou area, with tin-roofed rustic (imitation) wooden buildings. Mansions are three stories tall, while bayou guesthouses are a story shorter. Riverside's food court houses a working cotton press powered by a 32-foot waterwheel.

Each of Riverside's 2,048 rooms is 314 square feet. Most provide one king or two queen beds, a table and two chairs, a mini-fridge and coffeemaker, and two pedestal sinks outside the bathroom. Rooms in the Alligator Bayou section of Riverside feature brass bathroom fixtures, hickory-branch bedposts, Murphy beds, and quilted bedspreads. Rooms in the plantation-themed Magnolia Bend section of Riverside are more conventional, with light-green walls, chestnut-colored wood furnishings, olive carpets, and dark-blue bedding accents.

The Oak and Parterre buildings in Magnolia Bend contain exclusively Disney princess–themed rooms, similar in concept to the Disney-themed rooms at Caribbean Beach. Riverside's rooms are themed to *The Princess and the Frog,* with appearances by Tiana's other princess friends. These rooms cost around $70 more per night than other rooms.

Rooms in Alligator Bayou—along with those at Caribbean Beach—are unique among Disney's Moderate properties in that they sleep five people; the fifth is a fold-down, Murphy-style bed, more suitable for children than adults.

The main reader gripe about Riverside is its bus service. First from a Shildon, UK, woman:

We have stayed at POR three times and love it. The buses, however, are a nightmare. They run very erratically, and there never seem to be enough of them. Buses to water parks and MK were the worst.

From a Delmar, Delaware, mom:

Port Orleans Riverside has one of the worst bus services on property. Unfortunately, we forgot about that from our last stay here. One day a bus to a park takes 20 minutes; two days later, going to the exact same park, you will experience a long, tranquil drive around the loop, then make a stopover at French Quarter, followed by finally getting to the park about 45 minutes later or more. Utter madness!

A big fan of Port Orleans Riverside won't be going back:

I absolutely love Port Orleans Riverside. It is a gorgeous resort. I have stayed there four times since 1997. However, as lovely as it is, I doubt I will go back because each time I do, I am very disappointed with the bus service to and from the Magic Kingdom. The bus service to the Magic Kingdom is pretty bad. You have people trying to make it to early dining reservations and leaving early enough, but whoever schedules these buses doesn't seem to care. It won't change either, but it has been like this for years. The bus service coming back from the Magic Kingdom is nothing short of abominable. The lines are incredibly long. They send out the short buses, rather than the longer bendy buses. I waited 35+ minutes in a large crowd only to have to stand on this bus every single night. It is for this reason I will not go back to this beautiful resort.

Don't throw Port Orleans Riverside under the bus (pun intended). Simply rent a car or use a ride sharing service and get off the bus, Gus.

GOOD (AND NOT-SO-GOOD) ROOMS AT PORT ORLEANS RIVERSIDE RESORT *(See* tinyurl.com/por-roomviews *for photos.)* Riverside is so large that we use bicycles whenever we visit there. All told, there are 20 guest-room buildings (not counting flanking wings on two buildings). Divided into two sections, Alligator Bayou and Magnolia Bend, the resort is arrayed around two pine groves and a watercourse that Disney calls the Sassagoula River. Magnolia Bend consists of four three-story, grand plantation–style complexes named Acadian House, Magnolia Terrace, Oak Manor, and Parterre Place. Though Magnolia Bend is on the river, only about 15% of the guest rooms have an unobstructed view of the water. The vast majority of rooms overlook a courtyard or parking lot. Trees and other vegetation block the view of many rooms actually facing the river. The best views in Magnolia Bend are from the third-floor river side of Acadian House (Building 80), which overlooks the river and Ol' Man Island: rooms 8417–8419.

To the south are Magnolia Terrace (Building 85) and Oak Manor (Building 90), each in an H shape. They're nearer the front desk, restaurant, lounge, and shopping complex than Acadian House. Continuing south, Parterre Place (Building 95) has a number of rooms facing the river, but the views are blocked by trees or extend to the parking lot on the opposite shore. In general, with the few previous exceptions, if you want a nice river view, opt for Port Orleans French Quarter downriver.

Alligator Bayou, the other part of Port Orleans Riverside, forms an arch around the resort's northern half. Sixteen smaller, two-story guest-room buildings, set among pine groves and abundant gardens, offer a cozy alternative to the more-imposing structures of the Magnolia Bend section of Riverside and Port Orleans French Quarter. If you want a river view, ask for a second-story water-view room in Building 27 or 38. Building 14 also offers some river-view rooms and is convenient to shops, the front desk, and the restaurant, but it's in a noisy, high-traffic area. A good compromise for families is Building 18. It's insulated from traffic and noise by landscaping, but it's also next to a satellite swimming pool and within an easy walk of the lobby and restaurant.

Disney's Port Orleans Riverside map shows two lakes north of the river bend, suggesting additional water views in Alligator Bayou. But these are dried-up lakes now forested with pine. This area, however, is richly landscaped to complement the "pine islands," and though out of sight of water, it offers the most peaceful and serene accommodations in the Port Orleans resort. In this area, we recommend Buildings 26, 25, and 39, in that order. Note that these buildings are somewhat distant from the resort's central facilities, and there's no adjacent parking. In Alligator Bayou, avoid Buildings 15, 16, 17, and 24, all of which are subject to traffic noise from nearby Bonnet Creek Parkway.

Remember: All Port Orleans guest buildings have exterior corridors. When you look out your window, a safety rail will be in the foreground, and other guests will periodically walk past.

THE ANIMAL KINGDOM RESORTS

Disney's Animal Kingdom Lodge & Villas–Jambo House
(See tinyurl.com/ug-aklodge for extended coverage.)

Disney's Animal Kingdom Villas–Kidani Village
(See tinyurl.com/ug-kidani for extended coverage.)

ANIMAL KINGDOM LODGE & VILLAS: JAMBO HOUSE

STRENGTHS	WEAKNESSES
• Magnificent lobby	• Jambo House villas are smaller than those at Kidani Village
• Excellent on-site dining options	
• Large, beautiful feature pool	• Rooms are among the smallest of the Deluxe resorts
• On-site cultural and nature programs	
• Best theming of any Disney hotel	• Erratic bus service
	• No direct nonbus transportation to any theme park

ANIMAL KINGDOM VILLAS: KIDANI VILLAGE

STRENGTHS	
• Nice pool with excellent splash area	• Close to Jambo House amenities and restaurants
• Underground parking close to elevators	• Great fitness room
• Beautiful, understated lobby	**WEAKNESSES**
• Sanaa restaurant is an *Unofficial Guide* favorite	• Savanna views can be hit-or-miss
	• Erratic bus service
• Beautiful Grand Villas sleep 13	• No quick-service food other than pool bar

QUICK TAKE: *Animal Kingdom Lodge room ratings are among the highest of any Disney resort. They also have three of the five highest-rated sit-down restaurants, according to our reader surveys. If these resorts fit in your budget, they're the first places we suggest you consider.*

In the southwesternmost corner of the World and adjacent to Disney's Animal Kingdom theme park, Animal Kingdom Lodge opened in 2001. Designed by Peter Dominick of Wilderness Lodge fame, the resort fuses African tribal architecture with the rugged style of grand

Animal Kingdom Lodge & Villas

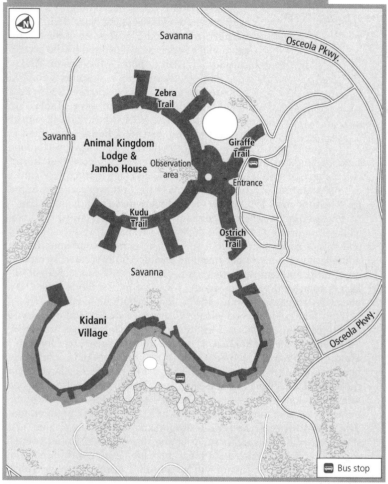

Bus stop

East African national-park lodges. Five-story thatched-roof guest-room wings fan out from a vast central rotunda housing the lobby. Public areas and about half of the rooms offer panoramic views of a private 43-acre wildlife preserve, punctuated with streams and elevated *kopje* (rock outcrops) and populated with some 200 free-roaming animals and 130 birds.

Most of the 972 guest rooms measure 344 square feet and boast hand-carved furnishings and richly colored soft goods. Standard amenities include a flat-panel TV, desk with two chairs, ceiling fan, mini-fridge, and coffeemaker. Behind each headboard sits faux mosquito netting. (Perhaps the tan curtains are supposed to be the folds of a safari tent.) Bathrooms have animal-themed wallpaper, two sinks, and a large mirror. Almost all rooms have full balconies.

The resort is divided into Jambo House, which has both regular hotel rooms and DDV units, and the all-DDV Kidani Village.

Jambo House offers fine dining in a casual setting at Jiko—The Cooking Place. Twin wood-burning ovens are the focal point of the restaurant, which serves meals inspired by the myriad cuisines of Africa. Boma—Flavors of Africa, the family restaurant, serves a buffet with food prepared in an exhibition kitchen featuring a wood-burning grill and rotisserie. Tables are under thatched roofs. The Mara, a quick-service restaurant with extended hours, and Victoria Falls, a delightful mezzanine lounge overlooking Boma, round out the hotel's food-and-beverage service. Other amenities include an elaborate swimming area, a village marketplace, and a 1-hour nighttime safari tour exclusively for Lodge guests ages 8 and up. The tour costs $75 per person and takes place nightly at 10 p.m.

Consisting of a separate building shaped like a backward 3, Kidani Village comprises 324 units, a dedicated savanna, a well-themed pool and splash zone, and Sanaa, a sit-down restaurant combining Indian and African cuisines. Other amenities include a fitness center; an arcade; a gift shop; and tennis, shuffleboard, and basketball courts. Kidani Village is connected to Jambo House by a half-mile walking trail; DDV guests at either resort can use the facilities at both buildings.

Both Jambo House and Kidani Village have studios and one-, two-, and three-bedroom villas. Most rooms at Kidani Village are larger, however, and the difference is anywhere from 50 square feet for a studio to more than 200 square feet for a two-bedroom unit. (The three-bedroom Grand Villas at Jambo House, 148 square feet larger than those in Kidani Village, are the exception.) Kidani's villas also have one more bathroom for one-, two-, and three-bedroom units. Because of the difference in area, one-bedroom units in Kidani Village can accommodate up to five people, and two-bedroom units can hold up to nine via a sleeper chair in the living room. At Jambo House, one-bedroom "value" rooms sleep four; standard, savanna, and Club Level rooms sleep five.

Having stayed at Kidani Village almost a dozen times, we think it's quiet and relaxed. The lobby and rooms have a smaller, more personal feel than Jambo House's. The exterior isn't anything special—essentially a set of green rectangles with oversize African-themed decorations attached. Kidani's distance from Jambo House makes it feel especially remote. The bus stops are a fair distance from the main building, too, and it's easy to head in the wrong direction when you're coming back from the parks at night.

Animal Kingdom Lodge & Villas is connected to the rest of Disney World by bus, but because of the resort's remote location, you should seriously consider having a car if you stay there.

From a Murfreesboro, Tennessee, mom who has a love–hate relationship with the place:

> Overall had a great trip to WDW. In regards to Animal Kingdom Lodge—found the setting unique and the staff to be exceptional and the common areas to be breathtakingly gorgeous. Loved all three

table service restaurants (including Sanaa in this). The location wasn't an issue since we had a car, and the pool area was fabulous. However, the rooms are really small for the price. We were especially dismayed at the commode/shower area. We had to literally sit down on the commode in order to have room to shut the door. I travel often for work, and the AKL bathrooms are literally the worst design I have seen in years. I have always loved visiting AKL and eating at Boma and Jiko—visiting AKL is always on every trip's to-do list. We wanted to love staying at AKL as well, but the room size and bathrooms dropped us from love to just like.

But a family of four from Lincoln, England, gives Animal Kingdom Lodge a mixed, though mostly positive, review:

We had a fab holiday, but we wouldn't recommend people paying the extra money to have a savanna room. The animals are scarce, and you don't really spend much time in your room. The pool and the kids' club were fantastic and the hotel stunning. The food court was fine, although we wished they'd change the menu, as after two weeks you're fed up of the same choices.

GOOD (AND NOT-SO-GOOD) ROOMS AT ANIMAL KINGDOM LODGE & VILLAS *(See* tinyurl.com/akl-roomviews *for photos.)* A glance at the resort map tells you where the best rooms and villas are. Kudu Trail and Zebra Trail, two wings branching from the rear of Jambo House, form a semicircle around the central wildlife savanna. Along each wing are seven five-story buildings, with accommodations on floors two through five. Five buildings on each wing form the semicircle, while the remaining two buildings jut away from the center. The best rooms—on floors three and four, facing into the circle—are high enough to survey the entire savanna yet low enough to let you appreciate the ground-level detail of this amazing wildlife exhibit; plus, these rooms offer the easiest access to the lobby and restaurants. Second-floor rooms really can't take in the panorama, and fifth-floor rooms are a little too high for intimate views of the animals. Most of the fourth-floor rooms in Jambo House are reserved for concierge guests, and the fifth and sixth floors house the DDV units.

Most rooms in the outward-jutting buildings, as well as rooms facing away from the interior, also survey a savanna, but one not as compelling as that of the inner circle. On the Zebra Trail, the first two buildings plus the first jutting building provide savanna views on one side and look onto the swimming complex on the other.

Less attractive still are two smaller wings, Ostrich Trail and Giraffe Trail, branching from either side of the lodge near the main entrance. Some rooms on the left side of Ostrich Trail (see map on page 213) overlook a small savanna. Rooms on the opposite side of the same buildings overlook the front entrance. Least desirable is Giraffe Trail, extending from the right side of the lobby: Its rooms overlook either the pool (water view) or the resort entrance (standard view). A Portage, Indiana, family begs to differ with our assessment, however:

We stayed in a pool-view room in Giraffe Trail and loved it. The view was beautiful, even without the animals (which you can see elsewhere). The proximity to the pool, lobby, and restaurants was *great, and we saved about $500 over what we would've spent on a savanna view.*

The best views in Kidani Village are the north-facing rooms near the bottom and middle of the backward 3. Try rooms 7X38–7X44, 7X46–7X52, 7X06–7X11, 7X68–7X82, and 7X61–7X67 (X = numbers 0–9). These overlook the savanna next to Jambo House's Kudu Trail rooms and beyond into undeveloped woods. West- and south-facing rooms in the bottom half of Kidani Village overlook the parking lot; west-facing rooms in the top half have either pool or savanna views. *(See* tinyurl.com/kidani-roomviews *for photos.)*

Disney's Coronado Springs Resort
(See **tinyurl.com/ug-coronado** *for extended coverage.)*

STRENGTHS	
• Most sophisticated room decor of the Moderate resorts	• Best public Wi-Fi at any Disney resort
• Setting is beautiful at night	**WEAKNESSES**
• Themed swimming area with waterslides	• Conventioneers may be off-putting to vacationing families
• Large feature pool	• Some rooms are a long distance from check-in, lobby, and restaurants
• On-site business center	• Multiple bus stops

QUICK TAKE: *Coronado Springs is undergoing an extensive but relatively contained expansion project that is expected to be completed in 2019. The Cabanas 9B building has been demolished to make way for a new 15-story tower, with 500 upscale rooms and suites and a concierge experience. Expect the percentage of guests here that are conference attendees to increase. Major landscaping, as well as a refurbishment of Coronado's remaining rooms, will also be done. The resort's lobby, restaurants, and pools remain open. Our walks around the resort did not turn up any instances of guest inconvenience, and reader-survey results remain unchanged. We're not discouraging anyone from staying here.*

NEAR ANIMAL KINGDOM, Coronado Springs Resort is Disney's only midpriced convention property. Inspired by northern Mexico and the American Southwest, the resort is divided into three separately themed areas. The two- and three-story Ranchos call to mind Southwestern cattle ranches, while the two-story Cabanas are modeled after Mexican beach resorts. The multistoried Casitas embody elements of Spanish architecture found in Mexico's great cities. The lobby, part of the Casitas, features a mosaic ceiling and tiled floor.

The vast resort surrounds a 22-acre lake, and there are three small pools as well as one large swimming complex. The main pool features a reproduction of a Mayan step pyramid with a waterfall cascading down its side.

Most of the 1,915 guest rooms measure 314 square feet and contain two queen beds, a desk and chair, a mini-fridge, a coffeemaker,

Coronado Springs Resort

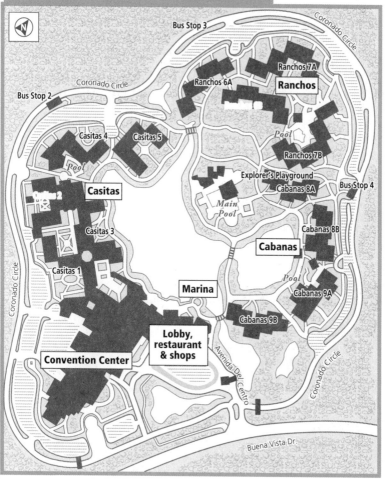

and a vanity outside the bathroom. Rooms are decorated with a subtle Southwestern theme, with turquoise accents. None of the rooms have their own balconies.

Coronado Springs completed a resort-wide room-refurbishment project in 2015. Updates included new interior paint, carpets, and bath vanities.

Perhaps because Coronado Springs is geared to conventions, getting work done here is easier than at any other Disney Moderate resort. A specially designed light fixture above the desk holds a down-pointing bulb and provides excellent illumination of the work area. Wi-Fi is available throughout the resort, and the business-center staff is friendly and knowledgeable.

Coronado Springs offers two full-service restaurants as well as Disney World's most interesting food court, plus Rix, a bar. Unfortunately, there's not nearly enough food service for a resort this large and remote. We suggest having a car to expand your dining options. The resort is connected to other Disney destinations by bus only. Walking time from the most remote rooms to the bus stop is 8–10 minutes.

Cabana 9B holds Coronado's Business Class rooms, with access to a private lounge for serving breakfast and snacks throughout the day. These rooms cost around $56 per night more than standard rooms, depending on the season.

Reader opinions concerning Coronado Springs are split. A family from Cumming, Georgia, was disappointed:

The convention center really interferes with a family vacation—everyone we met there was working and wanted to talk about work while we were trying to get away from work!

A Chester, Virginia, mother had a very different experience:

Coronado Springs was absolutely fabulous. The staff was friendly, the kids loved the pool, and we all loved Pepper Market. It was nice and quiet at night. There were many convention guests, but they did not interfere with our trip.

For a family from Kansas City, Kansas, Coronado Springs was their first accommodations in a Disney Moderate resort:

This was the first time we stayed at Coronado Springs. On our previous three trips, we stayed at Pop Century, and I was curious if the Moderate resorts were worth the extra money. At first, the size of the resort was daunting, and having the main building so far away from the rooms was a challenge. But we quickly settled into a routine and figured out the bus routes—for some of the buses, the main building was the last stop, and for other routes, the first. Maybe it was our bad luck, but finding the internal shuttle was like spotting a unicorn! The bus service was really the only major drawback. The room at Coronado was more spacious and came with a ceiling fan. The door separating the living area from the bath vanity was very useful because I was able to get ready in the morning without waking the kids. The kids really enjoyed the pool area, and I thought it was better themed than Pop Century. The size of the resort meant that we had more walking to and from the pool and main areas, but that also meant it felt less crowded. Overall, I thought the resort was worth the price difference.

A family from Indianapolis liked the swimming pools:

The pool at Coronado Springs was excellent—the kids loved the slide! Also utilized smaller pool close to our room—was good for kids to relax before bedtime.

Finally, a Canvey Island, England, reader was fair and balanced:

We stayed at Coronado Springs and were very satisfied overall. The Pepper Market food court was overly complicated (stamping tickets to pay at the end, multiple tickets per party), but the quality was good. The Maya Grill was a disappointment, overpriced for the quality of the food. The walk around the lake on a nice day is a delight.

As convention hotels go, Coronado Springs is kind of an odd duck. Whereas at comparable hotels everything is centrally located and the guest rooms are in close proximity to each other, the rooms here are spread around a huge lake. If you're assigned a room on the opposite side of the lake from the meeting area and restaurants, plan on an 11- to 15-minute hike every time you leave your room. If your organization books Coronado Springs for a meeting, consider having your meals catered—the restaurants simply don't have the capacity during a large convention to accommodate the breakfast rush or to serve a quick lunch between sessions.

GOOD (AND NOT-SO-GOOD) ROOMS AT CORONADO SPRINGS RESORT *(See* tinyurl.com/csr-roomviews *for photos.)* Coronado Springs encircles a large artificial lake called Lago Dorado. In addition to the main building (El Centro), which contains shopping venues, restaurants, and a conference center, there are three communities of accommodations. Moving clockwise around the lake, the Casitas are near the lobby, restaurants, shops, and convention center. Standard-view rooms face parking lots or a courtyard. Water-view rooms cover pools, the lake, and so on. For a good view of Lago Dorado, book one of these rooms:

3220–3287 (except 3224, 3225–3240, 3260–3265, 3266, and 3274–3280)

3320–3383 (except 3324, 3330–3335, 3360–3365, 3374–3380, and 3384–3387)

3420–3487 (except 3424, 3430–3435, 3460–3465, 3474–3479, and 3483–3486)

4461–4464

5202–5212

5303–5304, 5311–5312

5400–5413, 5423–5463 (except 5403–5404, 5411–5412, and 5450)

Next come the Ranchos, set back from the lake. The desert theme translates to lots of cactus and gravel, not much water or shade, and almost no good views. The Ranchos are a hike from everything but the main swimming area. Rooms 6X00–6X04 afford the best views.

Now come the Cabanas, which offer some very nice lake views. Cabana 9B (all Business Class rooms) is our favorite, near restaurants and the convention center, and only a moderate walk to the main pool. Rooms with the best views are 9500–9507, 9528–9543, 9554–9557, 9600–9611, and 9650–9656, with lake views, and 9640–9647, with a view of a small lagoon. Rooms overlooking the lake are subject to some generally tolerable traffic noise.

Other lake-view rooms we recommend include the following:

8129–8131 and 8142–8147

8500–8510, 8550–8553, and 8573 (except 8505, 8507, and 8509)

8600–8610, 8650–8653, and 8673 (except 8605, 8607, and 8609)

9150–9152 and 9253

Disney's All-Star Resorts: Movies, Music, and Sports

(See tinyurl.com/ug-allstars *for extended coverage.)*

STRENGTHS	WEAKNESSES
• Least expensive of the Disney resorts	• Most likely Disney resorts to host large school groups
• Rooms recently refurbished	
• Family suites at All-Star Music are less expensive than those at Art of Animation	• Rooms are small
	• No full-service dining; food courts often overwhelmed at mealtimes
• Convenient parking	
• Lots of pools	• All three resorts share buses during slower times of year; bus stops often crowded
• Lovely landscaping, if you know where to look (Music)	
• In-room pizza delivery	• Perhaps *Fantasia 2000* and *The Mighty Ducks* weren't the best choices to theme two entire sections around?

DISNEY'S ORIGINAL VERSION OF A BUDGET RESORT features three distinct themes executed in the same hyperbolic style. Spread over a vast expanse, the resorts comprise 30 three-story motel-style guest-room buildings. Although the three resorts are neighbors, each has its own lobby, food court, and registration area. All-Star Sports features huge sports equipment: bright football helmets, tennis rackets, and baseball bats—all taller than the buildings they adorn. Similarly, All-Star Music features 40-foot guitars, maracas, and saxophones, while All-Star Movies showcases giant popcorn boxes and icons from Disney films. The food courts were recently refurbished, and all three resorts offer in-room pizza delivery. Lobbies are loud (in both decibels and brightness) and cartoonish, with checkerboard walls and photographs of famous athletes, musicians, or film stars. There's even a photo of Mickey Mouse with Alice Cooper. Each resort has two main pools; Music's are shaped like musical instruments (the Piano Pool and the guitar-shaped Calypso Pool), and one of Movies' is star-shaped. All six pools feature plastic replicas of Disney characters, some shooting water pistols.

At 260 square feet, standard rooms at the All-Star Resorts are very small—the same size as those at Pop Century Resort and slightly smaller than Art of Animation's standard rooms.

unofficial **TIP**
The food courts at Sports and Music were recently overhauled and look fantastic.

All-Star rooms are so small, in fact, that a family of four attempting to stay in one room might redefine *family values* by week's end. Each room has two double beds or one king bed, mini-fridge (no coffeemaker), a separate vanity area, and a table and chairs. Bathrooms have curved shower rods, an improvement. Except for artwork and bathroom wallpaper, all three resorts' rooms are furnished identically. No rooms have balconies.

If you're planning to save for a Disney vacation, you may want to save enough for a bigger room at another resort if space is an important consideration. Also, the All-Stars are the noisiest Disney resorts, though guest rooms are well soundproofed and quiet. We still use a white-noise app on our phones when we stay here, though.

Due to the low staff-to-guest ratio, service is mediocre. Also, there are no full-service restaurants, and the bus ride from the remote All-Stars

All-Star Resorts

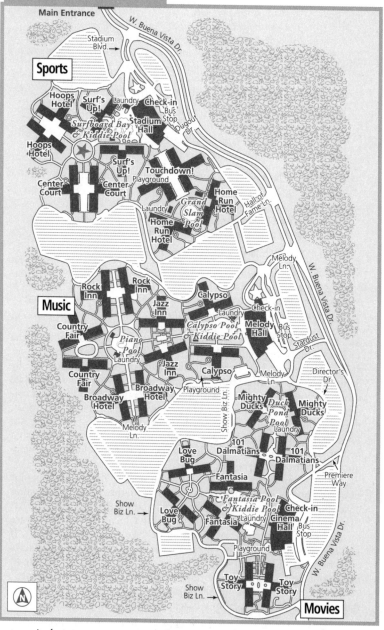

Main Entrance

W. Buena Vista Dr.

Stadium Blvd.

Sports

Hoops Hotel
Surf's Up!
Laundry
Check-in
Bus Stop
Stadium Hall
Dugout Dr.
Surfboard Bay & Kiddie Pool
Hoops Hotel
Surf's Up!
Touchdown!
Playground
Center Court
Center Court
Home Run Hotel
Laundry
Grand Slam Pool
Hall of Fame Ln.
Home Run Hotel

Melody Ln.
W. Buena Vista Dr.

Rock Inn
Rock Inn
Calypso
Check-in
Music
Jazz Inn
Calypso Pool & Kiddie Pool
Melody Hall
Bus Stop
Country Fair
Piano Pool
Stardust Dr.
Laundry
Country Fair
Jazz Inn
Calypso
Melody Ln.
Director's Dr.
Broadway Hotel
Playground
Broadway Hotel
Show Biz Ln.
Mighty Ducks
Duck Pond Pool
Mighty Ducks
Melody Ln.
Laundry
Love Bug
101 Dalmatians
101 Dalmatians
Fantasia
Premiere Way
Show Biz Ln.
Love Bug
Fantasia Pool & Kiddie Pool
Check-in
Laundry
Cinema Hall
Fantasia
Bus Stop
Playground
W. Buena Vista Dr.
Show Biz Ln.
Toy Story
Toy Story
Movies

to a sit-down restaurant at another resort is about 45 minutes one-way (there is, however, a McDonald's about a quarter-mile away). Bus service to the theme and water parks is pretty efficient. Walking time to the bus stop from the most remote guest rooms is about 8 minutes.

We receive a lot of letters commenting on the All-Star Resorts. From a family group of 13 from East Greenbush, New York:

The All-Star Resorts are perfectly family-oriented. Some nice touches that were not mentioned in your guide—a small amphitheater set up in the lobby to occupy the kids while you check in, and soft sidewalk material surrounding the kiddie pool. And the playground has two separate jungle gyms—one for older kids and one for younger kids.

A Baltimore family had a similarly positive experience:

We were pleasantly surprised by All-Star Movies. Yes, the rooms are small, but the overall magic there is amazing. The lobby played Disney movies, which is perfect if you get up early and the buses aren't running yet. Customer service was impeccable.

A Canadian family had a not-so-positive experience:

The guide didn't prepare us for the large groups of students who take over the resorts. They're very noisy and very pushy when it comes to getting on buses. Our scariest experience was when we tried getting on a bus and got mobbed by about 100 students.

From a Massachusetts family of four:

I would never recommend the All-Star for a family. It was like dormitory living. Our room was a long hike from the bus stop, and it was tiny—you needed to step into the bathroom, shut the door, then step around the toilet that blocked half the tub.

ALL-STAR MUSIC FAMILY SUITES In the Jazz and Calypso Buildings, the 192 suites measure roughly 520 square feet, slightly larger than the cabins at Fort Wilderness but slightly smaller than Art of Animation's Family Suites. Each suite, formed from the combination of two formerly separate rooms, includes a kitchenette with mini-refrigerator, microwave, and coffeemaker. Sleeping accommodations include a queen bed in the bedroom, plus a pullout sleeper sofa, a chair bed, and an ottoman bed. We're not sure we'd let adult friends (ones we want to keep, anyway) on the sofa bed or the chair or ottoman beds, but they're fine for children. A hefty door separates the two rooms.

The All-Star Music Family Suites also feature flat-panel TVs plus two bathrooms—one more than the Fort Wilderness cabins. The suites cost about 25% less than the cabins and about 20% less than the Art of Animation Family Suites, but they don't have the kitchen space or appliances to prepare anything more than rudimentary meals. If you're trying to save money by eating in your room, the cabins are your best bet. If you just want a little extra space and somewhere to nuke your Pop-Tarts in the morning, the All-Star suites are just fine.

Reader comments about the family suites are generally positive, though measured. First, from a North Carolina family of five:

It was so nice to have a place to unwind without the kids at night, along with two bathrooms and extra space for breakfast/snacks/drinks in the kitchen area. My only issue was that we weren't comfortable leaving the kids on the foldouts because they're right next to the front door, plus my husband and I didn't want to be confined

*to the bedroom from the time we put the kids to bed, so we slept on
a foldout. The first night was hell, but the second night we took the
mattresses off the pullout chair and ottoman and put them on top of
the mattress on the couch—MUCH better!*

From a Skokie, Illinois, family of five:

*We found the All-Star Music Family Suite to be very roomy for the
six of us. Our teenagers and preteen were quite comfortable on the
pullout sofa, chair, and ottoman. Having the two bathrooms was a
must, and the kitchen area was great; lots of shelf space for the food
we had delivered from Garden Grocer (they're excellent, by the way)
[see page 512]. Our only complaint is that from 7:30 a.m. until midnight there's always music playing—it can get annoying to always
have that beat going in the background. The rooms are soundproofed
but not enough; had to use earplugs.*

GOOD (AND NOT-SO-GOOD) ROOMS AT THE ALL-STAR RESORTS *(See*
tinyurl.com/asmo-roomviews, tinyurl.com/asmu-roomviews, *and* tiny
url.com/assp-roomviews *for photos.)* Although the layouts of All-Star
Resorts' Movies, Music, and Sports sections are different, the buildings
are identical three-story, three-winged structures. The T-shaped buildings are further grouped into pairs, generally facing each other, and
share a common subtheme. For example, there's a Toy Story pair in the
Movies section. In addition to being named by theme, such as *Fantasia,*
buildings are numbered 1–10 in each section. Rooms are accessed via a
motel-style outdoor walkway, but each building has an elevator.

Parking is plentiful, all of it in sprawling lots buffering the three
sections. A room near a parking lot means easier loading and unloading but also unsightly views of the lot during
your stay. The resort offers a luggage service,
but it often takes up to an hour for your bags
to arrive.

To avoid a parking-lot vista, request a
room facing a courtyard or pool. The trade-off
is noise. The sound of cars starting in the parking lot is no match for shrieking children or
hooting teenagers in the pool. But don't count
on a good view of the pool, even if your room faces it. The buildings'
themed facade decorations are placed on their widest face—the top
of the T—which is also the side facing the pool or courtyard. In some
cases, as with the surfboards in the Sports section, these significantly
obstruct the view. Floodlights are also trained on these facades, so if
you step out of your room at night to view the action below, looking
down may result in temporary blindness.

*un**official* **TIP**
Music 5654 may be the best
room at the All-Star Resorts.
This third-floor corner room
overlooks a small pond in a
wooded area behind the resort.
See tinyurl.com/music5654
for a photo of the view.

The sort of traveler you are should dictate the room you request.
If you choose an All-Star Resort because you'd rather spend time and
money at the parks, book a room near the bus stop, your link to the rest
of the World. Note that buses leave from the central public buildings of
each section, which are near the larger, noisier pools. If you're planning
to return to your room for an afternoon nap, request a room farther
from the pools. Also consider an upper-story room to minimize foot

traffic past your door. On the other hand, if you choose All-Star for its kid-friendly aspects, consider roosting near the action. A bottom-floor room provides easy pool access, and a room looking out on a courtyard or pool allows you to keep an eye on children playing outside.

For travelers without young children (infants excluded), the best bets for privacy and quiet are buildings that overlook the forest behind the resort, Buildings 2 and 3 in All-Star Sports and 5 and 6 in All-Star Music. Interior-facing rooms in these buildings (and their partners) also fill the bill because they overlook courtyards farthest from the large pools. The courtyards vary with theme but are generally only mildly amusing.

If you're traveling with children, opt for a section and building with a theme that appeals to your kids. Often, that will be a film, but it might be a sport. If you're staying in Home Run Hotel, don't forget the ball and gloves to maximize the experience (just keep games of catch away from the pool). Older elementary- and middle-school children probably will want to spend hotel time in or near the bigger pools. Periodically, cadres of teenagers—too cool for their younger siblings— effectively commandeer the smaller secondary pools. Playgrounds are tucked behind Building 9 in All-Star Music and behind Building 6 in All-Star Sports. Rooms facing these are ideal for families with children too young or timid for the often-chaotic larger pools. In All-Star Movies, the playground is nearer to the food court than to any rooms.

The following tip from a former All-Star Resorts cast member from Fayetteville, Georgia, illustrates just how big these resorts are:

Rooms at the far end of the Mighty Ducks building of All-Star Movies are closer to the All-Star Music food court, pool, and buses than to All-Star Movies' own facilities. Follow the walkway from the Ducks building north to All-Star Music's Melody Hall.

Disney's Pop Century Resort

(See tinyurl.com/ug-popcentury *for extended coverage.*)

STRENGTHS	WEAKNESSES
• Theming is fun for anyone over 35	• Theming may be lost on kids and teens
• Our favorite pool bar of the Value resorts	• Small rooms that are the same size as All-Stars' but slightly more expensive
• One bus stop	• Bus stops at theme parks are a long distance from park entrances
• Walking trail around Hour Glass Lake and connecting bridge to Art of Animation	
• Queen beds in refurbished rooms	
• Convenient parking	

ON VICTORY WAY near the ESPN Wide World of Sports Complex is Pop Century Resort. Originally designed to be completed in phases, the resort opened its first section in 2004. The second phase was canceled in favor of a new Value resort, Disney's Art of Animation (see page 227).

Pop Century is a near-clone of the All-Star Resorts; that is, it consists of four-story, motel-style buildings built around a central pool, food court, and registration area. Decorative touches make the difference. Where the All-Star Resorts display larger-than-life icons from

Pop Century Resort & Art of Animation Resort

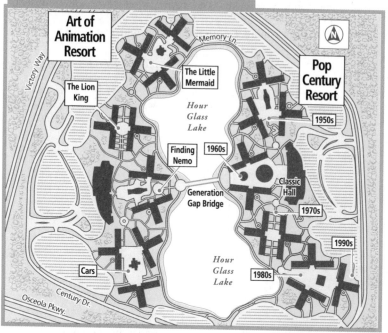

sports, music, and movies, and Art of Animation is inspired by Disney cartoons, Pop Century draws its icons from decades of the 20th century and their attendant popular culture: building-sized Big Wheels, hula hoops, and the like, punctuated by silhouettes of people doing the jitterbug and the twist.

The public areas at Pop Century Resort are marginally more sophisticated than the ones at the All-Star Resorts, with 20th-century period furniture and decor rolled up in a saccharine "those were the days" theme. A food court, a bar, a playground, pools, and so on emulate the All-Star Resorts model in size and location. A Pop Century departure from the All-Star precedent has merchandise retailers thrown in with the fast-food concessions in a combination dining-and-shopping area. This apparently is what happens when a giant corporation tries to combine selling pizza with hawking Goofy hats. (You just know the word *synergy* was used like cheap cologne in those design meetings.) As at the All-Star Resorts and Art of Animation, there's no full-service restaurant. The resort is connected to the rest of Walt Disney World by bus, but because of the limited dining options, we recommend having a car.

Running $118–$225 per night, guest rooms at Pop Century are small at 260 square feet. The decor is upbeat, with white bedspreads and blue walls. Wall art depicts pop memorabilia from decades past. Cherry-finish wood-inlaid furniture and blue-and-tan-patterned carpet provide an upscale touch, but these are not rooms you'd want to spend a lot of time in. Bathrooms are tiny and counter space a scarce commodity. Worst of all, we've received many complaints from readers that the soundproofing between rooms is inadequate. A lake separating Pop Century from the Art of Animation Resort offers water views not available at the All-Star Resorts.

A reader from Dublin, Georgia, thinks we underrate Pop:

I can't believe you don't like Pop Century. (1) There's a lake at a Value resort and a view of fireworks. (2) The courtyards have Twister games and neat pools for little children. (3) Pop's dinner entrées are among the best bargains and the best food anywhere. (4) The layout is convenient to the food court. (5) Bus transportation is better than anywhere else, including Grand Floridian! (6) Where else do the cast members do the shag to oldies?

But a Springfield, Illinois, dad gives Pop Century a mixed review:

We wanted something different from All-Star Movies, so we gave Pop Century a shot. Believe the noise complaints—they're true. It's like the walls were made of papier-mâché. Although the bus service was great and the pool (and splash pools) were nice for a Value resort, we'll be back at All-Star Movies the next time around.

A family from Spartanburg, South Carolina, was also disturbed by the noise:

The resort itself was great, but it was hard to actually nap when we came back to the resort each afternoon due to music and games on the loudspeakers. Do not face the 1960s pool if you want some R&R.

A hungry Schnecksville, Pennsylvania, reader thought the best thing about Pop Century was the Art of Animation (AOA) Resort next door:

We stayed at Pop but found our access to AOA to be invaluable. The AOA food court was by far superior to Pop's—it had separate lines at individual stations for things like make-your-own burgers or pasta bowls. At Pop, there were no separate lines like this, and the station with burgers, nuggets, and fries was always busy. Also, to get a grilled cheese, you had to get your bread from the bakery, take it to the hamburger line, and ask them to make you a grilled cheese.

A 40-something Florida mom loves Pop Century but highlights its deficiencies:

I was very, very happy with our experiences and pleasantly surprised they weren't as bad as you make them sound. For the money, the benefits far outweigh the fact that the rooms are uninspired. They're clean, you get bus service, and there is a food court open almost all the time, as well as an awesome arcade and nice pools. Yes, the pools are not that great, but if the pools were really nice, our kids wouldn't want to leave for the parks (LOL), so that's actually a plus for me. We don't want to be paying for resort services we won't have time to use.

In late spring 2017, we saw Disney hard at work remodeling all of the rooms in Building 8 to a new style. It starts from the ground up, literally: The carpet is replaced with a modern hardwood-floor look. The modern touches extend throughout the room. One feature we love is that the second bed in the room is a fold-down option, as at Art of Animation. When the bed isn't in use, it disappears into the wall, freeing up floor space (and turning into a desk). The bulky armoire–television stand is replaced by built-in shelving and a wall-mounted monitor. The bathroom overhaul is stylish and efficient, with lots more shelf space, plenty of storage, and a modern shower. We hope this spreads like kudzu across Disney's Value resorts.

GOOD (AND NOT-SO-GOOD) ROOMS AT POP CENTURY RESORT *(See* tinyurl.com/pop-roomviews *for photos.)* The best rooms for both view and convenience are the lake-view rooms in Buildings 4 and 5, representing the 1960s. Another option, though with a less compelling view, would be rooms in the same building facing east, toward the registration and food-court building. Next-best choices would be the east-facing rooms of Building 3 in the 1950s, and of Building 6 in the 1970s. Avoid south-facing rooms in 1980s Building 7 and 1990s Building 8. Both are echo chambers for noise from nearby Osceola Parkway. Finally, so-called preferred rooms at Pop Century, which are closer to the main pool and lobby, cost about $7–$17 more than others. They're definitely closer, but they probably save only 5 minutes of walking per day and subject you to more noise from guests walking past your room. We don't think these rooms are worth the extra cost. Finally, note that guest rooms don't have private patios or balconies.

Disney's Art of Animation Resort *(see map on page 225)*
(See tinyurl.com/ug-artofanimation *for extended coverage.)*

STRENGTHS	WEAKNESSES
• Exceptional theming, particularly *Cars* and *Lion King* areas	• Most expensive Value resort
• Best pool of the Value resorts	• Terrible in-room mobile reception
• Landscape of Flavors food court is an *Unofficial Guide* favorite	• The number of made-to-order meals at the food court can mean long waits in line
• Family Suites are innovatively designed and themed	• The resort's Family Suites are rarely discounted
• Interior hallways in some buildings	• Poor soundproofing
• Walking trail around Hour Glass Lake and connecting bridge to Pop Century	
• Just one bus stop	

OPENED IN MAY 2012, Disney's Art of Animation is a Value resort across Hour Glass Lake from Pop Century. It was originally designed to be part of Pop Century and represent the years 1900–1949, but recessions and a then-abundance of hotel capacity prevented Disney from ever completing construction. When the time came for a new Value resort, Disney switched the theme to its animated movies, which still fit in well with the pop-culture motif across the lake.

As at Pop Century, Art of Animation's standard rooms are housed in four-story buildings and exterior-facing walkups, with a series of themed swimming pools and a food court. However, the majority of the resort's accommodations are suites similar to those at Disney's All-Star Music Resort. All told, there are 864 standard rooms and 1,120 suites. The suites have interior hallways to the guest rooms instead of the exterior walkways found at Disney's other Value resorts.

Art of Animation's suites are around 565 square feet, about what you'd get by combining two standard rooms into one suite. Each suite has a master bedroom, a living room, two full bathrooms, and a kitchenette with mini-fridge, microwave, and coffeemaker. Sleeping accommodations include a queen bed in the bedroom, a sleeper sofa, and a living-room table that converts into a full-size bed. The bedroom and living room have flat-panel TVs.

Slightly larger than comparable rooms at other Value resorts, standard rooms are 277 square feet and include one king or two double beds, a flat-panel TV, a mini-fridge, and a table and chairs.

The theming incorporates characters from four Disney films: *Cars, Finding Nemo, The Lion King,* and *The Little Mermaid.* All but the *Little Mermaid*–themed rooms are suites. As at Pop Century, large, colorful icons stand in the middle of each group of buildings; here, though, they represent film characters rather than pop-culture touchstones. An interesting departure from the other Value resorts is the outside paint schemes: Rather than using pastels, Disney has decorated the exteriors with giant murals stretching the length of each structure. The *Cars* buildings, for example, each display a four-story panoramic vista of the American desert, with the movie's iconic characters in the middle, while the *Lion King* buildings capture a single verdant jungle scene. It's a great idea.

Three of the four sets of themed buildings have pools; the *Lion King* complex has a playground instead. Like the other Value resorts, Art of Animation has a central building—here called Animation Hall—for check-in and bus transportation; it also holds the resort's food court, Landscape of Flavors; a gift shop; and a video-game arcade.

Speaking of check-in, the wall behind the front desk is a dazzling rainbow of colors from floor to ceiling. In sharp contrast to the faded paints and photos at, say, the All-Stars, Art of Animation's backlight displays and wall art are bright and vibrant and should stand up well to Florida's weather.

Most comments concerning Art of Animation have been positive. A Collingswood, New Jersey, reader says:

> Art of Animation I was skeptical about. From pics it looked like it was going to be a child's dream but not necessarily an adult's. I was wrong—it's incredible! For a Value resort, it feels more like a Deluxe. The room was awesome; great layout and having two bathrooms was so nice. The Big Blue Pool and the Cozy Cone Pool are great. Landscape of Flavors impressed me too—so many options for fresh, delicious, comfort food as well as exotic fare.

Readers complain, however, about the long walk from the *Little Mermaid*–themed buildings to the food court and front desk. Mobile reception was also singled out as a problem. A woman from Houston related the following:

There was no AT&T service inside the building where our rooms were. There was plenty of service outside the building, but the moment we stepped inside it was like a vacuum. It was very upsetting.

Noise and soundproofing are likewise issues. A Guyton, Georgia, mom comments:

The room was very poorly soundproofed. I heard snoring and bathroom noises from other rooms that I should not have been able to hear. One afternoon my toddler and I returned to the room for a nap—I suppose housekeeping was cleaning the room above ours, but it sounded like someone was bowling up there.

GOOD (AND NOT-SO-GOOD) ROOMS AT ART OF ANIMATION The quietest suites are south- and east-facing rooms in Buildings 3 (*Cars*), 4 (*Finding Nemo*), and 6 (*The Lion King*). The quietest standard rooms are east-facing rooms in Building 8 and south-facing rooms in Building 7 (both *The Little Mermaid*). Avoid northwest-facing rooms in Building 1 and southwest-facing rooms in Building 10, which face the Disney bus route and Art of Animation's bus stops.

INDEPENDENT HOTELS OF THE DISNEY SPRINGS RESORT AREA

THE SEVEN HOTELS of the Disney Springs Resort Area (DSRA) were created back when Disney had far fewer of its own resorts. The hotels—the **Best Western Lake Buena Vista Resort Hotel, B Resort & Spa, DoubleTree Suites by Hilton Orlando,** the **Hilton Orlando Buena Vista Palace,** the **Hilton Orlando Lake Buena Vista,** the **Holiday Inn in the Walt Disney World Resort,** and **Wyndham Lake Buena Vista Resort**—are chain affairs with minimal or nonexistent theming, though the Hilton Orlando Buena Vista Palace is fairly upscale. Several of the larger properties have shifted their focus to convention and business travelers.

The main advantage to staying in the DSRA is being in Disney World and next to Disney Springs. Guests at the Hilton, Wyndham Lake Buena Vista Resort, Buena Vista Palace, and Holiday Inn are an easy 5- to 15-minute walk from the Marketplace on the east side of Disney Springs. Guests at B Resort & Spa, the Best Western Lake Buena Vista, and DoubleTree Suites are about 10 minutes farther by foot. Disney transportation can be accessed at Disney Springs, though the buses take a notoriously long time to leave due to the number of stops throughout the complex. Although all DSRA hotels offer shuttle buses to the theme parks, the service is provided by private contractors and is somewhat inferior to Disney transportation in frequency of service, number of buses, and hours of operation. Get firm details in advance about shuttle service from any DSRA hotel you're considering. All these hotels are easily accessible by car and are only marginally farther from the Disney parks than several of the Disney resorts; DSRA hotels are also quite close to Typhoon Lagoon water park.

DSRA hotels, even the business- and convention-focused ones, try to appeal to families. Some have pool complexes rivaling those at any Disney resort, whereas others offer a food court or all-suite rooms. A few sponsor character meals and organized kids' activities; all have counters for buying Disney tickets, and most have Disney gift shops.

AMENITIES AT THE DSRA RESORTS					
HOTEL	CHILDREN'S PROGRAMS	DINING	KID-FRIENDLY	POOL(S)	RECREATION
Best Western LBV Resort	None	★★½	★★★	★★½	★★
B Resort & Spa	None	★★★½	★★½	★★½	★★★
DoubleTree Suites	None	★★	★★★	★★½	★★½
Hilton Orlando BV Palace	★★★★	★★	★★★½	★★★½	★★★★
Hilton Orlando LBV	None	★★½	★★½	★★★	★★½
Holiday Inn WDW Resort	None	★★	★★	★★★	★★
Wyndham LBV Resort	★★½	★★½	★★★	★★★	★★★

A Difficult Value Proposition

With the exception of the B Resort & Spa, we find it difficult to recommend these hotels. The rooms at many are in need of refurbishment. Further, for much of the year there's little price difference between these rooms and those at Disney's Value resorts, especially when Disney offers discounts. If you're driving, note that the traffic near Disney Springs is an absolute gridlock throughout the evening, too.

ADDITIONAL FEES AT THE DSRA RESORTS				
HOTEL	SELF-PARKING	RESORT FEE	INTERNET	TOTAL PER DAY
Best Western LBV Resort	$8	$14	Free	$22
B Resort & Spa	$20	$28	Free	$48
Doubletree Suites	$20	None	$10	$30
Hilton Orlando BV Palace	Free	$25	Free	$25
Hilton Orlando LBV	$17	$24	Free	$41
Holiday Inn WDW Resort	$12	None	Free	$12
Wyndham LBV Resort	$8	$18	Free	$26

Speaking of prices, all of the DSRA resorts tack on daily charges for self-parking, Internet access, or some cockamamy "resort fee." These fees add $12–$48 per night to your stay, plus tax.

Heaven knows Disney's Deluxe resorts are overpriced, but it's hard to see how any DSRA property can compete with the value proposition of Disney's inexpensive hotels, which offer free airport transportation, better bus service, free parking, and extra time at the theme parks. We suspect most readers who choose the DSRA resorts do so either because they've earned enough rewards points to qualify for a free stay or the Disney resorts are sold out. We'd be hard-pressed to think of another reason to stay at these hotels, especially if we had a car.

Descriptions of each DSRA resort follow. Also take a peek at the combined website for the DSRA hotels at disneyspringshotels.com. Finally, check the comparative charts above.

B Resort & Spa ★★★½

LOCATED WITHIN WALKING DISTANCE of shops and restaurants and situated 5 miles or less from the Disney parks, the 394-room B Resort & Spa targets couples, families, groups, and business travelers.

1905 Hotel Plaza Blvd.
☎ 407-828-2828 or
866-759-6832
tinyurl.com/bresortlbv

Decorated in cool blues, whites, and grays, guest rooms and suites afford views of downtown Orlando, area lakes, and theme parks. Along with B Resorts–exclusive Blissful Beds, each room is outfitted with sleek modern furnishings and a large interactive flat-screen TV. Additional touches include a mini-fridge and gaming consoles (available on request). Some rooms are also equipped with bunk beds, kitchenettes, or wet bars.

Our most recent stay at B Resort was in early 2015, and we enjoyed it quite a bit. Our standard room was spotlessly clean, and the room decor is fun without being faddish. The bathroom is spacious, with plenty of storage. The glass shower is well designed and has good water pressure. There's absolutely nothing wrong with this hotel at this price point, except for the terrible traffic you have to endure every night because of Disney Springs. And that's a shame because it's not the hotel's doing. If the B were on the other side of Disney Springs, we'd gladly stay here again.

A mom from Tennessee also likes the B Resort, especially when it's on sale:

The vibe of the B Resort was great—like a knockoff of the W, very bright and modern. The restaurant was great, and the zero-entry pool was good. The resort has a more adult feel, but I never felt out of place with my son. I found a deal on Orbitz for around $310 for three nights, with taxes and fees. If choosing between the B and Pop Century for a short stay, I'd take the B Resort hands-down.

Amenities include free Wi-Fi, a spa, a beauty salon, and a fitness center. The main restaurant, American Kitchen, serves a modern upscale take on classic comfort food in regional styles. Guests can also choose from a poolside bar and grill; The Pickup, a grab-and-go shop off the lobby that serves breakfasts, snacks, picnic lunches, and ice cream; and 24/7 in-room dining.

Other perks: a zero-entry pool with interactive water features; a kids' area; loaner iPads; Monscierge, a touchscreen concierge and destination guide in the lobby; and more than 25,000 square feet of meeting and multiuse space. Though not served by Disney transportation, B Resort provides bus service to the parks and other Disney venues. A resort fee of $28 per day applies.

Best Western Lake Buena Vista Resort Hotel ★★★

THE 18-STORY, 325-ROOM Best Western Lake Buena Vista has relatively few of the extras common to most other DSRA properties. The rooms are dull. Parking is a hike from many rooms, and to get to them you pass through hallways and areas that could use a good scrubbing. The most surprising thing was the attitude of general indifference from several of the staff when we needed help checking in.

2000 Hotel Plaza Blvd.
☎ 407-828-2424 or
800-348-3765
lakebuenavista
resorthotel.com

A breakfast buffet and dinner service of American fare are available in the Trader's Island Grill, while the Marketplace offers sandwiches and snacks. The poolside Flamingo Cove Lounge provides its own menu of pub standards as well as alcoholic refreshment. The pool is small though pleasantly landscaped, and there's a kiddie pool as well. Other amenities include a fitness room and game room. Although there are no organized children's programs, the resort can arrange child care.

DoubleTree Suites by Hilton Orlando   ★★★½

2305 Hotel Plaza Blvd.
☎ 407-934-1000
doubletreeguestsuites.com

THIS GIANT WHITE BUNKER of a hotel is the only all-suite establishment on Disney property. What it lacks in atmosphere and creative attributes, it makes up for in convenience and comfort. Within walking distance of Disney Springs, the 229 suites are spacious for a family, although the decor is startling, with no apparent theme. No rooms have balconies, though ground floors offer patios.

Amenities include a safe, hair dryer, refrigerator, microwave, coffeepot, fold-out bed, and two TVs (bedroom and living room).

Children will enjoy their own check-in desk, the free chocolate-chip cookie, and the small playground. The heated pool, children's pool, and whirlpool spa are moderate in size; a minus is that traffic noise from Interstate 4 can be heard faintly from the pool deck. The tiny fitness center (more like a fitness closet), pool table, four tennis courts, and outdoor bar are adjacent to the pool. High-speed Internet and a business center in the lobby are convenient for those on working holidays. The Market (open 7 a.m.–midnight) offers groceries, drinks, ice cream, and sundaes for those late-night munchies; the EverGreen Cafe serves breakfast, lunch, and dinner. Babysitting is available.

Hilton Orlando Buena Vista Palace   ★★★½

1900 E. Buena Vista Dr.
Lake Buena Vista
☎ 407-827-2727 or
866-397-6516
buenavistapalace.com

NOTE: *The Buena Vista Palace underwent a major renovation in late 2016 after it was bought by Hilton. Look for an updated profile in the e-book version of the* Guide.

The Hilton Orlando Buena Vista Palace is upscale and convenient. Surrounded by an artificial lake and plenty of palms, the spacious pool area comprises three heated pools, the largest of which is partially covered; a whirlpool and sauna; a basketball court; and a sand volleyball court. A pool concierge will fetch your favorite magazine or fruity drink. On Sunday, the resort hosts a character breakfast with Disney friends (extra costs apply). The 897 guest rooms are posh and spacious; each comes with desk, coffeemaker, hair dryer, satellite TV with pay-per-view movies, iron and board, and mini-fridge. There are also 117 suites. In-room babysitting is available. One lighted tennis court, a fitness center, an arcade, and a playground round out amenities. Two restaurants and a mini-market are on-site. *Note:* All these amenities and services come at a price—a $25-per-night resort fee will be added to your bill.

Hilton Orlando Lake Buena Vista   ★★★★

1751 Hotel Plaza Blvd.
☎ 407-827-4000
hilton-wdwv.com

ALTHOUGH THE HILTON'S resort fees are outrageous and the decor is dated, the rooms are comfortable and nicer than some others in the DSRA. On-site dining includes Covington Mill Restaurant, offering sandwiches and pasta; Andiamo, an Italian bistro; and Benihana, part of the Japanese steakhouse–sushi bar chain. Covington Mill hosts a Disney-character breakfast on Sundays. The two pools are matched with a children's spray pool and a 24-hour fitness center. An exercise room and a game room are on-site, as is a 24-hour market. Babysitting is available, but there are no organized children's programs.

A Denver family of five found the Hilton's shuttle service lacking:

> The transportation, provided by a company called Mears, was unreliable. They did a better job of getting guests back to the hotel from the park than getting them to the park from the hotel. Shuttles from the hotel were randomly timed and went repeatedly to the same parks—skipping others and leaving guests to wait for up to an hour.

Holiday Inn in the Walt Disney World Resort ★★★½

COMPLETELY RENOVATED IN 2010, the Holiday Inn is modern and comfortable. The layout remains the same, with tower rooms grouped around an atrium and wing rooms overlooking the pool. The feel of the hotel is modern and contemporary yet relaxed and comfortable. Disney Springs is just a short walk away.

1805 Hotel Plaza Blvd.
☎ 407-828-8888
or 888-465-4329
hiorlando.com

The totally upgraded rooms feature pillow-top beds with triple sheeting and firm or soft pillows. Each room has a 32-inch flat-panel HDTV and free high-speed Internet. The bathrooms are clean and well designed—the nicest in any DSRA resort. Amenities include granite countertops and showerheads with a choice of comfort sprays.

The Palm Breezes Restaurant and Bar serves breakfast, lunch, and dinner at reasonable prices. A breakfast buffet is available, as well as à la carte items. The Grab n Go Outlet in the lobby offers quick snacks and sandwiches. Other amenities include a large and well-kept zero-entry pool, along with a Jacuzzi in the pool area. A separate entrance brings you into the convention center, ballroom, and meeting room areas, with a business center nearby.

Wyndham Lake Buena Vista Resort   ★★★½

THE MAIN REASON TO STAY at the Wyndham is the short walk to Disney Springs. The lobby is bright and airy and check-in service friendly. Rooms are larger than most and have in-room refrigerators. Pool-facing rooms in the hotel's wings have exterior hallways that overlook the pool

1850 Hotel Plaza Blvd.
☎ 407-828-4444
wyndhamlakebuena
vista.com

and center courtyard; these hallways can be noisy during summer months. Elevators are available, but they're unusually slow—it's probably faster to walk to the second and third floors, assuming you're up for the exercise. Disney-character breakfasts take place on Tuesdays, Thursdays, and Saturdays at LakeView Restaurant.

CAMPING AT WALT DISNEY WORLD

DISNEY'S FORT WILDERNESS RESORT & CAMPGROUND is a spacious area for tent and RV camping. Fully equipped, air-conditioned prefabricated log cabins are also available for rent.

Tent/Pop-Up campsites provide water, electricity, and cable TV and run $58–$124 a night depending on season. **Full Hook-Up** campsites have all the previous amenities, accommodate large RVs, and run $78–$146 per night. **Preferred Hook-Up** campsites for tents and RVs add sewer connections and run $91–$162 per night. **Premium** campsites add an extra-large concrete parking pad and run $97–$170 a night.

All sites are level and provide picnic tables, waste containers, grills, and free Wi-Fi. Fires are prohibited except in the grills. Pets are permitted in some Premium and Preferred loops.

Campsites are arranged on loops accessible from one of three main roads. There are 28 loops, with Loops 100–2100 for tent and RV campers and Loops 2200–2800 offering cabins at $336–$568 per night. RV sites are roomy by eastern-US standards, with the Premium and Full Hook-Up campsites able to accommodate RVs more than 45 feet long, but tent campers will probably feel a bit cramped. (Note that tent stakes cannot be put into the concrete at the Premium sites.) On any given day, 90% or more of campers are RVers.

Fort Wilderness offers arguably the most recreational facilities and activities of any Disney resort. Among them are two video arcades; nightly campfire programs; Disney movies; a dinner theater; two swimming pools; a beach; walking paths; bike, boat, canoe, golf-cart, and water-ski rentals; horseback riding; wagon rides; and tennis, basketball, and volleyball courts. There are two convenience stores, a restaurant, and a tavern. Comfort stations with toilets, showers, pay phones, ice machine, and laundry facilities are within walking distance of all campsites.

If you're in the mood to walk, look for the path near Pioneer Hall that leads to the Wilderness Lodge area. This flat, paved walkway is about 0.75 mile long and is a great place to see live deer and other woodland creatures. It also provides easy access to the dining opportunities at the Wilderness Lodge, great if you're looking to branch out from the options at the Fort but don't want to deal with the vagaries of the Disney transportation system.

Access to the Magic Kingdom is by boat from Fort Wilderness Landing and to Epcot by bus, with a transfer at the Transportation and Ticket Center (TTC) to the Epcot monorail. Boat service may be suspended during thunderstorms, in which case Disney will provide buses. An alternate route to the Magic Kingdom is by internal bus to the TTC, then by monorail or ferry to the park. Transportation to all other Disney destinations is by bus. Motor traffic within the campground is permitted only when entering or exiting. Get around within the campground by bus, golf cart, or bike, the latter two available for rent.

For tent and RV campers, there's a fairly stark trade-off between sites convenient to pools, restaurant, trading posts, and other amenities, and those that are most scenic, shady, and quiet. RVers who prefer to be near guest services, the marina, the beach, and the restaurant and tavern should go for Loops 100, 200, 700, and 400 (in that order). Loops near the campground's secondary facility area with pool, trading post, bike and golf-cart rentals, and campfire program are 1400, 1300, 600, 1000, and 1500, in order of preference. If you're looking for a tranquil, scenic setting among mature trees, we recommend Loops 1800, 1900, 1700, and 1600, in that order, and the backside sites on the 700 loop. The best loop of all, and the only one to offer both a lovely setting and proximity to key amenities, is Loop 300. The best loops for tents and pop-up campers are 1500 and 2000, with 1500 being nearest a pool, a convenience store, and the campfire program.

With the exception of Loops 1800 and 1900, avoid sites within 40 yards of the loop entrance. These sites are almost always flanked by one of the main traffic arteries within Fort Wilderness. Further, sites on the outside of the loop are almost always preferable to those in the center of the loop. RVers should be forewarned that all sites are back-ins and that although most sites will accommodate large rigs, the loop access roads are pretty tight and narrow.

Fort Wilderness Cabins

STRENGTHS	WEAKNESSES
• Informality	• Isolated location
• Children's play areas	• Complicated bus service
• Best recreational options at WDW	• Confusing campground layout
• Special day and evening programs	• Lack of privacy
• Campsite amenities	• Very limited on-site dining options
• Shower and toilet facilities	• Crowding at beaches and pools
• *Hoop-Dee-Doo Musical Revue* show	• Small baths in cabins
• Convenient self-parking	• Extreme distance to store and restaurant facilities from many campsites
• Off-site dining via boat at the Magic Kingdom	

Rental cabins offer a double bed and two bunk beds in the only bedroom, augmented by a lightly-padded pullout sofa bed in the living room. There's one rather small bathroom with shower and tub.

The prefab log cabins (classified as Moderate resorts in the Disney hierarchy) are warm and homey, but the stem-to-stern interior wood paneling and smallish windows make for rather dark accommodations at night. Neither the lighting fixtures provided nor the wattage of their bulbs is up to the job of lighting the cabins once the sun goes down.

All cabins offer air-conditioning, televisions with DVD players and/or VCRs, fully equipped kitchens, and dining tables. Housekeeping is provided daily. Most readers are crazy about the cabins. Some representative comments follow. A Wappingers Falls, New York, family writes:

> We stayed at Fort Wilderness in a cabin because (1) we wanted a separate bedroom area; (2) we wanted a kitchen; (3) our kids are very lively, and the cabins were apart from each other so we wouldn't disturb other guests; and (4) we thought the kids might meet other children to play with. The cabins worked out just right for us. The kids had a ball chasing the little lizards and frogs, kicking around pinecones, sitting on the deck to eat ice pops, and sleeping in bunk beds.

A mother of two from Albuquerque, New Mexico, offers this:

> We stayed in a cabin and liked having all the space and the full kitchen. However, the pool nearest our cabin (a quarter-mile away!) never even had a lifeguard. I had hoped to be able to send the kids to

Continued on page 238

Fort Wilderness Resort & Campground

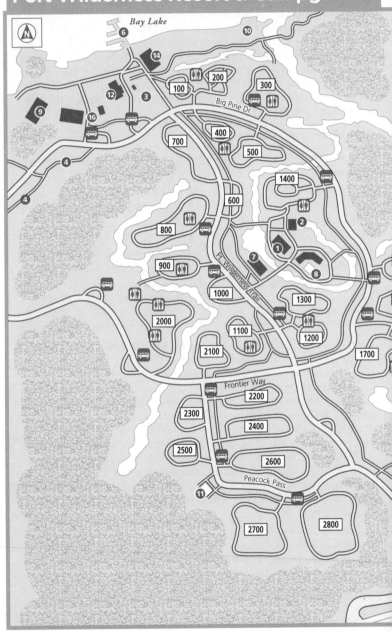

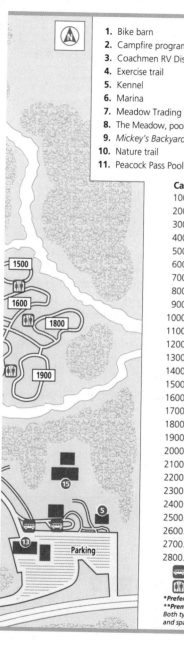

1. Bike barn
2. Campfire program
3. Coachmen RV Display
4. Exercise trail
5. Kennel
6. Marina
7. Meadow Trading Post
8. The Meadow, pool, and tennis courts
9. *Mickey's Backyard BBQ*
10. Nature trail
11. Peacock Pass Pool
12. Pioneer Hall
    Crockett's Tavern
    Guest Services
    Hoop-Dee-Doo
      Musical Revue
    Trail's End Restaurant
13. Reception Outpost
14. Settlement Trading Post
15. Tri-Circle-D Livery
    (horseback riding)
16. Tri-Circle-D Ranch

Campsite Loops
100. Bay Tree Lake*
200. Palmetto Path*
300. Cypress Knee Circle*
400. Whispering Pine Way**
500. Buffalo Bend**
600. Sunny Sage Way**
700. Cinnamon Fern Way**
800. Jack Rabbit Run**
900. Quail Trail**
1000. Raccoon Lane**
1100. Possum Path**
1200. Dogwood Drive**
1300. Tumblewood Turn**
1400. Little Bear Path and Big Bear Path**
1500. Cottontail Curl*
1600. Timber Trail*
1700. Hickory Hollow*
1800. Conestoga Trail*
1900. Wagon Wheel Way*
2000. Spanish Moss Lane
2100. Bobcat Bend
2200. Arrowhead Way
2300. Shawnee Bend
2400. Settler's Bend
2500. Cedar Circle
2600. Moccasin Trail
2700. Heron Hollow
2800. Willow Way

🚌 Bus stop
🚻 Comfort station and laundry facility

*Preferred Hook-Up campsites
**Premium campsites
Both types of sites have power, water, sewer, cable TV,
and space for large RVs.

Continued from page 235

> *swim when we needed some time to ourselves, but with the distance and lack of lifeguards, there was no way to do that.*

A mother of two from Mechanicsville, Virginia, puts Fort Wilderness on a pedestal:

> *The most important thing—the family time. This is the only resort where you're encouraged to go outside and play! You can bike, swim, visit two arcades, hike the nature trail, ride a horse, rent a boat, play volleyball, go to the beach, attend a character sing-along and marshmallow roast followed by a classic Disney movie, enjoy multiple playgrounds, play tennis, rent a golf cart, walk around at night to see the festively decorated campsites, take a romantic carriage ride, take your first pony ride, and see a wild turkey. Don't forget the view of the fireworks from the beach or the up-close water light parade.*
>
> *With all of this stuff, much of it free or very affordable, who needs the parks? We visited last June and never set foot in a park.*

Bus service at Fort Wilderness leaves a lot to be desired—so much so, in fact, that we wouldn't stay there unless we had our own car. To go anywhere, you first have to catch an internal bus that makes many, many stops. If your destination is outside Fort Wilderness, you then have to transfer to a second bus. To complicate things, buses serving destinations outside the campground depart from two locations, the Reception Outpost and Pioneer Hall. This means you have to keep track of which destinations each transfer center serves.

A recommendation from a Rochester, New York, dad:

> *If you're staying at Fort Wilderness, we highly recommend getting a golf cart. There's a lot going on at the campground, and the bus system can be cumbersome. Also, our 3-year-old wasn't always up for the walk—just getting from our cabin to the main loop was a lot for her.*

If you rent a cabin or camp in a tent or RV, particularly in fall or spring, keep abreast of local weather conditions.

A number of independent campgrounds and RV parks are convenient to Walt Disney World. Visit campflorida.com/region/central-florida for listings.

HOW *to* EVALUATE *a* WALT DISNEY WORLD TRAVEL PACKAGE

HUNDREDS OF WALT DISNEY WORLD package vacations are offered each year. Some are created by the Walt Disney Travel Company, others by airlines, independent travel agents, and wholesalers. Almost all include lodging at or near Disney World plus theme park admissions. Packages offered by airlines include air transportation.

Prices vary seasonally; mid-March–Easter, summer, and holiday periods are the most expensive. Off-season, there are plenty of empty rooms, and you can negotiate great discounts, especially at non-Disney properties. Similarly, airfares and rental cars are cheaper off-peak.

Almost all package ads are headlined "5 Days at Walt Disney World from $645" (or such). The key word is *from:* The rock-bottom price includes the least desirable hotels; if you want better or more-convenient digs, you'll pay more—often much more.

Packages offer a wide selection of hotels. Some, like the Disney resorts, are very dependable. Others run the gamut of quality.

Checking two or three independent sources is best. Also, before you book, ask how old the hotel is and when the guest rooms were last refurbished. Locate the hotel on a map to verify its proximity to Disney World. If you won't have a car, make sure that the hotel has adequate shuttle service.

Packages with non-Disney lodging are much less expensive. But guests at Disney-owned properties get Extra Magic Hours privileges, the opportunity to make dining and FastPass+ reservations far in advance, free parking, and access to Disney transportation. These privileges don't apply to guests at the Disney Springs Resort Area hotels (see page 229).

Packages should be a win–win proposition for both buyer and seller. The buyer makes only one phone call and deals with one salesperson to set up the whole vacation (transportation, rental car, admissions, lodging, meals, and even golf and tennis). The seller, likewise, deals with the buyer only once. Some packagers also buy airfares in bulk on contract, not unlike a broker playing the commodities market. By buying a large number of airfares in advance, the packager saves significantly over posted fares. The practice is also applied to hotel rooms. Because selling packages is efficient and the packager often can buy package components in bulk at discount, the seller's savings in operating expenses are sometimes passed on to the buyer, making the package not only convenient but also an exceptional value.

In practice, however, the seller may not pass on those savings. Packages sometimes are loaded with extras that cost the packager almost nothing but run the package's price sky-high. Savings passed on to customers are still somewhere in Fantasyland.

Choose a package that includes features you're sure to use. You'll pay for all of them whether you use them or not. If price is more important than convenience, call around to see what the package would cost if you booked its components on your own. If the package price is less than the à la carte cost, the package is a good deal. If costs are about equal, the package probably is worth it for the convenience. Much of the time, however, you'll find you save significantly by buying the components individually.

CUT TO THE CHASE

IT'S MUCH FASTER TO BOOK a Disney resort room online than it is to call the Disney reservations number (☎ 407-W-DISNEY). If you call, you'll be subjected to about 5–10 minutes of recorded questions (many just fishing for nonrelevant personal information). If you actually

DISNEY LODGING FOR LESS

Mary Waring, *former webmaster at* **MouseSavers** *(mousesavers .com; see page 40), knows more about Disney hotel packages than anyone on the planet. Here are her money-saving suggestions.*

- **BOOK "ROOM-ONLY."** It's frequently a better deal to book a room-only reservation instead of buying a vacation package. Disney likes to sell vacation packages because they're easy and profitable. When you buy a package, you're typically paying a premium for convenience. You can often save money by putting together your own package. It's not hard: Just book room-only at a resort and buy passes, meals, and extras separately.

  Disney now prices its standard packages at the same rates as if you had purchased individual components separately at full price. However, what Disney doesn't tell you is that components can usually be purchased separately at a discount—and those discounts are not reflected in the brochure prices of Disney's packages. (Sometimes you can get special-offer packages that do include discounts; see the next section.)

  Keep in mind that Disney's packages often include extras you're unlikely to use. Also, packages require a $200 deposit and full payment 30 days in advance; plus, they have stringent change and cancellation policies. Generally, booking room-only requires a deposit of one night's room rate with the remainder due at check-in. Your reservation can be changed or canceled for any reason until five days before check-in.

- **USE DISCOUNT CODES TO REDUCE YOUR ROOM-ONLY OR PACKAGE RATE.** Disney uses these codes to push unsold rooms at certain times of year and occasionally offers packages that include resort discounts or value-added features. Check a website like mousesavers.com to learn about codes that may be available for your vacation dates. Some codes are available to anyone, while others are just for Florida residents, Annual Pass holders, and so on.

  Discount codes aren't always available for every hotel or every date, and they typically don't appear until two to six months in advance. The good news is that you can usually apply a code to an

want to make a reservation, slog on through. (When the question "Have you called us before?" pops up, answer "yes" unless you want to be corralled into an additional survey for "first-timers.") If you just want to ask a question or speak to a live person, touch 0 to bypass all the recorded stuff.

WALT DISNEY TRAVEL COMPANY MAGIC YOUR WAY PACKAGES

DISNEY'S MAGIC YOUR WAY travel-package program mirrors the admission-ticket program Here's how it works: You begin with a base existing room-only reservation. Simply call the Disney Reservation Center at ☎ 407-W-DISNEY (934-7639) (or contact a Disney-savvy travel agent) and ask whether any rooms are available at your preferred hotel for your preferred dates using the code.

- **BE FLEXIBLE.** Buying a room or package with a discount code is a little like shopping for clothes at a discount store: If you wear size XX-small or XXXX-large, or you like green when everyone else is wearing pink, you're a lot more likely to score a bargain. Likewise, resort discounts are available only when Disney has excess rooms. You're more likely to get a discount during less-popular times (such as value season) and at larger or less-popular resorts. Animal Kingdom Lodge and Old Key West Resort seem to have discounted rooms available more often than the other resorts do.

- **BE PERSISTENT.** This is the most important tip. Disney allots a certain number of rooms to each discount. Once the discounted rooms are gone, you won't get that rate unless someone cancels. Fortunately, people change and cancel reservations all the time. If you can't get your preferred dates or hotel with one discount code, try another one (if available) or keep calling back first thing in the morning to check for cancellations—the system resets overnight, and any reservations with unpaid deposits are automatically released for resale.

- **SPRING FOR "FREE DINING."** One of Disney's biggest package bargains, this promotion has been offered since 2005 during less-busy times of year. When you purchase a full-price room and full-price tickets for each person in the room, you get a Disney Dining Plan for your entire stay. The trick is to choose one of Disney's cheapest rooms and enjoy all that free food: If you choose a Value resort, you get the Quick-Service Dining Plan; if you choose a Moderate resort, you get the standard Disney Dining Plan. You can also book a Value resort and pay the difference to upgrade from Quick-Service to the regular plan. Free Dining is always offered throughout September (a slow time due to heat, humidity, hurricane season, and kids going back to school); sometimes it's offered in late August or at other times during the year.

package room and tickets. Tickets can be customized to match the number of days you intend to tour the theme parks and range in length from 2 to 10 days. As with theme park admissions, the package program offers strong financial incentives to book a longer stay. "The longer you play, the less you pay per day," is the way Disney puts it, borrowing a page from Sam Walton's concept of the universe. An adult 1-Day Base Ticket for the Magic Kingdom (with tax) costs $114–$132, depending on the day of your visit, whereas if you buy a 7-Day Base Ticket, the average cost per day drops to $62.38 You can purchase options to add on to your Base

Tickets, such as hopping between theme parks; playing minigolf; or visiting water parks or ESPN Wide World of Sports.

With Magic Your Way packages, you can avoid paying for features you don't intend to use. You need not purchase a package with theme park tickets for the entire length of your stay. With Magic Your Way you can choose to purchase as many days of admission as you intend to use. On a one-week vacation, for example, you might want to spend only five days in the Disney parks, saving a day each for Universal Studios and SeaWorld. With Magic Your Way you can buy only five days of admission on a seven-day package. Likewise, if you don't normally park-hop, you can purchase multiday admissions that don't include the Park Hopper feature. Best of all, you can buy the various add-ons at any time during your vacation.

Before we deluge you with a boxcar of options and add-ons, let's define the basic components of Disney's Magic Your Way package:

- One or more nights of accommodations at your choice of any Disney resort. Rates vary with lodging choice: The Grand Floridian is usually the most expensive, and the All-Star, Pop Century, and Art of Animation Resorts are the least expensive.
- Base Ticket for the number of days you tour the theme parks (must be at least 2-Day Base Tickets for packages)
- Unlimited use of the Disney transportation system
- Free theme park parking
- Official Walt Disney Travel Company luggage tag (one per person)

Magic Your Way Dining Plans

Disney offers dining plans to accompany its ticket system. They're available to all Disney resort guests except those staying at the Swan, the Dolphin, the hotels of the Disney Springs Resort Area, and Shades of Green. Guests must also purchase a Magic Your Way package from Disney (not through an online reseller), have Annual Passes, or be members of the Disney Vacation Club (DVC) to participate in the plan. Except for DVC members, a three-night minimum stay is typically also required. Overall cost is determined by the number of nights you stay at a Disney resort.

You must purchase a Disney package vacation to be eligible for a dining plan, as a family of five from Waldron, Michigan, learned:

> We read through the Unofficial Guide and noticed that it said not to book a package during slow season. We were overwhelmed with the decisions that we had to make, so we booked the resort first, then the tickets, and then we wanted the dining plan. Well, they wouldn't add the dining plan on because we had already booked everything.

MAGIC YOUR WAY PLUS DINING PLAN This plan provides, for each member of your group, for each night of your stay, one counter-service meal, one full-service meal, and two snacks at participating Disney dining locations and restaurants, including room service at some Disney resorts (type "Disney Dining Plan Locations" into your favorite search engine to find sites with the entire list).

The plan also includes one refillable drink mug per person, per package, but it can be filled only at Disney resort counter-service restaurants. For guests ages 10 and up, the price for 2018 is $75.59, tax included; for guests ages 3–9, the price is $25.80 per night, tax included. Children younger than age 3 eat free from an adult's plate.

For instance, if you're staying for three nights, you'll be credited with three counter-service meals, three full-service meals, and six snacks for each member of your party. All those meals will be put into a group meal account. Meals in your account can be used by anyone in your group, on any combination of days, so you're not required to eat every meal every day. This means that, say, you can skip a full-service meal one day and have two on another day.

The counter-service meal includes

- A main course (a sandwich, dinner salad, pizza, or the like) or a complete combo meal (such as a hamburger and fries) plus beverage; breakfast is typically a combination platter with eggs, bacon or sausage, potatoes, a biscuit, and a drink

The full-service sit-down meals include

- A main course or entrée with beverage
- A dessert (except breakfast)

If you're dining at a buffet, the full-service meal includes the buffet and beverage. Tax is included in the dining plan, but tips are not. Beverage choices include unlimited soda, coffee, or tea or, for adults, one beer, wine, cocktail, milkshake, smoothie, or specialty hot chocolate.

The definition of *snacks* is detailed enough to read like a nuclear-disarmament specification:

- **All single-serving nonalcoholic beverages not in a souvenir cup or with a souvenir attachment.** The serving size must be less than 1 liter, and beverages served at recreation counters are excluded from the plan.

- **All soups served in counter-service locations,** including Disney resort food courts.

- **All items that are eligible as snacks and are on the menu as single items but have additional options at a separate price.** What the heck does that mean? If you want a pretzel with cheese sauce, then together they count as one snack.

- **All ice-cream novelties.** Also all hand-scooped ice cream not served in a souvenir container, including ice-cream sundaes consisting of up to two scoops.

- **All counter-service items identified as sides** or additions that are not considered entrées.

- **Fresh-popped popcorn.** Pre-bagged popcorn is not considered a snack. *Oh?*

- **Counter-service breakfast items that can be considered part of an entrée and that are also offered as separate sides,** such as cereal with milk; French toast sticks; create-your-own oatmeal or quinoa; grits; bacon; sausage; eggs; potatoes; or biscuits, with or without gravy. When in doubt, ask a cast member what else might count.

Disney's top-of-the-line restaurants (referred to as Disney Signature restaurants in the plan), along with Cinderella's Royal Table, all the dinner shows, regular room service, and in-room pizza delivery, count as two full-service meals on the standard (Plus) dining plan. If you dine at one of these locations, two full-service meals will be deducted from your account for each person dining.

In addition to the preceding, the following rules apply:

- Everyone staying in the same resort room must participate in the Disney Dining Plan.

- Children ages 3–9 must order from the kids' menu, if available. This rule is occasionally relaxed at Disney's counter-service restaurants, enabling older kids to order from the adult (ages 10+) menu.

- Alcoholic and specialty beverages are included in the plan starting in 2018.

- A full-service meal can be breakfast, lunch, or dinner. The greatest savings occur when you use your full-service-meal credits for dinner.

- The meal plan expires at midnight **on the day you check out** of your Disney resort. **Unused meals are nonrefundable.**

- Neither the Disney Dining Plan nor Disney's Free Dining can be added to a discounted room-only reservation.

QUICK-SERVICE DINING PLAN This plan includes meals, snacks, and drinks at most counter-service eateries in Walt Disney World. The cost (including tax) is $52.49 per day for guests ages 10 and up, $21.75 per day for kids ages 3–9. The plan includes two counter-service meals and two snacks per day, in addition to one refillable drink mug per person, per package (eligible for refills only at counter-service locations in your Disney resort).

MAGIC YOUR WAY DELUXE DINING PLAN This plan offers a choice of full- or counter-service meals for three meals a day at any participating restaurant. In addition to the three meals a day, the plan also includes two snacks per day and a refillable drink mug. The Deluxe Plan costs $116.24 for adults and children ages 10 and up and $39.90 for children ages 3–9 for each night of your stay (prices include tax).

Not only does the Deluxe Dining Plan cost a lot of money, it costs a lot of time, as a dad from Hudson Falls, New York, explains:

> *The Deluxe Dining Plan gave us a chance to try new restaurants, but it felt like most of our trip revolved around food: get to the restaurant, wait to be seated, order drinks, wait, get drinks, wait, order meals, wait, get meals, wait, order dessert, wait, get dessert, wait, get the check, wait, give the waitstaff your room card, wait, figure out the tip, and wait. We lost 4.5–6 hours a day just on eating, plus the travel time.*

In addition to food, all the plans include sweeteners, such as a free round of miniature golf, discounts on spa treatments and salon services, and deals on recreational activities like watersports.

Disney ceaselessly tinkers with the dining plans' rules, meal definitions, and participating restaurants. Here are some recent examples:

- You can exchange a sit-down meal credit for a counter-service meal, though doing this even once can negate any savings you get from using a plan in the first place.

- At sit-down restaurants, you can substitute dessert for a side salad, cup of soup, or fruit plate.

- You may exchange one sit-down or counter-service meal credit for three snacks, as long as you do so within the same transaction. It is not a good deal to exchange a sit-down credit for three snacks.

- Counter-service restaurants do not differentiate between adult and child meal credits. If you have two adult credits and two child credits on your account, you may purchase four adult counter-service meals with those credits.

- Finally, you can use your meal credits to pay for the meals of people who are not on any dining plan.

THINGS TO CONSIDER WHEN EVALUATING THE PLUS DINING PLAN The dining plan has been one of the most requested of Disney's package add-ons since its introduction; families report that their favorite aspect is the peace of mind that comes from knowing their meals are paid for ahead of time, rather than having to keep track of a budget while they're in the parks. Families also enjoy the communal aspect of sitting down together for a full meal, without having to worry about who's picking up the food or doing the dishes.

Costwise, however, it's difficult for many families to justify using the plan. If you prefer to always eat at counter-service restaurants, you'll be better off with the Quick-Service plan. You should also avoid the Plus plan if you have finicky eaters, you're visiting during holidays or summer, or you can't get reservations at your first- or second-choice sit-down restaurants. In addition, if you have children ages 10 and up, be sure that they can eat an adult-sized dinner at a sit-down restaurant every night; if not, you'd probably come out ahead just paying for everyone's meals without the plan.

If you opt for the plan, skipping one full-service meal during a visit of five or fewer days can mean the difference between saving and losing money. In our experience, having a scheduled sit-down meal for every day of a weeklong vacation can be mentally exhausting, especially for kids. One option might be to schedule a meal at a Disney Signature restaurant, which requires two full-service credits, and have no scheduled sit-down meal on another night in the middle of your trip, allowing everyone to decide on the spot if they're up for something formal.

As already noted, many of the most popular restaurants are fully booked as soon as their reservation windows open. If you're still interested in the dining plan, book your restaurants as soon as possible, typically 180 days before you visit. Then decide whether the plan makes economic sense. For more on Advance Reservations—the term is Disney-speak (hence the capital letters) and not exactly what it implies—see Part Four.

If you're making reservations to eat at Disney hotels other than your own, a car allows you to easily access all the participating restaurants. When you use the Disney transportation system, dining at the various resorts can be a logistical nightmare. Those without a car may want to weigh the immediate services of a taxi or ride sharing—typically $8–$12 each way across Disney property, versus a 50- to 75-minute trip on Disney transportation each way.

When Disney offers Free Dining discounts (typically in September), they generally charge rack rate for the hotel. You should work out the math, but Free Dining is typically a good deal for families who have two children under age 10, are staying at a Value resort, and book lots of character meals. Light eaters and childless couples, especially those staying at Deluxe resorts, may find it cheaper to take a room discount and pay for food separately.

For an in-depth discussion of the various plans, including number crunching (with algebra, even!), visit TouringPlans.com (scroll down and click "Dining" on the homepage, then "Disney Dining Plan").

Readers who tried the Disney Dining Plan had varying experiences, but frustration seems to be a common refrain. A New Hampshire family comments:

> *Dining plans are NOT for us. Keeping track of the meals, figuring out what you can and can't buy, and rushing around on the last day trying to use up what's left is just too stressful. We'd rather just buy what we want, when and where we want it.*

A reader from The Woodlands, Texas, laments that the plan has altered the focus of her vacation:

> *I want to have fun. I don't want to be locked into a tight schedule, always worrying about where we need to be when it's time to eat, and I don't want to eat when I'm not hungry just because I have a reservation somewhere.*

On the upside, here's what a Tennessee mother of a 3-year-old has to say:

> *We LOVED the dining plan. It was wonderful to not have to stress every day about trying to keep up with a budget for food. The plan turned out to be a fantastic deal for us, especially because we did four character meals that would have cost at least $400 otherwise.*

A Belmont, Massachusetts, dad is a fan of the Quick Service Dining Plan:

> *If you intend to eat Disney food, the counter-service meal plan is a good option. The full-service restaurants seemed overpriced, and the necessity of reservations months in advance seemed a bar to flexibility. You get two counter-service meals (entrée/combo and drink) and two snacks (food item or drink) per person per day, and even though kids' meals are cheaper, there's no distinction when you order—kids can order [more-expensive] adult meals.*

But a mom from Orland Park, Illinois, comments on the difficulty of getting Advance Reservations:

> *It's impossible to get table reservations anywhere good. We found ourselves taking whatever was open and were unhappy with every sit-down meal we had, except for lunch at Liberty Tree Tavern. I don't enjoy planning my day exclusively around eating at a certain restaurant at a certain time, but that is what you must do six months in advance if you want to eat at a good sit-down restaurant in Disney.*

Echoing the mom above is a reader from San Jose, California—who *wasn't* on the dining plan:

> *I was told by a Disney rep to make all my reservations 90 days out because the restaurants are booked by people on the dining plan. In fact, I was told that most of the sit-down restaurants don't even take*

walk-ins anymore. Sure enough, even though I was well over 90 days away from my vacation, a lot of my restaurant choices were unavailable. I had to rearrange my entire schedule to fit the open slots at the restaurants I didn't want to miss.

Many readers report that Disney cast members are more knowledgeable about the dining plan than they used to be. A Washington, DC–area couple writes:

The kinks are worked out, and everyone at the parks we talked to seemed to get it, but we still spent $40 or more at most sit-down dinners on extra drinks and tips.

But a mom from Texarkana, Arkansas, begs to differ:

As a first-time visitor with kids who had read multiple books, blogs, and other resources, I was still confused by our dining plan once we were there. We had a 2-year-old, who was supposed to be able to eat free, plus a 5-year-old and four adults. Some restaurants—all in the parks, our resort, or Disney Springs—would let me order my 2-year-old a free kids' meal, but others would not. Either the staff is completely confused about the dining plan or the inconsistencies are on purpose. Either way, it made the dining part of our trip very frustrating!

The dining plan left a family of five from Nashville, Tennessee, similarly dazed and confused:

What was annoying was the inconsistency. You can get a 16-ounce chocolate milk on the kids' plan, but only 8 ounces of white milk at many places. At Earl of Sandwich, you can get 16 ounces of either kind. A pint of milk would count as a snack (price $1.52), but they wouldn't count a quart of milk (price $1.79) because it wasn't a single serving. However, in Animal Kingdom, my husband bought a water-bottle holder (price $3.75) and used a snack credit.

From a Lansdale, Pennsylvania, mom:

The gratuities alone on two-point meals for the Deluxe Dining Plan were nearly what we would pay for a comparable meal outside of the park. We used one point for lunch at sit-down restaurants and two points for dinner at a Signature restaurant daily. With four adults, we ended up with over $500 in payments to restaurants after already paying for the Deluxe Dining Plan. The dining plans used to be a good deal, but not any longer.

A Land O' Lakes, Florida, dad bumped into this problem:

We had some trouble with our Deluxe Dining Plan being "invalidated" after checkout, though it was supposed to be valid until midnight of our checkout date. That was annoying because calls to the resort were needed to verify the meals left on our passes for The Crystal Palace and for some snacks later.

Another reader encountered the problem in reverse:

While your park tickets are activated on the day of your arrival, it turns out that your dining plan is not activated until someone at the hotel actually checks you in. Nothing in Disney's e-mails or literature tells people this. We were unable to use our dining plan for breakfast or snacks until the Wilderness Lodge decided it was time to check us in. Fortunately, we had a credit card that we could use for breakfast and for snacks. Then we had to spend an hour dealing with the front desk to reverse the credit card charges and deduct our meal credits. It was a horrible experience, and it's the main reason we will never stay at Wilderness Lodge again.

Reader Tips for Getting the Most Out of the Plan

A mom from Radford, Virginia, shares the following tip:

Warn people to eat lunch early if they have dinner reservations before 7 p.m. Disney doesn't skimp on food—if you eat a late lunch (where, by the way, they feed you the same ungodly amount of food), you WILL NOT be hungry for dinner.

And this Lawrence, Kansas, mom offers another:

The quick-service meals aren't really designated for kids or adults when they ring you up and subtract the food from your plan. I wish I'd have known early on that if they couldn't see I had a child under age 9, I could have ordered a regular meal and gotten more food. We figured that out toward the end and started ordering bigger meals for our 7-year-old (we saved the leftovers to share later).

A mom from Brick Township, New Jersey, found that the dining plan streamlined her touring:

We truly enjoyed our Disney trip, and this time we purchased the dining plan. This was great for the kids because we did a character-dining experience every day. This helped us in the parks because we didn't have to wait in line to see the characters. Instead, we got all of our autographs during our meals.

A Saskatoon, Saskatchewan, father of three says you have to watch vendors like a hawk:

We had a problem with a vendor who charged us meal service for each of the ice cream bars we purchased. This became evident at our final sit-down meal, when we didn't have any meal vouchers left. Check the receipts after every purchase!

DOING THE MATH

COMPARING A MAGIC YOUR WAY PACKAGE with purchasing the package components separately is a breeze.

1. Pick a Disney resort and decide how many nights you want to stay.
2. Next, work out a rough plan of what you want to do and see so you can determine the admission passes you'll require.
3. When you're ready, call the Disney Reservation Center (DRC) at ☎ 407-W-DISNEY (934-7639) and price a Magic Your Way package with tax for your selected resort and dates. The package will include

both admissions and lodging. It's also a good idea to get a quote from a Disney-savvy travel agent (see page 132).

4. Now, to calculate the costs of buying your accommodations and admission passes separately, call the DRC a second time. This time, price a room-only rate for the same resort and dates. Be sure to ask about the availability of any special deals. While you're still on the line, obtain the prices, with tax, for the admissions you require. If you're not sure which of the various admission options will best serve you, consult our free Ticket Calculator at **TouringPlans.com.**

5. Add the room-only rates and the admission prices. Compare this sum to the DRC quote for the Magic Your Way package.

6. Check for deals and discounts on packages and admission.

Regarding the economics of the dining plan, it's illustrative to know how the cost of one day on the plan is spent on each component. We'll spare you the math, but an approximate value for each item across every 2018 Disney Dining Plan is as follows:

- Each counter-service meal is worth **$19.42.**
- Each table-service meal is worth **$40.41.**
- Every snack and specialty beverage is worth around **$3.10.**
- The refillable mug is worth **$5–$6,** depending on trip length.

THROW ME A LINE!

IF YOU BUY A PACKAGE FROM DISNEY, don't expect reservationists to offer suggestions or help you sort out your options. Generally, they respond only to your specific questions, ducking queries that require an opinion. A reader from North Riverside, Illinois, complains:

> My wife made two telephone calls, and the representatives from WDW were very courteous. However, they only answered the questions posed and were not eager to give advice on what might be most cost-effective. I feel a person could spend 8 hours on the phone with WDW reps and not have any more input than you get from reading the literature.

If you can't get the information you need from Disney, get in touch with a good travel agent. Chances are that the agent can help you weigh your options.

Purchasing Room-Only Plus Passes Versus a Package

SUE PISATURO of **Small World Vacations** (smallworldvacations.com), a travel agency that specializes in Disney, also thinks there's more involved in a package-purchase decision than money.

> Should you purchase a Walt Disney World package or buy all the components of the package separately? There's no single answer to this confusing question.
>
> A Walt Disney World package is like a store-bought prepackaged kids' meal, the kind with the little compartments filled with meat, cheese, crackers, drink, and dessert: You just grab the package and go. It's easy, and if it's on sale, why bother doing it yourself? If it's not on sale, it still may be worth the extra money for convenience.

Purchasing the components of your vacation separately is like buying each of the meal's ingredients, cutting them up into neat piles and packaging the lunch yourself. Is it worth the extra time and effort to do it this way? Will you save money if you do it this way?

You have two budgets to balance when you plan your Disney World vacation: time and money. Satisfying both is your ultimate goal. Research and planning are paramount to realizing your Disney vacation dreams. Create your touring plans before making a final decision with regard to the number of days and options on your theme park passes. Create your dining itinerary (along with Advance Reservations, if possible) to determine if Disney's dining plan can save you some money.

Dining Plans for Non-Disney Hotels

Disney has begun to experiment with a dining-inclusive package for area hotels not owned by Disney itself. Booking for this experimental package is available until December 1, 2017, for travel dates through December 31, 2017. The **Quick-Service Dining Gift Card Package** is available for guests staying at the Walt Disney World Swan and Dolphin hotels, the Four Seasons Resort Orlando at Walt Disney World, and some Disney Springs Resort Area hotels, with a minimum three-day theme park ticket. Guests of these properties may add on a discounted prepaid gift card, which may be used for dining at quick-service restaurant locations or food carts in Walt Disney World. For each theme park admission ticket day, adult guests will be charged $35 but will receive a $40 dining card credit. Child guests (ages 3–9) will be charged $12.50 but will receive a $15 dining card credit. This is a 12.5% discount for adults and a 16.7% discount for children. Guests should be aware that using less than the full value of the discount card will effectively result in a smaller discount, or even a possible overcharge, for quick-service meals.

HOTELS *outside*
WALT DISNEY WORLD

SELECTING AND BOOKING A HOTEL OUTSIDE WALT DISNEY WORLD

LODGING COSTS OUTSIDE DISNEY WORLD vary incredibly. If you shop around, you can find a clean motel with a pool within 5–20 minutes of the World for as low as $50 a night with tax. Because of hot competition, discounts abound, particularly for AAA and AARP members.

There are four primary out-of-the-World areas to consider:

1. INTERNATIONAL DRIVE AREA This area, about 15–25 minutes northeast of the World, parallels I-4 on its eastern side and offers a wide selection of hotels and restaurants. Prices range from $56 to $400 per night. The chief drawbacks are terribly congested roads, countless traffic signals, and inadequate access to westbound I-4. While I-Drive's biggest bottleneck is its intersection with Sand Lake Road, the mile between Kirkman and Sand Lake Roads is almost always gridlocked. We provide tips for avoiding this traffic in Part Seven (see "Sneak Routes," page 488).

Regarding traffic on International Drive (known locally as I-Drive), a convention-goer from Islip, New York, weighed in with this:

> When I visited Disney World with my family last summer, we wasted huge chunks of time in traffic on International Drive. Our hotel was in the section between the big McDonald's at Sand Lake Road and [now-closed] Wet 'n Wild at Universal Boulevard. There are practically no left-turn lanes in this section, so anyone turning left can hold up traffic for a long time.

Traffic aside, a man from Ottawa, Ontario, sings the praises of his I-Drive experience:

> International Drive is the place to stay when going to Disney. Your description of this location failed to point out that there are several discount stores, boutiques, restaurants, mini-putts, and other entertainment facilities, all within walking distance of remarkably inexpensive accommodations and a short drive away from WDW.

I-Drive hotels are listed in the ***Orlando Official Visitors Guide,*** published by Visit Orlando. To obtain a copy, call ☎ 800-972-3304 or 407-363-5872, or check visitorlando.com.

2. LAKE BUENA VISTA AND THE I-4 CORRIDOR A number of hotels are along FL 535 and west of I-4 between Disney World and I-4's intersection with Florida's Turnpike. They're easily reached from the interstate and are near many restaurants, including those on International Drive. The *Orlando Official Visitors Guide* (see above) lists most of them. For some traffic-avoidance tips, see "The I-4 Blues" (page 472) in Part Seven, Arriving and Getting Around. This area includes Disney's new Value-priced Flamingo Crossings resort area (see page 280).

3. US 192 (IRLO BRONSON MEMORIAL HIGHWAY) This is the highway to Kissimmee, to the southeast of Disney World. In addition to large full-service hotels, many small, privately owned motels often offer a good value. Several dozen properties on US 192 are nearer Disney parks than are more expensive hotels inside the World. The number and variety of restaurants on US 192 have increased markedly, compensating for the area's primary shortcoming. Locally, US 192 is called Irlo Bronson Memorial Highway. The section to the west of I-4 and the Disney Maingate is designated Irlo Bronson Memorial Highway West, while the section from I-4 running southeast toward Kissimmee is Irlo Bronson Memorial Highway East.

The combined east and west sections have numbered mile markers that simplify navigation if you know which marker is closest to your destination. Though traffic is heavy on Irlo Bronson west of the Maingate, it doesn't compare with the congestion east of the Maingate and I-4 between Mile Markers 8 and 13. This section can—and should—be

Continued on page 256

Hotel Concentrations Around Walt Disney World

1. International Drive Area
2. Lake Buena Vista Resort Area and the I-4 Corridor
3. US 192–Kissimmee Resort Area
4. Universal Orlando Area

Orlando

Lake Apopka

Winter Garden

Pine Hills

Winter Park

Orlando

Lake Butler

Lake Tibet

Universal Orlando

Walt Disney World

Lake Buena Vista

Conway

Lake Conway

Orlando International Airport

Central Florida GreeneWay

Kissimmee

East Lake Tohopekaliga

International Drive & Universal Areas

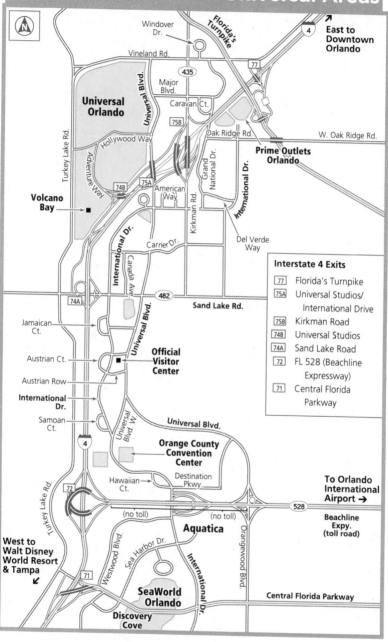

Windover Dr.

Florida's Turnpike

4 → East to Downtown Orlando

Vineland Rd.

77

435

Major Blvd.

Universal Blvd.

Universal Orlando

Caravan Ct.

75B

Turkey Lake Rd.

Hollywood Way

Oak Ridge Rd.

W. Oak Ridge Rd.

Adventure Way

74B

75A

American Way

Prime Outlets Orlando

Grand National Dr.

Kirkman Rd.

International Dr.

Volcano Bay ■→

International Dr.

Canada Ave.

Carrier Dr.

Del Verde Way

482

74A

Sand Lake Rd.

Jamaican Ct.

Austrian Ct.

Universal Blvd.

Official Visitor Center ■

Austrian Row

International Dr.

Samoan Ct.

4

Universal Blvd. W.

Universal Blvd.

Orange County Convention Center

Hawaiian → Ct.

Destination Pkwy.

72

To Orlando International Airport →

528

(no toll)

(no toll)

Aquatica

Orangewood Blvd.

Beachline Expy. (toll road)

Turkey Lake Rd.

West to Walt Disney World Resort & Tampa ↙

71

Westwood Blvd.

Sea Harbor Dr.

International Dr.

SeaWorld Orlando

Discovery Cove

Central Florida Parkway

Interstate 4 Exits

77	Florida's Turnpike
75A	Universal Studios/ International Drive
75B	Kirkman Road
74B	Universal Studios
74A	Sand Lake Road
72	FL 528 (Beachline Expressway)
71	Central Florida Parkway

Lake Buena Vista Resort Area & the I-4 Corridor

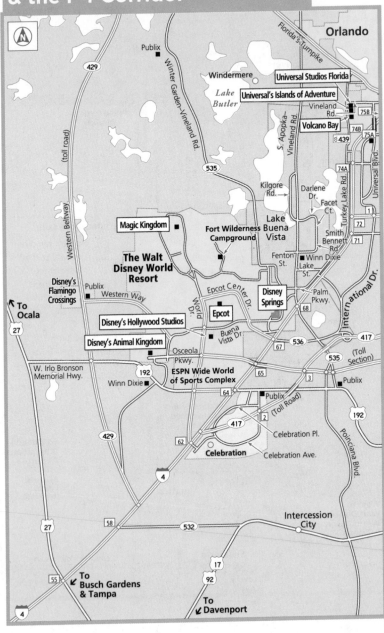

US 192–Kissimmee Resort Area

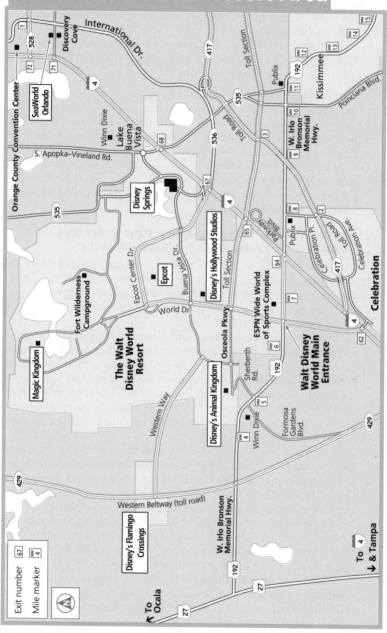

Continued from page 251

avoided by using **Osceola Parkway,** a toll road that parallels Irlo Bronson to the north and terminates in Walt Disney World at the entrance to Animal Kingdom.

Hotels on US 192 and in Kissimmee are listed in the *Kissimmee Visitor's Guide.* Order a copy by calling ☎ 800-327-9159, or view it online at experiencekissimmee.com.

4. UNIVERSAL STUDIOS AREA In the triangular area bordered by I-4 on the southeast, Vineland Road on the north, and Turkey Lake Road on the west are Universal Orlando and the hotels most convenient to it. Running north–south through the middle of the triangle is Kirkman Road, which connects to I-4. On the east side of Kirkman are a number of independent hotels and restaurants. Universal hotels, theme parks, and CityWalk are west of Kirkman. Traffic in this area is not nearly as congested as on nearby International Drive, and there are good interstate connections in both directions.

DRIVING TIME TO THE PARKS FOR VISITORS LODGING OUTSIDE WALT DISNEY WORLD

OUR HOTEL INFORMATION CHART on pages 291–306 shows the commuting time to the Disney theme parks from each hotel listed. Those commuting times represent an average of several test runs. Your actual time may be shorter or longer depending on traffic, road construction (if any), and delays at traffic signals.

The commuting times in our Hotel Information Chart show conclusively that distance from the theme parks is not necessarily the dominant factor in determining commuting times. Among those we list, the hotels on Major Boulevard opposite the Kirkman Road entrance to Universal Orlando, for example, are the most distant (in miles) from the Disney parks. But because they're only one traffic signal from easy access to I-4, commuting time to the parks is significantly less than for many closer hotels.

Note that times in the chart differ from those in the Door-to-Door Commuting Times chart in Part Seven. The latter compares using the Disney transportation system with driving your own car *inside* Walt Disney World. These times include actual transportation time plus tram, monorail, or other connections required to get from the parking lots to the entrance turnstiles. The hotel chart's commuting times, by contrast, represent only the driving time to and from the entrance of the respective parking lot of each park, with no consideration for getting to and from the parking lot to the turnstiles.

Add to the commuting times in the Hotel Information Chart a few minutes for paying your parking fee and parking. Once you park at the Transportation and Ticket Center (Magic Kingdom parking lot), it takes 20–30 minutes more to reach the Magic Kingdom via monorail or ferry. To reach Epcot from its parking lot, add 7–10 minutes. At Disney's Hollywood Studios and Animal Kingdom, the lot-to-gate transit is 5–12 minutes. If you haven't purchased your theme park admission in advance, tack on another 10–20 minutes.

HOTEL SHOPPING ON THE INTERNET: WELCOME TO THE WILD WEST

UNMATCHED AS AN EFFICIENT and timely distributor of information, the Internet has become the primary resource for travelers seeking to shop for and book their own air travel, hotels, rental cars, entertainment, and travel packages. It's by far the best direct-to-consumer distribution channel in history.

INTERNET ECONOMICS 101 The evolution of selling travel on the web has radically altered the way airlines, hotels, cruise lines, rental-car companies, and the like do business. Before the Internet, they depended on travel agents or direct contact with customers by phone. Transaction costs were high because companies were obligated to pay commissions and fund labor-intensive in-house reservations departments. With the advent of the Internet, inexpensive e-commerce transactions became possible: Airlines and rental-car companies began using their own websites to effectively cut travel agents out of the sales process. Hotels also developed websites but continued to depend on wholesalers and travel agents as well.

It didn't take long before independent websites sprang up that sold travel products from a wide assortment of suppliers, often at deep discounts. These sites, called **online travel agencies** (**OTAs**), include such familiar names as **Travelocity, Orbitz, Priceline, Expedia, Hotels.com,** and **Hotwire.** Those mentioned and others like them attract huge numbers of customers shopping for hotels.

OTAS AND THE MERCHANT MODEL In the beginning, hotels paid OTAs about the same commission that they paid travel agents, but then the OTAs began applying the thumbscrews, forcing hotels to make the transition from a simple commission model to what's called a merchant model. Under this model, hotels provide an OTA with a deeply discounted room rate that the OTA then marks up and sells. The difference between the marked-up price and the discounted rate paid to the hotel is the OTA's gross profit. If, for example, a hotel makes $120 rooms available to an OTA at a 33% discount, or $80, and the OTA sells the room at $110, the OTA's gross profit is $30 ($110 − $80).

The merchant model, originally devised for wholesalers and tour operators, has been around since long before the Internet. Wholesalers and tour operators, then and now, must commit to a certain volume of business, commit to guaranteed room allotments, pay deposits, and bundle the discounted rates with other travel services so that the actual hotel rate remains hidden within the bundle. This is known as *opaque pricing*. The merchant model costs the hotel two to three times the normal travel-agent commission—considered justifiable because the wholesalers and tour operators also promote the hotel through brochures, websites, trade shows, print ads, and events.

OTAs now demand the equivalent of a wholesale commission or higher but are subject to none of the requirements imposed on wholesalers and tour operators. For instance, they don't have to commit to a specified volume of sales or keep discounted room rates opaque. In return, hotels give up 20%–50% of gross profit and are rewarded by having their rock-bottom rates plastered all over the Internet, with corresponding damage to their image and brand. (This last is why it's very rare to see a Disney hotel advertised on an OTA site at a price lower than what you can obtain from Disney itself.)

What's more, doing business with OTAs is very expensive for hotels. The cost for a hotel to sell a multiday booking on its own website is $10–$12, including site hosting and analytics, marketing costs, and management fees. This is 10–20 times cheaper than the cost of the same booking through an OTA. Let's say a hotel sells a $100 room for six nights on its own website. Again, the booking would cost the hotel around $12, or $2 per night. If an OTA books the same room having secured it from the hotel at a 30% discount, the hotel receives $70 per night from the OTA. Thus the hotel's cost for the OTA booking is $30 per night, or $180 for six nights—15 times as costly as selling the room online with no middleman.

In the hotel industry, occupancy rates are important, but simply getting bodies into beds doesn't guarantee a profit. A more critical metric is *revenue per available room* (**RevPAR**). For a hotel full of guests booked through an OTA, RevPAR will be 20%–50% lower than for the same number of guests who booked the hotel directly, either through the hotel's website or by phone.

It's no wonder, then, that hotels and OTAs have a love–hate relationship. Likewise, it's perfectly understandable that hotels want to maximize direct bookings through their own websites and minimize OTA bookings. Problem is, the better-known OTAs draw a lot more web traffic than a given hotel's (or even hotel chain's) website. So the challenge for the hotel becomes how to shift room-shoppers away from the OTAs and channel them to its website. A number of hotel corporations, including Choice, The Hotel Group (Hilton, DoubleTree, Marriott, Comfort Inn), Hyatt, InterContinental, and Wyndham, have risen to that challenge by forming their own OTA called **Room Key** (roomkey.com). The participating chains hope that working together will generate enough visitor traffic to make Room Key competitive with the Expedias and Travelocities of the world.

MORE POWER TO THE SHOPPER Understanding the market dynamics we've described gives you a powerful tool for obtaining the best rates for the hotel of your choice. It's why we tell you to shop the web for the lowest price available and then call your travel agent or the hotel itself to ask if they can beat it. Any savvy reservationist knows that selling you the room directly will both cut the hotel's cost and improve gross margin. If the reservationist can't help you, ask to speak to his or her supervisor. (We've actually had to explain hotel economics to more than a few clueless reservation agents.)

As for travel agents, they have clout based on the volume of business they send to a particular hotel or chain and can usually negotiate a rate even lower than what you've found on the Internet. Even if the agent can't beat the price, he or she can often obtain upgrades, preferred views, free breakfasts, and other deal sweeteners. When we bump into a great deal on the web, we call our agent. Often she can beat the deal or improve on it, perhaps with an upgrade. *Reminder:* Except for special arrangements agreed to by you, the fee or commission due to your travel agent will be paid by the hotel.

THE SECRET The key to shopping on the Internet is, well, shopping. When we're really hungry for a deal, there are a number of sites that we always check out:

OUR FAVORITE ONLINE HOTEL RESOURCES
mousesavers.com Best site for hotels in Disney World
hotelcoupons.com Self-explanatory
experiencekissimmee.com Primarily US 192–Kissimmee area hotels
orlandovacation.com Great rates for condos and home rentals
visitorlando.com Good info; not user-friendly for booking

We scour these sites for unusually juicy hotel deals that meet our criteria (location, quality, price, amenities). If we find a hotel that fills the bill, we check it out at other websites and comparative travel search engines such as **Kayak** (kayak.com) and **Mobissimo** (mobissimo.com) to see who has the best rate. (As an aside, Kayak used to be purely a search engine but now sells travel products, raising the issue of whether products not sold by Kayak are equally likely to come up in a search. Mobissimo, on the other hand, only links potential buyers to provider websites.) Your initial shopping effort should take about 15–20 minutes, faster if you can zero in quickly on a particular hotel.

Next, armed with your insider knowledge of hotel economics, call the hotel or have your travel agent call. Start by asking about specials. If there are none, or if the hotel can't beat the best price you've found on the Internet, share your findings and ask if the hotel can do better. Sometimes you'll be asked for proof of the rate you've discovered online—to be prepared for this, go to the site and enter the dates of your stay, plus the rate you've found to make sure it's available. If it is, print the page with this information and have it handy for your travel agent or for when you call the hotel. (*Note:* Always call the hotel's local number, not its national reservations number.)

INDEPENDENT AND BOUTIQUE HOTEL DEALS While chain hotels worry about sales costs and profit margins, independent and so-called boutique hotels are concerned about discoverability—making themselves known to the traveling public. The market is huge and it's increasingly hard for these hotels to get noticed, especially when they're competing with major chains. Independent and boutique hotels work on the premise that if they can get you through the front door, you'll become a loyal customer. For these hotels, substantially discounting rates is part of their marketing plan to build a client base. Because such hotels get lost on the big OTA sites and on search engines like Kayak and Google, they've jumped on the flash-sale bandwagon. Offering almost irresistible rates on daily-coupon sites like **Groupon** and **LivingSocial,** the independents can get their product in front of thousands of potential guests.

These offers are very generous but also time-limited. If you're in the market, though, you'll be hard-pressed to find better deals. While an OTA such as Expedia generally obtains rooms at a 20%–35% discount off the hotel's published rate, flash sites cut deals at an extra-deep discount. This allows their subscribers to bid on or secure coupons for rooms that are often as much as 50% lower than the hotel's standard rate and that frequently include perks such as meals, free parking, waived resort fees, shopping vouchers, spa services, and entertainment. On Groupon's homepage, click "Getaways" or just wait for Getaway coupons by e-mail as part of your free subscription. On LivingSocial you have to specifically subscribe to "Adventures" and "Escapes"; otherwise, you'll receive only non-travel-related offers.

ANOTHER WRINKLE Finally, a quick word about a recent trend: bidding sites. On these sites you enter the type of accommodation you desire and your travel dates, and hotels will bid for your reservation. Some sites require that you already have a confirmed booking from a hotel before you can bid. A variation is that you reserve a room at a particular hotel (including Disney hotels) for a set rate. If the rate drops subsequently, you get money back; if the rate goes up, your original rate is locked in.

TripAdvisor's **Tingo** (tingo.com) and Montreal-based **BackBid** (backbid.com) each claim to be able to beat rates offered by hotel websites and OTAs.

AIRBNB If you've traveled at all over the past few years, you've probably heard of Airbnb (airbnb.com), which hooks up travelers with owner-hosted alternative lodging all over the world, from spare bedrooms in people's homes to private apartments, vacation homes, and even live-in boats. It's also rattled the hotel industry because it's not subject to most of the regulations and taxes that dedicated hotels must observe.

We use Airbnb extensively in our personal and professional travel, including for most of our work in New York City and Washington, DC. But we find Airbnb not to be as useful in Orlando for a couple of reasons. One is the enormous supply of vacation-home rentals and hotel rooms, which keeps prices down for lodging around Disney. Second are Disney's incentives for staying on property, including free airport transportation and extra time in the parks. Airbnb users seem to agree: While Orlando is one of the country's biggest travel destinations, it's not one of Airbnb's top 10 markets.

Be Careful Out There: Hotel Scams

In a very convincing scam that's metastasizing to hotels all over the country, a guest receives a phone call, purportedly from the front desk, explaining that there has been a system failure and that the hotel needs the guest's credit card information again to expedite checkout.

Here's what you need to know: (1) A hotel won't ask you to provide sensitive information over the phone, and (2) a hotel won't call you in the middle of the night. If this happens to you, hang up and call hotel security.

Another scam involves websites that look very polished and official and may even include the logos of well-known hotel brands. The scammers will happily sell you a room, paid for in advance with your credit card, and e-mail you credible looking confirmation documents. Problem is, they never contact the hotel to make the booking. In a variation, they actually make the booking but fail to pay the hotel, leaving you to pay when you arrive. To be safe, never click a pop-up that routes you to a third-party hotel site, regardless of how good the deal sounds.

CONDOMINIUMS AND VACATION HOMES

VACATION HOMES ARE FREESTANDING, while condominiums are essentially one- to three-bedroom accommodations in a larger building housing a number of similar units. Because condos tend to be part of large developments (frequently time-shares), amenities such as swimming pools, playgrounds, game arcades, and fitness centers often rival those found in the best hotels. Generally speaking, condo developments don't have restaurants, lounges, or spas.

With a condo, if something goes wrong, there will be someone on hand to fix the problem. Vacation homes rented from a property-management company likewise will have someone to come to the rescue, though responsiveness varies from company to company. If you rent directly from an owner, correcting problems is often more difficult, particularly when the owner doesn't live in the same area as the rental home.

In a vacation home, all the amenities are contained in the home. Depending on the specific home, you might find a small swimming pool, a hot tub, a two-car garage, a family room, a game room, and even a home theater. Features found in both condos and vacation homes include full kitchens, laundry rooms, TVs, DVD players, and frequently stereos. Interestingly, though almost all freestanding vacation homes have private pools, very few have backyards. This means that, except for swimming, the kids are pretty much relegated to playing in the house.

The Price Is Nice

The best deals in lodging in the Walt Disney World area are vacation homes and single-owner condos. Prices range from about $65 a night for two-bedroom condos and town homes to $200–$500 a night for three- to seven-bedroom vacation homes. Forgetting about taxes to keep the comparison simple, let's compare renting a vacation home to staying at one of Disney's Value resorts. A family of two parents, two teens, and two grandparents would need three hotel rooms at Disney's All-Star Resorts. At the lowest rate obtainable, that would run you $110 per night, per room, or $330 total. Rooms are 260 square feet each, so you'd have a total of 780 square feet. Each room has a private bath and a television.

Renting at the same time of year from **All Star Vacation Homes** (no relation to Disney's All-Star Resorts), you can stay at a 2,053-square-foot, four-bedroom, three-bath vacation home with a private pool 3 miles from Walt Disney World for $289—slightly more economical than Disney's Value resorts, with a few bonuses: With four bedrooms, each of the teens can have his or her own room. Further, for the dates we checked, All Star Vacation Homes was running a special in which they threw in a free rental car with a one-week home rental.

But that's not all—the home comes with the following features and amenities: a flat-screen LED TV with a DVD player (assorted games and DVDs available for complimentary checkout at the rental office); a heatable private pool; five additional flat-screen TVs and DVD players (one in each bedroom and one in the game room); a fully equipped kitchen; a game room with an air-hockey table and video-game console; a hot tub; a full-size washer and dryer; a fully furnished private patio; and a child-safety fence.

Continued on page 264

Rental-Home Developments Near WDW

Abbey/West Haven 7
Acadia Estates 10
Ashley Manor 7
Aviana 7
Aylesbury 8
Bahama Bay 9
Bass Lake Estates 5
Bass Lake US 27 9
Bella Piazza 9
Bella Trae 7, 8
BellaVida 9
Bentley Oaks 7
Blue Heron Beach 1
Briargrove 7
Bridgewater
    Crossing 7
Bridgewater Town Ctr. 7
Buenaventura Lakes 4
Calabay Parc 9
Calabay Tower Lake 8
Calabria 9
Cane Island 5
ChampionsGate 7, 8
Chatham Park 5
Clear Creek 5
Club Cortile 5
Country Creek 5
Countryside Manor 6
Creekside 5
Crescent Lakes 6

Crystal Cove 5
Cumbrian Lakes 5
Cypress Lakes 3
Cypress Pointe Forest 7
Davenport Lakes 9
Doral Woods 6
Eagle Pointe 5
Emerald Island 10
Encantada 9
Esprit/Fairways 9
Fiesta Key 5
Flamingo Lakes 3
Florida Pines 9
Floridays 2
Formosa Gardens 10
Four Corners 9
Glenbrook 9
Golden Oaks 1
Grand Palms 9
Grand Reserve 7
Greater Groves 9
Hamilton Reserve 5
Hamlet at West Haven 7
Hampton Lakes 9
Happy Trails 9
Highgate Park 9
High Grove 9

Highland Park 10
Highlands Reserve 9
Hillcrest Estates 9
Indian Creek 10
Indian Point 5
Indian Ridge 10
Indian Ridge Oaks 10
Indian Wells 1
Island Club West 9
Laguna Bay 5
Lake Berkley 5
Lake Davenport 9
Lake Wilson
    Preserve 7
Lakeside 4
Legacy Dunes 9
Legacy Park 9
Liberty Village 5
Lighthouse Key Resort 9
Lindfields 9
Loma Linda 7
Loma Vista 4
Lucaya Village Resort 5
Magic Landings 4
Manors at Westridge 9
Marbella 8
Meadow Woods 4

Millbrook Manor 9
Mission Park 9
Montego Bay 5
Oak Island Cove 10
Oak Island Harbor 10
Oakpoint 7
Orange Lake 10
Orange Tree 9
The Palms 9
Paradise Woods 7
Pines West 8
Pinewood 7
Providence 4
Regal Palms 9
Remington Golf Club 4
Remington Point 4
Ridgewood Lakes 8
Robbins Rest 7

Rolling Hills 10
Royal Oaks 5
Royal Palm Bay 5
Royal Palms 8
Runaway Beach Club 5
Sanctuary at
    West Haven 7
Sandy Ridge 10
Santa Cruz 7
Seasons 5
Shire at West Haven 7
Silver Creek 9
Solana 9
Southern Dunes 8
St. James Park 6

Lake Buena Vista 535

Walt Disney World

536

Celebration

545

Western Way

192

27

Citrus Ridge

Bunker Hill

429 (toll road)

192

417

4

Zone 9

Zone 10

Zone 1

Intercession City

17

Loughman

Zone 8

27

Zone 7

Zone 6

4

0 — 3 mi
0 — 3 km

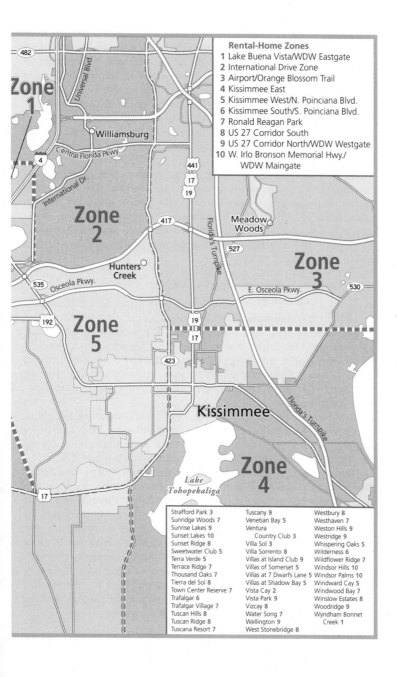

Rental-Home Zones

1 Lake Buena Vista/WDW Eastgate
2 International Drive Zone
3 Airport/Orange Blossom Trail
4 Kissimmee East
5 Kissimmee West/N. Poinciana Blvd.
6 Kissimmee South/S. Poinciana Blvd.
7 Ronald Reagan Park
8 US 27 Corridor South
9 US 27 Corridor North/WDW Westgate
10 W. Irlo Bronson Memorial Hwy./
   WDW Maingate

Strafford Park 3
Sunridge Woods 7
Sunrise Lakes 9
Sunset Lakes 10
Sunset Ridge 8
Sweetwater Club 5
Terra Verde 5
Terrace Ridge 7
Thousand Oaks 7
Tierra del Sol 8
Town Center Reserve 7
Trafalgar 6
Trafalgar Village 7
Tuscan Hills 8
Tuscan Ridge 8
Tuscana Resort 7

Tuscany 9
Venetian Bay 5
Ventura
   Country Club 3
Villa Sol 3
Villa Sorrento 8
Villas at Island Club 9
Villas of Somerset 5
Villas at 7 Dwarfs Lane 5
Villas at Shadow Bay 5
Vista Cay 2
Vista Park 9
Vizcay 8
Water Song 7
Wellington 9
West Stonebridge 8

Westbury 8
Westhaven 7
Weston Hills 9
Westridge 9
Whispering Oaks 5
Wilderness 6
Wildflower Ridge 7
Windsor Hills 10
Windsor Palms 10
Windward Cay 5
Windwood Bay 7
Winslow Estates 8
Woodridge 9
Wyndham Bonnet
   Creek 1

Continued from page 261

One thing we like about All Star Vacation Homes is that its website, allstarvacationhomes.com, offers detailed information, including a dozen or more photos of each specific home. When you book, the home you've been looking at is the actual one you're reserving. If you want to see how the home previously described is furnished, for instance, go to the homepage, scroll down to the very bottom of the page and look for a small search window that says, "Search by property name or ID." Enter **2-8137 SP-WP** in the search window. You'll be taken to another page with a description of the home, a slide show, a floor plan, and additional information.

On the other hand, some vacation-home companies, like rental-car agencies, don't assign you a specific home until the day you arrive. These companies provide photos of a typical home instead of making information available on each of the individual homes in their inventory. In this case, you have to take the company's word that the typical home pictured is representative and that the home you'll be assigned will be just as nice.

How the Vacation-Home Market Works

In the Orlando–Walt Disney World area, there are more than 26,000 rental homes, including stand-alone homes, single-owner condos (that is, not time-shares), and town homes. The same area has about 116,000 hotel rooms. Almost all the rental homes are occupied by their owners for at least a week or two each year; the rest of the year, owners make the homes available for rent. Some owners deal directly with renters, while others enlist the assistance of a property-management company.

Incredibly, about 700 property-management companies operate in the Orlando–Kissimmee–Walt Disney World market. Most are mom-and-pop outfits that manage an inventory of 10 homes or fewer (probably fewer than 70 companies oversee more than 100 rental homes).

Homeowners pay these companies to maintain and promote their properties and handle all rental transactions. Some homes are made available to wholesalers, vacation packagers, and travel agents in deals negotiated either directly by the owners or by property-management companies on the owners' behalf. A wholesaler or vacation packager will occasionally drop its rates to sell slow-moving inventory, but more commonly the cost to renters is higher than when dealing directly with owners or management companies: Because most wholesalers and packagers sell their inventory through travel agents, both the wholesaler/packager's markup and the travel agent's commission are passed along to the renter. These costs are in addition to the owner's cut and/or the fee for the property manager.

Along similar lines, logic may suggest that the lowest rate of all can be obtained by dealing directly with owners, thus eliminating an intermediary. Although this is sometimes true, it's more often the case that property-management companies offer the best rates. With their marketing expertise and larger customer base, these companies can produce a higher occupancy rate than can the owners themselves.

What's more, management companies, or at least the larger ones, can achieve economies of scale not available to owners regarding maintenance, cleaning, linens, even acquiring furniture and appliances (if a house is not already furnished). The combination of higher occupancy rates and economies of scale adds up to a win–win situation for owners, management companies, and renters alike.

Location, Location, Location

The best vacation home is one that is within easy commuting distance of the theme parks. If you plan to spend some time at SeaWorld and the Universal parks, you'll want something just to the northeast of Walt Disney World (between the World and Orlando). If you plan to spend most of your time in the World, the best selection of vacation homes is along US 192 to the south of the park.

Walt Disney World lies mostly in Orange County but has a small southern tip that dips into Osceola County, which, along with Polk County to the west of the World, is where most vacation homes and single-owner condos and town houses are. Zoning laws in Orange County (which also includes most of Orlando, Universal Studios, SeaWorld, Lake Buena Vista, and the International Drive area) used to prohibit short-term rentals of homes and single-owner condos, but in recent years the county has loosened its zoning restrictions in a few predominantly tourist-oriented areas.

By our reckoning, about half the rental homes in Osceola County and all the rental homes in Polk County are too far away from Walt Disney World for commuting to be practical. That said, an entrance to Walt Disney World off the FL 429 four-lane toll road halves the commute from many of the vacation-home developments arrayed around the intersection of US 192 and US 27. FL 429 runs north–south from I-4 south of Walt Disney World to Florida's Turnpike. You might be able to save a few bucks by staying farther out, but the most desirable homes to be found are in Vista Cay and in developments no more than 4 miles from Disney World's main entrance on US 192 (Irlo Bronson Memorial Highway), in Osceola County.

To get the most from a vacation home, you need to be close enough to commute in 20 minutes or less to your Walt Disney World destination. This will allow for naps, quiet time, swimming, and dollar-saving meals you prepare yourself. Though traffic and road conditions are as important as the distance from a vacation home to your Disney destination, we recommend a home no farther than 5 miles away in areas northeast of Walt Disney World and no farther than 4.5 miles away in areas south of the park. Bear in mind that rental companies calculate distance from the vacation home to the absolute nearest square inch of Disney property, so in most instances you can expect to commute another 3 or more miles within Walt Disney World to reach your ultimate destination.

Shopping for a Vacation Home

The only practical way to shop for a rental home is on the web. This makes it relatively easy to compare different properties and rental companies; on the downside, there are so many owners, rental companies, and individual homes to choose from that you could research yourself into a stupor. Three main types of websites serve the home-rental game: those for property-management companies, which showcase a given company's homes and are set up for direct bookings; individual owner sites; and third-party listings sites, which advertise properties available through different owners and sometimes management companies as well. Sites in the last category will usually refer prospective renters to an owner's or management company's site for reservations.

We've found that most property-management sites are not very well designed and will test your patience to the max. You can practically click yourself into old age trying to see all the homes available or figure out where on earth they are. Nearly all claim to be "just minutes from Disney." (By that reasoning, we should list our homes; they're also just minutes from Disney . . . 570 minutes, to be exact!)

Many websites list homes according to towns (such as Auburndale, Clermont, Davenport, Haines City, and Winter Garden) or real estate developments (including Eagle Pointe, Formosa Gardens, Indian Ridge, and Windsor Palms) in the general Disney area, none of which you're likely to be familiar with. The information that counts is the distance of a vacation home or condo from Walt Disney World; for that you often must look for something like "4 miles from Disney" embedded in the home's description. If you visit a site that lists homes by towns or real estate developments, begin by looking at our map on pages 262 and 263, which shows where all these places are in relation to Walt Disney World. If the map is unhelpful in determining distance, we suggest that you find another location for your stay.

The best websites provide the following:

- Numerous photos and in-depth descriptions of individual homes
- Overview maps or text descriptions that reflect how far specific homes or developments are from Walt Disney World
- The ability to book the rental home of your choice on the site
- An easy-to-find phone number for bookings and questions

The best sites are also easy to navigate, let you see what you're interested in without your having to log in or divulge any personal information, and list memberships in such organizations as the Better Business Bureau and the Central Florida Vacation Rental Managers Association (visit cfvrma.com for the association's code of ethics).

Recommended Websites

After checking out dozens upon dozens of sites, here are the ones we recommend. All of them meet the criteria listed above. If you're stunned that there are so few of them, well, so were we. (For the record, we elected not to list some sites that met our criteria but whose homes are too far away from Walt Disney World.)

All Star Vacation Homes (allstarvacationhomes.com) is easily the best of the management-company sites, with easily accessible photos and plenty of details listed. All their rental properties are within either 4 miles of Walt Disney World or 3 miles of Universal Studios.

#1 Dream Homes (floridadreamhomes.com) has a good reputation for customer service and now has photos of and information about the homes in its online inventory.

Orlando's Finest Properties (orlandosfinestproperties.com) represents both homeowners and property-management companies. Offering a broad inventory, the Orlando's Finest Properties website features links to vacation home rental companies.

Vacation Rentals by Owner (vrbo.com) is a nationwide vacation-homes listings service that puts prospective renters in direct contact with owners. The site is straightforward and always lists a large number of rental properties in Celebration, Disney's planned community situated about 8–10 minutes from the theme parks. Two similar listings services with good websites are **Vacation Rentals 411** (vacationrentals411.com) and **Last Minute Villas** (lastminutevillas.net).

Visit Orlando (visitorlando.com) is the website to visit if you're interested in renting a condominium at one of the many time-share developments (click on "Places to Stay"). You can call the developments directly, but going through this site allows you to bypass sales departments and escape their high-pressure invitations to sit through sales presentations. The site also lists hotels and vacation homes.

Making Contact

Once you've found a vacation home you like, check the website for a Frequently Asked Questions (FAQ) page. If there's not one, here are some of the things you'll want to ask the owner or rental company.

1. How close is the property to Walt Disney World?
2. Is the home or condominium that I see on the Internet the one I'll get?
3. Is the property part of a time-share development?
4. Are there any specials or discounts available?
5. Is everything included in the rental price, or are there additional charges? What about taxes?
6. How old is the property I'm interested in? Has it been refurbished recently?
7. What is the view from the property?
8. Is the property near any noisy roads?
9. What is your smoking policy?
10. Are pets allowed (or not)?
11. Is the pool heated?
12. Is there a fenced backyard where children can play?
13. How many people can be seated at the main dining table?
14. Is there a separate dedicated telephone at the property?
15. Is high-speed Internet access available?
16. Are linens and towels provided?
17. How far are the nearest supermarket and drugstore?
18. Are child-care services available?
19. Are there restaurants nearby?
20. Is transportation to the parks provided?
21. Will we need a car?
22. What is required to make a reservation?
23. What is your change/cancellation policy?

24. When is checkout time?
25. What will we be responsible for when we check out?
26. How will we receive our confirmation and arrival instructions?
27. What are your office hours?
28. What are the directions to your office?
29. What if we arrive after your office has closed?
30. Whom do we contact if something goes wrong during our stay?
31. How long have you been in business?
32. Are you licensed by the state of Florida?
33. Do you belong to the Better Business Bureau and/or the Central Florida Vacation Rental Managers Association?

We frequently receive letters from readers extolling the virtues of renting a condo or vacation home. This endorsement by a New Jersey family of five is typical:

I cannot stress enough how important it is if you have a large family (more than two kids) to rent a house for your stay! We had visited WDW several times in the past by ourselves when we were newlyweds. Fast-forward 10 years later, when we took our three kids, ages 6 years, 4 years, and 20 months. We stayed at Windsor Hills Resort, which I booked through globalresorthomes.com. I was able to see all the homes and check availability when I was reserving the house. This development is 1.5 miles from the Disney Maingate. It took us about 10 minutes to drive there in the a.m., and we had no traffic issues at all.

THE BEST HOTELS FOR FAMILIES OUTSIDE WALT DISNEY WORLD

WHAT MAKES A SUPER FAMILY HOTEL? Roomy accommodations, in-room fridge, great pool, complimentary breakfast, child-care options, and programs for kids are a few of the things the *Unofficial Guide* hotel team researched in selecting the top hotels for families from among hundreds of properties in the Disney World area. Some of our picks are expensive, others are more reasonable, and some are a bargain. All understand a family's needs.

Though all of the following hotels offer some type of shuttle to the theme parks, some offer very limited service. Call the hotel before you book and ask what the shuttle schedule will be when you visit. Because families, like individuals, have different wants and needs, we haven't ranked these properties; they're listed by zone and alphabetically.

INTERNATIONAL DRIVE & UNIVERSAL AREAS

CoCo Key Water Resort–Orlando ★★★½

7400 International Dr. Orlando
☎ 407-351-2626 or 877-875-4681
cocokeyorlando.com

Rate per night $75–$180. **Pools** ★★★★. **Fridge in room** Yes. **Shuttle to parks** Yes (Aquatica, SeaWorld, Universal, and Volcano Bay, free; Disney World, $18/person round-trip). **Maximum number of occupants per room** 4. **Special comments** $28/day resort fee for use of the water park; day guests may use the water park for $24.95/person Monday–Thursday ($26.95 on weekends and $21.95 for Florida residents).

NOT FAR FROM THE UNIVERSAL ORLANDO theme parks, CoCo Key combines a tropical-themed hotel with a canopied water park featuring three pools and 14 waterslides, as well as poolside food and arcade entertainment. A full-service restaurant serves breakfast and dinner; a food court offers family favorites such as burgers, chicken fingers, and pizza.

A unique feature of the resort is its cashless payment system, much like that on a cruise ship. At check-in, families receive bar-coded wristbands that allow purchased items to be easily charged to their room.

The spacious guest rooms include 37-inch flat-panel TVs, free Wi-Fi, granite showers and countertops, and plentiful outlets for electronics.

DoubleTree by Hilton Orlando at SeaWorld ★★★★½

Rate per night $129–$291. **Pools** ★★★½. **Fridge in room** Standard in some rooms; available in others for $10/day. **Shuttle to parks** No. **Maximum number of occupants per room** 4. **Special comments** Good option if you're visiting SeaWorld or Aquatica. Pets welcome (1 pet per room, 25-pound limit, $75); $19.95/day resort fee.

10100 International Dr. Orlando
☎ 407-352-1100 or 800-327-0363
doubletreeorlando idrive.com

ON 28 LUSH, TROPICAL ACRES with a Balinese feel, the DoubleTree is adjacent to SeaWorld and Aquatica water park. The 1,094 rooms and suites—classified as resort or tower—are suitable for business travelers or families. We recommend the tower rooms for good views and the resort rooms for maximum convenience. Laguna serves steak and seafood, along with breakfast; you can also get a quick bite at The Market or the pool bar. Relax and cool off at one of the three pools (there are two more just for kids), or indulge in a special spa treatment. A fitness center, minigolf course and putting green, children's day camp, and game area afford even more diversions. The resort is about a 15-minute drive to Walt Disney World, a 12-minute drive to Universal, or a short walk to SeaWorld.

Hard Rock Hotel ★★★★½

Rate per night $259–$464. **Pool** ★★★★. **Fridge in room** Yes. **Shuttle to parks** Yes (Universal, SeaWorld, Discovery Cove, Aquatica, and Volcano Bay). **Maximum number of occupants per room** 5 (double-queen) or 3 (king). **Special comments** Character breakfast Tuesday; character dinner Saturday. Pets welcome ($50/night).

5800 Universal Blvd. Orlando
☎ 407-503-2000 or 888-464-3617
hardrockhotels.com /orlando

FOR YOUNGER ADULTS and families with older kids, the Hard Rock Hotel is the hippest place to lay your head. It's both Universal Orlando's least-expansive (but second-most-expensive) on-site deluxe resort and the closest resort to Universal's theme parks. The exterior has a California Mission theme, with white stucco walls, arched entryways, and rust-colored roof tiles. Inside, the lobby is a tribute to rock-and-roll style, all marble, chrome, and stage lighting. The lobby's walls are decorated with enough concert posters, costumes, and musical instruments to start another wing of Cleveland's Rock and Roll Hall of Fame; ask the front desk for information about a self-guided memorabilia tour.

The eight floors hold 650 rooms and 29 suites, with the rooms categorized into standard, deluxe, and club-level tiers. Standard rooms are 375 square feet, slightly larger than rooms at Disney's Moderate resorts and a bit smaller than most Disney Deluxe rooms. The Hard Rock Hotel completed a top-to-bottom "remastering" of its rooms in early 2015, giving the formerly masculine decor a major makeover, with light-gray walls and linens, pastel furniture, and colorful retro-inspired accents.

Standard rooms are furnished with two queen beds, with smooth, plush, comfortable linens and more pillows than you'll know what to do with. Rooms also include a flat-panel LCD television, a refrigerator, a coffeemaker, and an alarm clock with a 30-pin iPhone docking port.

A six-drawer dresser and separate closet with sliding doors ensure plenty of storage space. In addition, most rooms have a reading chair and a small desk with two chairs. An optional rollaway bed, available at an extra charge, allows standard rooms to sleep up to five people.

Each room's dressing area features a sink and hair dryer. The bathroom is probably large enough for most adults to get ready in the morning while another person gets ready in the dressing area.

Deluxe rooms with king beds are around 500 square feet and can accommodate up to three people with an optional rollaway bed rental. These rooms feature a U-shaped sitting area in place of the second bed, and the rest of the amenities are the same as in standard rooms. Deluxe queen rooms are also 500 square feet and can hold up to five people using a pullout sofa.

Situated in the middle of the resort's C-shaped main building, the 12,000-square-foot pool includes a 250-foot waterslide, a sand beach, and underwater speakers so you can hear the music while you swim. Adjacent to the pool are a fountain play area for small children, a sand-volleyball court, hot tubs, and a poolside bar. The Hard Rock also has a small, functional fitness center. Like all Universal Orlando Resort hotels, the Hard Rock has a business center and video arcade.

On-site dining includes The Kitchen, a casual full-service restaurant open for breakfast, lunch, and dinner, featuring American food such as burgers, steaks, and salads. The Palm Restaurant is an upscale steakhouse available for dinner only. And, of course, the Hard Rock Cafe is just a short distance away at Universal CityWalk.

While not exactly cheap (it charges $22 per night for self-parking), Hard Rock is a good value compared to, say, Disney's Yacht & Beach Clubs. What you're paying for at the Hard Rock is a short walk to the theme parks and Universal Express Unlimited first, and the room second.

Holiday Inn Resort Orlando Suites–Waterpark ★★★½

14500 Continental Gateway
Orlando
☎ 407-387-5437
hisuitesorlando.com

Rate per night $129–$500. **Pools ★★★★**. **Fridge in room** Yes. **Shuttle to parks** Yes. **Maximum number of occupants per room** 8. **Special comment** $25/day resort fee.

FOLLOWING A $30 MILLION RENOVATION, the hotel formerly known as the Nickelodeon Suites Resort is now the Holiday Inn Resort Orlando Suites–Waterpark. Sadly, all of the Nickelodeon experiences are gone: no Double Dare, no getting slimed, no characters. The resort that remains, however, is still impressive—and newly renovated.

The 777 suites come in one, two, and three-bedroom varieties and each suite contains a mini-fridge, a microwave, a flat-screen TV, and high-speed Internet. The resort also has two water parks with 13 slides, a 4-D Experience,

Laser Challenge, and a 3,000-square-foot arcade, along with cabanas, a poolside bar, and casual dining.

Loews Portofino Bay Hotel ★★★★½

Rate per night $294–$479. **Pools** ★★★★. **Fridge in room** Minibar; fridge available for $15/day. **Shuttle to parks** Yes (Universal, SeaWorld, Discovery Cove, Aquatica, and Volcano Bay). **Maximum number of occupants per room** 5 (double-queen) or 3 (king). **Special comments** Character dinner on Friday. Pets welcome ($50/night).

5601 Universal Blvd. Orlando
☎ 407-503-1000 or 888-464-3617
loewshotels.com /universal-orlando

UNIVERSAL'S TOP-OF-THE-LINE HOTEL evokes the Italian seaside city of Portofino, complete with a man-made Portofino Bay past the lobby. To Universal's credit, the layout, color, and theming of the guest-room buildings are a good approximation of the architecture around the harbor in the real Portofino (Universal's version has fewer yachts, however).

Inside, the lobby is decorated with pink marble floors, white-wood columns, and arches. The space is both airy and comfortable, with side rooms featuring seats and couches done in bold reds and deep blues.

Most guest rooms are 450 square feet, larger than most at Disney's Deluxe resorts, and have either one king bed or two queen beds. King rooms sleep up to three people with an optional rollaway bed; the same option allows queen rooms to sleep up to five. Two room-view options are available: Garden rooms look out over the landscaping and trees (many of these are the east-facing rooms in the resort's east wing; others face one of the three pools); bay-view rooms face either west or south and overlook Portofino Bay.

Rooms come furnished with a 32-inch LCD flat-panel TV, a refrigerator, a coffeemaker, and an alarm clock with a 30-pin iPhone docking port. Other amenities include a small desk with two chairs, a comfortable reading chair with lamp, a chest of drawers, and a standing closet. As at all Universal on-site hotels, Wi-Fi is free in guest rooms and the lobby, though you can pay $15 per day for higher speeds. Beds are large, plush, and comfortable.

Guest bathrooms at Portofino Bay are the best on Universal property. The shower has enough water pressure to strip paint from old furniture, not to mention an adjustable spray nozzle that varies the water pulses to simulate everything from monsoon season in the tropics to the rhythmic thumps of wildebeest hooves during migrating season. We love it.

Portofino Bay has three pools, the largest of which, the Beach Pool, is on the west side of the resort. Two smaller quiet pools sit at the far end of the east wing and to the west of the main lobby. The Beach Pool has a zero-entry design and a waterslide themed after a Roman aqueduct, plus a children's play area, hot tubs, and a poolside bar and grill. The Villa Pool has private cabanas for that Italian Riviera feeling. Rounding out the luxuries are the Mandara Spa, a complete fitness center, a business center, and a video arcade.

On-site dining includes three sit-down restaurants serving Italian cuisine: a deli, a pizzeria, and a café serving coffee and gelato. Some of the food prices go well beyond what we'd consider reasonable, even for a theme park hotel.

While we think Portofino Bay has some of Universal's best rooms, the prices put it on par with the Ritz-Carlton—something its good points can't quite justify. On the other hand, the Ritz isn't a short walk from The Wizarding World of Harry Potter.

Loews Royal Pacific Resort   ★★★★½

6300 Hollywood Way
Orlando
☎ 407-503-3000 or
888-464-3617
loewshotels.com
/universal-orlando

Rate per night $234–$404. **Pools** ★★★★. **Fridge in room** Yes. **Shuttle to parks** Yes (Universal, SeaWorld, Discovery Cove, Aquatica, and Volcano Bay). **Maximum number of occupants per room** 5 (double-queen) or 3 (king). **Special comments** Microwaves available for $15/day. Character breakfast on Sunday; character dinners on Monday, Wednesday, and Thursday. Pets welcome ($50/night).

YOU MAY BE TEMPTED, as we were initially, to write off the Royal Pacific as a knockoff of Disney's Polynesian Village Resort. There are similarities, but the Royal Pacific is attractive enough, and has enough strengths of its own, for us to recommend that you try it for yourself.

Guests enter the lobby from a walkway two stories above an artificial stream that surrounds the resort. Once you're inside, the lobby's dark teak-wood accents contrast nicely with the enormous amount of light coming in from the windows and three-story A-frame roof. Palms line the walkway through the lobby, and through these you see that the whole lobby surrounds an enormous outdoor fountain.

The 1,000 guest rooms are spread among three Y-shaped wings attached to the main building. Standard rooms are 335 square feet—about the size of a room at Disney's Moderate resorts—and feature one king or two queen beds. King rooms sleep up to three people with an optional rollaway bed; queen rooms sleep five with that rollaway bed. The beds, fitted with 300-thread-count sheets, are very comfortable.

Rooms have modern monochrome wall treatments and carpets, accented with boldly colored floral graphics. Amenities include a 32-inch flat-panel LCD TV, a refrigerator, a coffeemaker, and an alarm clock with a 30-pin iPhone docking port. Other amenities include a small desk with two chairs, a comfortable reading chair, a chest of drawers, and a large closet.

A dressing area with sink is separated from the rest of the room by a wall. Next to the dressing area is the bathroom, with a tub, shower, and toilet. While they're acceptable, the bathroom and dressing areas at the Royal Pacific are our least favorite in the Universal resorts.

As at the Hard Rock, the Royal Pacific's zero-entry pool includes a sand beach, a volleyball court, a play area for kids, a hot tub, and cabanas for rent, plus a poolside bar and grill.

Amenities include a 5,000-square-foot fitness facility, a business center, a video arcade, two full-service restaurants, three bars, and a luau. Of the table-service restaurants, only Islands Dining Room is open for breakfast. Emeril Lagasse's Tchoup Chop, the other table-service option, is open for lunch and dinner (reservations recommended).

Loews Sapphire Falls Resort   ★★★★

6601 Adventure Way
Orlando
☎ 407-503-5000 or
888-464-3617
loewshotels.com
/universal-orlando

Rate per night $179–$229. **Pools** ★★★★. **Fridge in room** Yes. **Shuttle to parks** Yes (Universal, SeaWorld, Discovery Cove, Aquatica, and Volcano Bay). **Maximum number of occupants per room** 5 (double-queen) or 3 (king). **Special comments** Microwaves available for $15/day. Character breakfast on Saturday. Pets welcome ($50/night).

UNIVERSAL'S FIFTH ON-SITE LOEWS HOTEL brought a sunny Caribbean island vibe to the Moderate market when its 1,000 rooms opened in summer 2016. Sandwiched between Royal Pacific and Cabana Bay—physically and pricewise—Sapphire Falls sports all the amenities of Universal's three deluxe hotels, including water-taxi transportation to the parks, with the crucial exception of complimentary Express Passes.

Water figures heavily here; the namesake falls form the scenic centerpiece of the resort. The 16,000-square-foot, zero-entry main pool features a white-sand beach, a waterslide, children's play areas, a fire pit, and cabanas for rent. A fitness room holds a sauna and hot tub. For dinner, Amatista Cookhouse offers table-service Caribbean dining, with an open kitchen and waterfront views. Club Katine serves tapas-style small plates near the pool bar's fire pit. New Dutch Trading Co. is an island-inspired grab-and-go marketplace, and Strong Water Tavern in the lobby has rum tastings and tableside ceviche.

Sapphire Falls also contains 131,000 square feet of meeting space and a business center. Walkways connect to a parking structure, which in turn connects to the meeting facilities at Royal Pacific, making the new sister properties ideal for conventions.

The rooms range from 364 square feet in a standard queen or king to 529 square feet in the 36 Kids' Suites, up to 1,358 square feet in the 15 Hospitality Suites. All rooms have a flat-panel HDTV, mini-fridge, and coffeemaker.

Universal's Cabana Bay Beach Resort ★★★★

Rate per night $119–$210 standard rooms, $174–$294 suites. **Pools ★★★★. Fridge in room** Suites only. **Shuttle to parks** Yes (Universal, SeaWorld, Discovery Cove, Aquatica, and Volcano Bay). **Maximum number of occupants per room** 4 for standard rooms, 6 for suites.

6550 Adventure Way
Orlando
☎ 407-503-4000 or
888-464-3617
loewshotels.com
/universal-orlando

OPENED IN SPRING 2014, Cabana Bay is Universal's first on-site hotel aimed at the value and moderate markets. The theme is mid-century modern, with lots of windows, bright colors, and period-appropriate lighting and furniture. We think the resort would be right at home in the deserts of Palm Springs or Las Vegas.

Kids will love the two large and well-themed pools (one with a lazy river), the amount of space they have to run around in, the video arcade, and the vintage cars parked outside the hotel lobby. Adults will appreciate the sophisticated kitsch of the decor, the multiple lounges, the business center, and the on-site Starbucks. We think Cabana Bay is an excellent choice for price- and/or space-conscious families visiting Universal.

The hotel's closest competitor in the Orlando area is Disney's Art of Animation Resort, and the two share many similarities. Both have standard rooms and family suites. At 430 square feet per suite, Cabana Bay suites are about 135 square feet smaller than comparable suites at A of A and have only one bathroom. We found them well appointed for two to four people per room (though not for the six Loews claims as its capacity). Rack rates for the suites are about $140–$300 per night less than Art of Animation's.

Each family suite has a small bedroom with two queen beds, divided from the living area and kitchenette by a sliding screen; a foldout sofa in the living area offers additional sleeping space. (Standard rooms also have two queen beds.) The bath is divided into three sections: toilet, sink area, and shower room with additional sink. The kitchenette has a microwave, coffeemaker, and mini-fridge. A bar area allows extra seating for quick meals, and a large closet has enough space to store everyone's luggage. Built-in USB charging outlets for your devices are a thoughtful touch.

Recreational options include the 10-lane Galaxy Bowl (about $15 per person with shoe rental), poolside table tennis and billiards, and a large Jack LaLanne fitness center. (Fitness centers aren't found at any Disney Value or Moderate resort except Coronado Springs.) Outdoor movies are shown nightly near the pool.

In addition to the Starbucks, a food court with seating area shows 1950s TV clips. Swizzle Lounge in the lobby, two pool bars, in-room pizza delivery, and the Galaxy Bowl round out the on-site dining options. You'll find more restaurants and clubs nearby at the Royal Pacific Resort and Universal CityWalk.

Unlike the other Universal resorts, Cabana Bay offers no watercraft service to the parks—it's either take the bus or walk. In November 2014, a new pedestrian bridge opened connecting Cabana Bay to CityWalk and the rest of Universal Orlando, but we still recommend the bus service for most people. Cabana Bay guests are eligible for early entry at Universal but do not get a complimentary Universal Express pass.

Cabana Bay has proved so popular that Universal added two additional towers that enlarge the resort by 400 more guest rooms. The new rooms, which opened in 2017, offer views of Volcano Bay, the new Universal water park that opened in 2017.

Day guests who want to check out Cabana Bay should take the bus there from the parking hub—the garden walk's gate requires a key card for hotel access. Take care when driving into and out of the hotel's driveway on Adventure Way. If you miss the entrance or make a right when exiting, you'll find yourself on a one-way road to I-4 West toward Disney, and you won't be able to make a U-turn until the FL 528 expressway.

LAKE BUENA VISTA & I-4 CORRIDOR

B Resort & Spa ★★★½

Rate per night $89–$329. **Pools** ★★★½. **Fridge in room** Yes. **Shuttle to parks** Yes (Disney only). **Maximum number of occupants per room** 4 plus child in crib. **Special comments** $28/night resort fee. *See full profile on page 231.*

Four Seasons Resort Orlando at Walt Disney World Resort ★★★★★

10100 Dream Tree Blvd.
Lake Buena Vista
☎ 407-313-7777
or 800-267-3046
fourseasons.com
/orlando

Rate per night $545–$845. **Pools** ★★★★★. **Fridge in room** Yes. **Shuttle to parks** Yes (Disney only). **Maximum number of occupants per room** 4 (3 adults or 2 adults and 2 children). **Special comments** The best pool complex in Walt Disney World.

WITH 444 GUEST ROOMS, the Four Seasons Resort Orlando is simultaneously the largest hotel in the Four Seasons chain and the smallest on Disney property. It's also the best deluxe resort in the area, with comfort, amenities, and personal service that far surpass anything Disney's Deluxes offer. If you're trying to fit a couple of days of relaxing nonpark time into your vacation, this is the hotel to choose.

Standard guest rooms average around 500 square feet and feature either one king bed with a sleeper sofa or two double beds (a crib is available in double rooms). Amenities include two flat-panel televisions, a coffeemaker, a small refrigerator, a work desk with two chairs, a personal digital video recorder (DVR) to record TV shows, and Bluetooth speakers for your personal audio. In keeping with the room's gadget-friendly spirit, each nightstand has four electrical outlets and two USB ports.

Bathrooms have glass-walled showers, a separate tub, marble vanities with two sinks, mosaic-tile floors, hair dryers, lighted mirrors, and a TV in the mirror above the sink.

Most rooms have an 80-square-foot balcony with table and chairs—perfect for your morning coffee or an evening nightcap. Standard-view rooms look out onto the resort's lawns, gardens, and nearby homes in Golden Oak. Lake-view rooms—which overlook the lake, the Tom Fazio–designed Tranquilo Golf Club (formerly Osprey Ridge), or the pool—cost about $100 more per night than standard-view rooms. Park-view rooms, on floors 6–16, cost about $200 more per night than standard-view rooms and offer views of the Magic Kingdom's nightly fireworks. (Suites are available with views of Epcot, too.)

The resort's 5-acre pool area is the best on Walt Disney World property, and it's the least crowded. It features an adult pool, a family pool, an 11,000-square-foot lazy river, and a splash zone with two 242-foot waterslides. To put this in perspective, the Four Seasons' pool area is about twice as large as Stormalong Bay at the Yacht & Beach Club Resorts but with only a third as many guests. Private pool cabanas are available for rent for around $200/day.

Capa, a Spanish-themed rooftop restaurant, serves seafood and steaks (open nightly, 6–10 p.m.; dress is resort casual, and reservations are recommended). Ravello, on the first floor, serves American breakfasts (6:30–11 a.m.) and Italian dinners (5:30–10 p.m.; reservations are recommended, and dress is smart casual). PB&G (Pool Bar and Grill) serves barbecued meats and salads by the main pool (11 a.m.–6 p.m.).

At the hotel's Disney Planning Center, Disney cast members can help with reservations or any other Disney needs. Disney will also deliver your in-park purchases to the Four Seasons, but staying at the Four Seasons does not qualify guests for Extra Magic Hours, 60-day FastPass+ reservations, or use of Magical Express from the airport.

The hotel has a full-service spa and fitness center, as well as a beautiful late-checkout lounge that allows use of the showers and bathrooms in the spa.

Hilton Orlando Buena Vista Palace ★★★½

Rate per night $139–$342. **Pools** ★★★½. **Fridge in room** Yes. **Shuttle to parks** Yes (Disney only). **Maximum number of occupants per room** 4. **Special comments** Sunday character brunch available; $25/night resort fee. *See full profile on page 232.*

Hilton Orlando Lake Buena Vista ★★★★

Rate per night $161–$278. **Pools** ★★★½. **Fridge in room** Minibar; mini-fridge available free on request. **Shuttle to parks** Yes (Disney theme and water parks only). **Maximum number of occupants per room** 4. **Special comments** Sunday character breakfast; $27/night resort fee. *See full profile on page 232.*

Hilton Orlando Bonnet Creek ★★★★

14100 Bonnet Creek
Resort Lane
Orlando
☎ 407-597-3600
hiltonbonnetcreek.com

Rate per night $119–$249. **Pool** ★★★★½. **Fridge in room** Yes. **Shuttle to parks** Yes. **Maximum number of occupants per room** 4. **Special comments** $30/night resort fee.

THE HILTON BONNET CREEK is one of our favorite non-Disney hotels in Lake Buena Vista, and the value for the money beats anything in Disney's Deluxe category. Behind Caribbean Beach and Pop Century Resorts, this Hilton is much nicer than the one in the Disney Springs Resort Area.

Standard rooms measure around 414 square feet—comparable to Disney's Deluxe resorts—and have either one king bed or two queen beds. The beds' mattresses and linens are very comfortable. Other features include a 37-inch flat-panel TV, a spacious work desk, an armoire, a small reading chair with floor lamp, a nightstand, and a digital clock. A coffeemaker, a small refrigerator, and an ironing board and iron are all standard, along with free wired and wireless Internet.

Bathrooms include tile floors with glass showers. Unfortunately, the layout isn't as up-to-date as other hotels'—where many upscale hotel bathrooms have two sinks, the Hilton's has only one. And where modern bathroom configurations often include a dressing area separate from the bath and a separate water closet for the commode, everything is in the bathroom here.

The Hilton's public areas are stylish and spacious. Families will enjoy the huge zero-entry pool, complete with waterslide, as well as the 3-acre lazy river. Even better, the Hilton staff run arts-and-crafts activities poolside during the day, allowing parents to grab a quick swim and a cocktail. Pool-facing cabanas are also available for rent at around $300 per day or $150 per half-day. A nice fitness center sits on the ground floor.

The Hilton participates in the Waldorf Astoria's Kids Club next door, for children ages 5–12. A daytime program is available 10:30 a.m.–2:30 p.m., and an evening program is available 6–10 p.m. on Friday and Saturday. Price is $75 for the first child, $25 for each additional child.

There are more than a dozen restaurants and lounges between the Hilton and the Waldorf Astoria, with cuisine including an upscale steakhouse, Italian, sushi, tapas, a coffee bar, an American bistro, and breakfast buffet choices. Hours are usually 7–11:30 a.m. for breakfast, 11:30 a.m.–5 p.m. for lunch, and 5–10 p.m. for dinner. Reservations are recommended for the fancy places.

Marriott Village at Lake Buena Vista ★★★

8623 Vineland Ave.
Orlando
☎ 407-938-9001
or 877-682-8552
marriottvillage.com

Rate per night $74–$189. **Pools** ★★★. **Fridge in room** Yes. **Shuttle to parks** Disney only. **Maximum number of occupants per room** 4 (Courtyard and Fairfield) or 5 (SpringHill). **Special comments** Free Continental breakfast at Fairfield and SpringHill.

THIS GATED HOTEL COMMUNITY INCLUDES a 388-room Fairfield Inn (★★★½), a 400-suite SpringHill Suites (★★★), and a 312-room Courtyard (★★★½). Whatever your budget, you'll find a room here to fit it. If you need a bit more space, book SpringHill Suites; if you're looking for value, try the Fairfield Inn; if you need limited business amenities, reserve at the Courtyard. Amenities at all three properties include fridge, cable TV, iron and board, hair dryer, and microwave. Cribs and roll-away beds are available at no extra charge at all locations. Swimming pools at all three hotels are attractive and medium-sized, featuring children's interactive splash zones and whirlpools; in addition, each property has its own fitness center. The incredibly convenient Village Marketplace food court includes Pizza Hut, Village Grill, Village Coffee House, and a 24-hour convenience store. Bahama Breeze and Golden Corral full-service restaurants are within walking distance. Other services and amenities include a Disney planning station and ticket sales, an arcade, and a Hertz car-rental desk. Shoppers will find the Orlando Premium Outlets adjacent. You'll get plenty of bang for your buck at Marriott Village.

Sheraton Vistana Resort Villas   ★★★★

Rate per night $127–$254. **Pools** ★★★½. **Fridge in room** Yes. **Shuttle to parks** Yes (Disney only). **Maximum number of occupants per room** 4–8. **Special comments** Though time-shares, the villas are rented nightly as well.

8800 Vistana Centre Dr. Orlando
☎ 407-239-3100 or 866-208-0003
tinyurl.com/vistanaresort

THE SHERATON VISTANA is deceptively large, stretching across both sides of Vistana Centre Drive. Because Sheraton's emphasis is on selling the time-shares, the rental angle is little known. But families should consider it; it's one of Orlando's best off–Disney World properties.

The spacious villas come in one-bedroom, two-bedroom, and two-bedroom-with-lock-off models (which can be reconfigured as one studio room and a one-bedroom suite). Decorated in beachy pastels, each villa has a full kitchen (including fridge/freezer, microwave, oven/range, dishwasher, toaster, and coffeemaker, with an option to prestock with groceries and laundry products), a washer and dryer, TVs in the living room and each bedroom (one with DVD player), a stereo with CD player in some villas, a separate dining area, and a private patio or balcony in most.

Grounds offer seven swimming pools (three with bars); four playgrounds; two restaurants; game rooms; fitness centers; a minigolf course; sports-equipment rentals (including bikes); and courts for basketball, volleyball, tennis, and shuffleboard. A mind-boggling array of activities for kids (and adults) ranges from crafts to games and sports tournaments.

Of special note: Vistana is highly secure, with locked gates bordering all guest areas, so children can have the run of the place without parents worrying about them wandering off. The one downside: noise, both above (from being on the flight path of a helicopter tour company) and below (from International Drive). Bring a white-noise machine or app for better sleep.

Staybridge Suites Orlando Lake Buena Vista   ★★★★½

Rate per night $130–$260. **Pool** ★★★. **Fridge in room** Yes (full kitchen). **Shuttle to parks** Yes. **Maximum number of occupants per room** 4 (1-bedroom suites) or 8 (2-bedroom suites). **Special comments** Highest-rated off-site resort by *Unofficial Guide* readers in 2016; AAA Three Diamond Award; no resort fees; free hot breakfast and afternoon reception.

8751 Suiteside Dr. Lake Buena Vista
☎ 407-238-0777
sborlando.com

WE FOUND THIS GEM through our reader surveys, which named this Staybridge Suites the best off-site hotel near Walt Disney World in 2016. Having stayed there, we agree. The Staybridge is so inexpensive we'd recommend the two-bedroom suites for families as small as two or three people.

The best value is the two-bedroom suites. We paid $136 (with tax) for ours, less than you'd pay for a Value resort most of the year. For that we got two separate bedrooms on opposite ends of the suite. One bedroom has a king bed; the other, two doubles. A sleeper sofa is standard in both the one- and two-bedroom layouts.

Each bedroom has its own full bathroom. Between the bedrooms are a living room, dining area, and full kitchen with dishwasher, range, microwave, and fridge as well as plates, cups, glasses, cutlery, and basic pots and pans. There's a big-screen TV in the living room and smaller ones in each bedroom.

Other amenities include free Wi-Fi, a free hot-breakfast bar, and an afternoon reception with free drinks and snacks. Service was excellent. Be aware that the Staybridge is popular enough that it's unlikely your room will be ready much before the 4 p.m. check-in time.

Located about 0.5 mile from the Disney Springs Resort Area, just around the corner on South Apopka–Vineland Road, the Staybridge is about a 10-minute drive to the Disney Springs parking garages and about 19 minutes to the Magic Kingdom parking lot. Nearby are two shopping centers, both easily walkable from your room.

Waldorf Astoria Orlando   ★★★★½

14200 Bonnet Creek Resort Ln, Orlando
☎ 407-597-5500 or 800-425-3673
waldorfastoria3
.hilton.com/

Rate per night $179–$424. **Pool** ★★★★. **Fridge in room** Yes. **Shuttle to parks** Yes (Disney only) **Maximum number of occupants per room** 4, plus child in crib. **Special comments** Good alternative to Disney Deluxe resorts; $30/night resort fee.

THE WALDORF ASTORIA is between I-4 and Disney's Pop Century Resort, near the Hilton Orlando at the back of the Bonnet Creek Resort property. Getting here requires a GPS or good directions, so be prepared with those before you travel. Once you arrive, however, you'll know the trip was worth it. Beautifully decorated and well manicured, the Waldorf is more elegant than any Disney resort. Service is excellent, and the staff-to-guest ratio is far lower than at Disney properties.

At just under 450 square feet, standard rooms feature either two queen beds or one king. A full-size desk allows you to get work done if it's absolutely necessary, and rooms also have flat-panel televisions, high-speed Internet, and Wi-Fi. The bathrooms are spacious and gorgeous, with cool marble floors, glass-walled showers, separate tubs, and enough counter space for a Broadway makeup artist.

Amenities include a fitness center, a spa, a golf course, six restaurants, and two pools (including one zero-entry pool for kids). Shuttles service the Disney parks about every half-hour, but check with the front desk for the exact schedule when you arrive. Runners will like the relative solitude—it's about a 1-mile round-trip to the nearest busy road.

Wyndham Bonnet Creek Resort   ★★★★½

9560 Via Encinas
Lake Buena Vista
☎ 407-238-3500
wyndhambonnet
creek.com

Rate per night $179–$370. **Pool** ★★★★. **Fridge in room** Yes. **Shuttle to parks** Yes (Disney only, $8/person). **Maximum number of occupants per room** 4–12 depending on room/suite. **Special comments** A non-Disney suite hotel in Disney World.

THIS CONDO HOTEL lies on the south side of Buena Vista Drive, about a quarter-mile east of Disney's Caribbean Beach Resort. It's part of a luxury-hotel complex on the same site that includes a 500-room Waldorf Astoria (see previous profile), a 400-room Wyndham Grand, and a 1,000-room Hilton (see page 276). The development is surrounded on three sides by Disney property and on one side by I-4.

One- and two-bedroom condos have fully equipped kitchens, washers and dryers, jetted tubs, and balconies. Activities and amenities include two outdoor swimming pools, a lazy river float stream, a children's activities program, a game room, a playground, and miniature golf. Free scheduled transportation serves all the Disney parks. One-bedroom units are furnished with a king bed in the bedroom and a sleeper sofa in the living area; two-bedroom condos have two double beds in the second bedroom, a sleeper sofa in the living area, and an additional bath.

US 192 AREA

Clarion Suites Maingate ★★★

Rate per night $99–$169. **Pool** ★★★. **Fridge in room** Yes. **Shuttle to parks** Yes (Disney, Universal, and SeaWorld). **Maximum number of occupants per room** 6 for most suites. **Special comments** Free Continental breakfast served daily for up to 2 guests; additional breakfast $5.99 in advance, $6.99 day of; $10/day resort fee.

THIS PROPERTY HAS 150 SPACIOUS one-room suites, each with double sofa bed, microwave, fridge, coffeemaker, TV, hair dryer, and safe. The suites are clean and contemporary, with muted deep-purple and beige tones and plenty of bathroom counter space. The heated pool is large and has plenty of chairs. A kiddie pool, whirlpool, and poolside bar complete the courtyard. Other amenities include an arcade and a gift shop. But Maingate's big plus is its location next to a shopping center with everything a family could need: You'll find 10 dining options, including Outback Steakhouse, Red Lobster, and Chinese, Italian, and Japanese eateries; a Winn-Dixie Marketplace; a liquor store; a bank; a dry cleaner; and an information center with park passes for sale, among other services—all a short walk from your room.

7888 W. Irlo Bronson Memorial Hwy. Kissimmee
☎ 407-390-9888 or 888-390-9888
clarionsuites kissimmee.com

Gaylord Palms Resort & Convention Center ★★★★½

Rate per night $257–$339. **Pool** ★★★★. **Fridge in room** Yes. **Shuttle to parks** Yes (Disney, free; other parks, $21/person round-trip). **Maximum number of occupants per room** 4. **Special comments** Probably the closest you'll get to Disney-level extravagance out of the World. Resort fee of $22/day plus parking fee of $22/day.

6000 W. Osceola Pkwy. Kissimmee
☎ 407-586-0000
gaylordpalms.com

THIS UPSCALE RESORT, with its colossal convention facility, caters to business clientele, but it's still a nice (if pricey) family resort. Hotel wings are defined by the three themed glass-ceilinged atriums they overlook. Key West's design is reminiscent of island life in the Florida Keys; Everglades is an overgrown spectacle of shabby swamp chic; and the immense, central St. Augustine recalls

Spanish Colonial Florida. Lagoons, streams, and waterfalls connect all three, and walkways and bridges abound. A fourth wing, Emerald Bay Tower, overlooks the Emerald Plaza shopping and dining area of the St. Augustine atrium. These rooms are the nicest and most expensive; they're mostly used by convention-goers. Though rooms have fridges, alarm clocks with CD players, and other perks such as high-speed Internet, they work better as retreats for adults than for kids. However, children will enjoy the themed areas and the family pool (with water-squirting octopus). In-room child care is available (see page 454).

Orange Lake Resort   ★★★★½

8505 W. Irlo Bronson
Memorial Hwy.
Kissimmee
☎ 407-239-0000 or
888-657-3529
orangelake.com

Rate per night $107–$159. **Pools** ★★★★. **Fridge in room** Yes. **Shuttle to parks** Yes, for a fee (varies based on your destination). **Maximum number of occupants per room** Varies. **Special comments** This is a time-share property, but if you rent directly through the resort as opposed to the sales office, you won't have to listen to time-share sales pitches; $7.95/night resort fee.

YOU COULD SPEND YOUR ENTIRE VACATION never leaving this prop-erty, about 6–10 minutes from the Disney theme parks. From its 10 pools and two mini–water parks to its golfing opportunities (36 holes of championship greens plus two 9-hole executive courses), Orange Lake offers an extensive menu of amenities and recreational opportunities. If you tire of lazing by the pool, try waterskiing, wakeboarding, tubing, fishing, or other activities on the 80-acre lake. There's also a live alligator show, exercise programs, organized competitive sports and games, arts-and-crafts sessions, and miniature golf. Karaoke, live music, a Hawaiian luau, and movies at the resort cinema are some of the evening options.

The 2,412 units are tastefully decorated and comfortably furnished, rang-ing from suites and studios to three-bedroom villas, all with fully equipped kitchens. If you'd rather not cook on vacation, try one of the seven restau-rants scattered across the resort: two cafés, three grills, one pizzeria, and a fast-food eatery. Babysitters are available to come to your villa, accompany your family on excursions, or take your children to attractions for you.

We reevaluated the Orange Lake Resort in early 2016 after a reader noticed several negative reviews of the property on TripAdvisor.com, most mentioning room cleanliness. Our test room—a one-bedroom villa with washer and dryer and full kitchen for $136/night with tax—was spotless, as were the rooms we got to peek into around the resort. As far as suites go, we like the **Staybridge Suites Orlando Lake Buena Vista** (see page 277) a bit better, but we'd stay at Orange Lake again.

DISNEY'S FLAMINGO CROSSINGS

SpringHill Suites   ★★★★

13279 Flamingo Crossings
Blvd., Winter Garden
☎ 407-507-1200
tinyurl.com/fc-springhill

Rate per night $120–$170. **Pool** ★★★★. **Fridge in room** Yes. **Shuttle to parks** No. **Maximum number of occupants per room** 3 (1-bedroom suites) or 5 (2-bedroom suites), plus infant in crib.

TownePlace Suites ★★★★

Rate per night $200–$250. **Pool** ★★★★. **Fridge in room** Yes. **Shuttle to parks** No. **Maximum number of occupants per room** 3 (1-bedroom suites) or 5 (2-bedroom suites), plus infant in crib.

13295 Flamingo Crossings Blvd., Winter Garden
☎ 407-507-1200
tinyurl.com/fc-townplace

A FEW YEARS AGO, Disney sold some land on the far western side of its Disney property to hotel developers, who named it Flamingo Crossings. Located as it is at the intersection of US 429 and Western Way, we're not exaggerating when we say it's less than 60 seconds from Disney property by car. Follow Western Way for a few minutes and you'll end up at Disney's Coronado Springs Resort.

Two hotels have opened so far, both Marriott brands: **TownePlace Suites,** an extended-stay hotel, and **SpringHill Suites,** each with about 250 rooms. (A third hotel, as yet unnamed, is said to be opening at some point.) The hotels are adjacent and share parking, a huge pool complex, and a gym. Other amenities include sports-practice fields and facilities—a nod to the sports groups that participate in events at the ESPN Wide World of Sports Complex. Our stays here in early 2016 confirmed this target market: The lobby is constantly awash with color-coordinated teens either prepping for or unwinding from some event.

Despite the potential for noise, our rooms were very quiet. They were also spotless. Our two-bedroom suite had a small, full kitchen, while our studio had a microwave and coffeemaker. Both had only one bathroom, and we think the two-bedroom units could have used a second.

Besides being close to Disney property, the Flamingo Crossings hotels are about a 10-minute drive to a wide variety of suburban stores on US 192, including a Publix, a Super Target, and tons of restaurants.

If you have a car or aren't doing events at Wide World of Sports, we think the **Staybridge Suites Orlando Lake Buena Vista** (see page 277) or **Orange Lake Resort** (see previous page) offer better value for the money.

HOTELS *and* MOTELS:
Rated and Ranked

IN THIS SECTION, WE COMPARE HOTELS in four main areas outside Walt Disney World (see page 250) with those inside the World.

In addition to Disney properties, we rate hotels in the four lodging areas defined earlier in this chapter. Additional hotels can be found at the intersection of US 27 and I-4, on US 441 (Orange Blossom Trail), and in downtown Orlando. Most of these require more than 30 minutes of commuting to Disney World and thus are not rated. We also haven't rated lodging east of Siesta Lago Drive on US 192.

WHAT'S IN A ROOM?

EXCEPT FOR CLEANLINESS, state of repair, and decor, travelers pay little attention to hotel rooms. There is, of course, a clear standard of quality that differentiates Motel 6 from Holiday Inn, Holiday Inn from Marriott, and so on. Many guests, however, fail to appreciate that some rooms are better engineered than others. Making the room usable to its occupants is an art that combines both form and function.

Beyond decor, how "livable" is the room? In Orlando, for example, we've seen some beautifully appointed rooms that aren't well designed for human habitation. Even more than decor, your room's details and layout will make you feel comfortable and at home.

ROOM RATINGS

TO EVALUATE PROPERTIES FOR THEIR QUALITY, tastefulness, state of repair, cleanliness, and size of their standard rooms, we have grouped the hotels and motels into classifications denoted by stars—the overall star rating. Star ratings in this guide apply only to Orlando-area properties and don't necessarily correspond to ratings awarded by *Frommer's,* Mobil, AAA, or other travel critics. Because stars have little relevance when awarded in the absence of recognized standards of comparison, we have tied our ratings to expected levels of quality established by specific American hotel corporations.

Overall star ratings apply only to room quality and describe the property's standard accommodations. For most hotels, a standard accommodation is a room with one king bed or two queen beds. In an all-suite property, the standard accommodation is either a studio or a one-bedroom suite. Ratings are assigned without regard to amenities such as restaurant(s), recreational facilities, and entertainment.

In addition to stars (which delineate broad categories), we use a numerical rating system—the room-quality rating. Our scale is 0–100, with 100 being the best possible rating and zero (0) the worst. Numerical ratings show the difference we perceive between one property and another. For instance, rooms at both the Rosen Inn at Pointe Orlando and Stay Sky Suites I-Drive Orlando are rated three and a half stars (★★★½). In the supplemental numerical ratings, the former is a 75 and the latter an 82. This means that within the ★★★½ category, Stay Sky Suites has slightly nicer rooms than the Rosen Inn Pointe Orlando.

The location column identifies the area around Walt Disney World where you'll find a particular property. **WDW** means the property is inside Walt Disney World. A **1** means it's on or near International Drive. Properties on or near US 192 (a.k.a. Irlo Bronson Memorial Highway, Vine Street, and Space Coast Parkway) are indicated by a **3,** and those in the vicinity of Universal Orlando as **4.** All others are marked with **2** and for the most part are along FL 535 and the I-4 corridor, though some are in nearby locations that don't meet any other criteria.

Names of properties along US 192 also designate location (for example, Holiday Inn Maingate West). The consensus in Orlando seems to be that the main entrance to Disney World is the broad interstate-type road that runs off US 192. This is called the **Maingate.** Properties along US 192 call themselves Maingate East or West to differentiate their positions along the highway. So, driving southeast from Clermont or Florida's Turnpike, the properties before you reach the Maingate turnoff are called Maingate West, while the properties after you pass the Maingate turnoff are called Maingate East.

LODGING AREAS (see map on page 252)	
WDW Walt Disney World	
1 International Drive	**3** US 192 (Irlo Bronson Memorial Highway)
2 Lake Buena Vista and I-4 Corridor	**4** Universal Orlando Area

Cost estimates are based on the hotel's published rack rates for standard rooms. Each **$** represents $50. Thus a cost symbol of **$$$** means that a room (or suite) at that hotel will be about $150 a night; amounts over $200 are indicated by **$ x 5** and so on.

OVERALL STAR RATINGS		
★★★★★	Superior rooms	Tasteful and luxurious by any standard
★★★★	Extremely nice rooms	What you'd expect at a Hyatt Regency or Marriott
★★★	Nice rooms	Holiday Inn or comparable quality
★★	Adequate rooms	Clean, comfortable, and functional without frills—like a Motel 6
★	Super-budget	These exist but are not included in our coverage

We've focused on room quality and excluded consideration of location, services, recreation, or amenities. In some instances, a one- or two-room suite is available for the same price or less than that of a single standard hotel room.

If you've used an earlier edition of this guide, you'll notice that new properties have been added and many ratings and rankings have changed, some because of room renovation or improved maintenance or housekeeping. Lax housekeeping or failure to maintain rooms can bring down ratings.

Before you shop for a hotel, consider this letter from a man in Hot Springs, Arkansas:

> We canceled our room reservations to follow the advice in your book and reserved a hotel highly ranked by the Unofficial Guide. We wanted inexpensive, but clean and cheerful. We got inexpensive, but also dirty, grim, and depressing. The room spoiled the holiday for me aside from our touring.

This letter was as unsettling to us as the bad room was to the reader—our integrity as travel journalists is based on the quality of the information we provide. When rechecking the hotel, we found our rating was representative, but the reader had been assigned one of a small number of threadbare rooms scheduled for renovation.

Be aware that some hotel chains use the same guest-room photo in promotional literature for all their hotels and that, consequently, the rooms at a specific property may bear no resemblance to the photo in question. When you or your travel agent calls, ask how old the property is and when the guest room you're being assigned was last renovated. If you're assigned a room that is inferior to your expectations, demand to be moved.

THE TOP 30 BEST DEALS

	HOTEL	LODGING AREA	OVERALL QUALITY	ROOM QUALITY	COST ($ = $50)
1	Rodeway Inn Maingate	3	59	★★½	$-
2	Radisson Resort Orlando-Celebration	3	86	★★★★½	$$-
3	Orange Lake Resort	3	94	★★★★½	$$+
4	Motel 6 Orlando-I-Drive	1	66	★★★	$
5	Super 8 Kissimmee/Maingate	3	70	★★★	$+
6	Staybridge Suites Orlando Lake Buena Vista	2	90	★★★★½	$$$+
7	Shades of Green	WDW	91	★★★★½	$$+
8	Maingate Lakeside Resort	3	67	★★★	$+
9	Westgate Vacation Villas	2	90	★★★★½	$$$-
10	Legacy Vacation Club Orlando	3	80	★★★½	$$-
11	Legacy Vacation Club Lake Buena Vista	2	85	★★★★	$$+
12	Courtyard Orlando Lake Buena Vista at Vista Centre	2	89	★★★★	$$+
13	Galleria Palms Kissimmee Hotel	3	76	★★★½	$$-
14	Four Points by Sheraton Orlando Studio City	1	90	★★★★½	$$$-
15	Extended Stay America Convention Center/Westwood	1	84	★★★	$$+
16	Las Palmeras by Hilton Grand Vacations	1	87	★★★★	$$+
17	Barefoot'n Resort	3	85	★★★★	$$+
18	Hilton Grand Vacations Club at SeaWorld	1	95	★★★★	$$$
19	Westgate Town Center	2	93	★★★★	$$$
20	Hilton Garden Inn Lake Buena Vista/ Orlando	2	88	★★★★	$$+
21	Westgate Lakes Resort & Spa	2	92	★★★★½	$$$
22	Extended Stay America Orlando Theme Parks	4	75	★★★½	$$
23	WorldQuest Orlando Resort	1	88	★★★★	$$$-
24	Palms Hotel & Villas	3	76	★★★½	$$
25	Wyndham Cypress Palms	3	87	★★★★	$$$-
26	Monumental Hotel	1	70	★★★	$$-
27	Marriott's Grande Vista	1	92	★★★★½	$$$+
28	Courtyard Orlando LBV in Marriott Village	2	82	★★★½	$$+
29	La Quinta Inn Orlando-Universal Studios	4	65	★★★★	$$-
30	Buena Vista Suites	1	83	★★★★	$$$-

A WORD ABOUT TOLL-FREE TELEPHONE NUMBERS

AS WE'VE REPEATED SEVERAL TIMES in this chapter, it's essential to communicate with the hotel directly when shopping for deals and stating your room preferences. Most toll-free numbers are routed directly to a hotel chain's central reservations office, and the customer-service agents there typically have little or no knowledge of the individual hotels in the chain or of any specials those hotels may be offering. In our Hotel Information Chart (pages 291–306), therefore, we list the toll-free number only if it connects directly to the hotel in question; otherwise, we provide the hotel's local phone number. We also provide local numbers for the Disney resorts in the Hotel Information Chart and in the Walt Disney World Phone Numbers chart on pages 32 and 33, but note that Disney hotels must be booked through the Disney Reservation Center (☎ 407-W-DISNEY or 934-7639). After you've reserved your room, you can check online to make sure the reservation is in order.

THE 30 BEST HOTEL VALUES

IN THE CHART OPPOSITE, we look at the best combinations of quality and value in a room. Rankings are calculated without consideration for location or the availability of restaurant(s), recreational facilities, entertainment, and/or amenities.

A reader wrote to complain that he had booked one of our top-ranked rooms in terms of value and had been very disappointed in the room. We noticed that the room the reader occupied had a quality rating of ★★½. Remember that the list of top deals is intended to give you some sense of value received for dollars spent. A ★★½ room at $60 may have the same *value* as a ★★★★ room at $120, but that doesn't mean the rooms will be of comparable *quality*. Regardless of whether it's a good deal, a ★★½ room is still a ★★½ room.

$80 IS THE NEW $50 One of our major research projects over the last two editions was to find hotels with clean, safe, functional rooms that we could recommend to you for less than $50 per night with tax.

Dear reader, we found exceedingly few—they're listed opposite and following. And we learned something along the way.

At the $50 price point, we frequently had to make compromises in either safety or functionality, or both. At one motel on International Drive, we were greeted with a sign advising that copies of our driver's licenses would be shared with local police(!). At another motel, our door lock was made of plastic and didn't include a deadbolt—we had to pack our belongings into the car every time we left the room. At a third, our game of "spot the meth lab" became "spot the one that's *not* a meth lab." We were too scared to stay the night.

Most of the rooms we checked at this price point had some sort of mechanical problem, from balky toilets to water shooting out of the bathroom sink faucet whenever you turned it on. On the upside, the staff we met were uniformly helpful, and most were downright cheerful.

Ultimately, we decided that **$80 per night** (with tax) is the bare minimum you should expect to pay for a clean, safe, not-sketchy hotel room near Disney property—the $50 rooms that made it into the book are rare exceptions to the rule and aren't really representative when it comes to quality.

If you find something cheaper than $80 per night that meets our criteria and isn't already listed here, please let us know.

How the Hotels Compare

HOTEL	LODGING AREA	OVERALL QUALITY	ROOM QUALITY	COST ($ = $50)
Four Seasons Resort Orlando at Walt Disney World Resort	WDW	★★★★★	98	$- x 19
Omni Orlando Resort at ChampionsGate	2	★★★★★	96	$$$$+
Hilton Grand Vacations Club at SeaWorld	1	★★★★½	95	$$$$+
Rosen Centre Hotel	1	★★★★½	95	$$$$$-
Disney's Animal Kingdom Villas (Kidani Village, studios)	WDW	★★★★½	95	$- X 11
Bay Lake Tower at Disney's Contemporary Resort (studios)	WDW	★★★★½	95	$+ X 13
Orange Lake Resort	3	★★★★½	94	$$$-
Westgate Town Center	2	★★★★½	94	$$$$+
Gaylord Palms Resort & Convention Center	3	★★★★½	94	$$$$$$
The Ritz-Carlton Orlando, Grande Lakes	1	★★★★½	94	$- X 7
Waldorf Astoria Orlando	2	★★★★½	93	$$$$$-
Hard Rock Hotel	4	★★★★½	93	$+ X 8
Disney's Contemporary Resort	WDW	★★★★½	93	$+ X 10
Disney's Grand Floridian Resort & Spa	WDW	★★★★½	93	$+ X 15
The Villas at Disney's Grand Floridian Resort & Spa	WDW	★★★★½	93	$+ x 21
DoubleTree by Hilton Orlando at SeaWorld	1	★★★★½	92	$$$-
Westgate Lakes Resort & Spa	2	★★★★½	92	$$$-
Marriott's Grande Vista	1	★★★★½	92	$$$+
Hilton Orlando	1	★★★★½	92	$$$$$-
Hyatt Regency Grand Cypress	2	★★★★½	92	$$$$$-
Loews Portofino Bay Hotel	4	★★★★½	92	$+ X 8
Disney's Polynesian Village Resort	WDW	★★★★½	92	$- X 13
Disney's Polynesian Villas & Bungalows (studios)	WDW	★★★★½	92	$+ X 13
Shades of Green	WDW	★★★★½	91	$$$-
Vacation Village at Parkway	3	★★★★½	91	$$$-
The Grove Resort and Spa	3	★★★★½	91	$$$$$$-
Disney's Animal Kingdom Villas (Jambo House, studios)	WDW	★★★★½	91	$+ X 10
Holiday Inn Orlando SW–Celebration Area	3	★★★★½	90	$$+
Four Points by Sheraton Orlando Studio City	1	★★★★½	90	$$$-
Hyatt Regency Orlando	1	★★★★½	90	$$$-
Rosen Plaza Hotel	1	★★★★½	90	$$$-
Caribe Royale All-Suite Hotel & Convention Center	1	★★★★½	90	$$$
Cypress Pointe Resort	2	★★★★½	90	$$$+
Staybridge Suites Lake Buena Vista	2	★★★★½	90	$$$+
Liki Tiki Village	3	★★★★½	90	$$$$-
Renaissance Orlando at SeaWorld	1	★★★★½	90	$$$$-
Bohemian Celebration Hotel	2	★★★★½	90	$$$$+
Marriott's Harbour Lake	2	★★★★½	90	$$$$+

How the Hotels Compare (continued)

HOTEL	LODGING AREA	OVERALL QUALITY	ROOM QUALITY	COST ($ = $50)
Polynesian Isles Resort Phase 1 (Diamond Resorts)	3	★★★★½	90	$$$$+
Orlando World Center Marriott Resort	2	★★★★½	90	$$$$$−
Westgate Vacation Villas	2	★★★★½	90	$$$$$
Wyndham Bonnet Creek Resort	2	★★★★½	90	$$$$$+
Walt Disney World Dolphin	WDW	★★★★½	90	$$$$$$−
Walt Disney World Swan	WDW	★★★★½	90	$$$$$$−
Loews Royal Pacific Resort	4	★★★★½	90	$+ X 7
Disney's Old Key West Resort (studios)	WDW	★★★★½	90	$+ X 9
Disney's Saratoga Springs Resort & Spa (studios)	WDW	★★★★½	90	$+ X 9
Boulder Ridge Villas at Disney's Wilderness Lodge (studios)	WDW	★★★★½	90	$ X 11
Disney's Beach Club Resort	WDW	★★★★½	90	$ X 11
Disney's Beach Club Villas (studios)	WDW	★★★★½	90	$− X 12
Disney's BoardWalk Villas (studios)	WDW	★★★★½	90	$− X 12
Treehouse Villas at Disney's Saratoga Springs Resort & Spa	WDW	★★★★½	90	$− x 23
DoubleTree Universal	4	★★★★	89	$$$−
Courtyard Orlando Lake Buena Vista at Vista Centre	2	★★★★	89	$$$$
Sheraton Vistana Resort Villas	2	★★★★	89	$$$$+
Disney's Animal Kingdom Lodge	WDW	★★★★	89	$+ X 9
Disney's BoardWalk Inn	WDW	★★★★	89	$+ X 11
Disney's Yacht Club Resort	WDW	★★★★	89	$ X 11
Sheraton Lake Buena Vista Resort	2	★★★★	88	$$$−
Rosen Shingle Creek	1	★★★★	88	$$$$
WorldQuest Orlando Resort	1	★★★★	88	$$$$
Hilton Grand Vacations at Tuscany Village	1	★★★★	88	$$$$+
Hilton Orlando Bonnet Creek	1	★★★★	88	$$$$+
Floridays Resort Orlando	1	★★★★	88	$$$$$+
Wyndham Cypress Palms	3	★★★★	87	$$+
Mystic Dunes Resort & Golf Club	3	★★★★	87	$$$−
Hilton Orlando Lake Buena Vista	WDW	★★★★	87	$$$$
Las Palmeras by Hilton Grand Vacations	1	★★★★	87	$$$$$−
Radisson Resort Orlando-Celebration	3	★★★★	86	$$−
Embassy Suites Orlando-Lake Buena Vista Resort	2	★★★★	86	$$$$−
Hilton Orlando Buena Vista Palace	WDW	★★★★	86	$$$$−
Marriott's Cypress Harbour	1	★★★★	86	$$$$$$−
Marriott's Imperial Palms	1	★★★★	86	$+ X 7
Disney's Fort Wilderness Resort (cabins)	WDW	★★★★	86	$− X 9
Disney's Wilderness Lodge	WDW	★★★★	86	$+ X 9
Legacy Vacation Club Lake Buena Vista	2	★★★★	85	$$+
Hawthorn Suites Lake Buena Vista	2	★★★★	85	$$$

How the Hotels Compare (continued)

HOTEL	LODGING AREA	OVERALL QUALITY	ROOM QUALITY	COST ($ = $50)
Residence Inn Orlando at SeaWorld	2	★★★★	85	$$$+
Homewood Suites by Hilton Orlando Theme Parks	1	★★★★	85	$$$+
SpringHill Suites Orlando at Flamingo Crossings	2	★★★★	85	$$$$-
Wyndham Orlando Resort I-Drive	1	★★★★	85	$$$$
Homewood Suites by Hilton LBV-Orlando	2	★★★★	85	$$$$+
Sonesta ES Suites	1	★★★★	85	$$$$$-
Marriott's Royal Palms	1	★★★★	85	$$$$$+
Extended Stay America Convention Center–Westwood	1	★★★★	84	$$$-
The Point Universal Orlando Resort	1	★★★★	84	$$$-
Star Island Resort & Club	3	★★★★	84	$$$-
Hyatt Place Orlando Lake Buena Vista	2	★★★★	84	$$$+
Hyatt Place Orlando/Universal	4	★★★★	84	$$$$-
TownePlace Suites Orlando at Flamingo Crossings	2	★★★★	84	$$$$-
Homewood Suites by Hilton Near Universal	1	★★★★	84	$$$$+
Loews Sapphire Falls Resort	4	★★★★	84	$$$$$-
Disney's Port Orleans Resort–French Quarter	WDW	★★★★	84	$$$$$+
Extended Stay America Orlando Lake Buena Vista	2	★★★★	83	$$+
Buena Vista Suites	1	★★★★	83	$$$-
Residence Inn Orlando Lake Buena Vista	2	★★★★	83	$$$
Embassy Suites Orlando I-Drive/Jamaican Court	1	★★★★	83	$$$$-
Universal's Cabana Bay Beach Resort	4	★★★★	83	$$$$-
Disney's Coronado Springs Resort	WDW	★★★★	83	$$$$$-
Disney's Port Orleans Resort–Riverside	WDW	★★★★	83	$$$$$+
Holiday Inn Resort Lake Buena Vista	2	★★★½	82	$$
Clarion Inn & Suites Universal	$	★★★½	82	$$+
CoCo Key Water Resort–Orlando	1	★★★½	82	$$$-
Stay Sky Suites I-Drive Orlando	1	★★★½	82	$$$-
Holiday Inn Resort Orlando Suites–Waterpark	1	★★★½	82	$$$
Radisson Hotel Orlando Lake Buena Vista	2	★★★½	82	$$$
Castle Hotel	1	★★★½	82	$$$+
Parkway International Resort	3	★★★½	82	$$$+
Hilton Garden Inn Orlando I-Drive North	1	★★★½	82	$$$+
B Resort	WDW	★★★½	82	$$$$-
Melià Orlando Suite Hotel at Celebration	2	★★★½	82	$+ X 7
Quality Suites Lake Buena Vista	2	★★★½	81	$$+
Homewood Suites by Hilton I-Drive	1	★★★½	81	$$$-
SpringHill Suites Orlando Kissimmee	3	★★★½	81	$$$-
Westgate Towers	2	★★★½	81	$$$$+
Hawthorn Suites Orlando Convention Center	1	★★★½	80	$$-

How the Hotels Compare (continued)

HOTEL	LODGING AREA	OVERALL QUALITY	ROOM QUALITY	COST ($ = $50)
Hampton Inn & Suites Orlando–South Lake Buena Vista	3	★★★½	80	$$+
Legacy Vacation Club Orlando	3	★★★½	80	$$+
Courtyard Orlando Lake Buena Vista in Marriott Village	2	★★★½	80	$$$-
Fairfield Inn & Suites Near Universal Orlando Resort	4	★★★½	80	$$$-
Hilton Garden Inn Orlando at SeaWorld	1	★★★½	80	$$$$-
Residence Inn Orlando Convention Center	1	★★★½	80	$$$$-
SpringHill Suites Orlando Convention Center	1	★★★½	80	$$$$-
Disney's Art of Animation Resort	WDW	★★★½	80	$$$$
Disney's Caribbean Beach Resort	WDW	★★★½	80	$$$$$-
Holiday Inn in the Walt Disney World Resort	WDW	★★★½	79	$$$-
Courtyard Orlando I-Drive	1	★★★½	78	$$$$
Best Western Orlando Gateway Hotel	1	★★★½	77	$$+
Crowne Plaza Universal Orlando	1	★★★½	77	$$$+
Galleria Palms Kissimmee Hotel	3	★★★½	76	$+
Grand Lake Resort	1	★★★½	76	$$+
Quality Suites Royale Parc Suites	3	★★★½	76	$$+
Wingate by Wyndham Universal Studios	4	★★★½	76	$$$-
Delta Hotels by Marriott Lake Buena Vista	2	★★★½	76	$$$
Best Western Plus Universal Inn	4	★★★½	75	$$
Extended Stay America Deluxe Orlando Theme Parks	4	★★★½	75	$$+
Holiday Inn & Suites Orlando Universal	4	★★★½	75	$$+
Extended Stay America Orlando Theme Parks	4	★★★½	75	$$$-
Hampton Inn & Suites Sea World	1	★★★½	75	$$$-
Rosen Inn at Pointe Orlando	1	★★★½	75	$$$
DoubleTree Suites by Hilton Orlando Disney Springs	WDW	★★★½	75	$$$+
Hawthorn Suites Orlando I-Drive	1	★★★½	75	$$$+
Embassy Suites Orlando I-Drive	1	★★★½	75	$$$$+
Wyndham Lake Buena Vista Resort	WDW	★★★½	75	$$$$$-
Quality Inn at International Drive	1	★★★	74	$+
Quality Suites Turkey Lake	2	★★★	74	$$-
Hampton Inn South of Universal	1	★★★	74	$$$-
Best Western Lake Buena Vista Resort Hotel	WDW	★★★	74	$$$
Holiday Inn Express & Suites Orlando–International Drive	1	★★★	74	$$$
Clarion Suites Maingate	3	★★★	74	$$$+
Fairfield Inn & Suites Orlando International Drive	1	★★★	74	$$$+
High Point Resort	3	★★★	73	$$+
Disney's All-Star Movies Resort	WDW	★★★	73	$$$+
Disney's All-Star Music Resort	WDW	★★★	73	$$$+

How the Hotels Compare *(continued)*

HOTEL	LODGING AREA	OVERALL QUALITY	ROOM QUALITY	COST ($ = $50)
Disney's All-Star Sports Resort	WDW	★★★	73	$$$+
Baymont Inn & Suites Celebration	3	★★★	72	$$-
La Quinta Inn Orlando Universal Studios	4	★★★	72	$$-
Sunsol International Drive	1	★★★	72	$$-
Extended Stay America Orlando Convention Center	1	★★★	72	$$
Ramada Plaza Resort and Suites Orlando I-Drive	1	★★★	72	$$$+
Allure Resort	1	★★★	71	$$
Rosen Inn Near Universal	1	★★★	71	$$
Disney's Pop Century Resort	WDW	★★★	71	$$$+
Festiva Orlando Resort	3	★★★	71	$$$$-
Super 8 Kissimmee/Maingate	3	★★★	70	$+
Comfort Suites Universal	4	★★★	70	$$+
Monumental Hotel	1	★★★	70	$$$-
Hampton Inn I-Drive/Convention Center	1	★★★	70	$$$$
Monumental Movieland Hotel	1	★★★	68	$
Red Lion Kissimmee	3	★★★	68	$$$-
Westgate Palace	1	★★★	68	$$$$+
Hampton Inn Universal	4	★★★	67	$$$+
The Enclave Hotel & Suites	1	★★★	67	$$$$
Motel 6 Orlando–I-Drive	1	★★★	66	$+
Comfort Inn I-Drive	1	★★★	66	$$+
Comfort Inn Maingate	3	★★★	65	$$-
Ramada Convention Center I-Drive	1	★★★	65	$$-
Rosen Inn International Hotel	1	★★★	65	$$
Best Western I-Drive	1	★★★	65	$$$-
Clarion Inn Lake Buena Vista	2	★★½	64	$$-
Clarion Inn & Suites at I-Drive	1	★★½	64	$$+
Silver Lake Resort	3	★★½	64	$$$$-
InTown Suites Orlando Universal	1	★★½	63	$
Country Inn & Suites Orlando Universal	1	★★½	63	$$-
The Floridian Hotel & Suites	1	★★½	63	$$+
Ramada Gateway Kissimmee *(Garden rooms)*	3	★★½	62	$$-
Avanti Resort Orlando	1	★★½	62	$$$$+
Celebration Suites	3	★★½	61	$+
Super 8 Kissimmee	3	★★½	60	$+
Red Roof Inn Orlando Convention Center	1	★★½	60	$$-
Rodeway Inn Maingate	3	★★½	59	$-
Extended Stay Orlando Convention Center	1	★★½	58	$$+
Days Inn International Drive	1	★★	55	$$-
Destiny Palms Maingate West	3	★★	55	$$-

Hotel Information Chart

Allure Resort ★★★
8444 International Dr.
Orlando, FL 32819
☎ 407-345-0505
allureresortidrive.com

LOCATION	1
ROOM RATING	71
COST ($ = $50)	$$
DAILY RESORT FEE	$11

Commuting times to parks (in minutes):

MAGIC KINGDOM	27:00
EPCOT	14:00
ANIMAL KINGDOM	20:00
DHS	17:00

Avanti Resort Orlando ★★½
8738 International Dr.
Orlando, FL 32819
☎ 407-313-0100
avantiresort.com

LOCATION	1
ROOM RATING	62
COST ($ = $50)	$$$$+
DAILY RESORT FEE	$10

Commuting times to parks (in minutes):

MAGIC KINGDOM	28:00
EPCOT	14:00
ANIMAL KINGDOM	20:00
DHS	18:00

B Resort & Spa ★★★½
1905 Hotel Plaza Blvd.
Lake Buena Vista, FL 32830
☎ 407-828-2828
bresortlbv.com

LOCATION	WDW
ROOM RATING	82
COST ($ = $50)	$$$$–
DAILY RESORT FEE	$28

Commuting times to parks (in minutes):

MAGIC KINGDOM	15:45
EPCOT	11:00
ANIMAL KINGDOM	15:00
DHS	12:45

Bay Lake Tower at Disney's Contemporary Resort (studios) ★★★★½
4600 N. World Dr.
Lake Buena Vista, FL 32830
☎ 407-824-1000
tinyurl.com/baylaketower

LOCATION	WDW
ROOM RATING	95
COST ($ = $50)	$+ X 13
DAILY RESORT FEE	None

Commuting times to parks (in minutes):

MAGIC KINGDOM	on monorail
EPCOT	11:00
ANIMAL KINGDOM	17:15
DHS	14:15

Baymont Inn & Suites Celebration ★★★
7601 Black Lake Rd.
Celebration, FL 34747
☎ 407-396-1100
tinyurl.com/baymontcelebration

LOCATION	3
ROOM RATING	72
COST ($ = $50)	$$–
DAILY RESORT FEE	$8

Commuting times to parks (in minutes):

MAGIC KINGDOM	8:30
EPCOT	8:15
ANIMAL KINGDOM	5:30
DHS	7:45

Best Western I-Drive ★★★
8222 Jamaican Ct.
Orlando, FL 32819
☎ 407-345-1172
tinyurl.com/bwidrive

LOCATION	1
ROOM RATING	65
COST ($ = $50)	$$$–
DAILY RESORT FEE	$10

Commuting times to parks (in minutes):

MAGIC KINGDOM	8:30
EPCOT	8:15
ANIMAL KINGDOM	11:15
DHS	10:45

Best Western Lake Buena Vista Resort Hotel ★★★
2000 Hotel Plaza Blvd.
Lake Buena Vista, FL 32830
☎ 407-828-2424
lakebuenavistaresorthotel.com

LOCATION	WDW
ROOM RATING	74
COST ($ = $50)	$$$
DAILY RESORT FEE	$14

Commuting times to parks (in minutes):

MAGIC KINGDOM	16:00
EPCOT	11:15
ANIMAL KINGDOM	15:15
DHS	13:00

Best Western Orlando Gateway Hotel ★★★½
7299 Universal Blvd.
Orlando, FL 32819
☎ 407-351-5009
bworlando.com

LOCATION	1
ROOM RATING	77
COST ($ = $50)	$$+
DAILY RESORT FEE	$4.50

Commuting times to parks (in minutes):

MAGIC KINGDOM	29:00
EPCOT	13:00
ANIMAL KINGDOM	19:00
DHS	18:00

Best Western Plus Universal Inn ★★★½
5618 Vineland Rd.
Orlando, FL 32819
☎ 407-226-9119
tinyurl.com/bwuniversal

LOCATION	4
ROOM RATING	75
COST ($ = $50)	$$
DAILY RESORT FEE	$1.50

Commuting times to parks (in minutes):

MAGIC KINGDOM	17:30
EPCOT	13:00
ANIMAL KINGDOM	16:00
DHS	15:30

Bohemian Celebration Hotel ★★★★½
700 Bloom St.
Celebration, FL 34747
☎ 407-566-6000
celebrationhotel.com

LOCATION	2
ROOM RATING	90
COST ($ = $50)	$$$$+
DAILY RESORT FEE	None

Commuting times to parks (in minutes):

MAGIC KINGDOM	13:30
EPCOT	13:00
ANIMAL KINGDOM	13:00
DHS	12:30

Boulder Ridge Villas at Disney's Wilderness Lodge (studios) ★★★★½
901 Timberline Dr.
Lake Buena Vista, FL 32830
☎ 407-824-3200
tinyurl.com/wlvillas

LOCATION	WDW
ROOM RATING	90
COST ($ = $50)	$ X 11
DAILY RESORT FEE	None

Commuting times to parks (in minutes):

MAGIC KINGDOM	N/A*
EPCOT	10:00
ANIMAL KINGDOM	15:15
DHS	13:30

Buena Vista Suites ★★★★
8203 World Center Dr.
Orlando, FL 32821
☎ 407-239-8588
bvsuites.com

LOCATION	1
ROOM RATING	83
COST ($ = $50)	$$$–
DAILY RESORT FEE	$11

Commuting times to parks (in minutes):

MAGIC KINGDOM	9:15
EPCOT	4:30
ANIMAL KINGDOM	7:30
DHS	8:15

**Primary transportation to Boulder Ridge Villas is by ferry rather than by car.

Hotel Information Chart *(continued)*

Caribe Royale All-Suite Hotel & Convention Center ★★★★½			Castle Hotel ★★★½			Celebration Suites ★★½		
8101 World Center Dr. Orlando, FL 32821 ☎ 407-238-8000 **cariberoyale.com**			8629 International Dr. Orlando, FL 32819 ☎ 407-345-1511 **castlehotelorlando.com**			5820 W. US 192* Kissimmee, FL 34746 ☎ 407-396-7900 **suitesatoldtown.com**		
LOCATION	1		LOCATION	1		LOCATION	3	
ROOM RATING	90		ROOM RATING	82		ROOM RATING	61	
COST ($ = $50)	$$$		COST ($ = $50)	$$$+		COST ($ = $50)	$+	
DAILY RESORT FEE	$22		DAILY RESORT FEE	None		DAILY RESORT FEE	$11	
Commuting times to parks *(in minutes):*			Commuting times to parks *(in minutes):*			Commuting times to parks *(in minutes):*		
MAGIC KINGDOM	9:15		MAGIC KINGDOM	22:30		MAGIC KINGDOM	11:15	
EPCOT	4:45		EPCOT	17:45		EPCOT	11:00	
ANIMAL KINGDOM	7:45		ANIMAL KINGDOM	20:45		ANIMAL KINGDOM	9:15	
DHS	8:15		DHS	20:15		DHS	10:30	

Clarion Suites Maingate ★★★			CoCo Key Water Resort–Orlando ★★★½			Comfort Inn I-Drive ★★★		
7888 W. US 192* Kissimmee, FL 34747 ☎ 407-390-9888 **clarionsuiteskissimmee.com**			7400 International Dr. Orlando, FL 32819 ☎ 407-351-2626 **cocokeyorlando.com**			8134 International Dr. Orlando, FL 32819 ☎ 407-313-4000 **tinyurl.com/comfortidrive**		
LOCATION	3		LOCATION	1		LOCATION	1	
ROOM RATING	74		ROOM RATING	82		ROOM RATING	66	
COST ($ = $50)	$$$+		COST ($ = $50)	$$$-		COST ($ = $50)	$$+	
DAILY RESORT FEE	$10		DAILY RESORT FEE	$28		DAILY RESORT FEE	$9	
Commuting times to parks *(in minutes):*			Commuting times to parks *(in minutes):*			Commuting times to parks *(in minutes):*		
MAGIC KINGDOM	10:00		MAGIC KINGDOM	21:00		MAGIC KINGDOM	20:00	
EPCOT	9:15		EPCOT	16:30		EPCOT	15:30	
ANIMAL KINGDOM	7:00		ANIMAL KINGDOM	19:00		ANIMAL KINGDOM	18:30	
DHS	9:00		DHS	19:30		DHS	18:00	

Courtyard Orlando I-Drive ★★★½			Courtyard Orlando Lake Buena Vista at Vista Centre ★★★★			Courtyard Orlando Lake Buena Vista in Marriott Village ★★★½		
8600 Austrian Ct. Orlando, FL 32819 ☎ 407-351-2244 **tinyurl.com/courtyardidrive**			8501 Palm Pkwy. Lake Buena Vista, FL 32836 ☎ 407-239-6900 **tinyurl.com/courtyardlbv**			8623 Vineland Ave. Orlando, FL 32821 ☎ 407-938-9001 **tinyurl.com/courtyardlbvmarriott village**		
LOCATION	1		LOCATION	2		LOCATION	2	
ROOM RATING	78		ROOM RATING	89		ROOM RATING	80	
COST ($ = $50)	$$$$		COST ($ = $50)	$$$$		COST ($ = $50)	$$$-	
DAILY RESORT FEE	None		DAILY RESORT FEE	None		DAILY RESORT FEE	None	
Commuting times to parks *(in minutes):*			Commuting times to parks *(in minutes):*			Commuting times to parks *(in minutes):*		
MAGIC KINGDOM	21:45		MAGIC KINGDOM	13:15		MAGIC KINGDOM	12:00	
EPCOT	17:00		EPCOT	8:30		EPCOT	7:15	
ANIMAL KINGDOM	20:00		ANIMAL KINGDOM	11:30		ANIMAL KINGDOM	10:15	
DHS	19:30		DHS	11:00		DHS	9:45	

Delta Hotels by Marriott Lake Buena Vista ★★★½			Destiny Palms Maingate West ★★			Disney's All-Star Movies Resort ★★★		
12490 Apopka-Vineland Rd. Lake Buena Vista, FL 32836 ☎ 407-387-9999 **tinyurl.com/deltaorlando**			8536 W. US 192* Kissimmee, FL 34747 ☎ 407-396-1600 **destinypalmsmaingate.com/web**			1901 W. Buena Vista Dr. Lake Buena Vista, FL 32830 ☎ 407-939-7000 **tinyurl.com/allstarmovies**		
LOCATION	2		LOCATION	3		LOCATION	WDW	
ROOM RATING	76		ROOM RATING	55		ROOM RATING	73	
COST ($ = $50)	$$$		COST ($ = $50)	$$-		COST ($ = $50)	$$$+	
DAILY RESORT FEE	None		DAILY RESORT FEE	$4		DAILY RESORT FEE	None	
Commuting times to parks *(in minutes):*			Commuting times to parks *(in minutes):*			Commuting times to parks *(in minutes):*		
MAGIC KINGDOM	19:00		MAGIC KINGDOM	13:45		MAGIC KINGDOM	6:15	
EPCOT	4:00		EPCOT	13:15		EPCOT	5:45	
ANIMAL KINGDOM	10:00		ANIMAL KINGDOM	11:00		ANIMAL KINGDOM	4:15	
DHS	9:00		DHS	13:00		DHS	5:15	

*Irlo Bronson Memorial Highway

Clarion Inn & Suites at I-Drive ★★½
9956 Hawaiian Ct.
Orlando, FL 32819
☎ 407-351-5100
tinyurl.com/clarionidrive

LOCATION	1
ROOM RATING	64
COST ($ = $50)	$$+
DAILY RESORT FEE	$4

Commuting times to parks (in minutes):
MAGIC KINGDOM	19:30
EPCOT	14:15
ANIMAL KINGDOM	17:15
DHS	16:45

Clarion Inn & Suites Universal ★★★½
5827 Caravan Ct.
Orlando, FL 32819
☎ 407-351-3800
tinyurl.com/clarionuniversal

LOCATION	$
ROOM RATING	82
COST ($ = $50)	$$+
DAILY RESORT FEE	None

Commuting times to parks (in minutes):
MAGIC KINGDOM	27:00
EPCOT	20:00
ANIMAL KINGDOM	19:00
DHS	17:00

Clarion Inn Lake Buena Vista ★★½
8442 Palm Pkwy.
Lake Buena Vista, FL 32836
☎ 407-996-7300
clarionlbv.com

LOCATION	2
ROOM RATING	64
COST ($ = $50)	$$-
DAILY RESORT FEE	None

Commuting times to parks (in minutes):
MAGIC KINGDOM	13:15
EPCOT	8:30
ANIMAL KINGDOM	11:30
DHS	11:00

Comfort Inn Maingate ★★★
7675 W. US 192*
Kissimmee, FL 34747
☎ 407-396-4000
comfortinnkissimmee.com

LOCATION	3
ROOM RATING	65
COST ($ = $50)	$$-
DAILY RESORT FEE	$10

Commuting times to parks (in minutes):
MAGIC KINGDOM	8:30
EPCOT	8:00
ANIMAL KINGDOM	5:30
DHS	7:30

Comfort Suites Universal ★★★
5617 Major Blvd.
Orlando, FL 32819
☎ 407-363-1967
tinyurl.com/csuniversal

LOCATION	4
ROOM RATING	70
COST ($ = $50)	$$+
DAILY RESORT FEE	None

Commuting times to parks (in minutes):
MAGIC KINGDOM	17:45
EPCOT	13:15
ANIMAL KINGDOM	16:15
DHS	15:15

Country Inn & Suites Orlando Universal ★★½
7701 Universal Blvd.
Orlando, FL 32819
☎ 407-313-4200
countryinns.com/orlandofl_universal

LOCATION	1
ROOM RATING	63
COST ($ = $50)	$$-
DAILY RESORT FEE	None

Commuting times to parks (in minutes):
MAGIC KINGDOM	21:00
EPCOT	16:15
ANIMAL KINGDOM	19:15
DHS	18:45

Crowne Plaza Universal Orlando ★★★½
5800 Universal Blvd.
Orlando, FL 32819
☎ 407-355-0550
cporlando.com

LOCATION	1
ROOM RATING	77
COST ($ = $50)	$$$+
DAILY RESORT FEE	None

Commuting times to parks (in minutes):
MAGIC KINGDOM	25:00
EPCOT	11:00
ANIMAL KINGDOM	17:00
DHS	15:00

Cypress Pointe Resort ★★★★½
8651 Treasure Cay Ln.
Orlando, FL 32836
☎ 407-597-2700
cypresspointe.net

LOCATION	2
ROOM RATING	90
COST ($ = $50)	$$$+
DAILY RESORT FEE	$6

Commuting times to parks (in minutes):
MAGIC KINGDOM	12:00
EPCOT	14:00
ANIMAL KINGDOM	13:00
DHS	12:00

Days Inn International Drive ★★
5858 International Dr.
Orlando, FL 32819
☎ 407-351-4410
daysinnorlando
internationaldrive.com

LOCATION	1
ROOM RATING	55
COST ($ = $50)	$$-
DAILY RESORT FEE	$5

Commuting times to parks (in minutes):
MAGIC KINGDOM	17:00
EPCOT	13:00
ANIMAL KINGDOM	20:00
DHS	18:00

Disney's All-Star Music Resort ★★★
801 W. Buena Vista Dr.
Lake Buena Vista, FL 32830
☎ 407-939-6000
tinyurl.com/allstarmusicresort

LOCATION	WDW
ROOM RATING	73
COST ($ = $50)	$$$+
DAILY RESORT FEE	None

Commuting times to parks (in minutes):
MAGIC KINGDOM	6:15
EPCOT	5:45
ANIMAL KINGDOM	4:15
DHS	5:15

Disney's All-Star Sports Resort ★★★
1701 W. Buena Vista Dr.
Lake Buena Vista, FL 32830
☎ 407-939-5000
tinyurl.com/allstarsports

LOCATION	WDW
ROOM RATING	73
COST ($ = $50)	$$$+
DAILY RESORT FEE	None

Commuting times to parks (in minutes):
MAGIC KINGDOM	6:15
EPCOT	5:45
ANIMAL KINGDOM	4:15
DHS	5:15

Disney's Animal Kingdom Lodge ★★★★
2901 Osceola Pkwy.
Lake Buena Vista, FL 32830
☎ 407-938-3000
tinyurl.com/aklodge

LOCATION	WDW
ROOM RATING	89
COST ($ = $50)	$+ X 9
DAILY RESORT FEE	None

Commuting times to parks (in minutes):
MAGIC KINGDOM	8:15
EPCOT	6:15
ANIMAL KINGDOM	2:15
DHS	6:00

Hotel Information Chart *(continued)*

Disney's Animal Kingdom Villas
(Jambo House, studios) ★★★★½
2901 Osceola Pkwy.
Lake Buena Vista, FL 32830
☎ 407-938-3000
tinyurl.com/akjambo

LOCATION	WDW
ROOM RATING	91
COST ($ = $50)	$+ X 10
DAILY RESORT FEE	None

Commuting times to parks *(in minutes)*:

MAGIC KINGDOM	8:15
EPCOT	6:15
ANIMAL KINGDOM	2:15
DHS	6:00

Disney's Animal Kingdom Villas
(Kidani Village, studios) ★★★★½
3701 Osceola Pkwy.
Lake Buena Vista, FL 32830
☎ 407-938-7400
tinyurl.com/akkidani

LOCATION	WDW
ROOM RATING	95
COST ($ = $50)	$- X 11
DAILY RESORT FEE	None

Commuting times to parks *(in minutes)*:

MAGIC KINGDOM	8:15
EPCOT	6:15
ANIMAL KINGDOM	2:15
DHS	6:00

Disney's Art of Animation Resort
★★★½
1850 Animation Way
Lake Buena Vista, FL 32830
☎ 407-938-7000
tinyurl.com/artofanimationresort

LOCATION	WDW
ROOM RATING	80
COST ($ = $50)	$$$$
DAILY RESORT FEE	None

Commuting times to parks *(in minutes)*:

MAGIC KINGDOM	12:00
EPCOT	10:00
ANIMAL KINGDOM	12:00
DHS	3:00

Disney's BoardWalk Villas *(studios)*
★★★★½
2101 N. Epcot Resorts Blvd.
Lake Buena Vista, FL 32830
☎ 407-939-6200
tinyurl.com/boardwalkvillas

LOCATION	WDW
ROOM RATING	90
COST ($ = $50)	$- X 12
DAILY RESORT FEE	None

Commuting times to parks *(in minutes)*:

MAGIC KINGDOM	7:15
EPCOT	5:30
ANIMAL KINGDOM	7:00
DHS	3:00

Disney's Caribbean Beach Resort
★★★½
900 Cayman Way
Lake Buena Vista, FL 32830
☎ 407-934-3400
tinyurl.com/caribbeanbeachresort

LOCATION	WDW
ROOM RATING	80
COST ($ = $50)	$$$$$-
DAILY RESORT FEE	None

Commuting times to parks *(in minutes)*:

MAGIC KINGDOM	8:00
EPCOT	6:00
ANIMAL KINGDOM	7:15
DHS	4:15

Disney's Contemporary Resort
★★★★½
4600 N. World Dr.
Lake Buena Vista, FL 32830
☎ 407-824-1000
tinyurl.com/contemporarywdw

LOCATION	WDW
ROOM RATING	93
COST ($ = $50)	$+ X 10
DAILY RESORT FEE	None

Commuting times to parks *(in minutes)*:

MAGIC KINGDOM	on monorail
EPCOT	11:00
ANIMAL KINGDOM	17:15
DHS	14:15

Disney's Old Key West Resort
(studios) ★★★★½
1510 North Cove Rd.
Lake Buena Vista, FL 32830
☎ 407-827-7700
tinyurl.com/oldkeywest

LOCATION	WDW
ROOM RATING	90
COST ($ = $50)	$+ X 9
DAILY RESORT FEE	None

Commuting times to parks *(in minutes)*:

MAGIC KINGDOM	10:45
EPCOT	6:00
ANIMAL KINGDOM	14:30
DHS	10:30

Disney's Polynesian Village Resort
★★★★½
1600 Seven Seas Dr.
Lake Buena Vista, FL 32830
☎ 407-824-2000
tinyurl.com/wdwpolynesian

LOCATION	WDW
ROOM RATING	92
COST ($ = $50)	$- X 13
DAILY RESORT FEE	None

Commuting times to parks *(in minutes)*:

MAGIC KINGDOM	12:00
EPCOT	8:00
ANIMAL KINGDOM	16:15
DHS	12:30

Disney's Polynesian Villas & Bungalows
(studios) ★★★★½
1600 Seven Seas Dr.
Lake Buena Vista, FL 32830
☎ 407-824-2000
tinyurl.com/polynesianvillas

LOCATION	WDW
ROOM RATING	92
COST ($ = $50)	$+ X 13
DAILY RESORT FEE	None

Commuting times to parks *(in minutes)*:

MAGIC KINGDOM	12:00
EPCOT	8:00
ANIMAL KINGDOM	16:15
DHS	12:30

Disney's Saratoga Springs Resort & Spa
(studios) ★★★★½
1960 Broadway
Lake Buena Vista, FL 32830
☎ 407-827-1100
tinyurl.com/saratogawdw

LOCATION	WDW
ROOM RATING	90
COST ($ = $50)	$+ X 9
DAILY RESORT FEE	None

Commuting times to parks *(in minutes)*:

MAGIC KINGDOM	14:45
EPCOT	8:45
ANIMAL KINGDOM	18:15
DHS	14:30

Disney's Wilderness Lodge
★★★★
901 Timberline Dr.
Lake Buena Vista, FL 32830
☎ 407-824-3200
tinyurl.com/wildernesslodge

LOCATION	WDW
ROOM RATING	86
COST ($ = $50)	$+ X 9
DAILY RESORT FEE	None

Commuting times to parks *(in minutes)*:

MAGIC KINGDOM	N/A**
EPCOT	10:00
ANIMAL KINGDOM	15:15
DHS	13:30

Disney's Yacht Club Resort
★★★★
1700 Epcot Resorts Blvd.
Lake Buena Vista, FL 32830
☎ 407-934-7000
tinyurl.com/yachtclubwdw

LOCATION	WDW
ROOM RATING	89
COST ($ = $50)	$ X 11
DAILY RESORT FEE	None

Commuting times to parks *(in minutes)*:

MAGIC KINGDOM	7:15
EPCOT	5:15
ANIMAL KINGDOM	6:45
DHS	4:00

*Irlo Bronson Memorial Highway

Disney's Beach Club Resort
★★★★½
1800 Epcot Resorts Blvd.
Lake Buena Vista, FL 32830
☎ 407-934-8000
tinyurl.com/wdwbeachclub

LOCATION	WDW
ROOM RATING	90
COST ($ = $50)	$ X 11
DAILY RESORT FEE	None

Commuting times to parks (in minutes):
MAGIC KINGDOM	7:15
EPCOT	5:15
ANIMAL KINGDOM	6:45
DHS	4:00

Disney's Beach Club Villas (studios)
★★★★½
1800 Epcot Resorts Blvd.
Lake Buena Vista, FL 32830
☎ 407-934-8000
tinyurl.com/beachclubvillas

LOCATION	WDW
ROOM RATING	90
COST ($ = $50)	$- X 12
DAILY RESORT FEE	None

Commuting times to parks (in minutes):
MAGIC KINGDOM	7:15
EPCOT	5:15
ANIMAL KINGDOM	6:45
DHS	4:00

Disney's BoardWalk Inn ★★★★
2101 N. Epcot Resorts Blvd.
Lake Buena Vista, FL 32830
☎ 407-939-6200
tinyurl.com/boardwalkinn

LOCATION	WDW
ROOM RATING	89
COST ($ = $50)	$+ X 11
DAILY RESORT FEE	None

Commuting times to parks (in minutes):
MAGIC KINGDOM	7:15
EPCOT	5:30
ANIMAL KINGDOM	7:00
DHS	3:00

Disney's Coronado Springs Resort
★★★★
1000 W. Buena Vista Dr.
Lake Buena Vista, FL 32830
☎ 407-939-1000
tinyurl.com/coronadosprings

LOCATION	WDW
ROOM RATING	83
COST ($ = $50)	$$$$$-
DAILY RESORT FEE	None

Commuting times to parks (in minutes):
MAGIC KINGDOM	5:30
EPCOT	4:00
ANIMAL KINGDOM	4:45
DHS	4:45

Disney's Fort Wilderness Resort
(cabins) ★★★★
4510 N. Fort Wilderness Trail
Lake Buena Vista, FL 32830
☎ 407-824-2837
tinyurl.com/ftwilderness

LOCATION	WDW
ROOM RATING	86
COST ($ = $50)	$- X 9
DAILY RESORT FEE	None

Commuting times to parks (in minutes):
MAGIC KINGDOM	13:15
EPCOT	8:30
ANIMAL KINGDOM	20:00
DHS	14:00

Disney's Grand Floridian Resort & Spa ★★★★½
4401 Floridian Way
Lake Buena Vista, FL 32830
☎ 407-824-3000
tinyurl.com/grandflresort

LOCATION	WDW
ROOM RATING	93
COST ($ = $50)	$+ X 15
DAILY RESORT FEE	None

Commuting times to parks (in minutes):
MAGIC KINGDOM	on monorail
EPCOT	4:45
ANIMAL KINGDOM	11:45
DHS	6:45

Disney's Pop Century Resort ★★★
1050 Century Dr.
Lake Buena Vista, FL 32830
☎ 407-938-4000
tinyurl.com/popcenturywdw

LOCATION	WDW
ROOM RATING	71
COST ($ = $50)	$$$+
DAILY RESORT FEE	None

Commuting times to parks (in minutes):
MAGIC KINGDOM	8:30
EPCOT	6:30
ANIMAL KINGDOM	6:15
DHS	5:00

Disney's Port Orleans Resort–French Quarter ★★★★
2201 Orleans Dr.
Lake Buena Vista, FL 32830
☎ 407-934-5000
tinyurl.com/portorleansfq

LOCATION	WDW
ROOM RATING	84
COST ($ = $50)	$$$$$+
DAILY RESORT FEE	None

Commuting times to parks (in minutes):
MAGIC KINGDOM	12:00
EPCOT	8:00
ANIMAL KINGDOM	16:15
DHS	12:30

Disney's Port Orleans Resort–Riverside ★★★★
1251 Riverside Dr.
Lake Buena Vista, FL 32830
☎ 407-934-6000
tinyurl.com/portorleansriverside

LOCATION	WDW
ROOM RATING	83
COST ($ = $50)	$$$$$+
DAILY RESORT FEE	None

Commuting times to parks (in minutes):
MAGIC KINGDOM	12:00
EPCOT	8:00
ANIMAL KINGDOM	16:15
DHS	12:30

DoubleTree by Hilton Orlando at SeaWorld ★★★★½
10100 International Dr.
Orlando, FL 32821
☎ 407-352-1100
doubletreeorlandoidrive.com

LOCATION	1
ROOM RATING	92
COST ($ = $50)	$$$-
DAILY RESORT FEE	$20

Commuting times to parks (in minutes):
MAGIC KINGDOM	17:45
EPCOT	13:00
ANIMAL KINGDOM	16:00
DHS	15:30

DoubleTree Suites by Hilton Orlando Disney Springs ★★★½
2305 Hotel Plaza Blvd.
Lake Buena Vista, FL 32830
☎ 407-934-1000
doubletreeguestsuites.com

LOCATION	WDW
ROOM RATING	75
COST ($ = $50)	$$$+
DAILY RESORT FEE	None

Commuting times to parks (in minutes):
MAGIC KINGDOM	13:00
EPCOT	8:30
ANIMAL KINGDOM	12:30
DHS	10:00

DoubleTree Universal ★★★★
5780 Major Blvd.
Orlando, FL 32819
☎ 407-351-1000
doubletreeorlando.com

LOCATION	4
ROOM RATING	89
COST ($ = $50)	$$$-
DAILY RESORT FEE	None

Commuting times to parks (in minutes):
MAGIC KINGDOM	19:00
EPCOT	14:15
ANIMAL KINGDOM	17:15
DHS	16:45

**Primary transportation to Wilderness Lodge is by ferry rather than by car.

Hotel Information Chart *(continued)*

Embassy Suites Orlando I-Drive ★★★½	
8978 International Dr.	
Orlando, FL 32819	
☎ 407-352-1400	
embassysuitesorlando.com	
LOCATION	1
ROOM RATING	75
COST ($ = $50)	$$$$+
DAILY RESORT FEE	None
Commuting times to parks *(in minutes)*:	
MAGIC KINGDOM	28:00
EPCOT	13:00
ANIMAL KINGDOM	19:00
DHS	18:00

Embassy Suites Orlando I-Drive/ Jamaican Court ★★★★	
8250 Jamaican Ct.	
Orlando, FL 32819	
☎ 407-345-8250	
tinyurl.com/jamaicancourt	
LOCATION	1
ROOM RATING	83
COST ($ = $50)	$$$$-
DAILY RESORT FEE	None
Commuting times to parks *(in minutes)*:	
MAGIC KINGDOM	20:15
EPCOT	15:30
ANIMAL KINGDOM	18:30
DHS	18:00

Embassy Suites Orlando– Lake Buena Vista Resort ★★★★	
8100 Lake St.	
Orlando, FL 32836	
☎ 407-239-1144	
embassysuiteslbv.com	
LOCATION	2
ROOM RATING	86
COST ($ = $50)	$$$$-
DAILY RESORT FEE	$20
Commuting times to parks *(in minutes)*:	
MAGIC KINGDOM	12:45
EPCOT	8:00
ANIMAL KINGDOM	11:00
DHS	10:30

Extended Stay America Orlando Convention Center ★★★	
6451 Westwood Blvd.	
Orlando, FL 32821	
☎ 407-352-3454	
tinyurl.com/extendedstayocc	
LOCATION	1
ROOM RATING	72
COST ($ = $50)	$$
DAILY RESORT FEE	None
Commuting times to parks *(in minutes)*:	
MAGIC KINGDOM	17:30
EPCOT	12:45
ANIMAL KINGDOM	15:45
DHS	15:30

Extended Stay America Orlando Lake Buena Vista ★★★★	
8100 Palm Pkwy.	
Orlando 32836	
☎ 407-239-4300	
tinyurl.com/extendedlbv	
LOCATION	2
ROOM RATING	83
COST ($ = $50)	$$+
DAILY RESORT FEE	None
Commuting times to parks *(in minutes)*:	
MAGIC KINGDOM	13:45
EPCOT	9:00
ANIMAL KINGDOM	12:00
DHS	11:30

Extended Stay America Orlando Theme Parks ★★★½	
5620 Major Blvd.	
Orlando, FL 32819	
☎ 407-351-1788	
tinyurl.com/extendeduniversal	
LOCATION	4
ROOM RATING	75
COST ($ = $50)	$$$-
DAILY RESORT FEE	None
Commuting times to parks *(in minutes)*:	
MAGIC KINGDOM	18:00
EPCOT	14:15
ANIMAL KINGDOM	18:00
DHS	16:00

Festiva Orlando Resort ★★★	
7503 Atlantis Way	
Kissimmee, FL 34747	
☎ 407-396-4005	
festiva-orlando.com	
LOCATION	3
ROOM RATING	71
COST ($ = $50)	$$$$-
DAILY RESORT FEE	$10
Commuting times to parks *(in minutes)*:	
MAGIC KINGDOM	21:00
EPCOT	11:00
ANIMAL KINGDOM	10:00
DHS	9:00

Floridays Resort Orlando ★★★★	
12562 International Dr.	
Orlando, FL 32821	
☎ 407-238-7700	
floridaysresortorlando.com	
LOCATION	1
ROOM RATING	88
COST ($ = $50)	$$$$$+
DAILY RESORT FEE	$15
Commuting times to parks *(in minutes)*:	
MAGIC KINGDOM	14:30
EPCOT	9:45
ANIMAL KINGDOM	12:45
DHS	12:15

The Floridian Hotel & Suites ★★★½	
7531 Canada Ave.	
Orlando, FL 32819	
☎ 407-212-3021	
floridianhotelorlando.com	
LOCATION	1
ROOM RATING	63
COST ($ = $50)	$$+
DAILY RESORT FEE	$5
Commuting times to parks *(in minutes)*:	
MAGIC KINGDOM	20:15
EPCOT	15:45
ANIMAL KINGDOM	18:45
DHS	18:15

Gaylord Palms Resort & Convention Center ★★★★½	
6000 W. Osceola Pkwy.	
Kissimmee, FL 34746	
☎ 407-586-0000	
gaylordpalms.com	
LOCATION	3
ROOM RATING	94
COST ($ = $50)	$$$$$$
DAILY RESORT FEE	$22
Commuting times to parks *(in minutes)*:	
MAGIC KINGDOM	9:00
EPCOT	8:45
ANIMAL KINGDOM	7:00
DHS	8:15

Grand Lake Resort ★★★½	
7770 W. US 192*	
Kissimmee, FL 34747	
☎ 407-396-3000	
dailymanagementresorts.com	
LOCATION	1
ROOM RATING	76
COST ($ = $50)	$$+
DAILY RESORT FEE	None
Commuting times to parks *(in minutes)*:	
MAGIC KINGDOM	9:15
EPCOT	8:30
ANIMAL KINGDOM	6:15
DHS	8:30

The Grove Resort and Spa ★★★★½	
14501 Grove Resort Ave.	
Orlando, FL 34787	
☎ 407-545-7500	
groveresortorlando.com	
LOCATION	3
ROOM RATING	91
COST ($ = $50)	$$$$$-
DAILY RESORT FEE	$22.50
Commuting times to parks *(in minutes)*:	
MAGIC KINGDOM	20:00
EPCOT	18:00
ANIMAL KINGDOM	15:00
DHS	16:00

*Irlo Bronson Memorial Highway

The Enclave Hotel & Suites ★★★
6165 Carrier Dr.
Orlando, FL 32819
☎ 407-351-1155
enclavesuites.com

LOCATION	1
ROOM RATING	67
COST ($ = $50)	$$$$
DAILY RESORT FEE	None

Commuting times to parks (in minutes):

MAGIC KINGDOM	20:45
EPCOT	16:15
ANIMAL KINGDOM	19:15
DHS	18:45

Extended Stay America Convention Center–Westwood ★★★★
6443 Westwood Blvd.
Orlando, FL 32821
☎ 407-351-1982
tinyurl.com/extendedstay westwood

LOCATION	1
ROOM RATING	84
COST ($ = $50)	$$$-
DAILY RESORT FEE	None

Commuting times to parks (in minutes):

MAGIC KINGDOM	17:30
EPCOT	12:45
ANIMAL KINGDOM	15:45
DHS	15:30

Extended Stay America Deluxe Orlando Theme Parks ★★★½
5610 Vineland Rd.
Orlando, FL 32819
☎ 407-370-4428
tinyurl.com/esvineland

LOCATION	4
ROOM RATING	75
COST ($ = $50)	$$+
DAILY RESORT FEE	None

Commuting times to parks (in minutes):

MAGIC KINGDOM	18:00
EPCOT	14:15
ANIMAL KINGDOM	18:00
DHS	16:00

Extended Stay Orlando Convention Center ★★½
8750 Universal Blvd.
Orlando, FL 32819
☎ 407-903-1500
tinyurl.com/esccuniversal

LOCATION	1
ROOM RATING	58
COST ($ = $50)	$$+
DAILY RESORT FEE	None

Commuting times to parks (in minutes):

MAGIC KINGDOM	26:00
EPCOT	18:00
ANIMAL KINGDOM	18:00
DHS	16:00

Fairfield Inn & Suites Near Universal Orlando Resort ★★★½
5614 Vineland Rd.
Orlando, FL 32819
☎ 407-581-5600
tinyurl.com/fairfielduniversal

LOCATION	4
ROOM RATING	80
COST ($ = $50)	$$$-
DAILY RESORT FEE	None

Commuting times to parks (in minutes):

MAGIC KINGDOM	17:30
EPCOT	12:45
ANIMAL KINGDOM	15:45
DHS	15:15

Fairfield Inn & Suites Orlando International Drive ★★★
8214 Universal Blvd.
Orlando, FL 32819
☎ 407-396-6300
tinyurl.com/fairfieldinnidrive

LOCATION	1
ROOM RATING	74
COST ($ = $50)	$$$+
DAILY RESORT FEE	$20

Commuting times to parks (in minutes):

MAGIC KINGDOM	27:00
EPCOT	12:00
ANIMAL KINGDOM	18:00
DHS	17:00

Four Points by Sheraton Orlando Studio City ★★★½
5905 International Dr.
Orlando, FL 32819
☎ 407-351-2100
fourpointsorlandostudiocity.com

LOCATION	1
ROOM RATING	90
COST ($ = $50)	$$$-
DAILY RESORT FEE	None

Commuting times to parks (in minutes):

MAGIC KINGDOM	20:30
EPCOT	15:45
ANIMAL KINGDOM	18:45
DHS	18:15

Four Seasons Resort Orlando at Walt Disney World Resort ★★★★★
10100 Dream Tree Blvd.
Lake Buena Vista, FL 32836
☎ 407-313-7777
fourseasons.com/orlando

LOCATION	WDW
ROOM RATING	98
COST ($ = $50)	$- x 19
DAILY RESORT FEE	None

Commuting times to parks (in minutes):

MAGIC KINGDOM	9:00
EPCOT	8:00
ANIMAL KINGDOM	15:00
DHS	8:00

Galleria Palms Kissimmee Hotel ★★★½
3000 Maingate Ln.
Kissimmee, FL 34747
☎ 407-396-6300
galleriakissimmeehotel.com

LOCATION	3
ROOM RATING	76
COST ($ = $50)	$+
DAILY RESORT FEE	$10

Commuting times to parks (in minutes):

MAGIC KINGDOM	8:15
EPCOT	7:30
ANIMAL KINGDOM	5:15
DHS	7:15

Hampton Inn & Suites Orlando–South Lake Buena Vista ★★★½
4971 Calypso Cay Way
Kissimmee, FL 34746
☎ 407-396-8700
tinyurl.com/hamptonsouthlbv

LOCATION	3
ROOM RATING	80
COST ($ = $50)	$$+
DAILY RESORT FEE	None

Commuting times to parks (in minutes):

MAGIC KINGDOM	21:00
EPCOT	15:00
ANIMAL KINGDOM	17:00
DHS	15:00

Hampton Inn & Suites Sea World ★★★½
7003 Sea Harbor Dr.
Orlando, FL 32821
☎ 407-778-5900
tinyurl.com/hamptoninnseaworld

LOCATION	1
ROOM RATING	75
COST ($ = $50)	$$$-
DAILY RESORT FEE	None

Commuting times to parks (in minutes):

MAGIC KINGDOM	12:00
EPCOT	12:00
ANIMAL KINGDOM	14:00
DHS	12:00

Hampton Inn I-Drive/ Convention Center ★★★
8900 Universal Blvd.
Orlando, FL 32819
☎ 407-354-4447
tinyurl.com/hamptonocc

LOCATION	1
ROOM RATING	70
COST ($ = $50)	$$$$
DAILY RESORT FEE	None

Commuting times to parks (in minutes):

MAGIC KINGDOM	21:30
EPCOT	17:00
ANIMAL KINGDOM	20:00
DHS	19:30

Hotel Information Chart (continued)

Hampton Inn South of Universal ★★★
7110 S. Kirkman Rd.
Orlando, FL 32819
☎ 407-345-1112
tinyurl.com/hamptonkirkman

LOCATION	1
ROOM RATING	74
COST ($ = $50)	$$$-
DAILY RESORT FEE	None

Commuting times to parks (in minutes):

MAGIC KINGDOM	21:15
EPCOT	16:45
ANIMAL KINGDOM	19:45
DHS	19:15

Hampton Inn Universal ★★★
5621 Windhover Dr.
Orlando, FL 32819
☎ 407-351-6716
tinyurl.com/hamptonuniversal

LOCATION	4
ROOM RATING	67
COST ($ = $50)	$$$+
DAILY RESORT FEE	None

Commuting times to parks (in minutes):

MAGIC KINGDOM	19:00
EPCOT	14:15
ANIMAL KINGDOM	17:15
DHS	16:45

Hard Rock Hotel ★★★★½
5800 Universal Blvd.
Orlando, FL 32819
☎ 407-503-2000
hardrockhotels.com/orlando

LOCATION	4
ROOM RATING	93
COST ($ = $50)	$+ X 8
DAILY RESORT FEE	None

Commuting times to parks (in minutes):

MAGIC KINGDOM	21:45
EPCOT	17:00
ANIMAL KINGDOM	20:00
DHS	19:30

High Point Resort ★★★
2951 High Point Blvd.
Kissimmee, FL 34747
☎ 407-396-9600
highpointresortorlando.com

LOCATION	3
ROOM RATING	73
COST ($ = $50)	$$-
DAILY RESORT FEE	None

Commuting times to parks (in minutes):

MAGIC KINGDOM	21:00
EPCOT	11:00
ANIMAL KINGDOM	8:00
DHS	9:00

Hilton Garden Inn Orlando at SeaWorld ★★★½
6850 Westwood Blvd.
Orlando, FL 32821
☎ 407-354-1500
tinyurl.com/hgiseaworld

LOCATION	1
ROOM RATING	80
COST ($ = $50)	$$$$-
DAILY RESORT FEE	None

Commuting times to parks (in minutes):

MAGIC KINGDOM	15:30
EPCOT	11:00
ANIMAL KINGDOM	14:00
DHS	13:30

Hilton Garden Inn Orlando I-Drive North ★★★½
5877 American Way
Orlando, FL 32819
☎ 407-363-9332
tinyurl.com/hiltonidrive

LOCATION	1
ROOM RATING	82
COST ($ = $50)	$$$+
DAILY RESORT FEE	None

Commuting times to parks (in minutes):

MAGIC KINGDOM	21:15
EPCOT	16:30
ANIMAL KINGDOM	19:30
DHS	19:00

Hilton Orlando Bonnet Creek ★★★★
14100 Bonnet Creek Resort Ln.
Orlando, FL 32821
☎ 407-597-3600
hiltonbonnetcreek.com

LOCATION	1
ROOM RATING	88
COST ($ = $50)	$$$$+
DAILY RESORT FEE	$30

Commuting times to parks (in minutes):

MAGIC KINGDOM	8:00
EPCOT	6:00
ANIMAL KINGDOM	7:15
DHS	4:15

Hilton Orlando Buena Vista Palace ★★★★
1900 E. Buena Vista Dr.
Lake Buena Vista, FL 32830
☎ 407-827-2727
buenavistapalace.com

LOCATION	WDW
ROOM RATING	86
COST ($ = $50)	$$$$-
DAILY RESORT FEE	$25

Commuting times to parks (in minutes):

MAGIC KINGDOM	16:00
EPCOT	11:15
ANIMAL KINGDOM	15:15
DHS	13:00

Hilton Orlando Lake Buena Vista ★★★★
1751 Hotel Plaza Blvd.
Lake Buena Vista, FL 32830
☎ 407-827-4000
hilton-wdwv.com

LOCATION	WDW
ROOM RATING	87
COST ($ = $50)	$$$$
DAILY RESORT FEE	$27

Commuting times to parks (in minutes):

MAGIC KINGDOM	15:15
EPCOT	10:30
ANIMAL KINGDOM	14:30
DHS	12:15

Holiday Inn Orlando SW– Celebration Area ★★★★½
5711 W. US 192*
Kissimmee, FL 34746
☎ 407-396-4222
hicelebration.com

LOCATION	3
ROOM RATING	90
COST ($ = $50)	$$$
DAILY RESORT FEE	$15

Commuting times to parks (in minutes):

MAGIC KINGDOM	12:15
EPCOT	12:00
ANIMAL KINGDOM	10:15
DHS	11:30

Holiday Inn Resort Lake Buena Vista ★★★½
13351 FL 535
Orlando, FL 32821
☎ 407-239-4500
hiresortlbv.com

LOCATION	2
ROOM RATING	82
COST ($ = $50)	$$
DAILY RESORT FEE	$16.95

Commuting times to parks (in minutes):

MAGIC KINGDOM	10:45
EPCOT	6:00
ANIMAL KINGDOM	9:00
DHS	8:30

Holiday Inn Resort Orlando Suites– Waterpark ★★★½
14500 Continental Gateway
Orlando, FL 32821
☎ 407-387-5437
hisuitesorlando.com

LOCATION	1
ROOM RATING	82
COST ($ = $50)	$$$
DAILY RESORT FEE	$25

Commuting times to parks (in minutes):

MAGIC KINGDOM	9:45
EPCOT	5:00
ANIMAL KINGDOM	8:00
DHS	7:30

*Irlo Bronson Memorial Highway

Hawthorn Suites Lake Buena Vista ★★★★	
8303 Palm Pkwy. Orlando, FL 32836 ☎ 407-597-5000 hawthornlakebuenavista.com	
LOCATION	2
ROOM RATING	85
COST ($ = $50)	$$$
DAILY RESORT FEE	$13
Commuting times to parks (in minutes):	
MAGIC KINGDOM	20:15
EPCOT	15:30
ANIMAL KINGDOM	18:30
DHS	18:00

Hawthorn Suites Orlando Convention Center ★★★½	
6435 Westwood Blvd. Orlando, FL 32821 ☎ 407-351-6600 hawthornorlando conventioncenter.com	
LOCATION	1
ROOM RATING	80
COST ($ = $50)	$$-
DAILY RESORT FEE	$5
Commuting times to parks (in minutes):	
MAGIC KINGDOM	17:30
EPCOT	12:45
ANIMAL KINGDOM	15:45
DHS	15:30

Hawthorn Suites Orlando I-Drive ★★★½	
7975 Canada Ave. Orlando, FL 32819 ☎ 407-345-0117 tinyurl.com/hawthornidrive	
LOCATION	1
ROOM RATING	75
COST ($ = $50)	$$$+
DAILY RESORT FEE	None
Commuting times to parks (in minutes):	
MAGIC KINGDOM	20:00
EPCOT	15:15
ANIMAL KINGDOM	18:15
DHS	17:45

Hilton Grand Vacations at Tuscany Village ★★★★	
8122 Arrezzo Way Orlando, FL 32821 ☎ 407-465-2600 tinyurl.com/hgvtuscany	
LOCATION	1
ROOM RATING	88
COST ($ = $50)	$$$$$+
DAILY RESORT FEE	$25
Commuting times to parks (in minutes):	
MAGIC KINGDOM	16:15
EPCOT	14:00
ANIMAL KINGDOM	17:00
DHS	16:30

Hilton Grand Vacations Club at SeaWorld ★★★★½	
6924 Grand Vacations Way Orlando, FL 32821 ☎ 407-465-0100 tinyurl.com/seaworldhgv	
LOCATION	1
ROOM RATING	95
COST ($ = $50)	$$$$+
DAILY RESORT FEE	$25
Commuting times to parks (in minutes):	
MAGIC KINGDOM	17:00
EPCOT	12:30
ANIMAL KINGDOM	16:30
DHS	15:30

Hilton Orlando ★★★★½	
6001 Destination Pkwy. Orlando, FL 32819 ☎ 407-313-4300 thehiltonorlando.com	
LOCATION	1
ROOM RATING	92
COST ($ = $50)	$$$$$-
DAILY RESORT FEE	$27
Commuting times to parks (in minutes):	
MAGIC KINGDOM	24:00
EPCOT	17:00
ANIMAL KINGDOM	16:00
DHS	14:00

Holiday Inn & Suites Orlando Universal ★★★½	
5905 Kirkman Rd. Orlando, FL 32819 ☎ 407-351-3333 hiuniversal.com	
LOCATION	4
ROOM RATING	75
COST ($ = $50)	$$+
DAILY RESORT FEE	None
Commuting times to parks (in minutes):	
MAGIC KINGDOM	19:00
EPCOT	14:15
ANIMAL KINGDOM	17:15
DHS	16:45

Holiday Inn Express & Suites Orlando–International Drive ★★★	
7276 International Dr. Orlando, FL 32819 ☎ 407-351-4100 tinyurl.com/hiexpressidrive	
LOCATION	1
ROOM RATING	74
COST ($ = $50)	$$$
DAILY RESORT FEE	None
Commuting times to parks (in minutes):	
MAGIC KINGDOM	27:00
EPCOT	19:00
ANIMAL KINGDOM	18:00
DHS	17:00

Holiday Inn in the Walt Disney World Resort ★★★½	
1805 Hotel Plaza Blvd. Lake Buena Vista, FL 32830 ☎ 407-828-8888 hiorlando.com	
LOCATION	WDW
ROOM RATING	79
COST ($ = $50)	$$$-
DAILY RESORT FEE	$12
Commuting times to parks (in minutes):	
MAGIC KINGDOM	15:30
EPCOT	10:45
ANIMAL KINGDOM	12:30
DHS	14:45

Homewood Suites by Hilton I-Drive ★★★½	
8745 International Dr. Orlando, FL 32819 ☎ 407-248-2232 tinyurl.com/homewoodidrive	
LOCATION	1
ROOM RATING	81
COST ($ = $50)	$$$-
DAILY RESORT FEE	None
Commuting times to parks (in minutes):	
MAGIC KINGDOM	28:00
EPCOT	13:00
ANIMAL KINGDOM	18:00
DHS	17:00

Homewood Suites by Hilton LBV-Orlando ★★★★	
11428 Marbella Palm Ct. Orlando, FL 32836 ☎ 407-239-4540 tinyurl.com/homewoodsuiteslbv	
LOCATION	2
ROOM RATING	85
COST ($ = $50)	$$$$+
DAILY RESORT FEE	None
Commuting times to parks (in minutes):	
MAGIC KINGDOM	18:00
EPCOT	12:00
ANIMAL KINGDOM	18:00
DHS	14:00

Homewood Suites by Hilton Near Universal ★★★★	
5893 American Way Orlando, FL 32819 ☎ 407-226-0669 tinyurl.com/homewooduniversal	
LOCATION	1
ROOM RATING	84
COST ($ = $50)	$$$$+
DAILY RESORT FEE	None
Commuting times to parks (in minutes):	
MAGIC KINGDOM	18:00
EPCOT	14:00
ANIMAL KINGDOM	20:00
DHS	20:00

Hotel Information Chart *(continued)*

Homewood Suites by Hilton Orlando Theme Parks ★★★★
6940 Westwood Blvd.
Orlando, FL 32821
☎ 407-778-5888
tinyurl.com/homewoodorlando

LOCATION	1
ROOM RATING	85
COST ($ = $50)	$$$+
DAILY RESORT FEE	None

Commuting times to parks *(in minutes)*:

MAGIC KINGDOM	22:00
EPCOT	14:00
ANIMAL KINGDOM	13:00
DHS	14:00

Hyatt Place Orlando Lake Buena Vista ★★★★
8688 Palm Parkway
Orlando, FL 32836
☎ 407-778 5500
orlandolakebuenavista.place .hyatt.com

LOCATION	2
ROOM RATING	84
COST ($ = $50)	$$$+
DAILY RESORT FEE	None

Commuting times to parks *(in minutes)*:

MAGIC KINGDOM	18:00
EPCOT	13:00
ANIMAL KINGDOM	12:00
DHS	14:00

Hyatt Place Orlando/Universal ★★★★
5895 Caravan Ct.
Orlando, FL 32819
☎ 407-351-0627
orlandouniversal.place.hyatt.com

LOCATION	4
ROOM RATING	84
COST ($ = $50)	$$$$-
DAILY RESORT FEE	None

Commuting times to parks *(in minutes)*:

MAGIC KINGDOM	19:00
EPCOT	14:15
ANIMAL KINGDOM	17:45
DHS	16:45

La Quinta Inn Orlando Universal Studios ★★★
5621 Major Blvd.
Orlando, FL 32819
☎ 407-313-3100
tinyurl.com/lquniversal

LOCATION	4
ROOM RATING	72
COST ($ = $50)	$$-
DAILY RESORT FEE	None

Commuting times to parks *(in minutes)*:

MAGIC KINGDOM	18:00
EPCOT	13:15
ANIMAL KINGDOM	16:15
DHS	16:00

Las Palmeras by Hilton Grand Vacations ★★★★
9501 Universal Blvd.
Orlando, FL 32819
☎ 407-313-2200
tinyurl.com/laspalmerashilton

LOCATION	1
ROOM RATING	87
COST ($ = $50)	$$$$$-
DAILY RESORT FEE	$25

Commuting times to parks *(in minutes)*:

MAGIC KINGDOM	19:45
EPCOT	15:00
ANIMAL KINGDOM	18:15
DHS	17:30

Legacy Vacation Club Lake Buena Vista ★★★★
8451 Palm Pkwy.
Lake Buena Vista, FL 32836
☎ 407-238-1700
legacyvacationresorts.com

LOCATION	2
ROOM RATING	85
COST ($ = $50)	$$+
DAILY RESORT FEE	$4

Commuting times to parks *(in minutes)*:

MAGIC KINGDOM	13:15
EPCOT	8:30
ANIMAL KINGDOM	11:30
DHS	11:00

Loews Royal Pacific Resort ★★★★½
6300 Hollywood Way
Orlando, FL 32819
☎ 407-503-3000
loewshotels.com/universal-orlando

LOCATION	4
ROOM RATING	90
COST ($ = $50)	$+ X 7
DAILY RESORT FEE	None

Commuting times to parks *(in minutes)*:

MAGIC KINGDOM	20:00
EPCOT	15:15
ANIMAL KINGDOM	18:15
DHS	17:45

Loews Sapphire Falls Resort ★★★★
6601 Adventure Way
Orlando, FL 32819
☎ 407-503-5000
loewshotels.com/universal-orlando

LOCATION	4
ROOM RATING	84
COST ($ = $50)	$$$$$-
DAILY RESORT FEE	None

Commuting times to parks *(in minutes)*:

MAGIC KINGDOM	20:00
EPCOT	15:00
ANIMAL KINGDOM	17:00
DHS	14:00

Marriott's Cypress Harbour ★★★★
11251 Harbour Villa Rd.
Orlando, FL 32821
☎ 407-238-1300
tinyurl.com/cypressharbourvillas

LOCATION	1
ROOM RATING	86
COST ($ = $50)	$$$$$-
DAILY RESORT FEE	None

Commuting times to parks *(in minutes)*:

MAGIC KINGDOM	17:45
EPCOT	13:15
ANIMAL KINGDOM	17:45
DHS	16:15

Marriott's Royal Palms ★★★★
8404 Vacation Way
Orlando, FL 32821
☎ 407-238-6200
tinyurl.com/marriottsroyalpalms

LOCATION	1
ROOM RATING	85
COST ($ = $50)	$$$$$+
DAILY RESORT FEE	None

Commuting times to parks *(in minutes)*:

MAGIC KINGDOM	9:45
EPCOT	5:00
ANIMAL KINGDOM	8:00
DHS	7:30

Melià Orlando Suite Hotel at Celebration ★★★½
225 Celebration Pl.
Celebration, FL 34747
☎ 407-964-7000
tinyurl.com/meliacelebration

LOCATION	2
ROOM RATING	82
COST ($ = $50)	$+ X 7
DAILY RESORT FEE	$15/$20

Commuting times to parks *(in minutes)*:

MAGIC KINGDOM	20:00
EPCOT	12:00
ANIMAL KINGDOM	12:00
DHS	10:00

Monumental Hotel ★★★
12120 International Dr.
Orlando, FL 32821
☎ 407-239-1222
monumentalhotelorlandofl.com

LOCATION	1
ROOM RATING	70
COST ($ = $50)	$$$-
DAILY RESORT FEE	$6.75

Commuting times to parks *(in minutes)*:

MAGIC KINGDOM	14:45
EPCOT	10:00
ANIMAL KINGDOM	13:00
DHS	12:30

*Irlo Bronson Memorial Highway

Hyatt Regency Grand Cypress
★★★★½
1 Grand Cypress Blvd.
Orlando, FL 32836
☎ 407-239-1234
grandcypress.hyatt.com

LOCATION	2
ROOM RATING	92
COST ($ = $50)	$$$$$-
DAILY RESORT FEE	$30

Commuting times to parks (in minutes):

MAGIC KINGDOM	13:30
EPCOT	8:45
ANIMAL KINGDOM	11:45
DHS	11:15

Hyatt Regency Orlando ★★★★½
9801 International Dr.
Orlando, FL 32819
☎ 407-284-1234
orlando.regency.hyatt.com

LOCATION	1
ROOM RATING	90
COST ($ = $50)	$$$-
DAILY RESORT FEE	$22

Commuting times to parks (in minutes):

MAGIC KINGDOM	19:30
EPCOT	15:15
ANIMAL KINGDOM	18:15
DHS	17:45

InTown Suites Orlando Universal
★★½
5615 Major Blvd.
Orlando, FL 32819
☎ 407-370-3734
tinyurl.com/intownsuitesorlando

LOCATION	1
ROOM RATING	63
COST ($ = $50)	$
DAILY RESORT FEE	None

Commuting times to parks (in minutes):

MAGIC KINGDOM	28:00
EPCOT	20:00
ANIMAL KINGDOM	19:00
DHS	19:00

Legacy Vacation Club Orlando
★★★½
2800 N. Poinciana Blvd.
Kissimmee, FL 34746
☎ 407-997-5000
legacyvacationresorts.com

LOCATION	3
ROOM RATING	80
COST ($ = $50)	$$+
DAILY RESORT FEE	$4

Commuting times to parks (in minutes):

MAGIC KINGDOM	16:30
EPCOT	16:15
ANIMAL KINGDOM	14:30
DHS	15:30

Liki Tiki Village ★★★★½
17777 Bali Blvd.
Winter Garden, FL 34787
☎ 407-239-5000
likitiki.com

LOCATION	3
ROOM RATING	90
COST ($ = $50)	$$$$-
DAILY RESORT FEE	$16

Commuting times to parks (in minutes):

MAGIC KINGDOM	9:00
EPCOT	8:45
ANIMAL KINGDOM	5:15
DHS	8:15

Loews Portofino Bay Hotel
★★★★½
5601 Universal Blvd.
Orlando, FL 32819
☎ 407-503-1000
loewshotels.com/universal-orlando

LOCATION	4
ROOM RATING	92
COST ($ = $50)	$+ X 8
DAILY RESORT FEE	None

Commuting times to parks (in minutes):

MAGIC KINGDOM	21:45
EPCOT	17:15
ANIMAL KINGDOM	20:15
DHS	19:45

Marriott's Grande Vista ★★★★½
5925 Avenida Vista
Orlando, FL 32821
☎ 407-238-7676
tinyurl.com/marriottsgrandevista

LOCATION	1
ROOM RATING	92
COST ($ = $50)	$$$+
DAILY RESORT FEE	None

Commuting times to parks (in minutes):

MAGIC KINGDOM	15:00
EPCOT	12:45
ANIMAL KINGDOM	15:45
DHS	15:15

Marriott's Harbour Lake ★★★★½
7102 Grand Horizons Blvd.
Orlando, FL 32821
☎ 407-465-6100
tinyurl.com/harbourlake

LOCATION	2
ROOM RATING	90
COST ($ = $50)	$$$$+
DAILY RESORT FEE	None

Commuting times to parks (in minutes):

MAGIC KINGDOM	18:00
EPCOT	13:30
ANIMAL KINGDOM	18:00
DHS	16:30

Marriott's Imperial Palms ★★★★
8404 Vacation Way
Orlando, FL 32821
☎ 407-238-6200
tinyurl.com/imperialpalmvillas

LOCATION	1
ROOM RATING	86
COST ($ = $50)	$+ X 7
DAILY RESORT FEE	None

Commuting times to parks (in minutes):

MAGIC KINGDOM	9:45
EPCOT	5:00
ANIMAL KINGDOM	8:00
DHS	7:30

Monumental Movieland Hotel
★★★
6233 International Dr.
Orlando, FL 32819
☎ 407-351-3900
monumentalmovielandhotel.com

LOCATION	1
ROOM RATING	68
COST ($ = $50)	$
DAILY RESORT FEE	$2.50

Commuting times to parks (in minutes):

MAGIC KINGDOM	27:00
EPCOT	12:00
ANIMAL KINGDOM	18:00
DHS	17:00

Motel 6 Orlando–I-Drive ★★★
5909 American Way
Orlando, FL 32819
☎ 407-351-6500
tinyurl.com/motel6idrive

LOCATION	1
ROOM RATING	66
COST ($ = $50)	$+
DAILY RESORT FEE	None

Commuting times to parks (in minutes):

MAGIC KINGDOM	20:15
EPCOT	16:00
ANIMAL KINGDOM	19:00
DHS	18:30

Mystic Dunes Resort & Golf Club
★★★★
7600 Mystic Dunes Ln.
Kissimmee, FL 34747
☎ 407-396-1311
mystic-dunes-resort.com

LOCATION	3
ROOM RATING	87
COST ($ = $50)	$$$-
DAILY RESORT FEE	$12

Commuting times to parks (in minutes):

MAGIC KINGDOM	10:45
EPCOT	10:30
ANIMAL KINGDOM	7:45
DHS	10:00

Hotel Information Chart (continued)

Omni Orlando Resort at ChampionsGate ★★★★★
1500 Masters Blvd.
ChampionsGate, FL 33896
☎ 407-390-6664
tinyurl.com/omnichampionsgate

LOCATION	2
ROOM RATING	96
COST ($ = $50)	$$$$+
DAILY RESORT FEE	$25

Commuting times to parks (in minutes):
MAGIC KINGDOM	15:30
EPCOT	15:00
ANIMAL KINGDOM	15:00
DHS	14:30

Orange Lake Resort ★★★★½
8505 W. US 192*
Kissimmee, FL 34747
☎ 407-239-0000
tinyurl.com/orangelakeresort
orlando

LOCATION	3
ROOM RATING	94
COST ($ = $50)	$$$-
DAILY RESORT FEE	$7.95

Commuting times to parks (in minutes):
MAGIC KINGDOM	8:45
EPCOT	8:30
ANIMAL KINGDOM	5:30
DHS	8:00

Orlando World Center Marriott Resort ★★★★½
8701 World Center Dr.
Orlando, FL 32821
☎ 407-239-4200
marriottworldcenter.com

LOCATION	2
ROOM RATING	90
COST ($ = $50)	$$$$$-
DAILY RESORT FEE	$25

Commuting times to parks (in minutes):
MAGIC KINGDOM	9:45
EPCOT	5:00
ANIMAL KINGDOM	8:00
DHS	7:30

Quality Inn at International Drive ★★★
8300 Jamaican Ct.
Orlando, FL 32819
☎ 407-351-1660
tinyurl.com/qualityinndrive

LOCATION	1
ROOM RATING	74
COST ($ = $50)	$+
DAILY RESORT FEE	$5.95

Commuting times to parks (in minutes):
MAGIC KINGDOM	21:45
EPCOT	17:15
ANIMAL KINGDOM	20:15
DHS	19:45

Quality Suites Lake Buena Vista ★★★½
8200 Palm Pkwy.
Orlando, FL 32836
☎ 407-465-8200
qualitysuiteslbv.com

LOCATION	2
ROOM RATING	81
COST ($ = $50)	$$+
DAILY RESORT FEE	None

Commuting times to parks (in minutes):
MAGIC KINGDOM	13:45
EPCOT	9:15
ANIMAL KINGDOM	12:15
DHS	11:45

Quality Suites Royale Parc Suites ★★★½
5876 W. US 192*
Kissimmee, FL 34746
☎ 407-396-8040
royaleparcsuitesorlando.com

LOCATION	3
ROOM RATING	76
COST ($ = $50)	$$+
DAILY RESORT FEE	$11

Commuting times to parks (in minutes):
MAGIC KINGDOM	11:15
EPCOT	11:00
ANIMAL KINGDOM	9:15
DHS	10:30

Ramada Convention Center I-Drive ★★★
8342 Jamaican Ct.
Orlando, FL 32819
☎ 407-363-1944
tinyurl.com/ramadaidrive

LOCATION	1
ROOM RATING	65
COST ($ = $50)	$$-
DAILY RESORT FEE	$4

Commuting times to parks (in minutes):
MAGIC KINGDOM	20:15
EPCOT	15:30
ANIMAL KINGDOM	18:30
DHS	18:00

Ramada Gateway Kissimmee
(Garden) ★★½
7470 W. US 192*
Kissimmee, FL 34747
☎ 407-966-4410
ramadagateway.com

LOCATION	3
ROOM RATING	62
COST ($ = $50)	$$-
DAILY RESORT FEE	None

Commuting times to parks (in minutes):
MAGIC KINGDOM	5:00
EPCOT	9:00
ANIMAL KINGDOM	9:00
DHS	7:00

Ramada Plaza Resort and Suites Orlando I-Drive ★★★
6500 International Dr.
Orlando, FL 32819
☎ 407-345-5340
tinyurl.com/ramadaplazaidrive

LOCATION	1
ROOM RATING	72
COST ($ = $50)	$$$+
DAILY RESORT FEE	None

Commuting times to parks (in minutes):
MAGIC KINGDOM	17:00
EPCOT	20:00
ANIMAL KINGDOM	19:00
DHS	18:00

Residence Inn Orlando at SeaWorld ★★★★
11000 Westwood Blvd.
Orlando, FL 32821
☎ 407-313-3600
tinyurl.com/residenceinnseaworld

LOCATION	2
ROOM RATING	85
COST ($ = $50)	$$$+
DAILY RESORT FEE	None

Commuting times to parks (in minutes):
MAGIC KINGDOM	15:45
EPCOT	11:15
ANIMAL KINGDOM	14:15
DHS	13:45

Residence Inn Orlando Convention Center ★★★½
8800 Universal Blvd.
Orlando, FL 32819
☎ 407-226-0288
tinyurl.com/resinnconvention
center

LOCATION	1
ROOM RATING	80
COST ($ = $50)	$$$$-
DAILY RESORT FEE	None

Commuting times to parks (in minutes):
MAGIC KINGDOM	22:00
EPCOT	17:30
ANIMAL KINGDOM	20:30
DHS	20:00

Residence Inn Orlando Lake Buena Vista ★★★★
11450 Marbella Palm Ct.
Orlando, FL 32836
☎ 407-465-0075
tinyurl.com/residenceinnlbv

LOCATION	2
ROOM RATING	83
COST ($ = $50)	$$$
DAILY RESORT FEE	None

Commuting times to parks (in minutes):
MAGIC KINGDOM	15:40
EPCOT	11:00
ANIMAL KINGDOM	14:00
DHS	13:30

*Irlo Bronson Memorial Highway

Parkway International Resort
★★★½
6200 Safari Trail
Kissimmee, FL 34746
☎ 407-396-6600
parkwayresort.com

LOCATION	3
ROOM RATING	82
COST ($ = $50)	$$$+
DAILY RESORT FEE	$9
Commuting times to parks *(in minutes)*:	
MAGIC KINGDOM	8:30
EPCOT	8:15
ANIMAL KINGDOM	6:15
DHS	7:45

**The Point Universal Orlando
Resort** ★★★★
7389 Universal Blvd.
Orlando, FL 32819
☎ 407-956-2000
thepointorlando.com

LOCATION	1
ROOM RATING	84
COST ($ = $50)	$$$-
DAILY RESORT FEE	$13
Commuting times to parks *(in minutes)*:	
MAGIC KINGDOM	23:00
EPCOT	17:00
ANIMAL KINGDOM	23:00
DHS	19:00

**Polynesian Isles Resort Phase 1
(Diamond Resorts)** ★★★★½
3045 Polynesian Isles Blvd.
Kissimmee, FL 34746
☎ 407-396-1622
polynesianisle.com

LOCATION	3
ROOM RATING	90
COST ($ = $50)	$$$$+
DAILY RESORT FEE	$10
Commuting times to parks *(in minutes)*:	
MAGIC KINGDOM	14:30
EPCOT	14:15
ANIMAL KINGDOM	12:30
DHS	14:00

Quality Suites Turkey Lake ★★★
9350 Turkey Lake Rd.
Orlando, FL 32819
☎ 407-351-5050
qualitysuitesorlandofl.com

LOCATION	2
ROOM RATING	74
COST ($ = $50)	$$-
DAILY RESORT FEE	$4.50
Commuting times to parks *(in minutes)*:	
MAGIC KINGDOM	26:00
EPCOT	11:00
ANIMAL KINGDOM	17:00
DHS	16:00

**Radisson Hotel Orlando
Lake Buena Vista** ★★★½
12799 Apopka–Vineland Rd.
Orlando, FL 32836
☎ 407-597-3400
tinyurl.com/radissonlbv

LOCATION	2
ROOM RATING	82
COST ($ = $50)	$$$
DAILY RESORT FEE	None
Commuting times to parks *(in minutes)*:	
MAGIC KINGDOM	13:45
EPCOT	9:00
ANIMAL KINGDOM	12:00
DHS	11:30

**Radisson Resort Orlando-
Celebration** ★★★★
2900 Parkway Blvd.
Kissimmee, FL 34747
☎ 407-396-7000
tinyurl.com/radissonoc

LOCATION	3
ROOM RATING	86
COST ($ = $50)	$$-
DAILY RESORT FEE	$20
Commuting times to parks *(in minutes)*:	
MAGIC KINGDOM	8:30
EPCOT	8:00
ANIMAL KINGDOM	6:30
DHS	7:45

Red Lion Kissimmee ★★★
7300 W. US 192*
Kissimmee, FL 34747
☎ 407-396-7300
redlion.com/orlando

LOCATION	3
ROOM RATING	68
COST ($ = $50)	$$$-
DAILY RESORT FEE	$8
Commuting times to parks *(in minutes)*:	
MAGIC KINGDOM	17:00
EPCOT	8:00
ANIMAL KINGDOM	8:00
DHS	6:00

**Red Roof Inn Orlando
Convention Center** ★★½
9922 Hawaiian Ct.
Orlando, FL 32819
☎ 407-352-1507
tinyurl.com/redroofidrive

LOCATION	1
ROOM RATING	60
COST ($ = $50)	$$-
DAILY RESORT FEE	$4
Commuting times to parks *(in minutes)*:	
MAGIC KINGDOM	19:00
EPCOT	14:15
ANIMAL KINGDOM	17:15
DHS	16:45

Renaissance Orlando at SeaWorld
★★★★½
6677 Sea Harbor Dr.
Orlando, FL 32821
☎ 407-351-5555
tinyurl.com/renorlandoseaworld

LOCATION	1
ROOM RATING	90
COST ($ = $50)	$$$$-
DAILY RESORT FEE	$25
Commuting times to parks *(in minutes)*:	
MAGIC KINGDOM	16:45
EPCOT	12:15
ANIMAL KINGDOM	15:15
DHS	14:45

**The Ritz-Carlton Orlando,
Grande Lakes** ★★★★½
4012 Central Florida Pkwy.
Orlando, FL 32837
☎ 407-206-2400
grandelakes.com

LOCATION	1
ROOM RATING	94
COST ($ = $50)	$- X 7
DAILY RESORT FEE	$35
Commuting times to parks *(in minutes)*:	
MAGIC KINGDOM	23:00
EPCOT	18:15
ANIMAL KINGDOM	21:30
DHS	20:45

Rodeway Inn Maingate ★★½
5995 W. US 192*
Kissimmee, FL 34747
☎ 407-396-4300
rodewayinnmaingate.com

LOCATION	3
ROOM RATING	59
COST ($ = $50)	$-
DAILY RESORT FEE	$4
Commuting times to parks *(in minutes)*:	
MAGIC KINGDOM	11:15
EPCOT	11:00
ANIMAL KINGDOM	9:15
DHS	10:30

Rosen Centre Hotel ★★★★½
9840 International Dr.
Orlando, FL 32819
☎ 407-996-9840
rosencentre.com

LOCATION	1
ROOM RATING	95
COST ($ = $50)	$$$$$-
DAILY RESORT FEE	None
Commuting times to parks *(in minutes)*:	
MAGIC KINGDOM	19:45
EPCOT	15:15
ANIMAL KINGDOM	18:15
DHS	17:45

Hotel Information Chart (continued)

Rosen Inn at Pointe Orlando
★★★½
9000 International Dr.
Orlando, FL 32819
☎ 407-996-8585
roseninn9000.com

LOCATION	1
ROOM RATING	75
COST ($ = $50)	$$$
DAILY RESORT FEE	None

Commuting times to parks (in minutes):
MAGIC KINGDOM	28:00
EPCOT	12:00
ANIMAL KINGDOM	19:00
DHS	17:00

Rosen Inn International Hotel
★★★
7600 International Dr.
Orlando, FL 32819
☎ 407-996-1600
roseninn7600.com

LOCATION	1
ROOM RATING	65
COST ($ = $50)	$$
DAILY RESORT FEE	$25

Commuting times to parks (in minutes):
MAGIC KINGDOM	19:45
EPCOT	15:00
ANIMAL KINGDOM	18:00
DHS	17:30

Rosen Inn Near Universal ★★★
6327 International Drive
Orlando, FL 32819
☎ 407-996-4444
roseninn6327.com

LOCATION	1
ROOM RATING	71
COST ($ = $50)	$$
DAILY RESORT FEE	None

Commuting times to parks (in minutes):
MAGIC KINGDOM	26:00
EPCOT	19:00
ANIMAL KINGDOM	18:00
DHS	16:00

Sheraton Lake Buena Vista Resort
★★★★
12205 S. Apopka–Vineland Rd.
Orlando, FL 32836
☎ 407-239-0444
sheratonlakebuenavistaresort.com

LOCATION	2
ROOM RATING	88
COST ($ = $50)	$$$-
DAILY RESORT FEE	$24

Commuting times to parks (in minutes):
MAGIC KINGDOM	13:45
EPCOT	9:00
ANIMAL KINGDOM	12:00
DHS	11:30

Sheraton Vistana Resort Villas
★★★★
8800 Vistana Centre Dr.
Orlando, FL 32821
☎ 407-239-3100
tinyurl.com/vistanavillas

LOCATION	2
ROOM RATING	89
COST ($ = $50)	$$$$+
DAILY RESORT FEE	None

Commuting times to parks (in minutes):
MAGIC KINGDOM	11:15
EPCOT	6:30
ANIMAL KINGDOM	9:30
DHS	9:00

Sonesta ES Suites ★★★★
8480 International Dr.
Orlando, FL 32819
☎ 407-352-2400
tinyurl.com/sonestaorlando

LOCATION	1
ROOM RATING	85
COST ($ = $50)	$$$$$-
DAILY RESORT FEE	$8

Commuting times to parks (in minutes):
MAGIC KINGDOM	28:00
EPCOT	13:00
ANIMAL KINGDOM	19:00
DHS	18:00

Star Island Resort & Club ★★★★
5000 Ave. of the Stars
Kissimmee, FL 34746
☎ 407-997-8000
star-island.com

LOCATION	3
ROOM RATING	84
COST ($ = $50)	$$$-
DAILY RESORT FEE	$13

Commuting times to parks (in minutes):
MAGIC KINGDOM	15:45
EPCOT	15:15
ANIMAL KINGDOM	14:15
DHS	13:30

Stay Sky Suites I-Drive Orlando
★★★½
7601 Canada Ave.
Orlando, FL 32819
☎ 407-581-2151
stayskysuitesidriveorlando.com

LOCATION	1
ROOM RATING	82
COST ($ = $50)	$$$-
DAILY RESORT FEE	None

Commuting times to parks (in minutes):
MAGIC KINGDOM	20:15
EPCOT	15:45
ANIMAL KINGDOM	18:45
DHS	19:15

Staybridge Suites
Lake Buena Vista ★★★★½
8751 Suiteside Dr.
Orlando, FL 32836
☎ 407-238-0777
tinyurl.com/staybridgelbv

LOCATION	2
ROOM RATING	90
COST ($ = $50)	$$$+
DAILY RESORT FEE	None

Commuting times to parks (in minutes):
MAGIC KINGDOM	14:15
EPCOT	9:30
ANIMAL KINGDOM	12:30
DHS	12:00

Treehouse Villas at Disney's
Saratoga Springs Resort & Spa
★★★★½
1960 Broadway
Lake Buena Vista, FL 32830
☎ 407-827-1100
tinyurl.com/saratogawdw

LOCATION	WDW
ROOM RATING	90
COST ($ = $50)	$- x 23
DAILY RESORT FEE	None

Commuting times to parks (in minutes):
MAGIC KINGDOM	12:45
EPCOT	7:15
ANIMAL KINGDOM	16:45
DHS	12:30

Universal's Cabana Bay
Beach Resort ★★★★
6550 Adventure Way
Orlando, FL 32819
☎ 407-503-4000
loewshotels.com/universal-orlando

LOCATION	4
ROOM RATING	83
COST ($ = $50)	$$$$-
DAILY RESORT FEE	None

Commuting times to parks (in minutes):
MAGIC KINGDOM	20:00
EPCOT	15:00
ANIMAL KINGDOM	17:00
DHS	14:00

Vacation Village at Parkway
★★★★½
2975 Arabian Nights Blvd.
Kissimmee, FL 34747
☎ 407-396-9086
dailymanagementresorts.com

LOCATION	3
ROOM RATING	91
COST ($ = $50)	$$$-
DAILY RESORT FEE	$25

Commuting times to parks (in minutes):
MAGIC KINGDOM	8:30
EPCOT	8:15
ANIMAL KINGDOM	6:45
DHS	7:45

*Irlo Bronson Memorial Highway

Rosen Plaza Hotel ★★★★½
9700 International Dr.
Orlando, FL 32819
☎ 407-996-9700
rosenplaza.com

LOCATION	1
ROOM RATING	90
COST ($ = $50)	$$$-
DAILY RESORT FEE	None

Commuting times to parks (in minutes):
MAGIC KINGDOM	27:00
EPCOT	13:00
ANIMAL KINGDOM	19:00
DHS	17:00

Rosen Shingle Creek ★★★★
9939 Universal Blvd.
Orlando, FL 32819
☎ 866-996-9939
rosenshinglecreek.com

LOCATION	1
ROOM RATING	88
COST ($ = $50)	$$$$
DAILY RESORT FEE	None

Commuting times to parks (in minutes):
MAGIC KINGDOM	24:00
EPCOT	17:00
ANIMAL KINGDOM	16:00
DHS	14:00

Shades of Green ★★★★½
1950 W. Magnolia Palm Dr.
Lake Buena Vista, FL 32830
☎ 407-824-3400
shadesofgreen.org

LOCATION	WDW
ROOM RATING	91
COST ($ = $50)	$$$-
DAILY RESORT FEE	None

Commuting times to parks (in minutes):
MAGIC KINGDOM	3:30
EPCOT	4:45
ANIMAL KINGDOM	9:30
DHS	6:15

SpringHill Suites Orlando at Flamingo Crossings ★★★★
13279 Flamingo Crossings Blvd.
Winter Garden, FL 34787
☎ 407-507-1200
tinyurl.com/fc-springhill

LOCATION	2
ROOM RATING	85
COST ($ = $50)	$$$$-
DAILY RESORT FEE	None

Commuting times to parks (in minutes):
MAGIC KINGDOM	18:00
EPCOT	16:00
ANIMAL KINGDOM	10:00
DHS	15:00

SpringHill Suites Orlando Convention Center ★★★½
8840 Universal Blvd.
Orlando, FL 32819
☎ 407-345-9073
tinyurl.com/shsconventioncenter

LOCATION	1
ROOM RATING	80
COST ($ = $50)	$$$$-
DAILY RESORT FEE	None

Commuting times to parks (in minutes):
MAGIC KINGDOM	22:30
EPCOT	17:50
ANIMAL KINGDOM	20:45
DHS	20:20

SpringHill Suites Orlando Kissimmee ★★★½
4991 Calypso Cay Way
Kissimmee, FL 34746
☎ 407-997-1300
tinyurl.com/springhillkiss

LOCATION	3
ROOM RATING	81
COST ($ = $50)	$$$-
DAILY RESORT FEE	None

Commuting times to parks (in minutes):
MAGIC KINGDOM	22:00
EPCOT	9:00
ANIMAL KINGDOM	11:00
DHS	10:00

Sunsol International Drive ★★★
6859 American Way
Orlando, FL 32819
☎ 407-203-2664
sunsolhotels.net/internationaldrive

LOCATION	1
ROOM RATING	72
COST ($ = $50)	$$-
DAILY RESORT FEE	$9

Commuting times to parks (in minutes):
MAGIC KINGDOM	31:00
EPCOT	17:00
ANIMAL KINGDOM	22:00
DHS	20:00

Super 8 Kissimmee/Maingate ★★★
5875 W. US 192*
Kissimmee, FL 34746
☎ 407-396-8883
tinyurl.com/super8maingate

LOCATION	3
ROOM RATING	70
COST ($ = $50)	$+
DAILY RESORT FEE	None

Commuting times to parks (in minutes):
MAGIC KINGDOM	8:30
EPCOT	8:00
ANIMAL KINGDOM	7:45
DHS	5:45

TownePlace Suites Orlando at Flamingo Crossings ★★★★
13295 Flamingo Crossings Blvd.
Winter Garden, FL 34787
☎ 407-507-1200
tinyurl.com/fc-townplace

LOCATION	2
ROOM RATING	84
COST ($ = $50)	$$$$-
DAILY RESORT FEE	None

Commuting times to parks (in minutes):
MAGIC KINGDOM	18:00
EPCOT	16:00
ANIMAL KINGDOM	10:00
DHS	16:00

The Villas at Disney's Grand Floridian Resort & Spa ★★★★½
4401 Floridian Way
Lake Buena Vista, FL 32830
☎ 407-824-3000
tinyurl.com/grandfloridianvillas

LOCATION	WDW
ROOM RATING	93
COST ($ = $50)	$+ x 21
DAILY RESORT FEE	None

Commuting times to parks (in minutes):
MAGIC KINGDOM	on monorail
EPCOT	4:45
ANIMAL KINGDOM	11:45
DHS	6:45

Waldorf Astoria Orlando ★★★★½
14200 Bonnet Creek Resort Ln.
Lake Buena Vista, FL 32830
☎ 407-597-5500
waldorfastoriaorlando.com

LOCATION	2
ROOM RATING	93
COST ($ = $50)	$$$$$$-
DAILY RESORT FEE	$30

Commuting times to parks (in minutes):
MAGIC KINGDOM	8:00
EPCOT	6:00
ANIMAL KINGDOM	7:15
DHS	4:15

Walt Disney World Dolphin ★★★★½
1500 Epcot Resorts Blvd.
Lake Buena Vista, FL 32830
☎ 407-934-4000
swandolphin.com

LOCATION	WDW
ROOM RATING	90
COST ($ = $50)	$$$$$$-
DAILY RESORT FEE	$25

Commuting times to parks (in minutes):
MAGIC KINGDOM	6:45
EPCOT	5:00
ANIMAL KINGDOM	6:15
DHS	4:00

Hotel Information Chart *(continued)*

Walt Disney World Swan
★★★★½
1200 Epcot Resorts Blvd.
Lake Buena Vista, FL 32830
☎ 407-934-3000
swandolphin.com

LOCATION	WDW
ROOM RATING	90
COST ($ = $50)	$$$$$$-
DAILY RESORT FEE	$25

Commuting times to parks *(in minutes)*:
MAGIC KINGDOM	6:30
EPCOT	4:45
ANIMAL KINGDOM	6:15
DHS	4:00

Westgate Lakes Resort & Spa
★★★★½
10000 Turkey Lake Rd.
Orlando, FL 32819
☎ 407-345-0000
westgateresorts.com/lakes

LOCATION	2
ROOM RATING	92
COST ($ = $50)	$$$-
DAILY RESORT FEE	$13

Commuting times to parks *(in minutes)*:
MAGIC KINGDOM	17:30
EPCOT	14:30
ANIMAL KINGDOM	19:15
DHS	18:00

Westgate Palace ★★★
6145 Carrier Dr.
Orlando, FL 32819
☎ 407-996-6000
westgateresorts.com/palace

LOCATION	1
ROOM RATING	68
COST ($ = $50)	$$$$+
DAILY RESORT FEE	$10

Commuting times to parks *(in minutes)*:
MAGIC KINGDOM	20:45
EPCOT	16:15
ANIMAL KINGDOM	19:15
DHS	18:45

Westgate Towers ★★★½
7600 W. US 192*
Kissimmee, FL 34747
☎ 407-396-2500
westgateresorts.com/towers

LOCATION	2
ROOM RATING	81
COST ($ = $50)	$$$$+
DAILY RESORT FEE	None

Commuting times to parks *(in minutes)*:
MAGIC KINGDOM	8:45
EPCOT	8:30
ANIMAL KINGDOM	5:45
DHS	8:00

Westgate Town Center ★★★★½
7700 Westgate Blvd.
Kissimmee, FL 34747
☎ 407-396-2500
westgateresorts.com/town-center

LOCATION	2
ROOM RATING	94
COST ($ = $50)	$$$$+
DAILY RESORT FEE	$11

Commuting times to parks *(in minutes)*:
MAGIC KINGDOM	8:45
EPCOT	8:30
ANIMAL KINGDOM	5:45
DHS	8:00

Westgate Vacation Villas
★★★★½
7700 Westgate Blvd.
Kissimmee, FL 34747
☎ 407-239-0510
**westgateresorts.com
/vacation-villas**

LOCATION	2
ROOM RATING	90
COST ($ = $50)	$$$$$
DAILY RESORT FEE	$11

Commuting times to parks *(in minutes)*:
MAGIC KINGDOM	8:45
EPCOT	8:30
ANIMAL KINGDOM	5:45
DHS	8:00

**Wingate by Wyndham
Universal Studios** ★★★½
5661 Windhover Dr.
Orlando, FL 32819
☎ 407-226-0900
wingateorlando.com

LOCATION	4
ROOM RATING	76
COST ($ = $50)	$$$-
DAILY RESORT FEE	None

Commuting times to parks *(in minutes)*:
MAGIC KINGDOM	31:00
EPCOT	16:00
ANIMAL KINGDOM	22:00
DHS	21:00

WorldQuest Orlando Resort
★★★★
8849 Worldquest Blvd.
Orlando, FL 32821
☎ 407-387-3800
worldquestorlando.com

LOCATION	1
ROOM RATING	88
COST ($ = $50)	$$$$
DAILY RESORT FEE	$16

Commuting times to parks *(in minutes)*:
MAGIC KINGDOM	17:00
EPCOT	11:00
ANIMAL KINGDOM	17:00
DHS	13:00

Wyndham Bonnet Creek Resort
★★★★½
9560 Via Encinas
Lake Buena Vista, FL 32830
☎ 407-238-3500
wyndhambonnetcreek.com

LOCATION	2
ROOM RATING	90
COST ($ = $50)	$$$$$+
DAILY RESORT FEE	None

Commuting times to parks *(in minutes)*:
MAGIC KINGDOM	8:00
EPCOT	6:00
ANIMAL KINGDOM	7:15
DHS	4:15

Wyndham Cypress Palms ★★★★
5324 Fairfield Lake Dr.
Kissimmee, FL 34746
☎ 407-397-1600
cypresspalms.com

LOCATION	3
ROOM RATING	87
COST ($ = $50)	$$+
DAILY RESORT FEE	None

Commuting times to parks *(in minutes)*:
MAGIC KINGDOM	15:15
EPCOT	15:00
ANIMAL KINGDOM	14:45
DHS	14:45

**Wyndham Lake Buena Vista
Resort** ★★★½
1850 Hotel Plaza Blvd.
Lake Buena Vista, FL 32830
☎ 407-828-4444
wyndhamlakebuenavista.com

LOCATION	WDW
ROOM RATING	75
COST ($ = $50)	$$$$$-
DAILY RESORT FEE	$10/$20

Commuting times to parks *(in minutes)*:
MAGIC KINGDOM	15:15
EPCOT	10:45
ANIMAL KINGDOM	14:45
DHS	12:15

Wyndham Orlando Resort I-Drive
★★★★
8001 International Dr.
Orlando, FL 32819
☎ 407-351-2420
wyndham.com/hotels/MCOWD

LOCATION	1
ROOM RATING	85
COST ($ = $50)	$$$$
DAILY RESORT FEE	$20

Commuting times to parks *(in minutes)*:
MAGIC KINGDOM	19:45
EPCOT	15:00
ANIMAL KINGDOM	18:15
DHS	17:30

*Irlo Bronson Memorial Highway

PART FOUR

DINING *in* AND *around* WALT DISNEY WORLD

READER SURVEYS *plus* EXPERT OPINIONS: OUR APPROACH *to* DINING

WE RECEIVED MORE THAN 122,000 SURVEYS about Disney World restaurants in 2016, and we're on track to get even more in 2017. To put that in perspective, we think that's more surveys than Yelp and TripAdvisor have for the World over their entire lifetimes. *Combined.*

What makes the *Unofficial Guide* different from Yelp and others is that we display those surveys alongside comprehensive reviews written by culinary experts. With those critical analyses, you get a consistent evaluation of the entire range of Disney dining options from people who have tried every restaurant, kiosk, and food stand in the World. We (Bob and Len) will weigh in occasionally, too. Here's how to use the reader surveys and our critical reviews together.

• If a restaurant has earned 90% or better in our reader surveys and at least four stars (sit-down) or a B or better (counter-service) from our critics, make plans to visit; there's a strong chance you'll enjoy your meal. In the Magic Kingdom, for example, **Be Our Guest** and **Columbia Harbour House** both fit this profile.

• Avoid restaurants that have earned 80% or less in our reader surveys and either three stars or less (sit-down) or a C or lower (counter-service) from our critics. It's probably not worth your time or money. **Fresh Mediterranean Market** at the Dolphin Hotel is an example.

• For restaurants where our reader surveys disagree with our critical analysis, read the review for an explanation. An example is **STK** at Disney Springs. This upscale steakhouse has good food and friendly service, earning three and a half stars from our critics. However, STK insists on having a DJ spin pop music in its dining room at a volume more appropriate to Coachella than Walt Disney World. Families seem to hate this, as evidenced by STK's 60% survey rating. But if you're looking for a little Black Eyed Peas with your steak and fries, the music might appeal to you. Just know what you're getting into.

DINING *outside*
WALT DISNEY WORLD

unofficial **TIP**
Readers rate all of Universal's CityWalk sit-down restaurants higher than Disney's average sit-down.

UNOFFICIAL GUIDE RESEARCHERS love good food and invest a fair amount of time scouting new places to eat. And because food at Walt Disney World is so expensive, we (like you) have an economic incentive for finding palatable meals outside the World. Alas, the surrounding area isn't exactly a culinary mecca. If you thrive on fast food and the fare at chain restaurants (Denny's, T.G.I. Friday's, Olive Garden, and the like), you'll be as happy as an alligator at a chicken farm. But if you're in the market for a superlative dining experience, you'll find the pickings outside the World of about the same quality as those inside, only less expensive. Plus, some ethnic cuisines aren't represented in WDW restaurants.

Among specialty restaurants both in and out of the World, location and price will determine your choice. Our recommendations for specialty and ethnic fare served outside of the World are summarized in the table that starts on page 310.

Better restaurants outside the World cater primarily to adults. That's a plus, however, if you're looking to escape children or you want to eat in peace and quiet.

DINING AT UNIVERSAL CITYWALK

DINING AND SHOPPING are the focus at CityWalk, whose restaurants tend to cater more to adult tastes than the theme park restaurants do. Probably the best of the bunch is **Emeril's Orlando,** but each restaurant has a couple of decent options if you know what to look for. One thing all of them have in common is noise: Your fussy toddler will have to fight to be heard in some of these places. Some of the restaurants use **OpenTable** (opentable.com) for online reservations, and you can make reservations for the other venues at universalorlando.com via **NexTable,** making it easy to get seats before you go park-hopping.

ANTOJITOS ☎ 407-224-3663; tinyurl.com/antojitoscitywalk. The name means "little cravings," the Mexican equivalent of Spain's small-plate *tapas,* so it's only natural that the best dishes are the appetizers. Try the empanada trio (beef, chicken, and mushroom) and the *esquites asados,* roasted corn-off-the-cob with queso fresco and mayo. Antojitos carries more than 200 tequila brands, too, and makes a tasty margarita.

BOB MARLEY—A TRIBUTE TO FREEDOM ☎ 407-224-3663; tinyurl.com/bobmarleytribute. Set in a replica of the reggae singer's Jamaica home, the building is filled with memorabilia and photos showcasing his career and life. The Caribbean-inspired dishes—beef patties, yucca fries, oxtail stew, and such—aren't particularly memorable, but the laid-back atmosphere makes it worth a visit.

BUBBA GUMP SHRIMP CO. ☎ 407-903-0044; bubbagump.com/locations/orlando. A seafood-and-cocktails eatery, part of an international chain inspired by *Forrest Gump.* Shrimp and/or crab in almost everything,

In or Out of the World for These Cuisines?

AMERICAN Good selections both in and out of the World.

BARBECUE Better out of the World.

BUFFETS A toss-up—Disney buffets are expensive but offer excellent quality and variety. Out-of-World buffets aren't as upscale but are inexpensive.

CHINESE Better out of the World.

FRENCH Toss-up; good but expensive both in and out of the World.

GERMAN Passable but not great, in or out of the World.

ITALIAN Tie on quality; better value out of the World.

JAPANESE/SUSHI Teppan Edo in the Japan Pavilion at Epcot is tops for teppanyaki (table grilling). For sushi and sashimi, try **Tokyo Dining**, also in Japan, or visit **Morimoto Asia** at Disney Springs.

MEXICAN La Hacienda de San Angel at Epcot is good but expensive, with more-affordable food right next door at the quick-service **La Cantina de San Angel**. For decent Tex-Mex, try **El Patron** outside the World.

MIDDLE EASTERN More choice and better value out of the World.

SEAFOOD Toss-up.

STEAK/PRIME RIB Try **The Boathouse** at Disney Springs or **The Capital Grille** on International Drive out of the World. For more-affordable but nevertheless-delicious wads o' meat, try one of the **Black Angus** steakhouses on International Drive or on West Irlo Bronson Memorial Highway in Kissimmee (closed at press time for renovations).

with particular highlights of "Mama Blue's" gumbo and journey-worthy seafood "hush pups."

THE COWFISH ☎ 407-224-3663; tinyurl.com/thecowfish. *Unofficial Guide* readers say this is the best restaurant at CityWalk. An unusual combination of burger joint and sushi bar, Cowfish is a small chain (four locations) out of North Carolina. We've eaten at three of them, and they offer tasty food at reasonable prices. We like the burgers a bit more than the sushi. Try the Crab Rangoon dip appetizer and the bacon coleslaw as a side. The servers are friendly, but food delivery is painfully slow at peak times because the kitchen is undersized for the multistory dining rooms.

EMERIL'S ORLANDO ☎ 407-224-2424; emerilsrestaurants.com/emerils -orlando. Not to be confused with Emeril Lagasse's fancier and more expensive Asian-inspired Tchoup Chop at the nearby Royal Pacific Resort, this is the Florida outpost of Emeril's original restaurant in New Orleans. The cuisine—some of CityWalk's best—is Louisiana style with creative flair. Request the off-menu surf-and-turf po'boy for an insider treat. The smoked-mushroom appetizer is outstanding, and the banana cream pie will renew your faith in humanity.

HARD ROCK CAFE ☎ 407-351-7625; hardrock.com/cafes/orlando. The best meals we've had here have consisted of drinks and appetizers or desserts. The entrées—burgers, sandwiches, steaks, and such—aren't especially memorable. More remarkable is the collection of music

Continued on page 313

Where to Eat Outside Walt Disney World

AMERICAN

• **THE RAVENOUS PIG*** 565 W. Fairbanks Ave., Winter Park; ☎ 407-628-2333; theravenouspig.com; moderate–expensive. New American cuisine with an award-winning menu that changes depending on seasonal ingredients. Check out its nearby sister restaurant at **thecaskandlarder.com.**

• **SEASONS 52** 7700 W. Sand Lake Rd., Orlando; ☎ 407-354-5212; seasons52.com; moderate–expensive. Delicious, creative New American food that's low in fat and calories. Extensive wine list.

• **SLATE** 8323 Sand Lake Rd., Orlando; ☎ 407-500-7528; slateorlando.com; moderate–expensive. Combines intimacy and casual dining with greater success than many Restaurant Row establishments. Grab a quick bite from the extensive menu or try heartier fare from the copper-clad wood oven.

BARBECUE

• **BUBBALOU'S BODACIOUS BAR-B-QUE** 5818 Conroy Rd., Orlando (near Universal Orlando); ☎ 407-295-1212; bubbalous.com; inexpensive. Tender, smoky barbecue; tomato-based Killer Sauce.

• **4 RIVERS SMOKEHOUSE** 874 W. Osceola Pkwy., Kissimmee, and six area locations; ☎ 844-474-8377; 4rsmokehouse.com; inexpensive. Award-winning brisket, plus fried pickles and okra, cheese grits, and collards.

CARIBBEAN

• **BAHAMA BREEZE** 8849 International Dr., Orlando; ☎ 407-248-2499; 8735 Vineland Ave.; ☎ 407-938-9010; bahamabreeze.com; moderate. A creative and tasty version of Caribbean cuisine from the owners of the Olive Garden and Red Lobster.

CHINESE

• **KIM WU** 4914 S. Kirkman Rd., Orlando; ☎ 407-293-0752; moderate–expensive. Upscale American-style Chinese dishes. Popular lunch buffet.

CUBAN/SPANISH

• **COLUMBIA** 649 Front St., Celebration; ☎ 407-566-1505; columbiarestau rant.com; moderate. Authentic Cuban and Spanish creations, including paella and the famous 1905 Salad.

• **CUBA LIBRE** 9101 International Drive at Pointe Orlando; ☎ 407-226-1600, cubalibrerestaurant.com; moderate. Upscale, like Columbia above, Cuba Libre specializes in ceviches, tapas, and classic Cuban main courses ranging from $19 to $36. Salsa dancing until 2 a.m. on Fridays and Saturdays.

• **HAVANA'S CAFÉ** 8544 Palm Pkwy., Orlando; ☎ 407-238-5333, havanas cubancuisine.com; moderate. Authentic homemade Cuban cuisine that's much tastier and cheaper than Bongos at Disney Springs.

ETHIOPIAN

• **NILE ETHIOPIAN RESTAURANT** 7048 International Dr., Orlando; ☎ 407-354-0026; nile07.com; inexpensive–moderate. Authentic stews and delicious vegetarian dishes. Bob's favorite Orlando/WDW-area restaurant.

FRENCH

• **URBAIN40** 8000 Via Dellagio Way, Orlando; ☎ 407-872-2640; urbain40 .com; moderate–expensive. Splendid interpretations of classic Lyonnais dishes with locally inspired twists, in a great 1940s New York–inspired room.

* *20 minutes or more from Walt Disney World*

GREEK

• **TAVERNA OPA** 9101 International Dr., Orlando; ☎ 407-351-8660; opa orlando.com; moderate. Try traditional Greek standouts like *pastitsio, boureki, moussaka*, and lamb *kleftiko,* along with kebobs and seafood specialties cooked on a wood fire. Live entertainment many nights. Great for late-night dining.

INDIAN

• **TABLA CUISINE** 5827 Caravan Ct., Orlando; ☎ 407-248-9400; tabla cuisine.com; moderate. Within the Clarion Inn on I-Drive, but don't let that keep you away from one of the better Indian restaurants in the area. The menu also includes Chinese and Thai dishes.

ITALIAN

• **ANTHONY'S COAL-FIRED PIZZA** 8031 Turkey Lake Rd., Orlando; ☎ 407-363-9466; acfp.com; inexpensive. Pizzas, eggplant, pastas, beer, and wine.

• **BICE ORLANDO RISTORANTE** Loews Portofino Bay Hotel, Universal Orlando Resort, 5601 Universal Blvd., Orlando; ☎ 407-503-1415; bice -orlando.com; expensive. Authentic Italian and great wines.

• **PEPERONCINO CUCINA** 7988 Via Dellagio Way, Orlando; ☎ 407-440-2856; peperoncinocucina.com; moderate. Calabrian chef Barbara Alfano runs a tight and authentic kitchen, creating pastas and wood-fired pizza worthy of the name.

JAPANESE/SUSHI

• **AMURA** 7786 W. Sand Lake Rd., Orlando; ☎ 407-370-0007; amura.com; moderate. A favorite sushi bar for locals. The tempura is popular, too.

• **HANAMIZUKI** 8255 International Dr., Orlando; ☎ 407-363-7200; hana mizuki.us; moderate–expensive. Pricey but authentic.

• **NAGOYA SUSHI** 7600 Dr. Phillips Blvd., Suite 66, in the very rear of The Marketplace at Dr. Phillips; ☎ 407-248-8558; nagoyasushi.com; moderate. A small, intimate restaurant with great sushi and an extensive menu.

LATIN

• **SOFRITO LATIN CAFE** 8607 Palm Pkwy., Lake Buena Vista; ☎ 407-778-4205; sofritocafe.com; inexpensive. Located at the corner of FL 535 and Palm Parkway, Sofrito specializes in comfort foods from Cuba, Colombia, Argentina, Chile, Puerto Rico, Peru, Dominican Republic, and Venezuela. The restaurant is modern but somewhat sterile. The best play is to order takeout for pickup or delivery.

MEXICAN

• **CHEVYS FRESH MEX** 12547 FL 535, Lake Buena Vista; ☎ 407-827-1052; chevys.com; inexpensive–moderate. Conveniently located across from the FL 535 entrance to WDW.

• **EL PATRON** 12167 S. Apopka-Vineland Rd., Orlando; ☎ 407-238-5300; elpatronorlando.com; inexpensive. Family-owned restaurant serving freshly prepared Mexican dishes. Full bar.

• **EL TENAMPA MEXICAN RESTAURANT** 4563 W. Irlo Bronson Memorial Hwy., Kissimmee; ☎ 407-397-1981; inexpensive. Family-owned, with an extensive menu of authentic Mexican regional fare in a small, colorful room. Try their steak dish called Arrachea Tenampa.

(Continued on next page)

Where to Eat Outside WDW *(continued)*

MOROCCAN

• **MERGUEZ** 11951 International Dr., Orlando; ☎ 407-778-4343; merguez restaurant.com; inexpensive. Bright, informal setting with adjacent alfresco option. Excellent and representative Moroccan specialties. Awesome *bastillas* and tagines. Couscous, following the Moroccan custom, is served only on Friday. No alcohol sold.

NEW WORLD

• **NORMAN'S** 4012 Central Florida Pkwy., in the Ritz-Carlton Orlando; ☎ 407-393-4333; normans.com; expensive. Norman Van Aken, dean of New World cuisine, offers a menu that changes often—but you'll always find his sinfully delicious conch chowder. World-class wine menu.

PERUVIAN

• **EL INKA GRILL** 7600 Dr. Phillips Blvd., Orlando; ☎ 407-930-2810; elinka grill.com; moderate. El Inka Grill features 13 different ceviche and *tiradito* (thin raw fish marinated in citrus juice) preparations, including three ceviches that are grilled. Traditional Peruvian beef, fish, and chicken entrées run $17–$22 and most come with several sides. Portions are generous.

SEAFOOD

• **BONEFISH GRILL** 7830 W. Sand Lake Rd., Orlando; ☎ 407-355-7707; bonefishgrill.com; moderate. Casual setting along busy Restaurant Row on Sand Lake Road. Choose your fish, and then choose a favorite sauce to accompany. Also steaks and chicken.

• **CELEBRATION TOWN TAVERN** 721 Front St., Celebration; ☎ 407-566-2526; thecelebrationtowntavern.com; moderate. Popular hangout for locals, with New England–style seafood. Clam chowder is a big hit.

• **OCEAN PRIME** 7339 W. Sand Lake Rd., Orlando; ☎ 407-781-4880; ocean-prime.com; expensive. Elegant supper-club ambience; classic fare focusing on fresh seafood and perfectly cooked meats. Outdoor dining and piano bar.

STEAK/PRIME RIB

• **BULL & BEAR** 14200 Bonnet Creek Resort Ln., in the Waldorf Astoria Orlando; ☎ 407-597-5500; waldorfastoriaorlando.com/dining/bull-and-bear; expensive. Classic steakhouse with a clubby ambience.

• **THE CAPITAL GRILLE** Pointe Orlando, 9101 International Dr., Orlando; ☎ 407-370-4392; thecapitalgrille.com; expensive. Dry-aged steaks, good wine list, and classic decor.

• **TEXAS DE BRAZIL** 5259 International Dr., Orlando; ☎ 407-355-0355; texasdebrazil.com; expensive. All you can eat in a Brazilian-style *churrascaria*. Filet mignon, sausage, pork, chicken, lamb, and more. Ages 2 and under are free, ages 3–5 are $5, and ages 6–12 are half-price. Salad bar with 40-plus options.

• **VITO'S CHOP HOUSE** 8633 International Dr., Orlando; ☎ 407-354-2467; vitoschophouse.com; moderate. Upscale meatery with a taste of Tuscany.

THAI

• **THAI SILK** 6803 S. Kirkman Rd. at International Drive, Orlando; ☎ 407-226-8997; thaisilkorlando.com; moderate. Housed in an unassuming strip-mall location and acclaimed by Orlando dining critics for its authentic Thai dishes. Delicious vegetarian options; impressive wine list.

• **THAI THANI** 11025 International Dr., Orlando; ☎ 407-239-9733; 600 Market St., Suite 110, Celebration; ☎ 407-566-9444; thaithani.net; moderate. Specializes in Thai duck preparations. Some Chinese stir-fry.

Continued from page 309

memorabilia, including a 1959 pink Cadillac revolving over the bar. It's the biggest such collection on display anywhere in the Hard Rock chain.

HOT DOG HALL OF FAME ☎ 407-363-8000; tinyurl.com/hotdoghof. The menu is inspired by the food from baseball stadiums around the US—Kayem dogs from Boston, Sabretts from New York—served on bleacher seating with broadcasts of live and classic baseball games.

JIMMY BUFFETT'S MARGARITAVILLE ☎ 407-224-2155; margaritaville orlando.com. A boisterous tribute to the head Parrothead. The focal point is a volcano that spews margarita mix instead of lava. The food is Floridian–Caribbean, so expect lots of seafood, jerk seasoning, and Key lime pie. If you're not a Buffett fan, it isn't worth a special trip.

NBC SPORTS GRILL & BREW ☎ 407-224-3663; tinyurl.com/nbcgrill. Features 90 big-screen HDTVs and more than 100 beers, including specialty drafts not available elsewhere. Besides the televisions, the decor is intended to evoke a luxury skybox but is more like "sports bar industrial" with dark concrete floors and exposed-ductwork ceilings painted black. *Bonus:* Some dining tables are playable games (such as Foosball) with glass tops for the food. As for the food, it's decent but not memorable. If you must eat a meal, try the crab Scotch eggs, fish sandwich, or grilled steak. Otherwise, stick with the pretzels and beer.

PAT O'BRIEN'S ☎ 407-224-2102; patobriens.com/patobriens/orlando. Dueling pianos in the Lounge, a full menu in the Courtyard restaurant, those rum-filled Hurricanes throughout. Behind a facade that replicates the New Orleans original, "Pat's" offers NOLA classics (try the jambalaya) and massive sandwiches. The brick courtyard is a slice of the Big Easy, but noise levels are high during outdoor concerts nearby.

RED OVEN PIZZA BAKERY ☎ 407-224-4233; tinyurl.com/redoven pizza. Artisan pizza baked in a 900°F oven. Choose from five white and five red Neapolitan-style pies, made with San Marzano tomatoes, organic extra-virgin olive oil, buffalo mozzarella, fine-ground "00" flour, and filtered water. Pizzas run $9–$14 and serve two people.

TOOTHSOME CHOCOLATE EMPORIUM ☎ 407-224-3663; tinyurl.com /toothsomekitchen. Candies, cakes, and ice-cream concoctions, plus a savory menu of steaks, salads, and sandwiches, served inside a whimsical Wonka-esque steampunk confectionery factory. Very highly rated by *Unofficial Guide* readers, perhaps more for the theme than the food.

VIVO ITALIAN KITCHEN ☎ 407-224-2318; tinyurl.com/vivocitywalk. CityWalk's third-highest-rated restaurant in our latest reader survey. Surprisingly good house-made pasta (squid ink seafood is outstanding), interesting cocktails, and a 2-pound cannoli for dessert. Sit by the open kitchen and watch the show.

A food court on CityWalk's upper level offers serviceable quick bites: **Bread Box Handcrafted Sandwiches, BK Whopper Bar, Moe's Southwest Grill, Panda Express, Menchie's Frozen Yogurt,** and **Fusion Bistro Sushi & Sake Bar.**

STRONG WATER TAVERN ☎ 888-430-4999; loewshotels.com/sapphire -falls-resort. It's at Universal's Sapphire Falls Resort, not CityWalk. But if you're a fan of rum and tasty tapas, it might be worth a trip. The menu features dozens of rums, mostly from the Caribbean, in individual glasses or regional flights. The Caribbean-influenced, small-plates menu leans toward seafood but also includes pork, goat, and lamb at a quality better than you'd expect at a mid-priced hotel. We're told all dishes are prepared on request from fresh ingredients.

BUFFETS AND MEAL DEALS OUTSIDE WALT DISNEY WORLD

BUFFETS, RESTAURANT SPECIALS, and discount dining abound in the area surrounding Walt Disney World, especially on US 192 (a.k.a. Irlo Bronson Memorial Highway) and along International Drive. Local visitor magazines, distributed free at non-Disney hotels and other places, are packed with advertisements and coupons for seafood feasts, Chinese buffets, Indian buffets, breakfast buffets, and a host of other specials. For a family trying to economize, some of the come-ons are mighty sweet. But are the places good? Is the food fresh, tasty, and appealing? Are the restaurants clean and inviting? Armed with little more than a roll of Tums, the *Unofficial* research team tried all the eateries that advertise heavily in the tourist magazines. Here's what we discovered.

CHINESE SUPER BUFFETS If you've ever tried preparing Chinese food, especially a stir-fry, you know that split-second timing is required to avoid overcooking. It's no surprise, then, that Chinese dishes languishing on a buffet lose their freshness, texture, and flavor in a hurry.

For the past few editions of this guide, we found several Chinese buffets that we felt comfortable recommending; unfortunately, we would return the next year only to discover that their quality had slipped precipitously. We then searched for new buffets to replace the ones we deleted, and we can tell you that wasn't much fun. At the end of the day, **Ichiban Buffet** (5269 W. Irlo Bronson Memorial Highway, ☎ 407-396-6668; 5529 International Drive, ☎ 407-930-8889; ichibanbuffet .com), **Kim Wu** (4904 S. Kirkman Road; ☎ 407-293-0752), and **Hokkaido Chinese and Japanese Buffet** (12173 S. Apopka–Vineland Road; 407-778-5188; hokkaidobuffetorlando.com) are the only ones we've elected to list. Ichiban is our pick, with Japanese hibachi and sushi, plus traditional and American-style Chinese dishes, including steamed snow-crab legs (for an extra charge), raw oysters, and grilled head-on shrimp. The Irlo Bronson location *was* our favorite, but its quality has declined of late; its new I-Drive location has picked up the banner, for now. Kim Wu, another local favorite, is convenient to Universal Orlando, but the buffet is available only during lunch Monday–Friday.

INDIAN BUFFETS Indian food works better on a buffet than Chinese food; in fact, it actually improves as the flavors marry. In the Disney World area, most Indian restaurants offer a buffet at lunch only—not too convenient if you're spending your day at the theme parks. If you're out shopping or taking a day off, these Indian buffets are worth trying: **Aashirwad Indian Cuisine** (5748 International Drive, at the corner of International Drive and Kirkman Road; ☎ 407-370-9830; aashirwad restaurant.com); **Ahmed Halal Indian Restaurant** (11301 S. Orange Blossom Trail, Suite 104; ☎ 407-856-5970; ahmedindianrestaurant.com);

and **Woodlands Pure Vegetarian Indian Cuisine** (6040 S. Orange Blossom Trail; 407-854-3330; woodlandsusa.com).

CHURRASCARIAS A number of these South American–style meat emporiums have sprung up along International Drive. Our picks are **Café Mineiro** (6432 International Drive; ☎ 407-248-2932; cafemineirosteak house.com), a Brazilian steakhouse north of Sand Lake Road, and **BoiBrazil Churrascaria** (5668 International Drive; ☎ 407-354-0260; boibrazil.com). Both offer good value. More expensive are the Argentinean *churrasco* specialties at **The Knife** (12501 FL 535; ☎ 321-395-4892; theknife restaurant.com); be sure to try the sweetbreads, an Argentine specialty rarely found in the United States. If you prefer chain restaurants, the pricey **Texas de Brazil** and **Fogo de Chão** also have locations in Orlando.

SEAFOOD AND LOBSTER BUFFETS These affairs don't exactly fall under the category of inexpensive dining. The main draw (no pun intended) is all the lobster you can eat. The problem is that, after a few minutes on the buffet line, lobsters make better tennis balls than dinner, so try to grab your lobster immediately after a fresh batch has been brought out.

Two lobster buffets are on International Drive, and another is on US 192. Although all three do a reasonable job, we prefer **Boston Lobster Feast** (6071 W. Irlo Bronson Memorial Highway; ☎ 407-396-2606; 8731 International Drive, five blocks north of the Convention Center; ☎ 407-248-8606; bostonlobsterfeast.com). The International Drive location is cavernous and noisy, which is why we prefer the Irlo Bronson location, where you can actually have a conversation over dinner. The I-Drive location has ample parking, while the Irlo Bronson restaurant does not. At about $45 for early birds (before 6 p.m.) and $49 after 6 p.m., dining is expensive at both locations.

SALAD BUFFETS The most popular of these in the Walt Disney World area is **Sweet Tomatoes** (6877 S. Kirkman Road; ☎ 407-363-1616; 12561 S. Apopka–Vineland Road; ☎ 407-938-9461; 3236 Rolling Oaks Blvd., off US 192 near the FL 429 western entrance to Disney World; ☎ 407-966-4664; souplantation.com). During lunch and dinner, you can expect a line out the door, but fortunately it moves fast. The buffet features prepared salads and an extensive array of ingredients for building your own. In addition to salads, Sweet Tomatoes offers a variety of soups, a modest pasta bar, a baked-potato bar, an assortment of fresh fruit, and ice-cream sundaes. Dinner runs $12.39 for adults, $6.39 for children ages 7–12, and $4.39 for children ages 3–6. Lunch is $9.99 for adults on weekdays, $10.39 for adults on weekends, and the same prices as dinner for children. Check hotel lobbies for discount coupons.

BREAKFAST AND ENTRÉE BUFFETS Most chain steakhouses in the area, including **Ponderosa, Sizzler,** and **Golden Corral,** offer entrée buffets. Among them, they have 15 locations in the Walt Disney World area. All serve breakfast, lunch, and dinner. At lunch and dinner, you get the buffet when you buy an entrée, usually a steak; breakfast is a straightforward buffet (that is, you don't have to buy an entrée). As for the food, it's chain-restaurant quality but decent all the same. Prices are a bargain, and you can get in and out at lightning speed—important at breakfast when you're trying to get to the parks early. Some locations offer lunch and dinner buffets at a set price without your having to buy an entrée.

unofficial **TIP**
Most chain-restaurant breakfast buffets have a number of locations in the Disney World area, but their operating hours aren't always the same, so call before you go.

Though you can argue about which chain serves the best steak, we think **Golden Corral** wins the buffet contest hands-down, with at least twice as many offerings as its three competitors. While the buffets at Golden Corral and Ponderosa are pretty consistent from location to location, the buffet at the Sizzler (7602 W. Irlo Bronson Memorial Highway; ☎ 407-390-9615) varies a good deal from Sizzler locations out West. In addition to the steakhouses, WDW-area **Shoney's** also offer breakfast, lunch, and dinner buffets.

Local freebie visitor magazines are full of discount coupons for all of the previous restaurants.

A New Hampshire reader notes:

> You mention quite a few buffets for off-site dining, but it would have been nice to know their normal morning business hours. Some buffets (like Ponderosa) didn't open until 8 a.m. for breakfast. This is way too late if you're trying to get to the park at opening time.

DISNEY BUFFETS VS. OFF-SITE BUFFETS Most off-site buffets are long on selection but don't compare favorably to Disney buffets in terms of quality; likewise, the setting and ambience of Disney buffets is generally superior. If you're trying to save money, however, non-Disney buffets offer excellent value. Though some dishes may be below par, you should find enough that's palatable to put together a more-than-acceptable meal. Just start with small samples to sort out the winners and losers, then go back for larger portions of your favorites.

MEAL DEALS Discount coupons are available for a wide range of restaurants. A meat eater's delight is the Feast for Four at **Sonny's Real Pit Bar-B-Q.** For $44 per family of four, you get sliced pork and beef, plus chicken, ribs, your choice of three sides (choose from beans, slaw, and fries, among others), garlic bread or corn bread, and soft drinks or tea, all served family-style. The closest Sonny's location to Walt Disney World and Universal is at 7423 S. Orange Blossom Trail in Orlando (☎ 407-859-7197; sonnysbbq.com). No coupons are available (or needed) for Sonny's, but they're available for other "meateries."

COUPONS Find discounts and two-for-one coupons for many of the restaurants mentioned in freebie visitor guides available at most hotels outside Walt Disney World. The **Visit Orlando Official Visitors Center** (8723 International Drive; ☎ 407-363-5872; visitorlando.com; open daily, 8:30 a.m.–6:30 p.m., except Christmas) offers a treasure trove of coupons and free visitor magazines. In Kissimmee, visit the **Osceola County Welcome Center and History Museum** (4155 W. Vine St.; ☎ 407-396-8644; osceolahistory.org). Online, check out couponsalacarte.com and orlandocoupons.com for printable coupons.

THE GREAT ORLANDO PIZZA SCAM Plenty of reputable local pizza joints deliver to hotels in and around the theme parks; many Disney and Universal resorts offer pizza delivery as well. But for a few years now, con artists have been distributing flyers advertising delivery to hotel guests—they ask for your credit card number over the phone, but the pizza never arrives. Disregard any such flyers you find.

DINING *in* WALT DISNEY WORLD

THIS SECTION AIMS TO HELP YOU find good food without going broke or tripping over a culinary land mine. More than 140 restaurants operate within the World, including around 110 full-service establishments, more than 30 of which are inside the theme parks. Disney restaurants offer exceptional variety, serving everything from Moroccan lamb to Texas barbecue. Most restaurants are expensive, and many serve less-than-distinguished fare, but there are good choices in every area of Walt Disney World.

GETTING IT RIGHT

ALTHOUGH WE WORK HARD to be fair, objective, and accurate, many readers, like this woman from Charleston, West Virginia, think we're too critical of Walt Disney World restaurants:

> *Get a life! It's crazy and unrealistic to be so snobbish about restaurants at a theme park. Considering the number of people Disney feeds each day, I think they do a darn good job. Also, you act so surprised that the food is expensive. Have you ever eaten at an airport? HELLO IN THERE? . . . Surprise, you're a captive! It's a theme park!*

And a mom from Erie, Pennsylvania, strikes a practical note:

> *Most of the food at Walt Disney World is OK. It's true that you pay more than you should, but it's more convenient to eat in Walt Disney World than to run around trying to find cheaper restaurants somewhere else.*

*un*official **TIP**
Our research team has eaten at every restaurant, kiosk, bar, cart, and food stand in Walt Disney World many times.

As you may infer from these comments, researching and reviewing restaurants is no straightforward endeavor—to the contrary, it's fraught with peril. We've read dining reviews by writers who turn up their noses at everything but four-star French restaurants. We've read reviews devoid of criticism, written by "experts" unwilling to risk offending the source of their free meal. Finally, we've seen reviews that are wholly based on surveys submitted by diners whose credentials for evaluating fine dining are mysterious at best and questionable at least.

How, then, do we go about presenting the best possible dining coverage? At the *Unofficial Guide,* we begin with highly qualified culinary experts and then balance their opinions with those of our readers— which, by the way, don't always coincide. (Likewise, the coauthors' assessments don't always agree with those of our dining experts.)

In the spirit of democracy, we encourage you to fill out our online reader survey at touringplans.com/walt-disney-world/survey. If you'd like to share your dining experience in greater depth, we also invite you to write us at the address on page 14 or send us an e-mail at unofficial guides@menasharidge.com.

WHAT'S NEW?

THE THREE THINGS YOU NEED TO KNOW about Disney dining are location, location, and location. In this case, the locations are the **Animal Kingdom Lodge,** the **Grand Floridian Resort,** and **Disney Springs** (formerly Downtown Disney).

Two of Animal Kingdom Lodge's three sit-down restaurants placed in the top five in our most recent reader survey of Disney's 110-plus sit-down restaurants. **Jiko—The Cooking Place** (page 382), the resort's most upscale restaurant, came in first overall, for the second year in a row. **Sanaa** (#3, page 396) serves more-casual fare inspired by Indian cuisine. We think Indian food is a bit underrepresented at Disney World, so Sanaa is a good place to get your fix. The third restaurant, **Boma** (page 367), a family-friendly buffet with gentle introductions to the spices of African cooking, came in sixth. If dining is an integral part of your vacation experience and Animal Kingdom Lodge is within your budget, this is our top hotel recommendation.

Close behind the restaurants at Animal Kingdom Lodge are those at Disney's Grand Floridian Resort, starting with **Victoria & Albert's** (#8, page 407). V&A's is Disney's flagship restaurant, with impeccable, approachable service and the most inventive food on the property. Also making the top 10 is the **Grand Floridian Cafe** (#10, page 379), serving high-quality meals in a relaxed early-20th-century-Florida setting. Another advantage of staying at the Grand Floridian is monorail access to the **California Grill** (#9, page 369), at Disney's Contemporary Resort, and the Polynesian Resort's **Kona Cafe** (#12, page 384).

Perhaps the most surprising development in Disney dining over the past year has been how highly our readers have judged the new restaurants at Disney Springs, where there have been far more hits than misses. Tops among the newcomers are **Chef Art Smith's Homecomin'** (page 371), featuring fresh, Florida-inspired seafood and the best fried chicken on the property, and **The Boathouse** (page 366), which specializes in seafood but whose steaks are better (and cheaper) than many dedicated steak places nearby. If you're looking for a lighter meal, don't let the long lines at **Blaze Pizza** (page 350) deter you—the pizzas get cooked in less than 3 minutes and eaten almost as fast; you'll find a seat in no time. Tourists from the Great White North will rejoice in the high ratings of **The Daily Poutine** (page 350), serving Canada's national dish of fried potatoes covered in savory sauces. It's our recommendation—as professionals—that you follow up these meals with a stop at **Amorette's Patisserie** (page 349), which creates small, beautiful desserts and pastries whose style does not compromise on taste.

Scheduled to open at Disney Springs in late 2017 are an Orlando outpost of the L.A.-based **Edison,** an industrially themed restaurant and live-music venue, and **Wine Bar George,** the brainchild of wine guru/Master Sommelier George Miliotes. **Portobello** is reopening in summer 2017 under a new name—but we didn't know what it was at press time. Opening in 2018 are **Wolfgang Puck Bar & Grill** and **Jaleo,** from celebrity chef José Andrés, replacing Wolfgang Puck Grand Cafe.

A final note for this edition: We're justifiably critical when Disney markets a good restaurant as "outstanding," "world class," or some other hyped-up adjective. But we'd be remiss if we didn't point out

Advance Reservations: The Official Line

YOU CAN RESERVE THE FOLLOWING up to 180 days in advance:

AFTERNOON TEA AND CHILDREN'S PROGRAMS at the Grand Floridian Resort & Spa

ALL DISNEY TABLE-SERVICE RESTAURANTS and character-dining venues

FANTASMIC! DINING PACKAGE at Disney's Hollywood Studios

HOOP-DEE-DOO MUSICAL REVUE at Fort Wilderness Resort & Campground

MICKEY'S BACKYARD BBQ at Fort Wilderness Resort & Campground

SPIRIT OF ALOHA DINNER SHOW at the Polynesian Village Resort

Guests staying at Walt Disney World resorts—these do not include the Swan, the Dolphin, Shades of Green, or the hotels of the Disney Springs Resort Area—can book dining 180 days before they arrive and can make dining reservations for the entire length of their stay (up to 10 days).

how truly friendly and accommodating Disney's restaurant staff is. Here's an example to illustrate:

In early 2017, we re-reviewed Victoria & Albert's, the high-end gourmet restaurant at the Grand Floridian. Along with the meal, we ordered the wine parings with each dish—vino that's hand-selected by the restaurant's sommelier to complement the course being served.

You've probably heard news stories of blind taste tests showing that even experts often can't tell the difference between $10 and $100 bottles of wine. About halfway through the meal, we wondered whether all the "this Chardonnay's delicate sweetness pairs well with the food's acidity" talk was actually provable. So we asked the sommelier to bring a small glass of wine that, in his expert opinion, absolutely, positively did not go with the veal were eating.

There was consternation. The manager arrived and whispered, "I understand you have a request, sir?" We explained. A wine menu the size of a Gutenberg Bible was consulted. A glass of white wine was procured, and with it a description of exactly what would happen when we drank it. One sip stripped the taste from our mouths. Now, Victoria & Albert's does not stock bad wines. This was a simple, inexpensive demonstration that (1) the kind of wine paired with your food matters and (2) the V&A staff are experts such pairings.

That request might have been viewed as boorish in other restaurants, but Disney was happy to do it. It demonstrates how committed the staff is to making sure you're satisfied with your meal.

DISNEY DINING 101

DISNEY DINING PLANS

DISNEY OFFERS SEVERAL DINING PLANS. If you choose to sign up for a plan, you must do so when you book your Disney resort room or package vacation; for this reason, we explore the topic in depth in Part Three, Accommodations (see page 242).

WAITER, THESE PRICES ARE GIVING ME HEARTBURN!

INCREASES IN DISNEY'S TICKET COSTS are always sure to grab headlines, but most people don't notice that Disney's restaurant prices rise

THE REALITY OF GETTING LAST-MINUTE DINING RESERVATIONS

IF YOUR VACATION is more than 180 days out and you want to dine at a popular venue such as Be Our Guest Restaurant or Cinderella's Royal Table, following our advice starting on the next page will get you the table you want more than 80% of the time.

The longer you wait, the more effort you'll have to put in to find a reservation. For example, if you're trying for breakfast at Cinderella's Royal Table within the next seven days, your chance of finding any table the first time you check is less than 3%, based on our tests. But if you have the time and patience to visit Disney's website around 30 times over the next week—nope, not a typo—you have a 50/50 shot at finding a last-minute cancellation.

Besides Cinderella's Royal Table and Be Our Guest, the list below shows the restaurants whose capacity and demand make finding a last-minute reservation very difficult. If you're planning a trip within the next 30 days, see page 322 for alternatives.

- **Victoria & Albert's (Grand Floridian)** One of Disney World's best restaurants, with excellent food, exquisite service, and few tables.
- **Chef Art Smith's Homecomin' (Disney Springs)** Exceptional fried chicken, desserts you'd slap your siblings to get more of, *and* the best cocktails in Disney Springs.
- **Le Cellier Steakhouse (Canada/Epcot, dinner)** Consistently rated as one of Disney World's best steak places. Dinner is popular because a clockwise tour of World Showcase puts you near Canada in the evening.
- **Via Napoli (Italy/Epcot)** The best pizza in Walt Disney World is probably enough reason to go, but reader comments suggest that the waitstaff are easy on the eyes as well.
- **Rose & Crown Dining Room (UK/Epcot, dinner)** Serves good, familiar food and is a prime location for watching *IllumiNations*.
- **The Plaza Restaurant (Magic Kingdom)** The Plaza serves decent sandwiches in blessed air-conditioned comfort, but its small size makes it a difficult reservation to snag.

about as fast. For example, while the cost of a one-day theme park ticket has increased about 57% since 2010, the average entrée price at Le Cellier has gone from around $30 to just under $47—an increase of 55%. For reference, the average meal cost in a U.S. restaurant went up 4% during the same time, according to Zagat. Plus, Disney sometimes levies a "dining surcharge" during the summer and other busy times of year. Factoring in the surcharge, an adult breakfast at The Crystal Palace has increased almost 65% during the same time.

This comment from a New Orleans mom spells it out:

Disney keeps pushing prices up and up. For us, the sky is NOT the limit. We won't be back.

BEHIND THE SCENES AT ADVANCE RESERVATIONS

ALTHOUGH THEY'RE CALLED Advance Reservations, most reservations at Disney World don't guarantee you a table at a specific time, as they would at your typical hometown restaurant. Disney restaurants operate on what they call a template system. Instead of scheduling Advance Reservations for actual tables, reservations fill time slots. The number of slots available is based on the average length of time that guests occupy a table at a particular restaurant, adjusted for seasonality.

Here's a rough example of how it works: Let's say Coral Reef Restaurant at Epcot has 40 tables for four and 8 tables for six, and that the average length of time for a family to be seated, order, eat, pay, and depart is 40 minutes. Add 5 minutes to bus the table and set it up for the next guests, and the table is turning every 45 minutes. The restaurant provides Disney's central dining-reservations system (**CDRS**) with a computer template of its capacity, along with the average time the table is occupied. Both Disney World's dining website (disneyworld.disney.go.com/dining) and its dining hotline (☎ 407-WDW-DINE, 939-3463) use CDRS to process your reservation requests.

Thus, when you use the website to make Advance Reservations for four people at 6:15 p.m., CDRS removes one table for four from its overall capacity for 45 minutes. The template on the system indicates that the table will be unavailable for reassignment until 7 p.m. (45 minutes later). So it goes for all tables in the restaurant, each being subtracted from overall capacity for 45 minutes, then listed as available again, then assigned to other guests and subtracted again, and so on throughout the meal period. CDRS tries to fill every time slot for every seat in the restaurant or come as close to filling every slot as possible. No seats—repeat, none—are reserved for walk-ins.

Templates are filled differently depending on the season and restaurant. All Disney restaurants now charge a no-show fee; this has reduced the no-show rate to virtually zero, and these restaurants are booked every day according to their actual capacity.

A couple of tips: Only one person needs to dine at the restaurant for Disney to consider your reservation fulfilled, even if you have a reservation for more people. Also, while Disney says it requires 24 hours' notice, you can cancel up until midnight of the day before your meal. The upside to the no-show fee is that it's easier to book most restaurants closer to the date of your visit, as the fee discourages tentative plans.

With Advance Reservations, your wait will usually be less than 20 minutes during peak hours, and often less than 10 minutes. If you're a walk-in, especially during busier seasons, expect to either wait 40–75 minutes or be told that no tables are available.

GETTING ADVANCE RESERVATIONS AT POPULAR RESTAURANTS

BREAKFAST AND DINNER AT THE MAGIC KINGDOM'S **Be Our Guest Restaurant**, in Fantasyland, and the 8 a.m. breakfast slots at **Cinderella's Royal Table,** in Cinderella Castle, are two of the hardest-to-get reservations in Walt Disney World. Why? Be Our Guest has arguably the best food in the park, awesome special effects, and good word of mouth; Cinderella's Royal Table is Disney's tiniest character-meal restaurant, accommodating only about 130 diners at a time. You'll have to put in some effort to secure an Advance Reservation at these places.

Good Restaurants with Last-Minute Availability

IF YOU CAN'T GET A RESERVATION FOR	TRY
Cinderella's Royal Table (86% thumbs-up rating) or Be Our Guest Restaurant (90%), both in the Magic Kingdom	The Crystal Palace (Magic Kingdom, 91% thumbs-up), Akershus Royal Banquet Hall (Norway/Epcot, 88%), or Tusker House (Animal Kingdom, 93%) for theme park character meals. In the Magic Kingdom, the Jungle Navigation Co. Ltd. Skipper Canteen (81%) makes a great last-minute option, especially if you're hungry at off-peak hours.
Victoria & Albert's (Grand Floridian, 94%)	Our first choice for an adult night out would be Jiko—The Cooking Place (Animal Kingdom Lodge, 97% thumbs-up), with excellent food and an extensive wine list. If you're staying at a Magic Kingdom resort or you're in the mood for seafood, try Narcoossee's (Grand Floridian, 88%). The Contemporary Resort's California Grill (93%) is highly rated but very loud at dinner.
Le Cellier Steakhouse (Canada/Epcot, 88%)	If you're in the mood for steak near Epcot, try the Yachtsman Steakhouse (Yacht Club, 90%). For good steaks elsewhere, The Boathouse (Disney Springs, 90%) gets top marks.
Via Napoli (Italy/Epcot, 91%)	The nearby Tutto Italia Ristorante (Italy/Epcot 88%) and Tutto Gusto Wine Cellar (Italy/Epcot, 93%, no reservations) serve Italian appetizers and wine. A short walk from Epcot, the BoardWalk Inn's Trattoria al Forno (87%) serves Italian comfort food.
Rose & Crown Dining Room (UK/Epcot, 91%)	A tough call. Spice Road Table (Morocco/Epcot, 87%) probably has more empty tables and a better view of *IllumiNations*, but the food and service are below average. La Hacienda de San Angel (Mexico/Epcot, 87%) has better food, but you may not have a great view of the fireworks.
The Plaza Restaurant (Magic Kingdom, 85%)	Jungle Navigation Co. Ltd. Skipper Canteen (see above).
T-REX (Disney Springs, 81%)	The Rainforest Cafe (Disney Springs, 76%) is an option if you're looking to entertain small children. But if you're just looking for a good meal, almost anything at Disney Springs is a better choice.

The easiest and fastest way to get a reservation is to go to disney world.disney.go.com/dining starting at 6 a.m. Eastern time, a full hour before phone reservations open. To familiarize yourself with how the site works, try it out a couple of days before you actually make reservations. You'll also save time by setting up an account online before your 180-day booking window, making sure to enter any credit card information needed to guarantee your reservations.

If you live in California and have to get up at 3 a.m. Pacific time to make a reservation, Disney couldn't care less: There's no limit to the number of hoops they can make patrons jump through if demand exceeds supply.

Disney's website is usually within a few seconds of the official time as determined by the U.S. Naval Observatory or the National Institute of Standards and Technology, accessible online at time.gov. Using this site, synchronize your computer to the second the night before your 180-day window opens.

Early on the morning you want to make reservations, take a few moments to type the date of your visit into a word processor in MM/DD/YYYY format (for example, 11/16/2017 for November 16, 2017). Select the date and copy it to your computer's clipboard by

unofficial **TIP**

If you wonder why Disney makes everything so insanely complicated, so do we. We also wonder why people put up with it. Some excellent non-Disney restaurants are listed on starting on page 308.

pressing the **Ctrl** and **C** keys simultaneously (**Command-C** on Mac) or right-clicking your mouse and selecting "Copy"). This will save you from having to type in the date when the site comes online.

Next, start trying Disney's website about 3 minutes before 6 a.m. You'll see a text box where you can specify the date of your visit. Click the text box and press **Ctrl-A,** then **Ctrl-V** (substitute **Command** for **Ctrl** on Mac) to paste the date; then press the tab key on your keyboard. (You can also click on the blue calendar icon to flip through a month-by-month calendar, or you can select the entire date in the text box, right-click your mouse, and select "Paste," but these are slower.) You'll also see a place to specify the time of your meal and your party size; you can fill these in ahead of time, too.

Above the "Party Size" widget is a text box with the words "Search Within Dining." Start typing your restaurant name in that text box. As soon as you start typing, the website will start guessing which restaurant you want and offer a list of suggestions. It's faster if you just type a few letters—*be our* or *cin* is enough for the site to know you mean Be Our Guest or Cinderella's Royal Table, respectively. Click on the desired restaurant in the list of suggestions. Finally, click "Find a Table" or hit the Enter key on your keyboard—both submit your request to CDRS.

If your date isn't yet available, a message will appear saying, "There is a problem searching for reservations at this time" or something similar. If this happens, refresh the browser page and start over. If you don't see an error message, however, the results returned will tell you whether your restaurant has a table available.

Note that while you're typing, other guests are trying to make Advance Reservations too, so you want the transaction to go down as quickly as possible. Flexibility on your part counts—it's much harder to get seating for a large group, so give some thought to breaking your group into numbers that can be accommodated at tables for four. Also make sure that you have your credit card out where you can read it.

Advance Reservations for Cinderella's Royal Table character meals, the *Fantasmic!* Dining Package, the *Hoop-Dee-Doo Musical Revue,* the *Spirit of Aloha Dinner Show,* and *Mickey's Backyard BBQ* require complete prepayment with a credit card at the time of the booking. The name on the booking can't be changed after the Advance Reservation is made. Reservations may be canceled, with the deposit refunded in full, by calling ☎ 407-wDW-DINE at least 24 hours (Cinderella's) or 48 hours (*Fantasmic!* and the dinner shows) before seating time.

If you don't have access to a computer at 6 a.m. on the morning you need to make reservations, be ready to call ☎ 407-wDW-DINE at 7 a.m. Eastern time and follow the prompts to speak to a live person. You may still get placed on hold if call volume is higher than usual, and you'll be an hour behind the early birds with computers. Still, you'll be well ahead of those who couldn't make it up before sunrise.

Also, if you're on the Disney Dining Plan and you want to book the *Fantasmic!* package, Cinderella's Royal Table, or one of the dinner shows, you may be better off reserving by phone. The online system may not recognize your table-service credits, but you can book and pay with a credit card and then call ☎ 407-wDW-DINE after 7 a.m. and have them credit the charge for the meal back to your card (a potential hassle if you get an uncooperative cast member). When you get to Walt Disney World, you'll use credits from your dining plan to "pay" for the meal. (Sometimes the online system has glitches and shows no availability; in this case, call after 7 a.m. to confirm if the online system is correct.)

NEVER, NEVER, NEVER, NEVER GIVE UP Not getting what you want the first time you try doesn't mean the end of the story. A mom from Cincinnati advises persistence in securing Advance Reservations:

> I was crushed when I called and tried to reserve Chef Mickey's and couldn't. I decided not to give up and would go online once or twice a day to check reservations for Chef Mickey's and the other restaurants I wanted. It took me about a week, but sooner or later I ended up booking every single reservation I wanted except 'Ohana.

LAST-MINUTE ADVANCE RESERVATIONS Because Advance Reservations require a credit card, and because a fee is charged for failing to cancel in time, you can often score a last-minute reservation. This is attributable to reservation-holders who are tired or have last-minute conflicts calling in at the last moment to avoid paying the $10-per-head penalty. As long as the reservation-holder calls to cancel before midnight the day before, he or she won't be charged. So your best shot at picking up a canceled reservation is to repeatedly call or visit disneyworld.disney .go.com/dining as often as possible between 10 and 11 p.m.

***STILL* CAN'T GET AN ADVANCE RESERVATION?** Go to the restaurant on the day you wish to dine, and try for a table as a walk-in (most full-service restaurants take walk-ins between 2:30 and 4:30 p.m.). This is a long shot, though you may be able to swing it during the least busy times of year or on cold or rainy days during busier seasons. If you try to walk in then, your chances are best during the last hour of serving.

Disney full-service restaurants in the theme parks can be very hard-nosed about walk-ins, as a Fayetteville, Georgia, reader relates:

> We walked up to the Hollywood & Vine check-in podium at DHS to try for walk-in seating because it was an off time—3:30 p.m.—and we could see that the restaurant was virtually empty. But we were turned away for lack of availability. So we walked to Guest Services, obtained a reservation, walked back to the podium, and were immediately checked in. NOT guest-friendly, and not a good Disney experience. I do wish Disney sit-down restaurants would allow at least some walk-ins at slow times. Personally I don't want to book every meal 60 days in advance.

Landing an Advance Reservation for Cinderella's Royal Table at dinner is somewhat easier than at breakfast or lunch, but the price is a whopping $79 for adults and $47 for children ages 3–9. If you're unable to lock up a table for breakfast or lunch, a dinner reservation will at least get your kids inside the castle.

NO-SHOW FEES As noted earlier, Disney charges a per-person penalty if you fail to show up for an Advance Reservation the day of the meal. A $10 no-show fee is enforced at all Disney sit-down restaurants; at **Victoria**

& Albert's, it's $25 for the main dining room, $50 for Queen Victoria's Room and the Chef's Table (the latter two also require 48 hours' notice to cancel an Advance Reservation).

DRESS

DRESS IS INFORMAL at most theme park restaurants, but Disney has a "business casual" dress code for some of its resort restaurants: khakis, dress slacks, jeans, or dress shorts with a collared shirt for men, and capris, skirts, dresses, jeans, and dress shorts for women. Restaurants with this dress code are **Jiko—The Cooking Place** at Animal Kingdom Lodge & Villas, **Flying Fish** at the BoardWalk, **California Grill** at the Contemporary Resort, **Monsieur Paul** at Epcot's France Pavilion, **Cítricos** and **Narcoossee's** at the Grand Floridian Resort & Spa, **Artist Point** at Wilderness Lodge & Boulder Ridge Villas, **Yachtsman Steakhouse** at the Yacht Club Resort, **Todd English's bluezoo** and **Shula's Steak House** at the Dolphin Hotel, and **Il Mulino New York Trattoria** at the Swan Hotel. **Victoria & Albert's** at the Grand Floridian is the only Disney restaurant that requires men to wear a jacket to dinner.

NOISE AT RESTAURANTS

RESTAURANTS ARE NOISY in and out of the World. A Palmyra, Pennsylvania, reader using the Disney Dining Plan shared this:

We ate four times at WDW Signature Dining restaurants. The food was always good, and the check, with wine and tip, was always at least $150. However, the noise, especially at Le Cellier and Il Mulino, was overwhelming. WDW seems to have really skimped on the acoustics, even in Cítricos and the California Grill. We couldn't even eat in Bongos due to the noise, so we ate outside and had three competing bands to deal with.

STOP THE ASSEMBLY LINE!

HEAVEN FORBID that you request something a little different at Disney counter-service restaurants. A couple from northeast Georgia did and shared their experience:

We had a few times where we just couldn't communicate with a cast member. The "mac and cheese ON the hot dog" example was one. I've never seen or heard of macaroni and cheese ON a hot dog. And no matter how I tried to explain it to the cashier or the person at the food counter that my children didn't want the mac and cheese at all, whether on the side or in a bowl (and certainly not ON the hot dog), they couldn't get it. I still had to pay for the mac and cheese; then, when I saw it on the hot dogs, it took literally 10 minutes to get other hot dogs.

FOOD ALLERGIES AND SPECIAL REQUESTS

IF YOU HAVE SPECIAL DIETARY NEEDS, make them known when you make your Advance Reservations. For more information, see Part Six, Special Tips for Special People. A Phillipsburg, New Jersey, mom reports her family's experience:

Walt Disney World Buffets and Family-Style Restaurants

RESTAURANT	LOCATION	CUISINE	MEALS SERVED	CHARACTERS
Akershus Royal Banquet Hall	Epcot	American (B), Norwegian (L, D)	B, L, D	Yes
Biergarten Restaurant	Epcot	German	L, D	No
Boma—Flavors of Africa	Animal Kingdom Lodge	American (B), African (D)	B, D	No
Cape May Cafe	Beach Club Resort	American	B, D	Yes (B)
Captain's Grille	Yacht Club Resort	American	B*, L, D	No
Chef Mickey's	Contemporary Resort	American	B, Br, D	Yes
Cinderella's Royal Table	Magic Kingdom	American	B*, L, D	Yes
The Crystal Palace	Magic Kingdom	American	B, L, D	Yes
Fresh Mediterranean Market	Dolphin Hotel	Mediterranean/ American	B, L	No
Garden Grill Restaurant	Epcot	American	B, L, D	Yes
Garden Grove	Swan Hotel	American	B***, L, D***	Yes (B**, D)
Hollywood & Vine	Disney's Hollywood Studios	American	B, L, D	Yes
Hoop-Dee-Doo Musical Revue	Fort Wilderness	American	D	No
Liberty Tree Tavern	Magic Kingdom	American	L, D*	No
Mickey's Backyard BBQ	Fort Wilderness	American	D	Yes
1900 Park Fare	Grand Floridian	American	B, D	Yes
'Ohana	Polynesian Village	Polynesian	B, D	Yes (B)
Spirit of Aloha Dinner Show	Polynesian Village	American	D	No
Trail's End Restaurant	Fort Wilderness	American	B***, L, D***	No
Tusker House Restaurant	Disney's Animal Kingdom	American (B), African (L, D)	B, L, D	Yes
The Wave . . . of American Flavors	Contemporary Resort	American	B****, L, D	No
Whispering Canyon Cafe	Wilderness Lodge	American	B, L, D	No

*   Serves family-style meals only at the meal(s) indicated.
** Character-breakfast buffet served only on weekends.
*** Serves buffet-style meals only at the meal(s) indicated.
**** Serves breakfast buffet 7:30–11:45 a.m.

My 6-year-old has many food allergies. When making my Advance Reservations, I indicated these to the clerk. When we arrived at the restaurants, the staff was already aware of my child's allergies and assigned our table a chef who double-checked the list of allergies with us. The chefs were very nice and made my son feel very special.

A FEW CAVEATS

BEFORE YOU BEGIN EATING your way through the World, you need to know a few things:

1. Theme park restaurants rush their customers to make room for the next group of diners. Dining at high speed may appeal to a family with young, restless children, but for people wanting to relax, it's more like eating in a pressure chamber than fine dining.

2. Disney restaurants have comparatively few tables for parties of two, and servers are generally disinclined to seat two guests at larger tables. If you're a duo, you might have to wait longer—sometimes much longer—to be seated.

3. At full-service Disney restaurants, an automatic gratuity of 18% is added to your tab for parties of six or more—even at buffets where you serve yourself.

4. If you're dining in a theme park and cost is an issue, make lunch your main meal. Lunch entrées are similar to dinner entrées, but they're significantly cheaper.

WALT DISNEY WORLD RESTAURANT CATEGORIES

IN GENERAL, food and beverage offerings at Walt Disney World are defined by service, price, and convenience:

FULL-SERVICE RESTAURANTS Full-service restaurants are in all Disney resorts (except the All-Star Resorts, Art of Animation, Port Orleans French Quarter, and Pop Century), all major theme parks, and Disney Springs (Marketplace, The Landing at Town Center, and West Side). Disney operates most of the restaurants in the theme parks and its hotels, while contractors or franchisees operate the restaurants in hotels of the Disney Springs Resort Area (DSRA); the Swan and Dolphin hotels; and some in Disney's Animal Kingdom, Epcot, the BoardWalk, and Disney Springs. Advance Reservations (see pages 320–324) are recommended for most full-service restaurants except those in the DSRA. The restaurants accept American Express, Diners Club, Japan Credit Bureau, MasterCard, and Visa.

BUFFETS AND FAMILY-STYLE RESTAURANTS Many of these have Disney characters in attendance, and most have a separate children's menu featuring dishes such as hot dogs, burgers, chicken nuggets, pizza, macaroni and cheese, and spaghetti and meatballs. In addition to the buffets, several restaurants serve a family-style, all-you-can-eat, fixed-price meal.

Advance Reservations are required for character buffets and recommended for all other buffets and family-style restaurants. Most credit cards are accepted. As noted earlier, an automatic 18% gratuity is added

Disney Resort Food Courts: READER-SURVEY RATINGS

RESORT	FOOD COURT	THUMBS-UP RATING	NOTES
Art of Animation	Landscape of Flavors	89%	These ratings are about average for this kind of restaurant.
Pop Century	Everything POP	89%	
Port Orleans French Quarter	Sassagoula Floatworks & Food Factory	88%	
Port Orleans Riverside	Riverside Mill Food Court	87%	
All-Star Movies	World Premiere Food Court	86%	
Coronado Springs	Pepper Market	85%	
Fort Wilderness Campground	Trail's End To Go	85%	
All-Star Sports	End Zone Food Court	83%	These ratings are significantly lower than average.
All-Star Music	Intermission Food Court	82%	
Caribbean Beach	(closed for renovation)	N/A	

to the bill for parties of six or more, but when the tipping is at *your* discretion, a North Carolina reader urges generosity with waitstaff:

> *I've seen diners leave a dollar or two per person at buffets. I've also heard of people protesting Disney's prices by leaving a small tip or none at all. This is unacceptable—these servers keep your drinks full, keep your plates clean, and check on you constantly. They deserve at least 15%–18%. If you can't afford to tip, you shouldn't eat there.*

If you want to eat a lot but don't feel like standing in yet another line, then consider one of the all-you-can-eat family-style restaurants. These feature platters of food brought to your table in courses by a server. You can eat as much as you like—even go back to a favorite appetizer after you finish the main course. The food tends to be a little better than what you'll find on a buffet line.

See the table on page 326 for a list of buffets and family-style restaurants in the World.

FOOD COURTS Featuring a number of counter-service eateries under one roof, food courts can be found at the Moderate resorts (Coronado Springs, Caribbean Beach, Port Orleans) and Value resorts (All-Star, Art of Animation, and Pop Century).

If you're staying at one of Disney's Value or Moderate resorts, chances are you'll eat once or twice a day at your hotel's food court.

The closest thing to a food court at the theme parks is **Sunshine Seasons** at Epcot; see the next page and the full profile on page 354. Advance Reservations are neither required nor available at these restaurants.

COUNTER SERVICE Counter-service fast food is available in all the theme parks and at the BoardWalk and Disney Springs. The food compares in quality with Captain D's, McDonald's, or Taco Bell but is more expensive, though often served in larger portions.

FAST CASUAL Somewhere between burgers and formal dining are the establishments in Disney's "fast casual" category, including two in the theme parks: **Be Our Guest** in the Magic Kingdom (breakfast and lunch service, reservations recommended) and **Sunshine Seasons** in Epcot. Fast-casual restaurants feature menu choices a cut above what you'd normally see at a typical counter-service location. At Sunshine Seasons, for example, you can choose from rotisserie chicken or pork, tasty noodle bowls, or large sandwiches made with artisanal breads. Entrées cost about $1–$2 more on average than traditional counter service, but the variety and food quality more than make up the difference.

VENDOR FOOD Vendors abound at the theme parks, Disney Springs, and the BoardWalk. Offerings include popcorn, ice-cream bars, churros (Mexican pastries), soft drinks, bottled water, and (in theme parks) fresh fruit. Prices include tax; many vendors are set up to accept credit cards, charges to your room at a Disney resort, and the Disney Dining Plan. Others take only cash (look for a sign near the cash register).

HARD CHOICES

DINING DECISIONS WILL DEFINITELY affect your Walt Disney World experience. If you're short on time and you want to see the theme parks, avoid full service. Ditto if you're short on funds. If you do want full service, arrange Advance Reservations—as explained on page 320, they won't actually reserve you a table, but they can minimize your wait.

Integrating Meals into the *Unofficial Guide* Touring Plans

Arrive before the park of your choice opens. Tour expeditiously, using your chosen plan (taking as few breaks as possible), until about 11 or 11:30 a.m. Disney World's restaurants are busiest at 12:30 p.m. and 6:30 p.m. Once the park becomes crowded around midday, meals and other breaks won't affect the plan's efficiency. If you intend to stay in the park for evening parades, fireworks, or other events, eat dinner early enough to be finished in time for the festivities.

Character Dining

A number of restaurants, primarily those that serve all-you-can-eat buffets and family-style meals, offer character dining. At character meals, you pay a fixed price and dine in the presence of one to five Disney characters who circulate throughout the restaurant, hugging children (and sometimes adults), posing for photos, and signing autographs. Character breakfasts, lunches, and dinners are served at restaurants in and out of the theme parks. For an extensive discussion of character dining, see the section starting on page 447 in Part Five, Walt Disney World with Kids.

FULL-SERVICE DINING FOR FAMILIES WITH YOUNG CHILDREN

DISNEY RESTAURANTS OFFER an excellent (though expensive) opportunity to introduce young children to the variety and excitement of ethnic food. No matter how formal a restaurant appears, the staff is accustomed to fidgety, impatient, and often boisterous children. **Les Chefs de France** at Epcot, for instance, may be the

*un*official **TIP**
Look for the **Mickey Check** icon on healthy menu items such as fresh fruit and low-fat milk.

only French restaurant in the US where most patrons wear shorts and T-shirts and at least two dozen young diners are attired in basic black . . . mouse ears.

Almost all Disney restaurants offer kids' menus, and all have booster seats and high chairs. Servers understand how tough it is for children to sit still for an extended period of time, and they'll supply little ones with crackers and rolls and serve your dinner much faster than in comparable restaurants elsewhere. Reader letters suggest that being served too quickly is more common than having a long wait.

Good Walt Disney World Theme Park Restaurants for Children

In Epcot, preschoolers most enjoy **Biergarten Restaurant** in Germany, **San Angel Inn** in Mexico, and **Coral Reef Restaurant** at the Seas with Nemo & Friends Pavilion in Future World. The Biergarten combines a rollicking and noisy atmosphere with good basic food, including roast chicken. A German oompah band entertains, and kids can often participate in Bavarian dancing. San Angel Inn is in the Mexico village marketplace. From the table, children can watch boats on the Gran Fiesta Tour drift beneath a smoking volcano. With a choice of chips, tacos, and other familiar items, picky kids usually have no difficulty finding something to eat. (Be aware, though, that the service here is sometimes glacially slow.) Coral Reef, with tables beside windows looking into The Seas' aquarium, offers a satisfying mealtime diversion for all ages. If your children don't eat fish, Coral Reef also serves beef and chicken.

Biergarten offers reasonable value, plus good food. Coral Reef and San Angel Inn are overpriced, though the food is pretty good.

Be Our Guest and **Cinderella's Royal Table,** both in Fantasyland, are the hot tickets in the Magic Kingdom, but reservations are often unobtainable. (At present, there are no characters at Be Our Guest.) We think the best kids' fare is served at the **Liberty Tree Tavern.**

At Disney's Hollywood Studios, all ages enjoy the atmosphere and entertainment at **Hollywood & Vine,** the **Sci-Fi Dine-In Theater Restaurant,** and the **50's Prime Time Cafe.**

The four full-service restaurants at Disney's Animal Kingdom are **Tusker House Restaurant** (actually a character buffet); **Rainforest Cafe,** a great favorite of children; **Yak & Yeti Restaurant;** and **Tiffins,** a new, upscale location.

QUIET, ROMANTIC PLACES TO EAT

RESTAURANTS WITH GOOD FOOD and a couple-friendly ambience are rare in the theme parks. Only a handful of dining locales satisfy both requirements: **Coral Reef Restaurant,** an alfresco table at **Tutto Italia Ristorante,** the terrace at the **Rose & Crown Dining Room,** and the upstairs tables at the France Pavilion's **Monsieur Paul,** all in Epcot; **Tiffins** on Discovery Island at Disney's Animal Kingdom; and the corner booths at **The Hollywood Brown Derby** in Disney's Hollywood Studios. Waterfront dining (though not necessarily quiet or romantic) is available at **Paddlefish** at Disney Springs, and **Narcoossee's** at the Grand Floridian.

unofficial **TIP**
The **California Grill** atop the Contemporary Resort has the best view at Walt Disney World.

Victoria & Albert's at the Grand Floridian is the World's showcase gourmet restaurant; expect to pay big bucks. Other good choices for couples include **Artist Point** at Wilderness Lodge, **Yachtsman Steakhouse** at the Yacht Club, **Shula's Steak House** at the Dolphin, **Jiko—The Cooking Place** at Animal Kingdom Lodge, and **Flying Fish** at the BoardWalk.

Eating later in the evening and choosing a restaurant we've mentioned will improve your chances for intimate dining; nevertheless, children—well behaved or otherwise—are everywhere at Walt Disney World, and there's no way to escape them. These honeymooners from Slidell, Louisiana, write:

> *We made dinner reservations at some of the nicer Disney restaurants. We made sure to reserve past dinner hours, and we tried to stress that we were on our honeymoon. But in every restaurant we went to, we were seated next to large families. It's very difficult to enjoy a romantic dinner when there are small children crawling around under your table. Our suggestion: Seat couples without children together and families with kids elsewhere.*

FAST FOOD IN THE THEME PARKS

BECAUSE MOST MEALS DURING a Disney World vacation are consumed on the run while touring, we'll tackle counter-service and vendor foods first. Plentiful in all theme parks are hot dogs, burgers, chicken sandwiches, salads, and pizza. They're augmented by special items that relate to the park's theme or the part of the park you're touring. In Epcot's Germany, for example, counter-service bratwurst and beer are sold. In Frontierland in the Magic Kingdom, vendors sell smoked turkey legs.

Counter-service prices are fairly consistent from park to park. You can expect to pay the same for your coffee or hot dog at Disney's Animal Kingdom as you will at Disney's Hollywood Studios.

Getting your act together regarding counter-service restaurants in the parks is more a matter of courtesy than necessity. A mother from Fort Wayne, Indiana, points out that indecision can be as maddening as outright discourtesy, especially when you're hungry:

> *Every fast-food restaurant has menu signs the size of billboards, but do you think anybody reads them? People waiting in line spend enough time in front of these signs to memorize them and still don't have a clue what they want when they finally get to the counter. Folks, PULEEEZ get your orders together ahead of time!*

A North Carolina reader offers a tip for helping things along:

> *Many counter-service registers serve two queues each, one to the left and one to the right of each register. People are not used to this and will instinctively line up in one queue per register, typically on the right side, leaving the left vacant. We had register operators wave us up to the front several times to start a left queue instead of waiting behind others on the right.*

Healthful Food at Walt Disney World

Health-conscious choices such as fresh fruit are available at most fast-food counters and even from vendors. People who have diabetes, vegetarians,

THE COST OF COUNTER-SERVICE FOOD	
BAGEL OR MUFFIN	$2.99-$3.99
BROWNIE	$3.99-$7.99
BURRITO	$3.99-$6.49
CAKE OR PIE	$3.99-$5.59
CEREAL WITH MILK	$2.49-$3.99
CHEESEBURGER WITH FRIES	$5.99-$14.99
CHICKEN BREAST SANDWICH	$9.19-$11.99
CHICKEN NUGGETS WITH FRIES	$5.99-$9.29
CHILDREN'S MEAL (various)	$5.49-$5.99
CHIPS	$2.99-$3.25
COOKIE	$2.50-$3.99
FRIED-FISH BASKET WITH FRIES	$7.99-$9.49
FRENCH FRIES	$2.99
FRUIT (whole)	$1.99-$3.59
FRUIT CUP / FRUIT SALAD	$3.79-$3.99
HOT DOG	$5.75-$12.29
ICE CREAM / FROZEN NOVELTIES	$4-$9.95
NACHOS WITH CHEESE	$3.99-$7.69
PB&J SANDWICH	$5.49 (kids' meal)
PIZZA (personal)	$9.19-$10.99
POPCORN	$3.50-$5.50
PRETZEL	$2.95-$6
SALAD (entrée)	$7.99-$11.69
SALAD (side)	$3.29
SMOKED TURKEY LEG	$10.50-$13.29
SOUP / CHILI	$3.69-$7.99
SUB / DELI SANDWICH	$7.50-$11.49
TACO SALAD	$8.19
VEGGIE BURGER	$8.59-$9.99

THE COST OF COUNTER-SERVICE DRINKS		
DRINKS	**SMALL**	**LARGE**
BEER	$5.75-$8.25	$7.50-$12.50
BOTTLED WATER (one size)	$3-$4.50	$3-$4.50
COFFEE (one size)	$2.29	$7.99
LATTE (one size)	$3.99	$3.99-$5.19
FLOAT, MILKSHAKE, OR SUNDAE (one size)	$4.49-$6	$4.49-$6
FRUIT JUICE	$2.59-$2.99	$3.29-$3.79
HOT TEA AND COCOA (one size)	$2.09-$2.29	$2.09-$2.29
MILK	$1.79	$2.39-$3.29
SOFT DRINKS, ICED TEA, AND LEMONADE	$2.59-$2.99	$4.50

Refillable souvenir mugs cost $16.95 with tax (free refills) at Disney resorts and around $11 at the water parks. Each person on a Disney Dining Plan gets a free mug, refillable at their Disney resort.

dieters, those requiring kosher meals, and anyone trying to eat healthfully should have no trouble finding something to eat.

Disney World for Java Junkies

Starbucks can be found on the Magic Kingdom's Main Street, in Epcot's Future World, on Hollywood Boulevard in the Studios, on Discovery Island in Animal Kingdom, and in Disney Springs.

Beyond Counter Service: Tips for Saving Time and Money

Even if you confine your meals to quick-service fare, you lose a lot of time getting food in the theme parks. Here are some ways to minimize the time you spend hunting and gathering:

1. Eat breakfast before you arrive. Restaurants outside the World offer some outstanding breakfast specials; plus, some hotels provide small refrigerators in their guest rooms, or you can rent a fridge or bring a cooler. Both options will save a ton of time.

2. After a good breakfast, buy snacks from vendors in the parks as you tour, or stuff some snacks in a fanny pack.

3. All theme park restaurants are busiest between 11:30 a.m. and 2:15 p.m. for lunch and 6 and 9 p.m. for dinner. For shorter lines and faster service, don't eat during these hours, especially 12:30–1:30 p.m.

4. Many counter-service restaurants sell cold sandwiches. Buy a cold lunch minus drinks before 11:30 a.m., and carry it in small plastic bags until you're ready to eat (within an hour or so of purchase). Ditto for dinner. Buy drinks at the appropriate time from any convenient vendor.

5. Most fast-food eateries have more than one service window. Check the lines at all windows before queuing up: Sometimes a window that's staffed but out of the way will have a much shorter line or none at all. Note, however, that some windows may offer only certain items.

6. If you're short on time and the park closes early, stay until closing and eat dinner outside Disney World before returning to your hotel. If the park stays open late, eat dinner about 4 or 4:30 p.m. at the restaurant of your choice. You should sneak in just ahead of the dinner crowd.

Our readers use variations on these tips with great success. One Missouri mom writes:

We arrived at WDW with our steel Coleman cooler well stocked with milk and sandwich fixings. I froze a block of ice in a milk bottle, and we replenished it daily with ice from the resort ice machine. I also froze small packages of deli-type meats for later in the week. We ate cereal, milk, and fruit each morning, with boxed juices.

Each child had a belt bag of his own, which he filled from a special box of "goodies" each day with things like packages of crackers and cheese and packets of peanuts and raisins. Each child also had a small, rectangular plastic water bottle that could hang on the belt. We filled these at water fountains before getting into lines.

We left the park before noon, ate sandwiches, chips, and soda in the room, and napped. We purchased our evening meal in the park, at a counter-service eatery. We budgeted for both morning and evening snacks from a vendor but often didn't need them.

A Whiteland, Indiana, mom suggests:

If you're traveling with younger kids, take a supply of small paper or plastic cups to split drinks, which are both huge and expensive.

DISNEY DINING SUGGESTIONS

FOLLOWING ARE OUR SUGGESTIONS for dining at each of the major theme parks. If you want to try a full-service restaurant at one of the parks, be aware that the restaurants continue to serve after the park's official closing time.

THE MAGIC KINGDOM

OF THE PARK'S SEVEN full-service restaurants, **Be Our Guest** in Fantasyland is the best, followed by **Liberty Tree Tavern** in Liberty Square and **The Plaza Restaurant** on Main Street. **Skipper Canteen** opened in 2015 to average ratings. **Cinderella's Royal Table** in the castle and **The Crystal Palace** on Main Street serve a decent but expensive character buffet. Avoid **Tony's Town Square Restaurant** on Main Street.

AUTHORS' FAVORITE COUNTER-SERVICE RESTAURANTS

- **Be Our Guest Restaurant** (breakfast, lunch) *Fantasyland*
- **Columbia Harbour House** *Liberty Square*

These two restaurants' menus offer the most variety within the Magic Kingdom. Be Our Guest serves a tasty tuna niçoise salad (with seared tuna), a grilled ham-and-cheese sandwich that's better than you'd expect, and a savory braised-pork entrée. Columbia Harbour House's offerings include lobster rolls, chicken potpie, and a delicious hummus sandwich on multigrain bread. Beyond these, the Magic Kingdom's fast-food eateries are undistinguished, not to mention about twice as expensive as McDonald's, for about the same quality. On the positive side, portions are large, sometimes large enough for children to share. Check our mini-profiles of the park's counter-service restaurants (starting on page 347) before you queue up.

Our dining recommendations for a day at the Magic Kingdom:

1. Obtain an Advance Reservation for lunch at Be Our Guest. See page 321 for details.

2. Take the monorail to one of the hotels for lunch. The trip takes very little time, and because most guests have left the hotels for the parks, the resorts' restaurants are often not crowded. The food is better than the Magic Kingdom's, the service is faster, the atmosphere is more relaxed, and mixed drinks are available.

3. Full-service restaurants that accept Advance Reservations fill quickly in the summer and during holidays. To obtain Advance Reservations, visit disneyworld.disney.go.com/reservations/dining, call ☎ 407-939-3463, or hotfoot it to your chosen restaurant as soon as you enter the park. Advance Reservations are explained starting on page 321, and Magic Kingdom full-service and counter-service restaurants are profiled later in this chapter.

4. A good rule at any full-service restaurant is to keep it simple. Order sandwiches or basic dishes, such as roast turkey and mashed potatoes.

Here are some comments from readers about Magic Kingdom full-service and counter-service restaurants. First, regarding Cinderella's Royal Table, two perspectives from two different readers:

READER 1: *Our whole family did Cinderella's Royal Table for lunch. Our two little boys (ages 3 and 4) loved it even more than their 6-year-old sister. They loved all the princesses paying special attention to them because they were the only guys in the whole place. My 3-year-old left with his face covered in lipstick and even managed to propose to Cinderella—who, sadly, mentioned she was already married.*

READER 2: *The food was OK, but the characters spent a lot of time at each table—so much time that we only got to meet Snow White and Belle. Wasn't worth the trouble of getting the seating.*

There are two things everyone agrees on concerning Be Our Guest: The food is good, and it's hard to get into. Readers love the venue but not so much the cost. There are also issues with reservations. First, from a Burlington, Ontario, dad:

The best thing about the vacation: eating lunch at Be Our Guest. The atmosphere and quality of food were unlike any quick-service I'd ever had at Disney.

From a Kansas City, Missouri, mom:

Be Our Guest must be the new Cinderella's Royal Table. I tried to get a dinner reservation when we first planned our vacation four months ahead, and I couldn't get one.

A family of four from Papillion, Nebraska, offered this caution about reservations:

Please ensure people understand that Be Our Guest reservations may still lead to a long wait time. We had 11 a.m. reservations, which we canceled because we checked in and were told we would have at least a 45-minute wait. Those aren't reservations in my mind.

A Raleigh, North Carolina, reader had a disappointing experience at Be Our Guest:

We did breakfast at Be Our Guest, and I don't see what all the fanfare is about. The portions were very small, and we still spent about $28 per person. I had the croissant doughnut—$24! Came with a drink and that's it. And it's all self-serve for silverware and drinks. The line for $3 coffee was always five to six people deep. I felt like I needed a FastPass just to get a cup of joe.

A mom from Mansfield, Massachusetts, is scratching her head about empty tables during peak lunch hours:

When we checked in, they were turning people away who did not have reservations, as well as people with later lunch reservations who tried to check in early. Once we ordered, we took a quick tour of the seating situation (fearing the worst), only to find about 50% of the tables were unoccupied. While we ate, we noticed the room never filled up. Between the hours of noon and 1 p.m. on a Saturday afternoon, the restaurant was half-empty!

The Crystal Palace gets mixed reviews. A sampling:

The food quality and selection were the worst I've seen in 10 years of going there, and the characters were stretched way too thin—only two came to our table in an hour and a half.

Of all the restaurants we visited, I can't rave enough about The Crystal Palace and Liberty Tree Tavern. The food was great, and the service was wonderful.

Like the previous reader, the following reader really liked Liberty Tree Tavern:

Didn't expect much here but made a reservation based on your book. What a surprise! The food was great as well as the atmosphere.

So did this Broussard, Louisiana, couple—though their enthusiasm isn't exactly unqualified:

We booked a reservation for dinner at Liberty Tree Tavern. What we didn't realize is that it was a set menu. The food was excellent—like Thanksgiving dinner—but the price was crazy! Dinner for two with drinks and tip ran us close to $100. Definitely not what we were expecting.

EPCOT

SINCE THE BEGINNING, dining has been an integral component of Epcot's entertainment product. World Showcase has many more restaurants than attractions, and Epcot has added bars, tapas-style eateries, and full-service restaurants faster than any park in memory.

FULL-SERVICE RESTAURANTS IN EPCOT	
FUTURE WORLD	
Coral Reef Restaurant **The Seas**	Garden Grill Restaurant **The Land**
WORLD SHOWCASE	
Akershus Royal Banquet Hall **Norway**	Rose & Crown Dining Room **United Kingdom**
Biergarten Restaurant **Germany**	San Angel Inn Restaurante **Mexico**
Le Cellier Steakhouse **Canada**	Spice Road Table **Morocco**
Les Chefs de France **France**	Teppan Edo **Japan**
La Hacienda de San Angel **Mexico**	Tokyo Dining **Japan**
Monsieur Paul **France**	Tutto Gusto Wine Cellar **Italy**
Nine Dragons Restaurant **China**	Tutto Italia Ristorante **Italy**
Restaurant Marrakesh **Morocco**	Via Napoli **Italy**

For the most part, Epcot's restaurants have always served decent food, though the World Showcase restaurants have occasionally been timid about delivering honest representations of their host nations' cuisine. That seems to be changing faster in some areas (Mexico) than others (Morocco), but we're hopeful that we see a trend. It's still true that the less adventuresome diner can find steak and potatoes on virtually every menu, but the same kitchens will serve up the real thing for anyone willing to ask.

Many Epcot restaurants are overpriced, particularly **Monsieur Paul** (France) and **Coral Reef Restaurant** (The Seas). Combining attractive ambience and well-prepared food with good value are **Rose & Crown** (UK), **Via Napoli** (Italy), **Biergarten Restaurant** (Germany), and **La Hacienda de San Angel** (Mexico). Biergarten (along with **Restaurant Marrakesh** in Morocco) also features live entertainment.

unofficial **TIP**
Epcot has 18 full-service restaurants: 2 in Future World and 16 in World Showcase. With a couple of exceptions, these are among the best restaurants at Walt Disney World, in or out of the theme parks.

Eating at Epcot can be a consummate hassle, but an afternoon without Advance Reservations for dinner in World Showcase is like not having a date on the day of the prom. Each pavilion (except United States) has a beautifully seductive ethnic restaurant or two. To tour these exotic settings and not partake is almost beyond the limits of willpower. And while the fare isn't always compelling, the overall experience is exhilarating.

AUTHORS' FAVORITE COUNTER-SERVICE RESTAURANTS

- **Les Halles Boulangerie–Pâtisserie** *France*
- **Kringla Bakeri og Kafe** *Norway*
- **Sunshine Seasons** *The Land*
- **Tangierine Cafe** *Morocco*

Les Halles Boulangerie–Pâtisserie sells pastries, sandwiches, and quiches. The pastries are made on-site (the bread is baked upstairs), and the sandwiches are as close to actual French street food—in taste, size, and price—as you'll get anywhere in Epcot. (We had one of those *Ratatouille* flashback scenes while eating one, only ours was in the Marais.) Another favorite is the chicken-and-lamb *shawarma* platter at Morocco's **Tangierine Cafe.** Besides juicy lamb, it comes with some of the best tabbouleh we've tasted in Florida.

In addition to these, we recommend the following ethnic counter-service specialties:

GERMANY	**Sommerfest** for bratwurst and grapefruit beer
JAPAN	**Katsura Grill** for noodle dishes, teriyaki, and tempura
UNITED KINGDOM	**Rose & Crown Pub** for Guinness, Harp, and Bass beers; **Yorkshire County Fish Shop** for fresh fish and chips

Unofficial Guide readers have diverse opinions of Epcot's full-service restaurants. Concerning Coral Reef Restaurant in The Seas with Nemo & Friends:

Tried Coral Reef for the first time, despite reviews. Waited 40 minutes beyond our reserved time, and the food was mediocre and pricey. Next time I'll cook a burger next to my daughter's goldfish bowl.

Another reader, however, had a positive experience:

We were surprised by how much everyone loved Coral Reef. We had great service, and the food was awesome. We had a booth directly in front of the tank and didn't even request it!

Le Cellier is one of the most coveted reservations in Epcot:

Le Cellier is one of the hardest restaurants for which to get Advance Reservations [see page 321]. It wasn't available any of the 10 days of my trip, and I called more than 90 days in advance.

The filet mignon I got at Le Cellier may indeed have been the best steak I've ever had—and it had better have been for that price.

A mom from Marlborough, Connecticut, really enjoyed Tokyo Dining at the Japan Pavilion:

Tokyo Dining has become our favorite restaurant at Walt Disney World. The food is very good and reasonably priced, and the views over the World Showcase Lagoon are incredible.

Finally, a couple of pointed comments about Nine Dragons in China:

I've had better Chinese at our local strip mall.

I think they should rename it Nine Tums.

Drinking Around the World (Showcase)

A popular adult pastime at Epcot is to make a complete circuit of the World Showcase, sampling the exceptional alcoholic drinks native to each nation represented. Perhaps knowing this, Disney has added stand-alone bars to six pavilions.

LA CAVA DEL TEQUILA, MEXICO Inside the pyramid, La Cava stocks more than 100 kinds of tequila and mezcal (similar to tequila, with a smoky flavor), almost a dozen kinds of margaritas, and various light appetizers. La Cava seats just over 50 people but is far more popular than that. On weekends and during special events such as the Food & Wine Festival or Cinco de Mayo, expect a wait to get a table.

La Cava is Len's favorite bar in Walt Disney World. Two things set it apart: First, a dedicated tequila expert is on hand most days to explain the different types of tequila and provide tasting notes. (Her name is Hilda, and she's from the town of Tequila in Jalisco, Mexico—tell her Len sent you.) Second, the team that runs La Cava is very engaged with the Disney community on social media, which makes it easy to ask questions about the drinks and menus. As of this writing, folks who follow @cavadeltequila on Twitter get a discount on a shot.

SAKE BAR, JAPAN It isn't much more than a small circular table at the far end of the retail space on the first floor of the Japan Pavilion. A decent and affordable selection of sakes can be purchased from a shelf right next to the bar-table. Frankly, we're amazed that this hasn't been expanded into a proper dedicated room.

SPICE ROAD TABLE, MOROCCO Offering waterside food and drinks, Spice Road Table (see page 398) is an uncrowded spot for *IllumiNations* dining. Unique cast-member costuming, a highly detailed interior, and an open-air patio are the highlights of the setting and atmosphere. Choose from beer, wine, cocktails, and tapas-style small plates. The food is expensive and of average quality, and the service is slow.

TUTTO GUSTO WINE CELLAR, ITALY Tutto Gusto (see page 405) serves wine, spirits, and small plates in a setting reminiscent of an underground wine cellar. Perhaps learning from La Cava, which opened first, Tutto Gusto has seating for 113. Our favorite spot is a small room to the right just inside the entrance, with a fireplace, a couple of comfy chairs, and tables big enough to hold your food and drinks.

The menu is divided into three sections. The "small plates" section offers four choices that each serve two people: combinations of cured meats and salamis, cheeses, olives, veggies, and seafood. Prices start at $24 each. Besides these, there's a selection of sandwichlike panini available, but the bread isn't as good as you'd expect. The best, and most reasonably priced, thing on the menu is the pasta (try the hand-made cavatappi). When it comes to dessert, the cannoli are some of the best we've ever had. The wine list is extensive. Service is good.

We revisited Tutto Gusto for this edition of the book. We still think the charcuterie selections are overpriced at $24–$29, even if they serve two people. However, the service and food quality are good, and the place was packed with vacationers (not locals) returning to a favorite, "secret" spot. Expect a 15- to 60-minute wait to get in around dinner-time, depending on the time of year.

LES VINS DE FRANCE, FRANCE Les Vins is a small retail space that offers a variety of French wines, including Chardonnay, Merlot, Sauvignon Blanc, Cabernet Sauvignon, Pinot Noir, and Syrah, plus cocktails with France's Grey Goose vodka. You'll not be the first to call the Orange—a mix of Grey Goose and Grand Marnier—*une petit coup de pouce de maman.*

WEINKELLER, GERMANY Decorated in stone, dark woods, heavy chandeliers, and thick wood tables, Weinkeller serves wines by the glass (around $6) and in flights of three 2-ounce pours (about $10). If you like sweet white wines, this is the place to be. Selections usually include a couple of Rieslings, a Liebfraumilch, dessert wines, and ice wines. The bar has no seating and serves only a cheese plate, but the wine pours are generous—and that counts for something.

In addition to the preceding, the UK Pavilion has had the **Rose & Crown Pub** for years. But with the growing popularity of watering holes in World Showcase, we wouldn't be surprised if Disney added a few more.

DISNEY'S ANIMAL KINGDOM

WITH ANIMAL KINGDOM'S new nighttime attractions and entertainment, Disney has added another sit-down restaurant, a counter-service, and several smaller food windows to accommodate larger, later crowds. We recommend that you tour early after a good breakfast, then graze on vendor food until dinner. Then try **Yak & Yeti** for a moderately priced (for Disney), moderately paced meal, or **Tiffins** if you have a little more time and money. A nightcap at the **Nomad Lounge,** next door to Tiffins and on the way to Pandora, is a lovely way to end your day at the park.

Animal Kingdom isn't particularly exotic. You'll find a lot of counter-service fast food, along with **Tusker House,** a buffet-style restaurant; **Yak & Yeti,** a table-service restaurant, in Asia; and **Tiffins,** the upscale international gourmet room on Discovery Island. You'll also find plenty of traditional theme park food—hot dogs, burgers—but even the fast food is superior to typical Disney fare. Our two counter-service favorites are **Flame Tree Barbecue** on Discovery Island, with its water-front dining pavilions, and **Yak & Yeti Local Food Cafes** (just outside the full-service Yak & Yeti) for casual Asian dishes, from egg rolls to crispy honey chicken.

The park's new *Avatar*-themed **Satu'li Canteen** (not open at press time) is Pandora's answer to Chipotle's rice bowls. You'll pick a base of starch, grain, or lettuce; a protein; and garnishes. Also new is the **Pongu Pongu Lounge,** serving drinks inspired by the film.

Harambe Market, to the right as you approach Kilimanjaro Safaris, has four windows, each serving a different specialty, such as spice-rubbed ribs, batter-fried sausages, and chicken or beef kebabs. Beer and South African wines are also available.

Tiffins, opened in 2016 with traces of Adventurers Club mementos inside, is Animal Kingdom's entry into higher-end dining and a precursor to the park's eventual evening hours.

A Whitestone, New York, dad thinks we sell Tusker House short:

You really underestimate Tusker House. It was easily the best buffet, and the characters at lunch ended up making it a great meal.

A Cambridge, England, reader loved the full-service Yak & Yeti:

Our meal was the best we had in the World—in fact, some of the best Asian cuisine we had tried since our travels in Southeast Asia—yet we were dismayed to see tables of Americans ordering burgers.

A Laurel, Maryland, couple rave about Tiffins:

This is one of the best restaurants in all of Disney World. It's pricey of course, but the food is spectacular and the setting is very quiet and relaxing. It serves fixed price meals that include an appetizer, main course, and dessert.

A reader from Delaware agrees:

We ate at Tiffins in Animal Kingdom and it was outstanding, from the service to the decor (including the Nomad Lounge) to the food; best meal ever at WDW, even better than California Grill.

Another full-service restaurant in Animal Kingdom, **Rainforest Cafe,** has entrances both inside and outside the park, meaning you don't have to buy park admission to eat there. Both Rainforest Cafes (the other is at Disney Springs) accept Advance Reservations.

AUTHORS' FAVORITE COUNTER-SERVICE RESTAURANTS

- **Flame Tree Barbecue** *Discovery Island*
- **Yak & Yeti Local Food Cafes** *Asia*

DISNEY'S HOLLYWOOD STUDIOS

DINING AT HOLLYWOOD STUDIOS is less ethnic than at Epcot and possibly less interesting than at any other park. The park has five restaurants where Advance Reservations are recommended or required: **The Hollywood Brown Derby, 50's Prime Time Cafe, Sci-Fi Dine-In Theater Restaurant, Mama Melrose's Ristorante Italiano,** and the **Hollywood & Vine** buffet. The upscale Brown Derby is by far the best restaurant at the

Studios. For simple Italian food, including pizza, Mama Melrose's is fine; just don't expect anything fancy. At the Sci-Fi Dine-In, you eat in little cars at a simulated drive-in movie from the 1950s. Though you won't find a more entertaining restaurant in Walt Disney World, the food is hit-or-miss. Somewhat better is the 50's Prime Time Cafe, where you sit in Mom's time-warp kitchen and scarf down meat loaf while watching clips of classic sitcoms. It's just as fun, and the food is a step up. The best way to experience either restaurant is to stop in for dessert or a drink between 2:30 and 4:30 p.m. Hollywood & Vine features singing and dancing characters from the Disney Channel during breakfast and lunch.

AUTHORS' FAVORITE COUNTER-SERVICE RESTAURANTS

• **Trolley Car Cafe (Starbucks)** *Sunset Boulevard*

If you want to know the state of counter-service at Hollywood Studios, consider this:

- Disney closed the two highest-rated restaurants in all of DHS, with no replacements.
- The park has as many open restaurants rated "much worse than average" as "above average."

The best counter-service restaurant still open here is the **Trolley Car Cafe (Starbucks)** on Hollywood Boulevard. Note that Disney made $3.5 billion in profits in the second quarter of 2017. They have the money and talent to build better restaurants. In this case, they choose not to.

We receive considerable mail from readers recounting their DHS dining experiences. The 50's Prime Time Cafe, for instance, is always a hot topic. First, from a Maryland reader:

50's Prime Time Cafe was fun, but the food was mediocre at best. If my mom cooked that way, I would've run away from home.

But a West Newton, Massachusetts, family loved it:

We decided to go against your recommendation and give it a shot. We're so glad we did! For the five of us (ages 16–20), it was a blast. "Leroy," our waiter and "big brother" for the meal, came and sat at our table and helped us set our places so we wouldn't get in trouble with "Mom." When one member of our party cursed, "Mom" arrived to punish him, making him clear the table onto her tray, which he did shamefully. It was a total kick that we talked about for the rest of the trip.

If you arrive at the Studios without having arranged Advance Reservations for meals, you can make them at the restaurants. **The Hollywood Brown Derby,** expensive but tasty, is usually among the last to fill. The companion Hollywood Brown Derby Lounge is far less crowded and offers a small-plate and dessert menu, including the famous grapefruit cake.

WALT DISNEY WORLD DINNER THEATERS

SEVERAL DINNER-THEATER SHOWS play nightly at Walt Disney World. When you make a reservation, you'll receive a confirmation number and be told to pick up your tickets at a Disney-hotel Guest

Relations desk. Unlike Advance Dining Reservations, your seating times for dinner shows are guaranteed. Unless you cancel your tickets at least 48 hours before your reservation time, your credit card will still be charged the full amount. Dinner-show reservations can be made 180 days in advance; call ☎ 407-939-3463. While getting reservations for the *Spirit of Aloha Dinner Show* isn't terribly tough, booking the *Hoop-Dee-Doo Musical Revue* is a trick of the first order.

A couple from Bismarck, North Dakota, explains:

> *I'm glad we made our reservations so early (a year in advance). I was able to reserve space for us at* Spirit of Aloha *at the Polynesian Village and the* Hoop-Dee-Doo Musical Revue. *At both of these, they seat you according to when you made your reservation. At the* Hoop-Dee-Doo Musical Revue, *we had a front-center table. We were so close to the stage, we could see how many cavities the performers had!*

If you can't get reservations and want to see one of the shows:

1. Call ☎ 407-939-3463 at 9 a.m. each morning while you're at Disney World to make a same-day reservation. There are three performances each night, and for all three combined, only 3–24 people total will be admitted with same-day reservations.

2. Arrive at the show of your choice 45 minutes before showtime (early and late shows are your best bets) and put your name on the standby list. If someone with reservations fails to show, you may be admitted.

Borrowing a page from Las Vegas strip joints where nearsighted old coots are charged extra to sit way up front, Disney offers tiered seating for *Hoop-Dee-Doo* and *Spirit of Aloha*. The best seats are in **Category 1.** Next comes **Category 2,** with seats off to the side or behind Category 1. Finally, **Category 3** seats are at the Orlando Greyhound station, where you watch the show on a video feed. Just making sure you're still with us—actually, they're farther still to the side or back, or on another level from the stage. Both shows offer good views from almost all seats, so you can decide if sitting closer to the action is worth the extra bucks.

Hoop-Dee-Doo Musical Revue

Pioneer Hall, Fort Wilderness Campground ☎ 407-939-3463. **Showtimes** 4, 6:15, and 8:30 p.m. nightly. **Cost** *Category 1:* $72 adults, $43 children ages 3–9.; *Category 2:* $69 adults, $39 children; *Category 3:* $64 adults, $34 children. Prices include tax and gratuity. **Duration of show** 2 hours. **Discounts** Seasonal. **Type of seating** Tables of various sizes to fit the number in each party, set in an Old West–style dance hall. **Menu** All-you-can-eat barbecue ribs, fried chicken, salad, baked beans, and cornbread; Unlimited beer, wine, sangria, and soft drinks. Vegetarian, vegan, and gluten-free options available; mention dietary needs when making reservations.

unofficial **TIP**
To make reservations for the *Hoop-Dee-Doo Musical Revue,* call as soon as you're certain of the dates of your visit. The earlier you call, the better your seats will be.

DESCRIPTION AND COMMENTS *Hoop-Dee-Doo* is the longest-running show at Walt Disney World and a nostalgic favorite for many families. If you've ever thought *Country Bear Jamboree* would benefit from free-flowing beer and wine and barbecue, this is the show for you.

Audience participation includes sing-alongs, hand-clapping, and a finale where you may find yourself onstage. During the meal, the music continues (softly). The food itself is OK—*Hoop-Dee-Doo* shares a kitchen with local favorite Trail's End (page 403)—and you can't complain about the portion size.

Give special consideration to transportation when planning your evening at Fort Wilderness. There is no parking at Pioneer Hall, which is accessible only by boat (the Magic Kingdom and the loop between Fort Wilderness, Wilderness Lodge, and the Contemporary) and the Fort Wilderness internal bus system. After the show, resort buses at the Pioneer Hall stop will take you back to your resort.

Mickey's Backyard BBQ

Fort Wilderness Campground ☎ 407-939-3463. **Showtimes** Vary seasonally. **Cost** *Category 1:* $72 adults, $47 children ages 3–9; *Category 2:* $62 adults; $37 children. Prices include tax and gratuity. **Type of seating** Picnic tables. **Menu** Smoked chicken, barbecue pork ribs, burgers, hot dogs, corn, beans, mac and cheese, salads and slaw, bread, and watermelon and ice-cream bars for dessert. **Vegetarian alternatives** On request. **Beverages** Unlimited beer, wine, lemonade, and iced tea.

DESCRIPTION AND COMMENTS *Mickey's Backyard BBQ* combines all-you-can-eat picnic fare with a country-and-Western band, characters, and an after-dinner dance party for all. Because this is an outdoor affair, we recommend sticking to fall and spring for your visits, though it's offered year-round. The food, like that at *Hoop-Dee-Doo,* comes from the Trail's End Restaurant kitchen and is consistently good. The same caveats for transportation to *Hoop-Dee-Doo* apply here as well. Allow plenty of time to get to the Fort Wilderness Pavilion, where this show is held. It's a short walk past the Tri-Circle-D ranch from the Settlement Depot bus stop to the barbecue.

From a Rhode Island dad:

Mickey's Backyard BBQ was a surprise hit. It was easy to get there from the Magic Kingdom, and we went back there later for Extra Magic Hours. The food at the BBQ was nice, and watching little kids line dance with the characters was about the most adorable thing I've ever seen.

Spirit of Aloha Dinner Show

Disney's Polynesian Village Resort ☎ 407-939-3463. **Showtimes** Tuesday–Saturday, 5:15 and 8 p.m. **Cost** *Category 1:* $78 adults, $46 children ages 3–9.; *Category 2:* $74 adults, $44 children; *Category 3:* $66 adults, $39 children. All prices include tax and gratuity. **Discounts** Seasonal. **Type of seating** Long rows of tables, with some separation between individual parties. The show is performed on an outdoor stage, but all seating is covered. Ceiling fans provide some air movement, but it can get warm, especially at the early show. **Menu** Tropical fruit, roasted chicken, island pork ribs, mixed vegetables, rice, and pineapple bread; vegetarian alternatives on request. Chicken tenders, PB&J sandwiches, mac and cheese, and hot dogs are also available for children. Beverages include beer, wine, and soft drinks.

unofficial **TIP**
Spirit of Aloha is particularly susceptible to cancellations due to weather.

DESCRIPTION AND COMMENTS This show features South Seas–island native dancing followed by an all-you-can-eat "Polynesian-style" meal. The dancing is interesting and largely authentic, and the dancers are attractive but definitely PG-rated in the Disney tradition. We think the show has its moments and the meal is adequate, but neither is particularly special.

The show follows (tenuously) the "girl leaves home for the big city, forgets her roots, and must rediscover them" theme. The performers are uniformly attractive ("Studmuffins!" said a female *Unofficial* researcher when asked about the men), and the dancing is very good. The story, however, never really makes sense as anything other than a slender thread between musical numbers. Our show lasted for more than 2 hours and 15 minutes.

The food does little more than illustrate how difficult it must be to prepare the same meal for hundreds of people simultaneously: The roasted chicken is better than the ribs, but neither is anything special. We conditionally recommend *Spirit of Aloha* for special occasions, when the people celebrating get to go onstage. But go to the early show and get dessert somewhere else in the World.

A well-traveled couple from Fond du Lac, Wisconsin, comments:

Spirit of Aloha was a beautiful presentation, better than some shows we have seen in Hawaii! The food, however, lacked in all areas. The fruit platter was chintzy, the honey-roasted chicken was a bit fatty, and the pineapple cake was dry.

MORE READER COMMENTS ABOUT WALT DISNEY WORLD DINING

EATING IS A POPULAR TOPIC among *Unofficial Guide* readers. In addition to participating in our annual restaurant survey, many readers share their thoughts. The following comments are representative.

Here's a 13-year-old girl from Omaha, Nebraska, who doesn't get bent out of shape over one bad meal:

Honestly, when was the last time you came home from Disney World and said, "Gosh, my vacation really sucked because I ate at a bad restaurant?" Disney World is Disney World, no matter what.

A Canadian mom raises a caution about the California Grill:

We ate dinner on our last night at the California Grill. It was wonderful, but it took 3 hours. This is not a great place to take your kids. We were there from 7 to 10 p.m., and it was just too much for them.

From a reader in the United Kingdom:

We had the most fantastic meal at California Grill, and I'd definitely recommend it. Being central London–living foodie-types, we're very hard to please, but the meal there really was second to none.

An Albuquerque, New Mexico, couple is very enthusiastic about Artist Point at Wilderness Lodge:

Our meal at Artist Point was one of the best we've ever experienced. Our steaks were so good we're still talking about them months later.

A couple from Egg Harbor City, New Jersey, offers advice concerning Crockett's Tavern at Fort Wilderness Campground:

We absolutely love the nachos at Crockett's Tavern in Fort Wilderness. We always go there on our arrival day and talk about our plans for the week. On this most recent trip, although the line for the Trail's End restaurant was very long, we were immediately seated at the bar inside and ordered the nachos (the couple next to us was able to order the buffet dinner from the bar also). When we left, people who were waiting in line outside at our arrival were still waiting in line. If you are a small group of adults and there is room at the bar, go for it.

The Trail's End buffet, also at Fort Wilderness, has its advocates, such as this mom from Melbourne, Florida:

My family went to Trail's End for the buffet dinner one evening before the Chip and Dale's Campfire Sing-A-Long, and it was honestly one of the best meals we had the whole trip. If you like home-brewed tea, this is one of the few places in DW that serves it. We are already suckers for Southern cooking and hospitality, and this place didn't disappoint. Not to be missed are the banana pudding and apple cobbler.

Sanaa, in the Kidani Village section of Animal Kingdom Lodge, really impressed an Ellicott City, Maryland, family:

Sanaa is a beautiful restaurant with delicious and inexpensive (for Disney) food that you can't find anywhere else in Walt Disney World. We had a fabulous adults-only evening here, but I would bring children, too, for an early dinner overlooking the savanna.

A Texas mother of a teen ran into Disney cost cuts:

We had previously been to 1900 Park Fare for dinner and enjoyed it. This time we did not. There were way less food choices (they had sushi last year). It's way too expensive for bad food.

A mom from Columbus, Ohio, loved the character meal at Chef Mickey's:

While Akershus had the best food and the prettiest location for a character meal, our favorite character dinner was Chef Mickey's. The kids were comfortable there, and the characters really spent time with our family getting pictures, being silly, and having fun. It was a great experience for the whole family. Was the food above and beyond? No. But the look on my 4-year-old's face when she saw Mickey was amazing.

This reader tried several character meals, commenting:

The Crystal Palace (Magic Kingdom): a HUGE hit with my kids! We met Eeyore, Pooh, Tigger, and Piglet. The food was great too—lots of choices, and all done very well.

Chef Mickey's (Contemporary Resort): By far the best dining experience we had. And with it being Chef Mickey's, you of course get to meet Mickey, Minnie, Pluto, Goofy, and Donald. A must-do!

Hollywood & Vine (Hollywood Studios): We didn't care for this one at all—if it hadn't been for meeting the Disney Junior characters (Sofia the First, Jake, Handy Manny, and Doc McStuffins), we probably wouldn't have picked this one. The food was subpar, but the worst was the seating and organization of the characters: Most of the tables were booths, which made it very hard for children to get in and out to meet the characters and/or go to the buffet to get food. There was no rhyme or reason to which way the characters were going, and the handlers were nowhere to be found.

Evidently, Hollywood & Vine is also slow, as a Salinas, California, mom reports:

We were able to finish most of [our breakfasts] before the parks opened, but the Hollywood Studios breakfast took too long due to the characters not visiting people when they needed to do a little show. We ended up leaving without seeing all of the characters after 2 hours.

One mom in Columbia, South Carolina, was unimpressed with all of the character dinners:

WDW is becoming grossly overpriced. Major piece of advice: Unless your kids love character dining, skip ALL the sit-down restaurants. We ate at several, and NONE was worth what we paid.

A mother of three from Jamaica, New York, waited 2 hours and 40 minutes for a table at the Rainforest Cafe and still had a good time:

The Rainforest Cafe was an absolute delight. Our 6-year-old sat right next to a gorilla that ranted every few minutes, our 10-month-old loved the huge fish tanks, and they both loved the food. Our wait for a table was over 2 hours, but it was worth it.

But a Richardson, Texas, family had this to say:

It was wild, wet, and loud, and the service was the worst in WDW.

(Most negative reader comments concerning Rainforest Cafe pertain to the Disney Springs location, not the one at Animal Kingdom.)
We also get lots of comments about the dinosaur-themed T-REX restaurant at Disney Springs. A Dartmouth, Nova Scotia, mom writes:

Terrible experience! Overpriced, bad food, VERY LOUD—we couldn't even hear each other.

But what was a negative for the previous parent was a blessing for a Beaverton, Oregon, mother of two:

The best place for your kids to have a tantrum is T-REX. No one can hear them screaming!

And finally, Raglan Road at Disney Springs was a big hit with another mom of two, this one from Los Angeles:

Cannot say enough about this amazing Irish pub. The ambience, the food, and the entertainment were all absolutely top-notch. I feel like its presence could be overshadowed by other, more flashy restaurants at Disney Springs, but it was a HUGE highlight of our trip.

COUNTER-SERVICE *Mini-Profiles*

TO HELP YOU FIND palatable fast food that suits your tastes, we provide thumbnail profiles of the theme park counter-service restaurants, listed alphabetically by park. They're rated for quality, portion size, and value. (The average thumbs-up rating for all Disney counter-service restaurants is 89%, with a standard deviation of 6%.) Any restaurant with a rating below 80% should be approached with caution. Value ratings range from A to F, as follows:

A	Exceptional value; a real bargain
B	Good value
C	Fair value; you get exactly what you pay for
D	Somewhat overpriced
F	Extremely overpriced

THE MAGIC KINGDOM

Aloha Isle

QUALITY Excellent	VALUE B+	PORTION Medium	LOCATION Adventureland
READER-SURVEY RESPONSES 98% 👍	2% 👎	DISNEY DINING PLAN?	Yes

Selections Soft-serve; ice-cream floats; pineapple spears; juice.

Comments The pineapple Dole Whip soft-serve is a must-try. Formerly located across from the Swiss Family Treehouse, Aloha Isle is now next door to *Walt Disney's Enchanted Tiki Room.*

Be Our Guest Restaurant

QUALITY Excellent	VALUE B+	PORTION Medium	LOCATION Fantasyland
READER-SURVEY RESPONSES 90% 👍	10% 👎	DISNEY DINING PLAN?	Yes

Selections Breakfast: cured meats and cheeses, open-faced bacon-and-poached-egg sandwich with Brie, eggs Florentine in puff pastry, steel-cut oatmeal, scrambled egg whites with roasted tomatoes, signature croissant doughnuts. Lunch: tuna niçoise salad, croque monsieur, carved-turkey and roast-beef sandwiches, braised pork with mashed potatoes, veggie quiche, quinoa salad, potato leek or onion soup. Kids' meals include seared mahimahi, carved-turkey sandwich, slow-cooked pork, meat loaf, grilled cheese and tomato soup, or whole-grain macaroni with marinara.

Comments The best counter-service restaurant in the Magic Kingdom, and one of the best in all of Disney World. Our favorite breakfast selections are the open-faced bacon-and-egg sandwich with Brie and the fried doughnuts topped with banana-caramel sauce and chocolate ganache. For lunch we like the slow-cooked coq au vin–style pork with mushrooms, carrots, onions, and bacon. The croque monsieur sandwich is a grown-up version of grilled ham and cheese, with carved ham, Gruyère, and bécha-mel sauce and *pommes frites* on the side. If we're behaving, the generous seared-tuna niçoise salad hits the spot.

Note: Breakfast is served for just 2 hours (8–10 a.m.). Advance Reservations are available online at disneyworld.disney.go.com/dining. Disney has also rolled out advance lunch ordering via its My Disney Experience mobile app. See page 365 for a review of the sit-down-dinner service.

Casey's Corner

QUALITY Good	VALUE B	PORTION Medium	LOCATION Main Street, U.S.A.
READER-SURVEY RESPONSES 88% 👍	12% 👎	DISNEY DINING PLAN?	Yes

Selections Hot dogs, corn-dog nuggets, fries, and brownies.

Comments Best to stop at Casey's when it's extra-busy—that's the best guarantee of a fresh bun and hot fries. Len recommends the barbecue slaw dog; our dining insider favors the Polish sausage with grilled onions and stone-ground mustard, or the addictive corn-dog nuggets.

Columbia Harbour House

QUALITY Good	VALUE B	PORTION Medium	LOCATION Liberty Square
READER-SURVEY RESPONSES 93%👍 7%👎		DISNEY DINING PLAN? Yes	

Selections The kitchen, shared with Liberty Tree Tavern, has been recently upgraded. You can behave with the grilled salmon with couscous, tuna on multigrain bread, broccoli-peppercorn salad, or the Lighthouse Sandwich with hummus and broccoli slaw. Or you can indulge with fried shrimp or battered fish. The lobster roll falls somewhere in between. Other choices: fried chicken and fish nuggets; New England clam chowder; vegetarian chili; coleslaw; garden salad; and chocolate cake, seasonal cobbler, or strawberry yogurt for dessert. For kids: macaroni and cheese, PB&J sandwich, garden salad with chicken, chicken nuggets and fish, or tuna sandwich with grapes.

Comments No trans fats in the fried items, and the soups and sandwiches are a cut above most fast-food fare.

Cosmic Ray's Starlight Cafe

QUALITY Good	VALUE B	PORTION Large	LOCATION Tomorrowland
READER-SURVEY RESPONSES 82%👍 18%👎		DISNEY DINING PLAN? Yes	

Selections Rotisserie chicken and ribs; burgers (and veggie burgers); hot dogs; Greek salad; chicken, turkey, and vegetable sandwiches; chicken nuggets; bacon-Cheddar dog; barbecue pork sandwich; Angus bacon cheeseburger; chocolate or carrot cake. Kosher choices available upon request.

Comments The same menu items appear at all three ordering stations—a welcome change from years past. Generous toppings bar.

The Friar's Nook

QUALITY Good	VALUE B	PORTION Medium–large	LOCATION Fantasyland
READER-SURVEY RESPONSES 85%👍 15%👎		DISNEY DINING PLAN? Yes	

Selections Hot dogs, specialty macaroni and cheese (barbecue chicken, beef pot roast), veggies and chips with hummus, lemonade slush.

Comments We prefer the plain version of the mac and cheese, with crunchy panko topping. A little pricey, but filling.

Gaston's Tavern

QUALITY Good	VALUE C	PORTION Medium	LOCATION Fantasyland
READER-SURVEY RESPONSES 92%👍 8%👎		DISNEY DINING PLAN? Yes	

Selections Ham and cheese–stuffed pretzels, sliced fruit, mixed veggies with dip, hummus, croissants, and cinnamon rolls. Drinks include LeFou's Brew (frozen apple juice with toasted-marshmallow flavoring).

Comments The menu here changes more often than most Fantasyland locations, but the trend seems to be toward snacks, not meals.

Golden Oak Outpost *(open seasonally)*

QUALITY Good	VALUE B+	PORTION Medium–large	LOCATION Frontierland
READER-SURVEY RESPONSES 81%👍 19%👎		DISNEY DINING PLAN? Yes	

Selections Waffle fries, chicken breast nuggets, chocolate chip cookies.

Comments Served with apple slices or carrots.

The Lunching Pad

QUALITY Good	VALUE B–	PORTION Medium	LOCATION Tomorrowland
READER-SURVEY RESPONSES 82%👍 19%👎		DISNEY DINING PLAN? Yes	

Selections Ham and cheese–stuffed pretzel, frozen sodas, hot dogs.

Comments The frozen carbonated drinks—cola, cherry, blue raspberry—are a treat in summer's heat.

Pecos Bill Tall Tale Inn & Cafe

QUALITY Good   **VALUE** C   **PORTION** Medium-large   **LOCATION** Frontierland
READER-SURVEY RESPONSES 86% 👍 14% 👎   **DISNEY DINING PLAN?** Yes

Selections Steak or chicken fajita platter with rice and beans; spicy beef or chicken burrito; rice bowl with spicy beef, chicken, or veggies; salad with beef or chicken; chicken enchilada soup; churros, sopapillas, and yogurt for dessert.

Comments Bill has taken a page from Chipotle's Tex-Mex menu. The new items are an improvement over the old burgers, but they're more expensive than and not quite as good as Chipotle.

The Pinocchio Village Haus

QUALITY Fair   **VALUE** C   **PORTION** Medium   **LOCATION** Fantasyland
READER-SURVEY RESPONSES 81% 👍 19% 👎   **DISNEY DINING PLAN?** Yes

Selections Flatbread pizzas; Italian flatbread sub; chicken nuggets; fries; Caesar salad with chicken or shrimp; chicken Parmesan sandwiches; Caesar salad with shrimp; kids' meal of pizza, chicken nuggets, mac and cheese, or PB&J.

Comments An easy stop for families in Fantasyland, but it's usually crowded. Consider Columbia Harbour House (see previous page) instead; it's just a few minutes' walk away—and tastier.

Tomorrowland Terrace Restaurant *(open seasonally)*

QUALITY Fair   **VALUE** C   **PORTION** Medium-large   **LOCATION** Tomorrowland
READER-SURVEY RESPONSES 77% 👍 23% 👎   **DISNEY DINING PLAN?** Yes

Selections One-third-pound Angus bacon cheeseburger; chicken nuggets; chicken Caesar salad; lobster roll; chicken sandwich with bacon; citrus shrimp salad; chocolate cake, carrot cake, or yogurt for dessert.

Comments The lobster roll, served with homemade potato chips, is our favorite item on the menu. *The* place to grab an outdoor table and watch the Castle lit by fireworks.

Tortuga Tavern *(open seasonally)*

QUALITY Fair   **VALUE** B   **PORTION** Medium-large   **LOCATION** Adventureland
READER-SURVEY RESPONSES 81% 👍 19% 👎   **DISNEY DINING PLAN?** Yes

Selections Pulled pork, or grilled chicken sandwiches. Desserts are chocolate cake and gelato. Kids' meal is PB&J or mac & cheese.

Comments The smoked sausage is our favorite of the sandwiches.

DISNEY SPRINGS

Amorette's Patisserie

QUALITY Excellent   **VALUE** B   **PORTION** Small-medium   **LOCATION** Town Center
READER-SURVEY RESPONSES 93% 👍 7% 👎   **DISNEY DINING PLAN?** Yes

Selections Individually portioned and painstakingly decorated specialty cakes and pastries made by talented Disney pastry chefs; Disney themed, 10-plus-layer dome cakes; Champagnes.

Comments Perfect for those seeking Signature Dining–style "fancy" desserts, Amorette's impresses with seasonally themed specialties and mainstays like New York–style cheesecake topped with lemon curd, and opera cake dripping in coffee and chocolate. Don't miss out on the Petit Amorette's Cake, a smaller portion of their signature cake with 11 layers of red velvet and chocolate cakes, cherry and chocolate mousses, and raspberry jelly.

Blaze Pizza

QUALITY Excellent	VALUE A	PORTION Large	LOCATION Town Center
READER-SURVEY RESPONSES 96% 👍 4% 👎		DISNEY DINING PLAN? Yes	

Selections Specialty and build-your-own 11-inch pizzas with a selection of 20-plus fresh toppings (including vegan and gluten-free options); salads; *agua frescas.*

Comments Each fast-fired pizza is prepared in around 3 minutes after you select your toppings, Chipotle-style. Ignore the long line outside—it moves very quickly. Go light on the toppings for best results. If you can't get enough, splurge for the "high rise" dough, more like traditional pizza dough. Blaze and Via Napoli (Epcot) are the two best pizza places in the World, by a large margin.

B.B. Wolf's Sausage Co.

QUALITY Good-excellent	VALUE A-	PORTION Medium	LOCATION Marketplace
READER-SURVEY RESPONSES 85% 👍 15% 👎		DISNEY DINING PLAN? Yes	

Selections Sausage sandwiches (bratwurst and hot dogs much better than you can find in the parks); draft beers.

Comments Even with a small menu and limited outdoor seating, B.B. Wolf's is a worthy stop for a smaller meal or heavy snack on the go.

Cookes of Dublin

QUALITY Good-excellent	VALUE A-	PORTION Medium-large	LOCATION The Landing
READER-SURVEY RESPONSES 92% 👍 8% 👎		DISNEY DINING PLAN? Yes	

Selections Deep-fried meats and burgers, meat pies, fish and chips; specialty French-fry dips; salads.

Comments Wait times can be on the high side, but if you're looking for a quick-service version of Raglan Road's heavier Irish fare, this is the perfect stop. Even the pickiest eaters will like the excellent onion rings and chicken fingers.

D-Luxe Burger

QUALITY Good	VALUE C	PORTION Medium-large	LOCATION Town Center
READER-SURVEY RESPONSES 86% 👍 14% 👎		DISNEY DINING PLAN? Yes	

Selections Specialty burgers (The Southern, topped with a fried green tomato; veggie with tzatziki); hand-cut french fries with a variety of dipping sauces (curry ketchup and garlic ranch are zesty and unique); gelato shakes (spiked and nonalcoholic); floats.

Comments Burgers and fries take a little time, but the specialty options are worth the wait. Split a burger and regular fries unless you have a hearty appetite; otherwise, take advantage of any combos the restaurant offers for a better deal on sometimes-pricey meals.

The Daily Poutine

QUALITY Fair-good	VALUE B-	PORTION Small-medium	LOCATION Marketplace
READER-SURVEY RESPONSES 86% 👍 16% 👎		DISNEY DINING PLAN? Yes	

Selections Regional poutine variations—French fries with toppings such as traditional gravy and cheese curds, pulled pork and black beans, or Bolognese and mozzarella.

Comments As a heavy snack or light meal that's portable, these poutines aren't high quality, but they are filling and priced well for the portion size. Readers rate it among the best places in Disney Springs.

Earl of Sandwich

QUALITY Good	VALUE B-	PORTION Small-medium	LOCATION Marketplace
READER-SURVEY RESPONSES 93% 👍 7% 👎		DISNEY DINING PLAN? Yes	

Selections Hot sandwiches; salads; wraps; desserts (including brownie sandwiches with oodles of frosting in the middle).

Comments There's always a long line here, but it tends to move quickly. Sandwiches are served on fresh bread but aren't anything you can't find at your local deli or chain sub shop. Good stop for picky eaters or people on the go.

Frontera Cocina Walk-Up Window

QUALITY Good–excellent   **VALUE** B   **PORTION** Small–medium   **LOCATION** Town Center
READER-SURVEY RESPONSES 84% 👍 16% 👎 **DISNEY DINING PLAN?** No

Selections Tacos; guacamole and chips; margaritas.

Comments A small menu highlights a few of the full-service restaurant's best options in taco form. Split a guacamole order, and sample both taco varieties for a perfect (and economical) meal for two.

Morimoto Asia Street Food

QUALITY Good–excellent   **VALUE** C   **PORTION** Small–medium   **LOCATION** The Landing
READER-SURVEY RESPONSES 88% 👍 13% 👎 **DISNEY DINING PLAN?** No

Selections Steamed-bun tacos; *takoyaki* (octopus fritters); Morimoto's famous ribs; boba tea; specialty beers and cocktails.

Comments Offering smaller tastes of many of the full-service restaurant's options, Street Food is good for a snack but expensive if you try to make a full meal out of anything here. Sample the ribs and grab a drink if you want the best of Morimoto's flavors without splurging on a meal inside.

The Polite Pig

QUALITY Good–excellent   **VALUE** B-   **PORTION** Medium   **LOCATION** Town Center
READER-SURVEY RESPONSES Not enough to rate **DISNEY DINING PLAN?** Yes

Selections Southern barbecue staples (pulled pork, ribs, fried chicken); specialty veggie sides (barbecue cauliflower, smoked corn, whiskey-caramel Brussels sprouts); bourbon bar; cocktails and local beers on tap; homemade cakes and pies for dessert.

Comments A hybrid fast-casual/table-service restaurant, Polite Pig offers a bit more than your standard quick-service spot. Barbecue smoked on-site is the name of the game, but the side dishes are not to be missed. Skip the sandwiches and split a few entrées (the pulled pork and the ribs are our favorites) with sides; it's the best bang for your buck and offers a chance to try more of the outstanding appetizers (house-made giant pretzel, barbecue cracklins) and high-quality desserts.

The Smokehouse at House of Blues

QUALITY Fair   **VALUE** C   **PORTION** Small–medium   **LOCATION** West Side
READER-SURVEY RESPONSES 89% 👍 11% 👎 **DISNEY DINING PLAN?** Yes

Selections Barbecue standards (ribs, chicken, pulled pork); smokehouse nachos; bottled beers.

Comments Fast and convenient is the word here—nothing at Smokehouse is high-quality or better than your neighborhood barbecue restaurant, but there's rarely a line, and the food is served quickly.

YeSake

QUALITY Fair–good   **VALUE** B   **PORTION** Small–medium   **LOCATION** West Side
READER-SURVEY RESPONSES Not enough to rate **DISNEY DINING PLAN?** Yes

Selections Customizable wraps and rice/noodle bowls with Asian ingredients and world flavors; cocktails, sake, beer.

Comments On-the-go heavy snacks made to order with your choice of vegetables, proteins, and sauces. A better value than Morimoto Asia Street

Food for similar portions, though the flavors are not outside the box or anything special.

Wolfgang Puck Express

QUALITY Good **VALUE** C **PORTION** Medium-large **LOCATION** Marketplace, West Side
READER-SURVEY RESPONSES 91% 👍 9% 👎 **DISNEY DINING PLAN?** Yes

Selections Breakfast; pizza, sandwiches, pasta, salads; desserts; wine.

Comments Though expensive out-of-pocket, Wolfgang Puck Express offers a good bang for your buck for dining plan credit use. It's one of the only hot breakfast options in Disney Springs and is consistently busy at lunch and dinner for the simple but classic American menu.

EPCOT

L'Artisan des Glaces

QUALITY Excellent **VALUE** C **PORTION** Large **LOCATION** France
READER-SURVEY RESPONSES 96% 👍 5% 👎 **DISNEY DINING PLAN?** Yes

Selections Ice-cream flavors change but can include vanilla, chocolate, mint chocolate, pistachio, hazelnut, profiterole, caramel with salt, and coffee. Sorbet flavors can include strawberry, mango, melon, lemon, and pomegranate. Those over age 21 can enjoy two scoops in a martini glass, topped with Grand Marnier, rum, or whipped cream–flavored vodka.

Comments L'Artisan des Glaces serves some of the best ice cream at Walt Disney World, made on the spot. Our profiterole had chunks of chocolate-covered cookie pieces, and our white chocolate–coconut contained fresh shaved coconut. The chocolate macaron ice-cream sandwich is worth every calorie.

La Cantina de San Angel

QUALITY Good **VALUE** B **PORTION** Medium-large **LOCATION** Mexico
READER-SURVEY RESPONSES 89% 👍 11% 👎 **DISNEY DINING PLAN?** Yes

Selections Tacos with seasoned beef, chicken, or fried fish; fried cheese empanada; Mexican salad with cabbage, lettuce, black beans, and corn; grilled chicken with Mexican rice, corn, cascabel sauce, and pickled onions; guacamole and chips; churros and frozen fruit pops; *mucho* margaritas. For kids, empanadas or chicken tenders.

Comments A popular spot for a quick meal, with 150 covered outdoor seats. When it's extra busy, they open up the back of La Hacienda's dining room for air-conditioned seating.

Crêpes des Chefs de France

QUALITY Excellent **VALUE** B+ **PORTION** Medium **LOCATION** France
READER-SURVEY RESPONSES 90% 👍 10% 👎 **DISNEY DINING PLAN?** No

Selections Crepes filled with chocolate, strawberry preserves, ice cream, or sugar; ice cream; specialty beer (Kronenbourg 1664); espresso.

Comments These crepes rate high—even among French guests. Look for the kiosk at the front of the France Pavilion.

Electric Umbrella

QUALITY Fair **VALUE** B- **PORTION** Medium **LOCATION** Innovations East
READER-SURVEY RESPONSES 80% 👍 20% 👎 **DISNEY DINING PLAN?** Yes

Selections Angus bacon cheeseburger; French Dip burger; sausage-and-pepper sub; veggie flatbread; veggie naan-wich with tofu; "Energy" salad with chicken; chicken nuggets; child's plate with cheeseburger, mac and cheese, vegetarian flatbread, or chicken wrap; cheesecake, no-sugar-added brownie, chocolate cupcake.

Comments In a word, uninspired. Much better choices elsewhere.

Fife & Drum Tavern

QUALITY Fair	VALUE C	PORTION Large	LOCATION United States
READER-SURVEY RESPONSES 91%👍 10%👎		DISNEY DINING PLAN? Yes	

Selections Turkey legs, popcorn, soft-serve ice cream, frozen slushes, wine, beer, and alcoholic lemonade and root beer.

Comments Great place to grab a bite for a show at the America Gardens Theatre—and a deceptively sweet cocktail. Seating also available in and around the Liberty Inn, behind the Fife & Drum. Home of the Doofenslurper—frozen lemonade topped with passion-fruit sorbet foam.

Fountain View

QUALITY Fair	VALUE C	PORTION Small	LOCATION Future World Plaza
READER-SURVEY RESPONSES 90%👍 10%👎		DISNEY DINING PLAN? Yes	

Selections Coffee drinks and teas; breakfast sandwiches and pastries.
Comments Disney-themed Starbucks.

Les Halles Boulangerie–Pâtisserie

QUALITY Good	VALUE A	PORTION Small-medium	LOCATION France
READER-SURVEY RESPONSES 97%👍 3%👎		DISNEY DINING PLAN? Yes	

Selections The beautiful deli–bakery case is stocked with goodies such as tuna niçoise salad, sandwiches (ham and cheese; Brie, cranberry, and apple), imported-cheese plates, quiches, soups, and delicate pastries.

Comments Les Halles opens at 9 a.m.—2 hours before World Showcase—so it's a wonderful spot for a quiet breakfast (come in via International Gateway). Breads and pastries are made in the bakery above Chefs de France. For an authentic Parisian experience, grab a baguette and eat it while walking around France. Usually crowded starting at lunch and throughout the day.

Katsura Grill

QUALITY Good	VALUE B	PORTION Small-medium	LOCATION Japan
READER-SURVEY RESPONSES 84%👍 16%👎		DISNEY DINING PLAN? Yes	

Selections Basic sushi; udon noodle bowls (beef, curry, and tempura shrimp); chicken, beef, or salmon teriyaki; chicken curry; Japanese curry rice with beef; edamame; miso soup; green-tea cheesecake; green-tea, strawberry, and adzuki-bean ice cream; teriyaki chicken kids' plate; Kirin beer, sake, and plum wine.

Comments Possibly the loveliest spot to escape the Epcot crowd and have a quick meal outside.

Kringla Bakeri og Kafe

QUALITY Good-excellent	VALUE B	PORTION Small-medium	LOCATION Norway
READER-SURVEY RESPONSES 96%👍 4%👎		DISNEY DINING PLAN? Yes	

Selections Norwegian pastries and cakes; rice cream; sandwiches such as the Norwegian Club with lingonberry mayo; meatballs; vegetable torte; lattes and imported beers and wines.

Comments Try the ham-and-apple sandwich with Jarlsberg and Muenster. Ditto the rice cream (not a typo, by the way). Shaded outdoor seating.

Liberty Inn

QUALITY Fair	VALUE C	PORTION Medium	LOCATION United States
READER-SURVEY RESPONSES 86%👍 14%👎		DISNEY DINING PLAN? Yes	

Selections Angus bacon cheeseburger with Vermont Cheddar; Old Bay fried shrimp with rice; grilled-chicken BLT; grilled-chicken salad with cranberries, pecans, and apples; Southwest salad with chicken and black-bean salsa; hot dogs; grilled-veggie "chicken" salad with guacamole and corn salsa; chicken nuggets; child's plate of grilled chicken, fried shrimp, mac and cheese, or cheeseburger.

Comments They've freshened up the menu and revamped the kitchen. The surf and turf is a relative bargain at $14.99. Kosher items also available.

Lotus Blossom Cafe

QUALITY Fair	VALUE C	PORTION Medium	LOCATION China
READER-SURVEY RESPONSES 80%👍 20%👎		DISNEY DINING PLAN? Yes	

Selections Pork and vegetable egg rolls, pot stickers, Hong Kong–style vegetable curry (chicken optional), sesame chicken salad, shrimp fried rice with egg roll, orange chicken, beef-noodle soup bowl, caramel-ginger or lychee ice cream, plum wine, Tsingtao beer.

Comments The menu never changes, and the food remains mediocre.

Promenade Refreshments

QUALITY Fair	VALUE C	PORTION Large	LOCATION World Showcase Promenade
READER-SURVEY RESPONSES 83%👍 17%👎		DISNEY DINING PLAN? Yes	

Selections Chili dogs, hot dogs, kettle chips, beer.

Comments Seating is limited to nonexistent—be prepared to walk and chew.

Refreshment Cool Post

QUALITY Good	VALUE B–	PORTION Small	LOCATION Between Germany and China
READER-SURVEY RESPONSES 91%👍 10%👎		DISNEY DINING PLAN? Yes	

Selections Hot dogs, soft-serve ice cream in a cone, slushes, coffee or tea, draft Safari Amber beer ($9).

Comments Home of the Frozen Elephant—an adult slushy of frozen Coke and Amarula, a cream liqueur from South Africa.

Refreshment Port

QUALITY Good	VALUE B–	PORTION Medium	LOCATION Near Canada
READER-SURVEY RESPONSES 95%👍 5%👎		DISNEY DINING PLAN? Yes	

Selections Fried favorites—croissant doughnut, chicken nuggets, and fries—plus flavored coffees, hot chocolate, and soft-serve ice cream.

Comments Almost everyone in line is here for the trendy croissant doughnut.

Rose & Crown Pub

QUALITY Good	VALUE C+	PORTION Medium	LOCATION United Kingdom
READER-SURVEY RESPONSES 94%👍 6%👎		DISNEY DINING PLAN? No	

Selections Fish and chips; Scotch egg (hard-boiled, wrapped in sausage, and deep-fried); Indian-style chicken masala; bangers and chips; Guinness, Harp, and Bass beers, as well as other spirits.

Comments Most of the crowd is here to drink in an authentic British pub with ales, lagers, and stouts.

Sommerfest

QUALITY Fair	VALUE C	PORTION Medium	LOCATION Germany
READER-SURVEY RESPONSES 84%👍 16%👎		DISNEY DINING PLAN? Yes	

Selections Bratwurst, frankfurter with sauerkraut, *nudelgratin* (baked macaroni with Cheddar and Swiss), cold potato salad, apple strudel, Black Forest cake, German wine, beer, and schnapps shots.

Comments Indulge in a hearty sausage and a cold Pilsner in the courtyard. Skip the *nudelgratin*. Much of the food looks better than it tastes.

Sunshine Seasons

QUALITY Excellent	VALUE A	PORTION Medium	LOCATION The Land
READER-SURVEY RESPONSES 93%👍 7%👎		DISNEY DINING PLAN? Yes	

Selections Includes the following four areas: (1) wood-fired grills and rotisseries, with rotisserie half-chicken, slow-roasted pork chop, and wood-grilled fish with seasonal vegetables; (2) the sandwich shop with made-to-order sandwiches such as oak-grilled veggie flatbread, spicy fish tacos, and turkey and cheese on ciabatta; (3) the Asian shop, with noodle bowls and various stir-fry combinations; and (4) the soup-and-salad shop, with soups made daily and unusual creations such as the Power Salad (quinoa, almonds, and chicken). Breakfast includes the usual suspects: pastries, bacon, eggs, and the like.

Comments One of the best quick-service spots in Epcot. The breakfast panini (eggs, bacon, roast pork, and cheese) is an *Unofficial* favorite.

Tangierine Cafe

QUALITY Good	VALUE B	PORTION Medium	LOCATION Morocco
READER-SURVEY RESPONSES 93% 👍	7% 👎	DISNEY DINING PLAN? Yes	

Selections Chicken and lamb *shawarma;* hummus; tabbouleh; lentil salad; couscous salad; chicken, lamb, and falafel wraps; vegetarian hummus, tabbouleh, and lentils platter; child's burger or chicken tenders; Moroccan wine and beer; baklava.

Comments One of Epcot's top-rated restaurants, it's rarely busy, and the food is better than the blatantly touristy Restaurant Marrakesh inside. Grab a seat outdoors and people-watch along World Showcase Promenade.

Yorkshire County Fish Shop

QUALITY Good	VALUE B+	PORTION Medium	LOCATION United Kingdom
READER-SURVEY RESPONSES 94% 👍	6% 👎	DISNEY DINING PLAN? Yes	

Selections Fish and chips, Victoria sponge cake, Bass Pale Ale draft, and Harp Lager.

Comments There's usually a line for the crisp, hot fish and chips at this convenient fast-food window attached to the Rose & Crown Pub (see full-service profile on page 395). Outdoor seating overlooks the lagoon.

DISNEY'S ANIMAL KINGDOM

Creature Comforts

QUALITY Fair	VALUE C	PORTION Small	LOCATION Discovery Island near Africa
READER-SURVEY RESPONSES 96% 👍	4% 👎	DISNEY DINING PLAN? Yes	

Selections Coffee drinks and teas; breakfast sandwiches and pastries.

Comments Disney-themed Starbucks. The fare is largely the same as you'd find at any other, plus the occasional Animal Kingdom–themed treat.

Flame Tree Barbecue

QUALITY Excellent	VALUE B-	PORTION Large	LOCATION Discovery Island
READER-SURVEY RESPONSES 95% 👍	5% 👎	DISNEY DINING PLAN? Yes	

Selections St. Louis–style ribs; smoked half-chicken; pulled-pork sandwich; Jamaican jerk chicken salad; rib, chicken, and pork sampler; watermelon salad; fries with pulled pork and cheese; smoked-turkey sandwich; child's plate of baked chicken drumstick, chicken sandwich, hot dog, or PB&J sandwich; French fries and onion rings; Key lime or chocolate mousse; Safari Amber beer, Bud Light, Mandarin orange vodka lemonade, and wine.

Comments Expanded outdoor seating provides more shaded space overlooking the water. One of our favorites for lunch.

Harambe Market

QUALITY Good	VALUE B	PORTION Large	LOCATION Africa
READER-SURVEY RESPONSES 89% 👍	11% 👎	DISNEY DINING PLAN? Yes	

Selections Spice-rubbed Karubi ribs, beef and pork or tikka masala chicken sausages, grilled-chicken skewers, gyro flatbread, or grilled-vegetable stack, each served with a side of green papaya–carrot slaw and a black-eyed pea, corn, and tomato salad. Beer and South African wines are also available. Kids' menu includes child-size versions of the adult selections or a snack pack with yogurt, apple slices, carrot sticks, and crackers.

Comments Four separate stalls with Disney-created backstories. Plenty of shaded seating. Disney Imagineers modeled the marketplace setting after a typical real-life market in an African nation during the 1960s colonial era. We like the spice-rubbed Karubi ribs and chicken skewers.

Kusafiri Coffee Shop and Bakery

QUALITY	Good	VALUE	B	PORTION	Medium	LOCATION	Africa
READER-SURVEY RESPONSES		88% 👍	13% 👎	DISNEY DINING PLAN?	Yes		

Selections Cupcakes, turnovers, Danish, muffins, croissants, cookies, brownies, cake, fruit cups, yogurt, coffee, cocoa, and juice. Breakfast wrap (egg, sausage, spinach, and goat cheese) served until 10:30 a.m.

Comments The cinnamon roll is a favorite. Kosher items are available.

Pizzafari

QUALITY	Fair	VALUE	B	PORTION	Medium	LOCATION	Discovery Island
READER-SURVEY RESPONSES		80% 👍	20% 👎	DISNEY DINING PLAN?	Yes		

Selections Shrimp flatbread; cheese, pepperoni, sausage, or veggie personal pizza; meatball sub; Romaine salad with chicken or shrimp. For kids, mac and cheese, pasta with turkey marinara, cheese pizza, or PB&J. Chocolate mousse or tiramisu for dessert. Beer and wine available.

Comments The pizza is unimpressive but popular.

Restaurantosaurus

QUALITY	Good	VALUE	B+	PORTION	Medium–large	LOCATION	DinoLand U.S.A.
READER-SURVEY RESPONSES		87% 👍	13% 👎	DISNEY DINING PLAN?	Yes		

Selections Angus bacon cheeseburger; chicken nuggets; black-bean burger; chili-cheese hot dog; roasted chicken salad; grilled-chicken sandwich; kids' turkey wrap, corn-dog nuggets, cheeseburger, or PB&J.

Comments Good burger-toppings bar. Plenty of seating. Search for the pun-filled signs. May serve breakfast during peak seasons.

Royal Anandapur Tea Company

QUALITY	Good	VALUE	B	PORTION	Medium	LOCATION	Asia
READER-SURVEY RESPONSES		96% 👍	5% 👎	DISNEY DINING PLAN?	No		

Selections Wide variety of hot and iced teas and coffees (fantastic frozen chai); lattes, espresso, and cappuccino; pastries.

Comments Halfway between Expedition Everest and Kali River Rapids, this is the kind of small, eclectic, Animal Kingdom–specific food stand that you wish other parks had. Around 10 loose teas from Asia and Africa can be ordered hot or iced.

Satu'li Canteen

QUALITY	Too new to rate	VALUE	Too new to rate	LOCATION	Pandora
READER-SURVEY RESPONSES		95% 👍	5% 👎	DISNEY DINING PLAN?	Yes

Selections The signature item is the customizable "bowl." Start with a base of quinoa and vegetable salad, red and sweet potato hash, whole grain and rice, or romaine and kale salad. Then add wood-grilled chicken, slow-roasted beef, panko-breaded mahimahi, or chili-spiced fried tofu, and finish with a choice of dressings. The menu also offers steamed "pods"—*bao* buns with either cheeseburger or vegetable-curry filling, served with root-vegetable chips and crunchy vegetable slaw. The children's menu includes items for both adventurous and traditional palates.

Comments Located in the new Pandora section of Animal Kingdom, Satu'li Canteen is the first WDW eatery to offer Mobile Order, a new system that allows guests to order and pay for meals with the My Disney Experience app, bypassing lines at the restaurant itself.

Thirsty River Bar & Trek Snacks

QUALITY	Good	VALUE	B	PORTION	Medium	LOCATION	Asia
READER-SURVEY RESPONSES		91%👍	9%👎	DISNEY DINING PLAN?	Yes		

Selections Smoked-turkey sandwich; roasted-pork *bánh mì* sandwich with cilantro and Sriracha sauce; Thai papaya salad with shrimp, peanuts, and chiles; Asian noodle salad; hummus; fresh fruit and vegetables; ice-cream novelties; chips and other snacks. Full bar serving cocktails and a few beers and wines.

Comments Thirsty River has a couple of interesting sandwiches and many snacks and drinks. Try the Himalayan Ghost, a scary-smooth mix of vodka, guava juice, and lemonade.

Yak & Yeti Local Food Cafes

QUALITY	Fair	VALUE	B	PORTION	Large	LOCATION	Asia
READER-SURVEY RESPONSES		91%👍	9%👎	DISNEY DINING PLAN?	Yes		

Selections Crispy honey chicken with steamed rice, Korean stir-fry barbecue chicken, ginger chicken salad, Asian chicken sandwich, roasted-vegetable couscous wrap, teriyaki beef bowl, egg rolls, chicken fried rice. Kids' menu: chicken tenders, PB&J, or cheeseburger with fresh fruit.

Comments For filling up when you're in a hurry. A small but eclectic mix.

DISNEY'S HOLLYWOOD STUDIOS

ABC Commissary

QUALITY	Fair	VALUE	B-	PORTION	Medium-large	LOCATION	Commissary Lane
READER-SURVEY RESPONSES		77%👍	24%👎	DISNEY DINING PLAN?	Yes		

Selections Chimichurri steak; Mediterranean salad (chicken optional); chicken club sandwich; salmon Southwest burger; child's chicken nuggets, cheeseburger, or turkey sandwich; chocolate mousse; cupcakes; no-sugar-added strawberry parfait; wine and beer.

Comments You're bound to find something to like on this diverse menu, housed in a model of New York's Rockefeller Center. Indoors and centrally located but hard to find. Offers kosher meals.

Backlot Express

QUALITY	Fair	VALUE	C	PORTION	Medium-large	LOCATION	Echo Lake
READER-SURVEY RESPONSES		85%👍	15%👎	DISNEY DINING PLAN?	Yes		

Selections One-third-pound Angus bacon cheeseburger, with or without barbecue brisket on top; chicken nuggets; chicken and waffles; chicken salad; Parmesan and garlic fries; chili-cheese dog. Star Wars–themed desserts include Blue Milk Panna Cotta and Tie Fighter with Caramel Corn.

Comments Fun props—some actually used in movies—decorate this spacious eatery. Many menu items now have a Star Wars theme.

Catalina Eddie's

QUALITY	Fair	VALUE	B	PORTION	Medium-large	LOCATION	Sunset Boulevard
READER-SURVEY RESPONSES		84%👍	16%👎	DISNEY DINING PLAN?	Yes		

Selections Cheese and pepperoni pizzas, chicken pesto flatbread, Caesar salad, banana parfait, and vanilla cake with chocolate custard.

Comments Better rated now than in the last edition, when it was dead last among DHS counter-service joints, but still nothing to write home about.

Fairfax Fare

QUALITY Fair	VALUE B	PORTION Medium-large	LOCATION Sunset Boulevard
READER-SURVEY RESPONSES 86% 👍 14% 👎		DISNEY DINING PLAN? Yes	

Selections Barbecue chicken and ribs; pulled-pork sandwiches; "designer" hot dogs (barbecue pork and coleslaw, macaroni and cheese with truffle oil); chili dogs; loaded baked potatoes; Fairfax Salad with barbecue pork, bacon, and corn-tomato salsa; banana parfait; vanilla cake.

Comments If you're looking for meat, this is the place. Ask to have your bun warmed before your dog is served. Also open for breakfast.

Min and Bill's Dockside Diner

QUALITY Fair	VALUE C	PORTION Small-medium	LOCATION Echo Lake
READER-SURVEY RESPONSES 76% 👍 24% 👎		DISNEY DINING PLAN? Yes	

Selections Slow-roasted beef with mashed potatoes, corn, and carrots; chili-cheese hot dog with chips; macaroni and cheese with pulled pork; sushi veggie roll with edamame salad; chocolate cake for dessert. Kids' meal is a turkey sandwich with carrots and cookie.

Comments Stir the toppings into the warm mac and cheese for a hearty meal in a bowl. Limited seating at nearby picnic tables.

PizzeRizzo

QUALITY Poor	VALUE D	PORTION Large	LOCATION Muppet Courtyard
READER-SURVEY RESPONSES 81% 👍 19% 👎		DISNEY DINING PLAN? Yes	

Selections Personal pizzas, meatball subs, and salads, none of it good. The too-doughy pizza's one accomplishment is that it manages to be burnt on top and underdone below. The salads are how vegetables express ennui.

Comments The decor upstairs is better than the food downstairs. There, Rizzo's Deluxe Supreme Banquet Hall features an ongoing wedding reception, with a disco-heavy soundtrack.

Rosie's All-American Cafe

QUALITY Fair	VALUE C	PORTION Medium	LOCATION Sunset Boulevard
READER-SURVEY RESPONSES 82% 👍 18% 👎		DISNEY DINING PLAN? Yes	

Selections Cheeseburgers; fried green tomato sandwich on ciabatta bread; chicken nuggets; soups; child's turkey sandwich or chicken nuggets with carrot sticks or applesauce; strawberry shortcake, or vanilla cake with chocolate custard.

Comments A quick stop on the way to Tower of Terror or Rock 'n' Roller Coaster and close enough to eat with accompanying screams.

Trolley Car Cafe

QUALITY Fair	VALUE C	PORTION Small	LOCATION Sunset Boulevard
READER-SURVEY RESPONSES 94% 👍 6% 👎		DISNEY DINING PLAN? Yes	

Selections Coffee drinks and teas; breakfast sandwiches and pastries.

Comments Disney-themed Starbucks. The building is the real attraction: The pink-stucco Spanish Colonial exterior calls to mind old Hollywood; the industrial-style interior evokes a trolley-car switching station.

FULL-SERVICE RESTAURANTS
In Depth

THE PROFILES IN THIS SECTION, listed alphabetically, allow you to quickly check the cuisine, location, star rating, cost range, quality rating, and value rating of every full-service restaurant at WDW.

OVERALL RATING Ranging from one to five stars, this rating encompasses the entire dining experience: service, ambience, and food quality.

COST RANGE This tells you about how much you can expect to spend on a full-service entrée (appetizers, sides, soups/salads, desserts, drinks, and tips aren't included). Costs are categorized as **inexpensive** (less than $13), **moderate** ($13–$23), or **expensive** ($24 and up).

QUALITY RATING Food quality is rated from one to five stars, five being the best. Criteria are taste, freshness of ingredients, preparation, presentation, and creativity of food served. Price is not a consideration.

VALUE RATING If, on the other hand, you're looking for both quality *and* value, then you should check this rating, also expressed as stars.

PAYMENT All Disney restaurants take American Express, Carte Blanche, Diners Club, Discover, Japan Credit Bureau, MasterCard, and Visa.

NEW AND UPCOMING

The Edison *(opens late 2017)*
Town Center, Disney Springs; ☎ 407-939-3463

SUMMARY AND COMMENTS Themed to evoke a 1920s electric company, The Edison will feature classic American food and craft cocktails along with live music, cabaret performances, contortionists, palm readers, and DJs. Expect a strict dress code banning athletic wear and requiring collared shirts and dress shoes for men.

Jaleo *(opens 2018)*
West Side, Disney Springs; ☎ 407-939-3463

SUMMARY AND COMMENTS Replacing Wolfgang Puck Grand Cafe, Jaleo—chef José Andrés's seventh restaurant by this name—will feature such Spanish classics as tapas and paella.

Shutters at Old Port Royale *(reopens late 2017)*
Caribbean Beach Resort; ☎ 407-939-3463

SUMMARY AND COMMENTS A Disney resort mainstay, this steak-and-seafood spot closed in spring 2017 as part of the renovations at Caribbean Beach. Whether the menu changes with the new look remains to be seen.

Wine Bar George *(opens 2018)*
The Landing, Disney Springs; ☎ 407-939-3463

SUMMARY AND COMMENTS Owned by Master Sommelier George Miliotes—one of only 230 people in the world who have earned this designation—Wine Bar George will serve small plates and showcase wines from big names and noteworthy upstarts.

Wolfgang Puck Bar & Grill *(opens 2018)*
Town Center, Disney Springs; ☎ 407-939-3463

SUMMARY AND COMMENTS A full-fledged counterpart to Puck's L.A. and Las Vegas Bar & Grill locations, this one will serve familiar dishes including his signature pizzas. We hope the quality will be a step up from that of his disappointing Grand Cafe, which closed in 2017 to make way for Jaleo (see above) on the West Side.

Continued on page 363

WALT DISNEY WORLD Restaurants by Cuisine

CUISINE	LOCATION	OVERALL RATING	COST	QUALITY RATING	VALUE RATING
AFRICAN					
JIKO—THE COOKING PLACE	Animal Kingdom Lodge-Jambo House	★★★★½	Exp	★★★★½	★★★½
BOMA—FLAVORS OF AFRICA	Animal Kingdom Lodge-Jambo House	★★★★½	Exp	★★★★	★★★★½
SANAA	Animal Kingdom Villas-Kidani Village	★★★★	Exp	★★★★	★★★★
JUNGLE NAVIGATION CO. LTD. SKIPPER CANTEEN	Magic Kingdom	★★★½	Mod	★★★	★★★
TUSKER HOUSE RESTAURANT	Animal Kingdom	★★★	Mod	★★★	★★★
AMERICAN					
CALIFORNIA GRILL	Contemporary	★★★★★	Exp	★★★★★	★★★
BE OUR GUEST RESTAURANT	Magic Kingdom	★★★★	Exp	★★★★	★★★★
THE HOLLYWOOD BROWN DERBY	DHS	★★★★	Exp	★★★★	★★★
TIFFINS	Animal Kingdom	★★★★	Exp	★★★★	★★★
PADDLEFISH	Disney Springs	★★★★	Exp	★★★½	★★½
BOATWRIGHT'S DINING HALL	Port Orleans	★★★★	Mod	★★★	★★
ARTIST POINT	Wilderness Lodge	★★★½	Exp	★★★★	★★★
CAPE MAY CAFE	Beach Club	★★★½	Mod	★★★½	★★★★
CHEF ART SMITH'S HOMECOMIN'	Disney Springs	★★★½	Mod	★★★½	★★★½
LIBERTY TREE TAVERN	Magic Kingdom	★★★½	Mod	★★★	★★★
WHISPERING CANYON CAFE	Wilderness Lodge	★★★	Mod	★★★½	★★★★
CAPTAIN'S GRILLE	Yacht Club	★★★	Mod	★★★½	★★★
THE CRYSTAL PALACE	Magic Kingdom	★★★	Mod	★★★½	★★★
GEYSER POINT BAR & GRILL	Wilderness Lodge	★★★	Mod	★★★½	★★★
HOUSE OF BLUES RESTAURANT & BAR	Disney Springs	★★★	Mod	★★★½	★★★
50'S PRIME TIME CAFE	DHS	★★★	Mod	★★★	★★★
TUSKER HOUSE RESTAURANT	Animal Kingdom	★★★	Mod	★★★	★★★
CINDERELLA'S ROYAL TABLE	Magic Kingdom	★★★	Exp	★★★	★★
OLIVIA'S CAFE	Old Key West	★★★	Mod	★★★	★★
T-REX	Disney Springs	★★★	Mod	★★	★★
THE WAVE . . . OF AMERICAN FLAVORS	Contemporary	★★★	Mod	★★	★★
CHEF MICKEY'S	Contemporary	★★½	Exp	★★★	★★★
ESPN CLUB	BoardWalk	★★½	Mod	★★★	★★★
HOLLYWOOD & VINE	DHS	★★½	Mod	★★★	★★★
1900 PARK FARE	Grand Floridian	★★½	Mod	★★★	★★★
GRAND FLORIDIAN CAFE	Grand Floridian	★★½	Mod	★★★	★★
BEACHES & CREAM SODA SHOP	Beach Club	★★½	Inexp	★★½	★★½
FRESH MEDITERRANEAN MARKET	Dolphin	★★½	Mod	★★½	★★

AMERICAN *(continued)*					
SPLITSVILLE	Disney Springs	★★½	Mod	★★½	★★
RAINFOREST CAFE	Animal Kingdom and Disney Springs	★★½	Mod	★★	★★
GARDEN GROVE	Swan	★★	Mod	★★★	★★
TURF CLUB BAR & GRILL	Saratoga Springs	★★	Mod	★★★	★★
LAS VENTANAS	Coronado Springs	★★	Mod	★★½	★★
SCI-FI DINE-IN THEATER RESTAURANT	DHS	★★	Mod	★★½	★★
GARDEN GRILL RESTAURANT	Epcot	★★	Exp	★★	★★★
BIG RIVER GRILLE & BREWING WORKS	BoardWalk	★★	Mod	★★	★★
THE FOUNTAIN	Dolphin	★★	Mod	★★	★★
THE PLAZA RESTAURANT	Magic Kingdom	★★	Mod	★★	★★
TRAIL'S END RESTAURANT	Fort Wilderness Resort	★★	Mod	★★	★★
PLANET HOLLYWOOD OBSERVATORY	Disney Springs	★½	Mod	★★	★★
MAYA GRILL	Coronado Springs	★	Exp	★	★
BUFFET					
BOMA—FLAVORS OF AFRICA	Animal Kingdom Lodge-Jambo House	★★★★½	Exp	★★★★	★★★★½
CAPE MAY CAFE	Beach Club	★★★½	Mod	★★★½	★★★★
THE CRYSTAL PALACE	Magic Kingdom	★★★	Mod	★★★½	★★★
TUSKER HOUSE RESTAURANT	Animal Kingdom	★★★	Mod	★★★	★★★
THE WAVE . . . OF AMERICAN FLAVORS	Contemporary	★★★	Mod	★★	★★
CHEF MICKEY'S	Contemporary	★★½	Exp	★★★	★★★
HOLLYWOOD & VINE	DHS	★★½	Mod	★★★	★★★
1900 PARK FARE	Grand Floridian	★★½	Mod	★★★	★★★
GARDEN GROVE	Swan	★★	Mod	★★★	★★
AKERSHUS ROYAL BANQUET HALL	Epcot	★★	Exp	★★	★★★★
BIERGARTEN RESTAURANT	Epcot	★★	Exp	★★	★★★★
TRAIL'S END RESTAURANT	Fort Wilderness Resort	★★	Mod	★★	★★
CAJUN					
BOATWRIGHT'S DINING HALL	Port Orleans	★★★★	Mod	★★★	★★
CHINESE					
NINE DRAGONS RESTAURANT	Epcot	★★	Mod	★★	★★
CUBAN					
BONGOS CUBAN CAFE	Disney Springs	★★	Mod	★★	★★
COCKTAILS AND BAR BITES					
JOCK LINDSEY'S HANGAR BAR	Disney Springs	★★	Mod	★★½	★★½
ENGLISH					
ROSE & CROWN DINING ROOM	Epcot	★★★	Mod	★★★½	★★

WDW Restaurants by Cuisine *(continued)*

CUISINE	LOCATION	OVERALL RATING	COST	QUALITY RATING	VALUE RATING
FRENCH					
MONSIEUR PAUL	Epcot	★★★★	Exp	★★★★½	★★★
BE OUR GUEST RESTAURANT	Magic Kingdom	★★★★	Exp	★★★★	★★★★
LES CHEFS DE FRANCE	Epcot	★★★	Exp	★★★	★★★
GERMAN					
BIERGARTEN	Epcot	★★	Exp	★★	★★★★
GLOBAL					
PARADISO 37	Disney Springs	★★½	Inexp	★★★	★★★
GOURMET					
VICTORIA & ALBERT'S	Grand Floridian	★★★★★	Exp	★★★★★★	★★★★
INDIAN/AFRICAN					
SANAA	Animal Kingdom Villas-Kidani Village	★★★★	Exp	★★★★	★★★★
IRISH					
RAGLAN ROAD	Disney Springs	★★★★	Mod	★★★½	★★★
ITALIAN					
TUTTO ITALIA RISTORANTE	Epcot	★★★★	Exp	★★★★	★★★
VIA NAPOLI	Epcot	★★★★	Mod	★★★½	★★★
TUTTO GUSTO WINE CELLAR	Epcot	★★★½	Inexp	★★★★	★★
TRATTORIA AL FORNO	BoardWalk	★★★½	Mod	★★★½	★★
IL MULINO NEW YORK TRATTORIA	Swan	★★★	Exp	★★★	★★
MAMA MELROSE'S	DHS	★★½	Mod	★★★	★★
TONY'S TOWN SQUARE RESTAURANT	Magic Kingdom	★★½	Mod	★★★	★★
JAPANESE/SUSHI					
KIMONOS	Swan	★★★★	Mod	★★★★½	★★★
TEPPAN EDO	Epcot	★★★½	Exp	★★★★	★★★
MORIMOTO ASIA	Disney Springs	★★★½	Exp	★★★½	★★★★
TOKYO DINING	Epcot	★★★	Mod	★★★★	★★★
MEDITERRANEAN					
CÍTRICOS	Grand Floridian	★★★½	Exp	★★★★½	★★★
FRESH MEDITERRANEAN MARKET	Dolphin	★★½	Mod	★★½	★★
MEXICAN					
FRONTERA COCINA	Disney Springs	★★★½	Mod	★★★½	★★★
LA HACIENDA DE SAN ANGEL	Epcot	★★★	Exp	★★★½	★★½
SAN ANGEL INN RESTAURANTE	Epcot	★★★	Exp	★★★	★★
MAYA GRILL	Coronado Springs	★	Exp	★	★
MOROCCAN					
SPICE ROAD TABLE	Epcot	★★★★	Mod	★★★★	★★★

MOROCCAN *(continued)*					
RESTAURANT MARRAKESH	Epcot	★★★	Mod	★★½	★★
NORWEGIAN					
AKERSHUS ROYAL BANQUET HALL	Epcot	★★	Exp	★★	★★★★
PAN-ASIAN/POLYNESIAN					
TIFFINS	Animal Kingdom	★★★★	Exp	★★★★	★★★
MORIMOTO ASIA	Disney Springs	★★★½	Exp	★★★½	★★★★
'OHANA	Polynesian Village	★★★	Mod	★★★½	★★★
KONA CAFE	Polynesian Village	★★★	Mod	★★★	★★★★
TRADER SAM'S GROG GROTTO	Polynesian Village	★★★	Mod	★★★	★★★
YAK & YETI RESTAURANT	Animal Kingdom	★★	Exp	★★½	★★
SEAFOOD					
NARCOOSSEE'S	Grand Floridian	★★★★½	Exp	★★★½	★★
FLYING FISH	BoardWalk	★★★★	Exp	★★★★	★★★
PADDLEFISH	Disney Springs	★★★★	Exp	★★★½	★★½
ARTIST POINT	Wilderness Lodge	★★★½	Exp	★★★★	★★★
TODD ENGLISH'S BLUEZOO	Dolphin	★★★	Exp	★★★★	★★
THE BOATHOUSE	Disney Springs	★★★	Exp	★★★	★★½
CORAL REEF RESTAURANT	Epcot	★★½	Exp	★★	★★
STEAK					
SHULA'S STEAK HOUSE	Dolphin	★★★★	Exp	★★★★	★★
STK ORLANDO	Disney Springs	★★★½	Exp	★★★★	★★½
LE CELLIER STEAKHOUSE	Epcot	★★★½	Exp	★★★½	★★★
YACHTSMAN STEAKHOUSE	Yacht Club	★★★	Exp	★★★½	★★

Continued from page 359

FULL-SERVICE RESTAURANT PROFILES
Akershus Royal Banquet Hall ★★

NORWEGIAN/BUFFET	EXPENSIVE	QUALITY ★★	VALUE ★★★★
READER-SURVEY RESPONSES 88%👍 12%👎		DISNEY DINING PLAN? Yes	

Norway, World Showcase, Epcot; ☎ 407-939-3463

Reservations Required for breakfast and recommended for lunch and dinner. A credit card is required to reserve breakfast and lunch. **Dining Plan credits** 1 per person, per meal. **When to go** Anytime. **Cost range** Breakfast $50 (child $28), lunch $49 (child $30), dinner $58 (child $35). **Service** ★★★★. **Friendliness** ★★★★. **Parking** Epcot lot. **Bar** Full service. **Wine selection** Good. **Dress** Casual. **Disabled access** Yes. **Customers** Theme park guests. **Character breakfast** Daily, 8–11:10 a.m. **Character lunch** Daily, 11:55 a.m.–3:30 p.m. **Character dinner** Daily, 4:55–8:35 p.m.

SETTING AND ATMOSPHERE The inside of Akershus looks like every child's vision of a fairy-tale castle: high ceilings, stone archways, sumptuous purple carpets, regal banners flying. What's mildly surprising, given the attention to authenticity elsewhere in Epcot, is that it doesn't look more like the real Akershus Castle in Oslo, which has plain wooden floors; flat, simple ceilings; and painted brick arches. Disney's version is almost as ungodly expensive as the real thing, though, and you're apt to hear *norsk* spoken by your servers. Close enough for us. The saving grace is that most visitors don't realize it is in fact a restaurant and walk by.

HOUSE SPECIALTIES Breakfast: smorgasbord of smoked salmon, herring, mackerel, and goat cheese. Lunch and dinner: *koldtbord* ("cold board" of meats, cheeses, seafood, and salads), roasted chicken with potatoes, pan-seared salmon, house-made goat cheese ravioli, and *kjottkake* (beef-and-pork dumplings served with mashed potatoes, vegetables, and lingonberry sauce). For kids: macaroni in cheese sauce, pasta with grilled chicken, cheese pizza, salmon with rice, and meatballs with mashed potatoes.

OTHER RECOMMENDATIONS Carlsberg beer on tap, wine, Aquavit cocktails.

SUMMARY AND COMMENTS Akershus has never been on our "you've just gotta try this" list, but if you have kids who love princesses, they won't be disappointed. There was a time when the buffet was noteworthy, but these days all the attention in the kitchen goes to feeding families fast. As for the prices? You're paying for that princess face time.

Artist Point ★★★½

AMERICAN/SEAFOOD	EXPENSIVE	QUALITY ★★★★	VALUE ★★★
READER-SURVEY RESPONSES 90%👍	10%👎	DISNEY DINING PLAN? Yes	

Wilderness Lodge & Villas; ☎ 407-939-3463

Reservations Required. **Dining Plan credits** 2 per person, per meal. **When to go** Anytime. **Cost range** $35–$60 (child $9–$16). **Service** ★★★★★. **Friendliness** ★★★★★. **Parking** Hotel lot. **Bar** Full service. **Wine selection** All wines from the Pacific Northwest. **Dress** Dressy casual. **Disabled access** Yes. **Customers** Hotel guests, locals. **Hours** Daily, 5:30–9:30 p.m.

SETTING AND ATMOSPHERE A beautiful room in a stunning resort. Understated Arts and Crafts decor, taking inspiration from the Old Faithful Inn at Yellowstone National Park: massive landscape paintings, heavy wooden tables, cast-iron chandeliers. Get a table by the window, and you might see the geyser near the waterfront erupting every hour.

HOUSE SPECIALTIES The smoky portobello soup, a worthy starter, never leaves the menu. Ditto the cedar-plank salmon and kettle-steamed mussels. Time your visit for the May–June Copper River salmon season for a true delight.

OTHER RECOMMENDATIONS Artisanal cheese and charcuterie assortments, grilled buffalo strip steak, roasted Berkshire pork loin, diver scallops. For kids, baked salmon, grilled chicken, and pasta.

SUMMARY AND COMMENTS Don't be put off by the cavernous dining room—the food and friendly service warm it up. You can order from the Artist Point menu at the Territory Lounge next door, if you can't get in at Artist Point. If you have time, park at Fort Wilderness and take the boat to the lodge—the approach is gorgeous.

Beaches & Cream Soda Shop ★★½

AMERICAN	INEXPENSIVE	QUALITY ★★½	VALUE ★★½
READER-SURVEY RESPONSES 95%👍	5%👎	DISNEY DINING PLAN? Yes	

Beach Club Resort; ☎ 407-934-8000

Reservations Recommended. **Dining Plan credits** 1 per person, per meal. **When to go** Anytime. **Cost range** $9–$16. **Service** ★★★. **Friendliness** ★★★★. **Parking** Hotel lot. **Bar** Beer only. **Wine selection** None. **Dress** Casual. **Disabled access** Yes. **Customers** Resort guests. **Hours** Daily, 11 a.m.–11 p.m.

SETTING AND ATMOSPHERE Casual eats and retro soda-fountain decor. Guests in bathing suits and flip-flops queue up for the burgers, sandwiches (corned beef Reuben, seafood salad), and piles of hot fries.

HOUSE SPECIALTIES Burgers and fries; giant hot dogs; hand-scooped ice cream, including the gargantuan $29 Kitchen Sink dessert, with five flavors of ice cream slathered with toppings.

OTHER RECOMMENDATIONS Chef salad, roasted turkey on brioche, vegetarian falafel, root beer float.

SUMMARY AND COMMENTS Beaches & Cream exists mainly to give guests an excuse to eat all the things they're not supposed to. But hey, it's vacation—indulge! Seating is scarce during peak hours.

Be Our Guest Restaurant ★★★★

FRENCH/AMERICAN	EXPENSIVE	QUALITY ★★★★	VALUE ★★★★
READER-SURVEY RESPONSES	90%👍 10%👎	DISNEY DINING PLAN? Yes	

Fantasyland, Magic Kingdom; ☎ 407-939-5277

Reservations Accepted. **Dining Plan credits** 1 per person, per meal (Quick-Service credits for breakfast and lunch, Table-Service credit for dinner). **When to go** Breakfast, lunch, or dinner. **Cost range** Breakfast $22 (child $14), lunch $10.50–$16 (child $9.50–$11.50), dinner $19 (child $9–$11). **Service** ★★★★. **Friendliness** ★★★★. **Parking** Magic Kingdom lot. **Bar** Wine and beer only. **Wine selection** Solid wine list that's mostly French to match the restaurant's theme—from sparkling starters to a sweet Sauternes. A handful of popular California vintages are on the list. **Dress** Casual. **Disabled access** Yes. **Customers** Magic Kingdom guests. **Breakfast** Daily, 8–10 a.m. **Lunch** Daily, 10:30 a.m.–2:30 p.m. **Dinner** Daily, 4–9:30 p.m.

SETTING AND ATMOSPHERE Beast's Castle is so popular that they've added quick-service breakfast from 8 to 10 a.m., in one of three themed rooms inspired by *Beauty and the Beast:* the Grand Ballroom, the mysterious West Wing, and the pretty Rose Gallery. (Dinner reservations are still the most difficult to snag.) The rooms fill up fast, with a noise level to match the hordes (550 seats). The lights are dimmed at dinner, which offers table service and a tad more serenity. And grown-ups love a beverage menu that includes wine and beer. (See page 347 for counter-service profile.)

HOUSE SPECIALTIES Sustainable catch of the day.

OTHER RECOMMENDATIONS Grilled strip steak with *pommes frites.* For dessert, cupcakes and a no-sugar-added lemon-raspberry fruit puff.

SUMMARY AND COMMENTS It does a fine job of feeding the masses. If you already have a breakfast or lunch reservation, you can preorder online up to 30 days in advance. For a slightly less hectic experience, choose a table in the West Wing, which is smaller, darker, and a little quieter.

Biergarten Restaurant ★★

GERMAN/BUFFET	EXPENSIVE	QUALITY ★★	VALUE ★★★★
READER-SURVEY RESPONSES	92%👍 8%👎	DISNEY DINING PLAN? Yes	

Germany, World Showcase, Epcot; ☎ 407-939-3463

Reservations Accepted. **Dining Plan credits** 1 per person, per meal. **When to go** Lunch or dinner. **Cost range** $35–$60 (child $15–$23). **Service** ★★★★. **Friendliness** ★★★★. **Parking** Epcot lot. **Bar** Full service. **Wine selection** German. **Dress** Casual. **Disabled access** Yes. **Customers** Theme park guests. **Lunch** Daily, noon–3:10 p.m. **Dinner** Daily, 4–9 p.m.

SETTING AND ATMOSPHERE Biergarten is a hefty German buffet set inside a nighttime Teutonic town square. You're seated at long tables lined up in rows emanating like the moon's rays from a central dance floor and stage. A lederhosen-clad oompah band plays and encourages diners to sing and dance. (If you do, mercifully low light levels mean your friends' cell phone videos can't positively ID you.) Just as in the real Germany, table space is assigned community-style, so you may be seated with other families.

HOUSE SPECIALTIES Beet salad, various sausages, homemade spaetzle with gravy, *nudelgratin* (baked macaroni with cheese custard), and sauerbraten. There's also carved-to-order pork roast with German mustard and breaded pork schnitzel.

OTHER RECOMMENDATIONS *Rouladen* (thinly sliced beef rolled and stuffed with onions), braised red cabbage, potato dumplings (dinner only), and German beer.

ENTERTAINMENT AND AMENITIES Oompah band and German dancers perform starting around 1 p.m.

SUMMARY AND COMMENTS The quality of the food continues to dip, but the lively 25-minute dinner show (one every hour) and noisy dining room are part of the fun, especially for families. And kids, basically, love the place.

Big River Grille & Brewing Works ★★

AMERICAN	MODERATE		QUALITY ★★	VALUE ★★
READER-SURVEY RESPONSES	78%👍	22%👎	DISNEY DINING PLAN?	Yes

BoardWalk; ☎ 407-560-0253

Reservations Not accepted. **Dining Plan credits** 1 per person, per meal. **When to go** Lunch or dinner. **Cost range** $15–$35. **Service** ★★★. **Friendliness** ★★★★. **Parking** BoardWalk lot. **Bar** Full service. **Wine selection** Minimal. **Dress** Casual. **Disabled access** Yes. **Customers** Tourists. **Hours** Sunday–Thursday, 11 a.m.–11 p.m.; Friday–Saturday, 11 a.m.–11 p.m.

SETTING AND ATMOSPHERE Situated for prime people-watching on Disney's BoardWalk, the outdoor tables fill up fast on a pretty day. A minimalist interior focuses on the craft beer that is made on the premises, with glass walls allowing you to see the process as ales and lagers are microbrewed. The place is small—it seems like the huge copper brewing tanks take up more room than that allotted to the diners.

HOUSE SPECIALTIES Beer-cheese soup, flame-grilled meat loaf, pork ribs with Rocket Red barbecue sauce.

SUMMARY AND COMMENTS The food is just OK, but with the growing popularity of craft beer, Big River Grille is a hot spot on the BoardWalk. Their house brews include a light lager, a robust ale, and seasonal choices. Good late-night-dining choice.

The Boathouse ★★★

SEAFOOD	EXPENSIVE		QUALITY ★★★	VALUE ★★½
READER-SURVEY RESPONSES	90%👍	10%👎	DISNEY DINING PLAN?	Yes

The Landing, Disney Springs; ☎ 407-939-2628

Reservations Accepted. **Dining Plan credits** 2 per person, per meal. **When to go** Lunch or dinner. **Cost range** $12–$60 (child $10). **Service** ★★★. **Friendliness** ★★★★. **Parking** Disney Springs garage. **Bar** Full service. **Wine selection** Good. **Dress** Casual. **Disabled access** Yes. **Customers** Locals and Disney guests. **Hours** Daily, 11 a.m.–11 p.m.

SETTING AND ATMOSPHERE The first things you notice about The Boathouse, on the waterfront at Disney Springs, are the vintage Amphicars (amphibious autos produced in the 1960s) and the Italian water taxis floating next to the front door—a multimillion-dollar fleet of 19 rare boats from private collectors, museums, and boat shows around the world. The airy restaurant seats up to 600 (200 outdoors) in nautically themed dining rooms (two private). The three bars include one built over the water and attached to more than 300 feet of boardwalk and docks.

HOUSE SPECIALTIES Seafood of every sort: a raw bar with three to five varieties of fresh oysters and wild-caught Baja shrimp; lobster; fish and shellfish, including Florida seasonal varieties; jumbo lump crab cake; Florida-farmed caviar; filet mignon topped with jumbo lump crab. Baked Alaska.

SUMMARY AND COMMENTS Quality is hit-or-miss; some items are superb (fish buckets); some should be avoided (tuna burger). Expensive, but the servings are big enough to share, and the food is fresh—even the fries are hand-cut. While seafood is the star, the steaks are top-notch as well. Hop a ride in an Amphicar ($150 per car) or a water taxi ($75 per person, $50 kids 13 and up) before or after your meal.

From a Northampton, UK, couple who liked the food but not the tab:

The Boathouse, whilst delivering tasty food, was vastly overpriced—$39 for an 8-ounce steak and three small potatoes is a bit much.

Boatwright's Dining Hall ★★★★

AMERICAN/CAJUN	MODERATE	QUALITY ★★★	VALUE ★★
READER-SURVEY RESPONSES	88%👍 12%👎	DISNEY DINING PLAN?	Yes

Port Orleans Resort–Riverside; ☎ 407-939-7639

Reservations Accepted. **Dining Plan credits** 1 per person, per meal. **When to go** Early evening. **Cost range** Dinner $17–$35 (child $9). **Service** ★★★★½. **Friendliness** ★★★★★. **Parking** Hotel lot. **Bar** Full service. **Wine selection** Fair. **Dress** Casual. **Disabled access** Yes. **Customers** Hotel guests. **Hours** Daily, 5–10 p.m.

SETTING AND ATMOSPHERE Situated between River Roost Lounge and Riverside Mill Food Court, just off of Port Orleans Riverside's lobby, Boatwright's features a simply appointed open dining room bathed in golden wood finishes, with diners feasting on New Orleans–inspired classics underneath a large boat skeleton. Always busy and a tad noisy, the restaurant serves dinner daily.

HOUSE SPECIALTIES French onion soup, classically presented smothered in Gruyère cheese, is a hearty way to start a meal here if you aren't in the mood to share. Besides, you'll fight dining companions for the last forkful of Mardi Gras pimento cheese fritters before settling in for entrées. Even the vegetarian jambalaya will satisfy; it's just as flavorful as the traditional Andouille- and shrimp-packed version on the menu. Charleston-style creamy shrimp and grits is particularly outstanding, but be sure to save some room to share one of the many incredible desserts, such as peanut butter mousse cake, red velvet cheesecake, or classic Southern banana pudding.

OTHER RECOMMENDATIONS Colonel Peace's Pieces, a Southern-fried sampler of crawfish, shrimp, oysters, and okra, and the Turbodog Barbecued Ribs for something hearty. Voodoo Chicken and Waffles and a traditional warm-vinaigrette-topped spinach salad round out the savory favorites.

SUMMARY AND COMMENTS Exceeding expectations for a non–Signature Dining location in both food and service, Boatwright's might just be a true hidden gem of Disney dining. It can be tough to find a reservation here, but it's worth the visit (and wait prior to seating) when you do. Nothing here is over-the-top or fancy, but you'll get a truly satisfying meal with friendly and honest service.

Boma—Flavors of Africa ★★★★½

AFRICAN/BUFFET	EXPENSIVE	QUALITY ★★★★	VALUE ★★★★½
READER-SURVEY RESPONSES	94%👍 6%👎	DISNEY DINING PLAN?	Yes

Animal Kingdom Lodge & Villas–Jambo House; ☎ 407-934-7639

Reservations Recommended for dinner. **Dining Plan credits** 1 per person, per meal. **When to go** Breakfast or dinner. **Cost range** Breakfast $27 (child $15), dinner $46 (child $26). **Service** ★★★★½. **Friendliness** ★★★★. **Parking** Valet ($20) or hotel lot. **Bar** Full service. **Wine selection** All South African. **Dress** Casual. **Disabled access** Yes. **Customers** Hotel guests. **Breakfast** Daily, 7:30–11 a.m. **Dinner** Daily, 5–9:30 p.m.

SETTING AND ATMOSPHERE On the first floor of Animal Kingdom Lodge, Boma's huge dining room evokes an African marketplace, complete with thatched-roof ceilings. With so many tables and buffet dining stations, plus the massive open kitchen where guests can observe all the goings-on, the dining room can be loud during peak meal times. Still, large and small families alike find it welcoming.

HOUSE SPECIALTIES Boma's buffet takes guests to a culinary frontier full of rich flavors. Dishes represent regional cuisines from across Africa. Daily rotating entrées include carved spice-rubbed beef strip loin and orange almond-crusted salmon. Sides such as *fufu* (mashed sweet potatoes) topped with chakalaka (spiced tomato stew), peanut rice, and sweet-corn pudding are home runs. Cold prepared salads are ripe with fresh produce, ranging in flavor from sweet and sour (pickled watermelon rind) to savory (lentils and hearts of palm with goat cheese). Boma's signature dessert, the Zebra Dome—a thin layer of white cake supporting an orb of Amarula cream-liqueur mousse, smothered with white chocolate ganache and drizzled with dark chocolate—has a cult following.

OTHER RECOMMENDATIONS A rotating selection of specialty soups—the carrot-ginger soup and Cape Malay lamb curry in particular are must-tries. Specialty dips and condiments such as Kalamata olive hummus, tamarind barbecue sauce, coriander chutney, and Masai Mara sauce (think a Kenyan pesto) will tickle taste buds as complements to any dish or bread. For breakfast, *bobotie* (a savory quiche dish) and French toast bread pudding shine; made-to-order omelets and carved meats satisfy those in search of more American options.

SUMMARY AND COMMENTS In a World where buffets are a dime a dozen and sometimes feature lackluster food, it can be easy to discount Boma. This restaurant, though, really bucks the trend; fresh, seasonal, well-prepared offerings dominate each meal station here. And the value, at both breakfast and dinner, is almost impossible to beat. Advance Reservations are a must—walk-up tables here are few and far between.

Bongos Cuban Cafe ★★

CUBAN	MODERATE	QUALITY ★★	VALUE ★★
READER-SURVEY RESPONSES	68% 👍	32% 👎	DISNEY DINING PLAN? Yes

Disney Springs West Side; ☎ 407-828-0999

Reservations Recommended. **Dining Plan credits** 1 per person, per meal. **When to go** Lunch or dinner. **Cost range** $15–$45 (child $6–$10). **Service** ★★★★. **Friendliness** ★★★★. **Parking** Disney Springs garage. **Bar** Full service. **Wine selection** Moderate. **Dress** Casual. **Disabled access** Elevator to second level. **Customers** Fans of Cuban culture and cuisine; Disney guests. **Hours** Sunday–Thursday, 11 a.m.–11 p.m.; Friday–Saturday, 11 a.m.–11:55 p.m.

SETTING AND ATMOSPHERE Bongos is one of the Downtown Disney originals that have remained untouched during the transition to Disney Springs. The three-story pineapple icon and beautiful tropical decor—banana-leaf roof, banana-leaf ceiling fans, and palm tree–shaped columns—take diners on a trip to Havana. Hand-painted murals and mosaics lend an artistic air, and an open wraparound porch provides pleasant outdoor dining.

HOUSE SPECIALTIES Cuban sandwich, Cuban-style skirt steak, and *ropa vieja* (shredded beef in tomato sauce).

ENTERTAINMENT AND AMENITIES Latin music. *Fun fact:* At one time, Desi Arnaz Jr. led the band.

SUMMARY AND COMMENTS Gloria Estefan and her husband-producer, Emilio, created this large restaurant that marries salsa music with Cuban cuisine. The menu is long overdue for an update. Start with a mojito; then try a classic Cuban dish—it may not be as authentic as at Miami's Cuban restaurants, but if you're craving hearty dishes with beans, rice, fried sweet plantains, roast chicken or pork, or slow-cooked beef, Bongos fills the bill.

California Grill ★★★★★

AMERICAN	EXPENSIVE	QUALITY ★★★★★	VALUE ★★★
READER-SURVEY RESPONSES	93%👍 7%👎	DISNEY DINING PLAN? Yes	

Contemporary Resort; ☎ 407-939-3463

Reservations Required. **Dining Plan credits** 2 per person, per meal. **When to go** During evening fireworks. **Cost range** Brunch $80 (child $48), dinner $37–$69 (child $9–$18). **Service** ★★★★★. **Friendliness** ★★★★★. **Parking** Valet ($25) or hotel lot. **Bar** Full service. **Wine selection** Fantastic. **Dress** Dressy casual. **Disabled access** Yes. **Customers** Hotel guests and locals. **Dinner** Daily, 5–10 p.m. **Sunday brunch** 10 a.m.–1 p.m.

SETTING AND ATMOSPHERE The beautiful California Grill remains one of the top choices for Disney dining, both for its remarkable view from the 15th floor of the Contemporary Resort and for its bustling open kitchen, which turns out spectacular fare. It can be crowded and noisy, filled with families who want a view of the Magic Kingdom fireworks, so book a table early or late for a somewhat quieter experience. A showstopping wine display comprises 1,600 bottles in a climate-controlled case just off the elevator. If you don't have a reservation, ask for a seat at the sushi bar or in the lounge, where you can order appetizers (but not entrées).

HOUSE SPECIALTIES A new chef took over the kitchen in 2016, so expect a slowly revamped menu. Sushi, three-meat signature meatballs, Sonoma goat cheese ravioli; crispy rock-shrimp salad, pork two ways (grilled tenderloin and lacquered pork belly), oak-fired filet of beef, chocolate pudding cake. Outstanding wine list and craft cocktails.

ENTERTAINMENT AND AMENITIES Magic Kingdom fireworks are the star of the show, observed from the newly opened terrace—but only guests with reservations may watch from the 15th floor. California Grill now hosts an event on Sunday evenings called "Celebration at the Top—Savor, Sip, and Sparkle." Guests will enjoy tasting-size plates of some of the restaurants' offerings while watching the fireworks display. A selection of beer, wine, and cordials is included. The cost of this event is $99 (plus gratuity and tax) per person. Complimentary valet parking is included with this event. Make reservations by calling ☎ 407-WDW-DINE (939-3463).

SUMMARY AND COMMENTS In spite of the noise, California Grill is one of Walt Disney World's top dining experiences.

Cape May Cafe ★★★½

AMERICAN/BUFFET	MODERATE	QUALITY ★★★½	VALUE ★★★★
READER-SURVEY RESPONSES	91%👍 9%👎	DISNEY DINING PLAN? Yes	

Beach Club Resort; ☎ 407-934-3358

Reservations Recommended. **Dining Plan credits** 1 per person, per meal. **When to go** Breakfast or dinner. **Cost range** Breakfast $36 (child $21), dinner $48 (child $27). **Service** ★★★★★. **Friendliness** ★★★★★. **Parking** Hotel lot. **Bar** Full service. **Wine selection** Limited. **Dress** Casual. **Disabled access** Yes. **Customers** Epcot and hotel guests. **Breakfast** Daily, 7:30–11 a.m. **Dinner** Daily, 5–9 p.m.

SETTING AND ATMOSPHERE Just off the lobby at the Beach Club, Cape May Cafe features nautical New England decor in two dining rooms and lots of comfortable seating.

HOUSE SPECIALTIES The buffet includes shrimp, both peel-and-eat and fried; steamed mussels; calamari and clams (each offered on different days); salmon; chicken; corn on the cob; lots of salads; and a good dessert bar. The kids' bar includes chicken nuggets and mac and cheese.

ENTERTAINMENT AND AMENITIES Character breakfast with Goofy, Minnie, and Chip 'n' Dale.

SUMMARY AND COMMENTS Cape May's all-you-can-eat menu isn't terribly exciting, but you can get your money's worth in decent seafood. Advance Reservations are recommended. Because Cape May is within easy walking distance of the World Showcase entrance to Epcot, it's a convenient and affordable place to dine before *IllumiNations*.

Captain's Grille ★★★

AMERICAN	MODERATE	QUALITY ★★★½	VALUE ★★★
READER-SURVEY RESPONSES	83%👍 17%👎	DISNEY DINING PLAN?	Yes

Yacht Club Resort; ☎ 407-939-3463

Reservations Accepted. **Dining Plan credits** 1 per person, per meal. **When to go** Breakfast or lunch. **Cost range** Breakfast buffet $24 (child $13), lunch $13–$23 (child $9), dinner $16–$33 (child $9–$11). **Service** ★★★★. **Friendliness** ★★★★★. **Parking** Hotel lot. **Bar** Full service. **Wine selection** Good. **Dress** Casual. **Disabled access** Yes. **Customers** Hotel guests. **Breakfast** Daily, 7:30–11:25 a.m. **Lunch** Daily, 11:30 a.m.–2 p.m. **Dinner** Daily, 5–9 p.m.

SETTING AND ATMOSPHERE Set just off the main lobby of the Yacht Club Resort, Captain's Grille serves breakfast, lunch, and dinner in a casual, lightly nautical-themed atmosphere. The restaurant is rarely busy at lunch, often not requiring a reservation. It can be bustling and loud for breakfast and dinner.

HOUSE SPECIALTIES On the breakfast buffet, try the individual frittatas, bread pudding, and fresh biscuits and gravy. Or order the lump crab omelet or dark-chocolate waffles with espresso cream from the menu. For lunch, try the Yacht Club Burger, with meat blended in-house and cooked to order, lump crab cakes, and buttermilk rock shrimp tacos. Dinner's highlights are the Farmer's Market beet salad, New England clam chowder, beer-braised mussels, and Cabernet-braised short ribs.

OTHER RECOMMENDATIONS Captain's Grille excels when they stick to the simple dishes, such as the shaved-beef sandwich at lunch or the rosemary-brined pork tenderloin at dinner. Fluffy and tangy lemon-ricotta hot cakes are a mainstay on the breakfast menu and just tempting enough to make you reconsider the excellent breakfast buffet. House-made gelato and hazelnut-chocolate cake are standouts on the otherwise lackluster dessert menu.

SUMMARY AND COMMENTS Though the restaurant is rarely busy, the relaxed atmosphere of the dining room tends to melt into the service here, yielding a sometimes longer-than-expected meal in a simple space. Keep Captain's Grille in mind if you're in search of a generally satisfying plate of food away from the Florida heat and hustle of the theme parks.

Le Cellier Steakhouse ★★★½

STEAK	EXPENSIVE	QUALITY ★★★½	VALUE ★★★
READER-SURVEY RESPONSES	88%👍 13%👎	DISNEY DINING PLAN?	Yes

Canada, World Showcase, Epcot; ☎ 407-939-3463

Reservations Required. **Dining Plan credits** 2 per person, per meal. **When to go** Before 6 p.m. **Cost range** Lunch and dinner $35–$60 (child $9–$17). **Service** ★★★★. **Friendliness** ★★★★★. **Parking** Epcot lot. **Bar** Full bar. **Wine selection** Canadian wines are featured. **Dress** Casual. **Disabled access** Yes. **Customers** Theme park guests. **Lunch** Daily, 12:30 a.m.–3:55 p.m. **Dinner** Daily, 4–9 p.m.

SETTING AND ATMOSPHERE Walk past the Canada Pavilion's pretty gardens into this small, darkened dining room, intended to evoke the look and feel of a wine cellar. Given the escalated prices, it doesn't feel upscale, with heavy wooden tables and no linens, but the crowd doesn't seem to mind—the steaks make up for the ambience. Service is "cheerful Canadian," meaning servers will apologize to *you* if you spill something on *them*.

HOUSE SPECIALTIES Mushroom filet mignon, Canadian Cheddar soup.

OTHER RECOMMENDATIONS Rib eye, pan-seared salmon. An excellent selection of wines.

SUMMARY AND COMMENTS New chef Dee Foundoukis has stepped up the kitchen. They've scaled back the prices a bit—the rib eye is down to $54!—and the menu is the same for lunch and dinner, so go anytime you can get in (more about that on page 320). If you're looking for a good steak in a theme park setting—and authentic poutine—Le Cellier is the place to go.

Chef Art Smith's Homecomin'

AMERICAN	MODERATE		QUALITY ★★★½		VALUE ★★★½
READER-SURVEY RESPONSES	91%👍	9%👎	DISNEY DINING PLAN? Yes		

The Landing, Disney Springs; ☎ 407-560-0100

Reservations Recommended. **Dining Plan credits** 1 per person, per meal. **When to go** Lunch or dinner. **Cost range** $16–$41 (child $9–$12). **Service** ★★★★. **Friendliness** ★★★★. **Parking** Disney Springs garage. **Bar** Full service. **Wine selection** Modest. **Dress** Casual. **Disabled access** Yes. **Customers** Disney guests and locals. **Lunch and dinner** Sunday–Thursday, 11 a.m–midnight; Friday–Saturday, 11 a.m.–1 a.m.

SETTING AND ATMOSPHERE Florida farm-style decor with a reclaimed-wood-and-mason-jar vibe. Dining rooms chairs are covered in faux-burlap sacks. Florida born and raised, Art Smith is Oprah Winfrey's former private chef and is well known for his appearances on *Top Chef Masters* and *Iron Chef America*.

HOUSE SPECIALTIES The 200-seat Homecomin' focuses on Smith's takes on traditional Southern cooking, highlighting Florida's produce and seafood bounty with dishes he's known for: pimento cheese, deviled eggs, Low-country shrimp and grits, biscuits and sawmill gravy, and chicken and dumplings. Sweets from his bakery will be shipped in daily. Cocktails feature artisanal moonshine.

OTHER RECOMMENDATIONS Our kryptonite is the fried chicken and doughnuts (yes, you read that right), a platter of fried chicken served with house-made sugar doughnuts and KC Greens.

SUMMARY AND COMMENTS There's some menu overlap with the nearby House of Blues. We'd eat here for the calmer atmosphere and fresher food.

Chef Mickey's ★★½

AMERICAN/BUFFET	EXPENSIVE		QUALITY ★★★		VALUE ★★★
READER-SURVEY RESPONSES	85%👍	15%👎	DISNEY DINING PLAN? Yes		

Contemporary Resort; ☎ 407-939-3463

Reservations Required. **Dining Plan credits** 1 per person, per meal. **When to go** Early evening. **Cost range** Breakfast and brunch $43 (child $26), dinner $54 (child $32). **Service** ★★★★. **Friendliness** ★★★★★. **Parking** Valet ($25) or hotel lot. **Bar** Full service. **Wine selection** Fair. **Dress** Casual. **Disabled access** Yes.

Customers Theme park guests. **Character breakfast** Daily, 7–11:30 a.m. **Character brunch** Daily, 11:35 a.m.–2:30 p.m. **Character dinner** Daily, 5–9:30 p.m.

SETTING AND ATMOSPHERE Can you say *madhouse*? This big, open dining room with the monorail whizzing by overhead (inside the hotel) is a cacophony of children's and parents' voices. The food is secondary—everyone's here to meet Mickey and his pals, who promise a stop at every single table. The buffet circles the center of the room.

HOUSE SPECIALTIES Breakfast: pancakes, carved ham, pastries. Brunch: breakfast faves (Mickey waffles, etc.), plus lunch choices such as barbecue ribs and baked salmon. Dinner: carved beef and turkey, sundae bar.

OTHER RECOMMENDATIONS Salads and sushi. And Mom and Dad can have a cocktail for dinner—even tequila on the rocks.

ENTERTAINMENT AND AMENITIES Character visits.

SUMMARY AND COMMENTS The food takes a backseat to the characters, but you won't leave hungry, and the kids' buffet (mac and cheese, mini–corn dogs) will satisfy picky eaters. Best of all, nobody cares if the kids are loud.

Les Chefs de France ★★★

FRENCH	EXPENSIVE	QUALITY ★★★	VALUE ★★★
READER-SURVEY RESPONSES	88%👍 12%👎	DISNEY DINING PLAN?	Yes

France, World Showcase, Epcot; ☎ 407-827-8709

Reservations Recommended. **Dining Plan credits** 1 per person, per meal. **When to go** Lunch or dinner. **Cost range** Lunch $15–$30 (child $8–$10), dinner $19–$36 (child $8–$10). **Service** ★★★★★. **Friendliness** ★★★★★. **Parking** Epcot lot. **Bar** Beer. **Wine selection** Very good. **Dress** Casual. **Disabled access** Yes. **Customers** Theme park guests. **Lunch** Daily, noon–3 p.m. **Dinner** Daily, 5–9 p.m.

SETTING AND ATMOSPHERE Overheard outside this restaurant's very Parisian windows: "It's just like Julia Child!" Except it's not—it's like stepping into a busy bistro, and with young French students in the States for the Disney College Program making up much of the waitstaff, the sound of *français* feels oh so Continental. The smells are delicious, with baguettes from the on-site bakery on every table. White tablecloths and padded banquettes accentuate the classic bistro decor of the main dining room, where window tables make for fun people-watching on the World Showcase Promenade.

HOUSE SPECIALTIES Dishes inspired by the three great French chefs for whom the restaurant is named: Paul Bocuse, the late Gaston Lenôtre, and Roger Vergé. At lunch, try the prix fixe bowl of onion soup topped with Gruyère and a croque monsieur for the classic French experience; at dinner, duck breast with cherries, or grilled tenderloin of beef.

OTHER RECOMMENDATIONS Baked goat cheese salad, short ribs braised in Cabernet, crème brûlée.

SUMMARY AND COMMENTS This is a restaurant created by three of France's best chefs. Jérôme Bocuse, son of Paul Bocuse, runs the restaurant with executive chef Bruno Vrignon, who trained in Lyon with the elder Bocuse.

Cinderella's Royal Table ★★★

AMERICAN	EXPENSIVE	QUALITY ★★★	VALUE ★★
READER-SURVEY RESPONSES	86%👍 14%👎	DISNEY DINING PLAN?	Yes

Cinderella Castle, Fantasyland, Magic Kingdom; ☎ 407-939-3463

Reservations Required; must prepay in full. **Dining Plan credits** 2 per person, per meal. **When to go** Early. **Cost range** Character breakfast $61 (child $36), character lunch and dinner $80 (child $47). **Service** ★★★★. **Friendliness** ★★★★. **Parking** Magic Kingdom lot. **Bar** Limited selection of sparkling wine by the glass and bottle. **Dress** Casual. **Disabled access** Limited. **Customers**

Theme park guests. **Character breakfast** Daily, 7:55–10:15 a.m. **Character lunch** Daily, 11:30 a.m.–2:50 p.m. **Character dinner** Daily, 4–8 p.m.

SETTING AND ATMOSPHERE A recent spiffing-up of the medieval banquet hall included new carpet and new costumes for the servers, but most guests won't recognize the difference. It's still the top spot for dining in the theme parks. While the food is better than average, it's more about experiencing a character meal on the second floor of Cinderella Castle.

HOUSE SPECIALTIES All of the meals are fixed-price character affairs, and the kitchen is upping its game—at breakfast there's caramel apple–stuffed French toast; goat cheese quiche; poached lobster and shrimp topped with a poached egg and hollandaise; beef tenderloin and cheese frittata; or a healthy plate with scrambled egg whites, hot 10-grain cereal, Greek yogurt, house-made granola, walnut-sunflower bread, and fresh fruit. At lunch you'll find fish of the day, braised short ribs with parsnip mashed potatoes, gnocchi or rice with seasonal vegetables, and pan-seared chicken with goat cheese polenta. Dinner fare may include slow-roasted pork loin and flourless chocolate cake.

ENTERTAINMENT AND AMENITIES Assorted princesses attend all three meals.

SUMMARY AND COMMENTS It isn't cheap to eat here, but no matter—families can't seem to get enough of this "Disney magic." For more on reserving a spot at the Royal Table (and the travails thereof), see page 453.

Cítricos ★★★½

MEDITERRANEAN	EXPENSIVE	QUALITY ★★★★½	VALUE ★★★
READER-SURVEY RESPONSES 89%👍	11%👎	DISNEY DINING PLAN? Yes	

Grand Floridian Resort & Spa; ☎ 407-939-3463

Reservations Required. **Dining Plan credits** 2 per person, per meal. **When to go** Dinner. **Cost range** $33–$60 (child $9–$17). **Service** ★★★★★. **Friendliness** ★★★★★. **Parking** Valet ($25); self-parking is deceptively far away. **Bar** Full service. **Wine selection** Very good. **Dress** Dressy casual. **Disabled access** Yes. **Customers** Hotel guests and locals. **Dinner** Daily, 5:30–10 p.m.

SETTING AND ATMOSPHERE The golds and yellows of the Mediterranean color this stylish dining room on the second floor of the Grand Floridian. Diners enjoy the culinary magic of the full-view show kitchen.

HOUSE SPECIALTIES Sautéed Florida rock shrimp with tomato, lemon, feta, and white wine; crispy pan-fried veal chop; oak-grilled seasonal swordfish.

OTHER RECOMMENDATIONS Charcuterie platter, oak-grilled beef tenderloin, warm chocolate-banana torte.

SUMMARY AND COMMENTS If you can't get a reservation at Victoria & Albert's next door, this is the next best thing. The chefs appreciate local and seasonal produce and seafood, so the menu always has a few delicious surprises based on what's freshest. If you're flush with cash, reserve the Chef's Domain, a private room for up to 12 guests and a special menu.

Coral Reef Restaurant ★★½

SEAFOOD	EXPENSIVE	QUALITY ★★	VALUE ★★
READER-SURVEY RESPONSES 81%👍	19%👎	DISNEY DINING PLAN? Yes	

The Seas with Nemo & Friends, Future World, Epcot; ☎ 407-939-3463

Reservations Required. **Dining Plan credits** 1 per person, per meal. **When to go** Lunch. **Cost range** Lunch $16–$33 (child $11), dinner $20–$33 (child $11). **Service** ★★★★. **Friendliness** ★★★★. **Parking** Epcot lot. **Bar** Full service. **Wine selection** Good. **Dress** Casual. **Disabled access** Yes. **Customers** Theme park guests. **Lunch** Daily, 11:30 a.m.–3:30 p.m. **Dinner** Daily, 4–9 p.m.

SETTING AND ATMOSPHERE Though the decor could use a facelift, you can't beat the view in this darkened dining room, which faces one of the world's largest saltwater aquariums; tiered seating gives everyone a pretty good view of the multitude of fishes (and sometimes Mickey in a scuba suit). The ethereal entryway gives the impression that you're going under the sea; special light fixtures throw ripple patterns on the ceiling.

HOUSE SPECIALTIES Creamy lobster soup with tarragon and brandy, on the menu since the restaurant opened; seared rainbow trout; grilled New York strip steak; Chocolate Wave dessert. For kids: grilled fish or grilled chicken tenders, pork tenderloin.

SUMMARY AND COMMENTS Certainly the best restaurant in Future World, Coral Reef is a great escape from the Florida sun. Grab a souvenir fish guide and check out the 8,000 sea creatures that call this place home—but are probably not on the menu.

The Crystal Palace ★★★

AMERICAN/BUFFET	MODERATE	QUALITY ★★½	VALUE ★★★
READER-SURVEY RESPONSES 91%👍 9%👎		DISNEY DINING PLAN? Yes	

Main Street, U.S.A., Magic Kingdom; ☎ 407-939-3463

Reservations Required. **Dining Plan credits** 1 per person, per meal. **When to go** Anytime. **Cost range** Breakfast $32 (child $20); lunch and dinner $45 (child $27). **Service** ★★★. **Friendliness** ★★★★. **Parking** Magic Kingdom lot. **Bar** None. **Dress** Casual. **Disabled access** Yes. **Customers** Park guests. **Character breakfast** Daily, 8–10:45 a.m. **Character lunch/dinner** Daily, 11:30 a.m.–9 p.m.

SETTING AND ATMOSPHERE A breakfast or lunch visit to The Crystal Palace surrounds you with cool sunlight and decorative plants, along with a large, easy-to-navigate buffet area. The restaurant's white steel supports, arched ceilings, and glass roof (especially the atrium) are tributes to its namesake, built to house London's 1851 Great Exhibition—the first world's fair—and among the first structures to use plate glass in large quantities. Because of all the windows, the setting is less distinctive for dinner after dark.

HOUSE SPECIALTIES The buffet items change often but may include waffles and pancakes layered with fresh fruit for breakfast and, for lunch and dinner, charbroiled octopus, rainbow trout, shrimp and grits, pan-seared salmon in mushroom risotto, and seafood scampi. Dessert includes turtle cheesecake, a Baileys–Jack Daniel's mousse, and a sundae bar. The salads are exceptionally fresh. Kids get their own buffet with macaroni and cheese and chicken fingers.

ENTERTAINMENT AND AMENITIES Pooh and friends schmooze with the kids.

SUMMARY AND COMMENTS The best dining value in the Magic Kingdom—go hungry and fill up. The food is consistently good, but eating seems somehow secondary to the desire to get lots of photos with Pooh and his pals. If you time dinner right and can snag a table away from like-minded diners, there is a great view of Main Street parades in the conservatory.

ESPN Club ★★½

AMERICAN/SANDWICHES	MODERATE	QUALITY ★★★	VALUE ★★★
READER-SURVEY RESPONSES 82%👍 18%👎		DISNEY DINING PLAN? Yes	

BoardWalk; ☎ 407-939-1177

Reservations Not accepted. **Dining Plan credits** 1 per person, per meal. **When to go** Lunch or dinner. **Cost range** $13–$33 (child $9). **Service** ★★★. **Friendliness** ★★★★. **Parking** Valet ($25) or BoardWalk lot. **Bar** Full service. **Wine selection** Minimal. **Dress** Casual. **Disabled access** Yes. **Customers** Tourists. **Hours** Daily, 11 a.m.–1 a.m.; *note:* cover charge during big games.

SETTING AND ATMOSPHERE A sports bar to the nth degree, with more than 100 monitors, basketball-court flooring, sports memorabilia, and more television monitors than a network affiliate. The bar area features satellite sports-trivia video games. A large octagonal space with a wall of TVs serves as the main dining room.

HOUSE SPECIALTIES Burgers, burgers, and burgers. Sausage, potato pancake, and bacon burgers; Cuban burgers; ESPN surf and turf; seafood mac and cheese; ESPN house chili.

SUMMARY AND COMMENTS If you plan to watch a big sports event, go early—or run away—as the line often spills out the door and onto the sidewalks. It's incredibly noisy and fun, with large portions and decent quality. And don't worry about missing a play—there are even TVs in the restrooms.

50's Prime Time Cafe ★★★

AMERICAN	MODERATE		QUALITY ★★★		VALUE ★★★
READER-SURVEY RESPONSES	88%👍	12%👎	DISNEY DINING PLAN?	Yes	

Echo Lake, Disney's Hollywood Studios; ☎ 407-939-3463

Reservations Recommended. **Dining Plan credits** 1 per person, per meal. **When to go** Lunch or dinner. **Cost range** Lunch and dinner, $15–$30 (child $9). **Service** ★★★★★. **Friendliness** ★★★★★. **Parking** DHS lot. **Bar** Full service. **Wine selection** Limited. **Dress** Casual. **Disabled access** Yes. **Customers** Theme park guests. **Lunch** Daily, 11 a.m.–3:15 p.m. **Dinner** Daily, 3:30–8 p.m.

SETTING AND ATMOSPHERE Dine in a 1950s kitchen stocked with antique refrigerators, boomerang-patterned laminate tabletops, sunburst clocks, and decoupage art made from preserved fruit. Black-and-white TVs play vintage sitcom clips while you wait for your entrées; then you order dessert from a menu shown on GAF View-Master reels.

HOUSE SPECIALTIES Pot roast, chicken potpie, PB&J milkshake, and other retro fare. There's a nod to contemporary cuisine with a multigrain pasta, but it's hard to pass up fried chicken and meat loaf.

SUMMARY AND COMMENTS Though the restaurant is usually packed and noisy, the waitstaff makes it worthwhile, nagging you just like Mom did to "Take your elbows off the table!" and "Finish every last bite!" If the place is packed, grab a spot at the bar in the equally kitschy Tune-In Lounge next door—they serve food, and they will make you a PB&J shake or a Dad's Electric Lemonade (with vodka).

Flying Fish ★★★★

SEAFOOD	EXPENSIVE		QUALITY ★★★★		VALUE ★★★
READER-SURVEY RESPONSES	91%👍	9%👎	DISNEY DINING PLAN?	Yes	

BoardWalk; ☎ 407-939-3463

Reservations Recommended. **When to go** Dinner. **Cost range** $37–$64 (child $13–$17). **Service** ★★★★★. **Friendliness** ★★★★★. **Bar** Full service. **Wine selection** Extensive. **Parking** Valet ($25) or Boardwalk hotel lot. **Dress** Dressy casual. **Disabled access** Yes. **Customers** Hotel guests; locals. **Dinner** 5:30–10 p.m. Sunday–Thursday; 5:30–10:30 p.m. Friday–Saturday

SETTING AND ATMOSPHERE Situated at the heart of the BoardWalk, Flying Fish takes diners under the sea for an upscale modern seafood dinner enveloped by classy deep blue– and silver-rich restaurant decor. The open kitchen and showcase bar entertain guests seated near the front of the bustling restaurant, with diners enjoying a more muted experience in the rear of the main dining room.

HOUSE SPECIALTIES Maine lobster pasta with golden tomato sauce shines on the seafood-dominant menu, though landlubbers will be perfectly content with the Wagyu filet mignon. Soup and salad, rotating frequently throughout every season, are particularly solid ways to start any meal here, with both highlighting the freshest produce Florida has to offer. For more adventurous diners, the octopus and sea bass "paella" will hit all the high notes. Adroit bartenders craft specialty cocktails that pair with most meals, while a strong wine program complements every dish from start to finish. Complete your meal at Flying Fish with the visually striking and delicious Florida Reef dessert or the always-competent chef's selection of artisanal cheeses.

OTHER RECOMMENDATIONS House fish specials are different every day and are accompanied by the freshest seasonal vegetables you can find at Walt Disney World. Kurobuta pork belly with a shirred quail egg impresses as an appetizer, and plancha-seared Hokkaido scallops are sure to satisfy. If you're in search of a wider-reaching tasting menu, take advantage of the prix fixe Chef's Tasting and Wine Experience, allowing you a front-row seat to the open kitchen.

SUMMARY AND COMMENTS Long a mainstay of the Walt Disney World fine dining roster, Flying Fish impresses with both upscale food and attentive service. The kitchen can sometimes force a slower-paced meal here, even after reopening following an extensive refurbishment several months ago, but the food is always worth the wait. Enjoy a fancy night out on the BoardWalk with an aperitif at neighboring AbracadaBar before settling into the Flying Fish dining experience.

The Fountain ★★

AMERICAN	MODERATE	QUALITY ★★	VALUE ★★
READER-SURVEY RESPONSES 88%👍	12%👎	DISNEY DINING PLAN? No	

Dolphin Hotel; ☎ 407-934-1609

Reservations Not taken. **When to go** Lunch or dinner. **Cost range** $7.50–$16 (child $11). **Service** ★★★★. **Friendliness** ★★★★. **Bar** Beer and wine only. **Wine selection** Limited. **Parking** Hotel lot ($18). **Dress** Casual. **Disabled access** Yes. **Customers** Hotel guests. **Lunch and dinner** Daily, 11 a.m.–11 p.m.

SETTING AND ATMOSPHERE Informal soda-shop ambience.

HOUSE SPECIALTIES Build-your-own burgers and hot dogs (including black-bean and turkey burgers), milkshakes (we love the PB&J), and ice cream.

OTHER RECOMMENDATIONS Big salads including seared salmon and chicken Caesar. And the ice-cream panini sandwich.

SUMMARY AND COMMENTS Probably not the best choice for calorie counters.

Fresh Mediterranean Market ★★½

MEDITERRANEAN/AMERICAN	MODERATE	QUALITY ★★½	VALUE ★★
READER-SURVEY RESPONSES 57%👍	43%👎	DISNEY DINING PLAN? No	

Dolphin Hotel; ☎ 407-934-1609

Reservations Available but not necessary. **When to go** Breakfast or lunch. **Cost range** Breakfast (buffet or à la carte) $5–$26 (child $15), lunch $15–$18 (child $12). **Service** ★★★★. **Friendliness** ★★★★. **Parking** Hotel lot ($17). **Bar** Beer, wine, and limited cocktails. **Wine selection** Limited. **Dress** Casual. **Disabled access** Yes. **Customers** Hotel guests. **Breakfast** Daily, 6:30–10:35 a.m. **Lunch** Monday–Friday, 11:30 a.m.–2 p.m.; Saturday–Sunday, noon–2 p.m. Days of operation may vary according to hotel occupancy.

SETTING AND ATMOSPHERE A pleasant enough room with floor-level windows. Ask for a veranda table if you want to have a quiet conversation away from the action in the open kitchen.

HOUSE SPECIALTIES Breakfast: fresh fruit and vegetable juices, made-to-order omelets, "Paleo" cereal, and one of the few places in Orlando to get chipped beef on toast. Lunch: burgers, salads, and Sonoma County wines.

OTHER RECOMMENDATIONS Sangria with organic fruit juices.

SUMMARY AND COMMENTS The menu is as spartan as the setting, but if you're looking for healthful and organic choices, this is the spot.

Frontera Cocina ★★★½

MEXICAN	MODERATE	QUALITY ★★★½	VALUE ★★★
READER-SURVEY RESPONSES	84%👍 16%👎	DISNEY DINING PLAN? No	

Town Center, Disney Springs; ☎ 407-939-3463

Reservations Recommended. **When to go** Lunch or dinner. **Cost range** $14–$34 (children $9). **Service** ★★★★. **Friendliness** ★★★★. **Parking** Disney Springs garage. **Bar** Full service. **Wine selection** Modest. **Dress** Casual. **Disabled access** Yes. **Customers** Disney guests and locals. **Lunch and dinner** Sunday–Wednesday, 11 a.m.–10 p.m.; Thursday–Saturday, 11 a.m.–11 p.m.

SETTING AND ATMOSPHERE Though the exterior presents with muted beige walls and white accents meant to evoke classic Florida waterfront architecture, bright pops of color from the centerpiece chandelier and bar accents highlight the sleek, modern eatery's interior, made casual by exposed ductwork and cozy dark-wood furnishings. The open show kitchen and the "Wall of Fame" shelves ,packed with specialty liquors and wines, are bathed in natural sunlight from the large windows on nearly every wall, showcasing the springs and the patio from the back dining room.

HOUSE SPECIALTIES Traditional Yucatecan *sikil pak* (pumpkin seed dip), build-your-own carne asada tacos, ancho-marinated half chicken served with highly lauded *queso añejo* mashed potatoes, Frontera margarita and specialty agave flights, as well as the pecan pie bar (a family recipe from chef Rick Bayless's grandmother).

OTHER RECOMMENDATIONS Made-to-order guacamole, shrimp and bay scallop cóctel verde, mushroom torta with chipotle-garlic mojo, carnitas, red-chile chicken enchiladas, Mexican "Cola" (Avión blanco tequila, tamarind, Ancho Reyes chile liqueur, with a black ant salt rim), and Coconut-Lime Quattro Leches cake. The dessert menu is small; kids may be happier with a cupcake from nearby Sprinkles.

SUMMARY AND COMMENTS If you want Frontera Cocina food on the go, there's a takeaway window offering chips and guac, two kinds of tacos, soft drinks, beer, and margaritas.

Garden Grill Restaurant ★★

AMERICAN	EXPENSIVE	QUALITY ★★	VALUE ★★★
READER-SURVEY RESPONSES	93%👍 7%👎	DISNEY DINING PLAN? Yes	

The Land, Future World, Epcot; ☎ 407-560-6071

Reservations Required. **Dining Plan credits** 1 per person, per meal. **When to go** Anytime. **Cost range** Breakfast $32 (child $19); lunch and dinner $45 (child $27). **Service** ★★★★. **Friendliness** ★★★★★. **Parking** Epcot lot. **Bar** Wine, beer, and some mixed drinks. **Wine selection** Fair. **Dress** Casual. **Disabled access** Yes. **Customers** Theme park guests. **Character breakfast** 8-10:30 a.m. **Character lunch** 11:30 a.m.–3 p.m. **Character dinner** 4-8 p.m.

SETTING AND ATMOSPHERE With the popular Soarin' attraction nearby, the all-you-can-eat Garden Grill stays busy, even though the concept and the dining room have grown rather dated. Even so, it's a classic: The floor revolves slowly as you peer down into the unseen side of scenes from Living with the Land, the Land Pavilion's ride-through attraction (see page 585). At about the time you finish a meal, you've revolved once, past scenes of a desert, a rainforest, and a farm—an otherwise hidden view of inside the farmhouse. The constant crowing of a "rooster" and dog barks are questionable highlights. Much more exciting for kids are the Disney characters—Mickey, Chip 'n' Dale, and others make stops at tables for photo ops and greetings, a far easier way for the kids to get photos and autographs than standing in line outside, but way more expensive.

HOUSE SPECIALTIES Beef filet, turkey breast with stuffing and gravy, and sustainable fish of the day; buttermilk mashed potatoes, veggies, and salads made with ingredients from The Land's greenhouses. Dessert is a seasonal cobbler with vanilla-bean whipped cream. The kids' menu includes turkey breast with whole-grain rice pilaf, mac and cheese, chicken drumsticks, sweet potato sticks, and broccoli.

ENTERTAINMENT AND AMENITIES The view. Character dining at all three meals. Free nonalcoholic beverages included with meals.

SUMMARY AND COMMENTS The food is filling but chain-restaurant mediocre, giving new meaning to "all you can eat." Still, the retro-Disney setting is worth experiencing at least once. You won't be going back for seconds.

Garden Grove ★★

AMERICAN/BUFFET	MODERATE	QUALITY ★★★	VALUE ★★
READER-SURVEY RESPONSES	72% 👍	28% 👎	DISNEY DINING PLAN? No

Swan Hotel; ☎ 407-934-1609

Reservations Recommended. **When to go** Anytime. **Cost range** Breakfast $12–$23 (child $7–$14), lunch $14–$19 (child $9–$12), dinner $30–$37 (child $18); weekend Disney-character breakfast buffet $25 (child $16), Disney-character seafood buffet (Friday and Saturday nights) $36 (child $17). **Service** ★★★. **Friendliness** ★★★. **Parking** Valet ($26) or hotel lot ($18). **Bar** Full service. **Wine selection** Good. **Dress** Casual. **Disabled access** Yes. **Customers** Hotel guests, some locals, tourists. **Breakfast** Daily, 6:30–11:30 a.m. **Lunch** Daily, 11:30 a.m.–2 p.m. **Dinner** Daily, 5–9:30 p.m.

SETTING AND ATMOSPHERE Disney characters are the stars every night for dinner—and for breakfast on weekends—in this spacious dining room with a 25-foot faux oak tree in the center. At night, the lights are dimmed and the oak tree is illuminated with lanterns and twinkling lights.

HOUSE SPECIALTIES For lunch, burgers, short-rib salad, fish tacos. For dinner, a new concept with unlimited salad and soup for starters, a protein (beef, salmon, chicken) or vegetarian entrée, and finally an "endless" dessert buffet. The weekend seafood buffet features a raw bar, jumbo scallops, fried-seafood basket, paella, and salmon.

SUMMARY AND COMMENTS Garden Grove isn't worth a special trip if you aren't already staying at the Swan. But the room is pretty, the food is plentiful, and the character meals are a bargain compared with the ones at, say, Chef Mickey's.

Geyser Point Bar & Grill ★★★

AMERICAN	MODERATE	QUALITY ★★★½	VALUE ★★★
READER SURVEY RESPONSES	Too new to rate	DISNEY DINING PLAN? Yes	

Wilderness Lodge & Boulder Ridge Villas; ☎ 407-939-3463

Reservations Not accepted. **Dining Plan credits** Accepted on some items. **When to go** Anytime. **Cost range** Breakfast $7–$12 (child $5); lunch and dinner $9–$15 (child $7). **Service** ★★★½. **Friendliness** ★★★★. **Parking** Valet ($25); self-service free. **Bar** Full bar. **Customers** Hotel guests. **Wine selection** Fair. **Breakfast** 7–11 a.m. **Lunch/dinner** 11 a.m.–midnight.

SETTING AND ATMOSPHERE Picturesque views of the resort's geyser and pool area along with Bay Lake. Geyser Point is a hybrid quick-service restaurant and table-service lounge venue, with both sharing the same lovely seating area. The main food offerings are counter service, but there is a substantial bar menu with imaginative drinks and hearty snacks.

HOUSE SPECIALTIES A step up from most standard quick-service fare, lighter lunch and dinner options include a grilled salmon BLT and a veggie-packed grilled portobello mushroom salad. While a regular burger is available for those in search of classic flavors, the upgraded bison cheeseburger with Tillamook Cheddar and marionberry barbecue sauce impresses without being stuffy or overpriced.

OTHER RECOMMENDATIONS Crab cakes feature on the menu all day, with an adventurous crab cake eggs Benedict at breakfast and served on a hearty sandwich with Canadian bacon and spicy cabbage-carrot slaw at lunch and dinner. For dessert, sample a rich chocolate mousse brownie or a seasonally appropriate fruit pie.

SUMMARY AND COMMENTS Though portions are not always overwhelming in size, the quality of the food and the view of the resort area from any given table combine to create a more upscale-than-normal quick-service dining experience. Best of all, guests don't have to fuss with paper plates and trays of food in the busy dining area; ordered food is delivered to guests at their chosen tables on real dishes with nonplastic silverware (or neatly packaged in to-go containers, if so desired).

Grand Floridian Cafe ★★½

AMERICAN	MODERATE		QUALITY ★★★		VALUE ★★
READER-SURVEY RESPONSES	93%👍	7%👎	DISNEY DINING PLAN?	Yes	

Grand Floridian Resort & Spa; ☎ 407-939-3463

Reservations Accepted. **Dining Plan credits** 1 per person, per meal. **When to go** Anytime. **Cost range** Breakfast $11–$19 (child $8–$12), lunch $13–$25 (child $9), dinner $19–$33 (child $9). **Service** ★★★. **Friendliness** ★★★★. **Parking** Valet ($25); self-parking is far away. **Bar** Full service. **Wine selection** Good. **Dress** Casual. **Disabled access** Yes. **Customers** Hotel guests. **Breakfast** Daily, 7–11 a.m. **Lunch** Daily, 11:30 a.m.–2 p.m. **Dinner** Daily, 5–9 p.m.

SETTING AND ATMOSPHERE Light and airy decor with lots of sunlight, servers dressed in Victorian costumes, and pretty views of the pool and courtyard. Open three meals a day for casual dining.

HOUSE SPECIALTIES The expansive breakfast menu includes omelets, lobster hash, seasonal pancakes, and unique breakfast salads, including bacon and eggs on greens and quinoa. At lunch, the surf-and-turf burger is a standout, layering Angus beef and Maine lobster. Falafel fritters, deli sandwiches, penne pasta with shrimp or roasted chicken. For dinner, shrimp and sausage on mascarpone grits; strip steak; miso-glazed salmon. Add-ons of shrimp or scallops.

OTHER RECOMMENDATIONS Scrumptious desserts: chocolate fondue, mocha pot de crème, chocolate timbale, berry tarts.

SUMMARY AND COMMENTS A quick place to grab a tasty bite in a pleasantly themed room.

La Hacienda de San Angel ★★★

MEXICAN	EXPENSIVE		QUALITY ★★★½		VALUE ★★½
READER-SURVEY RESPONSES	87%👍	13%👎	DISNEY DINING PLAN?	Yes	

Mexico, World Showcase, Epcot; ☎ 407-939-3463

Reservations Required. **Dining Plan credits** 1 per person, per meal. **When to go** Dinner. **Cost range** $24–$59 (child $8.50–$9.50). **Service** ★★★★. **Friendliness** ★★★★★. **Parking** Epcot lot. **Bar** Full. **Wine selection** All Mexican. **Dress** Casual. **Disabled access** Yes. **Customers** Theme park guests. **Hours** Daily, 4–8:35 p.m.

SETTING AND ATMOSPHERE Right along the waterfront in Mexico, La Hacienda is a primo spot for watching fireworks through the tall windows. The interior has authentic touches of Mexico in its lighting and decor.

HOUSE SPECIALTIES The simplest dishes on the menu are the best: excellent guacamole, *queso fundido;* pork confit carnitas; the taco sampler with pork, beef, battered fish, and chicken; short ribs with chimichurri; fried-shrimp tacos with chipotle-lime aioli. The margaritas are the real deal— or just go for a flight of fine sipping tequila.

SUMMARY AND COMMENTS One word: tequila. Sampling lunches are held during Food & Wine Fest and are worth booking ahead. We're not too impressed with the pricey mixed grill, and we advise making a meal of appetizers and a signature cocktail, like the avocado margarita with a hibiscus–Himalayan salt rim. There is also a vegetarian menu if you ask.

Hollywood & Vine   ★★½

AMERICAN/BUFFET	**MODERATE**	**QUALITY** ★★★	**VALUE** ★★★
READER-SURVEY RESPONSES	80% 👍	21% 👎	**DISNEY DINING PLAN?** Yes

Echo Lake, Disney's Hollywood Studios; ☎ 407-939-3463

Reservations Recommended. **Dining Plan credits** 1 per person, per meal. **When to go** Anytime. **Cost range** Breakfast buffet $32 (child $20); lunch buffet $41 (child $25); dinner buffet $50 (child $30), depending on *Fantasmic!* seating. **Service** ★★★★. **Friendliness** ★★★★★. **Parking** DHS lot. **Bar** Full service. **Wine selection** Limited. **Dress** Casual. **Disabled access** Yes. **Customers** DHS guests. **Character breakfast** Daily, 8–10:20 a.m. **Character lunch** Daily, 11 a.m.–2:55 p.m. **Dinner** Daily, 5–9 p.m.; character dinner offered through at least early 2017.

SETTING AND ATMOSPHERE Just off Hollywood Boulevard, this 1930s-era diner has a sleek Art Deco design (think chrome and tile) that gets lost amid all the Disney-character frenzy, with little ones happy to see their favorite Disney Channel pals at breakfast and lunch. About every 30 minutes, Sofia the First, Doc McStuffins, Handy Manny, and Jake from *Jake and the Never Land Pirates* perform for cheering fans under the age of 6. Dinner is a Minnie-themed affair here through at least early 2017. Beginning May 14, guests can experience lunch with Minnie and friends too.

HOUSE SPECIALTIES Salads, soups, create-your-own pasta, fish of the day, carved and grilled meats, fresh fruits and breads, sundae bar, and chocolate fountain. Menu changes often.

SUMMARY AND COMMENTS It's family-friendly, so expect lots of noisy kids. Disney has experimented with offering Halloween and winter holiday-themed character meals here.

The Hollywood Brown Derby   ★★★★

AMERICAN	**EXPENSIVE**	**QUALITY** ★★★★	**VALUE** ★★★
READER-SURVEY RESPONSES	88% 👍	12% 👎	**DISNEY DINING PLAN?** Yes

Hollywood Boulevard, Disney's Hollywood Studios; ☎ 407-939-3463

Reservations Accepted. **Dining Plan credits** 2 per person, per meal. **When to go** Early evening. **Cost range** Lunch and dinner $18–$49 (child $7–$15). **Service** ★★★★★. **Friendliness** ★★★★★. **Parking** DHS lot. **Bar** Full service. **Wine selection** Very good. **Dress** Casual. **Disabled access** Yes. **Customers** Theme park guests. **Lunch** Daily, noon–3:25 p.m. **Dinner** Daily, 3:30–8 p.m.

SETTING AND ATMOSPHERE An oasis of civility in the middle of a theme park, this is a replica of the original Brown Derby (not the one shaped like a hat) in California. The sunken dining room has a certain elegance, with tuxedoed waiters, curved booths, and white linen. Tall palm trees in huge pots stand in the center of the room and reach for the high ceiling. Ask for a seat on the second-level gallery; it's much quieter and affords good people-watching in the hectic main space.

HOUSE SPECIALTIES Cobb salad (named for Bob Cobb, owner of the original restaurant), the famous grapefruit cake made from the original Brown Derby recipe, grilled Wagyu-beef burger, and original fettuccine Alfredo at lunch; beef Wellington, lamb "two ways" (chop and pulled), charred filet of beef and an odd tofu noodle bowl at dinner. Expensive add-ons of lobster tail or scallops that should be entrées but aren't. The kids' menu includes grilled black grouper, whole-grain penne pasta, and grilled chicken breast.

OTHER RECOMMENDATIONS Togarashi-pumpkinseed-crusted ahi tuna, crispy jumbo lump crab cake appetizer.

SUMMARY AND COMMENTS The Brown Derby is one of the top theme park restaurants at Disney World. It's expensive, yes, but also a wonderful way to relax and regenerate. The decor is so perfect you'll feel as if you're in a Fred Astaire–Ginger Rogers movie. Service is outstanding, as is the food.

If you don't have reservations, the patio lounge opens at noon and is first-come, first-served, with a menu of small plates and cocktails, and a good place to have a drink and wait until your table is ready. Shaded by big umbrellas, the outdoor tables are great spots for people-watching. The menu ($9–$29) is all small plates: Cobb salad, artisanal cheeses, charcuterie, Wagyu-beef sliders with Cognac-mustard aioli and Gouda cheese, and desserts. (You can also order from the regular menu.) Drink choices include various flights—martinis, margaritas, Champagnes, white and red wines, Scotches, and Grand Marnier vintages—along with wines by the glass or half-bottle and classic cocktails.

House of Blues Restaurant & Bar   ★★★

REGIONAL AMERICAN	MODERATE	QUALITY ★★★½	VALUE ★★★
READER-SURVEY RESPONSES	89%👍	11%👎	DISNEY DINING PLAN? Yes

Disney Springs West Side; ☎ 407-934-2583

Reservations Recommended. **Dining Plan credits** 1 per person, per meal. **When to go** Lunch or early dinner; Sunday gospel brunch. **Cost range** $13–$30 (child $7–$10), brunch $40 (child $22). **Service** ★★★★. **Friendliness** ★★★. **Parking** Disney Springs garage. **Bar** Full service. **Wine selection** Modest. **Dress** Casual. **Disabled access** Good. **Customers** Blues lovers. **Brunch** 2 seatings on Sunday: 10:30 a.m. and 1 p.m. **Lunch** Daily, 11:30 a.m.–4 p.m. **Dinner** Daily, 4:15 a.m.–10 p.m.

SETTING AND ATMOSPHERE Adjacent to Cirque du Soleil, House of Blues has a ramshackle look that's almost out of place in Disney Springs, but it's a solid stop for lunch or dinner before or after a show. And with its own separate concert hall, there's often great live music, including the lively Sunday gospel brunch. A quick-service window, along with the outdoor bar and seating (with live music in the evening), draws passersby. But if you have time for a sit-down meal, the fabulous folk art in the restaurant is worth a look. The enchanting, art-filled Voodoo Garden has been replaced with more indoor seating.

HOUSE SPECIALTIES Barbecue sandwiches (pulled pork, brisket, and chicken), ribs, and smoked turkey legs at The Smokehouse walk-up window. Inside, choose from flatbreads, burgers, shrimp and grits, ribs, New York strip steak, and Voodoo Shrimp simmered in amber beer.

OTHER RECOMMENDATIONS Jambalaya, tacos, mac and cheese, bourbon bread pudding.

SUMMARY AND COMMENTS The best food on the West Side in a fun, casual setting. If you want to take in one of the musical acts next door, see the show first so you can get a good seat; then come back afterward to eat.

Il Mulino New York Trattoria ★★★

ITALIAN	EXPENSIVE	QUALITY ★★★	VALUE ★★
READER-SURVEY RESPONSES 76%👍	25%👎	DISNEY DINING PLAN? No	

Swan Hotel; ☎ 407-934-1199

Reservations Accepted. **When to go** Dinner. **Cost range** $16–$45 (child $12–$16). **Service** ★★. **Friendliness** ★★. **Parking** Valet (free with validation) or hotel lot ($18). **Bar** Full service. **Wine selection** Good. **Dress** Dressy casual. **Disabled access** Yes. **Customers** Mostly hotel guests and conventioneers. **Hours** Daily, 5–11 p.m.

SETTING AND ATMOSPHERE A spin-off of the New York City restaurant, Il Mulino takes an upscale-casual, downtown NY approach to Italian cuisine, with family-style platters for sharing. Tables are dark wood, and an open kitchen creates a bustle. You can request private dining in one of the smaller rooms.

HOUSE SPECIALTIES The cuisine focuses on Italy's Abruzzi region, with hearty pastas and big cuts of meat. Try the spaghetti carbonara or the veal saltimbocca. Risottos are well made; spaghetti with baby shrimp, clams, mussels, and calamari is well made but overpriced.

OTHER RECOMMENDATIONS Charcuterie, mussels in white wine, pizzas, sautéed jumbo shrimp over cannellini beans, rib eye with sautéed spinach.

SUMMARY AND COMMENTS A predictable menu with a little bit of everything you would expect in a bustling Italian restaurant: pizza, pasta, meat, seafood. Il Mulino is perfect for conventioneers—and there appear to be many of them sharing the big tables—but adventurous eaters may want to go elsewhere.

Jiko—The Cooking Place ★★★★½

AFRICAN/FUSION	EXPENSIVE	QUALITY ★★★★½	VALUE ★★★½
READER-SURVEY RESPONSES 97%👍	3%👎	DISNEY DINING PLAN? Yes	

Animal Kingdom Lodge & Villas–Jambo House; ☎ 407-939-3463

Reservations Required. **Dining Plan credits** 2 per person, per meal. **When to go** Dinner. **Cost range** $35–$59.99 (child $9–$18). **Service** ★★★★★. **Friendliness** ★★★★★. **Parking** Valet ($25) or hotel lot. **Bar** Full bar. **Wine selection** All South African. **Dress** Dressy casual. **Disabled access** Good. **Customers** Hotel guests and locals. **Hours** Daily, 5:30–10 p.m.

SETTING AND ATMOSPHERE Bathed in a perpetual sunset, with metal birds soaring around, the main dining room is warm and inviting, accented by the central *jiko* ("cooking place" in Swahili), where chefs prepare many of the appetizers featured on the restaurant's seasonally rotating menu in view of a few lucky diners. As you enter, stop to gaze at the wine room. The bottles on display represent just a sample of the massive wine selection—the largest collection of South African wines available outside of the African continent.

HOUSE SPECIALTIES Guests flock to Jiko for several dishes, among them the grilled wild-boar tenderloin appetizer, African spice–infused flatbreads, maize-crusted Alaskan halibut with tomato-butter sauce, and oak-grilled filet mignon with South African red wine sauce and bobotie mac and cheese. The seasonally updated malva (mallow) pudding dessert highlights traditional African flavors on the sweet spectrum, but the pastry chefs also like to highlight local produce with such treats as peppercorn-infused strawberry shortcake and orange-ginger cheesecake.

OTHER RECOMMENDATIONS Botswana-style Seswaa short ribs and Moroccan lamb tagine bring on the spices, while luscious seasonal soup options like the curried butternut squash bisque start any meal off on the right foot. For those in search of vegan and vegetarian options, Jiko stands out as one of the few Disney Signature Dining locations to offer dedicated options that are both satisfying and flavorful. A large selection of specialty teas and Kenyan press-pot coffee complement the excellent dessert selections.

SUMMARY AND COMMENTS Tucked away in a quiet corner of Animal Kingdom Lodge, Jiko is one of the true hidden gems of fine dining in Walt Disney World. Superb service in a nonfussy atmosphere can be tough to pull off, but Jiko does that and more, welcoming guests into the cooking place for a meal packed with truly unique flavors. Families will enjoy the dining room's perpetual sunset, while solo diners or small parties may want to take advantage of the cooking place's seating for both dinner and a show.

Jock Lindsey's Hangar Bar ★★½

COCKTAILS AND BAR BITES	MODERATE	QUALITY	★★½	VALUE ★★½
READER-SURVEY RESPONSES	91% 👍	9% 👎	DISNEY DINING PLAN? No	

The Landing, Disney Springs; ☎ 407-939-3463

Reservations Not accepted. **When to go** Anytime. **Cost range** Appetizers $9–$16; cocktails $9.25–$21. **Service** ★★★★. **Friendliness** ★★★★. **Parking** Disney Springs garage. **Bar** Full service. **Wine selection** OK; beer selection is better. **Dress** Casual. **Disabled access** Yes. **Customers** Theme park guests. **Hours** Sunday–Thursday, 11:30 a.m.–midnight; Friday–Saturday, 11:30 a.m.–1 a.m.

SETTING AND ATMOSPHERE A 1930s-era airplane hangar converted into a bar. Lots of Indiana Jones movie references in the decor. Booth, bar, and table seating are available, all of it kid-friendly. Indoor and covered outdoor seating are available.

SUMMARY AND COMMENTS Definitely more bar than sit-down restaurant, Jock Lindsey's also serves appetizers. Our favorites are Dr. Elsa's Shrimp BLT flatbread, with shrimp, bacon, roasted tomatoes, and basil pesto, and the Sallah's Falafel. Skip the cheese-stuffed dates (served cold, as if they'd been refrigerated for a long while), pretzels (too dry), brats, and sliders (both unremarkable).

Jungle Navigation Co. Ltd. Skipper Canteen ★★★½

ASIAN/AFRICAN/LATIN	MODERATE	QUALITY · ★★★	VALUE ★★★
READER-SURVEY RESPONSES	81% 👍 19% 👎 –	DISNEY DINING PLAN? Yes	

Frontierland, Magic Kingdom; ☎ 407-939-3463

Reservations Recommended. **Dining Plan credits** 1 per person, per meal (table-service credit for lunch and dinner). **When to go** Lunch or dinner. **Cost range** Lunch and dinner $17–$35 (child $10–$13). **Service** ★★★★. **Friendliness** ★★★★. **Parking** Magic Kingdom lot. **Bar** Limited selection of beer and wine. **Dress** Casual. **Disabled access** Yes. **Customers** Magic Kingdom guests. **Lunch** Daily, 11 a.m.–2:55 p.m. **Dinner** Daily, 3–9:30 p.m.

SETTING AND ATMOSPHERE Posited as the home of off-duty Jungle Cruise skippers, Skipper Canteen offers guests an oasis from the theme park with three distinct dining rooms (and a boatload of corny jokes). The crew's mess hall features high ceilings, dark wooden fixtures, and souvenirs collected from skippers' travels bathed in stained glass window-tinted natural light. Behind a hidden bookcase (with highly amusing book titles), guests can visit the secret meeting room of the Society of Explorers and Adventurers, filled with posh fixtures, maps, and a beautiful collection of butterflies. The jungle room completes the dining set, with intimate seating near intricately carved wood bookshelves and colorful stained glass lamps.

HOUSE SPECIALTIES An eclectic menu features flavors from several world cuisines, with Asian influences in the *shu mai, char siu* pork (a house favorite), *shiriki* noodle salad, and Korean barbecue–inspired "Tastes Like Chicken" crispy fried chicken. South American influences samba into the grilled steak with chimichurri, as well as the house-made corn pancakes topped with mojo pork and avocado cream. The rich Kungaloosh chocolate cake with caramelized bananas will close out any meal with a smile.

OTHER RECOMMENDATIONS Veggie lovers rejoice at the curried veggie crew stew, a heartier vegetarian alternative to typical offerings. Skip's Beefy Baked Pasta, an Egyptian take on lasagna, uses a familiar form to introduce guests to mildly exotic flavors. Any dessert here is worth your time, with high-quality vanilla chiffon cakes with tropical flavors and a rice pudding with a zingy lemon curd. Even the kids' menu satisfies across the board, especially with a chocolate lava cake or fun sunflower seed-coated chocolate-dipped bananas.

SUMMARY AND COMMENTS A welcome addition to Magic Kingdom dining, Skipper Canteen breathes life into theme park dining with fresh flavors and fine service. The menu decidedly does not cater to simpler tastes and aims higher than it can sometimes achieve, but any in-park restaurant that tackles dining head on by serving whole fried fish and head-on prawns is worth a shot. More than a year after the restaurant's opening, the adventurous menu has stayed largely intact, thanks to the ever-diversifying tastes of park guests.

Kimonos ★★★★

JAPANESE	MODERATE	QUALITY ★★★★½	VALUE ★★★
READER-SURVEY RESPONSES 87%👍 13%👎		DISNEY DINING PLAN? No	

Swan Hotel; ☎ 407-934-1609

Reservations Accepted for parties of 6 or more. **When to go** Dinner. **Cost range** Sushi and rolls à la carte $5.25–$18. **Service** ★★★★★. **Friendliness** ★★★★★. **Parking** Valet ($26) or hotel lot ($18). **Bar** Full service. **Wine selection** Very good. **Dress** Casual. **Disabled access** Yes. **Customers** Hotel guests and locals. **Hours** Daily, 5:30–11 p.m.; bar opens at 5 p.m.

SETTING AND ATMOSPHERE Sushi and nightly karaoke—what a combo! Go early if you want a zen experience with sushi and sake in the serene setting: black-lacquered tabletops and counters, tall pillars rising to bamboo rafters with rice-paper lanterns, and elegant kimonos that hang outstretched on the walls and between the dining sections. The chefs will greet you with a friendly welcome, and you'll be offered a hot towel to clean your hands.

HOUSE SPECIALTIES Both cooked and raw sushi and hot dishes. Classic rolls include California, tuna, and soft-shell crab; the Kimonos roll features tuna, salmon, yellowtail, and wasabi mayo. Small plates include beef satay and chicken katsu.

SUMMARY AND COMMENTS The skill of the sushi artists is as much a joy to watch as is eating the wonderfully fresh creations. Karaoke starts at 9 p.m., with mostly the convention crowd at the microphone.

Kona Cafe ★★★

POLYNESIAN/PAN-ASIAN	MODERATE	QUALITY ★★★	VALUE ★★★★
READER-SURVEY RESPONSES 93%👍 7%👎		DISNEY DINING PLAN? Yes	

Polynesian Village Resort; ☎ 407-939-3463

Reservations Accepted. **Dining Plan credits** 1 per person, per meal. **When to go** Anytime. **Cost range** Breakfast $10–$16 (child $6–$8), lunch $13–$18 (child $9–$11), dinner $19–$34 (child $9–$11). **Service** ★★★★. **Friendliness** ★★★★★. **Parking** Valet ($25) or hotel lot. **Bar** Full service. **Wine selection** OK. **Dress** Casual. **Disabled access** Yes. **Customers** Mostly hotel guests; some locals. **Breakfast** Daily, 7:30–11:45 a.m. **Lunch** Daily, noon–2:45 p.m. **Dinner** Daily, 5–10 p.m.

SETTING AND ATMOSPHERE With the remake of the Polynesian Village Resort, Kona Cafe remains the hotel's coffee shop, open three meals a day. Right next to the monorail station, the casual, open dining room is an easy ride from the Magic Kingdom by boat or monorail should you want to escape the theme park for lunch or dinner.

HOUSE SPECIALTIES Breakfast: Tonga Toast—French toast layered with bananas—is still the most requested dish. Lunch: passable crab cakes, fish tacos, grilled ahi tuna sandwich, pan-Asian noodles with shrimp, beef, or vegetables; Angus beef and fried shrimp Kona burger; banana-chocolate crème brûlée. Dinner: sushi, tuna poke, pan-seared duck breast, grilled curry-crusted lamb chop, New York strip steak, and sustainable fish.

OTHER RECOMMENDATIONS Charcuterie and cheese, Kilauea torte (chocolate cake with a warm chocolate center), and Kona coffee served in a press pot.

SUMMARY AND COMMENTS The menu is themed to the island decor, and though the dining room isn't fancy, the food is on a higher plane than your average java joint's. An adjacent sushi bar serves the full restaurant menu for dinner and offers coffee and pastries during breakfast and lunch.

Liberty Tree Tavern ★★★½

AMERICAN	MODERATE		QUALITY ★★★		VALUE ★★★
READER-SURVEY RESPONSES	88%👍	12%👎	DISNEY DINING PLAN?	Yes	

Liberty Square, Magic Kingdom; ☎ 407-939-3463

Reservations Accepted. **Dining Plan credits** 1 per person, per meal. **When to go** Lunch or dinner. **Cost range** Lunch $14–$23 (child $9.50–$11), dinner $33 (child $19). **Service** ★★★★. **Friendliness** ★★★★. **Parking** Magic Kingdom lot. **Bar** Limited selection of beer, wine, and hard cider. **Dress** Casual. **Disabled access** Yes. **Customers** Theme park guests. **Lunch** Daily, 11 a.m.–2:55 p.m. **Dinner** Daily, 3:15–9:30 p.m.

SETTING AND ATMOSPHERE With individual rooms themed to historical figures in United States history (Betsy Ross, Ben Franklin, Thomas Jefferson, John Paul Jones, and George and Martha Washington), Liberty Tree Tavern feels like a quaint and cozy Colonial home nestled in a sprawling theme park. Appropriately creaky wood staircases flank the central lobby, which can be quite busy during popular mealtimes.

HOUSE SPECIALTIES Most guests come (and return) to Liberty Tree for the All-You-Care-to-Enjoy Patriot's Platter, with roasted turkey, prime rib, pork roast, mashed potatoes, stuffing, seasonal vegetables, and mac and cheese. It was recently updated to be made entirely in-house and is much tastier as a result. For those looking for something slightly smaller at lunch, stick to the New England clam chowder, Colony Salad with seared salmon, and Ooey Gooey Toffee Pudding (worth the splurge alone).

OTHER RECOMMENDATIONS The lunch menu is fairly compact, but several options are worth consideration: The Freedom Pasta, packed with fresh vegetables and served with grilled chicken or shrimp, is easy to share, even for two adults, and the Crab & Lobster dip makes for a filling starter.

SUMMARY AND COMMENTS Always a solid standby for families in search of classic American fare, the tavern serves up quality food with good service at a quick pace—a luxury in Magic Kingdom. Very popular for both lunch and dinner, reservations are sometimes hard to come by but are worth the effort to score: Even with new additions to Magic Kingdom dining, Liberty Tree Tavern still ranks as one of the top meals you can enjoy inside this park. Because of its location, dead-center on the parade route, a late lunch can be timed to end just as Festival of Fantasy passes.

Mama Melrose's Ristorante Italiano ★★½

ITALIAN	MODERATE		QUALITY ★★★	VALUE ★★
READER-SURVEY RESPONSES	88%👍	13%👎	DISNEY DINING PLAN?	Yes

Muppet Courtyard, Disney's Hollywood Studios; ☎ 407-939-3463

Reservations Required. **Dining Plan credits** 1 per person, per meal. **When to go** Lunch or dinner. **Cost range** $15–$33 (child $10–$11). **Service** ★★★. **Friendliness** ★★★★★. **Parking** DHS lot. **Bar** Full service. **Wine selection** Limited. **Dress** Casual. **Disabled access** Yes. **Customers** Theme park guests. **Lunch** Daily, 11:30 a.m.–3:15 p.m. **Dinner** Daily, 3:45–8 p.m.

SETTING AND ATMOSPHERE Tucked at the back of Disney's Hollywood Studios, Mama Melrose's is easy to miss. This casual restaurant is inspired by "red-sauce Italian" joints as much as New York and L.A. movie scenes: checkered tablecloths, red vinyl booths, and grapevines hanging from the rafters. Ambience is generally quiet unless it's peak season.

HOUSE SPECIALTIES Fresh mozzarella, penne alla vodka or campanelle pasta with chicken or shrimp, flatbread "pizzas," seasonal pastas, pork saltimbocca. Whole-wheat pasta available.

OTHER RECOMMENDATIONS Cioppino; charred strip steak; oak-fired mussels; tiramisu, Ghirardelli chocolate and cherry torte, and cannoli for dessert.

SUMMARY AND COMMENTS Because of Mama Melrose's out-of-the-way location, you can sometimes just walk in, especially in the evening, but this will change as Disney's new Star Wars attractions take up what was wasted space nearby. The food won't win any awards—the red sauce is a little heavy, for instance—but for family-style Italian, it's fine.

Maya Grill ★

MEXICAN/AMERICAN	EXPENSIVE		QUALITY ★	VALUE ★
READER-SURVEY RESPONSES	79%👍	21%👎	DISNEY DINING PLAN?	Yes

Coronado Springs Resort; ☎ 407-939-3463

Reservations Accepted. **Dining Plan credits** 1 per person, per meal. **When to go** Dinner. **Cost range** $20–$58 (child $7–$9.50). **Service** ★★★. **Friendliness** ★★★. **Parking** Hotel lot. **Bar** Full service. **Wine selection** Fair. **Dress** Casual. **Disabled access** Yes. **Customers** Hotel guests. **Hours** Daily, 5–10 p.m.

SETTING AND ATMOSPHERE The dining room, long in need of a redo, was designed to evoke the ancient world of the Maya, achieving "a harmony of fire, sun, and water." But the idea falls short. The kitchen is open to view—but so is the barren and starkly lit walkway outside.

HOUSE SPECIALTIES Overpriced Tex-Mex and Nuevo Latino dinner fare, such as a $58 rib eye, fajita skillet, and slow-cooked pork with corn tortillas.

SUMMARY AND COMMENTS Maya Grill at the relatively overlooked Coronado Springs is owned by the same folks who run the restaurants at the Mexico Pavilion in Epcot, but execution falls short here considering the high prices ($24 for shrimp tacos). Still, conventioneers keep it busy.

Monsieur Paul ★★★★

FRENCH	EXPENSIVE		QUALITY ★★★★½	VALUE ★★★
READER-SURVEY RESPONSES	86%👍	14%👎	DISNEY DINING PLAN?	YES

France, World Showcase, Epcot; ☎ 407-939-3463

Reservations Required. **Dining Plan credits** 2 per person, per meal on Plus and Deluxe Plans; 1 per person, per meal on Premium and Platinum Plans. **When to go** Late dinner. **Cost range** $39–$44 (child $13–$16). **Service** ★★★★. **Friendliness** ★★★★★. **Parking** Epcot or BoardWalk lot; enter through back gate. **Bar** Full service. **Wine selection** Good but pricey. **Dress** Casual.

Disabled access Elevator to second level. **Customers** Theme park guests. **Hours** Daily, 5:30–8:35 p.m.

SETTING AND ATMOSPHERE Light and modern, Monsieur Paul is tucked away upstairs at the France Pavilion. Access lies up a stairway (there's also an elevator) lined with photos of legendary French chef Paul Bocuse. His son, Jérôme, runs the restaurants started in 1982 in Epcot by his father and two other famous French chefs, Gaston Lenôtre and Roger Vergé, and can often be seen visiting tables in the dining room. Despite Monsieur Paul's relaxed ambience, this is definitely upscale cuisine, with sublime sauces and classic French preparations. Open only for dinner; request a table at the windows to watch the world go by on World Showcase Lagoon. Seats just 120.

HOUSE SPECIALTIES Chef Bocuse's black-truffle soup; red snapper in potato "scales"; classic *cassolette d'escargots;* roasted duck breast with oxtail-stuffed cabbage.

SUMMARY AND COMMENTS Monsieur Paul may be a bit formal and high-priced for many park guests, but if you can get past the sticker shock, this is *the* spot for a quiet dinner and conversation. Young chef Nicolas Lemoyne, who worked at l'Auberge du Pont de Collonges in Lyon, France, wows diners with classic French tastes, including Maine lobster with *pommes fondantes* in black-pepper sauce, and warm chocolate-almond cake with raspberry coulis. There's also a three-course fixed-price menu ($89 per person), along with a solid wine list. A rather grown-up kids' menu includes roasted chicken breast and filet mignon.

Morimoto Asia ★★★½

JAPANESE/PAN-ASIAN	EXPENSIVE	QUALITY ★★★½	VALUE ★★★★
READER-SURVEY RESPONSES	88%👍 13%👎	DISNEY DINING PLAN? Yes	

Disney Springs, The Landing; ☎ 407-939-6686

Reservations Accepted. **Dining Plan credits** 2 per person, per meal. **When to go** Lunch, dinner, late night. **Cost range** Lunch $9–$36 (child $12), dinner $12–$54 (child $12). **Service** ★★★★. **Friendliness** ★★★★. **Parking** Disney Springs Lot. **Bar** Wine, beer, sake, cocktails. **Wine selection** Wide range by the glass or bottle. **Dress** Casual. **Disabled access** Yes. **Customers** Theme park guests and locals. **Lunch** Daily, 11:30 a.m.–4:15 p.m. **Dinner** Daily, 5–10 p.m. **Forbidden Lounge late menu** Weeknights, 10 p.m.–midnight; weekends, 10 p.m.–1 a.m.

SETTING AND ATMOSPHERE Ultra-hip version of a big-city club with Japanese wood-tone highlights. Iron Chef Masaharu Morimoto has taken the Disney opportunity to open his first restaurant that expands beyond sushi and into a pan-Asian expedition, and in most cases he hits the mark. Quirky takes on Chinese, Japanese, and Korean dishes join a substantial sushi menu from the kitchen and upstairs sushi bar, where the chef makes frequent appearances. Fishing baskets and steel beads form the chandeliers, and a continuous white engineered-stone ribbon runs from the "secret" entrance to the Forbidden Lounge upstairs, creating the handrail, bar, and seating areas throughout the building and framing the glass-bottle lighting upstairs (a nod to the building's fictional beginnings as a bottling company). There are anime cartoons and graphic photographs throughout, framing the multi-compartmentalized open kitchen.

HOUSE SPECIALTIES Pork, shrimp, chicken, and veggie dim sum; 24-hour-marinated, house-carved Peking duck; kung pao chicken; Morimoto spare ribs; lo mein, pad Thai, and ramen noodles; sushi rolls and sashimi.

OTHER RECOMMENDATIONS Indonesian *goreng,* Korean *buri bop,* Singapore *laksa,* Chinese lobster *chow fun.*

SUMMARY AND COMMENTS Parts of the menu are so inventive and spot-on that you can forgive the massive misses, like the puzzling cream cheese–stuffed "krab" Rangoon cigars. The outdoor terrace upstairs has what might be the best view of the new Disney Springs lagoon, rising above the sometimes noisy crowd below. Look for the "unmarked" door on the side of the building to enter the Forbidden Lounge (not really a secret, but Disney Springs isn't on a spring, either) with its late-night menu until 11 p.m. If you're in a hurry and just want a quick bite, the walk-up window outside and to the left of the entrance serves sushi, rice bowls, and other snacks. Prices range from $6 to $15, and outdoor seating is available.

Narcoossee's ★★★★½

SEAFOOD	EXPENSIVE		QUALITY ★★★½		VALUE ★★
READER-SURVEY RESPONSES	88%👍	13%👎	DISNEY DINING PLAN?		Yes

Grand Floridian Resort & Spa; ☎ 407-939-3463

Reservations Required. **Dining Plan credits** 2 per person, per meal. **When to go** Sunday brunch, early evening. **Cost range** Brunch $69 (child $41); dinner $33–$75 (child $7–$17). **Service** ★★★★★. **Friendliness** ★★★★★. **Parking** Valet ($25); self-parking is deceptively far away. **Bar** Full service. **Wine selection** Good. **Dress** Dressy casual. **Disabled access** Yes. **Customers** Hotel guests and locals. **Dinner** Daily, 5:30–10 p.m. **Sunday brunch** 10 a.m.–2 p.m.

SETTING AND ATMOSPHERE Situated on the waterfront of Seven Seas Lagoon at the far end of Disney's Grand Floridian Resort, Narcoossee's may not amaze with its simple wood finishes and plain-bordering-on-sparse interiors, but the lagoon and Magic Kingdom views and wraparound porch certainly bring a bit of ambience. Though the restaurant is slightly cramped and occasionally loud, the dim lighting and finely appointed tableware make for a romantic date night or a classy brunch affair.

HOUSE SPECIALTIES It's hard to go wrong with any of the fresh seafood selections, but the flown-in-daily steamed Maine lobster and butter-poached twin lobster tails definitely top the list of must-try entrées. Local shrimp shines in seasonal pasta dishes and appetizer shrimp and grits. Asian-inspired ahi tuna or pan-seared Georges Bank day-boat scallops may also strike your fancy. For those sticking to land animals, the duck and filet mignon are excellent, but seafood really dominates the favorites here. For dessert, go for the perfectly executed crème brûlée.

OTHER RECOMMENDATIONS Maine lobster bisque and Prince Edward Island mussels start any meal off well, and the signature Narcoossee's Candy Bar will satisfy any chocolate lover. Don't miss the lobster mac and cheese and loaded mashed potatoes on the sides menu—both are worth the splurge. Sunday brunch is a must, with upscale takes on classic breakfast entrées and extravagant cocktails.

SUMMARY AND COMMENTS An oft-forgotten Signature restaurant, Narcoossee's outpaces upscale competitors around Walt Disney World in delivering both impeccable service and outstanding food. You'll certainly pay a hefty price for a meal here, but the high-quality, fresh ingredients shine on every dish. Servers expertly pace your meal to allow viewing opportunities for Magic Kingdom fireworks and the Electrical Water Pageant, so aim for a later reservation in the evening for both dinner and a show.

Nine Dragons Restaurant ★★

CHINESE	MODERATE		QUALITY ★★		VALUE ★★
READER-SURVEY RESPONSES	80%👍	20%👎	DISNEY DINING PLAN?		Yes

China, World Showcase, Epcot; ☎ 407-939-3463

Reservations Recommended. **Dining Plan credits** 1 per person, per meal. **When to go** Lunch or dinner. **Cost range** Lunch $16–$23 (child $8–$11), dinner

$15–$27 (child $8–$11). **Service** ★★★. **Friendliness** ★★★★. **Parking** Epcot lot. **Bar** Full service. **Wine selection** Minimal. **Dress** Casual. **Disabled access** Yes. **Customers** Theme park guests. **Lunch** Daily, noon–3:25 p.m. **Dinner** Daily, 3:30–8:50 p.m.

SETTING AND ATMOSPHERE Nine Dragons' attractive interior—subdued wood tones, colorful lanterns, beautiful backlit glass sculptures from China—and efficient service create a respite from the bustle of World Showcase. Ask for a window seat for a view of passersby on the promenade.

HOUSE SPECIALTIES Braised-pork-belly steamed buns; Shrimp Typhoon; kung pao shrimp; Beijing roast duck salad with egg roll skin and hoisin sauce dressing; five-spiced fish.

OTHER RECOMMENDATIONS Vegetarian stir-fry, noodle sampler with fresh vegetables and pork and chicken dipping sauces. Sticky rice pudding and ginger cake for dessert.

SUMMARY AND COMMENTS You can usually get a table without a wait in the spacious dining room, and while Nine Dragons gets a bad rep for being pricey, we think the food and service are above average.

1900 Park Fare ★★½

AMERICAN/BUFFET	MODERATE	QUALITY ★★★	VALUE ★★★
READER-SURVEY RESPONSES	92%👍 8%👎	DISNEY DINING PLAN?	Yes

Grand Floridian Resort & Spa; ☎ 407-939-3463

Reservations Recommended. **Dining Plan credits** 1 per person, per meal. **When to go** Breakfast or dinner. **Cost range** Breakfast $32 (child $20), dinner $50 (child $30). **Service** ★★★★. **Friendliness** ★★★★. **Parking** Valet ($25); self-parking is deceptively far away. **Bar** Full service. **Wine selection** Limited. **Dress** Casual. **Disabled access** Yes. **Customers** Hotel and resort guests. **Character breakfast** Daily, 8–11:50 a.m. **Character dinner** Daily, 4–9 p.m.

SETTING AND ATMOSPHERE Everyone is here to see the Disney characters—the food and decor are afterthoughts, though the tables are set with linen and service is first-rate in the bright, cavernous, high-ceilinged room. An antique band organ, "Big Bertha," periodically pumps out music to dine by.

HOUSE SPECIALTIES The buffet usually includes mojo roast pork loin, Mongolian beef stir-fry, Mississippi fried catfish, and Florida strawberry soup.

OTHER RECOMMENDATIONS Separate buffet for kids includes cheese ravioli, hot dogs, chicken tenders, and a taco bar.

ENTERTAINMENT AND AMENITIES Character dining with Mary Poppins, Winnie the Pooh, Tigger, and Alice at breakfast, and Cinderella, Prince Charming, and others at dinner.

SUMMARY AND COMMENTS A good, relatively inexpensive choice for character dining, but too bright and loud for adults without children.

'Ohana ★★★

POLYNESIAN	MODERATE	QUALITY ★★★½	VALUE ★★★
READER-SURVEY RESPONSES	91%👍 9%👎	DISNEY DINING PLAN?	Yes

Polynesian Village Resort; ☎ 407-939-3463

Reservations Recommended. **Dining Plan credits** 1 per person, per meal. **When to go** Breakfast or dinner. **Cost range** Character breakfast $35 (child $20), dinner $46 (child $26). **Service** ★★★★. **Friendliness** ★★★★★. **Parking** Hotel lot. **Bar** Full service. **Wine selection** Limited. **Dress** Casual. **Disabled access** Yes. **Customers** Resort guests. **Character breakfast** Daily, 7:30 a.m.–noon. **Dinner** Daily, 3:30–10 p.m.

SETTING AND ATMOSPHERE Columns of carved tiki gods support the raised thatched roof in the center of 'Ohana's main dining room, while the dining tables, arranged in rows, resemble long, segmented surfboards. The centerpiece of the main room is a large, open-pit grill, on which your food is prepared with flair *and* flare: From time to time, the chef will pour some liquid on the fire, causing huge flames to shoot up. This is usually in response to something one of the strolling entertainers has said, evoking a sign from the fire gods.

'Ohana is perfect for families with young children. At any given moment, there may be a hula-hoop contest or a coconut race, where kids are invited to push coconuts around the dining room with broomsticks.

HOUSE SPECIALTIES Skewer service is the specialty here—there's no menu. As soon as you're seated, the feeding frenzy begins. Starters include honey-glazed chicken wings, fried pork dumplings, pineapple-coconut bread, and mixed green salads. The main course is steak, sweet-and-sour chicken, and spicy grilled peel-and-eat shrimp, accompanied by stir-fried vegetables and egg noodles with pineapple in teriyaki sauce, all placed on a lazy Susan in the center of the table. Breakfast includes scrambled eggs, island-style fried potatoes, and Hawaiian pork sausages.

ENTERTAINMENT AND AMENITIES Strolling singers, games, and Disney characters at breakfast.

SUMMARY AND COMMENTS Our readers adore 'Ohana, which means "family." (Breakfast with Lilo and Stitch might be reason enough.) The fact that the food just keeps coming makes it all taste a little better. Request a seat in the main dining room, where the fire pit is.

Olivia's Cafe ★★★

AMERICAN	MODERATE	QUALITY ★★★	VALUE ★★
READER-SURVEY RESPONSES	88%👍 12%👎	DISNEY DINING PLAN?	Yes

Old Key West Resort; ☎ 407-939-3463

Reservations Accepted. **Dining Plan credits** 1 per person, per meal. **When to go** Lunch. **Cost range** Breakfast $12–$16 (child $6–$8), lunch and dinner $14.50–$33 (child $10–$11). **Service** ★★★★. **Friendliness** ★★★★. **Parking** Hotel lot. **Bar** Full service. **Wine selection** Limited. **Dress** Casual. **Disabled access** Yes. **Customers** Resort guests. **Breakfast** Daily, 7:30–10:30 a.m. **Lunch** Daily, 11:30 a.m.–4:55 p.m. **Dinner** Daily, 5–10 p.m.

SETTING AND ATMOSPHERE Old Key West was the first Disney Vacation Club. Many DVC members consider Olivia's their home kitchen, and their photos decorate the walls. The decor is Disneyfied Key West, with pastels, mosaic-tile floors, potted palms, and tropical trees in the center of the room. There is some outside seating, which looks out over the waterway. Tile, wood siding, and no tablecloths add up to one noisy dining room.

HOUSE SPECIALTIES Breakfast: crab-cake eggs Benedict, banana-bread French toast, and poached eggs with sweet potato hash. Lunch and dinner: conch fritters and conch chowder; Olivia's classic burger with applewood-smoked bacon; Plantation Key pork chop with smoked-Gouda fondue; slow-cooked prime rib; shrimp and rice; barbecue pork ribs.

OTHER RECOMMENDATIONS Catch of the day, banana-bread pudding sundae, Key lime tart.

SUMMARY AND COMMENTS Unless you're staying at Old Key West, you might not know Olivia's exists—all the more reason to visit. Service is super friendly, and the kitchen turns out tasty casual fare. Take a stroll on the boardwalk with a Rum Runner or frozen margarita after your meal.

Paddlefish ★★★★

AMERICAN/SEAFOOD	EXPENSIVE	QUALITY ★★★½	VALUE ★★½
READER-SURVEY RESPONSES	Too new to rate	DISNEY DINING PLAN?	Yes

The Landing, Disney Springs; ☎ 407-934-2628

Reservations Recommended. **Dining Plan credits** 2 per person, per meal. **When to go** Lunch or dinner. **Cost range** $12–$70 (child $9–$15). **Service** ★★★★½. **Friendliness** ★★★★★. **Parking** Disney Springs Lime Garage. **Bar** Full service. **Dress** Casual. **Disabled access** Yes. **Customers** Theme park guests, locals, fans of seafood. **Lunch** Daily, 11:30 a.m.–3:55 p.m. **Dinner** Daily, 4 p.m.–11 p.m.

SETTING AND ATMOSPHERE Formerly home to Fulton's Crab House, Paddlefish reopened in early 2017 with a modern aesthetic, making the stationary "steamship" seem more like a classy yacht than a classic paddleboat. Sleek design and muted colors inside don't distract from the views offered from the large picture windows at the sides and rear of the ship, overlooking her iconic paddlewheel. Outdoor seating on the first and third decks offers prime views of the area, but the true star of the restaurant is the rooftop bar, where you can enjoy an iconic Florida sunset alongside a drink and select appetizer options.

HOUSE SPECIALTIES Build-your-own seafood boils and tableside-prepared lobster guacamole are sure to impress any guests. The crab fries (hand-cut and perfectly fried) and yellow curry Maine mussels are solid choices for appetizers if you're in search of cooked, fresh seafood. Ahi poke and market-fresh oysters will cool you down and tickle your palate on hot summer days. The Atlantic halibut–based modern fish and chips is worth the splurge, but for something classier at dinner, consider the black cod en papillote (perfectly steamed in parchment) or the branzino for two, served tableside.

OTHER RECOMMENDATIONS Lobster corn dogs are more than just a novelty, while the crab cakes feature prominently on the restaurant's lunch, Sunday brunch, and dinner menus. Sandwiches and salads reign on the lunch menu, with a house burger that might be good enough to sway you from your Disney Springs go-to restaurants.

SUMMARY AND COMMENTS Seafood takes center stage here, with Paddlefish featuring some of the freshest selections available at Walt Disney World. While Boathouse has raised the bar for upscale-casual surf-and-turf dining, Paddlefish does so for a wider variety of seafood options. Service, even just after the restaurant's reopening, is stellar, with attentive and knowledgeable servers ready to guide you through the extensive menu. Though it's not quite as upscale-feeling as other Signature restaurants, given its sheer size, the restaurant's views and menus make it a great date night or family "fancy" dinner option while you're exploring all that Disney Springs has to offer.

Paradiso 37 ★★½

GLOBAL	INEXPENSIVE	QUALITY ★★★	VALUE ★★★
READER-SURVEY RESPONSES 76%👍	24%👎	DISNEY DINING PLAN? Yes	

Disney Springs; ☎ 407-934-3700

Reservations Accepted. **Dining Plan credits** 1 per person, per meal. **When to go** Lunch or dinner. **Cost range** $11–$35 (child $8). **Service** ★★★. **Friendliness** ★★★★. **Parking** Disney Springs garage. **Bar** Full service. **Wine selection** Limited. **Dress** Casual. **Disabled access** Yes. **Customers** Theme park guests, locals. **Hours** 11:30 a.m.–11 p.m.

SETTING AND ATMOSPHERE In keeping with all the development going on at Disney Springs, Paradiso recently expanded, nearly doubling its seating, adding more terrace dining, and installing a new outdoor performance stage along the waterfront. Ambience is festive and casual, with an open kitchen. Food is inspired by street foods of Central, South, and North America, from enchiladas to barbecue pork.

HOUSE SPECIALTIES Ceviche, jalapeño burger, Argentinean skirt steak, Chilean-style salmon, and the "mangled margarita," a combo of a margarita and sangria. (The *37* in the name refers to the number of tequilas on offer.)

OTHER RECOMMENDATIONS Quesadillas, burritos.

SUMMARY AND COMMENTS The drinks outshine the food, but Paradiso 37 is one of the few Disney spots that cook burgers medium-rare. And the joint boasts "the coldest beer in the world," served at a crisp 29°F–32°F.

Planet Hollywood Observatory at Disney Springs ★½

AMERICAN	MODERATE	QUALITY ★★	VALUE ★★
READER-SURVEY RESPONSES 68%👍	32%👎	DISNEY DINING PLAN?	Yes

Disney Springs; ☎ 407-827-7827

Reservations Accepted. **Dining Plan credits** 1 per person, per meal. **When to go** Lunch or dinner. **Cost range** $15–$50 (child $10). **Service** ★★★. **Friendliness** ★★★. **Parking** Disney Springs Orange Garage. **Bar** Full service. **Wine selection** Limited. **Dress** Casual. **Disabled access** Yes. **Customers** Tour groups, theme park guests. **Lunch** 11 a.m.–4:55 p.m. **Dinner** 5–11:45 p.m.

SETTING AND ATMOSPHERE Recently updated and renamed Planet Hollywood Observatory, the restaurant has a modernized design that highlights function over form, with far less of its iconic movie memorabilia on the walls. Wall projections and a house DJ take center stage in the typically loud and busy main dining room, but a new outdoor patio offers seating with a view of Disney Springs in a much quieter atmosphere. Stargazer Lounge, outside on the ground-floor rear of the restaurant, offers live music on select nights alongside a colorful constellation of alcoholic concoctions.

HOUSE SPECIALTIES The signature Chicken Crunch remains one of the solid options. Over-the-top burgers now reign supreme on the menu—thanks to celebrity chef Guy Fieri—with options including one topped with the restaurant's specialty mac and cheese, and The Mayor of Flavortown, topped with the fixings from an entire Reuben sandwich. Deep-fried lasagna, St. Louis–style barbecue ribs served on a mini-picnic table, and the High Roller appetizer sampler served on a (nonfunctioning) Ferris wheel round out the highlights of the all-day menu.

OTHER RECOMMENDATIONS Salads, nachos, pasta, and steaks, much like what you'd find at your neighborhood chain restaurant, make up much of the menu. Highly decorated milkshakes and individual desserts in jars occupy the tamer end of the dessert menu, but a 6-scoop ice-cream brownie sundae and 12-scoop mystery ice-cream and gelato challenge are also available to dare adventurous guests' palates and stomachs.

SUMMARY AND COMMENTS Long home to large tour groups and families with picky eaters in search of a simple meal, Planet Hollywood Observatory continues to serve a niche clientele in the newly revitalized Disney Springs. The food, though, even with a new injection of life from Fieri, still barely ekes by as passable but now features even higher price tags. With so many new options for simple but high-quality food just a few steps away at Homecomin', Blaze Pizza, and D-Luxe Burgers, the jury's out on whether Planet Hollywood Observatory is worth the price of a visit.

The Plaza Restaurant ★★

AMERICAN	MODERATE	QUALITY ★★	VALUE ★★
READER-SURVEY RESPONSES 85%👍	15%👎	DISNEY DINING PLAN?	Yes

Main Street, U.S.A., Magic Kingdom; ☎ 407-939-3463

Reservations Recommended. **Dining Plan credits** 1 per person, per meal. **When to go** Lunch or dinner. **Cost range** $12–$19 (child $9). **Service** ★★★★. **Friendliness** ★★★★. **Parking** Magic Kingdom lot. **Bar** No alcohol served.

Dress Casual. **Disabled access** Yes. **Customers** Theme park guests. **Hours** 11 a.m.–9:30 p.m.

SETTING AND ATMOSPHERE The Plaza, a quaint and cozy spot tucked away on a side street at the end of Main Street as you head to Tomorrowland, adds Art Nouveau touches to Main Street's Victorian theme. Decor aside, it's air-conditioned heaven on a sweltering Florida day.

HOUSE SPECIALTIES Chicken-strawberry salad, tuna salad on croissant, beef brisket–onion burger, grilled Reuben sandwich, ice-cream desserts such as the Plaza banana split or sundae.

OTHER RECOMMENDATIONS Plaza Club; veggie sandwich with fresh mozzarella, hummus, and basil pesto; beef brisket–onion burger. For kids, turkey sandwich, grilled chicken strips, grilled cheese, cheeseburger, PB&J.

SUMMARY AND COMMENTS While it's not on anyone's Disney-dining bucket list, The Plaza is a true blast from the past—it was one of the first restaurants at the Magic Kingdom when the park opened in 1971. So go and enjoy an old-fashioned indulgence like a hot-fudge sundae or banana split. The Plaza now accepts reservations only from 11 a.m. until noon. The rest of the day, the restaurant will serve walk-up guests only.

Raglan Road Irish Pub & Restaurant ★★★★

IRISH	MODERATE	QUALITY ★★★½	VALUE ★★★
READER-SURVEY RESPONSES	91%👍 9%👎	DISNEY DINING PLAN?	Yes

Disney Springs; ☎ 407-938-0300

Reservations Recommended. **Dining Plan credits** 1 per person, per meal. **When to go** Monday–Saturday after 8 p.m. **Cost range** Sunday brunch $12–$30, lunch $15–$27 (child $8–$12), dinner $15–$30 (child $8–$12). **Service** ★★★½. **Friendliness** ★★★★★. **Parking** Disney Springs garage. **Bar** Irish whiskeys and beers. **Wine selection** Better than a pub's but not extensive. **Dress** Casual. **Disabled access** Yes. **Customers** Tourists and locals. **Saturday and Sunday brunch** 10 a.m.–3 p.m. **Lunch and dinner** 11 a.m.–11 p.m., with pub grub available until closing (1 a.m.-ish).

SETTING AND ATMOSPHERE Many elements of this pub, including the bar, were handcrafted from hardwoods in Ireland and sent to the United States for reassembly ("lock, stock, and beer barrel," as the website advises). The venue is huge by Irish-pub standards, but the dark polished-wood paneling, as well as the snugs (small, private cubbyholes), preserves the feel of the traditional pub. The pentagonal main room sits beneath an impressive but very unpublike dome. In the middle of the room is a tall, tablelike platform accessible to Celtic dancers via a permanently attached short staircase. A modest bandstand is situated along the wall in front of a large pseudo-hearth. Branching from the cavernous domed center room are cozy dining areas and snugs.

HOUSE SPECIALTIES Celebrity chef Kevin Dundon, star of the Irish reality shows *Guerrilla Gourmet* and *Heat* as well as *Kevin Dundon's Modern Irish Food* on PBS, oversees the kitchen, which turns out classic Irish fare with a twist, and he is at the restaurant at least four times a year. The must-try appetizer or late-night snack is the Dalkey Duo: batter-fried cocktail sausages with a mustard dipping sauce. And while you could order a burger, we recommend branching out and trying something different—say, Kevin's Heavenly Ham (glazed loin of bacon with cabbage and potatoes), Cluck Curry (chicken curry with almond rice), or Sod the Stew (beef stew infused with a hint of Guinness). And of course, beer-battered fish and chips.

Brunch includes boxty (a "sandwich" of Irish ham and Cheddar between two hash-brown cakes, topped with a fried egg), omelets, pancakes, sausages, and the requisite Bloody Marys and mimosas.

ENTERTAINMENT AND AMENITIES Though you could consider a great selection of Irish lagers and stouts an amenity, the real draw here is the Celtic music. A talented band plays daily. Starting in the early evening with a couple of superb acoustic sets, the band sets up as the diners filter out and the pub crawlers settle in. Celtic dancers fill the stage and dance on the aforementioned table to some of the numbers. (Think *Riverdance*, not stripper pole.)

SUMMARY AND COMMENTS A night in a good Irish pub, Raglan Road included, is a joyous and uplifting experience. As the Irish say, it'll set you right up. A quick fish and chips can be had around the corner at Cookes of Dublin if you're in a hurry.

Rainforest Cafe ★★½

AMERICAN	MODERATE	QUALITY ★★	VALUE ★★
READER-SURVEY RESPONSES†	80%👍 21%👎	DISNEY DINING PLAN?	Yes

†Average of Animal Kingdom (83% 👍) and Disney Springs (76% 👍)

Disney's Animal Kingdom; ☎ 407-938-9100
Disney Springs Marketplace; ☎ 407-827-8500

Reservations Recommended. **Dining Plan credits** 1 per person, per meal. **When to go** After the lunch crunch, in late afternoon, and before dinner hour. **Cost range** $13–$33 (child $9). **Service** ★★★. **Friendliness** ★★★★. **Parking** Marketplace lot. **Bar** Full bar. **Wine selection** Limited. **Dress** Casual. **Disabled access** Yes. **Customers** Tourists, locals. **Hours** *Disney's Animal Kingdom:* Daily, 8:30 a.m.–8 p.m.; *Disney Springs Marketplace:* 11 a.m.–10:35 p.m. (Animal Kingdom location serves breakfast; Disney Springs location does not.)

SETTING AND ATMOSPHERE It's always packed, and there's usually a wait, but families flock to this now-familiar restaurant for big plates of food in a noisy dining room with lots to keep the kids entertained. Look for the giant volcano that can be seen, and heard, erupting all over the Marketplace; the smoke coming from the volcano is nonpolluting, in accordance with the restaurant's conservation theme. The dining room looks like a jungle—imagine all the silk plants in the world tacked to the ceiling—complete with animatronic elephants, bats, and monkeys (not the most realistic we've seen). There's occasional thunder and even some rainfall.

HOUSE SPECIALTIES House-made crab dip, Caribbean coconut shrimp, burgers, ribs, brownie cake with ice cream.

ENTERTAINMENT AND AMENITIES After the wait you endure, a chair and some sustenance are all the entertainment you'll need. If you're willing to pay to avoid the long wait, stop by the day before and buy a Landry's Select Club membership for $25. By presenting your card on the day you want to dine, you'll be seated much faster (and get 10% off retail and other benefits).

SUMMARY AND COMMENTS While we've never been impressed by the Rainforest Cafes, a lot of our readers rave about them. The shopping and the kid appeal must be the attractions because it certainly isn't the food (or service). But the semisecret entrance into Animal Kingdom, hidden past the Rainforest gift shop, might be the best reason for its existence.

Restaurant Marrakesh ★★★

MOROCCAN	MODERATE	QUALITY ★★½	VALUE ★★
READER-SURVEY RESPONSES	86%👍 14%👎	DISNEY DINING PLAN?	Yes

Morocco, World Showcase, Epcot; ☎ 407-939-3463

Reservations Accepted. **Dining Plan credits** 1 per person, per meal. **When to go** Lunch or dinner. **Cost range** Lunch $16–$25 (child $8), dinner $22–$46 (child $8). **Service** ★★★★½. **Friendliness** ★★★★★. **Parking** Epcot lot. **Bar**

Full service. **Wine selection** Limited. **Dress** Casual. **Disabled access** Yes. **Customers** Theme park guests. **Lunch** Daily, 11:30 a.m.–3:15 p.m. **Dinner** Daily, 3:30–9 p.m.

SETTING AND ATMOSPHERE Nestled in the far back corner of the Morocco pavilion, Restaurant Marrakesh is pretty easy to miss from the outside but definitely wows once you step inside. A continuation of the ornate decorations of the Fez House courtyard near the front of the pavilion, Marrakesh's interior is palatial, complete with stucco carving, intricate wood inlays, and colorful tile mosaics. Plush carpet and dim lighting date the decor a bit, but guests may be too busy enjoying the hourly belly-dancing and traditional-music shows to notice.

HOUSE SPECIALTIES Several "feast" options allow you to sample several of the restaurant's specialties, including the beef *brewat* roll (akin to an egg roll, with ground beef and hints of cinnamon), the roast lamb *meshoui* (a whole braised shank, served on the bone for an impressive presentation), and any variety of savory couscous. À la carte entrées, such as the Moga-dor fish tagine and lemon chicken, truly shine above the muted flavors of the chicken and beef kebabs.

OTHER RECOMMENDATIONS The goat cheese and olive spread with tabbouleh and red pepper sauce is a hidden gem to share before an entrée or as a midafternoon snack. Dessert isn't Marrakesh's strong suit, so stick to the baklava, or skip it in favor of alternate options at nearby Tangierine Cafe or Spice Road Table.

SUMMARY AND COMMENTS Restaurant Marrakesh rarely sees crowds outside of festival seasons with dining packages, so it's a good option if you're on the prowl for a prime walk-up or last-minute booking opportunity. Service is typically very attentive but can border on formal, which may be off-putting for those wanting a more casual meal. The menu, while generally satisfying, rarely changes and features only faint efforts at spice-packed authentic cuisine nowadays. For the same price point, you may be better off with the more diverse flavors offered at Spice Road Table.

Rose & Crown Dining Room ★★★

ENGLISH	MODERATE	QUALITY ★★★½	VALUE ★★
READER-SURVEY RESPONSES	91%👍 9%👎	DISNEY DINING PLAN? Yes	

United Kingdom, World Showcase, Epcot; ☎ 407-939-3463

Reservations Accepted. **Dining Plan credits** 1 per person, per meal. **When to go** Lunch or dinner. **Cost range** Lunch $18–$33 (child $10–$11), dinner $18–$33 (child $10–$11). **Service** ★★★★★. **Friendliness** ★★★★★. **Parking** Epcot lot. **Bar** Full bar with Bass, Guinness, and Harp beers on tap. **Wine selection** Limited. **Dress** Casual. **Disabled access** Yes. **Customers** Epcot guests. **Lunch** Daily, noon–3:20 p.m. **Dinner** Daily, 4–8 p.m.

SETTING AND ATMOSPHERE Pub in the front, dining room in the back. The pub hops with activity from open to close and has the look and feel of a traditional English watering hole: a large, cozy bar with rich wood appointments, beamed ceilings, and a hardwood floor. The adjoining dining room is rustic and simple.

HOUSE SPECIALTIES Fish and chips, bangers and mash (sausage and mashed potatoes), pan-roasted Scottish salmon, and shepherd's pie (the vegetarian version is delicious too), washed down with Bass ale.

OTHER RECOMMENDATIONS Trio of UK cheeses, Scotch egg (a hard-boiled egg with a deep-fried sausage coating), the requisite New York strip steak, and sticky toffee pudding for dessert.

SUMMARY AND COMMENTS At dinnertime, the Rose & Crown is packed with folks appropriating tables for *IllumiNations*. The food is good, so branch out and try something new—you can always get fish and chips at the adjacent walk-up window.

Sanaa ★★★★

INDIAN/AFRICAN	EXPENSIVE	QUALITY ★★★★	VALUE ★★★★
READER-SURVEY RESPONSES	95% 👍	5% 👎	DISNEY DINING PLAN? Yes

Animal Kingdom Villas–Kidani Village; ☎ 407-939-3463

Reservations Accepted. **Dining Plan credits** 1 per person, per meal. **When to go** Lunch or dinner. **Cost range** Lunch $15–$26 (child $11–$12), dinner $19–$35 (child $11–$12). **Service** ★★★★. **Friendliness** ★★★★. **Parking** Valet ($25) or garage. **Bar** Full service. **Wine selection** Good. **Dress** Casual. **Disabled access** Yes. **Customers** Theme park guests, locals, Disney Vacation Club guests. **Breakfast** Daily, 7–10 a.m. **Lunch** Daily, 11:30 a.m.–3 p.m. **Dinner** Daily, 5–9:30 p.m.

SETTING AND ATMOSPHERE A floor down from the Kidani Village lobby, Sanaa's casual dining room is inspired by African outdoor markets, with baskets, beads, and art on the walls. It's a cozy space, with 9-foot-tall windows that look out on the resort's savanna—giraffes, water buffalo, and other animals wander within yards of you as you dine.

HOUSE SPECIALTIES Starters include Indian-style breads (naan, onion *kulcha*, and *paneer paratha*) served with red-chile sambal, spicy jalapeño-lime pickle, coriander chutney, and cucumber raita; tandoori chicken; sustainable fish. For lunch: lamb kefta sliders and tandoori shrimp sandwich. For dinner: butter chicken, seafood curry, and sustainable fish. Diverse Old and New World wines pair beautifully with the food.

OTHER RECOMMENDATIONS Tanzanian chocolate mousse.

SUMMARY AND COMMENTS Sanaa (sah-**NAH**) is a favorite of Disney cast members and locals—the flavors are addicting. It's not as upscale as Jiko—The Cooking Place, the resort's fine-dining restaurant (page 382), offering instead a casual take on African–Indian fusion cuisine. If the dining room looks too crowded, the cozy bar room on the side is available for full-menu dining—just without the animals on parade. Sanaa serves a quick-service version of breakfast in the morning. Offerings include hot food such as eggs, waffles, and bacon, as well as a small section of grab-and-go cold foods.

San Angel Inn Restaurante ★★★

MEXICAN	EXPENSIVE	QUALITY ★★★	VALUE ★★
READER-SURVEY RESPONSES	85% 👍	15% 👎	DISNEY DINING PLAN? Yes

Mexico, World Showcase, Epcot; ☎ 407-939-3463

Reservations Accepted. **Dining Plan credits** 1 per person, per meal. **When to go** Lunch or dinner. **Cost range** Lunch $19–$30 (child $9–$10), dinner $25–$30 (child $9). **Service** ★★★. **Friendliness** ★★★. **Parking** Epcot lot. **Bar** Full service. **Wine selection** Limited. **Dress** Casual. **Disabled access** Yes. **Customers** Theme park guests. **Lunch** Daily, 11:30 a.m.–4 p.m. **Dinner** Daily, 4:30 p.m.–park closing.

SETTING AND ATMOSPHERE Step inside the Aztec pyramid in Mexico, navigate the busy marketplace, and end up at San Angel Inn, which overlooks a starry sky and the Gran Fiesta Tour boat ride. Its decor is inspired by the original San Angel Inn in Mexico City and is incredibly atmospheric—it really does feel like you're dining in an outdoor Mexican square.

HOUSE SPECIALTIES Appetizers include *tlacoyos de chilorio,* corn cakes topped with refried beans, pork, queso fresco, sour cream, and green-tomatillo sauce; and quesadillas *repozadas,* battered corn quesadillas stuffed with corn, *huitlacoche* (Mexican truffle), mushrooms, and queso fresco. Still on the menu is the classic mole poblano—chicken in a sauce made from several kinds of chiles and unsweetened Mexican chocolate.

OTHER RECOMMENDATIONS Chile relleno, carne asada, cheesecake with *cajeta* (caramel sauce).

ENTERTAINMENT AND AMENITIES Mariachi or marimba bands.

SUMMARY AND COMMENTS The prices are steep, but the menu goes beyond the typical tacos and such, offering regional dishes that are difficult to find in the States. Tables are uncomfortably close together for some folks; request a waterside table overlooking the boat ride for more room and a slightly quieter evening. The dining room is a cool, quiet respite from the theme park—but you might need a flashlight to read the menu.

Sci-Fi Dine-In Theater Restaurant ★★

AMERICAN	MODERATE	QUALITY ★★½	VALUE ★★
READER-SURVEY RESPONSES	86%👍 14%👎	DISNEY DINING PLAN? Yes	

Commissary Lane, Disney's Hollywood Studios; ☎ 407-939-3463

Reservations Recommended. **Dining Plan credits** 1 per person, per meal. **When to go** Lunch or dinner. **Cost range** $14–$32 (child $10–$11). **Service ★★★★★**. **Friendliness ★★★★★**. **Parking** DHS lot. **Bar** Full service. **Wine selection** Limited. **Dress** Casual. **Disabled access** Yes. **Customers** Theme park guests. **Lunch** Daily, 11 a.m.–3:55 p.m. **Dinner** Daily, 4–7:30 p.m.

SETTING AND ATMOSPHERE Walk through the doors and into the back of a simulated soundstage; then round the corner into a stage set that re-creates a drive-in from the 1950s, with faux classic cars instead of tables. Hop in, order, and watch campy black-and-white clips. Servers take your order from the driver's seat. Basically, the place is a hoot.

HOUSE SPECIALTIES Same menu at lunch and dinner, with everything from burgers to pasta and New York strip.

ENTERTAINMENT AND AMENITIES Cartoons and clips of vintage horror and sci-fi movies, such as *Attack of the 50 Foot Woman, Robot Monster,* and *The Blob.*

SUMMARY AND COMMENTS We consider the Sci-Fi an attraction, not a dining destination: The concept is fun, but the prices are too high for what you get. Stick with simple fare (the Reuben is delicious), fill up on appetizers, or just order a shake or hot-fudge sundae. If you must try Sci-Fi, we recommend making late-afternoon or late-evening Advance Reservations. Otherwise, try walking in around 11 a.m. or 3 p.m.

Shula's Steak House ★★★★

STEAK	EXPENSIVE	QUALITY ★★★★	VALUE ★★
READER-SURVEY RESPONSES	87%👍 13%👎	DISNEY DINING PLAN? No	

Dolphin Hotel; ☎ 407-934-1362

Reservations Required. **When to go** Dinner. **Cost range** $28–$130 (for the Australian lobster tail). *Note:* Everything is à la carte. **Service ★★★★**. **Friendliness ★★★★**. **Parking** Valet (free with validation) or hotel lot ($18). **Bar** Full service. **Wine selection** Good; expensive. **Dress** Dressy. **Disabled access** Yes. **Customers** Hotel guests and locals. **Dinner** Daily, 5–11 p.m.

SETTING AND ATMOSPHERE Shula's feels more like a men's club than a resort restaurant, but the appeal to conventioneers is obvious: dark woods; even darker lighting; large, gilt-framed black-and-white photographs of football players in action, and high prices that get passed on to expense accounts.

HOUSE SPECIALTIES In a word, meat—really expensive but very high-quality meat. Only certified Angus beef is served: filet mignon, porterhouse (including a 48-ounce cut), and prime rib. The restaurant's reputation is better than the somewhat pedestrian food.

OTHER RECOMMENDATIONS Barbecue shrimp stuffed with basil, seasonal oysters, 4-pound Maine lobster, catch of the day.

SUMMARY AND COMMENTS Shula's is classier than it is kitschy, though printing the menu on the side of a football and placing it on a kickoff tee in the center of the table is a bit much. We could also do without the rehearsed spiel from the waiters and the pretentious parading of raw beef and live lobster at each table. But if you have deep pockets and you're in the mood for red meat, Shula's has you covered.

Spice Road Table ★★★★

MOROCCAN	MODERATE	QUALITY ★★★★	VALUE ★★★
READER-SURVEY RESPONSES	87% 👍	13% 👎	DISNEY DINING PLAN? Yes

Morocco, World Showcase, Epcot; ☎ 407-939-3463

Reservations Recommended. **When to go** Anytime, but it's a primo spot for nightly fireworks. **Cost range** $23–$33 (child $9). **Service** ★★★★★. **Friendliness** ★★★★★. **Parking** Epcot lot. **Bar** Full service. **Wine selection** Limited. **Dress** Casual. **Disabled access** Yes. **Customers** Epcot guests. **Hours** Daily, 11:30 a.m.–9 p.m.

SETTING AND ATMOSPHERE A prime location for daytime people-watching and nighttime fireworks, Spice Road Table is situated directly along World Showcase Lagoon at the front of the Morocco pavilion. The outdoor covered patio features excellent dining in plein air when Florida weather cooperates, and indoor seating provides colorful pops of modern Moroccan decor. The central lobby is the restaurant's showcase bar, bathed in jewel tones and overlooking the pavilion's iconic waterwheel through peekaboo windows.

HOUSE SPECIALTIES Perfectly fried calamari, baked Brie, and grape leaves stuffed with bright, lemony rice stand out as favorites on the small-plates side of the menu. Hummus fries transform falafel into a more accessible but still authentic dish worthy of consideration. For those looking for full meals, the yellowfin tuna showcases well-prepared, bold flavors. Dessert stars include a rich chocolate mousse pyramid and a pistachio crème brûlée sure to impress.

OTHER RECOMMENDATIONS Lamb sliders with tzatziki offer a bit of punch and spice, as does the *merguez* sausage appetizer—a slightly smaller portion but easy to share. Grilled beef and chicken skewers may sound simple, but the accompanying chimichurri and roasted potatoes take the otherwise pedestrian dish to the next level. Coriander-crusted rack of lamb offers a more upscale take on the same flavors frequently featured at nearby Restaurant Marrakesh.

SUMMARY AND COMMENTS No longer just a quick stop for a snack, Spice Road Table has expanded its slate of small plates to include several entrées to satisfy those less willing to share with others. Appetizers and desserts still shine here, though, and pair excellently with the restaurant's extensive wine and cocktail lists. Service is just as attentive as the pavilion's other table service location, Restaurant Marrakesh, but the casual atmosphere seems more appropriate to the outdoor seating area and modern Epcot.

Splitsville ★★½

AMERICAN	MODERATE	QUALITY ★★½	VALUE ★★
READER-SURVEY RESPONSES	95% 👍	5% 👎	DISNEY DINING PLAN? Yes

Disney Springs West Side; ☎ 407-938-7467

Reservations Accepted. **Dining Plan credits** 1 per person, per meal. **When to Go** Anytime. **Cost range** $11–$26 (child $7–$8). **Service** ★★½. **Friendliness** ★★★.

Parking Disney Springs Orange Garage. **Bar** Full service. **Wine selection** Don't expect Lafite Rothschild. **Dress** Casual. **Disabled access** Yes. **Customers** Tourists. **Lunch** Daily, 10:30 a.m.–3:25 p.m. **Dinner** Daily, 3:30 p.m.–11:55 p.m.

SETTING AND ATMOSPHERE Splitsville is part of a multistate chain of "luxury lanes"—hybrid bowling alleys/restaurants. The decor is vaguely mid-century modern, with Sputnik lamps and other Space Age touches. It's loud, obviously, but there's plenty to see and room for rambunctious kids to roam while you wait for your food.

HOUSE SPECIALTIES The sushi—salmon, shrimp, tuna, crab, and various combinations thereof—is the best thing on the menu.

SUMMARY AND COMMENTS The menu is more spread-out than a 7/10 split: Burgers, sushi, pizza, seafood, barbecue, Mexican, and Italian are represented, plus nachos and other bar food. It would be a stretch for any kitchen to make half of these things well, let alone a kitchen in a bowling alley. We've tried almost everything on the menu, and while all of it was OK, the only thing we'd order again is the sushi.

STK Orlando ★★★½

STEAK	EXPENSIVE		QUALITY ★★★★		VALUE ★★½
READER-SURVEY RESPONSES	60%👍	40%👎	DISNEY DINING PLAN? No		

The Landing, Disney Springs; ☎ 407-917-7440

Reservations Required. **When to go** Lunch and dinner. **Cost range** $18–$98. **Service** ★★★★. **Friendliness** ★★★★. **Parking** Disney Springs garage. **Bar** Full service. **Wine selection** OK, though not encyclopedic. **Dress** Casual. **Disabled access** Yes. **Customers** Theme park guests. **Lunch** Daily, 11:30 a.m.–4 p.m. **Dinner** Sunday–Thursday, 5–11 p.m., Friday–Saturday, 5 p.m.–midnight.

SETTING AND ATMOSPHERE The turreted brick exterior, intended to evoke a turn-of-the-20th-century train station, couldn't be more different from the inside. A lower level houses a bar and seating area with a Las Vegas/Miami-ultralounge feel, complete with DJ and lots of noise. The quieter, less-glitzy upstairs has both indoor and outdoor seating, the latter with fantastic views of Disney Springs. The turret contains even more seating.

HOUSE SPECIALTIES Duh—steaks, from a $28 skirt steak to a $98, 32-ounce porterhouse and market-priced Wagyu beef. Sides include an indulgent mac and cheese, creamed spinach (natch), and Parmesan-truffle fries.

OTHER RECOMMENDATIONS "Lil'BRG" sliders, grilled octopus, crispy rock shrimp, upmarket beef short ribs with horseradish cream, and signature cocktails such as the strawberry cobbler (Belvedere vodka with muddled strawberries and a "rim" of graham cracker crumbs) and the Secret Affair (Purity vodka with lime, watermelon, and a rim of Tajín chili powder).

SUMMARY AND COMMENTS Featuring The Landing's only rooftop dining space overlooking the water, the massive STK—part of a growing international chain—aims to bring sexy to the Orlando steakhouse scene. The steaks aren't cheap, but they're excellent, particularly the fork-tender porterhouse. Try to get a seat upstairs, though, so you don't have to shout over your meal.

For our first reader survey that included STK, the restaurant garnered just 60% positive responses, putting it in 899th place among all 909 ranked restaurants at Walt Disney World. This is among the lowest we've ever seen for a new upscale-dining venue at Walt Disney World and may be a predictor of future changes at the venue.

Teppan Edo ★★★½

JAPANESE	EXPENSIVE		QUALITY ★★★★		VALUE ★★★
READER-SURVEY RESPONSES	92%👍	8%👎	DISNEY DINING PLAN? Yes		

Japan, World Showcase, Epcot; ☎ 407-939-3463

Reservations Recommended. **Dining Plan credits** 1 per person, per meal. **When to go** Lunch or dinner. **Cost range** $18–$56 (child $14–$15). **Service** ★★★★★. **Friendliness** ★★★★★. **Parking** Epcot lot. **Bar** Full service. **Wine selection** Limited. **Dress** Casual. **Disabled access** Via elevator. **Customers** Epcot guests. **Lunch** Daily, noon–3:45 p.m. **Dinner** Daily, 4–8:55 p.m.

SETTING AND ATMOSPHERE Six Japanese dining rooms with grills on tables and entertaining chefs chopping, slicing, and dicing.

HOUSE SPECIALTIES Chicken, shrimp, beef, scallops, and Asian vegetables stir-fried on a teppanyaki grill by a knife-juggling chef.

ENTERTAINMENT AND AMENITIES Watching the teppanyaki chefs.

SUMMARY AND COMMENTS A popular dining option for families—the communal tables are a fun way to meet other guests. You'll get plenty to eat, but the starters include sushi, tempura, ribs, edamame, and miso soup.

Tiffins ★★★★

PAN-ASIAN/AMERICAN	EXPENSIVE	QUALITY ★★★★	VALUE ★★★
READER-SURVEY RESPONSE	93%👍 7%👎	DISNEY DINING PLAN?	Yes

Discovery Island, Disney's Animal Kingdom; ☎ 407-939-3463

Reservations Recommended. **Dining Plan credits** 2 per person, per meal (Premium and Platinum plans: 1 per person, per meal). **When to go** Lunch and dinner. **Cost range** $29–$53. **Service** ★★★★. **Friendliness** ★★★★★. **Parking** Animal Kingdom lot. **Bar** Full bar. **Wine selection** Excellent. **Dress** Casual. **Disabled access** Yes. **Customers** Theme park guests. **Lunch** Daily, 11:30 a.m.–3:30 p.m. **Dinner** Daily, 4 p.m.–7 p.m.

SETTING AND ATMOSPHERE Located on Discovery Island, Tiffins is tucked behind the Pizzafari counter-service restaurant, on a walking path to the new land of Pandora. Inside, Tiffins is divided into three relatively small, quiet dining rooms, plus the Nomad Lounge bar. A wraparound porch, located behind the dining rooms, offers outdoor seating.

The decor is said to be inspired by the travel adventures of the Imagineers who built Animal Kingdom. You'll see artifacts from Asia and Africa lining the walls of one room, and giant butterflies in another. The main dining room's centerpiece is carved-wood sculptures. Yet with all of these, Tiffins still feels quiet and restrained.

HOUSE SPECIALTIES The standout appetizers are the marinated grilled octopus and black-eyed pea fritters. For mains, try the whole fried sustainable fish; spiced lamb chops; Wagyu strip loin; or duck. For dessert, the lime cheesecake or passion fruit tapioca is tasty.

OTHER RECOMMENDATIONS There are only a handful of things we wouldn't recommend, mostly because there are many other, better options. We'd skip the lobster curry soup and bread service appetizers. In the entrée section, the $29 roasted-vegetable curry is more like a stew, and while it's good (and spicy), it's very expensive for what it is. Vegetarians might be better off ordering two appetizers as a main course. Between the whole fish and the halibut, we'd order the whole fish.

SUMMARY AND COMMENTS Tiffins is a fairly new addition to Walt Disney World, but it's fast becoming a favorite. With both Tiffins and its companion bar, Nomad Lounge, garnering 93% positive reader response, our advice is to book a reservation soon, because once Animal Kingdom's Pandora starts to bring more foot traffic to the area, it will become a challenge to dine here. Overall, our meals here have been delicious, with consistent quality from the kitchen and the waitstaff. Tiffins would be right at home in any of Disney's Deluxe resorts.

As a Signature restaurant, Tiffins's prices are higher than at the other sit-down options in the park. However, the quality supports the prices, which are in line with what we're paying for comparable quality, service, and setting in our hometowns. If you're looking for a relaxing way to spend a couple of hours before seeing Animal Kingdom's nighttime entertainment, this is the place to do it.

One last thing: If you're uncomfortable looking your food in the eye, don't order the whole fried fish. It's delicious, but our fish's facial expression seemed to indicate that the deep fryer caught it by surprise.

Todd English's bluezoo ★★★

SEAFOOD	EXPENSIVE		QUALITY ★★★★	VALUE ★★
READER-SURVEY RESPONSES	88% 👍	12% 👎	DISNEY DINING PLAN?	No

Dolphin Hotel; ☎ 407-934-1111

Reservations Recommended. **When to go** Dinner. **Cost range** $32–$65 (child $12–$19). *Note:* Everything is à la carte. **Service** ★★★★. **Friendliness** ★★★. **Parking** Valet (free with validation) or hotel lot ($18). **Bar** Full service. **Wine selection** Excellent. **Dress** Dressy casual. **Disabled access** Yes. **Customers** Hotel guests, locals. **Hours** Daily, 5–11 p.m.

SETTING AND ATMOSPHERE A lovely yet slightly cold dining room swathed in blues with iridescent bubbles suspended from the lights. The name is courtesy of celebrity chef Todd English's son, who as a young boy saw an under-the-sea movie and said it looked like a "blue zoo." Open kitchen, raw bar, and a unique circular rotisserie that makes the fish being grilled on it seem to dance on the coals.

HOUSE SPECIALTIES "Dancing fish" (from the rotisserie), 2-pound Maine lobster in sticky soy glaze, 72-hour short ribs, beef tenderloin.

OTHER RECOMMENDATIONS New England–style clam chowder with salt-cured bacon, teppan-seared jumbo sea scallops, raw-bar platter.

SUMMARY AND COMMENTS English's stylish Florida outpost is frequented mainly by conventioneers who don't mind the high prices—$3 for a single oyster, $60 for the 2-pound lobster—or the expensive wine list. English's reputation should make for a finer dining experience than the ultimately disappointing menu delivers, but few of the seafood-centric dishes are actually as good as they could be.

Tokyo Dining ★★★

JAPANESE	MODERATE		QUALITY ★★★★	VALUE ★★★
READER-SURVEY RESPONSES	89% 👍	12% 👎	DISNEY DINING PLAN?	Yes

Japan, World Showcase, Epcot; ☎ 407-939-3463

Reservations Accepted. **Dining Plan credits** 1 per person, per meal. **When to go** Lunch. **Cost range** $9–$34 (child $13). **Service** ★★★★. **Friendliness** ★★★. **Parking** Epcot lot. **Bar** Full service. **Wine selection** Limited. **Dress** Casual. **Disabled access** Yes. **Customers** Theme park guests. **Lunch** Daily, noon–3:45 p.m. **Dinner** Daily, 4–8:55 p.m.

SETTING AND ATMOSPHERE Gracious service, modern Asian decor, and a beautifully lit sushi bar distinguish this restaurant. There are no seats at the sushi bar, but the sushi chefs are great entertainment for the entire dining room. Tables near the windows have a wonderful second-floor view of World Showcase.

HOUSE SPECIALTIES Tempura shrimp, chicken, and vegetables; panko oysters; sushi; bento box with sliced steak, sashimi, California roll, tempura shrimp, and vegetables served with sukiyaki beef rice.

SUMMARY AND COMMENTS The dining room is sleek, the sushi is super-fresh, and the overall experience is relaxing and congenial. Service is so outstanding and quintessentially Japanese that it may take a few minutes to adjust your attitude. Enjoy the refined attention.

Tony's Town Square Restaurant ★★½

ITALIAN	MODERATE	QUALITY ★★★	VALUE ★★
READER-SURVEY RESPONSES 77% 👍	23% 👎	DISNEY DINING PLAN?	Yes

Main Street, U.S.A., Magic Kingdom; ☎ 407-939-3463

Reservations Recommended. **Dining Plan credits** 1 per person, per meal. **When to go** Late lunch or early dinner. **Cost range** Lunch $15–$33 (child $9–$11), dinner $18–$34 (child $9–$11). **Service** ★★★★. **Friendliness** ★★★★★. **Parking** Magic Kingdom lot. **Bar** Limited selection of beer and wine. **Dress** Casual. **Disabled access** Yes. **Customers** Magic Kingdom guests. **Lunch** Daily, 11:30 a.m.–2:55 p.m. **Dinner** Daily, 3–9:30 p.m.

SETTING AND ATMOSPHERE Just inside the Magic Kingdom on Main Street, with a glass-windowed porch that's wonderful for watching the action outside, Tony's Town Square is a bit worn around the edges, but it's another rite of passage for Disney fans—you *must* have a plate of spaghetti in the restaurant that commemorates *Lady and the Tramp*.

HOUSE SPECIALTIES Sausage-and-pepperoni flatbread, spaghetti with meatballs, shrimp scampi, chicken Parmigiana, New York strip.

SUMMARY AND COMMENTS It's not haute cuisine, but Tony's does a decent job with pasta (multigrain and gluten-free options available).

Trader Sam's Grog Grotto ★★★

PAN-ASIAN	MODERATE	QUALITY ★★★	VALUE ★★★
READER-SURVEY RESPONSES 94% 👍	6% 👎	DISNEY DINING PLAN?	No

Disney's Polynesian Village Resort; ☎ 407-939-3463

Reservations Not accepted. **When to go** Dinner. **Cost range** $8.49–$15 (small plates only). **Service** ★★★. **Friendliness** ★★★★. **Parking** Polynesian Village lot or valet ($25). **Bar** Full service. **Wine selection** Good. **Dress** Casual. **Disabled access** Yes. **Customers** Locals and Disney guests. **Hours** Daily, 4 p.m.–midnight.

SETTING AND ATMOSPHERE Fans of Trader Sam's Enchanted Tiki Bar at the Disneyland Hotel couldn't wait for Disney World to get a version of its own. But while the two share nostalgic interactive props, animatronics (the ones here are a nod to the old 20,000 Leagues Under the Sea attraction), and even a few menu items, the Grog Grotto has its own vibe. Off the Polynesian Village's main lobby and featuring views of the marina and Seven Seas Lagoon, this tiki bar has its own lore built in: It was started by Trader Sam, Adventureland's famous "head" salesman, who welcomes you to his enchanted South Seas hideaway to explore a menu of "magical tropical drinks and food." (Trader Sam also makes an appearance at the new Jungle Navigation Co. Ltd. Skipper Canteen.)

HOUSE SPECIALTIES Cocktails are the big draw, with names like Castaway Crush, Tahitian Torch, and the over-the-top Uh-Oa!—Myers's and Bacardi rums mixed with various fruit juices and served in a communal tiki bowl with straws all around; there are also "No Booze Brews" for teetotalers.

OTHER RECOMMENDATIONS Small plates include chicken lettuce cups with hoisin-ginger sauce, Hawaiian poke with Sriracha aioli, kalua pork tacos with shredded cabbage and pickled vegetables, pan-fried dumplings with soy-sesame dipping sauce, roasted chicken and pork-pâté *bánh mì* sliders with pickled vegetables, salmon *oshizushi* (pressed sushi), corn-battered Portuguese sausages with curry ketchup, and the Headhunter Sushi Roll.

SUMMARY AND COMMENTS Trader Sam's is already a hit with Disneyphiles, so get there early—there are just 50 seats inside and 80 on the patio.

Trail's End Restaurant   ★★

AMERICAN/BUFFET	MODERATE	QUALITY ★★	VALUE ★★
READER-SURVEY RESPONSES 87% 👍	13% 👎	DISNEY DINING PLAN?	Yes

Fort Wilderness Resort & Campground; ☎ 407-939-3463

Reservations Recommended. **Dining Plan credits** 1 per person, per meal. **When to go** Breakfast or dinner. **Cost range** Breakfast $20 (child $11), brunch $23 (child $13), dinner $30 (child $17). **Service** ★★★. **Friendliness** ★★★. **Parking** Fort Wilderness lot. **Bar** Full-service bar next door. **Wine selection** Limited. **Dress** Casual. **Disabled access** Yes. **Customers** Fort Wilderness campers, theme park guests. **Breakfast** 7:30–11:30 a.m. **Brunch** (when offered) 7:30 a.m.–2 p.m. **Dinner** 4:30–9:30 p.m.

SETTING AND ATMOSPHERE At Fort Wilderness, next to the *Hoop-Dee-Doo Musical Revue,* Trail's End is what a restaurant would have looked like had America's settlers built one out of a log cabin. The interior, charming but a bit tired, features exposed log beams, oak tabletops, and walls hung with enough old-timey kitchen equipment to start a flea market.

HOUSE SPECIALTIES Breakfast and dinner are served buffet-style. Breakfast features eggs, sausage, bacon, waffles, and biscuits and gravy, along with fruit and pastries. The dinner menu (buffet or carryout) includes fried chicken, ribs, pasta, catch of the day, pizza, and chili.

OTHER RECOMMENDATIONS Fried green tomatoes and beans-and-greens soup at lunch.

SUMMARY AND COMMENTS With its "everything but the kitchen sink" philosophy, Trail's End offers something for everyone. Brunch is served occasionally. When no brunch is being served, breakfast extends until noon.

Trattoria al Forno   ★★★½

ITALIAN	MODERATE	QUALITY ★★★½	VALUE ★★
READER-SURVEY RESPONSES 87% 👍	13% 👎	DISNEY DINING PLAN?	Yes

Disney's BoardWalk; ☎ 407-939-3463

Reservations Accepted. **Dining Plan credits** 2 per person, per meal. **When to go** Breakfast or dinner. **Cost range** Breakfast $7–$14 (child $7–$10), dinner $17–$37 (child $10–$13). **Service** ★★★. **Friendliness** ★★★★. **Parking** Lot for Disney's BoardWalk and valet. **Bar** Full service. **Wine selection** Good; all Italian. **Dress** Casual. **Disabled access** Yes. **Customers** Locals and Disney guests. **Breakfast** Daily, 7:30–11 a.m. An all-new character breakfast debuted this spring. **Dinner** Daily, 5–10 p.m.

SETTING AND ATMOSPHERE The big dining room feels a little more personal, with three different "dining areas" and a private room at the back and an open kitchen for watching the action, including a wood-burning oven. Our favorite spot is the "formal dining room" right in front of the kitchen, where it's a little less noisy (and carpeted), or one of the booths at the back. Servers tend to be a little overattentive. There's also a quick-service window streetside to soothe the urgent pizza craving.

HOUSE SPECIALTIES For breakfast: poached egg over polenta with fennel sausage, red sauce, and Parmesan; waffle with espresso-mascarpone cream; cured Italian meats with hard-boiled egg, tomatoes, and cheeses. For dinner: thin-sliced cured meats; pizzas; linguine with clams; tagliatelle alla carbonara; T-bone steak; tiramisu and *bomboloni* (fried doughnuts).

SUMMARY AND COMMENTS The kitchen is doing things right—making mozzarella and ciabatta daily, rolling out fresh pasta (cavatelli), slicing cured meats with a beautiful Italian flywheel. The wine list is carefully curated, with labels from all of Italy's major regions and more than 30 available by the glass or *quartino*. Breakfast is one of the best on Disney property.

T-REX ★★★

AMERICAN	MODERATE	QUALITY ★★	VALUE ★★
READER-SURVEY RESPONSES 81% 👍	19% 👎	DISNEY DINING PLAN? Yes	

Disney Springs Marketplace; ☎ 407-828-8739

Reservations Recommended. **Dining Plan credits** 1 per person, per meal. **When to go** Lunch or dinner. **Cost range** $16–$34 (child $9). **Service** ★★★. **Friendliness** ★★★. **Parking** Disney Springs Orange Garage. **Bar** Full service. **Wine selection** Minimal. **Dress** Casual. **Disabled access** Yes. **Customers** Families. **Hours** Daily, 11 a.m.–10:30 p.m.; open until 11:30 p.m. Friday–Saturday.

SETTING AND ATMOSPHERE Sensory overload in a cavernous dining room with life-size robotic dinosaurs, giant fish tanks, bubbling geysers, waterfalls, fossils in the bathrooms, and crystals in the walls. Volume: loud and louder, with meteor showers and growling dinos.

HOUSE SPECIALTIES Gigantosaurus Burger, Pork-asaurus Sandwich.

SUMMARY AND COMMENTS Expect a wait unless there's an empty seat at the bar. But nobody's here just for the ordinary, overpriced food—it's non-stop "eatertainment," with kid-friendly food served in huge portions.

Turf Club Bar & Grill ★★

AMERICAN	MODERATE	QUALITY ★★★	VALUE ★★
READER-SURVEY RESPONSES 88% 👍	12% 👎	DISNEY DINING PLAN? Yes	

Saratoga Springs Resort & Spa; ☎ 407-939-3463

Reservations Accepted. **Dining Plan credits** 1 per person, per meal. **When to go** Dinner. **Cost range** Dinner $18–$35 (child $10–$11). **Service** ★★★. **Friendliness** ★★★★. **Parking** Lot. **Bar** Full service. **Wine selection** Good. **Dress** Casual. **Disabled access** Good. **Customers** Hotel guests. **Hours** Daily, 5–10 p.m.

SETTING AND ATMOSPHERE If you're looking for an out-of-the-way spot that's quiet with decent food, Turf Club is a good bet. When the weather is nice, ask for an outdoor table; you can spot golfers on the adjacent Lake Buena Vista Golf Course and look across the way to Disney Springs. Just off the lobby of Saratoga Springs Resort, the dining room is equestrian-themed.

HOUSE SPECIALTIES Signature grilled-romaine salad, prime rib, Turf Club pasta.

OTHER RECOMMENDATIONS Crispy free-range chicken breast with three-cheese mac and cheese, grilled lamb chops, sustainable fish.

SUMMARY AND COMMENTS Because this tucked-away spot caters mainly to the Disney Vacation Club crowd, it's rarely crowded. The cuisine won't wow you, but the grilled-romaine salad (with Caesar dressing, balsamic reduction, and roasted cherry tomatoes) is one of Disney's best.

Tusker House Restaurant ★★★

AMERICAN/AFRICAN/BUFFET	MODERATE	QUALITY ★★★	VALUE ★★★
READER-SURVEY RESPONSES 93% 👍	7% 👎	DISNEY DINING PLAN? Yes	

Africa, Disney's Animal Kingdom; ☎ 407-939-3463

Reservations Required for character meals. **Dining Plan credits** 1 per person, per meal. **When to go** Anytime. **Cost range** Breakfast $30 (child $18), lunch $38 (child $23), dinner $42 (child $25). **Service** ★★★. **Friendliness** ★★★. **Parking** Animal Kingdom lot. **Bar** Full-service bar next door. **Dress** Casual. **Disabled access** Yes. **Customers** Theme park guests. **Character breakfast** Daily, 8–10:55 a.m. **Character lunch** Daily, 11:00 a.m.–3:30 p.m. **Character dinner** Daily, 4 p.m.–7:30 p.m.

SETTING AND ATMOSPHERE Tusker House's character meals feature Mickey, Donald, Daisy, and Goofy. The setting—inside the Harambe Village square—is plainer than Disney's promotional photos would indicate, especially after dark. The food is surprisingly good, with spices and taste combinations you won't find at other spots. It's on par with the buffet at Boma in Animal Kingdom Lodge, only with a theme park outside and Disney characters within.

HOUSE SPECIALTIES Carved sirloin, rotisserie pork and chicken, chicken curry, seafood stew, spiced tofu.

OTHER RECOMMENDATIONS African- and Indian-influenced dishes such as chutney, couscous, and curry.

SUMMARY AND COMMENTS Tusker House appeals to kids who want to meet the Disney characters and grown-ups who appreciate the convenience and value of a buffet without the typical buffet boredom. You can try something different, such as beef bobotie at breakfast and curries and chutneys at lunch and dinner, but there are plenty of familiar tastes, too.

Tutto Gusto Wine Cellar ★★★½

ITALIAN	INEXPENSIVE	QUALITY ★★★★	VALUE ★★★
READER-SURVEY RESPONSES	93%👍 7%👎	DISNEY DINING PLAN? No	

Italy, World Showcase, Epcot; ☎ 407-560-8040

Reservations Not accepted. **When to go** Dinner. **Cost range** $8–$29 (no kids' meals). **Service** ★★★★. **Friendliness** ★★★½. **Parking** Epcot lot. **Bar** Full service. **Wine selection** Large and diverse. **Dress** Casual. **Disabled access** Yes. **Customers** Theme park guests. **Hours** Daily, 11:30 a.m.–9 p.m.

SETTING AND ATMOSPHERE Tucked away in the far corner of Italy, Tutto Gusto welcomes guests into an intimate space, complete with cozy fireplace-adjacent seating and unique wine-bottle chandeliers. A bit dark and cool, Tutto Gusto can be packed during the day with guests looking to take a break from the heat by sampling a glass of one of 200-plus wines.

HOUSE SPECIALTIES Wine flights ranging from three to six pours offer guests a taste of some of their most popular and interesting selections, but *quartinos* and full bottles are available for those wanting to settle in for a while longer. Customizable sharing plates featuring a wide variety of cheese, charcuterie, and marinated vegetables are perfect for a small bite to accompany your wine. Individually portioned desserts, such as the Caramellito, tiramisu, and strawberries with mascarpone, highlight classic Italian flavors with a sweet treat to end your visit.

OTHER RECOMMENDATIONS For those in search of a larger meal, pasta dishes with decadent lamb ragù or Calabrian chili and garlic–sautéed shrimp satisfy, along with house-made meatballs, creamy sweet-sausage ziti, or shrimp and lobster arancini. Small panini, served alongside mini wedge Caesar salads, present several of the restaurant's meat and cheese selections in a slightly more substantial way and are a nice light lunch option.

SUMMARY AND COMMENTS The perfect hiding place for those in search of a respite from World Showcase, Tutto Gusto serves up light fare and high-quality wines in a beautifully quaint space. There are several popular "off-menu" options that servers will helpfully explain: Meat and cheese selections can be ordered individually or as part of the main menu's sharing boards, and dishes from neighboring Tutto Italia can also be ordered at select times of day. The standing bar area typically has a shorter wait than for tables at peak times, for those looking to just grab one glass of wine or a refreshing cocktail on the go. Tutto Gusto is one of six standalone bars that have been added to select World Showcase pavilions, allowing guests to "drink around the world." For details, see page 338.

Tutto Italia Ristorante ★★★★

ITALIAN	EXPENSIVE	QUALITY ★★★★	VALUE ★★
READER-SURVEY RESPONSES	88%👍 12%👎	DISNEY DINING PLAN? Yes	

Italy, World Showcase, Epcot; ☎ 407-939-3463

Reservations Recommended. **Dining Plan credits** 1 per person, per meal. **When to go** Midafternoon. **Cost range** Lunch $17–$34 (child $10), dinner $24–$36 (child $10). **Service** ★★★★. **Friendliness** ★★★★. **Parking** Epcot lot. **Bar** Beer and wine only. **Wine selection** All Italian. **Dress** Casual. **Disabled access** Yes. **Customers** Theme park guests. **Lunch** Daily, 11:30 a.m.–3:30 p.m. **Dinner** Daily, 4:30–9 p.m.

SETTING AND ATMOSPHERE Tutto Italia feels like a big restaurant in Rome or Milan, with huge murals of a piazza along the wall behind the upholstered banquettes, but it can get noisy in the dining room, which is nearly always full. If the weather is pleasant, request a table on the piazza.

HOUSE SPECIALTIES *Fior di latte* mozzarella with roasted peppers and basil; fettuccine campagnole (with arugula, spinach, basil, and burrata cheese); pollo al forno; Black Angus rib eye; panna cotta and gelato for dessert.

OTHER RECOMMENDATIONS Any of the pastas (fettuccine, gnochetti, ravioli, spaghetti); fried calamari.

SUMMARY AND COMMENTS One of the best Epcot restaurants. Pricey, yes, but the service is polished and genuinely Italian (due to the genuinely Italian waiters), the cuisine is authentic, and the servings are ample.

Las Ventanas ★★

AMERICAN	MODERATE	QUALITY ★★½	VALUE ★★
READER-SURVEY RESPONSES	85%👍 15%👎	DISNEY DINING PLAN?	Yes

Coronado Springs Resort; ☎ 407-939-3463

Reservations Recommended. **Dining Plan credits** 1 per person, per meal. **When to go** Anytime. **Cost range** Breakfast $7–$20 (child $9), lunch $15–$17 (child $10), dinner $15–$28 (child $10). **Service** ★★★★. **Friendliness** ★★★★. **Parking** Coronado Springs. **Bar** Beer and wine only. **Dress** Casual. **Disabled access** Yes. **Customers** Coronado Springs guests. **Breakfast** Daily, 7–10:30 a.m. **Lunch** Daily, 11 a.m.–2 p.m. **Dinner** Daily, 4–10 p.m.

SETTING AND ATMOSPHERE Tucked discreetly inside one of the main hallways connecting Coronado's food court with its convention space, Las Ventanas is more refined and subdued than the nearby Pepper Market, with high ceilings, dark slate floors, and rust-colored walls.

HOUSE SPECIALTIES Huevos rancheros at breakfast; the ominous-sounding Huevos Divorciados. Prime rib and seared pork loin.

SUMMARY AND COMMENTS Las Ventanas isn't anything special, but it can be a welcome, quiet place for a simple breakfast. Stick to the basics (waffles, eggs, sandwiches, and burgers) and you'll be fine.

Via Napoli ★★★★

ITALIAN	MODERATE	QUALITY ★★★½	VALUE ★★★
READER-SURVEY RESPONSES	91%👍 10%👎	DISNEY DINING PLAN?	Yes

Italy, World Showcase, Epcot; ☎ 407-939-3463

Reservations Recommended. **Dining Plan credits** 1 per person, per meal. **When to go** Lunch or dinner. **Cost range** Entrées $18–$30, pizzas $18 (individual)–$48 (serves 3–5). **Service** ★★★★. **Friendliness** ★★★★. **Parking** Epcot lot. **Bar** Beer and wine only. **Dress** Casual. **Disabled access** Yes. **Customers** Theme park guests. **Lunch** Daily, 11:30 a.m.–4:25 p.m. **Dinner** Daily, 4:30–9 p.m.

SETTING AND ATMOSPHERE The three big pizza ovens, named after the three active Italian volcanoes, Etna, Vesuvius, and Stromboli, are the stars of the show in this loud, cavernous dining room with tile floors and stucco walls. There are enough staff and guests moving around that it feels like a bustling Italian market. Shaded outdoor seating is also available.

HOUSE SPECIALTIES The best pizza in Walt Disney World. The rest of the menu is average, with the possible exception of the salads.

SUMMARY AND COMMENTS Because the pizzas are cooked at infernolike temperatures, they don't stay in the oven for long and vegetable toppings stay crunchy. The Capricciosa (eggplant, artichokes, prosciutto, and mushrooms) and four-cheese pies are our favorites. Servers must attend so many diners that mistakes happen often; pay attention to what's put down in front of you, and errors will be corrected, usually in your favor.

Victoria & Albert's ★★★★★

GOURMET	EXPENSIVE	QUALITY ★★★★★		VALUE ★★★★
READER-SURVEY RESPONSES	94%👍	6%👎	DISNEY DINING PLAN?	No

Grand Floridian Resort & Spa; ☎ 407-939-3463

Reservations Mandatory; must confirm by noon the day of your seating; call at least 180 days in advance to reserve. **When to go** Anytime. **Cost range** Fixed price, 7-course $185 (pairing $250), 10-course $235 (pairing $340), Queen Victoria's Room $235 (pairing $340), Chef's Table $250 (pairing $355). **Service** ★★★★★. **Friendliness** ★★★★. **Parking** Valet (free); self-parking is deceptively far away. **Wine selection** 700 on the menu, 4,200 more in the cellar. **Dress** Jacket required for men, evening wear for women. **Disabled access** Yes. **Customers** Hotel guests, locals. **Hours** Variable seating starting at 5:45 p.m., plus 1 seating at 5:30 p.m. for the Chef's Table. *Note:* No children under age 10 admitted except at Chef's Table.

SETTING AND ATMOSPHERE With only 18 tables in the main dining room, Queen Victoria's Room with seating for 8, and the 10-seat Chef's Table, this is the top dining experience at Disney World. A winner of AAA's Five Diamond Award for 16 straight years—the only restaurant in Central Florida so honored—Victoria & Albert's is civilized, lavish, and expensive, with Frette linens, Riedel crystal, Christofle silver. Seats are booked six months in advance for the 6- to 10-course meals, and cancellations are rare.

HOUSE SPECIALTIES The menu changes daily, but you might find Minnesota elk tenderloin, Alaskan salmon, local free-range chicken, Florida sturgeon caviar, and Australian Kobe-style beef on chef Scott Hunnel's menu. Pastry chef Erich Herbitschek's desserts are divine.

ENTERTAINMENT AND AMENITIES A harpist or violinist entertains from the foyer. But the best show is in the kitchen when you book the Chef's Table, where Hunnel crafts a personalized menu.

SUMMARY AND COMMENTS Hunnel (a James Beard Foundation nominee) and his team prepare modern American cuisine with the best of the best from around the world. While the main dining room and Queen Victoria's Room are whisper-quiet, the convivial Chef's Table is a different experience altogether. For epicures, it's a bargain.

The Wave . . . of American Flavors ★★★

NEW AMERICAN/BUFFET		MODERATE	QUALITY ★★		VALUE ★★
READER-SURVEY RESPONSES	89%👍	11%👎	DISNEY DINING PLAN?	Yes	

Contemporary Resort; ☎ 407-939-3463

Reservations Accepted. **Dining Plan credits** 1 per person, per meal. **When to go** Anytime. **Cost range** Breakfast $6.50–$12.50 à la carte, $24 buffet (child $13); lunch $12–$20 (child $9); dinner $17.50–$34 (child $9). **Service** ★★★. **Friendliness** ★★★. **Parking** Valet ($25) or hotel lot. **Bar** Full service. **Wine selection** All New World screw-caps. **Dress** Casual. **Disabled access** Yes. **Customers** Hotel guests, locals. **Breakfast** Daily, 7:30–11:45 a.m. **Lunch** Daily, noon–2 p.m. **Dinner** Daily, 5–9:30 p.m.

SETTING AND ATMOSPHERE On the first floor of the Contemporary just past the front desk, you walk into The Wave's lounge, with the dining room to the left—the lounge is usually packed after 5 p.m., and it's hard to snag a seat. The adjoining dining room has the feel of an upscale coffee shop, with wooden tables and white-linen napkins.

HOUSE SPECIALTIES For breakfast: a generous buffet, organic Colombian press-pot coffee, mega-berry smoothie, sweet potato pancakes, make-your-own muesli. For lunch: lump crab–Florida rock shrimp cakes, build-your-own burger. For dinner: grilled Colorado lamb chops, sustainable fish, potato gnocchi with braised short rib, vegetarian curry stew.

OTHER RECOMMENDATIONS Pork belly with local eggs, charcuterie board, no-sugar-added crème brûlée.

SUMMARY AND COMMENTS While it's not a dining destination, the kitchen has stayed the course with healthful, locally sourced dining options. Organic beers and coffees, hip cocktails, and screw-cap wines from around the globe are part of the forward-thinking beverage lineup.

Whispering Canyon Cafe ★★★

AMERICAN	MODERATE	QUALITY ★★★½	VALUE ★★★★
READER-SURVEY RESPONSES	91% 👍	9% 👎 DISNEY DINING PLAN?	Yes

Wilderness Lodge & Boulder Ridge Villas; ☎ 407-939-3463

Reservations Accepted. **Dining Plan credits** 1 per person, per meal. **When to go** Anytime. **Cost range** Breakfast $11–$18 (child $6–$10), lunch $13–$23 (child $8–$14), dinner $19–$34 (child $8–$14). **Service** ★★★★. **Friendliness** ★★★★. **Parking** Hotel lot. **Bar** Full service. **Wine selection** Limited. **Dress** Casual. **Disabled access** Yes. **Customers** Hotel guests. **Breakfast** Daily, 7:30–11:15 a.m. **Lunch** Daily, 11:45 a.m.–2:30 p.m. **Dinner** Daily, 5–10 p.m.

SETTING AND ATMOSPHERE A big, open dining room just off the lobby with whimsical Wild West decor. Despite its name, Whispering Canyon Cafe is anything but quiet—OK, it's remarkably noisy—with servers encouraging diners to let loose and have fun (pony races, anyone?). Tables have a barrel-top lazy Susan where food is placed for an all-you-can-eat experience.

HOUSE SPECIALTIES For breakfast, the all-you-can-eat platter offers bacon, sausage, scrambled eggs, home fries, and buttermilk biscuits and gravy. For lunch and dinner, big skillets loaded with corn bread, pulled pork, smoked pork ribs, roasted chicken, sausage, mashed potatoes, baked beans, and corn on the cob are crowd-pleasers.

OTHER RECOMMENDATIONS New York strip steak, citrus-glazed rainbow trout, s'mores with marshmallow gelato.

SUMMARY AND COMMENTS Whispering Canyon is rowdy fun for families, and the all-you-can-eat skillets give hungry folks their money's worth.

Yachtsman Steakhouse ★★★

STEAK	EXPENSIVE	QUALITY ★★★½	VALUE ★★
READER-SURVEY RESPONSES	90% 👍	10% 👎 DISNEY DINING PLAN?	Yes

Yacht Club Resort; ☎ 407-939-3463

Reservations Required. **Dining Plan credits** 2 per person, per meal. **When to go** Dinner. **Cost range** Dinner $31–$125 (child $9–$17). **Service** ★★★★. **Friendliness** ★★★★. **Parking** Hotel lot. **Bar** Full service. **Wine selection** Very good. **Dress** Dressy casual. **Disabled access** Yes. **Customers** Hotel guests and locals. **Hours** Daily, 5–9:30 p.m.

SETTING AND ATMOSPHERE Wooden beams, white linens, and a view of the Yacht Club's sandy lagoon make Yachtsman feel light and airy rather than dark and masculine like the typical steakhouse. Beef is the star, of course, but there are other options on the menu, even vegetarian. The adjacent Crew's Cup Lounge is a fun place to start the evening.

HOUSE SPECIALTIES The 32-ounce porterhouse for two ($119) is a worthy splurge. Outstanding cheese and charcuterie selections, too.

OTHER RECOMMENDATIONS Day-boat sea scallops, potato and leek–stuffed anelli pasta, Caribbean red snapper, bison strip loin.

SUMMARY AND COMMENTS Yachtsman has a cult following of local meat lovers who don't mind the sky-high prices. The quality is outstanding: The dry-aged steaks are cut and trimmed on the premises, and vintages from every major wine-producing region of the world complement the menu.

Yak & Yeti Restaurant ★★

PAN-ASIAN	EXPENSIVE	QUALITY ★★½	VALUE ★★
READER-SURVEY RESPONSES 92%👍	8%👎	DISNEY DINING PLAN? Yes	

Asia, Disney's Animal Kingdom; ☎ 407-939-3463

Reservations Recommended. **Dining Plan credits** 1 per person, per meal. **When to go** Dinner. **Cost range** $18–$29 (child $9). **Service ★★★★**. **Friendliness ★★★★**. **Parking** Animal Kingdom lot. **Bar** Full service. **Wine selection** Limited. **Dress** Casual. **Disabled access** Yes. **Customers** Theme park guests. **Lunch** Daily, 11 a.m.–3:30 p.m. **Dinner** Daily, 4 p.m.–park closing.

SETTING AND ATMOSPHERE A rustic two-story Nepalese inn—with seating for hundreds. Windows on the second floor overlook the Asia section of the theme park. The Asian artifacts are more interesting than the food.

HOUSE SPECIALTIES Lo mein and curry noodle bowls; crispy honey tempura chicken; Kalbi flat-iron steak and coconut shrimp; chicken tikka masala; teriyaki mahimahi.

SUMMARY AND COMMENTS Yak & Yeti isn't as good as it used to be—with Chinese, Indian, Japanese, and Thai cuisines represented, there's just too much going on. The kitchen should pare down the menu and then fine-tune what's left. But sitting at the bar with a Pink Himalayan cocktail and dim sum basket is the perfect escape from Animal Kingdom madness.

PART FIVE

WALT DISNEY WORLD *with* KIDS

The ECSTASY *and the* AGONY

SO OVERWHELMING IS THE DISNEY MEDIA and advertising presence that any child who watches TV or shops with a parent is likely to get revved up about going to Walt Disney World. Parents, if anything, are even more susceptible. Almost all moms and dads brighten at the prospect of guiding their children through this special place. But the reality of taking a young child (particularly during the summer) can be closer to the agony than to the ecstasy.

An Ohio mother who took her 5-year-old one summer recalls:

I felt so happy and excited before we went. I guess it was all worth it, but when I look back I think I should have had my head examined. The first day we went to the Magic Kingdom, it was packed. By 11 in the morning, we had walked so far and stood in so many lines that we were all exhausted. Kristy cried about going on anything that looked or even sounded scary and was frightened by all of the Disney characters (they're so big!) except Minnie and Snow White.

We got hungry about the same time as everyone else, but the lines for food were too long and my husband said we'd have to wait. By 1 in the afternoon we were just plugging along, not seeing anything we were really interested in, but picking rides because the lines were short, or because whatever it was, was air-conditioned. At around 2:30, we finally got something to eat, but by then we were so hot and tired that it felt like we had worked in the yard all day. At the end, we were so P.O.'d and uncomfortable that we weren't having any fun.

Before you stiffen in denial, let us assure you that this family's experience is not unusual. Most young children are as picky about rides as they are about what they eat, and many preschoolers are intimidated by the Disney characters. Few humans (of any age) are mentally or physically equipped to march all day in a throng of 50,000 people in the hot Florida sun. And would you be surprised to learn that almost 60% of preschoolers said the thing they liked best about their Disney vacation was the hotel swimming pool?

But even somewhat older kids will surprise you, as this Windsor, Ontario, mom relates:

On day three, we were in World Showcase and our two girls suddenly stopped in their tracks between Italy and Germany. They looked around for a minute and we asked what was wrong. Turns out they'd finally seen something other than characters that appealed to them. "Could we just run around on that grass over there for a few minutes?" they asked. "We won't take too long." So away they went to chase each other on the grass for 10 minutes. Years later, that is what they remember about the trip. Ever since, we've tried to include time in each trip plan to "run around on that grass over there," wherever "there" might be.

unofficial TIP
When considering a trip to Walt Disney World, think about whether your kids are old enough to enjoy what can be a very fun but taxing trip.

With good planning and a sense of humor, you'll be e-mailing us messages like this one from a Harrisburg, Pennsylvania, mom:

I knew it would be fun for my daughter, but what I didn't expect was just how much fun it would be for me.

REALITY TESTING: WHOSE DREAM IS IT?

REMEMBER WHEN YOU WERE LITTLE and you got that nifty remote control car for Christmas, the one Dad wouldn't let you play with? Did you wonder who the car was really for? Ask yourself a similar question about your vacation to Walt Disney World. Whose dream are you trying to make come true: yours or your child's?

Young children read their parents' emotions. When you ask, "Honey, how would you like to go to Disney World?" your child will respond more to your smile and enthusiasm than to any notion of what Disney World is all about. The younger the child, the more this holds true. From many preschoolers, you could elicit the same excitement by asking, "Sweetie, how would you like to go to Cambodia on a dogsled?"

So is your happy fantasy of introducing your child to Disney magic a pipe dream? Not necessarily, but you have to be open to reality testing. For example, would you increase the probability of a successful visit by waiting a year or two? Will your child have sufficient endurance and patience to cope with long lines and large crowds?

RECOMMENDATIONS FOR MAKING THE DREAM COME TRUE

WHEN YOU'RE PLANNING A DISNEY WORLD VACATION with young children, consider the following:

AGE Although Walt Disney World's color and festivity excite all children and specific attractions delight toddlers and preschoolers, Disney entertainment is generally oriented to older children and adults. Children should be a fairly mature 7 years old to *appreciate* the Magic Kingdom and Disney's Animal Kingdom, a year or two older to get much out of Epcot or Disney's Hollywood Studios.

Readers continually debate how old a child should be or the ideal age to go to Disney World. A Rockaway, New Jersey, mom writes:

I found myself rereading your section "The Ecstasy and the Agony." Unfortunately, our experience was pure agony, with the exception of our hotel pool. It was the one and only thing our kids enjoyed. I had planned and saved for this trip for over a year, and I cried all week at the disappointment that our kids just wanted to swim.

A dad from Columbus, Ohio, felt like he was in a maternity ward:

We were shocked to see so many newborns as well. I could have sworn that one woman gave birth at the bus stop, her baby was so small.

A Lawrenceville, Georgia, mother of two toddlers advises maintaining children's normal schedule:

The first day, we tried your suggestion about an early start, so we woke the kids (ages 4 and 2) and hurried them to get going. BAD IDEA. This put them off-schedule for naps and meals the rest of the day.

WHEN TO VISIT Avoid the hot, crowded summer months, especially if you have preschoolers. Go in October, November (except Thanksgiving), early December, January, February, or May. If you have children of varied ages and they're good students, take the older ones out of school and visit during the cooler and less congested off-season.

Most readers who've tried Disney World at various times agree. A New Hampshire parent writes:

I took my grade-school children out of school for a few days to go during a slow time and would highly recommend it. We communicated with the teachers about a month before traveling to seek their preference for whether classwork and homework should be completed before, during, or after our trip. It's so much more enjoyable to be at Disney when your children can experience rides and attractions and all that is Disney rather than standing in line.

There's another side to this story, and we've received some well-considered letters from parents and teachers who don't think taking kids out of school is such a hot idea. From a father in Fairfax, Virginia:

My wife and I are disappointed that you seem to be encouraging families to take their children out of school to go to WDW. My wife is an eighth-grade teacher of chemistry and physics. She has parents pull their children, some honor-roll students, out of school for vacations, only to discover when they return that the students are unable to comprehend the material.

A Martinez, California, teacher offers this compelling analogy:

There are a precious 180 days for us as teachers to instruct our students, and there are 185 days during the year for Disney World. I have seen countless students during my 14 years of teaching struggle to catch up the rest of the year due to a week of vacation during critical instructional periods. The analogy I use with my students' parents is that it's like walking out of a movie after watching the first 5 minutes, then returning for the last 5 minutes and trying to figure out what happened.

But a teacher from Penn Yan, New York, sees things differently:

As a teacher and a parent, I disagree with the comments from teachers saying that it's horrible for a parent to take a child out for a vacation. If a parent takes the time to let us know that a child is going to be out, we help them get ready for upcoming homework the best we can. If the child is a good student, why shouldn't they go have a wonderful experience with their family?

If possible, have your child's teacher create special assignments relating to the educational aspects of Disney World. If your children can't afford to miss school, take your vacation as soon as the school year ends. Alternatively, try late August, before school starts.

BUILD NAPS AND REST INTO YOUR ITINERARY The parks are huge: Don't try to see everything in one day. Tour in the early morning and return to your hotel around 11:30 a.m. for lunch, a swim, and a nap. Even during off-season, when crowds are smaller and the temperature is more pleasant, the major parks' size will exhaust most children younger than age 8 by lunchtime. Return

*un*official **TIP**
If you must rent a car to make returning to your hotel practicable, do it.

to the park in late afternoon or early evening and continue touring. A family from Texas underlines the importance of naps and rest:

Probably the most important tip your guide gave us was going to the hotel to swim and regroup during the day. The parks became unbearable by noon—and so did my husband and boys. The hotel was an oasis that calmed our nerves! After about 3 hours of playtime, we headed out to a different park for dinner and a cool evening of fun.

Regarding naps, this mom doesn't mince words:

For parents of small kids: Take the book's advice, get out of the park, and take the nap, take the nap, TAKE THE NAP!

From a Pennsylvania mom:

Do not try to push through the day. A nap in a stroller in the Florida heat is not a nap. By 2 p.m., the park was exploding with crying children, and I saw a lot of little kids getting smacked and screamed at in the "happiest place on Earth."

If you plan to return to your hotel at midday and want your room made up, let housekeeping know. before you leave in the morning.

WHERE TO STAY The time and hassle involved in commuting to and from the theme parks will be less if your hotel is close by. This doesn't necessarily mean you have to lodge inside Disney World. Because the World is so geographically dispersed, many off-property hotels are closer to the parks than some Disney resorts (see our Hotel Information Chart in Part Three, showing commuting times from Disney and non-Disney hotels). Regardless of where you stay, it's imperative that you take young children out of the parks each day for a few hours of rest. Neglecting to relax can ruin the day—or the vacation—for everyone.

If you have young children, book a hotel that's within a 20-minute drive from the theme parks. It's true that you can revive somewhat by retreating to a Disney hotel for lunch or by finding a quiet restaurant in the parks, but there's no substitute for returning to the comfort of your hotel.

If you're traveling with children 12 years old and younger and you want to stay in Walt Disney World, we recommend the **Polynesian**

Village & Villas, **Grand Floridian & Villas**, or **Wilderness Lodge & Boulder Ridge Villas** (in that order), if they fit your budget. For less-expensive rooms, try **Port Orleans French Quarter**. The least expensive on-site rooms are available at the **All-Star Resorts**. In addition to standard hotel rooms, the **All-Star Music** and **Art of Animation Resorts** offer two-room Family Suites that can sleep as many as six and provide kitchenettes. Log cabins at **Fort Wilderness Resort & Campground** and the DVC resorts are another option for families who need a little more space. Outside the World, check our top hotels for families (see page 268), but know that many more good options exist.

BE IN TOUCH WITH YOUR FEELINGS When you or your kids get tired and irritable, call time-out. Trust your instincts. What would feel best? Another ride, an ice-cream break, or going back to the room for a nap?

LEAST COMMON DENOMINATORS Somebody is going to run out of steam first, and when he or she does, the whole family will be affected. Pushing the tired or discontented beyond their capacity will spoil the day for them—and you. Energy levels vary. Be prepared to respond to members of your group who poop out. *Hint:* "We've driven a thousand miles to take you to Disney World and now you're ruining everything!" is not an appropriate response.

BUILDING ENDURANCE Though most children are active, their normal play usually doesn't condition them for the exertion required to tour a Disney park. Start family walks four to six weeks before your trip to get in shape. A mother from Wescosville, Pennsylvania, reports:

> We had our 6-year-old begin walking with us a bit every day one month before leaving—when we arrived at Disney World, her little legs could carry her, and she had a lot of stamina.

From a Middletown, Delaware, mom:

> You recommended walking for six weeks prior to the trip, but we began months in advance, just because. My husband lost 10 pounds, my daughter never once complained, and we met a lot of neighbors!

A Tallahassee mother of two isn't convinced that our fitness recommendations are warranted:

> I suggest you retool your Physical Preparation section to address different levels of fitness/overall physical condition/age/health. So, for example, couch potatoes with weight issues are going to need lots of preparation. But not all those warnings and tips are going to apply to many of us. Thank you!!

Our response is to at least run a little test, say a six-mile hike, to establish your family's baseline level of fitness. Be safe. Many find out the hard way that they're not as fit as they think.

SETTING LIMITS AND MAKING PLANS To avoid arguments and disappointments, establish guidelines for each day and get everybody committed. Include the following:

1. Wake-up time and breakfast plans
2. When to depart for the park

3. What to take with you

4. A policy for splitting the group or for staying together, and what to do if the group gets separated or someone is lost

5. What you want to see, including plans in the event an attraction is closed or too crowded

6. A policy on what you can afford for snacks

7. How long you plan to tour in the morning and what time you'll return to your hotel to rest

8. When you'll return to the park and how late you'll stay

9. Dinner plans

10. A policy for buying souvenirs, including who pays (kids or parents)

11. Bedtimes

BE FLEXIBLE Any day at Disney World includes surprises; be prepared to adjust your plan. Listen to your intuition.

WHAT KIDS WANT According to the travel-research firm MMGY Global, 71% of children between the ages of 6 and 17 say they need a vacation because school and homework get them down. The chart below shows what kids want and don't want when taking a vacation. Kids surveyed have a lot in common about what they do want, not as much concerning what they don't.

WHAT DO KIDS WANT?	WHAT DO KIDS NOT WANT?
To go swimming/have pool time **85%**	To get up early **52%**
To eat in restaurants **78%**	To ride in a car **36%**
To stay at a hotel or resort **76%**	To play golf **34%**
To visit a theme park **76%**	To go to a museum **31%**
To stay up late **73%**	

Other high-ranking wants include throwing water balloons and eating ice cream.

MAINTAINING SOME SEMBLANCE OF ORDER AND DISCIPLINE OK, OK, wipe that smirk off your face. Order and discipline on the road may seem like an oxymoron to you, but you won't be hooting when your 5-year-old launches a tantrum in the middle of Fantasyland. Your willingness to give this subject serious consideration before you leave home may well be the most important element of your pre-trip preparation.

Discipline and order are more difficult to maintain when traveling than at home because everyone is, as a Boston mom puts it, "in and out"—in strange surroundings and out of the normal routine. For children, it's hard to contain excitement and anticipation that pop to the surface in the form of fidgety hyperactivity, nervous energy, and sometimes, acting out. Confinement in a car, plane, or hotel room only exacerbates the situation, and kids often tend to be louder than normal, more aggressive with siblings, and much more inclined to push the envelope of parental patience. Once you're in the theme parks, it doesn't get much better. There's more elbow room, but there are also overstimulation, crowds, heat, and miles of walking. All this, coupled with marginal or inadequate rest, can lead to a meltdown in the most harmonious of families.

Sound parenting and standards of discipline practiced at home, applied consistently, will suffice to handle most situations on vacation. Still, it's instructive to study the hand you're dealt when traveling. For starters, aside from being jazzed and ablaze with adrenaline, your kids may believe that rules followed at home are somehow suspended when traveling. Parents reinforce this misguided intuition by being inordinately lenient in the interest of maintaining peace in the family. While some of your home protocols (cleaning your plate, going to bed at a set time) might be relaxed to good effect on vacation, differing from your normal approach to discipline can precipitate major misunderstanding and possibly disaster.

Children, not unexpectedly, are likely to believe that a vacation to Walt Disney World is intended just for them. This reinforces their focus on their own needs and largely erases any consideration of yours. Such a mind-set dramatically increases their sense of hurt and disappointment when you correct them or deny them something they want. An incident that would hardly elicit a pouty lip at home could well escalate to tears or defiance when traveling. It's important before you depart on your trip, therefore, to discuss your vacation needs with your children, and to explore their wants and expectations as well.

unofficial **TIP**
Teaching your kids to tell you clearly what they want or need will help make the trip more enjoyable for everyone.

According to *Unofficial Guide* child psychologist Karen Turnbow, PhD, successful response to (or avoidance of) behavioral problems on the road begins with a clear-cut disciplinary policy at home. Both at home and on vacation the approach should be the same, and should be based on the following key concepts:

1. LET EXPECTATIONS BE KNOWN Discuss what you expect from your children, but don't try to cover every imaginable situation (that's what lawyers are for—just kidding). Address expectations regarding compliance with parental directives, treatment of siblings, resolution of disputes, schedules (including morning wake-up and bedtimes), courtesy and manners, staying together, and who pays for what.

2. EXPLAIN THE CONSEQUENCES OF NONCOMPLIANCE Detail very clearly and firmly the consequence of not meeting expectations. This should be very straightforward and unambiguous: "If you do X (or don't do X), this is what will happen."

3. WARNING You're dealing with excited, expectant children, not machines, so it's important to issue a warning before meting out discipline. It's critical to understand that we're talking about one unequivocal warning rather than multiple warnings or nagging. These last undermine your credibility and make your expectations appear relative or less than serious. Multiple warnings or nagging also effectively pass control of the situation from you to your child.

4. FOLLOW-THROUGH If you say you're going to do something, do it. *Period.* Children must understand that you mean business.

5. CONSISTENCY Inconsistency makes discipline a random event in the eyes of your children. Random discipline encourages random behavior, which translates to a nearly total loss of parental control. Long-term, both at home and on the road, your response to a given situation or transgression must be perfectly predictable. Structure and repetition, which are essential for a child to learn, cannot be achieved in the absence of consistency.

Although the previous methods are the five biggies, several corollary concepts and techniques are worthy of consideration as well.

Understand that whining, tantrums, defiance, sibling friction, and even holding up the group are ways in which children communicate with parents. Frequently the object or precipitant of a situation has little or no relation to the unacceptable behavior. A fit may on the surface appear to be about the ice cream you refused to buy little Robby, but there's almost always something deeper, a subtext that is closer to the truth (this is why ill behavior often persists after you give in to a child's demands). As often as not, the real cause is a need for attention. This need is so powerful in some children that they will subject themselves to certain punishment and parental displeasure to garner the attention they crave, even if it's negative.

To get at the root cause of the behavior in question requires both active listening and empowering your child with a "feeling vocabulary." Active listening is a concept that's been around a long time. It involves being alert not only to what a child says but also to the context in which it's said, to the words used and possible subtext, to the child's emotional state and body language, and even to what's *not* said. Sounds complicated, but it's basically being attentive to the larger picture and, more to the point, being aware that there *is* a larger picture.

Helping your child develop a feeling vocabulary involves teaching your child to use words to describe what's going on. The idea is to teach the child to articulate what's really troubling him, to be able to identify and express emotions and mood states in language. Of course, learning to express feelings is a lifelong learning experience, but it's much less dependent on innate sensitivity than on being provided with the tools for expression and being encouraged to use them.

Children are almost never too young to begin learning a feeling vocabulary. And helping your child to get in touch with—and to communicate—his or her emotions will stimulate you to focus on *your* feelings and mood states in a similar way. With persistence and effort, the whole family can achieve a vastly improved ability to communicate.

A Shelby, North Carolina, reader touts a resource for parents whose kids need a little help with their feeling vocabularies:

> I use a therapy technique at work called the **Alert Program** that helps kids develop self-regulation skills, including a feeling vocabulary. The website (**alertprogram.com**) provides an explanation and additional resources [some free, some for sale]. You can use many analogies to make it work, but an especially fun one is to use Disney characters: A child might feel like Winnie the Pooh if he's "just right," Tigger if he's hyper or needs a movement break, or Eeyore if he's feeling tired or sad.

Until you get the hang of active listening and a feeling vocabulary, be careful not to become part of the problem. There's a laundry list of not-so-adult responses to bad behavior that only make things worse: hitting, yelling, belittling, pleading, nagging, and inducing guilt.

Responding to a child appropriately in a disciplinary situation requires thought and preparation. Following are things to keep in mind and techniques to try when your world blows up while waiting in line for Dumbo.

1. BE THE ADULT It's well understood that children can push their parents' buttons faster and more skillfully than just about anyone or anything else. They've got your number, know precisely how to elicit a response, and are not reluctant to go for the jugular. Fortunately (or unfortunately), you're the adult, and to deal with a situation effectively, you've got to act like one. If your kids get you ranting and caterwauling, you effectively abdicate your adult status. Worse, you suggest by way of example that being out of control is an acceptable expression of hurt or anger. No matter what happens, repeat the mantra, "I am the adult in this relationship."

2. FREEZE THE ACTION Being the adult and maintaining control almost always translates to freezing the action, to borrow a sports term. Instead of responding in knee-jerk fashion (that is, at a maturity level closer to your child's than yours), freeze the action by disengaging. Wherever you are or whatever the family is doing, stop in place and concentrate on one thing, and one thing only: getting all involved to calm down. Practically speaking, this usually means initiating a time-out. It's essential that you take this action immediately. Grabbing your child by the arm or collar and dragging him toward the car or hotel room only escalates the turmoil by prolonging the confrontation and by adding a coercive physical dimension to an already volatile emotional event. For the sake of everyone involved, including the people around you (as when a toddler throws a tantrum in church), it's essential to retreat to a more private place. Choose the first place available. Firmly sit the child down and refrain from talking to him until you've both cooled off. This might take a little time, but the investment is worthwhile. Truncating the process is like trying to get on your feet too soon after surgery.

3. ISOLATE THE CHILD You'll be able to deal with the situation more effectively and expeditiously if the child is isolated with one parent. Dispatch the uninvolved members of your party for a snack break or have them go on with the activity or itinerary without you (if possible) and arrange to rendezvous later at an agreed time and place. In addition to letting the others get on with their day, isolating the offending child with one parent relieves him of the pressure of being the group's focus of attention and object of anger. Equally important, isolation frees you from the scrutiny and expectations of the others in regard to how to handle the situation.

4. REVIEW THE SITUATION WITH THE CHILD If, as discussed a few pages back, you've made your expectations clear, stated the consequences of failing to meet those expectations, and administered a warning, review the situation with the child and follow through with the discipline warranted. If, as often occurs, things are not so black-and-white, encourage the child to communicate his feelings. Try to uncover what occasioned the acting out. Lectures and accusatory language don't work well here, nor do threats. Dr. Turnbow suggests that a better approach (after the child is calm) is to ask, "What can we do to make this a better day for you?"

5. FREQUENT TANTRUMS OR ACTING OUT The preceding four points relate to dealing with an incident as opposed to a chronic condition. If a child frequently acts out or throws tantrums, you'll need to employ a somewhat different strategy.

Tantrums are cyclical events evolved from learned behavior. A child learns that he can get your undivided attention by acting out. When you respond, whether by scolding, admonishing, threatening, or negotiating, your response further draws you into the cycle and prolongs the behavior. When you accede to the child's demands, you reinforce the effectiveness of the tantrum and raise the cost of capitulation next time around. When a child thus succeeds in monopolizing your attention, he effectively becomes the person in charge.

To break this cycle, you must disengage from the child. The object is to demonstrate that the cause-and-effect relationship (that is, tantrum elicits parental attention) is no longer operative. This can be accomplished by refusing to interact with the child as long as the untoward behavior continues. Tell the child that you're unwilling to discuss his problem until he calms down. You can ignore the behavior, remove yourself from the child's presence (or vice versa), or isolate the child with a time-out.

Most children don't pick the family vacation as the time to start throwing tantrums. The behavior will be evident before you leave home, and home is the best place to deal with it. Be forewarned, however, that bad habits die hard, and that a child accustomed to getting attention by throwing tantrums will not simply give up after a single instance of disengagement. More likely, the child will at first escalate the intensity and length of his tantrums. By your consistent refusal over several weeks (or even months) to respond to his behavior, however, he will finally adjust to the new paradigm.

Children are cunning as well as observant. Many understand that a tantrum in public is embarrassing to you and that you're more likely to cave in than you would at home. Once again, consistency is the key, along with a bit of anticipation. When traveling, it's not necessary to retreat to the privacy of a hotel room to isolate your child. You can carve out space for a time-out almost anywhere: on a theme park bench, in a park, in your car, in a restroom, even on a sidewalk.

You can often spot the warning signs of an impending tantrum and head it off by talking to the child before he reaches an explosive emotional pitch. And don't forget that tantrums are about getting attention. Giving your child attention when things are on an even keel often preempts acting out.

6. SALVAGE OPERATIONS Kids are full of surprises, and sometimes those surprises are, well, not good. What if your sweet precious pulls a stunt so beyond the pale that it threatens to derail your entire trip? In the case of one Ohio boy visiting Disney World with his family, his offense resulted in his being grounded more or less for life. For starters, his parents split up the group: One parent escorted the miscreant back to the hotel room, where he was effectively confined for the duration. That evening, Mom and Dad arranged for in-room sitters for the rest of the stay. Expensive? Yep, but better than ruining the vacation for everybody else.

In another case, a child acted out at the Magic Kingdom, though the offense was of a milder order of magnitude. Because it was the family's last day at Disney World, the parents elected to place the misbehaver in time-out for the rest of their day in the park—one parent would monitor the culprit while the other parent and the siblings enjoyed the attractions. At agreed-upon times, the parents would switch places.

Parenting Advice: Readers Weigh In

Though the foregoing section was developed by top child psychologists, it rubs some readers, like this teacher from Corryton, Tennessee, the wrong way:

The one thing I don't like is the section on how to make your kids behave. As a preschool teacher, I can honestly say that people who need this advice won't take it anyway—so why bother?

But a North Carolina psychiatrist disagrees:

The section on child behavioral issues while traveling is one of the most concise and well-articulated presentations on this subject that I have encountered. I recommend it to many of my patients who are contemplating traveling with their children.

A New Hampshire father of two had this to say:

Your advice on touring with children was fabulous. Your book gave us confidence to do the parks without being deer caught in the headlights.

ABOUT THE *UNOFFICIAL GUIDE* TOURING PLANS

PARENTS WHO USE OUR TOURING PLANS are often frustrated by interruptions and delays caused by their children. Here's what to expect:

1. SPONTANEOUS CHARACTER ENCOUNTERS CAN WREAK HAVOC WITH THE TOURING PLANS. Our standard touring plans for young children include character meet and greets; more can be added with our touring plan software. Still, you're apt to see numerous Disney characters roaming the parks. This stops many children in their tracks. Attempting to haul your child away before he has satisfied his curiosity is likely to cause anything from whining to full-scale revolt. Either go with the flow or remind him of the specific time for photos and autographs. Be aware that lines for autographs can be as long as those for major attractions; our touring plans use FastPass+ (see page 94) to minimize waits in line.

2. OUR TOURING PLANS CALL FOR VISITING ATTRACTIONS IN A CERTAIN ORDER, OFTEN SKIPPING ATTRACTIONS ALONG THE WAY. Children don't like to skip *anything*! If something catches their eye, they want to see it right there and then. Some can be persuaded to skip attractions if parents explain their plans in advance, but other kids flip out at skipping something, particularly in Fantasyland. A mom from Charleston, South Carolina, writes:

We didn't have much trouble following the touring plans at Hollywood Studios and Epcot. The Magic Kingdom plan, on the other hand, turned out to be a train wreck. While we were on Dumbo, my 5-year-old saw eight dozen other things in Storybook Circus she wanted to do. Long story short: After Dumbo, there was no getting her out of there.

A mother of two from Burlington, Vermont, adds:

My kids were very curious about the castle because we had read Cinderella at home. Whenever I wanted to leave Fantasyland, I would just say, "Let's go to the castle and see if Cinderella is there." Once we got as far as the front door to the castle, it was no problem going out to the Central Plaza and then to another land.

3. IF YOU'RE USING A STROLLER, YOU WON'T BE ABLE TO TAKE IT INTO ATTRACTIONS OR ONTO RIDES. This includes rides such as the Walt Disney World Railroad that are included in the touring plans as in-park transportation. (An exception: Folding strollers are permitted on the railroad.) Stroller parking is available throughout the theme parks.

4. USE TECHNOLOGY TO GET BACK ON TRACK. Kids and touring plans are sort of like tossing back tequila shots: Sometimes unexpected things happen. Fortunately, we've built our Lines app (see page 29) to recover from such unforeseen events. If you find yourself out of sync with your plan and you're using Lines, just press the "Optimize" button when you're ready to get started again. Lines will redo your touring plan from that moment forward, using the current crowd conditions in the park.

While our touring plans help you make the most of your time at the parks, it's impossible to define what "most" will be. If you have two young children, you probably won't see as much as two adults will; if you have four children, you probably won't see as much as a couple with only two.

STUFF TO THINK ABOUT

OVERHEATING, SUNBURN, AND DEHYDRATION
These are the most common problems of younger children at Disney World. Carry and use sunscreen. Apply it on children in strollers, even if the stroller has a canopy. To avoid overheating, stop for rest regularly—say, in the shade, or in a restaurant or at a show with air-conditioning. Carry plastic bottles of water (bottles with screw caps are sold in all major parks for about $3).

unofficial **TIP**
Several companies, such as Neutrogena and California Baby, make sunscreens that won't burn your eyes. Look for a product *without* the active ingredient avobenzone, which is usually the culprit when it comes to stinging and burning.

BLISTERS AND SORE FEET In addition to wearing comfortable shoes, bring along blister bandages if you or your children are susceptible to blisters. These bandages (which are also available at First Aid, if you didn't heed our warnings) offer excellent protection, stick well, and won't sweat off. Remember that a preschooler may not say anything about a blister until it's already formed, so keep an eye on things during the day. For an expanded discussion, see page 507.

FIRST AID Each major theme park has a **First Aid Center**. In the Magic Kingdom, it's at the end of Main Street to your left, between Casey's Corner and The Crystal Palace. At Epcot, it's on the World Showcase side of Odyssey Center. At Disney's Hollywood Studios, it's in the Guest Relations Building inside the main entrance. At Disney's Animal Kingdom, it's in Discovery Island, on your left just before you cross the bridge to Africa, across from Creature Comforts. In all four parks, First Aid and the Baby Care Center are right next to each other. If you or your children have a medical problem, go to a First Aid Center. They're friendlier than most doctor's offices and are accustomed to treating everything from paper cuts to allergic reactions.

KIDS WITH ADHD Some parents of children prescribed Ritalin or similar medication let their child take a "drug holiday" when school lets out. If you've cut your child's dosage or discontinued her medication altogether, be aware that she might experience sensory overload at Disney World. Consult your child's physician before altering his or her drug regimen.

GLASSES AND SUNGLASSES If your kids (or you) wear them, attach a strap or string to the frames so the glasses will stay on during rides and can hang from the child's neck while indoors.

THINGS YOU FORGOT OR RAN OUT OF Rain gear, diapers, baby formula, sunburn treatments, memory cards, and other sundries are sold at all major theme parks and at Typhoon Lagoon, Blizzard Beach, and Disney Springs. If you don't see something you need, ask if it's in stock. Basic over-the-counter meds are often available free in small quantities at the First Aid Centers in the parks.

INFANTS AND TODDLERS AT THE THEME PARKS The major parks have **Baby Care Centers.** Everything necessary for changing diapers, preparing formulas, and warming bottles and food is available. Supplies are sold, and rockers and special chairs for nursing mothers are provided. At the Magic Kingdom, the Baby Care Center is next to The Crystal Palace at the end of Main Street. At Epcot, it's in the Odyssey Center, between Test Track in Future World and Mexico in World Showcase. At Disney's Hollywood Studios, it's in the Guest Relations Building, left of the main entrance. At Disney's Animal Kingdom, the Baby Care Center is behind First Aid, near the Discovery Island entrance to Africa. Dads are welcome at the centers and can use most services. In addition, many men's restrooms in the major parks have changing stations.

If your baby is on formula, this Wisconsin mom has a handy tip:

We got hot water from the food vendors and mixed the formula as needed. It eliminated keeping bottles cold and then warming them up.

Infants and toddlers are allowed in any attraction that doesn't have minimum height or age restrictions. But as a Minneapolis mother reports, some attractions are better for babies than others:

Theater and boat rides are easier for babies. Rides where there's a bar that comes down are doable, but harder—Peter Pan was our first encounter with this type of ride, and we had barely gotten situated when I realized my son might fall out of my grasp.

The same mom also advises:

We used a baby sling on our trip and thought it was great when standing in lines—much better than a stroller, which you have to park before getting in line (and navigate through crowds).

If you're a mother who wants to nurse during a theater attraction, note that most shows run about 17–20 minutes. Exceptions are *The Hall of Presidents* at the Magic Kingdom and *The American Adventure* at Epcot, which run 23 and 29 minutes, respectively.

We should pause to state unambiguously that mothers are free to nurse whenever and wherever they choose. A Georgia mom, not sure that all nursing mothers understand this, writes:

> *Women have the right to nurse in public without being criticized. It's not necessary to sit through all of* The Hall of Presidents *to feed your child. A lot of people read your books, and it would be nice to see you refer to breastfeeding as normal and not something that needs to be hidden or covered.*

A Lake Charles, Louisiana, mom is more blunt:

> *Don't tell me that men who'll do almost anything to see a boob will faint dead away at the sight of a nursing mother's breast. Ladies, feed your babies and tell the prudes to get over themselves!*

RUNNING OUT OF GAS When Bob was preparing to hike from the Colorado River to the rim of the Grand Canyon—a 5,000-foot ascent—a park ranger advised him to mix an electrolyte-replacement powder in his water and eat an energy-boosting snack at least twice every hour. While there's not much ascending to do at Walt Disney World, battling the heat, humidity, and crowds contributes to poop-out, especially where kids are concerned. Limiting calorie consumption to mealtimes just won't get it, as an experienced and wise grandma points out:

> *Children who get cranky during a visit often do so from all that time and energy expended without food. Feed them! A snack at any price goes a long way toward keeping little ones happy and parents sane!*

A mom from Blountville, Tennessee, says kids are not the only ones to need an energy boost:

> *BRING SNACKS into the park. I offered my kid a snack every hour or so, because I wanted to prevent the hunger meltdowns. I brought almonds for my husband and also made him eat a snack when the kids did. It's not just the kids who get grumpy when hungry!*

WILDLIFE Alligators can be found in almost all bodies of water in Florida, including those at Walt Disney World. Though alligator-related attacks are very rare, adults and especially children may become targets while swimming, wading, or sitting near the water's edge. Alligators are most active when feeding in the late afternoon and evening. If you happen to see an alligator in a nonthreatening situation, give it a wide berth—gators can run faster than you—and by no means feed it. Feeding alligators leads to them becoming habituated to humans and virtually guarantees their presence where you don't want them.

STROLLERS

STROLLERS ARE AVAILABLE for rent at all four theme parks and at Disney Springs (single stroller, $15 per day with no deposit, $13 per day for the entire stay; double stroller, $31 per day with no deposit, $27 per day for the entire stay; stroller rentals at Disney Springs require a $100 credit card deposit; double strollers not available at Disney Springs). Strollers are welcome at Blizzard Beach and Typhoon Lagoon, but no rentals are available. With multiday rentals, you can skip the rental line entirely after your first visit—just head over to the stroller-handout area,

show your receipt, and you'll be wheeling out of there in no time. If you rent a stroller at the Magic Kingdom and you decide to go to Epcot, Disney's Animal Kingdom, or Disney's Hollywood Studios, just turn in your Magic Kingdom stroller and present your receipt at the next park. You will be issued another stroller at no additional charge.

You can rent a stroller in advance; this allows you to bypass the payment line and go straight to the pickup line. Disney resort guests can pay ahead at their resort's gift shop, so hang on to your receipts!

Pick up strollers at the Magic Kingdom entrance, to the left of Epcot's Entrance Plaza and at Epcot's International Gateway, and at **Oscar's Super Service,** located just inside the entrance of Disney's Hollywood Studios. At Disney's Animal Kingdom, they're at **Garden Gate Gifts,** to the right just inside the entrance. Returning one is a breeze—you can ditch it anywhere in the park when you get ready to leave. To see what these strollers look like, Google "rental strollers at Walt Disney World."

Strollers are a must for infants and toddlers, but we have seen many sharp parents rent strollers for somewhat older children—the stroller spares parents from having to carry kids when they sag, and it provides a convenient place to tote water and snacks.

A family from Tulsa, Oklahoma, recommends springing for a double stroller:

> We rent a double for baggage room or in case the older child gets tired of walking.

But a New Lenox, Illinois, family advocates not leaving anyone out:

> If your kids are 8 or under, RENT STROLLERS for all of them! An 8-year-old will fit in a stroller, and you can fit up to four kids in two doubles. My husband suggested getting a stroller for our 6-year-old and the two "babies" (ages 4 and 3). We plowed through crowds, and the kids didn't get nearly as tired since they could be seated whenever they wanted.

We've always advocated using strollers for any child who will fit; however, a McKean, Pennsylvania, reader thinks the situation has gotten out of hand:

> I really think it is time to curtail the use of, or sign for a peace armistice with, the main battle tank of Disney touring—the stroller. Or crowd battering ram, or exit blocker. One bawling 12-year-old in a

double stroller—with gear enough to conquer Everest stuffed into this mini RV, cramming it's way into, around, or over you in Casey's Corner or other such place—is becoming the norm. There are ways to know if your child should not be in a stroller:

(1) If he/she drove the family to the park.

(2) If the first two digits of his/her birth year are 19 rather than 20.

(3) If your child's husband or wife wonders when their turn in the stroller is coming up.

(4) If they're "drinking around the world" with you.

(5) If you're at Disney to celebrate his/her parole, probation, divorce, or promotion at work.

If you go to your hotel for a break and intend to return to the park, leave your rental stroller in stroller parking near the park entrance, marking it with something personal like a bandanna. When you return, your stroller will be waiting.

Rental strollers are too large for all infants and many toddlers. If you plan to rent a stroller for your infant or toddler, bring pillows, cushions, or rolled towels to buttress him in.

Bringing your own stroller is OK. However, only collapsible strollers are allowed on monorails, parking-lot trams, and buses. Your stroller is unlikely to be stolen, but mark it with your name.

Having her own stroller was indispensable to this Mechanicsville, Virginia, mother of two toddlers:

> How I was going to manage to get the kids from the parking lot to the park was a big worry for me before I made the trip. I didn't read anywhere that it was possible to walk to the entrance of the parks instead of taking the tram, so I wasn't sure I could do it.
>
> Since I have two kids ages 1 and 2, it was easier to walk to the entrance of the park from the parking lot with the kids in my own stroller than to take the kids out of the stroller, fold the stroller (while trying to control the two kids and associated gear), load the stroller and the kids onto the tram, etc. No matter where I was parked, I could always just walk to the entrance.

A Secaucus, New Jersey, mom weighed all the considerations in exemplary type-A fashion:

> If your child is under age 2, bring your own stroller. Three reasons to bring your own: First, you have all the way from your car to the Transportation and Ticket Center to the monorail (or ferry) to the stroller rental without a stroller, but with your child, diaper bag, and own self and stuff in tow. Not half as bad as doing it in reverse when leaving, when you're exhausted and have added to your luggage with purchases and the toddler who might have walked in wants to be carried out. Second, the WDW stroller is simply too large for most children under age 2 to be comfortable without significant padding. The seat is so low that the child is forced to keep their legs straight out in front of them. Third, despite being soooo big, there's NO PLACE to store anything.
>
> Now, if your child is past needing a diaper bag, the WDW strollers seem like a pretty good deal. You won't need the storage space,

and they do maneuver very well. They seem especially good for children who no longer need a stroller at home (ages 4–6) but who won't make it walking all day.

If your child is 2 or 3, it's a toss-up. If you're a type-A mom, like me, who carries extra clothes, snacks, toys, enough diapers for three days, along with a pocketbook and extra-jackets-for-everyone-just-in-case, you've probably found a stroller that suits your needs and will be miserable with the WDW kind. If you're a type-B "we can get everything else we need at the park; I'll just throw a diaper in my back pocket" mom, you'll probably be tickled with the WDW strollers.

An Oklahoma mom, however, reports a bad experience with bringing her own stroller:

It's much easier to rent a stroller in the park. The one we brought was nearly impossible to get on the buses and was a hassle at the airport. I remember feeling dread when a bus pulled up—people look at you like you have a cage full of chickens.

PARKING YOUR STROLLER Well-marked stroller parking is available in all the "lands" of every park. If you leave your stroller in front of an attraction instead of a designated parking area, it will be moved.

STROLLER-RENTAL OPTIONS With Disney pricing its own stroller rentals so high, a number of Orlando rental companies have sprung up, able to undercut Disney's prices, provide more comfortable strollers, and deliver them to your hotel. Most of the larger companies offer the same stroller models (the Baby Jogger City Mini Single, for example), so the primary differences between the companies are price and service.

unofficial **TIP**
When you enter a show or board a ride, you must park your stroller, usually in an open area. Bring a cloth or towel to dry it if it rains before you return.

Regarding the latter, Disney currently allows just a handful of stroller companies to drop off and pick up at a Disney hotel without your having to be physically present to meet the delivery person, thus freeing you to run around the parks instead of waiting around at your hotel. The two companies reviewed below are part of the **Disney Featured Stroller Provider** program, a fact that they mention prominently on their websites. Before renting from another company, check to see if they're on the featured list too.

We had mom and TouringPlans.com blogger **Angela Dahlgren** rent strollers from different companies, use them in the parks, then return them. Her evaluations cover the overall experience, from the ease with which the stroller was rented to the delivery of the stroller, its condition upon arrival, usability in the parks, and the return process.

Kingdom Strollers (☎ 407-271-5301; kingdomstrollers.com) topped Angela's list, getting top marks for website ease of use, stroller selection, condition, and overall service. The stroller was also much easier to use than Disney's standard model, had more storage, and had an easier-to-use braking system. A rental of one to three nights costs $40; four to seven nights is $60. That makes the break-even point for choosing Kingdom Strollers over Disney somewhere around five days.

Angela also recommends **Orlando Stroller Rentals**, LLC (☎ 800-281-0884; orlandostrollerrentals.com), which has the same prices, plus an excellent website that allows you to easily compare the features of different strollers.

STROLLER WARS Sometimes strollers disappear while you're enjoying a ride or show. Disney staff will often rearrange strollers parked outside an attraction. This may be done to tidy up or to clear a walkway. Don't assume that your stroller is stolen because it isn't where you left it. It may be neatly arranged a few feet away—or perhaps more than a few feet away, as this Skokie, Illinois, dad reports:

> More than once, our stroller was moved out of visible distance from the original spot. On one occasion, it was moved to a completely different stroller-parking area near another ride, and no sign or cast member was around to advise where. We had to track a cast member down, and she had to call in to find out where it had been moved. Be prepared for this.

Sometimes, however, strollers are taken by mistake or ripped off by people not wanting to spend time replacing one that's missing. Don't be alarmed if yours disappears: You won't have to buy it, and you'll be issued a new one.

*un*official **TIP**
Don't try to lock your stroller to a fence, post, or anything else at WDW. You'll get in big trouble.

While replacing a stroller is no big deal, it's inconvenient. A Minnesota family complained that their stroller was taken six times in one day at Epcot and five times in a day at Disney's Hollywood Studios. Even with free replacements, petty larceny on this scale represents a lot of wasted time. Through our own experiments and readers' suggestions, we've developed a technique for hanging on to a rented stroller: Affix something personal (but expendable) to the handle. Evidently, most strollers are pirated by mistake (they all look alike) or because it's easier to swipe someone else's than to replace one that has disappeared. Because most stroller "theft" results from confusion or laziness, the average pram-pincher will hesitate to haul off a stroller containing another person's property. We tried several items and concluded that a bright, inexpensive scarf or bandanna tied to the handle works well as identification. A sock partially stuffed with rags or paper works even better (the weirder and more personal the object, the greater the deterrent).

A multigenerational family from Utah went a step further and made their stroller difficult to move:

> We decorated our stroller with electrical tape to make it stand out, and my son added a small cowbell to make it clang if moved.

STROLLERS AS LETHAL WEAPONS A middle-aged couple from Brunswick, Maine, lobbies for a temporary stroller ban:

> As an over-45 couple, we couldn't believe the number and sizes of strollers and those ubiquitous scooters. You had to be constantly vigilant or you would have your foot run over or path

*un*official **TIP**
Children under age 14 must be accompanied by someone age 14 or older when entering Disney World's theme parks and water parks.

slowed down. One day a week, in one theme park, there should be a "no wheels" day.

You'd be surprised at how many people are injured by strollers pushed by parents who are driving aggressively or in a hurry. Given the number of strollers, pedestrians, and tight spaces, mishaps are inevitable on both sides. A simple apology and a smile are usually the best remediation.

LOST CHILDREN

ALTHOUGH IT'S AMAZINGLY EASY to lose a child (or two) in the theme parks, it usually isn't a serious problem: Disney employees are schooled in handling the situation. If you lose a child in the Magic Kingdom, report it to a Disney employee, and then check at the Baby Care Center and at City Hall, where lost-children logs are kept. At Epcot, report the loss, then check at the Baby Care Center in the Odyssey Center. At Disney's Hollywood Studios, report the loss at the Guest Services Building, at the entrance end of Hollywood Boulevard. At Disney's Animal Kingdom, go to the Baby Care Center in Discovery Island. Paging isn't used, but in an emergency, an "all-points bulletin" can be issued throughout the park(s) via internal communications. If a Disney employee encounters a lost child, he or she will take the child immediately to the park's Baby Care Center.

Sew a label into each child's shirt that states his or her name, your name, the name of your hotel, and your cell phone number. You can also write the information on a strip of masking tape or attach a MagicBand to the child's clothing (but resist the urge to put it on like a dog collar).

An easier and trendier option is a temporary tattoo with your child's name and your phone number. Unlike labels, ID bracelets, or wristbands, the tattoos cannot fall off or be lost. Temporary tattoos last about two weeks, won't wash or sweat off, and are not irritating to the skin. They can be purchased online from **SafetyTat,** at safetytat.com, or from **Tattoos With A Purpose,** at tattooswithapurpose.com. Special tattoos are available for children with food allergies, hearing impairments, and autism.

unofficial **TIP**
We suggest that kids younger than 8 be color-coded by dressing them in purple T-shirts or equally distinctive clothes.

A Kingston, Washington, reader recommends recording vital info for each child on a plastic key tag or luggage tag and affixing it to the child's shoe. This reader also snaps a photo of the kids each morning to document what they're wearing. A Rockville, Maryland, mom shared a strategy one step short of a cattle brand:

Traveling with a 3-year-old, I was very anxious about losing him, so I wrote my cell phone number on his leg with a permanent marker. I felt much more confident that he'd get back to me quickly if he became lost.

One way to better keep track of your family is to buy each person a "Disney uniform"—in this case, the same brightly and distinctively colored T-shirt. A Yuma, Arizona, family tried this with great success:

We all got the same shirts (bright red) so that we could easily spot each other in case of separation (VERY easy to do). It was a lifesaver when our 18-month-old decided to get out of the stroller and wander off. As I've heard before, Dumbo seems to draw them in, and lo and behold, guess where we found him (still dragging his leash but with a nice cast member following him). No matter what precautions you may try, it seems there are always those opportunities to lose a child, but the recognizable shirts helped tremendously.

HOW KIDS GET LOST

CHILDREN GET SEPARATED FROM THEIR PARENTS every day at Disney theme parks under remarkably similar (and predictable) circumstances:

1. PREOCCUPIED SOLO PARENT The party's only adult is preoccupied with something like buying refreshments, reading a map, or using the restroom. Junior is there one second, gone the next.

2. THE HIDDEN EXIT Sometimes parents wait on the sidelines while two or more children experience a ride together. Parents expect the kids to exit in one place and the youngsters pop out elsewhere. Exits from some attractions are distant from entrances. Know exactly where your children will emerge before you allow them to ride by themselves.

3. AFTER THE SHOW At the end of many shows and rides, a Disney staffer announces, "Check for personal belongings and take small children by the hand." When dozens, if not hundreds, of people leave an attraction simultaneously, it's easy for parents to lose their children unless they have direct contact.

4. POTTY PROBLEMS Mom tells 6-year-old Tommy, "I'll be sitting on this bench when you come out of the restroom." Three possibilities: One, Tommy exits through a different door and becomes disoriented (Mom may not know there's another door). Two, Mom decides she also will use the restroom, and Tommy emerges to find her gone. Three, Mom pokes around in a shop while keeping an eye on the bench but misses Tommy when he comes out.

If you can't find a companion- or family-accessible restroom, make sure there's only one exit. The restroom on a passageway between Frontierland and Adventureland in the Magic Kingdom is the all-time worst for disorienting visitors. Children and adults alike have walked in from the Adventureland side and walked out on the Frontierland side (and vice versa). Adults realize quickly that something is wrong. Children, however, sometimes fail to recognize the problem.

Designate a distinctive meeting spot and give clear instructions: "I'll meet you by this flagpole. If you get out first, stay right here." Have your child repeat the directions back to you. When children are too young to leave alone, sometimes you have to think outside the box, as our Rockville, Maryland, mom did:

It was very scary for me at times, being alone with children who had just turned 1 and 2. I was at Epcot inside one of the buildings and I had to leave my kids with a WDW employee outside of the restroom because the stroller just wouldn't fit inside with me. Thinking about the incident now makes me laugh. The good news is that I found that most WDW bathrooms can accommodate a front-and-back double stroller inside the handicapped stall with you.

5. PARADES There are many parades and shows at which the audience stands. Children tend to jockey for a better view. By moving a little this way and that, the child quickly puts distance between you and him before either of you notices.

6. MASS MOVEMENTS Be on guard when huge crowds disperse after fireworks or a parade, or at park closing. With 20,000–40,000 people at once in an area, it's very easy to get separated from a child or others in your party. Use extra caution after the evening parade and fireworks in the Magic Kingdom, *Fantasmic!* at Disney's Hollywood Studios, *Rivers of Light* at Animal Kingdom, and *IllumiNations* at Epcot. Plan where to meet in the event you get separated.

7. CHARACTER GREETINGS When the Disney characters appear, children can slip out of sight. (See "Then Some Confusion Happened," page 445.)

8. GETTING LOST AT DISNEY'S ANIMAL KINGDOM It's especially easy to lose a child in Animal Kingdom, particularly at the Oasis entryway, on the Maharajah Jungle Trek, and on the Gorilla Falls Exploration Trail. Mom and Dad will stop to observe an animal. Junior stays close for a minute or so and then, losing patience, wanders to the exhibit's other side or to a different exhibit.

Especially in the multipath Oasis, locating a lost child can be maddening, as a Safety Harbor, Florida, mother describes:

> *Manny wandered off in the paths that lead to the jungle village while we were looking at a bird. It reminded me of losing somebody in the supermarket, when you run back and forth looking down each aisle but can't find the person you're looking for because they're running around too. I was nutso before we even got to the first ride.*

DISNEY, KIDS, *and* SCARY STUFF

DISNEY RIDES AND SHOWS are adventures, and they focus on themes of all adventures: good and evil, death, beauty and ugliness, fellowship and enmity. As you sample the attractions at Walt Disney World, you'll transcend the spinning and bouncing of midway rides to thought-provoking and emotionally powerful entertainment. All of the endings are happy ones, but the adventures' impact, given Disney's gift for special effects, often intimidates and occasionally frightens young children.

*un*official **TIP**
Monsters and special effects at Disney's Hollywood Studios are more real and sinister than those in the other parks.

There are attractions with menacing witches, burning towns, skeletons, and ghouls popping out of their graves, all done with humor, provided you're old enough to understand the joke.

If your child has difficulty coping with the ghouls of The Haunted Mansion, then think twice about exposing him at the Studios to battle scenes in Star Tours or machine-gun battles and the creature from *Alien* in The Great Movie Ride.

You can reliably predict that Walt Disney World will, at one time or another, send a young child into system overload. Be sensitive, alert, and prepared for almost anything, even behavior that is out of character for your child. Most children take Disney's macabre trappings in stride, and others are easily comforted by an arm around the shoulder or a squeeze of the hand. Parents who know that their children tend to become upset should take it slow and easy, sampling benign adventures like the Jungle Cruise, gauging reactions, and discussing with the children how they felt about what they saw.

Sometimes young children will rise above their anxiety to try to please their parents or siblings. This doesn't necessarily indicate a mastery of fear, much less enjoyment. If children leave a ride in apparently good shape, ask if they would like to go on it again (not necessarily now, but sometime). The response usually will indicate how much they actually enjoyed the experience.

Evaluating a child's capacity to handle the visual and tactile effects of Disney World requires patience, understanding, and experimentation. Each of us has our own demons. If a child balks at or is frightened by a ride, respond constructively. Let your children know that lots of people, adults and children, are scared by what they see and feel. Help them understand that it's OK if they get frightened and that their fear doesn't lessen your love or respect. Take pains not to compound the discomfort by making a child feel inadequate; try not to undermine self-esteem, impugn courage, or ridicule. Most of all, don't induce guilt by suggesting the child's trepidation might be ruining the family's fun. It's also sometimes necessary to restrain older siblings' taunting.

A reader from New York City expresses strong feelings about pressuring children:

> As a psychologist who works with children, I felt ethically torn watching parents force their children to go on rides they didn't want to ride. The Disney staff were more than willing to organize a parental swap to save these children from such abuse!

A visit to Disney World is more than an outing or an adventure for a young child. It's a testing experience, a sort of controlled rite of passage. If you help your little one work through the challenges, the time can be immeasurably rewarding and a bonding experience for you both.

THE FRIGHT FACTOR

WHILE EACH YOUNGSTER IS DIFFERENT, following are seven attraction elements that alone or combined could push a child's buttons and indicate that a certain attraction isn't age appropriate for that child:

1. THE NAME Young children will naturally be apprehensive about something called, say, The Haunted Mansion or Tower of Terror.

2. VISUAL IMPACT FROM OUTSIDE Splash Mountain, the Tower of Terror, and Big Thunder Mountain Railroad look scary enough to give

Continued on page 435

SMALL-CHILD FRIGHT-POTENTIAL CHART

This is a quick reference to identify attractions to be wary of, and why. The chart represents a generalization, and all kids are different. It relates specifically to kids ages 3–7. On average, younger children are more likely to be frightened than older ones.

The Magic Kingdom

SORCERERS OF THE MAGIC KINGDOM Loud but not frightening.

MAIN STREET, U.S.A.

MAIN STREET VEHICLES Not frightening in any respect.

WALT DISNEY WORLD RAILROAD Not frightening in any respect.

ADVENTURELAND

JUNGLE CRUISE Moderately intense, some macabre sights. A good test attraction.

PIRATES OF THE CARIBBEAN Slightly intimidating queuing area; intense boat ride with gruesome (though humorously presented) sights and a short, unexpected slide down a flume.

THE MAGIC CARPETS OF ALADDIN Much like Dumbo. A favorite ride of young children.

SWISS FAMILY TREEHOUSE Kids who are afraid of heights may want to skip it.

WALT DISNEY'S ENCHANTED TIKI ROOM A thunderstorm, loud volume level, and simulated explosions frighten some preschoolers.

FRONTIERLAND

BIG THUNDER MOUNTAIN RAILROAD Visually intimidating from outside, with moderately intense visual effects. The roller coaster is wild enough to frighten many adults, particularly seniors. Switching-off option provided (see page 439).

COUNTRY BEAR JAMBOREE Not frightening in any respect.

FRONTIERLAND SHOOTIN' ARCADE Frightening to kids who are scared of guns.

SPLASH MOUNTAIN Visually intimidating from the outside, with moderately intense visual effects. The ride culminates in a 52-foot plunge down a steep chute. Switching-off option provided (see page 439).

TOM SAWYER ISLAND AND FORT LANGHORN Some very young children are intimidated by dark walk-through tunnels that can be easily avoided.

LIBERTY SQUARE

THE HALL OF PRESIDENTS Not frightening, but boring for young ones.

THE HAUNTED MANSION Name raises anxiety, as do sounds and sights of waiting area. Intense attraction with humorously presented macabre sights. The ride itself is gentle.

LIBERTY BELLE RIVERBOAT Not frightening in any respect.

THE MUPPETS PRESENT . . . GREAT MOMENTS IN AMERICAN HISTORY
Not frightening in any respect. Your kids should love it.

FANTASYLAND

ARIEL'S GROTTO Not frightening in any respect.

DUMBO THE FLYING ELEPHANT A tame midway ride that's a great favorite of most young children.

THE BARNSTORMER May frighten some preschoolers.

ENCHANTED TALES WITH BELLE Not frightening in any respect.

IT'S A SMALL WORLD Not frightening in any respect.

MAD TEA PARTY Midway-type ride can induce motion sickness in all ages.

THE MANY ADVENTURES OF WINNIE THE POOH Frightens a few preschoolers.

PETER PAN'S FLIGHT Not frightening in any respect.

PETE'S SILLY SIDESHOW Not frightening in any respect.

PRINCE CHARMING REGAL CARROUSEL Not frightening in any respect.

PRINCESS FAIRYTALE HALL Long lines may have parents running for the hills.

FANTASYLAND *(continued)*
SEVEN DWARFS MINE TRAIN May frighten some preschoolers.
UNDER THE SEA: JOURNEY OF THE LITTLE MERMAID Animatronic octopus character frightens some preschoolers.

TOMORROWLAND
ASTRO ORBITER Visually intimidating from the waiting area, but the ride is actually relatively tame.
BUZZ LIGHTYEAR'S SPACE RANGER SPIN May frighten some preschoolers.
MONSTERS, INC. LAUGH FLOOR May frighten some preschoolers.
SPACE MOUNTAIN Very intense roller coaster in the dark; the Magic Kingdom's wildest ride and a scary roller coaster by any standard. Switching-off option provided (see page 439).
STITCH'S GREAT ESCAPE! Very intense (and smelly). May frighten children age 9 and younger. Switching-off option provided (see page 439).
TOMORROWLAND SPEEDWAY The noise of the waiting area slightly intimidates preschoolers; otherwise, not frightening.
TOMORROWLAND TRANSIT AUTHORITY PEOPLEMOVER Not frightening in any respect.
WALT DISNEY'S CAROUSEL OF PROGRESS Not frightening in any respect.

Epcot

FUTURE WORLD
JOURNEY INTO IMAGINATION WITH FIGMENT Loud noises and unexpected flashing lights startle younger children.
THE LAND: *THE CIRCLE OF LIFE* Not frightening in any respect.
THE LAND: LIVING WITH THE LAND Not frightening in any respect.
THE LAND: SOARIN' May frighten kids age 7 and younger, or anyone with a fear of heights. Otherwise a very mellow ride.
MISSION: SPACE Extremely intense space-simulation ride that has been known to frighten guests of all ages. Switching-off option provided (see page 439).
THE SEAS: SEABASE Not frightening in any respect.
THE SEAS: THE SEAS WITH NEMO & FRIENDS Very sweet but may frighten some toddlers.
THE SEAS: *TURTLE TALK WITH CRUSH* Not frightening in any respect.
SPACESHIP EARTH Dark, imposing presentation intimidates a few preschoolers.
TEST TRACK Intense thrill ride may frighten guests of any age. Switching-off option provided (see page 439).
UNIVERSE OF ENERGY: *ELLEN'S ENERGY ADVENTURE* Dinosaur segment frightens some preschoolers; visually intense, with some intimidating effects.

WORLD SHOWCASE
CANADA: *O CANADA!* Not frightening, but audience must stand.
CHINA: *REFLECTIONS OF CHINA* Not frightening in any respect.
FRANCE: *IMPRESSIONS DE FRANCE* Not frightening in any respect.
GERMANY: Not frightening in any respect.
ITALY: Not frightening in any respect.
JAPAN: Not frightening in any respect.
MEXICO: GRAN FIESTA TOUR Not frightening in any respect.
MOROCCO: Not frightening in any respect.
NORWAY: FROZEN EVER AFTER Tame, but a small drop at the end of the ride frightens some preschoolers.

Continued on next page

SMALL-CHILD FRIGHT-POTENTIAL CHART
(continued)

Epcot (continued)

WORLD SHOWCASE (continued)

NORWAY: ROYAL SOMMERHUS MEET AND GREET Not frightening in any respect.

UNITED KINGDOM Not frightening in any respect.

UNITED STATES: *THE AMERICAN ADVENTURE* Not frightening in any respect.

Disney's Animal Kingdom

THE OASIS Not frightening in any respect.

RAFIKI'S PLANET WATCH Not frightening in any respect.

DISCOVERY ISLAND

THE TREE OF LIFE/*IT'S TOUGH TO BE A BUG!* Very intense and loud, with special effects that startle viewers of all ages and potentially terrify little kids.

WILDERNESS EXPLORERS Not frightening in any respect.

AFRICA

FESTIVAL OF THE LION KING A bit loud, but otherwise not frightening.

GORILLA FALLS EXPLORATION TRAIL Not frightening in any respect.

KILIMANJARO SAFARIS A "collapsing" bridge and the proximity of real animals make a few young children anxious.

WILDLIFE EXPRESS TRAIN Not frightening in any respect.

ASIA

EXPEDITION EVEREST Can frighten guests of all ages. Switching-off option provided (see page 439).

FLIGHTS OF WONDER Swooping birds alarm a few small children.

KALI RIVER RAPIDS Potentially frightening and certainly wet for guests of all ages. Switching-off option provided (see page 439).

MAHARAJAH JUNGLE TREK Some children may balk at the bat exhibit.

RIVERS OF LIGHT Loud with special effects but generally not frightening.

DINOLAND U.S.A.

THE BONEYARD Not frightening in any respect.

DINOSAUR High-tech thrill ride rattles riders of all ages. Switching-off option provided (see page 439).

PRIMEVAL WHIRL A beginner roller coaster. Most children age 7 and older will take it in stride. Switching-off option provided (see page 439).

THEATER IN THE WILD/*FINDING NEMO—THE MUSICAL* Not frightening in any respect, but loud.

TRICERATOP SPIN A midway-type ride that will frighten only a small percentage of younger children.

PANDORA: THE WORLD OF AVATAR

AVATAR FLIGHT OF PASSAGE May frighten kids age 7 and younger or anyone with claustrophobia or a fear of heights.

NA'VI RIVER JOURNEY More focused on sights and sounds than excitement or speed. Not frightening in any respect.

Disney's Hollywood Studios

HOLLYWOOD BOULEVARD

THE GREAT MOVIE RIDE Intense in parts, with very realistic special effects and some visually intimidating sights. Frightens many preschoolers.

SUNSET BOULEVARD
FANTASMIC! Terrifies some preschoolers.
ROCK 'N' ROLLER COASTER The wildest coaster at Walt Disney World. May frighten guests of any age. Switching-off option provided (see page 439).
THEATER OF THE STARS/*BEAUTY AND THE BEAST—LIVE ON STAGE* Not frightening in any respect.
THE TWILIGHT ZONE TOWER OF TERROR Visually intimidating to young children; contains intense and realistic special effects. The plummeting elevator at the ride's end frightens many adults as well as kids. Switching-off option provided (see page 439).
ECHO LAKE
INDIANA JONES EPIC STUNT SPECTACULAR! An intense show with powerful special effects, including explosions, but young kids generally handle it well.
JEDI TRAINING: TRIALS OF THE TEMPLE Not frightening in any respect.
STAR TOURS—THE ADVENTURES CONTINUE Extremely intense visually for all ages; too intense for kids under age 8. Switching-off option provided (see page 439).
MUPPET COURTYARD
JIM HENSON'S MUPPET-VISION 3-D Intense and loud, but not frightening.
TOY STORY LAND
ALIEN SWIRLING SAUCERS *(OPENS 2018)* Like Mater's Junkyard Jamboree at Disney's California Adventure, which can induce motion sickness in riders of all ages.
SLINKY DOG DASH *(OPENS 2018)* Looks to be between The Barnstormer and Seven Dwarfs Mine Train in intensity; may frighten some preschoolers.
TOY STORY MANIA! Dark ride may frighten some preschoolers.
ANIMATION COURTYARD
DISNEY JUNIOR—LIVE ON STAGE! Not frightening in any respect.
STAR WARS LAUNCH BAY Not frightening in any respect.
VOYAGE OF THE LITTLE MERMAID Some children are creeped out by Ursula.
WALT DISNEY: ONE MAN'S DREAM Not frightening in any respect.

Continued from page 431

adults second thoughts, and they terrify many little kids. A Utah family of six reports the following:

> At 5 years old, my granddaughter was big enough and willing to go on almost everything. The problem was with the preliminary introductions to Haunted Mansion and Tower of Terror. Walking through and learning the stories before the actual rides were what frightened her and made her opt out without going in. The rides themselves would not have been bad; she loved Splash Mountain and Big Thunder Mountain, but she could SEE those rides before entering.

3. VISUAL IMPACT OF THE INDOOR-QUEUING AREA The caves at Pirates of the Caribbean and the dungeons and "stretch rooms" of The Haunted Mansion can frighten children.

4. THE INTENSITY Some attractions inundate the senses with sights, sounds, movement, and even smell. Animal Kingdom's *It's Tough to be a Bug!*, for example, combines loud sounds, lights, smoke, and animatronic insects with 3-D cinematography to create a total sensory experience.

A Johnston, Iowa, mom describes the situation well:

The 3-D and 4-D experiences are way too scary for even a very brave 5-year-old girl. The shows that blew things on her, shot smells in the air, had bugs flying, etc. scared the bejesus out of her. We escorted her crying from It's Tough to Be a Bug!, Mickey's PhilharMagic, *and* Stitch's Great Escape!

5. VISUAL IMPACT OF THE ATTRACTION Sights in various attractions range from falling boulders to lurking buzzards, from grazing dinosaurs to waltzing ghosts. What one child calmly absorbs may scare the pants off of another the same age.

6. DARK Many Disney World attractions operate indoors in the dark. For some children, this triggers fear. A child who gets frightened on one dark ride (The Haunted Mansion, for example) may be unwilling to try other indoor rides.

7. THE TACTILE EXPERIENCE Some rides are wild enough to cause motion sickness, wrench backs, and discombobulate guests of any age.

A BIT OF PREPARATION

WE RECEIVE MANY TIPS FROM PARENTS telling how they prepared their young children for the Disney experience. Common strategies are to acquaint children with the characters and stories behind the attractions by reading Disney books, watching Disney videos at home, and watching videos online that show the attractions. Of the latter, a Lexington, Kentucky, mom reports:

My timid 7-year-old daughter and I watched ride and show videos on YouTube, and we cut out all the ones that looked too scary.

A Gloucester, Massachusetts, mom solved the problem on the spot:

My 3½-year-old was afraid of The Haunted Mansion. We just pulled his hat over his face and quietly talked to him while we rode.

You can also watch one of Disney's free **vacation-planning videos** at tinyurl.com/disneyplanningvideos. As a YouTube supplement, these videos give your kids an adequate sense of what they'll see; note that you'll need to fill out a short survey to watch the videos. For more-immediate gratification, you can also watch the **Travel Channel**'s Walt Disney World specials on Hulu or Netflix streaming.

ATTRACTIONS THAT EAT ADULTS

YOU MAY SPEND SO MUCH ENERGY worrying about Junior that you forget to take care of yourself. The attractions listed below can cause motion sickness or other problems for older kids and adults:

POTENTIALLY PROBLEMATIC ATTRACTIONS FOR GROWN-UPS
THE MAGIC KINGDOM
• **FANTASYLAND** Mad Tea Party • **FRONTIERLAND** Big Thunder Mountain Railroad, Splash Mountain • **TOMORROWLAND** Space Mountain
EPCOT • **FUTURE WORLD** Mission: Space, Test Track
DISNEY'S ANIMAL KINGDOM
• **ASIA** Expedition Everest, Kali River Rapids • **DINOLAND U.S.A.** Dinosaur • **PANDORA** Avatar Flight of Passage

POTENTIALLY PROBLEMATIC ATTRACTIONS FOR GROWN-UPS	
DISNEY'S HOLLYWOOD STUDIOS	
• **ECHO LAKE** Star Tours—The Adventures Continue	
• **SUNSET BOULEVARD** Rock 'n' Roller Coaster, The Twilight Zone Tower of Terror	

A WORD ABOUT HEIGHT REQUIREMENTS

A NUMBER OF ATTRACTIONS REQUIRE children to meet minimum height and age requirements. (All Appeal by Age attraction ratings for preschoolers in the theme park chapters assume that the kids surveyed were tall enough to ride.) If you have children who don't meet the posted requirements, you have several options, including switching off (see page 439). If those kids are resentful of their taller (or older) siblings who do qualify to ride, a mom from Virginia has some advice:

> Height requirements can generate intense sibling jealousy. Frontierland was a real problem for us in that respect. Our petite 5-year-old, to her outrage, was left out while our 8-year-old went on Splash Mountain and Big Thunder Mountain with Grandma and Granddad, and the nearby alternatives weren't helpful (too long a line for rafts to Tom Sawyer Island, etc.). The best areas had a playground or other quick attractions for short people near the rides with height requirements, like The Boneyard near the Dinosaur ride at Animal Kingdom.

ATTRACTION AND RIDE RESTRICTIONS

THE MAGIC KINGDOM	
The Barnstormer	35" minimum height
Big Thunder Mountain Railroad	40" minimum height
Seven Dwarfs Mine Train	38" minimum height
Space Mountain	44" minimum height
Splash Mountain	40" minimum height
Stitch's Great Escape!	40" minimum height
Tomorrowland Speedway	32" to ride, 54" to drive unassisted
EPCOT	
Mission: Space	44" minimum height
Soarin'	40" minimum height
Test Track	40" minimum height
DISNEY'S ANIMAL KINGDOM	
Dinosaur	40" minimum height
Expedition Everest	44" minimum height
Kali River Rapids	38" minimum height
Avatar Flight of Passage	44" minimum height
Primeval Whirl	48" minimum height
DISNEY'S HOLLYWOOD STUDIOS	
Rock 'n' Roller Coaster	48" minimum height
Star Tours—The Adventures Continue	40" minimum height
The Twilight Zone Tower of Terror	40" minimum height

Continued on next page

ATTRACTION AND RIDE RESTRICTIONS (continued)

Alien Swirling Saucers (opens 2018)	Similar rides have a 32" height requirement.
Slinky Dog Dash (opens 2018)	Similar rides have a 35"–38" height requirement.
DISNEY SPRINGS	
Marketplace Carousel	42" minimum height
BLIZZARD BEACH WATER PARK	
Chair Lift	32" minimum height
Downhill Double Dipper slide	48" minimum height
Slush Gusher slide	48" minimum height
Summit Plummet slide	48" minimum height
T-Bar (in Ski Patrol Training Camp)	60" maximum height
Tike's Peak children's area	48" maximum height
TYPHOON LAGOON WATER PARK	
Bay Slides	60" minimum height
Crush 'n' Gusher	48" minimum height
Humunga Kowabunga slide	48" minimum height
Ketchakiddee Creek children's area	48" maximum height
Wave Pool	*Adult supervision required*

The reader makes a good point, although splitting up the group and then meeting later could prove more complicated than she imagines. If you split up, ask the Disney cast member (called a greeter) stationed at the entrance to the attraction(s) with a height requirement how long the wait will be. If you tack on 5 minutes for riding to the anticipated wait and then add 5 or so minutes to exit and reach the meeting point, you'll have a better sense of how long the younger kids (and their supervising adult) will have to do other stuff while the other members of your party ride.

Our guess is that even with a long line for the rafts, the reader would've had sufficient time to take her daughter to Tom Sawyer Island while the sibs rode Splash Mountain and Big Thunder Mountain with the grandparents. For sure, she had time to tour the Swiss Family Tree-house in adjacent Adventureland.

For more information, see the chart above and on the previous page.

WAITING-LINE STRATEGIES
for ADULTS *with*
YOUNG CHILDREN

CHILDREN HOLD UP BETTER THROUGH THE DAY if you limit the time they spend in lines. Arriving early and using our touring plans are two ways to greatly reduce waiting. Here are other ways to reduce stress for children:

1. LINE GAMES Anticipate that children will get restless in line, and plan activities to reduce the stress and boredom. In the morning, have waiting children discuss what they want to see and do during the day. Later, watch for and count Disney characters or play simple games such as 20 Questions. Lines move continuously; games requiring pen and paper are impractical. Waiting in the holding area of a theater attraction is a different story. Here, tic-tac-toe, hangman, drawing, and coloring make the time fly.

A Springfield, Ohio, mom reports on an unexpected but welcome assist from her brother:

> *I have a bachelor brother who joined my 5-, 7-, and 9-year-olds and me for vacation. Pat surprised all of us with a bunch of plastic animal noses he had in his hip pack. When the kids got restless or cranky in line, he'd turn away and pull out a pig nose or a parrot nose or something. When he turned back around with the nose on, the kids would majorly crack up.*

A Waco, Texas, dad broke out the bubbly:

> *I took bubbles along with us. My boys loved them and so did the other children waiting in line. (I bought wedding-size bottles that would fit into everyone's fanny pack.)*

2. SWITCHING OFF Several attractions have minimum height and/or age requirements. Some couples with children too small or too young forgo these attractions, while others take turns riding. Missing some of Disney's best rides is an unnecessary sacrifice, and waiting in line twice for the same ride is a tremendous waste of time.

ATTRACTIONS WHERE SWITCHING OFF IS COMMON	
THE MAGIC KINGDOM	**DISNEY'S ANIMAL KINGDOM**
• The Barnstormer • Big Thunder Mountain Railroad • Space Mountain • Splash Mountain • *Stitch's Great Escape!* • Tomorrowland Speedway	• Avatar Flight of Passage • Dinosaur • Expedition Everest • Kali River Rapids • Primeval Whirl
EPCOT	**DISNEY'S HOLLYWOOD STUDIOS**
• Mission: Space • Soarin' • Test Track	• Rock 'n' Roller Coaster • Star Tours— The Adventures Continue • The Twilight Zone Tower of Terror

Instead, take advantage of "switching off," also known variously as "The Baby Swap," "The Rider Swap," or "The Baby/Rider Switch." For switching off to work, there must be at least two adults. Adults and kids wait in line together. When you reach a cast member, say you want to switch off. The cast member will allow everyone, including young children, to enter the attraction. When you reach the loading area, one adult rides while the other exits with the kids. Then the riding adult disembarks and takes charge of the children while the other adult rides. (The nonriding adult also may be given a Rider Switch

Pass or lanyard.) A third member of the party, either an adult or an older child, can ride twice, once with each switching-off adult, so the grown-ups don't have to ride alone.

3. COMBINING THE FASTPASS+ SYSTEM WITH SWITCHING OFF On most FastPass+ attractions, Disney handles switching off somewhat differently. When you tell the cast member that you want to switch off, you'll get a special "rider exchange" FastPass good for three people. One parent and the nonriding child (or children) will at that point be asked to leave the line. When those riding reunite with those waiting, the waiting adult and two others from the party can ride using the special FastPass.

This eliminates confusion at the boarding area while sparing the nonriding adult and child the tedium of waiting in line.

4. LAST-MINUTE COLD FEET If your young child gets cold feet just before boarding a ride where there's no age or height requirement, you usually can arrange a switch-off with the loading attendant. (This happens frequently in Pirates of the Caribbean's dungeon waiting area.)

No law says you have to ride. If you reach the boarding area and someone is unhappy, tell an attendant you've changed your mind and you'll be shown the way out.

5. THROW YOURSELF ON THE GRENADE, MILDRED! For long-suffering parents who are determined to sacrifice themselves on behalf of their children, we provide a Magic Kingdom One-Day Touring Plan called the Dumbo-or-Die-in-a-Day Touring Plan for Parents with Small Children. This plan (see page 824) will ensure that you run yourself ragged. Designed to help you forfeit everything of personal interest for your children's pleasure, the plan guarantees you'll go home battered and exhausted, with extraordinary stories of devotion and perseverance. By the way, it really works. Anyone under age 8 will love it.

The DISNEY CHARACTERS

THE LARGE, FRIENDLY costumed versions of Mickey, Minnie, Donald, Goofy, and others—known as the Disney characters—provide a link between Disney animated films and the theme parks. To those emotionally invested, the characters in Disney films are as real as next-door neighbors, never mind that they're drawings on plastic. In recent years, theme park personifications of the characters also have become real to us. It's not a person in a mouse costume; it's Mickey himself. Similarly, meeting Belle or Elsa isn't an encounter with a pretty cast member but a real celebrity—a memory to be treasured.

unofficial **TIP**
Don't underestimate your child's excitement at meeting the Disney characters—but also be aware that very small children may find the large costumed characters a little frightening.

While Disney animated-film characters number in the hundreds, only about 250 have been brought to life in costume. Of these, fewer than a fifth mix with guests; the others perform in shows or parades. Originally confined to the Magic Kingdom, the Disney characters are now found in all major theme parks and at Disney Deluxe resorts that host character meals. Characters also often visit the Disney water parks and occasionally appear at Disney Springs.

We receive hundreds of reader comments telling us how much the Disney characters enhanced their theme park experience. This e-mail from a Wisconsin mom is representative:

unofficial **TIP**
Many kids take special delight in meeting the "face characters," such as Anna, Elsa, Tiana, and Cinderella, who can speak to them and engage them in a way that the mute animal characters can't.

> *I can't say enough about the characters and how they react to the children and just people in general. They are obviously highly trained in people skills and just add an extra dimension to the park.*

WDW CHARACTER-GREETING VENUES

THE MAGIC KINGDOM

MICKEY AND HIS POSSE

Chip 'n' Dale Frontierland

Daisy, Donald, Goofy, Minnie Pete's Silly Sideshow (FastPass+)

Mickey Town Square Theater (FastPass+)

Pluto Town Square

DISNEY ROYALTY (*Princesses, Princes, Suitors, and Such*)

Aladdin, Jasmine Adventureland

Anna and Elsa On float during the Festival of Fantasy Parade and *Mickey's Royal Friendship Faire* stage show

Ariel Ariel's Grotto (FastPass+)

Belle *Enchanted Tales with Belle* (FastPass+)

Cinderella, Aurora, Elena of Avalor, Rapunzel, Tiana Princess Fairytale Hall (FastPass+)

Gaston Fountain outside Gaston's Tavern

Merida Fairytale Garden

Snow White Outside the Town Square Theater exit

The Tremaines and the Fairy Godmother In Fantasyland near Cinderella Castle

FAIRIES

Tinker Bell Town Square Theater (FastPass+)

MISCELLANEOUS

ALICE IN WONDERLAND
Alice, the Mad Hatter Mad Tea Party

THE ARISTOCATS **Marie** Town Square

MARY POPPINS **Mary Poppins** Main Street, U.S.A., next to the Chappeau store

PETER PAN **Peter, Wendy** Fantasyland next to Peter Pan's Flight

TOY STORY **Buzz Lightyear** Tomorrowland

WINNIE THE POOH **Pooh, Tigger** Fantasyland near The Many Adventures of Winnie the Pooh

EPCOT

MICKEY AND HIS POSSE

Donald Mexico, at the Mexico Promenade

Minnie, Mickey Epcot Character Spot (FastPass+)

Pluto World Showcase Plaza

DISNEY ROYALTY

Aladdin, Jasmine Morocco   **Anna, Elsa, other Frozen characters** Norway   **Belle** France
Mulan China   **Snow White** Germany

MISCELLANEOUS

Alice, Mary Poppins and (occasionally) Bert United Kingdom

Joy and Sadness (*Inside Out*), Baymax (*Big Hero 6*) Innoventions West

WDW CHARACTER-GREETING VENUES

DISNEY'S ANIMAL KINGDOM

MICKEY AND HIS POSSE

Donald DinoLand U.S.A. to the left of the Dinosaur exit on Cretaceous Trail
Goofy, Pluto DinoLand U.S.A. near Primeval Whirl
Mickey, Minnie Adventurers Outpost, Discovery Island (FastPass+)

DISNEY ROYALTY

Pocahontas Discovery Island at Character Landing

MISCELLANEOUS

A BUG'S LIFE **Flik** Discovery Island

DISNEY JUNIOR **Doc McStuffins** Rafiki's Planet Watch at Conservation Station

THE JUNGLE BOOK **King Louie and Baloo** At Upcountry Landing across from
  Flights of Wonder   **Tarzan** Discovery Island behind the Tree of Life

THE LION KING **Rafiki** Rafiki's Planet Watch at Conservation Station

UP **Russell** By *It's Tough to Be a Bug!* (**Dug** may appear occasionally.)

DISNEY'S HOLLYWOOD STUDIOS

MICKEY AND HIS POSSE

Daisy, Donald At park entrance

Minnie, Sorcerer Mickey Commissary Lane between ABC Commissary and Sci-Fi Dine-In

Goofy Commissary Lane across from ABC Commissary

Pluto Animation Courtyard

DISNEY CHANNEL STARS

Doc McStuffins, Jake (*Jake and the Never Land Pirates*), Sofia the First
  Animation Courtyard near *Disney Junior—Live on Stage*!

MISCELLANEOUS

FROZEN **Chewbacca** Celebrity Spotlight in Echo Lake

STAR WARS **Chewbacca, Kylo Ren BB-8 (separate queue)** Star Wars Launch Bay
  Stormtroopers Animation Courtyard

TOY STORY **Buzz, Woody, Green Army Men** Pixar Place

BLIZZARD BEACH

FROZEN **Olaf, Kristoff** These two Frozen characters rotate in a regular meet and greet
  during the Frozen Games from the end of May to mid-August.

TYPHOON LAGOON

LILO & STITCH **Lilo, Stitch** Singapore Sal's, near the park entrance (spring and summer on
  a rotating basis)

CHARACTER WATCHING Watching characters is a pastime. Where families once were content to meet characters occasionally, they now pursue them relentlessly, armed with autograph books and selfie sticks. Mickey, Minnie, and Goofy are a snap to bag; other characters seldom come out, quite a few appear only in parades or stage shows, and still others appear only in a location consistent with their starring role. The Fairy

unofficial **TIP**
If you're using our Lines app in the parks, don't worry about losing time for meet and greets. Just tap "Optimize" after getting your autograph, and we'll tell you where to go next.

Godmother is often near Cinderella Castle in Fantasyland, while Buzz Lightyear appears close to his eponymous attraction in Tomorrowland.

A Brooklyn dad complains that character collecting has gotten out of hand:

> *This year, when we took our youngest child (who is now 8 years old), he had already seen his siblings' collection and was determined to outdo them. However, rather than random meetings, the characters are now available practically all day long at different locations, according to a printed schedule, which our son was old enough to read. We spent more time standing in line for autographs than we did for the most popular rides!*

A family from Birmingham, Alabama, found some benefit in their children's pursuit of characters:

> *We had no idea we'd be caught up in this madness, but after my daughters grabbed your guidebook to get Pocahontas to sign it (we had no blank paper), we quickly bought a Disney autograph book and gave in. It was actually the highlight of their trip, and my son even got into the act by helping get places in line for his sisters. It was an amazing, totally unexpected part of our visit.*

PREPARING YOUR CHILDREN TO MEET THE DISNEY CHARACTERS Almost all of the characters are quite large; several, like Buzz Lightyear, are huge. Small children don't expect this, and preschoolers especially can be intimidated.

Discuss the characters with your children before you go. On first encounter, don't thrust your child at the character. Allow the little one to deal with this big thing from whatever distance feels safe. If two

adults are present, one should stay near the youngster while the other approaches the character and demonstrates that it's safe and friendly. Some kids warm to the characters immediately; some never do. Most take a little time and several encounters.

There are two kinds of characters: "furs," or those whose costumes include face-covering headpieces (including animal characters and such humanlike characters as Captain Hook), and "face characters," those for whom no mask or headpiece is necessary. These include Anna and Elsa, Aladdin and Jasmine, Ariel, Belle, Cinderella, Mary Poppins, Merida, Prince Charming, Snow White, and Tiana, among others.

Only face characters speak. Because cast members couldn't possibly imitate the furs' distinctive cinema voices, Disney has determined that it's more effective to keep such characters silent. Lack of speech notwithstanding, headpiece characters are warm and responsive, and they communicate effectively with gestures. Tell children in advance that these characters don't talk. As an aside, Disney has been implementing technology for making some of the furs talk, most notably Mickey and Minnie.

Some character costumes are quite cumbersome and make it hard for the cast members inside to see well. (Eyeholes frequently are placed in the mouth of the costume or even on the neck or chest.) Children who approach the character from the back or side may not be noticed, even if the child touches the character. It's possible in this situation for the character to accidentally step on the child or knock him down. A child should approach a character from the front, but occasionally not even this works—Donald and Daisy, for example, have to peer around their bills. If a character appears to be ignoring your child, the character's handler will get its attention. Finally, some characters, such as Buzz Lightyear, can't sign autographs because of their costumes, but he sometimes uses a stamp; in any case, he will always gladly pose for photos.

It's OK for your child to touch, pat, or hug the character. Understanding the unpredictability of children, the character will keep his feet still, particularly refraining from moving backward or sideways. Most characters will pose for pictures or sign autographs. Costumes make it difficult for characters to wield a normal pen. If your child collects autographs, carry a pen the width of a Magic Marker.

"THEN SOME CONFUSION HAPPENED" Kids sometimes become lost at character encounters. Usually, there's a lot of activity around a character, with both adults and children touching it or posing for pictures. Most commonly, Mom and Dad stay in the crowd while Junior approaches the character. In the excitement and with the character moving around, Junior heads in the wrong direction to look for Mom and Dad. In the words of a Salt Lake City mom: "Milo was shaking hands with Dopey one minute, then some confusion happened and Milo was gone."

We recommend that parents with preschoolers stay with them when they meet characters, stepping back only to take a quick picture.

CHARACTER HOGS While we're on the subject of cameras, give other families a chance. Especially if you're shooting video, consider the perspective of this Houston mom:

One of the worst things to deal with is people who shoot about 3 minutes of their child with Mickey, asking everyone else to move. A photo takes about 2 seconds.

MEETING CHARACTERS FOR FREE

DISNEY HAS CREATED many permanent greeting locations intended to satisfy its guests' inexhaustible desire to meet characters. The chart on pages 442 and 443 lists them by park and character.

Meeting characters at the greeting locations may be free, but it can eat up of hours of time. A reader from Panama City, Florida, offers this advice:

Use FastPass+ for character greetings whenever you can. We did this for Ariel in Fantasyland and with Rapunzel at Princess Fairytale Hall, and we got in superfast!

This reader's comment highlights the point that you generally cannot rely on bumping into characters spontaneously as you walk around the park. A mom from Little Rock, Arkansas summarizes the issue:

We were disappointed in Disney's system of character greetings. You must find the schedule and wait in line to meet any characters. I miss the days when they would just appear—we once saw Jafar walking through Adventure Land all by himself! Now they are completely scheduled so you have to plan your visit and queue up with all the other visitors. I can't tell you how many times we tried to get in line only to be told the line was closed.

Meeting characters can be interesting, as the following anecdotes demonstrate. First from a Hamilton, Ohio, mom who wasn't awed by royalty:

For the first time in 28 years, I almost had a knock-down, drag-out with a princess. We went to the Princess Fairytale Hall to meet up with a couple of princesses the 6-year-old wanted to see. Rapunzel was very cool and chatty, posing for pictures, the whole deal. Cinderella was another story. While 6-year-old was smiling and waiting for a picture, I sat the 1-year-old baby girl on the floor so I could reach for my camera. All of a sudden, Cinderella goes ballistic, yelling (in the most un-princesslike voice), "Oh no, the little princess MUST have shoes! The little princess CANNOT be in the castle without shoes!" I'm like, "Listen, Cindy, the little princess is a year old. She can't walk yet, so she doesn't have shoes. Just smile for the picture and we'll be on our way." True story.

A Canadian mom found herself on duty for a character emergency:

If you have a child who is sensitive to other people's needs and is still of the age where the characters are real, make sure that you visit Donald immediately after watching PhilharMagic. My daughter was so worried about Donald Duck smashing through a wall [on film as part of the show] that we had to drop what we were going to do and stand in line at the circus tent just so she could kiss Donald and make sure he was OK. Fortunately "Donald" knew what she was talking about and played along with the doctoring.

Likewise, a family from Ontario discovered their daughter's depth of feeling for the seven dwarfs:

We got in line early for the Dwarfs (her favorites) at 5:50 p.m., still waited almost 2 hours before her turn in line ... and then she wouldn't leave. HUGE lineup, and she insisted on hugging and interacting with every dwarf—she squeezed herself between the seven of them and avoided my attempts to grab her and pull her away. There were very annoyed people behind us in line. Part of me feels bad that they waited the extra 2 minutes, the other part of me is angry that they wouldn't let a 3-year-old have her moment. She didn't care about the photo like the adults, she wanted to MEET her "Hi-Hoes." As it was, I eventually snagged her as she was screaming "GRUMPY! YOU HAVE TO BE HAPPY! BE HAPPY GRUMPY!" at the top of her lungs.

CHARACTER DINING

BECAUSE OF THE INCREDIBLE POPULARITY of character dining, reservations can be hard to come by if you wait until a couple of months before your vacation to book your choices. What's more, if you want to book a character meal, you must provide Disney with a credit card number. Your card will be charged $10 *per person* if you no-show or cancel your reservation less than 24 hours in advance; you may, however, reschedule with no penalty. See "Getting Advance Reservations at Popular Restaurants" (page 321) for the full story.

At very popular character meals like the breakfast at Cinderella's Royal Table, you're required to make a for-real reservation and guarantee it with a for-real deposit.

WHAT TO EXPECT

CHARACTER MEALS ARE BUSTLING AFFAIRS held in the largest full-service restaurants at the theme parks and on-property resorts, plus the Walt Disney World Swan and select hotels in the Disney Springs Resort Area and the Bonnet Creek Resort (including the Four Seasons).

Character breakfasts offer a fixed menu served individually, family-style, or on a buffet. The typical breakfast includes scrambled eggs; bacon, sausage, and ham; hash browns; waffles or French toast; biscuits, rolls, or pastries; and fruit. With family-style service, the meal is served in large skillets or platters at your table. The character breakfast at Akershus Royal Banquet Hall, for example, is served family-style and consists of typical breakfast fare such as eggs, bacon and sausage, and Danish pastries. Seconds (or thirds) are free. Buffets offer much the same fare, but you fetch it yourself.

Character dinners range from a set menu to buffets to ordering off the menu. Character-dinner buffets, such as those at 1900 Park Fare at the Grand Floridian and Chef Mickey's at the Contemporary Resort, separate the kids' fare from the grown-ups', though everyone is free to eat from both lines. Typically, the children's buffet includes hamburgers, hot dogs, pizza, fish sticks, chicken nuggets, macaroni and cheese, and peanut-butter-and-jelly sandwiches. Selections at the adult buffet usually include prime rib or other carved meat, baked or broiled Florida seafood, pasta, chicken, an ethnic dish or two, vegetables, potatoes, and salad.

CHARACTER-MEAL HIT PARADE

1. CINDERELLA'S ROYAL TABLE MAGIC KINGDOM

- **MEALS SERVED** Breakfast, lunch, and dinner • **SETTING** ★★★★
- **CHARACTERS** Cinderella, Ariel, Aurora, Jasmine, Snow White, Fairy Godmother (rare)
- **TYPE OF SERVICE** Fixed menu • **FOOD VARIETY & QUALITY** ★★★
- **NOISE LEVEL** Quiet • **CHARACTER–GUEST RATIO** 1:26

2. AKERSHUS ROYAL BANQUET HALL EPCOT

- **MEALS SERVED** Breakfast, lunch, and dinner • **SETTING** ★★★★
- **CHARACTERS** 4-6 characters chosen from among Ariel, Belle, Snow White, Aurora, Mary Poppins, and Cinderella
- **TYPE OF SERVICE** Family-style and menu (all you care to eat)
- **FOOD VARIETY & QUALITY** ★★★½ • **NOISE LEVEL** Quiet
- **CHARACTER–GUEST RATIO** 1:54

3. CHEF MICKEY'S CONTEMPORARY

- **MEALS SERVED** Breakfast, brunch, dinner • **SETTING** ★★★
- **CHARACTERS** Mickey, Minnie, Donald, Goofy, Pluto (sometimes Chip 'n' Dale)
- **TYPE OF SERVICE** Buffet
- **FOOD VARIETY & QUALITY** Breakfast and brunch ★★★   Dinner ★★★½
- **NOISE LEVEL** Loud • **CHARACTER–GUEST RATIO** 1:56

4. THE CRYSTAL PALACE MAGIC KINGDOM

- **MEALS SERVED** Breakfast, lunch, and dinner • **SETTING** ★★★
- **CHARACTERS** Pooh, Eeyore, Piglet, Tigger • **TYPE OF SERVICE** Buffet
- **FOOD VARIETY & QUALITY** Breakfast ★★½   Lunch and dinner ★★★
- **NOISE LEVEL** Very loud • **CHARACTER–GUEST RATIO** Breakfast, 1:67; lunch and dinner, 1:89

5. 1900 PARK FARE GRAND FLORIDIAN

- **MEALS SERVED** Breakfast, dinner • **SETTING** ★★★
- **CHARACTERS** *Breakfast:* Mary Poppins, Alice, Mad Hatter, Pooh, Tigger
  Dinner: Cinderella, Prince Charming, Lady Tremaine, the two stepsisters
- **TYPE OF SERVICE** Buffet • **FOOD VARIETY & QUALITY** Breakfast ★★★   Dinner ★★★½
- **NOISE LEVEL** Moderate • **CHARACTER–GUEST RATIO** Breakfast, 1:54; dinner, 1:44

6. THE GARDEN GRILL EPCOT

- **MEAL SERVED** Breakfast, lunch, dinner • **SETTING** ★★★★½
- **CHARACTERS** Mickey, Pluto, Chip 'n' Dale • **TYPE OF SERVICE** Family-style
- **FOOD VARIETY & QUALITY** ★★★½ • **NOISE LEVEL** Very quiet
- **CHARACTER–GUEST RATIO** 1:46

At all meals, characters circulate around the room while you eat. During your meal, each of the three to five characters present will visit your table, arriving one at a time to cuddle the kids (and sometimes the adults), pose for photos, and sign autographs.

Theresa Brown posted this great tip for getting the best photos at the independent Disney website AllEars.net:

We did several character meals. At first, we would only use our cameras to take pictures of our children with the characters after they had signed the autograph books and were posing with them.

7. TUSKER HOUSE RESTAURANT   DISNEY'S ANIMAL KINGDOM

- **MEALS SERVED** Breakfast, lunch, dinner • **SETTING** ★★★
- **CHARACTERS** Donald, Daisy, Mickey, Goofy • **TYPE OF SERVICE** Buffet
- **FOOD VARIETY & QUALITY** ★★★ • **NOISE LEVEL** Very loud
- **CHARACTER–GUEST RATIO** 1:112

8. CAPE MAY CAFE   BEACH CLUB

- **MEAL SERVED** Breakfast   **SETTING** ★★★ • **CHARACTERS** Goofy, Donald, Minnie
- **TYPE OF SERVICE** Buffet • **FOOD VARIETY & QUALITY** ★★½
- **NOISE LEVEL** Moderate • **CHARACTER–GUEST RATIO** 1:67

9. 'OHANA   POLYNESIAN VILLAGE

- **MEAL SERVED** Breakfast   **SETTING** ★★
- **CHARACTERS** Lilo and Stitch, Mickey, Pluto • **TYPE OF SERVICE** Family-style
- **FOOD VARIETY & QUALITY** ★★½ • **NOISE LEVEL** Moderate
- **CHARACTER–GUEST RATIO** 1:57

10. HOLLYWOOD & VINE   DISNEY'S HOLLYWOOD STUDIOS

- **MEALS SERVED** Breakfast, lunch, dinner • **SETTING** ★★½
- **CHARACTERS** *Breakfast and lunch:* Handy Manny, Sofia the First, Doc McStuffins, Jake (*Jake and the Never Land Pirates*); *Dinner:* Minnie's Seasonal Dining
- **TYPE OF SERVICE** Buffet • **FOOD VARIETY & QUALITY** ★★★
- **NOISE LEVEL** Moderate • **CHARACTER–GUEST RATIO** 1:71

11. GARDEN GROVE   SWAN

- **MEALS SERVED** Breakfast (Sat. and Sun.), dinner (nightly) • **SETTING** ★★★
- **CHARACTERS** Chip 'n' Dale, Goofy, Pluto • **TYPE OF SERVICE** Buffet
- **FOOD VARIETY & QUALITY** ★★★½ • **NOISE LEVEL** Moderate
- **CHARACTER–GUEST RATIO** 1:198, but frequently much better

12. TRATTORIA AL FORNO   DISNEY'S BOARDWALK

MEAL SERVED Breakfast   **SETTING** ★★★½

CHARACTERS Rapunzel, Flynn Ryder, Ariel, Prince Eric

TYPE OF SERVICE Fixed menu with several choices

FOOD VARIETY & QUALITY ★★★½

NOISE LEVEL Quiet   **CHARACTER–GUEST RATIO** 50:1

But after the second meal, we started snapping away as soon as the characters approached our table. We're so glad we did this, because we captured a very funny sequence of events while at 1900 Park Fare at the Grand Floridian. After that, we started snapping away at all of the character meals, and now that we're back, we see that the candid shots usually gave us better pictures than the posed ones! Of course, you want the posed pictures, but the candid ones just might end up being your favorite memories of the meals!

At some larger restaurants, including 'Ohana at the Polynesian Village Resort and Chef Mickey's at the Contemporary, character meals involve impromptu parades of characters and children around the room, group singing, napkin waving, and other organized madness.

Even without parades and such, character meals are pretty frenetic, as this mother of a 3-year-old attests:

*The character meals are NOT relaxing. I wish I had known how fran-
tic and rushed I would be. I was literally sprinting to the buffet to
throw food on my plate, so I wouldn't miss a character at our table.
I still HIGHLY recommend them, as the food was actually pretty
good, and the meals were the BEST part of our daughter's trip. But
just be prepared for it to be a semi-hectic affair.*

WHEN TO GO

ATTENDING A CHARACTER BREAKFAST usually prevents you
from arriving at the theme parks in time for opening. Because early
morning is best for touring and you don't want to burn daylight linger-
ing over breakfast, we suggest:

1. Schedule your in-park character breakfast for the first seating if the park opens
at 9 a.m. or later. You'll be admitted to the park before other guests (admission
is still required) through a special line at the turnstiles. Arrive early to be among
the first parties seated.

2. Go to a character dinner or lunch instead of breakfast. It'll be a nice break.

3. Schedule the last seating for breakfast. Have a light snack such as cereal or bagels
before you head to the parks for opening, hit the most popular attractions until
10:15 or so, and then head for brunch. The buffet should keep you fueled until
dinner, especially if you eat another light snack in the afternoon.

4. Go on arrival or departure day. The day you arrive and check in is usually good for
a character dinner. Settle at your hotel, swim, then dine with the characters. This
strategy has the added benefit of exposing your children to the characters before
chance encounters at the parks. Some children, moreover, won't settle down to
enjoy the parks until they have seen Mickey. Departure day also is good for a
character meal. Schedule a character breakfast on your checkout day before you
head for the airport or begin your drive home.

5. Go on a rest day. If you plan to stay five or more days, you'll probably take a day
or half-day from touring to rest or do something else. These are perfect days
for a character meal.

HOW TO CHOOSE A CHARACTER MEAL

MANY READERS ASK FOR ADVICE about character meals. This
question from a Waterloo, Iowa, mom is typical:

*Are all character breakfasts pretty much the same or are some better
than others? How should I go about choosing one?*

In fact, some *are* better, sometimes much better. When we evaluate
character meals, we look for the following:

1. THE CHARACTERS The meals offer a diverse assortment of characters.
Pick a meal that features your kids' favorites. Check out our Character-
Meal Hit Parade chart (see pages 448 and 449) to see which characters
are assigned to each meal. Most restaurants stick with the same charac-
ters. Even so, check the lineup when you call to make your Advance
Reservations.

2. ATTENTION FROM THE CHARACTERS At all character meals, characters circulate among guests, hugging children, posing for pictures, and
signing autographs. How much time a character spends with you and

your children depends primarily on the ratio of characters to guests. The more characters and fewer guests, the better. Because many character-meal venues never fill to capacity, the character-to-guest ratios in our Character-Meal Hit Parade chart have been adjusted to reflect an average attendance. Even so, there's quite a range. The best ratio is at Cinderella's Royal Table, where there's about 1 character to every 26 guests.

The worst ratio is theoretically at the Swan resort's Garden Grove, where there could be as few as 1 character for every 198 guests. We say "theoretically," however, because in practice there are far fewer guests at the Garden Grove than at character meals in Disney-owned resorts, and often more characters. (During one meal, friends of ours were literally the only guests in the restaurant for breakfast and had to ask the characters to leave them alone to eat.)

A Jerseyville, Illinois, mom gives the face characters high marks:

> Our 7-year-old daughter wanted to have dinner with Sleeping Beauty, so we scheduled a character dinner with the princesses in the Norway Pavilion. The princesses were so accessible and took their time with our child, answering questions and smiling for pictures. In fact, our daughter told us she "had the best day of her life," and parents want to hear that from their child.

An Indiana mother of two relates the importance of keeping tabs on the characters:

> For character meals, take note of which characters are there when you arrive, and mentally check them off as they visit your table. If the last one or two seem slow to arrive, seek out the "character manager" and let him or her know ASAP.

3. THE SETTING Some character meals are in exotic settings. For others, moving the event to an elementary-school cafeteria would be an improvement. Our chart rates each meal's setting with the familiar scale of zero (worst) to five (best) stars. Two restaurants, Cinderella's Royal Table in the Magic Kingdom and Garden Grill Restaurant in the Land Pavilion at Epcot, deserve special mention. Cinderella's Royal Table is on the first and second floors of Cinderella Castle in Fantasyland, offering guests a look inside the castle. Garden Grill is a revolving restaurant overlooking several scenes from the Living with the Land boat ride. Also at Epcot, the popular Princess Storybook Meals are held in the castlelike Akershus Royal Banquet Hall. Though Chef Mickey's at the Contemporary Resort is rather sterile in appearance, it affords a great view of the monorail running through the hotel. Themes and settings of the remaining character-meal venues, while apparent to adults, will be lost on most children.

4. THE FOOD Although some food served at character meals is quite good, most is average (palatable but nothing to get excited about). In variety, consistency, and quality, restaurants generally do a better job with breakfast than with lunch or dinner (if served).

Some restaurants offer a buffet, while others opt for "one-skillet" family-style service, in which all hot items are served from the same pot or skillet. Regarding the latter, a Texas mom notes:

The family-style meals are much better for character dining. At the buffet, you're scared to leave your table in case you miss a character or other action.

To help you sort everything out, we rate the food at each character meal in our chart using the five-star scale.

5. THE PROGRAM Some larger restaurants stage modest performances where the characters dance, head a parade around the room, or lead songs and cheers. For some guests, these activities give the meal a celebratory air; for others, they turn what was already mayhem into absolute chaos. Either way, the antics consume time the characters could spend with families at their table.

6. NOISE If you want to eat in peace, character meals are a bad choice. That said, some are much noisier than others. Our chart gives you an idea of what to expect.

7. WHICH MEAL? Although breakfasts seem to be most popular, character lunches and dinners are usually more practical because they don't interfere with early-morning touring. During hot weather, a character lunch can be heavenly.

8. COST Dinners cost more than lunches and lunches more than breakfasts. Prices for meals (except at Cinderella Castle) vary considerably from the least expensive to the most expensive restaurant. Breakfasts run about $27–$58 for adults and $15–$38 for kids ages 3–9. For character lunches, expect to pay $31–$61 for adults and $16–$38 for kids. Dinners are $31–$73 for adults and $16–$43 for children. Little ones age 2 years and younger eat free. The meals at the high end of the price range are at **Cinderella's Royal Table** in the Magic Kingdom and **Akershus Royal Banquet** Hall at Epcot. The reasons for the sky-high prices: (1) Cinderella's Royal Table is small but in great demand and (2) both Akershus and Cindy's are Disney-princess central.

9. ADVANCE RESERVATIONS Disney makes Advance Reservations for character meals 180 days before you wish to dine (Disney resort guests can reserve 180 days in advance, plus up to 10 additional days of your trip in advance); moreover, Disney resort guests can make Advance Reservations for all meals during their stay. Reservations for most character meals are easy to obtain even if you call only a couple of weeks before your trip. Cinderella's Royal Table and Be Our Guest are another story. For these, you'll need our strategy (see Part Four), as well as help from Congress and the Pope. If you don't get what you want at first, try again later, advises a London, England, mother of two:

When a booking window opens, many people overbook and then either get buyer's remorse or find alternative bookings and cancel. When my booking window first opened, I was able to book barely 20% of what I wanted, but within two to three weeks, I had 100%.

10. CHECKING IT TWICE Disney occasionally shuffles the characters and theme of a character meal. If your little one's heart is set on Pooh and Piglet, getting Hook and Mr. Smee is just a waste of time and money. Reconfirm all character-meal Advance Reservations three weeks or so before you leave home by calling ☎ 407-WDW-DINE.

11. "FRIENDS" For some venues, Disney has stopped specifying characters scheduled for a particular meal. Instead, they say it's a given character "and friends"—for example, "Pooh and friends," meaning Eeyore, Piglet, and Tigger, or some combination thereof, or "Mickey and friends" with some assortment chosen among Minnie, Goofy, Pluto, Donald, Daisy, Chip, and Dale.

12. THE BUM'S RUSH Most character meals are leisurely affairs, and you can usually stay as long as you want. An exception is Cinderella's Royal Table at the Magic Kingdom. Because Cindy's is in such high demand, the restaurant does everything short of pre-chewing your food to move you through, as this European mother of a 5-year-old can attest:

> We dined a lot, did three character meals and a few Signature restaurants, and every meal was awesome except for lunch with Cinderella in the castle. While I'd often read it wouldn't be a rushed affair, it was exactly that. We had barely sat down when the appetizers were thrown on our table, the princesses each spent just a few seconds with our daughter—almost no interaction—and the side dishes were cold. We were out of there within 40 minutes and felt very stressed. Considering the price for the meal, I cannot recommend it.

GETTING AN ADVANCE RESERVATION AT CINDERELLA'S ROYAL TABLE

ONCE UPON A TIME, breakfast was the only character meal served at Cinderella Castle in the Magic Kingdom. Reservations for every table were gone within minutes of becoming available each morning. Disney responded to this popularity by adding character lunches and dinners—and jacking up the price to around $60–$70 per adult. As a result, it's now much easier to get into Cinderella's Royal Table for some meals during your stay. Also, the opening of the wildly popular **Be Our Guest Restaurant** in Fantasyland has taken a lot of pressure off Cindy's. If you're visiting during peak periods or you've got to have a reservation at a specific, popular time, see our Advance Reservation tips starting on page 321.

DISNEY'S ROYAL ALTERNATIVES If you're unwilling to fund Cinderella's shoe habit or you simply weren't able to get an Advance Reservation before young Ariel graduates from college, rest assured there are other venues that will feed you in the company of princesses.

Akershus Royal Banquet Hall, in the Norway Pavilion of Epcot's World Showcase, serves family-style breakfast, lunch, and dinner. Disney tends to define *princess* quite loosely, so you may see any character who's ever donned a dress (with the exception of Cinderella) at this meal. Entrées are a combination of traditional buffet fare and Scandinavian-style dishes.

Dinner at the Grand Floridian's **1900 Park Fare** features the whole crew from *Cinderella,* including Lady Tremaine and the stepsisters (breakfast is a character buffet with Winnie the Pooh and friends). At $50 per adult and $30 for children age 9 and under, this is a far more economical option for diners wishing to get their princess on, and the wicked stepsisters are an absolute hoot. This meal is also a little more boy-friendly if you're entertaining a mixed crowd. Finally, remember that your own little princess may be feeding off your own excitement over eating in the Castle—she might be just as happy with a plastic crown purchased in the gift shop and a burger from Cosmic Ray's.

OTHER CHARACTER EVENTS

A CAMPFIRE AND SING-ALONG are held nightly (times vary with the season) near the Meadow Trading Post and Bike Barn at **Fort Wilderness Resort & Campground.** Chip 'n' Dale lead the songs, and a Disney film is shown. The program is free and open to resort guests (☎ 407-824-2900). Another character encounter at Fort Wilderness is *Mickey's Backyard BBQ,* held seasonally on Thursdays and Saturdays. See page 343 for details.

BABYSITTING

CHILD-CARE CENTERS Child care isn't available inside the theme parks, but two Magic Kingdom resorts connected by monorail or boat (Polynesian Village and Wilderness Lodge & Villas), four Epcot resorts (the Yacht & Beach Club Resorts, the Swan, and the Dolphin), and Animal Kingdom Lodge, along with the Hilton at Walt Disney World, have child-care centers for potty-trained children age 3 and older (see chart opposite). Services vary, but children generally can be left between 5 p.m. and midnight. Milk and cookies and blankets and pillows are provided at all centers, and dinner is provided at most. Play is supervised but not organized, and toys, videos, and games are plentiful. Guests at any Disney resort or campground may use the services.

The most elaborate of the child-care centers (variously called "clubs" or "camps") is **Lilo's Playhouse** at the Polynesian Village Resort. The rate for ages 3–12 is $58.58 for the "duration of the evening."

All the clubs accept reservations (some six months in advance!) with a credit card guarantee. Call the club directly, or reserve through Disney at ☎ 407-WDW-DINE. Most clubs require a 24-hour cancellation notice and levy a hefty penalty of 2 hours' time or $30 per child for no-shows. A limited number of walk-ins are usually accepted on a first-come, first-served basis.

unofficial **TIP**
Child-care clubs close at or before midnight. If you intend to stay out late, in-room babysitting is your best bet.

If you're staying at a Disney resort that doesn't offer a child-care club and you *don't* have a car, then you're better off using in-room babysitting. Trying to take your child to a club in another hotel by Disney bus means a 50- to 90-minute trip each way. By the time you've deposited your little one, it will almost be time to pick him or her up again.

IN-ROOM BABYSITTING Two companies provide in-room sitting in Walt Disney World and surrounding areas: **Kid's Nite Out** and **Fairy Godmothers** (no kidding). Kid's Nite Out also serves hotels in the greater Orlando area, including downtown. All three provide sitters older than age 18 who are insured, bonded, screened, reference-checked, police-checked, and trained in CPR. In addition to caring for your kids in your room, the sitters will, if you direct (and pay), take your children to the theme parks or other venues. Both services offer bilingual sitters. (See the chart on the next page for details.)

BABYSITTING SERVICES

KID'S NITE OUT	FAIRY GODMOTHERS
☎ 407-828-0920 or 800-696-8105 **kidsniteout.com**	☎ 407-277-3724 (24 hours)
HOTELS SERVED All Walt Disney World and Orlando-area hotels	**HOTELS SERVED** All WDW hotels and those in the general WDW area
SITTERS Men and women	**SITTERS** Mothers and grandmothers, female college students
MINIMUM CHARGES 4 hours	**MINIMUM CHARGES** 4 hours
BASE HOURLY RATES 1 child, $18 2 children, $21 3 children, $24 4 children, $26	**BASE HOURLY RATES** 1 child, $16 2 children, $16 3 children, $16 4 children or more, $18
EXTRA CHARGES Transportation fee, $10; starting before 8 a.m. or after 9 p.m., +$2 per hour; additional fee for holidays	**EXTRA CHARGES** Transportation fee, $16; starting after 10 p.m., +$2 per hour
CANCELLATION DEADLINE 24 hours before service	**CANCELLATION DEADLINE** 3 hours before service
FORM OF PAYMENT AE, D, MC, V; tips in cash	**FORM OF PAYMENT** Cash or traveler's checks for actual payment; tips in cash
THINGS SITTERS WON'T DO Transport children in private vehicle, take children swimming, give baths	**THINGS SITTERS WON'T DO** Transport children, give baths. Swimming is at sitter's discretion.

CHILD-CARE CLUBS*

HOTEL	NAME OF PROGRAM	AGES	PHONE
ANIMAL KINGDOM LODGE •	Simba's Cubhouse •	3-12 •	☎ 407-938-4785
DOLPHIN AND SWAN •	Camp Dolphin •	4-12 •	☎ 407-934-4241
POLYNESIAN VILLAGE RESORT •	Lilo's Playhouse •	3-12 •	☎ 407-824-2000
YACHT & BEACH CLUB RESORTS •	Sandcastle Club •	3-12 •	☎ 407-934-3750
WILDERNESS LODGE & VILLAS •	Cub's Den* •	3-12 •	☎ 407-824-1083

* Child-care clubs operate afternoons and evenings. Before 4 p.m., call the hotels rather than the numbers listed above. All programs require reservations; call ☎ 407-WDW-DINE (939-3463).

* Camp Dolphin offers 2 free hours if you're dining at Shula's, Il Mulino, or Bluezoo that evening. Cub's Den is closed through 2017 during renovations at Wilderness Lodge.

* Mandara Spa offers 2 free hours if you purchase a treatment for $75 or more.

SPECIAL PROGRAMS
for CHILDREN

SEVERAL CHILDREN'S PROGRAMS ARE AVAILABLE at Walt Disney World parks and resorts. While all are undoubtedly fun, we find them somewhat lacking in educational focus.

Many of Disney's Deluxe and DVC resorts offer a continuous slate of free children's activities from early morning through the evening, from storytelling and cookie decorating to hands-on activities themed to the resort. The Animal Kingdom Lodge's activities are representative: They're grouped into categories such as "Cultural Immersion," "Culinary Exploration," and "Animal Programs." Here's a recent sampling of offerings, from the dozens offered on this day:

11:30 a.m. Animal Enrichment: Help animal experts prepare and present interactive objects to the animals on the savanna.

Noon–12:30 p.m. Medallion rubbing in the Jambo House lobby

12:30–1 p.m. Meet a lobby greeter

1–1:30 p.m. Animal stamps activity

1–2 p.m. Cookie decorating

2–3 p.m. African face painting *or* pin trading *or* wildlife games

3:30–4:30 p.m. African Wonders interactive matching game *or* cultural tour of Sanaa

4:30–5 p.m. Music of the Savanna: Playing African instruments and learning about African music

There was plenty more after dinner, too. We think these programs offer an inexpensive alternative to the theme parks on your first or last day of travel, or whenever parents need a quiet break by the pool.

DISNEY'S FAMILY MAGIC TOUR This is a 1½- to 2-hour guided tour of the Magic Kingdom for the entire family. Even children in strollers (no younger than age 3) are welcome. The tour combines information about the Magic Kingdom with the gathering of clues that ultimately solve "diabolical" problems. There's usually a marginal plot such as saving Wendy from Captain Hook, in which case the character at the end of the tour is Wendy. The tour departs daily at 10 a.m. The cost is about $39 per person with tax, plus a valid Magic Kingdom admission. The maximum group size is 20 persons. Reservations can be made up to one year in advance by calling ☎ 407-wDW-TOUR (939-8687).

DISNEY'S PIRATE ADVENTURE Children ages 4–12 get to don bandannas, hoist the Jolly Roger, and set out on a boat trip to search for buried treasure by following a map. At the final port of call, the kids find the treasure (doubloons, beads, and rubber bugs!) and wolf down snacks. The treasure is split among the kids. The adventure costs about $40 per child with tax and is offered at Port Orleans Riverside (Bayou Pirate Adventure), the Grand Floridian (Pirate Adventure), the Yacht Club (Albatross Treasure Cruise), and the Caribbean Beach Resort (Islands of the Caribbean). All programs are offered daily, 9:30–11:30 a.m., weather permitting; call ☎ 407-wDW-PLAY (939-7529) for days offered and other information. Boys and girls alike really love this outing—many report it as the highlight of their vacation. *Note:* No parents allowed!

DISNEY'S THE MAGIC BEHIND OUR STEAM TRAINS Kids must be age 10 or older for this 3-hour tour, presented Monday–Saturday. At the 7:30 a.m. start time, join the crew of the Walt Disney World Railroad as they prepare their steam locomotives for the day. Cost is about $54 per person with tax, plus a valid Magic Kingdom admission. Call ☎ 407-wDW-TOUR for information and reservations.

MY DISNEY GIRL'S PERFECTLY PRINCESS TEA PARTY It certainly takes a princely sum to cover the tab on this Grand Floridian gathering, hosted by Rose Petal, an enchanted storytelling rose. Your little princess gets dressed up in her favorite regal attire and sips tea with Princess Aurora. For an additional fee, girls receive an 18-inch My Disney Girl doll dressed in a matching Princess Aurora gown plus accessories. Other loot includes a ribbon tiara, silver link bracelet, fresh rose, scrapbook set, and "Best Friend" certificate. A luncheon is served as well. The cost is about $334 with tax and tip for one adult and one child ages 3–11; add an additional adult for $99 or an additional child for $235. **Note: This event is not covered by the Disney Dining Plan.** The tea party is held every Sunday, Monday, and Wednesday–Friday, 10:30 a.m.–noon. Call ☎ 407-939-6983 for reservations and information.

WONDERLAND TEA PARTY Held at 1900 Park Fare restaurant in the Grand Floridian Monday–Friday afternoons at 2 p.m. for $43 per child (ages 4–12, with tax), the program consists of decorating (and eating) cupcakes and having lunch and tea with characters from Alice in Wonderland. Reservations can be made by calling ☎ 407-wdw-dine 90 days in advance.

BIRTHDAYS *and* SPECIAL OCCASIONS

IF SOMEONE IN YOUR FAMILY CELEBRATES A BIRTHDAY while you're at Disney World, don't keep it a secret. A Lombard, Illinois, mom put the word out and was glad she did:

> My daughter was turning 5 while we were there; our hotel asked me who her favorite character was and did the rest. We came back to our room on her birthday and there were helium balloons, a card, and a Cinderella photo autographed in ink! When we entered the Magic Kingdom, we received an "It's My Birthday Today" pin (FREE!), and at the restaurant she got a huge cupcake with whipped cream, sprinkles, and a candle. IT PAYS TO ASK!

PART SIX

SPECIAL TIPS *for* SPECIAL PEOPLE

WALT DISNEY WORLD *for* PEOPLE *with* BAD ATTITUDES

YOU'D BE AMAZED at how many people are dragged unwillingly to Walt Disney World by their friends and families. But for skeptics and cynics who've never visited, there's hope, as described by a 25-year-old woman from Williamstown, Massachusetts:

> My boyfriend is sort of anti-Disney, so to save our relationship and vacation, I steered us clear of some traditional must-sees. (It's a Small World, for example, might have sent him over the edge.) I made sure that Soarin' was one of the first rides we went on. He absolutely loved it, and it opened his mind to the rest of the Disney experience.

A Louisiana mom—the lone Disney fan in her family—chimed in with this:

> This year I DRAGGED two teenage boys and an outdoorsman, all Disney haters, to Orlando. None of them wanted to go, but after the trip, my 16-year-old son said, "Mom, I'll go with you again," and my husband said, "I'm shocked that I had a great time."

WALT DISNEY WORLD *for* SINGLES

DISNEY WORLD IS GREAT FOR SINGLES. It's safe, clean, and low-pressure. Safety and comfort are unsurpassed, especially for women traveling alone. Parking lots are well lit and constantly patrolled.

If you're looking for a place to relax without being hit on, Disney World is perfect. The bars, lounges, and nightclubs are among the most laid-back and friendly you're likely to find. Between the BoardWalk and Disney Springs, nightlife abounds; virtually every type of entertainment is available at a reasonable price. If you overimbibe and you're a Disney resort guest, Disney buses will return you safely to your hotel.

See "Tips for Going Solo" on pages 460 and 461 for more ways to enjoy Walt Disney World on your own.

WALT DISNEY WORLD
for COUPLES

MANY COUPLES THINK Walt Disney World is strictly for kids. Not so, an Evans City, Pennsylvania, woman attests:

> *I have many friends who think I was crazy to travel to Walt Disney World without my children (ages 9 and 12). I absolutely loved it! Instead of rushing from thrill ride to thrill ride with all the other hordes of people, we were able to slow down and enjoy all of the amazing details that make WDW the incredibly special place that it is. It is an entirely different, but equally magical, experience.*

So many couples tie the knot or honeymoon in the World that Disney has a dedicated department to help arrange the day of your dreams. **Disney's Fairy Tale Weddings & Honeymoons** (☎ 321-939-4610; disneyweddings.com) offers a range of ceremony venues and services, plus honeymoon planning and registries.

WEDDINGS, COMMITMENT CEREMONIES, AND VOWS RENEWALS

COUPLES WISHING TO GET HITCHED have three choices of Disney wedding packages. The **Memories Collection** includes the couple and up to four other people; the **Escape** and **Wishes Collections** are for the couple and up to 18 other people. The Memories and Escape Collections offer a variety of options, including the following:

- Fresh flowers
- A violinist
- Limousine transportation
- A professional Disney photographer and selection of prints
- Wedding planning website
- On-site wedding coordinator

The Escape Collection also includes a two-tier wedding cake, Champagne, and digital images of your event presized for sharing on social media. The officiant and marriage certificate are not included in any collection, but Disney keeps a list from which you can choose (or you can bring your own).

Many couples make a special trip to Disney World to plan their weddings in person, though it's entirely possible to make all arrangements by phone and online. While it may seem that a Disney wedding is the ultimate cookie-cutter event, many options exist for making your day personal and special. We think the best resource for planning a Disney wedding is *Passporter's Disney Weddings & Honeymoons,* by Carrie Hayward (available as a print book or e-book at passporter.com /weddings.asp).

TIPS FOR GOING SOLO

SINGLE CAN MEAN TRAVELING ALONE as well as unmarried, and being by yourself doesn't mean that you can't have a great time at Disney World. **Deb Wills,** creator of the all-things-Disney website **allears.net,** offers this advice:

- One of the best parts about traveling solo is that you can be your own boss. Sleep in, have leisurely morning coffee on the balcony, relax by the pool . . . or not. If you'd rather get up and go early, who's to stop you?

- Put some spontaneity into your day. If you're taking Disney transportation, get on the first park bus that arrives.

- Get on the resort monorail (not the Express!) at the Magic Kingdom, and visit each of the resorts it stops at. Each resort has its own theme and character, with lots to see and explore.

- Did you know that you can walk through the queues and view the preshows of the thrill rides even if you don't want to ride? Wander through at your own pace, then tell the cast member before boarding that you don't wish to ride, and you'll be shown to a nearby exit.

- If you *do* want to experience the thrill rides, take advantage of the single-rider lines for the Rock 'n' Roller Coaster, Expedition Everest, and Test Track. They can cut your wait time significantly.

- If you encounter folks taking photos of each other, ask if they'd like to be in one photo, then offer to snap the picture. This is a great way to make friends.

- Get your favorite Disney snack, find a bench, and people-watch. You'll be amazed at what you see: the honeymooning couple wearing bride-and-groom mouse ears, toddlers giving Mickey and the characters their first hugs, grandparents smiling indulgently as their grandchildren smear ice cream all over their faces. If you're missing the smiles of your own children, buy a couple of balloons and give them away. You'll help make the kids near you very, very happy.

LEGALITIES

TO MARRY IN THE WORLD, you need a marriage license, issued at any Florida courthouse. There is no waiting period. Florida residents must complete a 4-hour premarital counseling session to marry less than 3 days after obtaining their license; all weddings must occur within 60 days of getting the license. Blood tests aren't required, but both parties must present identification and their Social Security numbers. If you were widowed or divorced within 30 days of the wedding, you must present a certified copy of the deceased spouse's death certificate or your divorce decree.

unofficial **TIP**
Contact Disney as soon as you have a date in mind for your event—popular dates may not be available on short notice. If you wish to hold your ceremony inside a theme park, you're restricted to very early in the morning or late at night, when the park is closed to guests.

HONEYMOONS AND HONEYMOON REGISTRIES

HONEYMOON PACKAGES are adaptations of regular Disney World travel packages, though you may purchase add-ons such as flowers and in-room gifts to make your trip more special. Some couples who honeymoon at Walt Disney World create a registry that allows friends and family to bestow gifts of tours,

- Learn how some of the magic is created. Take a behind-the-scenes tour (see Part Fifteen) or one of the Deluxe hotel tours.

- Visit Animal Kingdom Lodge and relax at an animal-viewing area. Find an animal keeper; they'll gladly discuss care of the wild animals at the resort.

- Don't hesitate to strike up conversations with cast members or guests in line with you. International cast members in Epcot's World Showcase are happy to share stories about their homelands.

- Enjoy a leisurely shopping adventure around the World. Some stores (**Arribas Brothers** in Disney Springs and **Mitsukoshi Department Store** in the Japan Pavilion at World Showcase) have really neat displays and exhibits.

- Go to that restaurant you've always wanted to try but your picky eater has always declined. You don't have to order a full meal; try several appetizers or, better yet, just dessert.

- Special fun can be had at a Character Meal (no waiting in long lines). Which one has characters you love? Make an early or late reservation for fewer people and more character interaction. The Garden Grill in The Land is a hidden gem!

- Check the calendar for special events. The annual Flower and Garden Festival has lots of eye candy you can enjoy at your own pace.

- Use common sense about your personal security. I feel very comfortable and safe traveling alone at Disney World and have done so many times, but I still don't do things that I wouldn't do at home (like announce to anyone listening that I'm traveling solo). If you aren't comfortable walking to your room alone, ask at the front desk for a security escort. Use extra caution in the parking lots at night, just as you would at home.

spa packages, special dinners, and the like. For more information on honeymoon registries, visit disney.honeymoonwishes.com.

ROMANTIC GETAWAYS

DISNEY WORLD IS A FAVORITE GETAWAY FOR COUPLES, but not all Disney hotels are equally romantic. Some are too family-oriented; others swarm with convention-goers. For romantic (though expensive) lodging, we recommend **Animal Kingdom Lodge & Villas; Bay Lake Tower** at the Contemporary; the **Polynesian Village & Villas; Wilderness Lodge & Villas;** the **Grand Floridian Resort, Spa, & Villas; BoardWalk Inn & Villas;** and the **Yacht & Beach Club Resorts.** The Alligator Bayou section at **Port Orleans Riverside,** a Disney Moderate resort, also has secluded rooms.

CELEBRATING . . . EVERYTHING!

DISNEY WORLD IS ALL ABOUT CELEBRATING—marriages, birthdays, anniversaries, the works—but only if you let somebody know. A St. Louis newlywed offers this advice:

> *If you're celebrating, ask for Celebration Buttons when you check into your hotel or at any park's Guest Relations, then WEAR THEM!*

Cast members regularly congratulated us, and I'm relatively certain we were seated at better tables for dinner based solely on our buttons.

TIPS FOR VISITORS WHO NEED "ADULT TIME"

BELIEVE IT OR NOT, WALT DISNEY WORLD is a very popular destination for adults traveling without kids, either as solos, couples, or groups of friends. The self-contained universe of Disney World, with its easy transportation, security, and variety of dining, drinking, and entertainment options, makes it a fabulous place to vacation sans children (don't tell ours, but sometimes we prefer it that way).

Naturally, anyone who visits the Most Magical Place on Earth is well advised to be prepared to see children—lots of them—and it would be naive to think any other way. But that doesn't mean that you need to be around the little tykes every minute. Here are some tips.

- **Dine late.** Most families will try to eat dinner before 8 p.m. Have a late lunch and try for a reservation closer to the last seating at your restaurant. The exception to this is California Grill, where many people (families or not) will try to time their meal around the fireworks at the Magic Kingdom.

- **Dine at Victoria & Albert's.** V&A is the only restaurant on property that does not admit guests under age 10. Pricey? Yes. Worth it? Yep.

- **Go to the spa.** See page 774 for more info.

- **Linger in World Showcase.** We could spend hours poring over the details of the World Showcase pavilions. Favorites include the terra-cotta soldiers in China, the Bijtsu-kan Gallery in Japan, and the Gallery of Arts and History in Morocco.

- **Really take in the trails of Animal Kingdom.** The animal trails of the Asia, Africa, and Tree of Life at this park are peaceful and beautiful.

- **Stay up late.** Take a tip from a friend of this book, Tom Bricker, and don't leave the park until well past closing. There's something magical about having all of Main Street or Sunset Boulevard to yourself with the lights and background music still playing. Do make sure you don't miss the last bus to your resort, though, if you didn't drive.

- **Take a tour.** Many Walt Disney World tours have an age limit for how young a guest can be to experience them. See page 741 for details.

- **Spend the morning at the pool.** Most families hit the parks in the morning and come back to their hotels around lunch. Do the opposite and pretend the lifeguard is your personal cabana boy or girl.

- **Use the TouringPlans.com hotel-room finder** (see page 127) to scope out the quietest parts of your Disney resort.

WALT DISNEY WORLD
"At Large"

YOU'VE JUST SPENT A SMALL FORTUNE for your vacation. If you're a person of size, you don't want to worry about whether you'll have trouble fitting in the ride vehicles. Fortunately, Walt Disney World realizes that its guests come in all shapes and sizes and is quite accommodating. Deb Wills and Debra Martin Koma, experts on Walt Disney World travel for those with special challenges, offer these suggestions.

- Remember that you'll be on your feet for hours at a time, so wear comfortable, broken-in shoes. If you feel a blister starting, take care of it quickly. (Each theme park has a First Aid Center stocked with bandages and other necessities. For more on blister prevention, see page 507.)

- If you're prone to chafing, consider bringing an antifriction product (such as Bodyglide) designed to control or eliminate rubbing. You can find this and similar products at most pharmacies and sporting-goods stores.

- Not all attractions have the same kinds of vehicles or seating. Some have bench seats, while others have individual seats; some have overhead harnesses, while others have seat belts or lap bars. Learn what type of seating or vehicle each attraction has before you go so you know what to expect (check out tinyurl.com/allears-ride-gallery for details). If the attraction has a seat belt, pull it all the way out before you sit down to make it easier to strap yourself in. Note that some attractions even have seat-belt extenders—ask a cast member about these.

- Several attractions (Expedition Everest, for example) offer a sample ride vehicle for you to try before you get in line. Ask a cast member for details.

- Front seats (such as those in the Rock 'n' Roller Coaster and Test Track) often have more legroom.

- In restaurants, look for chairs without arms. Ask a host if you don't see one.

- Request a resort hotel room with a king-size bed. It may cost a bit more, but the good sleep you'll get will be more than worth it.

WALT DISNEY WORLD *for* EXPECTANT MOTHERS

WHEN IT COMES TO PREGNANT WOMEN visiting Walt Disney World, the authors, alas, have no wisdom of their own to impart. (Try as they might, Bob and Len have never been in the family way.)

Enter **Debbie Grubbs,** a Colorado reader. During her fifth month of pregnancy, she waddled intrepidly all over the World, compiling observations and tips for expectant moms that she shares below.

Magic Kingdom: *Splash Mountain is a no-go, obviously, due to the drop—or so I thought. It turns out that the seat configuration in the "logs" has more to do with it than the drop. The seats are made so that your knees are higher than your rear, causing compression on the abdomen (when it's this large). This is potentially harmful to the baby.*

Big Thunder Mountain Railroad is also restricted for obvious reasons. It's just not a good idea to ride roller coasters when pregnant.

Mad Tea Party may be OK if you don't spin the cups. We didn't ride this one because my doctor advised me to skip rides with centrifugal [or centripetal] force. Dumbo in Fantasyland and the Astro Orbiter in Tomorrowland are OK, though.

Space Mountain is one of my favorite rides . . . but a roller coaster nonetheless.

Tomorrowland Speedway isn't recommended due to the amount of rear-ending by overzealous younger drivers.

(We also think Debbie would have passed on Seven Dwarfs Mine Train and its swinging cars.)

Disney's Animal Kingdom: *Both Dinosaur and Primeval Whirl are very jerky and should be avoided.*

(We think Debbie would've avoided Expedition Everest, too. The boat ride at Pandora might be fine, but Pandora's flight simulator is probably too much.)

Epcot: *Mission: Space and Test Track are restricted, as are all simulator rides; they're way too rough and jerky. [Nonmoving seats are available in some simulation attractions—ask a cast member.] Soarin' is fine.*

Disney's Hollywood Studios: *Tower of Terror is out of the question for the drop alone, and Star Tours is restricted because it's a simulator. Rock 'n' Roller Coaster is clearly off-limits.*

Water Parks: *Slides are off-limits, but not the wave pools and floating creeks (great for getting the weight off your feet).*

A mother of three from Bethesda, Maryland, adds:

Go to a golf shop and buy one of those walking sticks with a seat attached to it—I would've been a goner without one. They're lightweight and easy to carry. Also, a support garment (such as a BellyBra) is a must for relieving the weight on your lower back.

From a Branchburg, New Jersey, woman:

I would add that moms-to-be should be really mindful of the temperature, staying hydrated, and having realistic expectations for how much you'll be able to do. We averaged 5–7 miles of walking per day during our trip, and this may have been a bit too much for me (I was six months pregnant at the time). Once the temperatures started approaching 90, I found it difficult to catch my breath and my feet also began to swell. A midday nap or swim break was 100% required; I tried to skip it on a few days and I was miserable as a result. I was most frustrated at Epcot, where most of the headliner attractions are restricted for pregnant guests.

MORE TIPS FOR MOMS-TO-BE

IN ADDITION TO DEBBIE'S TIPS, here are a few of ours:

1. Discuss your Disney World plans with your obstetrician before your trip.

2. Start walking at home to build up your stamina for walking in the parks. Once in the World, however, try to use in-park transportation whenever you can so that you're not having to walk *all* the time.

3. Get as much rest as you need, even if you have to sacrifice time at the parks. (Staying at a Disney resort makes it easier to return to your room.)

4. Eat properly and hydrate throughout the day, especially when it's hot.

5. While there have been no confirmed cases of the Zika virus in the Orlando area to date, there have been cases in other parts of Florida. Disney has begun providing free insect repellent to all guests. Women who are or may become pregnant may want to take extra precautions.

WALT DISNEY WORLD
for SENIORS

unofficial TIP
There are few WDW attractions that we suggest seniors avoid.

SENIOR CITIZENS have much the same problems and concerns as all Disney visitors. Older guests do, however, get into predicaments caused by touring with younger people. Pressured by their grandchildren to endure a frantic pace, many seniors concentrate on surviving Disney World rather than enjoying it. Seniors must either set the pace or dispatch the young folks to tour on their own.

An older reader in Alabaster, Alabama, writes:

Being a senior is not for wussies, particularly at Walt Disney World. Things that used to be easy take a lot of effort, and sometimes your brain has to wait for your body to catch up. Half the time, your grandchildren treat you like a crumbling ruin, then they turn around and trick you into getting on a roller coaster in the dark. Tell seniors that they have to be alert and not trust anyone—not their children, not the Disney people, and especially *not their grandchildren. When your grandkids want you to go on a ride, don't follow along blindly like a lamb to the slaughter.* **He who hesitates is launched!**

Most seniors we interview enjoy Disney World much more when they tour with folks their own age. If, however, you're considering visiting with your grandchildren, we recommend making an orientation visit without them first. This way, it'll be easier to establish limits, maintain control, and set a comfortable pace later on.

If you're *determined* to take the grandkids, read carefully the sections of this book that discuss family touring. (*Hint:* The Dumbo-or-Die-in-a-Day Touring Plan has been known to bring grown-ups of all ages to their knees.)

And when it comes to attractions, we feel that personal taste trumps age. We hate to see seniors pass up a full-blown adventure like Splash Mountain because it's a so-called thrill ride—it gets its appeal more from music and visual effects than from the thrill of the ride. Use our attraction profiles to help you make informed decisions.

GETTING AROUND

unofficial TIP
Park maps issued to each guest on admission are coded to show which attractions accommodate wheelchairs.

MANY SENIORS LIKE TO WALK, but a 7-hour visit to a theme park includes 4–10 miles on foot. Not up to that? Consider renting a wheelchair or mobility vehicle.

Wheelchairs rent (minus tax) for $12 with no deposit required, $10 per day for multiday rentals, and free at your Disney resort ($315 deposit). Rentals are available at all Walt Disney World theme parks (see Parts Nine through Twelve for specific locations) and at Disney Springs. ECVs and ESVs cost $50 per day, plus a $20 refundable deposit ($100 at Disney Springs); call ☎ 407-824-5217 to reserve a vehicle. Wheelchairs are welcome at Disney's Blizzard Beach and Typhoon Lagoon water parks but are unavailable for rent.

Buena Vista Scooters (☎ 866-484-4797 or 407-938-0349; buena vistascooters.com) rents ECVs for $50 per day for one day or $30 per day for two or more days, with free delivery to and pickup from your Disney resort. For rentals of three or more days, **Apple Scooter** (☎ 321-726-6837; applescooter.com) is slightly less expensive, with the same fee delivery and pickup at Disney resorts.

Your wheelchair-rental deposit slip is good for a replacement wheelchair in any park during the same day. You can rent a chair at the Magic Kingdom in the morning, return it, go to any other park, present your deposit slip, and get another chair at no additional charge.

TIMING YOUR VISIT

RETIREES SHOULD MAKE THE MOST of their flexible schedules and go to Walt Disney World in the fall or spring (excluding holiday weeks), when the weather is nicest and the crowds are usually the thinnest. Crowds are also generally sparse from late January through early February. See Part One, page 41, for more information on the best times of year to visit.

LODGING

IF YOU CAN AFFORD IT, STAY IN WALT DISNEY WORLD. Rooms are among the Orlando–Kissimmee area's nicest, and transportation is always available to any Disney destination at no additional cost.

Disney hotels reserve rooms close to restaurants and transportation for guests of any age who can't tolerate much walking. They also provide golf carts to pick up and deliver guests at their rooms. Service can vary dramatically depending on the time of day and the number of guests requesting carts. At check-in time (around 3 p.m.), for example, the wait for a ride can be as long as 40 minutes.

Here are four reasons to consider staying in Disney World:

1. The quality of the properties is consistently above average.
2. Staying in the World guarantees transportation when you need it. Disney buses run about every 20 minutes. (If you miss the last bus, though, you may need to call an Uber, Lyft, or taxi.)
3. You get free parking in major theme parks' lots.
4. You get preferential tee times on resort golf courses.

Walt Disney World hotels are spread out. It's easy to avoid most stairs, but it's often a long hike to your room from parking lots or bus stops. Seniors intending to spend more time at Epcot and Hollywood Studios than at the Magic Kingdom or Animal Kingdom should consider the **BoardWalk Inn & Villas,** the **Dolphin, Swan,** or the **Yacht & Beach Club Resorts.**

The **Contemporary Resort** and **Bay Lake Tower** are good choices for seniors who want to be on the monorail system. So are the **Grand Floridian** and the **Polynesian Village,** though they cover many acres, necessitating a lot of walking. For a restful, rustic feeling, choose **Wilderness Lodge & Boulder Creek Villas.** If you want a kitchen and the comforts of home, book **Animal Kingdom Villas, Beach Club Villas, BoardWalk Villas, Grand Floridian Villas, Old Key West Resort, Saratoga Springs,** or **Polynesian Villas & Bungalows.** If you enjoy watching birds and animals, try **Animal Kingdom Lodge & Villas.** Try **Saratoga Springs** for golf.

RVers will find pleasant surroundings at **Disney's Fort Wilderness Resort & Campground.** Several independent campgrounds are within 30 minutes of Disney World (see page 238). None offer the wilderness setting or amenities that Disney does, but they cost less.

TRANSPORTATION

ROADS IN DISNEY WORLD CAN BE DAUNTING. Armed with a decent sense of direction and a great sense of humor, however, even the most timid driver can get around. (See Part Seven following.)

Parking for the disabled is available adjacent to each theme park's entrance; toll-plaza attendants will provide a dashboard ticket and direct you to the reserved spaces. Disney requires that you be recognized officially as disabled to use this parking, but temporarily disabled or injured persons also are permitted access.

SENIOR DINING

EAT BREAKFAST AT YOUR HOTEL RESTAURANT or have juice and rolls in your room. Carry snacks in a fanny pack supplemented by fruit, fruit juice, and soft drinks purchased from vendors. Make Advance Reservations for lunch before noon to avoid the crowds. Follow with an early dinner and be out of the restaurants, ready for evening touring and fireworks, long before the main crowd even thinks about dinner.

WALT DISNEY WORLD *for* GUESTS *with* SPECIAL NEEDS

DISNEY WORLD IS SO ATTUNED TO GUESTS with physical challenges that unscrupulous people have been known to fake a disability in order to take unfair advantage. If you have a disability, Disney World is prepared to meet your needs.

Each theme park offers a free booklet describing disabled services and facilities at disneyworld.disney.go.com/guest-services/guests-with -disabilities. Or get it when you enter the parks, at resort front desks, and at wheelchair-rental locations inside the parks. More-limited information is available online at disneyworld.disney.go.com/plain-text.

For specific requests, call ☎ 407-939-7807 (voice) or 407-939-7670 (TTY). When the recorded menu comes up, press 1. Limit your questions and requests to those regarding disabled services and accommodations (address other questions to ☎ 407-824-4321 or 407-827-5141 [TTY]). If you'll be staying at a Disney resort, let the reservation agent know of any special needs you have when you book your room.

Following and on the next page are equipment, services, and facilities available at Disney hotels; note that not all hotels offer all items.

• Accessible vanities	• Portable commodes
• Bed and bathroom rails	• Refrigerators
• Braille on signs and elevators	• Rubber bed padding
• Closed-captioned televisions	• Shower benches
• Double peepholes in doors	• Strobe-light smoke detectors

• Handheld showerheads	• Roll-in showers
• Knock and phone alerts	• TTYs
• Lowered beds	• Wheelchairs
• Phone amplifiers	• Widened bathroom doors

Service animals are welcome at all Disney resorts and theme parks.

Much of the Disney transportation system is disability-accessible. Monorails can be accessed by ramp or elevator, and all bus routes are served by vehicles with wheelchair lifts, though unusually wide or long wheelchairs (or motorized chairs) may not fit the lift. Watercraft accommodations for wheelchairs are iffier. If you plan to stay at Wilderness Lodge & Villas, Fort Wilderness Campground, or an Epcot resort, call ☎ 407-939-7807 (voice) or 407-939-7670 (TTY) for the latest information on watercraft accessibility.

Food and merchandise locations at theme parks, Disney Springs, and hotels are generally accessible, but some fast-food queues and shop aisles are too narrow for wheelchairs. At these locations, ask a cast member or member of your party for assistance.

VISITORS WITH DISABILITIES

WHOLLY OR PARTIALLY NONAMBULATORY guests may rent wheelchairs. Most rides, shows, attractions, restrooms, and restaurants accommodate the nonambulatory disabled. If you're in a park and need assistance, go to Guest Relations.

A limited number of electric carts, ECVs (electric convenience vehicles), and ESVs (electric standing vehicles) are available for rent. They give nonambulatory guests tremendous freedom and mobility.

All Disney lots have close-in parking for disabled visitors. Request directions when you pay your parking fee. All monorails and most rides, shows, restrooms, and restaurants accommodate wheelchairs.

Even if an attraction doesn't accommodate wheelchairs, ECVs, or ESVs, nonambulatory guests may ride if they can transfer from their wheelchair to the ride's vehicle. Disney staff, however, aren't trained or permitted to assist with transfers—guests must be able to board the ride unassisted or have a member of their party assist them. Either way, members of the nonambulatory guest's party will be permitted to ride with him or her.

Because the waiting areas of most attractions won't accommodate wheelchairs, nonambulatory guests and their parties should ask a cast member for boarding instructions as soon as they arrive at an attraction entrance.

Disabled guests and their families give Disney high marks for accessibility and sensitivity. An Arlington, Virginia, woman writes:

Disney is dynamite in its treatment of handicapped vacationers. My mom has mobility problems, and she was worried about getting around. Disney supplied a free wheelchair, every bus had kneeling steps for wheelchair users, and the cast members sprang into action when they saw us coming.

DIETARY RESTRICTIONS AND ALLERGIES Walt Disney World restaurants work hard to accommodate guests' special dietary needs. When you make a dining reservation online or by phone, you'll be asked about food allergies and the like. When you arrive at table-service restaurants and buffets, alert the host or hostess and your server.

Similarly, many counter-service restaurants have special allergy-friendly menus available upon request; just ask any cast member when you arrive at the restaurant. TouringPlans.com also maintains a list of Disney World restaurant menus, including most special offerings and prices—look for the words "allergy friendly" on the menu list at tinyurl.com/allergymenuswdw. For more information, e-mail special .diets@disneyworld.com or visit tinyurl.com/wdwspecialdiets.

An Idaho mom and her teenage daughter found Disney restaurants very responsive to their dietary needs:

> My daughter and I both have a gluten allergy. I have never felt so well cared for and safe eating anywhere else in the world. From our resort (both the food court and Boatwright's) to every single quick-service or sit-down restaurant, we had several choices, and we never waited longer than 8 minutes for our "special" orders.

To request kosher meals at table-service restaurants, call ☎ 407-WDW-DINE 48 hours in advance. All Disney menus have vegetarian options; vegans may have to talk to the chef. Vegetarians, vegans, and pescetarians should speak up when making dining reservations.

Folks with special diets *and* a sweet tooth should try the vegan, gluten-free, and kosher treats from **Erin McKenna's Bakery NYC,** with locations at Disney Springs, many Disney hotel food courts, and Animal Kingdom's Tewa Treats. Besides sweets, the bakery does a tasty line of savory focaccia every once in a while. You can also order special-occasion cakes and baked goods by phone or online (☎ 407-938-9044 or 855-462-2292; erinmckennasbakery.com/orlando).

For guests who are subject to allergic reactions that can be severe or life-threatening, Disney provides epinephrine injectors (**EpiPens**) at First Aid Centers and other locations throughout the parks. These locations are shown on guide maps. Nurses and emergency responders are trained in EpiPen use, but guests with known conditions should always travel with their own supplies.

SIGHT- AND/OR HEARING-IMPAIRED GUESTS Guest Relations at the parks provides free assistive-technology devices to visually and hearing-impaired guests ($25 refundable deposit, depending on the device). Sight-impaired guests can customize the given information (such as architectural details, restroom locations, and descriptions of attractions and restaurants) through an interactive audio menu that is guided by a GPS in the device. Hearing-impaired guests can benefit from amplified audio and closed-captioning for attractions loaded into the same device.

Braille guidebooks are available from Guest Relations at all parks ($25 refundable deposit), and Braille menus are available at some theme park restaurants. Some rides provide closed-captioning; many theater attractions provide reflective captioning.

Disney provides sign-language interpretations of live shows at the theme parks on certain designated days of the week:

THE MAGIC KINGDOM: Mondays and Thursdays
EPCOT: Fridays

DISNEY'S ANIMAL KINGDOM: Saturdays and Tuesdays
DISNEY'S HOLLYWOOD STUDIOS: Sundays and Wednesdays

Get confirmation of the interpreted-performance schedule a minimum of one week in advance by calling Disney World information at ☎ 407-824-4321 (voice) or 407-827-5141 (TTY). You'll be contacted before your visit with a show schedule that lists the names, dates, and times of the interpreted performances.

NONAPPARENT DISABILITIES We receive many letters from readers whose traveling companion or child requires special assistance but who, unlike a person in a wheelchair, is not visibly disabled. Autism, for example, can make it very difficult or impossible for someone to wait in line for more than a few minutes or in queues surrounded by a crowd.

A trip to Disney World can be nonetheless positive and rewarding for guests who are on the autism spectrum. And while any Disney vacation requires planning, a little extra effort to accommodate the affected person will pay large dividends.

Disney's PDF **Guide for Guests with Cognitive Disabilities** is available for download at tinyurl.com/cognitivedisabilitiesguide.

Disney's Disability Access Service (DAS)

THE DISABILITY ACCESS SERVICE (DAS) is designed to accommodate guests who can't wait in regular standby lines. Sign up for the service at the Guest Relations window of the first theme park you visit. You only need to sign up once; the service carries over to each subsequent park you visit. For clarity, we'll refer to the person signing up for the DAS service as the "DAS enrollee."

Bring the MagicBands or park tickets of everyone in your group to Guest Relations. All of your group's MagicBands/tickets will be linked to the DAS—this comes in handy in situations we'll describe below. It also helps to have the My Disney Experience (MDE) app loaded on your smartphone; the DAS works like FastPass+, and DAS reservations are displayed in MDE.

At Guest Relations, present identification, and describe your or your family member's limitations. You don't need to disclose a specific medical condition: What Disney is looking for is a description of how the condition affects you in the parks. Their goal is to get you the right level of assistance, not to obligate you to prove that you qualify.

Be as detailed as possible in describing limitations. For instance, if your child is on the autism spectrum and has trouble waiting in long lines or has sensory issues that make it difficult for him or her to stand or tolerate loud noises, let the cast member know each of these things.

The DAS also requires a photograph. Pictures are taken with an iPad (the cast member will come to you if you can't make it up to the counter.) If the DAS is for a child, you may use either the child's photo or substitute your own. Finally, you must agree to be bound by its rules.

The DAS may be used at any attraction or meet and greet with a FastPass+ line. Anyone with a linked MagicBand or ticket can present it outside the attraction; if the standby wait time is less than 10 minutes, you'll usually be escorted through the standby entrance or FastPass+ entrance. If the standby time is higher, a cast member will provide a time for you to return to ride—again, this is entered into MDE.

The return time will be the current wait time minus 10 minutes—if, say, you get to Splash Mountain at 12:20 p.m. and the standby time is 40 minutes, your return time will be 30 minutes later, at 12:50 p.m.

You may return at the specified time or at any time thereafter. The DAS enrollee must also return to ride. When you return, the enrollee will scan his or her MagicBand first, followed by the other members of your group. Everyone will be given access to the FastPass+ line.

The DAS is good for parties of up to six people. For parties of more than six, all members must be present when the card is used. The DAS is good (1) for the duration of your vacation or (2) for 14 days (60 days for Annual Pass holders), whichever is shortest.

You can also use FastPass+ while you're using the DAS. In fact, cast members will suggest you do so. It may take some extra planning on the front end, but using FastPass+ helps your DAS access.

FRIENDS OF BILL W.

FOR INFORMATION ON **Alcoholics Anonymous** meetings in the Walt Disney World area, including Celebration, Four Corners, Kissimmee, and St. Cloud, visit osceolaintergroup.org. For information on **Al-Anon** and **Alateen** meetings in the area, visit al-anonorlando.org.

INTERNATIONAL VISITORS

DISNEY HAS DEVELOPED A WIRELESS DEVICE called **Ears to the World** that provides synchronized narration in French, German, Japanese, Portuguese, or Spanish for more than 30 attractions in the theme parks. The wireless, lightweight headsets provide real-time translation and are available for a $25 refundable deposit at Guest Relations in all parks.

A mom from Minorca, Spain, offers advice to readers who are making the long haul to Walt Disney World:

> *You cannot predict how the time difference is going to affect you or the little people. Coming from Spain, we were looking at a 9-hour flight from the UK and a 6-hour time difference, and we spent our first few days in a haze after trying to do too much too soon.*

Londoner and *Unofficial* friend Andrew Dakoutros sent us this grab bag of tips and warnings for other Disney-bound Brits:

> *(1) Magical Express doesn't automatically take your bags from the carousel; (2) Jellyrolls [the piano bar at Disney's BoardWalk] doesn't accept UK driving licences as ID for entry [they accept passports]; (3) MagicBands are not mailed to UK addresses; (4) many MouseSavers codes [see page 40] can't be used from the UK; (5) the Twinings tea at The Tea Caddy [at Epcot] doesn't taste as good as in London.*
>
> *Additionally, you need to emphasise how hot Florida is and the importance of sunscreen. Most Britons holiday in Spain or Greece, where the sun is nowhere near as strong.*
>
> *Brits also like to go shopping, and at two stores in particular: Abercrombie and Hollister. We consider these luxury brands—prices in Florida are about 30% less than in the UK—so every holiday to the US tends to involve a visit to one of those two stores.*

PART SEVEN

ARRIVING *and* GETTING AROUND

▌ GETTING THERE

DIRECTIONS

YOU CAN DRIVE to any Walt Disney World destination via **World Drive** off US 192; via **Epcot Center Drive** off Interstate 4; via **FL 536** and **Osceola Parkway West** from FL 417/Central Florida GreeneWay (a toll road); or from the **Western Way** interchange off FL 429, also known as the Western Beltway (see all maps in this chapter).

FROM INTERSTATE 10 Take I-10 east across Florida to I-75 southbound at Exit 296A/Tampa, and then take Florida's Turnpike (a toll road) southbound at Exit 328 (on the left) toward Orlando. Take FL 429 (another toll road) to Exit 267A/Tampa southbound off the turnpike. Leave FL 429 at Exit 8, the Western Way interchange, in the direction of Walt Disney World, and follow the signs to your Disney destination. Also use these directions to reach hotels along US 192 (also known as Irlo Bronson Memorial Highway).

unofficial **TIP**
Interstate 4 is technically an east–west highway, but it actually runs diagonally (northeast– southwest) across Florida. In metro Orlando, it runs mostly north– south—and that can complicate getting your bearings if you're not familiar with the area. Most highways branching off I-4 run east and west here, not north and south as logic might suggest.

FROM INTERSTATE 75 SOUTHBOUND Take I-75 south onto Florida's Turnpike via Exit 328 (on the left) toward Orlando. Take FL 429 (toll) southbound off the turnpike. Leave FL 429 at Exit 8, the Western Way interchange, in the direction of Walt Disney World, and follow the signs to your Disney destination. Also use these directions to reach hotels along US 192 (Irlo Bronson Memorial Highway).

THE I-4 BLUES Over many years of covering Disney World, we've watched I-4 turn from a highway into a parking lot. The greatest congestion is between the Universal Orlando–International Drive area and downtown Orlando, but the section to the southwest serving the Disney World exits has also become a choke point, seemingly irrespective of the time of day. If you're going from Walt Disney World toward Orlando (east), the jam usually breaks up after you pass the FL 535 exit, but it gets congested again near Universal Orlando and northeast due to construction. As you head west toward Tampa, traffic eases up after the US 192 interchange.

In addition to extremely heavy traffic, I-4 is in the midst of two contiguous, six-year construction projects that affect the entire stretch of the highway from FL 434 north of Orlando, southwest past downtown Orlando, past the Universal Orlando exits, and past all the Walt Disney World exits. The projects extend to the intersection of US 27, southwest of Walt Disney World in Polk County. Optimistically scheduled to be completed in 2021, the project includes widening, paving, constructing new interchanges, improving existing interchanges, adding two express toll lanes in each direction, and adding access/egress ramps. There are also unrelated projects on I-4 extending southwest from Daytona and I-95; near Samford north of Orlando; and from US 27 to US 92 farther southwest. To summarize, I-4 is pretty much a mess from Tampa to Daytona.

If you're considering a hotel on or near I-Drive, try to find one toward the southern end of I-Drive. If the I-4 traffic becomes intolerable, it's pretty easy to commute from the Universal Orlando–International Drive area to Walt Disney World on (1) Turkey Lake Road, connecting to Palm Parkway and FL 535 on the northwest side of I-4; (2) the southernmost section of I-Drive, connecting to FL 536 on the southeast side of the interstate; or (3) Daryl Carter Parkway, which bridges I-4 just northeast of FL 535, connecting Palm Parkway and International Drive near the Orlando Vineland Premium Outlets.

MORE CONSTRUCTION PROJECTS on several intersecting highways important to tourists include FL 528 (Beachline Expressway) in the section that runs between Orlando International Airport (MCO) and I-4; West Sand Lake Road between Florida's Turnpike and I-4; and FL 536 between FL 535 and I-4.

AVOIDING I-4 CONSTRUCTION Following we offer alternative routes based on the assumption that construction in the affected areas will continue into 2018 and beyond. Before you take any of the recommended detours, however, verify using the links listed, that the construction zones are still active. If you're driving at very low traffic times, you might prefer to deal with the I-4 construction rather than take a detour. During the day, 6 a.m.–10 p.m., most projects try to keep all lanes open, though traffic sometimes slows to a crawl (as it does in the Disney World area even when there's no roadwork in progress). From 10 p.m. to 6 a.m., however, there are lane closures.

Real-time road conditions are available at i4exitguide.com/i-4 -traffic, and an interactive map showing all active construction projects in Florida can be found at fdot.gov/agencyresources/maps/projects. Info about construction in Orlando and the tourist areas is available at Central Florida Roads (cflroads.com), an FDOT website. For information and current conditions on area toll roads, see cfxway.com.

TECH TIP On long road trips, use a GPS device that's smart enough to accept traffic updates and route you around delays. TomTom GPS units, for example, have an accessory cable that picks up traffic signals from

I-4 & Walt Disney World Area

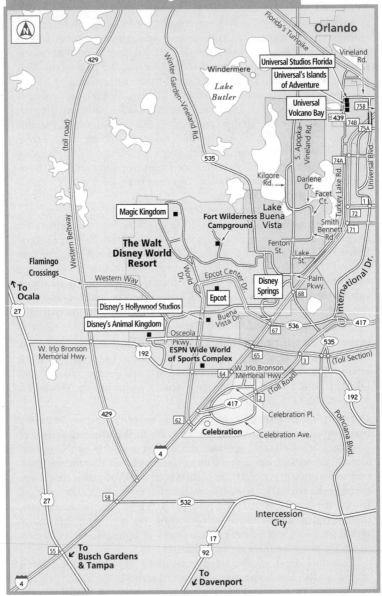

HD radio broadcasts. If you have a newer smartphone, the app Waze (free; iOS, Android, and Windows Phone; waze.com), also does this.

TRAVELING SOUTHWEST ON I-4, we recommend going around Orlando on FL 417/Central Florida GreeneWay (a toll road), exiting on West Osceola Parkway into Walt Disney World. In addition to construction in Orlando and the Disney World area, there's also construction between Daytona and Deland. To avoid this part of I-4, exit I-95 onto US 92 westbound, and turn south (left) onto US 17. When you hit I-4, take it west a short distance to FL 417, and bypass Orlando to the east. Be sure to have about $2 in quarters with you.

TRAVELING EAST ON I-4 It's pretty much impossible to miss the construction in Polk County, and there are no good workarounds. Construction in Polk County is more of a problem at night.

FROM I-95 SOUTHBOUND Exit I-95 onto US 92 westbound; turn south (left) onto US 17. When you hit I-4, take it west a short distance to FL 417; bypass Orlando to the east, exiting onto West Osceola Parkway and then into Walt Disney World. Have about $2 in quarters with you.

FROM I-95 NORTHBOUND Exit I-95 onto FL 44 toward Deland. At I-4, go southwest, exiting onto Saxon Boulevard. Take Saxon Boulevard west to US 17, and turn south (left). When you hit I-4 again, take it west a short distance to FL 417. Take FL 417, and bypass Orlando to the east. Be sure to have about $2 in quarters with you.

FROM SANFORD INTERNATIONAL AIRPORT Take East Airport Boulevard west to FL 417/Central Florida GreeneWay (a toll road), and bypass Orlando to the east, exiting on West Osceola Parkway and continuing into Walt Disney World. Be sure to have about $2 in quarters with you.

FROM ORLANDO INTERNATIONAL AIRPORT (MCO) There are two basic routes, but there is construction on the northern one, the Beachline Expressway (FL 528), between the airport and I-4. Until the roadwork is completed, take the other route. Exit the airport on Jeff Fuqua Boulevard and proceed south to FL 417/Central Florida GreeneWay (a toll road). Turn right up the ramp and take FL 417 northwest. Exit onto West Osceola Parkway and follow it to Walt Disney World. Be sure to have about $2 in quarters with you.

FROM MIAMI, FORT LAUDERDALE, AND SOUTHEASTERN FLORIDA Head north on Florida's Turnpike to Exit 249/Osceola Parkway West, and follow the signs.

FROM TAMPA AND SOUTHWESTERN FLORIDA Take I-75 northbound to I-4; then drive east on I-4, take Exit 64 onto US 192 West, and follow the signs.

Walt Disney World Exits off I-4

East to west (in the direction of Orlando to Tampa), five I-4 exits serve Walt Disney World:

EXIT 68 (FL 535/LAKE BUENA VISTA) primarily serves the Disney Springs Resort Area and Disney Springs, including the Marketplace and the West Side. It also serves non-Disney hotels with a Lake Buena Vista address. This exit puts you on a road with lots of traffic signals, especially near I-4. Avoid it unless you're headed to one of the preceding destinations.

EXIT 67 (FL 536/EPCOT/DISNEY SPRINGS) delivers you to a four-lane expressway into the heart of Disney World. It's the fastest and most convenient way for westbound travelers to access almost all Disney destinations except Disney's Animal Kingdom and ESPN Wide World of Sports Complex. Be alert for road construction.

EXIT 65 (OSCEOLA PARKWAY) is the best exit for westbound travelers to access Disney's Animal Kingdom, Animal Kingdom Lodge, Pop Century Resort, Art of Animation Resort, the All-Star Resorts, and ESPN Wide World of Sports Complex.

EXIT 64 (US 192/MAGIC KINGDOM) is the best route for eastbound travelers to all Disney destinations.

EXIT 62 (DISNEY WORLD/CELEBRATION) is the first Disney exit you'll encounter heading east. This four-lane, controlled-access highway connects to the Walt Disney World Maingate. Accessing Disney World via the next exit, Exit 64, also routes you through the main entrance.

ALTERNATIVE AIRPORTS

A SHORT DISTANCE northeast of Orlando is **Sanford International Airport (SFB; orlandosanfordairport.com).** Small, convenient, and easily accessible, it's low-hassle compared with the huge Orlando International Airport (MCO) and its block-long security-checkpoint lines.

The primary domestic carrier serving Sanford International is **Allegiant Air** (☎ 702-505-8888; allegiantair.com), with service from large and small airports throughout the East Coast and the Midwest. European carriers include **ArkeFly** (Netherlands; ☎ 855-808-4015; arke fly.nl), **Icelandair** (☎ 800-223-5500; icelandair.com), **Monarch** (UK: ☎ +44 (0) 1582 398 036; flymonarch.com), and **Thomson Airways** (UK: ☎ 0871 231 4691; thomson.co.uk). Finally, **SST Air** (☎ 407-288-8820; sstair.com) offers seasonal charter flights between Sanford and various cities in Brazil. Other airlines include **Jetairfly** (☎ +32 (0) 70 22 00 00; jetairfly.com); **National Airlines** (☎ 855-757-6999; nationalairlines .com); **OrangeAir** (☎ 888-359-2541; flyorangeair.com); **Surinam Air** (flyslm.com); and **TUI** (☎ 855-808-4015; tui.nl/vliegtickets).

A reader from Roanoke, Virginia, uses Sanford frequently, writing:

The 45-minute drive to WDW is more than made up for by avoiding the chaos at Orlando International, and it's stress-free.

From another reader:

I couldn't be happier with our car service out of Sanford. Bob Martinez of **Better Deal Transport** *(betterdealtransport.com) was our driver. It was $180 round-trip, no hidden fees, gratuity included. He was great—flexible, patient, and in touch through the day as we dealt with delays. That part of the experience couldn't have been better.*

Other readers, like this couple from White Township, New Jersey, prefer flying into Tampa instead:

We've found that flying from Newark to Tampa instead of Orlando saves us money and our sanity. It means significantly lower fares, fewer children on the plane, and shorter security lines.

Be aware, however, that it's an 77-mile drive from Tampa International Airport to the Magic Kingdom—about an hour and 15 minutes.

SECURITY AT ORLANDO INTERNATIONAL AIRPORT

THIS AIRPORT HANDLES ABOUT 35 MILLION PASSENGERS a year. It's not unusual to see lines from the checkpoints snaking out of the terminal and into the main shopping corridor and food court. A number of passengers have reported missing their flights even when they arrived at the airport 90 minutes before departure. System improvements have alleviated some, but by no means all, of the congestion. Most waits to clear security average less than 15 minutes, compared with 55 minutes or longer before the improvements. Check tinyurl. com/mcowaits for current security wait times.

unofficial **TIP**
We recommend arriving at MCO 90 minutes–2 hours before your scheduled departure.

GETTING TO DISNEY WORLD FROM THE AIRPORT

YOU CURRENTLY HAVE FIVE OPTIONS for getting from Orlando International Airport (**MCO**) to Walt Disney World:

1. TAXI Taxis carry four to eight passengers (depending on vehicle type). Rates vary according to distance. If your hotel is in the World, your fare will be about $60–$72, plus tip. For the US 192 Maingate area, it will cost about $55. To International Drive or downtown Orlando, expect to pay in the neighborhood of $38–$50.

2. SHUTTLE SERVICE Mears Transportation Group (☎ 855-463-2776; mearstransportation.com) provides your transportation if your vacation package includes airport transfers. Nonpackage travelers can also use the service. The shuttles collect passengers until they fill a van (or bus). They're then dispatched. Mears charges *per-person* rates (children under age 3 ride free). One-way and round-trip services are available. See the chart below for a fare breakdown.

You might have to wait at the airport until a vehicle fills. Once under way, the shuttle will probably stop several times to discharge passengers before reaching your hotel.

From your hotel to the airport, you're likely to ride in a van (unless you're part of a tour group, for which Mears might send a bus). Because shuttles make several pickups, you must leave much earlier than if you were taking a cab or returning a rental car.

FROM THE AIRPORT TO:	ONE-WAY ADULT/CHILD	ROUND-TRIP ADULT/CHILD
INTERNATIONAL DRIVE	$21/$16	$33/$25
DOWNTOWN ORLANDO (leaves hourly)	$20/$16	$32/$24
DSRA RESORTS–LAKE BUENA VISTA	$23/$18	$37/$28
US 192 MAINGATE AREA	$23/$18	$37/$28

3. TOWN-CAR SERVICE Like a taxi, town-car service will transport you directly from the airport to your hotel. The driver will usually be waiting for you in your airline's baggage-claim area. If saving time and hassle is worth the money, book a town car.

Each town-car service we surveyed offers large, well-appointed late-model sedans or limousines, which hold four passengers (to reserve a child's car seat, call ahead). Trunks easily hold golf bags.

Tiffany Towncar Service (☎ 888-838-2161 or 407-370-2196; tiffany towncars.com) provides a prompt, clean ride. The round-trip fee to a Disney or non-Disney resort in a town car is $130–$140 plus tip; one-way is about $75–$80.

Quicksilver Tours & Transportation (☎ 888-468-6939 or 407-299-1434; quicksilver-tours.com) offers 8-person limos and 10-person vans as well as 4-person town cars. Round-trip town-car rates range from $125 to $130, depending on location; round-trip van rates range from $140 to $145; round-trip limo rate is $240.

Mears Transportation Group (☎ 855-463-2776; mearstransporta tion.com) also offers a town-car service for around $180 round-trip.

4. RENTAL CARS Short- and long-term rentals are available. Most companies allow drop-off at certain hotels or subsidiary locations in the Disney area if you don't want the vehicle for your entire stay. Likewise, at any time during your stay, you can pick up a car at those hotels and locations. Check mousesavers.com for rental-car discount codes.

The preferred routes to Walt Disney World, Universal Orlando, Sea-World, I-Drive, and US 192 all involve toll roads. Some roads require exact change to enter or exit via automated gates, and manned toll booths will not accept any currency denomination larger than a $20 bill. So before you leave the airport, make sure you're armed with at least a couple of dollars in quarters and some ones, fives, and tens.

On the subject of toll roads, don't be surprised if your rental company tries to (aggressively) sell you, or slip in, a bunch of extras. Foreign visitors are especially targeted. An Egham, United Kingdom, reader reported this:

> They tried hard to sell us unnecessary extras, such as a $50 cash-less toll system, whereas the actual tolls to/from the theme park area came to $4.50. Also, they do seem to have slipped about $100 of extras past me, although I was never asked and never agreed to anything. The rental companies try to frighten tourists into buying the cashless toll system by saying that some tolls don't accept cash and there will be heavy fines if you go through one. Our experience was that it was not necessary and would have been a waste of money.

For most theme park visitors, the only tolls you'll have to pay are on roads from and to the airport.

5. RIDE-SHARING SERVICES **Lyft** (lyft.com), **Uber** (uber.com), and similar services use ordinary people and their cars as an informal taxi service. Customers use a mobile app to find drivers in their area and estimate the length and cost of the ride.

As of July 1, 2017, both Lyft and Uber can pick you up and drop you off at the airport. Pickup details were still being worked on as we were going to press; the proposed pickup location was going to be on the airport's second level, the same as where passengers are currently picked up by family and friends.

These services can also save you money commuting within the World. On a recent trip from Saratoga Springs Resort to the Magic Kingdom via Fort Wilderness, for example, Uber charged us $8.60, while the return taxi ride along the same route, in the same traffic, was $21.40. To avoid the potential hassle of a traffic stop, make sure your driver is city-compliant: Look for a blue sticker on the vehicle's windshield, and check that the driver is wearing an ID badge. A family from Elmhurst, Illinois, used Uber to escape the World:

> We took Uber between our WDW resort and Universal. It was really convenient and only cost about $14 each way for the three of us.

And from an Indianapolis, Indiana, couple:

> If you are using a touring plan to make the most of your day and have tight timelines, I can't recommend Uber enough. We used the monorail and buses during the day and evening, but when it came to making it to our breakfast reservations on time and getting over to Animal Kingdom for rope drop, Uber was immediately our first choice. We were able to get there without having to lose extra sleep getting to the bus stop early. We never waited for a car for longer than 4 minutes, and the drivers were friendly and quick.

DISNEY'S MAGICAL EXPRESS

THIS FREE BUS SERVICE shuttles guests of Disney-owned and -operated resorts between MCO and Walt Disney World. (The Swan, the Dolphin, Shades of Green, and the hotels of Bonnet Creek Resort and the Disney Springs Resort Area don't participate.) Magical Express also provides free luggage delivery to your resort, except between 10 p.m. and 5 a.m.—if your flight arrives between those hours, you'll need to pick up your stuff from baggage claim before boarding the bus.

First, register your flight information with your resort reservation, either at the time of booking or as soon as you've booked your flights, by calling ☎ 866-599-0951 or using mydisneyexperience.com.

US and Canadian travelers will receive their Magical Express paperwork in the mail 20–40 days before they arrive. The packet contains detailed instructions for getting around the airport, bus vouchers, and tags for checked luggage (one per traveler); **MagicBands** (see page 73) also work as bus vouchers. When it's time for your trip, you'll check your bags as you normally would and plan to see them again in your hotel room. If you've ever been on a cruise, the procedure is similar.

Non-Canadian international travelers won't get their vouchers or tags in the mail; they must go through Customs with bags in hand. Disney will collect the bags for transport at the Magical Express Welcome Center, where international guests will also receive their bus vouchers.

The Magical Express Welcome Center is on the B side of the airport's lower level. Look for signs once you reach the airport's main concourse.

If you already have your bus vouchers or MagicBands, just head straight to the bus check-in. A cast member will scan your vouchers/bands and direct you to a holding area for your resort's bus line. If you've lost or accidentally packed your vouchers/bands or you need other assistance, you'll be directed to the Welcome Center desk.

There's no seating inside the holding area, so if you know that a member of your party will have trouble standing for more than a very short time, let a cast member know. Lines generally move quickly, though, with waits to board rarely exceeding 20 minutes. Once on the bus, try to get a seat up front, since you'll be among the first to get off (and get in line at your hotel). Passengers must be at least 12 years old to ride unaccompanied by an adult.

Buses are shared among resorts—for example, a bus to Old Key West may also stop at Saratoga Springs or Port Orleans. Most of the time, Disney will try to fill a bus before sending it on its way. Each bus has 55 seats, and five buses may load at once. On more than one occasion, particularly for flights arriving very early in the morning or late at night, we've been the only passengers on our bus.

unofficial **TIP**
This is a good place to remind you of Disney's online check-in (see page 157), which will save you time registering at your hotel.

We've usually arrived at our resorts within 90 minutes of stepping off our plane. When you consider that you don't have to wait for your bags and that the trip takes 30 minutes regardless of who's driving, Magical Express is about as efficient an operation as you could hope for.

Your checked bags are picked up at the airport, sorted by destination, and sent directly on to your room—if it's ready. If not, bell services will hold your bags until you're able to get into your room. Because you may be separated from your checked bags for a few hours, remember the following:

- Don't check valuables such as cameras, laptops, or jewelry. This is good advice whether you use Magical Express or not.
- Likewise, don't check anything you'll need quick access to—MagicBands, phone chargers, travel documents, glasses, medication, and such.
- Pack swimsuits and sunscreen in your carry-on bag and enjoy the pool before your bags arrive.
- It's not necessary to check strollers and wheelchairs—these can be stored in your bus's luggage compartment.

If you booked your trip too late to get luggage tags, you can still use the delivery service: Just give the baggage-claim numbers that your airline gave you to the cast members at the Magical Express check-in desk, and they'll pick up and deliver your bags. We've done this before and it worked without a hitch.

THE TRIP HOME The day before you check out of your resort, you'll get a notification from Disney with your return information on it. This will include a time for you to board your bus back to MCO.

If you're checking bags, you'll need to pick up luggage tags separately at your resort lobby's Airline Check-in Desk. As of this edition, six airlines participate in advance check-in: **Alaska, American, Delta, JetBlue, Southwest,** and **United;** guests using these airlines for international flights may use the service as well. As this is also your airline check-in, you'll need to show ID just as you would at the airport. (When you drop off your bags, you'll also get your boarding passes if your flight leaves before noon, otherwise the passes will be delivered to your room on the morning of your departure.) If your airline charges a luggage fee, you'll need to prepay it and provide proof of payment when you drop off your bags. If you're confident your airline will waive the fees (because you've achieved frequent-flyer status, hold the airline's credit card, or something similar), bring proof of that as well when you drop off your bags.

As this Bloomington, Illinois, couple discovered, the major downside to using Magical Express for your return trip is that you'll board your bus only about 3 hours before your flight is scheduled to depart (4 hours for international flights):

On departure day, we stopped at three resorts after we were picked up, arriving at the last resort 50 minutes after we had departed ours. We were on the bus a total of 1 hour and 40 minutes, and our flight began boarding less than 15 minutes after we reached the gate. That's cutting it a little close in our opinion.

A group from Manchester, Connecticut, reports a similar experience:

Our flight out was at 8 a.m.—virtually impossible to get there from the hotel using Magical Express unless you leave at 5 a.m.! Next time we'll rent a car.

Magical Express Considered

What's our take on Magical Express? Well, when we see the word *free* attached to a travel package, our first question is, "What's the catch?" Disney is nothing if not crafty, and the goal of getting folks to use their bus service is to keep people and their wallets inside Walt Disney World. If seeing other area sights (such as Universal) or eating at off-site restaurants is a priority for you, consider renting a car at the airport or at one of the Disney on-site rental desks (see "Renting a Car" on the next page).

A reader from Cary, North Carolina, loved Magical Express:

I appreciated the Magical Express bus and luggage service to and from MCO and the resorts. Bypassing baggage claim on the way in and checking bags for flights at participating resorts make for a pleasant travel experience. I believe it's worth the price of paying for on-property accommodations alone.

The service is not without hiccups, as a mom from Des Moines, Iowa, explains:

We used the Magical Express from the airport. And while I was prepared for the luggage delivery to take a while, I was a little shocked to have them deliver the luggage at 2:30 a.m.! We had landed at the airport at 9 p.m. If I had any idea it would take that long, I would have picked up my luggage at the airport myself. Fortunately, I had packed PJs for my children in our carry-on, so they were able to go to sleep. The adults, however, not so much.

A dad from Ontario, Canada, warns:

On the return trip to the airport, [some international travelers'] bags don't automatically go on the Magical Express—you must get them using claim tickets and put them on the bus yourself. Had it not been for the bus driver, I would have left the resort without my baggage and arrived at the airport thinking all I had to do was show the driver my claim ticket.

A woman from Arlington, Tennessee, warns about unwarranted baggage fees on the return flight:

> [I am] so tired of the hassle at Magical Express luggage check-in [at the resort]. They are determined to collect fees for baggage to the point of it being insane. I had status on the airline and carry the AmEx Delta card. Didn't pay a dime for anyone in my traveling party to bring baggage to Disney, so why do they think I would pay to get the same baggage back home? If they had true visibility into the airlines' systems, they would see that our baggage was already checked in at $0 in fees.

Finally, *not* using Magical Express turned out to be liberating for this Mansfield, Texas, reader. His comments bolster our earlier assertion regarding why Disney offers Magical Express in the first place:

> We rented a car from the airport, which helped us decide to go to Universal for Harry Potter, which made us want to try Discovery Cove. Because we didn't use Magical Express, we ended up spending hundreds of dollars that could have been Disney's.

RENTING A CAR

READERS PLANNING TO STAY in Walt Disney World ask frequently if they'll need a car. If your plans don't include restaurants, attractions, or destinations outside Disney World, then the answer is a very qualified no. But take into account the thoughts of this reader from Washington:

> We rented a car and were glad we did. With a car we could drive to the grocery store to restock our snack supply. It also came in handy for our night out. I shudder at how long it might have taken us to get from the Caribbean Beach to the Polynesian Village to leave our kids at the child-care facility, then back to the Polynesian Village to get the kids, and then back to the Caribbean Beach.

A dad from Avon Lake, Ohio, adds:

> Although we stayed at the Grand Floridian, we found the monorail convenient only for the Magic Kingdom. Of the six nights we stayed, we used our car five days.

From an Ann Arbor, Michigan, mother of three:

> During our stay it was almost impossible to get into any of the Disney restaurants. Purely out of desperation, we rented a car so we could eat outside WDW. We had no problem finding good places to eat at a fraction of what you'd pay inside.

PLAN TO RENT A CAR

1. If your hotel is outside Walt Disney World.
2. If your hotel is in the World but you want to eat someplace other than the theme parks and your hotel.
3. If you plan to return to your hotel for naps or swimming during the day.
4. If you plan to visit other area theme parks or water parks (including Disney's).

Renting a Car at Orlando International Airport

MCO has two terminals: **A** and **B**. Airlines serving Orlando are assigned to one or the other. Each terminal has three levels and a parking garage.

Ticket counters are on Level Three. Baggage claim is on Level Two. Level One is where the car-rental counters are or where you can catch a courtesy vehicle to an off-site rental location.

Orlando is the largest rental-car market in the world. At last count, 31 companies vie for your business. Eleven—**Alamo, Avis, Budget, Dollar, Enterprise, E-Z Rent-A-Car, Firefly Car Rental, Hertz, National,** and **Thrifty**—have counters at each terminal. **Payless** and 19 other companies have locations near the airport and provide courtesy shuttles outside Level One at both terminals. We prefer renting inside the airport, though, because (1) you can complete your paperwork while you wait for your checked luggage to arrive at baggage claim and (2) it's just a short walk to the garage to pick up your car.

unofficial **TIP**
Orlando is one of the least expensive US cities in which to rent a car, with an average rate of $25 a day for the most affordable car. (New York is the most expensive city, at $76 a day.)

If you rent on-site, you'll return your car to the garage adjacent to the terminal where your airline is located. If you return your car to the wrong garage, you'll have to schlep your luggage from one side of the airport to the other to reach your check-in.

Most rental companies charge about $5–$8 a gallon to fill the gas tank. If you plan to drive a lot, prepay for a fill-up so you can return the car empty, or fill up near your hotel on your way back to the airport. If you're taking FL 417, turn right at the Boggy Creek Road exit—it's one exit past the airport exit—and drive about a mile to find the closest gas station to MCO. When you're finished refueling, retrace your route and pass under FL 417 to the airport.

How the Orlando Rental-Car Companies Stack Up

When it comes to renting a car, most *Unofficial Guide* readers are looking for the following, as reflected in the table below:

1. Quick, courteous, and efficient processing on pickup.
2. A nice, well-maintained, late-model automobile.
3. A car that is clean and odor-free.
4. Quick, courteous, and efficient processing on return.
5. If applicable, an efficient shuttle between the rental agency and airport.

COMPANY	PICKUP EFFICIENCY	CONDITION OF CAR	CLEANNESS OF CAR	RETURN EFFICIENCY	OVERALL RATING	SURVEY RANK
NATIONAL	A	A	A	A	A	1
ALAMO	B	A	A	B	A	2
ENTERPRISE	B	A	A	A	A	3
HERTZ	B	A	A	A	A	4
SIXT	C	B	A	B	B	5
AVIS	C	A	A	A	B	6
THRIFTY	B	B	B	B	B	7
BUDGET	C	B	B	A	B	8
DOLLAR	C	B	B	B	B	9
ADVANTAGE	D	B	B	B	B	10
E-Z RENT-A-CAR	C	B	C	B	B	11
FOX	F	D	C	C	D	12

DISCOUNT-CODE *Whac-A-Mole*

IN PAST EDITIONS OF THIS BOOK, we've published the best car-rental discount codes we could find. Then, within a few weeks of the book's release, the rental companies would discontinue the best of the ones we'd printed.

Fortunately, the website **autoslash.com** will automatically search for better car rates (including discounts as they're announced), e-mail you if it finds a lower rate, and optionally rebook you automatically at the lower rate if you want. The Autoslash site and search work both for existing car rental reservations and new requests. If you give Autoslash a try, let us know how it works.

On a scale from A (best) to F (worst), the table shows how readers rate the Orlando operations of each company. To participate in our survey, go to touringplans.com/walt-disney-world /survey.

This year, *Unofficial Guide* readers rated **National Car Rental** as the top rental company in Orlando for the eighth time in the past nine years. **Alamo,** the other winner, came in a close second. In fact, with the exception of Fox's and Advantage's car-pickup process (plus Sixt, in our experience), most of the major rental companies are delivering consistently good service.

Readers are spot-on about Fox's pickup process. Be prepared for the customer-service desk to assume you're going to steal the car; the voluminous paperwork is just there to help the bounty hunters find you. We think Fox's car-return folks are super, though.

At the Sixt office, the pace is glacial. During our last visit, we estimated that the five agents working could process no more than 15 car rentals per hour, combined. That, along with the customer service issues we've had, are enough for us to recommend going elsewhere.

If you rent a car, a 6%–7% sales tax, a $2.50-per-day airport-facility surcharge, and a vehicle-license-recovery fee of 45 cents–$2.02 per day will be added to your bill. Some companies, including Alamo, add fees for tire and battery wear, and something called a "Florida surcharge." Luckily, you can rent a car at your hotel on the day you actually need it.

The Insurance Thing

Anyone who rents a car should know what his or her auto insurance does and doesn't cover. If you have the slightest question about your coverage, call your agent. A corollary discussion pertains to added coverage from your credit card company if the rental fee is charged on the card. Usually, credit card coverage picks up deductibles and some ancillary charges that your auto-insurance policy doesn't cover. The tune is the same, however: Make sure you understand what is and isn't covered.

The Public-Transportation Alternative

Some hotel shuttles outside of Walt Disney World don't operate early enough to get you to the parks before opening. An alternative is the **LYNX** public bus system. If you're staying in downtown Orlando, on International Drive south of the Beachline Expressway, or along Palm Parkway in Lake Buena Vista, you can take the LYNX **#50 bus** to the Walt Disney World Transportation and Ticket Center (TTC). The bus runs outbound daily from 5:15 a.m. to 11:40 p.m. and inbound from 5:28 a.m. to 1:05 a.m. Precise hours of service vary depending on where along the route you are. Use the online trip planner at golynx.com or call ☎ 407-841-LYNX for travel information. A Slaughter, Louisiana, woman gives the service high marks:

> We stayed at a hotel that was on the LYNX #50 bus line. It was perfect for getting to and from the park without having to wait for the hotel shuttles to start, which would have had us arriving after park opening. For 8 bucks, we couldn't beat it!

The downside is that the trip on the #50 bus takes almost 2 hours terminal-to-terminal; figure about 50 minutes or so if you board south of the Beachline Expressway. The **#56 bus** runs from Kissimmee to the TTC along US 192 (Irlo Bronson Memorial Highway), a trip of 1.25 hours one-way. The closer you are to Disney World and the farther you are from downtown Kissimmee, the shorter the trip.

GETTING ORIENTED

A GOOD MAP

READERS FREQUENTLY COMPLAIN about the quality of signs and maps provided by Disney. While it's easy to find the theme parks, locating other Disney destinations can be challenging: Disney-supplied maps are often hard to read or lacking in detail. Your best bet, in addition to the maps in this guide, is a Walt Disney World road map created by **Alamo Rent A Car.** Get it from the front desk or concierge at the resorts.

A good, free map of the Orlando–Kissimmee–Disney World area is available at the **Car Care Center**, near the Magic Kingdom parking lot.

Google Maps has a detailed interactive map of Walt Disney World; see google.com/maps; an official resort map at disneyworld.disney.go .com/maps also offers excellent detail. The Disney official map provides resort detail only, while the Google Maps version includes nearby non-Disney hotels, businesses, and roads.

GPS COORDINATES FOR THE THEME PARKS

CHECK WHETHER YOUR GPS UNIT already includes Disney's theme parks. If not, use these coordinates to guide you. Supplement them with Disney's road signs, which will direct you to parking as you get close.

DESTINATION PARKING LOT	GPS ADDRESS	LATITUDE AND LONGITUDE
THE MAGIC KINGDOM	3111 World Dr. Lake Buena Vista, FL 32830	N28° 25.124' W81° 34.871'
EPCOT	200 Epcot Center Dr. Lake Buena Vista, FL 32830	N28° 22.869' W81° 32.964'
ANIMAL KINGDOM	2801 Osceola Pkwy. Lake Buena Vista, FL 32380	N28° 21.480' W81° 35.426'
DHS	351 S. Studio Dr. Lake Buena Vista, FL 32830	N28° 21.309' W81° 33.415'

(Continued on next page)

GPS COORDINATES FOR THE THEME PARKS (continued)		
DESTINATION PARKING LOT	**GPS ADDRESS**	**LATITUDE AND LONGITUDE**
BLIZZARD BEACH	1534 Blizzard Beach Dr. Lake Buena Vista, FL 32830	N28° 21.338' W81° 34.384'
TYPHOON LAGOON	1145 E. Buena Vista Dr. Lake Buena Vista, FL 32830	N28° 22.162' W81° 31.576'
DISNEY SPRINGS	1490 E. Buena Vista Dr. Lake Buena Vista, FL 32830	N28° 22.064' W81° 31.167'

FINDING YOUR WAY AROUND

WALT DISNEY WORLD IS LIKE ANY BIG CITY: It's easy to get lost here. Signs for the theme parks are excellent, but finding a restaurant or hotel is often confusing. The easiest way to orient yourself is to think in terms of five major areas, or clusters:

1. The first encompasses all hotels and theme parks around Seven Seas Lagoon. This includes the Magic Kingdom; hotels connected by the monorail; Shades of Green Resort; and the Palm, Magnolia, and Oak Trail Golf Courses.

2. The second includes developments on and around Bay Lake: Wilderness Lodge & Villas, Fort Wilderness Campground, and the Four Seasons Resort Orlando and Tranquilo Golf Club.

3. Cluster three contains Epcot, Disney's Hollywood Studios, the BoardWalk, ESPN Wide World of Sports, Epcot resort hotels, Pop Century Resort, Art of Animation Resort, and Caribbean Beach Resort.

4. The fourth cluster encompasses Disney Springs (including the Marketplace and West Side); Typhoon Lagoon water park; Lake Buena Vista Golf Course; the Disney Springs Resort Area; and the Port Orleans, Saratoga Springs, and Old Key West resorts.

5. The fifth cluster contains Disney's Animal Kingdom; Blizzard Beach water park; and Animal Kingdom Lodge & Villas, the All-Star Resorts, and Coronado Springs Resort.

HOW *to* TRAVEL *around the* WORLD *(or, The* Real *Mr. Toad's Wild Ride)*

TRYING TO COMMUTE around Walt Disney World can be frustrating. A Magic Kingdom street vendor, telling us how to get to Epcot, proposed, "You can take the ferry or the monorail to the Transportation and Ticket Center. Then you can get another monorail, or you can catch the bus, or you can take a tram out to your car and drive over there yourself." What he didn't say was that it would be easier to ride a mule than to take any conceivable combination from this transportation smorgasbord.

TRANSPORTATION TRADE-OFFS FOR GUESTS LODGING OUTSIDE WALT DISNEY WORLD

DAY GUESTS (those staying outside the World) can use the monorail, bus, and boat systems. Our most important advice for these guests is to park in the lot of the theme park (or other Disney destination) where they plan to finish their day. This is critical if you stay at a park until closing.

Moving Your Car from Lot to Lot on the Same Day

Once you've paid to park in any major theme park lot ($20 per day), show your receipt and you'll be admitted into another park's lot on the same day without further charge. Annual Pass holders and Disney resort guests park free in any theme park lot.

ALL YOU NEED TO KNOW ABOUT DRIVING TO THE THEME PARKS

1. POSITIONING OF THE PARKING LOTS The Animal Kingdom, Epcot, and DHS lots are adjacent to each park's entrance. The Magic Kingdom lot is adjacent to the Transportation and Ticket Center (TTC). From the TTC, take a ferry or monorail to the park's entrance. Electronic displays at each will show you which option is faster.

2. PAYING TO PARK Disney resort guests and Annual Pass holders park free. All others pay. If you pay to park and you move your car during that day, show your receipt and you won't have to pay at the new lot. The daily parking rate for motorcycles and standard cars is $20. There is also now a preferred parking option, with spots closer to the park entrances, available for $35 per day. Resort guests and annual pass holders continue to receive free regular parking but will incur an upcharge for preferred parking.

3. FINDING YOUR CAR WHEN IT'S TIME TO DEPART Jot down, text, or take a phone picture of the section and row where you park. If you're driving a rental car, note the license-plate number.

4. GETTING FROM YOUR CAR TO THE PARK ENTRANCE Each lot provides trams to the park entrance or, at the Magic Kingdom, to the TTC. If you arrive early in the morning, it may be faster to walk to the entrance (or TTC) than to take the tram. At the TTC, Disney has added digital wait-time boards, showing you how long the wait is to board the express monorail to the Magic Kingdom or board the ferry. Choose the shorter of the two lines.

5. GETTING TO DISNEY'S ANIMAL KINGDOM FOR PARK OPENING If you're staying on-property and are planning to be at this theme park when it opens, take a Disney bus from your resort instead of driving.

6. HOW MUCH TIME TO ALLOT FOR PARKING AND GETTING TO THE PARK ENTRANCE At Epcot and Disney's Animal Kingdom, figure about 15–20 minutes to pay, park, walk or ride to the entrance, and get through the security screening. At Disney's Hollywood Studios, allow 15–20 minutes; at the Magic Kingdom, 10–15 minutes to get to the TTC and another 25–35 to get through security and reach the park entrance via the monorail (most of which is waiting to board) or ferry (slower but usually less in demand). If you haven't purchased your theme park admission in advance, tack on another 10–20 minutes (and another $20 per ticket) before you actually enter the park.

7. COMMUTING FROM PARK TO PARK You can commute among the theme parks via Disney bus, to and from the Magic Kingdom and Epcot by monorail, or to and from Epcot and Disney's Hollywood Studios by boat or on foot. You can, of course, commute in your own car as well. Using Disney transportation or your car, allow 45–60 minutes one-way, entrance to entrance. If you plan to park-hop, leave your car in the lot of the park where you'll finish the day.

8. LEAVING THE PARK AT THE END OF THE DAY If you stay at a park until closing, expect the parking-lot trams, monorails, and ferries to be mobbed. (The Magic Kingdom has wait-time displays showing the lines for the monorail and ferry.) If the wait for the tram is unacceptable, walk to your car, or walk to the first stop on the tram route and wait there for a tram. When someone gets off, you can get on.

9. DINNER AND A QUICK EXIT One way to beat closing crowds at the Magic Kingdom is to arrange reservations for dinner at a restaurant in the Contemporary Resort. When you leave the Magic Kingdom for dinner, move your car from the TTC lot to the Contemporary lot. After dinner, walk (8–10 minutes) or take the monorail back to the Magic Kingdom. When the park closes and everyone else is fighting to board the monorail or ferry, you can stroll back to the Contemporary, claim your car, and get on your way. Use the same strategy at Epcot by arranging a reservation at an Epcot resort. When the park closes after *IllumiNations*, exit via the International Gateway and walk to the resort where you parked.

10. CAR TROUBLE All parking lots have security patrols. If you have a dead battery or minor automotive problem, the patrols will help you.

For more serious trouble, the **Car Care Center** (☎ 407-824-0976), near the Magic Kingdom parking lot, can help. Prices for most services are comparable to those at home. The facility stays busy, so expect to leave your car unless the fix is simple. Hours are Monday–Friday, 7 a.m.–7 p.m.; Saturday, 7 a.m.–4 p.m.; and Sunday, 8 a.m.–3 p.m.

11. SCORING A GREAT PARKING PLACE If you arrive at a park after noon or move your car from park to park, there will be empty parking spaces near the entrance vacated by early guests who have left. Instead of following Disney signage or being directed by staff to a distant space, drive to the front and hunt a space, or use the approach of a Coopersburg, Pennsylvania, couple:

> After leaving Epcot for lunch, we returned to find a fullish parking lot. We were unhappy because we had left a third-row parking spot. My husband told the attendant that we had left just an hour ago and that there were lots of spaces up front. Without a word of protest, he waved us to the front, and we got our same spot back!

GOOD FUZZ, BAD FUZZ

FOR AS LONG AS ANYONE CAN REMEMBER, Disney World security imposed little to no restraint on speeding drivers. However, we've been alerted to the increasing presence of Orange County law enforcement busting speeders on Disney World property. So for the lead-footed among you, there will be no more Fairy Godmother treatment, and the character with the flashing blue lights isn't Goofy.

SNEAK ROUTES

SNEAK ROUTE IS A WHITEWATER-PADDLING TERM for an easy way through tough rapids. Unfortunately, not all difficult rapids have a sneak route. For those that don't, there's only one way through: the hard way. As we research this guide, we're constantly looking for ways to avoid traffic snarls. For some roads and areas, there are no alternative routes. For others, we've discovered sneak routes.

THE LIGHTS OF DISNEY SPRINGS Although dozens of searchlights blaze at Disney Springs after dark, what we're talking about here are the many multifunction traffic signals on **Buena Vista Drive** in front of Disney Springs, which mark a traffic bottleneck of the first order. Heaven help you if you're traveling from Coronado Springs Resort to Disney Springs—you'll encounter up to 15 traffic signals in the 5-mile drive. In the evening especially, this commute can take up to half an hour. It wouldn't be so bad if only traffic to Disney Springs were affected, but because Buena Vista Drive is one of Walt Disney World's most important traffic arteries, the traffic jam is on the order of a blocked coronary ventricle.

Most traffic entering and exiting Walt Disney World from the FL 535 entrance must run this traffic-signal gauntlet, and so too must guests staying at the seven hotels of the Disney Springs Resort Area and Saratoga Springs Resort when traveling to Epcot, Disney's Hollywood Studios, the Magic Kingdom, Disney's Animal Kingdom, and Typhoon Lagoon. To avoid the bottlenecked area requires long but nearly traffic-free circumnavigation. Coming from the theme parks, you can bypass the mess by taking **I-4** or alternatively by looping around on **Bonnet Creek Parkway** and **Disney Vacation Club Way.** If you're going back to an Epcot or Magic Kingdom resort from Disney Springs, it may be faster to take I-4 West and follow the signs back to Disney property. Any way you look at it, though, it's a congested World after all.

The good news is that if you're coming by car from I-4 or on foot from the Disney Springs Resort Area, it's easier than ever to get to Disney Springs. Westbound I-4 now offers three exits to Disney Springs, including a new, direct exit to the Disney Springs parking garage (take Exit 67 Epcot/Disney Springs). Guests staying at a Disney Springs Resort Area hotel will find convenient pedestrian bridges linking the Marketplace to Hotel Plaza Boulevard and Buena Vista Drive.

INTERNATIONAL DRIVE (I-DRIVE) This is by far the most difficult area to navigate without long traffic delays. Most hotels on I-Drive are between **Kirkman Road** to the north and **FL 417 (Central Florida GreeneWay)** to the south. Between Kirkman Road and FL 417, three major roads cross I-Drive: From north to south on I-Drive (in the direction of Disney World), the first is **Universal Boulevard.** Next is **Sand Lake Road (FL 482),** pretty squarely in the middle of the hotel district. Finally, the **Beachline Expressway (FL 528)** connects I-4 and the airport.

unofficial **TIP**
To locate your I-Drive hotel, check iridetrolley.com or Google Maps (zoom way in for hotel names to appear).

The southern third of I-Drive can be accessed via **Central Florida Parkway,** connecting I-4 and Palm Parkway with the SeaWorld area of I-Drive, and by **Daryl Carter Parkway,** connecting Palm Parkway with the Orlando Vineland Premium Outlets.

I-Drive is a mess for a number of reasons: scarcity of left-turn lanes, long multidirectional traffic signals, and, most critically, limited access to westbound I-4 (toward Disney). From the Orange County Convention Center south to the Beachline Expressway and FL 417/Central Florida GreeneWay, getting on westbound I-4 is easy, but in the stretch where the hotels are concentrated (from Kirkman to about a mile south

Disney Springs Sneak Routes

Sneak route
(traffic is two-way
unless arrow
shows
one-way)

(area to avoid)

535

435

Winter Garden–Vineland Rd.

Vista Blvd.

S. Apopka–Vineland Rd.

Winn-Dixie

Palm Pkwy.

Port Orleans
Resort–Riverside

Buena Vista Dr.

The Crossroads
Shopping Ctr.

Port Orleans
Resort–French
Quarter

Disney
Vacation
Club Way

Treehouse
Villas

Saratoga
Springs
Resort
& Spa

Buena
Vista
Palace

Best Western

DoubleTree
Suites

Wyndham

B Resort

Holiday Inn

Old Key
West
Resort

Hotel Plaza Blvd.

Disney
Springs

Hilton

Bonnet Creek Pkwy.

Buena Vista Dr.

4

400

Epcot Center Dr.

Typhoon
Lagoon

Lake
Bryan

S. Apopka–Vineland Rd.

Bonnet
Creek Resort

Orlando
World Center
Marriott Resort

535

World Center Dr.

536

of Sand Lake), the only way most visitors know to access I-4 westbound
is to slog through the gridlock of the I-Drive–Sand Lake Road intersection en route to the I-4–Sand Lake Road interchange. A combination of
a long, long traffic signal, a sea of motorists, and insufficient turn lanes
makes this about as much fun as a root canal.

The object, then, is to access I-4 westbound *without* getting on Sand
Lake Road. If your hotel is north of Sand Lake, access **Kirkman Road**
by going north on I-Drive (in the opposite direction of the heaviest
traffic) to the Kirkman Road intersection and turning left, or by cutting over to Kirkman via eastbound **Carrier Drive**. In either case, take
Kirkman north over I-4 and, at the first traffic signal (at the entrance
to Universal Orlando), make a U-turn. This will put you directly onto
a westbound I-4 ramp. You can also go north on **Universal Boulevard**,
which parallels I-Drive to the east; after you cross I-4 onto Universal
property, stay left and follow the signs through two left turns to I-4—
the signs are small, so stay alert.

International Drive Area Sneak Routes

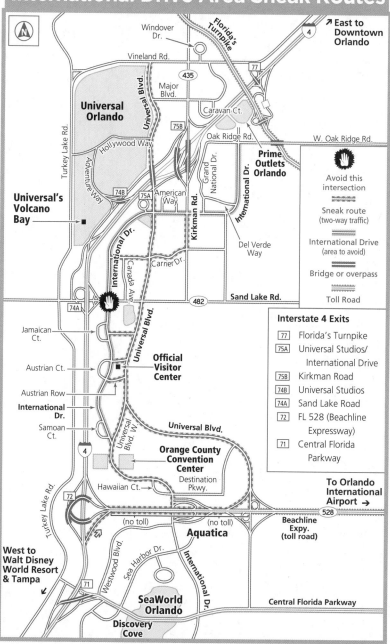

If your hotel is south of Sand Lake Road but north of Austrian Court, use **Austrian Row** to cut over to Universal Boulevard. Turn right (south) on Universal and continue until you intersect the **Beachline Expressway (FL 528)**; then take the Beachline west to I-4 (no toll).

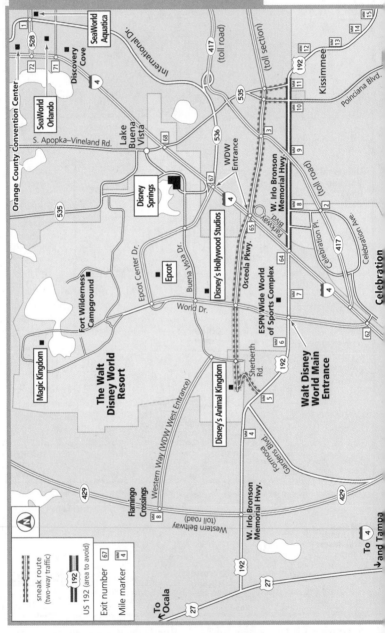

US 192–Kissimmee Resort Area Sneak Routes

US 192 (IRLO BRONSON MEMORIAL HIGHWAY) This road runs east–west along the southern border of Walt Disney World. From the Disney World entrance west on US 192/Irlo Bronson toward Clermont and east toward

I-4 Sneak Routes

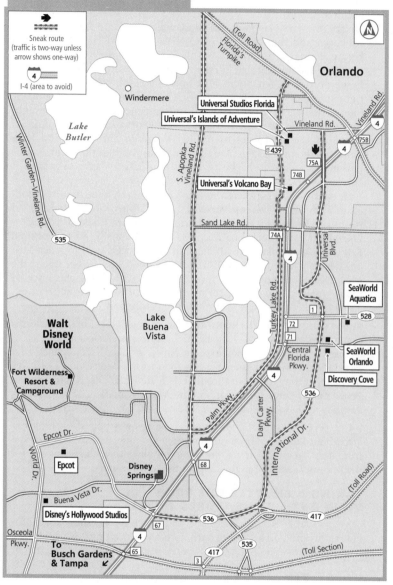

Sneak route
(traffic is two-way unless
arrow shows one-way)

I-4 (area to avoid)

Windermere

(Toll Road)

Florida's Turnpike

Orlando

Vineland Rd.

Vineland Rd.

Universal Studios Florida

Universal's Islands of Adventure

Vineland Rd.

439

75B

Lake
Butler

S. Apopka–
Vineland Rd.

75A

74B

Universal's Volcano Bay

Winter Garden–Vineland Rd.

Sand Lake Rd.

74A

535

Turkey Lake Rd.

Universal Blvd.

**SeaWorld
Aquatica**

1

528

Lake
Buena
Vista

72

**Walt
Disney
World**

71

Central
Florida
Pkwy.

**SeaWorld
Orlando**

**Fort Wilderness
Resort &
Campground**

Discovery Cove

4

536

Palm Pkwy.

Daryl Carter Pkwy.

International Dr.

Epcot Dr.

4

World Dr.

Epcot

**Disney
Springs**

68

Buena Vista Dr.

(Toll Road)

Disney's Hollywood Studios

536

417

Osceola
Pkwy.

4

67

**To
Busch Gardens
& Tampa**

65

417

3

535

(Toll Section)

Kissimmee is a concentration of hotels. The highway, though heavily used, has ample turn lanes. The downside is the many long, poorly timed multi-directional traffic signals. Even so, driving US 192 is easy compared with International Drive. Best of all, there are no godawful intersections like the one at I-Drive and Sand Lake Road.

Conspicuous mile markers are posted along US 192. If you know which marker is closest to your hotel, navigation is a snap. The main entrance (Maingate) to Disney World is between Mile Markers 6 and 7, and almost all US 192 hotels and restaurants are between Mile Markers 4 and 15. If your hotel is between Markers 5 and 8, no sneak routes are necessary; if it's between Markers 1 and 5, save time by entering Disney property via **Sherberth Road,** which runs into Disney's Animal Kingdom and the west end of Osceola Parkway. This road existed before Animal Kingdom or Osceola Parkway, but there are few signs on US 192 indicating that Sherberth affords a shortcut into and out of Disney property. After you turn onto Sherberth from US 192, bear right almost immediately at the fork. Continue until you reach a major intersection with Disney signage. Turn right and then continue straight to Osceola Parkway and most of Disney World, or go left to Animal Kingdom Lodge. To get to Animal Kingdom, turn right and look immediately for the turn lane that will take you into the theme park's parking lot. Osceola Parkway, a toll road, doesn't levy tolls until it crosses I-4 and leaves Disney property.

If your hotel is between Markers 8 and 15, save time (but pay modest tolls) by taking **Osceola Parkway** west to Disney World. If your hotel is between Markers 8 and 11, go north on **Poinciana Boulevard** to access Osceola. If your hotel is between Markers 11 and 15, go north on **FL 535 (Apopka–Vineland Road)** and turn west on Osceola to reach Disney's Animal Kingdom and Disney's Hollywood Studios. For Epcot, the Magic Kingdom, and Disney Springs, continue on FL 535 past Osceola to the intersection with **FL 536/World Center Drive;** then turn left on FL 536 and follow the signs to your Disney destination.

FL 535 (APOPKA–VINELAND ROAD) There are a number of hotels northeast and southwest of I-4 on FL 535 and on streets connecting to it. Though many guests commute to the parks through Disney property via Hotel Plaza Drive to Disney Springs and then via Buena Vista Drive, it's much easier to take I-4 west from FL 535 and enter Disney property on **Epcot Center Drive** for Epcot and the Magic Kingdom, or on **Osceola Parkway** for Disney's Hollywood Studios and Disney's Animal Kingdom.

I-4 Expect heavy traffic and possible delays westbound on I-4 from 7 to about 9:30 a.m. Eastbound toward Orlando, expect heavy traffic from 4 to 7 p.m. If you want to avoid I-4 altogether, check out our I-4 sneak routes, detailed in the map on the previous page.

TAKING A SHUTTLE BUS FROM YOUR OUT-OF-THE-WORLD HOTEL

MANY INDEPENDENT HOTELS and motels near Disney World provide trams and buses. They're fairly carefree, depositing you near theme park entrances and saving you parking fees. The rub is that they might not get you there as early as you desire (a critical point if you take our touring advice) or be available when you wish to return to your lodging. Each service is different; check details before you make reservations.

*un*official **TIP**
Warning: Most shuttles don't add vehicles at park-opening or -closing times. In the mornings, you may not get a seat.

Some shuttles go directly to Disney World, while others stop at other hotels en route. This can be a problem if your hotel is the second or third stop on the route. During periods of high demand, buses frequently fill up at the first stop, leaving little or no room for passengers at subsequent stops. Before booking, inquire how many hotels are on the route and the sequence of the stops. The different hotels are often so close together that you can easily walk to the first hotel on the route and board there. Similarly, if there's a large hotel nearby, it might have its own dedicated bus service that is more efficient. Use it instead of the service provided by your hotel. The majority of out-of-the-World shuttles work on a fixed schedule instead of arriving and departing somewhat randomly like the Disney buses. Knowing exactly when a bus will depart makes it easier to plan your day.

A multigenerational family from Seattle shares their experience:

We stayed at a hotel off-site and it was fine, but I think next time we'll stay in the World. The shuttles weren't all that convenient or frequent, so we ended up taking taxis more than we thought we would.

At closing or during a hard rain, more people will be waiting for the shuttle than it can hold, and some will be left behind. Most shuttles return for stranded guests, but guests may wait 20 minutes to more than an hour.

If you're depending on shuttles, leave the park at least 45 minutes before closing. If you stay until closing and you don't want the hassle of the shuttle, take Uber, Lyft, or a cab. Cab stands are near the Bus Information buildings at Disney's Animal Kingdom, Epcot, Disney's Hollywood Studios, and the TTC. If no cabs are on hand, a cast member will call one for you. If you're leaving the Magic Kingdom at closing, it's easier to take the monorail to a hotel and hail a cab from there rather than at the TTC.

unofficial **TIP**
If you want to go from resort to resort or almost anywhere else, you'll have to transfer at a bus hub.

THE DISNEY TRANSPORTATION SYSTEM

THE DISNEY TRANSPORTATION SYSTEM (**DTS**) is large, diversified, and generally efficient, but sometimes it's also overwhelmed, particularly at park-opening and -closing times. If you could be assured of getting on a bus, boat, or monorail at these critical times, we would advise you to leave your car at home. However, when huge crowds want to go somewhere at the same time, delays are unavoidable. In addition, some destinations are served directly, while many others require one or more transfers. Finally, it's sometimes difficult to figure how the buses, boats, and monorails interconnect.

Basically, Disney has a "hub and spoke" system. Hubs include the TTC, Disney Springs, and all four major theme parks (from 2 hours before official opening time to 1 hour after closing). With some exceptions, direct service is available from Disney resorts to the major theme parks and Disney Springs, as well as between parks.

If a hotel offers boat or monorail service, its bus service will be limited; you'll have to transfer at a hub for many destinations. If you're staying at a Magic Kingdom resort that's served by the monorail (**Contemporary and Bay Lake Tower, Grand Floridian & Villas, Polynesian Village & Villas**), you'll be able to commute efficiently to the Magic Kingdom. If you want to visit Epcot, you must take the monorail to the TTC and transfer to the Epcot monorail. (Guests at the Polynesian

Village & Villas can eliminate the transfer by walking 5–10 minutes to the TTC and catching the direct monorail to Epcot.)

If you're staying at an Epcot resort (**BoardWalk Inn & Villas, Dolphin, Swan, Yacht & Beach Club Resorts**), you can walk or commute by boat to Epcot's International Gateway (rear) entrance. Although direct buses link Epcot resorts to the Magic Kingdom and Disney's Animal Kingdom, there's no direct bus to Epcot's main entrance or Disney's Hollywood Studios. To reach the Studios from the Epcot resorts, you must take a boat or walk.

The **Caribbean Beach, Pop Century, Art of Animation, Saratoga Springs, Port Orleans, Coronado Springs, Old Key West, Animal Kingdom Lodge & Villas,** and **All-Star Resorts** offer direct buses to all theme parks. The rub is that you must sometimes walk a long way to bus stops or endure more than a half dozen additional pickups before actually heading for the park(s). Commuting in the morning from these resorts is generally easy, though you may have to ride standing. Returning in the evening, however, can be a different story. **Shades of Green** runs frequent shuttles from the resort to the TTC, where guests can transfer to their final destinations.

Hotels of the **Disney Springs Resort Area (DSRA)** provide shuttle service through an independent company. (The exception is the **Hilton**, which runs its own service.) The DSRA shuttles constitute a negative for guests at these hotels—the service is simply substandard. Before you book a DSRA hotel, check the nature and frequency of its shuttles.

Guests staying at **Fort Wilderness Resort & Campground** must use its buses to reach boat landings or the Settlement Depot and Reception Outpost bus stops. From these points, guests can travel directly by boat to the Magic Kingdom or by bus to other destinations. Except for going to the Magic Kingdom, the best way for Fort Wilderness guests to commute is in their own car.

The Express Transportation Bus

In late 2016, Disney introduced **Express Transportation,** the first fee-based transportation on the property, which promised expedited service between the four primary theme parks. The product is for annual pass holders and guests with park hopper tickets. Essentially, guests board and disembark buses backstage, eliminating the need to go through security screening and the park entrance gate at the destination park.

For single-day service, Express Transportation can be added for $15 per person. Multiday service costs $24 per person and is valid for seven consecutive days from the day of sale; Annual Pass holders may choose only the single-day option. Pickup locations will be found near the exit of **Buzz Lightyear's Space Ranger Spin** in Tomorrowland at the Magic Kingdom; east of **Spaceship Earth** at Epcot; near **Rock 'n' Roller Coaster** at Disney's Hollywood Studios; and near the entrance to **Kilimanjaro Safaris** at Disney's Animal Kingdom. Express Transportation is available from 10 a.m. until park close. Pickup will occur every 30 minutes.

The Disney Transportation System vs. Driving Your Own Car

To help you assess your transportation options, we've developed a chart (see pages 498 and 499) comparing the approximate commuting times from Disney resorts to various Walt Disney World destinations, using Disney transportation or your own car.

DISNEY TRANSPORTATION The times listed in the chart in the "Disney System" columns represent an average-case and worst-case scenario. For example, if you want to go from the Caribbean Beach Resort to Epcot, the chart indicates the times as 35 (49). The first number, 35, indicates how many minutes your commute will take on an average day. It assumes that buses run every 17 minutes, there are no major delays, and everything else is as usual. It represents the average time we observed during our research of the transportation system. For the pessimists, the number in parentheses (49) indicates the worst-case scenario. (*Example:* The bus is pulling away as you arrive at the stop, and you must wait 17 minutes for the next one.

When you finally board, the bus makes a number of additional stops before heading for Epcot. Once en route, the bus hits every red light.) When planning your transportation time, you'll do best to assume that your trip will take about the same time as the average in the chart (the first number). If you're running on a rigid schedule and you need to be sure of your arrival time, you can use the maximum time (the second number) to plan conservatively.

By far the biggest influence on your travel time between two points on the DTS is the amount of time you have to wait for your bus to arrive. Once you hop on your bus, the travel time is pretty consistent barring any unusual traffic problems; but your time waiting for the bus can vary greatly. Most cast members will tell you that buses run every 20 minutes. Our data indicates they run slightly more often—about every 15 minutes, an improvement of 1 minute over last year's numbers. Service at the Value and Moderate resorts is excellent: Our studies at Pop Century and the Port Orleans resorts showed an average wait of 13 minutes to catch a theme-park bound bus.

Bus schedules are also adjusted based on demand and fuel costs. We observed and timed almost 550 bus routes for this edition of the book: The intervals between any two buses arriving at a resort and headed for the same destination ranged from 1 minute to 43 minutes, although the average wait is, as noted, around 15 minutes. Still, if you've ever waited for an Epcot bus while three empty Disney Springs buses drive past, you know that Disney still has a lot of opportunity to optimize its bus-routing system.

The first number in the chart expresses the average transportation time, but our data shows that about 20% of the time your actual travel time will be less than half the average. So don't be surprised if your trip from Caribbean Beach Resort to Epcot takes only 15 minutes instead of the 35 (49) listed. Consider yourself lucky and enjoy the extra 20 minutes, doing something fun.

DRIVING YOUR OWN CAR The "Your Car" column in the chart indicates the average-case and worst-case scenarios for driving. To make these times comparable to DTS times, we added the time needed to get from your parked car to the park's entrance. While buses and monorails deposit guests at the park's entrance, those who drive must take a tram from their car to the gate or walk. At the Magic Kingdom, you must

Door-to-Door Commuting Times to and from the Disney Resorts and Parks

AVERAGE TIME (maximum time) IN MINUTES FROM	TO MAGIC KINGDOM		TO EPCOT		TO DHS	
	YOUR CAR	DISNEY SYSTEM	YOUR CAR	DISNEY SYSTEM	YOUR CAR	DISNEY SYSTEM
ALL-STAR RESORTS	37 (47)	20 (26)	18 (23)	25 (32)	16 (20)	17 (24)
ANIMAL KINGDOM	37 (48)	50 (68)	16 (17)	27 (38)	16 (17)	24 (34)
ANIMAL KINGDOM LODGE & VILLAS	39 (50)	19 (37)	19 (21)	27 (41)	18 (19)	22 (32)
ART OF ANIMATION RESORT	40 (51)	20 (30)	23 (28)	19 (30)	20 (24)	18 (28)
BEACH CLUB	36 (46)	23 (43)	16 (21)	18 (29*)	14 (18)	26 (37)
BLIZZARD BEACH	36 (46)	28 (39)	18 (23)	51 (70)	18 (22)	39 (54)
BOARDWALK INN & VILLAS	36 (46)	19 (31)	16 (21)	11 (22*)	14 (18)	26 (37)
CARIBBEAN BEACH	37 (47)	31 (43)	18 (23)	35 (49)	15 (19)	23 (33)
CONTEMPORARY-BAY LAKE	–	12 (17)	21 (26)	21 (29)	23 (27)	29 (39)
CORONADO SPRINGS	37 (47)	23 (32)	18 (23)	20 (28)	16 (20)	18 (26)
DHS	36 (46)	25 (35)	19 (24)	25 (35)	–	–
DISNEY SPRINGS	Bus service only back to your Disney resort					
DOLPHIN	35 (45)	20 (30)	15 (20)	24 (36*)	15 (19)	22 (32)
DISNEY SPRINGS RESORT AREA	41 (51)	69 (91)	21 (26)	47 (62)	20 (24)	45 (60)
EPCOT	36 (46)	26 (37)	–	–	19 (23)	21 (30)
FORT WILDERNESS	37 (47)	17 (27)	18 (23)	49 (67)	19 (23)	39 (54)
GRAND FLORIDIAN & VILLAS	–	7 (8)	18 (23)	33 (45)	20 (24)	23 (33)
MAGIC KINGDOM	–	–	26 (39)	33 (45)	22 (29)	24 (34)
OLD KEY WEST	36 (46)	24 (40)	18 (23)	24 (36)	18 (22)	25 (44)
POLYNESIAN VILLAGE	–	11 (14)	17 (22)	38 (53**)	19 (23)	28 (37)
POP CENTURY RESORT	40 (51)	26 (32)	23 (28)	23 (30)	20 (24)	18 (30)
PORT ORLEANS FRENCH QUARTER	37 (47)	24 (48)	19 (24)	27 (38)	19 (23)	22 (45)
PORT ORLEANS RIVERSIDE	38 (48)	17 (32)	20 (25)	23 (40)	20 (24)	17 (37)
SARATOGA SPRINGS	38 (48)	25 (41)	18 (23)	29 (43)	20 (24)	31 (45)
SHADES OF GREEN	28 (36)	35 (49)	18 (23)	33 (45)	20 (24)	20 (28)
SWAN	35 (45)	19 (43)	15 (20)	24 (36*)	15 (19)	22 (32)
TREEHOUSE VILLAS	37 (47)	27 (38)	18 (23)	27 (38)	19 (23)	25 (36)
TYPHOON LAGOON	37 (47)	41 (56)	18 (23)	51 (70)	15 (19)	62 (85)
WILDERNESS LODGE	–	15 (25)	20 (25)	38 (54)	22 (26)	29 (50)
YACHT CLUB	36 (46)	25 (40)	16 (21)	26 (57*)	14 (18)	34 (45)

\# Prior to 4 p.m., all transportation between the theme parks and Disney Springs requires a transfer at a nearby resort. After 4 p.m., buses run directly from the theme parks to Disney Springs. There are no buses from Disney Springs directly to the theme parks.

* This hotel is within walking distance of Epcot; time given is for boat transportation to the International Gateway (Epcot's rear entrance).

** By foot to Transportation and Ticket Center and then by Epcot monorail.

† Driving time vs. time on DTS. Driving times include time in your car, stops to pay tolls, time to park, and any transfers on Disney trams and monorails.

in Your Car Versus the Disney Transportation System †

TO ANIMAL KINGDOM		TO TYPHOON LAGOON		TO DISNEY SPRINGS		TO BLIZZARD BEACH	
YOUR CAR	DISNEY SYSTEM	YOUR CAR	DISNEY SYSTEM	YOUR CAR	DISNEY SYSTEM	YOUR CAR	DISNEY SYSTEM
11 (12)	19 (35)	12 (13)	48 (70)	13 (14)	29 (51)	6 (7)	49 (59)
–	–	17 (19)	65 (83)	19 (21)	–	10 (13)	41 (50)
9 (10)	17 (31)	19 (21)	64 (82)	22 (24)	32 (54)	11 (14)	47 (59)
14 (16)	18 (27)	12 (14)	46 (62)	15 (16)	29 (44)	10 (12)	42 (51)
17 (18)	26 (43)	9 (10)	49 (61)	10 (11)	25 (39)	12 (13)	48 (65)
10 (13)	26 (38)	13 (14)	80 (103)	14 (15)	–	–	–
17 (18)	20 (32)	9 (10)	44 (71)	10 (11)	25 (52)	12 (13)	40 (52)
17 (18)	31 (45)	6 (7)	46 (58)	7 (8)	30 (42)	12 (13)	60 (76)
20 (21)	25 (37)	17 (18)	47 (59)	16 (17)	37 (52)	15 (16)	62 (78)
11 (12)	18 (27)	12 (13)	37 (45)	13 (14)	27 (39)	6 (7)	44 (55)
16 (17)	20 (30)	8 (9)	77 (99)	9 (10)	–	11 (12)	56 (71)
Bus service only back to your Disney resort							
16 (17)	23 (35)	10 (11)	53 (67)	11 (12)	27 (39)	11 (12)	39 (48)
21 (22)	48 (64)	9 (10)	26 (29)	6 (7)	–	16 (17)	66 (81)
16 (17)	33 (48)	12 (13)	50 (62)	13 (14)	–	11 (12)	51 (65)
24 (25)	41 (57)	10 (11)	57 (72)	11 (12)	45 (63)	19 (20)	62 (78)
18 (19)	23 (35)	15 (16)	59 (75)	16 (17)	49 (68)	13 (14)	50 (64)
17 (18)	45 (63)	23 (31)	59 (75)	27 (36)	–	12 (13)	61 (77)
19 (20)	31 (57)	8 (9)	42 (53)	9 (10)	27 (40)	14 (15)	55 (70)
17 (18)	26 (43)	14 (15)	53 (72)	15 (16)	40 (59)	12 (13)	52 (69)
14 (16)	23 (29)	12 (14)	48 (68)	15 (16)	31 (50)	10 (12)	61 (71)
19 (20)	26 (41)	9 (10)	46 (68)	10 (11)	20 (33)	14 (15)	44 (55)
20 (21)	26 (42)	10 (11)	44 (61)	11 (12)	22 (33)	15 (16)	40 (48)
21 (22)	36 (49)	9 (10)	44 (55)	6 (7)	29 (44)	16 (17)	54 (69)
18 (19)	22 (33)	15 (16)	59 (75)	18 (20)	49 (68)	13 (14)	50 (64)
16 (17)	19 (44)	10 (11)	53 (67)	11 (12)	35 (46)	11 (12)	39 (48)
17 (19)	41 (59)	–	–	6 (7)	16 (24)	13 (14)	62 (80)
20 (21)	28 (40)	9 (10)	43 (54)	8 (9)	–	15 (16)	55 (70)
20 (21)	28 (53)	17 (18)	53 (71)	18 (19)	29 (51)	15 (16)	45 (62)
17 (18)	22 (38)	8 (10)	57 (69)	10 (12)	29 (59)	12 (13)	56 (68)

take a tram from the parking lot to the TTC, then catch a monorail or ferry to the entrance.

The Disney Transportation System for Teenagers

If you're staying at Disney World and have teens in your party, familiarize yourself with the Disney bus system. Safe, clean, and operating until 1 hour after the parks close (until 2 a.m. from Disney Springs), buses are a great way for teens to get around. Note that children under age 14 must be accompanied by someone age 14 or older to be admitted to the theme parks and water parks.

Walt Disney World Bus Service

Disney buses have an illuminated panel above the windshield that flashes the bus's destination. Theme parks also have designated waiting areas for each Disney destination. To catch the bus to the Caribbean Beach Resort from Disney's Hollywood Studios, for example, go to the bus stop and wait in the area marked TO THE CARIBBEAN BEACH RESORT. At the resorts, go to any bus stop and wait for the bus displaying your destination on the illuminated panel. Directions to Disney destinations are available when you check in or at your hotel's Guest Relations desk. Guest Relations can also answer questions about the transportation system.

Service from resorts to major theme parks is fairly direct. You may have intermediate stops, but you won't have to transfer. Service to the water parks and other Disney resorts almost always requires transfers or extra stops. Travel between your Disney hotel and Typhoon Lagoon requires a stop (and possibly a bus transfer) at Disney Springs. To travel between your Disney hotel and Blizzard Beach requires transfer at Animal Kingdom. If you're unlucky, this round-trip journey can take 2–3 hours per day. Our advice is to use Uber, Lyft, or a taxi to get from your Disney resort to a water park.

The fastest way to commute among resorts by bus is to take a bus from your resort to one of the major theme parks and then transfer there to a bus for your resort destination. This works, of course, only when the parks are open—actually, from 1 hour before opening until 1 hour after closing. (Disney buses stop taking passengers *to* the theme parks when they close, but they'll take passengers *from* the parks for an hour afterward.) If you're trying to commute to another resort for a late dinner during the off-season, when parks close early, you'll have to transfer at Disney Springs—which Disney, in its transportation instructions, lists somewhat disingenuously as the transfer point for *all* resort-to-resort commuting, hoping you'll stop and drop some dough en route. If the theme park buses are running, however, proceed to the park closest to your resort and transfer to the bus going to the resort where you'll be dining.

Despite what Disney's official schedule says, bus service to the theme parks begins about 7:30 a.m. on days when official park opening is 9 a.m. Generally, the buses run every 20 minutes. Buses to all four parks deliver you to the park entrance.

To be on hand for opening time (when official opening is 9 a.m.), catch direct buses to Epcot, Disney's Animal Kingdom, and Disney's Hollywood Studios between 7:30 and 8 a.m. Catch direct buses to the Magic Kingdom between 8 and 8:15 a.m. If you must transfer to reach your park, leave 15–20 minutes earlier. On days when official opening is 7 or 8 a.m., move up your departure time accordingly.

For your return bus trip in the evening, leave the park 40 minutes to an hour before closing to avoid the rush. If you're caught in the exodus, you may be inconvenienced, but you won't be stranded. Buses, boats, and monorails continue to operate for 1 hour after the parks close.

A mom from Ohio thinks Disney bus service needs some work:

WDW needs to do something about the buses to and from the parks. They are the WORST! Slow, infrequent, and too small. Thank

*goodness we rented a car. We drove everywhere after taking the ter-
rible buses three times. Zipped in and out and got around quickly.
They put more effort into the trams than the buses!*

A reader who stayed at Port Orleans reports:

*The Disney transportation system was wildly erratic, but we ended
up with more luck than not. For every time we had to wait a half-
hour at the bus stop, there were two or three times with no wait at all.*

If you're planning on riding a bus from Port Orleans Riverside to a
park around opening time, going to the West or North bus stop may
be your best option. These are the first stops on the route, and the bus
is sometimes full or standing-room-only before it gets to all the stops.

Not All Hubs Are Created Equal

All major theme parks, Disney Springs, and the TTC are hubs on the bus
system. If your route requires you to transfer at a hub, transfer at the closest park or the TTC, except at park closing time. Avoid Disney Springs as
a transfer point—traffic around the complex slows everything to a crawl.

As elsewhere in Walt Disney World, bus service at Disney Springs is
a crapshoot. This reader found himself in bus hell:

*I budgeted an HOUR for the return trip from Disney Springs to Ani-
mal Kingdom Lodge on the morning of our departure, and I STILL
found myself on the phone with Magical Express 30 minutes before
our bus was supposed to leave for the airport, asking when the next
bus after that would leave AKL. We barely made the backup bus. This
was NOT a "magical" ending to my vacation.*

Except at Fort Wilderness, no buses run between the TTC and the Disney resorts. If you're
commuting from resort to resort, you must transfer
at Disney Springs or one of the major theme parks
during park operating hours. If you're parked at
the TTC and you want to travel to a Disney resort,
go to the right of the Magic Kingdom entrance to
catch a bus to your destination.

When All Else Fails, Take Uber, Lyft, or (If You Must) a Cab

Sometimes depending on Disney transportation,
especially buses, is just too stressful if you absolutely have to be at a certain place at a certain time.
Happily, Uber, Lyft, and taxi service is available at
all resorts, the theme parks, Disney Springs, and many other Disney
World locations. Fares for short hauls within the World generally run
$7–$12 with Uber or Lyft, and $12–$25 for a cab. The time saved, plus
the peace of mind, makes the expenditure worthwhile to many guests,
including this Washington, DC, reader:

*I found Disney transportation unreliable when I really needed it at
park opening and closing times. My first night at Epcot, after Illumi-
Nations, the bus line was so long—and so stalled—that I decided it*

*un**official* **TIP**
Monorails run for 1 hour
after the Magic Kingdom
and Epcot close. If a train
is too crowded or you
need transportation
after the monorails have
stopped (for example,
during Evening Extra
Magic Hours), catch a bus
or boat. *Note:* As a safety
measure, Disney prohibits
guests from riding in the
front of a train.

made more sense to shell out for a cab than to wait another hour to get back to my hotel. Likewise at other busy times throughout the World. Even shelling out $80 or so for a few rides cost less than renting a car for a week.

Walt Disney World Monorail Service

Picture the monorail system as three loops. Loop A is an express route that runs counterclockwise connecting the Magic Kingdom with the TTC. Loop B runs clockwise alongside Loop A, making all stops, with service (in order) to the TTC, Polynesian Village & Villas, Grand Floridian & Villas, the Magic Kingdom, Contemporary Resort and Bay Lake Tower, and back to the TTC. The long Loop C dips southeast, connecting the TTC with Epcot. The hub for all loops is the TTC (where you usually park to visit the Magic Kingdom).

The monorail that serves the Magic Kingdom resorts usually starts running an hour and a half before official park opening. If you're staying at a Magic Kingdom resort and you wish to be among the first into the Magic Kingdom when official opening is 9 a.m., board the monorail at these times:

From the Contemporary Resort and Bay Lake Tower	7:45–8 a.m.
From the Polynesian Village Resort	7:50–8:05 a.m.
From the Grand Floridian Resort & Villas	8–8:10 a.m.

If you're a day guest, you'll be allowed on the monorail at the TTC between 8:15 and 8:30 a.m. when official opening is 9 a.m. If you want to board earlier, walk from the TTC to the Polynesian Village Resort and board there.

The monorail connecting Epcot and the TTC begins operating at 7:30 a.m. when Epcot's official opening is 9 a.m. To be at Epcot when it opens, catch the Epcot monorail at the TTC by 8:05 a.m.

While your Park Hopper pass suggests you can flit among parks, getting there is more complicated. For example, you can't go directly from the Magic Kingdom to Epcot. You must catch the express monorail (Loop A) to the TTC and transfer to the Loop C monorail to Epcot. If lines to board either monorail are short, you can usually reach Epcot in 30–40 minutes. But should you want to go to Epcot for dinner (as many do) and you're departing the Magic Kingdom in late afternoon, you may have to wait 30 minutes or longer to board the Loop A monorail. Adding this delay boosts your commute to 50–60 minutes.

Disney frequently changes the monorail's operating hours to allow for daytime inspection of the track and vehicles. When the monorail is closed, Disney provides bus or boat transportation to get you where you're going.

Walt Disney World Boat Service

Boats are a popular, third transportation option between some theme parks and resorts, as this reader from Ames, Iowa, reminds us:

You need to tell readers more clearly about the many different boat options. We stayed at Port Orleans French Quarter in December and took the ferry to Disney Springs several times. We also did a self-guided resort Christmas decorations tour and had fun taking different boats around the Magic Kingdom and Epcot resorts. These ferries were a much more pleasant option than buses for most legs of that tour.

The chart below shows the routes served by boats. Note that most routes stop at several resorts and that service may be suspended during thunderstorms. Strollers must be folded prior to boarding and stowed while on board the boat. Wheelchairs and scooters are permitted. Most routes run from approximately 45 minutes before park opening to 45 minutes after park closing.

WALT DISNEY WORLD BOAT ROUTES (ROUND-TRIP)
MAGIC KINGDOM —> FORT WILDERNESS —> MAGIC KINGDOM
MAGIC KINGDOM —> GRAND FLORIDIAN RESORT & VILLAS —> POLYNESIAN VILLAGE —> MAGIC KINGDOM
FORT WILDERNESS CAMPGROUND —> WILDERNESS LODGE —> CONTEMPORARY RESORT —> FORT WILDERNESS   *(NOTE: Walk or take the monorail from Contemporary to Magic Kingdom.)*
EPCOT —> BOARDWALK INN & VILLAS —> BEACH CLUB —> YACHT CLUB —> SWAN —> DOLPHIN —> EPCOT
DISNEY'S HOLLYWOOD STUDIOS —> BOARDWALK INN AND VILLAS —> BEACH CLUB RESORT AND VILLAS —> YACHT CLUB —> SWAN —> DOLPHIN —> DISNEY'S HOLLYWOOD STUDIOS
DISNEY SPRINGS —> SARATOGA SPRINGS —> OLD KEY WEST —> DISNEY SPRINGS
DISNEY SPRINGS —> PORT ORLEANS FRENCH QUARTER—> PORT ORLEANS RIVERSIDE —> DISNEY SPRINGS

Construction has started to link **Pop Century, Art of Animation,** and **Caribbean Beach** with Epcot and Disney's Hollywood Studios through an elevated, ski lift–like, enclosed gondola transportation system. Many details are still up in the air, but we've heard each gondola will be air-conditioned, hold around 10 guests, and open between late 2018 and mid-2019.

PART EIGHT

BARE NECESSITIES

MONEY, *Etc.*

CREDIT CARDS, MOBILE PAYMENTS, AND DISNEY GIFT CARDS

ACCEPTED THROUGHOUT WALT DISNEY WORLD are **American Express, Diners Club, Discover, Japan Credit Bureau, MasterCard,** and **Visa.** If you've got one of these credit cards linked to an iPhone 6 or newer, you can use **Apple Pay,** too. **Disney Gift Cards** can be used at most Disney-owned and-operated stores and restaurants, and for recreational activities, tickets, and parking. See disneygiftcard.com for details.

BANKING SERVICES

AT THE THEME PARKS, banking is limited to ATMs, which are marked on park maps and are plentiful throughout Walt Disney World; most MasterCard and Visa cards are accepted. To get cash with an American Express card, you must sign an agreement with Amex before your trip. ATMs are also at every Disney resort and throughout Disney Springs.

CURRENCY EXCHANGE

IN THE MAGIC KINGDOM, it's at **Guest Relations** in City Hall, on Main Street, U.S.A., at the park entrance. In Epcot, it's at Guest Relations on the west side of the Epcot Entrance Plaza. In the Studios or Animal Kingdom, exchange your euros, kroner, or zloty at Guest Relations to the left of the entrance turnstiles. Disney Springs' two Guest Relations locations are at the Marketplace and the West Side. Finally, all Disney resorts can do currency exchange at their front desks.

PROBLEMS *and* UNUSUAL SITUATIONS

ATTRACTIONS CLOSED FOR REPAIRS

FIND OUT IN ADVANCE what rides and attractions may be closed during your Disney World visit. To get the latest news on refurbishment schedules, check online at touringplans.com/closures or use our mobile app, **Lines.**

CAR TROUBLE

SECURITY PATROLS WILL HELP if you lock the keys in your parked car or find the battery dead. For more serious problems, the closest repair facility is the **Car Care Center,** near the Magic Kingdom parking lot (☎ 407-824-0976; open Monday–Friday, 7 a.m.–7 p.m.; Saturday, 7 a.m.–4 p.m., and Sunday, 8 a.m.–3 p.m.).

The nearest off-World repair center is **Maingate Citgo,** on US 192 west of I-4 (7424 W. Irlo Bronson Memorial Highway; ☎ 407-396-2721). Farther away but highly recommended by local *Unofficial Guide* researchers is **Riker's Automotive & Tire** (5700 Central Florida Parkway, near SeaWorld; ☎ 407-238-9800; rikersauto.com).

CELL PHONE SNAFUS

THIS WOMAN from Leawood, Kansas, spells out the problem:

> *In our group, we were using three different carriers, and we all had problems sending and receiving texts and making calls.*

The problem of signal strength is compounded by crowd noise and the ambient music played throughout the parks. Even if you manage to get a decent signal, it's an exasperating challenge to find someplace quiet enough to have a conversation. When possible, text instead of call. A woman from Washington, DC, adds this:

> *I was glad I brought a Mophie battery for my smartphone. The wireless in the parks is a big power drain.*

As you would expect, there are also Wi-Fi problems, as a Kennesaw, Georgia, woman points out:

> *I found the Wi-Fi horrible in all the parks. Dropped out continually, drained my battery, and wasn't strong enough to run their own app. Very disappointing.*

GASOLINE

THERE ARE THREE **Speedway** gas stations on Disney property. One station is adjacent to the Car Care Center on the exit road from the Transportation and Ticket Center (Magic Kingdom) parking lot. It's also convenient to the Shades of Green, Grand Floridian, and Polynesian Village resorts. Most centrally located is the station at the corner of Buena Vista Drive and Epcot Resorts Boulevard, near the BoardWalk Inn. A third station, also on Buena Vista Drive, is across from Disney Springs.

LOST AND FOUND

IF YOU LOSE (OR FIND) SOMETHING in the Magic Kingdom, go to **City Hall.** At Epcot, Lost and Found is behind Spaceship Earth. At Disney's Hollywood Studios, it's at **Hollywood Boulevard Guest Relations,** and at Disney's Animal Kingdom, it's at **Guest Relations** at the main entrance. If you discover you've lost something after you've left the parks, call ☎ 407-824-4245 (for all parks); see page 33 for the numbers to call while in the parks.

It's unusual for readers to send us tips about Lost and Found, but a mom from Indianapolis sent two!

If you lose something on a ride and it has medication in it, Disney cast members will shut down the ride for 45 seconds to try to retrieve it. If they can't find it or it didn't contain meds, you have to come back to Lost and Found for it at the end of the day.

Also, don't forget to write down [or take a picture of] the serial numbers on your passes (if you have them). With the serial number, a cast member can look up when it was last used, giving you an idea of where it was lost.

LOST MAGICBANDS Duplicates can be made at Guest Relations at any theme park or resort. There is no charge for resort guests.

LOST CARS Don't forget where you parked—write down your section and row, send yourself a text, or snap a picture with your phone or digital camera.

MEDICAL MATTERS

HEADACHE RELIEF Aspirin and other sundries are sold at the **Emporium** on Main Street, U.S.A., in the Magic Kingdom (behind the counter; you have to ask); at most retail shops in Epcot's Future World and World Showcase, Disney's Hollywood Studios, and Disney's Animal Kingdom; and at each Disney resort's gift shop.

ILLNESSES REQUIRING MEDICAL ATTENTION For the locations of the **First Aid Centers** in the theme parks, see the respective park chapters. Guests who use the service are generally very positive about it. This Hickory, North Carolina, reader's experience is representative:

We visited First Aid a time or two in the parks (my wife needed her blood pressure checked because she was worried about the heat and her pregnancy). We found trained medical staff, no wait, and all the friendliness and knowledge you would expect from Disney.

Off-property, there's a **Centra Care** walk-in clinic at 12500 S. Apopka–Vineland Road (☎ 407-934-CARE [2273]; open 8 a.m.–midnight during the week and 8 a.m.–8 p.m. weekends). Centra Care also offers 24-hour house calls and runs a free shuttle (☎ 407-938-0650).

A North Carolina family had a good experience at **Buena Vista Urgent Care** (8216 World Center Drive, Suite D; ☎ 407-465-1110):

We started day one needing medical care for our son, who has asthma and had developed croup. We found great care at Buena Vista Urgent Care. We waited 20 minutes, and then we were off to the parks.

The Medical Concierge (☎ 855-932-5252; themedicalconcierge .com) has board-certified physicians available 24-7 for house calls to your hotel room. They offer in-room X-rays and IV therapy service as well as same-day dental and specialist appointments. They also rent medical equipment. Insurance receipts, insurance billing, and foreign-language interpretation are provided. Walk-in clinics are also available.

DOCS (Doctors on Call Service; ☎ 407-399-DOCS; doctorsoncall service.com) also offers 24-hour house-call service. All physicians are certified by the American Board of Medical Specialties. A father of two from O'Fallon, Illinois, gives them a thumbs-up:

> *My wife's cold developed into an ear infection that required medical attention, and DOCS was able to respond in 40 minutes. The doctor had medicine with him and was very professional and friendly.*

Physician Room Service (☎ 407-238-2000; physicianroomservice .com) provides board-certified-doctor house calls to Disney World–area guest rooms for adults and children.

DENTAL NEEDS Call **Celebration Dental Group** (☎ 407-351-9704).

PRESCRIPTION MEDICINE Three drugstores nearby are **CVS** (8242 World Center Drive; ☎ 407-239-1442), **Walgreens** (12100 S. Apopka–Vineland Road; ☎ 407-238-0600), and **Turner Drugs** (1530 Celebration Blvd., Ste. 105A; ☎ 407-828-8125; turnerdrug.com). Turner Drugs charges $7.50 to deliver a filled prescription to your Disney hotel's front desk, $10–$15 for non-Disney hotels. The fee is charged to your hotel account.

SGT. BLISTERBLASTER'S GUIDE TO HAPPY FEET

1. ON YOUR FEET! Get up, La-Z-Boy rider: When you go to Walt Disney World, you'll have to walk a lot farther than to the refrigerator. You can log 5–12 miles a day at the parks, so now's the time to shape up them dogs. Start with short walks around the neighborhood. Increase your distance gradually until you can do 6 miles without CPR.

2. A-TEN-SHUN! During your training program, pay attention when those puppies growl. They'll give you a lot of information about your feet and the appropriateness of your shoes. Listen up! No walking in flip-flops, loafers, or sandals. Wear well-constructed, broken-in running or hiking shoes. If you feel a "hot spot," that means a blister is developing. The most common sites for blisters are heels, toes, and balls of the feet. If you develop a hot spot in the same place every time you walk (a clue!), cover it with a Johnson & Johnson blister bandage or cushion (in drugstores without a prescription) before you set out.

3. SOCK IT UP, TRAINEE! Good socks are as important as good shoes. When you walk, your feet sweat like a mule in a peat bog, and the moisture only increases friction. To minimize friction, wear a pair of socks made from material such as SmartWool or CoolMax, which wicks perspiration away from your feet (SmartWool socks come in varying thicknesses). To further combat moisture, dust your dogs with antifungal talcum powder.

4. WHO DO YOU THINK YOU ARE, IRON MAN? Don't be a hero. Take care of a foot problem the minute you notice it. Carry a small foot-emergency kit for your platoon. Include gauze, antibiotic ointment, disinfectant, moleskin or Johnson & Johnson blister bandages, scissors, a sewing needle or something else sharp (to drain blisters), and matches to sterilize the needle. Extra socks and talcum powder are optional.

5. BITE THE BULLET! If you develop a hot spot, cover it ASAP with a blister bandage. If you develop a blister, air out and dry your foot. Next, drain the fluid, but don't remove the top skin. Clean the area with disinfectant and place a blister bandage over the blister. The bandages come in several sizes, including specially shaped ones for fingers and toes; they're also good for covering hot spots. If you don't have blister bandages, don't cover the hot spot or blister with Band-Aids (they'll slip and wad up)—head to a park First Aid Center instead.

6. TAKE CARE OF YOUR PLATOON. If you have young, green troops in your outfit, they might not sound off when a hot spot develops. Stop several times a day and check their feet. If you forgot your emergency kit and a problem arises, stop by a First Aid Center. They have all the stuff you need to keep your command in action.

RAIN

WEATHER BAD? Go to the parks anyway. The crowds are lighter, and most attractions and waiting areas are under cover. Showers, especially during warmer months, are short.

Ponchos are about $9, umbrellas about $12. All ponchos sold at Disney World are made of clear plastic, so picking out somebody in your party on a rainy day can be tricky. Amazon sells an inexpensive orange poncho that will make your family pumpkin-colored beacons in a plastic-covered sea of humanity.

unofficial **TIP**
Raingear isn't always displayed in shops, so you have to ask for it.

A Wilmington, North Carolina, mom thinks high-quality raingear is worth the investment:

> *We're outdoor-sports people, so we have good raincoats. It rained every day on this trip, driving many people out of the parks and leaving others looking miserable. Meanwhile, we hardly noticed the rain from inside our high-end jackets.*

Some unusually heavy rain precipitated (no pun intended) dozens of reader suggestions for dealing with soggy days. The best came from this Memphis, Tennessee, mom:

1. Rain gear should include ponchos *and* umbrellas. When rain isn't beating down on your ponchoed head, it's easier to ignore.

2. If you're using a stroller, bring a plastic sheet or an extra poncho to protect it from rain. (Ponchos cover only Disney's single strollers.) Carry a towel in a plastic bag to wipe off your stroller after experiencing an attraction during a rainfall.

Unofficial Guide researcher Connie Wolosyk advises, "Wear a baseball cap under the poncho hood—without it, the hood never covers your head properly and your face always gets wet."

HOW TO LODGE A COMPLAINT WITH DISNEY

COMPLAINING ABOUT A LEAKY FAUCET or not having enough towels is pretty straightforward, and you'll usually find Disney folks highly responsive. But a more global gripe, or one beyond an on-site manager's ability to resolve, is likely to disappear in the labyrinth of Disney bureaucracy.

One of our readers' foremost gripes relates to Disney's unresponsiveness in fielding complaints. A Providence, Rhode Island, dad's remarks are typical:

> *It's all warm fuzzies and big smiles until you have a problem—then everybody plays* hide-and-seek. *The only thing you know for sure is it's never the responsibility of the Disney person you're talking to.*

A Portland, Maine, reader sums it up in classic New England style:

Lodging a complaint with Disney is like shouting at a brick.

Like most companies, Disney would rather hear from you when the news is good. Regarding complaints, Disney prefers to receive them in writing, but by the time you get home and draft a letter, it's often too late to correct the problem. And though Disney would have you believe that it's a touchy-feely outfit, it generally isn't a company that will make things right for you after the fact. You may receive a letter thanking you for writing and expressing regret without actually acknowledging responsibility (for example, "We're sorry you felt inconvenienced"—as if the perception somehow arose from your imagination). It's unlikely, though, that they'll offer to fix anything.

If you still want to lodge a complaint, write to **Walt Disney World Guest Communications** at PO Box 10040, Lake Buena Vista, FL 32830-0040 or wdw.guest.communications@disneyworld.com. If you're *really* steamed, you can fire off a letter to the following higher-ups:

Robert Iger, CEO	**Bob Chapek, Chairman**	**George Kalogridis, President**
The Walt Disney Company	Walt Disney Parks & Resorts	Walt Disney World
500 S. Buena Vista St.	500 S. Buena Vista St.	PO Box 10040
Burbank, CA 91521	Burbank, CA 91521	Lake Buena Vista, FL 32830

If Disney still doesn't respond, you can always go public:

Letters to the Editor, *Orlando Sentinel*
633 N. Orange Ave., MP-218
Orlando, FL 32801-1349
☎ 407-420-5000; fax 407-420-5286; insight@orlandosentinel.com

SERVICES

MESSAGES

MESSAGES LEFT at **City Hall** in the Magic Kingdom, **Guest Relations** at Epcot, **Hollywood Boulevard Guest Relations** at Disney's Hollywood Studios, or **Guest Relations** at Disney's Animal Kingdom can be retrieved at any of the four.

PET CARE

ACROSS FROM THE PORT ORLEANS RESORTS, the plush **Best Friends Pet Resort** accommodates up to 270 dogs in a variety of standard and luxury suites, some with private outdoor patios and play yards; the Kitty City pavilion houses up to 30 felines in two- and four-story cat condos. There's also a separate area just for birds and "pocket pets," such as hamsters. Encompassing more than 17,000 square feet of air-conditioned indoor space plus 10,000 square feet of covered outdoor runs and play areas, the resort is open to both Walt Disney World resort guests and visitors staying off-property. We sent Rosie, the *Unofficial Guide* research poodle, and it went great. We even got e-mailed photos of her during her stay. For more information, call ☎ 877-4-WDW-PETS (877-493-9738) or visit bestfriendspetcare.com. (*Note:* Pet parents must provide written proof of current vaccination from a vet, either at check-in or by fax at 203-706-4159.)

PHOTOS

FOR YEARS NOW, Walt Disney World has employed roving bands of photographers to take digital photos of families who don't use their own cameras. And Disney sells those pictures back to you through a website, where you can choose the images you want to keep, customize them with text and colorful borders, order photo CDs, and so on.

The latest iteration of the photo program, called **Memory Maker** (disneyworld.disney.go.com/memory-maker), adds to your package pictures taken of your family on rides such as Splash Mountain and the Tower of Terror. You can purchase Memory Maker for up to 30 days of photos for $149 if you purchase it in advance or for $169 if you purchase it in the park. Or you can purchase a Memory Maker One Day Entitlement for $59, which is available for purchase in the My Disney Experience mobile app only, allowing you to enjoy the benefits of Memory Maker for one-day Disney World park visits. A recent addition to the benefits for Disney World Annual Pass holders is the inclusion of free downloads of Memory Maker pictures. Because Memory Maker is linked to your My Disney Experience (MDE) account (see page 38), you're also able to see photos of friends and family you've linked to there. Additionally, you can now perform some basic photo editing within the app. Here's how to get started:

unofficial **TIP**
You must have a My Disney Experience account to buy a Memory Maker package.

1. Find a Memory Maker photographer to take your first picture. Photographers roam throughout the theme parks and water parks, including near park entrances, in restaurants (and during character meals), and around iconic attractions such as Splash Mountain.

2. The photographer will scan your RFID ticket or MagicBand. This links your pictures to your MDE account. Onboard ride-photo systems should automatically detect your MagicBand and link the photos to your account.

3. Visit the MDE website within 45 days of your trip to view your photos. You can add decorative borders and short captions to your pictures, too, as well as share photos online.

If you're already logged in to MDE, your purchase will be automatically linked to your account. If not, you'll be asked to do so (or sign up for MDE) to complete the purchase. The following ride photos will automatically link to your MDE account:

THE MAGIC KINGDOM Buzz Lightyear's Space Ranger Spin, Space Mountain, Splash Mountain
EPCOT Test Track
DISNEY'S ANIMAL KINGDOM Dinosaur, Expedition Everest
DISNEY'S HOLLYWOOD STUDIOS Rock 'n' Roller Coaster, The Twilight Zone Tower of Terror

You can download Memory Maker photos as many times as you want, subject to a few restrictions: First, if you prepurchase, you must do so at least three days before your trip in order to have all of your photos included. If you prepurchase fewer than three days before you arrive, you'll have to buy separately any photos taken during that three-day window. Next, Disney will store your photos for 45 days, so you'll need to download them promptly once you return home (you can also pay for extra time). Finally, once you've downloaded the first photo, you've got 30 days to download the rest. Disney grants you a limited license to reproduce the photos for personal use.

Because any two families can share a Memory Maker package via MDE, folks in the *Unofficial Guide* online community often split the cost with others traveling around the same time. It's a great way to get your photos at half-price. Visit tinyurl.com/share-memory-maker to find a partner on our discussion boards.

We get a lot of reader and website mail about the photo program, most of it positive. From a Loveland, Ohio, mom:

The PhotoPass option is awesome and so easy. Everywhere we went we would find Disney photographers and we got a lot of great pictures, which is nice since usually when you are on vacation you have one part of your family missing as he/she is taking the photo.

Honeymooners from Cambridge, Massachusetts:

My wife talked me into getting Memory Maker, and we both ended up being happy with the memories captured. Not having to carry a camera around was very convenient, especially when we went on water rides. Another advantage of it was having access to all the on-ride photos and videos, and the Tower of Terror video alone made the purchase worth it. The photographers were widespread and accommodating.

And a dad from Clear Spring, Maryland:

The Disney Memory Maker photo plan is definitely worth the cost. We had almost 300 pictures from various locations upon our return home—plus all of the professional shots of the parks. They were easy to download, and we can print them out as much as we want (or send to friends via social media).

But a Silver Spring, Maryland, dad reports a gap in the service:

I advance-purchased Memory Maker largely because we were planning several character meals, under the apparently incorrect assumption that photographers would be there. There was no sign of any photographer at any of the four character meals we did.

In addition to the in-park photographers, there is now a Memory Maker station at Disney Springs. There are no characters, but if you want a photographer to take a few snaps of your family, stop by. This can be a quick alternative to a formal posed photo session, and as a bonus, the pictures will be included with your existing photo package.

EXCUSE ME, BUT WHERE CAN I FIND . . .

RELIGIOUS SERVICES IN THE WALT DISNEY WORLD AREA? See allears .net/btp/church.htm for a complete list.

SOMEPLACE TO CHARGE MY CELL PHONE? Charging stations are available near the *Tangled*-themed restrooms in Fantasyland in the Magic Kingdom; they're built into the faux-wood posts near the seating area. Also try the seating area behind Big Top Treats in Storybook Circus; or the shopping area at the exit to Space Mountain. In Epcot, try the Innovation Plaza behind and to the right of Club Cool. If you prefer to charge on the go, we use **Mophie** and **New Trent** external batteries for our devices. Both are available at Amazon.com.

SOMEPLACE TO PUT ALL THESE PACKAGES? Lockers are located on the ground floor of the Main Street railroad station in the Magic Kingdom, to the right of Spaceship Earth in Epcot, and on the Transportation and Ticket Center's east and west ends. At DHS, lockers are to the right of the entrance at Oscar's Super Service. Animal Kingdom lockers are to the left inside the entrance. Cost is $8 a day for small lockers and $10 a day for large lockers. Lockers at Blizzard Beach and Typhoon Lagoon water parks cost the same.

unofficial **TIP**
Be aware that Package Pick-Up closes 2 hours before the park. Disney resort guests can have their purchases delivered to their hotel's gift shop.

Package Pick-Up is available at the theme parks. Ask the salesperson to send your purchases to Package Pick-Up; when you leave the park, they'll be waiting for you. Epcot has two exits, thus two Package Pick-Ups; specify the main entrance or the International Gateway. If you're staying at a Disney resort, you can also have packages delivered to your resort's gift shop for pickup the following day. If you're leaving within 24 hours, though, take them with you or use the in-park pickup location.

AN OLD-FASHIONED CAMERA? Camera Centers at the parks still sell disposable point-and-shooters with flash for around $18 plus tax ($21 for a waterproof version). Memory cards run $40–$60, so bring yours from home. Film developing is unavailable at Walt Disney World.

A GROCERY STORE? Publix locations on the west side of Disney World include **Water Tower Shoppes** (29 Blake Blvd., Celebration; ☎ 321-939-3100); **Orange Lake Town Center** (14928 E. Orange Lake Blvd., Kissimmee; ☎ 407-239-4989); and **Poinciana Place** (2915 Vineland Road, Kissimmee; ☎ 407-396-7525). Publix locations north of Disney World include **Lakeside Village Center** (7880 Winter Garden Vineland Road, Windermere; ☎ 407-343-7575). **Winn-Dixie** can be found at 7840 W. Irlo Bronson Memorial Highway in Kissimmee (closest to Disney World to the west; ☎ 407-397-2210) and 1957 S. Apopka–Vineland Road in Orlando (closest to Disney World to the east; ☎ 407-465-8600). Finally, the **Super Target** at 3200 Rolling Oaks Blvd. (☎ 407-321-3971) is the closest "Tarzhay" to the Western Way entrance.

We compiled a list of common vacation grocery items and then went shopping (no item was on sale). The chart opposite shows how prices at **Garden Grocer** (see below), the **Publix** at Water Tower Shoppes, the **Super Target** above, and the first **Winn-Dixie** above compare.

GROCERY MARKETS THAT DELIVER? If you don't have a car or you don't want to go to the store, **Garden Grocer** (gardengrocer.com) will shop for you and deliver your groceries. The best way to compile your order is on Garden Grocer's website before you leave home. If there's something you want that's not on their list of available items, they'll try to find it for you (including alcohol). Delivery arrangements are per your instructions. If you're staying at a hotel, you can arrange for your groceries to

ITEM	GARDEN GROCER	PUBLIX	SUPER TARGET	WINN-DIXIE
12 DOUGHNUTS (store brand)	$5.99	$5.98	$4.99	$4.00
MAXWELL HOUSE COFFEE (11.5 oz.)	$6.49	$4.79	$4.12	$3.79
COFFEE FILTERS (store brand, 200 count)	$2.49	$1.29	$1.34	$1.49
1 GALLON MILK (store brand)	$5.39	$3.69	$3.68	$4.05
TROPICANA ORANGE JUICE (59 oz.)	$5.99	$3.99	$3.69	$4.49
CHEERIOS (8.9 oz.)	$4.59	$3.59	$2.89	$3.49
COCA-COLA (12-pack, 12-oz. cans)	$6.99	$5.49	$5.49	$5.39
LAY'S POTATO CHIPS (10.5 oz.)	$5.39	$4.29	$3.99	$4.29
SUGAR (2 lbs., store brand)*	$4.19	$1.59	$2.09	$1.50
JIF PEANUT BUTTER (16 oz.)**	$3.99	$2.99	$2.99	$2.79
CHIPS AHOY! COOKIES (13.72 oz.)	$4.49	$3.79	$2.64	$3.59
BANANAS (4 lbs.)***	$0.49 each	$2.60.	$2.28.	$2.60
WONDER BREAD (store brand; 1 loaf)	$2.89	$2.79	$2.19	$2.69
BUDWEISER (12-pack, 12-oz. cans)	$15.99	$11.99	$11.99	$11.99
WELCH'S GRAPE JELLY (18 oz.)****	$3.49	$2.39	$2.12	$2.79
COLGATE TOOTHBRUSH	$2.59	$0.99	$0.94	$1.00
BANANA BOAT SPORT SPF 30 SUNSCREEN (8 oz.)	$10.99	$6.97	$6.49	$9.99
TOTALS	$97.82	$59.21	$63.92	$69.93

    * Super Target and Garden Grocer sell only 4-pound bags of sugar.

   ** Garden Grocer's price is for a 12-ounce jar.

  *** Garden Grocer also sells bananas in 10-pound bunches; total for Garden Grocer is based on 12 bananas (about 4 pounds).

**** Garden Grocer carries Welch's jelly only in the 30-ounce jar.

be left with bell services. If you can't get online, you can order by phone (☎ 866-855-4350). For orders of $200 or more, there's a $2 delivery fee; for orders less than $200, the delivery charge is $14; a minimum order of $40 is required. As of this writing, Garden Grocer doesn't deliver to the Swan or Dolphin, and delivery to the Yacht and Beach Club Resorts is limited to 4:30–5:30 p.m. Also note that Garden Grocer's delivery schedule may fill completely around holidays, at which point they'll stop accepting orders for delivery on those dates.

WINE, BEER, AND LIQUOR? Wine and beer are sold in grocery stores. The best range of adult beverages is sold at the **ABC Fine Wine & Spirits** store less than a mile north of the Crossroads shopping center (11951 S. Apopka–Vineland Road; ☎ 407-239-0775). We also like the **Publix** liquor store at Water Tower Shoppes (see previous page).

PART NINE

The
MAGIC KINGDOM

OPENED IN 1971, THE MAGIC KINGDOM was the first of Walt Disney World's four theme parks, much of it built by the same Disney staff who had built Disneyland almost two decades earlier. Such beloved attractions as **Cinderella Castle, Pirates of the Caribbean,** and **Splash Mountain** have helped define the basic elements of theme park attractions the world over. The remarkable achievement that Disney wrought in Orlando isn't that they could build a second, equally compelling theme park, but that they could do so on a much larger scale while keeping the fine details that make visiting a Disney park so completely immersive.

The Magic Kingdom is what springs to mind when most people think of Walt Disney World. The crown jewel of the World's parks, it sometimes receives as much attention, investment, and upgrades as the other three theme parks combined.

NOT TO BE MISSED AT THE MAGIC KINGDOM	
ADVENTURELAND	• A Pirate's Adventure • Pirates of the Caribbean
FANTASYLAND	• Peter Pan's Flight • *Mickey's PhilharMagic* • Seven Dwarfs Mine Train
FRONTIERLAND	• Big Thunder Mountain Railroad • Splash Mountain
LIBERTY SQUARE	• The Haunted Mansion
MAIN STREET, U.S.A.	• Meet Mickey Mouse at Town Square Theater
SPECIAL EVENTS	• *Happily Ever After* fireworks • *Once Upon a Time* show
TOMORROWLAND	• Buzz Lightyear's Space Ranger Spin • *Space Mountain*

ARRIVING

IF YOU DRIVE, the Magic Kingdom **Transportation and Ticket Center (TTC)** parking lot opens about 2 hours before the park's official opening. (For GPS coordinates, see page 485.) After paying a fee, you will be directed to a parking space, then transported by tram to the TTC. After that you'll catch either a monorail or a ferry to the park's entrance.

If you bring a stroller, a Ridgewood, New Jersey, family recommends the ferry (which starts operating 30–60 minutes before park opening):

The ferry from the TTC to the Magic Kingdom dock is a must if you're using a stroller. You can drive the stroller right onto the ferry and then just head to the back of the ferry to be the first ones off when it docks.

If you're staying at the Contemporary, Bay Lake Tower, Polynesian Village, or Grand Floridian Resort, you can commute to the Magic Kingdom by monorail (guests at the first two can walk to the park more quickly). If you're staying at Wilderness Lodge & Boulder Ridge Villas or Fort Wilderness Resort & Campground, you can take a boat or bus. Guests at other Walt Disney World resorts can reach the park by bus. All Disney lodging guests, regardless of conveyance, are deposited at the park's entrance, bypassing the TTC.

NEW SECURITY SCREENING PROCEDURES All visitors to the Magic Kingdom go through an airport-style security screening prior to entering the park. Disney changed the location of these screenings in 2017 as follows:

- Guests arriving by car will be screened at the TTC prior to boarding a monorail or ferry.
- Resort guests arriving by monorail or boat will be screened at their resort before boarding.
- Resort guests arriving by bus will be screened at the Magic Kingdom bus depot.
- Guests arriving on foot from the Contemporary or Bay Lake Tower will be screened along the walkway to the Magic Kingdom.

These changes get you into the parks faster by distributing the screening work to many more locations. They also prevent large clusters of guests from forming in the constrained area between the Magic Kingdom entrance turnstiles and train station tunnels, an important security concern.

NEW OPENING PROCEDURE In 2017, the Magic Kingdom began opening Main Street, U.S.A., to guests a full hour before the park's official opening time on days without morning Extra Magic Hours. Thus, if the park opens at 9 a.m., the Magic Kingdom will allow guests to enter the park and roam Main Street and the Central Plaza starting at 8 a.m.

Main Street's larger shops, such as the Emporium, are open early, in case you need sunscreen, ponchos, or aspirin. The Main Street Bakery Starbucks and the Plaza Ice Cream Parlor are also open for breakfast.

This extra hour has pros and cons. On the positive side, it's a chance to get great family photos of some of the park's most iconic places, bathed in gorgeous morning light, with relatively few crowds.

The downside—and this is significant—is that the extra hour creates large crowds in the Central Plaza to get in line for popular rides such as Seven Dwarfs Mine Train. On a recent visit, for example, we estimated a crowd of between 700 and 900 people packed into just one walkway between the Central Plaza and Fantasyland, all headed directly to Seven Dwarfs Mine Train. (Similar, smaller lines form on the walkways to Tomorrowland for Space Mountain, and Adventureland and Frontierland for Splash Mountain and Big Thunder.)

These groups rush to their rides as soon as the park opens. In the case of Seven Dwarfs, this created an immediate 60-minute standby wait whose line stretched back to Storybook Circus. Prior to this new

Continued on page 518

The Magic Kingdom

FP+ Attraction Offers FastPass+

Use FP+ FastPass+ Recommended

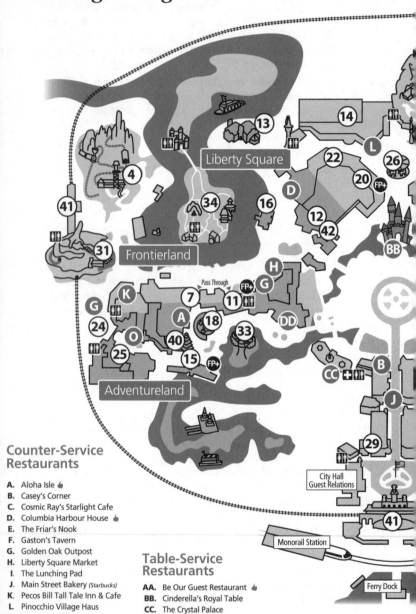

Liberty Square

Frontierland

Pass Through

Adventureland

City Hall
Guest Relations

Monorail Station

Ferry Dock

Counter-Service Restaurants

- **A.** Aloha Isle 👍
- **B.** Casey's Corner
- **C.** Cosmic Ray's Starlight Cafe
- **D.** Columbia Harbour House 👍
- **E.** The Friar's Nook
- **F.** Gaston's Tavern
- **G.** Golden Oak Outpost
- **H.** Liberty Square Market
- **I.** The Lunching Pad
- **J.** Main Street Bakery (Starbucks)
- **K.** Pecos Bill Tall Tale Inn & Cafe
- **L.** Pinocchio Village Haus
- **M.** Storybook Treats
- **N.** Tomorrowland Terrace (seasonal)
- **O.** Tortuga Tavern

Table-Service Restaurants

- **AA.** Be Our Guest Restaurant 👍
- **BB.** Cinderella's Royal Table
- **CC.** The Crystal Palace
- **DD.** Jungle Navigation Co. Ltd. Skipper Canteen
- **EE.** The Plaza Restaurant
- **FF.** Tony's Town Square Restaurant

First Aid Station   Happily Ever After/Once Upon a Time Viewing Area

FP+ FastPass+ Kiosks   Restrooms   Recommended Dining   ✅ Not to Be Missed

Fantasyland

Tomorrowland

Walkway to Resort Buses

11. Frontierland Shootin' Arcade
12. *The Hall of Presidents*
13. The Haunted Mansion ✅
14. It's a Small World FP+
15. *Jungle Cruise* FP+
16. *Liberty Belle* Riverboat
17. Mad Tea Party FP+
18. The Magic Carpets of Aladdin FP+
19. The Many Adventures of
    Winnie the Pooh FP+
20. *Mickey's PhilharMagic* ✅ FP+
21. *Monsters, Inc. Laugh Floor* FP+

22. Peter Pan's Flight ✅ Use FP+
23. Pete's Silly Sideshow FP+
24. A Pirate's Adventure ✅
25. Pirates of the Caribbean ✅ FP+
26. Prince Charming
    Regal Carrousel
27. Princess Fairytale Hall Use FP+
28. Seven Dwarfs Mine Train ✅
    Use FP+
29. Sorcerers of the Magic Kingdom
30. Space Mountain ✅ Use FP+
31. Splash Mountain ✅ Use FP+
32. *Stitch's Great Escape!* (seasonal)
33. Swiss Family Treehouse
34. Tom Sawyer Island
35. Tomorrowland Speedway FP+
36. Tomorrowland Transit
    Authority PeopleMover ✅
37. Town Square Theater
    (Meet and Greets) ✅ FP+
38. Under the Sea: Journey of
    the Little Mermaid FP+
39. *Walt Disney's*
    Carousel of Progress
40. *Walt Disney's*
    Enchanted Tiki Room
41. WDW Railroad (multiple stations)
42. *The Muppets Present . . . Great*
    Moments in American History

Attractions

1. Ariel's Grotto FP+
2. Astro Orbiter
3. The Barnstormer FP+
4. Big Thunder Mountain Railroad ✅ Use FP+
5. Buzz Lightyear's Space Ranger Spin ✅ FP+
6. Casey Jr. Splash 'N' Soak Station
7. *Country Bear Jamboree*
8. Dumbo the Flying Elephant FP+
9. *Enchanted Tales with Belle* Use FP+
10. Fairytale Garden

Continued from page 515

opening procedure, it would have taken 15–30 minutes for that kind of line to form.

MAGIC KINGDOM CONUNDRUM The decision you face is whether it's worth getting to the park 90 minutes before official opening to be at the front of this crowd. If you don't have FastPasses for Seven Dwarfs or Space Mountain, then arriving 90 minutes early could save you 90 minutes in line at just those two attractions, and give you shorter lines at any other rides you visit prior to 10 a.m. If you dislike waiting in line more than losing the same amount of sleep, go early, get some coffee and family photos, and then hop in line.

If you have FastPasses for one of the two rides, then arriving early allows you to see the other ride with what's likely to be the shortest waits of the day. And if you're lucky enough to have FastPasses for Seven Dwarfs and Space Mountain, then it's OK to arrive at the Magic Kingdom entrance 30 minutes before official opening.

Disney hasn't said whether this new opening process is permanent, but we think the additional hour of coffees and breakfasts sold on Main Street tilts the odds toward keeping it. There's no word either on whether the practice will spread to the other parks.

GETTING ORIENTED

AT THE MAGIC KINGDOM, stroller, wheelchair, and ECV/ESV rentals are in the train station; lockers are on the right, just inside the entrance. On your left as you enter **Main Street, U.S.A.,** is **City Hall,** the center for information, lost and found, guided tours, and entertainment schedules.

unofficial **TIP**
Only Starbucks sells coffee before 10 a.m. in Disney's theme parks.

The guide map found there lists all attractions, shops, and eating places; provides information about first aid, baby care, and assistance for the disabled; and gives tips for good photos. It lists times for the day's special events, live entertainment, Disney-character parades, and concerts, and it also tells when and where to find Disney characters.

The guide map is supplemented by a daily entertainment schedule, the **Times Guide.** In addition to listing performance times, the *Times Guide* provides info on Disney-character appearances and what Disney calls Special Hours, or operating hours for attractions and restaurants that open late or close early. The **My Disney Experience** app (see page 38) has this same information.

unofficial **TIP**
Because Cinderella Castle is so large, designate a very specific meeting spot, such as the entrance to Cinderella's Royal Table restaurant at the rear of the castle.

Main Street, U.S.A., ends at the **Central Plaza,** from which branch the entrances to five other "lands": **Adventureland, Frontierland, Liberty Square, Fantasyland,** and **Tomorrowland.**

Cinderella Castle, at the entrance to Fantasyland, is the Magic Kingdom's visual center. If you start in Adventureland and go clockwise around the Magic Kingdom, the castle spires will always be roughly on your right; if you start in Tomorrowland and go counterclockwise through the park, the spires will always be roughly on your left. The castle is an excellent meeting place if your group decides to split up or gets separated accidentally.

WHAT'S NEW AT THE MAGIC KINGDOM

THE PARK'S NEW SECURITY and opening procedures, and their impacts, are described on page 515. Beyond those, new shows include *The Muppets Present . . . Great Moments in American History* (page 536), a short outdoor comedy performance in Liberty Square; *Mickey's Royal Friendship Faire,* staged in front of Cinderella Castle several times per day; *Once Upon a Time* (page 556), an after-dark video-projection show played on Cinderella Castle; and *Happily Ever After* (page 554), a new fireworks show that replaces the Magic Kingdom's long-running and beloved *Wishes.*

Our Magic Kingdom touring plans reflect the latest developments. Check **TouringPlans.com** for updates.

FASTPASS+ ATTRACTIONS IN THE MAGIC KINGDOM

ADVENTURELAND
- Jungle Cruise
- The Magic Carpets of Aladdin
- Pirates of the Caribbean

FANTASYLAND
- Ariel's Grotto
- The Barnstormer
- Dumbo the Flying Elephant
- *Enchanted Tales with Belle*
- It's a Small World
- Mad Tea Party
- The Many Adventures of Winnie the Pooh
- *Mickey's PhilharMagic*
- Peter Pan's Flight
- Princess Fairytale Hall

- Seven Dwarfs Mine Train
- Under the Sea: Journey of the Little Mermaid

FRONTIERLAND
- Big Thunder Mountain Railroad
- Splash Mountain

LIBERTY SQUARE
- The Haunted Mansion

MAIN STREET, U.S.A.
- Town Square Theater Meet and Greets (Mickey, Tinker Bell)

TOMORROWLAND
- Buzz Lightyear's Space Ranger Spin
- *Monsters, Inc. Laugh Floor*
- Space Mountain
- Tomorrowland Speedway

WHILE THE MAGIC KINGDOM offers FastPass+ for about two dozen attractions, as listed above, our touring plan software identifies just 10 as frequently needing FastPass+: **(1) Peter Pan's Flight, (2) Seven Dwarfs Mine Train, (3) Big Thunder Mountain Railroad, (4) Splash Mountain, (5) *Enchanted Tales with Belle*, (6) Pirates of the Caribbean, (7) Jungle Cruise, (8) Space Mountain, (9) The Haunted Mansion, and (10) Buzz Lightyear's Space Ranger Spin.**

Why is Peter Pan's Flight listed first? First of all, it's really nobody's choice as the first attraction to visit. If you've got small children, you're probably headed to *Enchanted Tales with Belle* or Seven Dwarfs Mine Train; if you've got older kids, you're probably headed to Space Mountain or Seven Dwarfs. And no matter where you go first, you'll probably visit at least one other attraction nearby next. That means you're not getting to Peter Pan within the first 30 minutes the park is open.

Second, Peter Pan appears on virtually every Magic Kingdom touring plan. It's a classic, if simple, Disney ride with universal appeal.

Third, although it's not a headliner attraction, Peter Pan develops long lines throughout the day. Wait times during Christmas, for example, can exceed 150–180 minutes fairly often. The ride's hourly capacity is around 1,100 guests—a little more than half of Buzz Lightyear's and far less than half of Pirates of the Caribbean's.

Seven Dwarfs Mine Train, in the second spot, is usually the first Fast-Pass+ recommendation that our software suggests, often with a start time between 9 and 9:30 a.m. If you're doing a comprehensive tour of the Magic Kingdom that allows you to visit Space Mountain and Buzz Lightyear as soon as the park opens, then you can ride Seven Dwarfs Mine Train with little wait. It also puts you in a good position to ride a couple of secondary Fantasyland attractions before a 10 a.m. Peter Pan's Flight FastPass+ reservation—and that helps cut down on how much walking you have to do in the park.

Big Thunder and **Splash Mountains** are on the list, too. While they don't normally get a huge influx of guests immediately at park opening, lines of 20–40 minutes can develop around midmorning at Splash Mountain and Big Thunder Mountain as crowds make their way from Tomorrowland and Fantasyland.

Enchanted Tales with Belle makes the top five because it usually doesn't make sense to visit it first thing in the morning. Counting walking time to *Belle* and its elaborate preshow, you'd probably be committing about half an hour to that one attraction, whereas you could probably visit two or three other attractions in Fantasyland or Tomorrowland in the same amount of time.

Our software usually recommends **Pirates of the Caribbean** and the **Jungle Cruise** as day-of FastPasses that you'd get in the early afternoon inside the Magic Kingdom. Why? These aren't in the top tier of popular attractions in the park, and they've got enough capacity to move a lot of people per hour and thus moderate waits.

Space Mountain made the list because of **Seven Dwarfs Mine Train.** The latter is the newest headliner in the Magic Kingdom, and its low height requirement makes it a more family-friendly attraction than Space Mountain. Those two factors also make FastPass+ reservations much harder to get for Seven Dwarfs Mine Train than for Space Mountain. When FastPass+ isn't available for Seven Dwarfs, our touring plans usually suggest riding very early or very late, making a FastPass+ for Space Mountain the best possible alternative.

FastPass+ kiosk locations in the Magic Kingdom are as follows:

- In the walkway between Adventureland and Liberty Square, near the Diamond Horseshoe Saloon and Swiss Family Treehouse
- At the entrance to Jungle Cruise in Adventureland
- Outside *Mickey's PhilharMagic* in Fantasyland
- Near *Stitch's Great Escape!* in Tomorrowland

Same-Day FastPass+ Availability

The preceding tells you which attractions to focus on when making your *advance* FastPass+ reservations before you get to the park. Once you're in the park, you can make more FastPass+ reservations once the originals

MAGIC KINGDOM
When Same-Day FP+ Runs Out, by Crowd Level

ATTRACTION	LOW CROWDS*	MODERATE CROWDS*	HIGH CROWDS*
Ariel's Grotto	N/A	8 a.m.	N/A
The Barnstormer	3 p.m.	4 p.m.	3 p.m.
Big Thunder Mountain	N/A	8 a.m.	N/A
Buzz Lightyear's Space Ranger Spin	2 p.m.	3 p.m.	Noon
Dumbo the Flying Elephant	3 p.m.	5 p.m.	5 p.m.
Enchanted Tales with Belle	N/A	N/A	N/A
Festival of Fantasy parade	7 p.m.	9 p.m.	10 p.m.
The Haunted Mansion	3 p.m.	3 p.m.	Noon
It's a Small World	3 p.m.	5 p.m.	5 p.m.
Jungle Cruise	1 p.m.	2 p.m.	Noon
Monsters, Inc. Laugh Floor	2 p.m.	3 p.m.	2 p.m.
Mad Tea Party	3 p.m.	5 p.m.	5 p.m.
The Magic Carpets of Aladdin	2 p.m.	5 p.m.	4 p.m.
The Many Adventures of Winnie the Pooh	3 p.m.	5 p.m.	5 p.m.
Mickey's PhilharMagic	2 p.m.	3 p.m.	3 p.m.
Peter Pan's Flight	N/A	N/A	N/A
Pirates of the Caribbean	3 p.m.	4 p.m.	1 p.m.
Princess Fairytale Hall: Cinderella and Friends	N/A	N/A	N/A
Seven Dwarfs Mine Train	N/A	N/A	N/A
Space Mountain	1 p.m.	11 a.m.	N/A
Splash Mountain	N/A	9 a.m.	9 a.m.
Tomorrowland Speedway	1 p.m.	3 p.m.	1 p.m.
Town Square Mickey Mouse Meet and Greet	N/A	9 a.m.	N/A
Town Square Tinker Bell Meet and Greet	8 a.m.	9 a.m.	N/A
Under the Sea: Journey of the Little Mermaid	3 p.m.	5 p.m.	4 p.m.

* **LOW CROWDS** (Levels 1–3 on TouringPlans.com Crowd Calendar)
* **MODERATE CROWDS** (Levels 4–7 on TouringPlans.com Crowd Calendar)
* **HIGH CROWDS** (Levels 8–10 on TouringPlans.com Crowd Calendar)
N/A = no availability

have been used or have expired. How do you know which attractions are likely to have these day-of reservations? And when will they run out? Hush, *bubeleh*, the chart above has your answers.

You'll notice that many attractions have more day-of FastPass+ availability on days with moderate crowds than with low crowds. That seems backwards, but it's not: Disney can change how much of each ride's hourly capacity is dedicated to FastPass+ and increases this number on days of higher attendance. For example, on days of low crowds, Peter Pan's Flight might dedicate 75% of its hourly capacity to FastPass+ riders, 85% on days of moderate crowds.

DINING IN THE MAGIC KINGDOM

BELOW IS A QUICK RECAP of the Magic Kingdom's major restaurants, rated by readers from highest to lowest. See Part Four for details.

MAGIC KINGDOM RESTAURANT REFRESHER	
COUNTER-SERVICE	**FULL-SERVICE**
Aloha Isle (98% 👍), Adventureland	**The Crystal Palace** (B, L, D) (91% 👍), Main Street, U.S.A.
Columbia Harbour House (93% 👍), Liberty Square	**Be Our Guest** (D) (90% 👍), Fantasyland
Main Street Bakery (Starbucks) (93% 👍), Main Street, U.S.A.	**Liberty Tree Tavern** (L, D) (88% 👍), Liberty Square
Gaston's Tavern (92% 👍), Fantasyland	**Cinderella's Royal Table** (B, L, D) (86% 👍), Fantasyland
Be Our Guest (B, L) (90% 👍), Fantasyland	**The Plaza Restaurant** (L, D) (85% 👍), Main Street, U.S.A.
Casey's Corner (88% 👍), Main Street, U.S.A.	**Jungle Navigation Co Ltd. Skipper Canteen** (L, D) (81% 👍), Adventureland
Pecos Bill Tall Tale Inn and Cafe (86% 👍), Frontierland	**Tony's Town Square** (L, D) (77% 👍), Main Street, U.S.A.
The Friar's Nook (85% 👍), Fantasyland	
Cosmic Ray's (82% 👍), Tomorrowland	
The Lunching Pad (82% 👍), Tomorrowland	
The Pinocchio Village Haus (81% 👍), Fantasyland	

MAIN STREET, U.S.A.

BEGIN AND END YOUR VISIT ON MAIN STREET, which opens an hour or more before and closes 30 minutes–1 hour after the rest of the park. The Walt Disney World Railroad stops at Main Street Station; get on to tour the park or ride to Frontierland or Fantasyland.

Main Street is a Disneyfied turn-of-the-20th-century small-town American thoroughfare. Its buildings are real, not elaborate props. Attention to detail is exceptional: Furnishings and fixtures are true to the period. Along the street are shops, character-greeting venues, eating places, City Hall, and a fire station. Occasionally, horse-drawn trolleys, fire engines, and horseless carriages transport visitors along Main Street to the Central Plaza.

The circular area around the Central Plaza is a paved, landscaped viewing area for the large crowds that watch the evening parades and fireworks. And to disperse very heavy crowds, the areas behind the shops on either side of Main Street can become pedestrian walkways for guests to exit and enter the park during those parades and fireworks. The most frequently used arcade runs from just past Tony's Town Square Restaurant to the Tomorrowland side of The Plaza Restaurant; the other runs from near the First Aid Center next to The Crystal Palace, to the Fire Station near City Hall on Main Street.

Main Street Characters

DESCRIPTION AND COMMENTS Colorful characters, including the mayor of Main Street, roam the area for photos, autographs, and lively conversation.

Magic Kingdom Services

MOST PARK SERVICES are centered on Main Street, U.S.A., including:

Baby Care Center Next to The Crystal Palace, left around the Central Plaza (toward Adventureland)

Banking Services ATMs underneath the Main Street railroad station

Cell Phone Charging Space Mountain exit and behind Big Top Treats in Storybook Circus. Can drop at City Hall with cord for charging.

First Aid Center Next to The Crystal Palace, left around the Central Plaza (toward Adventureland)

Live Entertainment and Parade Information City Hall, at the railroad-station end of Main Street

Lost and Found City Hall

Lost Persons City Hall

Storage Lockers Underneath the Main Street railroad station

Walt Disney World and Local Attraction Information City Hall

Wheelchair, ECV/ESV, and Stroller Rentals Inside turnstiles at right as you face the train station

Not as engaging as the characters who populate Hollywood Boulevard in Disney's Hollywood Studios, but still fun.

TOURING TIPS Characters are usually available from park opening until around 2 p.m. They're fun to talk to if you're in the area, but don't make a special trip.

Sorcerers of the Magic Kingdom ★★★★

APPEAL BY AGE	PRESCHOOL ★★★½	GRADE SCHOOL ★★★★½	TEENS ★★★★
YOUNG ADULTS ★★★★		OVER 30 ★★★★	SENIORS ★★★

What it is Interactive video game. **Scope and scale** Minor attraction. **When to go** Before 11 a.m. or after 8 p.m. **Special comment** Long lines to play. **Authors' rating** Great idea; ★★★. **Duration of presentation** About 2 minutes per step, 4 or 5 steps per game. **Probable waiting time per step** 10–15 minutes.

DESCRIPTION AND COMMENTS Sorcerers of the Magic Kingdom combines aspects of role-playing games such as Dungeons and Dragons with Disney characters and theme park attractions. Your objective: to help the wizard Merlin keep evildoers from taking over the Magic Kingdom. Merlin sends you on adventures in different parts of the park to fight these villains. Each land hosts a different adventure within the game.

This free game is played with a set of trading cards. You'll need your park ticket or MagicBand to pick up your first set of cards and start the game. One card, known as your "key," is special because it links you to your game. You'll need to present your key card when you pick up a set of cards to start your next adventure.

DISNEY DISH WITH JIM HILL

SAVVY GAMESMANSHIP The number of guests who line up to play Sorcerers of the Magic Kingdom every day is only a bit less than the daily capacity of The Many Adventures of Winnie the Pooh. That's why Disney was quick to add the interactive Pirate's Adventure game to this theme park.

When you pick up your first set of cards, you'll view an instructional video explaining how to use them and the object of the game. Then you'll be sent to another location to start your first adventure. Each location in the park is associated with a unique symbol: an eye, a feather, a dragonfly, or something along those lines. Look for these symbols on the map to find the best route to your starting point.

Each adventure consists of four or five stops in a particular land. At each stop, another story will play on a video screen, outlining what your villain is trying to do. Merlin will ask you to cast a spell to stop the villain—to do so, hold one or more of your cards up to the video display. Cameras in the display read your card, deploy the spell, and show you the results.

The game has three levels: easy, medium, and hard. The easy version is the default and is appropriate for small children; holding up any one of your character cards is enough to defeat any villain. In more-advanced levels of the game, you need to display two or more character cards in specific combinations to defeat a particular villain. Different card combinations produce different spells, and only some spells work on certain characters in those advanced levels.

The audio at each step holds clues to which cards you should use against advanced villains. For example, if a villain says something like "Don't toy with me!" then you should look for cards with characters that are toys, such as the Toy Story characters; references to "being spotted" suggest using cards with characters from 101 Dalmatians; and so on.

The game launched with an initial series of around 70 unique cards; you can obtain 5 new ones per day. Don't worry if you play more than once and end up with duplicate cards—a small trading market exists within the park. Disney issues new card series over time.

An Anchorage, Alaska, couple offers these tips for playing the game:

(1) Unless you plan to stick with every member of your group every single minute, make sure they all get their own portal keys. (2) Every card has a "rarity," located above the card number. If you want to trade cards, only trade for similar rarities. The symbol designates its rarity: Planet (looks like a circle) is common, moon is uncommon, star is rare, lightning bolt is super-rare. You can only obtain lightning-bolt cards by buying card packs at the Emporium when they're in stock. They usually sell out by lunchtime, and the days they have them are random (to help increase scarcity). (3) When you're playing, be prepared for a LOT of people to come up to you and ask what you're doing. (4) Also, be prepared for people to walk in front of you when you're playing. This can cause the card reader to time out. (5) You can buy T-shirts with special designs on them that increase your power when you play at medium and hard levels.

This Stamford, Connecticut, reader stresses that Sorcerers of the Magic Kingdom takes a while to play:

Be warned—if you want to beat the game, it takes a lot longer than you think.

TOURING TIPS You'll probably encounter a couple of people ahead of you at each portal, especially if you play during the afternoon. One complete adventure should take about 30–60 minutes to play, depending on how crowded the park is. If the game sounds too confusing, A Pirate's Adventure in Adventureland (see page 527) is easier.

Town Square Theater Meet and Greets: Mickey Mouse, Tinker Bell and Friends *(FastPass+)* ★★★★½

APPEAL BY AGE	PRESCHOOL ★★★★★	GRADE SCHOOL ★★★★½	TEENS ★★★★½
YOUNG ADULTS ★★★★½		OVER 30 ★★★★½	SENIORS ★★★★½

What it is Character-greeting venue. **Scope and scale** Minor attraction. **When to go** Before 10 a.m. or after 4 p.m., or use FastPass+. **Special comment** Mickey and the fairies have 2 separate queues, requiring 2 separate waits in line. **Authors' rating** It all started with this mouse; ★★★★. **Duration of experience** 2 minutes per character. **Probable waiting time** 15–25 minutes. **Queue speed** Slow.

DESCRIPTION AND COMMENTS Children and teenagers rate character greetings among the highest of any Disney attractions, and there's no bigger celebrity than Mickey Mouse. The latest Mickey can even talk to you during your encounter—in six languages! Meet Mickey, along with Tinker Bell and her Pixie Hollow friends, throughout the day at the Town Square Theater on Main Street, to your right as you enter the park.

TOURING TIPS Lines usually recede after the afternoon parade. Oddly enough, meeting Mickey rarely requires FastPass+. If you don't have FastPasses, our touring plan software frequently puts meeting Mickey as the first step in the day. Mickey usually starts greeting guests at the park's official opening time, even if you're let into Main Street, U.S.A., early.

Transportation Rides

DESCRIPTION AND COMMENTS Trolleys, buses, and the like.

TOURING TIPS Will save you a walk to the Central Plaza. Not worth a wait.

Walt Disney World Railroad   ★★★★

APPEAL BY AGE	PRESCHOOL ★★★★½	GRADE SCHOOL ★★★★	TEENS ★★★★
YOUNG ADULTS ★★★★		OVER 30 ★★★★	SENIORS ★★★★½

What it is Scenic railroad ride around the perimeter of the Magic Kingdom; provides transportation to Frontierland and Fantasyland. **Scope and scale** Minor attraction. **When to go** Anytime. **Special comment** Main Street is usually the least congested station. **Authors' rating** Plenty to see; ★★★. **Duration of ride** About 20 minutes for a complete circuit. **Average wait in line per 100 people ahead of you** 8 minutes; assumes 2 or more trains operating. **Loading speed** Moderate.

DESCRIPTION AND COMMENTS This is a ride around the perimeter of the Magic Kingdom aboard a real steam-powered locomotive, with stops in Frontierland and Fantasyland. Views from the train include a peek into each land except Adventureland (where you're apt to see more of the behind-the-scenes infrastructure). While it's much faster to walk to any of the other stations, the train is more relaxing. The most scenic part of the tour is between the Frontierland and Main Street, U.S.A., stations. If you're in Frontierland and headed out of the park, it's a nice way to end your visit.

TOURING TIPS Save the train until after you've seen the featured attractions, or use it when you need transportation. On busy days, lines form at the Frontierland Station but rarely at the Main Street Station. Wheelchair access is available at the Frontierland and Fantasyland Stations.

Only folded strollers are permitted on the train, so you can't board with your rented Disney stroller. You can, however, obtain a replacement at your destination (keep your stroller name card and rental receipt with you).

Finally, note that the railroad shuts down immediately before and during parades; check your park guide map or *Times Guide* for parade times. Needless to say, this is not the time to queue up for the train.

ADVENTURELAND

ADVENTURELAND IS THE FIRST land located to the left of Main Street, U.S.A. It combines an African-safari theme with a tropical-island atmosphere.

Captain Jack Sparrow's Pirate Tutorial ★★★½

APPEAL BY AGE   PRESCHOOL ★★★★   GRADE SCHOOL ★★★★½   TEENS ★★★½
YOUNG ADULTS ★★★   OVER 30 ★★★½   SENIORS ★★★½

What it is Outdoor stage show with guest participation. **Scope and scale** Diversion.
When to go See *Times Guide* for show schedule. **Authors' rating** Sign us up;
★★★½. **Duration of presentation** About 20 minutes.

DESCRIPTION AND COMMENTS Outside Pirates of the Caribbean, Cap'n Jack
and a crew member teach would-be knaves the skills needed for a career
in piracy. Some kids go onstage to train in the finer points of dueling,
similar to *Jedi Training: Trials of the Temple* at Hollywood Studios (see
page 657). The show finishes with everyone taking the probably-not-
legally-binding pirate's oath and singing a rousing round of "A Pirate's
Life for Me." If you or your kids are fans of the Pirates ride or the movie
series, this show is worth a look as well.

TOURING TIPS The shows attract decent crowds, but the first and last show
seem to be the least popular. Standing-room-only and outdoors.

Jungle Cruise (FastPass+) ★★★★

APPEAL BY AGE   PRESCHOOL ★★★½   GRADE SCHOOL ★★★★   TEENS ★★★★
YOUNG ADULTS ★★★★   OVER 30 ★★★★   SENIORS ★★★★

What it is Outdoor safari-themed boat ride. **Scope and scale** Major attraction. **When
to go** Before 10:30 a.m., during the last 2 hours before closing, or use FastPass+. **Special comment** Fun to ride at night! **Authors' rating** A classic, but kinda long in the
tooth; ★★★½. **Duration of ride** 8–9 minutes. **Average wait in line per 100 people
ahead of you** 3½ minutes; assumes 10 boats operating. **Loading speed** Moderate.

DESCRIPTION AND COMMENTS One of the Magic Kingdom's largest attractions,
the Jungle Cruise is an outdoor, group boat ride through some of the
world's best-known tropical waterways. You'll pass through forest and jungle populated entirely by animatronic animals (some hostile) and natives.

Jungle Cruise was the park's signature ride when it opened at Disneyland. With the advent of modern, highly themed zoo environments (including Disney's Animal Kingdom), the Magic Kingdom's version would surely
have faded into obscurity were it not for one thing: The boat skippers tell
jokes. Actually, "jokes" is a stretch—the skippers tell *the* cheesiest, most
groan-inducing puns you've ever heard. If you're in the right frame of mind,
it's glorious. If not, heed this Pelham, Alabama, reader's warning:

*Jungle Cruise severely needs an update. Our tour guide indulged in annoying
comedy to make up for the lack of excitement. I would rather have been
eaten by the animatronic hippos.*

If, on the other hand, you like this sort of thing, the nearby **Jungle Navigation Co. Ltd. Skipper Canteen** restaurant (see page 383) serves tasty
food with the same kind of humor.

TOURING TIPS Jungle Cruise is a FastPass+ attraction. Before you make a
same-day reservation, however, ask a cast member what the estimated
wait in the standby line is. We think the ride is better at night.

The Magic Carpets of Aladdin (FastPass+) ★★★½

APPEAL BY AGE   PRESCHOOL ★★★★½   GRADE SCHOOL ★★★★   TEENS ★★★½
YOUNG ADULTS ★★★½   OVER 30 ★★★½   SENIORS ★★★½

What it is Elaborate midway ride. **Scope and scale** Minor attraction. **When to go**
Before 11 a.m. or after 7 p.m. **Authors' rating** A visually appealing children's ride;

DISNEY DISH WITH JIM HILL

A SWEET BUT NOT-SO-SPIRITED ADVENTURE Fans of the old Adventurers Club who wander around Skipper Canteen will notice that some of the artifacts lining the walls of this 222-seat eatery come from that now-defunct Pleasure Island nightclub. Sadly, the Kungaloosh! served here isn't the vodka-and-rum drink of old—instead, it's an African-inspired chocolate cake with caramelized bananas.

★★½. **Duration of ride** 1½ minutes. **Average wait in line per 100 people ahead of you** 16 minutes. **Loading speed** Slow.

DESCRIPTION AND COMMENTS The Magic Carpets of Aladdin is a spinning midway ride like Dumbo, except with magic carpets instead of elephants. A spitting camel sprays jets of water on carpet riders. Riders can maneuver their carpets up and down and side to side to avoid the water. The front seat controls vehicle height, while the backseat controls tilt—if you let the kids sit up front, prepare to get wet!

TOURING TIPS Like Dumbo, this ride has great eye appeal but extremely limited capacity (that is, it loads slowly). Try to get younger kids on during the first 30 minutes the park is open, or try just before park closing. Fast-Pass+ is almost never needed.

A Pirate's Adventure: Treasure of the Seven Seas
★★★★

APPEAL BY AGE   **PRESCHOOL** ★★★½   **GRADE SCHOOL** ★★★★½   **TEENS** ★★★★
YOUNG   ADULTS ★★★★   **OVER 30** ★★★★   **SENIORS** ★★★★

What it is Interactive game. **Scope and scale** Diversion. **When to go** Anytime. **Authors' rating** Simple, fast, and fun—especially at night; not to be missed; ★★★½. **Duration of experience** About 20 minutes to play the entire game.

DESCRIPTION AND COMMENTS Similar to Agent P's World Showcase Adventure at Epcot, A Pirate's Adventure features interactive areas with physical props and narrations that lead guests through a quest to find lost treasure, all within Adventureland.

Guests begin their journey at an old Cartography Shop near Golden Oak Outpost—this is the central hub for adventurers helping to locate missing treasure. Groups of up to six people are given a talisman (an RFID card) that will help them on their journey. The talisman activates a video screen that assigns your group to one of five different missions. Your group is then given a map and sent off to find your first location.

Once at the location, one member of the party touches the talisman to the symbol at the station, and the animation begins. Each adventure has four or five stops throughout Adventureland, and each stop contains 30–45 seconds of activity. No strategy or action is required: Watch what unfolds on the screen, get your next destination, and head off.

We like how well each station integrates into its surroundings, and how the stations' artifacts and props tie together the attraction and movie storylines. If you're not yet convinced to play, stand in Adventureland and watch the faces of the kids playing when they do something that triggers smoke, noise, or other effects. A Pirate's Adventure also serves as a good introduction to other interactive games, such as Sorcerers of the Magic Kingdom (see page 523).

DISNEY DISH WITH JIM HILL

ELEPHANTS ON ICE Jungle Cruise's 2017 "Jingle Cruise" holiday retheming will feature the following winter weather-related gag: The animatronic elephants in the bathing pool scene will be outfitted with oversize woolen hats and scarves, plus ice skates and hockey sticks. As soon as the temperature drops, the pachyderms will hit the ice and start knocking a puck around.

A Maryland mom writes:

The very best thing we did with our 4-year-old was A Pirate's Adventure. It was incredible. Located in its own building next to the arch in Adventureland, it was five scavenger hunts—we did all of them and it took 2 hours—our most fun 2 hours at the park! It's high-tech, magical, imaginative, active, and individualized. And you can keep the beautiful maps!

And from a New York City reader:

We highly recommend that families check out the Pirate's Adventure scavenger hunt at MK. Our girls (age 9) had a blast and were eager to complete all five stages of the journey. The maps were a fun challenge for them (easy enough to be just fun, but [challenging enough to] give them a sense that they were accomplishing something) and the surprises at each stage were lots of fun for all of us. The only caution I would add is that you should try to take part when there aren't too many other people participating. Waiting in line behind another group took the fun out of the excitement of finding a stop and seeing what happened when we activated it.

TOURING TIPS As we went to press, A Pirate's Adventure was offering a free Pirates of the Caribbean FastPass+ to groups who complete more than one mission. If you don't have a FastPass+ for POTC and the wait is 30 minutes or more, it's worth playing two games to get the FastPass. The effects are better at night. While we think everyone should try A Pirate's Adventure, it isn't a must if time is tight.

Pirates of the Caribbean *(FastPass+)* ★★★★½

APPEAL BY AGE	PRESCHOOL ★★★½	GRADE SCHOOL ★★★★	TEENS ★★★★½
YOUNG ADULTS ★★★★½		OVER 30 ★★★★½	SENIORS ★★★★½

What it is Indoor pirate-themed boat ride. **Scope and scale** Headliner. **When to go** Before 11 a.m., after 7 p.m., or use FastPass+. **Special comment** Frightens some children. **Authors' rating** Disney Audio-Animatronics at their best; not to be missed; ★★★★. **Duration of ride** About 7½ minutes. **Average wait in line per 100 people ahead of you** 3 minutes; assumes one FastPass+ line, one standby line. **Loading speed** Fast.

DESCRIPTION AND COMMENTS An indoor cruise through a series of sets that depict a pirate raid on an island settlement, from bombardment of the fortress to debauchery after the victory. Arguably one of the most influential theme park attractions ever created, the Magic Kingdom's version retains the elaborate queuing area, grand scale, and detailed scenes that have awed audiences since its debut in Disneyland in 1967. The successful Pirates of the Caribbean movies have boosted the ride's popularity, and guests' demands led to the addition of animatronic figures of the film's Captain Jack Sparrow and Captain Barbossa in scenes.

Speaking of debauchery, Pirates of the Caribbean displays a strong dose of political correctness. Even so, a Rockville, Maryland, mother was not prepared for what she saw:

I had no idea that it would be as visually violent and historically accurate as it was. I really didn't look forward to explaining to my son why those women had ropes around their necks and such.

TOURING TIPS Undoubtedly one of the park's most timeless attractions. Engineered to move large crowds in a hurry, Pirates is a good attraction to see in the late afternoon.

Swiss Family Treehouse ★★★½

APPEAL BY AGE	PRESCHOOL ★★★½	GRADE SCHOOL ★★★½	TEENS ★★★
YOUNG ADULTS ★★★	OVER 30 ★★★½		SENIORS ★★★½

What it is Outdoor walk-through treehouse. **Scope and scale** Minor attraction. **When to go** Anytime. **Special comment** Requires climbing a lot of stairs. **Authors' rating** Incredible detail and execution; ★★★. **Duration of tour** 10–15 minutes. **Average wait in line per 100 people ahead of you** 7 minutes.

DESCRIPTION AND COMMENTS An immense replica of the shipwrecked Swiss Family Robinson's arboreal abode. With its multiple stories and mechanical wizardry, it's the queen of all treehouses.

TOURING TIPS A self-guided walk-through tour involves a lot of stairs up and down, but no ropes, ladders, or anything fancy. Lookie-loos or people stopping to rest sometimes create bottlenecks that slow the crowd flow. Visit in late afternoon or early evening if you're on a one-day tour, or in the morning of your second day.

Walt Disney's Enchanted Tiki Room ★★★½

APPEAL BY AGE	PRESCHOOL ★★★½	GRADE SCHOOL ★★★½	TEENS ★★★
YOUNG ADULTS ★★★½	OVER 30 ★★★½		SENIORS ★★★★

What it is Audio-Animatronic Pacific-island musical-theater show. **Scope and scale** Minor attraction. **When to go** Before 11 a.m. or after 3:30 p.m. **Special comment** Frightens some preschoolers. **Authors' rating** Very, very . . . unusual; ★★★½. **Duration of presentation** 15½ minutes. **Preshow entertainment** Talking birds. **Probable waiting time** 15 minutes.

DESCRIPTION AND COMMENTS The current show here is a shortened version of the original attraction, which premiered at Disneyland in 1963. Starring four singing, wisecracking parrots—José, Fritz, Michael, and Pierre—*Enchanted Tiki Room* remains a favorite of many, including us. The show is a series of musical numbers sung by dozens of birds, plants, and tikis that come to life all around the large seating area.

Although most readers like the show, they caution that it may be frightening to younger children. Concerning the scary parts, a mother of three from Coleman, Michigan, is outspoken:

The Tiki Room show was very scary, with a thunder-and-lightning storm and a loud volcano. Can't Disney do anything without scaring young children?

TOURING TIPS Usually not too crowded. We go in the late afternoon, when we appreciate sitting in air-conditioned comfort with our brains in park. If you're a fan of the show, see it the next time you're there; we've heard rumors that the birds may be on the chopping block.

FRONTIERLAND

THIS "LAND" ADJOINS ADVENTURELAND as you move clockwise around the Magic Kingdom. Frontierland's focus is on the Old West, with stockade-type structures and pioneer trappings.

Big Thunder Mountain Railroad *(FastPass+)* ★★★★½

APPEAL BY AGE	PRESCHOOL ★★★★	GRADE SCHOOL ★★★★½	TEENS ★★★★½
YOUNG ADULTS ★★★★½		OVER 30 ★★★★½	SENIORS ★★★★

What it is Tame Western mining–themed roller coaster. **Scope and scale** Headliner. **When to go** Before 10 a.m., in the hour before closing, or use FastPass+. **Special comments** 40″ minimum height requirement; children younger than age 7 must ride with an adult. Switching-off option provided (see page 439). **Authors' rating** Great effects; relatively tame ride; not to be missed; ★★★★. **Duration of ride** About 3½ minutes. **Average wait in line per 100 people ahead of you** 2½ minutes; assumes 5 trains operating. **Loading speed** Moderate–fast.

DESCRIPTION AND COMMENTS Roller coaster through and around a Disney "mountain." The idea is that you're on a runaway mine train during the Gold Rush. We put this coaster at about a 5 on a "scary scale" of 10. Big Thunder contains first-rate examples of Disney creativity: a realistic mining town, falling rocks, and an earthquake, all humorously animated with swinging possums, petulant buzzards, and the like. Ride it after dark if you can. Seats in the back offer the best experience.

We love the interactive props in the queue. Spin a metal wheel and push on a dynamite plunger to trigger an "explosion" (of water, steam, or noise) near a passing train; watch "home movies" of the workers in the mines; see (and smell!) what some proverbial canaries experience underground; and more. Best of all, these toys are spaced just far apart for little kids to have something to do the entire time in line. Great thinking.

TOURING TIPS A superb Disney experience, but not too wild a roller coaster. Emphasis is more on the sights than on the thrill of the ride.

Nearby Splash Mountain affects traffic flow to Big Thunder Mountain Railroad—adventuresome guests ride Splash Mountain first, then go next door to ride Big Thunder. All this means large crowds in Frontierland all day and long waits for Big Thunder. The best way to experience both is to ride Seven Dwarfs Mine Train and Space Mountain one morning as soon as the park opens, then Splash Mountain and Big Thunder Mountain the next morning. If you have only one day, the order should be (1) Seven Dwarfs, (2) Splash Mountain, (3) Big Thunder, and (4) Space Mountain.

A Midwestern mom offers this tip to families with kids too short to ride:

If you're switching off on Thunder Mountain or Splash Mountain and have young kids to entertain, there's a fantastic little playground nearby where you can pass the time. It's completely covered and near the restrooms too! It's next to Splash Mountain, under the train tracks.

Guests experience Disney attractions differently. Consider this letter from a woman in Brookline, Massachusetts:

Being senior citizens and having limited time, my friend and I confined our activities to attractions rated as four or five stars for seniors. Because of your recommendation, we waited an hour to board Big Thunder Mountain Railroad, which you rated a 5 on a scary scale of 10. After living through 3½ minutes of pure terror, I will rate it a 15. We were so busy holding on and screaming and even praying for our safety that we didn't see any falling rocks, a mining town, or an earthquake. The Big Thunder Mountain Railroad should not be recommended for seniors or preschool children.

A woman from Vermont discovered that there's more to consider about Big Thunder than being scared:

Big Thunder Mountain Railroad was rated a 5 on the scary scale, but it was much higher on the lose-your-lunch meter. One more sharp turn and the kids in front of me would've needed a dip in Splash Mountain!

However, a reader from West Newton, Massachusetts, dubbed the ride "a roller coaster for people who don't like roller coasters."

Country Bear Jamboree ★★★½

APPEAL BY AGE	PRESCHOOL ★★★★	GRADE SCHOOL ★★★½	TEENS ★★★½
YOUNG ADULTS ★★★	OVER 30 ★★★½		SENIORS ★★★★

What it is Audio-Animatronic country hoedown. **Scope and scale** Major attraction. **When to go** Anytime. **Authors' rating** Old and worn but pure Disney; ★★★½. **Duration of presentation** 11 minutes. **Preshow entertainment** None. **Probable waiting time** It's not terribly popular but has a comparatively small capacity. Waiting time between noon and 5:30 p.m. on a busy day will average 11–22 minutes.

DESCRIPTION AND COMMENTS A charming cast of animatronic bears sings and stomps in a Western-style revue. It's an air-conditioned refuge on hot days, but the *Jamboree* has run for so long that the geriatric bears are a step away from assisted living. Reader comments tend to echo the need for something new. From a Sandy Hook, Connecticut, mom:

I know they consider it a classic, and kids always seem to love it, but could they PLEASE update it after half a century?

A woman from Carmel, Indiana, put her experience in perspective:

Here is a half-hour of my life that I can never get back.

But a Mississippi dad defends the show:

I find it interesting how my reactions and those of my family change to certain attractions. Take Country Bear Jamboree, for instance: In my 30s I considered it hokey and lame, yet I thoroughly enjoyed my daughter's intense love of it at ages 3 and 8 on two previous trips. This time, at age 54, I sat up fairly close with my wife and loved it—we even sang along! Of course, this was partly to embarrass my now-16-year-old daughter, who sat hunched down in the very last row. She says we have creeping senility, but I told her, "Just wait till you bring your kids!"

TOURING TIPS On hot and rainy days and during peak seasons, the *Jamboree* draws large crowds from midmorning on.

Frontierland Shootin' Arcade ★½

APPEAL BY AGE	PRESCHOOL ★★★	GRADE SCHOOL ★★★½	TEENS ★★★½
YOUNG ADULTS ★★★	OVER 30 ★★★		SENIORS ★★★½

What it is Electronic shooting gallery. **Scope and scale** Diversion. **When to go** Anytime. **Special comments** Costs $1 per play. **Authors' rating** Absolutely not a must; ★½.

DESCRIPTION AND COMMENTS One of a few attractions not included in Magic Kingdom admission. Would-be gunslingers get around 35 shots per $1 play. Each shot is followed by a short delay before the next shot can be taken—this prevents small children from accidentally using all 35 shots in 5 seconds. It's barely noticeable for adults. Despite our low rating, many

Unofficial Guide staff gladly spend a few bucks here when they visit the World. It's a small bit of you're-in-control interactivity in a park with a lot of sitting and watching.

TOURING TIPS Not a place to blow your time if you're on a tight schedule. The fun is entirely in the target practice—no prizes can be won.

Splash Mountain *(FastPass+)* ★★★★½

APPEAL BY AGE	PRESCHOOL ★★★★†	GRADE SCHOOL ★★★★½	TEENS ★★★★★
YOUNG ADULTS ★★★★½		OVER 30 ★★★★½	SENIORS ★★★★½

†Many preschoolers are too short to ride, and others freak out when they see it from the waiting line. Among preschoolers who actually ride, most love it.

What it is Indoor/outdoor water-flume adventure ride. **Scope and scale** Super-headliner. **When to go** As soon as the park opens, during afternoon or evening parades, just before closing, or use FastPass+. **Special comments** 40″ minimum height requirement; children younger than age 7 must ride with an adult. Switching-off option provided (see page 439). **Authors' rating** A soggy delight, and not to be missed; ★★★★★. **Duration of ride** About 10 minutes. **Average wait in line per 100 people ahead of you** 3½ minutes; assumes ride is operating at full capacity. **Loading speed** Moderate.

DISNEY DISH WITH JIM HILL

THIS IDEA *DIDN'T* MAKE A SPLASH When Tony Baxter came up with the Splash Mountain idea back in 1983, he wanted to name the ride "Zip-A-Dee-Doo-Dah River Run," tying it to the hit song from *Song of the South.* But then–Disney CEO Michael Eisner hated the name, preferring to keep the "mountain" theme going for Disney's thrill rides.

DESCRIPTION AND COMMENTS Splash Mountain tells the story of Br'er Rabbit, who goes off in search of adventure and finds it . . . along with a hungry fox and bear. Steep chutes and animatronics alternate with at least one special effect for each of the senses. The ride covers more than half a mile, splashing through swamps, caves, and backwoods bayous before climaxing in a five-story plunge and Br'er Rabbit's triumphant return home. More than 100 Audio-Animatronic characters, including Br'er Rabbit, Br'er Bear, and Br'er Fox, regale riders with songs, including "Zip-a-Dee-Doo-Dah."

TOURING TIPS This happy, adventuresome ride vies with Space Mountain in Tomorrowland and Seven Dwarfs Mine Train in Fantasyland as one of the park's most popular attractions. Crowds build faster the first hour the parks open, and waits of more than 2 hours can be expected once the park fills on busy days. Get in line no later than 10:30 a.m. during warmer months. Long lines will persist all day.

If you have only a day to see the Magic Kingdom, make FastPass+ reservations in advance for around 9:30 a.m. at Big Thunder Mountain Railroad and around 3:30 p.m. at Space Mountain. On the day of your visit, ride Seven Dwarfs Mine Train as soon as the park opens, then hotfoot it to Splash Mountain to ride immediately. Your FastPass+ reservation for Big Thunder will be valid by the time you're done, and you'll have experienced three of the park's four headliners in about an hour.

If you have two mornings, do the Fantasyland and Frontierland attractions—Seven Dwarfs Mine Train, Splash Mountain, and Big Thunder Mountain Railroad—on one day and Space Mountain the next. Spreading your visits over two mornings eliminates a lot of walking.

Other FastPass+ strategies combining the park's "mountains" with other headliners have been incorporated into our Magic Kingdom touring plans (see pages 819–824).

If you ride in the front seat, you almost certainly will get wet. Riders elsewhere get splashed but usually not doused. Since you don't know which seat you'll be assigned, go prepared. On a cool day, carry a plastic garbage bag and tear holes in the bottom and sides to make a water-resistant (not water-proof) sack dress (be sure to tuck the bag under your bottom). Or store a change of clothes, including footwear, in one of the park's rental lockers. Leave your camera or smartphone with a nonriding member of your group or wrap it in plastic. For any attraction where there's a distinct possibility of getting soaked, wear Tevas or some other type of waterproof sandal, and change back to regular shoes after the ride.

The scariest part of this adventure ride is the steep chute you see when standing in line, but the drop looks worse than it is. Despite reassurances, however, many children wig out when they see it. A mom from Grand Rapids, Michigan, recalls her kids' rather unique reaction:

We discovered after the fact that our children thought they would go under water after the drop and tried to hold their breath throughout the ride in preparation. They were really too preoccupied to enjoy the clever story.

Tom Sawyer Island and Fort Langhorn ★★★½

APPEAL BY AGE	PRESCHOOL ★★★★	GRADE SCHOOL ★★★★	TEENS ★★★½
YOUNG ADULTS ★★★½		OVER 30 ★★★½	SENIORS ★★★½

What it is Outdoor walk-through exhibit and rustic playground. **Scope and scale** Minor attraction. **When to go** Midmorning–late afternoon. **Special comment** Closes at dusk. **Authors' rating** The place for rambunctious kids; ★★★.

DESCRIPTION AND COMMENTS Tom Sawyer Island is a getaway within the park. It has hills to climb; a cave, windmill, and pioneer stockade (Fort Langhorn) to explore; a tipsy barrel bridge to cross; and paths to follow. You can watch riverboats chug past. It's a delight for adults and a godsend for children who have been in tow and closely supervised all day.

TOURING TIPS Tom Sawyer Island isn't one of the Magic Kingdom's more celebrated attractions, but it's one of the park's better-conceived ones. Attention to detail is excellent, and kids revel in its frontier atmosphere. It's a must for families with children ages 5–15. If your group is made up of adults, visit on your second day or on your first day after you've seen the attractions you most wanted to see.

Although children could spend a whole day on the island, plan on at least 20 minutes. Access is by raft from Frontierland; two operate simultaneously, and the trip is pretty efficient, although you may have to stand in line to board both ways. A St. Clair Shores, Michigan, family made an unplanned visit:

My 5-year-old son needed to run off some energy and he kept bumping into people in the crowded streets of Frontierland, so we veered from the touring plan and took the raft to Tom Sawyer Island. I thought it was a playground (we never bothered to head there before), but it was the coolest area to explore for our whole family! Unlike the Boneyard at Animal Kingdom, Tom Sawyer Island was truly an attraction. Very few people were there, which meant I got amazing pictures of my kids without strangers in the background, and the buildings, tunnels, and fort were so fun to explore! My kids asked to go back here the next day, and we did!

Walt Disney World Railroad

DESCRIPTION AND COMMENTS Stops in Frontierland on its circle tour of the park. See the description under Main Street, U.S.A. (page 525), for additional details.

TOURING TIPS Pleasant, feet-saving link to Main Street and Fantasyland, but the Frontierland Station is more congested than those stations.

LIBERTY SQUARE

LIBERTY SQUARE re-creates the United States at the time of the Revolutionary War. The architecture is Federal and Colonial. The **Liberty Tree**, a live oak more than 130 years old, lends dignity and grace to the patriotic setting.

The Hall of Presidents ★★★½ (closed until late 2017)

APPEAL BY AGE	PRESCHOOL ★★	GRADE SCHOOL ★★★	TEENS ★★★½
YOUNG ADULTS ★★★½	OVER 30 ★★★★		SENIORS ★★★★½

What it is Audio-Animatronic historical theater presentation. **Scope and scale** Major attraction. **When to go** Anytime. **Authors' rating** Impressive and moving; ★★★½. **Duration of presentation** Almost 23 minutes. **Preshow entertainment** None. **Probable waiting time** The lines for this attraction look intimidating once you're inside the lobby, but they're swallowed up as the theater exchanges audiences. It would be exceptionally unusual not to be admitted to the next show.

DESCRIPTION AND COMMENTS *The Hall of Presidents* combines a wide-screen theater presentation of the highlights and milestones in the United States' political history, with a short stage show including life-size animatronic replicas of every US president. Detail and costumes are masterful.

The last several presidents have had small speaking roles in the show. As we were going to press, Disney announced, putting initial rumors to rest, that Donald Trump will definitely have a speaking role. (We'd originally heard that Disney was considering reverting the show to its original format, with only George Washington and Abe Lincoln speaking.) Also per Disney, the show's mid-2017 reopening date has been pushed back to late 2017.

Regardless of who speaks, the inspirational, patriotic tone is a constant. For that reason, foreign visitors rate the show lower than do Americans.

We've had a high opinion of *Hall of Presidents* throughout its scripts. That said, we receive a lot of mail from readers who get more than entertainment from it. A New Jersey teen writes:

Mom and Dad both fell asleep during The Hall of Presidents. *Only I, a 15-year-old high school freshman, actually paid attention. It's not the most exciting thing in Disney World, but I find it very difficult to fall asleep when Morgan Freeman is speaking. His voice is way too awesome.*

A young mother in Marion, Ohio, adds:

The Hall of Presidents *is a great place to breast-feed.*

Finally, a woman in St. Louis writes:

We always go when my husband gets cranky so he can take a nice nap.

TOURING TIPS As the comments above show, a majority of readers are concerned about how to "stay woke" through this spectacle. *Resist* . . . the urge to relax. To quote our soon-to-be musical about James Buchanan, "Eternal vigilance is the price of liberty, fam."

The Haunted Mansion *(FastPass+)*   ★★★★½

APPEAL BY AGE   PRESCHOOL ★★★   GRADE SCHOOL ★★★★   TEENS ★★★★½
YOUNG ADULTS ★★★★½   OVER 30 ★★★★½   SENIORS ★★★★½

What it is Haunted-house dark ride. **Scope and scale** Major attraction. **When to go** Before 11 a.m. or during the last 2 hours before closing. **Special comment** Frightens some very young children. **Authors' rating** A masterpiece of detail and not to be missed; ★★★★½. **Duration of ride** 7-minute ride plus a 1½-minute preshow. **Average wait in line per 100 people ahead of you** 2½ minutes; assumes both "stretch rooms" operating. **Loading speed** Fast.

DISNEY DISH WITH JIM HILL

OLD-HAT IN A GOOD WAY As part of Disneyland's 60th-anniversary celebration, the long-gone-but-not-forgotten Hatbox Ghost returned to that theme park's Haunted Mansion. Walt Disney World's 50th anniversary is coming up in 2021, and according to what Imagineering insiders have recently told me, Disney World may get a hatbox-shaped birthday present at that time. But probably not sooner.

DESCRIPTION AND COMMENTS Only slightly scarier than a whoopee cushion, The Haunted Mansion serves up some of the Magic Kingdom's best visual effects. "Doom Buggies" on a conveyor belt transport you through the house from parlor to attic, then through a graveyard. The effects change tone with the setting: Those found in the house are generally spooky, while the graveyard effects, such as a ghostly opera singer wearing a Viking helmet, are there for laughs. Some kids become anxious about what they think they'll see; almost nobody actually gets scared.

Unofficial Guide writer Eve Zibart, a Haunted Mansion fan, says:

This is one of the best attractions in the Magic Kingdom, jam-packed with visual puns, special effects, hidden Mickeys, and lovely Victorian-spooky sets. It's not scary except in the sweetest of ways, and it will remind you of the days before ghost stories gave way to slasher flicks.

A Temple, Texas, mom isn't convinced when we say it isn't scary:

You say that the actual sights aren't really frightening. Well, what isn't frightening about a hanging corpse, a coffin escapee, and an axe-wielding skeleton bride?

A mom from Victoria, British Columbia, wishes that teens would shut their pieholes:

My 4-year-old daughter loved Space Mountain, but The Haunted Mansion really scared her. Our experience was that teenagers deliberately scream and pretend to be scared on this ride. This scares the crap out of the little ones.

Interactive elements in the left side of the outdoor queue ensure that guests have something to occupy them when lines are long. Features include a music-playing monument and a ship captain's tomb that squirts water.

TOURING TIPS Lines here ebb and flow more than those at most other Magic Kingdom hot spots because the Mansion is near *The Hall of Presidents* and the *Liberty Belle* Riverboat. These two attractions disgorge 700 and 450 people, respectively, when each show or ride ends, and many of these folks head straight for the Mansion. If you can't go before 11:30 a.m. or after 8 p.m., try to slip in between crowds.

If you're touring the Magic Kingdom in a single day, you'll find that Fast-Pass+ saves more time at other attractions than it does here. On the other hand, you may find it useful if you're touring over two or more days, or if the Mansion is your fourth FastPass.

Liberty Belle Riverboat ★★★½

APPEAL BY AGE	PRESCHOOL ★★★½	GRADE SCHOOL ★★★½	TEENS ★★★
YOUNG ADULTS ★★★½		OVER 30 ★★★½	SENIORS ★★★★

What it is Outdoor scenic boat ride. **Scope and scale** Major attraction. **When to go** Anytime. **Authors' rating** Slow, relaxing, and scenic; ★★½. **Duration of ride** About 16 minutes. **Average wait to board** 10–14 minutes.

DESCRIPTION AND COMMENTS Large-capacity paddle-wheel riverboat navigates the waters around Tom Sawyer Island and Fort Langhorn, passing settler cabins, old mining paraphernalia, an Indian village, and a small menagerie of animatronic wildlife. A beautiful craft, the *Liberty Belle* provides a lofty perspective of Frontierland and Liberty Square.

TOURING TIPS The riverboat, which departs roughly every half-hour, is a good attraction for the busy middle of the day. If you encounter huge crowds, chances are that the attraction has been inundated by a wave of guests coming from a just-concluded performance of *The Hall of Presidents.*

The Muppets Present . . . Great Moments in American History ★★★★½

APPEAL BY AGE	PRESCHOOL ★★★½	GRADE SCHOOL ★★★★	TEENS ★★★★
YOUNG ADULTS ★★★★½		OVER 30 ★★★★½	SENIORS ★★★★½

What it is Outdoor comedy show with the Muppets. **Scope and scale** Diversion. **When to go** Any performance. **Authors' rating** Liberty Square needs more of this; ★★★½. **Duration** 7–10 minutes.

DISNEY DISH WITH JIM HILL

PLUS-SIZE MISS PIGGY The team who fabricated the puppets for Liberty Square's *Great Moments in American History* deliberately made the Muppets bigger than the characters' TV versions, because most of the action here takes place on a second floor stage. This way, Fozzie and friends appear to be just the right size to Magic Kingdom visitors.

DESCRIPTION AND COMMENTS This wacky take on US history is hosted by James "J. J." Jefferson—the town crier of Liberty Square—and Sam the Eagle, the most patriotic of Muppets. Also starring Kermit, Miss Piggy, Fozzie, and Gonzo, the show is performed several times daily. There are multiple versions of the presentation—some with singing, some with storytelling—but all contain the Muppets' famous humor. We love it.

TOURING TIPS Performances typically take place every 30–50 minutes starting around 9:30 a.m. and ending around 5 p.m. No shows are scheduled in the 2 hours around parades (for example, 2–4 p.m. on days when the afternoon parade is at 3 p.m.).

FANTASYLAND

FANTASYLAND IS THE HEART OF THE MAGIC KINGDOM— a truly enchanting place spread gracefully like a miniature Alpine village beneath the steepled towers of Cinderella Castle.

Fantasyland is divided into three distinct sections. Directly behind Cinderella Castle and set upon a snowcapped mountain is **Beast's Castle,** part of a *Beauty and the Beast*–themed area. Most of this section holds dining and shopping, such as **Be Our Guest Restaurant** (see reviews in Part Four); **Gaston's Tavern,** a small quick-service restaurant; and a gift shop. The far-right corner of Fantasyland—including **Dumbo, The Barnstormer** kiddie coaster, and the Fantasyland train station—is called **Storybook Circus** as an homage to Disney's *Dumbo* film. These are low-capacity amusement park rides appropriate for younger children. A covered seating area with plush chairs, electrical outlets, and USB chargers is available behind **Big Top Souvenirs.**

DISNEY DISH WITH JIM HILL

BEAUTIFUL FIXTURE, BEASTLY PROBLEM The enormous chandelier that dangles over the Grand Ballroom in Be Our Guest Restaurant—12 feet tall and 11 feet wide, with 84 candles and 100 jewels—had to be partly disassembled at the last minute to fit through the restaurant's doors so that it could be installed.

The middle of Fantasyland holds the headliners, including **Under the Sea** and **Seven Dwarfs Mine Train.** The placement of these two attractions allows good traffic flow either to the left (toward Beast's Castle) for dining, to the right for attractions geared to smaller children, or back to the original part of Fantasyland for classic attractions such as **Peter Pan's Flight** and **The Many Adventures of Winnie the Pooh.**

The original part of Fantasyland also hosts the incredibly popular **Princess Fairytale Hall** meet and greet, with waits of 2 hours or more. Even so, Len's daughter, Hannah, thinks it's the best character-greeting venue in Walt Disney World.

Finally, when nature calls, don't miss the *Tangled*-themed **restrooms and outdoor seating,** near Peter Pan's Flight.

Ariel's Grotto (*FastPass+*) ★★★★

APPEAL BY AGE	PRESCHOOL ★★★★½	GRADE SCHOOL ★★★★½	TEENS ★★★½
YOUNG ADULTS ★★★★		OVER 30 ★★★★	SENIORS ★★★½

What it is Character-greeting venue. **Scope and scale** Minor attraction. **When to go** Before 10:30 a.m., during the last 2 hours before closing, or use FastPass+. **Authors' rating** Not as themed as other character greetings; ★★★. **Duration of experience** About 30–90 seconds. **Probable waiting time** 45 minutes. **Queue speed** Slow.

DESCRIPTION AND COMMENTS This is Ariel's home turf, next to the Under the Sea ride. In the base of the seaside cliffs under Prince Eric's Castle, Ariel (in mermaid form) greets guests from a seashell throne.

An older couple from San Antonio visited the Grotto but didn't find what they were expecting:

The description of Ariel's Grotto on the park map read, "Visit Ariel and all her treasures," which led us to believe it was some sort of walk-through gallery. Curious, we were ushered into Ariel's Treasure Room. Imagine our surprise when we saw a young woman dressed only in a clamshell bra and a fish tail. When we told her that we weren't interested in a photo opportunity—I could just imagine having a picture of a scantily clad woman on my desk—she looked hurt and said, "You don't want a picture of me?"

TOURING TIPS The Grotto may close an hour before the rest of the park. The greeting area is set up almost as if to encourage guests to linger, which keeps the line long. The queue isn't air-conditioned—which, if you ask us, is a rather literal-minded way to drive home the point that Ariel is hot.

The Barnstormer *(FastPass+)* ★★★

APPEAL BY AGE	PRESCHOOL ★★★★½	GRADE SCHOOL ★★★★	TEENS ★★★
YOUNG ADULTS ★★★		OVER 30 ★★★	SENIORS ★★★

What it is Small roller coaster. **Scope and scale** Minor attraction. **When to go** Before 11 a.m., during parades, during the last 2 hours before closing, or use FastPass+. **Special comment** 35" minimum height requirement. **Authors' rating** Great for little ones, but not worth the wait for adults; ★★. **Duration of ride** About 53 seconds. **Average wait in line per 100 people ahead of you** 7 minutes. **Loading speed** Slow.

DESCRIPTION AND COMMENTS The Barnstormer is a very small roller coaster. The ride is zippy but supershort. In fact, of the 53 seconds the ride is in motion, 32 seconds are consumed in leaving the loading area, being ratcheted up the first hill, and braking into the off-loading area. The actual time you spend careering around the track is 21 seconds.

A 42-year-old woman from Westport, Connecticut, warns adults that the ride may not be as tame as it looks:

A nightmare that should have gone in your "Eats Adults" section. It looked so innocent—nothing hidden in the dark, over quickly—but my 8-year-old son and I were terrified, and it took me hours to stop feeling nauseated.

Though the reader's point is well taken, The Barnstormer is a fairly benign introduction to the roller-coaster genre and a predictably positive way to help your children step up to more-adventuresome rides. Simply put, a few circuits will increase your little one's confidence and improve his or her chances for enjoying Disney's more adult attractions. (Seven Dwarfs Mine Train would be the next to try.)

TOURING TIPS The cars of this dinky coaster are too small for most adults and tend to whiplash taller people. Parties without children should skip this one. If you're touring with children, you have a problem: The ride is visually and aurally appealing, and most kids want to ride, subjecting the whole family to slow-moving lines. If The Barnstormer is high on your children's hit parade, try to ride within the first 2 hours that Fantasyland is open. This attraction is rarely a good use of FastPass+.

A Cary, North Carolina, mom offers a heads-up for solo parents:

There are some fussy rules for riding The Barnstormer. Each of the ride cars holds only two people, and every child under 7 must be accompanied by an adult. That means a single parent can't take two small children on the ride alone; you either need to rustle up another adult to help or skip it entirely.

Casey Jr. Splash 'N' Soak Station ★★★

APPEAL BY AGE	PRESCHOOL ★★★★½	GRADE SCHOOL ★★★★	TEENS ★★
YOUNG ADULTS ★★		OVER 30 ★★½	SENIORS ★★

What it is Opportunity to get wet. **Scope and scale** Diversion. **When to go** When it's hot. **Authors' rating** Great way to cool off; ★★★.

DESCRIPTION AND COMMENTS Casey Jr., the circus train from *Dumbo,* plays host to an absolutely drenching experience outside the Fantasyland Train Station in the Storybook Circus area. Expect a cadre of captive circus beasts to spray water on you in this elaborate water-play area.

TOURING TIPS Puts all other theme park splash areas to soaking shame. Bring a change of clothes and a big towel.

Dumbo the Flying Elephant *(FastPass+)* ★★★½

APPEAL BY AGE	PRESCHOOL ★★★★½	GRADE SCHOOL ★★★★	TEENS ★★★
YOUNG ADULTS ★★★	OVER 30 ★★★½		SENIORS ★★★½

What it is Disneyfied midway ride. **Scope and scale** Minor attraction. **When to go** Before 11 a.m., after 6 p.m., or use FastPass+. **Authors' rating** Disney's signature ride for children; ★★★½. **Duration of ride** 1½ minutes. **Average wait in line per 100 people ahead of you** 10 minutes. **Loading speed** Slow.

DESCRIPTION AND COMMENTS A tame, happy children's ride based on the lovable flying pachyderm. Parents and children sit inside small fiberglass "elephants" mounted on long metal arms, which spin around a central axis. Controls inside each vehicle allow you to raise the arm, making you spin higher off the ground. Despite being little different from rides at state fairs and amusement parks, Dumbo is the favorite Magic Kingdom attraction of many younger children.

As part of the Fantasyland expansion, Dumbo moved to the upper-right corner of the land. The attraction's capacity doubled with the addition of a second ride—a clone of the first. These two changes, along with the addition of the newer Fantasyland attractions, have drastically reduced waits to ride. If you do find yourself with a wait, Dumbo also includes a covered queue featuring interactive elements (read: things your kids can play with to pass the time in line).

From a Glenelg, Maryland, mother of two preschoolers:

The Dumbo waiting area is fantastic for young kids. That's right—what my kids look forward to most is not the actual Dumbo ride but the playground that Disney created as the waiting area.

TOURING TIPS If Dumbo is essential to your child's happiness, ride after dinner; not only are the crowds smaller at night, but the lighting and effects make the ride much prettier then. Or you can try to ride following the afternoon parade.

If you want to ride Dumbo twice with a minimal wait, have two adults get in line on the same side of Dumbo, and allow between 32 and 64 people to get between the first adult and child and the second adult. Pass the child to the second adult when the first ride is over.

Finally, with increased capacity and a remote location moderating its lines, Dumbo is almost never a good choice for one of your first three FastPasses.

Enchanted Tales with Belle *(FastPass+)* ★★★★

APPEAL BY AGE	PRESCHOOL ★★★★½	GRADE SCHOOL ★★★★½	TEENS ★★★
YOUNG ADULTS ★★★½	OVER 30 ★★★★		SENIORS ★★★★

What it is Interactive character show. **Scope and scale** Minor attraction. **When to go** As soon as the park opens, during the last 2 hours before closing, or use FastPass+. **Authors' rating** The prettiest meet-and-greet location in the park; ★★★★. **Duration**

of presentation About 20 minutes. **Preshow entertainment** A walk through Maurice's cottage and workshop. **Probable waiting time** 25 minutes. **Queue speed** Slow.

DESCRIPTION AND COMMENTS This multiscene *Beauty and the Beast* experience takes guests into Maurice's workshop, through a magic mirror, and into Beast's library, where the audience shares a story with Belle.

You enter the attraction by walking through Maurice's cottage, where you see mementos tracing Belle's childhood, including her favorite books, and lines drawn on one wall showing how fast Belle grew every year.

From there you'll enter Maurice's workshop at the back of the cottage. An assortment of Maurice's odd wood gadgets covers every inch of the floor, walls, and ceiling. Take a moment to peruse the gadgets, then focus your attention on the mirror on the wall to the left of the entry door.

Soon enough, the room gets dark and the mirror begins to sparkle. With magic and some really good carpentry skills, the mirror turns into a full-size doorway, through which guests enter into a wardrobe room. Once in the wardrobe room, the attraction's premise is explained: You're supposed to reenact the story of *Beauty and the Beast* for Belle on her birthday, and guests are chosen to act out key parts in the play.

Once the parts are cast, everyone walks into the castle's library and takes a seat. Cast members explain how the play will take place and introduce Belle, who gives a short speech about how thrilled she is for everyone to be there. The play is acted out within a few minutes, and all of the actors get a chance to take photos with Belle and receive a small bookmark as a memento.

During our visits, only those who were chosen to act in the play got to take photos with Belle. Also, those who took photos with Belle received a separate Memory Maker card for those photos.

Enchanted Tales with Belle is surely the prettiest and most elaborate meet-and-greet station in Walt Disney World. For the relative few who get to act in the play, it's also a chance to interact with Belle in a way that isn't possible in other character encounters. We also like how Disney "stages" guests in the cottage, workshop, and wardrobe rooms—it's a relatively efficient way to handle the wait in line, and it keeps guests from getting bored. Sure, it can still be a 30-minute wait for a 20-minute play, but it's the best of its kind in Orlando, and your kids will love it.

An enthusiastic review from an Austin, Texas, mom:

Enchanted Tales with Belle *surprised us with how well it was done. In the skit, my husband was a knight, my daughter was Mrs. Potts, and my son was silverware. It was so much fun, and the kids were so proud.*

TOURING TIPS *Enchanted Tales* has long lines from about an hour after the park opens. In fact, its popularity and low capacity have made it one of the hardest tickets at the Magic Kingdom, as a Lansing, Michigan, mom notes:

We found the wait for Enchanted Tales with Belle *was never below 40 minutes. But our girls completely loved it, and so did I.*

Since it's slow-loading, make *Enchanted Tales* the first thing on your touring plan if you want to see it. Alternatively, try to visit during the last 2 hours the park is open, or use FastPass+.

It's a Small World *(FastPass+)* ★★★½

APPEAL BY AGE	PRESCHOOL ★★★★½	GRADE SCHOOL ★★★★	TEENS ★★★
YOUNG ADULTS ★★★½	OVER 30 ★★★½		SENIORS ★★★★

What it is World brotherhood–themed indoor boat ride. **Scope and scale** Major attraction. **When to go** Before 11 a.m., during parades, after 7 p.m., or use FastPass+ **Authors' rating** Exponentially "cute"; ★★★½. **Duration of ride** About 11 minutes. **Average wait in line per 100 people ahead of you** 3½ minutes; assumes busy conditions with 30 or more boats operating. **Loading speed** Fast.

DESCRIPTION AND COMMENTS It's a Small World is a happy, upbeat indoor attraction with a mind-numbing tune that only a backhoe can remove from your brain. Small boats carry visitors on a tour around the world, with singing and dancing dolls showcasing the dress and culture of each nation. One of Disney's oldest entertainment offerings, Small World first unleashed its brainwashing song and lethally cute ethnic dolls on the real world at the 1964 New York World's Fair—the original exhibit was moved to Disneyland after the fair, and a duplicate was created for Walt Disney World when it opened in 1971.

Though it bludgeons you with its sappy redundancy, almost everyone enjoys It's a Small World—the first time, anyway. It stands, however, with *Enchanted Tiki Room* in the "What were they smokin'?" category.

A reader from Campbellton, New Brunswick, has developed a unique mechanism for coping with the annoying repetition of the theme song:

If, like me, you can't stand It's a Small World but get dragged on anyway, (1) ask to sit at the back of the boat, then (2) once you're in the building, pull out your iPhone and headphones and blast some heavy metal. You'd be amazed at how different and deceptively funny the ride becomes!

TOURING TIPS Cool off here when it's hot. Lines are usually 30 minutes or less, so you don't need FastPass+. If you wear a hearing aid, *turn it off*.

Mad Tea Party (*FastPass+*) ★★★★

APPEAL BY AGE	PRESCHOOL ★★★★½	GRADE SCHOOL ★★★★½	TEENS ★★★★
YOUNG ADULTS ★★★★		OVER 30 ★★★½	SENIORS ★★★

What it is Midway-type spinning ride. **Scope and scale** Minor attraction. **When to go** Before 11 a.m., after 5 p.m., or use FastPass+. **Special comment** You can make the teacups spin faster by turning the wheel in the center of the cup. **Authors' rating** Not worth the wait; ★★. **Duration of ride** 1½ minutes. **Average wait in line per 100 people ahead of you** 7½ minutes. **Loading speed** Slow.

DESCRIPTION AND COMMENTS Riders whirl feverishly in big teacups. *Alice in Wonderland*'s Mad Hatter provides the theme. Teenagers like to lure adults onto the teacups, then turn the wheel in the middle—making the cup spin faster—until the adults are plastered against the sides and on the verge of tossing their tacos. Don't even *consider* getting on this one with any person younger than 21.

A reader we've dubbed Melba the Human Centrifuge advises:

If you want to spin your teacup, don't put more than three people in one cup.

TOURING TIPS Mad Tea Party is notoriously slow-loading. Ride the morning of your second day if your schedule is more relaxed. Not a good choice for FastPass+.

The Many Adventures of Winnie the Pooh
(*FastPass+*) ★★★½

APPEAL BY AGE	PRESCHOOL ★★★★½	GRADE SCHOOL ★★★★	TEENS ★★★½
YOUNG ADULTS ★★★½		OVER 30 ★★★½	SENIORS ★★★★

What it is Indoor track ride. **Scope and scale** Minor attraction. **When to go** Before 10 a.m., in last hour park is open, or use FastPass+. **Authors' rating** As cute as the Pooh Bear himself; ★★★½. **Duration of ride** About 4 minutes. **Average wait in line per 100 people ahead of you** 4 minutes. **Loading speed** Moderate.

DESCRIPTION AND COMMENTS Pooh is sunny, upbeat, and fun. You ride a Hunny Pot through the pages of a huge picture book into the Hundred Acre Wood, where you encounter Pooh, Piglet, Eeyore, Owl, Rabbit, Tigger, Kanga, and Roo as they contend with a blustery day. There's even a dream sequence with Heffalumps and Woozles.

A 30-something couple from Lexington, Massachusetts, thinks Pooh has plenty to offer adults:

The attention to detail and special effects make it worth seeing even if you don't have children in your party. The Pooh dream sequence was great!

A Richmond, Indiana, mom loved Pooh's interactive queue:

The queue for The Many Adventures of Winnie the Pooh was amazing! There were so many things for little kids to do, and consequently fewer meltdowns! I wish there were more queues like that.

TOURING TIPS Pooh is a good choice for FastPass+ if you have small children and you're touring over two or more days.

Meet Merida at Fairytale Gardens   ★★★½

APPEAL BY AGE	PRESCHOOL ★★★★★	GRADE SCHOOL ★★★★½	TEENS ★★★½
YOUNG ADULTS ★★★½		OVER 30 ★★★½	SENIORS ★★★

What it is Storytelling session and character meet and greet. **Scope and scale** Diversion. **When to go** See *Times Guide* for schedule. **Authors' rating** Lovely lass, lovely locale; ★★★½. **Duration of presentation** About 10 minutes. **Probable waiting time** 1 hour or more. **Queue speed** Slow.

DESCRIPTION AND COMMENTS Merida, the flame-haired Scottish princess from *Brave,* greets guests in Fairytale Gardens, in front of Cinderella Castle on the Tomorrowland side, between the castle and Cosmic Ray's Starlight Cafe.

A mom from Shelby, North Carolina, saw red and liked it:

I was unaware that many of the princesses give red-lipstick kisses, and this delighted both of my children!

TOURING TIPS Princess meet and greets tend to be exceedingly popular, especially those involving princesses from recent movies, so expect long lines. If meeting Merida is a must-do for your family, get in line early in the morning.

Mickey's PhilharMagic (FastPass+)   ★★★★

APPEAL BY AGE	PRESCHOOL ★★★★	GRADE SCHOOL ★★★★½	TEENS ★★★★
YOUNG ADULTS ★★★★		OVER 30 ★★★★½	SENIORS ★★★★½

What it is 3-D movie. **Scope and scale** Major attraction. **When to go** Before 11 a.m., during parades, or use FastPass+. **Authors' rating** A zany masterpiece, not to be missed; ★★★★. **Duration of presentation** About 12 minutes. **Probable waiting time** 12–30 minutes.

DESCRIPTION AND COMMENTS The Magic Kingdom's 3-D movie, *Mickey's PhilharMagic* features an odd collection of Disney characters, mixing Mickey and Donald with Simba and Ariel as well as Jasmine and Aladdin. Presented in a theater large enough to accommodate a 150-foot-wide screen—huge by 3-D standards—the movie is augmented by an arsenal of special effects built into the theater. The plot involves Mickey, as the conductor of the PhilharMagic, leaving the theater to solve a mystery. In his absence, Donald attempts to take charge, with disastrous results.

Brilliantly conceived, furiously paced, and laugh-out-loud funny, *Mickey's PhilharMagic* will leave you grinning. And where other Disney 3-D movies are loud, in-your-face affairs, this one is softer and cuddlier. Things pop out of the screen, but they're really not scary. It's the rare child who is frightened—but there are always exceptions, as was the case with the 3-year-old child of this North Carolina mom:

Our family found PhilharMagic *way too violent (what seemed like minutes on end of Donald getting the crap kicked out of him by various musical instruments). I had to haul my screaming child out of the theater and submit to a therapeutic carousel ride afterwards.*

Happily, an Oregon mom has an easy way to nip the willies in the bud:

My advice to parents is simply to have their kids not wear the 3-D glasses. We took my daughter's off right away, and then she began giggling and having a good time watching the movie.

TOURING TIPS The theater is large, so don't be alarmed to see a gaggle of people in the lobby. *PhilharMagic* never needs FastPass+.

Peter Pan's Flight *(FastPass+)*   ★★★★

APPEAL BY AGE	PRESCHOOL ★★★★½	GRADE SCHOOL ★★★★	TEENS ★★★★
YOUNG ADULTS ★★★★		OVER 30 ★★★★	SENIORS ★★★★

What it is Indoor track ride. **Scope and scale** Minor attraction. **When to go** First or last 30 minutes the park is open, or use FastPass+. **Authors' rating** Nostalgic, mellow, and well done; not to be missed; ★★★★. **Duration of ride** A little over 3 minutes. **Average wait in line per 100 people ahead of you** 5½ minutes. **Loading speed** Moderate–slow.

DESCRIPTION AND COMMENTS Peter Pan's Flight is superbly designed and absolutely delightful, with a happy theme uniting some favorite Disney characters, beautiful effects, and charming music. This indoor ride begins in the Darling family's house before taking you on a relaxing trip in a "flying pirate ship" over old London and thence to Never-Never Land, where Peter saves Wendy from walking the plank and Captain Hook rehearses for *Dancing with the Stars* on the snout of the ubiquitous crocodile. There's nothing here that will jump out at you or frighten young children.

A themed queue for Peter Pan opened in 2015. Besides air-conditioning, the updated preshow area features a walk through the Darlings' street and home, where you'll see family portraits and various rooms of the house, play a few games, and get sprinkled with a bit of pixie dust.

TOURING TIPS Because Peter Pan's Flight is very popular, count on long lines all day. Fortunately, the new queue runs under the roof of the building, out of direct sun and rain, and has tons of new art and interactive games to help pass the time. Ride in the first 30 minutes the park is open, during a parade, just before the park closes, or use FastPass+.

Our touring plan software suggests using FastPass+ for Peter Pan's Flight more than any other Walt Disney World attraction (see page 519).

Pete's Silly Sideshow *(FastPass+)*   ★★★★

APPEAL BY AGE	PRESCHOOL ★★★★★	GRADE SCHOOL ★★★★½	TEENS ★★★★
YOUNG ADULTS ★★★★		OVER 30 ★★★★	SENIORS ★★★½

What it is Character-greeting venue. **Scope and scale** Minor attraction. **When to go** Before 11 a.m., during the last 2 hours before closing, or use FastPass+. **Authors' rating** Well themed with unique character costumes; ★★★½. **Duration of experience** 7 minutes per character. **Probable waiting time** 25 minutes. **Queue speed** Slow.

DESCRIPTION AND COMMENTS Pete's Silly Sideshow is a circus-themed character-greeting area in the Storybook Circus part of Fantasyland. The characters' costumes are distinct from the ones normally worn around the parks. Characters include Goofy as The Great Goofini, Donald Duck as The Astounding Donaldo, Daisy Duck as Madame Daisy Fortuna, and Minnie Mouse as Minnie Magnifique.

TOURING TIPS On non–Extra Magic Hour days, Pete's opens 45 minutes later than the rest of the park and usually closes at the same time as the first *Happily Ever After* fireworks show. The queue is indoors and air-conditioned. There's one queue for Goofy and Donald and a second queue for Minnie and Daisy; you can meet two characters at once, but you have to line up twice to meet all four. Rarely a good use of FastPass+.

Prince Charming Regal Carrousel ★★★½

APPEAL BY AGE	PRESCHOOL ★★★★½	GRADE SCHOOL ★★★★	TEENS ★★★½
YOUNG ADULTS ★★★½		OVER 30 ★★★½	SENIORS ★★★½

What it is Merry-go-round. **Scope and scale** Minor attraction. **When to go** Anytime. **Authors' rating** A beautiful ride for children; ★★★. **Duration of ride** About 2 minutes. **Average wait in line per 100 people ahead of you** 5 minutes. **Loading speed** Slow.

DESCRIPTION AND COMMENTS One of the most elaborate and beautiful merry-go-rounds you'll ever have the pleasure of seeing, especially when its lights are on.

A shy and retiring 9-year-old girl from Rockaway, New Jersey, thinks our rating of the carousel for grade-schoolers should be higher:

I want to complain. I went on the Prince Charming Regal Carrousel four times and I loved it! Raise those stars right now!

TOURING TIPS Unless young children in your party insist on riding, appreciate this attraction from the sidelines. While lovely to look at, the carousel loads and unloads very slowly.

Princess Fairytale Hall (*FastPass+*) ★★★

APPEAL BY AGE	PRESCHOOL ★★★★★	GRADE SCHOOL ★★★★½	TEENS ★★★★
YOUNG ADULTS ★★★★		OVER 30 ★★★½	SENIORS ★★★½

What it is Character-greeting venue. **Scope and scale** Minor attraction. **When to go** Before 10:30 a.m., after 4 p.m., or use FastPass+. **Authors' rating** You want princesses? Disney's got 'em! ★★★. **Duration of ride** 7–10 minutes (estimated). **Average wait in line per 100 people ahead of you** 35 minutes (estimated). **Loading speed** Slow.

DESCRIPTION AND COMMENTS Princess Fairytale Hall is Disney-princess central in the Magic Kingdom. Inside are two greeting venues, with each holding a small reception area for two princesses. Thus, there are four princesses meeting and greeting at any time, and you can see two of them at once. Signs outside the entrance tell you which line leads to which princess pair and how long the wait will be. Rapunzel usually leads one side, typically paired with Cinderella, Snow White, or another princess.

Around 5–10 guests at a time are admitted to each greeting area, where there's plenty of time for small talk, a photo, and a hug from each princess.

Enough time is given to each family, in fact, that we ran out of things to say to Rapunzel and shuffled quietly over to Snow White.

TOURING TIPS There have been some shake-ups in the princess contingent in residence at Fairytale Hall. In November 2016, Princess Elena of Avalor (a new Disney Channel character) has supplanted Sleeping Beauty in the greeting rotation. This follows the summer 2016 relocation of *Frozen*'s Anna and Elsa to the new Royal Sommerhus meet and greet at Epcot's Norway pavilion. The lines are now shorter than they were a year ago, but they can still be substantial. If your kids love princesses, even B-list ones, get Fairytale Hall out of the way first thing, or use FastPass+.

Seven Dwarfs Mine Train *(FastPass+)* ★★★★

APPEAL BY AGE PRESCHOOL ★★★★   GRADE SCHOOL ★★★★½ TEENS ★★★★½ YOUNG ADULTS ★★★★½   OVER 30 ★★★★½   SENIORS ★★★★

What it is Indoor/outdoor roller coaster. **Scope and scale** Major attraction. **When to go** As soon as the park opens, or use FastPass+. **Special comment** 38" minimum height requirement. **Authors' rating** Great family coaster; not to be missed; ★★★★. **Duration of ride** About 2 minutes. **Average wait in line per 100 people ahead of you** About 4½ minutes. **Loading speed** Fast.

DISNEY DISH WITH JIM HILL

MINING INSPIRATION FROM THE PAST In Seven Dwarfs Mine Train's main mine scene, the Imagineers built the animation of the marching Seven Short Dudes using rotoscoped images directly from the "Heigh-Ho" number in the movie.

DESCRIPTION AND COMMENTS In the pantheon of Disney coasters, Seven Dwarfs Mine Train fits somewhere between The Barnstormer and Big Thunder Mountain Railroad—that is, it's geared to older grade-school kids who've been on amusement park rides before. There are no loops, inversions, or rolls in the track, and no massive hills or steep drops; rather, the Mine Train's trick is that your ride vehicle's seats swing side-to-side as you go through turns. And—what a coincidence!—Disney has designed a curvy track with steep turns. There's also an elaborate indoor section showing the Seven Dwarfs' underground operation.

The exterior design includes waterfalls, forests, and landscaping and is meant to join together all of the surrounding Fantasyland's various locations, including France and Germany. The swinging effect is more noticeable the farther back you're seated in the train.

The Mine Train is the Magic Kingdom's newest headliner. As such, it generates a lot of reader comments. First, from a Rhode Island couple:

As far as new rides go, we give high marks to Seven Dwarfs Mine Train. It's faster than it looks in videos, and the animatronics are top-notch. It broke down during our FastPass+ window, so we were given an additional pass. On our next day in the Magic Kingdom, we rode it at night. Much like Big Thunder and Splash Mountain, this ride is even better at night!

From an Aurora, Illinois, woman:

It's a pretty easy coaster, somewhere between Big Thunder and The Barnstormer in intensity. I'd ride it just to see the mine scene over and over again!

A Chester, Virginia, mom offers a little cost–benefit analysis:

Seven Dwarfs Mine Train was a great ride, but not worth a 90-minute wait.

A mom from Horsham, Pennsylvania, felt let down:

Our family's rating of the 7 D Mine Train is two stars at most. The detail and activities in line were great, and I thought that the animation of the characters' faces was amazing. But we were all sadly disappointed in the ride—it's over so quickly, it really isn't worth your time. Realistically, if we only had to wait 15–20 minutes, we still would only give it two and a half stars at best.

A woman from White City, Saskatchewan, was particularly irked:

I do not agree with Seven Dwarfs Mine Train being a must see. [It] was a must waste: 1.5 hours of my time for 1.5 minutes of disappointment.

Finally, from a Philadelphia reader:

The Guide is correct in calling the Seven Dwarfs Minecart [sic] underwhelming, but we found it was much, much better at night. The lighting and track layout combined to make the ride feel a little faster, and it was generally more enjoyable. I see no reason to ride it in daylight again.

TOURING TIPS The new Magic Kingdom opening procedures (see page 515) mean that Seven Dwarfs has instant hourlong waits as soon as the park opens. Compounding that problem is that it's very difficult to get Fast-Pass+ reservations for the Mine Train. If they're available any time of day, grab them. If not, make FastPass+ reservations in advance for around 9:30 a.m. at Big Thunder Mountain Railroad and around 3:30 p.m. at Space Mountain. On the day of your visit, arrive at the Magic Kingdom 60 minutes before official opening and get in line along the walkway from the Central Plaza to Mad Tea Party. Ride Seven Dwarfs Mine Train as soon as the park opens, then hotfoot it to Splash Mountain to ride immediately. Your FastPass+ reservation for Big Thunder Mountain will be valid by the time you're done, and you'll have experienced three of the park's four headliners in about an hour. Avoid Extra Magic Hour mornings.

If you have two mornings, do the Fantasyland and Frontierland attractions—Seven Dwarfs Mine Train, Splash Mountain, and Big Thunder Mountain Railroad—on one day and Space Mountain the next. Spreading your visits over two mornings eliminates a lot of walking.

Other FastPass+ strategies combining the park's "mountains" with other headliners have been incorporated into our Magic Kingdom touring plans (see pages 819–824).

Under the Sea: Journey of the Little Mermaid
(FastPass+) ★★★★

| APPEAL BY AGE | PRESCHOOL ★★★★½ | GRADE SCHOOL ★★★★ | TEENS ★★★½ |
| YOUNG ADULTS ★★★★ | OVER 30 ★★★★ | | SENIORS ★★★★ |

What it is Dark ride retelling the film's story. **Scope and scale** Major attraction. **When to go** Before 10:30 a.m., during the last 2 hours before closing, or use Fast-Pass+. **Authors' rating** Colorful, but most effects are too simple for an attraction this big; ★★★½. **Duration of ride** About 5½ minutes. **Average wait in line per 100 people ahead of you** 3 minutes. **Loading speed** Fast.

DESCRIPTION AND COMMENTS Under the Sea takes riders through almost a dozen scenes retelling the story of *The Little Mermaid,* with animatronics, video effects, and a vibrant 3-D set the size of a small theater.

Guests board a clamshell-shaped ride vehicle running along a continuously moving track (similar to The Haunted Mansion's). Then the ride "descends" under water, past Ariel's grotto and on to King Triton's undersea kingdom. The most detailed animatronic is of Ursula, the octopus, and she's a beauty. Other scenes hit the film's highlights, including Ariel meeting Prince Eric, her deal with Ursula to become human, and, of course, the couple's happy ending.

The attraction's exterior is attractive, with detailed rock work, water, and story elements. (Our favorite effect is a "hidden Mickey"—the shape of Mickey's head and ears—that is created through a special alignment of the sun's shadow and the rock work, and only at noon on November 18, Mickey's birthday.) Our problems with the attraction are: (1) Most of the effects throughout the ride are simple and unimaginative, such as starfish that do nothing but spin on a central axis or lobsters that simply turn left and right, and (2) virtually the entire second half of the story is condensed into a handful of small scenes crammed together at the end of the ride.

A recent update to the ride brought improved lighting, a few more animatronic sea creatures in the main show scene, and more-realistic hair for some of the animatronics.

TOURING TIPS Expect moderate waits most of the day. If you can, ride early in the morning or late at night. Rarely a good choice for FastPass+.

Walt Disney World Railroad

DESCRIPTION AND COMMENTS The railroad stops in Fantasyland on its circle tour of the park. The leg from Fantasyland to Main Street, U.S.A., is the most scenic of the entire loop. See the description under Main Street, U.S.A. (page 525), for additional details.

TOURING TIPS Pleasant, feet-saving link to Main Street and Frontierland . . . but so crowded in the afternoon during times of peak attendance that you'll almost certainly find it faster to walk anywhere in the park.

TOMORROWLAND

AT VARIOUS POINTS IN ITS HISTORY, Tomorrowland's attractions presented life's possibilities in adventures ranging from the modern-day (If You Had Wings' round-the-world travel in the 1970s) to the distant future (Mission to Mars). The problem that stymied Disney repeatedly was that the future came faster and looked different than what they'd envisioned.

Today, Tomorrowland's theme makes the least sense of any area in any Disney park. Its current attractions are based on gas-powered race cars, rocket travel (two rides), a look back at 20th-century technology, two rides with aliens, and a comedy show with monsters. It's not so much a vision of the future as it is a collection of attractions that don't fit anywhere else in the park.

Astro Orbiter ★★★½

APPEAL BY AGE	PRESCHOOL ★★★★	GRADE SCHOOL ★★★★	TEENS ★★★½
YOUNG ADULTS ★★★½		OVER 30 ★★★	SENIORS ★★★

What it is Buck Rogers–style rockets revolving around a central axis. **Scope and scale** Minor attraction. **When to go** Before 11 a.m. or during the last hour before closing. **Special comment** Not as innocuous as it appears. **Authors' rating** Not worth the wait; ★★. **Duration of ride** 1½ minutes. **Average wait in line per 100 people ahead of you** 13½ minutes. **Loading speed** Slow.

DESCRIPTION AND COMMENTS Though visually appealing, the Astro Orbiter is still a slow-loading carnival ride. The fat little rocket ships simply fly in circles, albeit circles on a three-story platform above Tomorrowland. The best thing about the Astro Orbiter is the nice view when you're aloft.

TOURING TIPS Expendable on any schedule. If you ride with preschoolers, seat them first, then board. The Astro Orbiter flies higher and faster than Dumbo and frightens some young children. It also apparently messes with some adults. A mother from Lev HaSharon, Israel, writes:

It was a nightmare—people should be forewarned. I was able to sit through all the "Mountains," the "Tours," and the like without my stomach reacting even a little, but after Astro Orbiter I thought I would be finished for the rest of the day. Very quickly I realized that my only chance for survival was to pick a point on the toe of my shoe and stare at it (and certainly not lift my eyes out of the "jet") until the ride was over. My 4-year-old was my copilot; she loved it (go figure), and she had us up high the whole time.

Buzz Lightyear's Space Ranger Spin (FastPass+) ★★★★

APPEAL BY AGE PRESCHOOL ★★★★½ GRADE SCHOOL ★★★★½ TEENS ★★★★
YOUNG ADULTS ★★★★   OVER 30 ★★★★   SENIORS ★★★★

What it is Whimsical space travel–themed indoor ride. **Scope and scale** Minor attraction. **When to go** First or last hour the park is open, or use FastPass+. **Authors' rating** Surreal shooting gallery; ★★★★. **Duration of ride** About 4½ minutes. **Average wait in line per 100 people ahead of you** 3 minutes. **Loading speed** Fast.

DESCRIPTION AND COMMENTS This attraction is based on the space-commando character Buzz Lightyear from the Toy Story film series. The marginal storyline has you and Buzz trying to save the universe from the evil Emperor Zurg. The indoor ride is interactive to the extent that you can spin your car and shoot simulated laser cannons at Zurg and his minions. The first room's mechanical claw and red robot contain high-value targets, so aim for these.

TOURING TIPS Each car is equipped with two laser cannons and two score-keeping displays, enabling you to compete with your riding partner. A joystick allows you to spin the car to line up the various targets. Each time you pull the trigger, you release a red laser beam that you can see hitting or missing the target.

Most folks spend their first ride learning how to use the equipment (fire off individual shots as opposed to keeping the trigger depressed) and figuring out how the targets work. On the next ride, you'll be surprised by how much better you do. If you're hopeless at games of skill, check out our tips at **tinyurl.com/buzzfortheunskilled.**

Unofficial readers are unanimous in their praise of Buzz Lightyear. Some, in fact, spend several hours on it, riding again and again. The following comment from a Snow Hill, Maryland, dad is representative:

Buzz Lightyear was so much fun it can't be legal! We hit it first on early-entry day and rode it 10 times without stopping. The kids had fun, but it was Dad who spun himself silly trying to shoot the Z's.

Experience Buzz Lightyear after riding Space Mountain first thing in the morning, or use FastPass+.

Monsters, Inc. Laugh Floor *(FastPass+)* ★★★★

APPEAL BY AGE PRESCHOOL ★★★★ GRADE SCHOOL ★★★★½ TEENS ★★★★
YOUNG ADULTS ★★★★ OVER 30 ★★★★ SENIORS ★★★★

What it is Interactive animated comedy show. **Scope and scale** Major attraction.
When to go Before 11 a.m., after 4 p.m., or use FastPass+. **Special comment** Audience members may be asked to participate in skits. **Authors' rating** Good concept, but the jokes are hit-or-miss; ★★★½. **Duration of presentation** About 15 minutes.

DESCRIPTION AND COMMENTS We learned in Disney-Pixar's *Monsters, Inc.* that children's screams could be converted to electricity, which was used to power a town inhabited by monsters. During the film, the monsters discovered that kids' laughter worked even better as an energy source, so in this attraction the monsters have set up a comedy club to capture as many laughs as possible. Mike Wazowski, the one-eyed green monster, emcees the club's three comedy acts. Each act consists of an animated monster (most not seen in the film) trying out various bad puns, knock-knock jokes, and Abbott and Costello–like routines. Using the same cutting-edge technology as Epcot's *Turtle Talk with Crush,* behind-the-scenes Disney employees voice the characters and often interact with audience members during the skits. As with any comedy set, some performers are funny and some are not, but Disney has shown a willingness to experiment with new routines and jokes.

A Sioux Falls, South Dakota, mom is a big fan:

> *Laugh Floor was great. It's amazing how the characters interact with the audience—I got picked on twice without trying. Plus, kids can text jokes to Roz.*

TOURING TIPS The theater holds several hundred people, so there's no need to rush here first thing in the morning. Try to arrive late in the morning after you've visited other Tomorrowland attractions, or after the afternoon parade when guests start leaving the park. *Laugh Floor* is never a good choice for FastPass+.

Space Mountain *(FastPass+)* ★★★★

APPEAL BY AGE PRESCHOOL ★★½† GRADE SCHOOL ★★★★½ TEENS ★★★★★
YOUNG ADULTS ★★★★½ OVER 30 ★★★★½ SENIORS ★★★½

†*Some preschoolers love Space Mountain; others are frightened by it.*

What it is Roller coaster in the dark. **Scope and scale** Super-headliner. **When to go** When the park opens or use FastPass+. **Special comments** Great fun and action; much wilder than Big Thunder Mountain Railroad. 44″ minimum height requirement; children younger than age 7 must be

Motion Sickness

accompanied by an adult. Switching-off option provided (see page 439). **Authors' rating** An unusual roller coaster with excellent special effects; not to be missed; ★★★★. **Duration of ride** Almost 3 minutes. **Average wait in line per 100 people ahead of you** 3 minutes; assumes 2 tracks, with 1 dedicated to FastPass+ riders, dispatching at 21-second intervals. **Loading speed** Moderate–fast.

DESCRIPTION AND COMMENTS Totally enclosed in a mammoth futuristic structure, Space Mountain has always been the Magic Kingdom's most popular attraction. The theme is a space flight through dark recesses of the galaxy. Effects are superb, and the ride is the fastest and wildest in the Magic Kingdom. As a roller coaster, Space Mountain is much zippier than Big Thunder Mountain Railroad, but much tamer than the Rock 'n' Roller Coaster at Disney's Hollywood Studios or Expedition Everest at Disney's Animal Kingdom.

As a headliner, Space Mountain goes through periodic refurbishments to add effects and maintain ride quality. Past improvements include new lighting and effects, an improved sound system and soundtrack, and interactive games in the queue to help pass the time in line. Roller-coaster aficionados will tell you (correctly) that Space Mountain is a designer version of the Wild Mouse, a midway ride that's been around for almost 60 years. There are no long drops or swooping hills as there are on a traditional roller coaster—only quick, unexpected turns and small drops. Disney's contribution essentially was to add a space theme to the Wild Mouse and put it in the dark. And this does indeed make the Mouse seem wilder.

An Elburn, Illinois, reader recommends bracing yourself—literally:

They should require you to wear a neck brace on Space Mountain. That ride is painful.

TOURING TIPS People who can handle a fairly wild roller-coaster ride will take Space Mountain in stride. What sets Space Mountain apart is that cars plummet through darkness, with only occasional lighting. Half the fun of Space Mountain is not knowing where the car will go next.

Space Mountain is a favorite of many Magic Kingdom visitors ages 7–60. Each morning before opening, particularly during summer and holiday periods, several hundred Space Mountain junkies await the signal to head to the ride's entrance. To get ahead of the competition, be one of the first in the park. Proceed to the end of Main Street and wait at the entrance to Tomorrowland.

Couples touring with children too small to ride Space Mountain can both ride without waiting twice in line by taking advantage of "switching off." Here's how it works: When you enter the Space Mountain line, tell the first Disney attendant (Greeter One) that you want to switch off. The attendant will allow you, your spouse, and your small child (or children) to continue together and phone ahead to tell Greeter Two to expect you. When you reach Greeter Two (at the turnstile near the boarding area), you'll be given specific directions. One of you will proceed to ride, while the other stays with the kids. Whoever rides will be admitted by the unloading attendant to stairs leading back up to the boarding area. Here you switch off. The second parent rides, and the first parent takes the kids down the stairs to the unloading area where everybody is reunited and exits together. Switching off is also available at Big Thunder Mountain Railroad and Splash Mountain (and other attractions), and for FastPass+ users.

Seats are one behind another, as opposed to side by side—meaning that parents can't sit next to their kids who meet the height requirement.

If you don't catch Space Mountain first thing in the morning, use FastPass+ or try again during the 30 minutes before closing. To avoid overwhelming Space Mountain's air-conditioning system on hot days, would-be riders are sometimes held in line outside the entrance until the lines have subsided. The appearance from the outside is that the line is enormous when, in fact, most of the people waiting are those visible. This crowd-control technique, known as "stacking," discourages visitors from getting in line. (Stacking is also used at several Disney attractions during the hour before closing to ensure that the ride will be able to close on schedule.) Despite the apparently long line, the wait is usually no longer than if you had been allowed to queue inside.

Stitch's Great Escape! ★★ (seasonal)

APPEAL BY AGE	PRESCHOOL ★★	GRADE SCHOOL ★★½	TEENS ★★½
YOUNG ADULTS ★★		OVER 30 ★★	SENIORS ★★

What it is Theater-in-the-round sci-fi adventure show. **Scope and scale** Minor attraction. **When to go** Before 11 a.m. or after 6 p.m.; try during parades. **Special comments** Frightens children of all ages; 40" minimum height requirement. Switching-off option provided (see page 439). **Authors' rating** P.U.; ★★. **Duration of presentation** About 12 minutes. **Preshow entertainment** About 6 minutes. **Probable waiting time** 5–15 minutes.

DESCRIPTION AND COMMENTS *Stitch's Great Escape!* stars the havoc-wreaking little alien from the Disney animated feature *Lilo & Stitch*. In this show, Stitch is a prisoner of the galactic authorities and is being transferred to a processing facility en route to his final place of incarceration. He manages to escape by employing an efficient though gross trick, knocking out power to the facility in the process. (One wonders why aliens smart enough to master teleportation haven't yet invented a backup power source.) The rest of the show consists simply of Stitch lumbering around in the dark while cheap sound and odor effects are unleashed on the captive audience.

Unofficial Guide readers note *Stitch's Great Escape!* as the worst Magic Kingdom attraction. Guest response to it is so negative, in fact, that Disney has given up trying to improve it. This Norton Shores, Michigan, mom at least gave it a chance going in:

I love Lilo and Stitch *and am a huge fan of Stitch in particular. I got on the ride just knowing it would be great—then the lights went out. From that point on, it was just a big miserable fail. My 13-year-old actually heaved from the smell of Stitch's breath, and the bouncing [overhead restraints] jabbed us all painfully and repeatedly in the shoulders. The movie is still awesome, but the ride is a giant zit on the face of Disney that needs to be popped out of existence.*

A Las Vegas reader thinks he knows why an attraction that doesn't move has safety restraints:

Stitch's Great Escape! *has to be seen to understand just how awful an attraction can be. I had a glimmer of hope when they put the restraint on me. Looking back, I'm convinced the restraint was for the sole purpose of preventing the audience from leaving until they had been sufficiently tortured.*

Stitch's height requirement is 40 inches—the same as Big Thunder Mountain Railroad—in an attempt to keep out easily frightened younger children. The fact that Big Thunder is a roller coaster and that this ride doesn't move should be a warning to parents about its fright potential.

Stitch's Great Escape! is open seasonally. Expect it to be operational only during holidays and high crowd times.

TOURING TIPS *Stitch* is more than enough to scare the pants off many kids ages 6 and younger. *Parents, note:* You're held in your seat by overhead restraints that will prevent you from getting up to comfort your child if the need arises.

Tomorrowland Speedway *(FastPass+)* ★★★½

APPEAL BY AGE	PRESCHOOL ★★★★	GRADE SCHOOL ★★★★	TEENS ★★★½
YOUNG ADULTS ★★★		OVER 30 ★★★	SENIORS ★★★

What it is Drive-'em-yourself miniature cars. **Scope and scale** Major attraction. **When to go** Before 10 a.m., during the last 2 hours before closing, or use FastPass+. **Special comment** Kids must be 54" tall to drive unassisted, 32" with a parent. **Authors' rating** Boring for adults (★★); great for preschoolers. **Duration of ride** About 4¼ minutes. **Average wait in line per 100 people ahead of you** 4½ minutes; assumes 285-car turnover every 20 minutes. **Loading speed** Slow.

DISNEY DISH WITH JIM HILL

IS THE SPEEDWAY ABOUT TO BE SHANGHAIED? For the better part of 35 years now, the Imagineers have wanted to add a *TRON*-themed attraction to the Magic Kingdom. If all goes according to plan, a stateside version of Shanghai Disneyland's TRON Lightcycle Power Run should be running in time for WDW's 50th-anniversary celebration in 2021, at the soon-to-shutter Tomorrowland Speedway.

Motion Sickness

DESCRIPTION AND COMMENTS An elaborate miniature raceway with gasoline-powered cars that travel up to 7 mph. The raceway, with its sleek cars and racing noises, is quite alluring. The cars poke along on a guide rail, leaving the driver little to do, but teens and many adults still enjoy it.

TOURING TIPS This ride is visually appealing, and the 9-and-under crowd loves it (adults, not so much). If your child is too short to drive, ride along and allow him or her to steer the car while you work the foot pedal.

A mom from North Billerica, Massachusetts, writes:

I was truly amazed by the number of adults in line—the only reason I could think of for that would be an insane desire to go on absolutely every ride at Disney World. The cars aren't a whole lot of fun, and they tend to pile up at the end, so it takes almost as long to get off as it did to get on.

A dad from Pleasantville, New York, had this to say:

This is one attraction I wish they would replace with something better. It's boring and it smells bad.

The line for the speedway snakes across a pedestrian bridge to the ride's loading areas. Here's a tip for a shorter wait: Turn right off the bridge and then head to the first loading area rather than continuing to the second one.

Tomorrowland Transit Authority PeopleMover ★★★★

APPEAL BY AGE	PRESCHOOL ★★★★	GRADE SCHOOL ★★★★	TEENS ★★★★
YOUNG ADULTS ★★★★	OVER 30 ★★★★		SENIORS ★★★★½

What it is Scenic tour of Tomorrowland. **Scope and scale** Minor attraction. **When to go** Anytime, but especially during hot, crowded times of day (11:30 a.m.–4:30 p.m.). **Special comment** A good way to check out the line at Space Mountain and the Speedway. **Authors' rating** Scenic and relaxing; ★★★½. **Duration of ride** 10 minutes. **Average wait in line per 100 people ahead of you** 1½ minutes; assumes 39 trains operating. **Loading speed** Fast.

DESCRIPTION AND COMMENTS A once-unique prototype of a linear induction–powered mass-transit system, the PeopleMover has tramlike cars that carry riders on a leisurely tour of Tomorrowland, including a peek inside Space Mountain. In ancient times, the attraction was called the WEDway PeopleMover ("WED" = Walter Elias Disney).

A Delafield, Wisconsin, family offers only the faintest of praise:

Tomorrowland is best at night. With the lights, it turns boring rides like the PeopleMover into something less boring.

TOURING TIPS A relaxing ride where lines move quickly. It's a good choice during busier times of day.

Walt Disney's Carousel of Progress ★★★

APPEAL BY AGE	PRESCHOOL ★★★	GRADE SCHOOL ★★★½	TEENS ★★★½
YOUNG ADULTS ★★★½		OVER 30 ★★★★	SENIORS ★★★★½

What it is Audio-Animatronic theater production. **Scope and scale** Major attraction. **When to go** Anytime. **Authors' rating** Nostalgic, warm, and happy; ★★★. **Duration of presentation** 21 minutes. **Preshow entertainment** Documentary on the attraction's long history. **Probable waiting time** Less than 10 minutes.

DESCRIPTION AND COMMENTS *Walt Disney's Carousel of Progress* is a four-act play offering a nostalgic look at how electricity and technology changed the lives of an animatronic family during the 20th century. General Electric sponsored the first version of the show for the 1964 World's Fair in New York, in keeping with the fair's theme of progress. The first scene is set around 1900, the second around 1927, and the third in the late 1940s. The fourth scene is allegedly contemporary, but the script's references to "laser discs" and "car phones"—and the Smithsonian-eligible laptop on the kitchen counter—give away its last major revision in 1993.

Though dated, *Carousel of Progress* was almost entirely conceived and guided by Walt Disney himself, rare among Magic Kingdom attractions. It is the only Magic Kingdom attraction to display Walt's optimistic vision of a better future through technology and industry. If you're interested in the man behind the mouse, this show is a must-see.

TOURING TIPS *Carousel* handles big crowds effectively and is a good choice during busier times of day. Because of its age, it seems to have more minor operational glitches than most attractions, so you may be subjected to the same dialogue and songs several times. Look at it as extra air-conditioning.

LIVE ENTERTAINMENT *in* the MAGIC KINGDOM

BANDS, DISNEY-CHARACTER APPEARANCES, parades, ceremonies, and singing and dancing further enliven the Magic Kingdom. For specific events the day you visit, check the live-entertainment schedule in your guide map (free as you enter the park or at City Hall) or in the *Times Guide* available along with the guide map. WDW live-entertainment guru Steve Soares usually posts the Magic Kingdom's performance schedule about a week in advance at wdwent.com.

unofficial **TIP**
Note: If you're short on time, it's impossible to see Magic Kingdom feature attractions and the live performances.

Our one-day touring plans exclude live performances in favor of seeing as much of the park as time permits; parades and shows siphon crowds away from popular rides, thus shortening lines. Nonetheless, the color and pageantry of live events are integral to the Magic Kingdom—and a persuasive argument for a second day of touring. Here's a list of some regular performances and events that don't require reservations:

BAY LAKE AND SEVEN SEAS LAGOON ELECTRICAL WATER PAGEANT ★★★★ Usually performed at nightfall (9 p.m. at the Polynesian Village

Resort, 9:15 at the Grand Floridian Resort & Spa, and 10:15 at the Contemporary Resort) on Seven Seas Lagoon and Bay Lake, this is one of our favorites among the Disney extras, but it's necessary to leave the Magic Kingdom to view it. The pageant is a stunning electric-light show aboard small barges and set to nifty electronic music. Leave the Magic Kingdom and take the monorail to the Polynesian Village, the Grand Floridian, or the Contemporary.

CASTLE FORECOURT STAGE ★★★½ *Mickey's Royal Friendship Faire* debuted here in 2016, replacing the long-running *Dream-Along with Mickey* show. The cast includes Mickey, Minnie, Donald, and Goofy, with appearances by Anna, Elsa, Olaf, Rapunzel, Tiana, and others. Like its predecessors, the show is a bit of dialog stringing together several song-and-dance numbers involving the princesses.

The show is performed several times a day according to the season, with showtimes listed in the daily *Times Guide*. The Castle Forecourt Stage is elevated well above ground level, so good viewing spots are available all around Main Street's Central Plaza.

DISNEY-CHARACTER SHOWS AND APPEARANCES A number of characters are usually on hand to greet guests when the park opens. Because they snarl pedestrian traffic and stop most children dead in their tracks, this is sort of a mixed blessing. Most days, a character is on duty for photos and autographs 9 a.m.–10 p.m. next to City Hall. Mickey and Tinker Bell can be found in Main Street's Town Square Theater, to the right as you enter the park; Disney princesses are found in Fairytale Hall in Fantasyland. Check the daily *Times Guide* for character-greeting locations and times.

Knowing when and where characters appear is only half the battle, as a dad from Minster, Ohio, points out:

> One thing I didn't realize on day one was how early you have to be at the meeting place to meet the princesses at the Magic Kingdom. We had to arrive 30 minutes early to each princess. (Example: Snow White only shows up from 9:30 to 10:15 right by the main gate, so in order to get a meet with her, we had to line up at 9 a.m.) This was an entire day of princess-finding and picture-taking, and my 3-year-old loved it. We hated watching all the other parents who didn't know this little caveat walk away dejected with a crying child. We had the privilege of having two days to learn this rule.

FLAG RETREAT At 5 p.m. daily at Town Square (Walt Disney World Railroad end of Main Street). Sometimes performed with large college marching bands, sometimes with a smaller Disney band.

HAPPILY EVER AFTER FIREWORKS SHOW ★★★★★ Fireworks, music, and video projections combine in a multisensory production on the theme of *Happily Ever After*. Happily, the show is not just about princesses and romance, but includes messages about work and determination as part of a path to fulfillment. Images projected onto the castle include snippets from the usual suspects of *Frozen* and *Cinderella*, as well as scenes from *Hunchback of Notre Dame, Monsters, Inc., Cars,* and *Wreck-It Ralph,* among others. Like the previous evening fireworks, *Wishes, Happily Ever After* can be enjoyed from outside the park. However, due to the strong integration of the castle projections into the performance, be aware that you'll be missing a substantial portion of the show if you're not viewing from the Main Street area inside the Magic Kingdom.

DISNEY DISH WITH JIM HILL

TINK'S FIRST FLIGHT One of the most dramatic parts of the *Happily Ever After* show is seeing Tinker Bell fly over the Central Plaza. The first time this idea was tried was back in the summer of 1961, at Disneyland. Circus veteran Tiny Kline, then 70 years old, ziplined down from the Matterhorn into a giant "catcher's mitt" made of two bed mattresses. Walt Disney World got its own version of this on July 3, 1985.

A spot we'd previously recommended for *Wishes*, in the Tomorrowland Terrace area, was apparently so good that Disney decided to start charging people to use it. To view *Happily Ever After* from this location now costs $79 per adult and $47 per child. The viewing area is available starting 1 hour before the show, and the event includes a dessert buffet and nonalcoholic beverages. Reservations can be made 180 days in advance online or by calling ☎ 407-WDW-DINE (939-3463). If you make a reservation more than two weeks in advance, you'll be given a default reservation time of 6 p.m. for the dessert party and told to call back within two weeks of your trip for the actual time.

A St. Louis reader who went to the *Happily Ever After* dessert party pronounced it "meh":

> We did the fireworks dessert party at Tomorrowland Terrace against my better judgment. While the vantage point was pretty good and the desserts were tasty, it was definitely not worth the price.

FIREWORKS CRUISE For a different view, you can watch the fireworks from Seven Seas Lagoon aboard a chartered pontoon boat. The charter costs $320 for up to 8 people and just under $372 for 10 (tax included). Chips, soda, and water are provided; sandwiches and more-substantial food items may be arranged through reservations. Your Disney captain will take you for a little cruise and then position the boat in a perfect place to watch the fireworks. (A major indirect benefit of the charter is that you can enjoy the fireworks without fighting the mob afterward.)

Because this is a private charter rather than a public tour, only your group will be aboard. Life jackets are provided, but wearing them is at your discretion. To reserve a charter, call ☎ 407-WDW-PLAY (939-7529) at exactly 7 a.m. Eastern time about 180 days before the day you want to cruise. Because the Disney reservations system counts days in a somewhat atypical manner, we recommend that you phone about 185 days out to have a Disney agent specify the exact morning to call for reservations.

FERRYTALE FIREWORKS DESSERT CRUISE Disney added even more options to see *Happily Ever After* for an extra charge with Ferrytale Fireworks: A Sparkling Dessert Cruise. On this cruise, guests board one of the Walt Disney World ferries at the Transportation and Ticket Center for desserts, souvenir glow glasses, and a view of the fireworks. Unlike the dessert party at the Tomorrowland Terrace, this event includes alcoholic beverages for the adults. Unlike the pontoon cruise, this is not a private event for just your party. Pricing is $99 for adults and $69 for children. Reserve at ☎ 407-939-3463 or online through Disney Dining.

LET THE MAGIC BEGIN ★★ This 5-minute show takes place just before official park-opening time. A town crier, Mickey Mouse, and the Fairy Godmother officially open the Magic Kingdom for the day. Most of the characters that greet guests in the park appear onstage for about 2 minutes, but they only wave. There is no song, dance, or other show element. It's a cute diversion if you happen to be there, but it's entirely skippable if you don't want to sacrifice your position near the front of the pack to enter the main lands of the park.

MAGIC KINGDOM BANDS Banjo, Dixieland, steel drum, marching, and fife-and-drum bands play daily throughout the park.

MOVE IT! SHAKE IT! DANCE AND PLAY IT! STREET PARTY ★★★½ Starting at the Walt Disney World Railroad end of Main Street, U.S.A., and working toward the Central Plaza, this short walk incorporates about a dozen guests with a handful of floats, Disney characters (including Mickey, Minnie, and Goofy), and entertainers. The parade's soundtrack, updated in late 2014, includes recent pop hits by Disney and non-Disney artists, and there's a good amount of interaction between the entertainers and the crowd. Unless you're already on Main Street, however, or too pooped for anything else, we don't recommend making a special effort to see this parade.

ONCE UPON A TIME ★★★★ Like its predecessor, *Celebrate the Magic*, *Once Upon a Time* uses projection-mapping technology to cover every nook and cranny of Cinderella Castle in vibrant images that appear almost three-dimensional. The heartwarming show features *Beauty and the Beast*'s Mrs. Potts sharing bedtime stories with Chip. Here, guests go on a magical adventure through favorite Disney movies, including flying over London to Never-Never Land with Peter Pan, watching Winnie the Pooh fly toward the top of the castle with a colorful balloon, enjoying a whimsical tea party with the Mad Hatter, and more. The show culminates with classic scenes from *Beauty and the Beast*, including Belle waltzing with Beast, Beast's duel with Gaston, and Gaston's turning back into a prince. The conclusion includes a grand finale of additional appearances by beloved Disney characters.

TINKER BELL'S FLIGHT This nice special effect in the sky above Cinderella Castle heralds the beginning of the *Happily Ever After* fireworks show (when the park is open late).

TOMORROWLAND FORECOURT STAGE This two-story space behind the Astro Orbiter occasionally hosts DJ-led dance parties. We wouldn't make a special trip to see these, but they're fun if you're just passing by.

MAGIC KINGDOM HARD-TICKET *and* 24-HOUR EVENTS

THE MAGIC KINGDOM HOSTS special after-hours, holiday-themed events in September, October, November, and December, celebrating

Halloween and Christmas. These events require separate admission (see "The Walt Disney World Calendar" on page 50 in Part One for details) and can sell out. Space doesn't permit us to cover these events in the book, but we provide full details, including photos, best days to go, touring advice, and more, at blog.touringplans.com. Search for "Halloween Party" or "Christmas Party" to see the coverage.

DISNEY EARLY MORNING MAGIC PROGRAM   In 2016, Disney began a special extra-cost event called Early Morning Magic at the Magic Kingdom. For $73 per adult and $63 per child, guests receive a breakfast buffet at Pinocchio Village Haus and access to three Fantasyland attractions for 75 minutes before regular park opening. Offered on certain Tuesdays and Sundays in select months, Early Morning Magic's three attractions were Peter Pan's Flight, The Many Adventures of Winnie the Pooh, and Seven Dwarfs Mine Train. Regular park admission was also required.

PARADES

PARADES AT THE MAGIC KINGDOM ARE FULL-FLEDGED spectacles with dozens of Disney characters and amazing special effects. In addition to providing great entertainment, parades lure guests away from the attractions. If getting on rides appeals to you more than watching a parade, you'll find substantially shorter lines just before and during parades. Because the parade route doesn't pass through Adventureland, Tomorrowland, or Fantasyland, attractions in these lands are particularly good bets.

Be forewarned: The parade path disrupts pedestrian traffic throughout most of the Magic Kingdom. If you're on the left side of Main Street (facing the castle), anywhere in Adventureland, or anywhere from Pecos Bill's in Frontierland through the Liberty Tree Tavern in Liberty Square (that is, the side opposite the Rivers of America), you're cut off from the rest of the park.

If you're on the right-hand side of Main Street, however, you can walk counterclockwise around the Magic Kingdom from the Main Street train station, through all of Tomorrowland, all of Fantasyland, and the parts of Liberty Square and Frontierland that border the Rivers of America, ending at Splash Mountain in Frontierland.

If you plan to skip the parades in favor of attractions, plan on being on the "correct" side of the parade route 15 minutes before the parade starts. If you absolutely must cross the parade route, look for special crosswalks, typically near Casey's Corner on Main Street, U.S.A., and near the Liberty Tree Tavern in Liberty Square.

A Massachusetts mom recalls being trapped by the parade:

The only major glitch in my plan was that I thought the WDW Railroad (which I had been planning to use as our escape from the crowds) would reopen after the first parade. Maybe either Disney or the Unofficial Guide *should mention this, in case anyone else might be planning a similar escape route. [We do.]*

AFTERNOON PARADE

USUALLY STAGED AT 3 P.M., the afternoon parade features bands, floats, and marching Disney characters. The current production, **Festival** of Fantasy (★★★★), has floats that pay tribute to *The Little Mermaid*, *Brave,* and *Frozen,* among other Disney films. Many of the floats' pieces spin and swing to extremes not normally found in Disney parades: The *Tangled* platform has characters riding swinging wood hammers from one side of the street to the other. The most talked-about float is Maleficent (the villain from *Sleeping Beauty,* and the star of her own feature film) in dragon form—she spits actual fire at a couple of points along the route.

EVENING PARADE

DISNEY DISCONTINUED its long-running regular evening parade, the Main Street Electrical Parade, in October 2016; no word yet on a replacement. There are still evening parades during special events and parties such as **Mickey's Not-So-Scary Halloween Party** (page 52) and **Mickey's Very Merry Christmas Party** (page 54).

DISNEY DISH WITH JIM HILL

THE HEADLESS HORSEMAN IS A HER One Mickey's Not-So-Scary Halloween Party highlight has the Headless Horseman galloping through the park holding a flaming pumpkin in one hand. To make sure that the cast member perched high atop that horse can safely guide it through the park after dark, it's usually done by a female member of the Tri-Circle-D Ranch staff, who can look through a carefully concealed hole just above the Horseman's top coat button.

PARADE ROUTE AND VANTAGE POINTS

MAGIC KINGDOM PARADES circle Town Square, head down Main Street, go around the Central Plaza, and cross the bridge to Liberty Square. In Liberty Square, they follow the waterfront and end in Frontierland. Sometimes they begin in Frontierland and run the route in the opposite direction. Most guests watch from the Central Plaza or from Main Street. One of the best and most popular vantage points is the upper platform of the Walt Disney World Railroad station at the Town Square end of Main Street. This is also a good place for watching the *Happily Ever After* fireworks show, as well as for ducking out of the park ahead of the crowd when the fireworks end. The problem is, you have to stake out your position 30–60 minutes before the events begin.

Because most spectators pack Main Street and the Central Plaza, we recommend watching the parade from Liberty Square or Frontierland. Great vantage points frequently overlooked are as follows:

1. Sleepy Hollow snack-and-beverage shop, immediately to your right as you cross the bridge into Liberty Square. If you arrive early, buy refreshments and claim a table closest to the rail. You'll have a perfect view of the parade as it crosses Liberty Square Bridge, but only when the parade begins on Main Street.

2. The pathway on the Liberty Square side of the moat from Sleepy Hollow snack-and-beverage shop to Cinderella Castle. Any point along this path offers an unobstructed view as the parade crosses Liberty Square Bridge. Once again, this spot works only for parades coming from Main Street.

3. The covered walkway between Liberty Tree Tavern and the Diamond Horseshoe Saloon. This elevated vantage point is perfect (particularly on rainy days) and usually goes unnoticed until just before the parade starts.

Magic Kingdom Parade Route

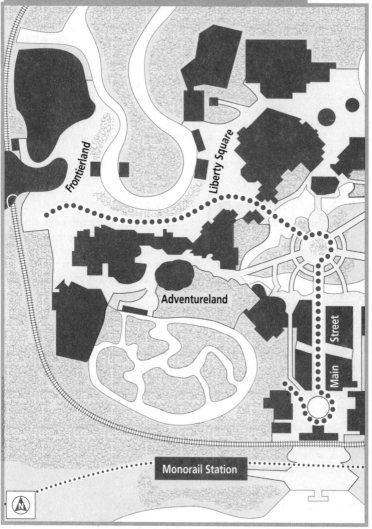

4. Elevated platforms in front of the Frontierland Shootin' Arcade, Frontier Trading Post, and the building with the sign reading FRONTIER MERCANTILE. These spots usually get picked off 10–12 minutes before parade time.

5. Benches on the perimeter of the Central Plaza, between the entrances to Liberty Square and Adventureland. Usually unoccupied until after the parade begins, they offer a comfortable resting place and an unobstructed (though somewhat distant) view of the parade as it crosses Liberty Square Bridge.

6. Liberty Square and Frontierland dockside areas; spots here usually go early.

7. The porch of Tony's Town Square Restaurant on Main Street provides an elevated viewing platform and an easy exit path when the fireworks are over.

Assuming it starts on Main Street (evening parades normally do), the parade takes 16–20 minutes to reach Liberty Square or Frontierland.

On evenings when the parade runs twice, the first parade draws a huge crowd, siphoning guests from attractions. Many folks leave the park after the early parade, with many more departing following the fireworks (which are scheduled on the hour between the two parades).

Continue to tour after the fireworks. This is a particularly good time to ride Splash Mountain and enjoy attractions in Adventureland. If you're touring Adventureland and the parade begins on Main Street, you won't have to assume your viewing position in Frontierland until 15 minutes after the parade kicks off (the time it takes the parade to reach Frontierland). If you watch from the Splash Mountain side of the street and head for the attraction as the last float passes, you'll be able to ride with only a couple of minutes' wait. You might even have time to work in a last-minute ride on Big Thunder Mountain Railroad.

VANTAGE POINTS FOR FIREWORKS

Plaza Gardens East and West were specifically constructed for fireworks viewing. Of the two, we prefer Plaza Gardens East (the same side of the park as Tomorrowland) because the configuration of light and audio poles is slightly less obtrusive when viewing the castle.

If those areas are full, then anywhere along Main Street is fine for the fireworks, especially if you plan to leave the park immediately afterward. Watching from the train-station end of Main Street is the easiest way to facilitate a quick departure.

Our two favorite spots if we intend to remain in the park are:

1. In Fantasyland between Seven Dwarfs Mine Train and *Enchanted Tales with Belle.* Some of the minor fireworks that float above the castle will be behind you, but all of the major effects will be right in front of you. The explosions are loud, and the echo off the back of Cinderella Castle is memorable.

2. On the bridge between the Central Plaza and Tomorrowland. It's a slightly sideways view of the fireworks, and there are a few trees that block some of the castle, but if Tinker Bell does her pre-fireworks flight from the castle, she'll fly directly over this area.

LEAVING THE PARK AFTER EVENING PARADES AND FIREWORKS

ARMIES OF GUESTS leave the Magic Kingdom after evening parades and fireworks. The Disney transportation system (buses, ferries, and monorail) is overwhelmed, causing long waits in boarding areas.

A mom from Kresgeville, Pennsylvania, recounts:

unofficial **TIP**
Digital displays at the Magic Kingdom exit show the wait to board the monorails and ferry—take the one with the shorter line.

Our family of five made the mistake of going to the Magic Kingdom the Saturday night before Columbus Day to watch the parade and fireworks. Afterwards, we lingered at The Crystal Palace to wait for the crowds to lessen, but it was no use. We started walking toward the gates and soon became trapped by the throng, not able to go forward or back. There was no way to get to the ferry to our hotel. Our group became separated, and it became a nightmare. We left the park at 10:30 p.m. and didn't get back to the Polynesian (less than a mile away) until after midnight. Even if they were to raise Walt Disney himself from cryogenic sleep and parade him down Main Street, I would never go to the Magic Kingdom on a Saturday night again!

An Oklahoma City dad offers this advice:

Never, never leave the Magic Kingdom just after the evening fireworks. Go for another ride—no lines because everyone else is trying to get out!

Congestion persists from the end of the early evening parade until closing time. Most folks watch the early parade and then the fireworks a few minutes later. If you're parked at the Transportation and Ticket Center (TTC) and are intent on beating the crowd, view the early parade from the Town Square end of Main Street, leaving the park as soon as the parade ends.

Here's what happened to a family from Cape Coral, Florida:

We tried to leave the park before the parade began, but Main Street was already packed and we didn't see any way to get out of the park—we were stuck. In addition, it was impossible to move across the street, and even the shops were so crowded it was virtually impossible to maneuver a stroller through them to get close to the entrance.

If you don't have a stroller (or are willing to forgo the $1 return refund for rental strollers), catch the Walt Disney World Railroad in Frontierland and ride to the park exit at Main Street. Again, don't cut it too close—the train stops running after the parade.

MAIN STREET PASSAGEWAYS Disney has built two pedestrian walkways behind the shops on either side of Main Street, U.S.A., specifically for guests who want to get in or out of the park without walking down the middle of Main Street. If you're on the Tomorrowland side of the park, a passageway runs from between The Plaza Restaurant and Tomorrowland Terrace, back behind the east side of Main Street, to Tony's Town Square Restaurant near the park exit. If you're on the Adventureland side of the park, the passageway runs from the First Aid area to the Main Street Fire Station near the park exit. However, these passageways aren't used every night, so there's no guarantee that they'll be available.

unofficial **TIP**
Be aware that the railroad shuts down during parades because the floats must cross the tracks when entering or exiting the parade route in Frontierland.

If the passageways aren't open and you're on the Tomorrowland side of the park, it's still possible for you to exit during a parade. Leaving Tomorrowland, cut through Tomorrowland Terrace. Before you reach Main Street, bear left into the side door of the corner shop. Once inside, you'll see that Main Street shops have interior doors allowing you to pass from one shop to the next without having to get on Main Street. Work your way from shop to shop until you reach Town Square (easy, because people will be outside watching the parade). At Town Square, bear left and move to the train station and the park exit.

This strategy won't work if you're on the Adventureland side of the park. You can make your way through Casey's Corner restaurant to Main Street and then work your way through the interior of the Main Street shops, but when you pop out of the Emporium at Town Square, you'll be trapped by the parade. As soon as the last float passes, however, you can bolt for the exit.

Another strategy for beating the masses out of the park (if your car is at the TTC lot) is to watch the early parade and then leave before the fireworks begin. Line up for the ferry; one will depart about every 8–10 minutes. Try to catch the ferry that will be crossing Seven Seas Lagoon while the fireworks are in progress. The best vantage point is on the top deck to the right of the pilothouse as you face the Magic Kingdom; the sight of fireworks silhouetting the castle and reflecting off Seven Seas Lagoon is unforgettable. While there's no guarantee that a ferry will load and depart within 3 or 4 minutes of the fireworks, your chances are about 50–50 of catching it just right. If you're in the front of the line for the ferry and don't want to board the boat that's loading, stop at the gate and let people pass you. You'll be the first to board the next boat.

Strollers, wheelchairs, and ECVs make navigating the crowds even more difficult. If you've got one of these, or you're staying at a Disney hotel not served by the monorail and you have to depend on Disney transportation, watch the early parade and fireworks, then enjoy the attractions until about 20–25 minutes before the late parade is scheduled to begin. Then leave the park using one of the strategies listed on the previous page, and catch the Disney bus or boat back to your hotel.

TRAFFIC PATTERNS *in* the MAGIC KINGDOM

WHEN WE RESEARCH THE MAGIC KINGDOM, we study its traffic patterns, asking:

1. WHICH SECTIONS OF THE PARK AND WHICH ATTRACTIONS DO GUESTS VISIT FIRST?
When the park opens, guest traffic to Fantasyland and Tomorrowland is heaviest, followed by Frontierland. Seven Dwarfs Mine Train pulls more people than ever into the back reaches of the park.

Our researchers tested the frequent claim that most people turn right into Tomorrowland and tour the Magic Kingdom in a counterclockwise sequence. We found the claim to be baseless.

2. HOW LONG DOES IT TAKE FOR THE PARK TO FILL UP? HOW ARE THE VISITORS DISPERSED IN THE PARK?
A surge of early birds arrives before or around opening time but is quickly dispersed throughout the empty

unofficial **TIP**
As the park fills up, visitors head for the top attractions before lines get long. This, more than anything else, determines morning traffic patterns.

park. After the initial wave is absorbed, there's a lull lasting about an hour after opening. Then the park is inundated for about 2 hours, peaking between 10 a.m. and noon. Arrivals continue in a steady but diminishing stream until around 2 p.m. The lines we sampled were longest between 1 and 2 p.m., indicating more arrivals than departures into the early afternoon. For touring purposes, most attractions develop long lines between 10 and 11:30 a.m.

ATTRACTIONS THAT GET CROWDED EARLY

FANTASYLAND • Peter Pan's Flight • Princess Fairytale Hall
• Seven Dwarfs Mine Train

FRONTIERLAND • Big Thunder Mountain Railroad • Splash Mountain

TOMORROWLAND • Buzz Lightyear's Space Ranger Spin • Space Mountain
• Tomorrowland Speedway

From late morning until early afternoon, guests are equally distributed through all the lands. However, guests concentrate in Fantasyland, Liberty Square, and Frontierland in late afternoon, with a decrease of visitors in Adventureland and Tomorrowland. Adventureland's Jungle Cruise and Tomorrowland's Buzz Lightyear and Space Mountain continue to be crowded, but most other attractions in those lands are readily accessible.

3. HOW DO MOST VISITORS TOUR THE PARK? Do first-time visitors tour differently from repeat guests? Many first-time visitors are guided by friends or relatives familiar with the Magic Kingdom. These tours may or may not follow an orderly sequence. First-time visitors without personal guides tend to be more orderly in their touring. Many first-time visitors, however, are drawn to Cinderella Castle upon entering the park, and thus they begin their rotation from Fantasyland. Repeat visitors usually head straightaway to their favorite attractions.

4. HOW DOES FASTPASS+ AFFECT CROWD DISTRIBUTIONS? In Part Two, we discuss which attractions' average wait times have been increasing or decreasing under FastPass+. When it comes to the Magic Kingdom, FastPass+ is moving guests from the right side of the park—Tomorrowland and Storybook Circus in Fantasyland—to Adventureland and the Liberty Square area, all on the left side of the park.

We've done our fair share of criticizing FastPass+, and there are still parts of it that are just plain goofy (see what we did there?). But as far as reaching its goal of more evenly distributing crowds throughout the park, FastPass+ has to be one of the big industrial-engineering-and-technology success stories of the past few years.

5. HOW DO SPECIAL EVENTS, SUCH AS PARADES AND LIVE SHOWS, AFFECT TRAFFIC PATTERNS? Parades pull huge numbers of guests away from attractions and provide a window of opportunity for experiencing the more popular attractions with less of a wait. Castle Forecourt Stage shows also attract crowds but only slightly affect lines.

6. WHAT ARE THE TRAFFIC PATTERNS NEAR AND AT CLOSING TIME? On our sample days, in busy times and off-season at the park, departures outnumbered arrivals beginning in midafternoon. Many visitors left in late afternoon as the dinner hour approached. When the park closed early, guests departed steadily during the 2 hours before closing, with a huge exodus at closing time. When the park closed late, a huge exodus began immediately after the early-evening parade and fireworks, with a second mass departure after the late parade, continuing until closing. Because Main Street and the transportation services remain open after the other five lands close, crowds leaving at closing mainly affect conditions on Main Street and at the monorail-, ferry-, and bus-boarding areas. In the hour before closing, the other five lands are normally uncrowded.

To get a complete view of the actual traffic patterns while you're in the park, use our mobile app, **Lines** (touringplans.com/lines). The app gives you current wait times and future estimates in half-hour increments for today and tomorrow. A quick glance shows how traffic patterns affect wait times throughout the day.

MAGIC KINGDOM TOURING PLANS

STARTING ON PAGE 819, our step-by-step touring plans are field-tested for seeing *as much as possible* in one day with a minimum of time wasted in lines. They're designed to help you avoid crowds and bottlenecks on days of moderate-to-heavy attendance. Understand, however, that there's more to see in the Magic Kingdom than can be experienced in one day. Since we first began covering the Magic Kingdom, four headliner attractions have been added and an entire land created and destroyed.

On days of lighter attendance (see "Selecting the Time of Year for Your Visit," page 41), our plans will save you time but won't be as critical to successful touring as on busier days.

To help with FastPass+, we've listed the approximate return times for which you should try to make reservations. (The plans should work with anything close to the times shown.) Because Disney limits how many FastPass+ reservations you can get, we've listed which attractions are most likely to need FastPass+, too. Check **TouringPlans.com** for the latest information.

CHOOSING THE APPROPRIATE TOURING PLAN

WE PRESENT FIVE MAGIC KINGDOM TOURING PLANS:

- Magic Kingdom One-Day Touring Plan for Adults
- Magic Kingdom Authors' Selective One-Day Touring Plan for Adults
- Magic Kingdom One-Day Touring Plan for Parents with Small Children
- Magic Kingdom Two-Day Touring Plan
- Magic Kingdom Dumbo-or-Die-in-a-Day Touring Plan for Parents with Small Children

If you have two days (or two mornings) at the Magic Kingdom, the Two-Day Touring Plan is *by far* the most relaxed and efficient. The two-day plan takes advantage of early morning, when lines are short and the park hasn't filled with guests. This plan works well year-round and eliminates much of the extra walking required by the one-day plans. No matter when the park closes, our two-day plan guarantees the most efficient touring and the least time in lines. The plan is perfect for guests who wish to sample both the attractions and the atmosphere of the Magic Kingdom.

If you have only a single day to visit but you wish to see as much as possible, then use the One-Day Touring Plan for Adults. Yes, it's exhausting, but it packs in the maximum. If you prefer a more relaxed visit, use the Authors' Selective One-Day Touring Plan. It includes the best the park has to offer (in the authors' opinion), eliminating the less-impressive attractions.

If you have children younger than age 8, adopt the One-Day Touring Plan for Parents with Small Children. It's a compromise, blending the preferences of younger children with those of older siblings and adults. The plan includes many children's rides in Fantasyland but omits roller-coaster rides and other attractions that may frighten young children or are off-limits because of height requirements. Or use the One-Day Touring Plan for Adults or the Authors' Selective One-Day Touring Plan for Adults, and take advantage of switching off, a technique whereby children accompany adults to the loading area of a ride with age and height requirements but don't board (see page 439).

unofficial TIP

Switching off allows adults to enjoy the more adventuresome attractions while keeping the group together.

The Dumbo-or-Die-in-a-Day Touring Plan for Parents with Small Children is designed for parents who are happy to just self-sacrificially stand around, sweat, wipe noses, pay for stuff, and watch the kids enjoy themselves. It's great!

"Not a Touring Plan" Touring Plans

For the type-B reader, these touring plans (see page 816) avoid detailed step-by-step strategies for saving every last minute in line. To paraphrase one of our favorite movies, they're more guidelines than actual rules. Use these to avoid the longest waits in line while having maximum flexibility to see whatever interests you in a particular part of the park.

For the Magic Kingdom, these "not" touring plans include advice for adults and parents with one day in the park, for anyone with two days, and for anyone with an afternoon and a full day to tour.

Two-Day Touring Plan for Families with Small Children

If you have young children and are looking for a two-day itinerary, combine the Magic Kingdom One-Day Touring Plan for Parents with Small Children with the second day of the Magic Kingdom Two-Day Touring Plan.

Two-Day Touring Plan for Early-Morning Touring on Day One and Afternoon–Evening Touring on Day Two

Many of you enjoy an early start at the Magic Kingdom on one day, followed by a second day with a lazy, sleep-in morning, resuming your touring in the afternoon and/or evening. If this appeals to you, use the Magic Kingdom One-Day Touring Plan for Adults or the Magic Kingdom One-Day Touring Plan for Parents with Small Children on your early day. Adhere to the touring plan for as long as it feels comfortable (many folks leave after the afternoon parade). On the second day, pick up where you left off. If you intend to use FastPass+ on your second day, make reservations well in advance, before they're all gone. Customize the remaining part of the touring plan to incorporate parades, fireworks, and other live performances according to your preferences.

MAGIC KINGDOM TOURING PLAN COMPANION

WE'VE CONSOLIDATED A GREAT DEAL OF INFORMATION about the Magic Kingdom in its Touring Plan Companion, on page 839 just after the touring plans. Like the plans, the companions are designed to clip out and take with you to the park. The Magic Kingdom Touring Plan Companion includes the best days to go, the best times to visit each attraction, the authors' rating, height requirements, small-child fright potential, and info on dining and cool places to take a break.

THE SINGLE-DAY TOURING CONUNDRUM

TOURING THE MAGIC KINGDOM IN A DAY is complicated by the fact that the premier attractions are at almost opposite ends of the park: Splash Mountain and Big Thunder Mountain Railroad in Frontierland, Space Mountain and Buzz Lightyear in Tomorrowland, and Under the Sea: Journey of the Little Mermaid and Seven Dwarfs Mine Train in the top center. It's virtually impossible to ride all six without encountering lines at one or another. If you ride Space Mountain and see Buzz Lightyear immediately after the park opens, for example, you won't have much of a wait, if any. By the time you leave Tomorrowland and hurry to Fantasyland, however, the line for Seven Dwarfs will be substantial. The same situation prevails if you ride the Fantasyland duo first: Seven Dwarfs Mine Train and Under the Sea, no problem; Space Mountain and Buzz Lightyear, however, have fair-sized lines. From 10 minutes after opening until just before closing, lines are long at these headliners.

unofficial **TIP**
Don't worry that other people will be following the plans and render them useless. Fewer than 4 in every 100 people in the park will have been exposed to this info.

The best way to ride all six without long waits is to use FastPass+ and tour over two mornings. Make midmorning FastPass+ reservations at Big Thunder for your first day. When you arrive, ride Seven Dwarfs Mine Train as soon as the park opens, then head directly for Splash Mountain. By the time you're done riding, your FastPass+ reservation should be ready for Big Thunder. On your second day, ride Space Mountain immediately after the park opens, then ride Buzz Lightyear.

If you have only a day to see the Magic Kingdom, make FastPass+ reservations in advance for around 9:30 a.m. at Big Thunder Mountain, and around 3:30 p.m. at Space Mountain. Then, on the day of your visit, ride Seven Dwarfs Mine Train as soon as the park opens, then ride Under the Sea, then hotfoot it to Splash Mountain. Your FastPass+ reservation for Big Thunder will be valid by the time you're done, and you'll have completed three of the park's four headliners in about an hour. Save Buzz Lightyear for around 3 p.m., when everyone is watching the parade, and hop on Space Mountain afterward.

PRELIMINARY INSTRUCTIONS FOR ALL MAGIC KINGDOM TOURING PLANS

BECOME FAMILIAR WITH THE MAGIC KINGDOM'S opening procedures, as described on pages 89 and 515. On days of moderate-to-heavy attendance, follow your chosen touring plan exactly, deviating from it only as follows:

1. When you're not interested in an attraction it lists. Simply skip that attraction and proceed to the next.

2. When you encounter a very long line at an attraction the touring plan calls for. If this is the case, skip the attraction in question and go to the next step, returning later to retry.

BEFORE YOU GO

1. Call ☎ 407-824-4321 or check **disneyworld.com** the day before you go to verify official opening time.

2. Purchase admission and make FastPass+ reservations before you arrive.

3. Get familiar with park-opening procedures (see previous section) and reread the plan you've chosen so you know what you're likely to encounter.

MAGIC KINGDOM ONE-DAY TOURING PLAN FOR ADULTS *(page 819)*

FOR Adults without young children.

ASSUMES Willingness to experience all major rides (including roller coasters) and shows.

This plan requires a lot of walking and some backtracking to avoid lines. Extra walking and morning hustling will spare you 4 or more hours of standing in line. How far you get depends on how quickly you move from ride to ride, how many times you rest or eat, how quickly the park fills, and what time the park closes.

MAGIC KINGDOM AUTHORS' SELECTIVE ONE-DAY TOURING PLAN FOR ADULTS *(page 820)*

FOR Adults touring without young children.

ASSUMES Willingness to experience all major rides (including roller coasters) and shows.

This plan includes only the attractions we think are best. It requires a lot of walking and some backtracking to avoid lines. How far you get depends on how quickly you move from ride to ride, how many times you rest or eat, how quickly the park fills, and what time the park closes.

MAGIC KINGDOM ONE-DAY TOURING PLAN FOR PARENTS WITH SMALL CHILDREN *(page 821)*

FOR Parents with children younger than age 8.

ASSUMES Periodic stops for rest, restrooms, and refreshments.

This plan represents a compromise between the observed tastes of adults and those of younger children. Included are many amusement park rides that children may have the opportunity to experience at fairs and amusement parks back home. Although these rides are included in the plan, omit them if possible. These cycle-loading rides often have long lines, consuming valuable touring time:

- **THE BARNSTORMER**
- **DUMBO THE FLYING ELEPHANT**
- **MAD TEA PARTY**
- **THE MAGIC CARPETS OF ALADDIN**

This time could be better spent experiencing the many attractions that better demonstrate the Disney creative genius and are found only in the Magic Kingdom. Instead, try either of the one-day plans for adults, and take advantage of switching off (see page 439). This allows parents and young children to enter the ride together; at the boarding area, one parent watches the children while the other rides. Families using this plan should review Magic Kingdom attractions in our Small-Child Fright-Potential Chart in Part Five (see pages 432–435).

This edition's updated touring plan requires less walking than in previous years, primarily due to the natural drop in popularity of some newer Fantasyland attractions, such as Under the Sea. The one short back-and-forth is to Tomorrowland after the midday break, to take advantage of FastPass+ at Buzz Lightyear instead of waiting in a longer line later.

If time is tight or you'd like a midday break longer than the 3–4 hours we've used as a default, skipping *Country Bear Jamboree* will save about 30 minutes of your day.

To Convert This One-Day Touring Plan into a Two-Day Touring Plan

Follow the one-day plan through lunch, including the suggested advance FastPass+ reservations. See Mickey Mouse on your way out of the park in Step 11. For Day 2, obtain advance, late morning FastPass+ reservations for Jungle Cruise, Pirates of the Caribbean, and Haunted Mansion. Start Day 2 with Buzz Lightyear and *Monsters, Inc. Laugh Floor,* then follow the plan's steps as shown.

MAGIC KINGDOM TWO-DAY TOURING PLAN
(pages 822 and 823)

FOR Those wishing to spread their Magic Kingdom visit over two days.

ASSUMES Willingness to experience all major rides and shows.

This two-day touring plan takes advantage of early-morning touring. Each day, you should complete the structured part of the plan by about 4 p.m. This leaves plenty of time for live entertainment. If the park is open late (after 8 p.m.), consider returning to your hotel at midday for a swim and a nap. Eat an early dinner outside Walt Disney World, and return refreshed to enjoy the park's nighttime festivities.

MAGIC KINGDOM DUMBO-OR-DIE-IN-A-DAY TOURING PLAN FOR PARENTS WITH SMALL CHILDREN
(page 824)

FOR Adults compelled to devote every waking moment to the pleasure and entertainment of their young children, or rich people who are paying someone else to take their children to the theme park.

PREREQUISITE This plan is designed for days when the Magic Kingdom doesn't close until 9 p.m. or later.

ASSUMES Frequent stops for rest, restrooms, and refreshments.

Name aside, this plan is no joke. Whether you're loving, guilty, masochistic, selfless, or insane, this itinerary will provide a youngster with about as perfect a day as is possible at the Magic Kingdom. Families using this plan should review Magic Kingdom attractions in our Small-Child Fright-Potential Chart in Part Five (see pages 432–435).

To Convert This One-Day Touring Plan into a Day-and-a-Half Touring Plan

The idea is to split the park in half so that Tomorrowland, Storybook Circus, and a few of the other Fantasyland attractions are on the second day. Here's how:

For the day of your afternoon visit, make FastPass+ reservations well in advance for Splash Mountain around 4 p.m., Pirates of the Caribbean around 5 p.m., and Jungle Cruise around 6:30 p.m. Work in the other rides, shows, and dinner around these, and end the day with the evening parade.

For your full-day visit, make FastPass+ reservations well in advance for Peter Pan's Flight around 10:30 a.m., *Enchanted Tales with Belle* around 6:30 p.m., and Buzz Lightyear around 8 p.m. Ride Seven Dwarfs Mine Train as soon as the park opens, then Winnie the Pooh on the way to Astro Orbiter and Tomorrowland Speedway. Visit Storybook Circus as you loop back to Under the Sea, then continue clockwise through Fantasyland before leaving the park for a midday break. Return to the park for dinner before your *Enchanted Tales* reservation, then see *Mickey's PhilharMagic*, the *Monsters, Inc.*, show in Tomorrowland, and Buzz Lightyear. See the parade and fireworks if you've not already done so.

PART TEN

EPCOT

WALT DISNEY'S ORIGINAL, 1960s-era vision for Epcot was a complete rethinking of the American city. Back then, it was EPCOT, an acronym meaning "**E**xperimental **P**rototype **C**ommunity of **T**omorrow." Among Walt's ideas for future city living were self-driving, electric cars and prefab, solar-powered homes electronically connected to a network of information services. Residents were to be employed by America's leading industries, working on cutting-edge products themselves designed to improve urban life. And they considered putting the entire city center inside an air-conditioned dome. These were no small plans.

After Walt died in 1966, the people who took over running his company considered his ideas too risky to implement. When it opened 16 years later, EPCOT Center was a two-part theme park: Half of its rides were based on a futuristic, semi-educational, better-living-through-technology look at the world, and half was a kind of permanent World's Fair (another of Walt's passions).

Public reaction to Epcot has always been mixed. Many visitors—then and now—are disappointed to find few Disney characters and little Magic Kingdom–style theming. Others, including at least one of this book's authors, consider the original Epcot to be the best theme park ever built. Most people fall in the middle, accepting both the park's high-tech presentations and its character-based rides for what they are.

EPCOT TODAY

EPCOT IS THE WALT DISNEY WORLD theme park most in need of refurbishment. A completely new attraction hasn't been built here in more than a decade, and just three headliner rides have been built in the past 20 years. Huge areas of the park sit closed and empty; Innoventions in Future World, for example, used to hold a dozen interesting attractions. Others, such as *The Circle of Life; Ellen's Energy Adventure;* half of The Seas and Imagination! Pavilions; and the Germany, Italy, United States, Japan, Morocco, France, and United Kingdom Pavilions in World Showcase haven't been meaningfully updated in 20–30 years. The tech-startup world uses the term *minimum viable product* to describe the least functionality that consumers will accept in a product; we think Disney management seems intent on finding the "minimum viable Epcot."

What Disney has invested in at Epcot is a series of seasonal "festivals" designed to sell food, alcohol, and merchandise. These festivals run 10 months of the year—only June and July didn't have them in 2017. While popular and mostly interesting, they're no substitute for compelling, technologically advanced attractions.

After Toy Story and Star Wars Lands open at Disney's Hollywood Studios in 2018 and mid-2019, respectively, Epcot may become the most expendable of Disney's parks for short vacations. Until then, though, there's enough at Epcot that visiting is still worth your time and money.

OPERATING HOURS

EPCOT HAS TWO THEMED AREAS, **Future World** and **World Showcase,** each with its own operating hours. Though the schedule changes throughout the year, Future World always opens earlier than World Showcase. While most of Future World's attractions stay open until the entire park closes, a few close around 7 p.m. most of the year.

World Showcase generally opens 2 hours later than Future World (generally 11 a.m.); the exceptions are Norway's Frozen-themed attractions, **Frozen Ever After** and the **Royal Sommerhus** meet and greet, and France's **Les Halles Boulangerie–Pâtisserie** bakery, all of which open with Future World and close with World Showcase. Besides these, a handful of other attractions in Epcot open late or close early. Check the *Times Guide* or the My Disney Experience app for specifics.

DINING IN EPCOT

HERE'S A QUICK RECAP of some of Epcot's top restaurants, rated by readers from highest to lowest. See Part Four for details.

EPCOT RESTAURANT REFRESHER	
COUNTER-SERVICE	**FULL-SERVICE**
Les Halles Boulangerie–Pâtisserie (97% 👍), France, World Showcase	**Garden Grill Restaurant** (93% 👍), The Land, Future World
L'Artisan des Glaces (96% 👍), France, World Showcase	**Tutto Gusto Wine Cellar** (93% 👍), Italy, World Showcase
Kringla Bakeri og Kafe (96% 👍), Norway, World Showcase	**Via Napoli** (91% 👍), Italy, World Showcase
Yorkshire County Fish Shop (94% 👍), United Kingdom, World Showcase	**Biergarten Restaurant** (92% 👍), Germany, World Showcase
Sunshine Seasons (93% 👍), The Land, Future World West	**Teppan Edo** (92% 👍), Japan, World Showcase
Tangierine Cafe (93% 👍), Morocco, World Showcase	**Rose & Crown Dining Room** (91% 👍), UK, World Showcase
Crêpes des Chefs de France (90% 👍), France, World Showcase	**Akershus Royal Banquet Hall** (88% 👍), Norway, World Showcase
Fountain View (Starbucks) (90% 👍), To the right of the big fountain in the back of Future World	**Le Cellier Steakhouse** (88% 👍), Canada, World Showcase
La Cantina de San Angel (88% 👍), Mexico, World Showcase	**La Hacienda de San Angel** (87% 👍), Mexico, World Showcase
Katsura Grill (84% 👍), Japan, World Showcase	**Monsieur Paul** (86% 👍), France, World Showcase
	Restaurant Marrakesh (86% 👍), Morocco, World Showcase

Continued on page 574

Epcot

Attractions

1. Agent P's World Showcase Adventure
2. *The American Adventure* ☑
3. *The Circle of Life*
4. Club Cool
5. Disney & Pixar Short Film Festival FP+
6. Epcot Character Spot FP+
7. Frozen Ever After FP+
8. Grand Fiesta Tour Starring the Three Caballeros
9. *IllumiNations: Reflections of Earth* ☑ FP+
10. *Impressions de France*
11. Innoventions East
12. Innoventions West
13. Journey Into Imagination with Figment FP+
14. Living with the Land ☑ FP+
15. Mission: Space ☑ Use FP+
16. *O Canada!*
17. *Reflections of China*

18. Royal Sommerhus *(Frozen meet and greet)* FP+
19. SeaBase
20. The Seas with Nemo & Friends Use FP+
21. Soarin' ☑ Use FP+
22. Spaceship Earth ☑ FP+
23. Test Track ☑ Use FP+
24. *Turtle Talk with Crush* ☑ FP+
25. Universe of Energy: *Ellen's Energy Adventure*

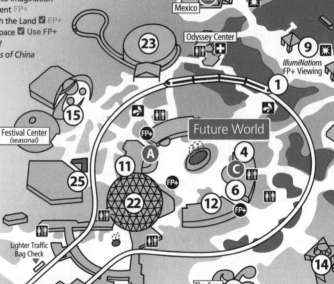

Future World

FP+ Attraction Offers FastPass+ ✚ First Aid Station ✷ *IllumiNations* Top Viewing Spot

Use FP+ FastPass+ Recommended (FP+) FastPass+ Kiosks 🚻 Restrooms 🍴 Recommended Dining

↘ "I Can't Believe It's Disney" Fountains ☑ Not to Be Missed

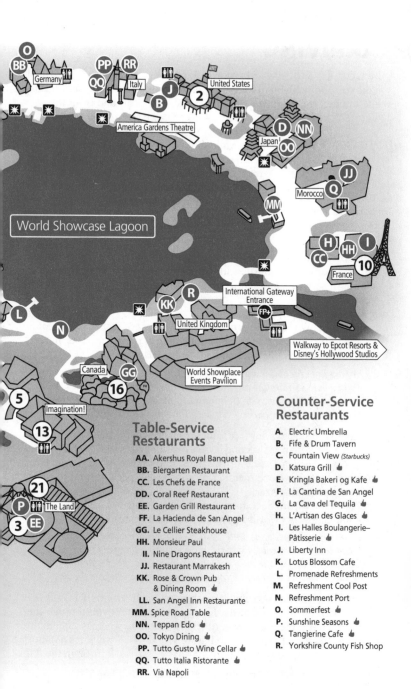

Table-Service Restaurants

AA. Akershus Royal Banquet Hall
BB. Biergarten Restaurant
CC. Les Chefs de France
DD. Coral Reef Restaurant
EE. Garden Grill Restaurant
FF. La Hacienda de San Angel
GG. Le Cellier Steakhouse
HH. Monsieur Paul
II. Nine Dragons Restaurant
JJ. Restaurant Marrakesh
KK. Rose & Crown Pub & Dining Room 🖐
LL. San Angel Inn Restaurante
MM. Spice Road Table
NN. Teppan Edo 🖐
OO. Tokyo Dining 🖐
PP. Tutto Gusto Wine Cellar 🖐
QQ. Tutto Italia Ristorante 🖐
RR. Via Napoli

Counter-Service Restaurants

A. Electric Umbrella
B. Fife & Drum Tavern
C. Fountain View *(Starbucks)*
D. Katsura Grill 🖐
E. Kringla Bakeri og Kafe 🖐
F. La Cantina de San Angel
G. La Cava del Tequila 🖐
H. L'Artisan des Glaces 🖐
I. Les Halles Boulangerie–Pâtisserie
J. Liberty Inn
K. Lotus Blossom Cafe
L. Promenade Refreshments
M. Refreshment Cool Post
N. Refreshment Port
O. Sommerfest 🖐
P. Sunshine Seasons 🖐
Q. Tangierine Cafe 🖐
R. Yorkshire County Fish Shop

Continued from page 571

■ ARRIVING

IF YOU'RE A GUEST AT ONE OF THE EPCOT RESORTS, it will take you about 20–30 minutes to walk the mile or so from your hotel to the International Gateway (back entrance of Epcot) and from there to Future World. Instead of walking, you can catch a boat from your Epcot resort hotel to the International Gateway and then walk about 8 minutes to Future World. To reach the front (Future World) entrance of Epcot from the Epcot resorts, either take a boat from your hotel to Disney's Hollywood Studios and transfer to an Epcot bus or take a cab.

unofficial **TIP**
Plan to arrive at the turnstiles 30–40 minutes before official opening time. Give yourself an extra 10 minutes or so to park and make your way to the entrance.

Arriving at the park by car is easy and direct (for GPS coordinates, see page 485). Epcot has its own parking lot, and, unlike at the Magic Kingdom, you don't have to take a monorail or ferry to reach the entrance. Trams service the parking lot, or you can walk to the front gate. Monorail service connects Epcot with the Transportation and Ticket Center, the Magic Kingdom (transfer required), and Magic Kingdom resorts (transfer required).

For unknown reasons, getting through entrance security at Epcot is more cumbersome and time-consuming than at the other parks. In fact, it's a royal pain, as this unidentified reader relates:

> *My biggest complaint was the amount of time it took to actually get into Epcot: 35 minutes at 10:30 a.m. to get bags checked (park had opened at 9) and another 10 minutes to get in. It took nowhere near as long at the other parks, even with the same crowd size.*

Take these delays into consideration if you're using one of the Epcot touring plans. A second, often overlooked, security checkpoint is on the other (east) side of the main checkpoint. If the main lines look too long, have one member of your group peek around to see if the east lines are shorter.

This reader from Sacramento, California, suggests using the International Gateway (World Showcase) entrance instead:

> *Thanks to MagicBands and FastPass+, the International Gateway entrance is convenient for getting into Epcot first thing in the morning. We entered by boat from the Dolphin and were met inside the gate by cast members who set up our FastPass+ reservations for the day.*

The downside to entering Epcot through the International Gateway (IG) at park opening is that the IG usually doesn't let you through the turnstiles until the park has officially opened, whereas the main entrance will have let guests into Future World's walkways. It's a minor disadvantage to guests headed to Soarin' or Test Track through the IG.

NOT TO BE MISSED AT EPCOT

FUTURE WORLD • Frozen Ever After • Living with the Land • Mission: Space
• Soarin' • Spaceship Earth • Test Track • *Turtle Talk with Crush*

WORLD SHOWCASE • *The American Adventure* • IllumiNations
• Meet Anna and Elsa at Norway

GETTING ORIENTED

EPCOT'S TWO THEMED AREAS are markedly different: **Future World** examines where mankind has come from and where it's going; **World Showcase** features the landmarks, cuisine, and culture of almost a dozen nations and is meant to be a sort of permanent World's Fair.

Navigating Epcot is unlike getting around at the Magic Kingdom. The Magic Kingdom is designed so that nearly every location is part of a discrete environment—Liberty Square and Main Street, U.S.A., for example. All environments are visually separated to preserve the integrity of the theme.

Epcot, by contrast, is visually open. And while it seems strange to see a Japanese pagoda and the Eiffel Tower on the same horizon, getting around is fairly simple. An exception is Future World, where the enormous **Innoventions East and West** buildings hide everything on their opposite sides.

At Epcot, the architectural symbol is **Spaceship Earth.** This shiny, 180-foot geosphere is visible from almost everywhere in the park. Like Cinderella Castle at the Magic Kingdom, Spaceship Earth can help you keep track of where you are in Epcot. But it's in a high-traffic area and isn't centrally located, so it isn't a good meeting place.

Any of the World Showcase pavilions make good meeting places, but be specific. "Hey, let's meet in Japan!" sounds fun, but each pavilion is a mini-town with buildings, monuments, gardens, and plazas. Pick a specific place in Japan—the sidewalk side of the pagoda, for example.

BABY SWAP (SWITCHING OFF) AT EPCOT

AT ALL DISNEY PARKS, attractions allow one parent to ride, and one to stay with a nonriding child. After one parent rides, he switches off with the other parent, who then goes to ride. If the child and nonriding parent must wait outside the attraction (as opposed to in the boarding area), the nonriding adult will be given a FastPass+ so he or she won't have to wait in the standby line. At Epcot, however, long FastPass+ waiting times require a family to spend an inordinate amount of time for both parents to ride. A Tulsa, Oklahoma, father of one elaborates:

Baby swap worked out really well on every ride in every park, except Epcot. The FastPass+ lines plus ride times for Soarin' (30 minutes), Mission: Space (30 minutes), and Test Track (45 minutes) were so long that it made baby swap very frustrating. Basically, in my experience, baby swap just does not work in Epcot, and they should allow you to stand in line together and swap at the ride boarding area.

DISNEY DISH WITH JIM HILL

WENT TO A GARDEN PARTY Disney's most advanced theater isn't at Cirque du Soleil—it's here at Epcot's America Gardens. Disney's show engineers say that's because this is the venue where celebrities appear when they're performing at Garden Rocks, the Eat to the Beat concert series, and doing readings at the Candlelight Processional.

FASTPASS+ ATTRACTIONS IN EPCOT

EPCOT OFFERS FASTPASS+ for 12 attractions in two tiers:

TIER A (Choose one per day)	
• Frozen Ever After	• Soarin'
• IllumiNations	• Test Track
TIER B (Choose two per day)	
• Disney & Pixar Short Film Festival	• Mission: Space
• Epcot Character Spot	• Spaceship Earth
• Journey into Imagination	• The Seas with Nemo & Friends
• Living with the Land	• Turtle Talk with Crush

Because the tiers limit the number and combinations of FastPass+ attractions you can experience, much of our Epcot touring strategy is dictated by the attractions in Tier A, which include **Frozen Ever After, Soarin',** and **Test Track.** Because you can't use FastPass+ for all three, your best bet is to visit one as the first step in a touring plan, then use FastPass+ for the others. Exceptions: **Living with the Land** and the **Disney & Pixar Short Film Festival** don't get crowds comparable to the others, so they're rarely a good use of FastPass+.

Epcot FastPass+ Strategy for Frozen Ever After

The opening of **Frozen Ever After** complicated touring Epcot for a couple of reasons. Because it's in the same FastPass+ tier as Soarin' and Test Track, you can obtain a FastPass for just one in advance. Frozen is also unlikely to have much day-of FastPass+ availability, because it's based on a hit film and it appeals to kids. Plus, its location in World Showcase makes it impractical as a detour while you're in Future World.

Even with Frozen Ever After in the Epcot lineup, our most frequent FastPass+ recommendation is still for **Spaceship Earth** around lunchtime (11 a.m. and 1 p.m.). Why? Like Peter Pan's Flight in the Magic Kingdom, Spaceship Earth is an attraction that families head to after they've done a couple of headliner thrill rides. Spaceship Earth's wait times can reach 30–40 minutes by late morning, making it one of the best FastPass+ choices in Tier B.

Our touring plan software gives **Mission: Space (Orange)** the second-highest number of FastPass+ recommendations. Waits here can easily exceed an hour or more, but its spot in Tier B means you can get a FastPass+ reservation for it without affecting your ability to get FastPass+ reservations at Tier A headliners.

Other Good FastPass+ Choices at Epcot

As noted previously, Spaceship Earth, Frozen Ever After, and Mission: Space are our most frequent recommendations for comprehensive tours of Epcot. Besides these, **The Seas with Nemo & Friends** is recommended frequently in our plans for parents with small children, as is **Journey into Imagination with Figment.** Waits at Journey into Imagination have—ironically—increased substantially with the introduction of FastPass+, making it a reasonable Tier B selection for parents with small children.

Attractions That Never Need FastPass+
In Our Epcot Touring Plans

These Epcot attractions never require FastPass+:

- Disney & Pixar Short Film Festival
- *Turtle Talk with Crush*
- Mission: Space (Green)

Waits for the **Disney & Pixar Short Film Festival** and *Turtle Talk with Crush* are almost always under 10 minutes, so they're not a good use of FastPass+. Similarly, the waits for the nonspinning **Mission: Space (Green)** are almost always lower than the spinning (Orange); the spinning version is more popular and that's what we have in our touring plans.

IllumiNations is a must-see, and FastPass+ gets you into a special viewing area for the show, but you still have to arrive a good 30–40 minutes in advance to get a good spot. Plus, there are so many other good viewing spots around World Showcase Lagoon that it's difficult to recommend FastPass+ for *IllumiNations;* the consequence is an hourlong wait at either Soarin', Test Track, or Frozen Ever After. The exceptions are if you're visiting World Showcase solely for dinner and *IllumiNations,* or if you've used your first three FastPass+ reservations and *IllumiNations* FastPasses are still available.

Two-Day Epcot FastPass+ Strategy

If you're visiting Epcot over two days, we suggest using FastPass+ at Soarin' one day and Frozen Ever After on the other day. On the day you visit Soarin', you'll have short lines if you head to Test Track as soon as the park opens. If you're unable to get to Epcot at park opening, remember that Test Track has a single-rider line. Test Track's single-rider line wait times are typically less than half those of the standby (non-FastPass+) wait times. If you're willing to split up your group, the single-rider line is a good way to shorten your wait at Test Track.

Look for Epcot FastPass+ kiosks in the following locations:

- At the Soarin' entrance, downstairs in The Land
- At the MyMagic+ Service Center, between Spaceship Earth and Innoventions East
- At the International Gateway entrance to the park
- In the Future World East walkway, on the way to Mission: Space
- In the Future World West walkway, on the way to The Land

Same-Day FastPass+ Availability

The preceding advice tells you which attractions to focus on when making your *advance* FastPass+ reservations before you get to the park. Once you're in the park, you can make more FastPass+ reservations once your advance reservations have been used or have expired. The chart on the next page shows which attractions are likely to have day-of FastPasses available, and the approximate times at which they'll run out. (For now, we're not sure Frozen Ever After will have day-of FastPasses.)

EPCOT
When Same-Day FP+ Runs Out, by Crowd Level

ATTRACTION	LOW CROWDS*	MODERATE CROWDS*	HIGH CROWDS*
Disney & Pixar Short Film Festival	3 p.m.	2 p.m.	2 p.m.
Epcot Character Spot	Noon	10 a.m.	8 a.m.
Frozen Ever After	N/A	N/A	N/A
IllumiNations	7 p.m.	7 p.m.	7 p.m.
Journey into Imagination	2 p.m.	2 p.m.	1 p.m.
Living with the Land	3 p.m.	3 p.m.	2 p.m.
Mission: Space (Orange)	4 p.m.	10 a.m.	N/A
The Seas with Nemo & Friends	4 p.m.	4 p.m.	3 p.m.
Soarin'	10 a.m.	N/A	N/A
Spaceship Earth	4 p.m.	3 p.m.	10 p.m.
Test Track	8 a.m.	N/A	N/A
Turtle Talk with Crush	4 p.m.	3 p.m.	1 p.m.

* **LOW CROWDS** (Levels 1–3 on TouringPlans.com Crowd Calendar)
* **MODERATE CROWDS** (Levels 4–7 on TouringPlans.com Crowd Calendar)
* **HIGH CROWDS** (Levels 8–10 on TouringPlans.com Crowd Calendar)
N/A = no availability

FUTURE WORLD

IMMENSE, GLEAMING FUTURISTIC STRUCTURES define the first themed area beyond Epcot's main entrance. Broad thoroughfares are punctuated with billowing fountains, all reflected in shiny space-age facades. Front and center is **Spaceship Earth,** flanked by **Innoventions East and West.** Pavilions dedicated to mankind's past, present, and future technological achievements ring the perimeter of Future World.

Spaceship Earth *(FastPass+)* ★★★★

APPEAL BY AGE	PRESCHOOL ★★★½	GRADE SCHOOL ★★★★	TEENS ★★★★
YOUNG ADULTS ★★★★	OVER 30 ★★★★		SENIORS ★★★★½

What it is Educational dark ride through past, present, and future. **Scope and scale** Headliner. **When to go** Before 10 a.m., after 4 p.m., or use FastPass+. **Special comment** If lines are long when you arrive, try again after 4 p.m. **Authors' rating** One of Epcot's best; not to be missed; ★★★★. **Duration of ride** About 16 minutes. **Average wait in line per 100 people ahead of you** 3 minutes. **Loading speed** Fast.

DESCRIPTION AND COMMENTS This ride spirals through the 18-story interior of Epcot's premier landmark, taking visitors past animatronic scenes depicting mankind's developments in communications, from cave painting to printing to television to space communications and computer networks. The ride shows an amazing use of the geosphere's interior.

Spaceship Earth's scenes are periodically refreshed. The most recent include a 1970s-era computer room and a home garage showing what looks suspiciously like the invention of the Apple personal computer (perhaps an homage to Steve Jobs, who before his death was Disney's largest individual shareholder). Interactive video screens on the ride vehicles allow you to customize the ride's ending animated video. A postshow area with games and interactive exhibits rounds out the attraction.

Epcot Services

EPCOT'S SERVICE FACILITIES, most located in Future World, include:

Baby Care Center On the World Showcase side of the Odyssey Center

Banking Services ATMs outside the main entrance, on the Future World bridge, and in World Showcase at the US Pavilion and International Gateway entrance

Cell Phone Charging Outlets available in The Seas, upstairs near the women's restroom; in The Land, upstairs near The Garden Grill; in Mexico, near the bench against the ramp that leads to the market; and in the Innoventions West hall behind Fountain View

Dining Reservations At Guest Relations, to the left of Spaceship Earth

First Aid Center Next to the Baby Care Center

Live-Entertainment Information At Guest Relations

Lost and Found At the main entrance at the gift shop

Lost Persons At Guest Relations and the Baby Care Center

Walt Disney World and Local Attraction Information At Guest Relations

Wheelchair, ECV, ESV, and Stroller Rentals Inside the main entrance and to the left, toward the rear of the Entrance Plaza; also at the International Gateway entrance

TOURING TIPS Because it's near Epcot's main entrance, Spaceship Earth attracts arriving guests throughout the morning. If you want to ride Soarin' and Test Track, try to get a FastPass+ reservation for around 1 p.m. You should be almost done with Future World's attractions by then and ready to head to World Showcase. Or, if you plan on spending the afternoon in Future World and don't want to use FastPass+, try Spaceship Earth after 3 p.m.

Innoventions East and West ★

APPEAL BY AGE	PRESCHOOL ★★★½		GRADE SCHOOL ★★★½	TEENS ★★★½
YOUNG ADULTS ★★★		OVER 30 ★★★		SENIORS ★★★

What it is Static and hands-on exhibits relating to products and technologies of the near future. **Scope and scale** Minor diversion. **When to go** On your second day at Epcot or after you've seen all the major attractions. **Special comment** Nothing to speak of, because there's next to nothing here to speak of. **Authors' rating** We're hoping for a spectacular refurbishment; ★.

Note: All of Innoventions West and almost all of Innoventions East are closed, with no reopening date announced. It's worth a visit only as an air-conditioned place to sit without fear of losing your kids.

CLUB COOL

DESCRIPTION AND COMMENTS Attached to the fountain side of Innoventions West, this Coca-Cola–sponsored retail space–soda fountain provides free unlimited samples of soft drinks from around the world. Some will taste strange to Americans (such as bitter-tasting **Beverly** from Italy and supersweet **Inca Kola** from Peru, which has been likened to liquid bubble gum), but others will please (such as raspberry-flavored **Sparletta Sparberry** from Zimbabwe and apricot-passionfruit-flavored **Vegita-Beta** from Japan).

Perhaps because it's free and indoors, kids and teens rate Club Cool higher than all Epcot offerings except Soarin' and Test Track. Unfortunately, at press time we hear that Club Cool may not be around for much longer, leaving even less of interest at Innoventions.

TOURING TIPS Club Cool can get crowded, so you may have to wait behind a person or two to dispense your drink during busier times. But because there's not much to do here, people don't usually spend more than a few minutes inside. Don't expect to go in here to fill a large cup with free soda—the machines dispense only an ounce or two at a time. Finally, watch out for sticky floors.

Epcot Character Spot *(FastPass+)* ★★★

APPEAL BY AGE	PRESCHOOL ★★★★★	GRADE SCHOOL ★★★★½	TEENS ★★★★
YOUNG ADULTS ★★★★		OVER 30 ★★★★	SENIORS ★★★★

What it is Character-greeting venue. **Scope and scale** Diversion. **When to go** Before 11 a.m., or use FastPass+. **Authors' rating** Indoors and air-conditioned; ★★★. **Duration of experience** 8 minutes. **Probable waiting time** 20–40 minutes. **Queue speed** Slow.

DESCRIPTION AND COMMENTS In Future World West, to the right of The Fountain restaurant, Epcot Character Spot offers your kids the chance to meet Disney characters indoors, in air-conditioned comfort. The characters on hand typically include Mickey Mouse, Minnie Mouse, Pluto, and Joy and Sadness from Pixar's *Inside Out*. You may also find Chip 'n' Dale nearby outside.

TOURING TIPS The Character Spot should be your first stop if you have small children. Make FastPass+ reservations for Soarin' for around 9:30 a.m. so you can proceed there directly after getting autographs. The venue typically stays open until 9 p.m., even when other Future World attractions close at 7 p.m., and usually until around 10:45 p.m. during evening Extra Magic Hours, when Epcot is open until 11 p.m. or later.

Universe of Energy: *Ellen's Energy Adventure* ★★★½

APPEAL BY AGE	PRESCHOOL ★★★	GRADE SCHOOL ★★★½	TEENS ★★★
YOUNG ADULTS ★★★		OVER 30 ★★★	SENIORS ★★★½

What it is Combination dark ride–theater presentation. **Scope and scale** Major attraction. **When to go** Anytime. **Special comment** Don't be dismayed by long lines—580 people enter the pavilion each time the theater changes audiences. **Authors' rating** Fun and informative, but showing its age; ★★★½. **Duration of presentation** About 26½ minutes. **Preshow entertainment** 8 minutes. **Probable waiting time** 14 minutes.

DESCRIPTION AND COMMENTS This attraction begins with a preshow film starring Ellen DeGeneres. While watching TV, Ellen dozes off and dreams that she's competing on *Jeopardy!* against her know-it-all former college roommate Judy (Jamie Lee Curtis). All of the categories deal with energy, and unfortunately for Ellen, Judy has a PhD in the subject.

Luckily, Ellen's next-door neighbor happens to be Bill Nye the Science Guy, who convinces Ellen—along with everyone else in the audience—to take a time-traveling crash course in the history of energy.

You move from the preshow hall to what appears to be an ordinary theater to watch another film, this one about energy sources. Then the seats divide into six 97-passenger traveling cars that carry you from the Big Bang (the beginning of Ellen's energy lessons) to the swamps and animatronic dinosaurs of a prehistoric forest. Special effects include the feel of warm, moist swamp air and the smell of sulfur from an erupting volcano.

The dialogue between DeGeneres and Nye is humorous and upbeat, but the script was written almost 20 years ago, when ExxonMobil was sponsoring the attraction. Don't expect to hear calls to action on climate change or carbon footprints, or much more than a passing reference to alternative energy sources.

For children, it's a toss-up. The dinosaurs frighten some preschoolers, and kids of all ages lose the thread during the educational segments.

A Zionsville, Indiana, reader agrees with us that *Ellen's Energy Adventure* is more than a little dated:

Ellen is genuinely funny, but this attraction is so old that the video quality is only slightly better than the Zapruder film's.

A Colorado couple thought it required too much time to experience:

We wished we hadn't used so much of our time at the Energy pavilion. The Energy presentation was way too long and old—the video was bad and the sound didn't match the video. It really didn't teach anything about what energy was or how it was produced.

TOURING TIPS Because the theater has a ride component, the line doesn't move while the show is in progress. When the theater empties, however, a large chunk of the line disappears as people are admitted for the next show. Because of this, waits are generally tolerable.

Mission: Space *(FastPass+)*   ★★★★

APPEAL BY AGE	PRESCHOOL ★★½	GRADE SCHOOL ★★★★	TEENS ★★★★½
YOUNG ADULTS ★★★★½		OVER 30 ★★★★	SENIORS ★★★★

Motion Sickness

What it is Space-flight-simulator ride. **Scope and scale** Super-headliner. **When to go** First or last hour the park is open, or use FastPass+. **Special comments** Not recommended for pregnant women or people prone to motion sickness or claustrophobia; 44" minimum height requirement; a gentler nonspinning version is also available. **Authors' rating** Impressive; not to be missed; ★★★★. **Duration of ride** About 5 minutes plus preshow. **Average wait in line per 100 people ahead of you** 4 minutes. **Loading speed** Moderate–fast.

DESCRIPTION AND COMMENTS Mission: Space was one of the most popular rides at Disney World until two guests died after riding it in 2005 and 2006. While neither death was linked directly to the attraction, the negative publicity caused many guests to skip it entirely. In response, Disney added a tamer nonspinning version of Mission: Space in 2006.

Disney's lawyers probably clocked as much time as the ride engineers in designing the "lite" version. Even before you walk into the building, you're asked whether you want your ride with or without spin. Choose the spinning version and you're on the Orange team; the Green team trains on the no-spin side. Either way, you're immediately handed the appropriate "launch ticket" containing the first of myriad warnings about the attraction, as this *Unofficial Guide* reader discovered:

I chose the more intense version and was handed the Orange launch ticket to read. Basically, it explained that if I had ever had a tonsillectomy or even a mild case of pattern baldness, I should take the less intense ride.

This San Antonio reader says you don't give up much by choosing the Green option:

I am 65 and have ridden the Orange version a number of times. On our latest trip, we went on the Orange version again and felt a little uncomfortable. My wife suggested that we try the Green version, which I mistakenly believed was some sort of boring mission-control exercise where we would sit behind a computer. The Green version gave us a great experience, including the feeling of lift-off and zero gravity, without the nausea.

Guests for both versions of the attraction enter the International Space Training Center, where they're introduced to the deep-space exploration program and then divided into groups for flight training. After orientation, they're strapped into space capsules for a simulated flight, where, of course, the unexpected happens. Each capsule accommodates a crew consisting of a group commander, pilot, navigator, and engineer, with a guest functioning in each role. The crew's skill and finesse (or, more often, lack thereof) in handling their respective responsibilities have no effect on the outcome of the flight.

The capsules are small, and both ride versions are amazingly realistic. The nonspinning version doesn't subject your body to g-forces, but it does bounce and toss you around in a manner roughly comparable to other Disney motion simulators. A Bradenton, Florida, mom found motion sickness to be the least of her problems:

I'd like to see warnings here about claustrophobia—I had no clue until the capsule closed that it would be so tight in there. I went into full panic mode.

We hear that Mission: Space may be getting either a new ride story or theming in late 2017, possibly to include characters from Disney's *Guardians of the Galaxy* film franchise.

TOURING TIPS Disney can reconfigure the ride's four centrifuges to either version based on guest demand. In general, the kinder, gentler version has a wait time of about half that of its more harrowing counterpart.

Having experienced the industrial-strength version of Mission: Space under a variety of circumstances, we've always felt icky when riding it on an empty stomach, especially first thing in the morning, so we looked around for an expert to tell us why. Because NASA is a codeveloper of Mission: Space and an authority on the effect of g-forces on the human body, we called them. Amazingly, a spokesman told us that NASA no longer does much high-g training these days. And the agency was reluctant to pass along anything resembling medical advice to the general public.

Fortunately, a longtime friend put us in touch with a real NASA astronaut who was willing to share (anonymously) some ideas on what causes the nausea, as well as some tips for preventing it. Our expert guesses, as we do, that low blood sugar is the culprit and suggests eating a normal meal 1–2 hours before experiencing the ride. Avoid milk and tomatoes; they're difficult to keep down and, as our contact noted with the voice of experience, particularly unpleasant if they come back up. A banana, we hear, is a good choice for your preflight meal. Another trick of the astronaut trade is to keep a piece of hard candy or a mint in your mouth; it's not clear, though, whether the candy helps keep blood-sugar levels high or is just a placebo. If all else fails, there are airsickness bags in each simulator.

Hit the john before you get in line—you'll think your bladder really has been to Mars and back before you get out of this one. We recommend securing a midmorning FastPass+ reservation for Mission: Space (Orange).

Few things delight our readers more than kibitzing about rides that can make you puke, and Mission: Space is at the top of this particular heap. From a Yakima, Washington, reader:

Mission: Space is awesome. A number of people we spoke to didn't ride because they were intimidated by the warnings about motion sickness.

A woman from Lisbon, Connecticut, used Mission: Space as her own personal relationship lab:

We now understand why husbands and wives will probably never go to space together after I (the "navigator") pushed his (the "pilot's") button during the flight. I couldn't help being a backseat driver—we could have crashed!

TEST TRACK PAVILION

DESCRIPTION AND COMMENTS Sponsored by Chevrolet, this pavilion consists of the **Test Track** attraction and **Inside Track,** a collection of transportation-themed exhibits and multimedia presentations. The pavilion is the last on the left before the World Showcase. Many readers tell us that Test Track "is one big commercial" for Chevrolet. We agree that promotional hype is more heavy-handed here than in most other business-sponsored attractions. But Test Track is nonetheless one of the most creatively conceived attractions in Disney World.

Test Track *(FastPass+)* ★★★★

APPEAL BY AGE	PRESCHOOL ★★★★	GRADE SCHOOL ★★★★★	TEENS ★★★★★
YOUNG ADULTS ★★★★½		OVER 30 ★★★★½	SENIORS ★★★★½

What it is Auto-test-track simulator ride. **Scope and scale** Super-headliner. **When to go** The first 30 minutes the park is open or just before closing, or use FastPass+. **Special comment** 40″ minimum height requirement. **Authors' rating** Not to be missed; ★★★★. **Duration of ride** About 4 minutes. **Average wait in line per 100 people ahead of you** 4½ minutes. **Loading speed** Moderate–fast.

DESCRIPTION AND COMMENTS Test Track takes guests through the process of designing a new vehicle and then "testing" their car in a high-speed drive through and around the pavilion.

Guests entering the pavilion walk past displays of sleek, futuristic concept cars and glossy video screens where engineers discuss the work of car design and consumers explain the characteristics of their perfect car.

After hearing about auto design, guests are admitted into the Chevrolet Design Studio to create their own concept car. Using a large touchscreen interface (like a giant iPad), groups of up to three guests drag their fingers to design their car's body, engine, wheels, trim, and color. The computer screen reflects each design decision's impact on the car's capability, efficiency, responsiveness, and power. (For example, designing a large truck with a huge V-8 engine increases the car's capability and power but drastically reduces its efficiency.) The entire creative experience takes 5–8 minutes.

Next, guests board a six-seat ride vehicle, attached to a track on the ground, for an actual drive through Chevrolet's test track. The idea here is that guests are taking part in a computer simulation designed to test their vehicle's performance characteristics. The vehicle's tests include braking maneuvers, cornering, and acceleration, culminating in a spin around the outside of the pavilion at speeds of up to 65 miles per hour.

The ride visuals are sleek and eye-catching, but trying to understand them as a coherent narrative is pointless. At various points during the ride, video screens show the virtual cars designed by the guests in your vehicle and a status update on how the vehicle's tests are progressing. Most guests figure out quickly that absolutely nothing in their car's design has any effect whatsoever on their ride experience.

Test Track's postshow area continues the design process by allowing guests to create commercials for their concept cars. Farther into the pavilion are displays of actual Chevys, many of which you can sit in. We've never heard of anyone attempting to buy a car from Test Track, but let us know if you have.

TOURING TIPS It's always been a challenge to keep Test Track running. When it's working properly, it's one of the park's better attractions—but for this London, Ontario, mom, such instances never materialized:

Test Track breaks down more than any ride I've ever seen. We went back there over and over again, got in line, and then had to get out. FastPass+ lines would have a 40-minute wait because no one got to ride at the proper time.

A repeat visitor from East Aurora, New York, suggests that all is not lost when the ride malfunctions:

If the ride breaks down, tell a cast member. They'll most likely give you a slip that allows you to skip the line and ride again. This happened to us twice during the busiest time of the year, and we rode again with no problem.

Be aware that FastPass+ reservations often run out by afternoon. In that case, try the single-rider line. Because most groups are unwilling to split up, this line is usually much shorter than the regular (standby) line.

IMAGINATION! PAVILION

DESCRIPTION AND COMMENTS Multiattraction pavilion on the west side of Innoventions West. Outside are an "upside-down" waterfall and one of our favorite Future World landmarks, the "jumping" water, a fountain that hops over the heads of unsuspecting passersby.

TOURING TIPS We recommend late-morning touring. See individual attractions for specifics.

Disney & Pixar Short Film Festival *(FastPass+)*   *zero stars*

What it is Trailers for upcoming Disney-Pixar films. **Scope and scale** Diversion. **When to go** If it's raining and you need shelter. **Authors' rating** No, just no; zero stars. **Duration of presentation** About 20 minutes. **Probable waiting time** About 13 minutes.

DESCRIPTION AND COMMENTS This theater has shown just three films in its 35-year history, all of them 3-D. *Magic Journeys,* a look inside childhood imaginations, ran from 1982 to 1986. *Captain EO,* an epic space opera and long-form music video starring Michael Jackson, ran from 1986 to 1994; and *Honey, I Shrunk the Audience,* a spin-off of Disney's Honey, I Shrunk the Kids films, for 17 years, 1994 to 2010.

Disney brought back *Captain EO* in 2010, ostensibly as a posthumous tribute to Jackson, but management no doubt recognized it as an opportunity to advertise a "new" attraction with built-in nostalgic appeal at minimal expense. In 2016, Disney decided to show previews for its upcoming films here, but these are exactly the same movie previews that you can see just about anywhere else for free, compared with the $110 it costs to get into Epcot these days.

TOURING TIPS Rarely crowded. Not a good use of FastPass+. Skip it. Seriously. We mean it.

Journey into Imagination with Figment *(FastPass+)*   ★★½

APPEAL BY AGE	PRESCHOOL ★★★★	GRADE SCHOOL ★★★½	TEENS ★★★
YOUNG ADULTS ★★★		OVER 30 ★★★	SENIORS ★★★

What it is Dark fantasy-adventure ride. **Scope and scale** Major attraction wannabe. **When to go** Anytime. **Authors' rating** ★★½. **Duration of ride** About 6 minutes. **Average wait in line per 100 people ahead of you** 2 minutes. **Loading speed** Fast.

DESCRIPTION AND COMMENTS Journey into Imagination takes you on a tour of the zany Imagination Institute. Sometimes you're a passive observer and sometimes you're a test subject as the ride provides a glimpse of the fictitious lab's inner workings. Stimulating all your senses and then some, it hits you with optical illusions, an experiment in which noise generates colors, a room that defies gravity, and other brain teasers. All along the way, Figment (a purple dragon) makes surprise appearances. After the ride, you can adjourn to an interactive exhibit area offering some basic imagery technology.

Reader responses to Figment and company are pretty consistent. From a Franklin, Tennessee, family of three:

Journey into Imagination should be experienced only if you're a HUGE Figment fan—we, on the other hand, hated it. My husband was convinced after our touring plan sent us to Figment that all touring plans were a waste of time.

The ride falls short of the promise suggested by its name. Will you go to sleep? No. (OK, *maybe.*) Will you find it amusing? Probably. Will you remember it tomorrow? Only Figment knows.

TOURING TIPS The standby wait for this attraction have increased significantly because of FastPass+, but it's rarely a good choice as a reservation. You can enjoy the interactive postshow exhibit without taking the ride, so save it for later in the day.

THE LAND PAVILION

DESCRIPTION AND COMMENTS The Land is a huge themed area containing three attractions and two restaurants. When the pavilion was built, its emphasis was on farming, but it now focuses on the environment.

TOURING TIPS This is a good place to grab a fast-food lunch. If you're coming here to see the attractions, however, stay away during mealtimes. Be forewarned that strollers aren't allowed inside the pavilion—those with babes in arms might want to bring an infant carrier.

The Circle of Life ★★★½

APPEAL BY AGE	PRESCHOOL ★★★½	GRADE SCHOOL ★★★½	TEENS ★★★
YOUNG ADULTS ★★★		OVER 30 ★★★	SENIORS ★★★½

What it is Film exploring humans' relationship with the environment. **Scope and scale** Minor attraction. **When to go** Anytime. **Authors' rating** Inspiring and enlightening; ★★★½. **Duration of presentation** About 20 minutes. **Preshow entertainment** Ecological slide show and trivia. **Probable waiting time** 10–15 minutes.

DESCRIPTION AND COMMENTS This playful yet educational film, starring Pumbaa, Simba, and Timon from Disney's animated feature *The Lion King,* spotlights the environmental interdependency of all creatures, demonstrating how easily the ecological balance can be upset. The message is sobering, but one that enlightens.

TOURING TIPS To minimize backtracking, visit after a ride on Living with the Land or after lunch at Sunshine Seasons.

Living with the Land *(FastPass+)* ★★★★

APPEAL BY AGE	PRESCHOOL ★★★½	GRADE SCHOOL ★★★★	TEENS ★★★½
YOUNG ADULTS ★★★★		OVER 30 ★★★★	SENIORS ★★★★½

What it is Indoor boat ride chronicling the past, present, and future of farming and agriculture in the United States. **Scope and scale** Major attraction. **When to go** Before 11 a.m., after 1 p.m., or use FastPass+. **Special comments** Go early in the morning and save other Land attractions (except for Soarin') for later in the day. The ride is on the pavilion's lower level. **Authors' rating** Informative without being dull; not to be missed; ★★★★. **Duration of ride** About 14 minutes. **Average wait in line per 100 people ahead of you** 3 minutes; assumes 15 boats operating. **Loading speed** Moderate.

DESCRIPTION AND COMMENTS The boat ride takes visitors through swamps, past inhospitable farm environments, and through a futuristic greenhouse where real crops are grown using the latest agricultural technologies. The greenhouse exhibits change constantly: Along with familiar fruits and grains such as tomatoes, corn, and rice, recent plantings include fluted pumpkins, hot peppers, and more-exotic foods such as Malabar nuts, pandan, caimito, and amaranth. This produce is used in restaurants throughout WDW.

Many Epcot guests assume that Living with the Land will be too dry and educational for their tastes. A woman from Houston writes:

I had a bad attitude about Living with the Land—I just didn't think I was up for a movie about wheat farming. Wow, was I surprised!

TOURING TIPS See this attraction before the lunch crowd hits The Land's restaurants. Living with the Land is rarely a good use of FastPass+. If you have a special interest in the agricultural techniques being demonstrated, take the **Behind the Seeds at Epcot** tour (see page 744).

Soarin' *(FastPass+)* ★★★★½

What it is Flight simulator ride. **Scope and scale** Super-headliner. **When to go** First 30 minutes the park is open, or use FastPass+. **Special comments** Entrance on the lower level of the Land Pavilion. May induce motion sickness; 40" minimum height requirement. Switching-off option provided (see page 439). **Authors' rating** Thrilling and mellow at the same time; not to be missed; ★★★★½. **Duration of ride** 5½ minutes. **Average wait in line per 100 people ahead of you** 4 minutes; assumes 2 concourses operating. **Loading speed** Moderate.

Motion Sickness

DESCRIPTION AND COMMENTS Soarin' is a thrill ride for all ages, as exhilarating as a hawk on the wing and as mellow as swinging in a hammock. If you've ever experienced flying dreams, you'll have a sense of how Soarin' feels.

Once you enter the main theater, you're secured in a seat not unlike those on inverted roller coasters. When everyone is in place, the rows of seats swing into position, making you feel as if the floor has dropped away, and you're suspended with your legs dangling. Thus hung out to dry, you embark on a simulated hang-glider tour, with IMAX-quality images projected all around you and with the flight simulator moving in sync with the movie. The images are well chosen and drop-dead beautiful. Special effects include wind, sound, and even smell. The ride itself is thrilling but perfectly smooth.

We think Soarin' is a must-experience for guests of any age who meet the height requirement—and yes, we've interviewed senior citizens who absolutely loved it—but this North Carolina mom has reservations:

Soarin' was VERY cool, but also on the scary side for people who are afraid of heights or who don't like that unsteady feeling. While we were "soaring" up, I was fine, but when we were going down, I had to keep telling myself, "This is only an illusion. I cannot fall out. This is only an illusion. . . . "

A new ride film debuted at Soarin' in summer 2016, featuring film clips from flights around the world. Instead of being geographically constrained to California, the new film (which was created for the debut of Shanghai Disneyland) glides around the globe from the Matterhorn (the one in

Switzerland, not Anaheim) and an arctic glacier to the Taj Mahal and Great Wall of China. The new visuals are stunningly sharp, thanks to laser IMAX projectors, and computer animated animals are employed to create clever transitions, an improvement over the original's jarring location changes. Jerry Goldsmith's memorable musical theme returned with updated orchestrations, as did Patrick Warburton's flight-attendant preshow, but there's a new trio of scents to inhale along the way; we're growing partial to Eau de Africa. The end result is a clear upgrade over what was already one of Walt Disney World's top-rated rides.

TOURING TIPS Having Soarin' opposite Test Track and Mission: Space in Future World takes some crowd pressure off both sides of the park. Keep in mind, however, that Test Track and Mission: Space serve up a little too much thrill for some guests. Soarin', conversely, is an almost platonic ride for any age. For that reason, it's at the top of the hit parade. See it before 9:30 a.m. or book FastPass+ reservations up to 60 days in advance; expect same-day reservations to be gone by 10 a.m. most days.

Along with the new film, a third theater was built to increase ride capacity by 50%, making both the FastPass+ and standby queues flow far more smoothly. The new version features a number of vertical landmarks like the Eiffel Tower that look comically distorted from many seats.

A Lewiston, Maine, dad gave the new Soarin' a big thumbs-up:

The new Soarin' is amazing! The picture is a lot more crisp and clear than in the past, and even if the "trip around the world" doesn't make a lot of sense, it's still stunning. However, sitting on the edge of the theater was strange—the Eiffel Tower in particular was very distorted.

From an Arlington, Texas, reader:

With my apologies to the French, the Eiffel Tower looks as if it could use a little Viagra.

Once directed to one of the three concourses, politely request to wait an extra cycle for seats in row B1 to have an ideal view.

THE SEAS WITH NEMO & FRIENDS PAVILION

FEATURING CHARACTERS FROM DISNEY-PIXAR'S *Finding Nemo* and *Finding Dory,* this area encompasses what was once one of America's top marine aquariums, a ride that tunnels through the aquarium, an interactive animated film, and a number of walk-through exhibits. While we think those exhibits need updating and reimagining, the tank alone makes this pavilion a must-visit.

SeaBase ★★★½

APPEAL BY AGE	PRESCHOOL ★★★★½	GRADE SCHOOL ★★★★½	TEENS ★★★★
YOUNG ADULTS ★★★★		OVER 30 ★★★★	SENIORS ★★★★

What it is A huge saltwater aquarium, plus exhibits on oceanography, ocean ecology, and sea life. **Scope and scale** Major attraction. **When to go** Before 11:30 a.m. or after 5 p.m., especially on Extra Magic Hours evenings. **Special comment** Watch for tank feeding times between 3 and 3:30 p.m. **Authors' rating** Excellent; ★★★½. **Average wait in line per 100 people ahead of you** 3½ minutes. **Loading speed** Fast.

DESCRIPTION AND COMMENTS SeaBase is among Future World's most ambitious offerings, housed in a 200-foot-diameter, 27-foot-deep main tank containing fish, mammals, and crustaceans in a simulation of an ocean ecosystem. Visitors can watch the activity through 8-inch-thick windows below the surface (including some in the Coral Reef restaurant). On entering, you're directed to the loading area for The Seas with Nemo & Friends (see next profile), an attraction that conveys you via a Plexiglas tunnel through SeaBase's main tank. You disembark at SeaBase Alpha, where you can enjoy the other attractions. (If the wait for Nemo & Friends is too long, head straight for the exhibits by going through the pavilion's exit, around back, and to the left of the main entrance.)

About two-thirds of the main aquarium is home to reef species, including sharks, rays, and a number of fish that you've seen in quiet repose on your dinner plate. The other third, separated by an inconspicuous divider, houses bottlenose dolphins and sea turtles. As you face the main aquarium, the most glare-free viewing windows for the dolphins are on the ground floor to the left by the escalators. For the reef species, it's the same floor on the right by the escalators. Stay as long as you like.

TOURING TIPS Experience the ride and *Turtle Talk* in the late morning before the park gets crowded, saving the excellent exhibits for later.

SeaBase is uncrowded during evening Extra Magic Hours, making it a perfect time to have large swaths of the aquarium to yourself. We try to stop by every late night we can.

The Seas with Nemo & Friends *(FastPass+)* ★★★

APPEAL BY AGE PRESCHOOL ★★★★½ GRADE SCHOOL ★★★★ TEENS ★★★½
YOUNG ADULTS ★★★½ OVER 30 ★★★½ SENIORS ★★★½

What it is Ride through a tunnel in SeaBase's main tank. **Scope and scale** Major attraction. **When to go** Before 10:30 a.m., after 3 p.m., or use FastPass+. **Authors' rating** ★★★. **Duration of ride** 4 minutes. **Average wait in line per 100 people ahead of you** 3½ minutes. **Loading speed** Fast.

DESCRIPTION AND COMMENTS The Seas with Nemo & Friends is a high-tech ride featuring characters from the animated hit *Finding Nemo*. The ride likewise deposits you at the heart of the pavilion, where the exhibits, *Turtle Talk with Crush*, and viewing platforms for the main SeaBase aquarium are.

Upon entering The Seas, you're given the option of experiencing the ride or proceeding directly to the SeaBase exhibit area. If you choose the ride, you'll be ushered to its loading area, where you'll be made comfortable in a "clamobile" for your journey through the aquarium. The attraction features technology that makes it seem as if the animated characters are swimming with live fish. Very cool. Almost immediately you meet Mr. Ray and his class and learn that Nemo is missing. The remainder of the odyssey consists of finding Nemo with the help of Dory, Bruce, Marlin, Squirt, and Crush. Unlike the film, however, the ride ends with a musical finale.

A mom from Asheville, North Carolina, thinks we underestimate the fright factor:

The Seas with Nemo & Friends is scary—sharks, jellyfish, and anglerfish, along with growling, and so on. My 8-year-old hated it!

TOURING TIPS The earlier you ride, the better (ditto for *Turtle Talk with Crush*). If waits are too much, come back after 3 p.m. or so, or use FastPass+.

Turtle Talk with Crush *(FastPass+)* ★★★★

APPEAL BY AGE PRESCHOOL ★★★★½ GRADE SCHOOL ★★★★½ TEENS ★★★½
YOUNG ADULTS ★★★★ OVER 30 ★★★★ SENIORS ★★★★

What it is Interactive animated film. **Scope and scale** Minor attraction. **When to go** Before 11 a.m., after 3 p.m., or use FastPass+. **Authors' rating** A real spirit-lifter; not to be missed; ★★★★. **Duration of presentation** 17 minutes. **Preshow entertainment** None. **Probable waiting time** 10–20 minutes.

DESCRIPTION AND COMMENTS *Turtle Talk with Crush* is an interactive theater show starring the 153-year-old surfer-dude turtle from *Finding Nemo*. Although it starts like a typical Disney-theme-park movie, *Turtle Talk* quickly turns into a surprise interactive encounter as the on-screen Crush begins to have actual conversations with guests in the audience. Real-time computer graphics are used to accurately move Crush's mouth when forming words, and he's voiced by a guy who went to the Jeff Spicoli School of Diction.

Disney added Dory (the blue tang, voiced by Ellen DeGeneres) and other characters from their film *Finding Dory* to this attraction in 2016.

A mom from Henderson, Colorado, has a crush on Crush:

Turtle Talk with Crush is a must-see. Our 4-year-old was picked out of the crowd by Crush, and we were just amazed by the technology. It was adorable and enjoyed by everyone from Grammy and Papa to the 4-year-old!

TOURING TIPS It's unusual to wait more than one or two shows to get in. If you find long lines in the morning, try back after 3 p.m. when more of the crowd has moved on to World Showcase, or use FastPass+.

The "Mom, I Can't Believe It's Disney!" Fountains
★★★★

APPEAL BY AGE	PRESCHOOL ★★★★★	GRADE SCHOOL ★★★★★	TEENS ★★★★
YOUNG ADULTS ★★★★		OVER 30 ★★★★	SENIORS ★★★★★

What it is Combination fountains and showers. **Scope and scale** Diversion. **When to go** When it's hot. **Special comment** Secretly installed by Martians during *Illumi-Nations*. **Authors' rating** Yes! ★★★★. **Duration of experience** As long as you like. **Probable waiting time** None.

DESCRIPTION AND COMMENTS These simple fountains—one on the walkway linking Future World to World Showcase, the other in Future World East, on the way to Test Track—aren't much to look at, but they offer a truly spontaneous experience: a rarity in Walt Disney World, where everything is controlled, from the snow peas in your stir-fry to how frequently the crocodile yawns in the Jungle Cruise.

Spouts of water erupt randomly from the sidewalk. You can frolic in the water or let it cascade down on you or blow up your britches. On a broiling Florida day, fling yourself into the fountain and cut loose. Dance, skip, sing, splash, cavort, stick your toes down the spouts, or catch the water in your mouth as it descends. You can do all of this with your clothes on or, depending on your age, with your clothes off.

TOURING TIPS We don't know if the fountains' creator has been drummed out of the corps by the Disney Tribunal of People Who Sit on Sticks (probably), but we're grateful for his courage in introducing one thing that's not super-controlled. We do know that your kids will be right in the middle of the fun before your brain sounds the alert. Our advice: Pack a few pairs of dry shorts and turn the kids loose. You might even want to bring a spare pair for yourself.

WORLD SHOWCASE

EPCOT'S OTHER THEMED AREA, World Showcase is an ongoing World's Fair encircling a picturesque 40-acre lagoon. The cuisine, culture, history, and architecture of almost a dozen countries (and one make-believe kingdom) are permanently displayed in individual national pavilions spaced along a 1.2-mile promenade. The pavilions replicate familiar landmarks and present representative street scenes from the host countries.

World Showcase has some of the loveliest gardens in the United States. In Germany, France, United Kingdom, Canada, and, to a lesser extent, China, they're sometimes tucked away and out of sight of pedestrian traffic on the World Showcase promenade. They're best appreciated during the day, as a Clio, Michigan, woman explains:

unofficial **TIP**
If you don't want to spring for the Passport Kit, the Disney folks will be happy to stamp an autograph book or just about anything else—even your forehead.

Visit World Showcase in the daylight in order to view the beautiful gardens. We were sorry we didn't do this because we were following the guide and riding rides that we could have done later in the dark.

DISNEY DISH WITH JIM HILL

"GIGANTIC" CHANGES COMING TO WORLD SHOWCASE? When Epcot first opened, Spain was supposed to be among the next three international pavilions built. Sadly, that didn't happen. But now that *Gigantic*—Disney's musical retelling of "Jack and the Beanstalk," set in Spain—is scheduled for November 2018, there's a lot of talk about adding a Spain Pavilion to World Showcase.

Some kids find World Showcase boring, so to make it more interesting, most Epcot retail shops sell **Passport Kits** for about $12. Each kit contains a blank "passport" and stamps for every World Showcase country. As kids accompany their folks to each country, they tear out the appropriate stamp and stick it in the passport. Disney has built a lot of profit into this little product, but guests—namely, parents—don't seem to mind the cost. As this dad from Birmingham, Alabama, relates, the Passport Kit helps get the kids through World Showcase with a minimum of impatience, whining, and tantrums:

Adding stamps from the Epcot countries was the only way I was able to see all the displays with cheerful children.

Children also enjoy **Kidcot Fun Stops**, which are usually nothing more than a large table set up somewhere in each pavilion. Tables are staffed by Disney cast members who stamp passports and lead modest craft projects relating to the host countries.

A mom from Billerica, Massachusetts, is a fan of the Fun Stops:

The Kidcot project at Epcot was amazing! Our 2- and 5-year-olds loved making masks and collecting stamps.

An adult version of passport-stamp collecting is known as **Drinking Around the World** (see page 338), an activity enthusiastically endorsed by a woman from party-hearty New Orleans:

We drank a beer in each country at Epcot—Dad was the designated driver—and posed for photos in each, and it quickly became hilarious, as were the progression-of-drunkenness photos that followed.

World Showcase offers some of the most diverse and interesting shopping in Walt Disney World. See Part Sixteen for details.

Agent P's World Showcase Adventure ★★★★

| APPEAL BY AGE | PRESCHOOL ★★½ | GRADE SCHOOL ★★★★ | TEENS ★★★½ |
| YOUNG ADULTS ★★★ | | OVER 30 ★★★½ | SENIORS ★★½ |

What it is Interactive scavenger hunt in select World Showcase pavilions. **Scope and scale** Minor attraction. **When to go** Anytime. **Authors' rating** One of our favorite additions to the parks; ★★★★. **Duration of presentation** Allow 30 minutes per adventure. **Preshow entertainment** None. **Probable waiting time** None.

DESCRIPTION AND COMMENTS In their eponymous Disney Channel show, Phineas and Ferb have a pet platypus named Perry. In the presence of humans, Perry doesn't do a whole lot. (To be fair, we're not experts on typical platypus behavior, but read on.) When the kids aren't looking, though, Perry takes on the role of Agent P, a fedora-wearing, James Bond–esque secret agent who battles the nefarious Dr. Doofenshmirtz to prevent world domination.

In Agent P's World Showcase Adventure, you're a secret agent helping Perry, and you receive a cell phone–like device before you're dispatched on a mission to your choice of seven World Showcase pavilions. (You can also use your own phone.) Once you arrive at the pavilion, the device's video screen and audio provide various clues to help you solve a set of simple puzzles necessary for defeating Doofenshmirtz's plan. As you discover each clue, you'll find special effects such as talking statues and flaming lanterns, plus live "secret agents" stationed in the pavilions just for this attraction. For example, in a prior version of the game you were instructed to utter the phrase "Danger is my cup of tea" to someone working behind the counter at the United Kingdom's tea shop; he or she would respond by handing you a Twinings tea packet on which was printed a clue to solve a puzzle.

Agent P makes static World Showcase pavilions more interactive and kid-friendly. The adventures have simple clues, fast pacing, and neat rewards for solving the puzzles. Len's teenage daughter, Hannah, will happily spend an entire afternoon in World Showcase playing this game and drinking Japanese sodas. Don't be surprised if, having completed one pavilion's adventure, your child wants to do the same.

TOURING TIPS Playing the game is free, and no deposit is required for the device. You'll need proof of park admission to sign up before you play, and you can choose both the time and location of your adventure. Register and pick up your devices at the Italy or Norway Pavilion, the International Gateway (near the UK Pavilion), or the east side of the main walkway from Future World to World Showcase.

If you don't use your own phone, each group can have up to three devices for the same adventure. Because you're working with a device about the size of a cell phone, it's best to have one device for every two people in your group.

A Tucker, Georgia, mother of a 7-year-old is a fan:

My daughter and I thoroughly enjoyed Agent P's World Showcase Adventure. The interactivity was clever and exciting, plus NO LINES!

A Granger, Indiana, mom discovered a practical dimension to Agent P:

A great activity if it's raining: Do the adventure in Mexico. It's all inside, and by the time you're done, the rain usually is, too.

A Massillon, Ohio, mom was surprised at how long it took to play:

At Epcot, our 9- and 6-year-olds really enjoyed the Agent P mission, but it took way longer than the 25 minutes we were told (at least for the UK, the country we chose). It ended up being fine, but people should be aware.

NOW, MOVING CLOCKWISE around the World Showcase promenade, here are the nations represented and their attractions:

MEXICO PAVILION

DESCRIPTION AND COMMENTS Pre-Columbian pyramids dominate the pavilion's architecture. One pyramid forms Mexico's facade; the other overlooks the restaurant and plaza alongside the **Gran Fiesta Tour** indoor boat ride.

The village scene inside the pavilion is beautiful and exquisitely detailed. A retail shop occupies most of the left half of the inner pavilion, while Mexico's Kidcot Fun Stop is in the first entryway inside the pyramid. On the opposite side of the main floor is **La Cava del Tequila,** a bar serving more than 100 varieties of tequila as well as margaritas and mezcal.

TOURING TIPS The pyramids contain many authentic and valuable artifacts—take the time to stop and see these treasures.

Gran Fiesta Tour Starring the Three Caballeros ★★½

APPEAL BY AGE	PRESCHOOL ★★★★	GRADE SCHOOL ★★★★	TEENS ★★★½
YOUNG ADULTS ★★★½	OVER 30 ★★★½		SENIORS ★★★½

What it is Scenic indoor boat ride. **Scope and scale** Minor attraction. **When to go** Before noon or after 5 p.m. **Authors' rating** Visually appealing, light, and relaxing; ★★½. **Duration of ride** About 7 minutes (plus 1½-minute wait to disembark). **Average wait in line per 100 people ahead of you** 4½ minutes; assumes 16 boats in operation. **Loading speed** Moderate.

DESCRIPTION AND COMMENTS The Gran Fiesta Tour incorporates animated versions of Donald Duck, José Carioca, and Panchito—an avian singing group called The Three Caballeros, from Disney's 1944 film of the same name—to spice up what's basically a slower-paced, Mexican-style It's a Small World.

The storyline has the Caballeros scheduled to perform at a fiesta when Donald suddenly goes missing; large video screens show him enjoying Mexico's sights and sounds while José and Panchito try to track him down. Everyone is reunited in time for a rousing concert near the end of the ride.

At the risk of sounding like the Disney geeks we are, we must point out that Panchito is technically the only Mexican Caballero—José Carioca is from Brazil and Donald is from Burbank. In any case, more of the ride's visuals seem to be on the left side of the boat, so have small children sit nearer the left to keep their attention, and listen for Donald's humorous monologue as you wait to disembark at the end of the ride.

A Fanwood, New Jersey, reader feels the ride is culturally insensitive:

The Gran Fiesta Tour was dreadful. If the idea was to rid the ride of derogatory Mexican stereotypes, the designers woefully missed the mark.

A Wilmington, Delaware, woman blames Gran Fiesta Tour's lack of pizzazz on . . . who else?

Donald Duck has ruined even the minimal value of the Mexico ride.

TOURING TIPS If the line looks longer than 5 minutes, grab a margarita (or several) at La Cava del Tequila and come back in 15.

"NORWAY" PAVILION

DESCRIPTION AND COMMENTS This pavilion encapsulates both everything we love about Epcot and everything we hate about corporate Disney. Parts of the pavilion—that is, those based on the actual country of Norway—are complex, beautiful, and diverse. Highlights include replicas of the 14th-century Akershus Castle in Oslo; a miniature version of a stave church built in 1212 in Gol, Norway (go inside—the doors open!); and various other buildings that accurately represent traditional Scandinavian architecture. We were even inspired to visit Norway specifically because of how great this pavilion *was*.

For years after it was built, Epcot's Norway sat in a state of mostly benign neglect. The boat ride, Maelstrom, was a relatively short and lightly themed float-through of the country's history. The postride film was imbued with the same "our spirit is our people" platitudes that are repeated, in one way or another, in every World Showcase presentation ever made. But at least it was based on an actual country, at an actual point in time.

Fast-forward to today and the monster hit that is 2013's *Frozen,* set in the mythical Scandinavian-ish kingdom of Arendelle. Disney's bean counters, who couldn't design a pavilion if given Walt's own cryogenically preserved brain, must have looked at all the money *Frozen* made, seen Epcot's need to attract more customers, and decided that whatever World Showcase *really* is, it should include a made-up country whose main attractions are a hastily repurposed boat ride and a chance to meet unionized laborers dressed as cartoon toffs. Frankly, we're surprised that Disney hasn't replaced the actual Norwegian staff with Orlando teens taught to *bork-bork-bork* like The Muppets' Swedish Chef . . . yet.

Don't get us wrong—a hit like *Frozen* comes along once every 20 years, and Disney has to make hay while the sun shines. It's putting a pretend kingdom smack in the middle of World Showcase that sticks in our craw. And it's not as if there weren't already an entire Disney theme park within walking distance with so many closed or outdated attractions that charging $100 for admission is essentially petty larceny with a better marketing department. This *Frozen* stuff—which, not to put too fine a point on it, is an offshoot of a film, made by The Walt Disney Studios, in Hollywood—should have gone in Disney's Hollywood Studios instead.

Frozen Ever After *(FastPass+)* ★★★★

APPEAL BY AGE	PRESCHOOL ★★★★½	GRADE SCHOOL ★★★★½	TEENS ★★★★
YOUNG ADULTS ★★★★		OVER 30 ★★★★	SENIORS ★★★★

What it is Indoor boat ride and Disney film–shilling vehicle. **Scope and scale** Major attraction. **When to go** Before noon., after 7 p.m., or use FastPass+. **Special comment** Expect long waits from the moment it opens. **Authors' rating** Don't let this one go (unless the line is over 2 hours); ★★★★. **Duration of ride** Almost 5 minutes. **Average wait in line per 100 people ahead of you** 4 minutes; assumes 12 or 13 boats operating. **Loading speed** Fast.

DESCRIPTION AND COMMENTS Frozen Ever After is a pleasant boat ride through *Frozen*'s Arendelle. The premise is that you've arrived just in time for Arendelle's "Winter in Summer" celebration, where Elsa will use her magical powers to make it snow during the hottest part of the year. Nearly every major and minor character from the film is represented, from Olaf the snowman to Sven the reindeer, along with much of the soundtrack's songs with brand-new lyrics.

If you've visited Epcot before, the flume ride's path is almost identical to the old Norway boat ride Maelstrom that Frozen Ever After replaced, with the addition of two introductory show scenes where the queue and loading area once were. (The former unloading area is now also used to load, and the old post-show theater became a beautifully detailed village queue, complete with Wandering Oaken's shop to walk through.) First There's a short, mild section where you're propelled backwards for a few seconds, followed by a short downhill and small splash that most kids should take it in stride. The original ride's Vikings and trolls went to the trash heap, replaced by detailed sets augmented with digital projection mapping, and over a dozen animatronics sporting video-screen faces (like Seven Dwarfs Mine Train) and demonstrating some of the most spookily sophisticated movements we've ever seen; watch the fluidity of Elsa's wrists and elbows during the pivotal "Let It Go" scene, and weep for a future of robotic massage parlors.

TOURING TIPS Epcot hasn't opened many major new rides in recent years, and this one is based on a wildly popular film (and upcoming sequel). While World Showcase traditionally opened at 11 a.m., Disney opens Frozen Ever After each morning as soon as the park opens. It should also be open for morning and evening Extra Magic Hours.

With an average throughput of around 900 guests per hour, and frequent breakdowns during its debut, Frozen Ever After is perhaps the biggest theme park mismatch between supply and demand since Universal's Pteranodon Flyers. Within minutes of rope drop, you can expect the standby queue to stretch halfway to China (literally), and 300-minute wait times have been posted—mostly because the sign counter doesn't go any higher. If the ride breaks down, the standby line may be sealed off entirely until FastPass+ guests can be processed.

Disney puts Frozen Ever After in the same FastPass+ tier as Soarin' and Test Track, so you'll have to choose between a long hike to World Showcase and back early in the morning, or long lines at one of those three attractions. First visit the attraction you couldn't get a FastPass+ for, then the ones you could. Even with a FastPass+, plan to wait 30 minutes or more upon returning, especially if the ride has experienced an outage earlier in the day. If you want to visit Norway's Sommerhus Meet and Greet, too, you're in a pickle because it doesn't offer FastPass+. Your only choice is between hours in line here or hours in line at other attractions.

Royal Sommerhus Meet and Greet ★★★★

APPEAL BY AGE	PRESCHOOL ★★★★★	GRADE SCHOOL ★★★★½	TEENS ★★★★
YOUNG ADULTS ★★★★	OVER 30 ★★★★		SENIORS ★★★★

What it is Meet and greet with the Frozen princesses. **Scope and scale** Minor attraction. **When to go** As soon as World Showcase opens, at lunch or dinner, or the last hour the park is open. **Authors' rating** Det beste tegnet hilsen i World Showcase! ★★★★. **Duration of greeting** About 3 minutes. **Probable waiting time** 15–25 minutes.

DESCRIPTION AND COMMENTS Royal Sommerhus is a character greeting for Anna and Elsa. While Frozen wasn't explicitly set in Norway, the Royal Sommerhus meet and greet features traditional Norwegian architecture and crafts. Having visited Norway, we think Disney did a decent job of capturing that look.

TOURING TIPS This meet and greet is designed to have multiple rooms with Anna and Elsa operating simultaneously. This, coupled with Epcot's

DISNEY DISH WITH JIM HILL

TINY WAIST, BIG PROBLEM The biggest challenge that the Imagineers faced while building a new home for Frozen Ever After was finding a way to snake all of the wiring and technology necessary to power Elsa's projected face through the figure's teeny-tiny waist. Because Imagineers wanted to stay true to the Ice Queen's distinctive look from the film, Elsa's midsection was no bigger than your average coffee can. But Disney eventually found a way to make this beloved character sing and move just like in the movie.

lower average attendance relative to the Magic Kingdom's, means that waits should be somewhat shorter than when Anna and Elsa held forth at Magic Kingdom's Princess Fairytale Hall. This attraction does not offer FastPass+.

CHINA PAVILION

DESCRIPTION AND COMMENTS A half-sized replica of the Temple of Heaven in Beijing identifies this pavilion. Gardens and reflecting ponds simulate those found in Suzhou, and an art gallery features a lotus-blossom gate and formal saddle roofline. The China Pavilion offers two restaurants: the **Lotus Blossom Cafe,** a fast-food eatery, and **Nine Dragons Restaurant,** a full-service establishment (Advance Reservations recommended) that serves lamentably lackluster Chinese food in a lovely setting. **The Joy of Tea,** a tea stand and specialty-drink vendor, will feed your caffeine addiction until you can make it to Morocco's espresso bar.

The pavilion also hosts exhibits on Chinese history and culture. Past exhibits have covered everything from China's indigenous peoples to the layout of Hong Kong Disneyland. The current exhibit displays scaled-down replicas of the terra-cotta "tomb warriors" buried with the Qin Dynasty emperor in the second century B.C. to guard him in the afterlife.

Reflections of China   ★★★½

APPEAL BY AGE	PRESCHOOL ★★★	GRADE SCHOOL ★★★	TEENS ★★★½
YOUNG ADULTS ★★★½		OVER 30 ★★★★	SENIORS ★★★★

What it is Film about the Chinese people and culture. **Scope and scale** Major attraction. **When to go** Anytime. **Special comment** Audience stands throughout performance. **Authors' rating** ★★★½. **Duration of presentation** About 14 minutes. **Preshow entertainment** None. **Probable waiting time** 10 minutes.

DESCRIPTION AND COMMENTS Pass through the Hall of Prayer for Good Harvest to view this Circle-Vision 360 film. Warm and appealing (albeit politically sanitized), it's a brilliant introduction to the people and natural beauty of China.

TOURING TIPS The pavilion is truly beautiful—serene yet exciting. *Reflections of China* plays in a theater where guests must stand, but the film can usually be enjoyed anytime without much waiting.

GERMANY PAVILION

DESCRIPTION AND COMMENTS Dominated by a clock tower with boy and girl figures and a fountain depicting St. George's victory over the dragon, the pavilion's *platz* (plaza) is encircled by buildings in traditional architectural styles. The main attraction is **Biergarten,** a buffet that serves rib-sticking

German food and beer (see Part Four, page 365). Yodeling, folk dancing, and oompah-band music are part of the mealtime festivities.

The biggest draw in Germany may be **Karamell-Küche** ("Caramel Kitchen"), offering small caramel-covered sweets including apples, fudge, and cupcakes. We love coming here for a midday snack to tide us over before dinner. Check out the large and elaborate model railroad just beyond the restrooms as you walk from Germany toward Italy.

TOURING TIPS The pavilion is pleasant and festive. Tour anytime.

ITALY PAVILION

DESCRIPTION AND COMMENTS The entrance to Italy is marked by an 83-foot-tall campanile (bell tower) modeled after the tower in St. Mark's Square in Venice. Left of the campanile is a replica of the 14th-century Doge's Palace, also in the famous square. The pavilion has a waterfront on the lagoon where gondolas are tied to striped moorings.

TOURING TIPS Streets and courtyards in Italy are among the most realistic in World Showcase. **Via Napoli** has some of the best pizza in Walt Disney World; **Tutto Gusto Wine Cellar** serves small plates along with libations. Because there's no film or ride, you can tour the pavilion at any hour.

UNITED STATES PAVILION
The American Adventure ★★★★

APPEAL BY AGE	PRESCHOOL ★★½	GRADE SCHOOL ★★★½	TEENS ★★★½
YOUNG ADULTS ★★★★	OVER 30 ★★★★		SENIORS ★★★★½

What it is Mixed-media and Audio-Animatronic theater presentation on US history. **Scope and scale** Headliner. **When to go** Anytime. **Authors' rating** Disney's best historical and patriotic attraction; not to be missed; ★★★★. **Duration of presentation** About 29 minutes. **Preshow entertainment** Voices of Liberty choral singing. **Probable waiting time** 25 minutes.

DESCRIPTION AND COMMENTS The United States Pavilion consists of a fast-food restaurant (the **Liberty Inn**) and a patriotic show.

The American Adventure is a composite of everything Disney does best. Housed in an imposing brick structure reminiscent of Colonial Philadelphia, the 29-minute show is a stirring, albeit sanitized, rendition of American history narrated by an animatronic Mark Twain (who carries a burning cigar) and Ben Franklin. Behind a stage almost half the size of a football field is a 28-by-155–foot rear-projection screen—the largest ever used—on which motion picture images are interwoven with onstage action.

Though the production rouses patriotic emotion in some viewers, others find it deadly dull. A man from Fort Lauderdale, Florida, writes:

I saw The American Adventure *about 10 years ago and snoozed through it. We tried it again since you said it was updated, and it was still ponderous. I kept checking my watch, waiting for it to be over. I'll try it again in 10 years.*

DISNEY DISH WITH JIM HILL

ADD SOME EDUCATION TO YOUR VACATION If you're looking to cram in some culture while tasting tapas at Epcot's International Food & Wine Festival, try one of Epcot's six galleries. The American Heritage Gallery at the American Adventure Pavilion currently features a selection of rare art and artifacts that shines a spotlight on African-American history.

An Erie, Pennsylvania, couple resented what they saw as Disney's squeaky-clean take on American history:

The American Adventure glosses over the dark points of American history. For example, it neatly cuts out the audio about who bombed Pearl Harbor (at Epcot, after all, Japan is right next door). Why not focus on the natural beauty of America, its ethnic diversity, its contributions to world society?

(To be fair, the presentation isn't as squeaky-clean as it once was—both Tiger Woods and Lance Armstrong are held up as heroes in the film.)

TOURING TIPS *The American Adventure* is the best patriotic attraction in the Disney repertoire. It usually plays to capacity audiences from around 1:30 to 3:30 p.m., but it isn't hard to get into: Because of the theater's large capacity, it's highly unusual not to be admitted to the next performance.

JAPAN PAVILION

DESCRIPTION AND COMMENTS A five-story, blue-roofed pagoda, inspired by a 17th-century shrine in Nara, sets this pavilion apart. A hill garden behind it features waterfalls, rocks, flowers, lanterns, paths, and rustic bridges. On the right, as one faces the entrance, a building inspired by the ceremonial and coronation hall at Kyoto's Imperial Palace contains restaurants and a branch of Japan's **Mitsukoshi** department store. Through the center entrance and to the left is **Bijutsu-kan Gallery,** exhibiting colorful displays on Japanese pop culture. Recent subjects have included everything from comics to Japan's culture of "cute."

TOURING TIPS Japan blends simplicity, architectural grandeur, and natural beauty. Tour anytime.

MOROCCO PAVILION

DESCRIPTION AND COMMENTS A bustling market, winding streets, lofty minarets, and stuccoed archways re-create the romance and intrigue of Marrakesh and Casablanca. The pavilion also has a museum of Moorish art and **Restaurant Marrakesh,** featuring North African specialties. **Spice Road Table** serves up tapas-style Mediterranean dishes and excellent views of *IllumiNations,* along with high prices. For a quick lunch, try **Tangierine Cafe,** one of Epcot's highest-rated restaurants.

A Northfield, Minnesota, mother of two exploring Morocco found, of all things, peace and quiet:

We found an awesome resting place in Morocco—an empty air-conditioned gallery with padded benches. No one came in during the 15 minutes that we rested there, which was quite a difference from the rest of the park! Look for the red doors on your left when you enter.

TOURING TIPS Morocco has neither a ride nor a theater. Tour anytime. You'll often find Jasmine and Aladdin doing meet and greets here.

FRANCE PAVILION

DESCRIPTION AND COMMENTS A replica of the Eiffel Tower is, *naturellement,* this pavilion's centerpiece. The streets recall La Belle Époque, France's "beautiful time" between 1870 and 1910. The restaurants, along with the bakery and ice-cream shop, are very popular—perhaps explaining why readers rank France as the best World Showcase pavilion.

Impressions de France ★★★½

APPEAL BY AGE	PRESCHOOL ★★½	GRADE SCHOOL ★★★	TEENS ★★★
YOUNG ADULTS ★★★★	OVER 30 ★★★★		SENIORS ★★★★½

What it is Film essay on France and its people. **Scope and scale** Major attraction. **When to go** Anytime. **Authors' rating** Exceedingly beautiful film; ★★★½. **Duration of presentation** About 18 minutes. **Preshow entertainment** None. **Probable waiting time** 15 minutes (at suggested times).

DESCRIPTION AND COMMENTS *Impressions de France* is an 18-minute movie projected over 200 degrees onto five screens. Unlike at China and Canada, the audience sits to view this well-made film showcasing France's people, cities, and natural wonders.

TOURING TIPS Usually begins on the hour and half-hour. France's streets are small and become congested when visitors queue for the film.

UNITED KINGDOM PAVILION

DESCRIPTION AND COMMENTS A hodgepodge of period architecture attempts to capture Britain's urban and rural sides. One street alone has a thatched-roof cottage, a four-story Tudor half-timber building, a pre-Georgian plaster building, a formal Palladian facade of dressed stone, and a city square with a Hyde Park bandstand (whew!).

The pavilion is composed mostly of shops. **The Rose & Crown Pub** and **Rose & Crown Dining Room** offer dining on the water side of the promenade. For fish and chips to go, try **Yorkshire County Fish Shop.**

TOURING TIPS There are no attractions here, so tour anytime. Alice in Wonderland and Mary Poppins meet fans in the character-greeting area; check the *Times Guide* for a schedule. Advance Reservations aren't required for the Rose & Crown Pub, making it a nice place to stop for a beer.

CANADA PAVILION

DESCRIPTION AND COMMENTS Canada's cultural, natural, and architectural diversity are reflected in this large, impressive pavilion. Thirty-foot-tall totem poles embellish an Indian village at the foot of a replica of a magnificent château-style hotel. **Le Cellier,** a steakhouse located on Canada's lower level, is one of Walt Disney World's highest-rated restaurants. Dinner almost always requires Advance Reservations; lunch is a bit easier to arrange.

DISNEY DISH WITH JIM HILL

BREWING NEW IDEAS Back in the late 2000s, Disney seriously considered an "Anne of Green Gables" store in the Hôtel du Canada, the iconic building of the Canada Pavilion, but the financial crisis put an end to those plans. Now that the economy is on the rebound, the latest idea is to use the space for a Canadian craft-brew pub that would offer Epcot visitors a terrific view of *IllumiNations.*

O Canada!   ★★★½

APPEAL BY AGE	PRESCHOOL ★★½	GRADE SCHOOL ★★★½	TEENS ★★★½
YOUNG ADULTS ★★★★		OVER 30 ★★★★	SENIORS ★★★★

What it is Film essay on Canada and its people. **Scope and scale** Major attraction. **When to go** Anytime. **Special comment** Audience stands to watch. **Authors' rating** Makes you want to catch the first plane up there; ★★★½. **Duration of presentation** About 15 minutes. **Preshow entertainment** None. **Probable waiting time** 9 minutes.

DESCRIPTION AND COMMENTS *O Canada!* showcases the country's natural beauty and the diversity of its people. Narrated by Martin Short, the film features scenes of Canada's stunning landscapes. Visitors leave the theater through **Victoria Gardens,** inspired by the famed Butchart Gardens of British Columbia.

Cast members often conduct a preshow Canadian-trivia quiz outside the theater. Helpful tips for Americans: Canada's capital is Ottawa; its $1 coin is nicknamed the Loonie, after the bird engraved on it; and the $2 coin is the Toonie—not, unfortunately, the Doubloonie.

TOURING TIPS This large-capacity attraction (guests must stand) gets fairly heavy late-morning attendance, as Canada is the first pavilion encountered as one travels counterclockwise around World Showcase Lagoon.

LIVE ENTERTAINMENT
in EPCOT

LIVE ENTERTAINMENT IN EPCOT is more diverse than in the Magic Kingdom. In World Showcase, it reflects the nations represented. Future World provides a perfect setting for new and experimental offerings. Information about live entertainment on the day you visit is contained in the Epcot guide map, often supplemented by a *Times Guide*. WDW live-entertainment guru Steve Soares usually posts the Epcot performance schedule about a week in advance at wdwent.com.

Here are some of the venues, performers, and performances you'll encounter:

AMERICA GARDENS THEATRE This large amphitheater, near the US Pavilion, faces World Showcase Lagoon. It hosts pop and oldies musical acts throughout much of the year, as well as Epcot's popular **Candlelight Processional** for the Christmas holidays, and sometimes the **Voices of Liberty** (see below).

AROUND WORLD SHOWCASE Impromptu performances take place in and around the pavilions. Among the acts are a strolling mariachi group in Mexico; a juggler in Italy; two singing groups (**Voices of Liberty** and **American Music Machine**) at the US Pavilion; traditional songs, drums, and dances in Japan; more traditional music in Morocco; acrobats in France; a Scottish folk group in the United Kingdom; and a band in Canada. Performances occur about every half-hour.

Live entertainment in World Showcase exceeded the expectations of this Ayden, North Carolina, reader:

My husband and I loved the Japanese drumming and the Chinese acrobats. These performances were much more indicative of foreign cultures than the rides.

A Vero Beach, Florida, couple love Voices of Liberty:

Voices of Liberty is one of our favorite acts. Their period costuming, rousing folk and patriotic songs, incredible a cappella sound, and heartwarming spirit bring forth a huge, sincere response from the audience.

(Note that Disney changes up VOL's song set seasonally. When they're not in the US Pavilion, their repertoire consists of tunes from Disney movies—including, yes, "Let It Go.")

DINNER AND LUNCH SHOWS Restaurants in World Showcase serve up healthy portions of live entertainment with the victuals. Find folk dancing and an oompah band in Germany, singing waiters in Italy, and belly dancers in Morocco. Shows take place only at dinner in Italy and Morocco but at both lunch and dinner in Germany. Advance Reservations are required.

DISNEY CHARACTERS Characters appear at the Epcot Character Spot (see page 580), elsewhere throughout the park (see page 442), and at the Showcase Plaza between Mexico and Canada. Times are listed in the *Times Guide*. Finally, **Garden Grill Restaurant** in The Land and **Akershus Royal Banquet Hall** in Norway offer character meals.

IN FUTURE WORLD A musical crew of drumming janitors works near the front entrance and at Innoventions Plaza (between the two Innoventions buildings and by the fountain) according to the daily entertainment schedule.

INNOVENTIONS FOUNTAIN SHOW Throughout the day, the fountain between the two Innoventions buildings comes alive with pulsating, arching plumes of water synchronized to a musical score.

IllumiNations: Reflections of Earth (FastPass+) ★★★★½

APPEAL BY AGE	PRESCHOOL ★★★★	GRADE SCHOOL ★★★★	TEENS ★★★★½
YOUNG ADULTS ★★★★½		OVER 30 ★★★★½	SENIORS ★★★★½

What it is Nighttime fireworks and laser show at World Showcase Lagoon. **Scope and scale** Super-headliner. **When to go** Stake out a viewing position 60–100 minutes before the show (45–90 minutes during less-busy periods); FastPass+ not recommended except as noted on page 603. **Special comments** Check *Times Guide* for showtimes; audience stands. **Authors' rating** Epcot's most impressive entertainment event; not to be missed; ★★★★½. **Duration of show** About 18 minutes.

DESCRIPTION AND COMMENTS Epcot's great outdoor spectacle integrates fireworks, laser lights, neon, and music in a stirring tribute to the nations of the world. It's the climax of every Epcot day, and not to be missed.

    IllumiNations has a plot and a theme, both fairly freighted with symbolism. The show kicks off with colliding stars that suggest the Big Bang, following which "chaos reigns in the universe." This display is soon replaced by twittering songbirds and various other manifestations signaling the nativity of the Earth. Next comes a brief history of time, from the dinosaurs to ancient Rome, all projected in images on a huge, floating globe. Man's art and inspiration then flash across the globe "in a collage of creativity." All this stimulates the globe to unfold "like a massive flower," bringing on the fireworks crescendo heralding the dawn of a new age.

    Word around the lagoon is that a new nighttime extravaganza will replace *IllumiNations* sometime in the next few years. While we don't know the plot, we're reasonably sure it'll contain lasers, fireworks, and music.

TOURING TIPS See the next several pages for our detailed advice on viewing spots and exit strategies.

Getting Out of Epcot After *IllumiNations* (Read This Before Selecting a Viewing Spot!)

IllumiNations ends the day at Epcot. When it's over, only a couple of gift shops remain open. Because there's nothing to do, everyone leaves at once. This creates a great snarl at Package Pick-Up, the Epcot monorail station, and the Disney bus stop. It also pushes to the limit the tram system hauling guests to their cars in the parking lot. It's important, then, to decide how quickly you want to leave the park after the show, and then pick your vantage point.

If you're staying at an Epcot resort (Swan, Dolphin, Yacht & Beach Club Resorts, and BoardWalk Inn & Villas), watch the show from somewhere on the southern (US Pavilion) half of World Showcase Lagoon; then leave through the International Gateway between France and the United Kingdom. You can walk or take a boat back to your hotel from the International Gateway.

If you're staying at any other Disney hotel and you don't have a car, the fastest way home is to join the mass exodus through the main gate after *IllumiNations* and catch a bus or the monorail.

Those who have a car in the Epcot lot have a more problematic situation. To beat the crowd, find a viewing spot at the end of World Showcase Lagoon nearest Future World (and the exits). Leave as soon as the show concludes, trying to exit ahead of the crowd (note that thousands of people will be doing exactly the same thing). To get a good vantage point between Mexico and Canada on the northern end of the lagoon, stake out your spot 60–100 minutes before the show (45–90 minutes during less-busy periods), or use FastPass+. Otherwise, you may squander more time holding your spot before *IllumiNations* than you would if you watched from the less-congested southern end of the lagoon and took your chances with the crowd upon departure.

More groups get separated and more kids get lost following *IllumiNations* than at any other time. In summer, you'll be walking in a throng of up to 30,000 people. If you're heading for the parking lot, anticipate this congestion and preselect a point in the Epcot entrance area where you can meet if someone gets separated from the group. We recommend the fountain just inside the main entrance.

For those with a car, the main problem is reaching the parking lot. Once you're there, traffic leaves the parking lot pretty well. If you paid close attention to where you parked, consider skipping the tram and walking. If you walk, watch your children closely and hang on to them for all they're worth—the parking lot is pretty wild at this time of night, with hundreds of moving cars.

Good Locations for Viewing *IllumiNations* and Other World Showcase Lagoon Performances

The best place to be for any presentation on World Showcase Lagoon is in a seat on the lakeside veranda of **La Cantina de San Angel** in Mexico.

DISNEY DISH WITH JIM HILL

MARK YOUR CALENDARS FOR 1-1-21 When will a new nighttime show replace *IllumiNations* at Epcot? Disney filed permits with the FAA in fall 2015 that indicated they'd like to use drones as part of a new nighttime show. Given the regulatory hurdles and testing that have to happen for that, it might be WDW's 50th anniversary celebration (kicking off on January 1, 2021) before we see something new.

Where to View *IllumiNations*

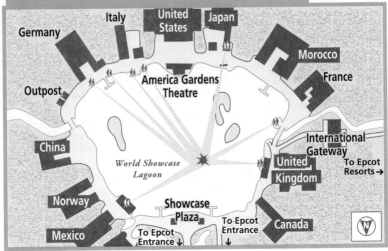

Come early—at least 90 minutes before *IllumiNations*—and relax with a cold drink or snack while you wait for the show.

A woman from Pasadena, California, nailed down the seat but missed the relaxation. She writes:

> Stake out a prime site for IllumiNations *at least an hour and a half ahead—and be prepared to defend it. We got a lakeside table at Cantina de San Angel at 6:30 p.m.; unfortunately, we had to put up with troops of people asking us to share our table and trying to wedge themselves between our table and the fence.*

La Hacienda de San Angel in Mexico, the **Rose & Crown Pub** in the United Kingdom, and **Spice Road Table** in Morocco also offer lagoon views. The views at Rose & Crown aren't quite as good as at the others.

If you want to combine dinner at these sit-down locations with *IllumiNations*, make an Advance Reservation for about 1 hour and 15 minutes before showtime. Report a few minutes early for your seating and tell the host that you want a table outside where you can watch the show. Our experience is that the staff will bend over backward to accommodate you. If you can't snag an outside table, eat inside and hang out until showtime. When the lights dim, indicating the start of *IllumiNations,* you'll be allowed to join the diners to watch the show.

Because most guests run for the exits after a presentation and islands in the southern (US Pavilion) half of the lagoon block the view from some places, the most popular spectator positions are along the northern waterfront from Norway and Mexico to Canada and the United Kingdom. Although the northern half of the lagoon unquestionably offers excellent viewing, it's usually necessary to claim a spot 60–100 minutes before *IllumiNations* begins.

For those who are late finishing dinner, can't use FastPass+, or don't want to spend an hour or more standing by a rail, here are some good viewing spots along the southern perimeter (moving counterclockwise from the United Kingdom to Germany) that often go unnoticed until 10–30 minutes before showtime:

1. **International Gateway Island** The pedestrian bridge across the canal near International Gateway spans an island that offers great viewing. This island normally fills 30 minutes or more before showtime.

2. **Second-Floor (Restaurant-Level) Deck of the Mitsukoshi Building in Japan** An Asian arch slightly blocks your sight line, but this covered deck offers a great vantage point, especially if the weather is iffy. Only La Hacienda de San Angel in Mexico is more protected. If you take up a position on the Mitsukoshi deck and find the wind blowing directly at you, you can be reasonably sure that the smoke from the fireworks won't be far behind.

3. **Gondola Landing at Italy** An elaborate waterfront promenade offers excellent viewing. Claim a spot at least 30 minutes before showtime.

4. **The Boat Dock Opposite Germany** Another good vantage point, the dock generally fills 30 minutes before *IllumiNations*. Note that this area may be exposed to more smoke from the fireworks because of Epcot's prevailing winds.

5. **Waterfront Promenade by Germany** Views are good from the 90-foot-long lagoonside walkway between Germany and China.

None of the viewing locations are reservable, and the good spots go early on busy nights. But speaking personally, we refuse to hold down a slab of concrete for 2 hours before *IllumiNations* as some people do. Most nights, you can find an acceptable vantage point 15–30 minutes before the show. Don't position yourself under a tree, an awning, or anything that blocks your overhead view.

A New Yorker who staked out his turf well in advance made this suggestion for staying comfortable until showtime:

> *Your excellent guide also served as a seat cushion while I waited seated on the ground. Make future editions thicker for greater comfort.*

IllumiNations and FastPass+

We don't recommend *IllumiNations* as a good use of one of your first three advance FastPass+ reservations, but if you have just one day to tour Epcot and you're using our standard touring plan, you should be able to pick up a same-day FastPass+ reservation for *IllumiNations* just after 2 p.m., after you've experienced all of Epcot's headliners.

Frozen Ever After in Norway makes for some tough FastPass+ choices. FastPasses for *IllumiNations* usually run out by 2 p.m., but it's unlikely that most guests will be finished with their Frozen Ever After FastPass+ experiences by then. However, plenty of excellent *IllumiNations* viewing locations can be found around World Showcase, so it's not as critical to have a FastPass+ for this nighttime show.

Readers confirm that even when you do have a FastPass+ reservation for *IllumiNations*, it doesn't work very well. These comments are representative:

> *It wasn't worth it to me. There were a LOT of people and a small amount of railing space, which everyone was jostling for. I'm vertically challenged (5'4"), and I couldn't see the globe very well.*

> *The lineup to get into the spot was INSANE. We went early and had to wait in line for about 20 minutes just to get into the viewing area.*

ILLUMINATIONS CRUISE

FOR A REALLY GOOD VIEW, you can charter a pontoon boat for $346 with tax. Captained by a Disney cast member, the boat holds up to 10 guests. Your captain will take you for a little cruise and then position the boat in a perfect place to watch *IllumiNations*. Chips, soda, and water are provided; sandwiches and more-substantial food items may be arranged through Disney reservations or Yacht Club Private Dining at ☎ 407-934-3160. Cruises depart from Bayside Marina. A major indirect benefit of the charter is that you can enjoy *IllumiNations* without fighting the mob afterward. Because this is a private charter rather than a tour, only your group will be aboard. Life jackets are provided, but you can wear them at your discretion. Because there are few boats, charters sell out fast. To reserve, call ☎ 407-WDW-PLAY (939-7529) at exactly 7 a.m. Eastern time 180 days before the day you want to charter. Because the Disney reservations system counts days in a somewhat atypical manner, we recommend phoning about 185 days out to have a Disney agent specify the exact morning to call for reservations. Similar charters are available on the Seven Seas Lagoon to watch the Magic Kingdom fireworks.

ILLUMINATIONS SPARKLING DESSERT PARTY Offered seasonally, this evening event features globally inspired sweet treats (Moroccan baklava, Italian cannoli, and the like), plus sparkling wine and soft drinks. Cost is $49 adults, $29 kids ages 3–9, tax included but park admission excluded. The location generally varies between the Port of Entry shop in World Showcase Plaza and the theater for *The American Adventure* in the US Pavilion; guests access a reserved viewing area near the party location, but keep in mind that there's no seating. Advance Reservations are recommended and can be made up to 180 days ahead; call ☎ 407-939-3463 or reserve online at disneyworld.disney.go.com/dining.

TRAFFIC PATTERNS
in EPCOT

IN THE MAGIC KINGDOM, Main Street, U.S.A., with its shops and eateries, serves as a huge gathering place when the park opens and funnels visitors to the Central Plaza, where entrances branch off to the lands. Thus, crowds are first welcomed and entertained (on Main Street), then distributed almost equally to the lands.

At Epcot, by contrast, Spaceship Earth, the park's premier landmark and one of its headliner attractions, is just inside the main entrance. When visitors enter the park, they almost irresistibly head for it. Hence, a bottleneck forms less than 75 yards from the turnstiles as soon as the park opens.

Early-morning crowds form at Test Track and Soarin' in Future World, and Frozen Ever After in Norway. Guests not visiting those are fairly equally distributed among the rest of Future World's attractions, most of which won't develop long waits until 11 a.m. or later.

Between 9 and 11 a.m., crowds build in Future World. Even when World Showcase opens (usually 11 a.m.), more people are entering

Future World than are leaving for the Showcase. Attendance continues building in Future World between noon and 2 p.m. World Showcase attendance builds rapidly as lunchtime approaches. Exhibits at the far end of World Showcase Lagoon report large audiences from about noon through 6:30 or 7:30 p.m.

The Magic Kingdom's premier attractions are situated on the far perimeters of its lands to distribute crowds evenly. Epcot's cluster of attractions in Future World holds the greater part of the throng in the smaller part of the park. World Showcase has just one major bottleneck—Norway's Frozen Ever After. Compared with Soarin' and Test Track, Frozen's long lines result more from a lack of ride capacity than guest demand. But with no attractions beyond Norway open in World Showcase until 11 a.m., most families who visit Frozen first head back to Future World.

The bottom line: Crowds build all morning and into early afternoon in Future World. Not until the evening meal approaches do crowds equalize in Future World and World Showcase. Evening crowds in World Showcase, however, don't compare in size with morning and midday crowds in Future World. Attendance throughout Epcot is normally lighter in the evening.

Some guests leave Epcot in the early evening, but most of them exit en masse after *IllumiNations*. Upward of 30,000 people head for the parking lot and monorail station at once. Still, this congestion doesn't compare with the post-fireworks gridlock at the Magic Kingdom. One primary reason for the easier departure from Epcot is that its parking lot is adjacent to the park, not separated from it by a lake as at the Magic Kingdom. At the Magic Kingdom, departing visitors form bottlenecks at the monorail to the Transportation and Ticket Center and main parking lot. At Epcot, they proceed directly to their cars.

To get a complete view of the actual traffic patterns while you're in the park, use our mobile app, **Lines** (touringplans.com/lines). The app gives you current wait times and future estimates in half-hour increments for today and tomorrow. A quick glance shows how traffic patterns affect wait times throughout the day.

EPCOT TOURING PLANS

TOURING EPCOT IS MUCH MORE STRENUOUS and demanding than touring the other theme parks. Epcot requires about twice as much walking. And, unlike the Magic Kingdom, Epcot has no effective in-park transportation; wherever you want to go, it's always quicker to walk. Our plans will help you avoid crowds and bottlenecks on days of moderate-to-heavy attendance, but they can't shorten the distance you have to walk. (Wear comfortable shoes.) On days of lighter attendance, when crowd conditions aren't a critical factor, the plans will help you organize your tour. We offer four touring plans:

- Epcot One-Day Touring Plan
- Epcot Authors' Selective One-Day Touring Plan
- Epcot One-Day Touring Plan for Parents with Small Children
- Epcot Two-Day Early-Riser Touring Plan

unofficial **TIP**
Visitors aware of the congestion at Spaceship Earth can take advantage of the excellent opportunities it provides for escaping waits at other Future World attractions.

The One-Day Touring Plan packs as much as possible into one long day and requires a lot of hustle and stamina. The Authors' Selective One-Day Touring Plan eliminates some lesser (in the authors' opinion) attractions and offers a somewhat more relaxed tour if you have only one day. The One-Day Touring Plan for Parents with Small Children gives little ones the best of Epcot while also building in needed rest time. Finally, the Two-Day Early-Riser Touring Plan is the most efficient, eliminating 90% of the backtracking and extra walking required by the other plans while still providing a comprehensive tour.

To help with FastPass+, we've listed the approximate return times for which you should attempt to make reservations. Check **Touring Plans.com** for the latest developments and information.

"Not a Touring Plan" Touring Plans

For the type-B reader, these touring plans (see page 817) avoid detailed step-by-step strategies for saving every last minute in line. For Epcot, these "not" touring plans include advice for adults and parents with one day in the park, for anyone with two days, and for anyone with an afternoon and a full day to tour.

BEFORE YOU GO

1. Call ☎ 407-824-4321 or check the day before you go to verify official opening time.
2. Make reservations at the Epcot full-service restaurant(s) of your choice 180 days before your visit.
3. Make FastPass+ reservations 60 or 30 days in advance.

EPCOT ONE-DAY TOURING PLAN FOR ADULTS
(page 825)

FOR Adults and children age 8 or older.

ASSUMES Willingness to experience all major rides and shows; Soarin', Test Track, and Frozen Ever After are in the same FastPass+ tier and you can choose only one in advance.

Touring Epcot requires a lot of walking regardless of whether you're using a plan or not. This plan uses a small amount of backtracking in order to avoid long waits in line.

The opening of Frozen Ever After complicates touring Epcot for a couple of reasons. Because it's in the same FastPass+ tier as Soarin' and Test Track, you can obtain only one FastPass in advance. It's also unlikely to have much day-of FastPass+ availability, because the attraction is based on a hit film and is one of the few things in Epcot specifically designed for children. Its location in World Showcase also makes it impractical as a detour while you're in Future World.

For those reasons, we think you'll save more time by choosing Frozen as an advance FastPass+ reservation rather than Soarin' or Test Track. As in years past, we suggest visiting Soarin' as soon as the park opens, and without FastPass+. Your next visit should be to Test Track, making use of the single-rider line there if possible. Your total wait in line for both attractions should be 40 minutes or less. For comparison, we estimate the wait at Frozen to be in the 60- to 90-minute range most of the day. When you factor in the backtracking involved in the alternatives, FastPass+ at Frozen seems to make the most sense.

We're recommending an evening FastPass+ reservation time for Frozen Ever After. If only early-afternoon times are available, take one and simply convert the counterclockwise tour of World Showcase to a clockwise tour.

If you get FastPass+ reservations for Frozen Ever After for 2–4 p.m., do a clockwise tour of World Showcase. We don't suggest FastPasses earlier than this because it will involve backtracking to Future World from World Showcase. And if no Frozen FastPasses are available, grab one for Test Track around 9:15 a.m.

Regardless of the time at which you obtain your Frozen FastPass, we think it's unlikely that any day-of FastPasses would be of much use, because of the backtracking from World Showcase you'd have to do to use them.

EPCOT AUTHORS' SELECTIVE ONE-DAY TOURING PLAN FOR ADULTS *(page 826)*

FOR All parties.

ASSUMES Willingness to experience major rides and shows.

This plan provides more time for leisurely meals and touring World Showcase. It eliminates the aging, lengthy *Ellen's Energy Adventure* and Journey into Imagination attractions and makes optional the not-really-Norwegian Frozen Ever After ride in Norway. Doing so allows use of an early-morning FastPass+ at Test Track.

Another advantage of this plan is that you'll be able to obtain day-of FastPasses right after you've experienced Spaceship Earth. It's still a long shot that day-of FastPasses will be available for Frozen Ever After, but a long shot is still a shot.

EPCOT ONE-DAY TOURING PLAN FOR PARENTS WITH SMALL CHILDREN *(page 827)*

FOR Parents with children younger than age 8.

ASSUMES Periodic stops for rest, restrooms, and refreshments.

This plan includes Epcot's two newest, child-friendly attractions: the Frozen Ever After boat ride and Royal Sommerhus meet and greet with Anna and Elsa, both at Norway. To make time available for those, we've dropped the dated, lengthy *Ellen's Energy Adventure* presentation from the morning in Future World. In addition to the Frozen attractions, this change may also allow you time for tours of one or two other World Showcase countries.

We're recommending a late-afternoon FastPass+ reservation time for Frozen Ever After. If only evening times are available, take one and simply convert the clockwise tour of World Showcase to a counterclockwise tour.

We don't suggest Frozen FastPasses for the morning because it will involve a special trip out to World Showcase, then a backtrack to Future World, essentially canceling much of the time saved in line. If no Frozen FastPasses are available, grab one for Soarin' at 9 a.m. and Epcot Character Spot at 10 a.m., and visit Norway in the last 2 hours the park is open.

EPCOT TWO-DAY EARLY-RISER TOURING PLAN
(pages 828 and 829)

FOR All parties.

ASSUMES Willingness to experience major rides and shows.

Touring Epcot over two days allows you to see all of the major attractions with minimal waits. Arriving early is a significant benefit, as is the ability to split Epcot's tiered FastPass+ headliners over two days.

This plan's basic strategy is to split the park into east and west, seeing the attractions on one side of the park on the first day and those on the other side on the second day. The single exception is visiting Test Track in Future World East on Day 1, when you're otherwise on the west side. That short morning walk to the other side of Future World enables you to use FastPass+ for Frozen Ever After at Norway on Day 2, allowing you to bypass the standby line.

PART ELEVEN

DISNEY'S ANIMAL KINGDOM

WITH ITS LUSH FLORA, WINDING STREAMS, meandering paths, and exotic setting, Disney's Animal Kingdom is a stunningly beautiful theme park. The landscaping alone conjures images of rainforest, veldt, and formal gardens. Soothing, mysterious, and exciting, every vista is a feast for the eye. Add to this loveliness a population of more than 1,700 animals, replicas of Africa's and Asia's most intriguing architecture, and a diverse array of singularly original attractions, and you have the most distinctive of all the Disney theme parks.

At 500 acres, Animal Kingdom is four times the size of the Magic Kingdom and almost twice the size of Epcot. But most of Animal Kingdom's geography is accessible only on guided tours or as part of attractions. The park consists of six "lands": **The Oasis, Discovery Island, DinoLand U.S.A., Africa, Asia,** and **Pandora—The World of Avatar.**

Its expansion notwithstanding, Animal Kingdom offers a limited number of attractions. To be exact, there are nine rides, several walk-through exhibits, an indoor theater, three amphitheaters, a conservation exhibit, and a children's playground.

Animal Kingdom's opening was seen as Disney taking dead aim at Busch Gardens in Tampa, a theme park known for its exceptional zoological exhibits. Up to that time, Disney had preferred the neatly controlled movements of Audio-Animatronic animals to the unpredictable behaviors of real critters. Unfortunately for Disney, however, the combination of creative natural-habitat zoological exhibits and roller coasters developed by Busch Gardens became immensely popular, and as any student of The Walt Disney Company can attest, there's nothing like a successful competitor to make the Disney folks change their tune. So, all press releases aside, Animal Kingdom was designed as a combination of natural-habitat zoological exhibits and thrill rides. Big surprise!

Even if the recipe was copied, the Disney version serves up more than its share of innovations. For starters, there's lots of space, thus allowing for the sweeping vistas that Discovery Channel viewers would expect in, say, an African veldt setting. Then there are the enclosures, natural in appearance, with few or no apparent barriers between you and the animals. The operative word, of course, is *apparent*. That flimsy stand of bamboo separating you from a gorilla is actually a neatly disguised

Continued on page 612

Disney's Animal Kingdom

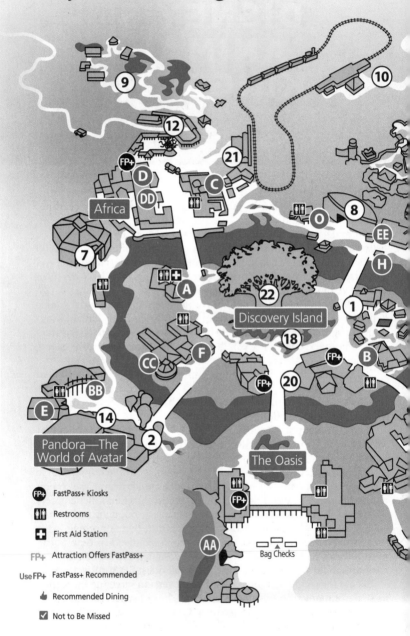

Africa

Discovery Island

Pandora—The World of Avatar

The Oasis

Bag Checks

FP+ FastPass+ Kiosks

♛ Restrooms

✚ First Aid Station

FP+ Attraction Offers FastPass+

Use FP+ FastPass+ Recommended

👍 Recommended Dining

☑ Not to Be Missed

Attractions

1. Adventurers Outpost Use FP+
2. Avatar Flight of Passage
3. The Boneyard
4. Conservation Station and Affection Section
5. Dinosaur ☑ Use FP+
6. Expedition Everest ☑ Use FP+
7. *Festival of the Lion King* ☑ FP+
8. *Flights of Wonder*
9. Gorilla Falls Exploration Trail
10. Habitat Habit!
11. Kali River Rapids Use FP+
12. Kilimanjaro Safaris ☑ Use FP+
13. Maharajah Jungle Trek
14. Na'Vi River Journey
15. Primeval Whirl FP+
16. *Rivers of Light* FP+
17. Theater in the Wild/ *Finding Nemo—The Musical* F
18. The Tree of Life/ *It's Tough to Be a Bug!*
19. TriceraTop Spin
20. Wilderness Explorers Sign-Up Station ☑
21. Wildlife Express Train

Rafiki's Planet Watch

Asia

DinoLand U.S.A.

Table-Service Restaurants

AA. Rainforest Cafe
BB. Satu'li Canteen
CC. Tiffins
DD. Tusker House Restaurant
EE. Yak & Yeti Restaurant

Counter-Service Restaurants

A. Creature Comforts *(Starbucks)*
B. Flame Tree Barbecue 👍
C. Harambe Market
D. Kusafiri Coffee Shop & Bakery
E. Pongu Pongu
F. Pizzafari
G. Restaurantosaurus
H. Royal Anandapur Tea Company
I. Thirsty River Bar & Trek Snacks
J. Yak & Yeti Local Food Cafes

Continued from page 609

set of steel rods embedded in concrete. The Imagineers even take a crack at certain animals' unwillingness to be on display: A lion that would rather sleep out of sight under a bush, for example, is lured to center stage with cool, climate-controlled artificial rocks.

Disney's Animal Kingdom has received mixed reviews since it opened in 1998. Guests complain loudly about the park layout, the necessity of backtracking through Discovery Island to access the various themed areas, congested walkways, and lack of shade. However, most of the attractions have been well received, as have the animal exhibits and the park's architecture and landscaping. We marvel at the fact that readers of similar backgrounds come away with such vastly differing opinions.

In truth, Animal Kingdom is a park to linger over and savor—two things that Disney, with its crowds, lines, and regimentation, has conditioned us not to do. But many people intuit that it must be approached in a different way, including this mother of three (ages 5, 7, and 9) from Hampton Bay, New York:

> To enjoy Animal Kingdom, you must have the right attitude. It's an educational experience, not a thrill park. We spoke to a cast member who played games with the kids—my daughter found a drawer full of butterflies, and the boys located a hidden ostrich egg and lion skull.

And though we offer a one-day touring plan for Animal Kingdom, a Cleveland reader argues for more time:

> I can't see how Animal Kingdom takes less than a day. There is so much to look at, animal-wise, architecturally, street performances— we kept going back at different times, and each time we saw the place literally in a new light or with different animals active.

These readers are right: Animal Kingdom's best features are its animals, nature trails, and cast members. The **Wilderness Explorers** scavenger hunt (see page 620) ties together all of the park's best elements, and it's part of our Animal Kingdom touring plan. It's a lot of fun to play, and you just might learn something along the way.

In 2016 Animal Kingdom rolled out two new attractions. The first is a nighttime version of its popular **Kilimanjaro Safaris** expedition, complete with new nocturnal species and high-tech wizardry to let you observe the grasslands at night. The second attraction is *Rivers of Light,* an evening water pageant that celebrates nature through floats, fountains, stunning visual displays, and music. See page 629 for more details.

Pandora—The World of Avatar is Disney World's newest land. Opened in May 2017, it completes a major expansion project that began when Disney signed *Avatar* filmmaker James Cameron to a development deal in 2011. Besides two new headliner rides—**Avatar Flight of Passage** and **Na'Vi River Journey**—Disney has brought to life the floating mountains and glow-in-the-dark plant life of Cameron's blockbuster film. Of course, you'll want to stay well into the evening to see all these new effects—and making Animal Kingdom a full-day park is exactly what Disney wanted to do. In addition, Pandora has an abundance of themed merchandise as well as two dining locations: a large quick-service restaurant and a walk-up bar. The quick-service restaurant, **Satu'li Canteen,**

offers an imaginative, themed menu that features an impressive array of customizable items. Ordering can be done on-site or in advance via the Disney World app.

ARRIVING

unofficial **TIP**
Arrive at the entrance turnstiles, admission in hand, 40 minutes before official opening during the summer and holiday periods, and 30 minutes before official opening the rest of the year.

DISNEY'S ANIMAL KINGDOM is off Osceola Parkway in the southwest corner of Walt Disney World and is not too far from Blizzard Beach, Coronado Springs Resort, and the All-Star Resorts. (For GPS coordinates, see page 485.) Animal Kingdom Lodge is about a mile away from the park on its west side. From I-4, take Exit 65, Osceola Parkway. Animal Kingdom has its own vast pay parking lot with close-in parking for the disabled. Once parked, you can walk to the entrance or catch a ride on one of Disney's trams.

If you're staying at a Disney resort and plan to arrive at Animal Kingdom before park opening, the Disney bus system is an option, but note that bus service is wildly erratic. To be safe, use your own car, or spring for a cab or ride-share service.

OPERATING HOURS

ANIMAL KINGDOM'S OPENING TIME corresponds to that of the other parks. Thus, you can expect a 9 a.m. opening during less busy times of the year and an 8 a.m. opening during holidays and high season. With the nighttime landscapes of Pandora and the *Rivers of Light* show, expect Animal Kingdom to be open until at least 10 p.m. during summer, and at least 8 p.m. in winter. That's a couple of hours after sundown, enough time to tour Pandora, take a nighttime Kilimanjaro Safaris ride, and possibly see *Rivers of Light*.

DISNEY DISH WITH JIM HILL

"LIGHT" TO BE SNUFFED OUT The current plan is to run *Rivers of Light* through summer 2020. For now, its replacement is a character-driven show involving Jon Favreau's *Lion King* reboot in 2019, and the sequel to 2016's Academy Award–winning *Jungle Book*. Look for it to debut in 2021 for WDW's 50th-anniversary celebration.

Animal Kingdom's standard opening procedure lets all guests through the turnstiles about 15–30 minutes before the official park opening. When this happens, you will usually find all of Pandora, plus Kilimanjaro Safaris, Expedition Everest, and TriceraTop Spin already open.

During slower or colder times of year, Disney may delay the daily opening of Kali River Rapids in Asia, as well as the Boneyard playground, the Wildlife Express Train, and Conservation Station. These procedures may change, so check the *Times Guide* or our app, **Lines,** for the schedule when you arrive. The rest of the attractions come online at official park opening time.

On holidays and other days of projected heavy attendance, Disney will open the park 30–60 minutes early.

Animal Kingdom currently holds two morning Extra Magic Hours sessions per week, although we don't think they save you that much time in line. Our advice is to get an extra hour of sleep and visit when early entry is not in effect.

Even with the extended hours, expect the Wildlife Express Train, Conservation Station, and Gorilla Falls Exploration Trail to close around 30–60 minutes before sunset. Thus, as days get shorter with the change of seasons, the attractions close earlier in the day.

Sleeping In and Seeing Animal Kingdom

The park's extended nighttime hours make it possible to arrive around noon and still see everything. This makes Animal Kingdom a great choice to visit after a long night at the Magic Kingdom or Epcot. See the section titled "Full-Day/Sleep-In Alternating Days" in Part Two (page 78) for more details and a late-arrival Animal Kingdom touring plan.

GETTING ORIENTED

AT THE ENTRANCE PLAZA ARE TICKET KIOSKS fronting the main entrance. To your right, before the turnstiles, is an ATM. After you pass through the turnstiles, wheelchair and stroller rentals are to your right. **Guest Relations**—park headquarters for information, guide maps, entertainment schedules (*Times Guides*), missing persons, and lost and found—is to the left. Nearby are restrooms, public phones, and lockers. Beyond the entrance plaza, you enter **The Oasis,** a lushly vegetated

Animal Kingdom Services

MOST OF THE PARK'S SERVICE FACILITIES are inside the main entrance and on Discovery Island, as follows:

Baby Care Center On Discovery Island

Banking Services ATMs at the main entrance, by the turnstiles, and near Dinosaur in DinoLand U.S.A.

Camera Memory Cards and Supplies Just inside the main entrance at Garden Gate Gifts, in Africa at Mombasa Marketplace, and at other retail shops throughout the park

Cell Phone Charging Outlets available at Pizzafari, Restaurantosaurus, Tusker House, and Conservation Station

Entertainment Information In the *Times Guide,* available at Guest Relations

First Aid Center On Discovery Island

Guest Relations/Information Inside the main entrance to the left

Lost and Found Inside the main entrance to the left

Lost Persons Can be reported at Guest Relations and the Baby Care Center

Storage Lockers Inside the main entrance to the left

Wheelchair, ECV/ESV, and Stroller Rentals Inside the main entrance, to the right network of converging pathways winding through a landscape punctuated with streams, waterfalls, and misty glades and inhabited by what Disney calls "colorful and unusual animals."

The park is arranged somewhat like the Magic Kingdom, in a hub-and-spoke configuration. The lush, tropical Oasis serves as Main Street, funneling visitors to **Discovery Island** at the center of the park. Dominated by the park's central icon, the 14-story hand-carved **Tree of Life**, Discovery Island is the park's retail and dining center. From Discovery Island, guests can access the respective themed areas of **Africa, Asia, DinoLand U.S.A.,** and **Pandora.** Discovery Island also hosts a theater attraction in The Tree of Life and a number of short nature trails.

Even if you dawdle in the shops and linger over the wildlife exhibits, you should easily be able to take in Animal Kingdom in one day.

FASTPASS+ ATTRACTIONS AT ANIMAL KINGDOM

FASTPASS+ IS OFFERED at 12 attractions:

AFRICA	DINOLAND U.S.A. *(continued)*
• *Festival of the Lion King*	• *Finding Nemo—The Musical*
• Kilimanjaro Safaris	• Primeval Whirl
ASIA	**DISCOVERY ISLAND**
• Expedition Everest	• *It's Tough to Be a Bug!*
• Kali River Rapids	• Meet Favorite Disney Pals at Adventurers Outpost
• *Rivers of Light*	**PANDORA**
DINOLAND U.S.A.	• Avatar Flight of Passage
• Dinosaur	• Na'Vi River Journey

THE MOST VALUABLE FASTPASSES AT ANIMAL KINGDOM

FASTPASS+ IS OFFERED AT A DOZEN Animal Kingdom attractions, but only eight of them ever require FastPass+ in our touring plans. This section explains why.

Kilimanjaro Safaris is the attraction that most frequently uses FastPass+ in our Animal Kingdom touring plans. Why? It's not a thrill ride, so it appeals to everyone, from small children to seniors. It's also very popular, so it appears in all our touring plans. Another advantage of using FastPass+ for Kilimanjaro is that you can choose whether to experience the standard daytime safari or try the nighttime version.

We recommend FastPass+ for the new Pandora attractions, **Avatar Flight of Passage** and **Na'Vi River Journey,** more than for any other Animal Kingdom attractions except Kilimanjaro Safaris. Both rides are in the same FastPass+ tier, so you have to choose one for your advance FastPass+. If you plan to ride Flight of Passage, we think that choice will save you the most time in line. If you're not riding Flight of Passage, get a FastPass+ for Na'Vi River Journey.

Expedition Everest appears next on our list of best FastPass+ attractions at Animal Kingdom. Because it's a popular ride, it appears in all of our 'tween, adult, and whole-family touring plans.

Animal Kingdom
When Same-Day FP+ Runs Out, by Crowd Level

ATTRACTION	LOW CROWDS*	MODERATE CROWDS*	HIGH CROWDS*
• Adventurers Outpost	9 a.m.	N/A	N/A
• Avatar Flight of Passage (too new to analyze)	—	—	—
• Dinosaur	1 p.m.	10 a.m.	N/A
• Expedition Everest	2 p.m.	Noon	N/A
• Festival of the Lion King	2 p.m.	11 a.m.	N/A
• Finding Nemo—The Musical	3 p.m.	2 p.m.	10 a.m.
• It's Tough to Be a Bug!	3 p.m.	3 p.m.	3 p.m.
• Kali River Rapids	4 p.m.	2 p.m.	N/A
• Kilimanjaro Safaris (daytime version)	2 p.m.	9 a.m.	N/A
• Na'Vi River Journey (too new to analyze)	—	—	—
• Primeval Whirl	3 p.m.	3 p.m.	1 p.m.
• Rivers of Light	N/A	N/A	N/A
* LOW CROWDS (Levels 1–3 on TouringPlans.com Crowd Calendar)			
* MODERATE CROWDS (Levels 4–7 on TouringPlans.com Crowd Calendar)			
* HIGH CROWDS (Levels 8–10 on TouringPlans.com Crowd Calendar)			
N/A = no availability			

Beyond those attractions, your choices for a best FastPass+ attraction depend on the ages of your family. The **Adventurer's Outpost** character meet and greet shows up on our Animal Kingdom touring plans for parents with small children. It's probably not going to be the first stop of your day, and using FastPass+ at the Outpost will generally save more time in line than using it at any other child-friendly attraction in our plans.

Similarly, **Rivers of Light, Kali River Rapids,** and **Dinosaur** are reasonable FastPass+ recommendations in some scenarios, such as days with late arrivals. The park's other FastPass-enabled attractions are good choices only in rare circumstances.

FastPass+ kiosk locations in Animal Kingdom are as follows:

- In front of the Disney Outfitters store on Discovery Island and across the walkway near Island Mercantile
- In front of the MyMagic+ Service Center, to the left of the entrance at The Oasis
- Near Kali River Rapids, Asia
- Near Harambe Market, Africa

Same-Day FastPass+ Availability

The preceding advice tells you which attractions to focus on when making your *advance* FastPass+ reservations before you get to the park. Once you're in the park, you can make more FastPass+ reservations once your advance reservations have been used or have expired. The chart on the previous page shows which attractions are likely to have day-of FastPasses available, and the approximate times at which they'll run out.

DINING IN ANIMAL KINGDOM

HERE'S A QUICK RECAP of Animal Kingdom's top few restaurants, rated by readers from highest to lowest. See Part Four, Dining In and Around Walt Disney World, for details.

ANIMAL KINGDOM RESTAURANT REFRESHER	
COUNTER-SERVICE	**FULL-SERVICE**
Creature Comforts (Starbucks) (96% 👍), Discovery Island	**Nomad Lounge** (*bar,* 92% 👍), Discovery Island
Royal Anandapur Tea Company (96% 👍), Asia (*coffee, tea, and pastries*)	**Tiffins** (93% 👍), Discovery Island
Flame Tree Barbecue (95% 👍), Discovery Island	**Tusker House Restaurant** (93% 👍), Africa
Satu'li Canteen (95% 👍), Pandora	**Yak & Yeti Restaurant** (92% 👍), Asia
Thirsty River Bar & Trek Snacks (91% 👍), Asia	
Yak & Yeti Local Food Cafes (91% 👍), Asia	

The OASIS

DESCRIPTION AND COMMENTS Though the functional purpose of The Oasis is the same as that of Main Street in the Magic Kingdom—that is, to funnel guests to the center of the park—it also serves as what Disney calls a "transitional experience." In plain English, this means that it sets the stage and gets you into the right mood to enjoy Disney's Animal Kingdom.

The minute you pass through the turnstiles, you'll know that this isn't just another central hub. Where Main Street, Hollywood Boulevard at the Studios, and the Epcot entrance plaza direct you like an arrow straight into the heart of the respective parks, The Oasis immediately envelops you in an environment replete with choices. There's no one broad thoroughfare but rather multiple paths. Each delivers you to Discovery Island at the center of the park, but the route you choose and what you see along the way are up to you. Nothing obvious clues you in about where you're going—there's no fairy-tale castle or giant golf ball to beckon you. Instead you'll find a lush, green, canopied landscape with streams, grottoes, and waterfalls.

The natural-habitat zoological exhibits in The Oasis are representative of those throughout the park. Although extraordinarily lush and beautiful, the exhibits are primarily designed for the comfort and well-being of the animals. A sign identifies the animal(s) in each exhibit, but there's no guarantee that they will be immediately visible. Because most habitats are large and provide ample terrain for the occupants to hide, you must linger and concentrate, looking for small movements in the vegetation. When you do spot the animal, you may make out only a shadowy figure, or perhaps only a leg or a tail.

TOURING TIPS The Oasis is a place to savor and appreciate, but it will be largely lost on Disney-conditioned guests who blitz through at warp speed to queue up for the big attractions. If you're a blitzer in the morning, plan to spend some time in The Oasis on your way out of the park. It usually closes 30–60 minutes after the rest of the park.

DISCOVERY ISLAND

DISCOVERY ISLAND COMBINES a profusion of tropical greenery with whimsical equatorial African architecture. Connected to the other lands by bridges, the island is the hub from which guests can access the park's various themed areas. A village is arrayed in a crescent around the base of Animal Kingdom's iconic landmark, **The Tree of Life.** Towering 14 stories above the village, it's this park's version of Cinderella Castle or Spaceship Earth. Flanked by pools, meadows, and exotic gardens populated by a diversity of birds and animals, The Tree of Life houses a theater attraction inspired by the Disney-Pixar film *A Bug's Life.*

As you enter Discovery Island over the bridge from The Oasis and the park entrance, you'll see The Tree of Life directly ahead, at 12 o'clock. The bridge to Asia is to the right of the tree at 2 o'clock, with the bridge to DinoLand U.S.A. at roughly 4 o'clock. The bridge connecting The Oasis to Discovery Island is at 6 o'clock, the bridge to Pandora—The World of Avatar is at 8 o'clock, and the bridge to Africa is at 11 o'clock.

Discovery Island is also the park's central headquarters for shopping and services. Here you'll find the **First Aid** and **Baby Care Centers,** plus FastPass+ kiosks. For Disney merchandise, try **Island Mercantile.** Counter-service food and snacks are available, as is upscale full-service dining at **Tiffins.**

DISCOVERY ISLAND TRAILS Winding behind The Tree of Life is a series of walking trails that include around a dozen animal-viewing opportunities, from otters and kangaroos to lemurs, storks, and porcupines. One end of the path begins just before the bridge from Discovery Island to Africa, on the right side of the walkway; the other is to the right of the entrance to The Tree of Life. In addition to the animals, you'll find verdant landscaping, waterfalls, and quiet spots to sit and reflect on your relationship with nature. Or nap. As we think Henry David Thoreau once said, "Not until we have dozed do we begin to understand ourselves."

Meet Favorite Disney Pals at Adventurers Outpost (FastPass+) ★★★½

APPEAL BY AGE	PRESCHOOL ★★★★½	GRADE SCHOOL ★★★★½	TEENS ★★★★
YOUNG ADULTS ★★★★		OVER 30 ★★★★	SENIORS ★★★★

What it is Character-greeting venue. Scope and scale Minor attraction. When to go First thing in the morning, after 5 p.m., or use FastPass+. Authors' rating Nicely themed (and air-conditioned); ★★★½. Duration of experience About 2 minutes. Probable waiting time About 20 minutes. Queue speed Fast.

DESCRIPTION AND COMMENTS An indoor, air-conditioned character-greeting location for Mickey and Minnie Mouse, Adventurers Outpost is decorated with photos, memorabilia, and souvenirs from the Mouses' world travels.

TOURING TIPS The Outpost features two greeting rooms with two identical sets of characters, so lines move fairly quickly. Good use of FastPass+ if you have kids too small to ride Expedition Everest or Dinosaur.

The Tree of Life / *It's Tough to Be a Bug!* / *The Awakening*
(FastPass+) ★★★★

APPEAL BY AGE   PRESCHOOL ★★★   GRADE SCHOOL ★★★★   TEENS ★★★★
YOUNG ADULTS ★★★★   OVER 30 ★★★★   SENIORS ★★★★

What it is 3-D theater show. **Scope and scale** Major attraction. **When to go** Anytime. **Special comment** The theater is inside the tree. **Authors' rating** Zany and frenetic and not to be missed; ★★★★. **Duration of presentation** About 8 minutes. **Probable waiting time** 12–20 minutes.

DESCRIPTION AND COMMENTS The Tree of Life, apart from its size, is quite a work of art—we think it's the most visually compelling structure in any Disney park. Although from afar it's certainly magnificent and imposing, it's not until you examine the tree at close range that you truly appreciate its rich detail. What appears to be ancient gnarled bark is, in fact, hundreds of carvings depicting all manner of wildlife, each integrated seamlessly into the trunk, roots, and limbs of the tree. New "roots" were added to the tree in 2015, including crocodile and ram's head carvings. Look for these along the Discovery Island walkway to Africa, on the front left side of the tree.

In sharp contrast to the grandeur of the tree is the subject of the attraction housed within its trunk. Called *It's Tough to Be a Bug!,* this humorous 3-D presentation is about the difficulties of being a very small creature. Lighthearted and whimsical, the show is similar to *Mickey's PhilharMagic* at the Magic Kingdom in that it combines a 3-D film with an arsenal of tactile and visual special effects. We rate *Bug* as not to be missed.

In 2016 Animal Kingdom introduced *The Awakening,* a new nighttime show at The Tree of Life. Shown several times per night, it combines digital video projections with music and other special effects. We've seen four different 3-minute shows. In each, special projection effects make it appear that some animals carved into the tree trunk have come alive. Other special effects happen in the tree's leaves and branches. It's similar to the Magic Kingdom's popular *Celebrate the Magic* show. We consider it not to be missed.

TOURING TIPS *It's Tough to Be a Bug!* is rarely crowded even on the busiest days. Go in the morning after Kilimanjaro Safaris, Kali River Rapids, Expedition Everest, and Dinosaur. If you miss the bugs in the morning, try again in the late afternoon.

Note that *It's Tough to Be a Bug!* is very intense, and the special effects will do a number on guests of all ages who are squeamish about insects. A mother of two from Williamsville, New York, shared this experience:

It's Tough to Be a Bug! was my girls' first Disney experience, and almost their last. The storyline was nebulous and difficult to follow—all they were aware of was the torture of sitting in a darkened theater being overrun with bugs. A constant stream of parents headed to the exits with terrorized children. Those who were left behind were screaming and crying as well. The 11-year-old refused to talk for 20 minutes after the fiasco, and the 3½-year-old wanted to go home—not back to the hotel, but home.

From a Louisville, Kentucky, family:

My 12-year-old-son and I were laughing at the comments made by concerned parents in the It's Tough to Be a Bug! *review, thinking it would be fun to watch families leave early with crying kids. And our particular show didn't disappoint, even in ways beyond my expectation, for, as the show progressed, my son became eerily quiet. In fact, it was only a matter of time that I found him hunkering down underneath his seat for survival after he saw the bugs coming at him and "feeling" their presence. Needless to say, he ended up being a good sport, and we were able to put it behind him after spending several hours with the on-site child psychologist. (Just kidding!)*

The Awakening runs several times per night starting around sunset. The best viewing spots are directly in front of the tree on Discovery Island, across from Island Mercantile.

Wilderness Explorers ★★★★

APPEAL BY AGE   **PRESCHOOL** ★★★★   **GRADE SCHOOL** ★★★½   **TEENS** ★★★½
YOUNG ADULTS ★★½   **OVER 30** ★★★★   **SENIORS** ★★★½

What it is Park-wide scavenger hunt and puzzle-solving adventure game. **Scope and scale** Diversion. **When to go** Sign up first thing in the morning and complete activities throughout the day. **Special comment** Collecting all 32 badges takes 3–5 hours, which can be done over several days. **Authors' rating** One of the best attractions in any Disney park; not to be missed; ★★★★.

DESCRIPTION AND COMMENTS Walt Disney World offers several interactive games in its theme parks, and Wilderness Explorers is the best of the bunch—a scavenger hunt based on Russell's Boy Scout–esque troop from the movie *Up*. Players earn "badges" (stickers given out by cast members) for completing predefined activities throughout the park. For example, to earn the Gorilla Badge, you walk the Gorilla Falls Exploration Trail to observe how the primates behave, then mimic that behavior back to a cast member to show what you've seen.

Register for the game near the bridge from The Oasis to Discovery Island. You'll be given an instruction book and a map showing the park location for each badge to be earned.

Cast members have been specially trained for this game and can tailor the activities based on the age of the child playing: Small children might get an explanation about what deforestation means, for example, while older kids may have to figure out why tigers have stripes. It's tons of fun for kids and adults, and we play it every time we're in the park.

The Wilderness Explorer program is a big hit with kids, as a Melbourne, Australia, mom relates:

I think you should tell people more about the Wilderness Explorer program at Animal Kingdom. My son loved collecting the badges. It was the highlight of his day, but people need to know how much time it consumes. Much time is spent collecting badges, but it is well worth the investment of time! It's educational, too!

TOURING TIPS Activities are spread throughout the park, including areas to which many guests never venture. You have to ride specific attractions to earn certain badges, so using FastPass+ for those will save time.

◼ AFRICA

THE LARGEST OF ANIMAL KINGDOM'S LANDS, Africa is entered through **Harambe,** a Disney-fied version of a modern rural African town. A market is equipped with modern cash registers; dining options consist of a sit-down buffet, limited counter service, and snack stands. What distinguishes Harambe is its understatement: Far from the stereotypical great-white-hunter image of an African town, Harambe is definitely (and realistically) *not* exotic. The buildings, while interesting, are architecturally simple. Though better maintained and more idealized than the real McCoy, Disney's Harambe would be a lot more at home in Kenya than the Magic Kingdom's Main Street would be in Missouri.

Harambe serves as the gateway to the African veldt habitat, Animal Kingdom's largest and most ambitious zoological exhibit. Access to the veldt is via the **Kilimanjaro Safaris** attraction, at the end of Harambe's main drag near the fat-trunked baobab tree. Harambe is also the departure point for the train to **Rafiki's Planet Watch** and **Conservation Station** (the park's veterinary headquarters), as well as the home of a long-running live theatrical show. Finally, a new walkway over by Festival at the Lion King connects Africa with Pandora.

Festival of the Lion King (*FastPass+*) ★★★★

APPEAL BY AGE	PRESCHOOL ★★★★½	GRADE SCHOOL ★★★★½	TEENS ★★★★½
YOUNG ADULTS ★★★★½		OVER 30 ★★★★½	SENIORS ★★★★★

What it is Theater-in-the-round stage show. **Scope and scale** Major attraction. **When to go** Before 11 a.m., after 4 p.m., or use FastPass+. Check your park map or *Times Guide* for showtimes. **Authors' rating** Upbeat, energetic, and spectacular; not to be missed; ★★★★. **Duration of presentation** 30 minutes. **Preshow entertainment** None. **When to arrive** 20–30 minutes before showtime.

DESCRIPTION AND COMMENTS Inspired by the Disney animated feature, *Festival of the Lion King* is part stage show, part parade, part circus; it is located behind and to the left of Tusker House. Guests sit in four sets of bleachers surrounding the stage and organized into cheering sections, which are called on to make elephant, warthog, giraffe, and lion noises. (You won't be alone if you don't know what a giraffe or warthog sounds like.) There's a great deal of strutting around, some acrobatics, and a lot of singing and dancing. By our count, every tune from *The Lion King* is belted out and reprised several times—if you didn't know the words to the songs before the show, you definitely will after.

Unofficial Guide readers are almost unanimous in their praise of *Festival of the Lion King.* This letter from a Naples, Florida, mom is typical:

Festival of the Lion King *was the best thing we experienced at Animal Kingdom. The singers, dancers, fire twirlers, acrobats, and sets were spectacular.*

TOURING TIPS *Festival of the Lion King* is a big draw, so try to see the first show in the morning or one of the last two shows at night. For midday performances, you'll need to queue up at least 35–45 minutes before showtime; to minimize waiting in the hot sun, don't hop in line until cast members give the word to do so. The bleachers can make viewing difficult for the height-deficient—if you have small children or short adults in your party, try to snag a seat higher up. Rarely a good use of FastPass+.

Gorilla Falls Exploration Trail ★★★★

APPEAL BY AGE	PRESCHOOL ★★★★	GRADE SCHOOL ★★★★	TEENS ★★★★
YOUNG ADULTS ★★★★		OVER 30 ★★★★	SENIORS ★★★★½

What it is Walk-through zoological exhibit. **Scope and scale** Major attraction. **When to go** Anytime. **Authors' rating** ★★★★. **Duration of tour** About 20–25 minutes.

DESCRIPTION AND COMMENTS As the trail winds between the domain of two troops of lowland gorillas, it's hard to see what, if anything, separates you from the primates. Also on the trail is a hippo pool with an underwater viewing area, plus a naked-mole-rat exhibit. A highlight is an exotic-bird aviary so craftily designed that you can barely tell you're in an enclosure.

TOURING TIPS The Gorilla Falls Exploration Trail is lush, beautiful, and jammed to the gills with people much of the time. Guests exiting Kilimanjaro Safaris can choose between returning to Harambe or walking the Gorilla Falls Exploration Trail. Many opt for the trail. Thus, when the Safaris are operating at full tilt, it spews hundreds of guests every couple of minutes onto the Exploration Trail. The animals, as well as their natural-habitat enclosures, are pretty nifty if you can fight your way close enough to see them.

Your only real chance for enjoying it is to walk through before 10 a.m.— that is, before the Safaris hit full stride—or after 4:30 p.m.

Another strategy, especially if you're more into the wildlife than the thrill rides, is to schedule a FastPass+ reservation for the Safaris 60–90 minutes after the park opens. That's long enough for an uncrowded, leisurely tour of the Gorilla Falls Exploration Trail and a quick snack before you go on safari.

Kilimanjaro Safaris (FastPass+) ★★★★★

APPEAL BY AGE PRESCHOOL ★★★★½ GRADE SCHOOL ★★★★½ TEENS ★★★★½
YOUNG ADULTS ★★★★½   OVER 30 ★★★★½   SENIORS ★★★★★

What it is Simulated ride through an African wildlife reservation. **Scope and scale** Super-headliner. **When to go** As soon as the park opens or in the 2 hours before closing, or use FastPass+. **Authors' rating** Not to be missed; ★★★★★. **Duration of ride** About 20 minutes. **Average wait in line per 100 people ahead of you** 4 minutes; assumes full-capacity operation with 18-second dispatch interval. **Loading speed** Fast.

DESCRIPTION AND COMMENTS Animal Kingdom's premier zoological attraction, Kilimanjaro Safaris offers an exceptionally realistic, albeit brief, imitation of an actual African photo safari. Thirty-two guests at a time board tall, open safari vehicles and are dispatched into a simulated African veldt habitat. Animals such as zebras, wildebeests, impalas, Thomson's gazelles, giraffes, and even rhinos roam apparently free, while predators such as lions, as well as potentially dangerous large animals like hippos, are separated from both prey and guests by all-but-invisible, natural-appearing barriers. Although the animals have more than 100 acres of savanna, woodland, streams, and rocky hills to call home, careful placement of water holes, forage, and salt licks ensures that the critters are hanging out by the road when safari vehicles roll by.

Having traveled in Kenya and Tanzania, I (Bob) can tell you that Disney has done an amazing job of replicating the sub-Saharan east-African landscape. The main difference that a Kenyan or Tanzanian would notice is that Disney's version is greener and, generally speaking, less barren. As on a real African safari, what animals you see, and how many, is pretty much a

---

DISNEY DISH WITH JIM HILL

TALL ORDER FOR A TOY Disney's zookeepers like to find fun new ways to keep their animals from getting bored. For the giraffes, they dangle a balloon from the ceiling of their barn. The giraffes use the balloon to practice sparring with their necks, something giraffes do in the wild to establish their place in their herd.

matter of luck. We've experienced Kilimanjaro Safaris more than 100 times and had a different experience on each trip.

Winding through the Safaris is Disney's **Wild Africa Trek,** a behind-the-scenes tour of Animal Kingdom that takes you into several of Kilimanjaro Safaris' animal enclosures. As you drive past the hippo pool or over the crocodile pool, look up for a series of rope bridges towering far above the ground—you may see Trekkers on tour. See page 745 of Part Fifteen for a complete description.

Animal Kingdom began nighttime safari tours in mid-2016 to coincide with the new nighttime shows and longer park hours. Before the first safari truck rolled into the setting sun, Disney spent more than a year acclimating the existing animals, and new nocturnal species such as hyenas, to life in a theme park. More impressive, though, was the baseball stadium–size wall of graphics displays they installed at the far end of the tour's savanna grasslands. When turned on late in the day, the displays are programmed to simulate the dusk of a setting sun for hours on end. It provides theme park guests enough light to see those animals still roaming around.

We tried the new nighttime safari as soon as it opened in mid-2016. The pace is slower, and some of the animals—rhinos, on our tour—were noticeably more active at night. But it was also almost impossible to see other animals, such as the hippos, crocs, and elephants. We think the nighttime safari is an excellent second visit to the attraction, after you've seen it during daylight.

A Wilmington, Delaware, man had a different experience:

Animal Kingdom at night was the hit of our trip, and the Kilimanjaro Safaris ride at night was great. We saw more animals in action than we had ever seen in the daytime, and the nighttime added just a hint of danger to the entire proceeding that made it fun. Also, we ate at Tiffins in the AK, and it was outstanding, from the service to the décor (including the Nomad Lounge) to the food—best meal ever at WDW, even better than California Grill.

TOURING TIPS Kilimanjaro Safaris is one of Animal Kingdom's busiest attractions, along with Expedition Everest and the two new Pandora attractions. From a touring standpoint, this is good news: By distributing guests evenly throughout the park, Expedition Everest makes it unnecessary to run to Kilimanjaro Safaris first thing in the morning. Our Animal Kingdom touring plan has you obtain FastPass+ reservations for the Safaris in the afternoon—while you wait for your FastPass+ return window, you'll have plenty of time to eat and tour the rest of Africa.

Waits for Kilimanjaro Safaris diminish in late afternoon, sometimes as early as 3:30 p.m. but more commonly somewhat later.

If you want to take photos, keep in mind that the vehicle isn't guaranteed to stop at any location, although the drivers try their best to do so when big animals are sighted. Be prepared to snap at any time. As for the ride, it's not that rough. Finally, the only thing that a young child might find scary is crossing an "old bridge" that seems to collapse under your truck.

RAFIKI'S PLANET WATCH

THIS AREA ISN'T REALLY a "land" or an attraction. Our best guess is that Disney uses the name as an umbrella for Conservation Station (the animal-care center), the petting zoo, and the environmental exhibits accessible from Harambe via the Wildlife Express Train. Presumably, Disney hopes that invoking Rafiki (a beloved character from *The Lion King*) will stimulate guests to make the effort to check out things in this far-flung outpost of the park.

Conservation Station and Affection Section ★★★½

What it is Behind-the-scenes educational exhibit and petting zoo. **Scope and scale** Minor attraction. **When to go** Anytime. **Special comments** Opens 30 minutes after the rest of the park. **Authors' rating** Not bad; ★★★½. **Probable waiting time** None.

DESCRIPTION AND COMMENTS Conservation Station is Animal Kingdom's veterinary and conservation headquarters. On the perimeter of the African section of the park, Conservation Station is, strictly speaking, a backstage working facility. Here guests can meet wildlife experts, observe some of the Station's ongoing projects, and learn about the behind-the-scenes operations of the park. The Station includes a rehabilitation area for injured animals and a nursery for recently born (or hatched) critters. Vets and other experts are on hand to answer questions.

While there are several permanent exhibits, including Affection Section (an animal-petting area), what you see at Conservation Station will largely depend on what's going on when you arrive. On most days when we've visited, there isn't enough happening to justify waiting in line twice (coming and going) for the train.

Most of our readers tell us that Conservation Station isn't worth the hassle. A Tinley Park, Illinois, mom writes:

Skip Conservation Station. Between the train ride to get to it and being there, we wasted a precious 1½ hours!

A Denver family had a better experience:

We really enjoyed Conservation Station. We saw a 13-foot python eating a rat!

And a reader from Kent in the United Kingdom was amused by both the goings-on and the other guests:

The most memorable part of Animal Kingdom for me was watching a veterinary surgeon and his team at Conservation Station perform an operation on a rat snake that had inadvertently swallowed a golf ball, presumably believing it to be an egg! This operation caused at least one onlooker to pass out.

You can access Conservation Station by taking the Wildlife Express Train directly from Harambe. To return to the center of the park, continue the loop from Conservation Station back to Harambe.

TOURING TIPS To enjoy Conservation Station, you have to invest a little effort and be inquisitive. Because it's so removed from the rest of the park, you'll never bump into it unless you take the train.

Habitat Habit!

DESCRIPTION AND COMMENTS On the pedestrian path between the train station and Conservation Station, Habitat Habit! consists of a tiny collection of signs about wildlife and a few animals. Park maps call it an attraction, which we find absurd.

Wildlife Express Train ★★

What it is Scenic railroad ride to Rafiki's Planet Watch and Conservation Station. **Scope and scale** Minor attraction. **When to go** Anytime. **Special comments** Opens 30 minutes after rest of park; last train departs at 4:30 p.m. **Authors' rating** Hohum; ★★. **Duration of ride** About 5–7 minutes one-way. **Average wait in line per 100 people ahead of you** 9 minutes. **Loading speed** Moderate.

DESCRIPTION AND COMMENTS This ride snakes behind the African wildlife reserve as it makes its loop connecting Harambe to Rafiki's Planet Watch and Conservation Station. En route, you see the nighttime enclosures for the animals that populate Kilimanjaro Safaris. Similarly, returning to Harambe, you see the backstage areas of Asia. Regardless of which direction you're heading, the sights aren't especially stimulating.

TOURING TIPS Most guests embark for Conservation Station after experiencing Kilimanjaro Safaris and the Gorilla Falls Exploration Trail. Thus, the train begins to get crowded between 10 and 11 a.m.

ASIA

CROSSING THE ASIA BRIDGE FROM DISCOVERY ISLAND, you enter Asia through the village of **Anandapur,** a veritable collage of Asian themes inspired by the architecture and ruins of India, Thailand, Indonesia, and Nepal. Situated near the bank of the Discovery River and surrounded by lush vegetation, Anandapur provides access to a gibbon exhibit and Asia's two feature attractions: the **Kali River Rapids** whitewater raft ride and **Expedition Everest.** Also in Asia is *Flights of Wonder,* a bird show.

Expedition Everest—yep, another mountain, and at 200 feet, the tallest in Florida—is a super-headliner roller coaster. You board an old mountain railway destined for the foot of Mount Everest and end up racing both forward and backward through caverns and frigid canyons en route to paying a social call on the Abominable Snowman. Expedition Everest is billed as a "family thrill ride," which means simply that it's more like Big Thunder Mountain Railroad than Rock 'n' Roller Coaster.

The nighttime *Rivers of Light* show (see page 629) combines music, water screens, video projections, and more on the Discovery River, with sections around Asia and DinoLand U.S.A.

Expedition Everest *(FastPass+)* ★★★★½

APPEAL BY AGE PRESCHOOL ★★½   GRADE SCHOOL ★★★★½   TEENS ★★★★★
YOUNG ADULTS ★★★★★   OVER 30 ★★★★★   SENIORS ★★★★

What it is High-speed outdoor roller coaster through Nepalese mountain village. **Scope and scale** Super-headliner. **When to go** Before 9:30 a.m. or after 3 p.m., or use FastPass+. **Special comments** 44" minimum height requirement; switching-off option provided (see page 439). **Authors' rating** Contains some of the park's most stunning visual elements; not to be missed; ★★★★½. **Duration of ride** 3½ minutes. **Average wait in line per 100 people ahead of you** Just under 4 minutes; assumes 2 tracks operating. **Loading speed** Moderate–fast.

DESCRIPTION AND COMMENTS The first true roller coaster in Animal Kingdom, Expedition Everest vies with Flight of Passage for the park's longest waits in line—and for good reason. Your journey begins in an elaborate waiting area modeled after a Nepalese village; then you board an old train headed for the top of Mount Everest. Throughout the waiting area are posted notes from previous expeditions, some with cryptic observations regarding a mysterious creature said to guard the mountain. These ominous signs are ignored (as if you have a choice!), resulting in a high-speed encounter with the Abominable Snowman himself.

The ride consists of tight turns (some while traveling backward), hills, and dips, but no loops or inversions. From your departure at the loading station through your first high-speed descent, you'll see some of the most spectacular panoramas available in Walt Disney World. On a clear day, you can see the buildings of Coronado Springs Resort, Epcot's Spaceship Earth, and possibly downtown Orlando. But look quickly, because you'll immediately be propelled, projectile-like, through the inner and outer reaches of the mountain. The final drop and last few turns are among the best coaster effects Disney has ever designed.

The coaster reaches a top speed of around 50 mph, just about twice that of Space Mountain, so expect to see the usual warnings for health and safety. The first few seats of these vehicles offer the best front-seat experience of any Disney coaster, indoor or out. If at all possible, ask to sit up front. Also, look for the animal poop on display in the FastPass+ return line—a deliberate attempt at verisimilitude, or did Disney run out of money for ride props and use whatever they could find? You decide.

As you might expect of a super-headliner attraction, Expedition Everest is the subject of much reader mail. A Seattle family rated Expedition Everest four thumbs up:

Expedition Everest is tremendous. It has enough surprises and runaway speed to make it one of the more enjoyable thrill rides in the whole Orlando area.

A Macon, Georgia, teen recruited the aged:

Expedition Everest was so smooooth! I went right out and brought my granny back to ride it. She didn't throw up or anything!

Beating the morning crowds to Expedition Everest is also a hot topic. From a Yonkers, New York, man:

At opening, we went toward DinoLand U.S.A. and followed the path around the lake to Everest. We arrived about 90 seconds ahead of the crowd being walked in and were the first to ride. Upon exiting, we noticed the line was already enormous.

A Brookfield, Connecticut, reader had great luck with the singles line:

The single-rider line at Expedition Everest is amazing! I rode seven times in a row. I think my longest wait was 3–5 minutes, but often I just walked on!

TOURING TIPS If you can get a FastPass+ for Flight of Passage but not Expedition Everest, then ride Expedition Everest as soon as the park opens. Other strategies for cutting your wait here include using the single-rider line, and riding during the last hour the park is open.

Flights of Wonder ★★★★

APPEAL BY AGE	PRESCHOOL ★★★★	GRADE SCHOOL ★★★★	TEENS ★★★★
YOUNG ADULTS ★★★★		OVER 30 ★★★★½	SENIORS ★★★★½

What it is Stadium show about birds. **Scope and scale** Major attraction. **When to go** Anytime. **Special comment** Performance times listed in handout park map or *Times Guide*. **Authors' rating** Unique; ★★★★. **Duration of presentation** 30 minutes. **Preshow entertainment** None. **When to arrive** 20–30 minutes before showtime.

DESCRIPTION AND COMMENTS *Flights of Wonder* is well paced and showcases a surprising number of bird species. The focus is on the natural talents and characteristics of the various species, so don't expect to see parrots riding bicycles—the birds' natural behaviors far surpass any tricks learned from humans. A Brattleboro, Vermont, reader found *Flights of Wonder* especially compelling, writing:

The ornithologist guide is not only a wealth of information but a talented, comedic entertainer. The birds are thrilling, and we especially appreciated the fact that their antics were not the results of training against the grain but actual survival techniques the birds use in the wild.

Flights of Wonder exceeded the expectations of a Colorado Springs family with two elementary-school-age kids:

A coworker with kids the same age as ours said her kids loved Flights of Wonder. *Midway through the show I stopped taking pictures of the birds and began taking pictures of the expressions of amazement and joy on the faces of my kids and husband.*

TOURING TIPS *Flights of Wonder* plays at the stadium near the Asia Bridge on the walkway into Asia. Though the stadium is covered, it's not air-conditioned; thus, early-morning and late-afternoon performances are more comfortable. To play it safe, get to the stadium about 10–15 minutes before showtime.

Kali River Rapids *(FastPass+)* ★★★½

Wet

What it is Whitewater raft ride. **Scope and scale** Headliner. **When to go** First or last hour the park is open, or use FastPass+. **Special comments** You're guaranteed to get wet; opens 30 minutes after the rest of the park; 38" minimum height requirement; switching-off option provided (see page 439). **Authors' rating** Short, scenic, and soaking; ★★★½. **Duration of ride** About 5 minutes. **Average wait in line per 100 people ahead of you** 5 minutes. **Loading speed** Moderate.

DESCRIPTION AND COMMENTS Whitewater raft rides have been a hot-weather favorite of theme park patrons for more than 25 years. The ride itself consists of an unguided trip down an artificial river in a circular rubber raft with a top-mounted platform seating 12 people. The raft essentially floats free in the current and is washed downstream through rapids and waves. Because the river is fairly wide, with numerous currents, eddies, and obstacles, there's no telling exactly where the raft will drift. Thus, each trip is different and exciting.

What distinguishes Kali River Rapids from other theme park raft rides is Disney's trademark attention to visual detail. Where many raft rides essentially plunge down a concrete ditch, Kali River Rapids flows through a dense rainforest and past waterfalls, temple ruins, and bamboo thickets, emerging into a cleared area where greedy loggers have ravaged the forest, and finally drifting back under the tropical canopy as the river cycles back to Anandapur. Along the way, your raft runs a gauntlet of raging cataracts, logjams, and other dangers.

The queuing area, which winds through an ancient Southeast Asian temple, is one of the most striking and visually interesting settings of any Disney attraction. And though the sights on the raft trip itself are also first-class, the attraction is marginal in two important respects. First, it's only about 3½ minutes on the water, and second, well . . . it's a weenie ride. Sure, you get wet, but otherwise the drops and rapids aren't all that exciting, as this Kansas family points out:

It was boiling hot, so we were happy about the prospect of being drenched. At the end, we all looked at each other and said, "Is that IT?" We couldn't believe we'd stood in line, sweating half to death, for 75 minutes just for that.

How wet do you get? A Plymouth, Michigan, reader has the answer:

Rather than just getting a little wet like on Splash Mountain, you get soaked—not the fun kind of wet. Poncho sales were brisk the day we were there.

TOURING TIPS Kali River Rapids is hugely popular on hot summer days. Ride during the first or last hour the park is open or use FastPass+. Again, you'll probably get drenched—we recommend wearing shorts to the park and bringing along a jumbo trash bag or can liner, as well as a smaller plastic bag. Before boarding the raft, take off your socks and punch a hole in your jumbo bag for your head. Though you can also cut holes for your arms, you'll probably stay drier with your arms inside the bag. Use the smaller plastic bag to wrap around your shoes. If you're worried about mussing your 'do, bring a third bag for your head.

A Shaker Heights, Ohio, family who donned our *couture de garbage* discovered that staying dry on Kali River Rapids is not without its social costs:

Cast members and the other people in our raft looked at us like we'd just beamed down from Mars. (One cast member asked whether we needed wet suits and snorkels.) Plus, we didn't cut arm holes in our trash bags because we thought we'd stay drier that way—problem was, once we sat down we couldn't fasten our seat belts. After a lot of wiggling and adjusting and helping each other, we finally got belted in, and off we went, looking like sacks of fertilizer with little heads poking out. Very embarrassing, but we stayed nice and dry.

A family from Humble, Texas, who rode early in the morning on a cool day, shares this:

Our plan hit a definite wall upon experiencing Kali River Rapids as number two on the schedule. We didn't read about the precautions for this ride in your book until after we rode. The 6-year-old and Mom were COMPLETELY drenched—so much so that we had to leave the park and go back to our room at Port Orleans to change clothes. Since the temperature was around 60 degrees that morning, we were pretty miserable by the time we got back to our room. Needless to say, our schedule was shot by then.

Using FastPass+ to ride later in the day would have been a better option in this case.

Kali River Rapids offers free 2-hour locker rental (to the left of the attraction entrance, near the restrooms). Store a change of clothes in these to keep dry. Alternatively, wear as little as the law and Disney allow. If you're wearing closed shoes, prop your feet up above the bottom of the raft—slogging around in wet shoes and socks is a surefire recipe for blisters.

Maharajah Jungle Trek ★★★★

APPEAL BY AGE	PRESCHOOL ★★★★	GRADE SCHOOL ★★★★	TEENS ★★★★
YOUNG ADULTS ★★★★		OVER 30 ★★★★	SENIORS ★★★★½

What it is Walk-through zoological exhibit. **Scope and scale** Headliner. **When to go** Anytime. **Special comment** Opens 30 minutes after the rest of the park. **Authors' rating** A standard-setter for natural-habitat design; ★★★★. **Duration of tour** About 20–30 minutes.

DESCRIPTION AND COMMENTS This walk is similar to the Gorilla Falls Exploration Trail but with an Asian setting and Asian animals. You start with Komodo dragons and work up to Malayan flying foxes. Next is a cave with fruit bats. Ruins of the maharajah's palace provide the setting for Bengal tigers. From the top of a parapet in the palace you can view a herd of blackbuck antelope and Asian deer. The trek concludes with an aviary.

Labyrinthine, overgrown, and elaborately detailed, the temple ruin would be a compelling attraction even without the animals. Throw in a few bats, bucks, and Bengals, and you're in for a treat. Most readers, such as this Washington, DC, couple, agree:

The Maharajah Jungle Trek was absolutely amazing. We were able to see all the animals, which were awake by that time (9:30 a.m.), including the elusive tigers. The part of the trek with the birds was fabulous; you could spot hundreds, some of which were eating on the ground a mere 3 feet away from us.

TOURING TIPS The Jungle Trek doesn't get as jammed up as the Gorilla Falls Exploration Trail and is a good choice for midday touring when most other attractions are crowded. The downside, of course, is that the exhibit showcases tigers, bats, and other creatures that might not be as active in the heat of the day as mad dogs and Englishmen.

Rivers of Light ★★★½

APPEAL BY AGE	PRESCHOOL ★★★½		GRADE SCHOOL ★★★★	TEENS ★★★★
YOUNG ADULTS ★★★★		OVER 30 ★★★★		SENIORS ★★★★½

What it is Nighttime spectacular. **Scope and scale** Major attraction. **When to go** Check your *Times Guide* for showtimes. **Authors' rating** Pleasant enough; ★★★½. **Duration of show** About 15 minutes.

DESCRIPTION AND COMMENTS *Rivers of Light* is Animal Kingdom's first nighttime spectacular. Set on the lagoon surrounded by Asia, DinoLand U.S.A., and Discovery Island, it uses water screens, fountains, lasers, music, boats, floats, and fire to show the colorful world of animals and nature.

The show begins with four lotus-flower lanterns floating on the lagoon. They're soon joined by shamans on what looks like a Chinese junk. The shamans conjure the forces of fire and water to reveal the majesty of the natural world, mostly as video projections on a huge water screen at the back of the lagoon. The highlight is the appearance of four immense, color-changing floats in the shape of a tiger, a turtle, an elephant, and an owl.

Rivers of Light's debut was scheduled for April 2016. However, technical issues and (we hear) needed story concept rewrites pushed the show's opening back by 10 months, to February 2017. Disney solved the technical problems by dropping the nonworking elements from the show, and the story problems by cutting out the slower parts. That reduced the show's running time by almost a third—from around 22 minutes to about 15. Unfortunately, those now-missing elements were critical to many scenes that now appear unclear and dull.

For example, the original show was supposed to include around a hundred small, floating lanterns with independent navigation systems to guide them around the lagoon. These lanterns, we're told, were going to change color and assemble themselves into different shapes on the water in response to the shamans' incantations—armadillos, amoebas, and so on.

However, Disney was never able to get the guidance systems working properly, so the entire effect was cut. The shamans' parts, however, and the rest of scene were left intact. What remains is a vast, empty, black lagoon stretching out in front of you, and a tiny shaman figure in the distance urgently gesturing about . . . something you don't see.

Beyond that, the wind patterns on the lagoon sometimes blur many of the videos projected onto the water screens. Our show notes include snippets such as "Lion? Grizzly? Rhino? Puppy?" written as we tried to determine what creature was on display. Disney seems to have addressed some of that concern by swapping out photorealistic images with big shadow puppets and abstract animal shapes, and that's an improvement. But the remaining images are often fuzzy enough to trigger a mental reminder to visit the eye doctor when you get home.

Another concern is the pacing. Because the floats and boats need to move into different positions for each scene, the onstage transitions are slow, especially for a generation raised on half-second quick-cut videos. It also points out how much Disney's other parks rely on fireworks to paper over the slower parts of their nighttime shows. And unlike *IllumiNations* (Disney's most ambitious and longest-running nighttime storytelling), *Rivers of Light* relies on too-familiar images and music to be memorable.

That said, the show's use of color, water, and animal imagery will appeal to younger children and anyone wanting something pretty to look at to wrap up a day at the park. Disney's hoping that's good enough for now.

Animal Kingdom offers a *Rivers of Light* dining package that combines dinner at one of the park's sit-down restaurants with guaranteed seats for the show. This is a worthwhile alternative if day-of FastPasses aren't available, especially if you were already planning to eat at Tiffins.

TOURING TIPS *Rivers of Light* is staged in the middle of the Discovery River, with seating split in two sections: on the shores of Asia in front of Expedition Everest, and along the banks of DinoLand U.S.A. in front of *Finding Nemo—The Musical*. Half of the show's 5,000 seats are reserved for Fast-Pass+, with very limited, partially obstructed viewing areas around the river. Arrive about 45 minutes in advance to get a standby seat.

To help meet demand, Disney may run two shows on busy nights, similar to the schedule for *Fantasmic!* at DHS. Still, *Rivers of Light* has half as many seats as *Fantasmic!*, despite Animal Kingdom's drawing more guests than the Studios. There may be many nights when people who want to see the show simply cannot. If seeing *Rivers of Light* is a must, use one of your three advance FastPasses, or get the dining package.

Finally, the area's prevailing winds are from the south and east, so mist from the show's fountains should head away from the seating areas. If the forecast calls for winds from the north or west, especially during colder months, bring ponchos or blankets just in case.

DINOLAND U.S.A.

THIS MOST TYPICALLY DISNEY of Animal Kingdom's lands is a cross between an anthropological dig and a quirky roadside attraction. Accessible via the bridge from Discovery Island, DinoLand U.S.A. is home to a children's play area, a nature trail, a 1,500-seat amphitheater, and **Dinosaur,** one of Animal Kingdom's three thrill rides.

Also in DinoLand are a couple of natural-history exhibits, including **Dino-Sue,** an exact replica of the largest, most complete *Tyrannosaurus rex* skeleton discovered to date. Named after fossil hunter Sue Hendrickson, the replica (like the original) is 40 feet long and 13 feet tall. It doesn't dance, sing, or whistle, but it will get your attention nonetheless.

The Boneyard ★★★

APPEAL BY AGE	PRESCHOOL ★★★★★	GRADE SCHOOL ★★★★½	TEENS ★★½
YOUNG ADULTS ★★½	OVER 30 ★★★		SENIORS ★★½

What it is Elaborate playground. **Scope and scale** Diversion. **When to go** Anytime. **Special comment** Opens 30 minutes after the rest of the park. **Authors' rating** Stimulating fun for children; ★★★. **Duration of visit** Varies. **Probable waiting time** None.

DESCRIPTION AND COMMENTS Arranged in the form of a rambling open-air dig site, this elaborately themed playground is particularly appealing to kids age 12 and younger, but visually appealing to all ages. It has a ropes course and caves to play in, as well as slides, swings, and climbing areas. It's decorated with dinosaur skeletons and has a sandpit where your kids can scrounge for bones and fossils.

TOURING TIPS Not the most pristine of Disney attractions, but certainly one where younger children will want to spend some time. And aside from being dirty, or at least sandy, The Boneyard gets mighty hot in the Florida sun. Keep your kids well hydrated, and drag them into the shade from time to time. Try to save the playground until after you've experienced the main attractions. Because The Boneyard is so close to the center of the park, it's easy to drop in whenever your kids get antsy. While the little ones clamber around on giant femurs and ribs, you can sip a tall cool one in the shade (still keeping an eye on them, of course).

As a Michigan family attests, kids love The Boneyard:

The highlight for our kids was The Boneyard, especially the dig site. They just kept digging and digging to uncover the bones of the woolly mammoth.

Be aware, however, that The Boneyard rambles over about a half-acre and is multistoried, making it easy to lose sight of a small child in the playground. Fortunately, there's only one entrance and exit. A mother of two from Stillwater, Minnesota, found the playground too large for her liking:

If you're a parent who likes to have your eyes on your kids at all times, you won't like The Boneyard. Kids climb to the top of the slides, then you can't see them and you don't know what chute they'll be exiting from.

From the mother of a 3-year-old:

If your child is quite young, make sure you have two people in the Boneyard— one to help them up all the stairs, the other to stay at the bottom and watch them as they exit the slide. By the time you get from the top of the structure to the bottom, they're off who-knows-where getting into mischief of one kind of another without adult supervision.

Dinosaur *(FastPass+)* ★★★★

APPEAL BY AGE	PRESCHOOL ★★½	GRADE SCHOOL ★★★★	TEENS ★★★★½
YOUNG ADULTS ★★★★½		OVER 30 ★★★★	SENIORS ★★★★

What it is Motion-simulator dark ride. **Scope and scale** Headliner. **When to go** Before 10:30 a.m., after 4:30 p.m., or use FastPass+. **Special comment** 40″ minimum height requirement; switching-off option provided (see page 439). **Authors' rating** Not to be missed; ★★★★. **Duration of ride** 3½ minutes. **Average wait in line per 100 people ahead of you** 3 minutes; assumes full-capacity operation with 18-second dispatch interval. **Loading speed** Fast.

DESCRIPTION AND COMMENTS Dinosaur is a combination track ride and motion simulator. In addition to moving along a cleverly hidden track, the ride vehicle also bucks and pitches (the simulator part) in sync with the visuals and special effects.

The plot has you traveling back in time on a mission of rescue and conservation. Your objective: to haul back a living dinosaur before the species becomes extinct. Whoever is operating the clock, however, cuts it a little close, and you arrive on the prehistoric scene just as a giant asteroid is hurtling toward Earth. General mayhem ensues as you evade carnivorous predators, catch Barney, and get the heck out of Dodge before the asteroid hits.

Dinosaur serves up nonstop action from beginning to end, with brilliant visual effects. Elaborate even by Disney standards, its tense, frenetic ride is embellished by the entire Imagineering arsenal of high-tech gimmickry.

To its credit, Disney is unafraid to keep Dinosaur a dark, fast ride. A mother from Kansasville, Wisconsin, liked it a lot:

Dinosaur is the best ride at WDW. Our group of 10, ranging in age from 65 (grandma) to 8 (grandson), immediately—and unanimously!—got back in line immediately after finishing.

That said, the menacing dinosaurs, along with the overall intensity of the experience, make Dinosaur a no-go for younger kids, as this Michigan family discovered:

Our 7-year-old son withstood every ride Disney threw at him, from Space Mountain to Tower of Terror. Dinosaur, however, did him in. By the end, he was riding with his head down, scared to look around.

TOURING TIPS Disney situated Dinosaur in such a remote corner of the park that guests have to poke around to find it. This, in conjunction with the overwhelming popularity of Pandora's new rides, plus Kilimanjaro Safaris and Expedition Everest, makes Dinosaur the easiest super-headliner attraction at Disney World to get on. Lines should be relatively light through midmorning, and more FastPasses should be available for day-of use.

Primeval Whirl (*FastPass+*) ★★★

APPEAL BY AGE	PRESCHOOL ★★★	GRADE SCHOOL ★★★★	TEENS ★★★★
YOUNG ADULTS ★★★½		OVER 30 ★★★½	SENIORS ★★★

What it is Small coaster. **Scope and scale** Minor attraction. **When to go** First or last hour the park is open or use FastPass+. **Special comment** 48" minimum height requirement; switching-off option provided (see page 439). **Authors' rating** "Wild mouse" on steroids; ★★★. **Duration of ride** Almost 2½ minutes. **Average wait in line per 100 people ahead of you** 4½ minutes. **Loading speed** Slow.

DESCRIPTION AND COMMENTS A small coaster with short drops and curves, Primeval Whirl runs through the jaws of a dinosaur, among other things. What makes this coaster different is that the cars also spin. You can't control the spinning—it starts and stops according to how the ride is programmed. Sometimes the spin is braked to a jarring halt after half a revolution, and sometimes it's allowed to make one or two complete turns. The complete spins are fun, but the screeching-stop half-spins are almost painful. If you subtract the time it takes to ratchet up the first hill, the actual ride time is about 90 seconds.

A Queens, New York, reader thinks Primeval Whirl is more evil than prime:

Primeval Whirl is a terrible ride on so many levels. My daughter nicknamed it "Primeval Hurl."

TOURING TIPS As with Space Mountain, Primeval Whirl is duplicated side-by-side, but with only one queue. When it runs smoothly, about 700 people per side can whirl in an hour—a goodly number for this type of attraction, but not enough to preclude long waits on busy-to-moderate days. If you want to ride, try to get on before 10 a.m.

Theater in the Wild / *Finding Nemo—The Musical*
(FastPass+) ★★★★

APPEAL BY AGE PRESCHOOL ★★★★½ GRADE SCHOOL ★★★★½ TEENS ★★★★
YOUNG ADULTS ★★★★   OVER 30 ★★★★½   SENIORS ★★★★½

What it is Enclosed venue for live stage shows. **Scope and scale** Major attraction.
When to go Anytime. **Special comment** Performance times are listed in the handout park map or *Times Guide*. **Authors' rating** Not to be missed; ★★★★. **Duration
of presentation** About 35 minutes. **When to arrive** 30 minutes before showtime.

DESCRIPTION AND COMMENTS *Finding Nemo—The Musical* is arguably the most
elaborate live show in any Disney World theme park. Incorporating dancing, special effects, and sophisticated digital backdrops of the undersea
world, it features on-stage human performers retelling Nemo's story with
colorful, larger-than-life puppets. To be fair, "puppets" doesn't adequately
convey the size or detail of these props, many of which are as big as a car
and require two people to manipulate.

A few scenes, such as one in which Nemo's mom is eaten, may be too
intense for some very small children. Some of the midshow musical numbers slow the pace, so the main concern for parents is whether the kids can
sit still for an entire show. With that in mind, we advise parents to catch a
pre-lunchtime performance—around 11:30 a.m. would be great. If the kids
get restless, you can either leave the show and have lunch, or head back to
your hotel for a break.

New Jersey drama critics have their own way with words, as this family
of five demonstrates:

The Finding Nemo *musical is da bomb! The musical was amazing! It's a flaw-
less package of puppetry, effects, music, and lots of Disney magic!*

TOURING TIPS To get a seat, show up 20–25 minutes in advance for morning
and late-afternoon shows, and 30–35 minutes in advance for shows
scheduled between noon and 4:30 p.m. Access to the theater is via a relatively narrow pedestrian path—if you arrive as the previous show is letting out, you'll feel like a salmon swimming upstream. *Finding Nemo* is
rarely a good use of FastPass+.

TriceraTop Spin ★★

APPEAL BY AGE PRESCHOOL ★★★★½ GRADE SCHOOL ★★★★ TEENS ★★★
YOUNG ADULTS ★★★   OVER 30 ★★★   SENIORS ★★★

What it is Hub-and-spoke midway ride. **Scope and scale** Minor attraction. **When to
go** Before noon or after 3 p.m. **Authors' rating** Dumbo's prehistoric forebear; ★★.
Duration of ride 1½ minutes. **Average wait in line per 100 people ahead of you**
10 minutes. **Loading speed** Slow.

DESCRIPTION AND COMMENTS Another Dumbo-like ride for young children.
Here you spin around a central hub until a dinosaur pops out of the top
of the hub. You would think Disney could come up with something a bit
more creative.

TOURING TIPS Come back later if the wait exceeds 20 minutes.

PANDORA—*The World of Avatar*

WHEN DISNEY ANNOUNCED IN 1994 that it was building Animal
Kingdom, one of the lands it was supposed to contain was called Beastly

Kingdom. The brainchild of a young Imagineer named Joe Rohde, it was envisioned as a land dedicated to mythological creatures, from unicorns and the Loch Ness Monster to flying dragons, all seen from hedge mazes, roller coasters and elaborate river voyages. Besides continuing the animal theme, Beastly Kingdom was going to be how Disney built traditional rides here, without having to worry about how to incorporate living things into the mix.

Rohde's plans for Beastly Kingdom were too ambitious to fit in the park's construction budget. The entire idea was quietly axed by 1996. When Animal Kingdom opened in 1998, the area that was to be Beastly Kingdom was called "Camp Minnie-Mickey." Instead of thrill rides and fantastic beasts, visitors got an elaborate *Festival of the Lion King* stage show, a modest amphitheater production about wildlife and nature featuring Pocahontas, and a jungle-themed meet-and-greet area. Rohde's dream got put in the warehouse of unbuilt Disney attractions.

Unbeknownst to Rohde, halfway around the world, a single mother in Edinburgh, Scotland, named Joanne was putting the finishing touches on her first book. Along with making her a billionaire, the book—*Harry Potter and the Sorcerer's Stone*—was to bring back the core of Rohde's Beastly Kingdom idea.

Part Thirteen of this book tells how Universal Orlando—Disney's direct competitor—opened Harry Potter's Hogsmeade Village in 2010 and Diagon Alley in 2014. Together they were the most ambitious, elaborate, and detailed theme park environments anyone had ever seen. To say that these lands, Harry Potter's devoted fans, and J. K. Rowling's prodigious output put the fear of God into Disney executives is to undersell just slightly their more immediate concern of lost tourism revenue.

The problem that Disney faced was that only a handful of writers like Rowling can produce globally beloved stories worth billions of dollars: Steven Spielberg, George Lucas, Peter Jackson, and James Cameron are on the short list. With Spielberg and Lucas nearing retirement, however, and Peter Jackson reportedly noncommittal, Disney signed Cameron to a theme park development deal for his *Avatar* film franchise in September 2011.

That deal puzzled many Disney theme park fans, including us. Yes, *Avatar* is the second-highest-grossing film of all time (adjusted for inflation, *Gone with the Wind* is No. 1), having earned more than $3 billion in ticket sales since its release in 2009. But it did so because of its then-revolutionary 3-D digital effects, not its writing. *Avatar,* we joked, was the film everyone saw about characters nobody liked. For Disney, whose motto had always been "It all begins with a story," building rides based on *Avatar* would be its own kind of alien experience.

Disney tapped Rohde, now an industry legend, to bring *Avatar* to life at Animal Kingdom. Camp Minnie-Mickey was demolished to make way, its *Festival of the Lion King* stage show moved to the park's Africa section. Five years of construction ensued—long enough for Universal to build a couple more hotels, several new rides, and an entire water park. Disney's $500 million gamble on the *Avatar* franchise seemed riskier by the day.

IS PANDORA BETTER THAN DIAGON ALLEY?

WITH PANDORA—THE WORLD OF AVATAR NOW OPEN, the obvious question is "Is it better than Diagon Alley?" We think the answer is "Yes, for some people." And that's as good as Disney could possibly have hoped for.

Before we begin, recall that sections of this book tell you not to visit Disney's Hollywood Studios while it's under construction because what's there isn't worth the price of admission. We're perfectly happy to criticize Disney's theme park decisions when warranted.

That said, let's start with Pandora's best feature: the environment. What Rohde and team have built here is more beautiful than nature generally produces on its own. (Anyone who has ever driven through Kansas knows what we mean.) The colors in Pandora are a bit more vibrant, the landscaping entirely more interesting, the sounds more alive, and the details more . . . *detailed* than what you probably see out your window right now. Pandora is intersected by perfectly placed waterfalls, too. And in the middle of it is a giant, floating mountain just like the ones you won't find outside Topeka.

These literally otherworldly features are grouped into views that are postcard-ready from any angle. There's always something stunning to see in the immediate foreground, in the middle distance, and far away. And that's true from anywhere you look inside the land. Diagon Alley is, without a doubt, a very detailed, visually rich urban setting. But it's space-constrained because of Universal's limited amount of land, so it doesn't have much visual depth. In contrast, Disney has the space to build a giant, multiplane viewing platform from every square foot of Pandora. And they did.

The exquisite detailing extends into the ride queues: The one for Na'Vi River Journey displays the weaving skills of Pandora's indigenous peoples, while the seemingly endless line for Avatar Flight of Passage goes through cave dwellings, nocturnal jungle scenes, and high-tech laboratories on its way to the ride experience. We'll be surprised if James Cameron puts polar ice caps on Pandora in *Avatar*'s sequels, if only because the encyclopedic terrain in Flight of Passage doesn't already show them.

IT'S THE END OF THE WORLD AS WE KNOW IT

WHETHER YOU THINK PANDORA is the most immersive theme park environment ever created will depend on how much you like Harry Potter. Even modest fans of the boy wizard are likely to prefer Diagon Alley's rich storylines and characters. But if you're not emotionally invested in Potter, or you prefer nature to city life, you may find Pandora the more appealing place to spend an afternoon and evening.

One thing is certain: The opening of Pandora marks the end of 20th-century Disney Imagineering. The days of "state of the art" meaning "passive rides"—even with cutting-edge technology and all the creative decorative techniques ever known—are over. The next generation of blockbuster theme park attractions, including what Disney is building for its Star Wars Land over at Hollywood Studios, starts with Pandora's scale and detail as a given.

On top of that, future rides are supposed to bring never-before-seen interactive effects: You'll be able to steer the *Millennium Falcon* in one ride, and if you crash it, the characters you interact with outside the ride will know that and make fun of you for it. It'll be a hyper-personalized, hyper-detailed adventure game, in a setting more lifelike than life itself. What Disney has done with Pandora is told Universal that they're playing that game to win.

Avatar Flight of Passage *(FastPass+)* ★★★★½

**APPEAL BY AGE   PRESCHOOL ★★★   GRADE SCHOOL ★★★★★   TEENS ★★★★★
YOUNG ADULTS ★★★★★   OVER 30 ★★★★★   SENIORS ★★★★½**

What it is Motion-simulator ride. **Scope and scale** Super-headliner. **When to go** Before 9:30 a.m., during the last 2 hours before closing, or use FastPass+. **Special comment** Disney's most advanced ride. **Authors' rating ★★★★½. Duration of ride** About 6 minutes. **Average wait in line per 100 people ahead of you** About 5 minutes **Loading speed** Moderate

DESCRIPTION AND COMMENTS Avatar Flight of Passage is Pandora's headliner ride and one of the most technologically advanced rides Disney has ever produced. It's a flight simulator in which you hop on the back of a winged, dragon-like Pandora banshee, for a spin around the planet's scenery.

Your journey begins with a long walk from the base of Pandora, up an inclined path, and into abandoned cave dwellings. Wall paintings and markings inside the caves tell the story of the Na'Vi, who first used them. From there, you walk through jungle and more rocks, until you reach the research laboratory of the humans who've settled on Pandora. Inside the lab are various experiments showing how the study of the planet's wildlife is progressing. Some of the effects are clever little engineering tricks—small, black, amoeba-like creatures scurrying about in the lab are probably made of ferrofluids (bits of metal suspended in a liquid) and moved about by specially shaped magnets. Even if you know how it's done, it's a joy to see the idea used.

The star of the preshow, however, is a Na'Vi avatar in suspended animation inside the lab. Encased in a giant, water-filled tube, the sleeping Na'Vi floats gently, its rest only briefly interrupted by the occasional finger twitch or leg movement. The people we toured with said it was either mesmerizing or vaguely unsettling.

Once through the queue, you're brought to a 16-person chamber room to prepare for your flight. A video plays, explaining the concept of an avatar—a way for you to project your consciousness onto another being, in this case a Na'Vi riding astride a banshee—and feel everything it feels. Your preparation includes a parasite decontamination procedure (Pandora is filled with critters, in case you hadn't noticed). A second part of the video seems to be chosen randomly from a few different scenes, so you're likely to get a different preshow experience the first few times you ride.

That done, you're led into an enclosed room with what looks like 16 stationary bicycles without pedals. You're handed 3-D goggles and told to approach the "bike," swing one leg over, mount it, and scoot as far forward as you can. The reason for doing this is that padded restraints will be deployed along your calves and lower back, ensuring you don't fall off during your flight. (The snug restraint system, coupled with the confined space of the room, causes some claustrophobic guests to exit before riding.)

The room goes dark, there's a flash of light, and suddenly your brain is "linked" to the Na'Vi surfing a banshee. You swoop up and down, left and right, on this flying dragon, going over the Pandora plains, through the mountains, and across its seas, all through a high-definition video projected onto a giant screen in front of you. As you fly, airbags at your legs inflate and deflate to simulate the banshee's breathing below you.

The flying effects are very well done; you can turn your head almost 90 degrees either way to survey the Pandora landscape while you're flying, and about 45 degrees up and down. Riders toward the middle of the room (seats 4–8 in one group and 9–12 in the other) have, we think, better range of vision. At any given time, Disney says, there are three levels of 16 riders flying with you. We didn't see anyone other than our immediate neighbors, but people at the far ends said they could see almost all of the riders when they turned their heads.

If you've experience Soarin' at Epcot, it's similar technology at work here, with the individual "bikes" replacing the grouped seats. The ebb and flow of the flight, too, reminds us of the Soarin' film pacing, right down to the finale over the Pandoran beach.

The video is clear and well synchronized with the ride vehicles. We heard no reports of motion sickness during our daylong visit, and that's unusual for most screen-based motion simulators. The problem with Flight of Passage, like the Na'Vi River Journey and the *Avatar* film, is that we're not really invested in the story of the banshee or the avatar. Technically, the ride is brilliant, and the visuals get your heart racing; Disney's Imagineers squeezed every bit they could out of the one *Avatar* film completed so far. But it has the emotional resonance of a Pac-Man video game.

TOURING TIPS We're told that if the entire queue is full, the wait to ride is between 4 and 5 hours. It's not worth that much time. However, this ride should be your first FastPass+ priority at Animal Kingdom.

As with Na'Vi River Journey, guests in wheelchairs and ECVs must transfer to the ride vehicles. As we went to press, the 3-D glasses were too big for many children. We expect Disney to offer different sizes soon.

Na'Vi River Journey *(FastPass+)* ★★★½

APPEAL BY AGE PRESCHOOL ★★★★½ GRADE SCHOOL ★★★★½ TEENS ★★★★
YOUNG ADULTS ★★★★   OVER 30 ★★★★   SENIORS ★★★★½

What it is Boat ride. **Scope and scale** Headliner. **When to go** Before 9:30 a.m., during the last 2 hours before closing, or use FastPass+. **Special comment** Very pretty but needs a plot; no height requirement. **Authors' rating** ★★★½. **Duration of ride** 4½ minutes. **Average wait in line per 100 people ahead of you** About 5 minutes. **Loading speed** Moderate.

DESCRIPTION AND COMMENTS The Na'Vi River Journey is a 4½-minute boat ride through the Pandora jungle. You begin by boarding one of two small, hewn rafts joined together. Each raft has two rows of seats, so four people go in each boat. That might seem small, but it's more likely a nod to authenticity: The Na'Vi are unlikely to have invented technology like fiberglass to make larger vessels as in, say, It's a Small World.

Off you go into the nighttime jungle, past glowing plants and exotic animals. To create these, Disney has used traditional, three-dimensional sets for the flora, coupled with video screens showing the movement of the fauna. Escape from Gringotts, the one ride at Diagon Alley, uses video screens for its action, too. But here again, Disney has one-upped Diagon Alley in that the screens directly in front of you in Na'Vi River Journey are semi-transparent, so you can see past them. And what's past them are more screens, with background scenes that also move. That means you're seeing action in the foreground and background simultaneously, all surrounded by densely packed landscaping.

Another bit of technology put to great use is video projection mapping like that used in the Magic Kingdom's nighttime show *Happily Ever After.* Here it's used to project three-dimensional bugs crawling on tree trunks in one of the middle scenes.

The big star, however, is the Shaman of Songs, displayed in the ride's culminating scene. This shaman is easily Disney's most lifelike animatronic ever created. Its arms move with such grace that the only reason to suspect it's a robot is that you don't know any real people who are that coordinated. (Disney has a history of building advanced but rather high-maintenance animatronics for Animal Kingdom. Expedition Everest's Yeti was built in a way that repairs to it require much of the surrounding ride's infrastructure to be removed. The Yeti hasn't run properly in almost a decade. We'll give River Journey an extra half-star next year if the shaman stays running.) Yet another nice touch is that the shaman's voice is off-pitch; Disney didn't make it sound like a professional singer.

The problem with Na'Vi River Journey is that you go in not knowing anything about the character and there's not enough story told during the ride to get you excited to meet the shaman. (If that doesn't make sense, imagine the same level of detail just described for a boat ride showing Obi-Wan Kenobi performing some heretofore unseen Jedi ritual that's officially part of the Star Wars canon. The line would stretch to Endor.) Despite that, there's enough to see in Na'Vi River Journey that it's worth reriding.

TOURING TIPS Disney seems to think that lines will not be too long once the initial opening hype dies down—the queue for the ride doesn't seem built to handle massive crowds. We'd ride it again if the waits are 20 minutes or less. Na'Vi River Journey offers FastPass+, but we don't yet think it's a good use.

Guests with disabilities must transfer to the boat—the small vessels can't accommodate wheelchairs or ECVs. Early riders have noted that Jake, the main character in *Avatar,* uses a wheelchair, and they think that Disney should have made different accommodations. We expect Disney to do so.

LIVE ENTERTAINMENT *in* ANIMAL KINGDOM

ANIMAL ENCOUNTERS Throughout the day, Disney staff conduct impromptu short lectures on specific animals at the park. Look for a cast member in safari garb holding a bird, reptile, or small mammal.

A small interactive event titled ***Winged Encounters—The Kingdom Takes Flight,*** featuring macaws and their handlers, takes place on Discovery Island in front of The Tree of Life. Guests can talk to the animal's trainers and see the birds fly around the middle of the park. The concept is similar to *Flights of Wonder* (see page 626) on a much smaller scale. Check the *Times Guide* for showtimes and the exact location.

STREET PERFORMERS You can find them most of the time at Harambe in Africa and at Anandapur in Asia. Far and away the most intriguing of these performers is a stilt walker named **DiVine** (★★★★). Bedecked in foliage and luxuriant vines, she blends so completely with Animal Kingdom's dense flora that you don't notice her until she moves. We've seen guests standing less than a foot away gasp in amazement as DiVine brushes them with a leafy tendril. Usually found on the path between Asia and Africa, DiVine is a must-see. Video of her is available on YouTube (search for "DiVine Disney's Animal Kingdom").

TRAFFIC PATTERNS *in* ANIMAL KINGDOM

THE PARK'S MAIN DRAWS are **Pandora, Kilimanjaro Safaris** in Africa, and **Expedition Everest** in Asia. Expect those attractions to be very busy from the moment the park opens, and for Pandora to be mobbed the entire day and night. Pandora, the Safaris, and Everest are at opposite sides of the park, which allows good guest distribution.

Pandora had just opened as we went to press, so the traffic patterns we've seen so far are atypical. But we think that one effect of Pandora's opening is that early-morning waits at DinoLand U.S.A., especially Dinosaur and Primeval Whirl, should be much lower.

As the day wears on, expect those who have experienced the headliner attractions to turn their attention to other rides and shows, and the crowds to become more equally distributed across the entire park. Less popular attractions don't experience high traffic until 11:30 a.m.

Many guests who arrive at park opening will have completed their tour of the park by late afternoon and will leave. Wait times at the headliner rides have traditionally dropped as the afternoon wears on. However, with the opening of the nighttime safaris and *Rivers of Light* show, we've noticed an uptick in ride wait times after sunset. We expect this to continue with Pandora open, as guests flock to see the land's "bioluminescent" landscaping.

Our mobile app, **Lines** (touringplans.com/lines), gives you current wait times and future estimates in half-hour increments for today and tomorrow. A quick glance shows how traffic patterns affect wait times throughout the day.

ANIMAL KINGDOM TOURING PLAN

THE PLAN ASSUMES THAT Na'Vi River Journey and Avatar Flight of Passage will continue to be in the same FastPass+ tier and that you'll be able to select only one of these. (If that assumption doesn't hold, use our free touring plan software to adjust the plan.)

"Not a Touring Plan" Touring Plans

For the type-B reader, these touring plans (see page 817) dispense with detailed step-by-step strategies for saving every last minute in line. For Animal Kingdom, these "not" touring plans include advice for adults and parents with one day in the park, for anyone with two days, and for anyone with an afternoon and a full day to tour.

BEFORE YOU GO

1. Call ☎ 407-824-4321 or check the day before you go to verify official opening time.

2. Make reservations at the Animal Kingdom full-service restaurant(s) of your choice 180 days before your visit.

3. Make FastPass+ reservations 60 or 30 days in advance.

DISNEY'S ANIMAL KINGDOM ONE-DAY TOURING PLAN *(page 830)*

THIS TOURING PLAN assumes a willingness to experience all major rides and shows. If you have children under age 8, refer to the Small-Child Fright-Potential Chart on pages 432–435. When you're following a printed touring plan, simply skip any attraction that you don't wish to experience.

Our touring plan includes a daytime ride on Kilimanjaro Safaris. The better visibility during daylight allows you to see more animals, at farther distances. It also provides a better perspective of the size and scope of the savanna. We think a nighttime ride on the Safaris is rewarding, too, if you have the time and energy. Use a day-of FastPass+ to avoid long waits.

PART TWELVE

DISNEY'S HOLLYWOOD STUDIOS

DHS: *A Brief History*

THE THEME PARK ORIGINALLY KNOWN AS DISNEY-MGM STUDIOS was hatched from a corporate rivalry and a twisted plot. At a time when Disney was weak and having to fight off "greenmail" (hostile-takeover bids), MCA—Universal's parent company at the time—announced plans to build an Orlando clone of its wildly successful Universal Studios Hollywood theme park. Behind the scenes, MCA was courting the billionaire Bass brothers of Texas, hoping to secure their investment in the project. The Basses, however, defected to the Disney camp and were front and center when CEO Michael Eisner suddenly announced that Disney, too, would build a movie theme park in Florida.

A construction race ensued, but Universal, in the middle of developing new attraction technologies, was no match for Disney, which could import proven concepts and attractions from its other parks. In the end, Disney-MGM Studios opened May 1, 1989, more than a year before Universal Studios Florida.

Back then, the park's soundstages and facilities produced many television shows and films, both live-action and animated. The Studios also hosted attractions that educated guests about TV and film production, the best known being a tram ride through and walking tour of the park's back lot. Others included shows on how sound effects were added to films, and reenactments of famous TV scenes using "green screen" technology and park guests as actors.

Disney purchased Pixar Animation Studios in 2006 after partnering with the company on a series of highly successful films, including *Toy Story; Monsters, Inc.; Finding Nemo;* and *The Incredibles.* The cost of continuing an association with MGM, coupled with Pixar's arguably greater popularity, probably influenced Disney's decision to drop the MGM name from the park in 2008 and replace it with *Hollywood.*

The *Studios* in "Disney's Hollywood Studios" is of little significance today. Movie and television production ceased long ago, and only a handful of aging attractions remain that offer a peek behind the

Continued on page 644

Disney's Hollywood Studios

Use FP+ Attraction Offers FastPass+   **FP+** FastPass+ Kiosks

     FP+ FastPass+ Recommended   Restrooms

     ☑ Not to Be Missed   ✚ First Aid Station

     👍 Recommended Dining

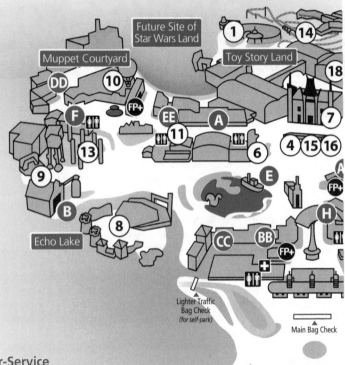

Future Site of Star Wars Land

Muppet Courtyard

Toy Story Land

Echo Lake

Lighter Traffic
Bag Check
(for self-park)

Main Bag Check

Counter-Service Restaurants

A. ABC Commissary 👍
B. Backlot Express 👍
C. Cataline Eddie's
D. Fairfax Fare
E. Min and Bill's Dockside Diner
F. PizzeRizzo
G. Rosie's All-American Cafe
H. Trolley Car Cafe *(Starbucks)*

Table-Service Restaurants

AA. The Hollywood Brown Derby 👍
BB. Hollywood & Vine
CC. 50's Prime Time Cafe
DD. Mama Melrose's Ristorante Italiano
EE. Sci-Fi Dine-In Theater Restaurant

Attractions

1. Alien Swirling Saucers *(scheduled to open 2018)*
2. *Beauty and the Beast—Live on Stage/ Theater of the Stars* FP+
3. *Disney Junior—Live on Stage!* FP+
4. Disney Movie Magic
5. *Fantasmic!* ☑ Use FP+
6. *For the First Time in Forever: A Frozen Sing-Along Celebration* FP+
7. The Great Movie Ride ☑ Use FP+
8. *Indiana Jones Epic Stunt Spectacular!* FP+
9. *Jedi Training: Trials of the Temple*
10. *Jim Henson's Muppet-Vision 3-D* ☑ FP+
11. Meet Mickey and Minnie Starring in Red Carpet Dreams
12. Rock 'n' Roller Coaster Starring Aerosmith ☑ Use FP+
13. Star Tours—The Adventures Continue ☑ Use FP+
14. Slinky Dog Dash *(scheduled to open 2018)*
15. *Star Wars: A Galactic Spectacular* fireworks
16. *Star Wars: A Galaxy Far Far Away* show
17. Star Wars Launch Bay
18. Toy Story Mania! ☑ Use FP+
19. The Twilight Zone Tower of Terror ☑ Use FP+
20. *Voyage of the Little Mermaid* FP+
21. *Walt Disney: One Man's Dream*

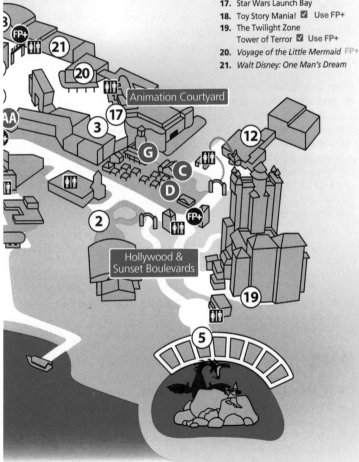

Continued from page 641

scenes. DHS is now simply an amusement park whose theme is movies and TV. We expect the park's name to change again before 2020.

DHS TODAY

TOY STORY LAND (see page 659), themed to the Pixar film franchise, opens sometime in 2018 with two new child-friendly rides. That's a warm-up for the opening of an as-yet-unnamed Star Wars–themed land by August 2019, with two major rides and at least one restaurant serving blue milk.

Until Toy Story Land opens, we don't think a visit to DHS is worth the cost of admission. About half the park's land and rides were demolished to make way for these new areas; those are still construction zones with nothing to see. Except for the evening fireworks, the handful of good attractions still open can be seen in as little as 4 hours. And of those, the *Indiana Jones Epic Stunt Spectacular!,* **The Great Movie Ride,** **Muppet-Vision 3-D,** and *Voyage of the Little Mermaid* haven't had significant updates in almost 25 years; it's been 18 for **Rock 'n' Roller Coaster.** The park's two best counter-service restaurants were closed without replacement in 2016, so the highest-rated place to eat quickly is now a Starbucks. The road construction around the park perimeter adds to the hassle. We understand this is all for a greater good; we're saying not to pay $120 for it until it's good. Try Universal Studios Florida instead.

An Aledo, Illinois, mom accepts that there are fewer attractions but thinks a visit is warranted if you have 'tweens and teens:

> I did notice in the Guide *that you advised readers to skip Hollywood Studios if they have a short trip. I respectfully disagree with that advice if visitors have teenage boys. Our two 12-year-olds' favorite parts of the trip were Rock 'n' Roller Coaster, Tower of Terror, Star Tours, and building their own light sabers in the gift shop! The recent closures do mean there are fewer options, but there was still plenty for them to do.*

DHS *at a* GLANCE

HOW MUCH TIME TO ALLOCATE

BECAUSE SO MANY ATTRACTIONS have closed, it's possible to see all of DHS is less than one full day. Even with the back third of the park still closed for Star Wars construction, there's far less ground to cover by foot, too. The one thing to watch out for is the park's perverse scheduling of live shows. That schedule often has show performances overlap, or allows too little time to get from one to another, as this West Chester, Pennsylvania, mom explains:

> *If I had it to do over, I'd skip the Studios. The shows were good, but we kept missing showtimes because either all the shows started at the same time or the walk between them was too long with little ones.*

Hollywood Studios Services

MOST PARK SERVICES are on Hollywood Boulevard, including:

Baby Care Center At Guest Relations; baby food and other necessities available at Oscar's Super Service

Banking Services ATM outside the park to the right of the turnstiles

Camera Supplies At The Darkroom on the right side of Hollywood Boulevard as you enter the park, just past Oscar's Super Service

Cell Phone Charging Outlets in the Hollywood Brown Derby lobby, inside Backlot Express, and near the restrooms next to Toy Story Mania!

First Aid Center At Guest Relations

Live Entertainment and Character Information Available free at Guest Relations and elsewhere in the park

Lockers To the right of the entrance, to the left of Oscar's Super Service

Lost and Found At Package Pick-Up, to the right of the park entrance

Lost Persons Report at Guest Relations

Wheelchair, ECV/ESV, and Stroller Rentals To the right of the entrance, at Oscar's Super Service

Our touring plan will help you stay a step ahead of the crowds, minimize your wait in line, and help with this show-schedule problem.

While we're on the subject of touring, here's more good news: You can sleep in, arrive around 11 a.m. or noon, and still see the entire park in one day, including *Fantasmic!* This works best when the park is open until 8:30 p.m. or later and you're able to get FastPass+ reservations for Toy Story Mania!, Star Tours, and either Slinky Dog Dash or Tower of Terror for the first 3 hours after you arrive. If you plan to stay at the Magic Kingdom late one night, following it up with a sleep-in morning and tour of the Studios is a good option.

DISNEY'S HOLLYWOOD STUDIOS IN THE EVENING

BECAUSE ALL OF DHS can be seen in as little as 4–6 hours, many guests who arrive early in the morning run out of things to do by 5 p.m. or so and leave. Their departure greatly thins crowds and makes the Studios ideal for evening touring. Lines for most attractions are bearable, and the park is cooler and more comfortable. The *Indiana Jones Epic Stunt Spectacular!* and productions at other outdoor theaters are infinitely more enjoyable during the evening than in the sweltering heat of the day.

DHS is the home of ***Fantasmic!*** (see page 650), a dazzling nighttime-entertainment event in the Disney repertoire. Staged most nights (sometimes twice a night), weather permitting, in its own theater behind The Twilight Zone Tower of Terror, *Fantasmic!* is not to be missed. It's also a crowd magnet, owing to DHS guests sticking around or guests from other parks arriving after dinner to see the show. Although the crowds thin in the late afternoon, they build again as showtime approaches, making *Fantasmic!* a challenge to get into. Also adversely affected are **Rock 'n' Roller Coaster** and, to a lesser extent, **The Twilight Zone Tower of Terror,** both nearby. Crowd levels elsewhere remain generally light, except at **Toy Story Mania!**

During summer 2017, Disney unveiled *The Music of Pixar Live!* This stage show was performed three times nightly at Theater of the Stars, the daytime home of the *Beauty and the Beast* show. A live orchestra played along with scenes from favorite Pixar films, and Pixar characters joined in the fun.

ARRIVING AT DISNEY'S HOLLYWOOD STUDIOS

DHS HAS ITS OWN PARKING LOT and is served by Disney transportation. If you drive, Disney's ubiquitous trams will convey you to the ticketing area and entrance gate. For GPS coordinates, see page 485.

GETTING ORIENTED AT DISNEY'S HOLLYWOOD STUDIOS

ON YOUR LEFT AS YOU ENTER, **Guest Relations** serves as the park headquarters and information center. Go there for a park map, a schedule of live performances (*Times Guide*), lost persons, baby-care facilities, and general information. To the right of the entrance are locker, stroller, and wheelchair rentals, Package Pick-Up, and lost and found.

As at the Magic Kingdom, you enter the park and pass down a main street. In this case, it's the **Hollywood Boulevard** of the 1930s and '40s. At the end of Hollywood Boulevard is a replica of the iconic **Grauman's Chinese Theatre**.

Though modest in size, the open-access areas of the Studios are confusingly arranged. As you face Grauman's Chinese Theatre, two themed areas—**Sunset Boulevard** and **Animation Courtyard**—branch off of Hollywood Boulevard to the right. Branching left off Hollywood Boulevard is **Echo Lake. Muppet Courtyard** holds *Muppet-Vision 3-D* and Mama Melrose's Ristorante Italiano, a full-service restaurant. **Pixar Place**'s attractions are behind the Chinese Theatre and to the left of Animation Courtyard. When Toy Story Land opens, the entrance to Toy Story Mania! will move from its current location to the opposite side of the building.

FASTPASS+ ATTRACTIONS IN DISNEY'S HOLLYWOOD STUDIOS

LIKE EPCOT, Disney's Hollywood Studios uses tiering (see page 100) to restrict the number of FastPass+ reservations you can have at its headliner attractions:

TIER A *(Choose one per day)*	
• *Beauty and the Beast—Live on Stage*	• Rock 'n' Roller Coaster
• *Fantasmic*	• Toy Story Mania!
• The Great Movie Ride	
TIER B *(Choose two per day)*	
• *Disney Junior—Live on Stage!*	• Star Tours—The Adventures Continue
• *For the First Time in Forever: A Frozen Sing-Along Celebration*	
• *Indiana Jones Epic Stunt Spectacular!*	• The Twilight Zone Tower of Terror
• *Jim Henson's Muppet-Vision 3-D*	• *Voyage of the Little Mermaid*
ENTERTAINMENT & PARADES	
• *The Comedy Warehouse Holiday Special* (seasonal)	

Disney's Hollywood Studios
When Same-Day FP+ Runs Out, by Crowd Level

ATTRACTION	LOW CROWDS*	MODERATE CROWDS*	HIGH CROWDS*
• Beauty and the Beast—Live on Stage	3 p.m.	3 p.m.	2 p.m.
• Disney Junior—Live on Stage!	2 p.m.	1 p.m.	10 a.m.
• Fantasmic!	6 p.m.	6 p.m.	6 p.m.
• For the First Time in Forever: A Frozen Sing-Along Celebration	2 p.m.	1 p.m.	11 a.m.
• The Great Movie Ride	3 p.m.	3 p.m.	1 p.m.
• Indiana Jones Epic Stunt Spectacular!	4 p.m.	3 p.m.	10 a.m.
• Jim Henson's Muppet-Vision 3-D	4 p.m.	4 p.m.	4 p.m.
• Rock 'n' Roller Coaster	2 p.m.	10 p.m.	N/A
• Star Tours—The Adventures Continue	3 p.m.	9 p.m.	N/A
• Toy Story Mania!	1 p.m.	N/A	N/A
• The Twilight Zone Tower of Terror	2 p.m.	8 p.m.	N/A
• Voyage of the Little Mermaid	3 p.m.	2 p.m.	Noon
* LOW CROWDS (Levels 1–3 on TouringPlans.com Crowd Calendar)			
* MODERATE CROWDS (Levels 4–7 on TouringPlans.com Crowd Calendar)			
* HIGH CROWDS (Levels 8–10 on TouringPlans.com Crowd Calendar)			
N/A = No availability			
Not open at press time: Slinky Dog Dash, Alien Swirling Saucers			

Note: Slinky Dog Dash wasn't open at press time, but we think it'll be a Tier A FastPass+ attraction. We think Alien Swirling Saucers will not offer FastPass+.

These restrictions mean that having a good touring plan is essential to avoid long lines. The good news is that while FastPass+ is offered at more than a dozen attractions at DHS, there are really only four that you need to be concerned with most of the year. Here's why:

Our print and online touring plans emphasize FastPass+ for **Toy Story Mania!** Families with children too small to ride Rock 'n' Roller Coaster or Tower of Terror should make a beeline to Toy Story Mania! first thing in the morning because lines grow quickly. Waits at Toy Story can reach 90 minutes or more on a busy day—in fact, the lines grow so fast that in about one-third of our touring plans, we recommend getting a FastPass+ reservation for 9–10 a.m., even when Toy Story is the first step in the plan. The two benefits to doing this are that (1) you'll shave off at least 10 minutes of waiting, and (2) you don't have to line up as early at park opening to join the mad rush to Toy Story.

Next, like Peter Pan's Flight in the Magic Kingdom, **Star Tours** isn't going to be anyone's first choice to visit. For teens and adults especially, the initial morning priorities will be Toy Story, Rock 'n' Roller Coaster, and Tower of Terror, possibly with The Great Movie Ride while they're in the area. This makes Star Tours a great choice for a mid- or late-morning FastPass+ reservation.

We really like how our touring plan software places **The Twilight Zone Tower of Terror** around midmorning in our plans. This lets you fit in a visit to *Beauty and the Beast—Live on Stage* around the Tower of

NOT TO BE MISSED AT DISNEY'S HOLLYWOOD STUDIOS
• *Fantasmic!* • *Jim Henson's Muppet-Vision 3-D* • Rock 'n' Roller Coaster
• Slinky Dog Dash *(opens 2018)* • Star Tours—The Adventures Continue
• Toy Story Mania! • The Twilight Zone Tower of Terror

Terror, so you don't have to backtrack later all the way down Sunset Boulevard just to see the show.

Finally, our software thinks **The Great Movie Ride** is a good Fast-Pass+ choice for day-of afternoon touring plans, after you've used your initial set of reservations.

So why isn't **Rock 'n' Roller Coaster** among our four musts? Because it's in the same FastPass+ tier as Toy Story Mania!, and you may choose only one of them. Because Toy Story almost always has the longer waits, it should be your FastPass+ choice. If you can get FastPass+ reservations for Toy Story, Star Tours, and Tower of Terror, our touring plan software will usually make Rock 'n' Roller Coaster your first stop, where you'll find the shortest waits of the day.

We don't think ***Fantasmic!*** is a good choice for FastPass+ in most cases. For one thing, your reservation doesn't guarantee you a seat: You still have to arrive 30–60 minutes beforehand to be guaranteed a good spot. If you arrive 5 minutes before the show starts, you're likely to be turned away even if you obtained a FastPass+. In addition, day-of FastPasses are often available for *Fantasmic!* until 4–7 p.m., even on days of moderate and high crowds. In those cases, you'll have plenty of time to snap one up after you've used your advance Fast-Passes on the park's rides. (If you'd rather not risk missing out on a *Fantasmic!* FastPass, consider the ***Fantasmic!* Dining Package** instead; it's described on page 651.)

FastPass+ kiosk locations at the Studios are as follows:

- At the wait-times board on the corner of Hollywood and Sunset Boulevards
- Near Toy Story Mania!, on Pixar Place
- Near *Muppet-Vision 3-D,* just off Streets of America

Same-Day FastPass+ Availability

The preceding advice tells you which attractions to focus on when making your *advance* FastPass+ reservations before you get to the park. In the park, you can make more reservations once your advance reservations have expired or been used. The chart on page 647 shows which attractions are likely to have day-of FastPasses available, and the approximate times at which they'll run out. Some attractions have more day-of FastPass+ availability on days with moderate crowds than with low crowds. That seems backwards, but it's not: Disney can change how much of each ride's hourly capacity is dedicated to FastPass+ and increases this number on days of higher attendance. For example, on low-crowd days *Muppet-Vision 3-D* might dedicate 50% of its hourly capacity to FastPass+ riders, perhaps 75% on days of moderate crowds.

DINING IN DISNEY'S HOLLYWOOD STUDIOS

HERE'S A QUICK RECAP of the Studios' top restaurants, rated by readers from highest to lowest. See Part Four for details.

DHS RESTAURANT REFRESHER	
COUNTER-SERVICE	**FULL-SERVICE**
Trolley Car Cafe (Starbucks) (94% 👍), Sunset Boulevard	**50's Prime Time Cafe** (88% 👍), Echo Lake
Fairfax Fare (86% 👍), Sunset Boulevard	**The Hollywood Brown Derby** (88% 👍), Hollywood Boulevard
Backlot Express (85% 👍), Echo Lake	**Mama Melrose's Ristorante Italiano** (88% 👍), Muppet Courtyard
	Sci-Fi Dine-in Theater Restaurant (86% 👍), Commissary Lane

DISNEY'S HOLLYWOOD STUDIOS ATTRACTIONS

HOLLYWOOD BOULEVARD

THIS PALM-LINED THOROUGHFARE re-creates Tinseltown's main drag during the Golden Age of Hollywood. Most service facilities are here, interspersed with eateries and shops. Merchandise includes Disney trademark items and movie-related souvenirs.

Hollywood characters and roving performers entertain on the boulevard, and other happenings pass this way. Introduced during the 2016 holiday season, *Jingle Bell, Jingle BAM!* is a nighttime spectacular involving projections, fireworks, seasonal music, and snow. The show is hosted by Wayne and Lenny, the comical elves from ABC's *Prep and Landing,* who search for Santa Claus, and features holiday scenes from *Mickey's Christmas Carol, Beauty and the Beast, Pluto's Christmas Tree, Bambi,* and *The Nightmare Before Christmas.*

The Great Movie Ride (*FastPass+*)   ★★★½

APPEAL BY AGE	PRESCHOOL ★★★	GRADE SCHOOL ★★★½	TEENS ★★★½
YOUNG ADULTS ★★★½	OVER 30 ★★★★		SENIORS ★★★★

What it is Indoor movie-history ride. **Scope and scale** Headliner. **When to go** Before 11 a.m., during dinner, after 8 p.m., or use FastPass+. **Special comments** Elaborate, with several surprises. **Authors' rating** The recent update is welcome but doesn't go far enough; ★★★½. **Duration of ride** About 19 minutes. **Average wait in line per 100 people ahead of you** 2 minutes; assumes all cars operating. **Loading speed** Fast.

DESCRIPTION AND COMMENTS Entering through a re-creation of Grauman's Chinese Theatre, guests board vehicles for a fast-paced tour of soundstage sets from classic films, including *Casablanca, Tarzan, The Wizard of Oz, Alien,* and *Raiders of the Lost Ark.* Each set is populated with Disney Audio-Animatronic characters, as well as the occasional human, all augmented by sound and lighting effects. One of Disney's larger and more ambitious dark rides, The Great Movie Ride encompasses 95,000 square feet and showcases some of the most famous scenes in filmmaking. Life-size animatronic sculptures of stars, including Gene Kelly, John Wayne, James Cagney, and Julie Andrews, inhabit some of the largest sets ever constructed for a Disney ride.

In early 2015, as part of an agreement with Turner Classic Movies, the Great Movie Ride's preshow film trailer and ride-film finale were updated with commentary from TCM host and film historian Robert Osborne. In addition, the finale was entirely reedited with a mix of classic clips, new scenes from previously featured films, and a handful of more-recent movies. (Refreshingly, this is the first Disney movie montage we've seen in a while that gives *Tangled* more screen time than *Frozen*.)

The updated preshow and finale are first-rate—it's the attraction's meat that merits a "meh." Don't strain yourself searching for signs of improved animatronics or new effects in old sets, much less any all-new scenes.

TOURING TIPS It's rare to see waits of more than 30 minutes at The Great Movie Ride except during peak season. For one thing, it's an interval-loading, high-capacity attraction; for another, many of the clips don't ring a bell with anyone under age 40. Actual wait times usually run about one-third shorter than the times posted. Great Movie Ride is a good option for day-of FastPasses.

SUNSET BOULEVARD

EVOKING THE 1940s, Sunset Boulevard—the first right off Hollywood Boulevard—provides another venue for dining, shopping, and street entertainment.

Fantasmic! (FastPass+) ★★★★½

APPEAL BY AGE	PRESCHOOL ★★★★	GRADE SCHOOL ★★★★½	TEENS ★★★★½
YOUNG ADULTS ★★★★½		OVER 30 ★★★★½	SENIORS ★★★★½

What it is Mixed-media nighttime spectacular. **Scope and scale** Super-headliner. **When to go** Check *Times Guide* for schedule; if 2 shows are offered, the second is less crowded. **Special comments** Disney's very best nighttime event. **Authors' rating** Not to be missed; ★★★★½. **Duration of presentation** 25 minutes. **Probable waiting time** 50–90 minutes for a seat, 35–40 minutes for standing room.

DESCRIPTION AND COMMENTS Off Sunset Boulevard behind the Tower of Terror, this mixed-media show is staged on an island opposite the 7,900-seat Hollywood Hills Amphitheater. By far the largest theater facility ever created by Disney, the amphitheater can accommodate an additional 2,000 standing guests for an audience of nearly 10,000.

Fantasmic! is the one of the most innovative outdoor spectacles we've seen at a theme park. Starring Mickey Mouse in his role as the Sorcerer's Apprentice from *Fantasia,* the production uses lasers, images projected on a shroud of mist, fireworks, lighting effects, and music in combinations so stunning you can scarcely believe what you're seeing. The plot is simple: good versus evil. The story gets lost in all the special effects at times, but no matter: It's the spectacle, not the storyline, that's powerful.

A Pearland, Texas, mom found *Fantasmic!* too intense for her young child:

Fantasmic! should come with a warning label. The characters' larger-than-life laser visages, loud and ominous music, and thundering explosions sent hordes of parents with screaming children fleeing for the exits.

We don't receive many reports of young children being terrified by *Fantasmic!*, but the reader's point is well taken. Spend some time preparing your kids for what they will see. You can mitigate the fright factor somewhat by sitting back a bit. Also, hang on to your kids after *Fantasmic!* and give them instructions for regrouping should you get separated.

TOURING TIPS *Fantasmic!* is presented one or more times most evenings, but Disney has been known to change the schedule, so verify before you go. *Fantasmic!* is to the Studios what *IllumiNations* is to Epcot or *Rivers of Light* is to Animal Kingdom. While it's hard to imagine a 10,000-person stadium running out of space, that's just what happens almost every time the show is staged. On evenings when there are two shows, the second will always be less crowded. If you attend the first (or only) scheduled performance, then arrive at least an hour in advance; if you opt for the second, arrive 50 minutes early.

Fantasmic! is a FastPass+ attraction, but we don't think it should be one of your first three choices. See page 648 for an in-depth explanation.

A Cross Junction, Virginia, woman offers this advance-planning tip:

Buy deli sandwiches outside the park, pack them with snacks and water in your backpack, and get a seat early.

A multigenerational family from Barrie, Ontario, makes this suggestion for guests who are short on nature's upholstery:

Bring pillows or towels to sit on. We were sitting on those benches from 6 p.m. for the 7:30 show, and boy, did our rears hurt by the end!

Rainy and windy conditions sometimes cause *Fantasmic!* to be cancelled. Unfortunately, Disney officials usually don't make a final decision about whether to proceed or cancel until just before showtime. We've seen guests wait stoically for over an hour with no assurance that their patience and sacrifice will be rewarded. We don't recommend arriving more than 20 minutes before showtime on rainy or especially windy nights. On nights like these, pursue your own agenda until 20 minutes or so before showtime, then head to the stadium to see what happens.

Exiting *Fantasmic!* via the show's single exit can be hair-raising, as this retired elementary-school teacher attests:

It was like a cattle stampede, but at a snail's pace! Twice I almost ran over toddlers whose mothers were too tired to carry them.

From a veteran of both Disneyland and Walt Disney World:

I visit Disneyland a lot, and their [crowd-control] cast members push the throngs of guests through the park like clockwork, even when it's bursting at the seams. At Disney World, it's basically every man for himself at the end of the spectacles as the cast members retreat, leaving very tired, very cranky guests to duke it out. Such is the case at Fantasmic!*—while I was very happy to see a backstage corridor wide open for a quick reroute, the presence of cast members was extremely rare. I was stunned!*

Finally, a couple from Alberta, Canada, sums it up for all of us:

For a show so deservedly hyped, I would hope WDW finds ways to make seeing it less stressful.

FANTASMIC! DINING PACKAGE If you eat lunch or dinner at **Hollywood & Vine, The Hollywood Brown Derby,** or **Mama Melrose's Ristorante Italiano,** you can obtain a voucher for the members of your dining party to enter *Fantasmic!* via a special entrance and sit in a reserved section of seats. In return for your patronage of the restaurant, you can avoid 30–90 minutes waiting in the regular line to be admitted. If you know you're going to eat dinner at one of these locations, the dining package is a better way to see *Fantasmic!* than using FastPass+.

You must call ☎ 407-WDW-DINE (939-3463) 180 days in advance and request the package for the night you want to see the show. *Note:* This is a real reservation, not an Advance Reservation, and it must be guaranteed with a credit card at the time of booking. There's no additional charge for the package itself, but there is a $10 charge for canceling a reservation with less than 48 hours' notice.

Included in the package are fixed-price menus for all three restaurants as follows; respective prices are for adults and kids ages 3–9: *Hollywood & Vine*: buffet dinner, $54/$33; *The Hollywood Brown Derby*: lunch and dinner, $63/$23; *Mama Melrose's*: lunch and dinner, $45/$18. Nonalcoholic drinks and tax are included; park admission and gratuity are not. Prices fluctuate according to season, so call WDW-DINE to find out the exact price for a particular date.

You'll receive your vouchers at the restaurant. After dinner, report to the Highlands Gate on Sunset Boulevard—between Theater of the Stars and the Once Upon a Time store—30–45 minutes before showtime. A cast member will collect your vouchers and escort you to the reserved-seating section of the amphitheater. Though you're required to arrive early, you can be seated immediately. The reserved seats are in the center of the stadium; you won't have assigned seats—it's first-come, first-served—so arrive early for the best choice. Finally, understand that if *Fantasmic!* is canceled due to weather or other circumstances, you won't receive a refund or even a voucher for another performance.

Weather notwithstanding, a Waldorf, Maryland, couple thinks the dining package is the only way to go:

> We booked dinner at Hollywood & Vine, got our passes for the package, and waltzed on in to the show. We felt like VIPs, and it was so relaxing to see the show without the rush of the crowds.

Dining packages are now also available for breakfast. Guests booking a package breakfast at Hollywood & Vine ($41.54 for guests ages 10 and up, $25.63 for guests 3-9) can receive a voucher for reserved seating at *Fantasmic!*

Rock 'n' Roller Coaster *(FastPass+)* ★★★★

| APPEAL BY AGE | PRESCHOOL ★½ | GRADE SCHOOL ★★★★½ | TEENS ★★★★★ |
| YOUNG ADULTS ★★★★★ | | OVER 30 ★★★★½ | SENIORS ★★★★ |

What it is Rock music–themed roller coaster. **Scope and scale** Headliner. **When to go** First 30 minutes the park is open, or use FastPass+. **Special comments** 48″ minimum height requirement; children younger than age 7 must ride with an adult. Switching-off option provided (see page 439). Note that this attraction has a single-rider line. **Authors' rating** Disney's wildest American coaster; not to be missed; ★★★★. **Duration of ride** Almost 1½ minutes. **Average wait in line per 100 people ahead of you** 2½ minutes; assumes all trains operating. **Loading speed** Moderate–fast.

Motion Sickness

DESCRIPTION AND COMMENTS Exponentially wilder than Space Mountain or Big Thunder Mountain Railroad in the Magic Kingdom, Rock 'n' Roller Coaster is an attraction for fans of high-speed thrill rides. Although the presence of Aerosmith and the synchronized music add measurably to the experience, the ride itself is the focus. Rock 'n' Roller Coaster's loops, corkscrews, and drops make Space Mountain seem like It's a Small World. What really makes this metal coaster unusual, however, is that first, it's in the dark (like Space Mountain, only with Southern California nighttime scenes instead of space), and second, you're launched up the first hill like a jet off a carrier deck. By the time you crest the hill, you'll have gone from 0 to 57 mph in less than 3 seconds. When you enter the first loop, you'll be pulling 5 g's— 2 more than astronauts used to experience at liftoff on a space shuttle.

Reader opinions of Rock 'n' Roller Coaster are predictably mixed, colored invariably by how the reader feels about roller coasters. First, from a mother of two from High Mills, New York:

You can't warn people enough about Rock 'n' Roller Coaster. My daughter and I refused to go on it at all. My 9-year-old son, who had no problems with any ride, including Tower of Terror, went on with my husband and came off so shaken he was "done for" the rest of the day. My husband just closed his eyes and hoped for the best.

And from a Longmont, Colorado, dad:

The first 15 seconds of this ride are spectacular. I've never experienced anything like the initial take-off.

From an Australian couple who traveled a long way to ride a coaster:

My wife and I are definitely not roller-coaster people. However, we found Rock 'n' Roller Coaster quite exhilarating—and because it's dark, we didn't always realize that we were being thrown upside down. We rode it twice!

TOURING TIPS Rock 'n' Roller Coaster is not for everyone—if Space Mountain or Big Thunder pushes your limits, stay away.

Expect long lines except in the first 30 minutes after opening and during the late-evening performance of *Fantasmic!* Ride as soon as possible in the morning, or use the single-rider line or FastPass+.

A good strategy for riding Rock 'n' Roller Coaster, Toy Story Mania!, and Tower of Terror with minimum wait is to make midmorning FastPass+ reservations for Toy Story Mania! and Tower of Terror up to 60 days in advance. Then, when you visit, rush first thing after opening to ride Rock 'n' Roller Coaster. If you can't make FastPass+ reservations before you arrive, ride Rock 'n' Roller Coaster or Toy Story Mania! first, an then find the nearest FastPass+ kiosk to make the other reservations.

Theater of the Stars / *Beauty and the Beast—Live on Stage* (FastPass+) ★★★★

What it is Live Hollywood-style musical featuring Disney characters, performed in an open-air theater. **Scope and scale** Major attraction. **When to go** Anytime; evenings are cooler. **Special comments** Check your *Times Guide* for showtimes. **Authors' rating** Excellent; ★★★★. **Duration of presentation** 25 minutes. **Preshow entertainment** None. **When to arrive** 25–35 minutes before showtime.

DESCRIPTION AND COMMENTS Theater of the Stars hosts live shows combining Disney characters with singers and dancers in upbeat and humorous Hollywood-style productions. The long-running *Beauty and the Beast* show, in particular, is outstanding. It combines a shortened (but complete) retelling of the story with all of the major musical numbers, with tons of characters and good set decoration.

To offer more entertainment options while the park is under construction, Disney ran a different evening show here for summer 2017, focused on music from Pixar's films. Disney hadn't extended the show's run beyond August 2017 as we were going to press, but we wouldn't be surprised if that changed or if similar shows were presented in the future.

The theater offers a clear field of vision from almost every seat. Best of all, a canopy protects the audience from the Florida sun (or rain), but the theater still gets mighty hot in the summer.

TOURING TIPS *Beauty and the Beast* usually runs from midmorning to around 4 p.m.; the show is so popular that you should arrive 25–35 minutes early to get a good seat.

The Twilight Zone Tower of Terror *(FastPass+)* ★★★★★

APPEAL BY AGE	PRESCHOOL ★★½	GRADE SCHOOL ★★★★	TEENS ★★★★½
YOUNG ADULTS ★★★★★		OVER 30 ★★★★½	SENIORS ★★★★

What it is Sci-fi-themed indoor thrill ride. **Scope and scale** Super-headliner. **When to go** First or last 30 minutes the park is open, or use FastPass+. **Special comments** 40" minimum height requirement. Switching-off option provided (see page 439). **Authors' rating** Walt Disney World's best attraction; not to be missed; ★★★★★. **Duration of ride** About 4 minutes plus preshow. **Average wait in line per 100 people ahead of you** 4 minutes; assumes all elevators operating. **Loading speed** Moderate.

DESCRIPTION AND COMMENTS The Tower of Terror is a different species of Disney thrill ride, though it borrows elements of The Haunted Mansion at the Magic Kingdom. The story is that you're touring a once-famous Hollywood hotel gone to ruin. As at Star Tours, the queuing area immerses guests in the adventure as they pass through the hotel's once-opulent public rooms. From the lobby, guests are escorted into the hotel's library, where Rod Serling, speaking from an old black-and-white television, greets the guests and introduces the plot.

The Tower of Terror is a whopper, at 13 stories tall. Breaking tradition in terms of visually isolating themed areas, it lets you see the entire Studios from atop the tower . . . but you have to look quick.

The ride vehicle, one of the hotel's service elevators, takes guests to see the haunted hostelry. The tour begins innocuously, but at about the fifth floor things get pretty weird. Guests are subjected to a full range of eerie effects as they cross into the Twilight Zone. The climax occurs when the elevator reaches the top floor—the 13th, of course—and the cable snaps.

The Tower of Terror is an experience to savor. Though the final plunges—yep, plural—are calculated to thrill, the meat of the attraction is its extraordinary visual and audio effects. There's richness and subtlety here, enough to keep the ride fresh and stimulating after many repetitions. Disney has also programmed random lift-and-drop sequences into the mix, making the attraction faster and keeping you guessing about when, how far, and how many times the elevator will fall.

A senior from the United Kingdom tried the Tower of Terror and liked it very much, writing:

I was thankful I had read your review of the Tower of Terror, or I would certainly have avoided it. As you say, it's so full of magnificent detail that it's worth riding even if you don't fancy the drops involved.

A reader from Washington state thinks the randomness is a net negative:

Did they make the Tower of Terror ride much more tame? Last time I went to WDW, it was almost 20 years ago, but I remember a HUGE drop initially. This time it was just kind of up, down, up, down, up, up, down. I couldn't hide the disappointment on my face, and the ride picture has me looking like I am still waiting for something cool to happen. Bummer.

The Tower has great potential for terrifying young children and rattling more-mature visitors. If you have teenagers in your party, use them as experimental probes. If they report back that they really, really liked the Tower of Terror, run like hell in the opposite direction.

DISNEY DISH WITH JIM HILL

THEATER FIT FOR A QUEEN The Imagineers went all-out in plussing up this oft-used theater. WDI started by projection-mapping the interior of the Hyperion Theater. They then had Walt Disney Animation Studios create all-new enhanced animation for this sing-along celebration. Toss in a few columns, a new blue-and-silver color scheme, and a grand reveal of Queen Elsa at the very end of this show, and you've got a showstopping theatrical presentation.

TOURING TIPS If you're on hand when the park opens and you want to ride Tower of Terror first, be aware that about 65% of the folks walking down Sunset Boulevard head for Rock 'n' Roller Coaster. If you're not positioned on the far right of the street, it will be hard to move through the crowd to make a right turn into Tower of Terror.

To save time once you're inside the queuing area, when you enter the library waiting room, stand in the far back corner across from the door where you entered and at the opposite end of the room from the TV. When the doors to the loading area open, you'll be the first admitted.

If you have young children (or anyone) who are apprehensive about this attraction, ask the attendant about switching off (see page 439).

Our touring plans on pages 831 and 832 incorporate an optimal strategy for riding Tower of Terror, Rock 'n' Roller Coaster, and Toy Story Mania! with minimum waits.

ECHO LAKE

AN ACTUAL MINIATURE LAKE near the middle of the Studios, to the left of Hollywood Boulevard, Echo Lake pays homage to its real-life California counterpart, which served as the backdrop to many early motion pictures. It also provides a visual transition from Hollywood Boulevard's retro theming to Streets of America's film-set ambience.

For the First Time in Forever: A Frozen Sing-Along Celebration (FastPass+)   ★★★

APPEAL BY AGE	PRESCHOOL ★★★★½	GRADE SCHOOL ★★★★½	TEENS ★★★★
YOUNG ADULTS ★★★★	OVER 30 ★★★★½		SENIORS ★★★★½

What it is Sing-along stage show retelling the story of *Frozen,* with appearances by Anna and Elsa. **Scope and scale** Minor attraction. **When to go** Arrive 15 minutes before the scheduled showtime. **Authors' rating** You'll learn all the words, whether you want to or not; ★★★. **Duration of presentation** 25 minutes.

DESCRIPTION AND COMMENTS This attraction started out as a hastily assembled stage show during the summer of 2014, when DHS was closing other attractions and needed something for guests to do. The show retells the plot of *Frozen* in 25 minutes. That's enough time to sing every song in the movie and have a quick visit from Anna and Elsa.

Scenes from the movie, projected on a drive-in movie–sized screen in the background, provide continuity and familiarize those who haven't seen the film with the characters and storyline. Live performers, including two "royal historians" and several characters from *Frozen,* lay down some stand-up comedy shtick to facilitate the narrative and add some corny and occasionally punchy humor. Most of the story is related at a leisurely pace, but the ending is presented in a nanosecond, leaving much of the audience stupefied. Of course, the finale features the meet and greet with Anna and Elsa and another rousing belting of "Let It Go."

If you're a fan of the movie, you probably won't notice the deficits described earlier. And even if you're not a fan, you'll enjoy the show's spirit as well as that of a theater full of enraptured children. Yes, it's contagious. Most readers view the sing-along favorably. First, a man from Pittsburgh:

The Frozen Sing-Along *show was the surprise hit! I was dreading having to attend this show, but it was hilarious! It felt like they took two of the comedians from* Monsters, Inc., *and dropped them live onstage. Don't judge a book by its cover; this show is an A+ for all ages.*

A mom from Houston, Texas, agrees:

A special shout-out to the attraction Frozen-Sing Along *at DHS. I reluctantly used a FastPass+, for my 7-year-old daughter. Glad we didn't skip it. It was a total hoot, akin to stand-up comedy, so both adults and elementary-aged kids thoroughly enjoyed it. My husband and I thought it was the highlight of our DHS visit! When we got home, my husband and 9-year-old son (who both had never seen the movie) watched* Frozen *with my daughter.*

A mom from Richmond, Virginia, says that even with *Frozen* overload, the sing-along is a definite upper:

The sing-along was fantastic—along with Fantasmic!, *it was the highlight of the day. Even if you're a bit sick of* Frozen, *the atmosphere and the humor involved make it a lot of fun.*

But a Connecticut reader was disappointed:

The new Frozen Sing-Along *show in Hollywood Studios was extremely disappointing. It claimed to be live action, but for most of the time the audience is watching scenes from the movie.*

TOURING TIPS FastPass+ gets you access to a preferred-seating section closer to the stage. The indoor theater is one of Disney's largest and most comfortable, with excellent sight lines from every seat. Crowd management when entering the theater is a little confusing, but once you're inside it sorts itself out.

Indiana Jones Epic Stunt Spectacular! (FastPass+) ★★★½

APPEAL BY AGE PRESCHOOL ★★★½ GRADE SCHOOL ★★★★½ TEENS ★★★★½
YOUNG ADULTS ★★★★ OVER 30 ★★★★ SENIORS ★★★★

What it is Movie-stunt demonstration and action show. **Scope and scale** Headliner. **When to go** First two shows or last show. **Special comment** Performance times posted on a sign at the entrance to the theater. **Authors' rating** Done on a grand scale; ★★★½. **Duration of presentation** 30 minutes. **Preshow entertainment** Selection of "extras" from audience. **When to arrive** 20–30 minutes before showtime.

DESCRIPTION AND COMMENTS Educational though somewhat unevenly paced, the popular production showcases professional stunt men and women who offer behind-the-scenes demonstrations of their craft. Sets, props, and special effects are very elaborate.

TOURING TIPS The Stunt Theater holds 2,000 people; capacity audiences are common. The first performance is always the easiest to see. If the first show is at 10 a.m. or earlier, you can usually walk in, even if you arrive 5 minutes late. For the second performance, show up about 15–20 minutes ahead of time; for the third and subsequent shows, arrive 20–30 minutes early. If you plan to tour during late afternoon and evening, attend the last performance of the day. To beat the crowd out of the stadium, sit on the far right (as you face the staging area) and near the top.

To be chosen from the audience to be an "extra" in the stunt show, arrive early, sit down front, and display unbridled enthusiasm. A woman from Richmond, Virginia, explains:

After the first performance, I realized the best way to get picked was to stand up, wave my arms, and shout when the "casting director" called for volunteers. (Sitting toward the front helps, too.)

Jedi Training: Trials of the Temple ★★★½

APPEAL BY AGE	PRESCHOOL ★★★★	GRADE SCHOOL ★★★★½	TEENS ★★★½
YOUNG ADULTS ★★★½		OVER 30 ★★★★	SENIORS ★★★★

What it is Outdoor stage show. **Scope and scale** Minor attraction. **When to go** First 2 shows of the day. **Special comments** To sign up your children to go onstage, visit the ABC Sound Studio building early in the morning, or look for cast members near the entrance just before and after park opening. Spots are first-come, first-served. **Authors' rating** A treat for young Star Wars lovers; ★★★½. **Duration of show** About 15 minutes. **When to arrive** 15 minutes before showtime.

DESCRIPTION AND COMMENTS *Jedi Training: Trials of the Temple* is staged several times daily to the left of the Star Tours building entrance, opposite Backlot Express. If you want your young Skywalkers-in-training to appear onstage, visit the sign-up area at the ABC Sound Studio building (across from Star Tours) as early in the morning as possible; also, cast members are sometimes stationed outside the entrance just before and after the park opens. Spots go quickly and are first-come, first-served.

A Windham, New Hampshire, mom describes a common conundrum:

Many families will have to choose between racing to Toy Story Mania! to ride or racing to sign up for Jedi Training: Trials of the Temple *(children MUST be present at sign-up). We hopped on Toy Story Mania!, then crossed the park to sign up for* Jedi. *By the time we got there, we were pushed to the 2:20 p.m. show, which eliminated the possibility of leaving for a nap after lunch.*

A Melbourne, Australia, mom laments the investment of time:

Our touring plans have been very accurate in the past. One thing that can quickly derail the plan is Jedi Training. *It requires that the kids be there more than 30 minutes before the show; add in the show and the time to sign up in the morning, and you are looking at a 90-plus-minute investment. That wasn't in the plan, but it was my son's favorite part of our last visit.*

Once onstage, these miniature Jedi are trained in the ways of The Force and do battle against the likes of Darth Vader, Kylo Ren, and the Seventh Sister Inquisitor (from the *Star Wars Rebels* TV show). If all this sounds too intense, it's not: Stormtroopers provide comic relief, and just as in the movies, the good guys always win.

TOURING TIPS Surprisingly popular, given that Disney hasn't promoted it at the same level of hype as other shows. In the summer, grab drinks at Backlot Express, right next door, about 20 minutes before the show starts.

If *Jedi Training: Trials of the Temple* is at the top of your child's hit parade, a mom from Camp Hill, Pennsylvania, suggests checking the weather forecast before you head to the park:

There are Jedi Training *shows throughout the day until 8 p.m., and the line to get signed up was huge! This show is a big draw for kids and parents. The only problem is that the show is on an outdoor stage and if there is rain, the show is canceled. One mom told me that this was the second day in a row she had tried to get her kids signed up. The day before, they were signed up, dressed in their Jedi robes, [but when] a few raindrops fell the show was canceled. Since all shows are filled, there is no chance to rebook that day. It seems that Disney needs to rethink this show and put it under some kind of cover; nothing makes for a more unhappy day than disappointing 15 little kids and even more parents after a lot of anticipation and waiting around.*

Star Tours—The Adventures Continue
(FastPass+) ★★★½

APPEAL BY AGE PRESCHOOL ★★★★ GRADE SCHOOL ★★★★½ TEENS ★★★★½
YOUNG ADULTS ★★★★½   OVER 30 ★★★★½   SENIORS ★★★★½

What it is Indoor space-flight-simulation ride. **Scope and scale** Headliner. **When to go** Before 10 a.m., after 6 p.m., or use FastPass. **Special comments** Expectant mothers and anyone prone to motion sickness are advised against riding. Too intense for many children younger than age 8; 40" minimum height requirement. **Authors' rating** A classic adventure; not to be missed; ★★★½. **Duration of ride** About 7 minutes. **Average wait in line per 100 people ahead of you** 5 minutes; assumes all simulators operating. **Loading speed** Moderate–fast.

Motion Sickness

DESCRIPTION AND COMMENTS Based on the Star Wars series, this was Disney's first modern simulator ride. Guests ride in a flight simulator modeled after those used for training pilots and astronauts. You experience dips, turns, twists, and climbs as your vehicle goes through an intergalactic version of the chariot race in *Ben-Hur*. The ride film, projected in high-definition 3-D, has more than 50 combinations of opening and ending scenes, including clips from *The Force Awakens*. You could ride Star Tours all day without seeing the same scenes twice.

An interactive show, *Jedi Training: Trials of the Temple* (see page 657), is staged several times daily to the left of the Star Tours building entrance.

TOURING TIPS Try to ride before 10 a.m., or use FastPass+. If you have young children (or anyone) who are apprehensive about this attraction, ask the attendant about switching off (see page 439). Watch for throngs arriving from performances of the *Indiana Jones Epic Stunt Spectacular!*—if you encounter a long line, try again later.

MUPPET COURTYARD

FORMERLY A WALK-THROUGH back-lot movie set, Muppet Courtyard is now a themed area with just one attraction and a single restaurant. The street sets, still intact, serve as a pedestrian thoroughfare.

Jim Henson's Muppet-Vision 3-D (FastPass+) ★★★★

APPEAL BY AGE PRESCHOOL ★★★★ GRADE SCHOOL ★★★★ TEENS ★★★★
YOUNG ADULTS ★★★★   OVER 30 ★★★★   SENIORS ★★★★

What it is 3-D movie starring the Muppets. **Scope and scale** Major attraction. **When to go** Anytime. **Authors' rating** Uproarious; not to be missed; ★★★★. **Duration of presentation** 17 minutes. **Preshow entertainment** Muppets on television. **Probable waiting time** 12 minutes.

DESCRIPTION AND COMMENTS *Muppet-Vision 3-D* provides a total sensory experience, with wild 3-D action augmented by auditory, visual, and tactile special effects. If you're tired and hot, this zany presentation will make you feel brand-new. Arrive early and enjoy the hilarious video preshow.

A New Brunswick, Canada, reader thinks the Muppets are heaven-sent:

I think Muppet-Vision 3-D is a godsend for five reasons: (1) It NEVER has a line (even on our visit on New Year's Day). (2) Everyone ages 1-100 gives the show high marks. (3) Between the preshow and the movie, it's half an hour seated comfortably in an air-conditioned theater. (4) Between the live actors and animatronics, it's so much more than just another silly 3-D movie. (5) IT'S THE MUPPETS! Who doesn't love these hysterical creatures and their 3-D shenanigans?

TOURING TIPS This show is popular, but capacity is almost always sufficient. Waits peak around lunchtime, and it's unusual to see a wait of more than 20 minutes except during holidays. Watch for throngs arriving from the *Epic Stunt Spectacular!*—if you do encounter a long line, try again later.

DISNEY DISH WITH JIM HILL

PUMPING UP PIXAR PLACE Disney wants to turn Hollywood Studios into a full-day theme park. To do that, a number of Pixar-themed rides are now in the works. Some will be simple spinners and flat rides similar to the ones that were recently installed at Hong Kong Disneyland and Walt Disney Studios in Paris. Others will be wildly ambitious, such as an indoor version of Radiator Springs Racers at Disney California Adventure. It's going to take almost five years to complete this Pixar Place expansion, but it should be a real winner once it's running.

PIXAR PLACE/TOY STORY LAND

THE WALKWAY BETWEEN *Voyage of the Little Mermaid* and the Backlot Express restaurant holds the popular Toy Story Mania! attraction. To emphasize the importance of the Toy Story franchise, this section of the park is called Pixar Place. When Toy Story Land opens in 2018, we expect the Pixar Place walkway to close and the entrance to Toy Story Mania! to relocate to Toy Story Land.

The 11-acre Toy Story Land is the first new land at Disney's Hollywood Studios in more than 20 years. The idea behind it is that you've been shrunk to the size of a toy and placed in Andy's backyard, where you get to play with other toys he's set up.

Toy Story Land's attractions are designed to appeal to young children. That's good; the park has needed more such rides for years. As we went to press, there were few details available about the two rides. The descriptions are what we've heard and sussed out with a case of Chivas and a roll of twenties.

Alien Swirling Saucers *(opens 2018)*

APPEAL BY AGE   NOT OPEN AT PRESS TIME

What it is Spinning car ride. **Scope and scale** Minor attraction. **When to go** As soon as the park opens. **Special comment** Height requirement likely to be around 32". **Authors' rating** N/A **Duration of ride** N/A. **Average wait in line per 100 people ahead of you** N/A. **Loading speed** N/A.

DESCRIPTION AND COMMENTS Alien Swirling Saucers is themed around *Toy Story*'s vending machine aliens and their obsession with The Claw. Like Mater's Junkyard Jamboree in Disney California Adventure, we expect about a dozen ride cars to move, whiplike, in a figure-eight pattern around two circular tracks embedded in the ground. We think there'll be two of those figure-eight tracks to boost the ride's hourly capacity. As far as the ride experience, if it's like Mater's, it'll be much milder than the Magic Kingdom's Mad Tea Party.

TOURING TIPS Expect long lines as soon as the ride opens. Ride during the first or last hour the park is open. We don't think FastPass+ will be offered for this ride.

Slinky Dog Dash *(opens 2018)*

What it is Outdoor roller coaster. **Scope and scale** Major attraction. **When to go** As soon as the park opens, or use FastPass+. **Special comment** Height requirement likely to be 32"–35". **Authors' rating** N/A, but we predict that it'll be not to be missed. **Duration of ride** N/A. **Average wait in line per 100 people ahead of you** N/A. **Loading speed** We think it'll be slow.

DESCRIPTION AND COMMENTS Slinky Dog Dash is a long, outdoor roller coaster designed to look like Andy built it out of Tinkertoys. The coaster's trains are themed (naturally) to *Toy Story*'s Slinky Dog. As for intensity, expect something along the lines of the Magic Kingdom's Barnstormer or Seven Dwarfs Mine Train—lots of turns, dips, and hills but no loops or high-speed curves—and not as forceful as Big Thunder Mountain Railroad.

TOURING TIPS Likely to be inundated as soon as the park opens and to stay that way all day. We expect Slinky Dog Dash to offer FastPass+; use it, or visit as soon as the park opens or right before the park closes.

It's likely that Disney will put Slinky Dog Dash and Toy Story Mania! in the same FastPass+ tier, meaning you'll be able to make an advance Fast-Pass+ reservation for only one of the two. If that happens, get a FastPass+ for whichever one you can, as early in the day as possible. When the park opens, head immediately for the other one and ride; then experience Alien Swirling Saucers.

Toy Story Mania! *(FastPass+)*   ★★★★½

What it is 3-D ride through indoor shooting gallery. **Scope and scale** Headliner. **When to go** As soon as the park opens, or use FastPass+. **Authors' rating** Not to be missed; ★★★★½. **Duration of ride** About 6½ minutes. **Average wait in line per 100 people ahead of you** 4½ minutes. **Loading speed** Fast.

DESCRIPTION AND COMMENTS Toy Story Mania! ushered in a new generation of Disney attraction: the "virtual dark ride." Since Disneyland opened in 1955, ride vehicles have moved past 2-D and 3-D sets often populated by Audio-Animatronic (AA) figures. Now, for Toy Story Mania!, the elaborate sets and endearing characters are gone. Instead, imagine long, empty corridors covered with reflective material. There's almost nothing there—until you put on your 3-D glasses. Instantly, the corridor is brimming with color and activity, thanks to projected computer-graphic (CG) images.

Conceptually, this is an interactive shooting gallery much like Buzz Lightyear's Space Ranger Spin (see page 548), but in Toy Story Mania!, your ride vehicle passes through a totally virtual midway, with booths offering such games as ring tossing and ball throwing. You use a cannon on your vehicle to play as you move from booth to booth. Unlike the laser guns in Buzz Lightyear, though, the pull-string cannons in Toy Story Mania! take advantage of CG image technology to toss rings, shoot balls, and even throw eggs and pies. Each booth is manned by a Toy Story character, who is right beside you in 3-D glory, cheering you on. In addition to 3-D imagery, you experience vehicle motion, wind, and water spray.

The ride begins with a training round, then continues through a number of "real" games in which you compete against your riding mate. The technology has the ability to self-adjust the level of difficulty, and there are plenty of easy targets for small children to reach. *Tip:* Let the string retract all the way back into the cannon before pulling it again.

Finally, a 6-foot-tall Mr. Potato Head occasionally interacts with and talks to guests in real time in the queuing area (similar to the *Turtle Talk with Crush* show at *Epcot*).

TOURING TIPS Because it's a ton of fun and it has a relatively low rider-per-hour capacity, Toy Story Mania! is the biggest bottleneck in Walt Disney World, surpassing even Test Track at Epcot. The only way to get aboard without a horrendous wait is to be one of the first through the turnstiles when the park opens and zoom to the attraction. Another alternative is to obtain FastPass+ reservations. But you'll need to act fast: Even on days of moderate attendance, all reservations for the day are usually gone by 11 a.m.

Families with children too small to ride Rock 'n' Roller Coaster or Tower of Terror make a beeline to Toy Story Mania! first thing in the morning, and waits can reach 90 minutes or more on a busy day. In fact, the lines grow so fast that in about a third of our touring plan variations, we recommend getting a FastPass+ reservation for 9–10 a.m., even when Toy Story is the first step in the plan. The two benefits to doing this are that you'll shave off at least 10 minutes of waiting, and you don't have to line up as early at the park entrance to join the mad run to Toy Story.

Readers generally love the ride but hate the wait. A Nashville, Tennessee, mom was mostly positive:

Toy Story Mania! was already swamped fairly early in the day. We had to resort to getting some of the last FastPass+ reservations, and it extended our day to wait until our return time came up. But oh my gosh, it was worth the wait!

But a woman from Aberdeen, Washington, was mostly frustrated:

We decided to risk the 70-minute wait for Toy Story Mania! because my family loves Pixar. The line is a nightmare—it took 2 hours to complete, because for every five regular-line people let into the ride, 40–50 FastPass+ people are let in. (Yes, I counted.)

Disney is adding a third track to Toy Story Mania!, which should be completed in 2016. It will be dedicated to standby guests, while the original two tracks will serve guests with FastPass+ reservations.

ANIMATION COURTYARD

THIS AREA IS TO THE RIGHT of The Great Movie Ride in the middle of the park. It holds two large theaters used for live stage shows, a walk-through display of Star Wars movie props, plus several character-greeting locations. We think it's just a big swath of asphalt in desperate need of some landscaping or a water feature.

Disney Junior—Live on Stage! (FastPass+)   ★★★★

APPEAL BY AGE	PRESCHOOL ★★★★½	GRADE SCHOOL ★★★★	TEENS ★★½
YOUNG ADULTS ★★½	OVER 30 ★★★		SENIORS ★★★

What it is Live show for children. **Scope and scale** Minor attraction. **When to go** Per the daily entertainment schedule. **Special comments** Audience sits on the floor. **Authors' rating** A must for families with preschoolers; ★★★★. **Duration of presentation** 20 minutes. **When to arrive** 20–30 minutes before showtime.

DESCRIPTION AND COMMENTS The show features characters from the Disney Channel's *Sofia the First, Doc McStuffins,* and *Jake and the Never Land Pirates,* among others. *Disney Junior* uses elaborate puppets instead of live characters onstage. A simple plot serves as the platform for singing, dancing, puppetry, and audience participation. The characters, who ooze love and goodness, rally throngs of tots and preschoolers to sing and dance along with them. All the jumping, squirming, and high-stepping is facilitated by having the audience sit on the floor so that kids can spontaneously erupt into motion when the mood strikes. Even for adults without children, it's a treat to watch the tykes rev up.

TOURING TIPS Staged in a huge building on the right side of the courtyard. Get here at least 25 minutes before showtime, pick a spot on the floor, and take a breather until the action begins.

Star Wars Launch Bay *(FastPass+)*   ★★

APPEAL BY AGE	PRESCHOOL ★★★★	GRADE SCHOOL ★★★★½	TEENS ★★★★½
YOUNG ADULTS ★★★★		OVER 30 ★★★★	SENIORS ★★★★

What it is Displays of a few Star Wars movie models and props, a movie trailer, and character greetings. **Scope and scale** Diversion. **When to go** Anytime. **Special comments** The movie trailer includes plot spoilers from the entire *Star Wars* oeuvre. **Authors' rating** This is not the entertainment you're looking for; ★★. **Probable waiting time** 20–30 minutes each for the movie trailer and character greetings.

DESCRIPTION AND COMMENTS It's no secret that Disney needs more things for guests to do at this park. Adding what's essentially a walk-through commercial and gift shop for their new Star Wars films seems to fill the bill. There are a few interesting models here for the serious Star Wars fan, but they're spread out over such a large space that it makes the whole building seem emptier.

Two character-greeting opportunities are available, usually Chewbacca and either Darth Vader, Kylo Ren, or BB-8. Waits in line for both usually run about 20–30 minutes. The line for the movie trailer—which, again, just summarizes the existing films—runs 15–30 minutes, too. If you're looking for a Star Wars character experience with little to no wait, look for a pair of Jawas located near the Cantina set. They roam about looking to trade small tokens with guests.

TOURING TIPS Visit first thing in the a.m. for shorter character-greeting lines.

Voyage of the Little Mermaid *(FastPass+)*   ★★★½

APPEAL BY AGE	PRESCHOOL ★★★★	GRADE SCHOOL ★★★★	TEENS ★★★½
YOUNG ADULTS ★★★½		OVER 30 ★★★½	SENIORS ★★★★

What it is Musical stage show featuring characters from the Disney movie *The Little Mermaid*. **Scope and scale** Major attraction. **When to go** Before 9:45 a.m., just before closing, or use FastPass+. **Authors' rating** Romantic, lovable, and humorous in the best Disney tradition; ★★★½. **Duration of presentation** 15 minutes. **Preshow entertainment** Taped ramblings about the decor in the preshow holding area. **Probable waiting time** Before 9:30 a.m., 10–30 minutes; after 9:30 a.m., 35–70 minutes.

DESCRIPTION AND COMMENTS *Voyage of the Little Mermaid* is a winner that appeals to every age. Sweet but not saccharine, its story is engaging, its special effects impressive, and its characters memorable.

We get a lot of mail from Europeans who complain about the "soppy sentimentality" of Americans in general and of Disney attractions in particular. These comments of a man from Bristol, England, are typical:

English cynicism made it hard for us at times to see Disney stories as anything other than gushing, namby-pamby, and full of stereotypes. Other Brits might also find the sentimentality cloying. Maybe you should prepare them for the need to rethink their wry outlook on life temporarily.

TOURING TIPS Except during the busiest holiday periods, it's unusual for any-one in line not to be admitted to the next showing of *Mermaid*. Typical waits are under 25 minutes most of the year.

When you enter the preshow lobby, stand near the doors to the theater. When they open, go inside, pick a row of seats and let 6–10 people enter the row ahead of you. The strategy is twofold: to obtain a good seat and be near the exit.

Walt Disney: One Man's Dream   ★★★

APPEAL BY AGE	PRESCHOOL ★★½	GRADE SCHOOL ★★★	TEENS ★★★½
YOUNG ADULTS ★★★★	OVER 30 ★★★★		SENIORS ★★★★½

What it is Tribute to Walt Disney. **Scope and scale** Minor attraction. **When to go** Any-time. **Authors' rating** Excellent; ★★★. **Duration of presentation** 25 minutes. **Preshow entertainment** Disney memorabilia. **Probable waiting time** For the film, 10 minutes.

DESCRIPTION AND COMMENTS Launched in 2001 to celebrate the 100th anni-versary of Disney's birth, *One Man's Dream* consists of an exhibit area showcasing Disney memorabilia and recordings, usually followed by a film documenting Disney's life. On display are various innovations in animation developed by Disney, along with early models and working plans for Walt Disney World and various Disney theme parks around the world. The stan-dard film provides a personal glimpse of Disney and offers insights regard-ing both his successes and failures. (Note that the Walt film is sometimes replaced by previews of upcoming Disney movies.)

TOURING TIPS Give yourself time here. Every minute spent among these extraordinary artifacts will enhance your visit, taking you back to a time when the creativity and vision that created Walt Disney World were per-sonified by one struggling entrepreneur.

There are occasional character greetings held in the back of the build-ing. Summer 2017 characters include Baby Groot and Star-Lord from *Guard-ians of the Galaxy*. Keep an eye out for unique photo ops here.

LIVE ENTERTAINMENT *in* DISNEY'S HOLLYWOOD STUDIOS

IN ADDITION TO THE MANY stage-show attractions, there are a number of other live-entertainment opportunities at Disney's Holly-wood Studios.

Currently, the focus is on Star Wars–related experiences. **The March of the First Order** is a minor parade–stage show hybrid. Captain Phasma and a legion of Stormtroopers walk in formation from the park entrance area to the Great Movie Ride and make a few proclamations from the stage. The "show" is quite minimal; it's mostly about the Empire march-ing around. The Stormtroopers' blasters and full-body uniforms are a thrill for Star Wars geeks, but they could be quite intimidating for a skittish child.

In *Star Wars: A Galaxy Far, Far Away,* newer characters such as Kylo Ren and BB-8 join Darth Maul and Chewbacca in scene reenactments.

Hollywood Studios' evening show is *Star Wars: A Galactic Spectacular.* This laser and fireworks presentation projects images and video from the Star Wars films onto a backdrop of the Chinese Theatre. The real thrill is listening to John Williams's soaring score while fireworks blast above you.

A new show, *Disney Movie Magic,* runs 30 minutes before the Star Wars fireworks. Projected onto the Chinese Theatre, it uses video projection technology to add special effects on top of clips from recent and classic Disney movie franchises. It's a nice diversion if you can't (or don't want to) see *Fantasmic!*

If you're in a more down-to-earth mood, keep an eye out for the **Citizens of Hollywood.** These "Streetmosphere" players wander the park and engage guests in interactive performances related to the glamour days of Hollywood.

CHARACTER GREETINGS On Commissary Lane, between the ABC Commissary and the Sci-Fi Dine-In Theater Restaurant is **Mickey and Minnie Starring in Red Carpet Dreams.** The idea is that you're visiting them both while they work on their latest films. Minnie's meet and greet is the set of her latest movie, a musical blockbuster; Mickey is decked out as the Sorcerer's Apprentice from *Fantasia.* See page 443 for additional character greetings in the Studios.

DISNEY'S HOLLYWOOD STUDIOS TOURING PLAN

WE PROVIDE TWO VERSIONS of our standard one-day plan for the Studios: one to use before Toy Story Land opens in 2018 (page 831) and one for after. (page 832). Each starts at 9 a.m. and allows for a leisurely lunch and dinner, plus free time after dinner to explore the park.

Until Toy Story Land opens, so many attractions are closed or in need of updates that it's possible to see everything worthwhile at the Studios in less than a full day. If you eat a quick-service lunch and dinner, you can show up around 11 a.m. and still see everything in the park. Try to get the same FastPass+ recommendations as shown on the standard plan, for the first 3 hours after your planned arrival time. Use our touring plan software as needed.

PART THIRTEEN

UNIVERSAL ORLANDO *and* SEAWORLD

UNIVERSAL ORLANDO

UNIVERSAL ORLANDO is a complete destination resort, with two theme parks; a brand-new water park; five (soon to be six) hotels; and a shopping, dining, and entertainment complex. A system of roads and two multistory parking facilities is connected by moving sidewalks to **City-Walk**, a shopping, dining, and nighttime-entertainment complex that also serves as a gateway to **Universal Studios Florida (USF)** and **Universal's Islands of Adventure (IOA)** theme parks, as well as **Universal's Volcano Bay** water park (see Part Fourteen, page 733, for a description).

Universal Orlando has developed into a world-class, multifaceted resort destination—one that we cannot cover comprehensively in the few dozen pages allocated in this book. For in-depth coverage of the Universal parks, consider *The Unofficial Guide to Universal Orlando,* by Seth Kubersky with Bob Sehlinger and Len Testa. This guide is the most comprehensive on Universal Orlando in print, with almost 400 pages devoted to the subject. Though we'll continue to cover Universal Orlando in this book, we strongly recommend the new guide for all of the tips, insights, elaborations, and attention to detail that we can't accommodate herein.

LODGING AT UNIVERSAL ORLANDO

UNIVERSAL HAS FIVE RESORT HOTELS, with a sixth opening in 2018. The 750-room **Portofino Bay Hotel** is a gorgeous property set on an artificial bay and themed like an Italian coastal town. The 650-room **Hard Rock Hotel** is an ultracool "Hotel California" replica, and the 1,000-room, Polynesian-themed **Royal Pacific Resort** is sumptuously decorated and richly appointed. These three resorts are on the pricey side, but guests get free Universal Express Unlimited passes for the length of their stay, including check-in and checkout day (see page 669 for details).

The retro-style **Cabana Bay Beach Resort,** Universal's largest hotel, has 2,200 moderate- and value-priced rooms, plus amenities (bowling alley, lazy river) not seen at comparable Disney resorts. **Loews Sapphire Falls Resort** has a Caribbean theme and is priced between the Royal Pacific and Cabana Bay Beach Resorts.

Continued on page 668

Universal Orlando

Universal's Islands of Adventure

To Tampa & Walt Disney World ←

Turkey Lake Rd.

Hollywood Way

The Wizarding World of Harry Potter–Hogsmeade

Universal's Cabana Bay Beach Resort

Universal's Volcano Bay

Loews Sapphire Falls Resort

Universal's Aventura Hotel *(opens 2018)*

Main Entrance

Loews Royal Pacific Resort

Universal CityWalk

Universal Blvd.

American Way

Hollywood Way

Parking Garages

Grand National Dr.

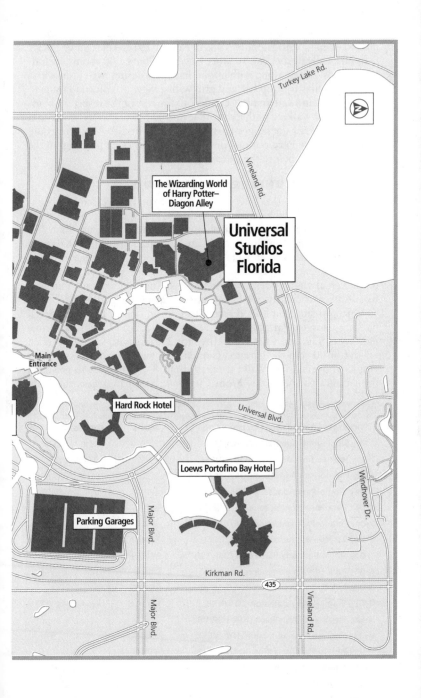

Continued from page 665

A sixth hotel, the value-priced **Universal's Aventura Hotel,** is scheduled to open next to Sapphire Falls in August 2018. Adjacent to Loews Sapphire Falls Resort, the 16-story tower will have 600 rooms, including 13 kids' suites, along with a food hall showcasing five cuisines and Universal's first rooftop bar and grill with a view of Volcano Bay.

Aventura and Cabana Bay connect to the rest of the resort via shuttle buses and walking paths; the other four hotels also offer water-taxi service. All hotel guests get Early Park Admission to The Wizarding World of Harry Potter at one or both theme parks (depending on the season) an hour before the general public.

ARRIVING AT UNIVERSAL ORLANDO

THE UNIVERSAL ORLANDO COMPLEX can be accessed from eastbound I-4 by taking Exit 75A and turning left at the top of the ramp onto Universal Boulevard. Traveling westbound on I-4, use Exit 74B and then turn right on Hollywood Way. Entrances are also off Kirkman Road to the east, Turkey Lake Road to the north, and Vineland Road to the west. Universal Boulevard connects the International Drive area to Universal via an overpass bridging I-4. Turkey Lake and Vineland Roads are particularly good alternatives when I-4 is gridlocked.

Once on-site, you'll be directed to park in one of two multitiered parking garages. Parking runs $20 for cars and $22 for RVs. Prime parking is $30, and valet is $40 (free for 2 hours with CityWalk lunch validation). From the garages, (sometimes) moving sidewalks deliver you to Universal CityWalk; it takes about 8–20 minutes to get from the garages to the parks. From CityWalk, you can access the main

UNIVERSAL ORLANDO ADMISSIONS *(online purchase)*		
TICKET TYPE (1-DAY PRICES = VALUE/ANYTIME)	ADULTS	CHILDREN (Ages 3–9)
1-Day Single-Park Admission (IOA/USF)	$117.15/$132.06	$111.82/$126.73
1-Day Park-to-Park Admission (IOA/USF)	$175.72/$190.63	$170.40/$185.31
1-Day Park-to-Park Admission (IOA/USF/VB)	$218.32/$233.23	$213/$227.91
2-Day Single-Park Admission (IOA/USF)	$211.94	$202.34
2-Day Park-to-Park Admission (IOA/USF)	$271.56	$260.91
2-Day Park-to-Park Admission (IOA/USF/VB)	$314.16	$303.51
3-Day Single-Park Admission (IOA/USF)	$239.61	$228.96
3-Day Single-Park Admission (IOA/USF/VB)	$276.89	$266.24
3-Day Park-to-Park Admission (IOA/USF)	$292.86	$282.21
3-Day Park-to-Park Admission (IOA/USF/VB)	$335.46	$324.81
4-Day Single-Park Admission (IOA/USF)	$244.94	$234.29
4-Day Single-Park Admission (IOA/USF/VB)	$287.54	$276.89
4-Day Park-to-Park Admission (IOA/USF)	$303.51	$292.86
4-Day Park-to-Park Admission (IOA/USF/VB)	$346.11	$335.46
5-Day Single-Park Admission (IOA/USF)	$255.59	$244.94
5-Day Single-Park Admission (IOA/USF/VB)	$298.19	$287.54
5-Day Park-to-Park Admission (IOA/USF)	$314.16	$303.51
5-Day Park-to-Park Admission (IOA/USF/VB)	$356.76	$346.11

entrances of both USF and IOA. Volcano Bay guests park in the same garages and are shuttled to the water park. Parking is free for everyone after 6 p.m. (except during Halloween Horror Nights).

Universal offers one- to five-day tickets for one or two theme parks; adding Volcano Bay to any two-park ticket costs $40 plus tax, regardless of length, and upgrading from one-park-per-day to Park-to-Park access costs $55. Universal charges $14 less for one-day tickets valid only during Value season; multiday tickets are valid anytime but expire 14 days after their first use. They also sell a range of two- and three-park annual passes, some of which include sizable discounts on hotels, food, and merchandise.

Prices in the chart opposite include sales tax; a single day's admission to Volcano Bay costs $71.35, also including tax. Buy your passes in advance at ☎ 800-711-0080 or universalorlando.com.

Be sure to check Universal Orlando's website for seasonal deals and specials. You can save as much as $20 by buying your tickets online. The **Official Ticket Center,** a ticket discounter (officialticketcenter.com), offers the most deeply discounted Universal tickets we know of. Tickets purchased through OTC include tax and free shipping. In addition, OTC often matches or beats the short-term deals Universal offers on its own website, such as a recent "buy two days, get two days free" special.

The main Universal Orlando information number is ☎ 407-363-8000. Reach Guest Services at ☎ 407-224-4233, or schedule a character lunch at universalorlando.com. The number for lost and found is ☎ 407-224-4244.

A WORD ABOUT CROWDS

YOU'VE PROBABLY READ about the huge crowds that inundate the Wizarding World outposts at both Universal parks. The reports are true, but they present an unbalanced view of the crowds at the Universal parks overall.

To get a quantitative grip on crowding, let's look at attendance figures compared with the size of the parks. On a day of average attendance, USF and Disney's Hollywood Studios see about the same number of guests per acre. However, USF has many more attractions than DHS. Therefore, the crowds are distributed among more attractions at USF, making it seem less crowded. Contrasting the Magic Kingdom with IOA, the latter averages about 200 guests per day, per acre, while the Magic Kingdom—the attendance leader of all the world's theme parks—registers around 500 guests per day, per acre. Depending on how you define *attractions,* however, the Magic Kingdom has about 42, versus 27 at Islands of Adventure. Even so, there are still one-and-a-half as many guests for each Magic Kingdom attraction as for each IOA attraction.

UNIVERSAL EXPRESS

SIMILAR TO DISNEY WORLD'S FASTPASS+, Universal Express is a system whereby any guest can "skip the line" and experience an attraction via a special queue with little or no waiting. While Disney's system requires scheduling your ride reservation hours or days ahead of time, Universal Express involves no planning; you simply visit any eligible operating attraction whenever you choose, with no return-time windows required. In addition, unlike FastPass+, Universal Express is not free for everyone.

Universal Express is a complimentary perk (valued at $89 per person, per day) for guests at Universal's top three hotels: Portofino Bay, Hard Rock, and Royal Pacific. Guests may use the Express lines all day long simply by flashing the pass they get at check-in. This perk far surpasses any benefit accorded to guests of Disney resorts and is especially valuable during peak season.

Day guests, along with guests staying at Cabana Bay, Sapphire Falls, and Aventura, can buy Universal Express for an extra $50–$160 (depending on the season), which provides line-jumping privileges at each Universal Express attraction at a given park. You can buy Universal Express for both theme parks and for either single (one ride only on each participating attraction) or unlimited use.

More than 90% of rides and shows are covered by Universal Express—a much higher percentage than those covered by FastPass+ at Walt Disney World; the notable exceptions are **Pteranodon Flyers** at IOA and **Kang & Kodos' Twirl 'n' Hurl** at USF. At press time, Universal announced that the two headliners at each park's Wizarding World of Harry Potter—**Harry Potter and the Forbidden Journey** (Hogsmeade, IOA) and **Harry Potter and the Escape from Gringotts** (Diagon Alley, USF)—were finally being added to the Express roster.

You can also buy Universal Express at the theme parks' ticket windows, just outside the front gates, but it's faster to buy once you're inside. Express Passes are sold at most park gift shops, as well as from freestanding kiosks that proliferate around the parks during peak seasons; Express is also available up to eight months in advance at universalorlando.com. You'll need to know when you plan on using it, though, because prices vary depending on the date.

IS UNIVERSAL EXPRESS WORTH IT? That depends on when you visit, hours of park operation, and crowd levels. Attendance has jumped at both parks since the opening of each Harry Potter land. However, the big-ticket rides in Hogsmeade and Diagon Alley don't (yet) participate in Universal Express, so you don't get to cut in line at Universal's most in-demand attractions. Still, if you want to sleep in and arrive at a park after opening, Express is an effective, albeit expensive, way to avoid long lines at the non-Potter headliner attractions, especially during holidays and busy times.

If, however, you arrive 30 minutes before park opening and you use our Universal Orlando touring plans (see pages 833–836), you should experience the lowest possible waits at both Universal Studios and Islands of Adventure. We encourage you to try the touring plans first, but if waits for rides become intolerable, you can always buy Express in the parks.

If you do use Express, bring a lanyard (or buy one from Universal for $9 and up) to wear the pass around your neck, lest you lose it.

SINGLES LINES

SEVERAL ATTRACTIONS HAVE THIS SPECIAL LINE for guests riding alone. As Universal employees will tell you, this line is often just as fast as the Express line. We recommend using the singles line whenever possible—it will decrease your wait and leave more time for repeating rides or just bumming around. Note, though, that some queues (particularly Forbidden Journey's and Escape from Gringotts's) are attractions in themselves and deserve to be experienced during your first ride.

LOCKERS

UNIVERSAL ENFORCES A MANDATORY locker system at its big thrill rides. On most rides, all bags, purses, and other objects too large to be secured in a pocket must be placed in a locker. A strict "no loose items" policy is enforced at The Incredible Hulk Coaster, Hollywood Rip Ride Rockit, and Dragon Challenge. At these rides, guests must pass through an airport-style security screening to ensure that no phones, keys, or even spare change enter the queue.

Lockers outside these attractions are free to use for an amount of time that depends on the length of the standby line. So if the line is 30 minutes, for example, and the ride itself is 10 minutes, you get 40 minutes plus a small cushion of about 15 minutes. The mandatory lockers then cost $3 for each half-hour after the free period, with a $20 maximum.

IOA's soaking water rides offer optional lockers that cost $4 for the first 90 minutes and $3 for each additional hour, up to $20. At the front of each park, there are also paid all-day lockers in standard and family sizes for $10–$12 that can be opened and relocked by the original user as many times as you like; just remember that only the person who used his or her finger to rent the locker can retrieve anything from it.

The locker banks are easy to find; each bank has a small computer in the center. When the sun is bright, the screen is almost impossible to read, so have someone block the sun or use a different computer. After selecting your language, you press your thumb onto the keypad and have your fingerprint scanned. We've seen people walk away cursing at this step, having repeated it over and over with no success. Don't press down too hard—the computer can't read your thumbprint that way. Instead, take a deep breath and place your thumb lightly on the scanner. Newer lockers scan your admission ticket instead of your thumb—a much more reliable method.

After you do your initial thumb scan, you'll receive a locker number. *Write it down!* When you return from your ride, go back to the same kiosk machine, enter your locker number, and then scan your thumb again.

UNIVERSAL DINING PROGRAMS

CITYWALK MEAL AND MOVIE DEAL This deal includes a ticket to any movie playing at the Universal Cineplex and a meal from a limited menu at participating Universal CityWalk restaurants. The package, which includes one entrée and a nonalcoholic drink, costs $21.95 for all ages. Buy your Meal and Movie Deal tickets at the CityWalk Guest Services ticket window or at all Destination Universal locations, or call ☎ 407-224-2691. Additional charges apply for IMAX, IMAX 3-D, and 3-D movies.

CHARACTER DINING A weekly character breakfast is offered at **Islands Dining Room** at the Royal Pacific Resort on Sundays ($27 adults, $15 kids ages 3–9, plus tax) and at **The Kitchen** at Hard Rock Hotel on Tuesdays ($21 adults, $16 kids ages 10–14, $12 ages 3–9, plus tax). For information and reservations, call ☎ 407-503-3463.

On select evenings, characters also make appearances during dinner at Islands Dining Room, The Kitchen, and **Trattoria del Porto** (Portofino Bay Hotel), as well as in the lobbies of the other resorts. Schedules change frequently, so contact the hotels directly for details.

At Universal Studios Florida, try the **Superstar Character Breakfast** at Cafe La Bamba, with characters from Universal's Superstar Parade. Guests can interact with Minions from *Despicable Me* and SpongeBob SquarePants, and even get an autograph from Dora and Diego. Later in the day, you get special VIP viewing access to the Superstar Parade; the private viewing area is near the bus stop by Revenge of the Mummy and Finnegan's Bar and Grill. A similar breakfast is held during the holiday season in Islands of Adventure with The Grinch. The breakfast costs $37.27 for adults and $22.36 for kids. After purchasing your dining experience online, you must call ☎ 407-224-7554 up to 24 hours before arriving to confirm your table. Separate theme park admission is required.

1-DAY COCA-COLA FREESTYLE SOUVENIR CUP This perk entitles you to one day of unlimited fountain soft drinks at all participating Coca-Cola Freestyle locations at both USF and IOA. Cost is $15.96 for one cup, $14.90 if ordered online or purchased in pairs at the park, $12.77 each for three or more, or $6.38 with a Universal Dining Plan. The price includes the first day of refills; each additional day costs $6.38.

UNIVERSAL'S CINEMATIC SPECTACULAR DINING EXPERIENCE First have dinner at Lombard's Seafood Grille; choose from an array of entrées, including fresh seafood, pasta, sandwiches, and more. Afterward, enjoy a spectacular view of *Universal's Cinematic Spectacular* nighttime show in an exclusive area at the restaurant's waterfront boardwalk. The experience is $47.47 per adult and $17.93 per child. After reserving and purchasing your dining experience online, you must call ☎ 407-224-7554 up to 24 hours before arriving to confirm your table. Separate theme park admission is required.

UNIVERSAL DINING PLAN This plan is available exclusively to guests who book a hotel package with Universal. The plan includes one counter-service meal (entrée and nonalcoholic beverage), one table-service meal (entrée, dessert, and nonalcoholic beverage), one snack (from a cart or counter-service location), and one additional beverage (also from a cart or counter-service location) each day. Select CityWalk locations and most in-park dining locations participate. Tips aren't included, and no substitutions may be made. Eligible menu items and restaurants are indicated by a Universal Dining Plan logo. Price per day is $59.63 for adults and $20.22 for children. To book your vacation package with the Universal Dining Plan, visit universalorlando.com.

The **Universal Quick Service Dining Plan** is available for all guests to buy from kiosks or restaurant cashiers. It provides one counter-service meal with drink, another soft drink, and one snack. The cost is $24.49 for adults and $15.97 for kids age 9 and younger, plus tax. It's valid at most counter-service eateries at all three parks (including Three Broomsticks in Hogsmeade, the Leaky Cauldron in Diagon Alley, and Fast Food Boulevard in Springfield: Home of the Simpsons) and a smattering at Universal CityWalk, but not at the hotels.

UNIVERSAL, KIDS, AND SCARY STUFF

THOUGH THERE'S PLENTY FOR YOUNGER CHILDREN to enjoy at the Universal Orlando parks, most major attractions can potentially make kids under age 8 wig out. At Universal Studios Florida, forget Hollywood Rip Ride Rockit, Men in Black Alien Attack, Revenge of the Mummy, The Simpsons Ride, *Terminator 2: 3-D*, and Transformers: The Ride 3-D. The first part of the E.T. Adventure ride is a little intense for a few preschoolers, but the end is all happiness and harmony. There are some scary visual effects on both the Hogwarts Express train that runs between the two parks and Harry Potter and the Escape from Gringotts dark ride–roller coaster, although both are billed as family rides. Interestingly, very few families report problems with *Universal Orlando's Horror Make-Up Show*. Anything we haven't listed is probably a safe bet.

At Volcano Bay, the Ko'okiri Body Plunge and Kala and Tai Nui Serpentine Body Slides feature a fall through a drop door before you plunge down twisting, winding tubes. The Maku Puihi Round Raft Rides and the Ohyah and Ohno Drop Slides are also not for the faint of heart.

At Universal's Islands of Adventure, watch out for The Amazing Adventures of Spider-Man, Doctor Doom's Fearfall, Dragon Challenge, Harry Potter and the Forbidden Journey, The Incredible Hulk Coaster, Jurassic Park River Adventure, and *Poseidon's Fury*. Skull Island is visually and psychologically intense; it may be too much for little ones. Popeye & Bluto's Bilge-Rat Barges is wet and wild, but most younger children handle it well. Dudley Do-Right's Ripsaw Falls is a toss-up, to be considered only if your kids like water-flume rides. *The Eighth Voyage of Sindbad* includes some explosions and startling special effects, but again, kids generally tolerate it well. Nothing else should pose a problem.

CHILD SWAP Switching off at Universal is similar to Disney's version but superior in several respects. The entire family goes through the whole line together before being split into riding and nonriding groups near the loading platform. The nonriding parent and child(ren) wait in a designated room, usually with some sort of entertainment (for example, Harry Potter and the Forbidden Journey at IOA shows the first 20 minutes of *Harry Potter and the Sorcerer's Stone* on a loop), a place to sit down, and sometimes restrooms with changing tables. At any theme park, the best tip we can give is to ask the greeter in front of the attraction what you're supposed to do.

BLUE MAN GROUP

UNIVERSAL STUDIOS FLORIDA'S Sharp Aquos Theater, near Universal CityWalk, is home to the Blue Man Group. The theater can be accessed from inside or outside USF; we recommend getting seats at least 15 rows back from the stage.

The three blue men are just that—blue—and bald and mute. Wearing black clothing and skullcaps slathered with bright-blue grease paint, they deliver a fast-paced show that uses music (mostly percussion) and multimedia effects to make light of contemporary art and life in the information age. The 1-hour, 45-minute production takes a whimsical look at how we use technology in our daily lives.

Tickets start at $63.90 for adults and $31.95 for children ages 3–9 and can be purchased online or at the Universal box office; tickets purchased at the box office cost $10 more.

UNIVERSAL CITYWALK

AT CITYWALK you'll find a variety of restaurants, clubs, shops, outdoor entertainment, a concert hall (**Hard Rock Live**), and the **Universal Cineplex 20** movie theater. CityWalk also has a number of combination restaurants and clubs. Open to families with kids until 9 p.m., many of these venues offer live entertainment.

The new kid on the block is the **Toothsome Chocolate Emporium & Savory Feast Kitchen.** Housed in a cavernous 19th-century-inspired steampunk building, this full-service restaurant, bar, and sweet shop is well worth a visit. Watch all manner of confections being created while you interact with the whimsical owner and her animatronic assistant. Chocolate is everywhere, from brownies to crepes. The "Savory Feast" part of the menu features steaks, sandwiches, and all-day brunch.

Entertainment options include **CityWalk's Rising Star,** a karaoke joint where singers are backed by a live band; reggae at **Bob Marley—A Tribute to Freedom;** a **Pat O'Brien's** dueling-pianos club; **Fat Tuesday,** specializing in New Orleans–style daiquiris; a **Hard Rock Cafe** and **Hard Rock Live** concert venue; **Jimmy Buffett's Margaritaville;** the **Red Coconut Club,** a two-story upscale cocktail lounge with live music and dancing; and a dance club called **The Groove,** with high-tech lighting and visual effects. If you want to go clubbing, $12.77 plus tax admits you to all of the clubs. For details, call Universal CityWalk information at ☎ 407-224-2691.

CityWalk is open daily, 11 a.m.–2 a.m. Parking, located in the same garages that serve the theme parks, runs $20 a day for cars and $22 for RVs, trailers, and other large rigs; regular parking is free after 6 p.m. If you're staying at a Universal resort, it's a short walk, but water taxis and buses are also available to transport you to CityWalk. To get back to your resort, try a pedicab, available for a modest tip. Call ☎ 407-224-FOOD (3663) for dinner reservations; visit universalorlando.com and select "At CityWalk" under "Events" for special events.

UNIVERSAL'S
ISLANDS *of* ADVENTURE

WHEN IOA OPENED IN 1999, it provided Universal with enough critical mass to actually compete with Disney. Doubly interesting is that the second Universal park is a direct competitor to Disney's Magic Kingdom, the most-visited theme park in the world. The park has more

NOT TO BE MISSED AT UNIVERSAL'S ISLANDS OF ADVENTURE

• The Amazing Adventures of Spider-Man	• Dragon Challenge
• Harry Potter and the Forbidden Journey	• Hogwarts Express
• The Incredible Hulk Coaster	• Jurassic Park River Adventure
• Popeye & Bluto's Bilge-Rat Barges	• Skull Island: Reign of Kong

kid-friendly rides and cartoon characters (like Fantasyland), thrill rides in a sci-fi city (like Tomorrowland), and a jungle river with robot creatures (like Adventureland). Its layout—a central entry corridor leading to a ring of connected lands—even mimics the classic Disneyland model, with one major exception: Instead of a hub and castle in the center, Universal built a large lagoon, whose estuaries separate the park's thematically diverse "islands" (actually peninsulas).

And though Universal played second fiddle to Disney for many years, times have changed: Universal's Islands of Adventure is a state-of-the-art park competing with a Disney park that is more than 45 years old and did not add a new super-headliner attraction for many years until the Fantasyland expansion of 2012–14.

In 2007 Universal's management made one bold bet: securing the rights to build a Harry Potter–themed area within IOA. Harry P. is possibly the only fictional character extant capable of trumping Mickey Mouse, and Universal went all-out, under J. K. Rowling's watchful and exacting eye, to create a setting and attractions designed to be the envy of the industry. The **Wizarding World of Harry Potter–Hogsmeade** opened at IOA in 2010 and was an immediate hit. And there is no sign of letting up: In summer 2016, IOA opened **Skull Island: Reign of Kong.** We applaud Universal Orlando for getting things done right, and at light speed, pun intended.

Disney and Universal officially downplay their fierce competition, pointing out that any new theme park or attraction makes Central Florida a more marketable destination. Behind closed doors, however, the two companies share a Pepsi-versus-Coke rivalry that keeps both working hard to gain a competitive edge. The good news is that all this translates into bigger and better attractions for you to enjoy.

BEWARE OF THE WET AND WILD

THOUGH WE DESCRIBE IOA as a direct competitor to the Magic Kingdom, there is one major qualification you should be aware of: Whereas most Magic Kingdom attractions are designed to be enjoyed by guests of any age, attractions at IOA are largely created for the under-40 set. The thrill rides here are serious with a capital *S*, making Space Mountain and Big Thunder Mountain look as delicate as Dumbo. In fact, seven out of the nine top

unofficial **TIP**
Consider yourself warned: several attractions at Islands of Adventure will drench you to the bone. Roller coasters are the real deal—not for the faint of heart or for little ones.

attractions at Islands are thrill rides, and of these, there are three that not only scare the doo-doo out of you but also drench you with water. Some of the water rides have People Dryers near the exit (they cost $5!), though they don't get you 100% dry.   *Continued on page 678*

Universal's Islands of Adventure

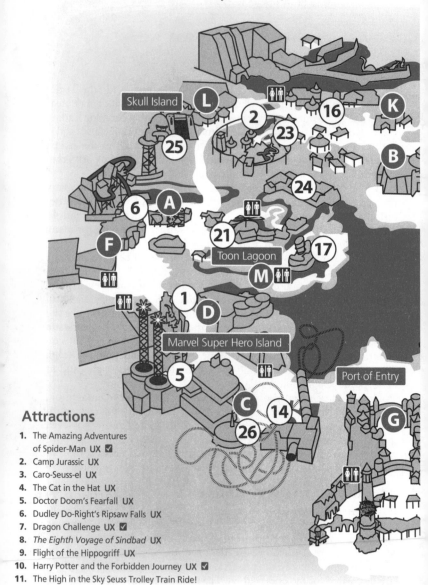

Attractions

1. The Amazing Adventures of Spider-Man UX ☑
2. Camp Jurassic UX
3. Caro-Seuss-el UX
4. The Cat in the Hat UX
5. Doctor Doom's Fearfall UX
6. Dudley Do-Right's Ripsaw Falls UX
7. Dragon Challenge UX ☑
8. *The Eighth Voyage of Sindbad* UX
9. Flight of the Hippogriff UX
10. Harry Potter and the Forbidden Journey UX ☑
11. The High in the Sky Seuss Trolley Train Ride!
12. Hogwarts Express–Hogsmeade Station ☑
13. If I Ran the Zoo
14. The Incredible Hulk Coaster UX ☑
15. Jurassic Park Discovery Center
16. Jurassic Park River Adventure UX ☑

17. Me Ship, *The Olive*
18. The Mystic Fountain
19. Ollivanders
20. One Fish, Two Fish, Red Fish, Blue Fish UX
21. Popeye & Bluto's Bilge-Rat Barges UX ☑

UX Attraction Offers Universal Express   ✚ First Aid Station

🚻 Restrooms   👍 Recommended Dining   ✅ Not to Be Missed

9

10

19

7

15

CC

12

Jurassic Park

The Wizarding World of Harry Potter–Hogsmeade

18

8

I

H

BB

The Lost Continent

22

Seuss Landing

11

J

13

3

E

AA

4

20

Table-Service Restaurants

AA. Confisco Grille
BB. Mythos Restaurant 👍
CC. Three Broomsticks 👍

Counter-Service Restaurants

A. Blondie's
B. The Burger Digs
C. Cafe 4
D. Captain America Diner
E. Circus McGurkus Cafe Stoo-pendous
F. Comic Strip Cafe
G. Croissant Moon Bakery
H. "Doc" Sugrue's Desert Kebab House
I. Fire Eater's Grill
J. Green Eggs and Ham *(seasonal)*
K. Pizza Predattoria
L. Thunder Falls Terrace 👍
M. Wimpy's *(seasonal)*

22. *Poseidon's Fury* UX
23. Pteranodon Flyers
24. Raptor Encounter
25. Skull Island: Reign of Kong UX
26. Storm Force Accelatron UX

Continued from page 675

For families, there are three interactive playgrounds as well as six rides that young children will enjoy. Of the thrill rides, only the two in Toon Lagoon are marginally appropriate for little ones.

GETTING ORIENTED AT ISLANDS OF ADVENTURE

BOTH UNIVERSAL THEME PARKS are accessed via the Universal CityWalk entertainment complex. Crossing CityWalk from the parking garages, you can bear right to Universal Studios Florida or left to Universal's Islands of Adventure.

Islands of Adventure is arranged much like Epcot's World Showcase (in a large circle surrounding a lake), but its themed areas are self-contained "lands" reminiscent of the Magic Kingdom. You first encounter the Moroccan-style **Port of Entry,** where you'll find Guest Services, lockers, stroller and wheelchair rentals, ATM banking, lost and found, and shopping. From Port of Entry, moving clockwise around the lagoon, you access **Marvel Super Hero Island, Toon Lagoon, Skull Island, Jurassic Park, The Wizarding World of Harry Potter–Hogsmeade, The Lost Continent,** and **Seuss Landing.**

ISLANDS *of* ADVENTURE ATTRACTIONS

MARVEL SUPER HERO ISLAND

WITH ITS FUTURISTIC AND RETRO-FUTURE design and comic-book signage, Marvel Super Hero Island offers shopping and attractions based on Marvel Comics characters.

The Amazing Adventures of Spider-Man
(Universal Express) ★★★★★

APPEAL BY AGE	PRESCHOOL ★½	GRADE SCHOOL ★★★★½	TEENS ★★★★½
YOUNG ADULTS ★★★★½		OVER 30 ★★★★½	SENIORS ★★★★

What it is Indoor adventure simulator ride based on Spider-Man. **Scope and scale** Super-headliner. **When to go** During the first 40 minutes the park is open. **Special comment** 40″ minimum height requirement. **Authors' rating** One of the best attractions anywhere; not to be missed; ★★★★★. **Duration of ride** 4½ minutes. **Probable waiting time per 100 people ahead of you** 5 minutes. **Loading speed** Fast.

DESCRIPTION AND COMMENTS The Amazing Adventures of Spider-Man, covering 1½ acres and combining moving ride vehicles, 3-D film, and live action, was enhanced in 2012 with a complete high-definition digital upgrade. It's frenetic, fluid, and astounding. The visuals are rich, and the ride is wild but not jerky. Though the attractions are not directly comparable, Spider-Man is technologically ahead of almost anything at Walt Disney World outside Pandora—which is to say that it will leave you in awe. In fact, it's considered by many to be the best theme park attraction on the planet.

The storyline is that you're a reporter for the *Daily Bugle* newspaper (where Peter Parker, also known as Spider-Man, works as a mild-mannered photographer), when it's discovered that evildoers have stolen—we promise we're not making this up—the Statue of Liberty. You're drafted on the spot by your cantankerous editor to go get the story. After speeding around and being thrust into a battle between good and evil, you experience a 400-foot "sensory drop" from a skyscraper roof all the way to the pavement. Spidey is less frantic and frenetic than the similar Transformers ride at USF and features more dialogue and humor.

TOURING TIPS If you were on hand for Early Park Admission, ride after experiencing The Wizarding World, Skull Island: Reign of Kong, and The Incredible Hulk Coaster. If you elect to bypass Wizarding World congestion, ride after Hulk.

Doctor Doom's Fearfall *(Universal Express)*   ★★★

APPEAL BY AGE	PRESCHOOL ★	GRADE SCHOOL ★★★★	TEENS ★★★½
YOUNG ADULTS ★		OVER 30 ★★★½	SENIORS ★★★

What it is Vertical ascent and free fall. **Scope and scale** Headliner. **When to go** First 40 minutes the park is open. **Special comment** 52″ minimum height requirement. **Authors' rating** More bark than bite; ★★★. **Duration of ride** 40 seconds. **Probable waiting time per 100 people ahead of you** 18 minutes. **Loading speed** Slow.

DESCRIPTION AND COMMENTS Here you're strapped into a seat with your feet dangling, blasted 200 feet up in the air, and then allowed to partially free-fall back down. The scariest part of the ride by far is the apprehension that builds as you sit, strapped in, waiting for the ride to launch; blasting up and falling down are actually pleasant.

TOURING TIPS We've seen glaciers that move faster than the line for Doctor Doom's Fearfall. If you want to ride without investing half a day, be on hand at park opening so you're one of the first to ride. Doctor Doom also has a singles line that's nearly always open.

The Incredible Hulk Coaster *(Universal Express)* ★★★★½

APPEAL BY AGE	PRESCHOOL ★	GRADE SCHOOL ★★★½	TEENS ★★★★★
YOUNG ADULTS ★★★★★		OVER 30 ★★★★½	SENIORS ★★★½

What it is Roller coaster. **Scope and scale** Super-headliner. **When to go** During the first 40 minutes the park is open. **Special comment** 54″ minimum height requirement. **Authors' rating** A coaster-lover's coaster; not to be missed; ★★★★½. **Duration of ride** 2¼ minutes. **Probable waiting time per 100 people ahead of you** 9 minutes. **Loading speed** Moderate.

DESCRIPTION AND COMMENTS The Hulk is one of the best coasters in Florida, providing a ride comparable to Montu at Busch Gardens. A major refurbishment in 2016 completely replaced the tracks and coaster trains; new on-ride and in-queue effects were also added. The trains feature lights that flash to a synchronized soundtrack composed by Fall Out Boy's Patrick Stump. Unfortunately, the reconstructed ride remains rougher than we'd hoped, though it's still a far cry from the side-to-side shaking of Rip Ride Rockit. You'll be shot like a cannonball from 0 to 40 mph in 2 seconds; then you'll be flung upside down 100 feet off the ground, which will, of course, induce weightlessness. Then it's a mere six rollovers, punctuated by two plunges into holes in the ground, before you're allowed to get out and throw up.

TOURING TIPS Skip the Wizarding World attractions in the early morning and ride The Incredible Hulk Coaster first thing. Alternatively, if you insist on going to Hogsmeade at rope drop (or if you're eligible for Early Park

Admission), ride immediately after you've enjoyed the Potter attractions. Stop by the electronic lockers near the entrance to deposit any items that might depart your person during the coaster's seven inversions.

Note that there's a separate line for those who want to ride in the first row. A singles line is also available during peak times.

Storm Force Accelatron *(Universal Express)* ★★½

APPEAL BY AGE	PRESCHOOL ★★★★★	GRADE SCHOOL ★★★★	TEENS ★★★★
YOUNG ADULTS ★★★½		OVER 30 ★★★	SENIORS ★★★

What it is Covered spinning ride. **Scope and scale** Minor attraction. **Special comment** May induce motion sickness. **When to go** During the first hour the park is open. **Authors' rating** Spiffed-up teacups; ★★½. **Duration of ride** 1½ minutes. **Probable waiting time per 100 people ahead of you** 21 minutes. **Loading speed** Slow.

DESCRIPTION AND COMMENTS Storm Force is a spiffed-up version of Disney's nausea-inducing Mad Tea Party. A storyline loosely ties this midway-type ride to the Marvel Super Hero Island area, but it offers no useful advice on keeping your lunch down.

TOURING TIPS Ride early or late to avoid long lines. If you're prone to motion sickness, skip it.

TOON LAGOON

THIS LAND TRANSLATES cartoon art into real buildings and settings. Whimsical and gaily colored, with rounded and exaggerated lines, Toon Lagoon is Universal's answer to Storybook Circus in the Magic Kingdom—but you have about a 60% chance of drowning at Universal's version. **Comic Strip Lane** is the main street of Toon Lagoon. Here you can visit the domains of Beetle Bailey, Hagar the Horrible, Krazy Kat, the Family Circus, and Blondie and Dagwood, among others your kids (or perhaps you) have never heard of. Shops and eateries tie in to the cartoon theme.

Dudley Do-Right's Ripsaw Falls *(Universal Express)* ★★★½

APPEAL BY AGE	PRESCHOOL ★½	GRADE SCHOOL ★★★★½	TEENS ★★★★½
YOUNG ADULTS ★★★★½		OVER 30 ★★★★	SENIORS ★★★★

What it is Flume ride. **Scope and scale** Major attraction. **When to go** Before 11 a.m. **Special comment** 44" minimum height requirement. **Authors' rating** A minimalist Splash Mountain; ★★★½. **Duration of ride** 5 minutes. **Probable waiting time per 100 people ahead of you** 9 minutes. **Loading speed** Moderate.

DESCRIPTION AND COMMENTS Inspired by the *Rocky and Bullwinkle* cartoons, this ride features Canadian Mountie Dudley Do-Right as he tries to save his girlfriend, Nell Fenwick, from the nefarious Snidely Whiplash. Storyline aside, it's a flume ride, with the inevitable big drop at the end.

TOURING TIPS Make no mistake—this ride *will* get you wet. This Livonia, Michigan, family enjoyed it:

We're far more enthusiastic about water rides than the Guide *is. We loved Dudley Do-Right more than Splash Mountain, even though we got soaked. (Forget ponchos—you'd need a biohazard suit to avoid getting drenched.)*

For those who don't enjoy it, coin-operated "People Dryers" are available, although this Cheyney, Pennsylvania, sees the whole thing as a soggy scam:

Their rides get you soaked, then they charge five bucks to dry you.

If you want to at least attempt to stay dry, arrive prepared with a poncho or at least a big garbage bag with holes cut out for your head and arms. Ride after experiencing the Marvel Super Hero rides and Skull Island.

Me Ship, *The Olive* ★★★

APPEAL BY AGE PRESCHOOL ★★★★★ GRADE SCHOOL ★★★½ TEENS ★★
YOUNG ADULTS ★★ OVER 30 ★★½ SENIORS ★★

What it is Interactive playground. **Scope and scale** Minor attraction. **When to go** Anytime. **Authors' rating** Colorful and appealing for kids; ★★★.

DESCRIPTION AND COMMENTS *The Olive* is Popeye's three-story boat come to life as an interactive playground. Younger kids can scramble around in Swee'Pea's Playpen, while older sibs shoot water cannons at riders trying to survive the adjacent Bilge-Rat Barges.

TOURING TIPS If you're into the big rides, save this for later in the day.

Popeye & Bluto's Bilge-Rat Barges
(Universal Express) ★★★★

APPEAL BY AGE PRESCHOOL ★½ GRADE SCHOOL ★★★½ TEENS ★★★★½
YOUNG ADULTS ★★★★★ OVER 30 ★★★★½ SENIORS ★★★★

What it is Whitewater raft ride. **Scope and scale** Major attraction. **When to go** Before 11 a.m. **Special comment** 42″ minimum height requirement. **Authors' rating** Bring your own soap; not to be missed; ★★★★. **Duration of ride** 4½ minutes. **Probable waiting time per 100 people ahead of you** 5 minutes. **Loading speed** Moderate.

Wet

DESCRIPTION AND COMMENTS This whitewater-raft ride for the whole family is engineered to ensure that everyone gets drenched; the ride even provides water cannons for highly intelligent nonparticipants ashore to fire at those aboard. The rapids are rougher and more interesting, and the ride longer, than Animal Kingdom's Kali River Rapids, but Disney wins for theming hands-down.

TOURING TIPS You'll get a lot wetter from the knees down on this ride, so use your poncho or garbage bag and ride barefoot with your britches rolled up. This ride often opens an hour after the rest of the park (usually at 10 a.m.). Experience the barges in the morning after the Marvel Super Hero attractions and Dudley Do-Right.

SKULL ISLAND

THIS IS BOTH AN ATTRACTION and an entire "island" unto itself, between Dudley Do-Right's Ripsaw Falls and Thunder Falls Terrace.

Skull Island: Reign of Kong *(Universal Express)* ★★★★½

APPEAL BY AGE PRESCHOOL ★★½ GRADE SCHOOL ★★★½ TEENS ★★★★½
YOUNG ADULTS ★★★½ OVER 30 ★★★★ SENIORS ★★★★★

What it is Indoor/outdoor truck safari with 3-D effects. **Scope and scale** Superheadliner. **When to go** Immediately after park opening or just before closing. **Special comments** 34″ minimum height requirement; switching-off option provided (see page 439). Despite the relatively low height requirement, this ride is very intense and may not be a good choice for little ones. **Authors' rating** The King has returned; not to be missed; ★★★★½. **Duration of ride** About 6 minutes. **Probable waiting time per 100 people ahead of you** 3 minutes. **Loading speed** Fast.

DESCRIPTION AND COMMENTS Skull Island: Reign of Kong is an original adventure set in the 1930s, casting guests as explorers with the 8th Wonder Expedition Company, which has set up its jungle base camp in an ancient temple inhabited by a hostile Kong-worshipping indigenous tribe. That may seem like a foolish place to pitch your tent, but it makes for a phenomenal queue experience, featuring both lifelike animatronic figures and live haunted house–style actors who startle unwitting guests.

Your transportation is an oversize 72-seat open-sided "expedition vehicle" helmed by one of five different animatronic tour guides. The ride begins with a short loop outside through the jungle (which may be bypassed in inclement weather), ending at the massive torch-framed doors in the center of Skull Island's imposing stony facade. You pass through a maze of caves, where you're swiftly assaulted by icky prehistoric bats, bugs, and beasties, brought to gruesome life through a mix of detailed physical effects and razor-sharp 3-D screens. You're then thrust into the center of a raging battle between vicious V-Rex dinosaurs and the big ape himself. Finally, just when you think it's all over, you'll have one last face-to-face encounter with the "eighth wonder of the world," only this time in the fur-covered flesh.

TOURING TIPS Skull Island is epic in every sense—including its lines. On the plus side, Kong draws some guests away from The Wizarding World of Harry Potter. Hit Skull Island first thing in the morning or immediately following the Hogsmeade attractions if you're using Early Park Admission. Finally, if you or your little one has a fear of darkness, insects, or man-eating monsters, you may want to forgo the monkey.

JURASSIC PARK

JURASSIC PARK (for anyone who's been asleep for 25 years) is a Steven Spielberg film franchise about a fictitious theme park with real dinosaurs. Jurassic Park at Universal's Islands of Adventure is a real theme park (or at least a section of one) with fictitious dinosaurs.

Camp Jurassic ★★★½

APPEAL BY AGE	PRESCHOOL ★★★★★	GRADE SCHOOL ★★★★★	TEENS ★★★½
YOUNG ADULTS ★★★★½		OVER 30 ★★★½	SENIORS ★★★

What it is Interactive play area. **Scope and scale** Minor attraction. **When to go** Anytime. **Authors' rating** Creative playground, confusing layout; ★★★½.

DESCRIPTION AND COMMENTS One of the best theme park playgrounds you'll find anywhere. A sort of dinosaur-themed Tom Sawyer Island minus the rafts, it allows kids to explore lava pits, caves, mines, and a rainforest. The playground is big enough for many kids to spend a solid hour just running around.

TOURING TIPS Camp Jurassic will fire the imaginations of the under-13 set—if you don't impose a time limit on the exploration, you could be here awhile.

Jurassic Park Discovery Center ★★½

APPEAL BY AGE	PRESCHOOL ★★★	GRADE SCHOOL ★★★½	TEENS ★★
YOUNG ADULTS ★★★½		OVER 30 ★★★	SENIORS ★★★½

What it is Interactive natural-history exhibit. **Scope and scale** Minor attraction. **When to go** Anytime. **Authors' rating** Definitely worth checking out; ★★½.

DESCRIPTION AND COMMENTS This interactive educational exhibit mixes fiction from the movie *Jurassic Park,* such as using fossil DNA to bring dinosaurs to life, with various skeletal remains and other paleontological displays. The best exhibit here lets guests watch an animatronic raptor being hatched, with a young witness getting to name the newborn. You never know quite when one will emerge, but ask an attendant if you should stick around.

TOURING TIPS The Discovery Center usually opens later than the rest of the park and may close earlier as well; typical hours are 10 a.m.–5 p.m. Tour after seeing the park's major rides and attractions, or on your second day in the park. Most folks can digest this exhibit in 10–15 minutes.

Jurassic Park River Adventure *(Universal Express)* ★★★★

APPEAL BY AGE	PRESCHOOL ★★½	GRADE SCHOOL ★★★★	TEENS ★★★★½
YOUNG ADULTS ★★★★½		OVER 30 ★★★★	SENIORS ★★★½

What it is Indoor-outdoor river-raft adventure ride based on the Jurassic Park movies. **Scope and scale** Super-headliner. **When to go** Before 11 a.m. **Special comment** 42″ minimum height requirement. **Authors' rating** Better than its Hollywood cousin; not to be missed; ★★★★. **Duration of ride** 6½ minutes. **Probable waiting time per 100 people ahead of you** 5 minutes. **Loading speed** Fast.

Wet

DESCRIPTION AND COMMENTS Guests board boats for a water tour of Jurassic Park. Everything is tranquil as the tour begins, and then, as word is received that some of the carnivores have escaped their enclosure, the tour boat is accidentally diverted into Jurassic Park's maintenance facilities. Here, the boat and its riders are menaced by an assortment of hungry meat-eaters. At the climactic moment, the boat and its passengers escape by plummeting over an 85-foot drop.

TOURING TIPS Though the boats make a huge splash at the bottom of the drop, you can stay relatively dry if you sit in an interior seat; sitting behind a larger person and keeping your arms down can help as well. Still, bring a poncho or plastic bag if you want to keep as dry as possible; paid lockers are located inside the queue. Also of note if you do get wet: Boy, does the water stink, as this Honolulu reader discovered:

The Jurassic Park ride is a lot of fun—so fun, in fact, that you won't realize how truly HEINOUS the water that drenches you during the climactic splash-down is until much later. We sat in the front row for the ride and got soaked. Three hours later, my girlfriend and I realized that we reeked.

Because Jurassic Park is situated next to The Wizarding World of Harry Potter–Hogsmeade, the boat will experience heavy crowds earlier in the day. Try to ride before 11 a.m. Unless your kids are fairly hardy, wait a year or two before you spring the River Adventure on them.

Pteranodon Flyers   ★★

APPEAL BY AGE PRESCHOOL ★★★½	GRADE SCHOOL ★★★★	TEENS ★★★★
YOUNG ADULTS ★★★½	OVER 30 ★★★	SENIORS ★★★★

What it is Suspended kiddie coaster. **Scope and scale** Minor attraction. **When to go** When there's no line. **Special comment** Adults and older children must be accompanied by a child between 36″ and 56″ tall. **Authors' rating** All sizzle, no steak; ★★. **Duration of ride** 1¼ minutes. **Probable waiting time per 100 people ahead of you** 28 minutes. **Loading speed** More sluggish than a hog in quicksand.

DESCRIPTION AND COMMENTS This ride swings you along a track that passes over a small part of Jurassic Park. Skip it—the next ice age will probably end before you reach the front of the line. And your reward for all that waiting? A 1-minute-and-15-second ride.

TOURING TIPS Photograph the pteranodon as it flies overhead. You're probably looking at something that will someday be extinct If your children
insist on riding, look for kiosks outside Camp Jurassic's entrance that dispense timed return tickets for the Flyers. You'll still have to wait awhile to
come back, but it beats stewing in the standby queue.

Raptor Encounter ★★★½

APPEAL BY AGE	PRESCHOOL ★★	GRADE SCHOOL ★★★★	TEENS ★★★★
YOUNG ADULTS ★★★½		OVER 30 ★★★½	SENIORS ★★★

What it is Photo op with lifelike dinosaur. **Scope and scale** Minor attraction. **When
to go** Check park map or attraction for appearance times. **Authors' rating** Clever
girl! Sure to scare the spit out of small kids; ★★★½. **Duration of encounter** About a
minute. **Probable waiting time per 100 people ahead of you** 30 minutes.

DESCRIPTION AND COMMENTS Several times per hour, blue siren lights around
Jurassic Park's sunken predator paddock signal the arrival of Zani, Rho,
Zulu, or Keelo, IOA's semi-tame velociraptor stars (actually amazingly
realistic puppets created by Michael Curry, a theatrical designer whose
credits also include Disney's *Lion King* and *Finding Nemo* musicals). A
game warden briefs one family at a time regarding proper safety procedures—convey calm assurance, move in slowly, don't smell like meat—
before they step up for a photo. Selfies are encouraged; just don't be
surprised if the dino snaps when you say, "Smile!"

TOURING TIPS The Raptor Encounter is quite popular, and with limited capacity and little shade, the wait can become unpleasant. Appearances begin
around 10 a.m. and run continuously until 6:45 p.m., with brief breaks
about every 20 minutes to rotate raptors. Ask a team member stationed
outside the paddock entrance approximately how long your wait will be
before queuing. Universal installed greenery at the exit to block passersby
from snapping photos, so if you want to see the dino, you'll have to deal
with the line. Don't try to touch the raptor, or you may come home minus
a hand; surreptitiously feeding your offspring to the dinosaurs is also dis-
couraged by management.

THE WIZARDING WORLD OF HARRY POTTER— HOGSMEADE

IN WHAT MAY PROVE TO BE THE COMPETITIVE COUP of all
time between archrivals Disney and Universal, the latter inked a deal
with Warner Brothers Entertainment to create a fully immersive Harry
Potter–themed environment based on the best-selling children's books
by J. K. Rowling and the companion blockbuster movies from Warner
Brothers. The project was blessed by Rowling, who demanded painstak-
ing accuracy from Universal regarding The Wizarding Worlds.

Passing beneath a stone archway, you enter the village of **Hogsmeade.**
Depicted in winter, the village setting is rendered in exquisite detail:
Stone cottages and shops have steeply pitched slate roofs; bowed multi-
paned windows; gables; and tall, crooked chimneys.

On most days of the year, from the slowest off-season through the
busiest summer weeks, you can enter and depart The Wizarding World
of Harry Potter–Hogsmeade as you please. The waits for the rides will
still be more than an hour at times, but gaining entry to the themed
area itself is not an issue.

On days when the park is busiest, access to Hogsmeade may be limited for part of the day. If barricades are placed at both entrance to The Wizarding World and timed return tickets are being distributed from kiosks outside Jurassic Park Discovery Center, we recommend waiting until the last hour or two the park is open, when the entry restrictions are usually removed.

WIZARDING WORLD-HOGSMEADE ATTRACTIONS

Dragon Challenge (Universal Express) ★★★★

APPEAL BY AGE	PRESCHOOL —	GRADE SCHOOL ★★★★½	TEENS ★★★★★
YOUNG ADULTS ★★★★½		OVER 30 ★★★★½	SENIORS ★★★★

What it is Roller coaster. **Scope and scale** Headliner. **When to go** Immediately after Harry Potter and the Forbidden Journey. **Special comment** 54″ minimum height requirement. **Authors' rating** Almost as good as the Hulk coaster; not to be missed; ★★★★. **Duration of ride** 2½ minutes. **Probable waiting time per 100 people ahead of you** 9 minutes. **Loading speed** Moderate.

Motion Sickness

DESCRIPTION AND COMMENTS The storyline here is that you're preparing to compete in the Triwizard Tournament from *Harry Potter and the Goblet of Fire*. As you wind through the long, long queue, you pass through tournament tents and dark passages that are supposed to be under the stadium. You'll see the Goblet of Fire on display and hear the distant roar of the crowd in the supposed stadium above you.

Riders board one of two coasters, Chinese Fireball or Hungarian Horntail, that are launched moments apart on tracks that are closely intertwined. The tracks are configured so that you get a different experience on each. The trains are dispatched sequentially instead of simultaneously, so it looks as if one train is chasing another.

Because this is an inverted coaster, your view of the action is limited unless you're sitting in the front row. Dragon Challenge is the highest coaster in the park and also claims the longest drop at 115 feet, plus five inversions. It's a smooth ride all the way. Coaster fans argue about which seat on which train provides the wildest ride. We prefer the front row of Horntail for the visuals and the last row of Fireball for added g-forces.

TOURING TIPS The queuing area is the longest, most convoluted affair we've ever seen, winding endlessly through a maze of faux subterranean passages before spitting you out at the loading areas for Fireball and Horntail. Visit the john before you get in line, and when you reach the loading areas, follow the person in front of you until your eyes adjust to the light. Waits rarely exceed 30 minutes before 11 a.m., so ride after experiencing Harry Potter and the Forbidden Journey. If you don't have time to ride both coasters, the *Unofficial* crew unanimously prefers Chinese Fireball. Rumor has it that Universal is considering slaying the dragons and replacing the entire ride and adjoining area with a new Harry Potter–themed ride. The coaster has an immense footprint, so its demise would free up enough real estate for a super-headliner, maybe two.

Flight of the Hippogriff (Universal Express) ★★★

APPEAL BY AGE	PRESCHOOL ★★★★	GRADE SCHOOL ★★★★½	TEENS ★★★½
YOUNG ADULTS ★★★½		OVER 30 ★★★½	SENIORS ★★★½

What it is Kiddie roller coaster. **Scope and scale** Minor attraction. **When to go** First 90 minutes the park is open. **Special comment** 36″ minimum height requirement. **Authors' rating** A good beginner coaster; ★★★. **Duration of ride** 1 minute. **Probable waiting time per 100 people ahead of you** 14 minutes. **Loading speed** Slow.

DESCRIPTION AND COMMENTS Below and to the right of Hogwarts Castle, next to Hagrid's Hut, the Hippogriff is short and sweet but not worth much of a wait. Potter nerds will want to ride to see Hagrid's Hut and a charming animatronic of Buckbeak.

TOURING TIPS Have your kids ride soon after the park opens while older sibs enjoy Dragon Challenge.

Harry Potter and the Forbidden Journey
(Universal Express) ★★★★★

APPEAL BY AGE	PRESCHOOL ★½	GRADE SCHOOL ★★★★½	TEENS ★★★★½
YOUNG ADULTS ★★★★½		OVER 30 ★★★★½	SENIORS ★★★½

What it is Motion-simulator dark ride. **Scope and scale** Super-headliner. **When to go** Immediately after park opening or in the last hours before closing. **Special comments** Expect *long* waits in line; 48″ minimum height requirement. **Authors' rating** Marvelous for Muggles and not to be missed; ★★★★★. **Duration of ride** 4¼ minutes. **Probable waiting time per 100 people ahead of you** 4 minutes. **Loading speed** Fast.

DESCRIPTION AND COMMENTS This ride provides the only opportunity at Universal Orlando to come in contact with Harry, Ron, Hermione, and Dumbledore as portrayed by the original actors. Half of the attraction is a series of preshows that sets the stage for the main event, a dark ride. To understand the storyline and get the most out of the attraction, it's critical to see and hear the entire presentation in each of the queue's preshow rooms. You can get on the ride in only 10–25 minutes using the single-rider line, but everyone should go through the main queue at least once.

From Hogsmeade you reach the attraction through the imposing Winged Boar gates and progress along a winding path. Entering the castle on a lower level, you walk through a sort of dungeon festooned with various icons and prop replicas from the Potter flicks, including the Mirror of Erised from *Harry Potter and the Sorcerer's Stone.* You later emerge back outside and into the Hogwarts greenhouses, which compose the larger part of the Forbidden Journey's queuing area. If you're among the first in the park and in the queue, you'll move through this area pretty quickly. Otherwise . . . well, we hope you like plants. The greenhouses aren't air-conditioned, but fans move the (hot) air around. Blessedly, there are water fountains but, alas, no restrooms—take care of that before getting in line for the attraction.

Having finally escaped horticultural purgatory, you reenter the castle, moving along its halls and passageways. One chamber you'll probably remember from the films is a multistory gallery of portraits, many of whose subjects come alive when they take a notion. You'll see for the first time the four founders of Hogwarts: Helga Hufflepuff holding her famous cup, Godric Gryffindor and Rowena Ravenclaw nearby, and the tall, moving portrait of Salazar Slytherin straight ahead. The founders argue about Quidditch and Dumbledore's controversial decision to host an open house at Hogwarts for Muggles (garden-variety mortals). Don't rush through the gallery—the conversation is essential to understanding the rest of the attraction.

Next up, after you've navigated some more passages, is Dumbledore's office, where the chief wizard appears on a balcony and welcomes you to Hogwarts. The headmaster's appearance is your introduction to Musion Eyeliner technology—a high-definition video-projection system that produces breathtakingly realistic, three-dimensional, life-size moving holograms. The technology uses a special foil that reflects images from HD projectors, producing holographic images of variable sizes and incredible clarity. After his welcoming remarks, Dumbledore dispatches you to the Defence Against the Dark Arts classroom to hear a presentation on the history of Hogwarts.

As you gather to await the lecture, Harry, Ron, and Hermione pop out from beneath an invisibility cloak. They suggest you ditch the lecture in favor of joining them for a proper tour of Hogwarts, including a Quidditch match. After some repartee among the characters and a couple of special effects surprises, it's off to the Hogwarts Official Attraction Safety Briefing and Boarding Instructions Chamber—OK, we made up the name, but you get the picture. The briefing and instructions are presented by animated portraits, including an etiquette teacher. Later on, even the famed Sorting Hat gets into the act. All this leads to the Room of Requirement, where hundreds of candles float overhead and you board the ride.

After all the high-tech stuff in your queuing odyssey, you'll naturally expect to be wowed by your ride vehicle. Surely it's a Nimbus 3000 turbobroom, a phoenix, a hippogriff, or at least the Weasleys' flying car. But no, what you'll ride one of the most technologically advanced theme park attractions in America is . . . a *bench*? Yep, a bench.

But as benches go, it's a doozy, mounted to a Kuka robotic arm that can be programmed to replicate all the sensations of flying, including broad swoops, steep dives, sharp turns, sudden stops, and fast acceleration. The ride vehicle moves you through a series of alternating sets and domes where scenes are projected all around you. The movement of the Kuka arm is synchronized to create the motion that corresponds to what is happening in the set or film. When everything works correctly, it's mind-blowing: You'll soar over Hogwarts Castle, narrowly evade an attacking dragon, spar with the Whomping Willow, get tossed into a Quidditch match, and fight off Dementors inside the Chamber of Secrets.

unofficial **TIP**
The only restrooms in The Wizarding World at IOA, labeled PUBLIC CONVENIENCES, are in the middle of Hogsmeade. Remember where they are—especially if you're planning to ride Forbidden Journey and you're prone to motion sickness.

TOURING TIPS Universal has toned down the Kuka programming to help reduce motion sickness, but we nonetheless recommend that you not ride on an empty stomach. If you start getting queasy, fix your gaze on your feet and try to exclude as much from your peripheral vision as possible. If you have a child who doesn't meet the minimum height requirement of 48 inches, a child-swapping option is provided at the loading area.

The seats accommodate a wide variety of body shapes and sizes. Each bench has specially modified seats at either end. Though these allow many more people to ride, it's possible that guests of size can't fit in them. The best way to figure out whether you can fit in a regular seat or one of the modified ones is to sit in one of the test seats outside the queue or just inside the castle. After you sit down, pull down on the safety harness as far as you can. One of three safety lights will illuminate: A green light indicates you can fit into any seat, a yellow light means you should ask for one of the modified seats on the outside of the bench, and a red light means the harness

unofficial **TIP**
Even if your child meets the height requirement, consider carefully whether Forbidden Journey is an experience he or she can handle—because the seats on the benches are compartmentalized, kids can't see or touch Mom or Dad if they get frightened.

can't engage enough for you to ride safely. For you to be cleared to ride, the overhead restraint has to click three times. If you don't pass muster, you'll be escorted to a place where you can wait for the rest of your party.

Upon entering Forbidden Journey's interior queue, riders with bags or loose items must secure them in a free locker. (Included in "loose items" is anything, including phones and coins, in pockets not secured by a button or Velcro.) If you don't need a locker, enter through Filch's gift shop and cut through the lockers to save as much as 30 minutes in line. If you do need to stow your stuff, be aware that the Forbidden Journey locker area is small, crowded, and confusing. It may make more sense to stash your things in the lockers beside Dragon Challenge and pay the fee if you go over time. Or have one member of your party hold your bags for you in the child-swap area.

The single-rider line is poorly marked, so relatively few guests use it. At Forbidden Journey, the wait in the single-rider line can be as much as one-tenth the wait in the standby line. Because the ride experience is individual (you can't see the other riders, including members of your party), the single-rider line is a great option. To get there, enter the right (no-bags) line and keep left all the way into the castle. After passing the locker area, take the first left into the unmarked single-rider line. If you use the single-rider line, however, you will miss much of the interior of the castle.

A good way to experience the castle *and* cut your waiting time is to tell the greeter at the castle entrance that you want to take the **castle-only tour.** This self-guided tour allows guests who don't want to experience the ride to view the many features of the castle via an alternative queuing lane. Pause as long as you desire in each of the various chambers and take in the preshows at your leisure without being herded along; at the end, if you want to ride, ask to be guided to the single-rider line.

Finally, Forbidden Journey takes Universal Express as of July 2017.

Hogwarts Express ★★★★½

APPEAL BY AGE	PRESCHOOL ★★★½	GRADE SCHOOL ★★★★½	TEENS ★★★★½
YOUNG ADULTS ★★★★★		OVER 30 ★★★★½	SENIORS ★★★★★

What it is Transportation attraction. **Scope and scale** Super-headliner. **When to go** Immediately after park opening until midafternoon. **Special comment** Park-to-Park ticket required to ride. **Authors' rating** Not to be missed; ★★★★½. **Duration of ride** 4 minutes. **Probable wait in line per 100 people ahead of you** 7 minutes. **Loading speed** Moderate.

DESCRIPTION AND COMMENTS See page 709 for a full review.

TOURING TIPS Because the Hogsmeade Station doesn't include the cool Platform 9¾ effect found at the King's Cross end, you'd expect waits for the one-way trip to be shorter here. Surprisingly, lines can be longer here than at USF on slower days, though King's Cross is the busier end during peak periods. Lines are usually less than 20 minutes through the morning but can build later in the day, so ride before midafternoon if experiencing the train is important. On peak days, guests wishing to take a same-day return trip may be relegated to a slower reride queue.

Note: You must have a Park-to-Park ticket to ride. Single-park tickets can be upgraded at Guest Services or at either train station.

Ollivanders ★★★★

APPEAL BY AGE	PRESCHOOL ★★★★	GRADE SCHOOL ★★★★½	TEENS ★★★½
YOUNG ADULTS ★★★★		OVER 30 ★★★★	SENIORS ★★★½

What it is Combination wizarding demonstration and shopping op. **Scope and scale** Minor attraction. **When to go** In the first or last 30 minutes of the day. **Special comments** Audience stands; identical to USF version but with a much slower line. **Authors' rating** Enchanting but inefficient; ★★★★. **Duration of presentation** 6 minutes. **Average wait in line per 100 people ahead of you** 7 minutes.

DESCRIPTION AND COMMENTS Next to the Owl Post is Ollivanders, a musty little shop stacked to the ceiling with boxes of magic wands. Inside you'll
find the same intimate wand-choosing ceremony found in the Diagon
Alley attraction of the same name (see page 710). It's great fun, but the
tiny shop can accommodate only about 24 guests at a time. After the
show, the whole group is dispatched to the Owl Post and Dervish and
Banges to make purchases. An interactive model, which triggers special
effects hidden inside shop windows throughout Hogsmeade and Diagon
Alley, costs $53.20; a basic model that doesn't do any tricks costs $46.81.

TOURING TIPS Due to the shop's very low capacity (about 150 guests per
hour), long lines for the show at Ollivanders form quickly upon park opening and last until just before the park closes. If you need to see this show,
and you can't go to the USF branch, go first thing in the morning or as
late as possible. If you just want to buy a wand, enter the store directly
rather than wait in the long outdoor queue; you can also buy the cheaper,
noninteractive version at an outdoor cart, usually set up between Filch's
Emporium of Confiscated Goods and the Flight of the Hippogriff exit,
with little to no wait.

Wizarding World Entertainment

Nearly every retail space sports some sort of animatronic or special effects
surprise. At **Dervish and Banges,** the fearsome *Monster Book of Monsters*
rattles and snarls at you as Nimbus 2001 brooms strain at their tethers
overhead. At the **Hog's Head** pub, the titular porcine part, mounted behind
the bar, similarly thrashes and growls. (The pub also serves The Wizarding
World's signature nonalcoholic brew, Butterbeer. Outdoor vendors also
sell it, but the wait at the Hog's Head is generally 10 minutes or less, versus
half an hour or more in the lines outside. Also, the outdoor vendors charge
a few cents more and don't honor Annual Pass discounts.)

Roughly across the street from the pub, you'll find benches in the
shade at the **Owlery,** where animatronic owls (complete with lifelike
poop) ruffle and hoot from the rafters. Next to the Owlery is the **Owl
Post,** where you can have mail stamped with a Hogsmeade postmark
before dropping it off for delivery (an Orlando postmark will also be
applied by the real USPS). You can't enter through the Owl Post's front
door on busy days, when it serves exclusively as an exit. Because it's so
difficult to get into the Owl Post, IOA sometimes stations a team member
outside to stamp your postcards with the Wizarding World postmark.

Street entertainment at the Forbidden Journey end of Hogsmeade
includes the ***Frog Choir*** (★★★), composed of four singers, two of
whom are holding large amphibian puppets sitting on pillows; and the
Triwizard Spirit Rally (★★★½), showcasing dancing and martial arts.
Performances run about 6–15 minutes.

THE LOST CONTINENT

THIS AREA IS AN EXOTIC MIX of Silk Road bazaar and ancient
ruins, with Greco-Moroccan accents. (And you thought your decorator

was nuts.) This is the land of mythical gods, fabled beasts, and expensive souvenirs. The best attraction in Lost Continent may be the **Mystic Fountain,** an interactive talking fountain in front of the *Sindbad* stadium. It's a fountain with an attitude, so keep your umbrella handy.

The Eighth Voyage of Sindbad *(Universal Express)* ★★½

APPEAL BY AGE	PRESCHOOL ★★	GRADE SCHOOL ★★★½	TEENS ★★★
YOUNG ADULTS ★★★	OVER 30 ★★½		SENIORS ★★½

What it is Theater stunt show. **Scope and scale** Major attraction. **When to go** Any time on the daily entertainment schedule. **Authors' rating** Explosively lame; ★★½. **Duration of presentation** 17 minutes. **Probable waiting time** 15 minutes.

DESCRIPTION AND COMMENTS A story about Sindbad the Sailor is the glue that (loosely) binds this stunt show featuring water explosions, 10-foot-tall circles of flame, and various other eruptions and perturbations. Not unlike an action movie that substitutes a mind-numbing succession of explosions, crashes, and special effects for plot and character development, the production is so vacuous and redundant (not to mention silly) that it's hard to get into the action.

TOURING TIPS See *Sindbad* (if you must) after you've experienced the rides and the better-rated shows.

Poseidon's Fury *(Universal Express)* ★★★½

APPEAL BY AGE	PRESCHOOL ★★	GRADE SCHOOL ★★★½	TEENS ★★½
YOUNG ADULTS ★★★	OVER 30 ★★★		SENIORS ★★★

What it is High-tech theater attraction. **Scope and scale** Headliner. **When to go** After experiencing all the rides. **Special comment** Audience stands throughout. **Authors' rating** Dumb but dazzling, ★★★½. **Duration of presentation** 17 minutes, including preshow. **Probable waiting time** 25 minutes.

DESCRIPTION AND COMMENTS The Greek god Poseidon tussles with an evil wizardish guy using fire, water, lasers, and smoke machines. The plot unfolds in installments as you pass from room to room and finally into the main theater. Though the premise is kind of silly, the technology at work here makes *Poseidon* by far and away the best of the Islands of Adventure theater attractions (it only has to compete with *Sindbad*).

TOURING TIPS Catch *Poseidon* after getting your fill of the rides. The attraction opens 1 or more hours after the rest of the park (usually at 10 a.m.) and closes 30 minutes or more before park closing. Frequent explosions, dark, and noise may frighten younger children.

SEUSS LANDING

A 10-ACRE THEMED AREA BASED on Dr. Seuss's famous children's books. As at the old Mickey's Toontown in the Magic Kingdom, all of the buildings and attractions replicate a whimsical, brightly colored cartoon style with exaggerated features and rounded lines. There are four rides at Seuss Landing; an interactive play area, **If I Ran the Zoo,** populated by Seuss creatures; and *Oh, the Stories You'll Hear!,* a live musical show.

Caro-Seuss-el *(Universal Express)* ★★★

APPEAL BY AGE	PRESCHOOL ★★★★★	GRADE SCHOOL ★★★★	TEENS ★★
YOUNG ADULTS ★★★★	OVER 30 ★★★½		SENIORS ★★★★

What it is Merry-go-round. **Scope and scale** Minor attraction. **When to go** Anytime. **Special comment** Ride is outside but covered. **Authors' rating** Wonderfully whimsical; ★★★. **Duration of ride** 2 minutes. **Average wait in line per 100 people ahead of you** 9 minutes. **Loading speed** Slow.

DESCRIPTION AND COMMENTS Totally outrageous, this full-scale, 56-mount merry-go-round is made up entirely of Dr. Seuss characters.

TOURING TIPS Waits usually aren't too long, even in the middle of the day.

The Cat in the Hat (Universal Express) ★★★½

APPEAL BY AGE	PRESCHOOL ★★★★★	GRADE SCHOOL ★★★★	TEENS ★★★
YOUNG ADULTS ★★★½		OVER 30 ★★★	SENIORS ★★★★

What it is Indoor cartoon dark ride. **Scope and scale** Major attraction. **When to go** Before 11:30 a.m. or after 4 p.m. **Special comment** 36″ minimum height requirement. **Authors' rating** Dr. S. would be proud; ★★★½. **Duration of ride** 3½ minutes. **Average wait in line per 100 people ahead of you** 5 minutes. **Loading speed** Moderate.

DESCRIPTION AND COMMENTS Guests ride on "couches" through 18 different sets inhabited by animatronic Seuss characters, including The Cat in the Hat, Thing 1 and Thing 2, and the beleaguered goldfish who tries to maintain order in the midst of bedlam.

TOURING TIPS Fun for all ages. Try to ride early or late in the day.

The High in the Sky Seuss Trolley Train Ride!
(Universal Express) ★★★½

APPEAL BY AGE	PRESCHOOL ★★★★★	GRADE SCHOOL ★★★★	TEENS ★★★
YOUNG ADULTS ★★★		OVER 30 ★★★½	SENIORS ★★★★½

What it is Elevated train. **Scope and scale** Major attraction. **When to go** Before 11:30 a.m. or just before closing. **Special comment** 40″ minimum height requirement. **Authors' rating** Relaxing; ★★★½. **Duration of ride** 3½ minutes. **Average wait in line per 100 people ahead of you** 9 minutes. **Loading speed** Molasses.

DESCRIPTION AND COMMENTS Trains putter along elevated tracks while a voice reads one of four Dr. Seuss stories over the train's speakers. As each train makes its way through Seuss Landing, it passes a series of animatronic characters in scenes that are part of the story being told. It's a charming little ride, but a bizarrely stringent minimum height requirement, raised in recent years to 40 inches, means that many in the Trolley's target demographic aren't allowed to ride.

TOURING TIPS The trains are small, fitting about 20 people, and the loading speed is glacial. Ride at the end of the day or first thing in the morning.

If I Ran the Zoo (Universal Express) ★★½

APPEAL BY AGE	PRESCHOOL ★★★★★	GRADE SCHOOL ★★★½	TEENS ★★★★
YOUNG ADULTS ★★★★½		OVER 30 ★★★	SENIORS ★★★★½

What it is Play area. **Scope and scale** Diversion. **When to go** Anytime. **Special comment** Kids may get wet. **Authors' rating** A nice break for parents; ★★½.

DESCRIPTION AND COMMENTS An interactive play area and outdoor maze, themed to Dr. Seuss rhymes and filled with the fantastic animals and gizmos from Seuss stories.

TOURING TIPS Tour anytime. Note that much of the play area is unshaded—bring cold drinks and hats for the little ones.

Oh! The Stories You'll Hear! ★★★

APPEAL BY AGE PRESCHOOL ★★★★ GRADE SCHOOL ★★★★ TEENS ★½
YOUNG ADULTS ★ OVER 30 ★★★ SENIORS ★★½

What it is Character-filled storytelling show. **Scope and scale** Minor attraction. **When to go** Scheduled showtimes. **Special comment** Audience stands during show. **Authors' rating** Warm and fuzzy; ★★★. **Duration of presentation** 9 minutes. **Probable waiting time** Negligible.

DESCRIPTION AND COMMENTS Featuring many of Dr. Seuss's most beloved characters (including The Lorax, The Grinch, Thing 1 and Thing 2, Sam I Am, and the Cat in the Hat), this festive singing and dancing show is staged in an outdoor area between One Fish, Two Fish, Red Fish, Blue Fish and The Cat in the Hat Ride. After each 9-minute show, the characters separate for individual meet and greets and autographs.

TOURING TIPS Shows run daily, usually starting by 10:30 a.m. and continuing every hour until about 4:30 p.m. on a schedule published in the park map. During inclement weather, the show takes place within the Circus McGurkus Cafe Stoo-pendous restaurant nearby.

One Fish, Two Fish, Red Fish, Blue Fish
(Universal Express) ★★★

APPEAL BY AGE PRESCHOOL ★★★★ GRADE SCHOOL ★★★★½ TEENS ★★★½
YOUNG ADULTS ★★½ OVER 30 ★★★ SENIORS ★★★

What it is Wet version of Dumbo the Flying Elephant. **Scope and scale** Minor attraction. **When to go** Before 10 a.m. **Special comment** Plan on getting wet. **Authors' rating** Who says you can't teach an old ride new tricks? ★★★. **Duration of ride** 2 minutes. **Average wait in line per 100 people ahead of you** 9 minutes. **Loading speed** Slow.

DESCRIPTION AND COMMENTS Imagine Dumbo with Seuss-style fish instead of elephants and you have half the story—the other half involves another opportunity to drown. Guests steer their fish up or down 15 feet in the air while traveling in circles. At the same time, they try to avoid streams of water projected from "squirt posts."

TOURING TIPS You'll get wetter than at a full-immersion baptism. Lines can build in the afternoon, so ride early while you'll still have time to dry off.

DINING *at* UNIVERSAL'S ISLANDS *of* ADVENTURE

OF IOA'S GUSTATORY OFFERINGS, we like **Three Broomsticks,** The Wizarding World of Harry Potter's counter-service restaurant, which serves Boston Market–style rotisserie chicken, plus fish-and-chips, shepherd's pie, and barbecue ribs; a similar menu (minus the Potter theming and crowds) is available at **Thunder Falls Terrace** in Jurassic Park. The **Hog's Head** pub, a short walk from Three Broomsticks, serves beer, wine, mixed drinks, and the obligatory Butterbeer. We're also fond of the gyros at **Fire Eater's Grill** and the sandwiches at **Blondie's.** Skip the green eggs at the **Green Eggs and Ham Cafe.**

IOA has two sit-down restaurants: **Confisco Grille,** in Port of Entry, and **Mythos Restaurant,** in The Lost Continent. Confisco is fine for pizza and drinks. Despite its Hellenic-sounding name, Mythos isn't a Greek restaurant; rather, like a typical Applebee's or Chili's, it serves something-for-everyone fare, including Italian risotto, Asian noodles, and Mexican fish tacos, plus steaks and burgers. Nothing on the menu stands out as either very good or very bad, so stick with appetizers and drinks.

ISLANDS *of* ADVENTURE TOURING PLANS

DECISIONS, DECISIONS

WHEN IT COMES TO TOURING IOA efficiently in a single day, you have two basic choices:

If you're intent on experiencing Forbidden Journey first thing, be at the turnstiles at least 30 minutes before the park opens. Once you're admitted, hurry to Hogsmeade and ride Forbidden Journey, Flight of the Hippogriff, and Dragon Challenge, *in that order*. Then head to other must-experience attractions before the park gets crowded. The catch? Ride difficulties could have you stuck in a long line while crowds—and more lines—spread to other areas of IOA.

Unless you have Early Park Admission at IOA, we recommend skipping Potterville first thing and enjoying other attractions, starting at Marvel Super Hero Island and then heading for Skull Island. The Wizarding World usually clears out in the afternoon and is often empty in the last hour, even on busy days, meaning you can ride Forbidden Journey with a minimal wait if you get in line shortly before closing time.

UNIVERSAL'S ISLANDS OF ADVENTURE ONE-DAY TOURING PLAN *(page 833)*

THIS TOURING PLAN is for guests without park-to-park tickets and is appropriate for groups of all sizes and ages. It includes thrill rides that may induce motion sickness or get you wet. If the plan calls for you to experience an attraction that doesn't interest you, simply skip it and go to the next step. Be aware that the plan calls for some backtracking. If you have young children in your party, customize the plan to fit their needs and take advantage of child swap at thrill rides.

THE BEST OF UNIVERSAL STUDIOS FLORIDA AND ISLANDS OF ADVENTURE IN ONE DAY
(pages 835 and 836)

THIS TOURING PLAN is for guests with One-Day Park-to-Park Tickets who wish to see the highlights of Universal Studios Florida and Islands of Adventure in a single day. The plan uses Hogwarts Express to get from one park to the other and then back again; you can walk back to the first park for the return leg if the line is too long. The plan includes a table-service lunch at Mythos (make reservations online a few days before your visit) and dinner at the Leaky Cauldron; during holiday periods, you may need to substitute a quick-service snack for one or both meals to fit in all of the plan's attractions.

UNIVERSAL STUDIOS FLORIDA

UNIVERSAL STUDIOS FLORIDA OPENED IN JUNE 1990. At the time, it was almost four times the size of Disney's Hollywood Studios, and much more of the facility was accessible to visitors. USF is spacious, beautifully landscaped, meticulously clean, and delightfully varied in its entertainment. Rides are exciting and innovative and, like many Disney attractions, focus on familiar and/or beloved movie characters or situations. In 2016 Universal Studios closed several attractions to make way for **Fast & Furious: Supercharged,** scheduled to open in 2018, and **Race Through New York Starring Jimmy Fallon,** which opened in 2017.

USF is laid out in a *P*-configuration, with the rounded part of the *P* sticking out disproportionately from the stem. Beyond the main entrance, a wide boulevard stretches past several shows and rides to the park's New York area. Branching off this pedestrian thoroughfare to the right are four streets that access other areas of the park and intersect a promenade circling a large lake. The area of USF open to visitors is a bit smaller than Epcot.

The park is divided into seven areas: **Hollywood, New York, Production Central, San Francisco, Woody Woodpecker's KidZone, World Expo,** and **The Wizarding World of Harry Potter—Diagon Alley. Springfield: Home of the Simpsons** is considered part of World Expo but is nonetheless a distinctive area all its own.

In most of USF, where one area begins and another ends is blurry, but no matter. Guests orient themselves by the major rides, sets, and landmarks and refer, for instance, to "New York," "the waterfront," "over by E.T.," or "by Mel's Diner." Because most USF attractions aren't thematically integrated into the areas of the park in which they reside, we present them alphabetically rather than by area.

USF offers all standard services and amenities, including stroller and wheelchair rental, lockers, diaper-changing and infant-nursing facilities, car assistance, and foreign-language assistance. Most of the park is accessible to disabled guests, and TDDs are available for the hearing-impaired. Almost all services are in the **Front Lot,** just inside the main entrance.

HOW MUCH TIME TO ALLOCATE

TOURING UNIVERSAL STUDIOS FLORIDA, including one meal and a visit to Diagon Alley, takes about 10–12 hours. Some theater attractions don't schedule performances until 11 a.m. or after. This means that early in the day, all park guests are concentrated among the limited number of attractions in operation.

NOT TO BE MISSED AT UNIVERSAL STUDIOS FLORIDA

- Harry Potter and the Escape from Gringotts
- Hogwarts Express
- Men in Black Alien Attack

- Ollivanders
- Revenge of the Mummy
- The Simpsons Ride

- *Terminator 2: 3-D*
- Transformers: The Ride 3-D
- *Universal Orlando's Horror Make-Up Show*

As a postscript, you won't have to worry about any of this if you use our Universal Studios touring plan. We'll keep you a step ahead of the crowd and make sure that any given attraction is running by the time you get there.

UNIVERSAL STUDIOS FLORIDA ATTRACTIONS

Animal Actors on Location! (Universal Express) ★★★

APPEAL BY AGE	PRESCHOOL ★★★★	GRADE SCHOOL ★★★★½	TEENS ★★★★
YOUNG ADULTS ★★★½		OVER 30 ★★★★	SENIORS ★★★★

What it is Animal tricks and comedy show. **Scope and scale** Major attraction. **When to go** After you've experienced all rides. **Authors' rating** Cute li'l critters; ★★★½. **Duration of presentation** 25 minutes. **Probable waiting time** None.

DESCRIPTION AND COMMENTS This show integrates video segments with live sketches, jokes, and animal tricks performed onstage. Live animals, some of which are veterans of TV and movies (and many of which were rescued from shelters), take part, and kids are invited to participate.

TOURING TIPS Sit in the center of the stadium about halfway up for the best chance to be picked. Check the entertainment schedule for showtimes.

The Blues Brothers Show ★★★½

APPEAL BY AGE	PRESCHOOL ★★★	GRADE SCHOOL ★★★½	TEENS ★★★½
YOUNG ADULTS ★★★½	OVER 30 ★★★★	SENIORS ★★★★	

What it is Rhythm and blues concert. **Scope and scale** Diversion. **When to go** Scheduled showtimes. **Special comment** A party in the street. **Authors' rating** Energetic; ★★★½. **Duration of presentation** 12 minutes. **Probable waiting time** None.

DESCRIPTION AND COMMENTS Staged on the corner of the New York area, across from the lagoon, *The Blues Brothers Show* features Jake and Elwood performing a few of the hit songs from the classic 1980 movie musical, including "Soul Man" and "Sweet Home Chicago." The brothers are joined onstage by Jazz the saxophone player and his girlfriend, Mabel the waitress, who belts an Aretha Franklin cover to start the show. The concert is a great pick-me-up, and the short run time keeps the energy high.

TOURING TIPS The audience stands on the street without cover or shade.

A Day in the Park with Barney (Universal Express) ★★★

APPEAL BY AGE	PRESCHOOL ★★★★★	GRADE SCHOOL ★★★	TEENS ★★
YOUNG ADULTS ★★★	OVER 30 ★★★	SENIORS ★★★	

What it is Live-character stage show. **Scope and scale** Major children's attraction. **When to go** Scheduled showtimes. **Authors' rating** A great hit with preschoolers; ★★★. **Duration of presentation** 20 minutes, plus 5-minute preshow and character greeting after the show. **Probable waiting time** None.

DESCRIPTION AND COMMENTS Barney, the cuddly purple dinosaur of public-television fame, leads a sing-along with the help of the audience and side-kicks Baby Bop and BJ. A short preshow gets the kids lathered up before they enter Barney's Park (the theater). Interesting theatrical effects

Continued on page 698

Universal Studios Florida

Attractions

1. *Animal Actors on Location!* UX
2. *The Blues Brothers Show*
3. *A Day in the Park with Barney* UX
4. Despicable Me Minion Mayhem UX
5. E.T. Adventure UX
6. Fast & Furious: Supercharged *(opens 2018)* UX
7. *Fear Factor Live* UX
8. Fievel's Playland
9. Harry Potter and the Escape from Gringotts UX ☑
10. Hogwarts Express–King's Cross Station ☑
11. Hollywood Rip Ride Rockit UX
12. Kang & Kodos' Twirl 'n' Hurl
13. Men in Black Alien Attack UX ☑
14. Ollivanders ☑
15. Revenge of the Mummy UX ☑

16. Race Through New York Starring Jimmy Fallon UX ☑
17. *Shrek 4-D* UX
18. The Simpsons Ride UX ☑
19. *Terminator 2: 3-D* UX ☑
20. Transformers: The Ride-3D UX ☑
21. *Universal Orlando's Horror Make-Up Show* UX ☑

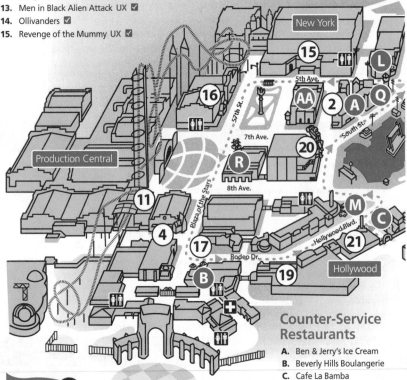

Counter-Service Restaurants

A. Ben & Jerry's Ice Cream
B. Beverly Hills Boulangerie
C. Cafe La Bamba
D. Chez Alcatraz
E. Duff Brewery
F. Fast Food Boulevard 👍
H. Florean Fortescue's Ice-Cream Parlour 👍

22. *Universal's Cinematic Spectacular: 100 Years of Movie Memories*

23. Woody Woodpacker's Nuthouse Coaster and Curious George Goes to Town

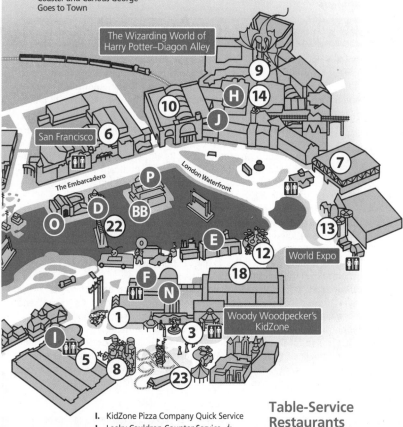

The Wizarding World of Harry Potter–Diagon Alley

San Francisco

The Embarcadero

London Waterfront

World Expo

Woody Woodpecker's KidZone

I. KidZone Pizza Company Quick Service
J. Leaky Cauldron Counter Service 👍
L. Louie's Italian Restaurant
M. Mel's Drive-In
N. Moe's Tavern
O. Richter's Burger Co.
P. San Francisco Pastry Company
Q. Starbucks Coffee
R. Universal Studios' Classic Monsters Cafe

Table-Service Restaurants

AA. Finnegan's Bar & Grill
BB. Lombard's Seafood Grille

UX Attraction Offers Universal Express   ✚ First Aid Station   🚻 Restrooms

👍 Recommended Dining   ✓ Not to Be Missed   • • • Parade Route

Continued from page 695

include wind, falling leaves, clouds and stars in the simulated sky, and snow. After the show, Barney poses for photos with parents and children inside the theater or in the indoor playground at the theater exit.

TOURING TIPS If your child likes Barney, this show is a must. There's also a great indoor play area nearby, designed especially for wee tykes.

Despicable Me Minion Mayhem *(Universal Express)* ★★★★

APPEAL BY AGE	PRESCHOOL ★★	GRADE SCHOOL ★★★★½	TEENS ★★★★
YOUNG ADULTS ★★★★½		OVER 30 ★★★★	SENIORS ★★★

What it is Motion-simulator 3-D ride. **Scope and scale** Major attraction. **When to go** Immediately after park opening or just before closing. **Special comment** Expect *long* waits in line. **Authors' rating** Great fun; ★★★★. **Duration of ride** 5 minutes. **Average wait in line per 100 people ahead of you** 7 minutes; assumes all simulators in use. **Loading speed** Moderate–slow.

DESCRIPTION AND COMMENTS Despicable Me Minion Mayhem involves high-tech motion simulators moving and reacting in sync with a cartoon projected on an IMAX-like screen. Though the simulators have been updated, the most significant upgrade is incorporated in the projection system, which employs high-definition 3-D digital technology.

The story combines elements from the animated movie *Despicable Me,* starring Gru, the archvillain, along with his adopted daughters and his diminutive yellow Minions. During the queue and preshow, you visit Gru's house and are then ushered into his lab, where you're turned into a Minion. Guests disembark the ride into a disco party with a Minion meet and greet before exiting through the obligatory gift shop.

TOURING TIPS Despicable Me Minion Mayhem is unfortunately situated at the very front of the park, within a few yards of the turnstiles. As a result, and because it's a popular attractions long lines develop as soon as the park opens. If you're among the first to enter and the wait is 20 minutes or less, get in line for Despicable Me, and then ride Hollywood Rip Ride Rockit, but if the line for Despicable Me exceeds 20 minutes, try late afternoon or the hour before the park closes. Stationary seating is available for those prone to motion sickness and for children less than 40 inches tall.

E.T. Adventure *(Universal Express)* ★★★½

APPEAL BY AGE	PRESCHOOL ★★★★	GRADE SCHOOL ★★★★	TEENS ★★★
YOUNG ADULTS ★★★		OVER 30 ★★★½	SENIORS ★★★★

What it is Indoor adventure ride based on the beloved movie. **Scope and scale** Major attraction. **When to go** Within 30 minutes of ride opening or late afternoon. **Special comment** 34″ minimum height requirement. **Authors' rating** A long, strange, happy trip; ★★★½. **Duration of ride** 4½ minutes. **Average wait in line per 100 people ahead of you** 5 minutes. **Loading speed** Moderate.

DESCRIPTION AND COMMENTS Guests board a bicycle-like conveyance to escape with E.T., The Extra-Terrestrial, from earthly law enforcement officials and journey to his home planet. Concerning the latter, where E.T. is reunited with family and friends, our Len Testa likens it to *The Wizard of Oz*'s Technicolor scene, only reenacted with a cave full of naked mole rats. (C'mon, Len, where's the love?)

Before you return home, E.T. bids each rider farewell by name. A Baton, North Carolina, reader with perhaps too much time on his hands got to wondering:

Why do the inhabitants of E.T.'s home planet, who presumably have never visited Earth, speak better English than he does?

Introduced in 1990, E.T. Adventure is showing its age: The human animatronics look like dime-store dummies, and some of E.T.'s pals are downright disturbing with their out-of-synch facial animation. Even so, E.T. is one of Universal's only family-friendly dark rides that relies on sets and robotics instead of screens, so we hope it sticks around for a long time to come.

TOURING TIPS Most preschoolers and grade-school children love E.T. Ride in the morning or late afternoon. On peak days, a time-saving single-rider line is occasionally opened.

Fast & Furious: Supercharged *(opens 2018)*

APPEAL BY AGE   NOT OPEN AT PRESS TIME

What it is Car chase 3-D motion simulator. **Scope and scale** Headliner. **When to go** After experiencing the other headliners.

DESCRIPTION AND COMMENTS While the details for USF's ride aren't yet final, we expect it to be similar to the version at Universal Studios Hollywood: Hydraulic platforms, 400-foot-long screens, and 34 ultra-HD 3-D projectors make it appear as if your ride vehicle is in the midst of a high-stakes car chase, pursuing an international crime cartel at 100-plus mph through a West Coast urban jungle.

After passing through an elaborate queue in an industrial warehouse, you stumble across an underground club. The feds crash the party, searching for a crucial crime witness hiding among the guests. After you board specially designed tramlike vehicles, the Fast & Furious crew, led by Vin Diesel as Dom Toretto and Dwayne "The Rock" Johnson as Luke Hobbs, come to your rescue and escort you on a virtual high-speed highway chase filled with computer-graphic car crashes and simulated explosions. The dialogue and visual effects are shockingly cheesy even by theme park standards (Len considers this part of the appeal), but it all goes by in such a nitro-fueled blur that it won't matter.

TOURING TIPS Supercharged is expected to use the same Virtual Line system as Race Through New York Starring Jimmy Fallon, so select your return time using the Universal smartphone app as soon as you enter the park, or grab a ticket from the ride's kiosks immediately after hitting Despicable Me.

Fear Factor Live *(Universal Express)*   ★★½

APPEAL BY AGE	PRESCHOOL	★	GRADE SCHOOL	★★	TEENS	★★★★
YOUNG ADULTS	★★★	OVER 30	★★★	SENIORS	★★	

What it is Live version of the gross-out-stunt TV show. **Scope and scale** Headliner. **When to go** 3–5 shows daily; crowds are smallest at the first and second-to-last shows. **Special comments** Too intense for kids age 8 and younger. Contestants for the stage show must be 18 years or older (photo ID required) and weigh at least 110 pounds. Anyone who doesn't wish to compete in the main show can sign up for the Critter Challenge or the Food Challenge; with an adult's permission, volunteers as young as age 16 can compete in the latter. **Authors' rating** *Ewwww;* ★★½. **Duration of presentation** 30 minutes. **Probable waiting time** None.

DESCRIPTION AND COMMENTS Open seasonally, *Fear Factor Live* is a stage version of the former NBC reality show that was recently revived for MTV. In the theme park iteration, six volunteers compete for a prize package that contains Universal swag ranging from park tickets to T-shirts.

The stage show consists of three different challenges. In the first, all six contestants are suspended two-and-a-half stories in the air and try to hang on to a bar as long as possible while heavy-duty fans blast their faces. Only four people go on to the next round.

Once the first two contestants are eliminated, it's time for a brief intermission called the Desert Hat Ordeal. Prepared with goggles and a mouthpiece, an audience member–lunatic who signed up for the Critter Challenge sits in a chair with a glass case over his or her head. A wheel is spun to determine the vermin that will be crawling over the volunteer's head: spiders, snakes, roaches, or scorpions. The prize: a free photo of the ordeal.

Back at the main competition, the four remaining contestants are split into two teams to compete in the Eel Tank Relay. One team member grabs beanbags out of a tank full of eels and throws them to his or her partner to catch in a bucket while audience members drench the contestants with high-powered water guns. The duo who buckets the most beanbags wins, going on to compete against each other in the final round.

As the stage is prepared for the finale, the folks who volunteered for the Food Challenge are split into two teams and invited to drink a mixture of curdled milk, mystery meat, and various live bugs that are all blended together onstage. The team that drinks the most of the mixture within the time limit wins a glamorous plastic mug that says I ATE A BUG.

The finale has the two remaining contestants scramble up a wall to retrieve flags, jump into a car that is lifted in the air, and then jump out of the car to retrieve more flags. When the required climbing, jumping, and flag-grabbing are accomplished, the first player to remove a rocket launcher from the backseat of the car and hit a target on the stage wall wins.

TOURING TIPS Contestants for the physical stunts are chosen early in the morning and between performances outside the theater; those demented enough to volunteer should arrive at least 75 minutes before showtime to sign papers and complete some obligatory training. The contestants for the Critter and Food Challenges are chosen directly from the audience.

Fievel's Playland ★★★

APPEAL BY AGE	PRESCHOOL ★★★★	GRADE SCHOOL ★★★★	TEENS —
YOUNG ADULTS —	OVER 30 —		SENIORS —

What it is Children's play area with waterslide. **Scope and scale** Minor attraction. **When to go** Anytime. **Authors' rating** A much-needed attraction for preschoolers; ★★★. **Probable waiting time** 20–30 minutes for the waterslide; otherwise, no waiting. **Loading speed** Slow for the waterslide.

DESCRIPTION AND COMMENTS This playground features ordinary household items reproduced on a giant scale, from a mouse's point of view. Younger kids can climb nets, walk through a huge boot, splash in a sardine-can fountain, seesaw on huge spoons, and climb onto a cow skull. Most of the playground is reserved for preschoolers, but a combination waterslide and raft ride is open to all ages. Except for that, there's no waiting in line here, and you can stay as long as you want.

TOURING TIPS The water ride is extremely slow to load and carries just 300 riders an hour. With an average wait of 20–30 minutes, the 16-second ride isn't worth the trouble, and, yes, you *will* get soaked. A lack of shade ensures that the playground is scorching during the summer.

Hollywood Rip Ride Rockit (Universal Express) ★★★★

What it is High-tech roller coaster. **Scope and scale** Headliner. **When to go** The first hour after park opening or after 5 p.m. **Special comments** 51″ minimum height requirement; expect long waits in line. **Authors' rating** Woo-hoo! (and ouch!); ★★★★. **Duration of ride** 2½ minutes. **Average wait in line per 100 people ahead of you** 6–8 minutes. **Loading speed** Moderate.

DESCRIPTION AND COMMENTS Rip Ride Rockit, a sit-down X-Car coaster, runs on a 3,800-foot steel track, with a maximum height of 167 feet and a top speed of 65 mph. (X-Car vehicles are more maneuverable than most other kinds and use less restrictive restraints, making for an exhilarating ride.)

You ascend—vertically—at 11 feet per second to crest the 17-story-tall first hill, the second-highest point reached by any roller coaster in Orlando (Mako at SeaWorld is higher). The drop is almost vertical, too, and launches you into Double Take, a loop inversion in which you begin on the inside of the loop, twist to the outside at the top (so you're upright), and then twist back inside the loop for the descent. Double Take stands 136 feet tall, and its loop is 103 feet in diameter at its widest point. You next hurtle into a stretch of track shaped like a musical treble clef. As on Double Take, the track configuration on Treble Clef is a first. Another innovation is Jump Cut, a spiraling negative-gravity maneuver: You feel like you're in a corkscrew inversion, but you never actually go upside down.

The ride starts in the Production Central area; weaves into the New York area near Race Through New York, popping out over the heads of guests in the square below; and then storms out and over the lagoon separating USF from IOA. Each row is outfitted with color-changing LEDs and high-end audio and video technology for each seat.

Like Rock 'n' Roller Coaster at Hollywood Studios, this coaster features a musical soundtrack. With Rip Ride Rockit, however, you get to choose the genre of music you want to hear as you ride: classic rock, country, disco, pop, or rap. The ride has dozens of hidden songs in its catalog: For example, press the Rip Ride Rockit logo on the number pad for 10 seconds, then enter 113 to hear Metallica's "For Whom the Bell Tolls." For the complete list, see tinyurl.com/rrrtrax or download the Pocket Rockit Setlist app for iOS or Android. When it's all over, Universal flogs photos and a DVD of your ride that intercuts stock coaster footage with clips of you screaming.

At nearly 10 years old, the "Triple R" isn't as smooth as it used to be, subjecting you to lots of side-to-side jarring. A Wisconsin reader warns:

I've ridden many coasters, including some over 400 feet tall and with speeds in excess of 120 mph, yet I've never ridden one as painful and as rough as Rip Ride Rockit. With the beating my head and neck took, I'll never ride it again.

TOURING TIPS Because the ride is so close to the USF entrance, it's a crowd magnet. Your only chance to ride without a long wait is to be one of the first to enter the park when it opens.

Kang & Kodos' Twirl 'n' Hurl ★★★

What it is Spinning ride. **Scope and scale** Minor attraction. **When to go** Before 11 a.m. or whenever there are 50 people or fewer in line. **Special comment** Rarely has long lines but loads slowly. **Authors' rating** The world's wittiest spinner; ★★★.

Duration of ride 1½ minutes. **Average wait in line per 100 people ahead of you** 21 minutes. **Loading speed** Slow.

DESCRIPTION AND COMMENTS The Twirl 'n' Hurl is Dumbo with Bart Simpson's sense of humor: Kang and Kodos are tentacled aliens who hold pictures of *Simpsons* characters; make the characters speak and spin by steering your craft to the proper altitude. All the while, Kang exhorts you (loudly) to destroy Springfield while haughtily insulting humans. Preschoolers enjoy the ride; older kids crack up over the snarky narration.

TOURING TIPS Twirl 'n' Hurl rarely attracts long lines, but slow loading speeds ensure a long wait. Try to ride before 11 a.m. If you want to enjoy the jokes without the wait, you can easily hear them from the sidelines.

Men in Black Alien Attack *(Universal Express)* ★★★★½

APPEAL BY AGE	PRESCHOOL ★★	GRADE SCHOOL ★★★★★	TEENS ★★★★★
YOUNG ADULTS ★★★★		OVER 30 ★★★★	SENIORS ★★★½

What it is Interactive dark thrill ride. **Scope and scale** Headliner. **When to go** During the first 2 hours the park is open or anytime using the single-rider line. **Special comments** May induce motion sickness; 42" minimum height requirement; switching-off option provided (see page 439). **Authors' rating** Buzz Lightyear's Space Ranger Spin on steroids; not to be missed; ★★★★½. **Duration of ride** 4½ minutes. **Average wait in line per 100 people ahead of you** 5 minutes. **Loading speed** Moderate–fast.

DESCRIPTION AND COMMENTS Based on the movie of the same name, the ride has a storyline in which you volunteer as a Men in Black (MIB) trainee. After an introduction warning that aliens "live among us" and articulating MIB's mission to round them up, Zed expands on the finer points of alien spotting and familiarizes you with your training vehicle and your weapon, an alien "zapper." Following this, you load up and are dispatched on an innocuous training mission that immediately deteriorates into a situation where only you are in a position to prevent aliens from taking over the universe. If you saw the movie, you understand that the aliens are mostly giant bugs and that zapping them makes them explode into myriad gooey body parts. Thus, the meat of the ride (no pun intended) consists of careening around Manhattan in your MIB vehicle and shooting aliens.

TOURING TIPS Each of the 120 or so alien figures has sensors that activate special effects and respond to your zapper—aim for the eyes and keep shooting until the aliens' eyes turn red. Targets above you score the most points; look for aliens behind second-story windows. Avoid a long wait and ride during the first 2 hours the park is open, or try the single-rider line if you don't mind splitting your group. For a special treat, ask an attendant for a free "immigration tour" of the queue.

Race Through New York Starring Jimmy Fallon *(Universal Express)* ★★★½

APPEAL BY AGE	PRESCHOOL ★	GRADE SCHOOL ★★★½	TEENS ★★★½
YOUNG ADULTS ★★★½		OVER 30 ★★★½	SENIORS ★★★½

What it is Comedic 3-D simulator ride. **Scope and scale** Headliner. **When to go** According to your Virtual Line return time. **Special comment** Requires free reservation to ride. **Authors' rating** A great leap forward for queue management, a small step sideways for 3-D simulators; ★★★½. **Duration of ride** 4 minutes. **Average wait in line per 100 people ahead of you** 5 minutes. **Loading speed** Moderate.

DESCRIPTION AND COMMENTS Housed in a replica of NBC's historic "30 Rock" offices in Manhattan, Race Through New York is the first Universal Orlando attraction to offer Virtual Line passes instead of a standby queue. Guests, except for those with Universal Express, are assigned a reservation time via Universal's mobile app or an automated kiosk. When your appointed time arrives, you return to the ride entrance, where you'll be directed to the first lobby of the NBC offices. An NBC page will hand you a color-coded card—hold on to it and take time to enjoy the lobby tributes to the previous hosts of *The Tonight Show*: Steve Allen (1954–1956), Jack Paar (1957–1962), Johnny Carson (1962–1992), Jay Leno (1992–2009 and 2010–2014), and Conan O'Brien (2009–2010).

When the lobby lights change to the color of your card, that's your cue to move to the next floor. Here, you await your ride in a fancy lounge outfitted with couches and touchscreen tables with video games inspired by *The Tonight Show Starring Jimmy Fallon*. The main attractions, however, are live appearances by some *Tonight Show* regulars: the Ragtime Gals, a male vocal quintet that performs tongue-in-cheek barbershop interpretations of pop hits, and Hashtag the Panda, a dancing "fur" character (celebrity guests who've worn the costume range from Chris Rock to Miley Cyrus).

When the color of the lights changes once more, it's time to make your way to Jimmy Fallon's studio. The Roots, Fallon's house band, rap the safety instructions before you enter a 72-seat theater with a large screen. Next, you'll don 3-D glasses and race against Fallon in his souped-up "Tonight Rider" roadster. Starting at the *Tonight Show* studio, the competition sends you careening through the streets and subways of New York and eventually to, yes, the moon. Fans create wind effects, and there are faint pizza smells in addition to the obligatory water spray. (Hey, it's Universal!)

The queue-less experience and preshow areas get a lot of points, and the ride itself has some of the sharpest visuals and smoothest movement in the Universal repertoire. But it breaks no new technical ground for the genre, and it relies on recognition of Fallon's stable of characters (like Ew! Girl and Tight Pants Man) for its jokes, which grow stale after several viewings.

Reserve your Virtual Line pass through the Universal smartphone app as soon as you arrive; shoot for early afternoon, when other attractions generally have their longest lines. You can also grab a ticket from the kiosks outside the attraction immediately after riding Despicable Me and Rip Ride Rockit. If return times have run out for the day, check at the attraction an hour or two before park closing to see if they're taking walk-ins.

Revenge of the Mummy *(Universal Express)* ★★★★½

APPEAL BY AGE	PRESCHOOL ★	GRADE SCHOOL ★★★	TEENS ★★★★½
YOUNG ADULTS ★★★★½		OVER 30 ★★★★½	SENIORS ★★★★

What it is Combination dark ride–roller coaster. **Scope and scale** Super-headliner. **When to go** The first 2 hours the park is open or after 4 p.m. **Special comments** 48" minimum height requirement; switching-off option provided (see page 439). **Authors' rating** Killer! Not to be missed; ★★★★½. **Duration of ride** 3 minutes. **Average wait in line per 100 people ahead of you** 7 minutes. **Loading speed** Moderate.

DESCRIPTION AND COMMENTS Revenge of the Mummy is an indoor dark ride based on the Mummy flicks, where guests fight off "deadly curses and vengeful creatures" while flying through Egyptian tombs and other spooky places on a high-tech roller coaster. The special effects are aging but still pretty good: video effects, animatronics, lighting, and enough fire-spewing gas vents to roast a chicken.

The ride begins slowly, passing through various chambers, including one where flesh-eating scarab beetles descend on you. Suddenly your vehicle stops, then drops backward and rotates. Next thing you know, you're shot at high speed up the first hill of the roller coaster. Though it's a wild ride by anyone's definition, the emphasis remains as much on the visuals, robotics, and special effects as on the ride itself.

TOURING TIPS Try to ride during the first 2 hours the park is open. If lines are long, the singles line is often faster than Universal Express. While most grade-schoolers we surveyed who were plucky enough to ride like the Mummy, one father feels we underestimate the fright factor:

This ride should NOT be recommended for grade-schoolers. My second-grader (who wasn't scared at all on Space Mountain) was terrified during this ride and cried afterward. Even I thought it was quite scary, and other adults on our ride echoed the same.

Shrek 4-D *(Universal Express)* ★★★½

APPEAL BY AGE	PRESCHOOL ★★★		GRADE SCHOOL ★★★★		TEENS ★★★½
YOUNG ADULTS ★★★½		OVER 30 ★★★½		SENIORS	★★★½

What it is 3-D movie. **Scope and scale** Headliner. **When to go** Anytime after experiencing the rides. **Authors' rating** The snarkiest 3-D show in town; ★★★½. **Duration of presentation** 20 minutes. **Probable waiting time** 16 minutes.

DESCRIPTION AND COMMENTS The preshow has the villainous Lord Farquaad describing his posthumous plan to reclaim his lost bride, Princess Fiona, who married Shrek. (The plan is posthumous since Lord Farquaad ostensibly died in the movie and it's his ghost making the plans, but whatever.) Guests then move to the main theater, don their 3-D glasses, and recline in seats equipped with "tactile transducers" and "pneumatic air propulsion and water spray nodules capable of both vertical and horizontal motion." As the 3-D film plays, guests are also subjected to smells relevant to the on-screen action (oh boy).

This attraction is a mixed bag. It's irreverent, frantic, laugh-out-loud funny, and iconoclastic. Concerning the last, the film takes a good poke at Disney, with Pinocchio, the Three Little Pigs, and Tinker Bell (among others) all sucked into the mayhem. But the 3-D video quality is dated by today's 4K HD standards, the story is incoherently disconnected from the clever preshow, and the bucking seats swiftly become a pain in the butt.

TOURING TIPS If you see lines longer than 20 minutes, try visiting during mealtimes or in the last 2 hours the park is open.

The Simpsons Ride *(Universal Express)* ★★★★

APPEAL BY AGE	PRESCHOOL ★		GRADE SCHOOL ★★★★		TEENS ★★★★
YOUNG ADULTS ★★★½		OVER 30 ★★★		SENIORS	★★½

What it is Mega-simulator ride. **Scope and scale** Super-headliner. **When to go** During the first 2 hours the park is open or after 4 p.m. **Special comments** 40" minimum height requirement; not recommended for pregnant women or people prone to motion sickness. **Authors' rating** Despicable Me Minion Mayhem with attitude; not to be missed; ★★★★. **Duration of ride** 4⅓ minutes, plus preshow. **Average wait in line per 100 people ahead of you** 5 minutes. **Loading speed** Moderate.

Motion Sickness

DESCRIPTION AND COMMENTS This attraction is a simulator ride similar to Star Tours at Disney's Hollywood Studios and Despicable Me Minion Mayhem at USF, but with a larger screen more like that of Soarin' at Epcot.

The attraction takes a humorous poke at thrill rides, dark rides, and live shows. Two preshows involve *Simpsons* characters speaking sequentially on different video screens in the queue; their comments help define the characters for guests who are unfamiliar with the TV show. The storyline has the conniving Sideshow Bob secretly arriving at Krustyland amusement park and plotting his revenge on Krusty the Clown and Bart, who, in a past *Simpsons* episode, revealed that Sideshow Bob had committed a crime for which he'd framed Krusty. Sideshow Bob gets even by making things go wrong with the attractions that the Simpsons (and you) are riding.

TOURING TIPS Like the show on which it's based, The Simpsons Ride has a definite edge—some parents may find the humor a little too coarse for younger children. Expect large crowds all day. Because the screen you sit in front of is a giant curved dome, sitting outside the central sweet spot may intensify motion sickness. For the best experience, ask the attendant at the bottom of the ramps for Level 2, and then ask the next attendant you see for Room 6.

Terminator 2: 3-D *(Universal Express)*   ★★★★

APPEAL BY AGE	PRESCHOOL ★½	GRADE SCHOOL ★★½	TEENS ★★★
YOUNG ADULTS ★★★★	OVER 30 ★★★½		SENIORS ★★★½

What it is 3-D thriller mixed-media presentation. **Scope and scale** Headliner. **When to go** After noon. **Special comments** One of the nation's best theme park theater attractions; very intense for some preschoolers and grade-schoolers. **Authors' rating** One of the best theme park attractions in the US; not to be missed; ★★★★. **Duration of presentation** 22 minutes, including 8-minute preshow. **Probable waiting time** 20–30 minutes.

DESCRIPTION AND COMMENTS The evil "cop" from *Terminator 2* battles Ahnuld Schwarzenegger's T-100 cyborg. In case you missed the Terminator flicks, here's a refresher: A bad robot arrives from the future to kill a nice boy. Another bad robot—who has been reprogrammed to be good—pops up to save the boy. The bad robot chases the boy and the good robot, menacing the audience in the process.

The attraction, like the films, is all action, and you really don't need to understand much. What's interesting is that it uses 3-D film and a theater full of sophisticated technology to integrate the real with the imaginary. Images seem to move in and out of the film, not only in the manner of traditional 3-D but also in actuality. Remove your 3-D glasses momentarily, and you'll see that the guy on the motorcycle is actually onstage.

TOURING TIPS Save *Terminator* until you've experienced all of the rides. Families with young children should know that the violence of the Terminator movies is largely absent from the attraction; there's suspense and action but not much blood and guts.

Transformers: The Ride 3-D   ★★★★½

APPEAL BY AGE	PRESCHOOL ★	GRADE SCHOOL ★★★★	TEENS ★★★★½
YOUNG ADULTS ★★★★½	OVER 30 ★★★★		SENIORS ★★½

What it is Multisensory 3-D dark ride. **Scope and scale** Super-headliner. **When to go** First 30 minutes the park is open or after 4 p.m. **Special comments** 40" minimum height requirement; single-rider line available. **Authors' rating** A breathtaking blur; not to be missed; ★★★★½. **Duration of ride** 4½ minutes. **Average wait in line per 100 people ahead of you** 5 minutes **Loading speed** Moderate–fast.

DESCRIPTION AND COMMENTS Hasbro's Transformers—those toy robots from the 1980s that you turned and twisted into trucks and planes—have been, er, transformed into director Michael Bay's blockbuster movie franchise and then to a theme park attraction befitting their pop-culture idols. Recruits to this cybertronic war enlist by entering the N.E.S.T. Base (headquarters of the heroic Autobots and their human allies). Inside, in the queue, video monitors catch you up on the backstory. Basically, the Decepticon baddies are after the Allspark, source of cybernetic sentience. Your job is to safeguard the shard. The vastly annoying top villain, Megatron, and his pals Starscream and Devastator threaten the mission, but don't worry—you have Sideswipe and Bumblebee on the bench to back you up.

The plot amounts to little more than a giant game of keep-away, and the uninitiated will likely be unable to tell one meteoric mass of metal from another, but you'll be too dazzled by the debris whizzing by to notice. The ride's mix of detailed set pieces and high-tech video projections brings these colossi to life in one very intense and immersive thrill ride.

Transformers: The Ride 3-D is a perfect example of an attraction that you can enjoy even if you have no clue about the story, but it doesn't hold up as well after repeated rides as The Amazing Adventures of Spider-Man, as it lacks that ride's humor, heart, and moving props.

TOURING TIPS This ride draws crowds—your only solace is that The Wizarding World of Harry Potter–Diagon Alley draws even larger throngs. Follow our touring plan to minimize waits. The single-rider line will get you on board faster, but as singles lines go, this is one of the slower ones and will close if it becomes backed up.

Universal Orlando's Horror Make-Up Show
(Universal Express) ★★★★½

APPEAL BY AGE	PRESCHOOL ★½	GRADE SCHOOL ★★★½	TEENS ★★★½
YOUNG ADULTS ★★★★½		OVER 30 ★★★★	SENIORS ★★★★½

What it is Theater presentation on the art of movie makeup. **Scope and scale** Major attraction. **When to go** Scheduled showtimes and after you've experienced all rides. **Special comment** May frighten some young children. **Authors' rating** A gory knee-slapper; not to be missed; ★★★★½. **Duration of presentation** 25 minutes. **Probable waiting time** None.

DESCRIPTION AND COMMENTS Lively, well-paced look at how makeup artists create film monsters, realistic wounds, severed limbs, and other assorted grossness. The *Horror Make-Up Show* is the sleeper attraction at Universal. Its humor and tongue-in-cheek style transcend the gruesome effects, and most folks (including preschoolers) take the blood and guts in stride.

TOURING TIPS Look for the second-story windows to the left of the theater marquee for a touching tribute to victims of the Pulse nightclub tragedy.

Woody Woodpecker's Nuthouse Coaster and Curious George Goes to Town ★★½

APPEAL BY AGE	PRESCHOOL ★★★★	GRADE SCHOOL ★★★★	TEENS ★★
YOUNG ADULTS ★★½		OVER 30 ★★½	SENIORS ★★½

What it is Kids' roller coaster. **Scope and scale** Minor attraction. **When to go** Anytime. **Special comment** 36" minimum height requirement; children 36"–48" must be accompanied by a supervising companion. **Authors' rating** A suitable starter thrill ride; ★★½. **Duration of ride** 1 minute. **Average wait in line per 100 people ahead of you** 8 minutes. **Loading speed** *Slooow.*

DESCRIPTION AND COMMENTS Woody Woodpecker's Nuthouse Coaster is a short, relatively low roller coaster for little kids. In terms of theme, size, and scariness, it's virtually identical to the Magic Kingdom's Barnstormer coaster: small enough for kids to enjoy but sturdy enough for adults, though its moderate speed might unnerve some smaller children (the minimum height to ride is 36 inches). The entire ride lasts about a minute, and at least 20 of those 60 seconds are spent cranking the train up the first (and only) lift hill.

TOURING TIPS Visit after you've experienced all the major attractions. If your young child has never before experienced a roller coaster, this would be an appropriate first attempt. Most of KidZone is rumored to be ripe for the wrecking ball—Universal has plans to build a new Super Nintendo Land featuring Mario and Donkey Kong.

THE WIZARDING WORLD OF HARRY POTTER-DIAGON ALLEY

WHEN UNIVERSAL OPENED The Wizarding World of Harry Potter at Islands of Adventure, it created a paradigm shift in the Disney–Universal theme park rivalry. Not only did Universal trot out some groundbreaking ride technology, but it also demonstrated that it could trump Disney's most distinctive competence: the creation of infinitely detailed and totally immersive themed areas.

It was immediately obvious that Universal would build on its Potter franchise success. Following much deliberation and consultation with Warner Bros. and author J. K. Rowling, the final design called for a London-waterfront street scene flanking Universal Studios Lagoon. The detailed facades, anchored by the **King's Cross** railroad station on the left and including **Grimmauld Place** and **Wyndham's Theatre,** recall West London scenes from the books and movies. **Diagon Alley,** secreted behind the London street scene, is accessed through a secluded entrance in the middle of the facade.

Enter Diagon Alley next to the Leicester Square marquee, in the approximate center of the building facades. As in the books and films, the unmarked portal is concealed within a magical brick wall that is ordinarily reserved for wizards and the like. (Unfortunately, the wall doesn't actually move, due to safety concerns.) The endless procession of Muggles (plain old humans) in shorts and flip-flops will leave little doubt where that entryway is.

When Early Park Admission is offered, USF admits eligible on-site resort guests 1 hour before the general public, with the turnstiles opening up to 90 minutes before the official opening time. Arrive at least 30 minutes before early entry starts; during peak season, we recommend showing up on the very first boat or bus from your hotel. If you're a day guest visiting on an Early Park Admission day, Diagon Alley will already be packed when you arrive.

Even when Early Park Admission isn't offered, all guests may enter Diagon Alley from the front gates up to 30 minutes before park opening, and hotel guests in IOA will arrive via Hogwarts Express a little after that, though Harry Potter and the Escape from Gringotts doesn't begin operating until close to official opening time.

WIZARDING WORLD–DIAGON ALLEY ATTRACTIONS

Harry Potter and the Escape from Gringotts
(Universal Express) ★★★★★

What it is Super-high-tech 3-D dark ride with roller coaster elements. **Scope and scale** Super-headliner. **When to go** Immediately after park opening or just before closing. **Special comment** Expect *looong* waits in line; 42" minimum height requirement. **Authors' rating** The ultimate realization of "Ride the Movies"; not to be missed; ★★★★★. **Duration of ride** 4½ minutes. **Probable waiting time per 100 people ahead of you** 4 minutes. **Loading speed** Moderate–fast.

DESCRIPTION AND COMMENTS Owned and operated by goblins, Gringotts Wizarding Bank is the Federal Reserve of the wizarding set and the scene of memorable sequences from the first and final Potter installments. The theme park adaptation is the centerpiece of Diagon Alley.

Like Forbidden Journey at IOA, Harry Potter and the Escape from Gringotts incorporates a substantial part of the overall experience into its elaborate queue, which (like Hogwarts Castle) even nonriders should experience. You enter through the bank's lobby, where you're critically appraised by glowering animatronic goblins. Your path takes you to a "security checkpoint" where your photo will be taken (to be purchased afterward as an identity lanyard in the gift shop, natch) and past animated newspapers and office windows where the scenario is set up.

Unlike Forbidden Journey, Gringotts doesn't rush you through its queue, but rather lets you experience two full preshows before approaching the ride vehicles. In the first, goblin banker Blordak and Bill Weasley (Ron's curse-breaking big brother) prepare you for an introductory tour of the underground vaults. Then you're off for a convincing simulated 9-mile plunge into the earth aboard an "elevator" with a bouncing floor and ceiling projections. All this is before you pick up your 3-D glasses and ascend a spiral staircase into the stalactite-festooned boarding cave where your vault cart awaits.

Visitors enter the bank at the exact moment that Harry, Ron, Hermione, and Griphook have arrived to liberate the Hufflepuff Cup Horcrux from Bellatrix Lestrange's vault. Only in this retelling of *Deathly Hallows: Part 2*'s iconic action scene, you (as Muggles opening new bank accounts) are ingeniously integrated into the action. Familiar film moments featuring the vaults' guardian dragon play out in the ride's background as Bellatrix and Voldemort appear to menace you with snakes and sinister spells, whereupon the heroic trio pauses its quest to save your hapless posteriors.

Gringotts's ornately industrial ride vehicles consist of two-car trains, each holding 24 people in rows of four. The ride merges Revenge of the Mummy's indoor-coaster aspects with The Amazing Adventures of Spider-Man's seamless integration of high-resolution 3-D film and massive sculptural sets, while adding a few new tricks such as independently rotating cars and motion-simulator bases built into the track.

As far as physical thrills go, Gringotts falls somewhere between Disney's Seven Dwarfs Mine Train and Space Mountain, with only one short (albeit unique) drop and no upside-down flips. It was designed to be less intense (read: less nauseating) than Forbidden Journey and therefore more appealing to families, with fewer height, weight, and size restrictions.

The ride feels noticeably different depending on the row you're seated in. The front row is closest to the action and has the scariest view of the drop; 3-D effects look better farther back. The sixth row gets the most coaster action, especially from the initial fall, but the screens are slightly distorted. The far right seat in row four is the sweet spot.

TOURING TIPS Though the interior line is gorgeous and air-conditioned, the mostly unshaded outdoor extended queue holds 4,000 guests—you don't want to be at the end of it. If you're a Universal resort guest and you qualify for Early Park Admission, take advantage. Or use Universal Express, which became available for both Wizarding World headliners at press time. When USF doesn't offer Early Park Admission, day guests who arrive before official opening may be allowed to queue for Gringotts before it begins running. Otherwise, try the attraction around lunchtime or in the late afternoon; wait times usually peak after opening but become reasonable later in the day. Just be aware that the queue may shutter to new arrivals before the park closes if the posted wait time exceeds the remaining operating hours by more than 60 minutes, or even earlier if the ride breaks down. Note that you must leave your bags in a free locker.

Hogwarts Express   ★★★★½

What it is Transportation attraction. **Scope and scale** Headliner. **When to go** Late morning or just before park closing. **Special comment** Requires a Park-to-Park ticket to ride. **Authors' rating** A moving experience; not to be missed; ★★★★½. **Duration of ride** 4 minutes. **Average wait in line per 100 people ahead of you** 7 minutes. **Loading speed** Moderate.

DESCRIPTION AND COMMENTS Just as in the novels and films, Diagon Alley at Universal Studios is connected to Hogsmeade at Islands of Adventure by the Hogwarts Express. The counterpart to Hogsmeade Station in IOA is USF's King's Cross station, a few doors down from Diagon Alley's hidden entrance. (*Note:* King's Cross has a separate entrance and exit from Diagon Alley; you can't go directly between them without crossing through the London Waterfront.)

The passage to Platform 9¾, from which Hogwarts students depart on their way to school, is concealed from Muggles by a seemingly solid brick wall, which you'll witness guests ahead of you dematerializing through. The train itself looks authentic to the *n*th degree, from the billowing steam to the brass fixtures and upholstery in your eight-passenger private cabin. Along your one-way Hogwarts Express journey, you'll see moving images projected beyond the windows of the car rather than the park's backstage areas, with the streets of London and the Scottish countryside rolling past outside your window. You experience a different presentation coming and going; plus, there are surprise appearances by secondary characters (Fred and George Weasley, Hagrid) and threats en route (Dementors, licorice spiders), augmented by sound effects in the cars.

TOURING TIPS Passengers need a valid Park-to-Park ticket. Disembarking passengers must enter the second park and, if desired, queue again for their return trip. You'll be allowed (nay, encouraged) to upgrade your 1-Park Base Ticket at the station entrance.

Park-to-Park ticket-purchasing Potterphiles should make the train their second stop of the day after Escape from Gringotts if going from Diagon Alley to Hogsmeade. Or, if Diagon Alley is your top priority of the day, enter IOA as early as possible and line up at the Hogsmeade Station for the train to London King's Cross. If the posted wait is 15 minutes or less, it's typically quicker to take the train than to walk to the other Wizarding World.

Ollivanders ★★★★

APPEAL BY AGE	PRESCHOOL ★★★★	GRADE SCHOOL ★★★★½	TEENS ★★★½
YOUNG ADULTS ★★★★		OVER 30 ★★★★	SENIORS ★★★½

What it is Combination wizarding demonstration and shopping op. **Scope and scale** Major attraction. **When to go** After riding Harry Potter and the Escape from Gringotts. **Special comment** Audience stands to watch the show. **Authors' rating** Enchanting; ★★★★. **Duration of presentation** 6 minutes. **Probable waiting time per 100 people ahead of you** 12 minutes.

DESCRIPTION AND COMMENTS Unlike the branch location in Hogsmeade at IOA (see page 688), the Diagon Alley Ollivanders is in its rightful location per the books, and in much larger digs. The shop has three separate choosing chambers, where wands choose a wizard (rather than the other way around).

TOURING TIPS Check out the self-sweeping broom (shades of *Fantasia*) while waiting for the show. If your young 'un is selected to test-drive a wand, be forewarned that you'll have to buy it if you want to take it home.

Wizarding World Entertainment

Take a moment to spot Kreacher (the house elf regularly peers from a second-story window above 12 Grimmauld Place) and chat with the Knight Bus conductor and his Caribbean-accented shrunken head. Look down the alley to the rounded facade of **Gringotts Wizarding Bank,** where a 40-foot fire-breathing Ukrainian Ironbelly dragon (as seen in *Harry Potter and the Deathly Hallows: Part 2*) perches atop the dome.

To the right of Escape from Gringotts is **Carkitt Market,** a canopy-covered plaza where short live shows are staged every half hour or so. *Celestina Warbeck and the Banshees* (★★★★) showcases the singing sorceress swinging to jazzy tunes titled and inspired by J. K. Rowling herself, and *Tales of Beedle the Bard* (★★★½) recounts the Three Brothers fable from *Deathly Hallows* with puppets crafted by Michael Curry (*Festival of the Lion King, Finding Nemo—The Musical*).

Intersecting Diagon Alley near the Leaky Cauldron is **Knockturn Alley,** a labyrinth of twisting passageways where the Harry Potter bad guys hang out. A covered walk-through area with a projected sky creating perpetual night, it features spooky special effects in the faux shop windows (don't miss the creeping tattoos and crawling spiders).

LIVE ENTERTAINMENT
at UNIVERSAL STUDIOS

IN ADDITION TO THE SHOWS profiled earlier, Universal offers a wide range of street entertainment. Costumed comic-book and cartoon characters roam the park for photo ops, along with movie star look-alikes. The handout park map notes times and places for character appearances and shows.

The Disney-like **Universal's Superstar Parade** (★★★½) features dancers and performers, four large and elaborate floats inspired by cartoons, and a very mixed bag of street-prowling Universal characters. The parade stops twice for a highly choreographed ensemble number. Though impressive in its scope and coordination, the performance is well-nigh impossible to take in from any given viewing spot.

The parade, marked on the park map, begins at the Esoteric Pictures gate in Hollywood between *Universal Orlando's Horror Make-Up Show* and Cafe La Bamba. It turns right, then immediately makes a hard left around Mel's Drive-In and follows the waterfront past Transformers toward San Francisco. From there, it turns left at Louie's Italian Restaurant and proceeds along 5th Avenue, past Revenge of the Mummy. At the end of 5th Avenue, the parade takes a left onto 57th Avenue/Plaza of the Stars and heads toward the front of the park, where it makes another left onto Hollywood Boulevard, from whence it disappears backstage through the gate where it entered. The best viewing spots are along 5th Avenue, on the front steps of faux buildings in New York.

Universal's Cinematic Spectacular: 100 Years of Movie Memories ★★★½ (seasonal when park is open late)

APPEAL BY AGE	PRESCHOOL ★★½	GRADE SCHOOL ★★½	TEENS ★★
YOUNG ADULTS ★★½	OVER 30 ★★★		SENIORS ★★½

What it is Fireworks, dancing fountains, and movies. **Scope and scale** Major attraction. **When to go** 1 show a day, usually at park closing. **Authors' rating** Good effort; ★★★½. **Special comments** Movie trailers galore; presented seasonally, when park is open late. **Duration of presentation** 15–20 minutes. **Probable waiting time** None.

DESCRIPTION AND COMMENTS This is USF's big nighttime event, shown on the lagoon in the middle of the Studios. The presentation runs through clips and music from the first 100 years of Universal's biggest movies; the scenes are projected onto three enormous "screens" made by spraying water from the lagoon into the air (similar to *Fantasmic!* at Disney's Hollywood Studios). Fireworks and colored lights are also used to good effect throughout the presentation, which is narrated by Morgan Freeman. It's an enjoyable way to end your day.

TOURING TIPS The Men in Black end of the lagoon is not recommended for viewing, but the terraced area near Mel's Drive-In at the opposite end affords a good look at the lasers and fireworks. The best spot is directly across the lagoon from Richter's Burger Co., where the sidewalk makes a small protrusion overlooking the water; we recommend arriving here at least 45 minutes ahead of time on peak attendance days, or 5–10 minutes prior during slower seasons. Before the show begins, be aware that not all of the movie clips may be suitable for young viewers.

DINING *at* UNIVERSAL STUDIOS FLORIDA

SPRINGFIELD: HOME OF THE SIMPSONS is home to a number of wacky *Simpsons*-inspired eateries: **Krusty Burger, The Frying Dutchman** for seafood, **Cletus' Chicken Shack, Luigi's Pizza, Lard Lad Donuts, Lisa's**

Teahouse of Horror, Bumblebee Man's Taco Truck, Duff Brewery, and Moe's Tavern. Serving sizes are large, and the food is a cut above typical theme park fare.

The best quick-service food in USF is served at the **Leaky Cauldron.** Diagon Alley's flagship restaurant serves authentically hearty British pub fare such as bangers and mash (sausages and mashed potatoes), cottage pie, toad-in-the-hole, Guinness stew, and a ploughman's platter for two of Scotch eggs and imported cheeses. When you're done, head over to **Florean Fortescue's Ice-Cream Parlour** and cap off your meal with some delicious Butterbeer ice cream.

USF's two sit-down restaurants are **Finnegan's Bar and Grill,** in New York, and **Lombard's Seafood Grille,** in San Francisco. Finnegan's serves typical bar food—burgers and wings—as well as fish-and-chips and other takes on Irish cuisine. Lombard's is the better restaurant, but it's not in the same stratosphere as, say, DHS's Hollywood Brown Derby.

Each week on select evenings, Universal characters show up for dinner at the three top-of-the-line resort hotels (see page 672).

UNIVERSAL STUDIOS FLORIDA TOURING PLANS

UNIVERSAL STUDIOS FLORIDA
ONE-DAY TOURING PLAN *(page 834)*

THIS PLAN IS FOR GUESTS without Park-to-Park tickets and includes every recommended attraction at USF. If a ride or show is listed that you don't want to experience (or isn't yet open, as may be the case for Fast & Furious: Supercharged), skip that step and proceed to the next. Move quickly from attraction to attraction, and if possible, hold off on lunch until after experiencing at least six rides.

THE BEST OF UNIVERSAL STUDIOS FLORIDA
AND ISLANDS OF ADVENTURE IN ONE DAY
(pages 835 and 836)

THIS TOURING PLAN is for guests with One-Day Park-to-Park Tickets who wish to see the highlights of Universal Studios Florida and Islands of Adventure in a single day. The plan uses Hogwarts Express to get from one park to the other and then back again; you can walk back to the first park for the return leg if the line is too long. The plan includes a table-service lunch at Mythos (make reservations online a few days before your visit) and dinner at the Leaky Cauldron; during holiday periods, you may need to substitute a quick-service snack for one or both meals to fit in all of the plan's attractions.

SEAWORLD ORLANDO

MANY READERS write us to extol the virtues of SeaWorld. The following comments are representative. From an English family:

STAR RATINGS FOR SEAWORLD ATTRACTIONS	
★★★★★	**Manta** (roller coaster)
★★★★★	**Mako** (in SeaWorld's own words, the tallest, longest, fastest coaster in Orlando)
★★★★½	**Antarctica: Empire of the Penguin** (motion-based trackless dark ride; you exit in a real penguin habitat)
★★★★½	*One Ocean* (high-tech Shamu and killer whale show)
★★★★	**Dolphin Cove** (2-acre outdoor dolphin habitat)
★★★★	*Dolphin Days* (show featuring dolphins and tropical birds)
★★★★	**Kraken** (roller coaster)
★★★½	*Clyde and Seamore Sea Lion High* (sea lion, walrus, and otter show)
★★★½	**Manta Aquarium** (more than 3,000 marine animals)
★★★½	**Shamu's Happy Harbor** (children's play area with two teacup-style rides, a children's roller coaster, a carousel, a net climb, a gently rocking boat, and a mild 20-foot drop tower)
★★★½	**Shark Encounter**
★★★½	**Wild Arctic** (simulation ride and Arctic-wildlife viewing)
★★★	*Blue Horizons* (theatrical spectacular that features dolphins, tropical birds, and acrobats)
★★★	**Pacific Point Preserve** (sea lion and seal viewing area)
★★★	*Pets Ahoy!* (show with performing birds, cats, dogs, and a pig)
★★★	**Shamu Underwater Viewing** (whale-viewing area)
★★★	**TurtleTrek** (3-D film about sea turtles; animal habitats)
★★½	**Journey to Atlantis** (combination roller coaster–flume ride)
★★½	**Stingray Lagoon**
★★	**Dolphin Nursery** (outdoor pool for expectant dolphins or mothers and calves)
★★	**Pelican Preserve**
★★	**Sky Tower** (400-foot tower with a bird's-eye view of Orlando)

The best-organized park is SeaWorld. The park map we got on arrival included the show schedule and told us which areas were temporarily closed due to construction. Best of all, there was almost no queuing. Overall, we rated this day so highly that it is the park we would most like to visit again.

A woman in Alberta, Canada, gives her opinion:

We chose SeaWorld as our fifth day at the "World." What a pleasant surprise! It was every bit as good (and in some ways better) than WDW itself. Well worth the admission, an excellent entertainment value, educational, well run, and better value for the dollar in food services.

Here's what you need to know: SeaWorld (☎ 407-545-5550 or 888-800-5447; seaworld.com/orlando) is a world-class marine-life theme park near the intersection of I-4 and the Beachline Expressway.

unofficial TIP
If you don't purchase your admission in advance, take advantage of the automatic admission machines to the right of the main entrance. If you have a credit card, the machines are faster than standing in line at the ticket windows.

It's about 10 miles east of Walt Disney World. Opening daily at 9 a.m. and closing between 6 and 10 p.m., depending on the season, SeaWorld charges $112.48 at the gate (prices include tax). If you purchase online, the same tickets will cost you about $20 less.

A number of multipark ticket options are available, including a three-park ticket that includes admission to any three of the following parks: SeaWorld Orlando, Aquatica Orlando, Busch Gardens Tampa Bay, and Adventure Island Tampa Bay.

Your three visits can be used at the same park or a combination of any of the parks listed above. The tickets, priced at $134.08, are valid one year from the date of purchase. The second and third visit must be redeemed within six months of your first visit.

For $252 plus tax, you can buy an annual pass that provides unlimited access to SeaWorld, Busch Gardens, and Aquatica. There are no blackout dates, and parking fees are waived. Florida residents can purchase the **Florida Platinum Pass,** which provides unlimited admission for one year to SeaWorld Orlando, San Diego, and San Antonio; Busch Gardens Tampa Bay and Williamsburg, Virginia; Adventure Island; Aquatica Orlando, San Diego, and San Antonio; Water Country USA (Virginia); and Sesame Place (Pennsylvania). The Florida Platinum Pass costs $336 plus tax and includes complimentary general parking to all of the parks above, as well as ride-again privileges at SeaWorld Orlando's Wild Arctic, Kraken, Manta, and Journey to Atlantis and at Busch Gardens Tampa Bay's Montu, Kumba, and SheiKra. Check SeaWorld's website for all ticket options. Parking is $19 per car, $24 per RV or camper.

unofficial TIP
Discount coupons for SeaWorld admission are available in the free visitor magazines found in most (but not Disney) hotel lobbies.

Figure 8–9 hours or more to see everything, 6 or so if you stick to the big deals. **Discovery Cove** (see next page) is directly across the Central Florida Parkway from SeaWorld. Parking at Discovery Cove is free.

SeaWorld is about the size of the Magic Kingdom and requires about the same amount of walking. In terms of size, quality, and creativity, it's unequivocally on par with Disney's major theme parks. Unlike Walt Disney World, SeaWorld primarily features stadium shows or walk-through exhibits. This means that you'll spend about 80% less time waiting in line during 8 hours at SeaWorld than you would for the same-length visit at a Disney park.

But you'll notice immediately as you check the performance times that the shows are scheduled so that it's almost impossible to see them back-to-back. A Cherry Hill, New Jersey, visitor confirms this rather major problem, complaining:

> *The shows were timed so that we were unable to catch all of the major ones in a 7-hour visit.*

FAVORITE EATS AT SEAWORLD		
LAND	SERVICE LOCATION	FOOD ITEM		
KEY WEST AT SEAWORLD **Captain Pete's Island Eats**	Hot dogs and fresh funnel cakes		
THE WATERFRONT **Voyager's Smokehouse**	Barbecue ribs and chicken		
SHARK ENCOUNTER **Sharks Underwater Grill**	Fish, pasta, and coconut chicken tenders; floor-to-ceiling glass allows guests to observe some 50 sharks and fish. *(Table service only.)*		
WILD ARCTIC **Mango Joe's**	Turkey, ham, or chicken salad sandwich; fruit salad		
FRONT GATE PLAZA **Sweet Sailin' Candy Shop**	Candies and hand-dipped chocolate turtles		
NEAR SEAPORT THEATER AND MANTA **Seafire Grill**	Tex-Mex rice bowl and fajitas		

Much of the year, you can get a seat for the stadium shows by showing up 10 or so minutes in advance. When the park is crowded, however, you need to be at the stadiums at least 20 minutes in advance (30 minutes in advance for a good seat).

unofficial TIP
You can't take food or drinks into SeaWorld or Aquatica.

All of the stadiums have splash zones, specified areas where you're likely to be drenched with ice-cold salt water by whales, dolphins, and sea lions.

Coming in summer 2018: **Infinity Falls,** a tropical rainforest–themed river-rapids ride featuring a vertical elevator that will lift rafts up to a 40-foot drop into the river. The 4-minute ride will be the centerpiece of a new rainforest area in the park that includes animals native to South America. The ride will have a 42-inch height restriction.

Finally, SeaWorld has four of the best roller coasters in Florida: **Mako, Journey to Atlantis, Manta,** and **Kraken.** If you're a coaster lover, be on hand before park opening and ride all four as soon as the park opens.

SeaWorld offers an all-day dining plan priced at $37.26 for adults and $21.29 for kids ages 3–9. Guests can eat at participating restaurant locations as often as once every hour until closing time.

In 2017, the **Seven Seas Food Festival** was held on 14 Saturdays from mid-February through mid-May. Asian, Latin, Polynesian, European, and Mediterranean dishes were served at food kiosks throughout the park; the quality and variety of the food was enhanced by the generous serving sizes. In addition to great food, weekly concerts featured legends such as Lynyrd Skynyrd, Styx, the Village People, the Commodores, and Grupo Manía. We hope SeaWorld will make the festival an annual event and add more days.

DISCOVERY COVE

unofficial TIP
With a focus on personal guest service and one-on-one animal encounters, Discovery Cove admits only 1,300 guests per day.

ALSO OWNED BY SEAWORLD, this intimate park is a welcome departure from the hustle and bustle of other Orlando parks. Its slower pace could be the overstimulated family's ticket back to mental health.

The main draw at Discovery Cove is the chance to swim with an **Atlantic bottlenose dolphin.** The 50-minute experience (30 minutes in the water) is open to visitors age 6 and up who are comfortable in the water. The experience begins with an orientation led by trainers and an opportunity for participants to ask questions. Next, small groups wade into shallow water to get an introduction to the dolphin in its habitat. The experience culminates with guests swimming into deeper water for closer interaction with the dolphin before being towed back to shore by the dolphin.

Other exhibits at Discovery Cove include the **Grand Reef,** the **Freshwater Oasis,** and the **Explorer's Aviary.** Snorkel or swim in the Grand Reef, which houses thousands of exotic fish and rays as well as an underwater shipwreck and hidden grottoes. The Freshwater Oasis is a swimming and wading experience where you can get up close and personal with otters and marmosets. In the Explorer's Aviary, you can touch and feed gorgeous tropical birds. The park is threaded by the **Wind-Away River,** in which you can float or swim, and dotted with beaches that serve as pathways to the attractions.

All guests are required to wear flotation vests when swimming, and lifeguards are omnipresent. You'll need your swimsuit, pool shoes, and a cover-up. On rare days when it's too cold to swim in Orlando, guests are provided with free wet suits. Discovery Cove also provides fish-friendly sunscreen samples; guests may not use their own sunscreen.

Discovery Cove is open 8 a.m.–5:30 p.m. daily; check-in begins at 7:15 a.m. Admission is limited, so purchase tickets well in advance; call ☎ 877-557-7404 or visit discoverycove.com. Prices vary seasonally from $276 per person to $361, including tax (no children's discount). Prices for Florida residents start at $233. Admission includes the dolphin swim; self-parking; Continental breakfast; a substantial lunch; snacks and drinks; use of beach umbrellas, lounge chairs, towels, lockers, and swim and snorkel gear; and unlimited admission to SeaWorld and Aquatica water park (see page 737) for 14 days surrounding your visit to Discovery Cove.

If you're not interested in the dolphin swim, you can visit Discovery Cove for the day for $180–$233 per person, plus tax, depending on the season. The ticket also gives you unlimited admission to Sea-World and Aquatica in Orlando for 14 consecutive days around the date of your reservation. For only $25 more you can add unlimited admission to Busch Gardens in Tampa Bay for 14 consecutive days. The passes are valid before or after your Discovery Cove visit.

For an additional $49–$69 per person, plus tax, depending on the season, you can experience **SeaVenture,** a 25-minute underwater stroll on the bottom of the Grand Reef aquarium. Participants wear diving helmets (large enough to accommodate eyeglasses), and no experience or scuba certification is necessary. Minimum age is 10 years.

PART FOURTEEN

The
WATER PARKS

YOU'RE SOAKING *in* IT!

DISNEY HAS TWO WATER PARKS, and there are two competing water parks in the area. At Disney World, **Typhoon Lagoon** is the more diverse splash pad, while **Blizzard Beach** takes the prize for the greater number of slides and the more bizarre theme. Outside the World are **Universal's Volcano Bay,** with parking at the Universal garages and shuttles to the entrance, and **Aquatica by SeaWorld,** on International Drive.

At both Disney water parks, the following rules and prices apply: One cooler per family or group is allowed, but no glass or alcoholic beverages are allowed; towels are $2; lockers are $13 for a small, $15 for a large; parking and life jackets are free. Admission, including tax, runs $62 for adults and $54 for children ages 3–9.

WATCH THE WEATHER

IF YOU BUY YOUR WALT DISNEY WORLD admission tickets before leaving home and you're considering the **Park Hopper Plus (PHP)** add-on (see page 67), you might want to wait until you arrive and have some degree of certainty about the weather during your stay. You can add the PHP option at any Disney resort or Guest Relations window at the theme parks. This is true regardless of whether you purchased your Base Tickets separately or as part of a package.

We get a lot of questions about the water parks during cold-weather months. Orlando-area temperatures can vary from the high 40s to the low 80s during December, January, and February. When it's warmer out, these months can serve up a dandy water-park experience, as this Batavia, Ohio, reader confirms:

> Going to Blizzard Beach in December was the best decision ever! They told us at the entrance that if the park didn't reach 100—yes, I said 100—people by noon, they would be closing. I guess they got to 101, because it stayed open but was virtually empty. There was no wait for anything all day! In June we waited in line for an hour for Summit Plummet, but in December it was just the amount of time it took to walk up the stairs. We had the enormous wave pool to ourselves. We did everything in the entire park and ate lunch in

less than 3 hours. It was perfect. The weather was slightly chilly at 71° and overcast with very light rain, but the water was heated, so we were fine.

EXTRA MAGIC HOURS

WHILE DISNEY ONCE OFFERED morning and evening Extra Magic Hours at its water parks, it's been several years since we last saw them on the operating schedule. It's Disney's prerogative to change its mind, however, especially during summer, so check the operating schedules a couple of days before you plan to go.

DISNEY'S WORLD OF SKIN

WE ONCE HAD TO COUNSEL a French exchange student working with us that it was very un-Disney to take off her top at the pool. A woman from Arkansas, however, thinks the French are gaining ground:

> *Warning to all visitors of the water parks! You will see more exposed bodies and inappropriate bathing attire than anywhere else in the world (with the possible exception of nude beaches). Apparently, bathing-suit retailers have magic mirrors that make men and women of any size/age look like supermodels. It was shocking to see so much inappropriately exposed skin and how casual people were about what they were exposing.*

BLIZZARD BEACH

BLIZZARD BEACH IS DISNEY'S MORE EXOTIC water-adventure park, and it arrived with its own legend. The story goes that an entrepreneur tried to open a ski resort in Florida during a particularly savage winter. Alas, the snow melted; the palm trees grew back; and all that remained of the ski resort was its alpine lodge, the ski lifts, and, of course, the mountain. Plunging off the mountain are ski slopes and bobsled runs transformed into waterslides. Visitors to Blizzard Beach catch the thaw—icicles drip and patches of snow remain. The melting snow has formed a lagoon (wave pool), which is fed by gushing mountain streams.

unofficial **TIP**
Picnic areas are scattered around the park, as are pleasant places for sunbathing.

Both Disney water parks are distinguished by their landscaping and the attention paid to executing their themes. As you enter Blizzard Beach, you face the mountain. Coming off the highest peak and bisecting the area at the mountain's base are two long slides. To the left of the slides is the wave pool. To the right are the children's swimming area and the ski lift. Surrounding the layout like a moat is a tranquil stream for floating in tubes.

unofficial **TIP**
If you're into slides, Blizzard Beach is tops among the Disney water parks.

On either side of the highest peak are tube, raft, and body slides. Including the two slides coming off the peak, Blizzard Beach has 19 slides. Among them is **Summit Plummet**, Disney World's longest speed slide, which begins with a 120-foot free fall, and the **Teamboat Springs** 1,200-foot-long water-bobsled run.

Blizzard Beach

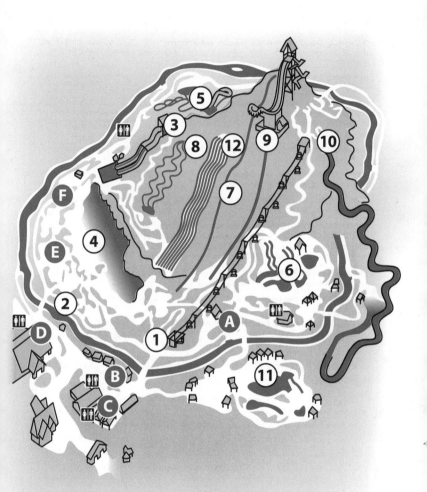

Attractions

1. Chairlift
2. Cross Country Creek
3. Downhill Double Dipper
4. Melt Away Bay
5. Runoff Rapids
6. Ski Patrol
7. Slush Gusher
8. Snow Stormers
9. Summit Plummet
10. Teamboat Springs
11. Tike's Peak
12. Toboggan Racers

Restaurants

A. Avalunch
B. Cooling Hut
C. Frostbite Freddy's
D. Lottawatta Lodge
E. Polar Pub
F. Warming Hut

Restrooms

BLIZZARD BEACH ATTRACTIONS

CHAIRLIFT UP MOUNT GUSHMORE Height requirement: 32". Great ride even if you go up just for the view. When the park is packed, use the singles line.

CROSS COUNTRY CREEK No height requirement. Lazy river circling the park; grab a tube.

DOWNHILL DOUBLE DIPPER Height requirement: 48". Side-by-side tube-racing slides. At 25 mph, the tube zooms through water curtains and free falls. It's a lot of fun, but it's rough.

MELT-AWAY BAY No height requirement. Wave pool with gentle, bobbing waves. Great for younger swimmers.

RUNOFF RAPIDS No height requirement. Three corkscrew tube slides from which to choose. The center slide is for solo raft rides; the other two slides offer one- or two-person tubes. The dark, enclosed tube gives you the feeling of being flushed down a toilet.

SKI PATROL TRAINING CAMP Height requirement: 60" for T-Bar. A place for preteens to train for the big rides.

SLUSH GUSHER Height requirement: 48". A 90-foot double-humped slide. Ladies, cling to those tops—all others, hang on for your lives.

SNOW STORMERS No height requirement. Three mat-slide flumes; down you go on your belly.

SUMMIT PLUMMET Height requirement: 48". A 120-foot free fall at 60 mph. Needless to say, this ride is very intense. Make sure your child knows what to expect. Being over 48 inches tall doesn't guarantee an enjoyable experience. If you think you'd enjoy washing out of a 12th-floor window during a heavy rain, then this slide is for you.

TEAMBOAT SPRINGS No height requirement. 1,200-foot group whitewater-raft flume. Wonderful ride for the whole family.

TIKE'S PEAK 48" and under only. Kid-size version of Blizzard Beach. This is the place for little ones.

TOBOGGAN RACERS No height requirement. Eight-lane race course. You go down the flume on a mat. Less intense than Snow Stormers.

One reader reports that the Blizzard Beach slides picked her husband's pocket:

> *Our family absolutely loved Summit Plummet, but it claimed all four of our park passes/room-key cards as its victims. My husband had the four cards in an exterior pocket of his swimsuit, secured closed by Velcro AND a snap. But after doing Summit Plummet and Slush Gusher twice apiece and Teamboat Springs once, he looked down, noticed the pocket flapping open, and found all four cards missing! So we had to cancel all the cards (they had charging privileges) and couldn't purchase any food or drinks while we were there (we didn't bring any cash because we planned to charge with our cards)!*

We've worn MagicBands at the water parks, and they're much more secure. The point is that anything in your pockets (cash, keys, etc.) may come out. A couple from Bowie, Maryland, came away with battle scars:

> *Summit Plummet gave me a bunch of bruises. Even my husband hurt for a few days. It wasn't a fun ride. Basically, you drop until you hit the slide, and that is why everyone comes off rubbing their butts. They say you go 60 mph on a 120-foot drop. I'll never do it again.*

For our money, the most exciting and interesting slides are the **Slush Gusher** and **Teamboat Springs** on the front right of the mountain, and **Runoff Rapids** on the back side of the mountain. Slush

Gusher is an undulating speed slide that we consider as exciting as the more vertical Summit Plummet without being as bone-jarring. On Teamboat Springs, you ride in a raft that looks like a children's round blow-up wading pool.

Runoff Rapids is accessible from a path that winds around the far left bottom of the mountain. The rapids consist of three corkscrew tube slides, one of which is enclosed and dark. As at Teamboat Springs, you'll go much faster on a two- or three-person tube than on a one-person tube. If you lean so that you enter curves high and come out low, you'll really fly. Because we like to steer the tube and go fast, we much prefer the open slides (where we can see) to the dark, enclosed tube. We thought crashing through the pitch-dark tube felt disturbingly like being flushed down a toilet.

The **Snow Stormers'** mat slides on the front of the mountain are fun but not as fast or as interesting as Runoff Rapids or **Downhill Double Dipper** on the far left front. **Toboggan Racers,** at the front and center of the mountain, consists of eight parallel slides where riders are dispatched in heats to race to the bottom. The ride itself is no big deal, and the time needed to get everybody lined up ensures that you'll wait extra long to ride. A faster, more exciting race venue can be found on the side-by-side slides of the undulating Downhill Double Dipper. Competitors here can reach speeds of up to 25 miles an hour.

A ski lift carries guests to the mountaintop (you can also walk up), where they can choose from Summit Plummet, Slush Gusher, or Teamboat Springs. For all other slides at Blizzard Beach, the only way to reach the top is on foot. If you're among the first in the park and don't have to wait to ride, the ski lift is fun and provides a bird's-eye view of the park. After riding once to satisfy your curiosity, however, you're better off taking the stairs to the top. The following attractions have a minimum height restriction of 48 inches: Slush Gusher, Summit Plummet, and Downhill Double Dipper.

The wave pool, called **Melt-Away Bay,** has gentle, bobbing waves. The float creek, **Cross Country Creek,** circles the park, passing through the mountain. The children's areas, **Tike's Peak** and **Ski Patrol Training Camp,** are creatively designed, nicely isolated, and—like the rest of the park—visually interesting.

The layout of Blizzard Beach (and Typhoon Lagoon, described next) is a bit convoluted. With slides on both the front and back of the mountain, it isn't always easy to find a path leading to where you want to go.

At the ski resort's now-converted base area are shops; counter-service food; restrooms; and tube, towel, and locker rentals. Blizzard Beach has its own parking lot but no lodging, though Disney's All-Star and Coronado Springs resorts are almost within walking distance. Guests at Disney resort hotels can commute to the park aboard Disney buses.

Because it's novel and has popular slides, Blizzard Beach fills early during hotter months. To stake out a nice sunning spot and to enjoy the slides without long waits, arrive at least 35 minutes before the official opening time (check disneyworld.com the night before you go).

TYPHOON LAGOON

TYPHOON LAGOON is comparable in size to Blizzard Beach. The park has 15 waterslides, some as long as 420 feet, and 2 streams. Most of the slides drop from the top of a 100-foot-tall artificial mountain. Landscaping and a typhoon-aftermath theme add interest and a sense of adventure to the wet rides.

Guests enter Typhoon Lagoon through a misty rainforest and then emerge in a ramshackle tropical town where concessions and services are situated. Special sets make every ride an odyssey as swimmers encounter bat caves, lagoons and pools, spinning rocks, formations of dinosaur bones, and many other imponderables.

Typhoon Lagoon has its own parking lot but no lodging. Disney resort guests can commute to the water park on Disney buses.

If you indulge in all features of Typhoon Lagoon, admission is a fair value. If you go primarily for the slides, you'll have only 2 early-morning hours to enjoy them before the wait becomes prohibitive.

Typhoon Lagoon provides water adventure for all ages. Activity pools for young children and families feature geysers, tame slides, bubble jets, and fountains. For the older and more adventurous are the enclosed **Humunga Kowabunga** speed slides, the corkscrew **Storm Slides,** and three whitewater raft rides: **Gangplank Falls, Keelhaul Falls,** and **Mayday Falls.** Billed as a "water roller coaster," **Crush 'n' Gusher** consists of a series of flumes and spillways that course through an

TYPHOON LAGOON ATTRACTIONS

BAY SLIDES Height requirement: 60″ and under only. A miniature two-slide version of Storm Slides, specifically designed for small children. Kids splash down into a far corner of the Surf Pool.

CASTAWAY CREEK No height requirement. Half-mile lazy river in a tropical setting with cool mists, waterfalls, and a tunnel through Mount Mayday. Wonderful!

CRUSH 'N' GUSHER Height requirement: 48″. Water roller coaster where you can choose from three slides: Banana Blaster, Coconut Crusher, and Pineapple Plunger, ranging from 410 to 420 feet long. This thriller leaves you wondering what exactly happened—if you make it down in one piece, that is; it's not for the faint of heart. If your kids are new to water-park rides, this is not the place to break them in, even if they're tall enough to ride.

GANGPLANK FALLS No height requirement. Whitewater-raft flume in a four-person tube.

HUMUNGA KOWABUNGA Height requirement: 48″. Speed slides that hit 30 mph. A five-story drop in the dark rattles even the most courageous rider. Women should ride this one in a one-piece swimsuit.

KEELHAUL FALLS No height requirement. Fast whitewater ride in a single-person tube.

KETCHAKIDDEE CREEK Height requirement: 48″ and under only. Toddlers and pre-schoolers love this area reserved only for them. Say "splish-splash" and have lots of fun.

MAYDAY FALLS No height requirement. Wild single-person tube ride. *Hang on!*

MISS ADVENTURE FALLS No height requirement. Gentle, family raft ride down a well-themed slide.

STORM SLIDES No height requirement. Three body slides plunge down and through Mount Mayday.

SURF POOL No height requirement. World's largest inland surf facility, with waves up to 6 feet high. Adult supervision is required. Monday–Friday, in the early morning before the park opens or in the evening after the park closes (hours vary), surfing lessons are offered (surfboard provided). Cost is $165 for 2½ hours; minimum age is 8; class size is 12. Call ☎ 407-WDW-PLAY (939-7529). The price doesn't include park admission.

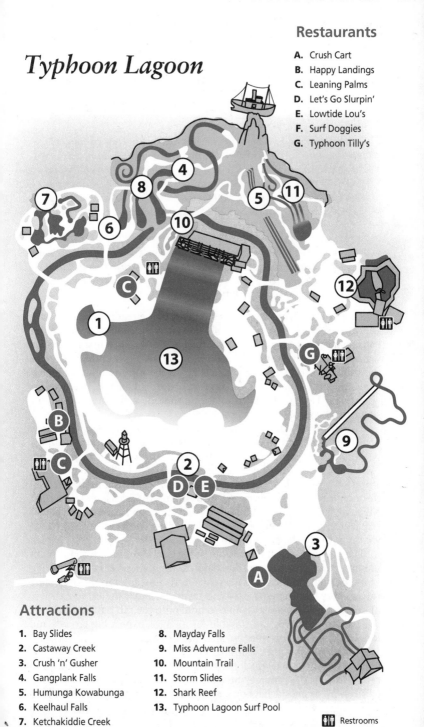

Typhoon Lagoon

Restaurants

A. Crush Cart
B. Happy Landings
C. Leaning Palms
D. Let's Go Slurpin'
E. Lowtide Lou's
F. Surf Doggies
G. Typhoon Tilly's

Attractions

1. Bay Slides
2. Castaway Creek
3. Crush 'n' Gusher
4. Gangplank Falls
5. Humunga Kowabunga
6. Keelhaul Falls
7. Ketchakiddie Creek
8. Mayday Falls
9. Miss Adventure Falls
10. Mountain Trail
11. Storm Slides
12. Shark Reef
13. Typhoon Lagoon Surf Pool

Restrooms

abandoned tropical fruit–processing plant. It features tubes that hold one or two people, and you can choose from three different routes: Banana Blaster, Coconut Crusher, and Pineapple Plunger, ranging from 410 to 420 feet long. Only Crush 'n' Gusher and the Humunga Kowabunga speed slides (where you can hit 30 miles an hour) have a minimum height requirement of 48 inches.

A Waterloo, Ontario, mom found Typhoon Lagoon more strenuous than she'd anticipated:

> I wish I'd been prepared for the fact that we'd have to haul the tubes up the stairs of Crush 'n' Gusher. My daughter was not strong enough to carry hers, so I had to lug them up by myself. I was EXHAUSTED by the end of the day, and my arms ached for a couple of days afterward. Had I known that was the case, I would have started lifting weights several months before our trip in preparation!

A New Jersey reader agreed:

> Thumbs WAY DOWN to the designer who made several places in the queue for Storm Slides where the stairs go DOWN then back UP then back DOWN then UP again—leading to all guests walking UP extra needless fights of stairs. BOO!

Those of you who share the sentiments of the readers quoted above will appreciate Typhoon Lagoon's newest attraction, **Miss Adventure Falls,** which opened in 2017 near Crush 'n' Gusher. In a first for Disney water parks, riders hop in a four-person, circular raft at the bottom of the slide, then ride a conveyor belt up to the top in about a minute. (The conveyor belt is, let's be honest, a not-bad shiatsu massage for your butt.) Though the rafts hold four, the ride works just as well for singles and couples.

The storyline—there's always a storyline—concerns Captain Mary Oceaneer, a treasure hunter who ran her ship aground and is stranded with her obstreperous parrot. You pass Captain Mary's ship and are fussed at by the parrot as you ascend. As if the bird wasn't enough, you also pass under a noisy dangling crate. The ride itself cascades through tunnels with twists, turns, dips, and the occasional waterfall. Miss Adventure Falls is a mild ride—mild enough that it has no height requirement. It's therefore not as exciting as Crush 'n' Gusher, which we think is still the best slide in the park.

The queuing area at the bottom of the conveyor is inadequate, making for major jam-ups on busy days. Getting guests off rafts arriving at the bottom, and loading guests from the queue onto the ascending rafts, is very labor-intensive for cast members and is subject to a variety of delays. Children must be able to hold onto the raft handles. Because the attraction is new and suitable for all ages, expect big crowds and long waits unless you ride just after park opening.

Slower metabolisms will also enjoy the meandering, 2,000-foot-long **Castaway Creek,** which floats tubers through hidden grottoes and rainforests. And, of course, the sedentary will usually find plenty of sun to sleep in. Typhoon Lagoon's **Surf Pool** is the world's largest inland surf facility, with waves up to 6 feet high (enough, so Disney says, to "encompass an ocean liner").

In spring 2017, Disney began testing a "virtual queue" system for some of the attractions at Typhoon Lagoon, allowing guests to avoid a long wait and instead arrive during an assigned 15-minute window. Guests wishing to ride Typhoon Lagoon's **Downhill Double Dipper** or **Slush Gusher** will receive a waterproof card attached to a wristband indicating their return time. This is akin to the old paper FastPass system. Stay tuned for updates as Disney tinkers with the process.

SURF POOL

WHILE BLIZZARD BEACH and Volcano Bay have wave pools, Typhoon Lagoon has a Surf Pool. Most people will encounter larger waves here than they have in the ocean. The surf machine puts out a wave about every 90 seconds (just about how long it takes to get back in position if you caught the previous wave). Perfectly formed and ideal for riding, each wave is about 5–6 feet from trough to crest. Before you join the fray, watch two or three waves from shore. Because each wave breaks in almost the same spot, you can get a feel for position and timing. Observing other surfers is also helpful.

The best way to ride the waves is to swim about three-fourths of the way to the wall at the wave-machine end of the pool. When the waves come—trust us, you'll feel and hear them—swim vigorously toward the beach and try to position yourself one-half to three-fourths of a body length below the breaking crest. The waves are so perfectly engineered that they'll either carry you forward or bypass you. Unlike ocean waves, though, they won't slam you down.

unofficial **TIP**
A final warning: The Surf Pool has a knack for stripping jewelry, loosening watchbands, and sucking stuff out of your pockets. Don't take anything out there except your swimsuit (and hang on to that).

A teenage girl from Urbana, Illinois, notes that the primary hazard in the Surf Pool is colliding with other surfers and swimmers:

> *The Surf Pool was nice except I kept landing on really hairy fat guys when the big waves came.*

A Gate City, Virginia, mom was caught off guard by the size and power of the waves:

> *I had forgotten how violent the wave pool is at Typhoon Lagoon. Thinking I'd be able to hold on to two young(ish) nephews is a mistake I made only once before getting them back to shallower water.*

A reader from Somerset, New Jersey, alerted us to another problem:

> *Typhoon Lagoon is a great family water park—our unexpected favorite. However, please tell your readers not to sit on the bottom of the wave pool—I got a horrible scratch/raspberry and saw about five others with similar injuries. The waves are stronger than they look.*

The best way to avoid collisions while surfing is to paddle out far enough that you'll be at the top of the wave as it breaks. This tactic eliminates the possibility of anyone landing on you from above and ensures maximum forward visibility. A corollary to this: The worst place to swim is where the wave actually breaks. You'll look up to see a 6-foot wall of water carrying eight dozen screaming surfers bearing

SOGGY TIPS FROM
A WATER-PUPPY FAMILY

A BOW, NEW HAMPSHIRE, FAMILY who are evidently working on a doctorate in Disney water parks were kind enough to share their knowledge:

If you're going to the water parks, train on your StairMaster prior to going, especially if you visit Blizzard Beach. For Runoff Rapids, you climb 125 stairs (yes, I counted). Imagine doing that three times in a row, trying to keep up with kids who want to go down the slide multiple times. In addition, there are at least (and here, I'm guessing) 300 stairs if you choose the Alpine Path instead of the chairlift to get to Summit Plummet. At Typhoon Lagoon, each slide, except Miss Adventure Falls, has approximately 60 steps, so at either park you have quite a bit of stairs to climb or go down.

We were at Blizzard Beach 15 minutes before park opening in late August, and we felt that this was plenty of time to beat the crowds. We noticed crowds building around 11 a.m. or so. If you are there at park opening, stash your things as quickly as possible (or send a member of your party to do so) while you take the chairlift to Summit Plummet. We were first in line for the chairlift, and we were at the top with no lines. The chairlift is definitely faster if you're one of the first in line, and you won't get winded from walking the Alpine Path. However, if you arrive later in the day, the line for the chairlift builds, and you'll be left having to climb the Alpine Path—great if you're in shape, but not so much if you're not!

Check the closing time of the water parks if you plan on arriving late afternoon. When Typhoon Lagoon closed at 8 p.m. and we arrived shortly after 2 p.m., lines tended to thin out by 4 p.m. However, when we tried that same tactic (arriving in the afternoon) when TL closed at 6 p.m., we noticed that the lines were still long, and it seemed like the crowd wasn't thinning at all. On those days, we wished that we had been there for park opening and left when crowds started to build.

We enjoyed the water parks, but we only stayed there about 3 hours max. Though the water parks are big (as in spread out), there weren't enough attractions to keep us there the entire day. Yes, they have slides,

down on you. This is the time to remember every submarine movie you've ever seen . . . *Dive! Dive! Dive!*

Either in the early morning before the park opens or in the evening after the park closes (hours vary), you can take surfing lessons, with an actual surfboard. Practice waves range from 3 to 6 feet tall. Most of the school's students are first-timers. Cost is $165 per person, and equipment is provided. For details, call ☎ 407-WDW-PLAY (939-7529).

but not as many as I expected a Disney park to have. When lines started to build around late morning, it became less fun to wait 15-plus minutes for a slide that takes less than 2 minutes to go down. Also, the less-popular attractions, such as the lazy river, got really busy, and there were hardly any tubes to be found.

Water shoes or water sandals are a good bet in the water parks, as the paths can get really hot in the summer, and only a few water jets are near the pathways to keep them cool. However, on some slides (such as the body slides), water shoes aren't allowed, so stash your water shoes at the base of the path where you exit, and grab them on your way out.

Some slides at Blizzard Beach, such as the Downhill Double Dipper, take FOREVER in line because you're waiting for a tube to make it from the pool up the conveyor belt to the slide stairs. Once the tube finally arrives, you still have to wait for both parties to go down together and to exit the pool. This process takes a long time. If this slide is important to you, make it one of the first things you do. The toboggan rides can also take a while because there is no clear system of who can take the mat when it finally arrives at the top (two mat rides are at the top of the mat conveyor belt: Toboggan Racers and Snow Stormers). Also, some slides aren't very comfortable. At TL, the Humunga Kowabunga should be called the Wedgie Maker. If your family is going to both water parks (like we did), I suggest skipping Gangplank Falls at Typhoon Lagoon and doing Teamboat Springs at Blizzard Beach instead. Not only is Teamboat Springs a LOT longer than Gangplank Falls, but it's also more fun.

Also, the wave pools at both parks are very different. At TL, it's "The Wave" pool. As in, there is only one, HUGE wave that you can try and bodysurf (good luck with that). At BB, it's more like "The Waves" pool, where waves are put out at a continual rate, at all times, like a gentle rocking motion, and there are tubes you can use. TL has no floatation device of any kind because, well, they'd be dangerous to everyone involved.

If you have something electronic (like a smartphone or key fob) that you need to stay dry at the water parks, purchase a waterproof container BEFORE going to the water park. The water parks only sell water-resistant containers, and even though the one we bought didn't seem to leak, it would have given us more peace of mind to have a waterproof bag/container.

TYPHOON LAGOON *versus* BLIZZARD BEACH

MANY WALT DISNEY WORLD GUESTS aren't interested in leaving the World. For them, the question is: Which is better, Typhoon Lagoon or Blizzard Beach? Our readers answer.

A mother of four from Winchester, Virginia, gives her opinion:

At Blizzard Beach, the family raft ride is great, but the kids' area is poorly designed. As a parent, when you walk your child to the top of a slide or the tube ride, they're lost to your vision as they go down because of the fake snowdrifts. There are no direct ways down to the end of the slides, so little ones are left standing unsupervised while parents scramble down from the top. The Typhoon Lagoon kids' area is far superior in design.

A couple from Woodridge, Illinois, writes:

We liked Blizzard Beach much more. It seems like they took everything from Typhoon Lagoon and made it better and faster. Summit Plummet was awesome—a total rush. The toboggan and bobsled rides were exciting—the bobsled really throws you around. The family tube ride was really good—much better and longer than the one at Typhoon Lagoon. Tube rides were great, especially in the enclosed tube. If you have time to go to only one water park, go to Blizzard Beach.

A hungry reader from Aberdeen, New Jersey, complains:

At Blizzard Beach, there's only one main place to get food (most of the other spots are more for snacks). At lunchtime, it took almost 45 minutes to get some sandwiches and drinks.

WHEN *to* GO

THE BEST WAY TO AVOID standing in lines is to visit the Disney World water parks when they're the least crowded. Our research, conducted over many weeks in the parks, indicates that tourists, not locals, make up the majority of visitors on any given day. And because weekends are popular travel days, the water parks tend to be less crowded then. In fact, of the weekend days we evaluated, the parks never reached full capacity; during the week, conversely, one or both parks closed every Thursday we monitored, and both closed at least once every other weekday. Therefore, we recommend going on a Monday or Friday.

unofficial **TIP**
During summer and holiday periods, Typhoon Lagoon and Blizzard Beach sometimes fill to capacity and close their gates before 11 a.m.

A mom from Manlius, New York, describes what *crowded* means:

Because we had the all-inclusive pass, we also visited Typhoon Lagoon, arriving before opening so we could stake out a shady spot. The kids loved it until the lines got long (11 a.m.–noon), but I hated it. It made Coney Island seem like a deserted island in the Bahamas. Floating on Castaway Creek was really unpleasant. Whirling around in a chlorinated, concrete ditch with some stranger's feet in my face, periodically getting squirted by water guns, passing under cascades of cold water, and getting hung up by the crowd is not at all relaxing for me. My husband and I then decided to bob in the Surf Pool. After about 10 minutes of being tossed around like corks in boiling water, he turned a little green around the gills, and we sought the peace of our shady little territory, which, in our absence, had become much, much smaller. The kids, however, loved the body slides and the surf waves.

A visitor from Middletown, New York, had a somewhat better experience at Typhoon Lagoon:

> On our second trip to Typhoon Lagoon, we dispensed with the locker rental (having planned to stay for only the morning when it was least crowded), and at park's opening just took right off for the Storm Slides before the masses arrived—it was perfect! We must have ridden the slides at least five times before any kind of line built up, and then we were also able to ride the tube and raft rides (Keelhaul and Mayday Falls) in a similar uncrowded, quick fashion because everyone else was busy getting their lockers!

If your schedule is flexible, a good time to visit the swimming parks is midafternoon to late in the day when the weather has cleared after a storm. The parks usually close during bad weather. If the storm is prolonged, most guests leave for their hotels. When Typhoon Lagoon or Blizzard Beach reopens after inclement weather has passed, you almost have a whole park to yourself.

PLANNING YOUR DAY
at DISNEY WATER PARKS

DISNEY WATER PARKS ARE ALMOST AS LARGE and elaborate as the major theme parks. You must be prepared for a lot of walking, exercise, sun, and jostling crowds. If your group really loves the water, schedule your visit early in your vacation. If you go at the beginning of your stay, you'll have more flexibility if you want to return.

To have a great day and beat the crowds, consider:

1. GETTING INFORMATION Call ☎ 407-WDW-MAGIC (939-6244) or check disneyworld.com the night before to verify when the park opens.

2. TO PICNIC OR NOT TO PICNIC Decide whether you want to carry a picnic lunch. Guests are permitted to take lunches and beverage coolers into the parks. However, alcoholic beverages and glass containers of any kind are forbidden.

3. GETTING STARTED If you're going to Blizzard Beach or Typhoon Lagoon, get up early, have breakfast, and arrive at the park 40 minutes before opening. If you have a car, drive instead of taking a Disney bus.

4. FOLLOW A GOOD TOURING PLAN We have two touring plans designed to help you avoid crowds and bottlenecks at Disney water parks (see pages 837 and 838). If you're attending on a day of moderate-to-heavy attendance (see the Crowd Calendar at our website, **TouringPlans.com**), consider using one of these tested plans. More are available on the site.

5. ATTIRE Wear your bathing suit under shorts and a T-shirt so you don't need to use lockers or dressing rooms. Regarding women's bathing suits, be advised that it's extremely common for women of all ages to part company with the top of their two-piece suit on the slides. Both the paths and beach sand get incredibly hot during the summer. Some form of foot protection is a must. Your socks will do in a pinch, but sandals that strap to your feet are best. Shops in the parks sell sandals,

Reef Runners, and other protective footwear that can be worn in and out of the water.

6. WHAT TO BRING You'll need a towel, sunscreen, and money. Because wallets and purses get in the way, lock them in your car's trunk, or leave them at your hotel. Carry your Disney resort ID (if you have one) and enough money for the day in a plastic bag or Tupperware container, or use your MagicBand to pay for stuff. Though nowhere is completely safe, we felt very comfortable hiding our plastic money bags in our cooler. Nobody disturbed our stuff, and our cash was much easier to reach than if we'd stashed it in a locker across the park. If you're carrying a wad or you worry about money anyway, rent the locker.

A Canadian reader offers another option if you don't feel comfortable stashing your valuables:

> As our admission was from an all-inclusive ticket [not a MagicBand], I was concerned about our passes being stolen or lost, yet I didn't want the hassle of a locker. I discovered that the gift shop sells water-resistant plastic boxes (with strings to go around your neck) in two sizes for around $5, with the smallest being just big enough for passes, credit cards, and a bit of money. I would've spent nearly as much on a locker rental, so I was able to enjoy the rest of the day with peace of mind.

7. WHAT *NOT* TO BRING Personal swim gear (fins, masks, rafts, and the like) isn't allowed. Everything you need is provided or available to rent. If you forget your towel, you can rent one (cheap!). If you forget your swimsuit or lotion, they're for sale. Personal flotation devices (life jackets) are available at no cost.

8. ADMISSION Buy your admission in advance or about 45 minutes before official opening. If you're staying at a Disney property, you may be entitled to a discount; bring your MagicBand or hotel or campground ID. Guests staying five or more days should consider the **Park Hopper Plus** add-on, which provides admission to either Blizzard Beach or Typhoon Lagoon.

9. LOCKERS Rental lockers are $13 per day for a small one and $15 per day for a large one. Small lockers are roomy enough for one person or a couple, but a family will generally need a large locker. Though you can access your locker freely all day, not all lockers are conveniently located.

Getting a locker at Blizzard Beach or Typhoon Lagoon is truly competitive. When the gates open, guests race to the locker-rental desk. The rental procedure is somewhat slow; if you aren't among the first in line, you can waste a lot of time waiting. We recommend skipping the locker. Carry a MagicBand or only as much cash as you'll need for the day in a watertight container that you can stash in your cooler. Ditto for personal items, including watches and eyeglasses.

unofficial **TIP**
When lines for the slides become intolerable, head for the surf or wave pool or the tube-floating streams.

10. TUBES Tubes for bobbing on the waves, floating in the creeks, and riding the tube slides are available for free.

11. GETTING SETTLED Establish your base for the day. There are many beautiful sunning and lounging spots scattered throughout both Disney swimming parks. Arrive early, and you can almost have your pick. The breeze is best along the beaches of the surf pools at Blizzard Beach and

Typhoon Lagoon. At Typhoon Lagoon, if there are children younger than age 6 in your party, choose an area to the left of Mount Mayday (ship on top) near the children's swimming area.

Also available are flat lounges (nonadjustable) and chairs (better for reading), shelters for guests who prefer shade, picnic tables, and a few hammocks. If you have money to burn, a handful of private, covered seating areas are available at both Disney water parks for up to six guests at $345 (including tax) per day. That includes your own lounge chairs, tables, towels, private lockers, a refillable drink mug, and an attendant who'll be at your beck and call. These seating areas are available by reservation at ☎ 407-WDW-PLAY (939-7529).

The best spectator sport at Typhoon Lagoon is the bodysurfing in the Surf Pool. It's second only to being out there yourself. With this in mind, position yourself to have an unobstructed view of the waves.

12. A WORD ABOUT THE SLIDES Waterslides come in many shapes and sizes. Some are steep and vertical, and some are long and undulating. Some resemble corkscrews, while others imitate the pool-and-drop nature of whitewater streams. Depending on the slide, swimmers ride mats, inner tubes, or rafts. With body slides, swimmers slosh to the bottom on the seat of their pants.

Modern traffic engineering bows to old-fashioned queuing. At the waterslides, it's just one person and one raft (or tube) at a time, and the swimmer on deck can't go until the person preceding him or her is safely out of the way. Thus, the slides' hourly capacity is limited compared with the continuously loading rides in the major theme parks. Because a certain interval between swimmers is required for safety, the only way to increase capacity is to increase the number of rides.

Though Typhoon Lagoon and Blizzard Beach are huge parks with many slides, they're overwhelmed almost daily by armies of guests. If your main reason for going to Typhoon Lagoon or Blizzard Beach is the slides and you hate long lines, be among the first guests to enter the park. Go directly to the slides, and ride as many times as you can before the park fills.

For maximum speed on a body slide, cross your legs at the ankles, and cross your arms over your chest. When you take off, arch your back so almost all of your weight is on your shoulder blades and heels (the less contact with the surface, the less resistance). Steer by shifting most of your upper-body weight onto one shoulder blade. For top speed on turns, weight the shoulder blade on the outside of each curve. If you want to go slowly, distribute your weight equally, as if you were lying on your back in bed. For curving slides, maximize speed by hitting the entrance to each curve high and exiting the curve low.

unofficial **TIP**
Because Florida is so flat, approaching weather can be seen from atop the slide platforms at the water parks. Leave the park early when you see a storm moving in, especially if you're riding the Disney buses.

Some slides and rapids have a minimum height requirement. Riders for Humunga Kowabunga at Typhoon Lagoon and for Slush Gusher and Summit Plummet at Blizzard Beach, for example, must be 4 feet tall. Pregnant women and persons with back problems or other health difficulties shouldn't ride.

13. LAZY RIVERS Each of the water parks we cover here offer mellow lazy rivers. A great idea, the floating streams are long, tranquil inner-tube rides that give you the illusion that you're doing something while you're being sedentary.

Disney's lazy rivers flow ever so slowly around the entire park, through caves, beneath waterfalls, past gardens, and under bridges. They offer a relaxing alternative to touring a park on foot.

Lazy rivers can be reached from several put-in and takeout points. There are never lines; just wade into the creek and plop into one of the inner tubes floating by. Ride the current all the way around, or get out at any exit. It takes 30–35 minutes to float the full circuit.

14. LUNCH If you didn't bring a picnic, you can buy food. Quality is comparable to fast food; prices (as you might expect) are a bit high.

15. BAD WEATHER Thunderstorms are common in Florida. On summer afternoons, storms can occur daily. Water parks close during a storm. Most storms, however, are short-lived, allowing the water park to resume normal operations. If a storm is severe and prolonged, it can cause a great deal of inconvenience. In addition to the park's closing, guests compete aggressively for shelter, and Disney resort guests may have to joust for seats on a bus back to the hotel.

You should monitor the local weather forecast the day before you go, checking again in the morning before leaving for the water park. Scattered thundershowers are to be expected, but moving storm fronts are to be avoided.

16. ENDURANCE The water parks are large and require almost as much walking as one of the theme parks. Add to this wave surfing, swimming, and all the climbing required to reach the slides, and you'll be pooped by day's end. Unless you spend your hours like a lizard on a rock, don't expect to return to the hotel with much energy. Consider something low-key for the evening. You'll probably want to hit the hay early.

17. LOST CHILDREN AND LOST ADULTS It's easier to lose a child or become separated from your party at one of the water parks than it is at a major theme park. Upon arrival, pick a very specific place to meet should you get separated. If you split up on purpose, set times for checking in. Lost-children stations at the water parks are so out of the way that neither you nor your lost child will find them without help from a Disney cast member. Explain to your children how to recognize cast members (by their distinctive name tags) and how to ask for help.

WATER-PARK TOURING PLANS

ONE-DAY TOURING PLANS for Blizzard Beach and Typhoon Lagoon can be found on pages 837 and 838, respectively. These plans are for parents with small children; touring plans for adults, along with our online reader survey, are available at TouringPlans.com. We'd love to hear from families who have tried these plans.

The plans presented here include all the slides, flumes, and rides appropriate for kids in both parks. Having brought our own children to these parks, we've also included tips on which slides to try first in case this is your child's first water-park experience. For example, at Typhoon Lagoon we suggest the family whitewater-rafting ride Miss Adventure Falls as the first attraction. If your child enjoys that, we list Gangplank Falls and then Keelhaul Falls as the next step up in water-slides. If that seems a bit much, however, the touring plan recommends the Ketchakiddee Creek play area as an alternative.

UNIVERSAL'S VOLCANO BAY

UNIVERSAL'S VOLCANO BAY (on Universal Orlando property next to Cabana Bay Beach Resort; universalorlando.com/theme-parks /volcano-bay.aspx) opened as Orlando's newest non-Disney water-park option on May 25, 2017. Unlike the former Wet 'n Wild, whose only themes appeared to be concrete and plastic, Volcano Bay features a scenic, man-made mountain and a colorful atmosphere that goes toe-to-toe with those of Typhoon Lagoon and Blizzard Beach. In fact, Universal bills this "water theme park" as its "third theme park," which is both technically correct and an act of marketing hubris on par with the initial advertising of The Wizarding World of Harry Potter as "a theme park within a theme park." Either way, the thrill, scope, and diversity of its 18 attractions make Volcano Bay an excellent alternative to the Disney swimming parks. Besides, contrary to what some Disney execs might have you believe, their water isn't any wetter.

Mears Transportation operates a shuttle between Walt Disney World and Universal Orlando that stops three times a day at Disney hotels. Cost is $20 for guests ages 3 and older. If you're staying outside Walt Disney World or Lake Buena Vista, or along US 192, you'll need a car or ride-share service. There is no guest parking at Volcano Bay itself; visitors will park in the same parking garages as other Universal theme park guests and pay the usual rates (see pages 668 and 669). Special shuttle buses transport guests along dedicated lanes to the front gate of Volcano Bay, which is also accessible on a walking path from the neighboring Cabana Bay Beach Resort.

Buy your Volcano Bay tickets at the Volcano Bay bus stop inside the parking structure, at any on-site hotel, at the park entrance, or at universalorlando.com. Buying your ticket and setting up an online account in advance will greatly speed your entry to the park. Admission is $71.36 per adult ($66.03 for kids ages 3–9) for one day or $42.60 as an upgrade to any multiday ticket. The park opens at 10 a.m. (with 9 a.m. early admission for all on-site hotel guests) and stays open as late as 10 p.m. during the summer. Disney water parks typically close by 7 or 8 p.m., but Volcano Bay is designed for nighttime operation, with special lighting effects activated after sunset.

*un*official **TIP**
Don't try to park at Cabana Bay if you're not staying there—you'll get hit with a $45/day fee.

Universal Orlando describes Volcano Bay's 28 acres as "a lush, tropical oasis that unfolds before you, instantly transporting you to a little-known Pacific isle." The park's icon, visible to passing cars on I-4, is a colossal volcano rising above a pristine beach, with majestic waterfalls transforming into blazing lava by night.

Universal's Volcano Bay

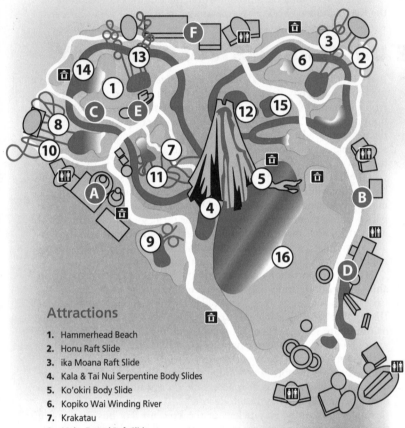

Attractions

1. Hammerhead Beach
2. Honu Raft Slide
3. ika Moana Raft Slide
4. Kala & Tai Nui Serpentine Body Slides
5. Ko'okiri Body Slide
6. Kopiko Wai Winding River
7. Krakatau
8. Maku Round Raft Slide
9. Ohyah & Ohno Drop Slides
10. Puihi Round Raft Slide
11. Punga Racers
12. Runamukka Reef
13. Taniwha Tubes
14. TeAwa The Fearless River
15. Tot Tiki Reef
16. Waturi Beach

Restaurants

A. Bambu
B. Dancing Dragons Boat Bar
C. The Feasting Frog
D. Kohola Reef Restaurant & Social Club
E. Kunuku Boat Bar
F. Whakawaiwai Eats

👫 Restrooms   🛅 Cabanas

Universal also boasts that it has eliminated two of the biggest hassles at water parks—long lines for slides and carrying tubes up stairs—by replacing queues with "Virtual Lines" and building conveyor belts for all the rafts. Every visitor is issued a waterproof "TapuTapu" wristband that you use to claim your place in the Virtual Lines, as well as reserve and open lockers and make payments throughout the park when linked to your credit card (with a secure PIN) using the Universal Orlando website or app. The TapuTapu bands also trigger special effects throughout Volcano Bay, such as controlling streams of water in Tot Tiki Reef or shooting water cannons at other guests who are enjoying the Kopiko Wai Winding River.

Tap your cleverly named TapuTapu band against a tiki totem outside a ride, and you'll be given an approximate time before you can return; your wait may be shorter than expected if other guests skip their return times, or longer if the attraction temporarily closes due to weather or technical problems. You can hold a reservation for just one ride at a time, and TapuTapu will alert you when it's time to return with a minimal wait. Reservations expire 1 hour from the time they're booked, and you can't get in another Virtual Line until you use or cancel your first ride.

In theory, this system should allow guests to enjoy the wave pool and lazy river instead of standing in hot queues, but the park's initial weeks were plagued by multihour waits for most of the slides, with popular attractions completely filling up for the day by midmorning. Sales of Universal Express passes, which provided immediate access to the slides except the Krakatau Aqua Coaster, were suspended at press time. We're not sure at this writing whether Express will return, so your best bet is to arrive as early as possible and secure a spot on Krakatau Aqua Coaster, followed by Ko'okiri Body Plunge, Honu, and Puihi (in that order). Also look for slides advertising RIDE NOW during early and late hours; you can hop on without losing your place in a Virtual Line.

VOLCANO BAY AT A GLANCE

VOLCANO BAY IS DIVIDED into four "Primary Areas" (a.k.a. lands), each with a unique theme, but because all of the areas sport the same lush South Seas scenery, it's impossible to tell where one section ends and another begins without a map.

The park's backstory is based on the fictional story of the Waturi, an ancient Polynesian people who set out on their outrigger canoes to find a new home. The Waturi visited many Polynesian islands, drawing elements from each culture, until they caught sight of the legendary fish Kunuku playing in the waves of Volcano Bay and settled there.

In practical terms, the park looks like an upscale resort in the South Pacific, with lush palm trees, tiki carvings, and thatched cabanas; as long as you're at ground level, you'd hardly guess there's a busy interstate only yards away. The Waturi legend also influenced the unpronounceable names of most of the attractions, but that's about as far as the theming goes on the slides—don't expect any indoor scenes or dark ride–style effects.

Guests enter the park at **Wave Village,** which is dominated by the **Waturi Beach** multidirectional wave pool and the **Reef** leisure pool.

VOLCANO BAY ATTRACTIONS

Krakatau

KRAKATAU AQUA COASTER Height requirement: 42", 49" if riding alone. Guest board a specially designed canoe that seats up to four. The ride uses linear induction motor technology, which launches the canoe uphill as well as downhill as you twist and turn around the volcano's blown-out interior. It's similar to Crush 'n' Gusher at Typhoon Lagoon, but far longer and more thrilling. Krakatau is the park's most popular ride, so get your TapuTapu reservation as early as possible.

KO'OKIRI BODY PLUNGE Height requirement: 48". Hop on this 125-foot slide, featuring a drop door with a 70-degree-angle descent, straight through the heart of the mountain. Drumbeats building up to the drop get your heart pounding, but the plunge itself is over before you have time to scream.

KALA AND TA NUI SERPENTINE BODY SLIDES Height requirement: 48". After falling through a drop door, two riders go down 124-foot body slides simultaneously. Their paths cross times as they hurtle down translucent intertwining tubes. The green side is like the Incredible Hulk Coaster of slides: It starts fast and somehow gets faster as it goes.

PUNGA RACERS Height requirement: 42", 49" if riding alone. Guests on racing mats shaped like manta rays go down enclosed slides across four lanes and through underwater sea caves.

Rainforest Village

MAKU AND PUIHI ROUND RAFT RIDES Height requirement: 42", 49" if riding alone. *Maku* and *Puihi* mean "wet" and "wild," and that's no exaggeration. North America's first "saucer ride," the six-person Maku raft plunges riders through bowl-like formations before ending up in a pool surrounded by erupting geysers. Puihi is the far more frightening slide of the pair: A six-person raft launches down into a dark, winding tunnel before shooting up a banked curve; riders glimpse the highway below and momentarily experience zero gravity prior to sliding back down.

OHYAH AND OHNO DROP SLIDES Height requirement: 48". Two short but intense twisting slides that launch guests 4 and 6 feet above the water at the end; Ohno is the taller of the two.

TANIWHA TUBES Height requirement: 42", 49" if riding alone. One tower sports four Easter Island–inspired waterslides with rafts for single or double riders. Along the way, tiki statues make sure that you don't stay dry. The slides are similar but not identical—ask for one with more-open-air sections if you get claustrophobic.

PUKA ULI LAGOON No height requirement. Tranquil leisure pool.

TEAWA THE FEARLESS RIVER No height requirement. A racing-torrent river where guests hang tight in their inner tubes amid roaring whitewater rapids as they surf beneath the slides inside Krakatau. If you're looking for a lazy river, this ain't it!

River Village

HONU AND IKA MOANA SLIDES Height requirement: 42", 49" if riding alone. Honu and Ika Mona are two separate slides attached to the same tower, where guests board multiperson animal-themed rafts (a sea turtle and a whale, respectively) before speeding down into a pool. Honu is a blue raft slide that sends you vertically up two giant sloped walls before sliding back down—it's the scariest group ride in the park. Ika Mona is a much gentler journey in and out of twisting green tunnels.

KOPIKO WAI WINDING RIVER No height requirement. A gentle, lazy river that passes through the park's landscape and into the volcano's hidden caves.

RUNAMUKKA REEF No height requirement. A three-story water playground for older children inspired by the coral reef, featuring twisting slides, sprinklers, and more.

TOT TIKI REEF No height requirement. A toddler play area with spraying Maori fountains, slides, and a kid-size volcano.

Wave Village

THE REEF No height requirement. Leisure pool with calm waters and its own waterfall. Relax and watch braver souls shoot down the Ko'okiri Body Plunge.

WAUTURI BEACH No height requirement. Features a multidirectional wave pool, situated at the foot of Krakatau Lagoon and fed by waterfalls cascading off the volcano's peak.

Paths from there lead clockwise to **Rainforest Village,** home to the park's densest collection of thrill rides, including **TeAwa the Fearless River,** and **River Village,** which features family-friendly attractions like the **Kopiko Wai** lazy river. The heart of the park is the *volcano* in Volcano Bay: 200-foot **Krakatau,** home to the signature **Krakatau Aqua Coaster** as well as three drop-capsule body slides, plus hidden caverns with cascading waterfalls and special effects triggered by your TapuTapu band.

Each area of the park offers amenities such as concierge locations and lockers ($8–$15 for all-day access). The themed restaurants and bars throughout Volcano Bay are particularly noteworthy, far exceeding what we've come to expect from water-park grub with light, refreshing meals perfect for a day at the beach. Caribbean and island-inspired foods are on the menu, and even less-adventurous fare like pizza and hot dogs has been upgraded with flatbreads and pretzel buns.

At **Bambu,** in Rainforest Village, we love the quinoa-edamame burger, topped with roasted shiitake mushrooms, lettuce, tomato, sriracha mayo, and a side of fries. Also at Rainforest Village is **The Feasting Frog;** try the taco sampler or tuna poke, both served with plantain chips. At River Village, **Whakawaiwai Eats** is home to the Hawaiian Pizza, with caramelized pineapple, diced ham, and pickled jalapeños. In Wave Village, at **Kohola Reef Restaurant and Social Club,** slow-smoked glazed Hawaiian ribs, served with boniato mash and sweet plantains, don't disappoint. For dessert, it's impossible to choose between chocolate lava cake and the pineapple upside-down cake . . . so order both! **Dancing Dragons Boat Bar** (Rainforest Village) and **Kunuku Boat Bar** (Wave Village) serve a variety of exotic drinks, but the signature cocktails are far too sugary for our taste. Stick with the locally brewed Volcano Blossom beer instead.

You can upgrade your visit with reserved padded loungers ($31.94 and up per pair), 6-person cabanas ($170.40 and up), or 16-person Family Suite cabanas ($319.49 and up). While they're not a necessity, we recommend the private loungers for their included shade canopy, locking storage box, and attendant to deliver food and drink orders. The cabanas get all that, plus towel service, free fruit and bottle water, and a private kiosk for making TapuTapu reservations.

Though Universal opened Volcano Bay before it was really ready for prime time, the park is still gorgeous, and it offers a good variety of activities even in a semi-incomplete state. If you can adjust your attraction-riding expectations to fit TapuTapu's quirks and relax into the park's immersive atmosphere, Volcano Bay may just be your slice of paradise alongside I-4.

AQUATICA *by* SEAWORLD

AQUATICA IS ACROSS INTERNATIONAL DRIVE from the back side of SeaWorld. From Kissimmee, Walt Disney World, and Lake Buena Vista, take I-4 East, exit onto the Central Florida Parkway, and then bear left on International Drive. From Universal Studios, take I-4 West to FL 528, and from there exit onto International Drive. Admission prices are actually a little higher than those of the Disney water parks if you purchase at the gate: $61 for adults and $56 for kids. Tickets purchased online are $20 cheaper, and off-season specials online can reduce admission to as little as $17. Standard parking is $14 ($19 for RVs, $17 for preferred parking). If you don't want to wait in a line to purchase tickets, buy them in advance at aquaticabyseaworld.com, or use the credit-card ticket machines to the left of Aquatica's main entrance.

Aquatica is comparable in size to the other water theme parks in the area. Attractively landscaped with palms, ferns, and tropical flowers, it's far less themed than Typhoon Lagoon, Blizzard Beach, and Volcano Bay. Promotional material suggests that Aquatica is unique by virtue of combining SeaWorld's signature marine-animal exhibits with the expected water-park assortment of wave pools, slides, and creek floats. Marine exhibits, however, start and end with a float-through tank of tropical fish and a pool of black-and-white Commerson's dolphins. Print, web, and television ads for the park show guests viewing the dolphins while descending through a see-through tube on the **Dolphin Plunge** body slide—a corkscrewing romp through a totally dark tube until you blast through the clear tube at the end. The reality, however, is that you're flushed through the clear tube so fast, and with so much water splashing around your face, that it's pretty much impossible to see anything. At Aquatica, the best option by far is to view the dolphins from the walkway surrounding the exhibit or from the subsurface viewing windows. In early 2016, SeaWorld said that the Commerson's dolphins will not be replaced once the current population passes away. There's no word on whether different dolphins (or other sea creatures) might be used in their place.

A Yorkshire, England, woman reacted to the Dolphin Plunge:

The slide had the longest queue in the park. We queued for the best part of an hour and all agreed that it was a waste of time! You can barely see through the transparent part of the tube where the dolphins are (if you're lucky!), the slide is short, and the see-through bit lasts about 2 seconds!

SeaWorld's promotional hype, along with the location of the Plunge just inside the park entrance and the slide's low carrying capacity (about 280 people an hour), ensures that the slide stays mobbed all day. To avoid a long wait, ride first thing after park opening.

Opened in 2014, the first new slide at Aquatica in years, **Ihu's Breakaway Falls,** artfully blends hanging (without a noose) and being flushed down a really big toilet. But first you have to climb the equivalent of 10 stories of stairs. Once you haul yourself to the top of the tower and are revived, you step into one of three tubes with plexiglass doors. At some undetermined time (Aquatica staff dither around to build your anxiety), a trapdoor opens under you, gallowslike, and down you go. Each tube offers a different ride, but all three include big vertical drops, pitched drops, and corkscrews (the toilet part). A fourth tube at the top of the tower provides a wild but less intimidating ride, with the usual sit-down-and-off-you-go launch.

Omaka Rocka is a wide-diameter, one-person enclosed tube ride. The name derives from the wave action inside the tube, which washes you alternately up one side of the tube and then the other.

Other slides include **Tassie's Twisters,** in which an enclosed tube slide spits you into an open bowl where you careen around the edge much in the manner of the ball on a roulette wheel. Close to the Dolphin Plunge, Tassie's Twisters should be your second early-morning stop. Next, head over to **Walhalla Wave** and **HooRoo Run,** both on the park's far right side. Both slides use circular rafts that can accommodate up to three people. Walhalla Wave splashes down an enclosed twisting tube, while HooRoo Run is an open-air run down a steep, straight, undulating slide. The same entrance serves both slides. Line up for Walhalla Wave (vastly more popular) on the right and HooRoo Run on the left. Make Walhalla Wave your third slide of the day, followed by HooRoo Run.

Then you pass along the right side of the children's adventure area, Walkabout Waters, to **Taumata Racer,** the park's highest-capacity slide with eight enclosed corkscrewing tubes. The remaining slide is **Whanau Way,** all the way across the park to the left of the entrance. Sporting one corkscrew and a few twists, Whanau Way employs tubes that can carry one or two people. Because it's hard to see from the park entrance, Whanau Way doesn't attract long lines until midmorning.

Taken as a whole, the slides at Aquatica aren't nearly as interesting, thrilling, or imaginative as those of its competitors, and aside from whisking you through a dolphin tank, they don't break any new ground. Also, all the slides except HooRoo Run launch you down a black hole, making every ride seem like the one before it. Dark slides are an essential part of every water-park lineup, but to have all slides dark save one makes for a very homogenized experience.

In addition to the slides, Aquatica offers side-by-side wave pools, **Cutback Cove** and **Big Surf Shores.** This arrangement allows one cove to serve up bodysurfing waves while the other puts out gently bobbing floating waves. A spacious beach arrayed around the coves is the park's primary sunning venue. Shady spots, courtesy of beach umbrellas, ring the perimeter of the area for the sun-sensitive.

Loggerhead Lane and **Roa's Rapids** are the two floating streams. The former is a slow and gentle tube journey that circumnavigates the Tassie's Twisters slide. Its claim to fame is a section of the float where a plexiglass tunnel passes through the Fish Grotto, a tank populated by hundreds of exotic tropical fish. Unique to Aquatica, Roa's Rapids is a much longer course with a very swift current. (The other water parks have floating creeks, but most are leisurely affairs where you can fall asleep in your tube.) Buoyancy vests are available, but most adults float or swim the stream. The name notwithstanding, there are no rapids, but the flow is constricted from time to time, considerably increasing the already fast speed of the current. There's only one place to get in and out, so if you miss the takeout, you're in for another lap.

When it comes to children's water attractions, Aquatica more than equals the other area parks. In the back of the park, to the right of the wave pools, is **Kata's Kookaburra Cove,** featuring a wading pool and slides for the preschool crowd. But the real pièce de résistance is **Walkabout Waters.** If you have children under age 10, this alone may be worth the price of admission. In a calf-deep 15,000-square-foot pool, it's an immense three-story interactive playground set with slides, stairs, rope bridges, landings, and more. Water pulsates, plops, sprays, and spritzes at you from every conceivable angle. Randomly placed plastic squirting devices allow kids to take aim at unsuspecting adults, but the kids disperse quickly when either of two huge buckets dumps hundreds of gallons of water down on the entire structure. It's impossible not to get wet. It's also impossible not to have fun.

As at the other water parks, Aquatica has lockers, towels, wheelchairs, and strollers to rent and gift shops to browse. The three restaurants are **WaterStone Grill,** offering specialty sandwiches, fried fish, wraps, and salads; **Banana Beach Buffet,** an all-you-can-eat venue dishing up burgers, hot dogs, and chicken; and **Mango Market,** a diminutive eatery serving pizza, wraps, and salads. WaterStone Grill and Mango Market serve beer.